WRITER'S CHOICE

GRAMMAR AND COMPOSITION

Artist unknown, Pompeii,
Portrait of a young woman,
first century A.D.

Consulting Author for Composition
Jacqueline Jones Royster

Grammar Specialist
Mark Lester

Visual-Verbal Learning Specialists
Ligature, Inc.

GLENCOE

McGraw-Hill

New York, New York   Columbus, Ohio   Woodland Hills, California   Peoria, Illinois

Glencoe/McGraw-Hill

A Division of The **McGraw·Hill** Companies

Cover, Mark E. Gibson/The Stock Market, (inset) Aaron Haupt.

Send all inquiries to:
Glencoe/McGraw-Hill
8787 Orion Place
Columbus, OH 43240

ISBN 0-02-635878-6
(Student's Edition)
ISBN 0-02-635879-4
(Teacher's Wraparound Edition)

Printed in the United States of America.

5 6 7 8 9 10   027/043   03 02 01 00

Contents of Teacher's Wraparound Edition

Teacher's Wraparound Edition

The Teacher's Wraparound Edition provides an effective resource for presenting the lessons in Writer's Choice. Each lesson plan has four parts: Focus, Teach, Assess, and Close. The margins offer additional information and strategies to meet a wide range of teaching situations.

TEACH provides varied strategies for addressing the needs of basic-to-average, LD, and advanced learners.

FOCUS clearly sets the objective with writing, thinking, speaking, and listening skills as well as motivating activities for the lesson.

Strategies and background information support critical thinking, cultural diversity, students learning English, cross-curricular connections, fine art, and civic literacy.

Teacher's Classroom Resources lists ancillaries that extend and support the lesson.

UNIT 3
Lesson 3.4

TEACH

Guided Practice

Using the Model
Point out that the graphic uses directional terms ("north," "east") and words showing proximity ("on top," "about") to orient readers rather than words that show distance. Other phrases that orient the reader are "along the east wall," "past the window," and "to the right/left." Students, too, can sketch scenes and label objects to help in ordering details.

Oral Reporting
Invite students to describe one of the following for a mock radio report: touring a giant cave; watching a parade; sitting in the highest seats at a game. Suggest that students freewrite for details and then use spatial order to organize the details into a script. Encourage students to tape-record their scripts for a "broadcast" to the class. Then have the class comment on whether they could clearly imagine what was being described.

Independent Practice

For further stimuli for descriptive writing, see *Fine Art Transparencies* 11–15.

Writing Process Transparencies, 11–13B
Writing Across the Curriculum, pp. 4–8
Cooperative Learning Activities, pp. 13–18

Skills Practice
Thinking and Study Skills, pp. 3, 9, 11, 14, 28–29
Sentence Combining Practice, pp. 28–29
Speaking and Listening Activities, pp. 14–15
Composition Practice, p. 21

120

Grammar
Editing Tip
As you edit, punctuate prepositional phrases correctly. For more information see Lesson 20.2, page 568.

Link the Detail
When you use spatial way to picture the scene next. Transition words, help to link details so created. Notice how the posts in Sarah Fisher's gram based on her des

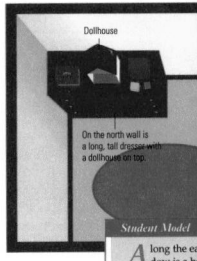

Dollhouse

On the north wall is a long, tall dresser with a dollhouse on top.

Student Model

A long the east dow is a be On the north wal house on top. To jewelry boxes, on the dollhouse is a box holds my hai

Notice how Sarah uses phrases like "on the north wall" to help you find your way around the room.

120 *Descriptive Writing: A Closer Look*

Enabling Strategies

Giving Directions
Students who are new to English may benefit from additional practice using directional and spatial order words and phrases. Have these students work in

order to describ Chinese playground.

UNIT 3
Lesson 3.4

Setting the Purpose

Lesson 3.4 teaches students how to describe a place by arranging details in spatial order.

FOCUS

Lesson Overview
Objective: To identify words and phrases that orient a reader in a particular scene
Skills: ordering details logically; linking details
Critical Thinking: recalling; identifying; organizing; drawing conclusions
Speaking and Listening: interpreting; questioning

Bellringer
When students enter the classroom, have this assignment on the board: *Imagine you're rafting in the middle of a wide river. Jot down details describing what you see, hear, and feel.*

Grammar Link to the Bellringer
As students discuss their answers to the Bellringer, write some of their descriptive details on the board. Have students indicate the ones with prepositional phrases.

Motivating Activity
Mark the details from the Bellringer activity, describing things that are near with an *A* and things that are far with a *B*. Ask students to draw conclusions about how you divided the details into groups. Mention that many writers arrange details from near to far or from far to near.

118

LESSON
3.4

Descriptive Writing
Using Spatial Order

A painter arranges details so that the viewer see an ordered picture. A writer describes details so that the reader imagine a scene clearly.

The Flemish painter Jan Vermeer arranged the details in this image so that the viewer's eye moves from behind the artist to the scene he is painting. Writers, like painters, arrange the details of a scene in a certain order and for particular reason.

Order Details
Logically

Writers can order details in several ways, depending on the point in space that seems a logic starting place. Details can be ordered from top to bottom, fr near to far, or from left to right When looking at a building, for example, you might first see nearby detail such as a decorative door frame. Then, farther the front of the building, you notice decorative stone faces above the windows. To describe this building, you could order these details from near to far.

Jan Vermeer, Allegory of the Art of Painting, c. 1665–1670

118 *Descriptive Writing: A Closer Look*

Literary Model

the place. In your journal write your description in that order.

3.4 U

About the Art

Jan Vermeer, *Allegory of the Art of Painting,* c. 1665–1670
Vermeer specialized in interior scenes, arranging the elements to achieve a balanced composition. This painting hangs in a museum in Vienna, Austria.

Teacher's Classroom

The following resources can be used for planning, instruction, practice, reinforcement, assessment, reteaching, enrichment, or evaluation.

Teaching Tools
Lesson Plans, p. 26

Resources

Transparencies
Fine Art Transparencies, 11–15
Writing Process Transparencies, 11–13B

Blackline Masters
Thinking and Study Skills, pp. 3, 9, 11, 14, 28–29

Writing Across the Curriculum, pp. 4–8
Cooperative Learning Activities, pp. 13–18
Sentence Combining Practice, pp. 28–29
Speaking and Listening Activities, pp. 14–15

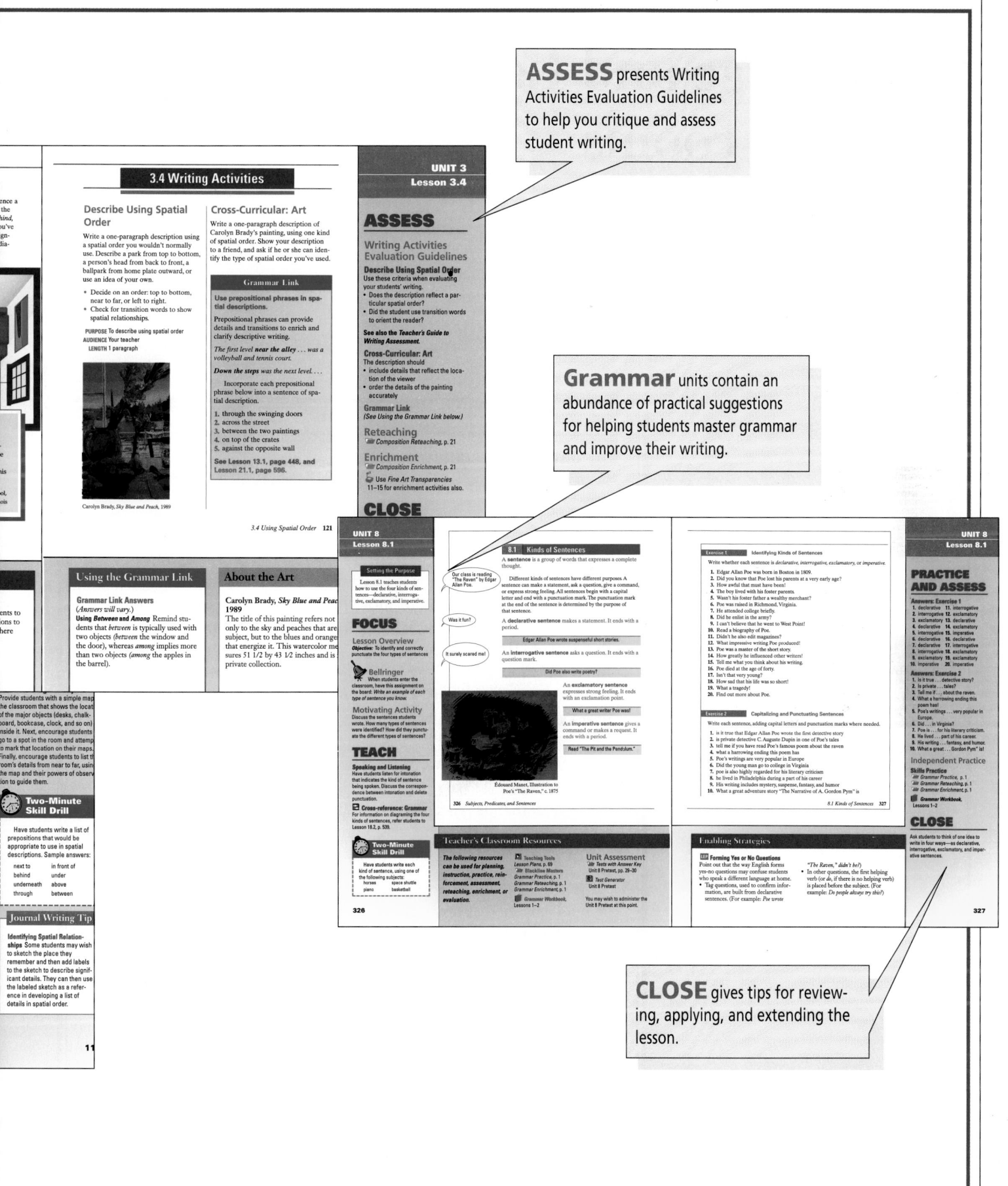

ASSESS presents Writing Activities Evaluation Guidelines to help you critique and assess student writing.

Grammar units contain an abundance of practical suggestions for helping students master grammar and improve their writing.

CLOSE gives tips for reviewing, applying, and extending the lesson.

Language and Learning in Classrooms

by Jacqueline Jones Royster
Associate Professor of English and Director of the University Writing Center at The Ohio State University

What Do Our Students Need to Learn?

The last thirty years or more have been tremendously exciting times in English Studies at all educational levels. We have made thought-provoking discoveries that encourage us to imagine *all manner of possibilities for language and learning* in our classrooms. As teachers whose concerns are systemically intertwined with reading and writing, we have been privileged to see other educators come to perceive the centrality of such concerns in their endeavors as well.

Likewise, we are more attuned now than ever before to the intense demands placed on our students. Even the young ones, seemingly, must contend with complex forces and lead complicated lives. To operate reasonably on a daily basis, they need to be able to:

• read varieties of text well.
• use language well (as speakers, listeners, readers, and writers) in gaining access to various and sundry information and in being critical and creative as they construct ideas meaningfully for different audiences and different purposes.
• reflect critically on their own uses of language and on the uses of others.
• recognize how language, particularly within a multimedia environment, impacts on their daily lives.

The intersection of these two points of understanding

Writer's Choice provides all manner of student-friendly invitations and instruction for frequent writing:
• Every four-page lesson includes a journal activity.
• Every four-page lesson ends with a full page of Writing Activities.
• Remarkable variety of writing activities includes writing based on Case Studies, on literature, and on content areas.

often becomes a point of anxiety for us, however. When we actually face our students, so widely divergent in backgrounds and ability levels, in the systems of support available to them, in their desires, motivation, and aspirations, and in their responses to the highly pressurized contexts in which we all live, we can feel very much at sea. These realities across communities—urban, suburban, rural—place considerable demands on us to be, above all else, *flexible and creative* in both our theoretical and pedagogical constructs.

What Is Our Task as Teachers?

Classroom teachers must operate now from a constant need to keep the conversations with our students open and viable, asking good questions and not just giving our own answers, looking from multidimensional, not just one-dimensional, points of view. The imperative is to think beyond the specifics of discrete skills and knowledge and easily countable measures of achievement. The imperative is to look qualitatively and dynamically at how language works, how students learn, how learning and achievement can break new ground. The imperative is to use our knowledge, experiences, expertise, and imagination to help our students:

- create a central place for reading and writing in their lives.
- function competently on their own and in the company of others.
- feel capable as human beings who can recognize and solve problems.
- live positive and productive lives.

Our task is to *structure classroom environments* that are content-rich, that incorporate students' participation as active learners, and that invite risk and experimentation. A basic goal becomes helping students to develop keen skills by which they make observations and articulate their visions. The impetus is toward structuring classroom experiences that allow them to think variously about their lives, the lives of others, and the wonderfully rich range of texts that continue to emerge from the human experience, and to *use their skills, knowledge, and understanding as they construct and reconstruct their perceptions of reality.* These efforts seem to stand at the center of our concerns. Ongoing developments in both theory and practice seem to reaffirm these values constantly, and most of us remain hopeful that, despite the hard work that is inevitably demanded, our students will learn to *manage the array of complex language and writing skills* they need to face future and unknown worlds.

Writer's Choice enables both students and teachers to be flexible and creative by providing an engaging array of options:
- Composition lessons in a unit may be used in order, or lessons may be linked to particular writing needs.
- Writer's Choice pages offer a variety of workable assignments and degrees of guidance.
- Grammar instruction is delivered through a wealth of exercises, the Grammar Links, literature-based Grammar Reviews, and the Troubleshooter.

Writer's Choice is a structured environment for problem solving and success:
- Manageable lessons address specific writing situations with workable strategies.
- Writing assignments and Writing Process in Action lessons give substantial contexts and criteria for self-evaluation.
- Complete unit on sentence combining is based on structured sentences.

Writer's Choice presents skills in context to help students construct a unified experience of language:
- Composition lessons use annotated models to show specific skills in action.
- Writing Process Tips integrate composition with grammar and vocabulary skills.
- Grammar Reviews integrate grammar, usage, and mechanics with literature.

Writer's Choice helps students manage the complexity of language and writing tasks:
- Complete instruction in the writing process
- Writing Process Tips throughout composition lessons for help with writing process
- Writing Assignments—realistic writing prompts with real world context
- Troubleshooter to help solve nine most common grammar, usage, and mechanics errors

The Middle School Concept

by Philip M. Anderson
Associate Professor, Department of Secondary Education and Youth Services, and Director of the English Education Program, Queens College, City University of New York

What Is Special About Middle School?

Anyone walking into a middle school can see what a special place it is: noisier, livelier, and simultaneously more disorienting and more interesting than either elementary or high school. Middle school students, while no longer children, are not ready to commit to the specialized, somewhat abstract, academic model of high school. But young adolescents ardently pursue knowledge about the world and *eagerly explore the possibilities* they now see before them.

Surveys of young adolescent educational interests reflect this *real-world consciousness*, reporting the following concerns:

- developing a personal identity
- dealing with questions encompassing morals and values
- securing a place of status in their peer group
- sorting out the maze of adult expectations
- anticipating their future lives (Paul S. George, et al., *The Middle School—and Beyond*, ASCD, 1992).

While some might perceive these social and psychological needs as impediments to academic learning, they embody powerful forces for motivating learning and ensuring interest in activities and outcomes. Meeting developmental needs (surveys of young adolescents' parents echo these concerns) provides a more productive learning environment for middle school students and more satisfying teaching conditions for their teachers.

How Is Middle School Organized?

The middle school is organized around student interests rather than administrative imperatives. Teachers of young

Writer's Choice is designed to capitalize on students' eagerness to explore possibilities:
- Wide variety of writing assignments gives students an array of choices and empowers them to draw on their own experiences.
- Contemporary design blends visual appeal with student-friendly text.
- Frequent Journal Writing activities provide opportunities for experimentation, reflection, and self-expression.

Writer's Choice reflects students' real-world consciousness:
- Case Studies of the writing process at work in real-world situations
- Student models by real student writers reflecting diverse populations
- Purpose, audience, and real-world context identified for writing assignments
- Readers Respond to the Model—actual student responses to literature
- Student Advisory Board ensuring student involvement in creation of the series

adolescents structure the curriculum to respond to students' individuated needs while providing enough structure to foster learning and promote social development. Interdisciplinary learning, the pragmatic approach of extracting from academic subjects as needed, supplies an essential ingredient.

Interdisciplinary curriculum in the middle school develops from central themes, or problems, drawn from young adolescent interests. Curriculum projects devised from these themes provide activities and an intellectual focal point for the students. The unifying theme invites cooperative learning, while the interdisciplinary projects evoke useful connections between the academic disciplines.

Cooperative learning, the other key feature of middle school organization, typically involves heterogeneous groups of students working toward a common goal. Studies of cooperative learning in the middle school report higher achievement levels, greater use of high-level thinking, and increased self-esteem. Cooperative learning models also heighten the social imperatives of the students as a means for teaching interdependence and advocating collaboration.

How Do Middle School Students Learn?

Middle school students learn best through active involvement. They need time to read, write, and explore. Writing activities should encourage personal response while maintaining enough structure for developing, expressing, and organizing ideas. Reading activities should extend information, yet allow students to shape meaning through a variety of responses.

Learning content at this age means connecting it with one's own experience. Students must draw on their prior knowledge to integrate new learning experiences. Young adolescents desire knowledge about life's possibilities and wish to measure themselves against their new interpretations and perceptions of the world.

Middle school students do not learn useful skills well in isolation. *Activities connecting reading, writing, speaking, listening, and viewing* are more likely to produce successful learning of skill and content. The connected world view young adolescents seek, and their nascent perceptions of the relationships among ideas and actions, are not served by sequestered drill and a fragmented curriculum.

Middle schools provide a vision of responsive and responsible education for all ages. The noise in a middle school is the sound of learning; the seeming disorder is the commotion of a construction site bent on building a better world.

Writer's Choice encourages and provides help with interdisciplinary writing:
- Writing assignments cover such curriculum areas as art, science, mathematics, music, and, of course, literature.
- Case Studies explore and model how today's professionals write in a variety of fields.
- *Writing Across the Curriculum* blackline masters provide practical help for writing in content areas.
- *Research Paper and Report Writing* blackline masters offer cross-curricular support.

Writer's Choice incorporates practical, carefully planned cooperative learning activities:
- Writing Activities often include a choice of a cooperative learning activity with clear, step-by-step guidance.
- Teacher's Wraparound Editions include additional optional cooperative activities, such as Pairs Check, Round-robin, and Think-Pair-Share.

Writer's Choice integrates reading, writing, speaking, listening, and viewing for a unified learning experience:
- Case Studies that connect the world of writing with the world of everyday experience
- Manageable lessons with Journal Writing activities for response and reflection
- Writing Activities at the end of every lesson, with a variety of contexts, curriculum areas, and degrees of guidance
- Literature selections and models
- Speaking and Listening activities
- Visual/verbal graphic devices that teach as well as invite response

Integrating the Language Arts

Writer's Choice encourages total language growth through reading, responding, writing, and reflecting:
- Manageable lessons with Journal Writing activities
- Writing Activities at the end of every lesson, with a variety of contexts, curriculum areas, and degrees of guidance
- Literature selections
- Shorter literature models
- Writing process instruction that demonstrates how thinking and writing go hand in hand

Writer's Choice encourages the exchange of perceptions:
- Student models by real student writers
- Readers Respond to the Model—real student responses to literature
- Peer Editing built into writing assignments
- Cooperative Learning activities
- Speaking and Listening activities

Writer's Choice embodies the interdependence of all language processes:
- Literature integrated into composition—through literature selections and models
- Grammar integrated into composition—through the Troubleshooter and the Grammar Links
- Composition integrated into grammar—through the Writing Applications
- Literature integrated into grammar—through selections in Grammar Reviews

by Denny Wolfe

Professor and Associate Dean of Darden College of Education at Old Dominion University in Norfolk, Virginia; formerly director of the Tidewater Writing Project

Why Integrate the Language Arts?

As English teachers, we have a unique responsibility: to assist students in their growth toward language maturity. Specifically, our challenge is to help students read, write, speak, and listen capably and effectively. To the extent we are successful in meeting this challenge, students learn to *think* critically and imaginatively.

Reading, writing, speaking, and listening are complementary processes. That is, growth in any one enhances growth in the others. We want students to achieve both *oracy* (speaking and listening competence) and *literacy* (reading and writing competence), and each feeds the other. Our curriculum, therefore, should function to give students *opportunities for total language growth*. By talking and by listening to others, students often are stimulated to read or write; during and after reading or writing, the *exchange of perceptions* through further oral and written activities both broadens and deepens students' understanding.

We must lead students toward a recognition of the *interdependence of all language processes*. Students can then become truly competent readers, writers, speakers, and listeners. The process works much like learning to drive a car. The competent driver must accomplish many tasks simultaneously—managing the steering wheel, operating the gas pedal, using the brake, looking ahead at the road, glancing behind through the rear-view mirror, paying attention to road signs. All of these are necessary to making the car work for us. Similarly, for language to work for us, we must use all the processes together, capitalizing on each to make the others meaningful.

How Can We Integrate the Language Arts?

One conception of the English curriculum is that it is about literature—in both print and nonprint forms—and that it is about experience. *The world of literature* and the world of students' experience must be drawn together if the English classroom is to be an exciting, dynamic place. When we as teachers attempt to draw these two worlds together, we create conditions for integrating the language arts.

For example, a poet may write about a sunset. Before asking students to read the poem (or hear it read), we can invite them to talk or to write about a sunset—a memorable experience, a place or a person they associate with a sunset, or a generic description of one. We might relate an experience or two of our own. Afterward, when students approach the poem, they have established a mindset for reading it, and they are potentially able to relate to it in special ways. Upon finishing the poem, they might talk in groups about how the poem is different from or similar to their own experiences. Or they may be invited to make journal entries. Such discussions or personal reflections in journals may lead to a full, even formal, piece of writing on some interesting aspect of the poem, perhaps drafted several times and finally released to the teacher. In these ways, students practice reading, writing, speaking, and listening to clarify and to enhance their thoughts and feelings about a literary experience.

How Do Students Benefit from Integrating the Language Arts?

When students engage in experiences that invite reading, writing, speaking, and listening to be used in concert, they gain a sense of the wholeness of English. They cease to think of these language processes as discrete—reading as one thing, writing another, and speaking and listening something else. They develop *a sense of community* as they talk together, share perceptions from their reading, and respond to each other's written drafts. Most importantly, they grow *toward full language maturity*, recognizing that each language process contributes to the development of all others. Finally, they become better thinkers, a major goal of all instruction.

Writer's Choice is literature-rich:
- Literature selections from the finest contemporary writers
- Annotated Literature models to take the mystery out of writing well
- Writing About Literature lessons with practical instruction for specific writing situations
- Literature-based Grammar Reviews

Writer's Choice helps students develop a sense of community through the use of language in their own lives, in the classroom, and in the world at large:
- Case Studies—writing in the real world
- Journal Writing—for response and reflection
- Peer Editing—for shared responses
- Cooperative Learning—reading, writing, speaking, listening, and thinking toward common goals
- Readers Respond—students talking to students

Writer's Choice provides a framework for each student's growth toward full language maturity:
- Choice among writing assignments empowers students to draw on their own experiences.
- Writing Process in Action includes criteria for students' self-evaluations.
- Grades 11 and 12 include *The Elements of Style* by William Strunk Jr. and E. B. White.

Multiculturalism

by Arnold Webb

Senior Research Associate, Research for Better Schools, Philadelphia, Pennsylvania

What Is Multiculturalism?

Multiculturalism is one of those words to which we educators nod knowingly when we hear it. We nod, secure in righteous affirmation of a concept that is second only to motherhood and with which no one would dare disagree. We also believe that we are all using essentially the same definitional parameters and, therefore, can communicate with each other on this issue from a common (and enlightened) conceptual base.

As comforting as the above notion may be, it is not entirely accurate. Perceptions concerning what constitutes meaningful multiculturalism in our classrooms range from fostering and stressing a common culture to celebrating and supporting cultural diversity. Hardcore adherents to each of these views believe strongly that their approach is the only viable way to *channel the dynamic cultural and ethnic mix in our classrooms* into areas that support and strengthen our democratic society.

I agree with Asa Hilliard, who said:

> I do not believe that it is necessary to choose between (cultural) commonality and uniqueness. This is a false dichotomy. Human minds and systems are powerful and flexible enough to handle both.

The truth is that both are essential. We must provide an environment in which children can understand the world around them and their place (and responsibility) in that society as citizens and as contributors to the perpetuation of democratic precepts and ideals. We cannot do this, however, without empowering every child to recognize and value his/her individual worth. That empowerment for many children can occur only when they are in an educational environment that provides opportunities for them

---

Writer's Choice helps you channel the cultural mix in your classroom:

- Student Advisory Board ensures student involvement in creation of the series.
- Student models reflect diverse population.
- Literature, grammar exercises, and fine art present cultural variety.

to understand and appreciate the unique historic and ongoing contributions of their ethnic and cultural heritage to their land of origin and to the American dream.

How Do We Strike the Right Balance?

How does a teacher strike a balance between providing youngsters with a positive sense of self-worth through pride in their cultural heritage and still engender appreciation of our unique shared culture as Americans? It is a daunting task, but it must be accomplished. Perhaps one might begin by taking a self-administered test and responding candidly to the following questions:

- What do I believe about the children I teach? What are the bases of my expectations of them?
- What do I know about the history, mores, and culture of my students?
- How is this knowledge utilized in my planning and teaching?
- Does the curriculum I teach reflect *the truths of a pluralistic society*? In what ways?
- What opportunities are provided in my classroom for children to know, understand, and *relate to classmates from other backgrounds and cultures*?
- What skills are my students learning that enable them to *contribute positively to an evolving, diverse, and demanding democracy*?

Your answers to the questions posed above should provide some private insights for you into the impact of multiculturalism in your own classroom. Do not believe for a moment, however, that you are alone in the struggle to celebrate diversity and to make multiculturalism a viable aspect of our educational systems.

In the final analysis, we teachers (all of us) must be responsive to the needs and exigencies of our changing society. For example, the 1990 Census revealed that one of every four Americans is a person of color. It is projected that by the year 2000, this figure will be one of every three. This demographic and economic imperative must be dealt with realistically in America's classrooms. Cultural and ethnic diversity is endemic, and we can shy away from its impact to our detriment, or we can build upon its strengths and benefit us all. What happens in our classrooms as we address this issue will markedly affect the rest of the nation's response. It's up to us!

Writer's Choice reflects the truths of a pluralistic society:
- Contemporary photographs
- Fine art
- Cultural Diversity annotations in Teacher's Wraparound Edition

Writer's Choice helps students relate to people of other backgrounds:
- Cultural diversity in Case Studies and topics of assignments and exercises
- Cultural diversity in models and literature

Writer's Choice empowers students to learn the skills of civic literacy:
- Civic Literacy annotations in Teacher's Wraparound Edition pinpoint skills and concepts.
- Case Studies exemplify variety of social roles and contributions.

Teaching Students with Different Abilities

by Beverly Ann Chin

Professor of English, University of Montana; Director of the Montana Writing Project

How Can We Teach Writing to Students with Different Abilities?

Our students bring a wide variety of experiences, attitudes, learning styles, cultures, and languages to our classrooms. The diversity of abilities is most apparent when we teach writing. Many students learn English as a second language and are developing basic skills in speaking, listening, reading, and writing. Other students speak standard English as a second dialect.

In our classrooms, we may have students who seem unable to put their ideas on paper, as well as students who view themselves as writers and initiate their own writing. We also have students who differ in their abilities to write for different purposes. For example, the student who enthusiastically creates a historical narrative on Spanish exploration in the 1500s may have difficulty organizing a persuasive editorial on Columbus Day celebrations. On the other hand, another student may find the persuasive editorial easier to write than the historical narrative.

We can teach writing to students with different abilities when we create learning environments that immerse students in reading, writing, speaking, listening, and viewing. By *placing our students at the center of the curriculum*, we engage them as active learners and language users. We can meet the needs, interests, and abilities of our individual students if we respect our students' languages and if we are flexible in our teaching strategies.

What Writing Strategies Work with Students of Different Abilities?

Here are some guidelines for teaching writing to students with different abilities:

Writer's Choice places students at the center of the curriculum by offering a coherent writing plan based on personal choice:

- Short, manageable lessons to meet specific writing needs and goals
- Wide variety of writing prompts with different degrees of guidance
- Journal writing and Portfolio keeping
- Alternative strategies for Basic Learners, Advanced Learners, and Limited English Proficiency Learners (Teacher's Wraparound Edition)

1. Provide *frequent opportunities* for students to write, read, and reflect. Students need to engage in authentic communication and to discover the personal and social nature of writing and reading. Students also need to read literature by authors of diverse backgrounds and cultures.

2. Help students discover the relationship between oral and written language. By encouraging students to "talk out" their ideas before and during the writing process, we help students *understand the connections* among speaking, writing, listening, and reading. We can also stimulate creative thinking by teaching students a variety of prewriting strategies.

3. Vary the instruction and management of writing workshops. Students differ in the amount and type of writing instruction they need. When we allow students to choose their writing topics, we help students become responsible for focusing the purpose and audience for their writing. By structuring small group, partnership, and individual writing activities, we address differences in learning styles as well as language abilities.

4. Emphasize fluency and quality of ideas before correctness. We need to model appropriate ways for students to respond to each other's writing. We also need to teach grammar, usage, and mechanics in the context of the students' writing. As students write for authentic purposes and audiences, students discover how the conventions of written language affect communication.

5. Encourage all students to display, present, and publish their writing. By creating an environment in which all students share their writing, we recognize each student as a valued and unique member of *our learning community*. Students also learn to take pride and ownership in their writing.

6. Evaluate writing process as well as progress. Students need to see and value their growth as writers. Through a portfolio, students document and reflect upon their growth as writers, readers, decision-makers, and risk-takers. Through observations, anecdotal records, and conferences with students, we can assess our students' development as language users and language learners.

7. Above all, appreciate the diversity of students in the classroom. When we teach writing as a tool for learning, thinking, and communicating, we enable our students to discover and define their individual and social identities. By engaging our students in meaningful language activities, we empower the students as problem-solvers, decision-makers, and lifelong learners.

Writer's Choice is a program of frequent writing opportunities:
- Personal Writing beginning each book
- Journal Writing for reflection and self-expression
- Writing prompts with a variety of student-friendly contexts
- Writing Process in Action lessons
- Opportunities to respond to literature

Writer's Choice helps students understand the connections among speaking, writing, listening, and reading through the sheer variety of language experiences:
- Case Studies
- Literature discussion
- Student models
- Writing Conferences
- Journal Writing
- Writing Across the Curriculum
- Speaking and Listening opportunities
- Peer responses
- Cooperative learning activities

Writer's Choice includes all students as members of a literate community:
- Choices among lessons and array of contexts for assignments enable all students to feel involved.
- Case Studies, Student Models, and Readers Respond encourage participation by example.
- *Practice, Reteaching,* and *Enrichment* blackline masters meet individual needs.

Journal Writing

by Charleen Silva Delfino
English Coordinator, East Side Union High School-District, San Jose, California; Director of the San Jose Area Writing Project

Journals—What Is Their Purpose?

In the 1960s, when I began teaching high school, journal writing looked very different from the journal writing I use today. Students were given little structure or purpose for their writing. Journals sounded more like diaries, and students were encouraged to keep writing for an assigned amount of time even if the same word was repeated over and over again. The journals were often boring to write and boring to read. The exception occurred when the students used the journal as a diary and told me more than I ever wanted to know about their romantic life. I soon abandoned journals.

Today, I find journal writing to be an *integral part* of all of my teaching. The big difference is that students have a very specific purpose for their journals—the purpose varies, but it is always present for me in my planning and for students in their writing. Journals are a form of personal writing, sometimes shared, but the main audience is always the writer himself or herself. I find that for special education students, second language students, and all less verbal students, journals help to develop fluency. For many students, any writing can be a painful activity. They know that the fewer words they write, the fewer chances they have of making a mistake. They don't view writing as an opportunity to express their opinions (often, they don't value their own opinions or feel anyone else does); rather, they see writing as a trap to demonstrate their weaknesses and to show what they don't know. Consistent use of journals that focus on content and not on form can help students develop the fluency they have lacked.

Are Journals Just for Special Students?

It is impossible for students to be wrong in a journal; consequently, they develop confidence in the student as a writer and as a learner. They help all students generate and validate ideas and beliefs. They enable students to explore ideas before

---

Writer's Choice makes journal writing an integral part of a complete composition program:
- Personal Writing Unit, including lessons on Writing as Self-Discovery, Keeping a Writer's Journal, and Keeping a Commonplace Book
- Journal Writing—a brief prompt halfway through each composition lesson
- Writing Process in Action includes suggestions for journal writing as a means for students to reflect on their writing experiences

writing a formal paper and to record impressions and reconstruct memories for personal writings. Journals enable students to bring prior knowledge and experiences to the study of a piece of literature and to respond as we read through a work of literature. Students may keep a double entry journal, recording words, phrases, or sentences that impress them on one side of a page, and then asking questions, responding, or debating them on the opposite side of the page. I often use journals to review previously learned materials and to check the effectiveness of a lesson. I also check on the effectiveness of my teaching by ending a class or starting the next one by asking what was the most interesting or important thing learned in the previous lesson. I can check for understanding in this manner as quickly as I can correct an objective test. Moreover, it is impossible for a student to fail a journal, and I have a better picture of my *students as learners.*

How Should We Respond to Student Journals?

No matter how effective journals may be, if responding to them becomes a burden, I won't use them. I never correct journals or other types of first draft writing. This decision saves me time and is based on sound teaching principles. When students write journals, I want them to concentrate on generating and exploring ideas and concepts; they can do this only if they are not concerned with form or correctness. Correctness is important, but not at this generating time. However, I do believe that it is important that students receive a response to their journals. Their ideas need to be validated. I vary the way I respond to all journals. Again, I never correct; sometimes, I read all journals and write one journal back to the whole class sharing some of the varying viewpoints I learned from my students. Other times, I use highlighters to identify key ideas in student journals that I found interesting, amusing, or challenging. Students can see that I have read their journals and know which part engaged me, yet I can read a whole class set in very little time.

Journals, as with all parts of the writing process, work most effectively in an atmosphere of trust and respect. The sharing of writing makes us vulnerable, but the sharing of personal writing where we are exploring new ideas makes us especially so. I have found that the best way for me to establish trust and a supportive atmosphere is for me to write with my students and to share my journals for their response. When they see me *thinking through new ideas, trying out various forms,* and exploring new concepts, I can truly establish a classroom that houses a community of writers who are trusting and open and willing to take risks.

Writer's Choice encourages journal writing as a tool for unifying students' educational experiences:
- Lessons on Writing to Learn, Keeping a Reader-Response Journal, and Using a Learning Log help students become more aware of themselves as learners.
- Cross-curricular writing prompts help students practice composition skills and transfer them to writing done in other classes and in the world of work.

Writer's Choice invites students to experiment, summarize, articulate, anticipate, synthesize, and evaluate:
- Journal Writing activities suggest a variety of relevant stimuli for helping students start out and set frameworks for problem solving, pose questions for follow-through, and engage higher-order thinking skills.

Portfolio Keeping

by Bonnie S. Sunstein

Associate Professor of English and Director of the Master of Arts in Teaching Program at Rivier College, Nashua, New Hampshire

How Do People Use Portfolios?

Artists, musicians, heads of state, and financiers use portfolios at intervals during their careers, gathering samples to represent depth and breadth in their work. They select different artifacts at different times, depending on who will be looking at their portfolios, and for what purposes. Over the last two centuries there is evidence that portfolios have appeared in tooled leather cases, carved wooden boxes, ornate display stands, and makeshift cloth carrying cases. The word *portfolio* derives from the Latin *portare* ("to carry") and *fogli* ("leaves or sheets of paper").

In the last decade, we've seen similarly colorful and energetic varieties of portfolios in schools and colleges. They appear on our classroom shelves in plastic boxes, shoe boxes, loose-leaf scrapbooks, neon-colored trapper-keepers, and metal drawers full of sedate manila folders. With homage to their heritage, all portfolios "carry" representative "leaves" of paper for the display of their owner's work. With portfolios, students can document their own histories as learners. They can *become their own authorities* rather than relying on external authorities to judge what's good or bad about their work. The use of portfolios to represent students' accomplishments is in its infancy, and the possibilities for learning from them are open and exciting.

How Can Portfolios Help Students and Teachers?

As students, teachers, classes, and whole school systems experiment with portfolios, we are shifting our thinking

---

Writer's Choice empowers students to become their own authorities:
- Reflection and Portfolio activities at the end of every composition unit
- Writing Portfolios for collecting student work

about the terms *assessment* and *evaluation*. For students, a collection of writing over time can offer insights as they *write reflectively about their own learning*. For teachers, portfolios enable us to include our students in our evaluation process. When we keep our own portfolios along with our students, our own written reflections point out the time we devote to our students and to our own personal literacy.

Because evaluation is inextricably tied to instruction, portfolios teach us more about our teaching. For whole classes, teachers and students can view progress over time and make more informed decisions about curriculum coverage. For school systems, large-scale use of portfolios can offer new kinds of information and raise questions we've never been able to ask before. In other words, portfolios can help us to evaluate where we've been, assess where we are, and project where we want to go next. When we collect our reading and writing for display and analysis, we connect our present to our past and our future.

What Goes into a Portfolio—and Why?

As this is being written, there are as many kinds of portfolios as there are people working with them, and that's a healthy sign. Some are distilled folders, holding samples of students' "best" work. Deciding what's "best" becomes a negotiation between a teacher and a student in which they decide what is important in writing. The decisions may offer surprises as we discover what issues we most value in our evaluations. Portfolios offer us a multidimensional look at ourselves.

Portfolios complete with students' reflections—commentaries about why the paper is included—offer *opportunities for metacognition*—thinking about their own thinking and documenting it. A "best" paper might be the one with the fewest errors or one that follows the teacher's assignment perfectly. But a "best" paper might be the one in which the student took a risk, worked out a nagging question, researched and synthesized a new idea, reached beyond the teacher's assignment. This paper might not have followed the assignment exactly, but it might represent a new moment in a student's thinking.

Portfolios are not writing folders redone; they are documented collections of literary decisions made at certain times among certain people. They reflect our philosophies of reflection, evaluation, and learning. Portfolio keeping is decision making, and making decisions involves asking tough questions—of ourselves and our students—about what we value in writing and reading.

Writer's Choice encourages students to write reflectively about their own learning:
- Student models of writing to learn
- Journal Writing
- Unit Review

Writer's Choice offers opportunities for metacognition:
- Writing activities point the way at each stage of the writing process.
- Criteria for self-evaluation accompany every Writing Process in Action.
- The Unit Review helps students ask the right questions about their work.

Vision, Values, and Assessment

by Jacqueline Jones Royster
Associate Professor of English and Director of the University Writing Center at The Ohio State University

What Should Our Perspective Be?

Any discussion of assessment in the language arts must realistically begin with an articulation of what, within the context of current trends and practices, we have determined to be worthy of attention in effective teaching and learning. With a clarification of vision and values, we are much better positioned to begin a more meaningful discussion of what to measure, why, how, and when. From this perspective, we turn away from images of ourselves as failure detectives and language-use police. Objectives for learning take a rightful place as the linchpins for teaching and translate reflexively into measures of learning and achievement.

This perspective emphasizes the importance of having an appropriate interface between the theoretical base on which a curriculum or course is fashioned, the pedagogical frame within which learning happens, and the mechanisms for monitoring and measuring learning and achievement. It brings into question what assessment should be about and do in the interest of the educational process. It encourages us to see assessment as critical throughout the learning process, not just at the end of it, and to recognize a need to think well beyond ordinary techniques of testing and evaluation.

A reconsideration of the role of assessment in learning makes it possible to examine particular mechanisms for exactly what and how much they can tell us about the learning process and achievement. Inevitably, we are drawn to a need to measure many values and expectations in determining learning quality. We are drawn to a need for *multiple measures*, both quantitative and qualitative, and *alternative mechanisms*. The imperative is twofold: 1) to bring to clarity a fully developed picture of students' abilities to perform and their capacity to activate and maximize learning; 2) to select a range of

---

Writer's Choice offers both students and teachers multiple measures and mechanisms for assessment:

- Writing Process in Action assignments encourage peer response and editing.
- Guidelines for Evaluation in the Teacher's Wraparound Edition provide specific suggestions for giving students feedback.
- An array of Tests accompanies the program.
- *Teacher's Guide to Writing Assessment* offers additional models and guidelines for assessment.

mechanisms that reaffirm the values in learning that we seek to engender and also mirror both the ways we teach and the ways our students learn.

What Is the Role of Portfolios?

One promising strategy for addressing this twofold imperative is a portfolio system. While there are several models of portfolio assessment—some more product-oriented, some more process-oriented—the key is to select a model that is well rooted in the values, needs, and concerns of the specific learning environment. A usable definition for *portfolio* is that it is an assembly of evidence, a collection, a repertoire of writing or writing-related performances that illustrates a particular set of values, concerns, and expectations. As artifacts of talents, abilities, and performance, therefore, portfolios serve as a multidirectional mechanism for curriculum evaluation and development, for teaching, and for learning. Several features seem worthy of noting:

1. Conceived as either a product or a process, portfolios facilitate the development of a community of discourse within which to engage in ongoing dialogue about knowledge, learning, and performance.

2. In inviting a consideration of multiple measures, interpretations, and reading over time and across tasks, purposes, and genres, portfolios become the embodiment of learning and pedagogy, so that the curriculum is less likely to be driven by assessment and more likely to be driven by learning.

3. As an organic tool, portfolios focus on the acquisition, development, and demonstration of particular strengths as these strengths constitute consensus definitions of learning and achievement.

4. Portfolios make room for students in their own learning, offering them opportunities to develop a sense of their responsibilities as learners and a sense of authority over what, indeed, they have managed to learn.

5. Portfolios provide systematic moments at which both teachers and students, independently and collaboratively, can engage in the type of talk and reflection that maximizes the capacity for assessment to filter itself more productively and positively throughout the learning process.

The challenge, therefore, is really to reconceive *testing and evaluation as a multidimensional measurement of learning and achievement.* The push is to defuse the adversarial nature of the testing relationship so that teachers are in a position to identify, reaffirm, and reward growth, development, and achievement.

Writer's Choice helps students establish, maintain, and assess portfolios:
- Criteria for self-evaluation accompany Writing Process in Action.
- Reflection and Portfolio activities within the Unit Review end each unit.

Writer's Choice provides instruments for testing and evaluation in addition to portfolios:
- Tests include both objective forms and holistic forms.
- Composition tests include criteria for the student's self-evaluation.
- Pretests and Mastery Tests cover Grammar, Usage, Mechanics, and Resources.
- Tests are available in both print form and as *Test Generator* software (IBM, Apple, Macintosh).

Writing Across the Curriculum

by Beverly Ann Chin

Professor of English, University of Montana; Director of the Montana Writing Project

What Is Writing Across the Curriculum?

Writing across the curriculum integrates subject area instruction with writing instruction. Teachers who implement a writing across the curriculum program view writing as a way to help students learn and think in different subject areas. When students write about specific subject area concepts, students *use writing as a means for discovering what they know, what they want to know, and what they've learned.* Through writing, we help students engage in the higher-level thinking skills of application, analysis, synthesis, and evaluation. We also encourage students to reflect on their feelings and progress as learners in the subject area.

In many writing across the curriculum programs, the terms "writing to learn" and "writing process" are intertwined. Writing to learn emphasizes the importance of writing as a tool for discovering ideas and gaining insights. When students engage in *writing to learn*, the writing becomes a vehicle for inquiry, hypothesis, and reflection. Often the writing is ungraded because the audience for the writing is the learner. The writing may or may not result in a "product."

Writing process refers to the recursive stages of prewriting, drafting, revising, editing, and publishing/presenting. Writing process teachers understand that students may vary in the amount of time needed for different writing projects. We also realize that all pieces of writing need not advance to the publishing stage. We value the learning that occurs in unfinished writing, and we celebrate the sharing that results from published writing.

Writing across the curriculum does not mean that "new" content is added to our subject areas. Rather, writing across the

---

Writer's Choice provides numerous opportunities for students to discover what they know, what they want to know, and what they've learned:

- Writing assignments cover art, science, social studies, mathematics, music, and, of course, literature.
- Case Studies explore and model how today's professionals write in the world of work.
- *Writing Across the Curriculum* blackline masters provide practical help for writing in content areas.
- *Research Paper and Report Writing* blackline masters offer cross-curricular support.

Writer's Choice encourages students to write to learn:

- Individual lessons cover such topics as Keeping a Learning Log, Writing to Learn, and Keeping a Reader-Response Journal.
- Annotations in the Teacher's Wraparound Edition identify points of intersection between English and other curriculum areas.

curriculum focuses our attention on "how" students learn and make sense of knowledge. When we use writing across the curriculum strategies in our teaching, students become better learners, and better communicators, in the different subject areas.

How Can We Help Our Students Use Writing to Learn in Different Subject Areas?

The most effective writing strategies are those that encourage students to write often and to reflect on their learning. One way of *inviting students to write* in any subject area is the journal. In the journal (or learning log), students enter their observations and feelings about subject area concepts. For example, in science, students record notes analyzing the data from an ongoing earth science experiment. In social studies, students create a chart on how different television stations report local news events during a one-week period. In English, students reflect on how an author creates suspense in an adventure novel they are reading. By making regular entries in their journals, students document their growth as thinkers.

The journal is also a place where students can do prewriting or drafting of an idea for a piece of writing. Students can share their journal ideas with classmates and use these ideas in future writing assignments.

Another important strategy in teaching writing across the curriculum is the creation of writing assignments that *reflect real-world writing*. When we write to communicate to other people, we have a clear purpose and audience for our writing. Writing assignments that incorporate writing purpose and audience create motivation for students to write. Helping students see themselves in different roles also gives students the opportunity to experiment with different voices. For example, an art writing assignment can ask students to imagine that they are museum curators. As museum curators, they must write a brochure that describes a new exhibit and that invites the community to see the exhibit. During a social studies unit on the California gold rush, students can imagine they are Chinese immigrants living in California in the mid-1800s. In a letter to their families in China, they describe their new life in the mining camps. Through these types of writing assignments, students reveal their insights into the subject area.

When we engage our students in writing across the curriculum, we motivate students to explore subject area knowledge as well as provide them with a powerful tool for lifelong learning.

Writer's Choice is a program of *invitation* and *instruction:*

- Journal Writing activities occur in every composition lesson.
- Annotated models invite student response.
- Case Studies and Literature selections invite student response.
- Guided Practice, Independent Practice, and Cross-Curricular activities invite the kinds of choices that generate student engagement.
- Writing Process in Action gives even more extended modeling and guidance.

Writer's Choice motivates students with real-world writing:

- Purpose, audience, and real-world context identified for writing assignments
- Case Studies of the writing process at work in real-world situations
- Student models by real student writers

Writing and Thinking

Writer's Choice is built on the belief that writing and thinking are closely connected:
- Clear, manageable lessons help students think through specific writing situations.
- Journal Writing activities support each composition lesson.
- A writing objective, as well as critical thinking and speaking and listening skills, is identified in the Teacher's Wraparound Edition for every writing lesson.

Writer's Choice involves students in the personal, active, and integrative processes of thinking:
- Student-friendly text and visuals
- Student models by real students
- Literature that engages contemporary readers
- Readers Respond to the Model pages that foster critical thinking
- Choices of assignments that enable students to draw on their own personal experiences and cross-curricular interests

by Philip M. Anderson
Associate Professor, Department of Secondary Education and Youth Services, and Director of the English Education Program, Queens College, City University of New York

How Can Writing Develop Thinking?

The *connections between writing and thinking* are not well established in schools. Allan Glatthorn's analysis of thinking skills programs found most rely on oral language, some ignoring written language altogether. Similarly, many "writing across the curriculum" programs give scant attention to thinking skills, instead restricting instruction solely to formal aspects of the term paper or note-taking techniques for lectures (in Frances Link, ed., *Essays on the Intellect*, ASCD, 1985).

Research conducted on thinking argues that cognitive processes must be taught, since they do not arise instinctively from social experience. Furthermore, students must strive to articulate tacit knowledge, i.e., personal knowledge residing below conscious levels of thinking (the phenomenon of "knowing more than we can say"). Tacit knowledge frequently establishes assumptions when we think about an issue or solve a problem.

In this regard, writing represents an important means for teaching thinking since it involves *personal, active, and integrative cognitive processes.* But, cognitive structures underlying writing need to be made explicit, allowing for a reciprocal relationship between growth in thinking and growth in writing.

How Can Thinking Be Taught During the Writing Process?

Many students perceive school writing as "knowledge telling"; they write all they know about a subject and stop. They expend little effort in expanding, analyzing, or reformulating that knowledge. As a result, academic writing frequently lacks coherence and rarely offers new understandings. However, teachers can remedy the situation by *emphasizing thinking,* and teaching cognitive structure, *throughout the recursive writing process.*

Journal writing provides a means for uncovering and examining tacit knowledge during prewriting. Reflection and reconstruction of ideas are encouraged when students articulate personal knowledge. Since the journal symbolizes recorded thought, opportunities to interact with one's own thinking over time are also accommodated.

Techniques such as graphic mapping (Venn diagram, e.g.) and thinking frames (compare/contrast, problem/solution, e.g.) enhance student thinking prior to writing and provide direction during the composing process. Structured prewriting assists student writers in organizing thought and determining means for completing the writing task.

Teachers can nurture student thinking during the writing process by "scaffolding" instruction. Scaffolding is a strategy in which teachers collaborate with students by carrying out parts of a task students temporarily need adult support to accomplish. Some forms of scaffolding include teacher modeling of process, frame categories and questions, changing misconceptions, and coaching (B. F. Jones, et al., *Teaching Thinking Skills: English/ Language Arts,* NEA, 1987).

Scaffolded instruction may employ face-to-face interaction, such as conferencing during revision. Peer and teacher dialogue with the student writer during revision, if more than mere editing, must focus on meaning and organization of thought.

But, scaffolding is also employed when the teacher clearly spells out the writing assignment by defining key features of structure and content. Students then can assess and construe the goals of the assignment, both discourse form and intellectual organization, providing an appropriate response within supportive guidelines provided by the teacher.

Finally, teaching students about the process of composing and the author's situation serves a metacognitive (i.e., conscious control of thinking strategies) function within writing instruction. Some research even suggests that misconceptions about the purpose and function of composing may be the primary culprit in poor writing achievement.

Process models of composing and cognitive process instruction are not incompatible components of the school curriculum. Each can advance the improvement of the other, resulting in students who can *think clearly and independently as well as effectively.*

Writer's Choice emphasizes thinking throughout the recursive writing process:
- Writing Process Tips recur throughout composition lessons.
- Writing Process in Action reinforces "revisiting" of previous thinking and writing.
- Case Studies exemplify the recursive writing process in the real world.

Writer's Choice fosters independent thinking and writing:
- Writing Process in Action includes criteria for self-evaluation.
- Reflection and Adding to Your Portfolio in each Unit Review focus students' thoughts about their writing.
- Troubleshooter helps students help themselves.
- *Thinking and Study Skills* blackline masters provide additional practice and activities.

Cooperative Learning

by **Charleen Silva Delfino**
English Coordinator, East Side Union High School District, San Jose, California;
Director of the San Jose Area Writing Project

Walking down the hallway, I heard voices coming out of F-22, and I smiled as I neared Mrs. Kennett's classroom. I knew that the noise I heard was the sound of eager students energetically discussing their friends' writing. Entering the room, I watched young writers asking questions, making suggestions, trying different options. When was the last time I had seen young people this engaged in the process of writing? Certainly, there weren't many models. Writing, especially in schools, is often a lonely enterprise entered into without great enthusiasm. What was different in F-22?

These students, representing many cultures—African American, Japanese, Hispanic, Filipino, Vietnamese, European American, Chinese—worked in groups of four responding to the historical fiction they had written based on a story of a family member who had moved to a new area. These stories were to be published in a class anthology about the immigrant experience. What was different? These students were engaged in a *practical cooperative learning activity*. They had a real audience and a real purpose for their writing. They had something to say because they cared about their own writing and they cared about the writing of the members of their group.

Isn't Cooperative Learning Just Group Work?

Certainly, cooperative learning is group work, but it is more than what is implied in "just group work." If a teacher tells students to get into groups and discuss their writing, the chances are very good that students will say something like, "I like your writing; it is really good." And then they will go on to discuss more pressing matters—like the dance Friday night or the bas-

---

Writer's Choice incorporates practical cooperative learning activities:

- Writing Activities often include a choice of a cooperative learning activity.
- Additional optional cooperative activities appear in Teacher's Wraparound Edition.
- Peer response and peer editing are encouraged.

ketball game after school. Students need to be *trained in a variety of ways of providing feedback* to each other about their writing. They need to learn how to ask questions that will give them the assistance they need. Certainly, this is not a natural gift that all students possess. They don't have the language to engage in these kinds of discussions (not many adults do either), but they can be trained.

Why Cooperative Learning?

Cooperative learning is not a panacea; it is not the answer to every problem. It is not the only method of instruction I employ, but it is certainly an important part of my classroom and my students' learning experience. With cooperative learning students need to be actively involved in their instruction; they are not passive participants in the learning process. Also, in the small group activities, students are more willing to participate and risk. If the group is constructed well, each student has a part and a contribution to make. The different learning styles and abilities of each student can be addressed. In heterogeneously grouped classes and classes with second language learners, these students' needs can be met. Students are forced to use the language to communicate with others.

What Makes Cooperative Learning Groups Work?

Careful planning is an essential step in making groups work. I have developed five rules that have made cooperative learning more successful for me:

1. Give clear directions, being sure that all students understand what is expected of them and what they are going to do.
2. Model with the whole class whatever you expect the students to do in their small groups.
3. Have students responsible for something concrete when they are finished.
4. Assign less time than you think they will need; it is easier to give more time than to take it away.
5. Vary the purpose and the activity of cooperative learning groups. Although students like some structure, too much repetition leads to boredom.

What is important is that learning be student-centered and that each student take an active role, making decisions and staying involved in the learning process.

Writer's Choice includes cooperative learning activities that fit a variety of purposes:
• Choices include brainstorming for prewriting, peer response for revision, responding to literature, responding to fine art, group problem-solving, and research for group writing.

Writer's Choice offers cooperative learning activities that are carefully planned and defined:
• Students are given clear, step-by-step guidance for cooperative activities.
• Teacher's Wraparound Edition provides detailed, concrete suggestions for additional cooperative activities, including round-robin, pairs check, three-step interview, think-pair-share, roundtable, partners, and co-op co-op.

Teaching Grammar and Usage

by Mark Lester
Professor of English, Eastern Washington University; formerly Chair of the Department of English as a Second Language, University of Hawaii

Why Do We Teach Grammar?

Children do not need to go to school to learn their native language, but they need to go to school to learn to think and talk about it. All native speakers of a language have a vast intuitive knowledge of the rules of their language. However, this knowledge is so deeply below the level of conscious awareness that native speakers cannot easily talk or even consciously think about how their own language works. Our language is a vehicle for conveying our thoughts; it is very difficult for us to learn to focus on the vehicle rather than on the meaning the vehicle conveys.

The study of grammar in school gives students the concepts and terms necessary for *talking and thinking about the vehicle of language*. A conscious knowledge of grammatical concepts and terms is also necessary for students to compare and contrast their use of language with other people's use of language and to explore alternative ways of expressing their own ideas.

How Can We Teach Grammar Effectively?

Research shows us that just teaching grammar terminology by itself is ineffectual. Grammar terminology is enormously abstract and loaded with hidden assumptions. Robert deBeaugrande compared grammar terminology to a ladder with the bottom rungs cut out—if you don't already know the concept underlying the terminology, the terminology itself will be of

Writer's Choice helps students learn to talk and think about the vehicle of language:
• Clear, manageable, two-page grammar lessons
• Visual/verbals that convey grammar concepts and examples graphically

little use to you. For example, the definition of preposition as "a word that shows the relationship of a noun or pronoun to some other word in a sentence" is incomprehensible unless you already know that a preposition is part of a prepositional phrase, that prepositions have noun or pronoun objects, and that prepositional phrases function as adjective or adverb modifiers. In order to grasp grammar terminology, students first need *numerous examples and extensive practice sessions* to grasp the concepts underlying the term.

Two techniques that help students grasp grammatical concepts are sentence combining and paraphrase tests. Sentence combining shows students how sentences with multiple phrases and clauses are built from underlying simple sentences. Sentence combining also allows students to compare and evaluate the grammatical and stylistic effect of different ways of combining the same simple sentences. Paraphrase tests that tap into students' unconscious knowledge of their language are practical ways of identifying grammatical concepts. For example, the definition of a noun as the name of "a person, a place, a thing, or an idea" doesn't really tell the student what a noun is. After all, even though *blue* is the name of a color and thus appears to fit the definition of a noun, *blue* still isn't a noun. However, learning that nouns typically follow the definite article *the* and can be made plural gives students two simple tests that they can use to see if a word is a noun. Since we cannot say *The sky is the blue* or *The sky is blues*, *blue* cannot be a noun in these sentences.

How Can We Teach Usage Effectively?

U sage is the way that we use grammar. Grammar provides a vocabulary that students and teachers need in order to talk about usage problems. For example, talking to a student about the subject-verb agreement errors in the student's paper would be very difficult if the student did not know what the terms *subject* and *verb* meant. However, just teaching grammar by itself to students does not necessarily help students with their usage problems. Not surprisingly, grammar taught in isolation from the students' usage problems is learned in isolation from usage problems.

Good grammar programs constantly *connect grammar to usage problems in the students' own writing*. Probably the most effective way of dealing with usage problems is the following: (a) collect examples of the error from the students' own papers; (b) have the students discuss the error, focusing on what the error is and how it can be corrected; and (c) back up the discussion with relevant exercises on grammar and usage.

Writer's Choice provides numerous examples and extensive practice in grammar and usage:
- Thematic exercises that are a natural part of every Grammar, Usage, and Mechanics lesson
- Alternative strategies for students of all ability levels provided in the Teacher's Wraparound Edition

Writer's Choice connects grammar and usage to students' own writing:
- Writing Process Grammar Tips in the composition units to further the integration of grammar and writing
- Grammar Reviews at the end of every grammar unit to integrate grammar, writing, and literature
- Troubleshooter that offers students a handy self-help guide to grammar, usage, and mechanics

Visual Learning

by Josef Godlewski
Executive Design Director, Ligature, Inc., Chicago and Boston

and Daniel Rogers
Executive Editorial Director, Ligature, Inc., Chicago and Boston

Why Are Visual Learning Strategies Important?

To be truly literate in a modern technological culture, we need to comprehend and use both verbal and visual literacies." This claim, made by Richard Sinatra and Josephine Stahl-Gemake in *Using the Right Brain in the Language Arts*, has important ramifications for the English classroom. Clearly, English teachers consider the development of verbal literacy as central to their mission, but what do we mean by visual literacy? Loosely defined, visual literacy encompasses a set of skills that enable an individual to decode and interpret images and visual representations of concepts, to use images and visual representations to communicate effectively, and to understand and enjoy the creative works of visual artists.

In a culture permeated by television, computer games, and other electronic media, students come to school with a rich experience in receiving and interpreting messages that are at once both visual and verbal. Rather than presenting a cause for alarm, this experience offers an opportunity for effective instructional materials and strategies to meet the learning needs of all students.

We can begin to use visual strategies to enhance instruction by first acknowledging that *presentations which effectively combine visual and verbal elements* are more compelling than text alone, particularly for students who have grown up in a video culture. We know from brain research that visual messages are processed largely in the brain's right hemisphere, while the processing of verbal messages takes place mainly in the left hemisphere. In essence, then, the compelling nature of video derives in large measure from its dual message that simultaneously stimulates

Writer's Choice enhances instruction by effectively combining visual and verbal elements:
- Sparkling visuals that grab and hold students' attention
- Computer graphics that clearly illustrate concepts and processes
- Visual Thinking annotations in the Teacher's Wraparound Edition with strategies for improving students' thinking and writing

two discrete regions of the brain. In the classroom, visuals that relate instructionally to the text can engage students' attention and serve as a gateway to a concept or skill to be explored verbally. This function of engagement and connection to personal experience is a necessary first step in the learning process.

An integrated combination of visual and verbal presentations can also provide greater access to concepts and skills for students of varied learning styles. For example, graphic organizers are a particularly powerful means of representing processes and relationships. Not just visual learners but all students can benefit from using a flow chart to represent the steps in a process or a Venn diagram to highlight similarities and differences.

In addition, *a memorable graphic representation of a key concept or relationship* provides a useful mnemonic tool for all learners. Again, brain research indicates that visual memories are formed and retrieved very differently from verbal memories. Thus, the association of an image with a particular concept can enhance students' ability to recall and apply that concept.

How Can Visuals Promote the Development of Student Writing?

Photographs and fine art can provide *points of entry to writing through visual exploration*. At the most basic level, students can write a personal response to a visual just as they would to a piece of literature. Similarly, they can describe what they see, narrate the story depicted, or write persuasively about their aesthetic judgment of the painting or photo.

At a more significant level, however, students can explore analogies between the writing process and the creative processes of photography and painting. Opportunities to explore the process of composing a photograph or other visual message can help students discover principles that they can apply to their written compositions. Like a writer, a photographer must select a subject, a focus, and a point of view. Similarly, both photographers and writers create a mood—one through the choice of lighting and camera angles, the other through the choice of words and sentence structure.

The ultimate payoff from these visual-verbal approaches to instruction lies in helping students become more effective communicators and more discerning recipients of communication. As they come to recognize the parallels between written and visual communication, they become better equipped to apply critical thinking skills both in their reading and writing and in their viewing.

Writer's Choice provides memorable graphic representations of key concepts and relationships:
- State-of-the-art graphics to help students see the connections between observing, thinking, and writing
- Visuals that offer an alternate mode of information delivery that is especially helpful for today's visually oriented students

Writer's Choice provides points of entry to writing through visual exploration:
- Fine art and contemporary photography for stimulating thinking and writing
- Fine Art Overhead Transparencies for additional writing prompts
- Writing Process Overhead Transparencies for easy-to-use graphic organizers and revision models

WRITER'S CHOICE

GRAMMAR AND COMPOSITION

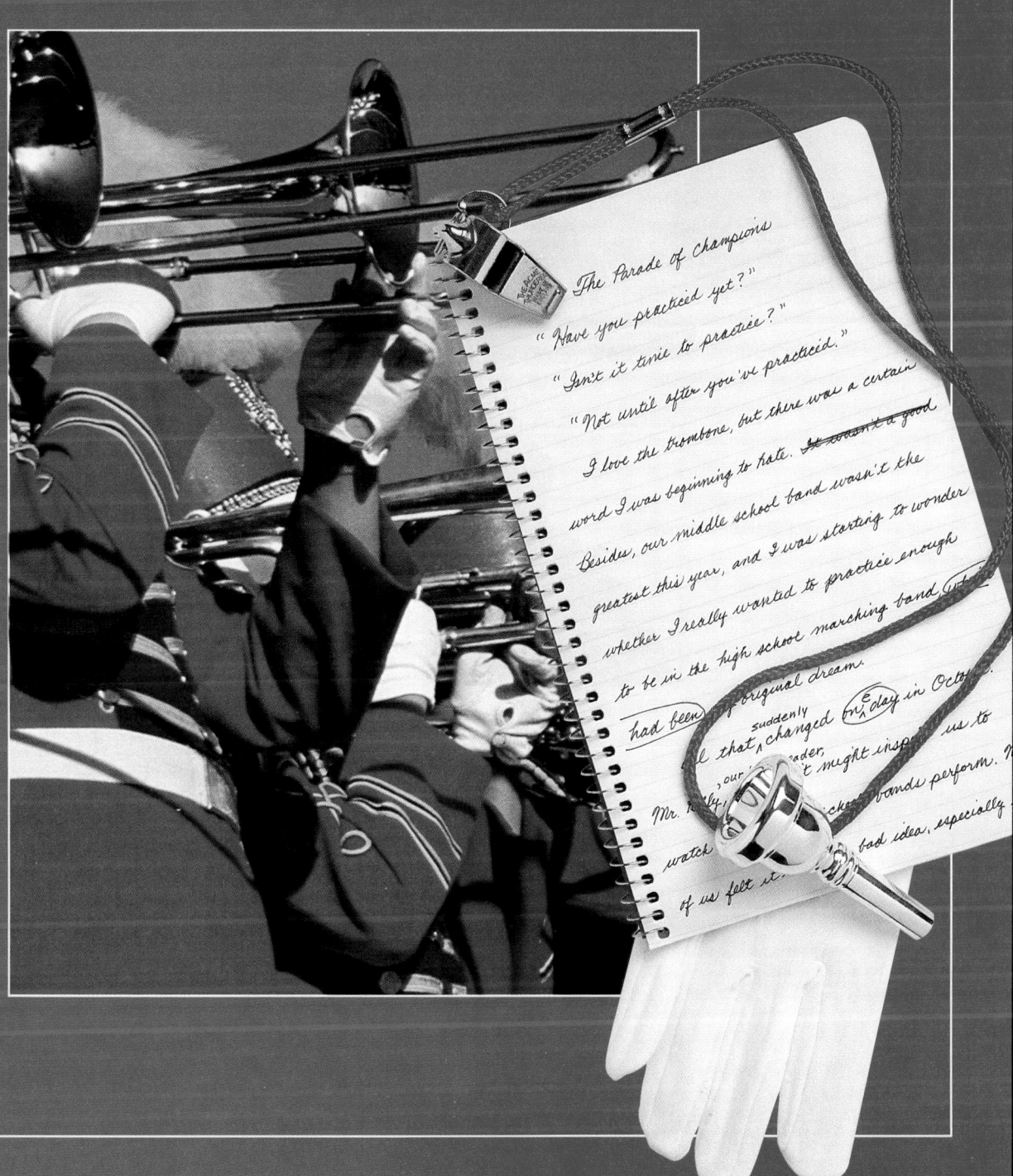

The Parade of Champions

"Have you practiced yet?"

"Isn't it time to practice?"

"Not until after you've practiced."

I love the trombone, but there was a certain word I was beginning to hate. It wasn't a good

Besides, our middle school band wasn't the greatest this year, and I was starting to wonder whether I really wanted to practice enough to be in the high school marching band that had been my original dream.

All that suddenly changed one day in October. Mr. _____, our _____ leader, _____ it might inspire _____ us to watch _____ bands perform. _____ bad idea, especially _____ of us felt it.

Student Advisory Board

Eliza Ali

Joshua Zapata

Nitida Wongthipkongka

Benjamin Rodriguez

Shanna Brechenfeld

Keianna Chatman

Alina Braica

Faris Karadsheh

Marinel A. Marty

Trina Chu

Paul Roustan

Tashaunda Jackson

WRITER'S CHOICE

GRAMMAR AND COMPOSITION

Thomas Hart Benton, *Cradling Wheat,* 1938

Consulting Author for Composition
Jacqueline Jones Royster

Grammar Specialist
Mark Lester

Visual-Verbal Learning Specialists
Ligature, Inc.

McGraw-Hill

New York, New York   Columbus, Ohio   Mission Hills, California   Peoria, Illinois

Consulting Author for Composition

Jacqueline Jones Royster is Associate Professor of English and Director of the University Writing Center at The Ohio State University. She is also on the faculty at the Bread Loaf School of English, Middlebury, Vermont. Dr. Royster's professional interests, besides improving the teaching of writing, include literacy studies and black feminist literature.

As Consulting Author, Dr. Royster guided the development of focused, modular lessons to engage middle school students in the writing process. She contributed to the articulation of the contents and objectives across all three levels, 6–8. Dr. Royster also prepared extensive critiques of lessons and features from initial outlines through all stages of development. In addition, Dr. Royster advised on elements of the accompanying teaching material, with special attention to assessment.

Grammar Specialist

Mark Lester is Professor of English at Eastern Washington University. He formerly served as Chair of the Department of English as a Second Language, University of Hawaii. He is the author of *Grammar in the Classroom* (Macmillan, 1990) and of numerous professional books and articles.

As Grammar Specialist, Dr. Lester reviewed student's edition material from Part 2: Grammar, Usage, and Mechanics and contributed extensively to the *Teacher's Wraparound Edition* for Part 2.

Composition Advisers

Philip M. Anderson is Associate Professor in the Department of Secondary Education and Youth Services at Queens College, City University of New York, where he is also Director of the English Education program.

Beverly Ann Chin is Professor of English at the University of Montana, where she is Director of Freshman Composition and Co-director of English Teacher Education. She is also Director of the Montana Writing Project and is active in NCTE, serving as President-Elect (1995–1996) and President (1996–1997).

Charleen Silva Delfino is District English Coordinator for the East Side Union High School District in San Jose, California. She is also Director of the Writing Project at San Jose University.

The advisers helped develop the tables of contents and determine pacing, emphasis, and activities appropriate for middle school students. They reviewed and commented on the manuscript for complete units.

Acknowledgments

Grateful acknowledgment is given authors, publishers, photographers, museums, and agents for permission to reprint the following copyrighted material. Every effort has been made to determine copyright owners. In case of omissions, the Publisher will make acknowledgments in future editions.
Continued on page 726

Humanities Consultant

Ronne Hartfield is Executive Director of Museum Education at the Art Institute of Chicago. Dr. Hartfield consults widely and is a nationally known expert in the areas of urban arts and multicultural education.

As Humanities Consultant, Dr. Hartfield suggested and critiqued works of fine art and folk art, pointing out esthetic matters (mentioned in the *Teacher's Wraparound Edition*) and suggesting activities for engaging the student's attention.

Visual-Verbal Learning Specialists

Ligature, Inc., is an educational research and development company with offices in Chicago and Boston. Ligature is committed to developing educational materials that bring visual-verbal learning to the tradition of the written word.

As visual-verbal and curriculum specialists, Ligature collaborated on conceiving and implementing the pedagogy of *Writer's Choice*.

Educational Reviewers

The reviewers read and commented upon manuscripts during the writing process. They also critiqued early drafts of graphic organizers and page layouts.

Toni Elaine Allison
Meridian Middle School
Meridian, Idaho

Geraldine Jackson
Mountain Gap Middle School
Huntsville, Alabama

Roslyn Newman
Woodland Middle School
East Meadow, New York

Amy Burton
Sterling Middle School
Fairfax, Virginia

Jeanne Kruger
Blair Middle School
Norfolk, Virginia

Evelyn Niles
Boys and Girls High School
Brooklyn, New York

Mary Ann Evans-Patrick
University of Wisconsin, Oshkosh
Oshkosh, Wisconsin

Diana McNeil
Pillans Middle School
Mobile, Alabama

Janet E. Ring
Dundee School District 300
Carpentersville, Illinois

Marie Hammerle
Oak Creek Elementary School
Cornville, Arizona

Linda Miller
Lake Travis Middle School
Austin, Texas

Kathleen Oldfield
Main Street School
Waterloo, New York

Randy Hanson
Mapplewood Middle School
Menasha, Wisconsin

Nadine Mouser
St. Thomas More School
Houston, Texas

Student Advisory Board

The Student Advisory Board was formed in an effort to ensure student involvement in the development of *Writer's Choice*. The editors wish to thank members of the board for their enthusiasm and dedication to the project.

The editors also wish to thank the many student writers whose models appear in this book.

Thanks are also due to *Merlyn's Pen* and *Cricket* for cooperation in providing student models.

Contents

Part 1 Composition

UNIT 1 Personal Writing

Grammar Link

Use the correct verb form when the subject of a sentence is an indefinite pronoun.

Some indefinite pronouns—*all, any, most, none,* and *some*—can be either singular or plural, depending on the phrase that follows.

What **are some** of the problems astro-nauts will face . . .?

Complete each sentence with the correct choice of verb.

1. All of the water (is, are) crucial.
2. None of the other planets (is, are) hospitable to human life.
3. Most of the problems (has, have)

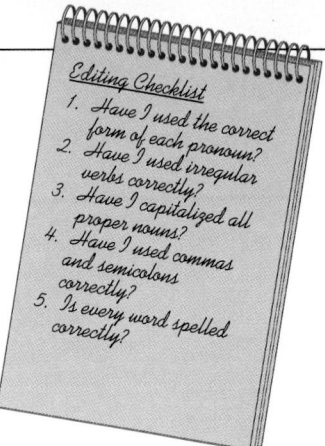

UNIT 2 The Writing Process

UNIT 3
Descriptive Writing

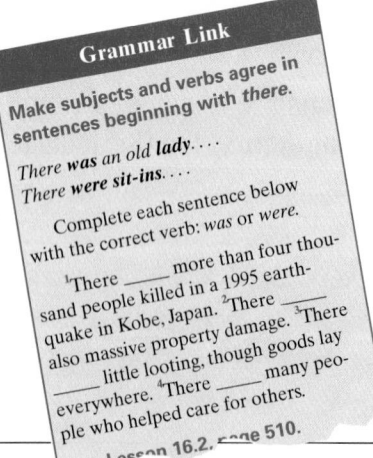

Grammar Link

Make subjects and verbs agree in
sentences beginning with *there*.

*There **was** an old lady. . . .*
*There **were** sit-ins. . . .*

Complete each sentence below
with the correct verb: *was* or *were*.

[1]There ____ more than four thousand people killed in a 1995 earthquake in Kobe, Japan. [2]There ____
also massive property damage. [3]There
____ little looting, though goods lay
everywhere. [4]There ____ many people who helped care for others.

See Lesson 16.2, page 510.

Editing Checklist
1. *Do all my subjects and verbs agree?*
2. *Do all my pronouns have clear antecedents?*
3. *Have I used commas correctly?*
4. *Have I used apostrophes correctly in possessive nouns?*
5. *Have I spelled every word correctly?*

UNIT 4 Narrative Writing

CONTENTS

UNIT 5 Expository Writing

Grammar Link

Avoid double negatives.

The injury means **no** more football, **no** more soccer, **no** more baseball, **or** anything!

This sentence is a strong negative statement, but if the author had ended it "no nothing," he would have confused his meaning with a double negative.

Revise each sentence below to eliminate double negatives.

1. Sometimes football players don't have no protective equipment.
2. How people dress isn't none of

UNIT 7 Troubleshooter 301

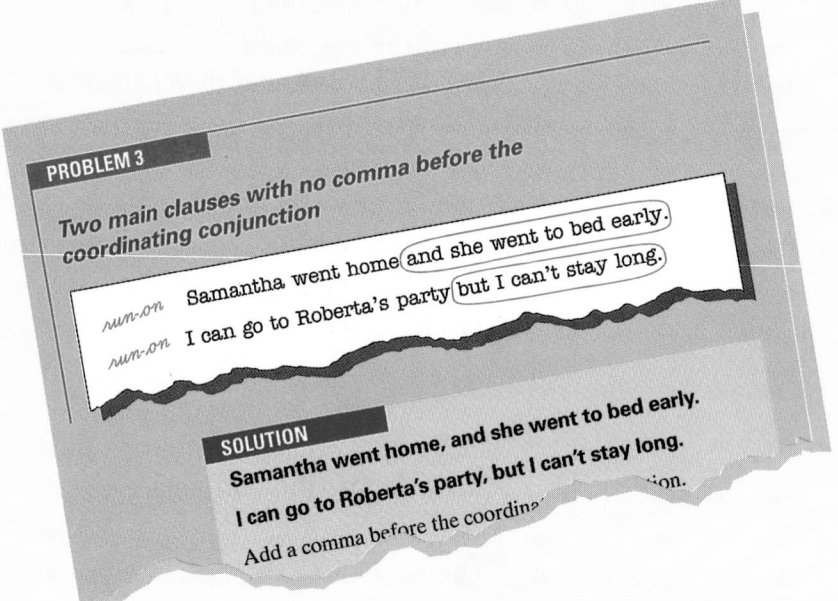

PROBLEM 3

Two main clauses with no comma before the coordinating conjunction

run-on   Samantha went home and she went to bed early.

run-on   I can go to Roberta's party but I can't stay long.

SOLUTION

Samantha went home, and she went to bed early.

I can go to Roberta's party, but I can't stay long.

Add a comma before the coordina... ...ion.

Part 2 Grammar, Usage, and Mechanics

Proofreading

Louis Armstrong was a **real** innovator in jazz.

Irregular Comparative and Superlative Forms		
Adverb	Comparative	Superlative
well	better	best
badly	worse	worst
little (amount)	less	least
far (distance)	farther	farthest

His music was **really** popular.

UNIT 13 Prepositions, Conjunctions, and Interjections 447

UNIT 14 Clauses and Complex Sentences 471

The team . . .

. . . **collect** cans and bottles at the shore.

Computers solve **problems**.

| Computers | solve | problems |

Computers process **data**.

| Computers | process | data |

Proofreading

We have a
picture of our
great **a**unt **M**eg.

Here is **G**reat
Aunt **M**eg
marching for
women's rights.

Part 3 Resources and Skills

UNIT 22 Library and Reference Resources 607

UNIT 23 Vocabulary and Spelling 629

Literature Models

Fine Art

Fine art—paintings, drawings, photos, and sculpture—is used to teach as well as to stimulate writing ideas.

Case Studies:
Writers at Work

Each case study focuses on a real writer working
on a real-life writing project. Come on backstage!

Indira Freitas Johnson

Artist
Proposal, *Johnson
Persuades with Proposals*
Pages 254–259

Laurence Yep

Memoir Writer
Memoir, *Yep Pieces
His Past Together*
Pages 4–9

Gary McLain (Eagle/Walking Turtle)

Travel Writer
Expository Writing, *McLain
Guides Travelers*
Pages 190–195

Bill Kurtis

Television Journalist
Documentary, *Kurtis
Explores Science*
Pages 42–47

Arthur Johnson

Historical Actor
Narrative, *Johnson
Interprets Ashby*
Pages 142–147

Julia Alvarez

Novelist
Novel, *Alvarez
Describes Home*
Pages 100–105

Part 1

Composition

The Morning After the Ice Storm

Outside my frosted window
The ground shines like metal.
Morning sunlight reflects o
The snow-covered rooftops and
Blinds me momentaril
Across the street m
Neighbor's ancient   k tree
Glistens in the   o bright
Light, its bra   hes wearing
Sleeves of ice

The ice fr   es all sounds,
all movements.

Part 1 Composition

2

UNIT

1 Personal Writing

Composition | **Lessons**

3

UNIT GOALS

The goal of Unit 1 is to help students, through example and instruction, to develop an ability to express their feelings and ideas through personal writing. The lessons show students how to express themselves in journals, learning logs, and other forms of personal writing.

Unit Assessment
📂 *Tests with Answer Key*
Unit 1 Choice A Test, p. 1
Unit 1 Choice B Test, p. 2
Unit 1 Composition Objective Test,
pp. 3–4

🔘 *Test Generator*
Unit 1 Choice A Test
Unit 1 Choice B Test
Unit 1 Composition Objective Test

You may wish to administer either the Unit 1 Choice A Test or the Unit 1 Choice B Test as a pretest.

Key to Ability Levels
Enabling Strategies have been coded for varying learning styles and abilities.

L1 Level 1 activities are within the ability range of Learning Disabled students.

L2 Level 2 activities are basic-to-average activities and are within the ability range of average students.

L3 Level 3 activities are challenging activities and are within the ability range of above-average students.

LEP LEP activities are within the ability range of Limited English Proficiency students.

FOCUS

Lesson Overview
Objective: To observe how a personal account is developed from events and responses from the writer's past
Skills: recalling experiences; observing; assembling a story; evaluating
Critical Thinking: analysis; synthesis; recalling; relating; defining and clarifying; visualizing; identifying
Speaking and Listening: note taking; discussing; questioning

Bellringer
When students enter the classroom, have this assignment on the board: *If you were writing a memoir about your life, what main events would you want to include? List the events and a phrase or two about each one.*

Grammar Link to the Bellringer
Discuss the Bellringer and the phrases that help readers picture events. Point out how these phrases can be written as appositives to add details to a sentence.

Motivating Activity
Invite students to describe times when they've tried to recapture a past event. Did the memory come back instantly, or after a while? Did it elude them completely? Did they use some kind of strategy to remember the event? Explain that writer Laurence Yep found a unique way to bring the memories back—by remembering smells.

Personal Writing
in the Real World

Yep Pieces His Past Together

F O C U S: Personal writing in the form of a memoir can help you look back and rethink your past.

▲ *Memoir author Laurence Yep*

Laurence Yep, award-winning writer of fantasies, went in a totally new direction when he decided to write *The Lost Garden*. This personal story, or memoir, of growing up in San Francisco challenged him to piece together his past. He began writing the book shortly after his father's death. "In a way, *The Lost Garden* was therapy," Yep explains. "It was my way to go back to these various places I used to go to with my father, and in some cases I tried to do it physically, but most of the time it was in my imagination and in my memory."

4   *Personal Writing: A Mirror of Myself*

Teacher's Classroom Resources

The following resources can be used for planning, instruction, practice, reinforcement, assessment, or evaluation.

🖋 **Teaching Tools**
Lesson Plans, p. 1

🖌 **Transparencies**
Writing Process Transparencies, 1–10

Writing a Memoir

Prewriting	Drafting	Revising

| Gathering Memories and Stepping Back | Assembling the Pieces | Testing the Fit |

"I think writers take bits and pieces of the world around them—things they see, things they remember, feelings they felt—and start assembling them in ways to create a world you can walk through and inhabit."

—Laurence Yep

Prewriting

GATHERING MEMORIES AND STEPPING BACK

People make memories by living; writers re-create memories by writing. To write a memoir, a writer must use senses other than sight to evoke, or call up, memories. "The layer of memory that is closest to the brain is not a layer of visual memories; it's the memory of smells. That's why a smell is more evocative than any visual detail," Yep explains.

Yep used memories of smells to help him mentally reconstruct his family's grocery store. The smell

▼ *Specific details—such as the jars of mango chutney in the Yep family's store—are powerful elements in a memoir.*

TEACH

Building Background

Warm-up:
Ask students to brainstorm a list of situations in which personal writing might be used.

Personal Reflection in Speaking:
Discuss times when people reveal what they are thinking and feeling to others, such as in conversations, speeches, some games, and meetings.

Personal Reflection in Writing:
Discuss any personal writing students have read. Ask questions such as
• What is the difference between personal writing and descriptions of a fictional character's feelings?
• What makes some personal writing interesting? What makes some personal writing not interesting?

Preview the Case Study
Have students scan the headings and captions of the Case Study to shape their expectations about what they will read. Remind students of any Laurence Yep books they have read. Then have students read the Case Study.

📁 **Blackline Masters**
Cooperative Learning Activities,
  pp. 1–6
Thinking and Study Skills,
  pp. 5, 13, 18
Case Studies: Writing in the Real World, pp. 1–4

Assessment
📁 *Teacher's Guide to Writing Assessment*

TEACH

Discussion Prompts

- What does Yep mean by saying, "the best writing is bringing out the specialness of ordinary things"? How can a writer make ordinary things seem special?
- Do you agree with Yep's differentiation between experiencing an event and understanding it? How would you put that idea in your own words? Do you have any examples?

▲ *Photos of the Pearl Apartments, where Yep lived as a boy, and the family store in San Francisco helped Yep when he was gathering memories.*

of crumbling plaster and wall materials brought back the hot summer afternoons he spent in a place that no longer exists. Smells brought back sights as one memory led to another.

"From there I drew a map of the whole store, as best I could, and as I did that, I started remembering certain corners of the store. I don't know if I put this in the description of the store, but we had three bottles of mango chutney that we had inherited from the former owner, and we never sold them," Yep recalls.

Photographs can also be helpful when gathering memories. During the writing of *The Lost Garden,* Yep kept several photographs of family members in front of him on his desk.

Daily events may seem to be great material for memoir

writir.g. But simply recalling experiences isn't enough. As Yep explains, "Really, the best writing is bringing out the specialness of ordinary things." When writing a memoir, a writer observes his or her own life from a distance. By stepping back, the writer is able to gain a new understanding of past events.

"People think that, because they've lived something, they actually understand it, when that's not true," says Yep. "What they've done is experience it, but understanding is quite another matter— it's the next step."

Yep explains, "What it requires, to understand something, is actually to step away from that experience, so you can look at things more objectively, and that's also one of the steps in writing."

6 *Personal Writing: A Mirror of Myself*

Cultural Diversity

Researching to Remember

Laurence Yep grew up in a Chinese-American community and thought he knew all about his people. However, when he began his novel *Dragonwings*, it surprised him that he had to do as much research as anyone else. Yep said, "I had to grow up again, but this time in the

1900s, developing a Chinese sense of reality." Yep had to do the same for *The Lost Garden*. Although this search for memories was much more personal, he found that the searching itself was still an important part of his writing.

▲ *Yep's memoir*
The Lost Garden
includes many photos
from his life.

Drafting

ASSEMBLING THE PIECES

Memoir writing can provide a writer with a map of the past. Yep's idea of writing as puzzle solving can help a writer see what to do when the pieces just don't fit. How does a writer solve that problem? Solving problems is the real fun of working puzzles, but it's frustrating when the puzzle pieces don't easily fit together.

In his writing Yep often begins with a memory, such as a scene or even a name. He makes an informal outline, which he uses as a guide. When problems arise, he accepts the fact that he may have to go back and start again.

As he says, "You realize that you've got to redesign the puzzle, that an outline is only a scaffolding inside of which you've got to build a ship. And sometimes you get the ship almost built, and you realize that this darned thing isn't going to float, and so you have to tear it down, and bring it down to the keel, and begin again."

Whether a writer solves puzzles or builds boats when writing, he or she should not be afraid to try something that might not work.

Case Study **7**

Technology Tip

Fitting Pieces Together

As Yep explains, putting the memory pieces together sometimes doesn't work the first or second time. Having notes and an organizational plan on the computer makes it easy to try different arrangements or add new material. Some programs even help students cut and paste graphic organizers. Suggest that students enter two or three different arrangements of their material into the computer and then call on partners' opinions before choosing the best arrangement.

TEACH

Discussion Prompts
• What might Yep mean when he talks about puzzle pieces not fitting together and having to start over again? Give an example of how this could happen when writing a memoir.
• How do you as a writer know when a scene you are building is not working? What are some signs that you may have to rework it or start over?

Cross-reference: Writing
For other ideas about writing about memories, refer students to Lesson 1.4, pp. 22–25.

TEACH

Guided Practice

L2 Discussion

Stimulate a discussion of the Case Study. You may want to invite students to talk about

- why personal writing can benefit from revision, even if the only audience will be the writer
- how writing is different when the intended audience is the writer
- the results or benefits that can come from taking the time to do personal writing

Independent Practice

- *Writing Process Transparencies,* 1–10
- *Case Studies: Writing in the Real World,* pp. 1–4
- *Cooperative Learning Activities,* pp. 1–6

Skills Practice

- *Thinking and Study Skills,* pp. 5, 13, 18

I was the Ch... a child who had been too... too Chinese to fit in elsewhere. I was... spoke more of West Virginia than of China. athletic family, the grandson of a Chinese grand...

When I wrote, I went from being a puzzle to a puzzle solver. I could reach into the box of rags that was my soul and begin stitching them together. Moreover, I could try out different combinations to see which one pleased me the most. I could take these different elements, each of which belonged to something else, and dip them into my imagination where they were melted down and cast into new shapes so that they became uniquely mine.

The first advice a beginning writer gets is to write about what you know, but that doesn't mean that the subject has to be in the same form you saw it. My first science-fiction novel, Sweet-

Revising

TESTING THE FIT

▲ *Writing allowed Yep, while growing up, to try out different ideas on paper.*

The first question raised about a finished piece of writing is "How good is it?" What is good writing? Since a memoir reflects a person's own experiences, thoughts, and actions, who is to decide if it's good?

Yep works to achieve certain qualities in his work. One quality is authenticity, the characteristic of being real or true. By asking friends or relatives for their feedback, a writer can see how well his or her point of view has been communicated. But, finally,

the writing is whatever the writer wants it to be.

"Writing is sort of a balanced view of things," he explains. Although his concerns for authenticity and balance suggest the writer's responsibilities to others, Yep also writes to please himself. He says, "You have to write for yourself. Writing is a way of exploring other selves and other worlds inside yourself. I think it can be very satisfying, whether you get a good mark on it or not."

8 *Personal Writing: A Mirror of Myself*

Beyond the Classroom

Personal Writing About Others

Point out that some writers for popular magazines, such as sports or teen magazines, write articles about events in people's lives that shaped their personality or that turned them toward a particular career. Ask students to discuss any such articles that they have read recently.

Responding to the Case Study

1. Discussion

Discuss these questions about Laurence Yep's writing.

- How did Yep use various senses to recall locations and personal experiences?
- What graphic aids did Yep look at or create to help him gather his memories?
- During drafting, does Yep always follow his outline, or does he tend to try new ideas and approaches? Explain why.
- When revising, how can writers test whether they have succeeded in communicating their point of view?

2. Personal Writing

Write a short paragraph describing a personal experience.

Think of an experience that made you feel happy or proud. In your mind, picture where you were and the time of year if that is important. Use all your senses to recall sights, smells, and sensations. Look at old photographs to help you remember. Make some notes. Then, to write the paragraph, begin with one sentence that tells what the experience was, where, and when. Add two more sentences that provide details of the experience.

Grammar Link

Use appositives to make your writing clearer and more interesting.

An appositive is a noun or a noun phrase placed next to another noun to identify it or add information about it.

Laurence Yep, **award-winning writer of fantasies,** *went in a totally new direction. . . .*

Write each sentence, adding an appositive to each italicized noun.

1. In this photo are my *cousins.*
2. I clearly remember the *scene.*
3. We used to live in *Burton.*
4. These *items* helped me gather details.
5. The memory sparked two *feelings.*

See Lesson 9.6, pages 358–359.

Case Study **9**

Using the Grammar Link

Grammar Link Answers

Answers will vary, but some samples are given below.

1. In this photo are my cousins, Marta and Gretel.
2. I clearly remember the scene, a wooded park in the city's center.
3. We used to live in Burton, a small city about fifty miles from here.
4. These items, faded photos and a forgotten diary, helped me gather details.
5. The memory sparked two feelings, sadness and regret.

Responding to the Case Study

1. Discussion

Students' responses may include

- smell helped him reconstruct memories of his family's grocery store; sight helped him draw a map
- photographs and a map he created
- tries new ideas and approaches—whatever it takes to make the pieces fit together tightly
- ask relatives or friends to read it

2. Personal Writing

Answers will vary. Look for

- one sentence that identifies the experience
- sensory details that make the experience seem real

See also the *Teacher's Guide to Writing Assessment.*

Grammar Link
(See Using the Grammar Link below.)

Reteaching

Ask students to produce a graphic organizer for one of their memories.

Enrichment

Invite students to write one or two memories that a familiar historical figure might have had.

CLOSE

Ask volunteers to share how they think their own personal writing might change after having read about Laurence Yep's process.

Closing Note

Students may be able to judge from experience how to use journals for future writing. You might provide copies of *The Lost Garden* to students.

Personal Writing
Writing for Yourself

In personal writing you express your own thoughts and feelings. Sometimes you write to share with others. At other times, you write just for yourself.

You can't wait to tell someone. It's such great news. You grab the phone and call a friend. "I have a brand-new baby sister!" you brag. In a brief note you tell another friend how excited you are about your new sister. These are personal thoughts and feelings, and your note is an example of personal writing.

Get Personal

Notes to yourself or letters to friends and family are personal writing. A private journal—a book for your most personal thoughts and feelings—is one of the best places for personal writing. What you write there is only for you. A classroom journal is another place for personal writing. Classroom journals are a tool for recording ideas and information, and they are often shared with classmates or teachers. Your classroom journals can also be an excellent source of ideas for writing assignments.

You can include more than just your writing in a journal. You might add photographs, magazine clippings, drawings, or even doodles.

Letters are another form of personal writing. Lonnel wrote the following letter to his sister Tamika, and he included the photograph on the right. Read the letter to see what personal experience Lonnel wanted to share.

Setting the Purpose

Lesson 1.1 guides students to express their experiences, thoughts, and feelings through personal writing.

FOCUS

Lesson Overview

Objective: To keep a journal as a place for personal writing
Skills: keeping a journal; writing letters
Critical Thinking: analyzing; synthesizing; recalling; summarizing; defining and clarifying; visualizing; generating new information
Speaking and Listening: discussing; explaining a process

Bellringer

When students enter the classroom, have this assignment on the board: *Have you ever considered keeping a journal or diary? Whether or not you currently keep one, what do you think of the idea?*

Grammar Link to the Bellringer

Ask students how it can help to practice correct punctuation while keeping a journal. Use the example of *its* and *it's*; if students practice using these words correctly, their usage can become second nature in all of the students' writing.

Motivating Activity

Ask students to imagine they've just received some exciting news. Whom do they want to tell? What will they say? How will they spread the news—over the phone, in a letter, or in some other way? Discuss why a journal can be a valuable place for reacting to news. How might it serve as a place for sorting out complex thoughts, ideas, and feelings?

Teacher's Classroom Resources

The following resources can be used for planning, instruction, practice, reinforcement, assessment, reteaching, enrichment, or evaluation.

Teaching Tools
Lesson Plans, p. 2

Transparencies
Fine Art Transparencies, 2–5
Writing Process Transparencies, 1–10

Blackline Masters
Thinking and Study Skills, pp. 3, 5, 22
Writing Across the Curriculum, p. 20
Cooperative Learning Activities, pp. 1–6

Dear Tamika,

It's a really nice day here at Bowen Lake. It's almost noon, and the woods and the lake are warm in the sun. I'm sitting on a rock on the top of a kind of hill—as much like a hill as anything they have around here. I haven't seen anyone for over an hour. Earlier two people in a canoe drifted by. They were far away, and I could hardly see them. I could hear their voices, though. It's quiet now. There's a kind of magic in being all alone with nature.

How's the family? Is Jason back from training camp? What's Mom's job like now that she's back at work? Send me news!

Your brother,
Lonnel

Journal Writing

Jot down the names of friends or family members to whom you might write a letter. Then list ideas of what to tell them. You can include both experiences and thoughts.

1.1 Writing for Yourself **11**

TEACH

Guided Practice

L2 Using the Model
Ask what words and phrases Lonnel might have used in his journal to capture the quiet atmosphere of the lake. Point out that journal entries may serve as raw material for any writing. Discuss examples of writing that could come from journal entries.

L1 Freewriting in Journals
Get students excited about journal writing by emphasizing that a journal can be a sounding board off which they bounce ideas and feelings. Students can also practice getting their thoughts for an assignment on paper without worrying about correct form. Have students identify and prepare for an upcoming assignment in this way.

Two-Minute Skill Drill

Have students write the first sentence of a journal entry about one of the following events:

getting a good or bad grade
meeting a new friend
trying out for a sport or play

Journal Writing Tip

Writing a Letter Discuss the difference between the communication of a phone call and a letter. How might thoughts and feelings sound different when one has time to choose the best, most fitting words?

Blackline Masters
Speaking and Listening Activities, pp. 21, 23
Composition Practice, p. 1
Composition Reteaching, p. 1
Composition Enrichment, p. 1

Unit Assessment
Teacher's Guide to Writing Assessment
Tests with Answer Key
Unit 1 Choice A Test, p. 1
Unit 1 Choice B Test, p. 2

Test Generator
Unit 1 Choice A Test
Unit 1 Choice B Test

You may wish to administer either the Unit 1 Choice A Test or the Unit 1 Choice B Test as a pretest.

TEACH

Guided Practice

L2 Using the Model

Invite a volunteer to identify Louisa May Alcott (author of *Little Women*, *Little Men*, and other books for young people). Then ask students what the author might mean by "I've begun to live." Why might she have referred to past entries as "rubbish"? Be sure students know that a garret is the unfinished part of a house just beneath the roof. *Behind-hand* means "behind schedule."

L3 Sharing Personal Writing

Set aside five to ten minutes of class time once a week to give a brief forum for those who wish to share personal writing with the class. Students might share journal entries by placing typed copies of them on a classroom bulletin board. Encourage students to respond in a number of creative ways, such as drawing pictures, creating diagrams, or writing short rhymes such as those that appear in autograph books.

Independent Practice

For further stimuli for personal writing, see *Fine Art Transparencies* 2–5.

Writing Process Transparencies, 1–10

Writing Across the Curriculum, p. 20

Cooperative Learning Activities, pp. 1–6

Skills Practice

Speaking and Listening Activities, pp. 21, 23

Thinking and Study Skills, pp. 3, 5, 22

Composition Practice, p. 1

Keep a Journal

Writing in a journal can help you explore and remember your private thoughts without worrying about what anyone else thinks. Once you've begun your journal, you'll get more out of it if you write in it regularly. The following journal entry was written by author Louisa May Alcott as a girl.

Her writing here sounds like a conversation with a close friend.

Do you think this writing could appear in a letter to a friend? Why?

> ### Literature Model
>
> I am in the garret with my papers round me, and a pile of apples to eat while I write my journal, plan stories, and enjoy the patter of rain on the roof, in peace and quiet. . . . Being behind-hand, as usual, I'll make note of the main events up to date, for I don't waste ink in poetry and pages of rubbish now. I've begun to *live*, and have no time for sentimental musing. . . .
>
> Norma Johnston, editor, *Louisa May: The World and Works of Louisa May Alcott*

Below are some journal entries and a postcard. The writer used a private journal to record thoughts and experiences. Some of them were shared in a postcard to a friend. Read both and see how alike and how different they are.

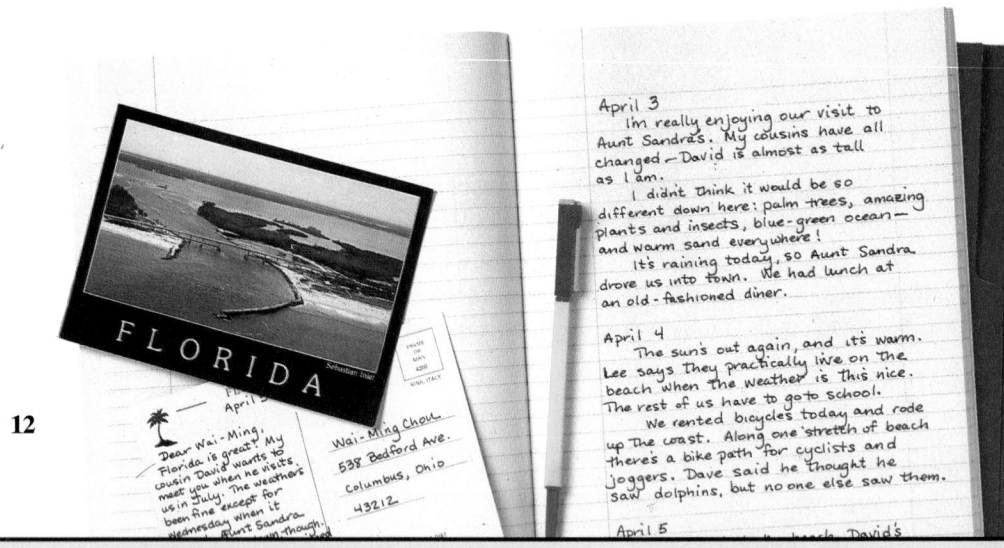

12

Enabling Strategies

LEP Writing in Both Languages

Encourage students learning English to write in their first language when they begin their journals. Ask them, however, to incorporate English into their writing as they learn it, even if at first the spellings are phonetic. Challenge students to use a new vocabulary word each time they write in their journal.

1.1 Writing Activities

Write a Letter

You can write to a friend who is distant or one whom you see often. Write about some experience you have had recently or about anything that's on your mind. Write as though you're talking to your friend.

- Express your thoughts and feelings.
- Include a doodle or drawing.

PURPOSE To write a personal letter
AUDIENCE A good friend
LENGTH 1 page

Artist unknown, Pompeii, *Portrait of a Young Woman*, first century A.D.

Cross-Curricular: History

The image on this page is from a wall painting found in the ruins of the ancient city of Pompeii. That city and its people were buried when Mount Vesuvius suddenly erupted in A.D. 79.

Look at the young woman in this painting. Write the entry she might have written in her personal journal the day of the catastrophe. Remember, life was going on peacefully. What might she have done on that day?

Grammar Link

Use the possessive pronoun *its* and the contraction *it's* correctly.

*The tree lost **its** leaves.*
***It's** getting colder every week.*

Complete each sentence with the correct word: *it's* or *its*.

1. It rained this morning, but _____ a beautiful afternoon.
2. My dog has injured _____ paw.
3. As I look at our house, I see _____ paint is cracking.
4. When _____ my turn to recite, I have to be ready.
5. Do you know _____ title?

See Lesson 7.8, pages 319–321.

1.1 Writing for Yourself **13**

ASSESS

Writing Activities Evaluation Guidelines

Write a Letter
Use these criteria when evaluating your students' writing.
- Have students explored personal concerns?
- Have students included a related drawing?

See also the *Teacher's Guide to Writing Assessment*.

Cross-Curricular: History
The journal entry should
- reflect the possible concerns or interests of a young woman
- sound like that of an ordinary day

Grammar Link
(See Using the Grammar Link below.)

Reteaching
📁 *Composition Reteaching*, p. 1

Enrichment
📁 *Composition Enrichment*, p. 1

 Use *Fine Art Transparencies* 2–5 for enrichment activities also.

CLOSE

Ask students to think about and share the part of the day that would be the best time for them to write a daily journal entry. Why would that time be best? What place would be best? Would they need to be in a "private" place? Would they prefer to listen to music while writing?

Using the Grammar Link

Grammar Link Answers
1. it's   4. it's
2. its   5. its
3. its

Differentiating Between *its* and *it's* Ask volunteers to share the strategies they use to remember the difference between these two words.

About the Art

Artist Unknown, Pompeii, *Portrait of a Young Woman*, first century A.D. The portrait, now in the Museo Nazionale, Naples, Italy, is from a Pompeian wall painting transferred to panel. The young woman's hair style dates the portrait to the reign of Claudius (A.D. 41–54).

13

LESSON

1.2

Personal Writing

Writing to Learn

FOCUS

Lesson Overview

Objective: To use a learning log to record questions and thoughts about what is being learned

Skills: analyzing; evaluating; writing to record

Critical Thinking: summarizing; identifying main idea; defining and clarifying; evaluating

Speaking and Listening: discussing

Bellringer

When students enter the classroom, have this assignment on the board: *Write down why, if you were an explorer in the Arctic, it would be important to keep a log of your findings and route.*

Grammar Link to the Bellringer

Have students underline the correct verb forms in these sample log entries.

1. All of the icy terrain (*is, are*) ahead of us.
2. Most of the vegetation (*has, have*) disappeared.

Motivating Activity

Ask students to imagine they have ideas for a new product or ways to improve an existing one. How would they keep track of their ideas? Where would they list the parts they've designed and keep the drawings they've made? Lead students to the conclusion that they might write questions and ideas related to schoolwork in a special binder or notebook. Elicit examples of entries that would be helpful in understanding their studies.

A learning log is another type of journal. In it you can keep a record of new facts or ideas you have learned in a class, as well as your thoughts and reactions to what you've learned. The example below was written after a science class. Read the entry and notice the clippings the writer included with it.

14　*Personal Writing: A Mirror of Myself*

Teacher's Classroom Resources

The following resources can be used for planning, instruction, practice, reinforcement, assessment, reteaching, enrichment, or evaluation.

Teaching Tools
Lesson Plans, p. 3

Transparencies
Fine Art Transparencies, 2–5
Writing Process Transparencies, 1–10

Record Your Progress

A learning log is a form of personal writing. It's for you. Writing in a log is an opportunity to become more involved in your learning and more aware of the progress you're making. For example, after reading a passage in your textbook, you can record your questions and thoughts in your learning log. Perhaps you'll raise these questions during your next class discussion. The chart below shows the kinds of entries you might put in your log. The goal is to make the information you study make sense to you.

Keeping a Learning Log	
Purpose	**Entry**
Summarize content.	Very hot stars are blue-white; cooler stars are orange or red.
Identify main ideas.	Sunspots are dark areas on the sun's surface that are cooler than surrounding areas.
Define problems, and ask questions.	I'm still not clear why our sun is called an average star.
Evaluate schoolwork.	The information on planets seemed easier than that on stars (because of the unit review?).

Journal Writing

What questions do you have about something you're learning now? Begin a learning log by writing down one or two of these questions.

1.2 Writing to Learn **15**

TEACH

Guided Practice

L2 Using the Graphic Organizer
Point out that graphic organizers help readers see at a glance the material to be learned. Explain that by citing four different purposes for writing, this chart illustrates one method of classifying. Ask students to suggest two or three other purposes and entries that could be added to the chart.

L2 Structuring Learning Logs
Suggest that students begin their logs by dividing each page into two vertical columns. Tell them to write quotations from their course work on the left side. Ask them to jot down their own reactions to each quote on the right—questions, conclusions, or even connections between the quote and a passage from another piece of reading.

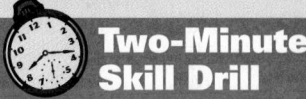

Two-Minute Skill Drill

Have students create a list of all the other subject-related learning logs they could write to help them. Ask them to include the topic they are presently studying in each class.

Journal Writing Tip

Writing Questions Reinforce that formulating and writing down questions about things that confuse them forces students to pinpoint the real sources of problems while they are trying to learn something new.

📂 **Blackline Masters**
Thinking and Study Skills, pp. 4, 5, 34–35
Writing Across the Curriculum, p. 20
Cooperative Learning Activities, pp. 1–6

Speaking and Listening Activities, pp. 21, 23
Composition Practice, p. 2
Composition Reteaching, p. 2
Composition Enrichment, p. 2

Assessment
📂 *Teacher's Guide to Writing Assessment*

TEACH

Guided Practice

L2 Using the Model

Students may need help in seeing how the writer of the learning log isolated the key ideas in the textbook passage. Ask whether a particular idea holds the passage together. Ask students to determine whether the other sentences connect in some way to the passage. Then encourage students to compare those ideas with the ones in the facsimile.

(Answer to model callout: It focuses on specific information the students may need for class discussion or a report.)

L2 Cooperative Learning

Students can practice their reasoning skills using the Co-op Co-op structure. Be sure that advanced learners are equally distributed among several small groups. Provide each group with a question from a classmate's learning log. Direct members to suggest strategies individually that the student might use to find the answer. After discussing strengths and weaknesses of the strategies, ask each group to share its strategies with the class.

Independent Practice

For further stimuli for personal writing, see *Fine Art Transparencies* 2–5.

Writing Process Transparencies, 1–10

Writing Across the Curriculum, p. 20

Cooperative Learning Activities, pp. 1–6

Skills Practice

Thinking and Study Skills, pp. 4, 5, 34–35

Speaking and Listening Activities, pp. 21, 23

Composition Practice, p. 2

16

Write and Think

Below is an example of how a learning log can be used. A student took the notes on the left as she read a textbook chapter on exploration of Mars. Then she wrote in her learning log. After a class discussion of this topic, she reread the textbook passage and looked over her notes. Then she used her learning log to rewrite the passage in her own words.

Text

Scientists are currently developing plans to further explore Mars. Because the distance between Earth and Mars is many millions of kilometers, it could take about three years to get to Mars and back. Because of the long duration of the flight, astronauts would face much more danger than they do in space shuttle missions.

How does the question help the student focus on things to learn?

Distance to Mars —
many millions of
kilometers
Length of Mars trip —
maybe three years
Danger — lowered
calcium in bones due
to near-zero gravity;
weak bones might
break once astronauts
land on Mars or
return to Earth.

Notes

What are some of the problems astronauts will face in exploring Mars?

One of the main problems is the length of the flight. Mars and Earth are many millions of kilometers apart. Traveling to the planet and back could take about three years. On the flight, astronauts' bones will lose calcium because of zero gravity. Once the crew reaches Mars or returns to Earth, their weak bones might fracture easily.

Learning Log

16 *Personal Writing: A Mirror of Myself*

Enabling Strategies

LEP Creating Learning Logs

Students who are learning English may have difficulty creating their first learning log. Fluent English speakers may act as tutors by trying to answer other students' questions and by showing them one or several models of actual learning logs that student tutors have created. Encourage students learning English to use sketches, diagrams, and other visuals as much as possible in their logs.

1.2 Writing Activities

Write a Learning Log Entry

Choose a difficult paragraph, page, or chapter from a homework assignment for another class. Then choose one of the options in the chart on page 15 and write a learning log entry: Either summarize the content, identify the most important ideas, state what you don't understand and ask a question about it, or write your opinion about what makes it difficult.

- Use the learning log entry you have created to try to make sense out of the information you are studying.
- During the next class of the subject for which you wrote the learning log entry, ask any question raised by the assignment.

PURPOSE To clarify a difficult section of a text-book

AUDIENCE Yourself

LENGTH 1 paragraph

COMPUTER OPTION

Consider keeping your learning log on the computer. As you review your entries, you can underline or bold-face key ideas. You can also keep an index or glossary of important words or ideas.

Grammar Link

Use the correct verb form when the subject of a sentence is an indefinite pronoun.

Some indefinite pronouns—*all, any, most, none,* and *some*—can be either singular or plural, depending on the phrase that follows.

*What **are some of the problems** astronauts will face? . . .*

Complete each sentence with the correct choice of verb.

1. All of the water (is, are) crucial.
2. None of the other planets (is, are) hospitable to human life.
3. Most of the problems (has, have) been anticipated.
4. Some of the constellations (is, are) difficult to spot.
5. Any of this (is, are) suitable.
6. None of it (is, are) complete.
7. Any of these questions (is, are) worthy of further research.
8. All of my notes (is, are) here.
9. Most of the work (requires, require) special skills.
10. Some of the confusion (is, are) due to the difficult terminology.

See Lesson 16.4, pages 514–515.

1.2 Writing to Learn **17**

Using the Grammar Link

Grammar Link Answers
1. All of the water is crucial.
2. None of the other planets are hospitable to human life.
3. Most of the problems have been anticipated.
4. Some of the constellations are difficult to spot.
5. Any of this is suitable.
6. None of it is complete.
7. Any of these questions are worthy of further research.
8. All of my notes are here.
9. Most of the work requires special skills.
10. Some of the confusion is due to the difficult terminology.

FOCUS

Lesson Overview

Objective: To identify and describe a personal wish or dream

Skills: writing a description; using vivid adjectives and adverbs

Critical Thinking: recalling; defining and clarifying; visualizing; analyzing; drawing conclusions; making decisions

Speaking and Listening: interpreting special clues; evaluating; discussing; asking questions

Bellringer

When students enter the classroom, have this assignment on the board: *Choose a career that sounds interesting to you. List three types of things you would do in that career.*

Grammar Link to the Bellringer

Ask one or two volunteers for their responses to the Bellringer activity and write them on the board. Ask the class to point out any sentence fragments in these responses and explain that sentence fragments are acceptable when writing for yourself.

Motivating Activity

Invite other students to share their responses to the Bellringer activity. Have them tell about potential future accomplishments by thinking about and discussing their lists of career-related tasks.

LESSON
1.3 Personal Writing
Writing About Wishes and Dreams

If I had a photograph of myself ten years from now, this is what I'd see. I am a tall, sleepy-eyed medical student in a white coat. I'm studying to be a heart surgeon. My white coat is rumpled because I slept in it on my break. I'm at a patient's bedside listening to his heart. He had heart surgery yesterday, and I was there in the operating room. During the operation I was

Journal writing is a good way to explore and record your wishes or dreams. Can you see yourself ten years from now? What will you look like? How will you have changed? What will you be doing? Where will you be? Read the journal entry at the left to see what one student wrote.

18 *Personal Writing: A Mirror of Myself*

Teacher's Classroom Resources

The following resources can be used for planning, instruction, practice, reinforcement, assessment, reteaching, enrichment, or evaluation.

Teaching Tools
Lesson Plans, p. 4

Transparencies
Fine Art Transparencies, 2–5
Writing Process Transparencies, 1–10

Look at Yourself

To imagine the future, it could be helpful to look at yourself as you are now. One way to do that is to use a cluster diagram like the one below. In your diagram you can record your interests, successes, failures, feelings, and reactions. You can even indicate how they relate to one another. Making connections may help you uncover interests you can combine as you begin to think about your future.

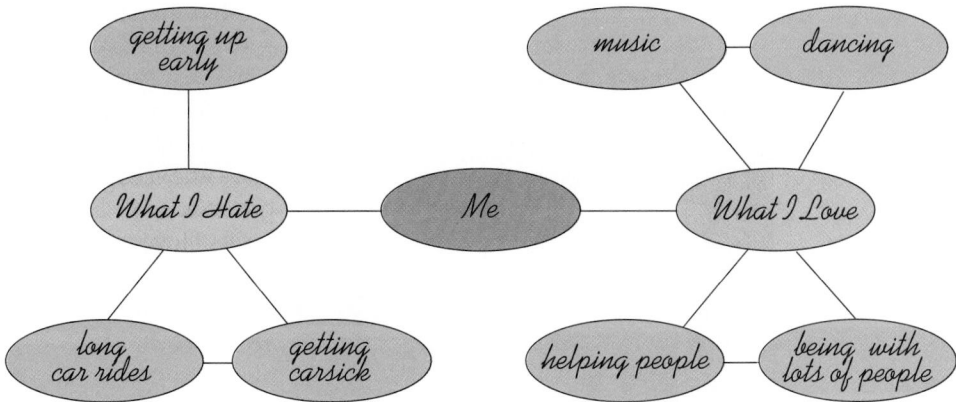

Journal Writing

In your journal make a *me* diagram—a cluster of magazine pictures that illustrates your interests. Below your diagram, write a paragraph entry explaining how the pictures show who you are.

TEACH

Guided Practice

L2 Using the Model
Ask students to study the cluster diagram to draw conclusions about the writer's hopes and dreams. For example, if he/she really hates getting up early, would a career as an early-morning newscaster be realistic? What else does the model reveal?

L2 Making a Cluster Diagram
Have students create their own cluster diagrams about themselves. When completed, ask volunteers to summarize what their diagrams reveal. Ask which subjects or careers might be compatible with their diagram.

 **Two-Minute Skill Drill**

List these headings on the board and have students write descriptive phrases relating to career choices they have considered and eliminated (encourage students to use a variety of adjectives and adverbs):

Reasons For   Reasons Against

Journal Writing Tip

Formulating Questions Suggest that students question themselves as they look at pictures in magazines: Why do I like this photo? Is it the color? the arrangement? Does something in the photo suggest who I am or want to be?

Encourage students to experiment with the format of their diagrams. For instance, suggest that they make such things as mobiles, videotapes, slide shows, and "movie" posters.

Blackline Masters
Thinking and Study Skills, pp. 2, 16, 22
Writing Across the Curriculum, p. 20
Cooperative Learning Activities, pp. 1–6

Speaking and Listening Activities, pp. 21, 23
Composition Practice, p. 3
Composition Reteaching, p. 3
Composition Enrichment, p. 3

Assessment
Teacher's Guide to Writing Assessment

19

TEACH

Guided Practice

L2 Using the Model

Read the model, or have a volunteer read it, emphasizing the author's sense of anticipation and wonder. Ask students whether they share Sylvia Plath's feelings. Do they ever feel "not completely molded"? Does the pace of growing up frustrate them? Are they excited about all the great things they might accomplish? Challenge students to respond to Plath's thoughts in their journals in a few concise sentences.

Independent Practice

For further stimuli for personal writing, see *Fine Art Transparencies* 2–5.

Writing Process Transparencies 1–10

Writing Across the Curriculum, p. 20

Cooperative Learning Activities, pp. 1–6

Skills Practice

Thinking and Study Skills, pp. 2, 16, 22

Speaking and Listening Activities, pp. 21, 23

Composition Practice, p. 3

Shape Your Future

You can explore your wishes and dreams in a number of ways. You could write a letter to a friend, relative, or favorite teacher. You could privately explore this topic in your journal. You might draw a picture of yourself as you want to be and include a few sentences describing your picture.

In the diary excerpt below, the poet Sylvia Plath reflects, at seventeen, on the future.

Literature Model

What is the best for me? What do I want? I do not know. I love freedom. I deplore constrictions and limitations. . . . I am not as wise as I have thought. I can see, as from a valley, the roads lying open for me, but I cannot see the end—the consequences. . . .

Oh, I love *now*, with all my fears and forebodings, for now I still am not completely molded. My life is still just beginning. I am strong. I long for a cause to devote my energies to. . . .

Sylvia Plath,
Letters Home

Enabling Strategies

LEP Choosing Words

Students who have difficulty with English may need extra assistance in choosing precise, descriptive words. Encourage these students to use a thesaurus and a dictionary as aids in writing about how their dreams have been affected by the circumstances that caused them to learn English. For example, if students were not born in the United States, what differences might there be in students' career goals if they were living in their country of origin?

1.3 Writing Activities

Write a Journal Entry

In your journal describe a childhood dream that has come true.

- Give details to make your images clear.
- Tell how you feel now and how you felt before.
- Explain what the fulfillment of this dream means to you.

PURPOSE To describe a childhood dream
AUDIENCE Yourself
LENGTH 2 paragraphs

Andy Warhol, *Chris Evert,* 1977

Cross-Curricular: Art

The painting on this page is of American tennis champion Chris Evert. The look of concentration and the tennis racket help characterize her. Suppose that someone were to photograph you in the future. Your appearance and an object you are holding will reflect the career dreams you have achieved. Write a paragraph in which you describe the photo and tell how it represents the future you.

Grammar Link

Avoid sentence fragments in formal writing.

Sentence fragments are acceptable in your personal journal. When you write for others, however, use complete sentences.

I am a tall, sleepy-eyed medical student in a white coat.

Revise each fragment below into a sentence by adding either a subject or a predicate.

1. My career in art.
2. Have enrolled in a pottery class.
3. Jennifer DuBerry, the instructor.
4. The wheel and the kiln.
5. Created an odd-looking vase.

See Lesson 8.2, pages 328–329.

1.3 Writing About Wishes and Dreams **21**

Using the Grammar Link

Grammar Link Answers
Answers will vary. Samples are given.
1. My career in art is taking off.
2. I have enrolled in a pottery class.
3. Jennifer DuBerry, the instructor, encourages me.
4. The wheel and the kiln are in the back of the room.
5. Another student created an odd-looking vase.

About the Art

Andy Warhol, *Chris Evert,* 1977
This portrait was produced as part of Warhol's Sports Figures Series. From a photo he took of Evert, Warhol made a silk-screen stencil and pulled the dark paint of the portrait across the bright pastel background.

Setting the Purpose

Lesson 1.4 encourages students to learn to use writing to record different aspects of their lives.

FOCUS

Lesson Overview

Objective: To write a first-person account of a personal turning point or other significant life event
Skills: identifying turning points; writing about personal life experiences
Critical Thinking: recalling; generating new information
Speaking and Listening: discussing

Bellringer

When students enter the classroom, have this assignment on the board: *Write a paragraph about a favorite memory from childhood.*

Grammar Link to the Bellringer
Have students circle *me, us, him, her,* and *them* when they are used in the Bellringer as the object of a verb or a preposition.

Motivating Activity

Ask volunteers to identify experiences they have had that changed them in some way, such as moving to a new home or meeting someone who greatly influenced them. Suggest that they explain how they changed. For example, the turning point might have changed their attitude about someone or something, sparked a new interest, or initiated a friendship.

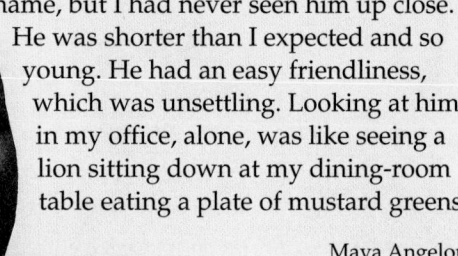

LESSON
1.4

P e r s o n a l   W r i t i n g
Writing One's Own Story

An autobiography is the story of a person's life written by that person. The passage below is autobiographical. Maya Angelou describes her first meeting with Martin Luther King Jr. Read it and see what her reaction was.

Literature Model

I walked into my office and a man sitting at my desk, with his back turned, spun around, stood up and smiled. Martin King said, "Good afternoon, Miss Angelou. You are right on time."

The surprise was so total that it took me a moment to react to his outstretched hand.

I had worked two months for the SCLC, sent out tens of thousands of letters and invitations signed by Rev. King, made hundreds of statements in his name, but I had never seen him up close. He was shorter than I expected and so young. He had an easy friendliness, which was unsettling. Looking at him in my office, alone, was like seeing a lion sitting down at my dining-room table eating a plate of mustard greens.

Maya Angelou,
The Heart of a Woman

22

Teacher's Classroom Resources

The following resources can be used for planning, instruction, practice, reinforcement, assessment, reteaching, enrichment, or evaluation.

Teaching Tools
Lesson Plans, p. 5

Transparencies
Fine Art Transparencies, 2–5
Writing Process Transparencies, 1–10

Identify Turning Points

You have had important moments, turning points, in your own life. Some may have even changed the course of your life. The diagram below shows turning-point events in one student's life. Study the diagram and its entries. Make a similar map for yourself. Put the important events in chronological order, the order in which they happened. If you need help recalling either the event or the timing, ask someone in your family. Save your diagram to use as you plan your own autobiographical writing.

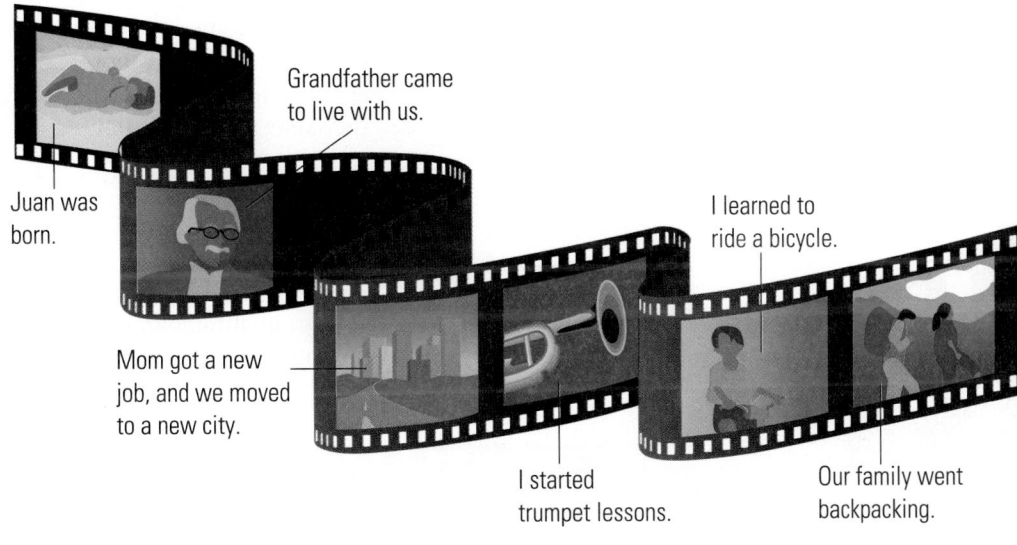

Juan was born.

Grandfather came to live with us.

Mom got a new job, and we moved to a new city.

I started trumpet lessons.

I learned to ride a bicycle.

Our family went backpacking.

Journal Writing

Look at the events in your diagram. Choose the one that is the most meaningful to you. Write about it in your personal journal.

1.4 Writing One's Own Story **23**

Blackline Masters
Thinking and Study Skills, pp. 5, 10, 17, 19
Writing Across the Curriculum, p. 20
Cooperative Learning Activities, pp. 1–6

Speaking and Listening Activities, pp. 21, 23
Composition Practice, p. 4
Composition Reteaching, p. 4
Composition Enrichment, p. 4

Assessment
Teacher's Guide to Writing Assessment

TEACH

Guided Practice

L2 Using the Model
Discuss with students what is unusual about the author's first contact with Dr. King. What does he do when he sees Maya? What does she do when he offers to shake her hand? Then call attention to the last sentence of the model. What does the lion image suggest about Dr. King? How do the dining table and mustard greens contrast with the lion?

L3 Making a Family Tree
Suggest that students produce a family tree. If their families have lived for a long time in one or two states, encourage them to use the genealogy department of the public library for research. If their families are far-flung, students might be able to interview older members by phone and use the resulting information to assemble a chart.

 **Two-Minute Skill Drill**

Write this list on the board and ask students to write down the numbers of the turning points:

1. going to the mall
2. graduating
3. moving to another state
4. finishing homework
5. falling in love
(Turning points: 2, 3, 5)

Journal Writing Tip

Personal Writing Encourage students to first get their event, feelings, and thoughts down on paper. They can go back to perfect spelling and grammar.

TEACH

Guided Practice

L2 Using the Model

Ask students to identify the turning point in this anecdote. Ask them why anecdotes are often used in auto-biographies (to entertain; to illustrate the subject's character).

If possible, find a few anecdotes in published autobiographies and share them with the class. Then tell students to use their journals to try out an anecdote in their own writing. *(Answer to model callout: He loves to cuddle up with his little sister; her eyes light up when she sees him; she says his name in a cute way.)*

L1 Writing About Turning Points

In a mini-workshop, meet for fifteen minutes two or three times a week and encourage students to discuss and write about turning points. Explain that you will not grade any of their writing. Emphasize that the goal of the workshop is that their ideas flow freely.

Independent Practice

For further stimuli for personal writing, see *Fine Art Transparencies*, 2–5.

Writing Process Transparencies, 1–10

Writing Across the Curriculum, p. 20

Cooperative Learning Activities, pp. 1–6

Skills Practice

Thinking and Study Skills, pp. 5, 10, 17, 19

Speaking and Listening Activities, pp. 21, 23

Composition Practice, p. 4

Write About Your Life

Choose a turning point in your life, and think about how you felt before and after that time. Consider which details would bring this event to life for someone else. A student wrote the journal entry below. Read it and notice the details he used to make clear how he felt.

> **Student Model**
>
> D uring cold, snowy days, I love to cuddle up with Shelly. As she lies against me, I feel as though I had just drunk a cup of hot chocolate. Whenever I walk into the room, her eyes light up brighter than the sun as she recognizes me. Then, she smiles her toothless grin and tries to say, "Barrwie." At those times, I love my little Shellster a lot. Since she was born, nothing has been the same; it's been better.
>
> Barry Rosenberg, Southfield, Michigan
> First appeared in *Stone Soup*

Which details show that Rosenberg's life has changed for the better?

The chart below shows the steps in autobiographical writing. It uses a turning point from the map on page 23. Notice the kinds of details the student uses to bring the experience to life.

Writing About Turning Points	
Steps in the Process	**Examples**
Choosing an event	start of trumpet lessons
Noting feelings about event	was happy about taking lessons admired the golden surface of the trumpet loved the bold trumpet sound
Writing about event	*Excited, I lifted the glittering trumpet to my lips. A thundering note marched out. I was sold on the trumpet for life.*

Enabling Strategies

LEP Increasing Vocabulary

Students who are learning English may have difficulty with the vocabulary needed to write about events in their lives. Give them the opportunity to relate their personal experiences orally to fluent English speakers before they begin to write. If there are key words they need for their writing, the fluent English-speaking students can help by writing these down for them.

Write About an Event

Choose an event from your life, and write an autobiographical composition. To plan and draft your composition, follow the steps outlined on page 24.

- Tell what happened.
- Explain how you felt before and after.
- Use details that make the event come to life for a reader.

PURPOSE To describe a turning point in your life
AUDIENCE Your teacher and classmates
LENGTH 1 page

Miriam Schapiro, *High Steppin' Strutter #1*, 1985

Cross-Curricular: Health

One way to feel good about yourself is to review events in your life that you feel positive about. In your journal complete the following sentence to help you identify these events: "I felt really proud of myself when. . . ." Write a one-page description of the incident or event.

Grammar Link

Use object pronouns—*me, us, him, her, them*—as the object of a verb or a preposition.

*. . . I had never seen **him** up close.*
*Looking at **him** in my office . . .*
*. . . at Jane and **him**.*

Write each sentence correctly.

1. The gift from Jem and she is here.
2. Jarmila chose he.
3. The news about Su and I is false.
4. Rodrigo met they at school.
5. The boys were kind to we.
6. Tino walked she to the door.
7. Tara wrote a thank-you letter to he.
8. The storm woke I last night.
9. The test was easy for she.
10. Don't call they too early tomorrow.

See Lesson 11.1, pages 402–403, and Lesson 11.3, pages 406–407.

Using the Grammar Link

Grammar Link Answers

1. from . . . her	6. walked her
2. chose him	7. to him
3. about . . . me	8. woke me
4. met them	9. for her
5. to us	10. call them

About the Art

Miriam Schapiro, *High Steppin' Strutter #1*, 1985
This 85-by-51-inch piece, a colored-paper collage enhanced with acrylic paint, responds to life—and Broadway musicals. The figure, which represents a dancer in a show, evokes the immense activity of the entire musical.

LESSON

1.5

Writing About Literature
Responding in a Journal

Poems are often a form of personal writing, and people's reactions to poetry can be very personal. What is your response to the poem below?

Setting the Purpose

Lesson 1.5 teaches students to write personal responses to literature in a journal.

FOCUS

Lesson Overview

Objective: To begin the habit of writing in a journal personal responses to one's reading

Skills: varying responses; responding to literature; using vivid language

Critical Thinking: analyzing; evaluating

Speaking and Listening: discussing; evaluating

Bellringer

When students enter the classroom, have this assignment on the board: *Write a paragraph describing the types of literature you most like to read. Explain why you prefer them.*

Grammar Link to the Bellringer
Ask students to circle any adjectives they used in the Bellringer.

Motivating Activity

Ask students to think about the last time they attended a movie with a group of friends. Was the number of interpretations the same as the number of people? Did the members of the group relate parts of the movie to their own knowledge or experience? If so, how? Point out that people have many different responses to literature also.

Literature Model

The Clouds Pass

The clouds pass in a blue sky
Too white to be true
Before winter sets in
The trees are spending all their money

I lie in gold
Above a green valley
Gold falls on my chest
I am a rich man.

Richard Garcia

Ray Vinella, *Aspen Grove*, 1960

A journal is a good place for responding to literature. Which images did you see most clearly in the poem? Record these in your journal. Also tell how you liked the poem.

Respond to Literature

The way you react to a poem can take many forms. Your response may be a quiet smile, a hearty laugh, or a flood of memories. Compare the following journal responses to Richard Garcia's poem to your own response.

26 *Personal Writing: A Mirror of Myself*

Teacher's Classroom Resources

The following resources can be used for planning, instruction, practice, reinforcement, assessment, reteaching, enrichment, or evaluation.

Teaching Tools
Lesson Plans, p. 6

Transparencies
Fine Art Transparencies, 2–5
Writing Process Transparencies, 1–10

Student Model

*I*n the poem "The Clouds Pass," Richard Garcia explains a great gift of nature. In autumn time nature gives the trees' leaves a beautiful golden color. Now these leaves are the money which the trees are dropping——spending.

Sarah Fisher, Solomon Schechter Day School,
Skokie, Illinois

This reader reacts to Garcia's poem with an explanation and with appreciation.

What aspects of the poem does this reader highlight?

An autumn afternoon. The air is crisp and cool, a hint of the frosty weather to come. But the sun is warm on my skin. Like the trees in Garcia's poem, I want to spend my "money" before winter arrives and sends me indoors. The warm, gold days of Indian summer make everyone feel rich. Garcia's poem celebrates Indian summer. It makes me feel lucky to be alive to enjoy this glorious time of year.

This reader responds to Garcia's poem with sensory descriptions.

What feelings does Garcia's poem raise for this reader?

Journal Writing

In your journal jot down the name of a poem that you've enjoyed. Close your eyes, and try to remember what you thought and felt as you read the poem. Record your answers in your journal.

1.5 Writing About Literature: Responding in a Journal **27**

TEACH

Guided Practice

L2 **Using the Models**

Suggest that students choose one of the model formats on student page 27 and respond to the poem on student page 26 in their journals. Encourage them to make their own connections with Garcia's ideas by expressing personal feelings about autumn. Students might also write poems as responses. *(Sample answer to model callout #1: nature as a gift; the image of the trees spending money)*
(Sample answer to model callout #2: warmth, enjoyment, and feeling lucky to be alive)

L2 **Understanding Creative License**

Point out that Garcia uses only one period—at the end of the poem. Ask students why Garcia might have done this. Suggest that the lack of punctuation allows the reader to group the words in different ways.

 **Two-Minute Skill Drill**

Choose one of these topics and create as many word pictures for it as you can.

sunset   an ice storm
summer   a starry sky

Journal Writing Tip

Feelings About Poetry Stress with students that there are no "right" or "wrong" answers when writing a personal response to a poem or any other piece of literature. Students should simply write their reactions, describing how the selection made them feel.

☞ **Blackline Masters**
Thinking and Study Skills,
  pp. 3, 4, 6, 9
Writing Across the Curriculum,
  p. 20
Cooperative Learning Activities,
  pp. 1–6

Speaking and Listening Activities, pp. 21, 23
Composition Practice, p. 5
Composition Reteaching, p. 5
Composition Enrichment, p. 5

Assessment
☞ *Teacher's Guide to Writing Assessment*

TEACH

Guided Practice

L2 Cooperative Learning

Students may enjoy using the round-robin strategy in small groups to respond to a poem they choose. Suggest that one group member read the poem aloud while the others concentrate on the images it brings to mind. Explain that each member should take one or more turns to share images, thoughts, and feelings evoked by the poem. Encourage students to comment on one another's responses.

L1 Using Photographs with Poetry

Encourage students to look through a portfolio of autumn photos and artwork in studying the Garcia poem. Suggest that they look for photos of large, lush trees with glowing, golden leaves. Encourage them to find pictures that go along with poems they choose to read and respond to.

Independent Practice

For further stimuli for personal writing, see *Fine Art Transparencies* 2–5.

Writing Process Transparencies, 1–10

Writing Across the Curriculum, p. 20

Cooperative Learning Activities, pp. 1–6

Skills Practice

Thinking and Study Skills, pp. 3, 4, 6, 9

Speaking and Listening Activities, pp. 21, 23

Composition Practice, p. 5

Vary Your Responses

Writing is one way to respond to literature or to explore your reactions to what you've read. You can express your thoughts and feelings in many ways. You could create an illustration, research and write about a topic contained in your reading, or write what one character might say to another. Which way is best for you? Begin by asking questions about the literature and how you felt about it. Look at some of the questions below to help you get started.

Questions to Help You Get Started

1. What did the literature make you think about?

2. How did it make you feel?

3. Which words brought pictures to mind?

4. What would you change about it?

Forms of Response

Write about how the literature makes you feel.

Write a poem expressing your feelings about the work.

Draw a picture of an image from the work.

Write a letter to the author.

Rewrite a passage with your own changes.

Make a cartoon based on the work.

Create a magazine ad for the work.

If the work is a poem, set it to music.

Dramatize a scene from the work.

Enabling Strategies

LEP Using Tutors

To help students who are learning English to write their literary responses, pair them with students who could serve as tutors. Encourage the tutors to read poems aloud to students and help the students with any questions about the language the poet uses. Also, suggest to the tutors that they encourage students to draw a picture, or pick one from a magazine, in response to a poem and then talk and write about the picture.

1.5 Writing Activities

Write a Response to Literature

Read the following poem or one of your choice, and write an entry about it in your journal. Use the questions below to help you explore your feelings and reactions.

Jukebox Showdown

Two men got into a fight with a jukebox
The air was night and warm
Splattered all over the avenue
Was screws and bolts
Broken 45's all over the place
The police came and arrested all three
The police asked the jukebox questions
Then dropped quarters in

Victor Hernández Cruz

- How did you feel when you finished reading the poem? What elements in the poem made you feel that way?
- What did you like best about the poem in general: its subject, its sound, its setting, the pictures it created in your mind? Explain.
- Did the poem tell you anything new or say something you haven't heard before?

PURPOSE To respond to a poem
AUDIENCE Yourself
LENGTH 2–3 paragraphs

Cooperative Learning

With a group of students, choose a poem from your literature book. Read the poem together, and discuss its meaning. Then write a journal response to the poem. Return to the group to share your responses.

Grammar Link

Use vivid adjectives in your writing.

Vivid adjectives help crystallize images in your reader's mind and make your meaning very precise.

*The air is **crisp** and **cool**, a hint of the **frosty** weather to come.*

Revise the sentences below, replacing the underlined adjectives with stronger, more vivid ones.

"The Clouds Pass" praises the yellow leaves of fall. The color of the leaves makes the speaker feel rich and happy.
When I read the poem, I shared the speaker's happy emotions. At the same time, the falling leaves make me sad. The poem is a good one.

See Lesson 3.3, pages 114–116.

1.5 Writing About Literature: Responding in a Journal   **29**

Using the Grammar Link

Grammar Link Answers
Answers will vary, but they should be vivid adjectives that can replace those underlined in the Grammar Link sentences. For example, students could replace *yellow* with *golden* or *glowing*.

About the Art

Ray Vinella, *Aspen Grove*, 1960 (See page 26.)
Vinella was born in Bari, Italy, and grew up in New York City. Best known for his impressionistic landscapes, Vinella has used many media, including oil, watercolor, egg tempera, and sculpture.

29

WRITING PROCESS IN ACTION

PERSONAL WRITING

Setting the Purpose

Students now have the opportunity to apply what they have learned about personal writing to an independent writing project. They will use the stages of the writing process to create and present a finished piece.

FOCUS

Lesson Overview
Objective: To write about a personal experience that involves shared feelings and emotions
Skills: using the five stages of the writing process: prewriting, drafting, revising, editing, presenting
Critical Thinking: recalling; synthesizing
Speaking and Listening: discussing, evaluating; explaining a process

Bellringer
When students enter the classroom, have this assignment on the board: *Make a list of friends and family members. For each name, note a memorable experience that you shared with that person.*

Grammar Link to the Bellringer
Remind students to capitalize all proper nouns in their lists.

Motivating Activity
Tell students about an experience that you shared with another person. Choose an unplanned experience if possible, such as dropping a friend's wedding cake in the parking lot of the reception hall. Explain how you felt, what you did, and how others reacted. Encourage volunteers to tell similar stories of their own.

In preceding lessons you've learned how to gather and organize your ideas to describe the events in an important personal experience. You've also learned how to describe the feelings you had because of that experience. You've also had the chance to write journal entries about your personal experiences. Now, in this lesson you will write about an experience you shared with someone else.

• Assignment •

Context	*You have decided to contribute to America, America, a publication of personal reflections and images from across the United States. Write about an experience you have shared with someone else.*
Purpose	*To share, in writing, a personal experience*
Audience	*A general audience of all ages*
Length	*2 paragraphs*

The following pages can help you plan and write your personal experience composition. Read through them, and then refer to them as you need to. But don't be tied down by them. You're in charge of your own writing process.

Teacher's Classroom Resources

The following resources can be used for planning, instruction, practice, reinforcement, assessment, reteaching, enrichment, or evaluation.

Teaching Tools
Lesson Plans

Transparencies
Writing Process Transparencies, 1–10

Prewriting

To come up with possible topics for this assignment, try to recall shared experiences that taught you something about life, another person, or yourself. This may help you focus on the people who are close to you and whom you see every day.

The options graphic at the right offers ways to tap into memories for ideas. The notebook gives an example of listing to generate ideas.

Drafting

Exploring your ideas thoroughly during prewriting helps drafting go smoothly. As you review your notes, consider details that will help the reader understand what happened. Write down your ideas just as they come to you. You can polish the good ones later.

Your writing may be clearest if you time-order events. Notice how Gary Soto uses time transitions:

Option A
Review journal entries.

Option B
Brainstorm with a friend.

Option C
Freewrite for ideas.

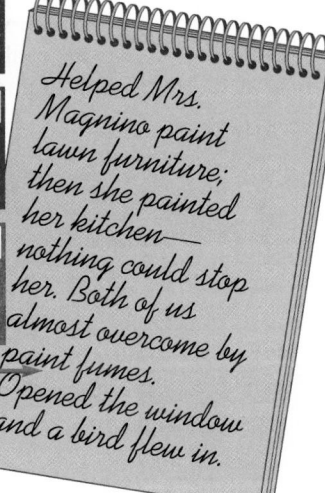

Helped Mrs. Magnino paint lawn furniture; then she painted her kitchen— nothing could stop her. Both of us almost overcome by paint fumes. Opened the window and a bird flew in.

Literature Model

*T*he next day I woke tired and started picking tired. The grapes rained into the pan, slowly filling like a belly, until I had my first tray and started my second. So it went all day, and the next, and all through the following week, so that by the end of the thirteen days the foreman counted out, in tens mostly, my pay of fifty-three dollars.

Gary Soto, *Living up the Street*

Writing Process in Action **31**

TEACH

Prewriting

L2 Developing Ideas for Personal Writing

One way for students to come up with ideas for personal experience writing is to make a list of people they interact with regularly. Then, next to each person's name, they might jot down briefly what happened the last time they saw each person. Would any of these incidents make a good story?

If nothing turns up, direct students to go back further into the past with each name. This mental process of linking people with events may trigger memories they can use in their writing.

Drafting

L2 Deciding on Details

Suggest that students having difficulty deciding what details to include or exclude ask themselves the following questions. Details that earn *yes* answers stay in, and those that are answered *no* should be omitted.

- Is it impossible to tell the story without this detail?
- Is this detail really a part of the experience?
- Does this detail have to be mentioned in order for the story to make sense?
- Would the story lose something important if you took out this detail?

📁 **Blackline Masters**
Thinking and Study Skills,
  pp. 3, 13, 18
Composition Practice, p. 6
Composition Reteaching, p. 6
Composition Enrichment, p. 6

📖 *Grammar Workbook*
Lesson 99

Assessment
📁 *Teacher's Guide to Writing Assessment*

TEACH

Revising

L2 Peer Editing

Students can work in writing conferences with peer editors before they revise their writing. Suggest that peer editors respond to the following:

• Is the description of the experience organized and clear?

• Does the language used convey vivid detail and the feelings of the writer?

You may want to duplicate the Peer Response forms in the *Teacher's Guide to Writing Assessment* for use in writing conferences.

Editing

L2 Peer Editing

After students edit their own work, have them edit another student's work. They can use the checklist on page 33.

Presenting

Before students present their personal writing, discuss how to prepare their papers for publication. Emphasize the importance of the final draft and that it must be neatly done.

Independent Practice

Writing Process Transparencies, 1–10

Skills Practice

Thinking and Study Skills, pp. 3, 13, 18

Composition Practice, p. 6

Grammar Workbook, Lesson 99

Journal Writing Tip

Reviewing the Writing Process Ask students what they will do differently the next time they do personal writing. Have them include these ideas in their journals.

Drafting Tip

For more information about putting events in order, see Lesson 1.4, pages 22–24.

Remember to focus on the shared experience and your own feelings. Review your prewriting notes, your journal, some old photos, anything that works. At this stage, don't edit—just write. You may find it helpful to review pages 10–13 and 18–21.

Revising

To begin revising, read over your draft to make sure that what you've written fits your purpose and audience. Then have a **writing conference.** Read your draft to a partner or small group. Use your audience's reactions to help you evaluate your work.

Question A

Have I put events in time order?

Question B

Have I included interesting details?

Question C

Have I shared my feelings about the experience?

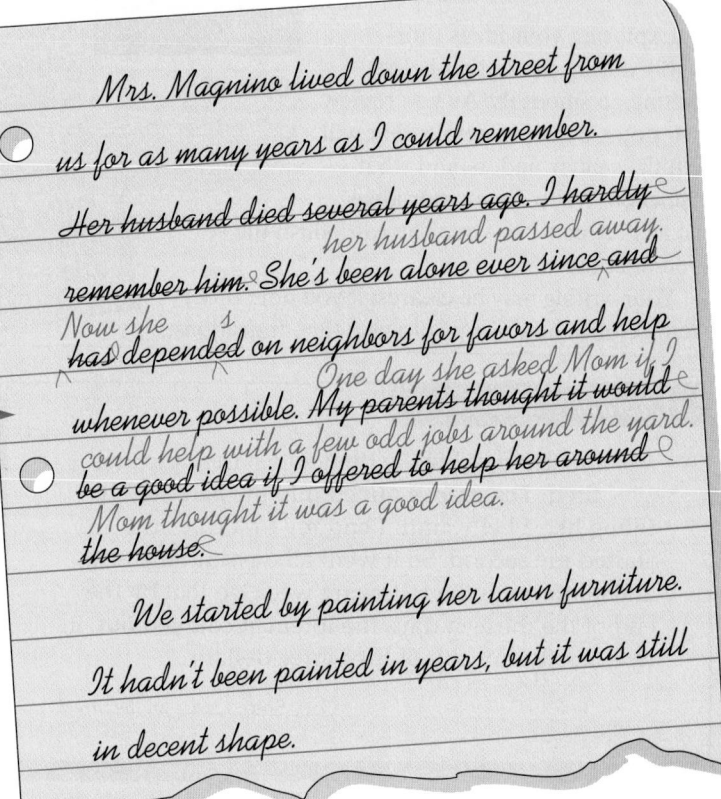

Mrs. Magnino lived down the street from us for as many years as I could remember. Her husband died several years ago. I hardly *her husband passed away.* remember him. She's been alone ever since and *Now she* *s* has depended on neighbors for favors and help whenever possible. *One day she asked Mom if I* My parents thought it would *could help with a few odd jobs around the yard.* be a good idea if I offered to help her around Mom thought it was a good idea. the house.

We started by painting her lawn furniture. It hadn't been painted in years, but it was still in decent shape.

32 *Personal Writing: A Mirror of Myself*

Enrichment and Extension

Follow-up Ideas

• Set aside time for students to celebrate the conclusion of their writing projects. Invite them to share their work.

• If students are sending their work out of the classroom for publication or sharing, make sure they keep photocopies.

Extending Personal Writing

• Brainstorm with students ways to apply their personal writing skills to other projects such as creating poems about turning points.

• Encourage students to look into contributing personal writing to a magazine or newspaper for publication.

Editing

You must complete one more step before you share your writing with others. In the editing stage carefully look over every sentence and word. Don't make your readers struggle through incorrect grammar or misspellings. **Proofread** for these errors, and use the standard proofreading symbols.

Use the editing checklist on the right to help you edit your writing. If certain grammar or punctuation rules give you problems, add them to the checklist. Then read through your work several times, looking for only one or two kinds of errors each time.

Editing Checklist
1. *Have I corrected any sentence fragments?*
2. *Do my verbs agree with their subjects?*
3. *Are all personal pronouns in the correct form?*
4. *Have I used standard spelling, capitalization, and punctuation?*

Presenting

Before you turn in your assignment, think of some suggestions you could give to the editors of *America, America* for the published version of your article. For example, you might suggest some footnotes to help readers with unfamiliar words or names. Maybe you have ideas for illustrations or photographs that could accompany your story. Turn your suggestions in with your writing.

▸ **Proofreading** ▸

For proofreading symbols, see page 81.

Journal Writing

Reflect on your writing process experience. Answer these questions in your journal: What do you like best about your personal experience writing? What was the hardest part of writing it? What did you learn in your writing conference? What new things have you learned as a writer?

Connections Across the Curriculum

Music
The lyrics of some contemporary songs focus on experiences shared with other people. Encourage students to bring in lyrics like these from notes that accompany cassette tapes or CDs. Ask them to read the lyrics aloud and discuss details that bring the experience to life.

ASSESS

Evaluation Guidelines
Use these criteria when evaluating your students' writing.
- Is the writing about an experience shared with another person?
- Is it an experience chosen for its humor, sorrow, irony, or other feeling or concept?
- Is it an experience from which the writer learned something about life or people?
- Is there a sense that the writer understands the meaning of the experience?
- Are details used to enhance the experience?
- Is the writing well organized and proofread?

Refer to the *Teacher's Guide to Writing Assessment* for further help with evaluating student writing.

Reteaching
📁 *Composition Reteaching,* p. 6

Enrichment
📁 *Composition Enrichment,* p. 6

CLOSE

Allow time for the students to discuss the entire writing process from prewriting through presenting and publication, if the entire process was completed. Allow them to read aloud what they wrote in their journals in order to spark general discussion. At the end of the discussion, ask if any students have thought of additional personal experiences that they would like to write about.

About the Author

Gary Soto grew up in the barrios of Fresno, California. Today he is a professor of Chicano Studies and English at the University of California at Berkeley.

Besides an autobiography, *Living up the Street*, Soto has written a number of books for young adults, including *Baseball in April, A Summer Life,* and *Taking Sides.* He has also written a book of poems for young people called *A Fire in My Hands.*

FOCUS

Lesson Overview

Objective: To understand that an autobiography may be an author's record of self-discovery
Skills: reading comprehension
Critical Thinking: identifying; generating new information
Speaking and Listening: discussing

Bellringer

When students enter the classroom, have this assignment on the board: *What have you done for work? List your paid and unpaid jobs, including any chores you do at home.*

Motivating Activity

Ask students if they have bought anything recently. How did they pay for it? If they had to earn the money, did they have any idea how much work was involved, or how long it would take?

UNIT
1

Personal Writing
Literature Model

Gary Soto from

Living up the Street

In Living up the Street, *Gary Soto writes about his growing-up years in Fresno, California. In the excerpt below, Soto describes the experience and feelings he had on his first job, picking grapes alongside his mother. As you read, pay special attention to the details Soto uses to make his experiences and feelings clear. Then try the Linking Writing and Literature activities on page 39.*

I cut another bunch, then another, fighting the snap and whip of vines. After ten minutes of groping for grapes, my first pan brimmed with bunches. I poured them on the paper tray, which was bordered by a wooden frame that kept the grapes from rolling off, and they spilled like jewels from a pirate's chest. The tray was only half filled, so I hurried to jump under the vines and begin groping, cutting, and tugging at the

34 *Personal Writing: A Mirror of Myself*

Teacher's Classroom Resources

The following resources can be used for planning, instruction, or practice.

Teaching Tools
Lesson Plans

Transparencies
Fine Art Transparencies, 1–5

Blackline Masters
Speaking and Listening Activities, pp. 24–25
Thinking and Study Skills, pp. 5, 9, 17

Assessment
Teacher's Guide to Writing Assessment

grapes again. I emptied the pan, raked the grapes with my hands to make them look like they filled the tray, and jumped back under the vine on my knees. I tried to cut faster because Mother, in the next row, was slowly moving ahead. I peeked into her row and saw five trays gleaming in the early morning. I cut, pulled hard, and stopped to gather the grapes that missed the pan; already bored, I spat on a few to wash them before tossing them like popcorn into my mouth.

So it went. Two pans equaled one tray—or six cents. By lunchtime I had a trail of thirty-seven trays behind me while Mother had sixty or more. We met about halfway from our last trays, and I sat down with a grunt, knees wet from kneeling on dropped grapes. I washed my hands with the water from the jug, drying them on the inside of my shirt sleeve before I opened the paper bag for the first sandwich, which I gave to Mother. I dipped my hand in again to unwrap a sandwich without looking at it. I took a first bite and chewed it slowly for the tang of mustard. Eating in silence I looked straight ahead at the vines, and

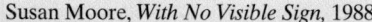

Susan Moore, *With No Visible Sign*, 1988

Literature Model **35**

UNIT 1
Literature
Model

TEACH

Guided Practice

L2 Guided Reading
- What literary devices does the author use to enrich his writing? (alliteration: "groping for grapes"; strong action verbs: *fighting, groped, tugging, raked;* simile: "they spilled like jewels from a pirate's chest")
- How does the author feel by lunchtime? What clues do you find? (He is tired or upset. He sat down with a grunt, took his sandwich out without looking at it, and ate in silence with his mother.)

About the Art

Susan Moore, *With No Visible Sign,* 1988

Susan Moore was born on March 27, 1953, in Coco Solo, Panama. She has exhibited her work in the United States and Italy. She has been visiting artist at Boston University and Yale Summer School of Art and Music. In 1989 she received a fellowship from the National Endowment for the Arts. Susan Moore's *With No Visible Sign* is oil pastel on paper and measures 74 inches by 67 inches. It is in the More Gallery in Philadelphia, Pennsylvania.

TEACH

Guided Practice

L2 Guided Reading

- Why is Gary Soto working in the fields? (He wants to earn money to buy new clothes for school.)
- How does Gary feel at the end of lunch? (He dreads going back to work.) What does he do to keep his mind and hands moving? (He daydreams about the pool, baseball, and girlfriends. He sings softly.)

only when we were finished with cookies did we talk.

"Are you tired?" she asked.

"No, but I got a sliver from the frame," I told her. I showed her the web of skin between my thumb and index finger. She wrinkled her forehead but said it was nothing.

"How many trays did you do?"

I looked straight ahead, not answering at first. I recounted in my mind the whole morning of bend, cut, pour again and again, before answering a feeble "thirty-seven." No elaboration,[1] no detail. Without looking at me she told me how she had done field work in Texas and Michigan as a child. But I had a difficult time listening to her stories. I played with my grape knife, stabbing it into the ground, but stopped when Mother reminded me that I had better not lose it. I left the knife sticking up like a small, leafless plant. She then talked about school, the junior high I would be going to that fall, and then about Rick and Debra, how sorry they would be that they hadn't come out to pick grapes because they'd have no new clothes for the school year. She stopped talking when she peeked at her watch, a bandless one she kept in her pocket. She got up with an "*Ay, Dios,*" and told me that we'd work until three, leaving me cutting figures in the sand with my knife and dreading the return to work.

Finally I rose and walked slowly back to where I had left off, again kneeling under the vine and fixing the pan under bunches of grapes. By that time, 11:30, the sun was over my shoulder and made me squint and think of the pool at the Y.M.C.A. where I was a summer member. I saw myself diving face first into the water and loving it. I saw myself gleaming like something new, at the edge of the pool. I had to daydream and keep my mind busy because boredom was a terror almost as awful as the work itself. My mind went dumb with stupid things, and I had to keep it moving with dreams of baseball and would-be girlfriends. I even sang, however softly, to keep my mind moving, my hands moving.

I worked less hurriedly and with less vision. I no longer saw that copper pot sitting squat[2] on our stove or Mother waiting for

1 **elaboration** (i lab'ə rā'shən) giving more details
2 **squat** (skwot) short and thick; low and broad

36 *Personal Writing: A Mirror of Myself*

Genre and Style

Reading Personal Writing

Living up the Street is an autobiography written in simple, direct language, such as "The next day I woke tired and started picking tired," to bring home the reality of hard work. Call students' attention to the figurative language that helps the reader share Soto's personal experiences, such as his description of the grapes filling a pan "like a belly." Ask students to find other examples.

Anthony Ortega, *Farmworkers de Califas*, 1990

it to whistle. The wardrobe that I imagined, crisp and bright in the closet, numbered only one pair of jeans and two shirts because, in half a day, six cents times thirty-seven trays was two dollars and twenty-two cents. It became clear to me. If I worked eight hours, I might make four dollars. I'd take this, even gladly, and walk downtown to look into store windows on the mall and long for bright madras[3] shirts from Walter Smith or Coffee's, but settling for two imitation ones from Penney's.

That first day I laid down seventy-three trays while Mother had a hundred and twenty behind her. On the back of an old envelope, she wrote out our numbers and hours. We washed at the pump behind the farm house and walked slowly back to our car for the drive back to town in the afternoon heat. That evening after dinner I sat in a lawn chair listening to music from a transistor radio while Rick and David King played catch. I joined them in a game of pickle, but there was little joy in trying to avoid their tags because I couldn't get the fields out of my mind: I saw

---

3 madras (mad′rəs) a fine, striped or plaid cotton cloth

Literature Model **37**

TEACH

Guided Practice

L2 Guided Reading
- What does the author mean when he says he worked with "less vision" in the final paragraph on page 36? Is he really seeing less? (He is not talking about sight, he is talking about his dreams. He no longer imagines that he will be able to buy his mother a copper pot, and he has adjusted his dreams of clothing to what he will actually be able to afford.)
- Why do you think the painting on page 37 was included with this passage? (The painting is of farmworkers, and the color and brushstrokes make one feel the heat and exhaustion that Gary Soto describes.)

About the Art

Anthony Ortega, *Farmworkers de Califas*, 1990

Anthony D. Ortega received his Bachelor of Arts degree and a Certificate in Latin American Studies from the University of Colorado. He has also studied at the Universidad de Veracruz in Xalapa, Mexico. He received the

AFKEY Award for Excellence in Art in 1991. Ortega is also a published writer.

His *Farmworkers de Califas* is mixed media and measures 30 by 42 inches. It is part of a private collection.

TEACH

Guided Practice

L2 Guided Reading
- What is the theme of the passage? (discovery)
- What important things does Gary learn about himself? (He cannot work as fast as his mother does in the fields, and he must give up his dreams in the face of hard work.) What does he discover about life? (He finds that hard work does not fulfill all dreams but produces such realities as fatigue, splinters, and mind-numbing boredom.)

Independent Practice

Fine Art Transparencies, 1–5

Skills Practice
Speaking and Listening Activities, pp. 24–25

Thinking and Study Skills, pp. 5, 9, 17

---

myself dropping on my knees under a vine to tug at a branch that wouldn't come off. In bed, when I closed my eyes, I saw the fields, yellow with kicked up dust, and a crooked trail of trays rotting behind me.

The next day I woke tired and started picking tired. The grapes rained into the pan, slowly filling like a belly, until I had my first tray and started my second. So it went all day, and the next, and all through the following week, so that by the end of thirteen days the foreman counted out, in tens mostly, my pay of fifty-three dollars. Mother earned one hundred and forty-eight dollars. She wrote this on her envelope, with a message I didn't bother to ask her about.

The next day I walked with my friend Scott to the downtown mall where we drooled over the clothes behind fancy windows, bought popcorn, and sat at a tier of outside fountains to talk about girls. Finally we went into Penney's for more popcorn, which we ate walking around, before we returned home without buying anything. It wasn't until a few days before school that I let my fifty-three dollars slip quietly from my hands, buying a pair of pants, two shirts, and a maroon T-shirt, the kind that was in style. At home I tried them on while Rick looked on enviously; later, the day before school started, I tried them on again wondering not so much if they were worth it as who would see me first in those clothes.

Writers and Writing

Triggering Memories
In *Living up the Street*, Gary Soto explains what triggered his memory of working in the fields. He saw the movie *Gandhi*, and the hard-working people shown in the film reminded him of his family.

Linking Writing and Literature
Readers Respond to the Model

How do Gary Soto's descriptions give a vivid picture of his experience and his feelings?

Explore Gary Soto's personal writing by answering the following questions. Then read how other students responded to his work.

1. Based on Soto's writing, how would you describe his job of picking grapes?

2. What feelings, interests, habits, and dreams does Soto have that are similar to those of many teenagers?

3. How is Soto's life different, or more difficult, than that of many teenagers?

4. Based on Soto's writing, what adjectives would you use to describe the setting of the grape fields?

5. While picking grapes, what does Soto look forward to buying with the money he will earn? What does he do once he has the money? In your opinion, why?

Since I am Hispanic (Puerto Rican), I put myself in the boy's place. I even enjoy some of the same things that he does. For example, I really like swimming, and I go to the YMCA pool, too.

I remembered well a number of the scenes from the selection. For example, I can still picture the boy's lunch with his mother and the grape picking. I think that, because the author kept my attention by describing these scenes in detail they stayed in my mind.

I would recommend this literature selection to a friend. I think it helps the reader see how some people have to struggle to make a little money.

Paul Roustan

I clearly remember the scene in which the boy gives up his dreams. He forgets about what he was going to buy, such as a copper teapot for his mother and stylish clothes for himself. He was hit with the reality of hard work. I liked the details about how tired he felt from working.

Joshua Zapata

Literature Model **39**

CLOSE

Post a piece of chart paper. Invite each student to share a response to the passage. Responses might be written or drawn.

ASSESS

Evaluation Guidelines for Discussion

As your students discuss the passage, either in small groups or as a class, encourage them to begin with a personal response. The student responses on this page might be used as a starting point.

Look for evidence that students

- have read the passage
- can state some of the writer's ideas in their own words
- understand the writer's point of view
- have connected the content to their own knowledge and experiences
- understand the ideas and implications of the passage

Some possible responses to the discussion questions on this page:

1. difficult, low-paying, hot, dusty, boring, tiring

2. He likes to swim; he's interested in girls and baseball; he'd like to have nice clothes; he likes to play pick-up games with his brothers and friends; he likes music.

3. He has to take a difficult job to make money to buy clothes for school; he and his family struggle to make the money they need.

4. dusty, yellow ground; low, thick, woody vines; hot sun overhead

5. He dreams of buying school clothes for himself and a copper pot for his mother. Once he has the money, he doesn't buy anything at first. Then, just before school starts, he buys only a few clothes and he does not buy the pot for his mother. I think he realizes that all his hard work cannot give him what he dreams of having.

REVIEW

Reflecting on the Unit
You may have students respond to Reflecting on the Unit in writing or through discussion.

Writing Across the Curriculum
Encourage students to express their true feelings and ideas in their writing and to include sensory language and details that will help bring their experiences alive.

Adding to Your Portfolio
Because this unit focuses primarily on personal writing, encourage students to select those pieces that best express their true feelings and ideas. Have students keep an eye out for samples that may contain ideas for future personal writing.

Portfolio Evaluation
If you grade the portfolio selections, you may want to award two marks—one each for content and form. Explain your assessment criteria before students make their selections. Commend
- experimentation with creative prewriting techniques
- clear, concise writing in which the main idea, audience, and purpose are evident
- successful revisions
- work that shows a flair for language

Unit 1 Review

 **Reflecting on the Unit**

Summarize.

- What is personal writing?
- Why is a journal a good place for personal writing?
- What is a learning log?

- How can you explore the future through personal writing?
- What kinds of events might you describe or explore in an autobiography?
- In what ways can you respond to a piece of literature?

 **Adding to Your Portfolio**

Choose a selection for your portfolio.
Look over the writing you did for this unit. Select a piece of writing for your portfolio. The writing you choose should show one or more of the following:

- your personal experiences: ideas, thoughts, feelings, activities, and memories
- discoveries you have made about yourself and the world in which you live
- your wishes or dreams for the future
- important events or turning points that have changed the direction of your life
- a personal response to a poem or other piece of literature

Reflect on your choice.
Attach a note to the piece you chose, explaining why you chose it and what you learned from writing it.

Set goals.
How can you improve your writing? What skill will you focus on the next time you write?

 **Writing Across the Curriculum**

Make a science connection.
Select a personal experience that happened in the natural world. To think of ideas, list places where you have contact with nature. Then write a journal entry describing an experience. Use sensory details to create a picture of the setting.

40 *Unit 1 Review*

Teacher's Classroom Resources

The following resources can be used for assessment or evaluation.

Unit Assessment
📂 *Tests with Answer Key*
Unit 1 Choice A Test, p. 1
Unit 1 Choice B Test, p. 2
Unit 1 Composition Objective Test, pp. 3–4

 Test Generator
Unit 1 Choice A Test
Unit 1 Choice B Test
Unit 1 Composition Objective Test

You may wish to administer one of these tests as a mastery test.

UNIT 2

Composition

The Writing Process

Lessons

41

UNIT GOALS

The goal of Unit 2 is to help students, through example and instruction, to develop an understanding of the recursive nature of the writing process and its five main stages: prewriting, drafting, revising, editing, and presenting.

Unit Assessment

Tests with Answer Key
Unit 2 Choice A Test, p. 5
Unit 2 Choice B Test, p. 6
Unit 2 Composition Objective Test, pp. 7–8

Test Generator
Unit 2 Choice A Test
Unit Composition Objective Test
Unit 2 Choice B Test

You may wish to administer either the Unit 2 Choice A Test or the Choice B Test as a pretest.

Key to Ability Levels

Enabling Strategies have been coded for varying learning styles and abilities.

L1 Level 1 activities are within the ability range of Learning Disabled students.

L2 Level 2 activities are basic-to-average activities and are within the ability range of average students.

L3 Level 3 activities are challenging activities and are within the ability range of above-average students.

LEP LEP activities are within the ability range of Limited English Proficiency students.

The Writing Process
in the Real World

Kurtis Explores Science

F O C U S: Like writing, the process of producing a documentary involves research, drafting a script, and editing the film.

▲ *Documentary producer Bill Kurtis*

One night back in 1987, TV journalist Bill Kurtis was filming a zoologist who was searching for a new species of bird in Peru. Kurtis said that suddenly "a light went on. In a flash I saw a series of stories following scientists into the field."

Today Kurtis heads Kurtis Productions, and his idea has become a television series called *The New Explorers*. Each program profiles a scientist—a hero to Kurtis—working on science's frontiers or bringing science to non-scientists. Sometimes it features people such as Chris Cheviarina and Jim Hicks—Mr. C and Uncle Jim. They're high school teachers "on a mission to teach physics you can actually understand."

42 *The Writing Process: Working Together*

Setting the Purpose

In the Unit 2 Case Study, students observe how a documentary producer gathers information, produces a rough cut, and then refines the television show. Students will explore and practice the writing process stages in the lessons that follow.

FOCUS

Lesson Overview

Objective: To identify attributes of an effective film documentary
Skills: researching; evaluating information; editing; organizing information
Critical Thinking: analyzing; synthesizing; evaluating; summarizing; building background; defining and clarifying; generating new information
Speaking and Listening: interviewing; formal speaking; informal speaking; introducing; explaining a process

Bellringer
When students enter the classroom, have this assignment on the board: *Write everything you know (or imagine) about what goes into producing a news show or documentary.*

Grammar Link to the Bellringer
Challenge students to replace any nondescript verbs from the Bellringer activity with more accurate, precise verbs.

Motivating Activity
Point out that creating a television documentary is like a cooperative learning project. Bill Kurtis, the producer, finds the topic and edits the final script. Associate producers seek leads to pursue; writers gather information and draft the script; film crews film the subject; and film editors cut and refine the film.

Teacher's Classroom Resources

The following resources can be used for planning, instruction, practice, reinforcement, assessment, or evaluation.

Teaching Tools
Lesson Plans, p. 9

Transparencies
Writing Process Transparencies, 1–10

Producing a Documentary

Prewriting	Drafting	Revising/Editing
Gathering Information	Creating a Rough Cut	Fine-tuning the Show

"I try to accomplish two things in **The New Explorers.** *One is to show that scientists are action-oriented, that science is an adventure. I also want to teach scientific ideas in a new way."*

—Bill Kurtis

Prewriting

GATHERING INFORMATION

Where did Kurtis find Uncle Jim and Mr. C, the heroes for "Rock 'n' Roll Physics"? "A staff member knew two teachers who began an amusement park physics program," said Kurtis.

Kurtis sensed a story. The teachers weren't scientists on the cutting edge. But it sounded as if they were turning physics into a high-voltage adventure. Kurtis sent his staff into action.

"We have associate producers," he said, "and they make some initial calls. Just like any journalist, we're asking, 'Is this a good story?'"

▼ *Bill Kurtis often travels when filming* The New Explorers. *His filming location might be the Amazon or an amusement park.*

📁 **Blackline Masters**
*Cooperative Learning
  Activities*, pp. 7–12
Thinking and Study Skills,
  pp. 1–2, 4, 8, 11, 13–19, 34–40
*Case Studies: Writing in the
  Real World*, pp. 5–8

Assessment
📁 *Teacher's Guide to
  Writing Assessment*

TEACH

Building Background

Warm-up:
Ask the class to list other products besides documentaries that might require the stages of prewriting, drafting, revising, editing, and presenting.

The Writing Process in Speaking:
Ask students to think of situations in which one of the stages mentioned above might be used in everyday language. For example, a person might revise a description or explanation if more accurate information becomes available.

The Writing Process in Writing:
Ask the class to list examples of writing that would require more than one draft to be clear and complete.
- How long does a piece of writing have to be to require all the stages of the writing process?
- How might even a poster or announcement benefit from the stages?
- In the business world, how often do you think articles, advertisements, or other products are presented without going through several stages and reviews?

Preview the Case Study
Invite students to skim the Case Study, noting the various types of reviews or refinements the documentary receives. Then have them read the Case Study more thoroughly and take notes about the details involved in each of the stages.

UNIT 2
Case Study

TEACH

Discussion Prompts

- Why do you suppose Kurtis chose to shoot the film or video before writing the script? What might be some benefits of this approach? When might it be better to write the script first?

- What do you think Kurtis was specifically looking for when he said, "I wanted to see how good they were on camera, how good the action was." What kinds of things could disappoint him during this stage and make him decide the show wouldn't work?

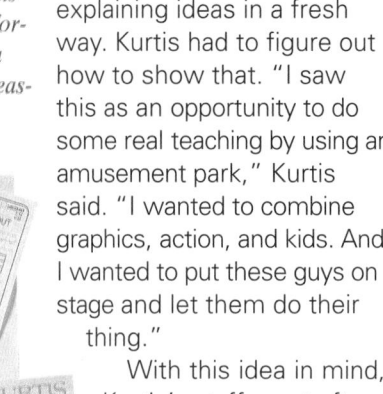

▼ *For Kurtis and his team, gathering information can mean a library trip just as easily as a field trip.*

The teachers were explaining ideas in a fresh way. Kurtis had to figure out how to show that. "I saw this as an opportunity to do some real teaching by using an amusement park," Kurtis said. "I wanted to combine graphics, action, and kids. And I wanted to put these guys on stage and let them do their thing."

With this idea in mind, Kurtis's staff went after more information. "We may go to the library," Kurtis said. "We may do interviews. Ultimately, we have to go out and shoot film or video."

In this case shooting takes place before the script for the show is written. The material gathered from the shoot will help during scriptwriting.

The first step in shooting "Rock 'n' Roll Physics" was catching the teachers in action. Kurtis sent a camera crew to Barrington High School outside Chicago. "I said, just follow the teachers and shoot everything they do," Kurtis explained. "I wanted to see how good they were on camera, how good the action was."

At this time, the physics class was wrestling with Newton's first law of motion. It states: An object in motion will remain in motion, and an object at rest will remain at rest, unless external force is applied.

What does Newton's first law of motion mean? In a school hallway the film crew caught Uncle Jim, Mr. C, and the class experimenting with a hovercraft. It was made of a chair, a vacuum cleaner, and a piece of plywood. The hovercraft zoomed down the hall; it became an object in motion! Mr. C yelled for students to grab the hovercraft before it crashed into a wall—in other words, to stop the moving object by applying force. There it was— Newton's first law in action.

44   *The Writing Process: Working Together*

Civic Literacy

Examining the Responsibilities of Teaching

Discuss why Kurtis picked the two science teachers as heroes. What qualities make a good teacher? What responsibilities does a teacher have? How do Mr. C and Uncle Jim fulfill those responsibilities? You might also discuss the responsibilities a documentary team has. What do they owe to their audience? What makes an effective documentary?

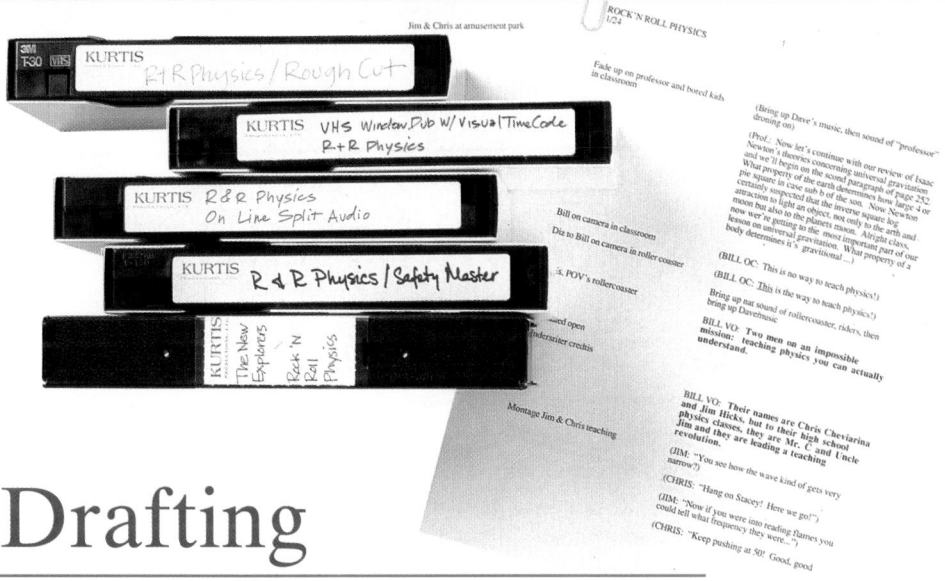

Drafting

CREATING A ROUGH CUT

With miles of film and heads full of physics, the team met to discuss the show. "We asked, 'How do we want to tell this story?'" Kurtis said.

Kurtis wanted to show the teachers bringing physics to life. So the producer pulled the best moments from the interviews. "These are the most important moments, because they're the ones that really grab you," Kurtis said.

Based on these moments, the script was drafted with a clear opener, a beginning, a middle, and an end. "You must be able to follow the story," Kurtis said. "You can't lose it along the way."

Next the script called for Kurtis to explain the show's subject and to introduce the heroes—the new explorers. "This is my getting-to-know-you section," Kurtis said. "I want viewers to get to know the heroes and their work. I want people to care about what they're doing."

High-energy scenes would take viewers from class to pool to parking lot to roller coaster. They would teach science, all right, but with color and action. "I like to change the pace often to keep the viewer's attention," Kurtis emphasized.

▲ *The script is used like an outline to guide the production of the documentary.*

Case Study **45**

TEACH

Discussion Prompts
- What do you think Kurtis means by important moments "that really grab you"? Can you give examples of what might be a "grabbing" moment and what might not be?
- How might one "change the pace" in a documentary? How does changing the pace keep the viewer's attention?

Connections Across the Curriculum

Science
Ask students to take on the role of documentary writers and explain how they would dramatize examples of a science principle they are currently studying for an audience of younger students.

TEACH

Guided Practice

L2 Discussion
Stimulate a discussion of the Case Study. You may want to invite students to talk about

- Kurtis's goals during the prewriting stage, how they were met.
- the goals during the drafting stage and the reasons for each goal.
- what the goals were during revising and editing, and how Kurtis would determine whether the goals were met.

Independent Practice

Writing Process Transparencies, 1–10
Case Studies: Writing in the Real World, pp. 5–8
Cooperative Learning Activities, pp. 7–12

Skills Practice
Thinking and Study Skills, pp. 1–2, 4, 8, 11, 13–19, 34–40

The ending would showcase students discussing the class and their teachers. Who could explain better why Uncle Jim and Mr. C's unusual teaching style works?

Revising/Editing

FINE-TUNING THE SHOW

The draft of the script was then revised, and fifty hours of video were cut down to four. Kurtis handed the script to the film editor, who related the best film images to the script. He created a rough cut, or draft, of the show.

With pictures and words combined, the show suddenly came to life. What did Kurtis and his team look for now? "Now we're television producers," he said. "Do we have an opening, a beginning, a climax, and a conclusion? Does the story work?"

"I'll tell you," he said, "on 'Rock 'n' Roll Physics' we looked at the rough cut and said, 'We need to do some work here.' Frankly, I wasn't understanding the science."

Kurtis thought bold graphics would help explain more clearly the difficult science concepts. To make better sense of Newton's first law, for instance, Kurtis looked for everyday examples. He wanted to show how objects in motion travel in a straight line unless another force stops them.

Besides adding graphics, the team re-edited the video. They cut some parts and expanded others. After nearly eight weeks of work, "Rock 'n' Roll Physics" was ready to go.

▼ *On location at an amusement park, Uncle Jim and Mr. C teach physics to their students.*

46　*The Writing Process: Working Together*

Visual Thinking

Creating a Flow Chart
Visual learners might benefit from a diagram illustrating the basic steps of writing a documentary. Help them create and illustrate a flow chart with steps such as the following:

1. Brainstorm: Decide what to tell about.
2. Narrow: Focus on one topic.
3. Draft: Create a first version.
4. Revise: Add or change material to make it more precise and clear.
5. Edit: Fix any mistakes; put the script and film together.

Responding to the Case Study

1. Discussion

Discuss these questions about Bill Kurtis's documentary writing.

- What framework, or basic plan, does Kurtis follow when drafting a script?
- What makes the story of Uncle Jim and Mr. C a good story?
- How was the script organized?
- What kinds of revisions were made to the rough cut? Why?

2. The Writing Process

Write the opening to a documentary.

The New Explorers introduces science "heroes" to viewers. What if *you* were making a documentary? What would you choose for a subject? Perhaps it would be about your favorite sport, music group, or hobby. Choose a subject you like that would be interesting to others, and write it down. Then think of a funny or exciting way to start your documentary, and write your opening.

Grammar Link

Use specific verbs to convey action.

Just as the teachers turned physics into a "high-voltage" adventure, you can charge up your writing with strong verbs.

*The hovercraft **zoomed** down the hall.*

Revise each sentence below by replacing the italicized verb with a more specific verb.

1. The class *made* a hovercraft.
2. Mr. C *said*, "Watch out!"
3. I really *like* this class.
4. I now *know* how Newton's first law of motion works.
5. I *walked* out of the room, ready to make my own video.

See Lesson 3.3, page 114.

Case Study **47**

ASSESS

Responding to the Case Study

1. Discussion
- a clear opener and a beginning, middle, and end
- They explained physics to students in a fresh, interesting, practical way.
- with high-energy scenes and frequent changes of pace
- cutting fifty hours of video to four; adding graphics and everyday examples to make explanations clearer; cutting some parts and expanding others to make it clear, informative, and interesting

2. The Writing Process
Answers will vary. Openings should intrigue listeners and introduce the people and topic in an inviting way.

See also *Teacher's Guide to Writing Assessment*.

Grammar Link
(See Using the Grammar Link below.)

Reteaching
Have students summarize how a documentary can be tailored to fit a specific purpose and to reach the audience.

Enrichment
Students might work together to review a television documentary, commenting on its use of graphics, action, and interviews to fulfill its intended purpose and to reach the audience.

CLOSE

Discuss how writers of documentary articles can compensate for having fewer visuals than are available with film. For example, the writers might rely more heavily on vivid sensory language to capture readers' interest and make ideas clear. **47**

Using the Grammar Link

Grammar Link Answers
Answers will vary, but some suggestions are given below.
1. constructed
2. yelled
3. enjoy
4. understand
5. rushed

Expanding the Vivid Verb Vocabulary Challenge groups of students to expand their vocabularies by using a thesaurus or synonym finder to collect more answers for the Grammar Link exercise. Challenge students to see how many words they can collect for each sentence.

FOCUS

Lesson Overview

Objective: To identify the goals of each writing process stage, and to learn techniques to fulfill these goals
Skills: prewriting; drafting; revising; editing; presenting
Critical Thinking: synthesizing; using main idea and details; establishing and evaluating criteria; visualizing; generating new information; identifying
Speaking and Listening: taking notes; discussing, evaluating

Bellringer

When students enter the classroom, have this assignment on the board: *Write down as many reasons as you can that tell why it helps to revisit something you've written.*

Grammar Link to the Bellringer
As students discuss the Bellringer question, point out that one benefit of revisiting is the chance to make the writing flow more naturally. For example, subject pronouns can be used if names are repeated unnecessarily.

Motivating Activity

Ask students how they would treat a cut finger. Elicit a process from them. First, they would wash the cut. Next, they would examine it to make sure that it was clean. Then, they would dry it and apply a bandage. Emphasize that they would repeat any step until they were satisfied with the outcome—much like the writing process.

The Writing Process
Working with the Writing Process

When the Camera Club decided to build a dark-room in the basement of their school, they made a plan. First they scouted a location; then they made a few sketches and lists.

Go Through a Process

Just as building doesn't begin with a hammer, writing doesn't begin with a pen. Both activities involve several stages—from the first idea to a finished product.

Prewriting   The prewriting stage begins with selecting and exploring a topic. One useful technique is to search your memory for experiences you'd like to share. Begin by looking at old photos of

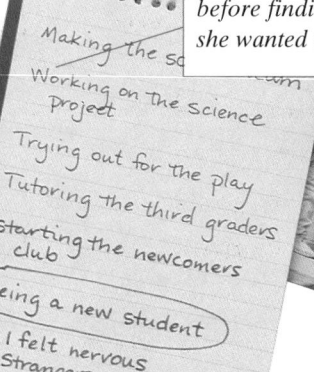

This writer made several prewriting notes before finding an idea she wanted to explore.

Making the s... ...m
Working on the science project
Trying out for the play
Tutoring the third graders
Starting the newcomers club
Being a new student
I felt nervous
Strangers, but friendly
Ms. Osaka broke the ice

48

Teacher's Classroom Resources

yourself and your friends, jotting down ideas as you go. Think about which ideas you'd enjoy writing about and which might interest others. Decide how to organize these ideas.

Drafting   When you draft, you turn your prewriting notes into sentences and paragraphs. You arrange your ideas in the order you chose in prewriting. New ideas will continue to come. Write them all down. Some will work, and some won't. Your draft may look messy, but don't worry. You can fix it later.

Revising   Step back and look over what you've written. Read it aloud to peer reviewers, and answer questions like the following: Are your ideas clear? Do they fit together? What other details might help your readers understand and enjoy what you've written?

Editing   In the editing stage, you examine each word, phrase, and sentence in your writing. This is the time to find and correct any errors in grammar, spelling, and punctuation. Your goal is a neat, error-free copy for others to read and enjoy.

Presenting   The presenting stage means sharing your writing with its audience. You can read a report aloud in class. You can work with others to publish a class poetry book. You can write a letter to the editor of the school newspaper. What other ways can you think of to present your work to readers?

> **Drafting**
> I felt nervous walking in that first morning. The halls were crowded. People seemed happy to [start] a new year. They

> **Revising**
> ○to Carver Junior High School
> I felt nervous walking in that first morning. The halls were crowded, People seemed happy to
> Friends greeted each other,
> together
> be starting a new year. They
> didn't seem to need to know a new
> especially
> person, and one from another
> faraway Japan ○
> country at that.

Journal Writing

Create your own chart to summarize and help you remember the writing process. Refer to it as you complete your writing assignments.

2.1 Working with the Writing Process   **49**

TEACH
Guided Practice

L2 Using the Model
Ask students to point out changes that the student made while revising. Ask them to speculate why each change was made. (The student added a specific location to the first sentence to identify the setting. Then the student made the third sentence more specific, giving details about actions.) Elicit that the addition of specific details made the writing clearer.

L1 Understanding Rewriting
Some students may be overwhelmed at the thought of writing and rewriting and then rewriting some more. They may feel discouraged if they can't get things "right" the first time. To encourage them, use analogies from outside the classroom. Architects revise plans continually until they meet the needs of the client. Even the Declaration of Independence went through many revisions.

Two-Minute Skill Drill

To help students differentiate between revising and editing, ask them to do both to the following sentence, using two different colors.

i haven't ever tried cooking things.

Journal Writing Tip

Summarizing the Steps You might direct students to note the tasks and goals of each stage. These "maps" will make the writing process easier to follow.

Unit Assessment

Composition Practice, p. 7
Composition Reteaching, p. 7
Composition Enrichment, p. 7

📁 *Teacher's Guide to Writing Assessment*
📁 *Tests with Answer Key*
   Unit 2 Choice A Test, p. 5
   Unit 2 Choice B Test, p. 6

💿 Test Generator
   Unit 2 Choice A Test
   Unit 2 Choice B Test

You may wish to administer either the Unit 2 Choice A Test or the Unit 2 Choice B Test as a pretest.

TEACH

Guided Practice

L2 Using the Model

You may wish to discuss the connotation of the term *small world* (coincidence) and the feelings that the student probably had. Ask students to suggest why this addition improved the piece. (It added details about feelings; it uses a figure of speech to make the writing more descriptive.)

L3 Identifying Problems

Ask students to refer to the chart and explain, through specific examples, why a writer might need to go back to a previous stage. For example, in a history report a writer might realize, while revising, that he or she had left out an important detail. To which stage might the writer return? (The writer would go back to the prewriting notes. If the information wasn't there, the writer would do further research.) Then ask students to examine selections from their own writing and make notes about stages they might return to in order to make important revisions.

Independent Practice

For further stimuli for writing, see *Fine Art Transparencies* 6–10.

Writing Process Transparencies, 1–10

Writing Across the Curriculum, pp. 4–8

Cooperative Learning Activities, pp. 7–12

Skills Practice

Thinking and Study Skills, pp. 1–2, 11, 13

Speaking and Listening Activities, pp. 6–7, 12, 23

Composition Practice, p. 7

Revising

How wrong I was! The first surprise ^icebreaker *came when I met Ms. Osaka,* ^the school librarian *I couldn't believe that she'd moved here just a year ago from Kushiro, my native city in Japan. Immediately, I understood the meaning of the term "small world."*

Be Flexible

Writing is a messy process. It needs to be messy, because ideas rarely flow in an orderly way. Novelist James A. Michener once said, "I have never thought of myself as a good writer. Anyone who wants reassurance of that should read one of my first drafts. But I'm one of the world's great rewriters."

At any stage in the writing process, a writer can have new and better ideas about how to say something, how to get the message across. Feel free to move backward and forward as you write. For example, if you get stuck while writing your draft because your notes are incomplete, go back to prewriting, and add to your notes. In editing, if a sentence doesn't say enough, rewrite and revise it until you're satisfied. One of this writer's best ideas, about a small world, came in a later revision.

The Writing Process

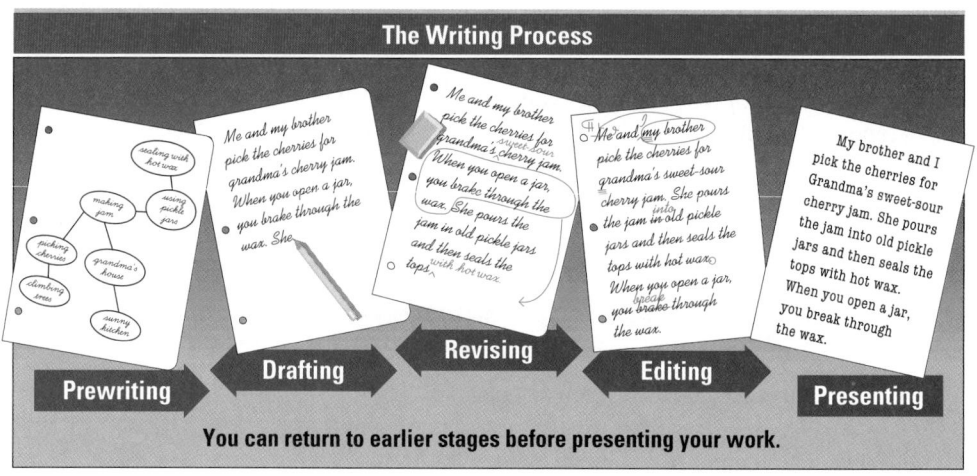

Prewriting ▸ **Drafting** ▸ **Revising** ▸ **Editing** ▸ **Presenting**

You can return to earlier stages before presenting your work.

50   *The Writing Process: Working Together*

Enabling Strategies

LEP Drafting and Revising

Students who have difficulties writing in English should be encouraged by the freedom that the early stages of the writing process afford. Point out that students should concentrate on ideas and details and not worry about spelling and mechanics until the editing stage, when help will be available from peer reviewers. Before students begin writing a paragraph, have a brainstorming session in which the students jot down their ideas and then try organizing them into a short informal outline.

2.1 Writing Activities

Write a Paragraph

How can the stages of creating a sculpture be like the stages of creating a piece of writing? Make some notes to yourself about how the process Oldenburg used to create his toothbrush sculpture is like the writing process. Then write a paragraph comparing the two processes.

- Point out how preparing for and finishing a piece of writing are like preparing for and finishing a sculpture.
- If you like, point out how the two processes are different.

PURPOSE To compare two creative processes
AUDIENCE Your classmates
LENGTH 1 paragraph

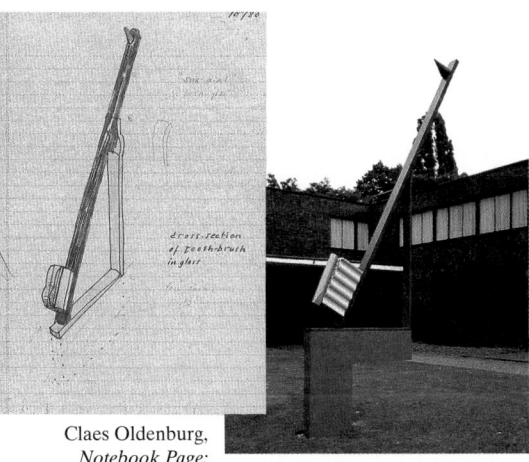

Claes Oldenburg, *Notebook Page: Cross-section of Toothbrush in Glass, 'sun dial,'* 1980

Claes Oldenburg, *Cross-section of a Toothbrush with Paste, in a Cup, on a Sink: Portrait of Coosje's Thinking,* 1983

Cooperative Learning

In a small group, brainstorm to create a list of public figures whom you consider important. You might list entertainers, athletes, writers, and political leaders. Together, explore reasons why you think each person is important. Finally, create a group list of ideas for an essay titled "What Makes an Important Person Important?" Using the list, have each member individually write one paragraph to answer the question. Combine your papers into a single report.

Grammar Link

Use subject pronouns—*I, we, she, he, they*—in the subject of a sentence.

*My brother and **I** pick the cherries for Grandma's sweet-sour cherry jam.*

Write each sentence, correcting errors in the use of pronouns.

[1] Me and her take piano lessons. [2] Us often play duets. [3] Me and you can sing this song. [4-5] In fact, me and Maria can play while you and him sing.

See Lesson 11.1, page 402, and Lesson 11.3, page 406.

2.1 Working with the Writing Process **51**

ASSESS

Writing Activities Evaluation Guidelines

Write a Paragraph
Use these criteria when evaluating your students' writing.
- Writing includes some details about the process the sculptor used.
- Writing addresses some points of comparison between the two processes.

See also the *Teacher's Guide to Writing Assessment.*

Cooperative Learning
Commend the following:
- prewriting notes that show a creative, thorough exploration of the topic
- a draft paragraph that shows effective use of the prewriting notes
- enough details to make the writer's ideas clear

Grammar Link
(See Using the Grammar Link below.)

Reteaching
📁 *Composition Reteaching,* p. 7

Enrichment
📁 *Composition Enrichment,* p. 7

🎨 Use *Fine Art Transparencies* 6–10 for enrichment activities also.

CLOSE

Have small groups discuss which of the five steps they have not used before and what those steps could contribute to their writing.

Using the Grammar Link

Grammar Link Answers
She and I take piano lessons. We often play duets. We [*or,* You and I] can sing this song. In fact, Maria and I can play while you and he sing.

Using Correct Subject Pronouns Have students make up paragraphs similar to that in the Grammar Link.

About the Art

Claes Oldenburg, *Notebook Page: Cross-section of Toothbrush in Glass, 'sun dial,'* 1980; *Cross-section of a Toothbrush with Paste, in a Cup, on a Sink: Portrait of Coosje's Thinking,* 1983.
During the 1960s American sculptor Claes Oldenburg became a leader in the Pop Art movement. He is famous for oversized sculptures of everyday objects.

FOCUS

Lesson Overview

Objective: To choose ideas and language for writing with a particular audience and purpose in mind
Skills: identifying audiences; understanding different purposes for writing; tailoring writing to an audience
Critical Thinking: analyzing; relating; categorizing; decision-making; defining and clarifying; visualizing
Speaking and Listening: discussing; asking questions

Bellringer

When students enter the classroom, have this assignment on the board: *Which type of books do you prefer to read—fiction or nonfiction? Why?*

Grammar Link to the Bellringer

As students discuss the differences in books that are written for different audiences, ask them also to comment on how the sentence structures might differ in these books.

Motivating Activity

Discuss students' responses to the Bellringer activity. Prompt them to use some classroom examples of books written for the two different audiences to compare tone, style, and purpose.

The Writing Process
Prewriting: Determining Audience and Purpose

The tools of a writer are words. The words must be chosen to suit the writer's purpose and audience.

The eighth graders at Carver Junior High School did many different kinds of writing. For example, they wrote an article about the Foods-of-the-World Festival. They wrote postcards during their class trip to Washington, D.C. They wrote a program for the talent show. They created posters advertising the craft fair. Finally, they made a memory book—a kind of yearbook—about their eighth-grade activities. Jot down one or two possible audiences for each of these pieces of writing.

Teacher's Classroom Resources

The following resources can be used for planning, instruction, practice, reinforcement, assessment, reteaching, enrichment, or evaluation.

Teaching Tools
Lesson Plans

Transparencies
Fine Art Transparencies, 6–10
Writing Process Transparencies, 1–10

Write for Your Readers

When writers know who their readers are, they can tailor their writing to their readers. How does the writer of the first article below signal that the audience is young readers?

Literature Model

Hollis Conway has always had long, skinny legs. When he was growing up in Shreveport, Louisiana, his minister called him Linky Legs.

Little did anyone know that those slender legs would one day launch Hollis over a high-jump bar set nearly eight feet off the ground! Hollis, now 24, is one of the best high jumpers in history.

Sports Illustrated for Kids

> *What words and ideas make this opening right for young readers?*

Literature Model

Low, smoky clouds rolled in off the Wasatch Mountains above Provo, Utah, last Saturday night as high jumper Hollis Conway prepared for his second attempt at an American record 7′ 9$\frac{3}{4}$″.

Merrell Noden, *Sports Illustrated*

> *What audience do you think this writer had in mind?*

Journal Writing

Find two magazines with similar content, one for teenagers and one for adults. Examine some articles, and make notes about how the words and ideas reflect each audience.

2.2 Prewriting: Determining Audience and Purpose **53**

📁 **Blackline Masters**
Thinking and Study Skills,
  pp. 2, 4, 13
Writing Across the Curriculum,
  pp. 4–5
Cooperative Learning Activities,
  pp. 7–12

Speaking and Listening
  Activities, pp. 6–7, 12, 23
Composition Practice, p. 8
Composition Reteaching, p. 8
Composition Enrichment, p. 8

Assessment
📁 *Teacher's Guide to Writing Assessment*

TEACH

Guided Practice

L2 Using the Model
Point out that the writer of the first model opens with the background to a childhood nickname and seems to suggest that Hollis's unexpected success can be a model for other skinny-legged kids who dream of being great athletes.

Ask students if it is possible to determine the intended audience by the tone and content of the second model. Is it different from the audience for first model? Suggest that the author was writing for a general audience of adult and teen sports fans. He helps readers picture the event by opening with a long, serious, fact-filled sentence describing a setting.

L1 Understanding Connotation
Help students to understand that writers need to make subtle changes in content and vocabulary in order to reach different audiences. Ask students to imagine that two family members, a parent and a younger sibling, volunteered to help make the same after-school snack on separate occasions. Ask volunteers to act out each situation and tape-record it. Then play the tape for the class. Ask students to listen for differences in content and vocabulary between the two skits. List these differences on the board.

Journal Writing Tip

Comparing Tone Encourage students to work together to summarize differences in approaches, stressing elements of content, vocabulary, and assumptions about the audience's prior knowledge.

TEACH

Guided Practice

L2 Using the Model

Lead students to understand that Ken's audience was probably his peers—other teens like himself. Ask students what his purpose was (to narrate, or tell a story about, a personal experience). Have students identify specific details and comparisons that Ken used to liven up his writing ("the grace of an antelope," "like an eagle"). Additionally, point out the use of direct quotations, emphasizing that they lend a real-life immediacy to the story.

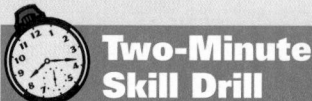

Two-Minute Skill Drill

Have students pitch an advertisement for sports equipment to the following audiences:

students   school principals

Have students consider how the purpose changes with each audience.

Independent Practice

For further stimuli for writing, see *Fine Art Transparencies* 6–10.

Writing Process Transparencies, 1–10

Writing Across the Curriculum, pp. 4–5

Cooperative Learning Activities, pp. 7–12

Skills Practice

Speaking and Listening Activities, pp. 6–7, 12, 23

Thinking and Study Skills, pp. 2, 4, 13

Composition Practice, p. 8

Know Your Purpose

The purpose of both passages about high jumping was to inform. The selection below has a different purpose—to narrate, or tell a story. Read this narrative about an exciting event in the writer's life. To consider two more purposes for writing, consult the chart below.

> ### Student Model
>
> *F*inally, it was my turn. . . . I ran as fast as I could, and approaching the first hurdle, I made it over but bumped my toe slightly. I was embarrassed. I ran on, afraid that I would repeat my error on the next hurdle. Perspiration rolled down my face.
>
> I leaped over the second hurdle with the grace of an antelope; I felt as if my feet had wings. My classmates cheered. I heard comments like "Boy, that kid's good!" and "Wow, look at him go!"
>
> I then flew over the third hurdle like an eagle and raced to the finish line. The gym teacher looked at his stopwatch in disbelief. "You got the highest score in the class, Ken!" he said. I felt good that I had done something better than everybody else.
>
> Ken Priebe, Grosse Pointe Woods, Michigan
> First appeared in *Cricket*

What purpose and audience do you think Ken had in mind? How does his writing reflect both?

Purposes for Writing	
To describe	Although short and thin, Ken was a fast runner.
To narrate	Finally, Ken leaped over the last hurdle.
To inform	Ken finished in first place because of his great efforts.
To persuade	Your contribution will help support the track team.

54   *The Writing Process: Working Together*

Enabling Strategies

LEP Adapting for Audiences

Students who have a limited English vocabulary may be unsure about which words are fit for specific audiences. Ask the class to brainstorm word characteristics to avoid with very young audiences, such as words with complex meanings or abstractions like *value* or *sympathy*. Elicit from students that highly specialized vocabulary or slang should be avoided unless the writer is certain the audience is familiar with the words. Ask the class to name other audiences, such as teenagers or government officials, for whom they would use a specific vocabulary.

2.2 Writing Activities

Collect Topic Ideas

What kind of writing would you like to do? Choose a topic for the piece you will develop through the stages of the writing process.

- Would you like to give information? Tell a story? Describe something? Persuade people about something?
- Choose three topics you might explore.
- Write down your audience for each topic.

PURPOSE To list topic ideas, to identify purpose and audience

AUDIENCE Yourself

LENGTH 1 page

Cooperative Learning

Brainstorm in a small group for writing ideas. How many ideas can you spin off from the painting on this page? List two ideas for each purpose listed in the chart on page 54. Use these ideas to get started.

- mealtimes at your house (describe)
- a story set in the past (narrate)
- what people should eat (persuade)

Share your ideas with the class. Add any you like to your own list.

Grammar Link

Avoid run-on sentences.

One way to correct a run-on sentence is to use a semicolon between the two main clauses.

I leaped over the second hurdle with the grace of an antelope; I felt as if my feet had wings.

Write five compound sentences, each punctuated with a semicolon.

See Lesson 7.2, pages 304–305, and Lesson 14.1, page 472.

Elizabeth Nourse, *Humble Ménage*, 1897

2.2 Prewriting: Determining Audience and Purpose **55**

Using the Grammar Link

Grammar Link Answers
Answers will vary, but some suggestions are given below.
1. At my house, dinner is a funny time; we laugh at least once every night.
2. We laugh because of the dog; he sits under the table at every meal.
3. The funny part is that the table is glass; he looks up at us while we eat.

About the Art

Elizabeth Nourse, *Humble Ménage*, 1897
This oil-on-canvas painting measures 39½ by 39½ inches. It is in the Grand Rapids Art Museum in Michigan. Nourse was interested in portraying strength of character as reflected in the everyday tasks of European peasants.

55

The Writing Process
Prewriting: Investigating a Topic

Once you have chosen your topic and decided on your purpose and your audience, you need to explore ideas about your topic. What will you include? What will you leave out?

The eighth graders had decided to make a memory book about their last year at Carver Junior High. Which activities would they include? Miguel said, "Let's brainstorm." In brainstorming, one idea sparked others, so the class listed all of them. Later they decided which ideas to include in their memory book.

56 *The Writing Process: Working Together*

FOCUS

Lesson Overview

Objective: To develop a selected topic by brainstorming and to gather information by interviewing

Skills: brainstorming; freewriting; clustering; listing; interviewing

Critical Thinking: synthesizing; categorizing; recalling; relating; visualizing; generating new information

Speaking and Listening: discussing; taking notes; informal speaking; interviewing

Bellringer

When students enter the classroom, have this assignment on the board: *For past papers when you were told to write about a topic, what stages did you go through to decide the information that you would include? List a few of these steps.*

Grammar Link to the Bellringer

Ask students to review their lists from the Bellringer activity for correct use of verb forms. Did they use the correct past tense? Have they used *have* and *has* correctly?

Motivating Activity

Discuss the different ways that people approach writing on a topic. Ask why some people prefer to write down their thoughts while others do not. What advantages and disadvantages does each method have? Talk about what could happen if a writer started writing before planning.

56

Teacher's Classroom Resources

The following resources can be used for planning, instruction, practice, reinforcement, assessment, reteaching, enrichment, or evaluation.

Teaching Tools
Lesson Plans, p. 12

Transparencies
Fine Art Transparencies, 6–10
Writing Process Transparencies, 1–10

Explore Your Topic

Once you have chosen a topic, you can explore it by brainstorming, freewriting, clustering, or listing. To freewrite, set a time limit—say, ten minutes—and write everything that comes to mind about the topic.

Don't let the pen stop moving. If you can't think of anything, keep writing the same word again and again. Often your best ideas—or at least the seed of them—will pop out.

Clustering and listing are also helpful techniques. Some students used clustering to explore ideas for the memory book. Kelly listed details for the class mural project. No matter which method you use, keep every idea for now.

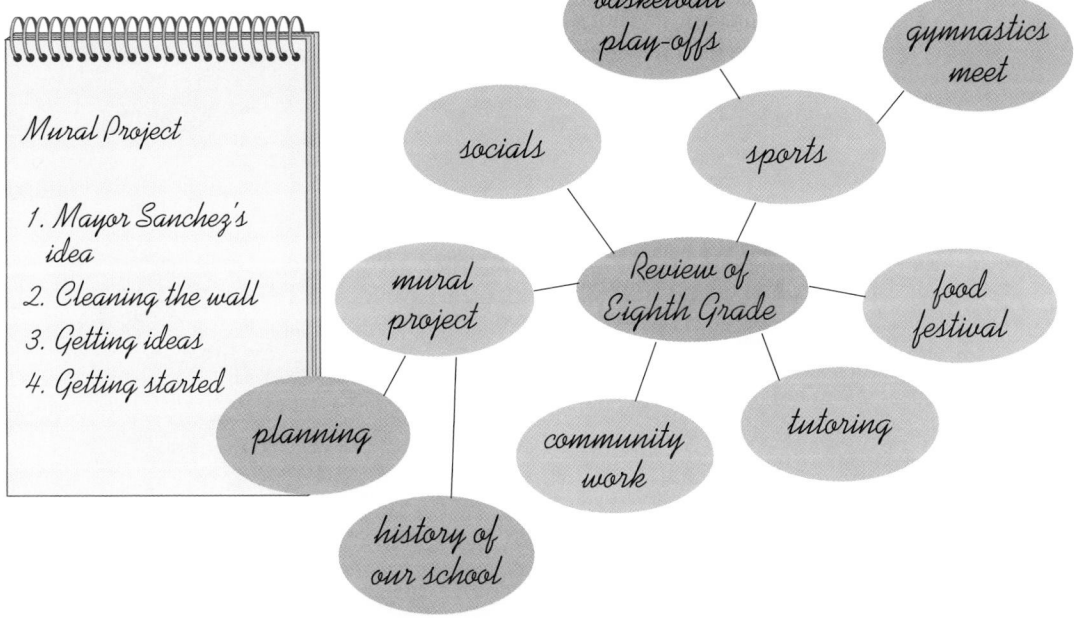

Mural Project

1. Mayor Sanchez's idea
2. Cleaning the wall
3. Getting ideas
4. Getting started

Journal Writing

What stands out as the most important event of the past school year? Set a timer for ten minutes. In your journal freewrite about why the event was important.

TEACH

Guided Practice

L2 **Using a Cluster Diagram**
Point out that the cluster diagram is an example of three levels of subtopic ideas. Explain that this form of graphic organizer is a kind of outline and is helpful because it shows how ideas are linked. Point out the three colors, and ask how they correspond to the three levels of information.

L1 **Focusing Freewriting**
Some students may have difficulty keeping a consistent focus during a ten-minute session of freewriting. You may want to provide some structure to boost their confidence. For example, you might suggest that they begin by dividing their papers into quarters and labeling the quarters with such headings as *Who? What? When? Where?* or *People, Events, Setting, Feelings.* Tailor the headings so they are appropriate to the broad topic students are brainstorming.

 **Two-Minute Skill Drill**

Challenge students to see how fast they can brainstorm five ideas for the following topics:

gardening   kite flying
checkers   pottery

Journal Writing Tip

Creative Thinking Encourage students to relax and let their ideas flow freely. Stress that freewriting is an opportunity for their imaginations to explore and play with ideas that during more disciplined, focused activities might not appear as easily.

📁 **Blackline Masters**
Thinking and Study Skills,
pp. 4, 8, 13, 34
Writing Across the Curriculum,
p. 5
Cooperative Learning Activities,
pp. 7–12

*Speaking and Listening
Activities,* pp. 6–7, 12, 23
Composition Practice, p. 9
Composition Reteaching, p. 9
Composition Enrichment, p. 9

Assessment
📁 *Teacher's Guide to Writing Assessment*

TEACH

Guided Practice

L2 Using the Model
Ask students to suggest other interesting questions or follow-up questions that the student might have asked Mayor Sanchez. Point out that, along with notes on Mayor Sanchez's answers, this student could also have written down exact quotations, which often makes writing livelier. They can also make the speaker's personality more vivid.

L2 Cooperative Learning
Students might use their Journal Activity freewriting as a starting place for practicing their interviewing skills. After forming groups, pair students and have partners interview each other regarding the most important event in the school year. Then each partner reports to the group information learned during the interview. Before students begin their interviews, encourage them to prepare strong fact-finding questions and follow-up questions, such as *Why, in your opinion, was this event special?* and *What do you feel you learned from it?*

Independent Practice

For further stimuli for writing, see *Fine Art Transparencies* 6–10.

Writing Process Transparencies, 1–10

Writing Across the Curriculum, p. 5

Cooperative Learning Activities, pp. 7–12

Skills Practice
Thinking and Study Skills, pp. 4, 8, 13, 34

Speaking and Listening Activities, pp. 6–7, 12, 23

Composition Practice, p. 9

Gather Facts and Details

Writers start with what they know, but they often need more information to help them shape their ideas. To find it, they tap a wide range of sources, such as books, magazines, and newspapers. Sometimes the best sources are people with special knowledge of the topic. For example, Ayako wondered, "Why was our class chosen to work on the mural? What do people think of it?" To find out, she interviewed the mayor.

To conduct a successful interview, come prepared with good open-ended questions, such as the ones Ayako listed. Listen well, and take notes carefully. With the interviewee's permission, you can use a tape recorder as well. Don't interrupt or rush ahead to the next question. Allow the person time to answer. Ask follow-up questions: "That's interesting. Can you say more about it?" After the interview reread your notes, and jot down what you learned.

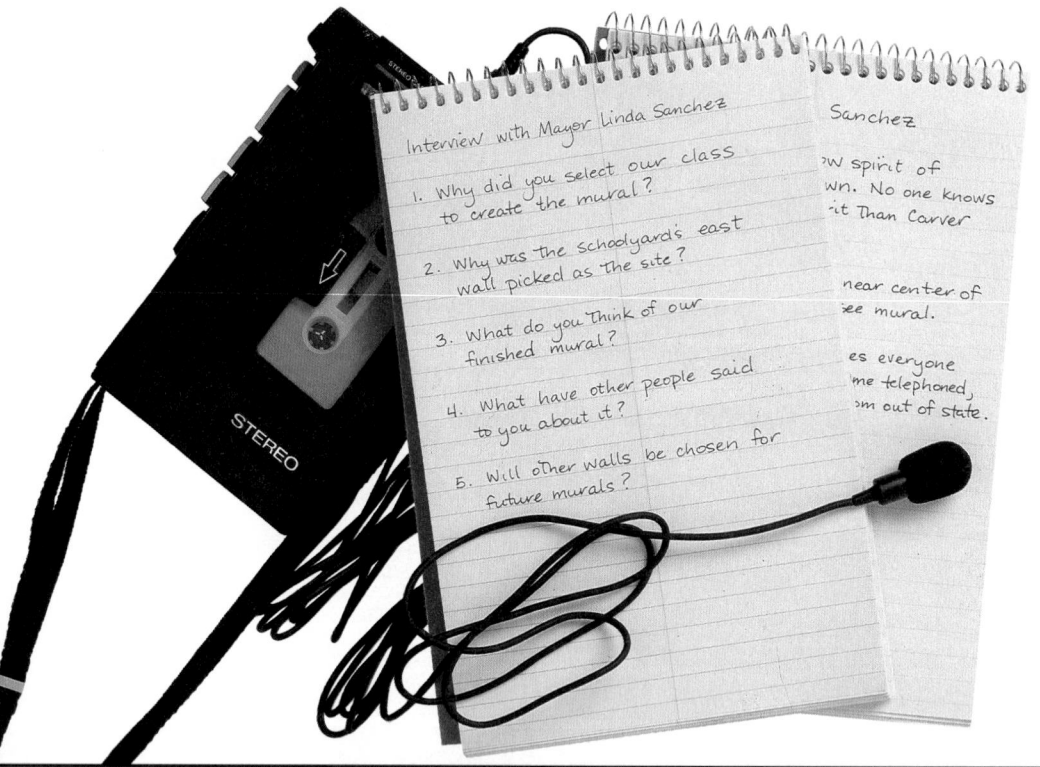

Enabling Strategies

LEP Double-checking Understanding
Students who are learning English may need extra encouragement to persist if they are feeling misunderstood during a brainstorming session or an interview. Urge students who are brainstorming in a group to ask questions if they are not clear about the suggestions of other students. For brainstorming sessions and interviews, students should try again if they think they were misunderstood.

2.3 Writing Activities

Investigate Your Topic

Look at your three best topic ideas. Choose two to explore and investigate. Do two of the following activities. You can do one for each idea or two for one of your ideas.

- Brainstorm ideas about the topic.
- Freewrite about the topic.
- List ideas about the topic.
- Cluster to explore the topic.
- Interview someone about your topic.

PURPOSE To create a set of prewriting notes about your topic
AUDIENCE Yourself
LENGTH 1–2 pages

COMPUTER OPTION

A computer allows you to do "invisible writing," which is an excellent freewriting technique. Choose a topic, and set a timer for ten minutes. Dim the screen, and begin to freewrite about your topic. Since you cannot see what you are writing, you will be able to let your ideas flow without interrupting your thoughts to make corrections.

Grammar Link

Use correct verb forms.

When you check your verbs, be especially alert to possible errors in the use of the *past* and *past participle* of irregular verbs.

*What **have** other people **said** to you about it?*

Write each sentence, using the past or past participle of the verb in parentheses.

1. Dylan had (rise) to his feet.
2. He (take) notes on our ideas.
3. All of us have (draw) on many sources.
4. We (seek) out new sources, too.
5. We had (speak) to many people.
6. Books and articles (give) us additional facts.
7. Then we (make) use of all that information.
8. We have (begin) to discover a unifying thread.
9. The thread has (spring) from somewhere.
10. It has (come) from our shared ideas.

See Lesson 10.11, page 388, and Lesson 10.12, page 390.

2.3 Prewriting: Investigating a Topic **59**

Using the Grammar Link

Grammar Link Answers
1. risen
2. took
3. drawn
4. sought
5. spoken
6. gave
7. made
8. begun
9. sprung
10. come

Explaining Past and Past Participle Verb Forms To help students understand when to use past and past participle verb forms, ask groups to write explanations in their own words and to present them to the class.

FOCUS

Lesson Overview

Objective: To organize ideas logically and to include supporting details
Skills: determining main idea; sequencing supporting details in a logical order; eliminating inappropriate details
Critical Thinking: identifying main idea and details; categorizing; defining and clarifying
Speaking and Listening: taking notes; discussing; asking questions

Bellringer

When students enter the classroom, have this assignment on the board: *List the steps you would follow to organize your own scrapbook. What would you include? What would you omit? Explain your choices.*

Grammar Link to the Bellringer

Ask students to review their lists for items naming specific people, places, events, months, or days. Have students correct any such words that do not begin with a capital letter.

Motivating Activity

Display a painting or photograph that contains many details, such as a busy urban scene. Have students suggest the main idea of the picture. Then ask what details support the main idea. What details would not belong in this picture? Point out that a piece of writing also has a main idea with supporting details. Details that do not support the main idea should be omitted.

The Writing Process
Prewriting: Organizing Ideas

Organizing ideas involves several steps—weeding out what doesn't belong, organizing the remaining ideas in a sensible way, and filling in missing details.

Rafael prepared to organize his ideas for the introduction to the class memory book. He gathered his notes and found resources such as back issues of the school newspaper, to help him fill in missing details.

Teacher's Classroom Resources

The following resources can be used for planning, instruction, practice, reinforcement, assessment, reteaching, enrichment, or evaluation.

📁 **Teaching Tools**
Lesson Plans, p. 13

📁 **Transparencies**
Fine Art Transparencies, 6–10
Writing Process Transparencies, 1–10

Weed Out What Doesn't Belong

Not all the ideas you gather on a topic belong in your writing. You have to decide what to keep and what to take out. First, think about what you want to say about your topic, and express that idea in one sentence. Then list the details, and cross out any that don't belong. Rafael asked himself which activities really helped to support his idea about "the activities our class did together." Notice how he weeded out some ideas.

Listing ideas   Topic

The activities our class did together made eighth grade a year to remember.

    talent show — April

    mural project — October

    tutoring   not a group activity

    craft fair — May

    Olympic Day — June

    ~~*parents' night*~~   *more for the parents*

    Foods-of-the-World Festival — December

    class trip — March

    visiting author   she talked, we listened

Journal Writing

Write a sentence expressing your opinion, either positive or negative, about a school activity. List details about the activity. Then think: Which details support my main idea? Which do not? Cross out the "weeds."

2.4 Prewriting: Organizing Ideas **61**

TEACH

Guided Practice

L2 Using the Model
Discuss with students why Rafael might have chosen to delete the items he did. Lead them to conclude that those events probably did not seem as important because the class members took a less active role in them. Therefore, they did not reflect and support his main idea—activities that made eighth grade "a year to remember"—as strongly as the others did.

L1 Writing the Main Idea
Some students may have difficulty summing up their main idea in one sentence. Suggest that they ask themselves two questions: What is my topic? What one point do I want to make about the topic? You may wish to give them some practice by asking them to complete such sentences as, *If I were writing about baseball, I would want to say ___.* Lead them to use the ending of the sentence as the basis for a main idea statement.

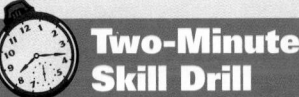

Two-Minute Skill Drill

Have students list the items they might include in a sports scrapbook.

Journal Writing Tip

Evaluating Ideas Stress that "weeding" should occur only after the list has been completed with every related idea that comes to mind. The purpose of cutting is to eliminate weak ideas and to emphasize the stronger ideas in their writing.

📂 **Blackline Masters**
Thinking and Study Skills,
  pp. 4, 11, 13–14
Writing Across the Curriculum,
  p. 6
Cooperative Learning Activities,
  pp. 7–12

Speaking and Listening
  Activities, pp. 6–7, 12, 23
Composition Practice, p. 10
Composition Reteaching, p. 10
Composition Enrichment, p. 10

Assessment
📂 *Teacher's Guide to Writing Assessment*

TEACH

Guided Practice

L2 Using the Model

Remind students that there is often more than one way to organize ideas. Ask what method Rafael chose to organize his notes (chronological order). What other method might he have chosen (order of importance)?

L2 Understanding Various Methods of Organization

Ask students to suggest ways to organize notes for a history report on the following topics. Discuss the options shown as well as others that may be suggested.

- the voyages of Magellan (chronological; spatial)
- the Battle of Gettysburg (chronological; spatial)
- five leading presidents (chronological; order of importance)

Remind students that the organizational plan will often depend on the purpose for writing. For example, if your purpose is to tell about the events in the Battle of Gettysburg, you might choose chronological order. However, if your purpose is to explain the strategy of the battle, you might choose spatial order to emphasize the battlefield layout and the movement of troops.

Independent Practice

📁 For further stimuli for writing, see *Fine Art Transparencies* 6–10.

📁 *Writing Process Transparencies,* 1–10

📁 *Writing Across the Curriculum,* p. 6

📁 *Cooperative Learning Activities,* pp. 7–12

Skills Practice

📁 *Thinking and Study Skills,* pp. 4, 11, 13–14

📁 *Speaking and Listening Activities,* pp. 6–7, 12, 23

📁 *Composition Practice,* p. 10

Organize Your ideas

Now you need to organize your ideas in a way that makes sense. How you do that depends on your purpose: are you going to describe, narrate, inform, or persuade?

To describe something, you sometimes arrange the details in order of location, or **spatial order.** You might start by describing what you see first; then move from left to right or from near to far. To narrate a story, you'd usually arrange the events in the order they happened, or **chronological order.** To explain, you could **compare and contrast** or use chronological order. If you plan to give persuasive reasons for an opinion, you might choose **order of importance.** You'd begin with your most important reason and then work toward your least important. On the other hand, you might do the opposite. Which order did Rafael choose?

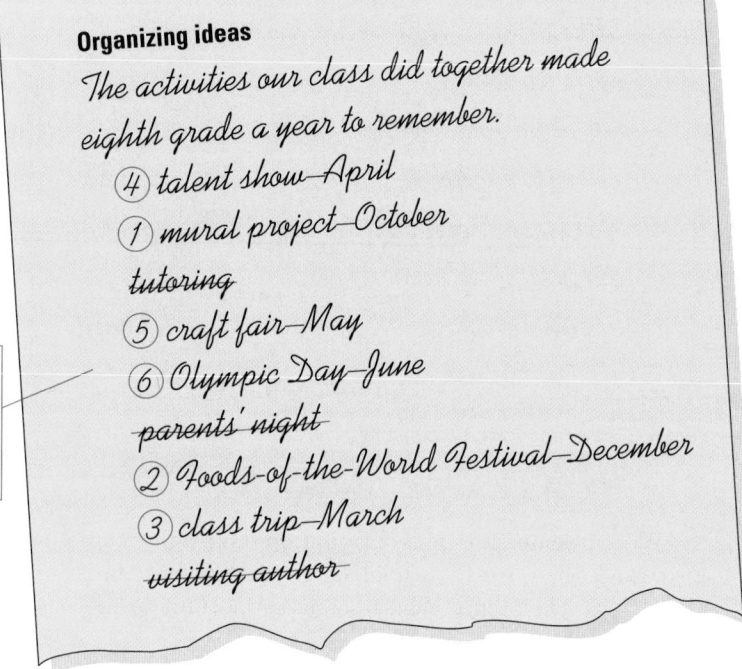

Organizing ideas

The activities our class did together made eighth grade a year to remember.
④ talent show—April
① mural project—October
~~tutoring~~
⑤ craft fair—May
⑥ Olympic Day—June
~~parents' night~~
② Foods-of-the-World Festival—December
③ class trip—March
~~visiting author~~

Could Rafael have chosen another order for these events? Explain your answer.

62   *The Writing Process: Working Together*

Enabling Strategies

LEP Organizing Ideas

Students learning English may experience difficulty understanding the various methods of organization. Prompt them to review the following:

- Chronological order: Ask students to think of events that occurred in a popular movie and to create a time line.

- Spatial order: Ask them what objects in their rooms at home are located above, below, or next to other objects.

- Order of importance: Ask students to rank three school events in order according to how important they think the event is, and to explain why.

2.4 Writing Activities

Organize Your Ideas

Look back at your prewriting notes. At this point, you should choose which topic you want to write about—you can change your mind later.

- Write one sentence stating your main idea.
- Look at your prewriting notes, and weed out any ideas that don't support your main idea.
- Add any ideas that you want to include.
- Decide how you will organize your writing.

PURPOSE To organize your ideas
AUDIENCE Yourself
LENGTH 1–2 pages

Cooperative Learning

In a small group, brainstorm to create a list of jobs you might like to have some-day. Each group member should copy the completed list. Individually each member should cross out the jobs that seem less attractive and number the remaining jobs in order of importance, with number one as the favorite. Then brainstorm about reasons for your choices. Working indi-vidually, each member should list reasons for choosing his or her favorite job, num-bering them in order of importance.

Grammar Link

Capitalize the specific names of people, places, institutions, events, months, and days.

Carver Junior High School

Olympic Day

April

Write the paragraph below, using capital letters correctly.

[1]One of my favorite relatives is uncle joe. [2]A veteran of the vietnam war, he is now principal of kennedy high school in hawaii. [3]I visited him last july. [4]One saturday and sunday we spent in oahu. [5]The pacific regatta was being held there. [6]The crew from the university of hawaii came in first. [7]They won a trophy donated by the royal savings bank. [8]Crew leader deana keolani thanked the organizers and sponsors. [9]That weekend we also visited the punchbowl, where victims of pearl harbor are buried. [10]Yes, I had a great month in the aloha state.

See Lesson 19.2, page 552; Lesson 19.3, page 554; and Lesson 19.4, page 556.

2.4 Prewriting: Organizing Ideas **63**

ASSESS

Writing Activities Evaluation Guidelines

Organize Your Ideas
Use these criteria when evaluating your students' writing.
- Do prewriting notes show a creative exploration of the topic?
- Is there a strong, clear main idea statement?
- Does the list of details support the main idea?
- Are the notes logically organized?

See also the *Teacher's Guide to Writing Assessment.*

Cooperative Learning
Consider the following:
- Did all group members participate?
- Did each group member listen to, and consider, the ideas of others?
- Did each group member list sensible reasons in the order of importance?

Grammar Link
(See Using the Grammar Link below.)

Reteaching
📁 *Composition Reteaching*, p. 10

Enrichment
📁 *Composition Enrichment*, p.10

CLOSE

Ask students to list five things they would like to accomplish in the future. Ask them to number the items in an ideal chronological order, and then to number the items in order of impor-tance. Discuss how the ordering of items compares. How does each item's importance affect its chrono-logical rank? What other factors affect the chronological plan?

Using the Grammar Link

Grammar Link Answers
1. Uncle Joe
2. Vietnam War, Kennedy High School, Hawaii
3. July
4. Saturday, Sunday, Oahu
5. Pacific Regatta
6. University of Hawaii
7. Royal Savings Bank
8. Deana Keolani
9. Punchbowl, Pearl Harbor
10. Aloha State

Capitalizing Proper Nouns Have students write a paragraph describing the topic they have chosen in this lesson, using as many specific names of people, places, institutions, events, months, and days as they can.

LESSON

2.5

The Writing Process
Drafting: Writing It Down

Drafting is putting your notes into sentences and paragraphs that work together to make an effective piece of writing.

FOCUS

Lesson Overview

Objective: To use prewriting notes to prepare a first draft

Skills: preparing a first draft; varying sentence types

Critical Thinking: defining and clarifying; synthesizing; identifying main idea

Speaking and Listening: note taking; evaluating; questioning

🔔 Bellringer

When students enter the classroom, have this assignment on the board: *Imagine that you've been asked to write a record of your day for inclusion in a time capsule. Jot down two or three things that you might like to share with others.*

Grammar Link to the Bellringer

Have students write an imperative sentence to get the attention of the person opening the time capsule.

Motivating Activity

Ask volunteers to share their responses to the Bellringer activity. To encourage students, use the analogy of mixing and using homemade modeling clay. The first step, which is similar to the prewriting stage of organizing (or "mixing") ideas, is to mix flour, salt, water, and oil. Then you knead the clay into a rough shape, the beginning of a figure. This is comparable to the drafting stage of writing. The figure is far from perfect, but it is beginning to take shape. Later you'll have a chance to refine the figure, just as writers revise first drafts.

This mural artist used sketches to help her decide what to include and how to arrange and rearrange all the mural parts. Rafael is at a similar point in the writing process. His next step is drafting. He'll turn his prewriting notes into the sentences and paragraphs that will work together to introduce the class memory book.

Start Your Draft

One place to begin drafting is at the beginning, with an introduction. Leads, or openings, are important. A writer must create interest and make readers want to keep reading. Try out some techniques that professionals use in writing leads. For example, ask a question, present an unusual detail, or use a dramatic quotation. Be sure to state the main idea clearly and to explain what will follow. Here's a first draft that Rafael wrote as an introduction to the memory book.

64   *The Writing Process: Working Together*

Teacher's Classroom Resources

The following resources can be used for planning, instruction, practice, reinforcement, assessment, reteaching, enrichment, or evaluation.

🔧 **Teaching Tools**
Lesson Plans, p. 14

✏️ **Transparencies**
Fine Art Transparencies, 6–10
Writing Process Transparencies, 1–10

Was it worth the wait? Turn the pages to see for yourself. Remember how hard it was to decide what to include in our memory book? We finally picked the great activities our eighth-grade class did together. Join us as we relive the mural project, the Foods-of-the-World Festival, the D.C. trip, the talent show, the craft fair, and the Olympic Day.

What does Rafael accomplish in his first and last sentences?

Not all writers begin at the beginning. Some start in the middle, on a part that seems easier to write. Others tackle their conclusion first. Drafting means trying options and taking chances. You may get stuck. To get unstuck, try one of these strategies.

Ways to Get Unstuck

| Draw a picture about your topic. | Have a healthful snack. | Freewrite in your journal. | Take a walk, or ride your bike. |

Journal Writing

What strategies have helped you start drafting or get unstuck? What new strategies could you try? In your journal make a list to refer to when you're stuck.

2.5 Drafting: Writing It Down **65**

TEACH

Guided Practice

L2 Using the Model
Have students read aloud page 64 and Rafael's first draft on page 65. Point out that Rafael's lead sentence asks a question to draw readers in. His last sentence tells what will follow. Discuss how such techniques hold a reader's interest.

Explain that many famous writers have expressed how difficult it can be to face an empty page. Read students the words of novelist William Faulkner: "Get it down. Take chances. It may be bad, but it's the only way you can do anything really good." Point out the illustrations of tricks a writer can use to get unstuck, and ask students to suggest additional ways: (pretend you're writing to a friend; play soft music).

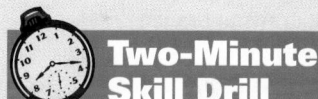

Two-Minute Skill Drill

Write this lead sentence on the board and have students rewrite it in two different ways; for example, as a question or a dramatic quotation.

I passed my pilot's test today.

Journal Writing Tip

Critical Thinking Suggest that students work with a partner to share and evaluate their strategies. You might list the strategies on the board and discuss them with the class. Ask students which new strategies might work for them. They can revise their lists or expand them to include these strategies.

📁 **Blackline Masters**
Thinking and Study Skills, pp. 4, 13
Writing Across the Curriculum, pp. 4–6
Cooperative Learning Activities, pp. 7–12

Speaking and Listening Activities, pp. 6–7, 12, 23
Composition Practice, p. 11
Composition Reteaching, p. 11
Composition Enrichment, p. 11

Assessment
📁 *Teacher's Guide to Writing Assessment*

TEACH

Guided Practice

L2 Using the Model

Discuss the model, pointing out the false start and the spelling error. Emphasize that at this point neatness doesn't count and students will not be marked for errors. Ask students to react to Rafael's draft. What additions might they like to see? Would more details about the mural make the paragraph more interesting? Clearer? Urge students to keep such thoughts in mind as they write.

L3 Drafting Practice

Students might practice drafting by writing brief summaries of short stories, novels, or movies. Ask them to write as quickly as possible, using notes or just their memories.

Students might want to share their drafts with the class. Later they can use these drafts to practice revising and editing before presenting their summaries as a guide to popular literature and entertainment.

Independent Practice

For further stimuli for writing, see *Fine Art Transparencies* 6–10.

Writing Process Transparencies, 1–10

Writing Across the Curriculum, pp. 4–6

Cooperative Learning Activities, pp. 7–12

Skills Practice

Thinking and Study Skills, pp. 4, 13

Speaking and Listening Activities, pp. 6–7, 12, 23

Composition Practice, p. 11

Let It Flow

As you draft, use your prewriting notes. They'll remind you of your purpose, audience, and plan of organization. Let your ideas flow freely. Don't interrupt the flow of ideas by thinking about grammar or spelling or even about writing in paragraphs. You'll have a chance to make changes later.

> *Later, the writer will correct spelling errors in this line. When the ideas are flowing, keep going!*

How can we forget The mural project began the year. The idea was to capture the spirit of our school and community in paint strokes. Barb and Deji led us in forming comitees, and then we all got into the act. Four paint-soaked months later our beautiful mural was done, ready for all to see.

66   *The Writing Process: Working Together*

Enabling Strategies

LEP Generating Ideas

Remind students who may struggle with English grammar and spelling that the goal of the drafting stage is to let their ideas flow as comfortably and freely as possible. Suggest that if students get stuck, they write a few words in their first or native language. They just need to keep the ideas flowing. Later, they will have plenty of time to make sure that they've translated the words into English and fixed any mistakes.

2.5 Writing Activities

Write a Draft

Use your prewriting notes to help you draft your piece. Skip every other line to leave room for changes. Don't worry about correctness. At this stage, you are still exploring what you want to say.

• Start with a lead or in the middle of your piece.
• Let your ideas flow.

PURPOSE To create a draft
AUDIENCE Yourself
LENGTH 1–2 pages

Diego Rivera, *Allegory of California*, 1931

Cross-Curricular: Music

Draft song lyrics to go with the mural on this page. First make notes about what your purpose is and what parts of the mural you want to write about. Then draft your lyrics. If you like, set your lyrics to music for the class.

Grammar Link

Use various kinds of sentences: declarative, interrogative, imperative, and exclamatory.

Was it worth the wait?
Turn the page to see for yourself.

Write a paragraph, following the directions below.

1. Write an interrogative sentence. Ask your readers if they ever organized a class event. (You choose the event.)
2. Write an imperative sentence. Tell readers to create a committee.
3. Write a declarative sentence. Explain the committee's job.
4. Write an exclamatory sentence. Warn the committee of what's ahead.
5. Write an interrogative sentence. Ask about the event.

See Lesson 8.1, page 326.

2.5 Drafting: Writing It Down **67**

See Lesson 8.1, page 326.

ASSESS

Writing Activities Evaluation Guidelines

Write a Draft
Use these criteria when evaluating students' writing:
• Is the main idea clear?
• Is there an introduction that tells what will follow?
• Are sentence types varied?
• Does the draft make interesting points?

See also the *Teacher's Guide to Writing Assessment*.

Cross-Curricular: Music
Prewriting notes should include
• a purpose statement
• a creative list of ideas based on the mural

The draft of the lyrics should use the prewriting notes and follow the form of song lyrics.

Grammar Link
(See Using the Grammar Link below.)

Reteaching
📁 *Composition Reteaching,* p. 11

Enrichment
📁 *Composition Enrichment,* p. 11
✎ Use *Fine Art Transparencies* 6–10 for enrichment activities also.

CLOSE

Review with students that the purpose of making and using prewriting notes is to generate ideas that can be expanded into a first draft. Discuss the need to focus on ideas, rather than on how neatly or correctly the ideas are recorded. Students may profit by making several drafts and then selecting the best ideas and expressions from each.

Using the Grammar Link

Grammar Link Answers
Paragraphs will vary. Be sure that students understand and have used the various kinds of sentences—declarative, interrogative, imperative, and explanatory—in their paragraphs.

About the Art

Diego Rivera, *Allegory of California*, 1931 The artist painted this mural, which measured 143 ¾ square feet, on a wall of the Pacific Stock Exchange in San Francisco. The model for the central female figure, representing the spirit of California, was American tennis star Helen Wills Moody.

Setting the Purpose

Lesson 2.6 teaches students how to revise their writing and make it clearer, more complete, and more interesting.

FOCUS

Lesson Overview

Objective: To review and revise a piece of writing for clarity, completeness, and interest

Skills: revising a draft; reviewing a draft with a peer

Critical Thinking: analyzing; defining; identifying

Speaking and Listening: discussing; reading aloud and listening to a draft

Bellringer

When students enter the classroom, have this assignment on the board: *Plan a perfect day. List everything you want to do, and revise your list until you have it just the way you want it.*

Grammar Link to the Bellringer
Have students read through their lists and underline the nouns. Invite them to consider whether they could have chosen more exact nouns.

Motivating Activity

Ask students whether they got their lists perfect on the first try, or if they changed some things. Let them see that revisions make writing better and reflect what a person really wants to communicate. Students can use this plan for a future writing assignment.

Revising: Taking a Fresh Look

No one should expect to create perfect writing without revising. The word revise *means "take a fresh look" at your writing and refine it. After you've finished your first draft, put it aside for a time—at least a day, if possible. When you see it again, you can tell better how it will sound to readers.*

After some recipe revisions suggested by his family, Ben's contribution to the Foods-of-the-World Festival was just right.

Revise for Clarity and Sense

Begin by reading aloud. Ask yourself, Is this clear? Does it make sense? Have I chosen the right words? The revising stage is a good time to consider whether you've used the best words. You might use a thesaurus to help you find words that say exactly what you mean. Examine the suggested revisions on the facing page. Then study the chart to help you revise.

68   *The Writing Process: Working Together*

Teacher's Classroom Resources

The following resources can be used for planning, instruction, practice, reinforcement, assessment, reteaching, enrichment, or evaluation.

Teaching Tools
Lesson Plans

Transparencies
Fine Art Transparencies, 6–10
Writing Process Transparencies, 1–10

Eighth-grade eating habits may have been changed forever by this event. Foods from places like Puerto Rico, India, and China expanded our taste experiences. *Spicy dishes* ~~Food~~, such as tacos and curries made peanut butter sandwiches seem like kids' stuff. Who can forget the parade of taste sensations that marched across our tongues at the Foods-of-the-World Festival? ~~Jenny Diaz covered the tables with blue and white tablecloths and put a colorful bouquet on each one.~~

How did the writer improve the paragraph by changing "food" to "spicy dishes"?

Moving this topic sentence to the beginning will help the writer focus on the main idea.

Questions for Revising

1. Is my writing clear? Does it make sense?
2. What is my purpose, and do I accomplish it?
3. Do I consider my audience?
4. Have I chosen the best, most precise words?
5. Do I say enough about it?

Journal Writing

Review your journal for entries about recent events in your life. Choose one entry that interests you. To strengthen it, make at least two major revisions. Refer to the chart above for ideas.

2.6 Revising: Taking a Fresh Look **69**

TEACH

Guided Practice

L2 Using the Model
Point out that if the writer had not moved the question to the beginning, the phrase *by this event* would be unclear. Also point out that the addition of specific foods improved the writing by adding interesting details. Ask students why removing the final sentence is important. (Since the sentence introduces a new idea, it should appear in a later paragraph.)

L2 Creating Interest
Some students may be discouraged about reworking a piece they feel is finished. Let them know that even great writers revise their work over and over again until they are satisfied. Challenge students to look for vague and uninteresting phrasing. Use the sentence *I went to the place* as an example. Suggest improvements, such as *I raced to the ticket counter,* pointing out how the use of specific, vivid verbs and nouns makes the sentence more interesting. Invite students' suggestions.

Two-Minute Skill Drill

Write these words on the board and have students write a more specific word for each:

flower   gem

eat   red

Journal Writing Tip

Understanding Significance
Remind students that everything that happens to them matters. Encourage them to view this activity as a chance to share the story of an important event.

📁 **Blackline Masters**
Thinking and Study Skills,
  pp. 1, 4, 13, 14
Writing Across the Curriculum,
  pp. 7–8
Cooperative Learning Activities,
  pp. 7–12

Speaking and Listening
  Activities, pp. 6–7, 12, 23
Composition Practice, p. 12
Composition Reteaching, p. 12
Composition Enrichment, p. 12

Assessment
📁 *Teacher's Guide to Writing Assessment*

TEACH

Guided Practice

L2 Using the Model
Discuss the peer reviewer's comments and the changes that the writer made. Stress that the writer obviously thought about what the peer reviewer said and made improvements based on those comments but still retained the right to make the final decisions. Remind students that the comments of the peer reviewer are meant to be helpful suggestions, not criticisms. Ask students whether they think the changes improve the writing and whether they would do anything to improve it further.

L1 Revising by Listening
Students who have difficulty analyzing and evaluating written material might benefit from tape-recording the draft or having someone else read it aloud. Suggest that they listen, reading along on a copy of the draft and making changes or additions on the copy whenever a better idea or a more precise phrase comes to mind.

Independent Practice

For further stimuli for writing, see *Fine Art Transparencies* 6–10.

Writing Process Transparencies, 1–10

Writing Across the Curriculum, pp. 7–8

Cooperative Learning Activities, pp. 7–12

Skills Practice
Thinking and Study Skills, pp. 1, 4, 13, 14

Speaking and Listening Activities, pp. 6–7, 12, 23

Composition Practice, p. 12

Ask a Peer to Review Your Work

One way to identify trouble spots in your work is to read it to others and ask for their comments. These peer reviewers will help you see your writing from the point of view of your audience. You can return the favor by listening to their work. As a peer reviewer, comment first on what is successful about the piece—in other words, say what works well for you. Then suggest any changes you think would help readers understand better. Read the paragraph below, comparing the peer reviewer's comments with the writer's revisions.

You made the food festival sound like fun.

Maybe you should list the ingredients.

Does the sentence about learning to cook belong?

I am confused by the last sentence.

We sampled delicious treats from several countries, but among the highlights *of the festival* were the pot stickers from the kitchen of Ms. Yu, our teacher. Ms. Yu used *an old family recipe* a way that had been passed down to her from her mother. ~~Her mother taught her how to cook.~~ Ms. Yu offered everyone a fortune cookie. Reading our fortunes aloud added a touch of humor to the event. Our greatest fortune came *when Ms. Yu gave us* with the recipe for those yummy pot stickers.

You can follow all or some or none of your peer reviewer's suggestions. Notice that the writer of the paragraph above made two of the three suggested changes. A peer reviewer's comments can help you decide what changes to make, but as the writer you're in charge.

70 *The Writing Process: Working Together*

Enabling Strategies

LEP Revising Together
Students learning English might work through the entire revision process with their peer reviewers. They could restate each of the reviewer's comments to ensure understanding. The reviewer might assist the writer by giving suggestions, encouraging the writer to keep thinking, and offering assistance in using a dictionary or thesaurus if necessary.

2.6 Writing Activities

Revise Your Draft

Look again at the draft you have written. Make sure some time has gone by—at least a day—before you begin to revise it.

- Put yourself in the place of your audience, and read over your draft, using the questions on page 69.
- Read your paper to a peer reviewer or reviewers, and discuss your paper with them.
- Decide what changes you want to make to your paper.

PURPOSE To revise your draft, to have a writing conference
AUDIENCE Yourself, your peer reviewers
LENGTH 1 page of comments

COMPUTER OPTION

Revising on a computer allows you to move text around and to try out different words and phrases. If you save versions of your drafts in separate files, you can "undo" changes that are not quite right by quitting and going back to the previous version. Some word-processing packages will allow you to undo your last change with an "undo" command.

Grammar Link

Use specific nouns in your writing.

Spicy **dishes**, such as **tacos** and **curries**, made peanut butter **sandwiches** seem like **kids' stuff**.

Rewrite the sentences below, replacing each italicized noun with a more specific noun.

1. *Others* and I went shopping yesterday.
2. All of us found just what we needed at the *store*.
3. Jenny bought a *tool* for her father's birthday.
4. George bought a *book* and immediately sat down to read it.
5. A lovely little *plant* charmed Kathleen.
6. The twins were lured toward a display of *clothes*.
7. The *pets* in the window snagged Jemal's attention.
8. As for me, I bought *footwear*.
9. The *employees* rang up our purchases.
10. After shopping, we treated ourselves to *food*.

See Lesson 3.3, page 114.

Using the Grammar Link

FOCUS

Lesson Overview

Objective: To revise a piece of writing for unity and clarity

Skills: choosing skills to support a main idea; using transitions

Critical Thinking: analyzing; defining and clarifying; focusing

Speaking and Listening: oral reporting; discussing

Bellringer

When students enter the classroom, have this assignment on the board: *Rewrite the following sentences, using commas to make the meaning clearer:*

You know Carrie I like your new track shoes. After all the practices we've had I've worn mine out.

Grammar Link to the Bellringer
Invite students to share their answers to the Bellringer activity. Point out that the use of commas in sentences helps make the meaning clearer.

Motivating Activity

Expand on ways that writers can convey messages clearly. Using students' history or science text, select paragraphs with a clear topic sentence and supporting details. Point out the relationships among the ideas and the clarity achieved by words or phrases that signal connections (*therefore, as a result, because*), time (*before, after, next, finally*), or location (*above, across, nearby*).

LESSON
2.7

The Writing Process
Revising: Writing Unified Paragraphs

As a writer, you want to make sure that each paragraph has a single, clear focus and that all of its sentences hang together.

Alicia wanted to write about the class visit to the Washington Monument. When she looked at photos of the class trip, she found two of the monument. Which do you think she chose? Why?

72 *The Writing Process: Working Together*

Teacher's Classroom Resources

The following resources can be used for planning, instruction, practice, reinforcement, assessment, reteaching, enrichment, or evaluation.

Teaching Tools
Lesson Plans, p. 16

Transparencies
Fine Art Transparencies, 6–10
Writing Process Transparencies, 1–10

Check for Unity

A paragraph is unified if all its sentences work together to express one main idea. That main idea is usually expressed in a topic sentence, which may appear at the beginning or the end or even in the middle of the paragraph. In revising, decide whether the main idea would be clearer if you added or revised a topic sentence. Make sure that all the details support the main idea. What unifies the paragraphs below?

Literature Model

There are two levels on which to enjoy a tour through black history in the nation's capital: Visit those neighborhoods that stand now and those monuments erected in memory of past struggles and accomplishments. Then, as you drive or walk around the city, try to imagine what once was.

Since 1790, when Congress ordered that a federal city be built on the Potomac River, blacks have made rich and varied contributions. Benjamin Banneker, a black surveyor, assisted Pierre L'Enfant, the city's designer, in laying out the new capital. When the temperamental L'Enfant was dismissed, taking his design notes with him, Banneker's memory was invaluable.

Patrice Gaines-Carter,
"Washington as a Mecca of Black History"

> *The details explain the "two levels" introduced in the topic sentence.*

> *Why does the writer begin a new paragraph here?*

Journal Writing

List ten or more ideas about your town or city. Review your list, and write topic sentences for paragraphs that could include two or more of the ideas.

2.7 Revising: Writing Unified Paragraphs **73**

TEACH

Guided Practice

L2 Using the Model
Ask students to identify the two levels introduced in the topic sentence (present and past). Point out that the writer begins a new paragraph to introduce a new topic, the rich and varied contributions of African Americans.

L2 Ordering with Paragraphs
Draw an analogy between a piece of writing and a numbered list of steps. Point out the similarity between a paragraph break and the next number on the list. Emphasize that without the numbers, steps are not easy to understand. The same is true of running text; without the paragraph breaks, all the thoughts run together and lose their focus.

Two-Minute Skill Drill

Have students rewrite these sentences as a paragraph, using time transition words to unify the writing.

1. This is what I do in the morning.
2. The alarm clock rings at 6 a.m.
3. I shower.
4. I make my breakfast.
5. I let the dog out when I leave.

Journal Writing Tip

Connecting Information Have students make cluster diagrams to connect visually related ideas. This may help them translate their ideas into topic sentences.

📂 **Blackline Masters**
Thinking and Study Skills,
  pp. 1, 4, 11, 13–14
Writing Across the Curriculum,
  pp. 7–8
Cooperative Learning Activities,
  pp. 7–12

Speaking and Listening Activities, pp. 6–7, 12, 23
Composition Practice, p. 13
Composition Reteaching, p. 13
Composition Enrichment, p. 13

Assessment
📂 *Teacher's Guide to Writing Assessment*

TEACH

Guided Practice

L2 Using the Model

Ask students to point out sentences that indicate a transition in time or place. Ask what key words and phrases the writer used to make such transitions clear. Point out the paragraph break. Help students understand that the first paragraph told about the first destination, and the next paragraph, the second destination. Ask how to rephrase the final sentence to emphasize the cause-and-effect relationship. (Sample: *Because* the statue was huge, I thought about what a great president Lincoln was.)

L1 Recognizing Cause and Effect

If students have difficulty recognizing cause-and-effect relationships, use a chain of events from popular culture. For example, a singer records a CD. The CD sells many copies. Then the singer becomes famous. Finally, the singer wins a Grammy. Ask the class to identify the cause and effect of each event. Then ask them to think of other examples. Elicit answers that use transition words.

Independent Practice

For further stimuli for writing, see *Fine Art Transparencies,* 6–10.

Writing Process Transparencies, 1–10

Writing Across the Curriculum, pp. 7–8

Cooperative Learning Activities, pp. 7–12

Skills Practice

Thinking and Study Skills, pp. 1, 4, 11, 13–14

Speaking and Listening Activities, pp. 6–7, 12, 23

Composition Practice, p. 13

Connect Ideas

The ideas in a paragraph must relate in clearly understandable ways. Writers connect their ideas, using words and phrases called transitions. Notice the transitions in the following passage.

Transitions

Time

| after | before | finally |
| first | next | at once |

Place

| above | across | beside |
| below | next to | near |

Cause and Effect

| as a result | because |
| since | therefore |

Using Transition Words

After our long bus ride, we were glad to reach our hotel in downtown Washington, D.C. The next morning found us revived and ready for our tour. The first stop was the Washington Monument. After waiting in line for an hour, we took the minute-long elevator ride to the top. When we got there, we looked out across the city. How awesome it was!

Our next stop was the Lincoln Memorial. Since Lincoln is one of my heroes, I took some photos of the seated statue. The statue's huge size reminded me of what a great president Lincoln was.

You don't think about transitions as you draft. When you revise, however, be sure that you've made smooth connections between ideas. In descriptive writing you may use spatial transitions, such as *nearby* and *on one side.* In narrative writing you may arrange ideas chronologically and use time transitions, such as *first* and *then.* When writing to explain, you can use cause-and-effect transitions, such as *therefore* and *as a result.*

74 *The Writing Process: Working Together*

Enabling Strategies

LEP Using Transition Words

Match students who are learning English with students who are fluent in English. Instruct the students who are learning English to act out how to do something—take a picture, make a snack, or work on a hobby. Instruct the observers to state aloud what they see their partners doing. For example, the partner of someone demonstrating taking a picture might say, "First, you take the camera out of its case. Then, you focus the camera. Finally, you shoot the picture."

2.7 Writing Activities

Check for Unified Paragraphs

Take another look at your draft. Are there ways you can make it ever clearer for your audience? Ask yourself these questions about your paragraphs:

- Does each paragraph focus on one main idea?
- Do all the details support the main idea?
- Where could I use transition words to connect ideas?

PURPOSE To revise your draft for unity

AUDIENCE Yourself

LENGTH Necessary changes on your draft

Monika Steinhoff, *La Plazuela, La Fonda (Hotel)—Santa Fe, New Mexico*, 1984

Cross-Curricular: Art

Examine the painting on this page. Notice how the artist draws the viewer in through a series of doorways and windows. Draft a paragraph that describes the painting. In revising, make sure that you have used transitions to help your reader.

Grammar Link

Use commas to set off introductory elements and word groups that interrupt the sentence.

After waiting in line for an hour, we took the . . . ride to the top.
Then, as you . . . walk around the city, try to imagine what once was.

Write each sentence, adding commas where necessary.

1. Rudely awakened by the alarm clock I slowly opened my eyes.
2. Mario you see had set it an hour early.
3. With a sudden burst of energy I jumped out of bed.
4. Yes I wanted to pound my brother.
5. No luck—he as he no doubt had planned was gone.

See Lesson 20.2, page 568, and Lesson 20.3, page 570.

2.7 Revising: Writing Unified Paragraphs **75**

Using the Grammar Link

Grammar Link Answers
1. Rudely awakened by the alarm clock, I slowly opened my eyes.
2. Mario, you see, had set it an hour early.
3. With a sudden burst of energy, I jumped out of bed.
4. Yes, I wanted to pound my brother.
5. No luck—he, as he no doubt had planned, was gone.

About the Art

Monika Steinhoff, *La Plazuela, La Fonda (Hotel)—Santa Fe, New Mexico,* 1984
This 24-by-28-inch oil painting is housed in a private collection. Monika Steinhoff, an American artist, is known for her colorful watercolors, oils, graphics, and batiks.

FOCUS

Lesson Overview

Objective: To write sentences of varying structure and length
Skills: sentence combining; improving paragraphs; gearing writing to an audience; using adverbs and adjectives
Critical Thinking: defining and clarifying; analyzing
Speaking and Listening: public speaking; listening for rhythm

Bellringer

When students enter the classroom, have this assignment on the board: *Combine these sentences and add more detail in order to make the description more interesting to the reader:*

The man entered the room. He looked at the jurors before taking his seat.

Grammar Link to the Bellringer

Have students underline the adverbs and circle the adjectives they used in rewriting the Bellringer sentences.

Motivating Activity

Display a picture of an urban skyline showing various building sizes and styles. Note that variety makes the scene interesting. If all the buildings were alike, they would be dull. Paragraphs can also be dull, especially if each sentence has the same structure. Explain that a major goal in revising is to ensure that sentences don't endlessly repeat the same pattern. Then invite students to share their answers to the Bellringer activity.

LESSON

2.8

The Writing Process
Revising: Writing Varied Sentences

A good writer tries to produce a pleasing rhythm in his or her sentences. Varying the length and structure of your sentences gives your writing this rhythm.

Kim and Emily arranged the acts for a class talent show. Rather than opening with three vocal solos in a row, they inserted a comedy act and a dance routine between two singers' solos. The variety gave a pleasing rhythm to the show.

In much the same way, a writer strives to produce a pleasing rhythm in his or her sentences. When you revise, read your sentences aloud, and listen to them. What will they sound like to your readers? Do they seem to plod along like three vocal solos in a row? Or do they flow smoothly, with the rhythm of a well-planned talent show?

76

Teacher's Classroom Resources

The following resources can be used for planning, instruction, practice, reinforcement, assessment, reteaching, enrichment, or evaluation.

Teaching Tools
Lesson Plans

Transparencies
Fine Art Transparencies, 6–10
Writing Process Transparencies, 1–10

Vary Sentence Structure

One way to give your writing a pleasing rhythm is to vary your sentence structure. Instead of always beginning with a subject, start some sentences with an adverb, a prepositional phrase, a participial phrase, or a subordinate clause. Rafael realized that he'd used the same basic pattern—a subject followed by a predicate—over and over again. Notice how he achieved a better rhythm by varying his sentence beginnings.

> To open the show,
> ~~The opening act was Maria.~~ She sang the song
> "Memory" from the musical Cats. Everyone was
> surprised at the emotion Maria put into her
> song. Since She's usually so quiet, Raoul performed
> next. His comedy act drew peals of laughter
> from the audience. ~~We weren't surprised by that.~~
> Raoul is funny, even when he's not on stage.
>   and Kim
> For the next act Shanti performed a dance
> routine to rap music. ~~Kim danced with her.~~

How did Rafael change his first sentence?

What else did Rafael do to vary his sentences?

Journal Writing

Read several paragraphs of your writing aloud. How do they sound? Examine the sentence patterns. Look especially at your sentence beginnings. If necessary, revise your work to vary the structure and patterns of sentences.

2.8 Revising: Writing Varied Sentences **77**

Blackline Masters
Thinking and Study Skills, pp. 1, 4, 13–14
Writing Across the Curriculum, p. 7
Cooperative Learning Activities, pp. 7–12

Speaking and Listening Activities, pp. 6–7, 12, 23
Composition Practice, p. 14
Composition Reteaching, p. 14
Composition Enrichment, p. 14

Assessment
Teacher's Guide to Writing Assessment

TEACH

Guided Practice

L2 Using the Model
Lead students to see that Rafael changed his first sentence to begin with an infinitive phrase. Have students read the original sentences and the revised sentences aloud to emphasize the improvement in rhythm. Other improvements that Rafael made include beginning two sentences with adverb clauses, and combining sentences to create a simple sentence with a compound subject.

L2 Varying Sentence Pace
Students who have difficulty "hearing" the flow of their sentences might benefit from tape-recording their work and listening to the recordings as they read along, marking places that might be improved by varying either sentence structure or length.

Two-Minute Skill Drill

Write the following sentences on the board. Have students add adverb phrases that could make the sentences more interesting.

The man walks slowly up the stairs. He is old and tired.

Journal Writing Tip

Focusing Encourage students to experiment freely with sentence structure and patterns. Ask partners or small groups to discuss the results of their sentence revising and to decide which revisions flow most smoothly and why.

TEACH

Guided Practice

L2 Using the Model
Point out that the last two sentences contrast sharply, resulting in a pleasing rhythm. Read these sentences aloud to show how the short final sentence also serves to add emphasis.

L1 Varying Rhythm of Sentences
Point out that varying sentence length and sentence patterns is a trick that many public speakers use to add punch and interest to their speeches. If possible, play tapes of political speakers and stand-up comedians as examples. Stress that it's very important for written materials to have varied sentences. Unlike a speaker, a writer can't rely on a tone of voice to achieve rhythm and variety.

L3 Varying Rhythm of Sentences
Students might enjoy experimenting with sentence structure. Ask them to select one complex or compound-complex sentence from their writing or that of an author such as Toni Morrison. Encourage them to rewrite the sentence as many times as possible by changing the structure or length or by using adverbs or adverb clauses.

Independent Practice

For further stimuli for writing, see *Fine Art Transparencies,* 6–10.

Writing Process Transparencies 1–10

Cooperative Learning Activities, pp. 7–12

Skills Practice
Thinking and Study Skills, pp. 1, 4, 13–14

Speaking and Listening Activities, pp. 6–7, 12, 23

Composition Practice, p. 14

78

Vary Sentence Length

Good writers avoid the monotony of many long sentences in a row and the choppiness of many short ones. The narrator of the selection below is a young boy traveling by train from Mexico to California. Notice the sentence rhythm. Then study the graphic to see how you can "cut and paste" to revise your sentences for length.

> *Which sentences vary widely in length? How does this variety affect the writing?*

Literature Model

*D*uring the afternoon dark clouds had piled up over us, rolling over the desert from the mountains. At sunset the first drops fell on our canvas roof. The rain picked up and the train slowed down. It was pouring when we began to pass the adobe huts of a town. We passed another train standing on a siding, the deck of our flatcar flooded and the awnings above us sagging with rainwater and leaking. It was night.

Ernesto Galarza, *Barrio Boy*

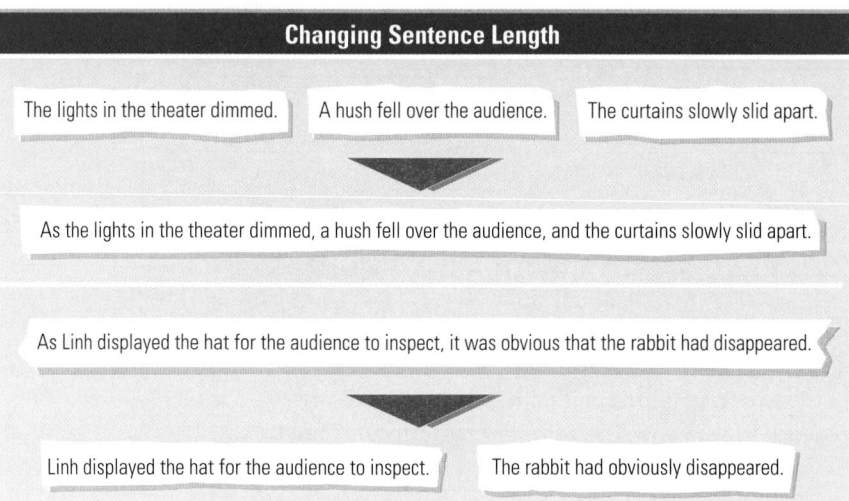

Changing Sentence Length

The lights in the theater dimmed. | A hush fell over the audience. | The curtains slowly slid apart.

As the lights in the theater dimmed, a hush fell over the audience, and the curtains slowly slid apart.

As Linh displayed the hat for the audience to inspect, it was obvious that the rabbit had disappeared.

Linh displayed the hat for the audience to inspect. | The rabbit had obviously disappeared.

78   *The Writing Process: Working Together*

Enabling Strategies

LEP Sentence Combining
Students struggling with English grammar and sentence structure may benefit from using sentence-combining flashcards. Each sentence card would have printed on it a sentence similar to those in the diagram at the bottom of the student page.

Other flashcards would have words that are used to introduce phrases and subordinate clauses printed on them. There would be three sets of word cards: one for words that tell when, one for words that tell why, and one for words that tell where.

2.8 Writing Activities

Revise for Sentence Variety

Now look at your sentences. Are there ways you can make them more varied? Ask yourself these questions:

- Do I have a mixture of long and short sentences?
- Do I have variety in the order of my words and phrases?
- Can I combine sentences to express my ideas more clearly?

Revise your sentences.

PURPOSE To revise for sentence variety
AUDIENCE Yourself
LENGTH Changes on the draft

COMPUTER OPTION

All word-processing programs include an editing feature that allows you to cut and paste easily. This is especially useful when combining two or three short sentences into one long one or when breaking a long sentence into two or three shorter ones. Use this feature to delete sentence parts or move them.

Grammar Link

Use adverb clauses to achieve sentence variety.

You can often combine the ideas in two simple sentences into one sentence. One effective method is to state the idea in one of the sentences in an adverb clause.

Even when he's not on stage, *Raoul is funny.*

When the adverb clause comes first in a sentence, use a comma after it.

Combine each of the pairs of sentences below by turning one of the sentences into an adverb clause. Use commas where necessary.

1. Sophia called. I went to meet her.
2. There was a sale. We walked to the mall.
3. It was raining. We took our umbrellas.
4. The prices were low. We did not buy anything.
5. We spotted the bus at the bus stop. We climbed aboard.

See Lesson 14.5, page 480; Lesson 20.3, page 570; and Lesson 21.4, page 602.

2.8 Revising: Writing Varied Sentences **79**

ASSESS

Writing Activities Evaluation Guidelines

Revise for Sentence Variety
Use these criteria when evaluating your students' writing:
- Is the length of sentences varied?
- Do some sentences begin with adverbial phrases or clauses?
- Have short choppy sentences been combined into longer ones?
- Are varied sentence types used for interest and rhythm?

See also the *Teacher's Guide to Writing Assessment*.

Computer Option
Ensure that students who use computers know how to access and use the editing functions available through individual word-processing programs. As appropriate, have students practice using the cut and paste functions.

Grammar Link
(See Using the Grammar Link below.)

Reteaching
📂 *Composition Reteaching,* p. 14

Enrichment
📂 *Composition Enrichment,* p. 14

CLOSE

Discuss the role of rhythm in music, stressing the pacing of phrases and the underlying beat. Play recordings of various types. Remind students that written materials also have a rhythm and a flow, which can be achieved by varying sentence structure and length.

Using the Grammar Link

Grammar Link Answers
Answers will vary. Sample answers follow.
1. When Sophia called, I went to meet her.
2. Because there was a sale, we walked to the mall.
3. Since it was raining, we took our umbrellas.
4. Although the prices were low, we did not buy anything.
5. When we spotted the bus at the bus stop, we climbed aboard.

The Writing Process
Editing: Fine-tuning Your Work

Setting the Purpose

Lesson 2.9 teaches students how to perfect their writing during the editing and proofreading phase of the writing process.

FOCUS

Lesson Overview

Objective: To edit a piece of writing using standard proofreading marks

Skills: identifying and correcting errors in spelling, mechanics, and grammar

Critical Thinking: identifying; evaluating

Speaking and Listening: discussing

Bellringer

When students enter the classroom, have this assignment on the board: *List all the things you try to correct when you edit your work.* (Students should include sentence structure, mechanics—spelling, capitalization, and punctuation—and grammar.)

Grammar Link to the Bellringer

Have students proofread for any errors in the following paragraph. Corrections are in parentheses.

I realy (really) *wanted to dance with Lisa. All night long I looked for my chance* (chance. When) *when it finaly* (finally) *came I was to* (too) *nervous to ask her. Its* (It's) *hard to be a teenage* (teenager).

Motivating Activity

Ask students' opinions about how they would feel if their names were spelled incorrectly on a sports trophy or on their high school diploma. Discuss the importance of editing and proofreading in relation to job applications and other real-life situations.

During the editing stage, the goal is to get your writing ready to share with others. You want your finished product to be as nearly perfect as possible.

After all that hard work on the memory book, the first thing people see shouldn't be a misspelled word on the cover. Correcting spelling may seem like a little thing, but it's important to do before the book reaches its audience. To begin the editing process, ask a peer reviewer to look over your piece of writing. A fresh pair of eyes will often catch mistakes you have overlooked.

80   *The Writing Process: Working Together*

Teacher's Classroom Resources

The following resources can be used for planning, instruction, practice, reinforcement, reteaching, assessment, enrichment, or evaluation.

Teaching Tools
Lesson Plans, p. 18

Transparencies
Fine Art Transparencies, 6–10
Writing Process Transparencies, 1–10

Check Your Sentences

Your first step is editing your sentences. Read them over carefully to check word choice and to identify any sentence fragments or run-on sentences. Examine the following edited paragraph. The writer has identified errors and marked them with proofreading symbols.

Proofreading			
Symbol	**Meaning**	**Symbol**	**Meaning**
∧	Insert	⊙	Period
⸮	Delete	⌃	Comma
⌣	Reverse	≡	Capital letter
¶	New paragraph	/	Lower-case letter

Lydia displayed
At the craft fair, Several items of jewelry made from ordinary office supplies. One of the most beautiful pieces was a pin in the shape of a skyscraper⊙ it was made out of neon-colored paper clips, gold staples, and the cap from a portable pencil sharpener.

> *The writer has broken the sentence into two shorter ones. Is there another way to correct this run-on sentence?*

Journal Writing

In your journal freewrite for five minutes about any topic that interests you. Let your work sit for a few hours. When you return to it, fix the errors that you find.

2.9 Editing: Fine-tuning Your Work   **81**

📁 **Blackline Masters**
Thinking and Study Skills,
  pp. 25–27
Writing Across the Curriculum,
  pp. 7–8
Cooperative Learning Activities,
  pp. 7–12

Speaking and Listening Activities, pp. 6–7, 12, 23
Composition Practice, p. 15
Composition Reteaching, p. 15
Composition Enrichment, p. 15

Assessment
📁 *Teacher's Guide to Writing Assessment*

TEACH

Guided Practice

L2 Using the Model
Point out that the writer made the first correction to fix a sentence fragment. Another way to correct the run-on sentence is the following: *One of the most beautiful pieces was a sky-scraper-shaped pin fashioned from neon-colored paper clips, gold staples, and the cap from a portable pencil sharpener.*

L2 Discussing Quality Control
Mention to students that checking a nearly completed product for mistakes and flaws is important not only for writers but also for businesses. For example, the lack of a final check in factory inspections of a product could severely endanger the consumer. Discuss how writers have a similar obligation to themselves and their readers: to make sure that a finely written piece is not marred by errors.

 Two-Minute Skill Drill

Write this paragraph on the board and have students use proofreading symbols to correct errors.

I have always wanted to travell my brother has gone too many countries but I havent. I would most like to visit swisserland.

Journal Writing Tip

Freewriting Remind students that freewriting is a valuable step in the writing process because it allows them to get ideas down on paper without worrying about errors. Ask volunteers to share their freewriting by reading to the class.

TEACH

Guided Practice

L2 Using the Model

Lead students to see that the two circled words were misspelled. In discussing the misspellings, you might point out this useful mnemonic device for spelling the second word: The princi*pal* is our *pal.*

L2 Cooperative Learning

In groups of three, students assume the roles of author, sentence checker, and mechanics checker, using a Simultaneous Roundtable format. Each student should bring a revised draft to the group. Each author passes it to the sentence checker, the person on his or her left. The author considers the sentence checker's marks, making necessary corrections. Next, the author passes the draft to the mechanics checker, the person on his or her right. Once again, the writer makes necessary corrections.

Independent Practice

For further stimuli for writing, see *Fine Art Transparencies,* 6–10.

Writing Process Transparencies, 1–10

Writing Across the Curriculum, pp. 7–8

Cooperative Learning Activities, pp. 7–12

Skills Practice

Thinking and Study Skills, pp. 25–27

Speaking and Listening Activities, pp. 6–7, 12, 23

Composition Practice, p. 15

Proofread for Mechanics and Grammar

After editing for sentence structure, proofread for errors in mechanics—spelling, capitalization, and punctuation—and in grammar. Once you've proofread your draft, prepare a clean final copy. Read your work over one more time. If you find a small mistake, correct it neatly.

Why did the writer circle "staggerd" and "principle"?

What is the meaning of each proofreading mark used in this paragraph?

> After the minimarathon had ended and the last few runners had (staggerd) into the schoolyard, the closing ceremonies for Olympic Day began. Justin, our star musician, had composed a song just for this day. The words reflected the spirit of the events. With the winning athletes leading the parade, we marched into the School auditorium, singing Justin's song. Ms. tsao, our (principle) handed out ribbons as we all cheered.

"Mind if we check the ears?"

Some writers proofread as they draft and revise. Most writers, however, concentrate on getting their ideas down during these stages and leave proofreading for a later stage.

82 *The Writing Process: Working Together*

Enabling Strategies

LEP Using Homonyms

Students learning English may need extra help with such troublesome homonyms as *their, there, they're; its, it's;* and *to, too, two.* Remind students that homonyms are words that sound the same but have different meanings. You might suggest that they set aside a section of their journals for a glossary of such terms.

Edit Your Writing

After revising the draft of your paper, you are satisfied that it says what you want it to in the best possible way. Now you are ready for the editing stage of the writing process. During this stage, you will proofread your paper, checking carfully for errors in mechanics and grammar.

- Carefully reread your sentences, checking for word choice, and looking for sentence fragments and run-on sentences.
- Use the proofreading symbols in the chart on page 81.
- Check your paper word-for-word, looking for one kind of error at a time.

PURPOSE To edit for correctness
AUDIENCE Yourself
LENGTH Changes on the draft

COMPUTER OPTION

The ability of your word-processing program to check spelling can be useful, but do not leave it all up to the computer. Your program probably won't alert you if you've written *form* instead of *from* or *their* instead of *there*. After using your computer to find obvious misspellings, proofread for errors only humans can identify.

Grammar Link

Use proofreading symbols to edit your writing.

When you edit a piece of writing, you may recognize run-on sentences or sentence fragments. You may spot errors in capitalization or punctuation. You may notice missing words or extra words. Proofreading symbols provide a convenient way to indicate necessary corrections.

Ms. tsao, our principle, handed out ribbons as we all cheered

First copy the passage below, just as it is written. Then use proofreading symbols to edit it.

[1]Sean took also a booth at the craft fair, this was a chance for him to display his pottery. [2]Including several vases. [3]He was thrilled when he sold three Pieces, a vase a pot with a lid and a bowl bowl. [4]Sean been practicing with irish designs in his work. [5]The bowl he sold is a copy of an ancient Ceremonial piece.

See Lessons 7.1–7.9, pages 302–322.

2.9 Editing: Fine-tuning Your Work **83**

ASSESS

Writing Activities Evaluation Guidelines

Edit Your Writing
Use these criteria when evaluating your students' editing:
- attention to grammar, usage, and mechanics
- correct use of proofreading marks

If errors still exist, urge the student to make a troubleshooter's list in his or her journal for mistakes that are difficult to catch.

See also the *Teacher's Guide to Writing Assessment.*

Grammar Link
(See Using the Grammar Link below.)

Reteaching
Composition Reteaching, p. 15

Enrichment
Composition Enrichment, p. 15

CLOSE

Have students write two or three sentences that need editing. Ask them to trade sentences with a partner. After editing and proofreading each other's work, they can return the sentences and briefly discuss their edits.

Using the Grammar Link

Grammar Link Answers
The corrected paragraph appears below. Students may select different options for some corrections. Check that proofreading marks are used correctly.

(1) Sean also took a booth at the craft fair. This was a chance for him to display his pottery, (2) including several vases. (3) He was thrilled when he sold three pieces—a vase, a pot with a lid, and a bowl. (4) Sean had been practicing with Irish designs in his work. (5) The bowl he sold is a copy of an ancient ceremonial piece.

Lesson 2.10 teaches students to draw conclusions about where, how, and in what format to publish a piece of writing.

FOCUS

Lesson Overview

Objective: To present the final copy of a piece of writing to the intended audience
Skills: formatting; revising; editing; finalizing
Critical Thinking: analyzing; establishing and evaluating criteria; visualizing
Speaking and Listening: formal speaking; informal speaking; note taking; asking questions; evaluating

Bellringer

When students enter the classroom, have this assignment on the board: *Write sentences about five or more qualities needed to play a team sport or to play in a band.*

Grammar Link to the Bellringer
Have students underline the subjects of their Bellringer sentences, indicating which are singular and which are plural.

Motivating Activity

Ask students to discuss their answers to the Bellringer activity and to share other experiences they've had in working to improve at playing a sport or a musical instrument. Ask whether they felt rewarded for their hard work. Lead students to understand that a writer's reward for the often difficult and long process of prewriting, drafting, revising, and editing is publication of the work. A writer takes pride in presenting his or her work to an appreciative audience.

The Writing Process
Presenting: Sharing What You've Written

Now that you've invested so much time, energy, and talent in your writing, you'll want to share it. Who will want to read it? What is the best way to present it to them?

These pages of pictures are from the eighth-grade memory book, *This Unforgettable Year.* Who in Carver Junior High School will probably want a copy? What audience might the memory book have outside the school?

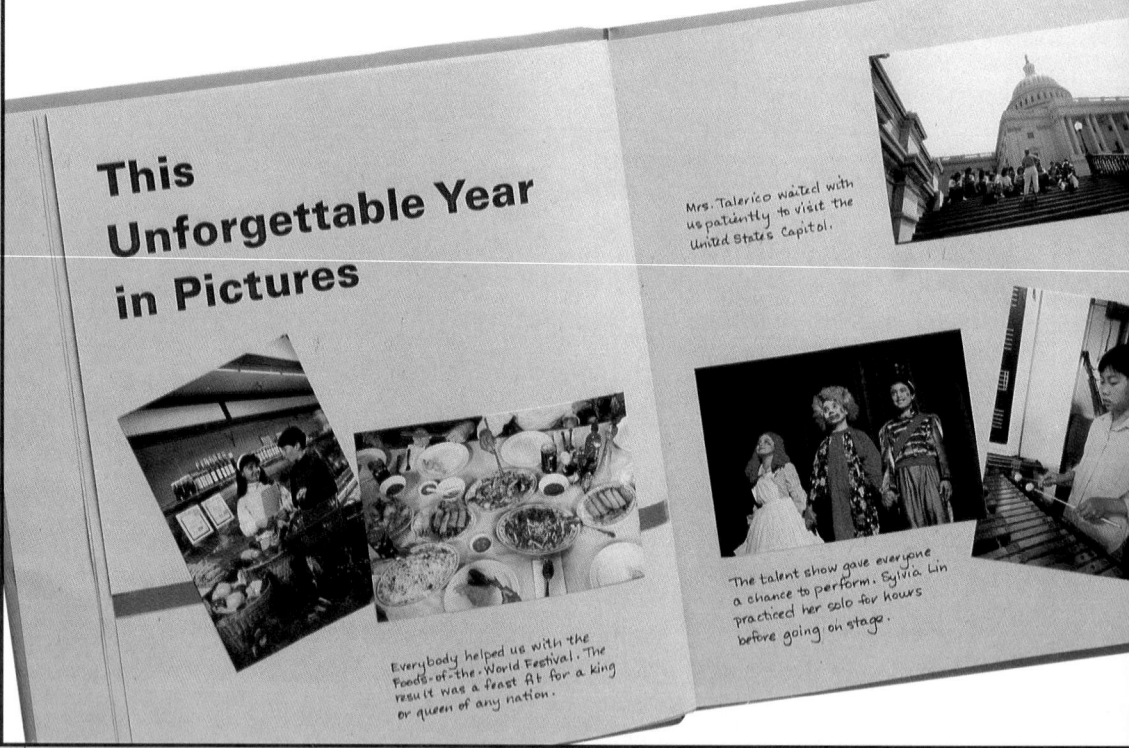

This Unforgettable Year in Pictures

Mrs. Talerico waited with us patiently to visit the United States Capitol.

Everybody helped us with the Foods-of-the-World Festival. The result was a feast fit for a king or queen of any nation.

The talent show gave everyone a chance to perform. Sylvia Lin practiced her solo for hours before going on stage.

Teacher's Classroom Resources

The following resources can be used for planning, instruction, practice, reinforcement, assessment, reteaching, enrichment, or evaluation.

Teaching Tools
Lesson Plans, p. 19

Transparencies
Fine Art Transparencies, 6–10
Writing Process Transparencies, 1–10

Present Your Writing at School

The best audiences you'll ever find are at school. Here are some ways to share your writing. Submit a piece to the school newspaper. Write the text for a bulletin-board display, or create a poster to promote an activity. Some classes exchange letters with students in other countries. Others publish an anthology of poems and stories, a memory book, or a yearbook.

> *This is the final revision of a page from* This Unforgettable Year.

Who can forget the parade of taste sensations that marched across our tongues at the Foods-of-the-World Festival? This event may have changed eighth-grade eating habits forever. Foods from places such as Puerto Rico, India, and China expanded our taste experiences. Spicy dishes, such as tacos and curries, made peanut butter sandwiches seem like kids' stuff.

Among the highlights of the festival were the pot stickers from the kitchen of Ms. Yu, our teacher. Ms. Yu used an old family recipe passed down to her from her mother. These traditional treats tickled our taste buds and made us all want to travel to China. To add to our pleasure, Ms. Yu offered everyone a fortune cookie. Reading our fortunes aloud added a touch of humor. Our greatest fortune came when Ms. Yu gave us the recipe for those yummy pot stickers.

Journal Writing

In your journal list opportunities for presenting your writing in your school. Choose two you would like to try. Find out where and how to submit your work.

2.10 Presenting: Sharing What You've Written **85**

Assessment
📁 *Teacher's Guide to Writing Assessment*

TEACH

Guided Practice

🄻2 Using the Model
Review with students the methods described in the introduction to the model for presenting writing to an audience. Explain that many magazines provide opportunities for students to publish original articles, stories, and poems. Two examples are *Cricket* and *Merlyn's Pen: The National Magazine of Student Writing.* Ask students to suggest a publication or format for the student model.

🄻2 Motivating Students
Encourage students as they refine their writing by pointing out that professional writers often have to fight discouragement. Margaret Mitchell received twenty-six rejection notices from publishers before one accepted *Gone with the Wind.* This book has become one of America's best sellers.

 **Two-Minute Skill Drill**

Write these sentences on the board, and have students write the verb that agrees in number with the subject:

1. One of my friends (skydive, skydives).
2. In *Time Out of Mind*, there (was, were) a land where trees touched the sky.
3. Many national holidays (is, are) celebrated on a Monday.

Journal Writing Tip

Acquiring Information Provide a place in the classroom for students to share information on publication tips and leads.

85

TEACH

Guided Practice

L1 Promoting Composition

Do not let visual learners or students with limited writing skills feel discouraged about submitting their work to an audience. Explain that students can present their work through the written word, an oral presentation, a taped presentation, or even have others take part in the presentation. Then discuss what audio-visual equipment is available for student use and how students might display a diverse range of finished products.

L3 Promoting Composition

Encourage better writers to explore opportunities for writing assignments at local newspapers. Many such publications hire student writers to cover school or neighborhood league sports competitions. In addition, check young people's magazines and local community organizations for essay, poetry, and short story competitions for young people. Provide entry forms for interested students, and offer guidance on the rules about topic restrictions and length limitations.

Independent Practice

For further stimuli for writing, see *Fine Art Transparencies,* 6–10.

Writing Process Transparencies, 1–10

Writing Across the Curriculum, pp. 7–8, 23–24

Cooperative Learning Activities, pp. 7–12

Skills Practice

Thinking and Study Skills, pp. 1, 19, 21

Speaking and Listening Activities, pp. 6–7, 12, 23

Composition Practice, p. 16

Present Your Writing to Others

How can you "publish" your writing outside school? One of the best ways is to write letters to friends and family members. If you have ideas about a local problem, write a letter to the editor. If you are interested in a hobby or sport, find a specialty magazine, and exchange ideas with fellow enthusiasts. Two excellent magazines, *Merlyn's Pen* and *Stone Soup*, consist of stories, poems, and other writing by students your age.

Contests offer still another opportunity for presenting your writing. The National Council of Teachers of English and other local and national organizations sponsor writing contests for young people. Your teacher or librarian may know about local groups, such as civic and veterans organizations, that sponsor essay contests. You can find other ideas in the collage below.

Enabling Strategies

LEP Sharing Information

Students who are new to English might enjoy making informal presentations to the class regarding non-English newspapers or magazines that they read.

Encourage these students to bring examples to class and to explain such differences in format as left-to-right vs. right-to-left reading and writing.

2.10 Writing Activities

Present Your Writing

You have taken your writing through prewriting, drafting, revising, and editing, and now it's time for the payoff—presenting, publishing, or sharing your writing!

- Prepare your work in the format that is best for your audience and purpose.
- Make your paper as neat and attractive as you can.
- Give it a send-off!

PURPOSE To present your finished work
AUDIENCE Your chosen audience
LENGTH Whatever is appropriate for your purpose

Cooperative Learning

In a small group, plan a class newsletter. Brainstorm ideas for articles and stories related to school activities and events. Have one member of the group record your ideas. Once the group has decided what activities and events to include, each member should choose a writing assignment. When all members have completed their writing, come together to revise and edit each piece. Then work together to lay out the newsletter. If possible, duplicate a copy for each class member, or present your completed newsletter as part of a classroom bulletin-board display.

Grammar Link

Make subjects and verbs agree.

Occasionally the subject of a sentence comes after the verb, but subject and verb must still agree.

Among the highlights of the festival **were** the **pot stickers** *from the kitchen of Ms. Yu, our teacher.*

Write each sentence, underlining the subject and using the correct form of the verb in parentheses.

1. There (is, are) many unusual sights on this camping trip—too many for Soraya.
2. Outside our tent (sits, sit) two fat raccoons, begging for a handout.
3. At the crossroads (stands, stand) a huge bull moose, watching us unconcernedly.
4. Here (comes, come) three baby porcupines and their mother.
5. There (goes, go) Soraya, fleeing the dangers of the woods for the safety of the city.

See Lesson 16.2, page 510.

2.10 Presenting: Sharing What You've Written **87**

ASSESS

Writing Activities Evaluation Guidelines
Present Your Writing
Use these criteria when evaluating your students' presentations:
- Is the presentation appropriate for the selected audience?
- Does it reflect thorough editing?
- Is it presented attractively?
- Are the ideas clear and presented in a sensible order?

See also the *Teacher's Guide to Writing Assessment.*

Cooperative Learning
Use the following evaluation criteria:
- Did each group member participate?
- Did group members consider the opinions and input of others?
- Does the newsletter show effective use of proofreading and editing?
- Is the publication appropriate to its purpose and audience?

Grammar Link
(See Using the Grammar Link below.)

Reteaching
📁 *Composition Reteaching,* p. 16

Enrichment
📁 *Composition Enrichment,* p. 16

CLOSE

Challenge students to explore publishing opportunities for student writers and artists within the community. For example, they might inquire at local libraries about opportunities to write book reviews or make posters about children's books. They might ask local organizations about contests open to young people. Provide a forum for sharing results.

Using the Grammar Link

Grammar Link Answers
1. <u>sights</u>, are
2. <u>raccoons</u>, sit
3. <u>moose</u>, stands
4. <u>porcupines</u> and <u>mother</u>, come
5. <u>Soraya</u>, goes

Collective Nouns as Subjects Remind students that collective nouns may take singular or plural verbs, depending on whether the reference is to the group as a whole or to the individuals of the group: *Class* is *dismissed* but *The class* have *all gone to their homes.*

87

Setting the Purpose

Students now have the opportunity to apply what they have learned about the the writing process to an independent writing project. They will use the stages of the writing process to create and present a finished piece.

FOCUS

Lesson Overview

Objective: To retell an exciting personal experience in a way that engages and involves a specific audience

Skills: using the five stages of the writing process: prewriting, drafting, revising, editing, and presenting; creating suspense; writing varied sentences; writing unified paragraphs

Critical Thinking: recalling; generating new information

Speaking and Listening: reading aloud and listening to a draft; discussing

Bellringer

When students enter the classroom, have this assignment on the board: *In a few sentences, summarize the plot of an exciting book, movie, or television show that you've seen or read.*

Grammar Link to the Bellringer

Have students look at what they just wrote and circle the pronouns and underline the verbs.

Motivating Activity

Invite a few volunteers to share their plot summaries. Tell students that when good writing comes to life, it can seem like a movie in a reader's mind. Tell them that this project will enable them to create a "movie of the mind" for their readers.

In preceding lessons you've learned about the stages of the writing process and how writers go back and forth between stages before they present their writing in final form. You've also practiced what you've learned about the writing stages. In this lesson you're invited to relive an exciting event you've experienced by writing about it.

• Assignment •

Context	*This year the theme of your school newspaper's annual writing contest is "And You Were There." Entries must portray an exciting event experienced by the writer.*
Purpose	*To involve readers with your account of an exciting event*
Audience	*Readers of your school newspaper*
Length	*2 paragraphs*

The following pages can help you plan and write your experience. Read through them, and then refer to them as you need to. But don't be tied down by them. You're in charge of your own writing process.

88   *The Writing Process: Working Together*

Teacher's Classroom Resources

The following resources can be used for planning, instruction, practice, reinforcement, assessment, reteaching, enrichment, or evaluation.

Teaching Tools
Lesson Plans, p. 21

Transparencies
Writing Process Transparencies, 1–10

Prewriting

What have you done recently that was exciting? Did you compete in a race or a chess match? Did you attend a concert or a pep rally? Did you have your artwork shown at an exhibit?

Use one of the options at the right, or an idea of your own, to begin thinking about a topic. Once you've decided on a topic, develop your ideas by listing, brainstorming, or interviewing.

Prewriting Tip

Look at pages 56–58 for suggestions on using brainstorming to develop a topic.

Prewriting Tip

Pages 60–62 tell you how to use lists to make sure your supporting details fit your main idea.

Drafting

You can make an account of an event exciting by creating suspense. One way to create suspense is to emphasize time pressures. For example, in the brainstorming example on the right, the writer focused on guests fighting the snow to get to a wedding on time. In the example below, the author uses time pressures to create suspense throughout his account of a basketball game.

Option A
Look at old programs and photos.

Option B
Read through your journal.

Option C
Brainstorm ideas.

Person skiing through very heavy snow. Brother Michael's wedding. Big snowstorm night before. Cars snowed in, buses late. People got to Village Hall any way they could.

Literature Model

We came out in the second half and played it pretty cool. Once we came within one point, but then they ran it up to five again. We kept looking over to Mr. Reese to see what he wanted us to do and he would just put his palms down and nod his head for us to play cool. There were six minutes to go when Mr. Reese put me and another guy named Turk in.

Walter Dean Myers, "The Game"

Writing Process in Action **89**

TEACH

Prewriting

L2 Developing Ideas for Writing

Some students may feel that their personal experiences are not exciting enough to be the source of action-packed writing. Point out that any experience that stands out in one's memory as an event that taught something; changed a person's thoughts or feelings; or seemed very funny, fast-paced, or even frightening contains the seeds of a great story.

Drafting

L2 Avoiding Writer's Block

Remind students that some people freeze up when confronted by a writing assignment. Tell students that at this point, they are just trying to get their ideas flowing. If possible, take the class to a special quiet location. Experiment with changes that make drafting as comfortable and fun as possible.

L1 Mapping the Event

Provide each student with a "draft map"—a large three-step flow chart containing three boxes. Ask students to use the map to jot down specific notes regarding the material they will put in the beginning, middle, and end of their accounts. Students should first organize their notes in the order in which they will appear in the account and then transfer the notes to the chart.

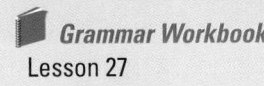 **Blackline Masters**
Thinking and Study Skills,
pp. 1–3, 5, 11, 17, 22
Composition Practice, p. 17
Composition Reteaching, p. 17
Composition Enrichment, p. 17

Grammar Workbook
Lesson 27

Assessment
Teacher's Guide to Writing Assessment

TEACH

Revising

L2 Peer Editing

Students can work in writing conferences with peer editors before they revise their writing. Suggest that peer editors respond to the following questions:

- Can I picture the scene and action?
- Can I understand the feelings?
- Do I understand why this event is important?

You may want to duplicate the Peer Response forms in the *Teacher's Guide to Writing Assessment.*

Editing

L2 Peer Editing

After students have edited their own work, have them edit another student's writing. Remind them to refer to the Editing Checklist on page 90.

Presenting

Before students present their independent writing, discuss how to prepare their papers for publication. Emphasize the importance of the final draft and that it must be neatly done.

Independent Practice

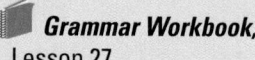 *Writing Process Transparencies,* 1–10

Skills Practice

Thinking and Study Skills, pp. 1–3, 5, 11, 17, 22

Composition Practice, p. 17

Grammar Workbook, Lesson 27

Journal Writing Tip

Reflecting Remind students that taking the time to reflect on their writing can give them valuable new insights.

Drafting Tip

For more information about using transitions to show the passage of time, see Lesson 2.7, page 74.

Revising Tip

Read your writing aloud to check its rhythm. For more help with sentence variety, see Lesson 2.8, pages 76–78.

As you write your draft, think about ways to emphasize the time element to create suspense. For example, in a movie, a hero needs to defuse a bomb. Suspense is created by repeatedly showing the bomb's timer ticking away the seconds.

Remember, in the drafting stage you need to let your writing flow to get your ideas down. You can make changes later. See pages 64–67 for more help with drafting.

Revising

To begin revising, read over your draft to make sure that what you have written fits your purpose and your audience. Then have a writing conference. Read your draft to a partner or small group. Use your audience's reactions to help you evaluate your work so far. The following questions can help you and your listeners.

Question A
Is my account clear?

Question B
Have I varied my sentences?

Question C
Have I written unified paragraphs?

> "I can't imagine where she is," Michael said into
> counted the eighth ring of his call to Anika's.
> the receiver as he paced back and forth.
> and the wedding was scheduled for noon.
> It was eleven thirty. I wanted to ask if they'd had
> , knowing that she was probably stuck in the snow,
> a fight, but I kept my mouth shut.
> ^ from the front door of the Village Hall,
> Just then I heard Kenny yell, "Hey, everyone,
> As I reached the door,
> you've got to see this!" I couldn't believe my eyes.
>
> It was Anika in her wedding dress, skiing down
> the street to the hall. It was 11:45. The guests who
> had made it to the hall applauded when Anika
> came inside, shaking the snow from her dress.

90

Enrichment and Extension

Follow-up Ideas

- Set aside time to celebrate the conclusion of students' writing projects. Encourage them to share their finished pieces with the class or in small groups.
- Make photocopies of work sent out for sharing or publication.

Extending the Writing Process

- Brainstorm with students ways they can use their expertise in the writing process in other subject areas, such as report writing in history or science.
- Encourage students to extend their use of the writing process to projects undertaken outside of school.

Editing

A careful editing job shows your readers that you care about your work and that you don't want errors to distract them from your ideas. The Editing Checklist will help you catch errors you might otherwise overlook. Usually writers **proofread** for only one kind of error at a time. If you do the same, you will probably do a better job of finding your mistakes. Use a dictionary and the Grammar, Usage, and Mechanics part of this book to help you with your editing.

Presenting

Make sure your account of an exciting event is neatly written or typed on clean white paper before you submit it to "And You Were There."

As an alternative way of presenting your writing, you might like to give an oral presentation. Let the excitement of the event come through in your voice, facial expressions, and gestures. You might want to include recorded background noise or music for your presentation. For example, you might want to record the sound of a crowd cheering or booing if your account is of a sports event.

Editing Checklist
1. Have I used the correct form of each pronoun?
2. Have I used irregular verbs correctly?
3. Have I capitalized all proper nouns?
4. Have I used commas and semicolons correctly?
5. Is every word spelled correctly?

Proofreading

For proofreading symbols, see page 81.

Journal Writing

Reflect on your writing process experience. Answer these questions in your journal: What do I like best about my article? What was the hardest part of writing it? What did I learn in my writing conference? What new things have I learned as a writer?

Writing Process in Action **91**

ASSESS

Evaluation Guidelines

Use the following questions to evaluate students' finished writing.
- Is the writing clear?
- Does the student use vivid words?
- Do supporting details fit the main idea?
- Is there an effective building of suspense and/or time pressures?
- Is the sequence of events sensible and clear?
- Are the pacing and flow smooth?
- Are there sentences of varying lengths?
- Are the paragraphs unified?
- Are there indications of careful editing for errors in grammar, spelling, and mechanics?

Refer to the *Teacher's Guide to Writing Assessment* for further help with evaluating student writing.

Reteaching
📁 *Composition Reteaching,* p. 17

Enrichment
📁 *Composition Enrichment,* p. 17

CLOSE

Ask students to discuss the following questions:
- How did writing about their experiences lead them to view those experiences differently?
- What new conclusions did they form about their experiences?

Cooperative Learning

Getting Help with Suspense
Ask students to work together in a think-pair-share activity. Have each student bring a draft of suspense writing or an excerpt from a suspense novel to the activity. Partners should consider how the writer might make better use of the action or include more vivid sensory details in the draft. Encourage writers to consider the ideas but to make their own decisions.

About the Author

African American author Walter Dean Myers was born in 1937 in West Virginia. He grew up in New York City, where he played basketball on playgrounds in Harlem. Even as a child, Myers was a constant writer, filling notebooks and journals with observations and ideas. He has written several highly successful books for young people.

FOCUS

Lesson Overview

Objective: To read an account of a suspense-filled athletic event
Skills: reading comprehension
Critical Thinking: identifying attributes; analyzing; making inferences
Speaking and Listening: discussing

Bellringer

When students enter the classroom, have this assignment on the board: *What do you do as part of a team? Write what makes you a good team member.*

Motivating Activity

Students who play basketball might provide the class with an overview of the game. Ask them to discuss the role of a system, practice, and teamwork, especially when they feel they are up against superior teams.

UNIT
2
The Writing Process
Literature Model

WALTER DEAN MYERS

THE GAME

With New York City's 116th Street as the setting, Walter Dean Myers's narrator, Stuff, reports the play-by-play action at the year's most important neighborhood basketball game in this chapter from Fast Sam, Cool Clyde, and Stuff. *As you read, pay special attention to how the author gets you interested in the story. Then try the activities in Linking Writing and Literature on page 97.*

W e had practiced and practiced until it ran out of our ears. Every guy on the team knew every play. We were ready. It meant the championship. Everybody was there. I never saw so many people at the center at one time. We had never seen the other team play but Sam said that he knew some of the players and that they were good. Mr. Reese told us to go out and play as hard as we could every moment we were on the floor. We all shook hands in the locker

92 *The Writing Process: Working Together*

Teacher's Classroom Resources

The following resources can be used for planning, instruction, or practice.

🔧 **Teaching Tools**
Lesson Plans, p. 20

📖 **Transparencies**
Fine Art Transparencies, 6–9

room and then went out. Mostly we tried to ignore them warming up at the other end of the court but we couldn't help but look a few times. They were doing exactly what we were doing, just shooting a few lay-ups and waiting for the game to begin.

They got the first tap and started passing the ball around. I mean they really started passing the ball around faster than anything I had ever seen. Zip! Zip! Zip! Two points! I didn't even know how they could *see* the ball, let alone get it inside to their big man. We brought the ball down and one of their players stole the ball from Sam. We got back on defense but they weren't in a hurry. The same old thing. Zip! Zip! Zip! Two points! They could pass the ball better than anybody I ever saw. Then we brought the ball down again and Chalky missed a jump shot. He missed the backboard, the rim, everything. One of their players caught the ball and then brought it down and a few seconds later the score was 6–0. We couldn't even get close enough to foul them. Chalky brought the ball down again, passed to Sam cutting across the lane, and then walked. They brought the ball down and it was 8–0.

They were really enjoying the game. You could see. Every time they scored they'd slap hands and carry on. Also, they had some cheerleaders. They had about five girls with little pink skirts on and white sweaters cheering for them.

Clyde brought the ball down this time, passed into our center, a guy named Leon, and Leon turned and missed a hook. They got the rebound and came down, and Chalky missed a steal and fouled his man. That's when Mr. Reese called time out.

"Okay, now, just trade basket for basket. They make a basket, you take your time and you make a basket—don't rush it." Mr. Reese looked at his starting five. "Okay, now, every once in a while take a look over at me and I'll let you know when I want you to make your move. If I put my hands palm down, just keep on playing cool. If I stand up and put my hands up like this"—he put both hands up near his face—"that means to make your move. You understand that?"

Everyone said that they understood. When the ball was back in play Chalky and Sam and Leon started setting picks from the outside and then passed to Clyde for our first two

Literature Model **93**

TEACH

Guided Practice

L2 Guided Reading
- What emotion is the author trying to convey when he reveals that the players on his team "tried to ignore" the other team, but then "couldn't help but look a few times"? (He may be trying to convey a mixture of nervousness, pride, and perhaps a brave front, curiosity, and a need to evaluate the opponents' skills.)
- Why do you think the author uses the words "Zip! Zip! Zip!" in the story? (The speed of the action is emphasized by the repeated use of this short word whose sound suggests its sense.)

Blackline Masters
Speaking and Listening Activities, pp. 12, 17–18, 23
Thinking and Study Skills, pp. 3–5, 11, 17–18, 34

Assessment
Teacher's Guide to Writing Assessment

TEACH

Guided Practice

L2 Guided Reading

- Why is the narrator surprised to be put in the game? (He may feel he is not one of the best players.)
- How is he feeling? (He feels nervous.) How can you tell? (His heart is beating very fast.)
- Predict what might happen to the narrator in the game. Then read on to see if your prediction is correct.

Red Grooms, *Fast Break*, 1983–1984

points. They got the ball and started passing around again. Zip! Zip! Zip! But this time we were just waiting for that pass underneath and they knew it. Finally they tried a shot from outside and Chalky slapped it away to Sam on the break. We came down real quick and scored. On the way back Mr. Reese showed everybody that his palms were down. To keep playing cool.

They missed their next shot and fouled Chalky. They called time out and, much to my surprise, Mr. Reese put me in. My heart was beating so fast I thought I was going to have a heart attack. Chalky missed the foul shot but Leon slapped the ball out to Clyde, who passed it to me. I dribbled about two steps and threw it back to Leon in the bucket. Then I didn't know what to do so I did what Mr. Reese always told us. If you don't know what to do then, just move around. I started moving toward the corner and then I ran quickly toward the basket. I saw Sam coming at me from the other direction and it was a play. Two guards cutting past and one of the defensive men gets picked off. I ran as close as I could to Sam, and his man got

94 *The Writing Process: Working Together*

About the Art

Red Grooms, *Fast Break*, 1983–1984
Fast Break by Red Grooms is an example of Pop Art, an art movement that became well known in the 1960s. Some of the more famous pop artists include Jasper Johns, Roy Lichtenstein, Marisol, Claes Oldenburg, Robert Rauschenberg, and Andy Warhol.

picked off. Chalky threw the ball into him for an easy lay-up. They came down and missed again but one of their men got the rebound in. We brought the ball down and Sam went along the base line for a jump shot, but their center knocked the ball away. I caught it just before it went out at the corner and shot the ball. I remembered what Mr. Reese had said about following your shot in, and I started in after the ball but it went right in. It didn't touch the rim or anything. Swish!

One of their players said to watch out for 17—that was me. I played about two minutes more, then Mr. Reese took me out. But I had scored another basket on a lay-up. We were coming back. Chalky and Sam were knocking away just about anything their guards were throwing up, and Leon, Chalky, and Sam controlled the defensive backboard. Mr. Reese brought in Cap, and Cap got fouled two times in two plays. At the end of the half, when I thought we were doing pretty well, I found out the score was 36–29. They were beating us by seven points. Mr. Reese didn't seem worried, though.

"Okay, everybody, stay cool. No sweat. Just keep it nice and easy."

We came out in the second half and played it pretty cool. Once we came within one point, but then they ran it up to five again. We kept looking over to Mr. Reese to see what he wanted us to do and he would just put his palms down and nod his head for us to play cool. There were six minutes to go when Mr. Reese put me and another guy named Turk in. Now I didn't really understand why he did this because I know I'm not the best basketball player in the world, although I'm not bad, and I know Turk is worse than me. Also, he took out both Sam and Chalky, our two best players. We were still losing by five points, too. And they weren't doing anything wrong. There was a jump ball between Leon and their center when all of a sudden this big cheer goes up and everybody looks over to the sidelines. Well, there was Gloria, BB, Maria, Sharon, Kitty, and about four other girls, all dressed in white blouses and black skirts and with big T's on their blouses and they were our cheerleaders. One of their players said something stupid about them but I liked them. They looked real good to me. We controlled the jump and Turk drove right down the lane and made a lay-up. Turk actually

Literature Model **95**

TEACH

Guided Practice

L2 Guided Reading
- What did the author do the first time he went into the game? (First he dribbled, then he passed the ball to Leon. Then he ran toward the basket and helped Sam and Chalky with a lay-up. Next he caught the ball and scored. He scored once more before being taken out of the game.)
- How does the author usually feel about the coach's decisions? (He feels confident.) How does he feel when the coach puts him and Turk in during the last six minutes? (He doesn't understand the decision. He wonders about taking out the best players and replacing them with others who aren't as good.)

Genre and Style

Reading First-person Narrative
Walter Dean Myers uses first-person narrative to relate this personal experience. The narrator, Stuff, is the main character of his book. All story events and emotions come from Stuff's point of view. The first-person narrative genre creates a realism that brings the reader right onto the playing court. Reading the action is like seeing a film, with Stuff's eyes and ears acting as the camera going up and down the court to follow each play.

TEACH

L2 Guided Reading

- Did the coach really want someone to foul the other team player when he called out "Foul him!"? (No) What was the coach's plan? (He wanted to trick the player into trying a quick shot as he was being fouled. He would be more apt to miss his shot.)
- Do you think the coach had a lot to do with the team's success? Why or why not? (Students might mention his relaxed, confident attitude and his decisions regarding whom to put in the game and when.)

Independent Practice

Skills Practice

📁 *Speaking and Listening Activities,* pp. 12, 17–18, 23
📁 *Thinking and Study Skills,* pp. 3–5, 11, 17–18, 34

made the lay-up. Turk once missed seven lay-ups in a row in practice and no one was even guarding him. But this one he made. Then one of their men double-dribbled and we got the ball and I passed it to Leon, who threw up a shot and got fouled. The shot went in and when he made the foul shot it added up to a three-point play. They started down court and Mr. Reese started yelling for us to give a foul.

"Foul him! Foul him!" he yelled from the sidelines.

Now this was something we had worked on in practice and that Mr. Reese had told us would only work once in a game. Anybody who plays basketball knows that if you're fouled while shooting the ball you get two foul shots and if you're fouled while not shooting the ball you only get one. So when a guy knows you're going to foul him he'll try to get off a quick shot. At least that's what we hoped. When their guard came across the mid-court line, I ran at him as if I was going to foul him. Then, just as I was going to touch him, I stopped short and moved around him without touching him. Sure enough, he threw the ball wildly toward the basket. It went over the base line and it was our ball. Mr. Reese took me out and Turk and put Sam and Chalky back in. And the game was just about over.

We hadn't realized it but in the two minutes that me and Turk played the score had been tied. When Sam and Chalky came back in they outscored the other team by four points in the last four minutes. We were the champs. We got the first-place trophies and we were so happy we were all jumping around and slapping each other on the back. Gloria and the other girls were just as happy as we were, and when we found that we had an extra trophy we gave it to them. Then Mr. Reese took us all in the locker room and shook each guy's hand and then went out and invited the parents and the girls in. He made a little speech about how he was proud of us and all, and not just because we won tonight but because we had worked so hard to win. When he finished everybody started clapping for us and, as usual, I started boo-hooing. But it wasn't so bad this time because Leon starting boo-hooing worse than me.

You know what high is? We felt so good the next couple of days that it was ridiculous. We'd see someone in the street and we'd just walk up and be happy. Really.

96 *The Writing Process: Working Together*

Enrichment and Extension

Writing a First-person Account

Point out that this story is filled with authentic and well-written characters, exciting action and suspense, and a feeling of teamwork and triumph. It is also very real. Stress that often the best, most realistic stories come, as this one did, from an actual experience the writer had. Encourage students to try writing a first-person account of an event that made them proud.

Linking Writing and Literature
Readers Respond to the Model

How does Walter Dean Myers interest you in the story?

Explore how Walter Dean Myers interests readers by answering these questions. Then read what other students liked about his story.

1. Walter Dean Myers told the story through the words of one of the players, Stuff. Why do you think Myers did this?

2. What details about the other team create interest and suspense at the beginning of the story?

3. What details about the players on Stuff's team added to the suspense of the game?

4. Which character in the story did you like the best? Why?

My favorite character was Mr. Reese, the coach. He trusted his players, and he didn't show favoritism. I remember the scene in which he let some less able players get on the court. I was surprised because the team was behind, but their coach had confidence in them. The writer made Mr. Reese seem real by showing how happy he was and how proud of his players. It was his spirit that the players drew upon.
Keianna Chatman

The story made me feel as if I was part of the game. The coach, Mr. Reese, was my favorite character. When the team was losing by several points, he told them to keep cool, and he kept them steady. He also kept them together. Without teamwork, a team would have nothing.
Benjamin Rodriguez

97

ASSESS

Evaluation Guidelines for Discussion

As your students discuss the passage, either in small groups or as a class, encourage them to begin with a personal response. The student responses on this page might be used as a starting point.

Look for evidence that students
• have read the passage
• can state some of the writer's ideas in their own words
• understand the writer's point of view
• have connected the content to their own knowledge and experiences
• understand the ideas and implications of the passage.

Some possible responses to the discussion questions on this page:

1. Telling the story through Stuff's eyes makes the events seem very real and immediate.

2. Interest and suspense were created through the descriptions of the team's speed in passing and their accurate shooting, "They could pass the ball better than anybody I ever saw," "We couldn't even get close enough to foul them."

3. Suspense was added through the players' initial inability to score frequently, their slower pace, and the fact that the coach put in two of the less talented players with six minutes left.

4. Answers will vary. Students should be able to support their answers with examples from the story.

CLOSE

Discuss the changes in the feelings of the players from the beginning of the game to the end.

REVIEW

Reflecting on the Unit

You may have students respond to Reflecting on the Unit in writing or through discussion.

Writing Across the Curriculum

Have students use examples of their writing from other classes, such as a social studies report, to talk about the following issues: Which prewriting technique did you find the most helpful (in writing your report)? What problems did you have in drafting your writing, and how did you solve them? What revising changes did you make that produced the most marked result? Did certain editing changes come up again and again?

Adding to Your Portfolio

Point out to students that portfolios have traditionally been a collection of designs or drawings that artists use as personal records and as a way to show prospective clients samples of their work.

Portfolio Evaluation

If you plan to grade the portfolio selections, you may want to award two marks—one for content and one for form. Explain your assessment criteria before students make their selections. Commend

- experimentation with creative prewriting techniques
- clear, concise writing in which the main idea, audience, and purpose are evident
- successful revisions
- work that shows a flair for language

Unit 2 Review

Reflecting on the Unit

Summarize what you have learned in this unit by answering the following questions:

- What are the stages of the writing process?
- Why should the writing process be flexible?
- What is involved in the prewriting stage?
- What does drafting mean?
- What does revising a piece of writing involve?
- What kinds of errors are corrected in the editing stage?
- What does presenting mean?

Adding to Your Portfolio

Choose a selection for your portfolio. Look over the writing you did for this unit. Choose a piece of writing to put into your portfolio. The piece you choose should show one or more of the following:

- connections to ideas found and explored in prewriting
- words and ideas that reflect a specific audience and purpose
- an opening that interests readers and explains what will follow
- revisions that you made after you and a peer reviewed it
- a pleasing sentence rhythm
- editing for sentence structure, grammar, and mechanics

Reflect on your choice.
Attach a note to the piece you chose, explaining briefly why you chose it and what you learned from writing it.

Set goals.
How can you improve your writing? What skill will you focus on the next time you write?

Writing Across the Curriculum

Make a science connection.
Think about an important scientific first or discovery that interests you. Write a paragraph about the event as if you were there working with the scientists. Try to help readers sense your scientific team's excitement about the event or discovery.

98 *The Writing Process: Working Together*

Teacher's Classroom Resources

The following resources can be used for assessment or evaluation.

Unit Assessment
📁 *Tests with Answer Key*
Unit 2 Choice A Test, p. 5
Unit 2 Choice B Test, p. 6
Unit 2 Composition Objective Test, pp. 7–8

💿 *Test Generator*
Unit 2 Choice A Test
Unit 2 Choice B Test
Unit 2 Composition Objective Test

You may wish to administer one of these tests as a mastery test.

UNIT

3

Composition

Descriptive Writing

Lessons

99

UNIT GOALS

The goal of Unit 3 is to help students, through example and instruction, to develop an understanding of descriptive writing. The unit's six lessons focus on using sensory details, precise language, and spatial order in describing people, places, and things and analyzing biographical passages in literature.

Unit Assessment

📁 *Tests with Answer Key*
Unit 3 Choice A Test, p. 9
Unit 3 Choice B Test, p. 10
Unit 3 Composition Objective Test,
  pp. 11–12

💿 *Test Generator*
Unit 3 Choice A Test
Unit 3 Choice B Test
Unit 3 Composition Objective Test

You may wish to administer either the Unit 3 Choice A Test or the Unit 3 Choice B Test as a pretest.

Key to Ability Levels

Enabling Strategies have been coded for varying learning styles and abilities.

L1 Level 1 activities are within the ability range of Learning Disabled students.

L2 Level 2 activities are basic-to-average activities and are within the ability range of average students.

L3 Level 3 activities are challenging activities and are within the ability range of above-average students.

LEP LEP activities are within the ability range of Limited English Proficiency students.

Setting the Purpose

In the Unit 3 Case Study students examine an award-winning novelist's use of descriptive writing. Students will explore and practice descriptive writing in the lessons that follow.

FOCUS

Lesson Overview
Objective: To describe a subject using clear, appropriate details
Skills: experimenting with words; noticing details; revising
Critical Thinking: analyzing; synthesizing; contrasting; recalling; evaluating; comparing; defining and clarifying
Speaking and Listening: discussing

Bellringer
When students enter the classroom, have this assignment on the board: *Write down some images and details you associate with the word* home. *What do you see, hear, smell, taste, and feel?*

Grammar Link to the Bellringer
Challenge students to turn their lists into several sentences using adjective clauses. For example, a student might write *The Fosters decided not to live in a home that always smelled like a donut shop*.

Motivating Activity
Ask students how often they think writers draw from personal experiences to describe people, settings, and other elements of their stories. Can students give examples of how real experiences might be used in a fictional account? How difficult would it be to write a story without using any information experienced first-hand?

Descriptive Writing
in the Real World

Alvarez Describes Home

F O C U S: Writing description helps to recall memories and to share and clarify experiences.

Writer Julia Alvarez was ten years old when her family moved from the Dominican Republic to the United States. Her first language was Spanish. While learning English, she found out that words often have meanings that are more complex and more descriptive than their dictionary definitions. Julia Alvarez grew up to write *How the García Girls Lost Their Accents*, an award-winning novel about immigrant experiences similar to her own. Writing allows Alvarez to bring back memories and to describe what makes her feel at home. As she explains, "Entering the world of the imagination, that's a portable homeland . . . I can take out my pad of paper in the Dominican Republic, here in Vermont, in California, in Turkey—and it's the same blank page. It's the same sense of creating a world, of making meaning, wherever you go."

▲ *Novelist Julia Alvarez*

100   *Descriptive Writing: A Closer Look*

Teacher's Classroom Resources

The following resources can be used for planning, instruction, practice, reinforcement, assessment, or evaluation.

Teaching Tools
Lesson Plans, p. 22

Transparencies
Writing Process Transparencies, 11–13B

Writing a Description

Prewriting	Drafting	Revising

sheep... grazing... powder puffs... **cumulus**... clouds... looking at a sheep farm

Playing with Words   Discovering Details   Seeing What Works

"*I began to write because it was a way to master words. It was also a way to make a home in words, in language. And you know, I always say that I left the Dominican Republic, and I landed not in the United States, but in the English language.*"

Julia Alvarez

▼ *Alvarez says that "writing became my new place" when she moved from the Dominican Republic.*

Prewriting

PLAYING WITH WORDS

"Much of writing is play-fulness with words. It's try-ing things out," Alvarez says. "You're not probably going to get it right the first time. So just let yourself get *some* of it right."

Learning to create vivid description takes time and practice for every writer. The writer must learn to notice the things of the world and to describe those things in fresh ways. To help herself do this,

Case Study **101**

TEACH

Building Background

Warm-up:
Have students list as many occasions as they can think of where descriptions are used.

Description in Speaking:
Ask the class to list specific occasions where people use descriptions in speaking, such as when telling friends about something they saw or experienced.

Description in Writing:
Discuss any descriptions students have read. Use prompts such as:
• What kinds of things are described in advertisements?
• How might a description by a newspaper reporter differ from a description by a television news reporter?

Preview the Case Study

Have students preview the case study's title and focus. Ask the students to read the case study. They may want to take notes as they read about the specific descriptive tricks Alvarez uses as a successful novelist.

📁 **Blackline Masters**
Cooperative Learning Activities,
 pp. 13–18
Thinking and Study Skills,
 pp. 3–6, 9, 22
*Case Studies: Writing in the
 Real World,* pp. 9–12

Assessment
📁 *Teacher's Guide to Writing
 Assessment*

TEACH

Discussion Prompts

• Julia Alvarez says that when people say they can't describe something, they may be trying to describe something too big. What might be some other reasons people have difficulty describing something?

• How can a writer use small details to create a large effect? Can you give an example from your own experience?

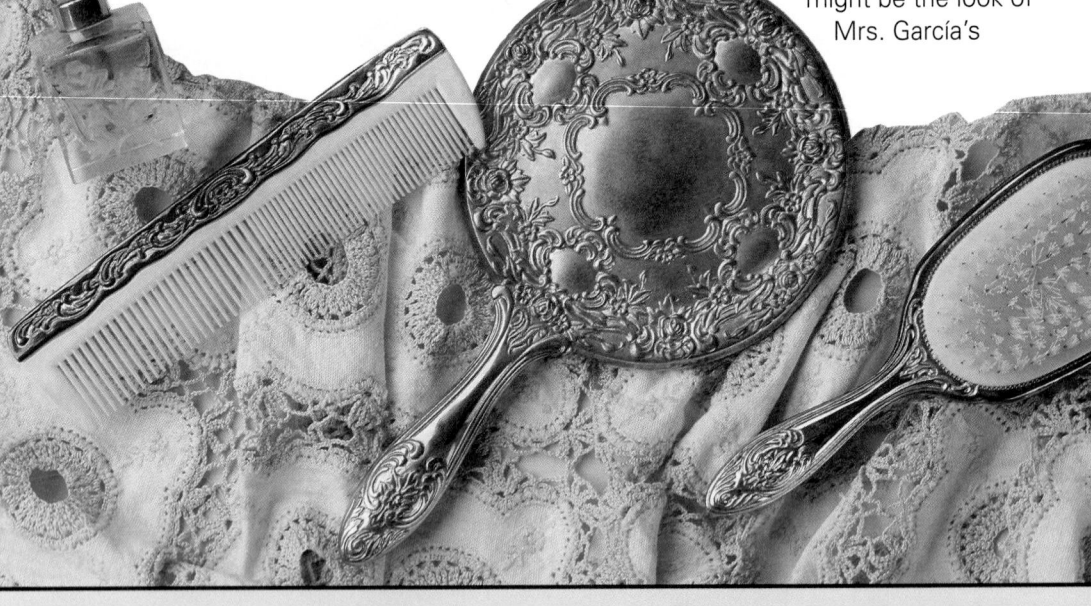

Alvarez plays a word game. In her journal she'll describe what she sees in daily life. She might look at the sheep grazing near her house and think of different images to describe them, such as powder puffs and cumulus clouds. As she explains, "What's great is that maybe two weeks down the line—maybe two years down the line—wouldn't you know it, but I'll have a character looking at a sheep farm!"

Drafting

DISCOVERING DETAILS

People often say that something important is "beyond words." Yet Julia Alvarez finds the words to describe complicated experiences of feelings and memories. "I think when somebody says that they can't describe something, they're trying for the big thing, instead of the little details that, of course, they can describe," she says.

Alvarez creates large effects with small details. She notices the intimate details that bring a reader close to a character or experience. The detail might be the feel of sun shining on top of a character's head. Or it might be the look of Mrs. García's

Cultural Diversity

Adjusting to America

In *How the García Girls Lost Their Accents*, Alvarez writes about an American family originally from the Dominican Republic and now living in New York City. The title refers to the process by which the four sisters in the family become Americanized. Mention that many U.S. writers who first came to this country as immigrants write about their early adjustments as a way of commenting on the positives and negatives of becoming an American.

> Sandi leaned her elbows on the vanity and watched her mother comb her dark hair in the mirror. Tonight Mami was turning back into the beauty she had been back home. Her face was pale and tragic in the lamplight; her bright eyes shone like amber held up to the light. She wore a black dress with a scoop back and wide shoulders so her long neck had the appearance of a swan gliding on a lake. Around her neck sparkled her good necklace that had real diamonds.

neck while she is combing her hair. When writing the description of Mrs. García in the chapter "Floor Show," Alvarez wanted to give a picture of what the mother looked like. Alvarez says, "I was trying to get a sense of the glamour and beauty of the mother, as seen from a little girl's eyes. I wanted to show that there was something beautiful and mysterious about the mother."

▲ *In this passage from* How the García Girls Lost Their Accents, *Alvarez describes the mother through the eyes of young Sandi.*

Revising

SEEING WHAT WORKS

Playing with words and finding details in memories and observations can be fun. Revising those early notes and journal entries can also be exciting and satisfying. As Alvarez explains, "That's part of the fun— when it all falls into place. You know, I'll discover something, and then all of a sudden, I'll have to go back and redo the beginning."

Alvarez sometimes reads her work out loud after she writes a few sentences. In this way she does some revising as she goes along.

Case Study **103**

TEACH

Discussion Prompts

- In the passage shown, how well do you think Alvarez accomplished her goal of showing that "there was something beautiful and mysterious about the mother"? How much more or less effective would it be if she simply wrote, "There was something beautiful and mysterious about mother"?
- While Alvarez sometimes reads her work after writing a few sentences, other writers find that they cannot stop to analyze until they have written much more than that. Which type of writer are you? Why?

Cooperative Learning

Creating a Collective Description

Ask groups of students to select a piece of art from this textbook. Each student should study the group's selection silently for a few minutes, then choose a detail of the picture to write a description of. When every group member has described one detail in the picture, the group can work together to compile the descriptions into one art review. Afterward, they might discuss the descriptions, commenting on the details that capture the look and feel of the art.

TEACH

Guided Practice

L2 Discussion
Stimulate a discussion of the case study. You may want to invite students to talk about
- how a writer can know if a description is working or not
- Alvarez's claim that the imagination is a "portable homeland"
- what can happen when a well-crafted description helps one see similarities between one's own world and the world of a stranger

Independent Practice

Writing Process Transparencies, 11–13B
Case Studies: Writing in the Real World, pp. 9–12
Cooperative Learning Activities, pp. 13–18

Skills Practice
Thinking and Study Skills, pp. 3–6, 9, 22

Still, details sometimes surprise her, and the direction a description takes may differ from what she imagined when she started writing. Alvarez says, "As you revise and revise, you happen upon things that you see are working. Then you polish them, or bring in new things to enhance them."

Having someone else read a description out loud can also help a writer to hear what needs revising. "What you write gets coated with your voice," Alvarez explains. "Having somebody else read out loud to you, you hear all the places that it's really off, in a way you can't hear it when you're writing."

Revision also demands that a writer think of her or his readers. The writer must revise and revise until the description fully brings an outsider into the private world of memories. As Alvarez says, "I know it's a process! And that certain things that get you started in a description later have to go."

104

Civic Literacy

Understanding Citizenship
Alvarez writes that when she came to the United States, she "landed…in the English language." This statement is especially true for new immigrants who must prove an ability to read, write, and speak basic English in order to obtain U.S. citizenship. Other requirements include being at least eighteen years of age and a legal U.S. resident for at least five years; demonstrating a basic understanding of American history, government, and law; and completing an oath of allegiance to the United States.

Responding to the Case Study

1. Discussion
Discuss these questions about Julia Alvarez's writing.

- What did Julia Alvarez learn about words and language when she had to learn English as an older child?
- How does the author use word games to help herself write?
- Why does she use details in her writing?
- What are some tips Julia Alvarez offers for revising?

2. Descriptive Writing
Write a descriptive portrait of someone you know.

Choose someone you know to describe. Make a list of details you notice about the person. Perhaps he laughs a certain way. Perhaps she always wears a certain kind of jacket. What kinds of feelings about the person do you want to convey to your readers?

Grammar Link

Use adjective clauses to describe a noun or a pronoun.

An adjective clause often begins with a relative pronoun—*who, whom, whose, which,* or *that.*

*Around her neck sparkled her good necklace **that had real diamonds.***

Incorporate each adjective clause below into a sentence. Start by thinking of a noun or a pronoun for each to modify.

1. who was shouting
2. which had been lost
3. whose hands were like ice
4. that won the game
5. that they liked the best

See Lesson 14.3, page 476, and Lesson 21.3, page 600.

Case Study **105**

ASSESS

Responding to the Case Study

1. Discussion
Students' responses may include the following:

- words have meanings that are more complex and descriptive than their dictionary definitions
- she tries to think of different images to describe the things she sees in everyday life
- to create large effects, to describe complicated experiences of feelings and memories, to bring readers close to a character or experience
- read your writing aloud; have others read your work aloud to you; think of your readers

2. Descriptive Writing
Answers will vary.

Grammar Link
(See Using the Grammar Link below.)

Reteaching
Students could read a description and write about any details in it that spark their own memories.

Enrichment
Have students describe the photograph on this page, conveying the mood of the art in their descriptions.

CLOSE

Invite the class to write a description of twentieth-century eighth-grade life for an audience living two hundred years from now.

Closing Note
Some examples of excellent descriptive writing are found in *Pilgrim at Tinker Creek* by Annie Dillard, *Out of Africa* by Isak Dinesen, and *One Writer's Beginnings* by Eudora Welty.

Using the Grammar Link

Grammar Link Answers
Answers will vary, but some suggestions are given below.

1. The boy who was shouting at us lives next door.
2. The book, which had been lost for days, was found in the car.
3. The woman, whose hands were like ice, put on the new gloves.
4. Theirs is the team that won the game.
5. The song that they liked the best was the one my brother wrote.

FOCUS

Lesson Overview

Objective: To rely on memory or observation to compose a description of a person, place, or thing
Skills: observing; using prior knowledge; using metaphors; taking notes while listening
Critical Thinking: recalling; generating new information
Speaking and Listening: discussing

🔔 Bellringer

When students enter the classroom, have this assignment on the board: *Write a short description of your favorite season.*

Grammar Link to the Bellringer

Have students review their descriptions and improve on any adjectives that can be made more vivid.

Motivating Activity

Invite students to read their descriptions aloud. Make four lists (one for each season) of the adjectives they used on the board. Then challenge the class to make each list as long as possible.

LESSON

3.1 Descriptive Writing
Writing Descriptions

A good description re-creates sights, sounds, and other impressions. Read the passage below, and share a hot summer night with Lorraine Hansberry.

Lorraine Hansberry recalls the sights, the sounds, the smells, and the feelings of her Chicago childhood. The reader can hear doors slamming and can sniff freshly cut lemons in the steamy night air.

Literature Model

*E*venings were spent mainly on the back porches where screen doors slammed in the darkness with those really very special summertime sounds. And, sometimes, when Chicago nights got too steamy, the whole family got into the car and went to the park and slept out in the open on blankets. Those were, of course, the best times of all because the grownups were invariably reminded of having been children in rural parts of the country and told the best stories then. And it was also cool and sweet to be on the grass and there was usually the scent of freshly cut lemons or melons in the air. And Daddy would lie on his back, as fathers must, and explain about how men thought the stars above us came to be and how far away they were.

Lorraine Hansberry, "On Summer"

106 *Descriptive Writing: A Closer Look*

Teacher's Classroom Resources

The following resources can be used for planning, instruction, practice, reinforcement, assessment, reteaching, enrichment, or evaluation.

📙 **Teaching Tools**
Lesson Plans, p. 23

📑 **Transparencies**
Fine Art Transparencies, 11–15
Writing Process Transparencies, 11–13B

📂 **Blackline Masters**
Thinking and Study Skills, pp. 3, 5, 12, 22, 33–34
Writing Across the Curriculum, pp. 4–8
Cooperative Learning Activities, pp. 13–18

Observe Details

Descriptive writing often starts with a memory or an observation—something that catches your attention. The details that make someone or something stay in your mind become the raw material for creating a description. Notice how writer Nicholasa Mohr brings to life details about Puerto Rico through the observation of one of her characters.

Literature Model

*S*he saw the morning mist settling like puffs of smoke scattered over the range of mountains that surrounded the entire countryside. Sharp mountainous peaks and curves covered with many shades of green foliage that changed constantly from light to dark, intense or soft tones, depending on the time of day and the direction of the rays of the brilliant tropical sun. Ah, the path, she smiled, following the road that led to her village. Lali inhaled the sweet and spicy fragrance of the flower gardens that sprinkled the countryside in abundance.

Nicholasa Mohr, *In Nueva York*

What words does the writer use to help you see the changing mountains?

Mohr draws you into her memories with a walk along the path.

Journal Writing

Think about how Nicholasa Mohr brings her village to life. List at least five words that the author uses to describe it. Then choose a memory of your own. Write at least five specific details.

3.1 Writing Descriptions **107**

Sentence Combining Practice,
pp. 28–29
Speaking and Listening
Activities, pp. 14–15
Composition Practice, p. 18
Composition Reteaching, p. 18
Composition Enrichment, p. 18

Unit Assessment

📁 *Teacher's Guide to Writing*
Assessment

📁 *Tests with Answer Key*
Unit 3 Choice A Test, p. 9
Unit 3 Choice B Test, p. 10
Unit 3 Composition Objective
Test, pp. 11–12

💿 *Test Generator*
Unit 3 Choice A Test
Unit 3 Choice B Test
Unit 3 Composition Objective
Test, pp. 11–12

You may wish to administer
either the Unit 3 Choice A Test
or Choice B Test as a pretest.

TEACH

Guided Practice

L2 **Using the Models**
Ask students whether Hansberry's description on page 106 creates a vivid image for them. Invite students who enjoy art to draw or paint the settings they imagine as you read the model aloud. Ask students to list the strongest details in Hansberry's description. Then direct students' attention to the model on page 107. Suggest that students rewrite the description, omitting the descriptive language. (She saw the mist and the mountains. When she saw the path, she smiled. Lali inhaled the smell of the garden.) Ask how omitting the descriptive language changes the passage.

L2 **Promoting Discussion**
Ask students to describe some memorable places they have seen. Invite listeners to ask questions about the description. Finally, ask what details the listeners found most vivid. Did the details cover all aspects of the place?

 **Two-Minute Skill Drill**

List the following words on the board and have students write a vivid adjective for each.

school	best friend
family member	favorite teacher

Journal Writing Tip

Using Descriptive Detail
Encourage pairs of students to read their descriptive details to one another. Ask the listeners to restate the writer's memories as a way of testing how accurately the writer conveyed the memory.

107

TEACH

Guided Practice

L1 Transcribing Descriptions
Many students with learning disabilities enjoy relaying descriptions orally but have difficulty putting their words into writing. Encourage these students to make an audiotape as the first draft of a description. Suggest that they then transcribe their tapes and begin revising their descriptions to create clear and vivid images.

L3 Describing Utopia
Ask students to draw on their prior knowledge to envision a utopian society. Have them write a description of one aspect of the society. They may wish to describe the lifestyle, living space, or structure of the society.

Independent Practice

For further stimuli for descriptive writing, see *Fine Art Transparencies* 11–15.

Writing Process Transparencies, 11–13B

Writing Across the Curriculum, pp. 4–8

Cooperative Learning Activities, pp. 13–18

Skills Practice
Thinking and Study Skills, pp. 3, 5, 12, 22, 33–34
Sentence Combining Practice, pp. 28–29
Speaking and Listening Activities, pp. 14–15
Composition Practice, p. 18

Grammar
Editing Tip

When you edit, use verb tenses consistently. For more information, see Lessons 10.5–10.9, pages 376–385.

Notice Descriptive Writing

Good descriptive writing involves using your senses to observe, selecting precise details, and organizing your ideas. You probably read descriptions more often than you realize. The chart below shows some examples of descriptive writing. In the model that follows the chart, Michael Lim describes an unusual fish.

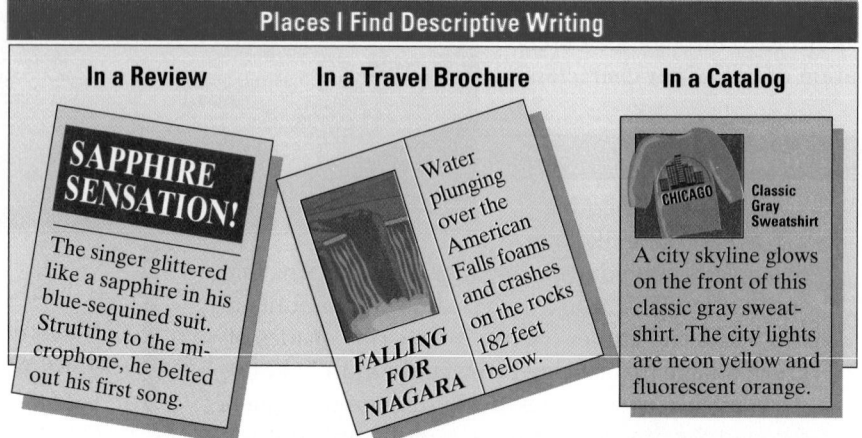

Places I Find Descriptive Writing

In a Review

SAPPHIRE SENSATION!
The singer glittered like a sapphire in his blue-sequined suit. Strutting to the microphone, he belted out his first song.

In a Travel Brochure

Water plunging over the American Falls foams and crashes on the rocks 182 feet below.
FALLING FOR NIAGARA

In a Catalog

CHICAGO — Classic Gray Sweatshirt
A city skyline glows on the front of this classic gray sweatshirt. The city lights are neon yellow and fluorescent orange.

The writer includes details such as the color and shape of the fish to help the reader see it.

> **Student Model**
>
> *A* t the bottom of the pool, in the very center, was a fish, lying quietly. . . . The fish was a blazing yellow with streaks of almost metallic blue running down its sides, resembling a slender torpedo in shape. It was at least several feet long, streamlined, its head and tail tapered down from its thicker body. The fish's fins and tail were the same blue as its streaks, only translucent.
>
> Michael Lim,
> The American International School, Vienna, Austria
> First appeared in *Merlyn's Pen*

108 *Descriptive Writing: A Closer Look*

Enabling Strategies

LEP Starting with a Drawing
Students struggling to describe something in English may be assisted by breaking the process down into three steps. First they can draw an image. Then they can collaborate with a classmate to label its details. Finally—still with assistance from a classmate—they can use their labels as outlines for writing their descriptions.

3.1 Writing Activities

Write a Description of a Person

Picture in your mind a person with whom you enjoy spending time. List words or phrases that capture the person's appearance and personality. Use these details in a written description.

- Choose details that will bring life to your description.
- Use your senses to help you choose details.

PURPOSE To describe a person by using details
AUDIENCE Yourself
LENGTH 1–2 paragraphs

Artist unknown, Mughal, *Fantastic Birds*, c. 1590

Cross-Curricular: Art

You think that one of the birds in the painting on this page would look great on a T-shirt. Write to a friend who is a designer, and ask if your idea is a good one. Describe the bird carefully, including as many details as possible—its color, the shape of the feathers and beak, the position of its body. Look for other details, such as what it is doing.

> **Grammar Link**
>
> **Use vivid adjectives to describe people, places, and things.**
>
> *Sharp mountainous* peaks . . .
>
> . . . the *brilliant tropical* sun.
>
> Complete each sentence below with one or two vivid adjectives.
>
> 1. They enjoyed the _____ dinner.
> 2. The _____ players left the arena.
> 3. It was late on a _____ summer evening.
> 4. She smiled when she heard the _____ music.
> 5. We neared the _____ mountains.
>
> See Lesson 3.3, page 114, and Lesson 12.1, page 424.

3.1 Writing Descriptions **109**

Using the Grammar Link

Grammar Link Answers
Answers will vary. Samples are given.
1. spicy   3. quiet   5. towering
2. talented 4. jazzy

Vivid Adjectives Ask students to list vivid adjectives they might use to describe themselves in a positive light.

About the Art

Artist unknown, Mughal, *Fantastic Birds*, c. 1590
Fantastic Birds was painted during the reign of India's Mughal Emperor Akbar the Great (1556–1605). It is painted with pigments bound by glue or gum, measures 6 5/8 by 5 inches, and is in the Ehrenfeld Collection.

109

Setting the Purpose

Lesson 3.2 teaches students to add sensory details to their writing to bring descriptions to life.

FOCUS

Lesson Overview

Objective: To use sensory details to describe a person, place, or thing
Skills: using sensory details; using observations to write descriptions
Critical Thinking: analyzing; recalling
Speaking and Listening: discussing; describing

Bellringer

When students enter the classroom, have this assignment on the board: *Turn to page 110. Imagine that you've stepped into the painting. Write a description of the scene, using as many sensory words as you can.*

Grammar Link to the Bellringer

Have students underline the possessive nouns in their writing.

Motivating Activity

Ask volunteers to share their descriptions. Which senses did students refer to in their passages? Ask whether, when they consider all five senses, they can add additional details to what they've written.

Descriptive Writing
Collecting Sensory Details

We use our sight, hearing, smell, touch, and taste to experience the world. These sensory details help bring a description to life.

Imagine that you've stepped into the painting below. What do you see, hear, feel, smell, and taste?

Thomas Hart Benton, *Cradling Wheat*, 1938

Use Sensory Detail

Artists use color, shape, and pattern to pull you into a painting. Writers do the same thing with sensory language— language that appeals to the senses. Sensory language

110   *Descriptive Writing: A Closer Look*

About the Art

Thomas Hart Benton, *Cradling Wheat*, 1938
This work, measuring 31 by 38 inches, exemplifies the artist's use of strongly contrasting colors and forms. It is painted in tempera and oil on board and is located at the St. Louis Art Museum.

Teacher's Classroom

The following resources can be used for planning, instruction, practice, reinforcement, assessment, reteaching, enrichment, or evaluation.

Teaching Tools
Lesson Plans

Literature Model

These walks, with the sound of cowbells tinkling in the woods by the river, and bobwhites, like fat little hens, calling their names, filled me with joy as I searched for flowers whose names Mother taught me: shy kitten's ears with grayish white, soft-haired pointed petals which grew flat to the ground and which I stroked, pretending they really were kitten's ears; buttercups and Johnny-jump-ups to be gathered by the handful; stalks of foxgloves with pink bell-shaped flowers which I picked and fitted over my fingers, pretending I was a fox wearing gloves; robin's eggs, speckled and shaped like a broken eggshell, which had such a strong odor Mother tactfully placed my bouquet in a mason jar on the back porch "so they will look pretty when Daddy comes in."

Beverly Cleary, *A Girl from Yamhill*

Prewriting Tip

Before you take notes for a description, close your eyes and concentrate on the senses of taste, touch, hearing, and smell.

What words does Cleary use to appeal to different senses?

describes how something looks, sounds, feels, smells, or tastes. In the passage above, Beverly Cleary takes us with her by engaging our senses.

Cleary, like all good writers, tries to engage her reader's senses when she writes a description. You can hear the tinkling cowbells and see grayish white kitten's ears. You can feel the velvet touch of petals and smell the nasty odor of robin's-eggs flowers. The writer takes you with her by telling exactly what she experienced.

Journal Writing

In your journal, list words and phrases describing a meal you remember: the food you ate and the people you were with. Use words and phrases from all five senses.

TEACH

Guided Practice

L2 Using the Model
Among the senses that Beverly Cleary touches on in this passage is the sense of smell. Mention that some people think smell is the sense most closely linked with our earliest memories. To test this hypothesis, have students close their eyes while you present various olfactory stimuli, such as baby powder, vanilla, lawn clippings, coffee beans, and damp wool. After each presentation, encourage students to freewrite about what the smells made them think of.

L3 Observing a Scene
Let students test their powers of observation by examining a place, such as the corner of the classroom, and listing every detail applying to each of the five senses. Students may use their list to write a short description. Afterward they may compare their descriptions to discern any details they may have overlooked.

Two-Minute Skill Drill

List these words on the board and have students write two sensory details about each.

waterfall   highway   desert

Journal Writing Tip

Observing Have students read their lists of sensory details aloud to see if they create the scene of the meal for the other students. If not, encourage revisions of details.

Resources

Transparencies
Fine Art Transparencies, 11–15
Writing Process Transparencies, 11–13B

Blackline Masters
Thinking and Study Skills,
pp. 3, 9, 12, 22

Writing Across the Curriculum,
   pp. 4–8, 20
Cooperative Learning Activities,
   pp. 13–18
Sentence Combining Practice,
   pp. 28–29
*Speaking and Listening
Activities,* pp. 14–15

Composition Practice, p. 19
Composition Reteaching, p. 19
Composition Enrichment, p. 19

Assessment
*Teacher's Guide to
Writing Assessment*

TEACH

Guided Practice

L2 Writing Poetry

Invite students to apply sensory details to poetry writing. Remind them that poetry is a sensory-rich form of writing often composed of concise, vivid details. Ask students to identify these details and then attempt their own carefully detailed poems. The exercise can help students recognize the importance of description across the spectrum of writing.

L2 Using the Model

The chart on page 112 and the student model show examples of how a student might move from an initial impression to a detailed written description. Encourage reluctant writers by pointing out that the resulting descriptions are only a few sentences long. Point out also that these are descriptions of familiar observations. With student input, make a list of familiar objects and invite students to use sensory details to describe them aloud.

Independent Practice

For further stimuli for descriptive writing, see *Fine Art Transparencies* 11–15.

Writing Process Transparencies, 11–13B

Writing Across the Curriculum, pp. 4–8, 20

Cooperative Learning Activities, pp. 13–18

Skills Practice

Thinking and Study Skills, pp. 3, 9, 12, 22

Sentence Combining Practice, pp. 28–29

Speaking and Listening Activities, pp. 14–15

Composition Practice, p. 19

Use Observations to Write Descriptions

Writing a good description begins with careful observation. This first step may be difficult if you are not used to looking at things closely. The chart shows how you can move from observing details to writing descriptions. In the model Jessica Griffiths uses details she observed to describe a familiar day.

From Observing to Writing	
Impressions	**Description**
New (short) haircut Relaxed smile	Mr. Marshall greets students with a relaxed smile. His thick black hair, which was rather long last year, is clipped neatly above his ears.
Slamming lockers Squeaky new shoes	As the hallways fill with students, locker doors slam with a staccato beat. New shoes squeak as they skid across the freshly polished floor.
Shiny pencil sharpener Smelly pencil shavings	On the first day of school, the shiny pencil sharpener doesn't get a rest. It grinds pencils to a sharp point. The strong smell of shavings fills the air.

Student Model

What sounds of the first day of school does the writer describe?

The writer combines sounds and scents to create this description.

The first day of school is always exciting and a bit scary. Students greet old friends, and teachers chat in the hallways. The squeak of new shoes and the scuffling of sneakers on the linoleum floor mingle with the girls' giggling. Slamming lockers echo in the long corridors. The scent of bubble gum contrasts with the sharp smell of erasers and lead shavings. Pencil sharpeners grinding are a reminder that class has started. Late students hurry to their classrooms. A new school year has begun.

Jessica Griffiths, Springman Junior High School, Glenview, Illinois

112 *Descriptive Writing: A Closer Look*

Enabling Strategies

LEP Simplifying Poetry

Students who are learning English can write poems with just one word per line. They should start by deciding what to write about. Then they can make a list of words that relate to their subject.

For example, if a student chooses the word *ocean*, he or she might think of the sensory details *wet, water, crashing, blue, waves, salty*. Finally, they can arrange their words in an order that appeals to them.

3.2 Writing Activities

Write a Description of a Walk

Think of a walk you take often. It could be down the halls of your school, through the hallway of your home, or on a path through a forest or by a lake. List sensory details from your walk.

Use the details to write a paragraph describing your walk. Have a friend read your description. Ask the person to tell you if your description is vivid and appeals to all the senses. Taking into account your friend's suggestions, revise your writing so it comes to life.

- Use details from your five senses: sight, hearing, taste, touch, and smell.
- Use your details to flesh out your description.

PURPOSE To describe a familiar walk using sensory details
AUDIENCE A friend
LENGTH 1 paragraph

Cooperative Learning

In a group, list names of characters from television or books. Select characters familiar to everyone in the group. List details that describe each character. Then choose a character to describe individually, but don't tell other group members which character you chose. Share your description, and challenge the group to guess the character you described. Discuss additional details that could bring the character into sharper focus, and revise.

Grammar Link

Use apostrophes correctly in possessive nouns.

Use an apostrophe plus *s* to form the possessive of a singular noun and of a plural noun that does not end in *s*. Use an apostrophe alone to form the possessive of a plural noun that ends in *s*.

...shy **kitten's** ears....

...the **mice's** squeaks.

...the **girls'** giggling.

Write each sentence, using apostrophes where necessary.

1. The childrens tears were salty on their tongues.
2. The suns rays warmed my skin.
3. When Al opened the carton, both boys noses wrinkled in disgust.
4. Loud, angry voices from the teachers room echoed in the hall.
5. Not a ripple disturbed the lakes placid surface.

See Lesson 20.7, page 578.

3.2 Collecting Sensory Details **113**

Using the Grammar Link

LESSON
3.3

Descriptive Writing
Using Precise Language

Setting the Purpose

Lesson 3.3 teaches students that taking time to choose precise words can make their descriptions more vivid.

FOCUS

Lesson Overview

Objective: To choose precise and lively nouns, adjectives, verbs, and adverbs for a vivid description
Skills: distinguishing between precise and general wording
Critical Thinking: analyzing; synthesizing; contrasting; evaluating; comparing; decision-making; identifying
Speaking and Listening: discussing

Bellringer

When students enter the classroom, have this assignment on the board: *What words would you use to describe your pet or a pet you know?*

Grammar Link to the Bellringer
Ask how many students used nouns and adjectives to describe pets. How many used verbs or adverbs? Challenge students to turn their lists into sentences, using verbs and adverbs that describe their pets well.

Motivating Activity

Ask students which of the posters on page 114 would be more helpful for identifying Harry. Why? You might have students discuss specific instances in which they had to create their own descriptions, such as when inquiring whether a shopkeeper carried a particular item. Under what circumstances is it sometimes difficult to think of precise descriptions?

LOST
During Storm

Small dog, smooth coat.
Some black marks.
Funny-looking tail.
Please call 555-3454
if you see our dog.

Harry the beagle is
LOST

Mixed brown, black,
and white coat.
Pink nose
with small black marks.
All-black ears.
Tail bent slightly.
Please call 555-3454.

Precise language is exact language; it says what the writer means and creates an image in the reader's mind. On a poster for a lost dog, precise language gets results.

Choose Precise Nouns and Adjectives

A good description includes specific nouns and exact adjectives. A precise noun, *beagle* or *Harry*, is more informative than a general noun, *dog*. The adjectives *brown, black*, and *white* describe the dog's coat more precisely than the vague adjective *smooth*. The difference between a general and a precise description is like the difference between the dogs in the pictures on the next page. Notice the precise words that Sarah Burch used in the next model.

114 *Descriptive Writing: A Closer Look*

Teacher's Classroom Resources

The following resources can be used for planning, instruction, practice, reinforcement, assessment, reteaching, enrichment, or evaluation.

Teaching Tools
Lesson Plans, p. 25

Transparencies
Fine Art Transparencies, 11–15
Writing Process Transparencies, 11–13B

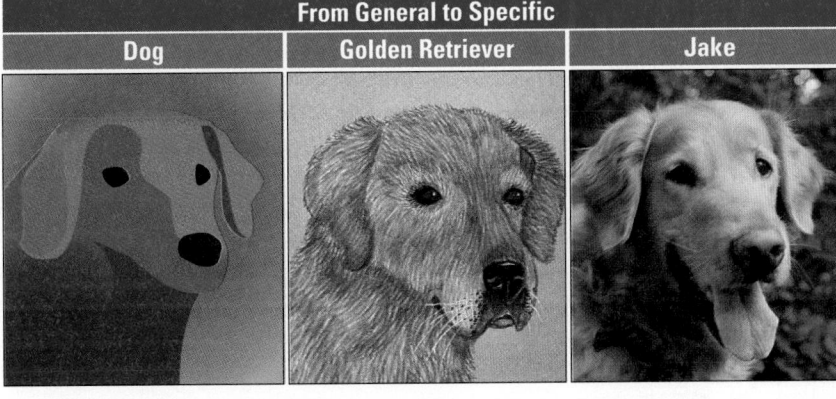

From General to Specific		
Dog	Golden Retriever	Jake

Student Model

As the sound of thunder rumbles through the foggy November rain, you sit next to the roaring fire in your cozy living room. Waiting patiently for the wicked storm to pass, you notice clouds of varying shapes and textures highlighted by zig-zags of lightning. Branches plunge to the ground as winds gust violently. Rain forms muddy puddles along the rutty driveway. The crackling birch in the fireplace and the constant glow of the embers comfort you throughout the ferocious storm.

Sarah Burch, Springman Junior High School,
Glenview, Illinois

What adjectives does the writer use to contrast the scenes inside and outside the house?

Journal Writing

Imagine that you have lost an object that is important to you. Make a list of precise words that describe the lost object. Then use the words to write a notice asking for help in locating the object.

3.3 Using Precise Language **115**

TEACH

Guided Practice

L2 Using the Model
Ask students to point out words the writer uses, such as *roaring, cozy, crackling,* and *constant,* to describe the inside scene. How do these descriptive words make the outside scene seem even more harsh than it otherwise might be?

L3 Tracking Increasing Specificity
Challenge students to research the scientific classifications of an organism, starting with the kingdom and ending with the species. Ask them to describe, in writing, the defining characteristics of the organism at each stage of classification. In this way they should be able to take an organism, such as a baboon, and describe first the characteristics shared by all animals (the power of locomotion, nonphotosynthetic metabolism) and last the characteristics specific to the species (large head; long, sharp teeth; grayish-brown hair).

Two-Minute Skill Drill

Write the following nouns on the board and have students write two progressively precise nouns or adjective-noun combinations for each. Refer to the dog illustrations as an example.

bird	clothes	tape
plant	covering	ball

Journal Writing Tip

Relevant Details Encourage students to think about details that will differentiate their object from others like it.

📁 **Blackline Masters**
Thinking and Study Skills,
  pp. 3, 6, 9, 12, 25–29
Writing Across the Curriculum,
  pp. 15, 20, 23
Cooperative Learning Activities,
  pp. 13–18

Sentence Combining Practice,
  pp. 28–29
Speaking and Listening
  Activities, pp. 14–15
Composition Practice, p. 20
Composition Reteaching, p. 20
Composition Enrichment, p. 20

Assessment
📁 *Teacher's Guide to Writing Assessment*

TEACH

Guided Practice

L2 Using the Model
In the story about Attila, lead students to see that *mercilessly, impatiently, fiercely,* and *restlessly* are examples of precise adverbs. Ask volunteers to explain why *whirls* is a more precise word than *circles.* (It conveys speed in addition to circular motion.)

L1 Demonstrating Differences
Ask small groups of students to actively demonstrate synonyms for a common verb such as *walk.* The differences among words such as *march, pace, hike,* and *stroll* should be easy to see. More subtle words such as *ramble, promenade,* and *saunter* may require discussion. Finally, ask each student to compose a short sentence for the verb he or she enacted.

Independent Practice

For further stimuli for descriptive writing, see *Fine Art Transparencies* 11–15.

Writing Process Transparencies, 11–13B

Writing Across the Curriculum, pp. 15, 20, 23

Cooperative Learning Activities, pp. 13–18

Skills Practice
Thinking and Study Skills, pp. 3, 6, 9, 12, 25–29

Sentence Combining Practice, pp. 28–29

Speaking and Listening Activities, pp. 14–15

Composition Practice, p. 20

116

Presenting Tip

Before reading your finished writing aloud, use a dictionary to check the pronunciation of any words you are not sure how to pronounce.

Choose Precise Verbs and Adverbs

Just as precise nouns and adjectives help create a vivid description, precise verbs and adverbs energize descriptive writing. Your choice of words will depend on the impression you want to make. For example, you might decide on the verb *devour* or *gobble,* rather than *eat,* to describe the action of eating hungrily.

Notice how the writer concentrated on finding more precise verbs and more vivid adverbs as she revised her description of her guinea pig.

Find examples of precise, well-chosen adverbs.

Why does "whirls" create a clearer picture of Attila than "circles"?

"Stalks" is more exact than "walks."

> Attila is a guinea pig with an attitude. From his tiny white ears to his short black legs, Attila wages war mercilessly. Mealtime is his battlefield. At dinnertime he fixes his beady eyes on me as he ~~eats~~ *devours* his well-prepared guinea pig salad. Then his plump, black-and-white body tenses. He waits impatiently for the main course. Attila ~~scratches angrily~~ *claws fiercely* at the cage. He ~~circles~~ *whirls* around the cage. All night long Attila ~~walks~~ *stalks* restlessly near his plate. The next morning the battle begins again.

116 *Descriptive Writing: A Closer Look*

Enabling Strategies

LEP Developing Choices
Encourage students to list words for which they would like to develop a personal vocabulary of synonyms. For example, a student might know there are synonyms for the word *cold,* but may not know many in English. Have groups work together, using dictionaries and thesauruses, to develop each other's lists. A proficient English speaker should be a part of (or accessible to) each group.

3.3 Writing Activities

Write a Description from an Animal's Point of View

Using precise words, write a description of an object from an animal's point of view. Choose your own topic or one of these:

- a canoe as it might seem to a whale
- a pizza slice as it appears to an ant
- a ball of yarn from the point of view of a cat playing with it

As you write, pay attention to the words you use.

- Use specific nouns and adjectives.
- Check for precise verbs and adverbs.

PURPOSE To use precise words to create vivid and energetic descriptions
AUDIENCE Your classmates
LENGTH 1–2 paragraphs

Cooperative Learning

A small group can revise the piece of writing found at the top of the next column. One person in the group should list more precise nouns. The second should list more vivid adjectives. The third should list stronger verbs. The fourth should list more intense adverbs. The group should then decide which suggestions to use in the revision. Finally, one member of the group can make a copy that includes all the changes.

The football players ran quickly onto the wet field for their first game of the season. Their uniforms were bright yellow. Every player's jaw tensed with determination. Each pair of eyes looked eager to begin the game. At kickoff the team yelled loudly and started to play.

Grammar Link

Use vivid adverbs to describe verbs, adjectives, and other adverbs.

*Attila wages war **mercilessly**.*

*Attila claws **fiercely** at the cage.*

For each sentence below, list three different adverbs that could be used to complete it.

1. The horse trotted _____ around the paddock.
2. Jamila approached the foul line _____ tentatively.
3. Quentin searched _____ for his lost notebook.
4. The _____ graceful dancers moved to the beat of the music.
5. The car traveled _____ down the street.

See Lesson 3.3, page 116, and 12.5, page 432.

3.3 Using Precise Language **117**

ASSESS

Writing Activities Evaluation Guidelines

Write a Description from an Animal's Point of View
Use these criteria when evaluating your students' writing.
- Is it clear what animal's perspective is being described?
- Did the student select details appropriate to the animal's size? (An ant and an elephant would likely notice different details.)

See also the *Teacher's Guide to Writing Assessment*.

Cooperative Learning
Assess the paragraph based on
- the value of specific improvements made to the text
- the inclusion of revisions for each part of speech indicated in the instructions

Grammar Link
(See Using the Grammar Link below.)

Reteaching
Composition Reteaching, p. 20

Enrichment
Composition Enrichment, p. 20

CLOSE

Play a game—either as a class or in small groups—in which students are given a general word for which they must find a more precise replacement. For example, *color* could be replaced by *red*. Extra points might be given to students who, in turn, find an even more precise word.

Using the Grammar Link

Grammar Link Answers
Answers will vary, but some suggestions are given below.
1. nervously, gracefully, quickly
2. very, a bit, quite
3. frantically, lazily, randomly
4. extremely, highly, very
5. wildly, crazily, slowly

Modifying Adjectives and Adverbs Challenge groups of students to write a paragraph using sentences with adverbs that modify adjectives or other adverbs. Remind them of adverbs that do not end in -*ly*, such as *sometimes*, *soon*, *there*, *everywhere*, and *straight*.

117

LESSON
3.4

Descriptive Writing
Using Spatial Order

A painter arranges details so that the viewer sees an ordered picture. A writer describes details so that the reader imagines a scene clearly.

Jan Vermeer, *Allegory of the Art of Painting*, c. 1665–1670

The Flemish painter Jan Vermeer arranged the details in this image so that the viewer's eye moves from behind the artist to the scene he is painting. Writers, like painters, arrange the details of a scene in a certain order and for a particular reason.

Order Details Logically

Writers can order details in several ways, depending on the point in space that seems a logical starting place. Details can be ordered from top to bottom, from near to far, or from left to right. When looking at a building, for example, you might first see a nearby detail such as a decorative door frame. Then, farther up the front of the building, you notice decorative stone faces above the windows. To describe this building, you could order these details from near to far.

118 *Descriptive Writing: A Closer Look*

FOCUS

Lesson Overview
Objective: To identify words and phrases that orient a reader in a particular scene
Skills: ordering details logically; linking details
Critical Thinking: recalling; identifying; organizing; drawing conclusions
Speaking and Listening: interpreting; questioning

Bellringer
When students enter the classroom, have this assignment on the board: *Imagine you're rafting in the middle of a wide river. Jot down details describing what you see, hear, and feel.*

Grammar Link to the Bellringer
As students discuss their answers to the Bellringer, write some of their descriptive details on the board. Have students indicate the ones with prepositional phrases.

Motivating Activity
Mark the details from the Bellringer activity, describing things that are near with an *A* and things that are far with a *B.* Ask students to draw conclusions about how you divided the details into groups. Mention that many writers arrange details from near to far or from far to near.

About the Art

Jan Vermeer, *Allegory of the Art of Painting,* **c. 1665–1670**
Vermeer specialized in interior scenes, arranging the elements to achieve a balanced composition. This painting hangs in a museum in Vienna, Austria.

Teacher's Classroom

The following resources can be used for planning, instruction, practice, reinforcement, assessment, reteaching, enrichment, or evaluation.

Teaching Tools
Lesson Plans, p. 26

Three Kinds of Spatial Order		
Top to Bottom	Near to Far	Left to Right

Sometimes a scene lends itself to a particular kind of spatial order. Notice how Laurence Yep uses top-to-bottom spatial order to describe a Chinese playground.

Literature Model

*I*n those days, it consisted of levels. The first level near the alley that became known as Hang Ah Alley was a volleyball and a tennis court. Down the steps was the next level with a sandbox (which was usually full of fleas), a small director's building, a Ping-Pong table, an area covered by tan bark that housed a slide, a set of bars, and a set of swings and other simple equipment.

Laurence Yep, *The Lost Garden*

Which words in the description identify the spatial order as top to bottom?

Journal Writing

Imagine that you are at a place you remember well. Choose one type of spatial order to describe the details of the place. In your journal write your description in that order.

3.4 Using Spatial Order **119**

TEACH

Guided Practice

L2 Using the Model
Help students recognize that the following words indicate top-to-bottom spatial order: "The first level" and "Down the steps."

L2 Prewriting Activity
Provide students with a simple map of the classroom that shows the location of the major objects (desks, chalkboard, bookcase, clock, and so on) inside it. Next, encourage students to go to a spot in the room and attempt to mark that location on their maps. Finally, encourage students to list the room's details from near to far, using the map and their powers of observation to guide them.

Two-Minute Skill Drill

Have students write a list of prepositions that would be appropriate to use in spatial descriptions. Sample answers:

next to	in front of
behind	under
underneath	above
through	between

Journal Writing Tip

Identifying Spatial Relationships Some students may wish to sketch the place they remember and then add labels to the sketch to describe significant details. They can then use the labeled sketch as a reference in developing a list of details in spatial order.

Resources

Transparencies
Fine Art Transparencies, 11–15
Writing Process Transparencies, 11–13B

Blackline Masters
Thinking and Study Skills, pp. 3, 9, 11, 14, 28–29

Writing Across the Curriculum, pp. 4–8
Cooperative Learning Activities, pp. 13–18
Sentence Combining Practice, pp. 28–29
Speaking and Listening Activities, pp. 14–15

Composition Practice, p. 21
Composition Reteaching, p. 21
Composition Enrichment, p. 21

Assessment
Teacher's Guide to Writing Assessment

TEACH

Guided Practice

L2 Using the Model

Point out that the graphic uses directional terms ("north," "east") and words showing proximity ("on top," "about") to orient readers rather than words that show distance. Other phrases that orient the reader are "along the east wall," "past the window," and "to the right/left." Students, too, can sketch scenes and label objects to help in ordering details.

L3 Oral Reporting

Invite students to describe one of the following for a mock radio report: touring a giant cave; watching a parade; sitting in the highest seats at a game. Suggest that students freewrite for details and then use spatial order to organize the details into a script. Encourage students to tape-record their scripts for a "broadcast" to the class. Then have the class comment on whether they could clearly imagine what was being described.

Independent Practice

For further stimuli for descriptive writing, see *Fine Art Transparencies* 11–15.

Writing Process Transparencies, 11–13B

Writing Across the Curriculum, pp. 4–8

Cooperative Learning Activities, pp. 13–18

Skills Practice

Thinking and Study Skills, pp. 3, 9, 11, 14, 28–29

Sentence Combining Practice, pp. 28–29

Speaking and Listening Activities, pp. 14–15

Composition Practice, p. 21

Grammar
Editing Tip

As you edit, punctuate prepositional phrases correctly. For more information see Lesson 20.2, page 568.

Link the Details

When you use spatial order, you must give your audience a way to picture the scene as you move from one detail to the next. Transition words, such as *under, to the right,* and *behind,* help to link details so that readers can follow the path you've created. Notice how transition words act as directional signposts in Sarah Fisher's description of a room and in the diagram based on her description.

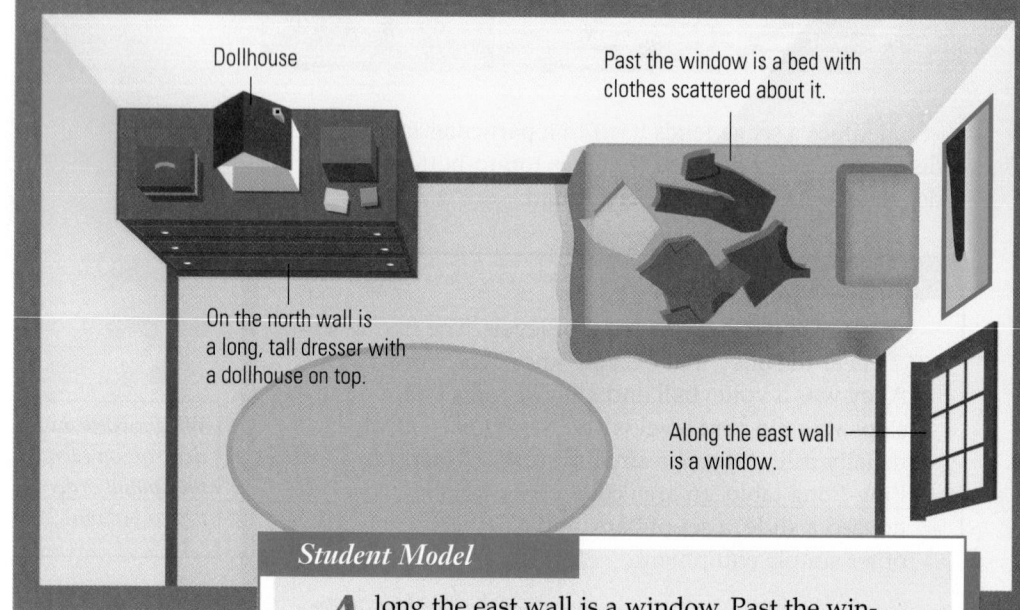

Dollhouse

Past the window is a bed with clothes scattered about it.

On the north wall is a long, tall dresser with a dollhouse on top.

Along the east wall is a window.

Notice how Sarah uses phrases like "on the north wall" to help you find your way around the room.

> *Student Model*
>
> **A**long the east wall is a window. Past the window is a bed with clothes scattered about it. On the north wall is a long, tall dresser with a dollhouse on top. To the right of the dollhouse are three jewelry boxes, one big and two small. To the left of the dollhouse is a purple box with a pink handle. This box holds my hair accessories and small gift boxes.
>
> Sarah Fisher, Solomon Schechter Day School,
> Skokie, Illinois

120   *Descriptive Writing: A Closer Look*

Enabling Strategies

LEP Giving Directions

Students who are new to English may benefit from additional practice using directional and spatial order words and phrases. Have these students work in pairs with English-proficient students to role-play asking and giving directions to some well-known location near where they live.

3.4 Writing Activities

Describe Using Spatial Order

Use an unusual spatial order to write a one-paragraph description. Describe a park from top to bottom, a person's head from back to front, a ballpark from home plate outward, or use an idea of your own.

- Stay with the order you have chosen; be consistent.
- Check for transition words to show spatial relationships.

PURPOSE To describe, using spatial order
AUDIENCE Your teacher
LENGTH 1 paragraph

Carolyn Brady, *Sky Blue and Peach*, 1989

Cross-Curricular: Art

Write a one-paragraph description of Carolyn Brady's painting, using one kind of spatial order. Show your description to a friend, and ask if he or she can identify the type of spatial order you've used.

Grammar Link

Use prepositional phrases in spatial descriptions.

Prepositional phrases can provide details and transitions to enrich and clarify descriptive writing.

*The first level **near the alley** . . . was a volleyball and tennis court.*

***Down the steps** was the next level. . . .*

Incorporate each prepositional phrase below into a sentence of spatial description.

1. through the swinging doors
2. across the street
3. between the two paintings
4. on top of the crates
5. against the opposite wall

See Lesson 13.1, page 448, and Lesson 21.1, page 596.

3.4 Using Spatial Order **121**

ASSESS

Writing Activities Evaluation Guidelines

Describe Using Spatial Order
Use these criteria when evaluating your students' writing.
- Does the description reflect a particular spatial order?
- Did the student use transition words to orient the reader?

See also the *Teacher's Guide to Writing Assessment.*

Cross-Curricular: Art
The description should
- include details that reflect the location of the viewer
- order the details of the painting accurately

Grammar Link
(See Using the Grammar Link below.)

Reteaching
📂 *Composition Reteaching*, p. 21

Enrichment
📂 *Composition Enrichment*, p. 21

🖐 Use *Fine Art Transparencies* 11–15 for enrichment activities also.

CLOSE

Ask students to review the descriptive words they wrote as part of Lesson 3.1, Lesson 3.2, and journal activities. Direct them to highlight any words they have listed that indicate spatial order. If some students do not find examples of such words, ask others to provide examples for students to include in their journals.

Using the Grammar Link

Grammar Link Answers
(*Answers will vary.*)
Using *Between* and *Among* Remind students that *between* is typically used with two objects (*between* the window and the door), whereas *among* implies more than two objects (*among* the apples in the barrel).

About the Art

Carolyn Brady, *Sky Blue and Peach*, 1989
The title of this painting refers not only to the sky and peaches that are its subject, but to the blues and oranges that energize it. This watercolor measures 51 1/2 by 43 1/2 inches and is in a private collection.

LESSON

3.5

Descriptive Writing
Describing a Thing

Lesson 3.5 teaches students to group details in a logical order to describe a particular thing.

FOCUS

Lesson Overview

Objective: To identify significant attributes of an object for a vivid description

Skills: choosing and organizing details; using sensory language; drafting; revising

Critical Thinking: asking questions, recalling; visualizing; categorizing; classifying

Speaking and Listening: taking notes; listening in class; discussing informally

Bellringer

When students enter the classroom, have this assignment on the board: *In a paragraph or two, describe your favorite childhood toy.*

Grammar Link to the Bellringer

Ask students to scan their responses to the Bellringer and underline all the pronouns they used to refer to the toy. You might ask questions such as these: Did you refer to the toy as both *it* and *they*? Or, did you sometimes refer to the toy as *it* and sometimes as *he* or *she*? Use their responses to lead a discussion about clear pronoun references.

Motivating Activity

To focus students' attention on the significant objects in their lives, present them with this scenario: Suppose there is a fire in your home. What single object would you attempt to rescue? Why is the object important?

Describing a thing involves creating a clear image of that particular thing in the reader's mind. The reader can picture the object's size and shape; more important, the reader knows what makes it special.

A packed suitcase bulges before you. You're in a new place, about to unpack and start a new life. Your thoughts turn to the things you couldn't bring with you. You picture some of the treasures you left behind. How can you describe something that is important to you? In the student model below, notice how Amanda Morgan describes a well-loved bear.

Student Model

*T*eddy is no placid-looking bear. He is stubborn looking. He is very well loved (as bears often get), and he is beginning to come apart at the seams. Mom tried to fix this tragic problem by sewing him up with bright red-and-blue yarn. The yarn is faded and looking a bit tattered itself, for the surgery was done about nine years ago.

Amanda Morgan, Neskowin, Oregon
First appeared in *Treasures: Stories and Art by Students in Oregon*

Teacher's Classroom Resources

The following resources can be used for planning, instruction, practice, reinforcement, reteaching, enrichment, or evaluation.

Teaching Tools
Lesson Plans, p. 27

Transparencies
Fine Art Transparencies, 11–15
Writing Process Transparencies, 11–13B

Choose the Details

The process of writing a good description begins with choosing an object that has meaning for you. It may be right in front of your eyes, or it may be stored in your memory. Once you decide on your subject, note details that will help you describe it. If you're looking at the object, jot down the details you observe. If you're remembering something, list details that make it memorable for you.

Asking yourself questions can help you choose details. For example, you might ask how something appears at different times of the day, what senses you use to observe it, or to what you might compare it. The questions below, although linked to a specific object, may help you think of other questions you can ask yourself to remember descriptive details.

> 1. How old is my bike?
>   My brother bought it new three years ago.
> 2. What condition is it in?
>   worn but well cared for; cracked seat
> 3. What color is my bike?
>   mostly metallic blue with gray tires
> 4. What memories about my bike come to mind?
>   the first time I rode it down our street after moving here; riding in the rain with Chris

Journal Writing

Write three or four questions about the appearance of something that is important to you. Answer your questions in your journal, making sure to record specific details.

3.5 Describing a Thing **123**

TEACH

Guided Practice

L2 Using the Model
Have students review the model on page 122. Ask them why the well-worn teddy bear is special to Amanda Morgan. (She loved the bear as a little girl and likes its stubborn look.)

L2 Using the Model
Draw students' attention to the questions and answers on this page. Point out that one reason the bike is important is that the writer links it to enjoyable experiences. In this case, the writer associates the bike with exploring his new neighborhood and having a good time with a friend.

L1 Choosing an Object
If students have trouble thinking of an object with personal significance, point out that it might simply be something beautiful or unusual, such as a rock they found and kept because it has a striking color or shape. Ask students to think of a little treasure they may have found and kept and then to jot down words and phrases that describe it. Remind them to use all five senses in their description. Then have students circle the details they think best describe the object.

Journal Writing Tip

Formulating Questions Ask students to include at least one question about memories or experiences. Remind them to write questions that call for more than just a yes or no answer.

Blackline Masters
Thinking and Study Skills, pp. 3, 7, 9, 11, 14, 20
Writing Across the Curriculum, pp. 4–8
Cooperative Learning Activities, pp. 13–18

Sentence Combining Practice, pp. 28–29
Speaking and Listening Activities, pp. 14–15
Composition Practice, p. 22
Composition Reteaching, p. 22
Composition Enrichment, p. 22

Assessment
Teacher's Guide to Writing Assessment

TEACH

Guided Practice

L2 Using the Model
Ask students why Silko might compare the colors of the rock to those in a sunset. (The comparison helps readers imagine the intense hues.)

L3 Cooperative Learning
Have pairs of students scan the literature models in their books to find one example of each of the three principles listed on this page. For selected examples, lead students in a discussion of why other approaches would or would not work as well.

Two-Minute Skill Drill

Tell students to imagine going for a walk on a winter evening. Have them describe the walk, listing details that appeal to each sense.

Independent Practice

For further stimuli for descriptive writing, see *Fine Art Transparencies* 11–15.

Writing Process Transparencies, 11–13B

Writing Across the Curriculum, pp. 4–8

Cooperative Learning Activities, pp. 13–18

Skills Practice

Thinking and Study Skills, pp. 3, 7, 9, 11, 14, 20

Sentence Combining Practice, pp. 28–29

Speaking and Listening Activities, pp. 14–15

Composition Practice, p. 22

124

Organize the Details

As you list the important details that describe a thing, consider ways to group these details. The thing itself may suggest a certain kind of grouping. The chart below shows three principles you can use to group details.

Grouping Details by Different Principles	
Principle	**Examples**
Shape/Color	Baggy blue-gray sweater, ankle-length denim skirt
Appearance/Function	Porch chair, rusted and bent, but still comfortable
Whole/Parts	Broken checkerboard, a bag of dominoes

Revising Tip

As you revise a description, be sure that the details you have included help the reader follow the spatial order you are using.

As you draft your description, use sensory details to bring your subject to life. Remember to use precise language, follow spatial order, and include transitions. Notice how Leslie Marmon Silko describes sandstone. She uses a *simile*—a comparison between two dissimilar things linked by the word *like* or *as*—while grouping her details around the color of sandstone.

What precise adjectives does the writer use?

Literature Model

*B*ut this time there was something about the colors of the sandstone. The reddish pink and orange yellow looked as if they had been taken from the center of the sky as the sun went down. She had never seen such intense color in sandstone. She had always remembered it being shades of pale yellow or peppered white—colors for walls and fences. But these rocks looked as if rain had just fallen on them.

Leslie Marmon Silko, "Private Property"

124 *Descriptive Writing: A Closer Look*

Enabling Strategies

LEP Visualizing an Object
Students new to English may be intimidated when they try to craft vivid, organized descriptions. Have them begin by drawing or photographing the object that they choose to describe. Next, ask them to write short, vivid, descriptive labels in their first language. Help them organize their labels by some logical grouping. Finally, have them work with a native speaker of English to translate their labels and select adjectives and similes that make sense.

3.5 Writing Activities

Write a Description of a Childhood Treasure

Think of something that was important to you in your childhood, such as a book or a stuffed animal. Write a description of it to share with a friend. Before you revise the rough draft of your description, ask your friend to read and comment on the draft.

- List details that make the object memorable.
- Group the details by shape/color, appearance/function, or whole/parts.

PURPOSE To write an effective description of an object

AUDIENCE A friend

LENGTH 1–2 paragraphs

▨▨ COMPUTER OPTION ▨▨

Create two computer vocabulary files, one listing words that describe or name sensory details, the other listing transition words. In your file of sensory details, you might list adjectives that describe colors, shapes, textures, smells, and sizes. Refer to the lists as you draft a description.

Grammar Link

Be sure that each pronoun clearly refers to its antecedent.

The antecedent is the word or group of words to which a pronoun refers. A pronoun must agree with its antecedent in number and gender.

*But these **rocks** looked as if rain had just fallen on **them.***

Complete the sentences below with appropriate pronouns.

1. When Sam's mother asked to see his report, ____ showed ____ to ____.
2. The principal posted the announcements so that we could read ____.
3. The students weren't expecting the fire drill buzzer, so ____ were startled when ____ heard ____.
4. Since my younger sister knows I'm good in math, ____ asked ____ to help ____ with the word problems.
5. Sarah said that ____ does not know who will be at the party.

See Lesson 11.1, page 402, and Lesson 11.2, page 404.

3.5 Describing a Thing **125**

Using the Grammar Link

FOCUS

Lesson Overview

Objective: To respond to a biography by making connections between the subject's life and one's own life

Skills: forming impressions about a personal account; using details in responding to a biography

Critical Thinking: synthesizing; categorizing; recalling; identifying main idea; summarizing; building background

Speaking and Listening: discussing

Bellringer

When students enter the classroom, have this assignment on the board: *If you were paid a million dollars to write a biography about anyone, who would be your subject? Why?*

Grammar Link to the Bellringer

Have students pretend that they are beginning their biographies. Suggest that they open with a quotation that captures the essence of their subject. After students write their imaginary quotations, discuss how they punctuated them.

Motivating Activity

Invite students to name people they have enjoyed reading about in biographies. Ask what they learned about the subject's personality or achievements. Discuss why people enjoy stories about real people. Do they find inspiration in stories of goals accomplished or difficulties overcome?

LESSON

3.6

Writing About Literature
Describing the Subject of a Biography

In a biography a writer, or biographer, tells the true story of a person's life. In the following passage, Lisa Aldred creates a verbal snapshot of the young boy who would later become Supreme Court Justice Thurgood Marshall.

Literature Model

He "was a jolly boy who always had something to say." But, she added, Thurgood showed a serious side as well. "I can still see him coming down Division Street every Sunday afternoon about one o'clock," she said. "He'd be wearing knee pants with both hands dug way into his pockets and be kicking a stone in front of him as he crossed over to Dolphin Street to visit his grandparents at their big grocery store on the corner. He was in a deep study, that boy, and it was plain something was going on inside him."

Lisa Aldred, *Thurgood Marshall*

A biographer's purpose is to make the subject of the biography come to life on the page. In this model biographer Lisa Aldred uses the words of a family friend, Odell Payne, to give us a vivid glimpse of the serious side of young Thurgood Marshall—future Supreme Court Justice.

126 *Descriptive Writing: A Closer Look*

Teacher's Classroom Resources

The following resources can be used for planning, instruction, practice, reinforcement, assessment, reteaching, enrichment, or evaluation.

Teaching Tools
Lesson Plans

Transparencies
Fine Art Transparencies, 11–15
Writing Process Transparencies, 11–13B

Form Strong Impressions

By telling what a person did and said, a biographer can bring the person to life on the pages. Descriptions of the subject's physical appearance and personality help the reader form impressions of the person. Here are some students' reactions to young Thurgood Marshall.

> *The description of the boy reminds me of my cousin Wilma. She used to spend hours skipping stones at the pond. I once crept up behind her. She didn't even notice me. Like Thurgood, Wilma was always "in a deep study." Sometimes that annoyed me, though!*

How is Thurgood like this student's cousin Wilma?

> *I just read a book my grandfather should read. It tells about the early life of Thurgood Marshall, who was a Supreme Court justice. Grandfather's always telling me to pay attention. If he reads the book, he'll know I'm just "in a deep study."*

This student has a good impression of Thurgood because he sees some of his own traits in the famous man.

Journal Writing

Describe someone you know well doing something he or she does often. Concentrate on using this action to illustrate your subject's personality.

3.6 Describing the Subject of a Biography **127**

TEACH

Guided Practice

L2 Using the Model
Explain that Thurgood Marshall was a justice of the Supreme Court, appointed in 1967. Earlier, as attorney for the NAACP, Marshall argued numerous civil rights cases before the Supreme Court. In 1954, in the case of *Brown v. Board of Education of Topeka, Kansas,* he persuaded the justices that segregation in public schools was unconstitutional. Marshall died in 1993.

Ask students to think of a time when someone might have described them as being "in a deep study." What were they thinking about at the time? (Responses might include pondering a personal problem, daydreaming about the future, reflecting on a memory, or analyzing a school assignment.)

L3 Cooperative Learning
Ask students to locate a biography of someone who interests them and read about the person's early life. Then assemble students in groups of three. Ask each student to share a passage that gives a verbal snapshot of the biography subject. The passage should describe something the person did or said that reveals a side of his or her personality. After each reading, listeners can offer their impressions of the person.

Journal Writing Tip

Inferring You may wish to offer the following examples of how actions can reflect someone's personality. A student who plays chess every day at lunch probably has an analytical mind. A person who volunteers to read to children at a daycare center is probably a caring, patient person who likes children.

TEACH

Guided Practice

L2 Using the Model

Point out that Andrea Gaines chose to write about Madison by imagining herself to be one of his college classmates. If students are asked to write a profile of a biography subject, suggest that they try a similar approach, putting themselves in the time period in which the person lived and taking the role of a friend.

Two-Minute Skill Drill

If students were to profile a biography subject by taking the role of someone nearby, how might their perspective change in each of the following roles?

parent	spouse
son	daughter
neighbor	co-worker

Independent Practice

For further stimuli for descriptive writing, see *Fine Art Transparencies* 11–15.

Writing Process Transparencies, 11–13B

Writing Across the Curriculum, p. 15

Cooperative Learning Activities, pp. 13–18

Skills Practice

Thinking and Study Skills, pp. 5, 6, 9, 19, 35, 37

Sentence Combining Practice, pp. 28–29

Speaking and Listening Activities, pp. 14–15

Composition Practice, p. 23

Grammar
Editing Tip

As you edit, be sure that you have correct subject-verb agreement in your sentences. For more information see Lessons 16.1–16.5, pages 508–517.

Focus on the Subject

A good biography paints a portrait of the subject, including his or her appearance, personality, and attitudes. With precise language, sensory details, clear organization, and strong transitions, the subject of a biography comes into sharp focus. After reading Jean Fritz's *The Great Little Madison*, Andrea Gaines wrote the imaginary letter below. Notice how she uses details that paint a portrait of the young Madison.

Student Model

October 16, 1769

Dear Aunt Winnefred,

How are you?

What details of Madison's appearance does Andrea provide?

Sorry I haven't written you lately, but I've been busy here at Princeton. This is only my first year here, but I feel as though I have a number of friends already. One of them is a quiet sophomore, James Madison. He's kind of short and thin, and has a very low voice. His handsome face glows with energy.

What details of Madison's personality does Andrea point out?

He throws himself into everything he does, whether it's reading books, protesting British taxes, or joining student fun.

I must run to class. I'll write to you later about my other friends.

Your loving niece,
Susan

Andrea Gaines,
Martha M. Ruggles
Elementary School,
Chicago, Illinois

Eighteenth-century Princeton University

128 *Descriptive Writing: A Closer Look*

Enabling Strategies

LEP Building Descriptive Vocabulary

To help students build their vocabulary of words that describe inner traits and outer appearance, ask the class to brainstorm two lists under the headings *Inside* and *Outside*. Ask for an explanation of each word suggested. Discuss how much of a contrast there can be between what is going on inside of a person and how he or she appears on the outside.

3.6 Writing Activities

Joan Brown, *The Night Before the Alcatraz Swim*, 1975

Write a Descriptive Response

Respond to a biography about a political figure. You may use the excerpt from *Thurgood Marshall*, or choose another biography that interests you. Think of creative ways to respond, as Andrea Gaines does on the previous page. Include your own description of the subject, as you see him or her.

- Use vivid details and precise language to describe your impression of the subject.
- Make sure your description brings the subject to life.

PURPOSE To write a descriptive response
AUDIENCE Your teacher and classmates
LENGTH 2 paragraphs

Grammar Link

Use quotation marks and other punctuation correctly in direct quotations.

"A painting, as well as a book, can be a biography," said the art teacher.

Write each sentence, adding quotation marks and other punctuation where necessary.

1. The student asked Did Joan Brown really swim to Alcatraz?
2. She tried said the teacher but she did not make it to the island.
3. The ship in the painting passed by her and the wake nearly caused her to drown explained the teacher.
4. How did she know to put the ship there if this was painted the night before the swim asked the student.
5. The teacher answered She painted this after she attempted to swim to the island.

See Lesson 20.6, page 576.

3.6 Describing the Subject of a Biography **129**

129

UNIT 3
WRITING PROCESS IN ACTION
DESCRIPTIVE WRITING

Setting the Purpose

Students now have the opportunity to apply what they have learned about descriptive writing to an independent writing project. They will use the stages of the writing process to create and present a finished piece.

FOCUS

Lesson Overview

Objective: To describe a favorite activity or hobby

Skills: using the five stages of the writing process: prewriting, drafting, revising, editing, presenting; communicating a special interest; peer reviewing

Critical Thinking: synthesizing; recalling; patterning; summarizing; building background; defining and clarifying; identifying main idea

Speaking and Listening: note taking; informal speaking; reading aloud; discussing; questioning

Bellringer

When students enter the classroom, have this assignment on the board: *Write down a hobby of yours, and give one reason you enjoy it.*

Grammar Link to the Bellringer Have students look over their writing, and make sure any pronouns they used have clear antecedents. For example, if a student wrote, "I like it because..." can the reader identify what *it* is?

Motivating Activity

Remind students that a hobby is any activity they enjoy in their spare time. Lead a discussion about hobbies, recording students' favorites on the board. If a hobby is named more than once, record students' different reasons for liking it. Encourage students to be specific in describing the places, people, and things connected with their hobbies.

In preceding lessons you've learned about using memories and observations in descriptive writing. You've learned about sensory details, about using precise language, and about how to order details. You've written a variety of descriptions. Now, in this lesson, you'll have a chance to describe the people, places, and things that are part of something you enjoy doing.

• Assignment •

Context	You are writing an article for the magazine _Popular Hobbies._ This magazine contains descriptions of the people, places, and things associated with various student hobbies.
Purpose	To describe people, places, and things related to your favorite hobby
Audience	Student readers of _Popular Hobbies_
Length	1 page

The following pages can help you plan and write your descriptions. Read through them, and then refer to them as you need to. But don't be tied down by them. You're in charge of your own writing process.

130   *Descriptive Writing: A Closer Look*

Teacher's Classroom Resources

The following resources can be used for planning, instruction, practice, reinforcement, assessment, reteaching, enrichment, or evaluation.

Teaching Tools
Lesson Plans, p. 30

Transparencies
Writing Process Transparencies, 11–13B

Prewriting

Start by thinking about the people, places, and things that go with your favorite hobby. To explore your answers, you might use one or all the options at the right. Perhaps you'll observe and take notes, use your journal to recall details, or freewrite.

Option A
Observe and take notes on details.

Option B
Review your journal.

Option C
Explore your ideas through freewriting.

I zoom along the smooth path by the park. People picnic, play radios, and eat things like fried chicken. I remember my bike rides by the songs I hear and food that I smell.

Drafting

Look over your prewriting, and think about ways of organizing your material into clear images. You might start with the most important details or with the details closest to you. Just use the order that makes the most sense to you, and let the writing flow. Notice how David Weitzman sets the scene at an old-time harvest.

Literature Model

*I*t was like the Fourth of July. Kids clambered up and slid down the hay stacks, played tag and skip-to-my-lou. Some of the men were pitching horseshoes and you could hear the thump of shoes fallen too short and the solid clank of a ringer. The women looked after all the little kids and put out lunches on big tables—heaps of potato salad, sandwiches, cakes and cookies, and frosty pitchers of iced tea.

David Weitzman, *Thrashin' Time*

Drafting Tip

For more information about using sensory details, see Lessons 3.1 and 2, pages 106–112.

A description rich in detail and sensory language can give your readers a clear picture of the world of your hobby.

Writing Process in Action **131**

TEACH

Prewriting

L2 Developing Ideas for Descriptive Writing
If students decide to make notes of their observations for prewriting, suggest that they try the following procedure to give them a head start on organizing their draft. Divide a blank sheet of paper into three sections. Label the sections *People, Places,* and *Things,* and record notes in the appropriate sections. Some students may wish to organize their notes in other ways (such as by the five senses) and should be encouraged to do so until they find the method that works best for them.

Independent Practice

Skills Practice
Thinking and Study Skills, pp. 5, 11, 17

Drafting

L2 Using Prewriting Notes
If students used the note-taking method described above, they might begin their draft by writing a paragraph for each section of notes.

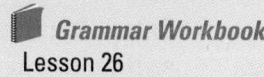 **Blackline Masters**
Thinking and Study Skills, pp. 5, 11, 17
Sentence Combining Practice, pp. 28–29
Composition Practice, p. 24
Composition Reteaching, p. 24
Composition Enrichment, p. 24

Grammar Workbook
Lesson 26

Assessment
Teacher's Guide to Writing Assessment

TEACH

Revising

L2 Peer Editing

Students can work in writing conferences with peer editors before they revise their writing. You may want to duplicate the Peer Response forms in the *Teacher's Guide to Writing Assessment*. Suggest that peer editors respond to the following questions:

- Does the writing include transition words that make it easier to follow?
- How might the order of details be improved?

Editing

L2 Peer Editing

After students have edited their own work, have them edit another student's writing. Remind them to refer to the Editing Checklist on the student page.

Presenting

Before students present their descriptive writing, discuss how to prepare their papers for publication. Emphasize the importance of the final draft and that it must be neatly done.

Independent Practice

📋 *Writing Process Transparencies*, 11–13B

Skills Practice

📁 *Thinking and Study Skills*, pp. 5, 11, 17
📁 *Sentence Combining Practice*, pp. 28–29
📁 *Composition Practice*, p. 24
📖 **Grammar Workbook**, Lesson 26

Journal Writing Tip

Reviewing the Process Suggest that students discuss which prewriting strategies were helpful.

Revising

Begin by rereading the assignment. Have you written what's been asked for? As soon as you're satisfied that you have, you can move on.

Now it's time to look at your draft and make it better. But first put your draft aside for a day, if possible. During this time, you might go back and review pages 68–79.

To begin revising, read over your draft to make sure that what you have written fits your purpose and your audience. Then have a writing conference. Read your draft to a partner or small group. Use your audience's reactions to help you evaluate your work.

Look at the revision below and use questions like the ones shown to guide your own revisions. Remember, revising is where many great writers do their best work, so work with care.

Vocabulary
Revising Tip

Check that your description uses specific nouns and verbs and vivid modifiers. For more information see Lesson 3.3, pages 114–116.

Question A
Have I used all my senses?

Question B
Are my images crisp and clear?

Question C
Are my details specific and linked with transitions?

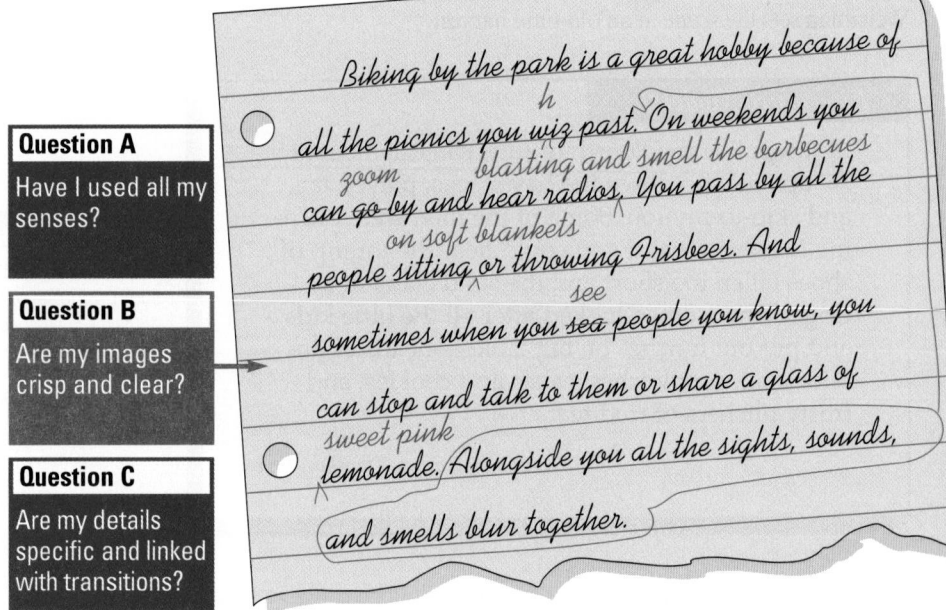

Biking by the park is a great hobby because of all the picnics you wiz past. On weekends you zoom blasting and smell the barbecues can go by and hear radios. You pass by all the on soft blankets people sitting or throwing Frisbees. And see sometimes when you sea people you know, you can stop and talk to them or share a glass of sweet pink lemonade. Alongside you all the sights, sounds, and smells blur together.

132 *Descriptive Writing: A Closer Look*

Enrichment and Extension

Follow-up Ideas

- Students' descriptions of hobbies can be collected, illustrated, bound, and placed in the school library.
- If students send their work out of the classroom for publication or sharing, make sure photocopies are retained.

Extending Description

- Brainstorm with students ways they can use their expertise in descriptive writing in other subject areas, such as describing the hobbies and pastimes of another country or era.

Editing

Edit your description to correct any mistakes. Read it several times, using the questions in this checklist. Ask a different question each time through. For example, you might **proofread** for capitalization and punctuation on your first pass and spelling on your second pass. Afterward, have someone else review your work. Other people can often see your mistakes better than you can.

Editing Checklist

1. *Have I correctly used apostrophes in possessive nouns?*
2. *Do my pronouns have clear antecedents?*
3. *Have I correctly punctuated quotations?*
4. *Have I spelled every word correctly?*

Presenting

Make a clean copy of your description. If possible, use a computer or word processor to give your work a professional look. Now you are ready to send your work to *Popular Hobbies*. You may want to include a drawing or photograph to illustrate your description. Do not feel that you have to include an illustration, though. Even without a picture, your description should be detailed enough so that your readers should be able to imagine the people, places, and things related to the hobby you have chosen.

Proofreading

For proofreading symbols, see page 81.

Journal Writing

Reflect on your writing process experience. Answer these questions in your journal: What did you like best about your description? What was the hardest part of writing it? What did you learn in your writing conference? What new things have you learned as a writer?

ASSESS

Evaluation Guidelines

Use the following criteria to evaluate students' finished writing.

- Does the writing focus on details that describe people, places, and things related to the student's hobby?
- Does the opening make the reader want to know more?
- Does the writing include precise nouns, verbs, adjectives, and adverbs?
- Are sensory details included?
- Are the details organized clearly, using spatial order or another appropriate sequence?
- Are apostrophes used correctly in possessive nouns?
- Is other punctuation used correctly?
- Do pronouns have clear antecedents?
- Does the final version contain proper spelling?

Refer to the *Teacher's Guide to Writing Assessment* for further help with evaluating student writing.

Reteaching
📁 *Composition Reteaching,* p. 24

Enrichment
📁 *Composition Enrichment,* p. 24

CLOSE

After students have presented their work, ask them to think about their descriptions from a reader's point of view. They should ask themselves, "What about this description would someone want to read?" Have them find at least two parts that capture their attention, then summarize in a sentence or two what made them the most powerful passages.

Enabling Strategies

LEP Illustrating a Hobby

Invite students to draw a series of pictures illustrating their hobbies. Students should first decide how to organize their drawings. When the drawings are complete, students can label each picture in their first language, then translate the labels into English.

About the Author

David Weitzman, a native of the Midwest, is also the author of *Windmills, Bridges, & Old Machines; My Backyard History Book;* and *Superpower: The Making of a Steam Locomotive.* He is an illustrator as well as a writer. In *Thrashin' Time* Weitzman's colorful prose is accompanied by large black-and-white line engravings that show the parts of the steam thresher in intricate detail.

FOCUS

Lesson Overview

Objective: To examine how a professional writer uses description to bring to life a memorable experience from the past
Skills: reading comprehension
Critical Thinking: inferring; analyzing
Speaking and Listening: discussing; performing

Bellringer

When students enter the classroom, have this assignment on the board: *Describe a new machine and its impact on your life and the lives of people around you.*

Motivating Activity

Have students share their descriptions. Let them know that in every generation, technology changes people's lives.

UNIT

3

Descriptive Writing
Literature Model

David Weitzman
from

Thrashin' Time

In Thrashin' Time: Harvest Days in the Dakotas *David Weitzman describes farm life in 1912 North Dakota through the eyes of young Peter Anders. As you read the following passage, pay special attention to the way Peter describes an autumn day when the whole neighborhood gathers to see a steam traction engine for the first time. Then try the activities in Linking Writing and Literature on page 139.*

Anna and I began pestering Pa to take us over to see the new engine. But it didn't take much doing. I could tell he wanted to go as much as we did. Pa glanced again at the smoke billowing into the sky. "Ya, sure, we can go. I'll finish up a bit here. Peter, you go hitch the horses up to the wagon. Maggie, if you and Anna put up a picnic, we'll go have us a look at that steam engine."

134 *Descriptive Writing: A Closer Look*

Teacher's Classroom Resources

The following resources can be used for planning, instruction, or practice.

Teaching Tools
Lesson Plans, p. 30

Transparencies
Fine Art Transparencies, 11–15

We got there to find that a lot of folks had come in wagons and buggies to gather 'round and watch the thrashin'.[1] Steam engines were still new in these parts. And there it was, the engine with its dark blue boiler, shiny brass whistle, red wheels all decorated with yellow stripes, gears spinning and rods going back and forth, rocking gently in time to the puffs of smoke from the stack—*tucka-tucka-tucka-tucka-tucka*. The sounds, that's what I liked. *Tucka-tucka-tucka-tucka* and the little steam engine going *ss—ss—ss—ss—ss—ss—ss*. The engine was quieter than I thought it would be. It was almost alive like the horses working everywhere 'round it. And the horses. Why, I'll betcha there were sixty head, big horses—Belgians and Percherons[2]—coming and going that afternoon. Teams pulled bundle wagons heaped tall with sheaves of wheat in from the fields, pulled wagons of yellow grain away from the separator to the silo. Another team hauled the water wagon, and another wagon brought loads of cord wood to keep the engine running sunup to sundown.

David Weitzman, from *Thrashin' Time*, 1991

It was like the Fourth of July. Kids clambered up and slid down the hay stacks, played tag and skip-to-my-lou. Some of the men were pitching horseshoes and you could hear the thump of shoes fallen too short and the solid clank of a ringer. The women looked after all the little kids and put out lunches on big tables—heaps of potato salad, sandwiches, cakes and

1 **thrashin'** (thrash' in) [or threshing (thresh'ing)] separating grain or seeds from a plant
2 **Belgians** (Bel' jənz) **and Percherons** (Pur' chə ronz') large, powerful horses used to drag heavy loads

Literature Model **135**

TEACH

L2 Guided Reading

• Weitzman writes, "*Teams pulled bundle wagons heaped tall with sheaves of wheat in from the fields, pulled wagons of yellow grain away from the separator to the silo.*" Based on this sentence, what can you infer about the task performed by the threshing machine? (It takes in stalks of wheat, separates the grain from the stalk, and collects the grain.)

• What sensory details does the author include about the engine on this page? (He includes the look and sound of the engine.)

Blackline Masters
Speaking and Listening Activities, p. 23
Thinking and Study Skills, pp. 3–6

Assessment
Teacher's Guide to Writing Assessment

TEACH

L2 Guided Reading

- What details does the author use to re-create the festive day? (Lots of people had come, children were playing, men were pitching horseshoes, and women had put out lots of food.)
- Why didn't some of the farmers like the steam thresher? What reasons did they give for preferring to use horses? (Horses are cheaper to own, reproduce themselves, use available fuel from the land, and provide fertilizer. Also, steam threshers can be dangerous and unreliable.)

cookies and frosty pitchers of iced tea. Dogs napped in the dark cool under the wagons, not paying any mind to the puppies tumbling all over them. The older boys stood around together, pretending they were chewing plugs of tobacco, hawking and spitting, like the thrashermen, only theirs wouldn't come brown. The men stood around the engine and the separator, puffing on their pipes, thumbs hooked under their suspenders. They inspected every part of that machine, pointing to this and that, looked up and down the belt stretching between the engine and the separator in a long figure eight. Most of them had never seen a steam traction engine before.

Some of the older folks didn't like the new machine. "The old ways is the best ways," one of them said, tugging on his whiskers. "All this talk about steam engines is just a bunch of gibble-gabble," agreed another, "I'll stick to my oxen and horses." Others told of hearing all about engines exploding, killing and maiming[3] the thrashin' crews, of careless engineers starting fires that burned up the farmer's whole crop and his barn besides. "Horses live off the land," Mr. Bauer said, "and don't need wood or coal. No, nothin' but some hay and oats and we don't have to buy that! What's more they give you foals." He reached over and rubbed his hand down the neck of a stout gray Percheron mare hitched to a grain wagon. "All you get from steam engines is debt." Mr. Bjork agreed, "and what would we do for fertilizer? Steam engines don't make much manure, you know." Everyone laughed. "More trouble than they're worth. Why last year Silas McGregor had to come borrow my oxen to pull his engine out of the mud. Wouldn't have one of those smoke-snortin' strawburners on my place," old Mr. Erstad scoffed, turning and waving away the scene.

But Mr. Torgrimson, now I could tell he was enjoying it. We were looking at the steam engine there up on the boiler, the connecting rod whizzing back and forth and the flywheel spinning so that the spokes were just a red blur. He was smiling and his eyes just twinkled. Then he pointed the stem of his pipe at the engine, squinted in a thoughtful way and rocked

3 **maiming** (mām′ ing) causing an injury so as to cripple or cause the loss of some part of the body

Genre and Style

Reading Descriptive Writing

In *Thrashin' Time* David Weitzman uses descriptive writing to draw the reader into the world of a turn-of-the-century midwestern grain farmer. He describes the physical presence of the steam thresher, using details of sight and sound. He also gives readers a sense of the significance of the machine through the words and thoughts of the different farmers. The details are so plentiful and vivid that readers experience the scene almost as if they were there.

back and forth on his heels. "You know, Peter, that's a wonderful thing, the steam engine. You're witnessin' the beginnin's of real scientific farmin'." He couldn't take his eyes off that engine. "I read about a steam outfit—over Casselton way it was—that thrashed more than six thousand bushels in one day! Imagine that, six thousand bushels in just one day! Why you and your Ma and Pa all workin' together couldn't do more'n twenty or thirty in the same time."

Mr. Torgrimson was the one who told me all about bonanza farming, where a bunch of engines would start out together, side-by-side, before daybreak, each pulling a fourteen-bottom plow almost as wide as our house. "They go all day, Peter, breakin' up thousands of acres of prairie grasslands before they rest at night—some even have head lamps so they can just keep going all night. The holdin's are so big, young fellow, that they go on 'n on for days like that 'fore they reach their line and turn 'round and plow back to where they started. Day after day, week after week they go up and back. Then they sowed all that land to wheat and thrashed one hundred and sixty-two thousand—here, I'll just write that number in the dust so you can see how big it is—162,000 bushels of wheat that season."

Thomas Hart Benton, *July Hay*, 1943

Literature Model **137**

TEACH

L2 Guided Reading

- Weitzman reproduces the speech of the farmers by dropping the ending or beginning sound of certain words. Look through this page and find examples of both. What is missing from words ending in *-ing*? (the final *g*) What effect does this have on the writing? (It makes the dialogue sound more realistic.)
- Why do you think the author includes the statistics about threshing on this page? (He uses numbers to describe how efficient steam threshing is.) If a steam outfit can process 6,000 bushels per day, and a family without a steam thresher can process thirty bushels per day, how many times more work can the machine do than the family? (200 times more)

About the Art

Thomas Hart Benton, *July Hay*, 1943

Thomas Hart Benton (1889–1975) frequently painted pictures of small town and rural life in the South and Midwest. Many of his paintings were an outgrowth of a sketching expedition he made in the late 1920s. In states from West Virginia to New Mexico, Benton gathered images of cotton pickers, cowboys, steel workers, and preachers. The tempera-and-oil painting *July Hay* is based on a drawing he made during his travels. It measures 38 by 26 3/4 inches and is located at the Metropolitan Museum of Art in New York City.

TEACH

L2 Guided Reading

- Why does Peter's father think the horses wouldn't be against steam power? (They wouldn't have to do the hard work of threshing anymore.)
- What are the different opinions people have of the steam engine? (Some are against it and want to stay with the old ways, some are for it because of increased productivity, and some have not made up their minds.)

Independent Practice

✎ For further stimuli for descriptive writing, see *Fine Art Transparencies* 11–15.

Skills Practice

📁 *Speaking and Listening Activities,* p. 23

📁 *Thinking and Study Skills,* pp. 3–6

I could tell Pa liked the engine too. He got up on the wagon and pitched bundles for a while, and then stood on the engine platform talking to the engineer, Mr. Parker. When he got down, he came over and put his hand on my shoulder, all the time looking at the engine, shaking his head like he couldn't believe his eyes. "Parker's got some machine there, by jippers, quite an outfit. What do you think about all this, Peter, steam power instead of horse power?"

I wasn't sure. "If the engine took the place of the horses, I think I'd miss Annie and Lulu and Quinn. Wouldn't you, Pa?"

"I would, but, you know, horse-power thrashin' is awful hard on them, son. Sure, I'd miss them, but we work them hard all year plowin' and diskin',[4] and seedin' and mowin'. Then just when they're so tuckered out, about to drop and needin' a good rest, we put them to thrashin'. You and I both have seen too many good horses broken, seen them drop, die of the heat and tiredness right there in the traces. And for all their work we might get a hundred bushels, maybe two in a day. I don't know, Peter, maybe steam power is a better thing. I just don't know." Pa chuckled and his eyes got all crinkled and wrinkled with laugh lines the way they do. "I do know one thing though. If you asked the horses, I betcha they wouldn't be against this new steam power the way some folks 'round here are."

4 **diskin'** (disk′ in) breaking up soil with a disk-shaped tool

138   *Descriptive Writing: A Closer Look*

Cultural Diversity

Immigrating to North Dakota

The farmers who discuss the steam thresher have Norwegian and German last names. In the late 1800s the largest group of immigrants to settle in the Dakota Territory was from Norway. Many also came from Germany. They were attracted to the flat, treeless land that could be easily plowed and seeded. Today many persons of German and Norwegian ancestry still live in North Dakota.

Linking Writing and Literature
Readers Respond to the Model

How does David Weitzman use descriptive writing to bring a different time to life?

Think about David Weitzman's descriptions as you answer these questions. Then read what other students liked about his descriptions.

1. What surprised you most about the steam engine that David Weitzman described? How does Weitzman's use of details add to your new image of the steam engine?
2. Did any details of his descriptions of the setting and the people who had come to see the steam engine stand out for you? Which ones?
3. How are the details organized in these descriptions? Can you think of another way they could have been organized?

I liked the scene in which the older people argued about the steam engine. They talked about the disadvantages of modern technology. Mr. Torgrimson was different, though. The invention thrilled him, and he thought about all the advantages of the invention.

I remember most clearly Mr. Torgrimson's talking with Peter about bonanza farming. He went on and on about how all that work could be done. He was my favorite character because he seemed more thoughtful.

I would end the story differently. I would have the father choose whether he wanted the steam engine or horses.
Marinel A. Marty

The author gave a good, detailed look at the steam engine. I enjoyed reading different points of view about the steam engine. I also liked reading the thoughts and feelings of the narrator.
Nitida Wongthipkongka

Literature Model **139**

Writers and Writing

Recollecting the Past
Although *Thrashin' Time* is told through the eyes of a young boy, it is based on the recollections of several real Dakotans. One reviewer said of the story, "It has the taste of historical truth, precise as to agricultural detail, precise as to ethnic background, precise as to the weight of labor." Challenge students to find examples of each kind of detail.

ASSESS

Evaluation Guidelines for Discussion
As your students discuss the passage, either in small groups or as a class, encourage them to begin with a personal response. The student responses on this page might be used as a starting point.

Look for evidence that students
- have read the passage
- can state some of the writer's ideas in their own words
- understand the writer's point of view
- have connected the content to their own knowledge and experiences
- understand the ideas and implications of the passage

Some possible responses to the discussion questions on this page:
1. The colors of the engine were the most surprising. His vivid adjectives and nouns and the description of the sound make it much clearer.
2. The comparison to the Fourth of July stood out, as did the description of the men standing around talking about the machine.
3. The festive atmosphere was ordered according to who was doing each activity. The men were ordered according to what opinion they professed. Additionally, that passage was in time order.

CLOSE

Students might be interested in acting out the threshing event described in the passage. Help students to choose parts and rehearse dialogue. As a group the class might also write dialogue for additional characters so that everyone has a speaking part.

REVIEW

Reflecting on the Unit

You may have students respond to Reflecting on the Unit in writing or through discussion.

Writing Across the Curriculum

Before students begin, encourage them to use precise language and vivid sensory details in order to create the image of life before electricity.

Adding to Your Portfolio

Before choosing pieces for their portfolio, students may first find it helpful to list criteria, such as vivid sensory details, appropriate transitions, and an ordering principle (spatial, chronological, or other) that creates a clear picture. Have students use the list when evaluating their pieces of writing.

Portfolio Evaluation

If you grade the portfolio selections, you may want to award two marks—one each for content and form. Explain your assessment criteria before students make their selections. Commend

- experimentation with creative prewriting techniques
- clear, concise writing in which the main idea, audience, and purpose are evident
- successful revisions
- work that shows a flair for language

140

Unit 3 Review

 **Reflecting on the Unit**

Summarize what you have learned in this unit by answering the following questions.

- How does descriptive writing begin?

- How do sensory details improve descriptive writing?

- What does describing an object involve?

- What kind of language improves a description?

- Why is clear spatial order important to descriptive writing?

- How can a biographer bring a person to life?

 **Adding to Your Portfolio**

Choose a selection for your portfolio. Look over the writing you did for this unit. Choose a piece of writing for your portfolio. The writing you choose should show one or more of the following:

- personal memories or observations
- vivid word pictures
- sensory details that appeal to more than one of the five senses
- precise language
- details in a clear spatial order
- an effective choice of details

Reflect on your choice. Attach a note to the piece you chose, explaining briefly why you chose it and what you learned from writing it.

Set goals. How can you improve your writing? What skill will you focus on the next time you write?

 **Writing Across the Curriculum**

Make a history connection. Think about your favorite hobby, and imagine that you are living before electricity was used in homes. How would living then affect the people, places, or things that are part of your hobby? Would your hobby exist? If not, what hobby might you have instead? Write a paragraph explaining how you might have spent your time.

Teacher's Classroom Resources

The following resources can be used for assessment or evaluation.

Unit Assessment

📁 *Tests with Answer Key*
Unit 3 Choice A Test, p. 9
Unit 3 Choice B Test, p. 10
Unit 3 Composition Objective Test, pp. 11–12

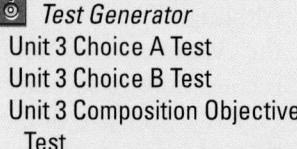 *Test Generator*
Unit 3 Choice A Test
Unit 3 Choice B Test
Unit 3 Composition Objective Test

You may wish to administer one of these tests as a mastery test.

UNIT 4

Composition

Narrative Writing

Lessons

141

UNIT GOALS

The goal of Unit 4 is to help students, through example and instruction, to develop an ability understand and use effective narrative writing techniques. Lessons focus on the elements of narrative writing, including characters, events, setting, chronological order, point of view, and dialogue.

Unit Assessment
📁 *Tests with Answer Key*
Unit 4 Choice A Test, p. 13
Unit 4 Choice B Test, p. 14
Unit 4 Composition Objective Test,
  pp. 15–16

💿 *Test Generator*
Unit 4 Choice A Test
Unit 4 Choice B Test
Unit 4 Composition Objective Test

You may wish to administer either the Unit 4 Choice A Test or the Unit 4 Choice B Test as a pretest.

Key to Ability Levels
Enabling Strategies have been coded for varying learning styles and abilities.

L1 Level 1 activities are within the ability range of Learning Disabled students.

L2 Level 2 activities are basic-to-average activities and are within the ability range of average students.

L3 Level 3 activities are challenging activities and are within the ability range of above-average students.

LEP activities are within the ability range of Limited English Proficiency students.

Setting the Purpose

In the Unit 4 Case Study, students examine how an actor researches and communicates the story of a character's life—reflecting narrative writing in a real-life situation. Students will explore and practice narrative writing in the lessons that follow.

FOCUS

Lesson Overview

Objective: To explore how people, places, and events of the past can be recreated in a historical narrative
Skills: researching; creating a character; acting; answering questions
Critical Thinking: analysis; synthesis; summarizing; making inferences; building background; visualizing
Speaking and Listening: informal speaking; interviewing; discussing; explaining a process

Bellringer
When students enter the classroom, have this assignment on the board: *If you could meet any historical character, whom would you choose? Write several phrases that identify the person.*

Grammar Link to the Bellringer
Point out that students can use the phrases from the Bellringer as non-essential details (appositives) in a sentence set off by commas, such as *Arthur Johnson, a narrative writer, brings history alive.* Have students use appositives in sentences.

Motivating Activity
Ask students about times when they've played the role of someone else—in skits and plays, at costume parties, and so on. How did they portray the character's personality? How successful were they?

142

Narrative Writing
in the Real World

Johnson Interprets Ashby

F O C U S: Characters in a narrative are believable when placed in a realistic setting and presented with personal challenges.

A s an interpreter of African American history for Colonial Williamsburg, Arthur Johnson draws twentieth-century visitors into the 1700s. As carriages slowly creak past the old brick buildings, visitors come upon Johnson spinning the story of Matthew Ashby. The six-foot five-inch bearded giant in colonial work clothes begins by explaining what he's up to. "I'm getting some runners and putting them up and getting these barrels on the cart here," Ashby grins. "You see, Mr. Prentis has given me some credit for taking these barrels and boxes down to Queen Anne's Port. That's what I do. I'm a carter, a carter by trade. I take anything, anywhere, anytime."

◄ *History interpreter Arthur Johnson*

142 *Narrative Writing: Bringing History to Life*

Teacher's Classroom Resources

The following resources can be used for planning, instruction, practice, reinforcement, assessment, or evaluation.

Teaching Tools
Lesson Plans

Transparencies
Writing Process Transparencies, 14–16B

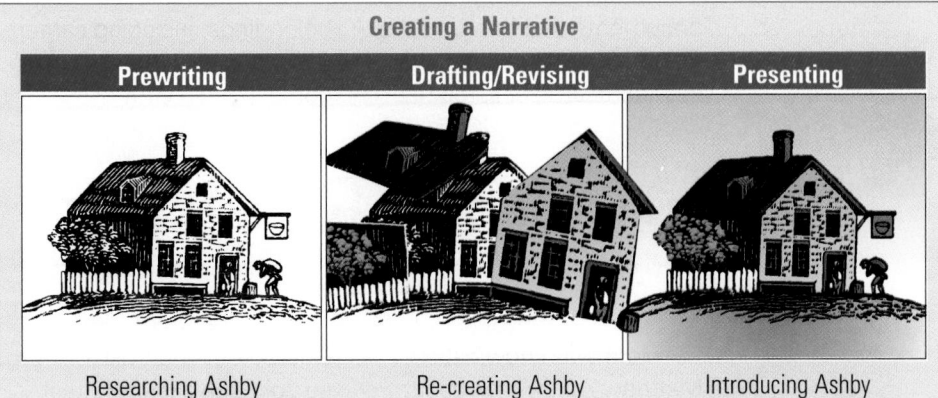

Creating a Narrative

Prewriting	Drafting/Revising	Presenting
Researching Ashby	Re-creating Ashby	Introducing Ashby

Prewriting

RESEARCHING MATTHEW ASHBY

At Williamsburg every restored building and costumed character is based on historical fact. Matthew Ashby was one of many African Americans who made up 50 percent of Williamsburg's population in the 1700s. "He was born free sometime in the 1720s," Johnson says. "As a teenager, he worked with a slave by the name of Joe who took care of horses and carted his master's property. Ashby learned his work from Joe."

Ashby met his wife, Ann, when she was a slave and married her in 1762. During this time, Ashby worked hard as a carter, earned a good rep-utation in Williamsburg, and won freedom for Ann and their two children in 1769.

Johnson learned these facts from a report based on

> *"I think a lot of people who come to Williamsburg don't understand that Williamsburg represents more than the lives of the rich and famous. . . . I like talking about the fact that ordinary people sustained, survived, and moved on."*
>
> — Arthur Johnson

Case Study **143**

Building Background

Warm-up:
Ask the class to generate a list of situations in which stories are told.

Narration in Speaking:
Remind students that they hear stories being told throughout the day, such as in conversations, on the radio, and on television.

Narration in Writing:
Talk about the different kinds of stories students have read. Ask
- How do you identify a story?
- What should every story have in it?
- What do you think makes a good story?
- Who else besides a novelist writes stories?

Preview the Case Study

After students look through the pictures in the Case Study, ask what kind of story they think the Case Study will feature. What do they think the title "Johnson Interprets Ashby" means? Have students read the Case Study.

📂 **Blackline Masters**
Case Studies: Writing in the Real World, pp. 13–16
Cooperative Learning Activities, pp. 19–24
Thinking and Study Skills, pp. 3, 5, 9, 23–24, 34–37

Assessment
📂 *Teacher's Guide to Writing Assessment*

TEACH

Discussion Prompts

- By using documents recounting the lives of southern people who lived during the 1700s, what other kinds of details about Ashby might Johnson have been able to figure out?
- What might have been missing in Johnson's performance had someone else done all the research on Ashby's character?

documents that survived the Revolutionary War. Ashby's will, for example, listed his belongings, including carpenter's tools, a harness for two horses, and a cart.

Drafting/Revising

RE-CREATING ASHBY

▼ *Arthur Johnson prepares for his role as Matthew Ashby.*

More was known about Matthew Ashby than about most free blacks of the 1700s, yet the historical record was thin. How did Johnson flesh out Matthew Ashby's character? He began with historical reports, as well as original records and documents.

"With a skeleton of facts, we can add meat to a character, based on what we know about the period," Johnson explains. Historians know a free-black community once existed outside Williamsburg, so Johnson assumed that Ashby lived there.

The record shows that Ashby succeeded in Williamsburg. "When Ashby petitioned for his family's freedom, the council said . . . we're going to free his wife and children," Johnson says.

Cultural Diversity

Fostering Awareness

Matthew Ashby was one of the thousands of African Americans who had their freedom. Many earned a living by using skills they had learned as slaves. Although technically "free," they were generally not given the rights and freedoms that the Constitution assures citizens of the United States. Free African Americans were not allowed to vote, and they were often subject to harsh local laws.

Day by day Johnson reviewed the facts he had learned. He tried to see the world as Ashby did. Then, in front of a mirror, Johnson practiced speaking as Ashby may have spoken. Later, he practiced in front of his wife. She listened, commented, and encouraged Johnson.

All this work enabled Johnson to become Matthew Ashby, to tell stories about this eighteenth-century man's life. For example, Johnson—in character as Ashby—recalls the day he "jumped the broom," or got married.

"I'll never forget when I got married," Ashby said. "For me it was a great, great day. You see, that night the preacher had come around. His name was Gowan. It seemed like all of my friends were around, such as Adam, who gave me a bucket.

"Gowan said a few words to Ann and me. And it seemed like when he told us to jump over that broom—and we jumped—Ann let me jump the farthest, to let me know that she would be with me no matter what."

While practicing to be Ashby, Johnson had to remember to stay in character. "Matthew wouldn't say a word like *cool*," Johnson says. Nor would he recognize modern things like videocams. What would Ashby do if a visitor asked to take his picture? "In the eighteenth century there were no cameras," Johnson explains. "So Matthew would say, 'Sir, I don't know what you're talking about. And whatever that is you're holding up to your eye, please, you might want to take it down.'"

▼ *In character as Ashby, Johnson performs Ashby's daily tasks as a carter.*

145

TEACH

Discussion Prompts
- What kinds of things might Johnson have tried to in his efforts "see the world as Ashby did"?
- How would it benefit Johnson to practice speaking in front of the mirror?

Connections Across the Curriculum

History
Remind students to keep chronology in mind as they write their historical narratives, avoiding *anachronisms*—details that are out of their proper time in history. Ashby's reaction to a camera is consistent with that of a person living in the 1700s. If Ashby showed a knowledge of the camera, visitors to Williamsburg would notice the anachronism, and realism would be forfeited. As students exchange drafts during revision, have them check each other's writing for anachronisms.

TEACH

Guided Practice

L2 Discussion
Stimulate a discussion of the Case Study. You may want to invite students to talk about
- how Johnson's mode of storytelling enables him to reach audiences he wouldn't reach through a book
- whether Johnson ever has to revise his presentation of Ashby and what might need to change
- how often students tell stories in casual conversations from what they've learned or researched

⇄ Cross-reference: Writing
For instruction and practice of writing dialogue, refer students to Lesson 4.4, pp. 160–163.

Independent Practice

📓 *Writing Process Transparencies* 14–16B
🗂 *Case Studies: Writing in the Real World*, pp. 13–16
🗂 *Cooperative Learning Activities,* pp. 19–24

Skills Practice
🗂 *Thinking and Study Skills,* pp. 3, 5, 9, 23–24, 34–37

▼ *As Ashby, Johnson involves Williamsburg visitors in his work. A visitor strolling by might be tossed a bundle and told to take it to Mr. Prentis.*

Presenting

INTRODUCING MATTHEW ASHBY

Once Johnson felt sure of his character, he took Ashby and his narratives public. Ashby works at Prentis & Company on Duke of Gloucester Street, Williamsburg's main thoroughfare. There he loads and unloads goods for Mr. Prentis.

To draw an audience, Ashby calls to visitors strolling by. "Good day," Ashby hollers. "Do you mind if we borrow your children? We need some help on the wagon."

Through his work he shows how eighteenth-century people used their minds to lift and carry loads. Johnson explains, "You had to know physics in the sense that you had to use levers and fulcrums. You had to know how to move a barrel that weighed half a ton."

When everything is loaded, Ashby relaxes and answers questions. "How long have you been doing this?" "When do you get up?" "Where do you live?"

From Ashby's answers, visitors learn about him and the lives of free blacks. Visitors learn what it took to survive in eighteenth-century Williamsburg. "I feel I can relate to Matthew Ashby because Ashby would be a survivor whether he was in the eighteenth century or the twentieth century."

146 *Narrative Writing: Bringing History to Life*

Beyond the Classroom

Considering Career Opportunities
Students interested in history and travel might enjoy discussing Arthur Johnson's job and others like it. Point out that Johnson's is only one of many kinds of career opportunities in the travel industry, many of which require a knowledge of history or geography. Such jobs are found in various locations, from a major historic site to a single house, such as the home of a famous poet or a former president.

Responding to the Case Study

1. Discussion
Discuss these questions about Arthur Johnson's work.
- What historical documents did Johnson research when interpreting the character of Matthew Ashby?
- What kinds of historical characters does Arthur Johnson particularly enjoy bringing to life in his narratives?
- How does Johnson stay in the eighteenth-century character of Ashby when performing in front of twentieth-century tourists?

- How does Johnson involve his audience in the daily activities of Ashby's work as a carter?

2. Narrative Writing
Write a narrative about a historical character.
Select a character—someone you know or a historical character. For prewriting activities, jot down questions about the person's character, as well as the time and place he or she lives or lived. Then draft a brief narrative paragraph showing the person's character.

Grammar Link

Use appositives to add information.

Use commas to set off an appositive that adds extra, nonessential information to a noun.

Arthur Johnson, **an interpreter of African American history for Colonial Williamsburg,** . . .

Use an appositive to combine the sentences.

1. Matthew Ashby was a free African American. He worked in Williamsburg.
2. He learned his trade from Joe. Joe was a local carter.
3. Ashby was an employee at Prentis & Co. He loaded and unloaded goods.
4. He married his wife in 1762. Her name was Ann.

See Lesson 9.6, page 358, and Lesson 21.2, page 598.

Case Study **147**

ASSESS

Responding to the Case Study

1. Discussion
Students' responses will vary but may include the following:
- original records and documents that survived the Revolutionary War; Ashby's will; historical reports
- ordinary people
- by remembering the language and tools Ashby was familiar with
- by asking for help with his work

2. Narrative Writing
Answers will vary. Students' drafts should reflect answers to the questions they asked during prewriting, if the questions were not too difficult to research. Encourage students to make inferences from their research when they do not find specific answers.

See also *Teacher's Guide to Writing Assessment.*

Grammar Link
(See Using the Grammar Link below.)

Reteaching
Have students choose two historical characters who were friends. Ask them to make an outline for a narrative about the two.

Enrichment
Students might want to make a videotape of their narratives. They could read their narratives aloud or turn them into scripts for short plays.

CLOSE

Have students write down clues that someone from the next century might use to draw conclusions about them and their daily activities.

Using the Grammar Link

Grammar Link Answers
Answers will vary, but some suggestions are given below.
1. Matthew Ashby, a free African American, worked in Williamsburg.
2. He learned his trade from Joe, a local carter.
3. An employee at Prentis & Company, Ashby loaded and unloaded goods.
4. He married his wife, Ann, in 1762.

Using Commas with Appositives Review the rule for using commas only with nonessential appositives. Have groups write sentences with either essential or nonessential appositives, then exchange papers to verify that commas are used only with nonessential appositives.

FOCUS

Lesson Overview

Objective: To develop an introduction for a historical narrative focusing on a person, an event, and a setting
Skills: exploring and narrowing topics; relating details; drawing attention
Critical Thinking: analyzing; recalling; evaluating; building background; visualizing
Speaking and Listening: discussing

Bellringer

When students enter the classroom, have this assignment on the board: *List several kinds of story characters that you enjoy reading about. What kinds of characters do you not enjoy reading about?*

Grammar Link to the Bellringer

Ask students to consider how they could best turn their Bellringer lists into complete sentences or paragraphs. Have them share their ideas with the class. How many different structures or solutions did the class think of using?

Motivating Activity

After students discuss the kinds of characters that do and do not interest them, ask them what kinds of character traits are most appealing. For example, many readers like to see how a character is similar to them; if the character does not have any traits they can relate to, they may lose interest.

Narrative Writing
Writing the Stories of History

Jacob Lawrence, *Frederick Douglass Series, No. 21, The Fugitive*, 1938–1939

A narrative is a story or account of an event. A historical narrative is a story about people and events in history.

In any time period you can find exciting stories of real people who changed the world. The 1800s, for example, gave us the great anti-slavery fighter Frederick Douglass. Like a story, Jacob Lawrence's painting presents one event in Douglass's life. A person, a place, an event—the basic elements of a story are all here.

Find Your Inspiration

Some writers get their ideas for historical narrative from an event; others, from a person. Writer Victoria Ortiz was inspired by a woman from the 1800s. Ortiz was a civil rights worker in Mississippi when she became interested in Sojourner Truth. In the biography she wrote, Ortiz tells how Sojourner spoke strongly for the abolition of slavery and for women's rights. An uneducated former slave, Sojourner lectured with wit and power. On the next page is a paragraph from Victoria Ortiz's book. Read it to see how she showed the character of Sojourner Truth.

148   *Narrative Writing: Bringing History to Life*

Teacher's Classroom Resources

The following resources can be used for planning, instruction, practice, reinforcement, assessment, reteaching, enrichment, or evaluation.

Teaching Tools
Lesson Plans

Transparencies
Fine Art Transparencies, 16–20
Writing Process Transparencies, 14–16B

Blackline Masters
Thinking and Study Skills, pp. 4, 13, 35, 37
Writing Across the Curriculum, p. 14
Cooperative Learning Activities, pp. 19–24

Literature Model

Ohe of the first times Sojourner was present at a Woman's Rights Convention was in October, 1850, in Worcester, Massachusetts. As she later retold the experience to Harriet Beecher Stowe, Sojourner sat for a long time listening to Frederick Douglass, Lucy Stone, Wendell Phillips, William Lloyd Garrison, and Ernestine Rose speak about women's rights. She soon became intrigued, and when called upon to speak she presented her position quite concisely: "Sisters, I aren't clear what you be after. If women want any rights more than they got, why don't they just take them and not be talking about it?" For Sojourner, it was obvious that action was more effective than words.

Victoria Ortiz, *Sojourner Truth: A Self-Made Woman*

Note that Sojourner Truth was a real person involved in a real event in history.

Why do you think some of the same people were advocates of both abolition and women's rights?

To find a topic for a historical narrative, think about people, places, times, and events in history that interest you. A person, a setting, an event—any one of these can spark an idea for a historical narrative.

Once you have an idea, explore and narrow it. Focusing on one point allows you to explore a topic in depth. For example, if you decide to write about a person, you may need to narrow your topic to a single event in his or her life. It is the details, such as Sojourner's statement on women's rights, that bring history to life.

*Activist
Sojourner Truth*

Journal Writing

Create a chart entitled Story Ideas from History. Make three columns, headed Person, Event, and Setting. Skim your history textbook for ideas for historical narratives. List each idea under the appropriate heading.

4.1 Writing the Stories of History **149**

TEACH

Guided Practice

L2 Using the Model

In this unit students read both factual and fictionalized models. To remind students of the difference, point out that the characters and the event in Ortiz's account are real. Even Sojourner's actual words were written down at the time she gave her speech. Ortiz names other historical figures who were present. When students answer the question about the two causes, they may suggest that people interested in human rights would support both causes because both involved a struggle for freedom.

L3 Exploring a Topic

Some students might want to find a biography of Sojourner Truth, either Ortiz's or another, and read a longer speech by Truth on the topic of women's rights. There is one in which she repeats "Ain't I a woman?" To spark interest, read the following passage from that speech: "That man over there says women need to be helped into carriages and lifted over ditches, and to have the best place everywhere. Nobody ever helps me into carriages, over mud puddles, or gets me any best place . . . And ain't I a woman?"

Journal Writing Tip

Brainstormer Topics Students might benefit from a brainstorming session in which they refresh one another's memories about events in history that they could use in their charts. You might even ask the social studies teacher to spend a few minutes brainstorming with the students, reminding them of characters and events they have studied.

Unit Assessment

Speaking and Listening Activities, pp. 12, 21
Composition Practice, p. 25
Composition Reteaching, p. 25
Composition Enrichment, p. 25

📁 *Teacher's Guide to Writing Assessment*
📁 *Tests with Answer Key*
Unit 4 Choice A Test, p. 13
Unit 4 Choice B Test, p. 14

💿 *Test Generator*
Unit 4 Choice A Test
Unit 4 Choice B Test

You may wish to administer either the Unit 4 Choice A Test or the Unit 4 Choice B Test as a pretest.

TEACH

Guided Practice

L2 Using the Model
Point out that the paragraph about Chávez contains the basic elements of a narrative introduction (person, setting, and event—including a problem the person faces). Discuss these elements, referring to the chart below the model. Note that the introduction raises a question: Will Chávez's meeting with the grape growers help the workers? Have students suggest how the writer could go on to add life and color to the narrative. (For example, the writer could tell readers about personal experiences that made Chávez care about the farm workers' plight.)

Two-Minute Skill Drill

Have students suggest an event and setting to write about for each of the following characters:

Nelson Mandela   Mother Teresa
Louisa May Alcott   Albert Einstein

Independent Practice

For further stimuli for narrative writing, see *Fine Art Transparencies,* 16–20

Writing Process Transparencies, 14–16B

Writing Across the Curriculum, p. 14

Cooperative Learning Activities, pp. 19–24

Skills Practice

Thinking and Study Skills, pp. 4, 13, 35, 37

Speaking and Listening Activities, pp. 12, 21

Composition Practice, p. 25

150

Vocabulary
Drafting Tip

As you draft, remember that concrete nouns and colorful adjectives strengthen the descriptions of people and settings, bringing history to life.

Hook Your Readers

Realistic details are especially important in writing about a historical event. Often writers uncover valuable details through research. Sometimes, however, a writer also needs to make up likely details to keep a narrative realistic and exciting. When you're ready to draft your historical narrative, you can use realistic details in your introduction to interest your reader immediately.

A good introduction often presents a person, a setting, and an event. One writer chose the persons and event below for a historical narrative. Read the paragraph that introduces the narrative, and think about the question in the box.

What question does this introduction raise? How does this question make readers want to keep on reading?

> It's a bright August morning in 1962. Many of the major grape growers of southern California have come to Delano City Hall to hear a man named César Chávez. He has come to talk with the people who have the power to improve the lives of his followers. The outcome will have a serious effect on the farm workers' future.

Introducing a Historical Narrative	
Persons	César Chávez, the grape growers
Event	A meeting to discuss the problems of farm workers
Setting	A bright August morning in 1962 at the City Hall in Delano, California

150   *Narrative Writing: Bringing History to Life*

Enabling Strategies

LEP Understanding the Words
To recognize the significance of Sojourner Truth's speech on page 149, students must understand it. Read it aloud and ask students to express the idea in their own words. Stress that although Sojourner was an uneducated former slave who didn't always use standard grammar, her language was powerful and effective. Be sure students understand the idea Ortiz alludes to in her last sentence (the idea that actions speak louder than words).

4.1 Writing Activities

Write an Introduction

Consult the Story Ideas from History chart in your journal, and plan a historical narrative for younger students to read.

- Make prewriting notes, and draft your introduction.
- Interest your readers with details about the person or setting.

PURPOSE To introduce a historical narrative
AUDIENCE Fifth-grade students
LENGTH 1–2 paragraphs

Cooperative Learning

In a group brainstorm historical periods that have exciting stories. Pick a historical period, and brainstorm story ideas. Each member should list persons, settings, and events, including problems the persons faced.

Work individually to write a narrative introduction to one event. Share your introductions. Later you can reread the introductions, choose one you like, and complete the narrative.

Grammar Link

Use complete sentences for clarity.

Your notes for a historical piece will often be in the form of sentence fragments, but use complete sentences in your narrative.

For Sojourner, it was obvious that action was more effective than words.

Revise the fragments below into paragraphs about scientist Robert Goddard. Use complete sentences.

1. As boy, read H. G. Wells, dreamed of space flight.
2. Wrote article on rocketry in 1919—largely ignored.
3. Launched first liquid propellant rocket in 1926—tiny.
4. Flight of two and a half seconds.
5. Vision of lunar landing ridiculed.
6. When real lunar landing—gained wider recognition.
7. Also predicted orbiting space station and probe to Mars.
8. Goddard ahead of time.
9. Speculated about journeys to distant solar systems.
10. Some day true?

See Lesson 8.2, page 328.

4.1 Writing the Stories of History **151**

ASSESS

Writing Activities Evaluation Guidelines

Write an Introduction
Use these criteria when evaluating your students' writing.
- introduction builds on ideas found in prewriting
- details about the person or setting make you want to read on
- complete sentences
- well-ordered paragraphs

See also the *Teacher's Guide to Writing Assessment.*

Cooperative Learning
Each individual should complete
- prewriting notes, based on the group's brainstorming session, suggesting persons, settings, and events for narratives about American history
- an introduction to a narrative, using the prewriting notes

Grammar Link
(See Using the Grammar Link below.)

Reteaching
📁 *Composition Reteaching*, p. 25

Enrichment
📁 *Composition Enrichment*, p. 25

CLOSE

For writing ideas and additional models, ask students to work together to help you compile a bibliography of young-adult historical fiction that is readily available in the school or public library.

Using the Grammar Link

Grammar Link Answers
Answers will vary. A sample is given below.

As a boy, Robert Goddard read H. G. Wells and dreamed about space flight. In 1919 he wrote an article on rocketry that was largely ignored. He launched the first liquid propellant rocket, a tiny one, in 1926. Its flight lasted two and a half seconds. Goddard's vision of a lunar landing was ridiculed, but when a real lunar landing took place, he gained wider recognition. Goddard also predicted an orbiting space station and a probe to Mars.

FOCUS

Lesson Overview

Objective: To develop a historical narrative using chronological order
Skills: choosing a time frame; using chronological order; using transitions
Critical Thinking: analyzing; comparing; ordering
Speaking and Listening: listening for transitions; discussing

🔔 Bellringer

When students enter the classroom, have this assignment on the board: *Write in order the events of your day so far.*

Grammar Link to the Bellringer

Have students look over what they just wrote and tell the class of any indefinite pronouns they included.

Motivating Activity

Point out that photos in an album make more sense if they've been arranged in the order in which they were taken. Invite students to give examples of other activities in which time order is important (playing video games, using a recipe, following a class schedule). Ask students to discuss the risks of not paying attention to time order.

LESSON

4.2 Narrative Writing
Using Chronological Order

Any story makes better sense if the writer thinks about time order, or chronology. A story is in chronological order when the events are presented in the time order in which they occurred.

Movies, television, and videotapes allow us to tell stories in words and images. Suppose you use pictures alone, or pictures with words, to tell a story—in a comic strip, a slide series, a videotape, or even a photo album. In what order would you arrange your pictures to tell a story?

Choose a Time Frame

When you write a narrative, you have to decide on a time frame—when your story will begin and end. The chart on the next page shows that time spans for narratives vary widely. Some narratives cover decades, even centuries. A short narrative may cover days, hours, or even minutes.

In *Homesick: My Own Story,* Jean Fritz tells about her childhood in China and her teen years in the United States. Fritz presents realistic pictures of life in China and America in the early 1900s. The following excerpt tells about a time just before Fritz began eighth grade in her first American school. As you read it, notice how she relates some of one day's events in chronological order. What details suggest that the setting is long ago?

Teacher's Classroom Resources

The following resources can be used for planning, instruction, practice, reinforcement, assessment, reteaching, enrichment, or evaluation.

🖋 **Teaching Tools**
Lesson Plans, p. 33

📖 **Transparencies**
Fine Art Transparencies, 16–20
Writing Process Transparencies, 14–16B

Literature Model

*T*he next day Aunt Margaret took me to Caldwell's store on Main Street and bought me a red-and-black-plaid gingham [cotton] dress with a white collar and narrow black patent leather belt that went around my hips. She took me to a beauty parlor and I had my hair shingled [a close-cut style].

When I got home, I tried on my dress. "How do I look?" I asked my grandmother.

"As if you'd just stepped out of a bandbox [a box for hats and collars; means 'perfectly groomed']."

I wasn't sure that was the look I was aiming for. "But do I look like a regular eighth grader?"

"As regular as they come," she assured me.

Jean Fritz, *Homesick: My Own Story*

What words used here would not be used today in describing a well-dressed eighth grader?

Time Spans for Historical Narratives

A Day

One Lifetime

Two Centuries

Journal Writing

Freewrite about two time periods, one that covers one recent day and one that covers two days. Include details and events that you would include in a narrative.

4.2 Using Chronological Order **153**

TEACH

Guided Practice

L2 Using the Model
Point out that the event in the model belongs to a longer narrative with a bigger time frame. Invite students to find words that help make the time sequence clear (*The next day* and *When I got home*). Ask which words indicate that the setting is in the past (the early 1900s), not in the present (*gingham, shingled,* and *bandbox*).

L1 Ordering Events in Time
List on the board, in random order, three to five events from an era in American history that students are studying or have recently studied. Ask students to number these events in time order. Then list the events in chronological order on the board.

Two-Minute Skill Drill

List these words and phrases on the board, and have students order them from earliest to latest.

late yesterday	last year
tomorrow	later today
early yesterday	next week

Journal Writing Tip

Organizing Graphically
Students may wish to make a graphic representation of a time period before writing about it. Invite them to choose one of their time periods, think about its significant events, then sketch it as a cartoon strip of four or five frames. (Stick figures are fine.)

📁 **Blackline Masters**
Thinking and Study Skills, pp. 5, 11, 13
Writing Across the Curriculum, p. 14
Cooperative Learning Activities, pp. 19–24
Speaking and Listening Activities, pp. 12, 21

Composition Practice, p. 26
Composition Reteaching, p. 26
Composition Enrichment, p. 26

Assessment
📁 *Teacher's Guide to Writing Assessment*

TEACH

Guided Practice

L2 Using the Model

To answer the question, call on a volunteer to read the model aloud while the other students read silently. Then ask students to identify the transitions that tie the events together (*In 1838, In an 1867 referendum, Late one night that year, later,* and *of 1871*). Have students compare the time frames in the chart on page 153 with the one represented in the model on this page. (*The time frame in Ben's narrative is roughly 33 years—not as long as a typical lifetime but closer to it than to the other time frames.*) Stress that narratives can cover as much or as little time as the writer chooses. Remind students that choosing a time frame is a prewriting activity for a narrative.

L3 Retelling with Cartoons

As an option to writing, encourage students to produce their own cartoon narratives. Students might research the steps leading to an important scientific discovery, the history of exploration of a continent, or the events in the life of a scientist. Original cartoon strips could be gathered into a class comic book and displayed in the library or in a central reference area.

Independent Practice

✏ For further stimuli for narrative writing, see *Fine Art Transparencies* 16–20.

✏ *Writing Process Transparencies* 14–16B

📂 *Writing Across the Curriculum*, p. 14

📂 *Cooperative Learning Activities*, pp. 19–24

Skills Practice

📂 *Thinking and Study Skills*, pp. 5, 11, 13

📂 *Speaking and Listening Activities*, pp. 12, 21

📂 *Composition Practice*, p. 26

154

Prewriting Tip

When you are organizing your notes, be sure to put them in an order that would make sense to your reader.

Make Time Order Clear

Ben Aylesworth researched the history of Wheaton, Illinois, a city near his home. He visited the Wheaton History Center and the Wheaton Public Library, where he read about his topic. He also interviewed his grandmother. Finally, Ben decided to focus on one event in the city's history and to relate the stages of that event in chronological order.

As he drafted, Ben used good transitions, such as *later* and *afterward*, to clarify the order of events. In writing a narrative, vary your transitions. If you always use *first, next,* and *finally,* your writing may sound dull. Find the transitions in the model below.

Lester Schrader, *Theft of the Records*, mid- to late nineteenth century

What transitions does Ben use to make the chronological order clear?

Student Model

How would you feel if citizens of a rival town stole your town's records, forever changing its history? In 1838 Naperville held the county records of the new DuPage County. Naperville and nearby Wheaton were fierce rivals. Both wanted the county seat. In an 1867 referendum Wheaton narrowly won the county seat, but the records stayed in Naperville.

Late one night that year, some young Wheaton men broke into the Naperville courthouse and stole the county records. An alarm sounded, and they dropped some of the papers. Later, fearing another raid, Naperville officials moved the remaining records to Chicago for safekeeping. But these were destroyed in the Great Chicago Fire of 1871. Wheaton has been the county seat ever since that famous midnight raid.

Ben Aylesworth, Hadley Junior High School,
Glen Ellyn, Illinois

154 *Narrative Writing: Bringing History to Life*

Enabling Strategies

LEP Using Sequence

To practice English transition words, some students might find it helpful to list chronologically some events in their everyday lives, such as what they do between supper and bedtime. Have students practice using transition words that link these actions, such as: *first, after that, when I finished, next, later, finally,* and *soon.* Another possibility for practice in time sequencing is a description of a family holiday celebration.

4.2 Writing Activities

Write a Narrative

A future historian will want to know about special events in your school and community. Plan and write a narrative about one annual event, such as a concert, a game or tournament, or a holiday parade and picnic.

- Choose an event, and list its stages.
- Arrange the stages in chronological order.
- In drafting and revising, use appropriate transitions.

PURPOSE To narrate the story of a school or community event
AUDIENCE Future historians
LENGTH 1–2 paragraphs

Cooperative Learning

In a small group, plan and write a historical narrative about your town or city. Pool what you know about your topic. Then work together to write the narrative of an event in your community's history. Focus on one incident, and arrange the details, or stages of the event, in chronological order. Include transitions to make the order of the events clear. Review one another's narratives, and revise your own as needed.

Grammar Link

Use the correct verb—singular or plural—when the subject is an indefinite pronoun.

Some indefinite pronouns (like *one* and *each*) are singular and require a singular verb. Some (like *both* and *many*) are plural and take a plural verb.

Both want the county seat.

Choose the correct verb to complete each sentence.

1. Many of the families (has, have) lived in the Park Cities for several generations.
2. Everyone in the community (knows, know) the brilliantly lit pecan tree on Armstrong Parkway.
3. Each of the other old pecan trees in the Park Cities (was, were) damaged or destroyed by an ice storm in 1965.
4. Only one of the trees (was, were) left standing.
5. Ever since, few in the town of Park Cities (has, have) taken pecan trees for granted.

See Lesson 16.4, page 514.

4.2 Using Chronological Order **155**

ASSESS

Writing Activities Evaluation Guidelines

Write a Narrative
Use these criteria when evaluating your students' writing.
- It retells an annual event in the school or community.
- It includes details to make the event understandable for someone in the future.
- The stages of the event are arranged in chronological order.
- Appropriate transitions make the time order clear.
- Indefinite pronouns are used correctly.

See also the *Teacher's Guide to Writing Assessment.*

Cooperative Learning
Observe each group in action, and see that each member takes part in the planning and writing. Narratives should cover these points:
- the topic is an event in the history of the city or town
- events are presented in clear chronological order
- appropriate transitions link events

Grammar Link
(See Using the Grammar Link below.)

Reteaching
📁 *Composition Reteaching*, p. 26

Enrichment
📁 *Composition Enrichment*, p. 26

CLOSE

Have the class make a school calendar that includes the first and last days of school, vacations, holidays, exam periods, and school events.

Using the Grammar Link

Grammar Link Answers
1. have
2. knows
3. was
4. was
5. have

Subject-Verb Agreement Ask students to rewrite each Grammar Link sentence using the form of the verb they did not choose. Students will need to supply new indefinite pronouns to agree with the new verbs.

Narrative Writing
Establishing Point of View

In narratives the point of view is important. Some stories are told by a main character in the first person—using "I" or "we." Others are told by an observer in the third person—using "he," "she," or "they."

In the story below, Justin Hoest speaks in the voice of a fictional grandfather in the early 2000s, telling his grandson about the 1960s civil rights movement.

Student Model

L et me start in the beginning. I was born in Birmingham, Alabama, in 1952. Back then, in southern states, it was segregated. There were separate water fountains, waiting rooms, stores, schools. Everywhere, some people were trying to keep segregation, and others were trying to stop it. The times were troubled.

"Martin Luther King Jr. came to Birmingham when I was ten. I met him some years later during the Selma marches. He helped organize demonstrations. There were sit-ins like in Nashville, and ➡

Note that although the story is fictional, it is set in a real time and place.

156   *Narrative Writing: Bringing History to Life*

FOCUS

Lesson Overview

Objective: To write a narrative that uses either a first-person or a third-person point of view
Skills: writing from a point of view; using pronouns to reflect point of view
Critical Thinking: analyzing; identifying; comparing; classifying
Speaking and Listening: discussing; explaining a process

Bellringer

When students enter the classroom, have this assignment on the board: *Write either I or he or she to indicate who you think is speaking these sentences:*

1. *My dream is to fly a plane.* (I)
2. *They rowed to shore.* (he or she)
3. *There were several people injured.* (he or she)

Grammar Link to the Bellringer

Ask students to underline the simple subjects once and the verbs twice in the Bellringer sentences. (1. <u>dream</u>, <u>is</u>; 2. <u>they</u>, <u>rowed</u>; 3. <u>people</u>, <u>were</u>)

Motivating Activity

Select a familiar incident from American history, such as the landing of the *Mayflower* or Paul Revere's ride. Ask a volunteer to relate what happened. Call on another to tell about the same event, pretending that he or she had participated in the action. Ask what pronouns the second student used that the first did not (first-person pronouns such as *I* and *we*). Explain that students will try out both ways of telling the stories of history.

156

Teacher's Classroom Resources

The following resources can be used for planning, instruction, practice, reinforcement, assessment, reteaching, enrichment, or evaluation.

Teaching Tools
Lesson Plans, p. 34

Transparencies
Fine Art Transparencies, 16–20
Writing Process Transparencies, 14–16B

adults would picket up and down the streets. We'd go to the meeting house in the evening. We would sing all night, or so it seemed. Everyone would dress in nice clothes, and the church smelled so good with the fresh candles burning.

Song filled the place:

I'm so glad; I'm fightin' for my rights;
I'm so glad; I'm fightin' for my rights;
Glory, Hallelujah!

"Finally my day came. We were clapping and singing. Some of us were carrying signs. The day was bright, but there was a menacing dark cloud lingering in the sky. We weren't scared, only nervous. Our feet on the hard pavement made a sound that represented the whole movement."

Justin Hoest, Maplewood Middle School,
Menasha, Wisconsin

Why do you think Justin chose to have the grandfather tell his own story?

Presenting Tip

When you present your narrative, you can accompany your writing with photos or recordings.

Use the First Person

In telling his story, Justin has chosen a first-person point of view. That is, he lets the grandfather tell the story using the pronouns *I* and *me*. First-person narratives describe just what the narrator witnesses and thinks. The reader sees all the events through the narrator's eyes and views them as the narrator views them.

A reporter is getting a first-person account of the game.

Journal Writing

Make column headings that name three important events in American history. In ten minutes create as many fictional characters as you can think of under each heading. They may be participants, like the grandfather, or just observers.

4.3 Establishing Point of View **157**

TEACH

Guided Practice

L2 Using the Model
Ask students to read the model silently. Then ask them whether a participant or an observer is telling the story. (*The grandfather, a participant, is the narrator.*) In explaining why Justin had the grandfather tell his own story, students will probably note that he wanted to bring the events to life by having an eyewitness relate them. Also, the pronouns *me, we*, and *our* show that the grandfather is telling his own story. As a lead-in to the section called Using the First Person, remind students that these pronouns are called first-person pronouns.

Two-Minute Skill Drill

Have students study the photo on page 156. Ask them to tell what pronouns would be used in narrating the scene as a first-person account from the point of view of

- Martin Luther King Jr.
- one of the children
- the photographer

Journal Writing Tip

Classifying As students prepare to begin this activity, you might put an example on the board. As a column heading, write *Operation Desert Storm*. Then start the list with a fictional character, such as Hakim, a Muslim child whose life is changed as a result of the conflict. Ask for volunteers to suggest two or three more characters you can create under the same heading.

📁 **Blackline Masters**
Thinking and Study Skills, pp. 5, 9, 13
Writing Across the Curriculum, p. 14
Cooperative Learning Activities, pp. 19–24

Speaking and Listening Activities, pp. 12, 21
Composition Practice, p. 27
Composition Reteaching, p. 27
Composition Enrichment, p. 27

Assessment
📁 *Teacher's Guide to Writing Assessment*

157

TEACH

Guided Practice

L2 Using the Model

You might begin by reading the poem aloud to students. Afterward, make sure students understand that the Island Queen is England, her daughter is the American colonies, and the event is the Boston Tea Party. Invite volunteers to review for the class what happened in Boston and why. (*England imposed a tax on tea, and the colonies protested by dumping the tea into Boston Harbor.*)

L3 Writing Narrative Poems

Ask students to work in groups to write narrative poems or ballads about other events in American history using the poem on this page as a model. Later, students might sing their poems to the class, possibly with guitar accompaniment; or they could choose a group member to perform a dramatic reading. Alternatively, one student might read the poem aloud as others pantomime the action.

Independent Practice

🖋 For further stimuli for narrative writing, see *Fine Art Transparencies* 16–20.

🖋 *Writing Process Transparencies,* 14–16B

📁 *Writing Across the Curriculum,* p. 14

📁 *Cooperative Learning Activities,* pp. 19–24

Skills Practice

📁 *Thinking and Study Skills,* pp. 5, 9, 13

📁 *Speaking and Listening Activities,* pp. 12, 21

📁 *Composition Practice,* p. 27

Grammar
Editing Tip

In editing your narrative, check to make sure you've used subject and object pronouns correctly. For more on using pronouns, see page 406.

Try the Third Person

Many short stories and other narratives are told from an observer's third-person point of view, using the pronouns *he, she, it,* and *they.* The following narrative poem uses the pronoun *she,* since the main characters are the Island Queen and her daughter. If you know something about the history of the American Revolution, you might be able to figure out who these characters are.

Literature Model

*T*here was an old lady lived over the sea
    And she was an Island Queen.
Her daughter lived off in a new country,
With an ocean of water between;
The old lady's pockets were full of gold
But never contented was she,
So she called on her daughter to pay her a tax
Of three pence a pound on her tea.

The tea was conveyed to the daughter's door,
All down by the ocean's side;
And the bouncing girl pour'd out every pound
In the dark and boiling tide;
And then she called out to the Island Queen,
"O mother, dear mother," quoth she,
"Your tea you may have when 'tis steep'd enough
But never a tax from me."

Traditional

Formats

Journal

Ballad

Letters

What point of view would you choose for a narrative? A short story, an imaginary journal or letter, a song, or a narrative poem can be in the first-person point of view. The main character is then the *I* of the story. Or you can tell your story in the third person. The main character is *he* or *she.* Most writers decide on their point of view in prewriting. Then they use imagination to bring the history to life.

158   *Narrative Writing: Bringing History to Life*

Enabling Strategies

LEP Recognizing Point of View

As the class learns to recognize the first-person point of view, you might ask students learning English to tell what pronouns they use in their original language to refer to themselves. Explain that these are called first-person pronouns. Then read aloud a few simple passages from stories in the students' literature book, and ask them to identify the first-person pronouns.

4.3 Writing Activities

Janet Fish, Charles, Drummer, Lorna, Roxanne and Jonathan, *1986*

Write a Narrative Paragraph

Look at what's happening in the painting above. Write a narrative paragraph as told by one of the people in the painting. Don't identify yourself in the writing—see if your classmates can guess who is telling the story.

- Use a first-person point of view, using *I* and *me* correctly.
- Tell what you and others are doing.

PURPOSE To use the first-person point of view
AUDIENCE Classmates
LENGTH 1 paragraph

Grammar Link

Make subjects and verbs agree in sentences beginning with *there*.

*There **was** an old **lady**....*
*There **were** sit-ins....*

Complete each sentence below with the correct verb: *was* or *were*.

[1]There _____ more than four thousand people killed in a 1995 earthquake in Kobe, Japan. [2]There _____ also massive property damage. [3]There _____ little looting, though goods lay everywhere. [4]There _____ many people who helped care for others.

See Lesson 16.2, page 510.

4.3 Establishing Point of View **159**

ASSESS

Writing Activities Evaluation Guidelines

Write a Narrative Paragraph
Use these criteria when evaluating your students' writing.

- The paragraph is about an event or action that could be happening in the painting.
- The writer uses a first-person point of view, with pronouns such as *I, me, we, us, my, our.*
- Specific details are included to help readers identify the speaker.
- All subjects and verbs agree in number.

See also the *Teacher's Guide to Writing Assessment.*

Grammar Link
(See Using the Grammar Link below.)

Reteaching
Composition Reteaching, p. 27

Enrichment
Composition Enrichment, p. 27

Use *Fine Art Transparencies* 16–20 for enrichment activities also.

CLOSE

Ask students to discuss any difficulty they continue to have distinguishing first-person and third-person point of view. Have students share any strategies that help them.

Using the Grammar Link

Grammar Link Answers
1. were
2. was
3. was
4. were

About the Art

Janet Fish, *Charles, Drummer, Lorna, Roxanne and Jonathan,* 1986
This painting depicts a group enjoying some time together. It is a 60-by-132-inch oil-on-canvas painting that is in the Robert Miller Gallery in New York City.

160

Setting the Purpose

Lesson 4.4 teaches students to explore using realistic dialogue to portray characters.

FOCUS

Lesson Overview

Objective: To capture the flavor of real speech in dialogue

Skills: characterizing through dialogue; writing realistic dialogue

Critical Thinking: analyzing; recalling; evaluating; visualizing

Speaking and Listening: note taking; discussing

Bellringer

When students enter the classroom, have this assignment on the board: *Write down several things you can learn about a person by listening to the way he or she talks to others.*

Grammar Link to the Bellringer

As students discuss their answers to the Bellringer, ask for examples of revealing statements that people might make. Write each suggestion on the board, asking for the student's directions on how to punctuate it.

Motivating Activity

Give students a chance to experience some of the challenges of writing a genuine-sounding dialogue. As they make up some dialogue for the two characters in Anthony Ortega's *Two Little Old Men*, ask them to note any difficulties they encounter or questions they have and what they like and dislike about what they have written.

LESSON

4.4

Descriptive Writing
Writing Realistic Dialogue

Dialogue can make a story come to life—or fall flat on its face.

Study the picture below. What do you think the two figures might be saying? How do you think they might be saying it? Jot down your ideas.

Anthony Ortega, *Two Little Old Men*, 1984

Now read two openers that were written for a story. Which one would be more likely to catch your interest? Why?

Jenny said she saw Joseph walking home.

Jenny burst in, shouting, "Hey, everybody, Joseph's come home!"

160 *Narrative Writing: Bringing History to Life*

Teacher's Classroom Resources

The following resources can be used for planning, instruction, practice, reinforcement, assessment, reteaching, enrichment, or evaluation.

Teaching Tools
Lesson Plans, p. 35

Transparencies
Fine Art Transparencies, 16–20
Writing Process Transparencies, 14–16B

Let Characters Speak for Themselves

Dialogue—direct quotations of spoken words or conversations—is a way of revealing character. What does the following conversation reveal about Hideyo and his mother?

Literature Model

Mother opened her mouth and could not close it for several seconds.

"Most of my classmates have enlisted," said Hideyo, serious for once. "I have decided to go to help our country."

"You cannot go, Hideyo!" Mother told him. "You must talk with Father. You just cannot make such a decision alone."

"Mother, I have already sent in my application," said Hideyo. "I will take the written and physical examinations!"

"How could you?" Mother moaned. "Why didn't you tell me?"

"I am eighteen. Big enough to make my own decision."

Yoko Kawashima Watkins, *So Far from the Bamboo Grove*

> *The mother's words tell you she loves her son and fears for his life.*

> *What does the dialogue reveal about Hideyo?*

Letting characters speak for themselves is easy when you write about someone you know well. Ask yourself, "What would this person say here?" After you draft some dialogue, it helps to put it aside for a day or so. Then, when you reread it, you can ask yourself if it sounds authentic. If it does not, see how to improve it.

Journal Writing

Listen to the speech of others, and jot down bits of conversation you hear. Next to each quotation identify the speaker—a bus driver, for instance, or a relative.

Grammar
Editing Tip

As you edit your dialogue, check your punctuation, capitalization, and paragraphing. For more about writing dialogue, see Lesson 20.6, page 576.

TEACH

Guided Practice

L2 Using the Model

To demonstrate how dialogue can reveal character, have students use the dialogue to answer these questions:

- What has Hideyo done?
- How does his mother react?
- Why does she react that way?

(*The dialogue shows that Hideyo respects his mother who loves him and fears for his safety, but Hideyo is determined to serve his country by enlisting.*)

L1 Listening to Speech

Be sure students understand that written dialogue can include sentence fragments, slang, and grammatically incorrect expressions. Dialogue should sound authentic, so students should learn to listen to actual speech. Some writers carry notebooks to record individual ways of speaking. Others simply listen and remember. By developing an ear for spoken language, a writer can create realistic dialogue.

Two-Minute Skill Drill

Ask students to write a sentence—as if part of a dialogue—that might be spoken by each of these speakers.

| a sibling | a parent |
| a manager | a waitress |

Journal Writing Tip

Identifying Attributes Urge students to analyze conversations they hear for pronunciation and word choice. They may notice that some people pronounce and choose words differently than they themselves would.

TEACH

Guided Practice

L2 Using the Model

Have students read the passage and find two quotations that are not attributed to a speaker (*lines 5 and 9*). With students, discuss why the speaker of those lines is obvious. Why might a writer purposefully not have every paragraph include a phrase such as *he said*? How can students know when it is safe to leave out such identifiers?

L3 Cooperative Learning

Ask pairs of students to create a dialogue with visual depictions representing the three elements pictured on this page. Have each pair trade dialogues and act them out, using the visuals as guides. Pairs can then discuss how tone of voice, facial expression, and body language can be represented in dialogues (*word choice, context, punctuation, and so on*).

Independent Practice

For further stimuli for narrative writing, see *Fine Art Transparencies* 16–20.

Writing Process Transparencies 14–16B

Writing Across the Curriculum, p. 14

Cooperative Learning Activities, pp. 19–24

Skills Practice

Thinking and Study Skills, pp. 3, 6, 34

Speaking and Listening Activities, pp. 12, 21

Composition Practice, p. 28

Make Conversation

Your dialogue will sound natural if your characters talk the way real people do. Below is a natural-sounding dialogue between a brother and sister. What did the writer do to make this conversation sound realistic?

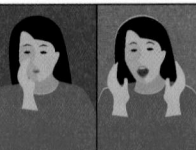

Tone of Voice

Facial Expression

Body Language

> "I can too run!" Antonio glared at her, arms locked stubbornly over his chest.
>
> "I didn't say you can't run, 'Tonio," Gina retorted. "I just said I can run faster than you!"
>
> "Yeah, well, I can run farther!"
>
> Gina rolled her eyes. "In your dreams, <u>fratello</u>!" she crowed. "You can't even run without tripping on something!"
>
> "Can too!"
>
> "Think about it, 'Tonio! Remember last year's Fourth of July picnic? Who wanted to run barefoot and then stepped on a wasp four seconds into the race? Not me!" Gina roared.

Did you notice the slang, sentence fragments, contractions, and descriptions of facial expressions and body language? Without these, the conversation would sound stiff and unnatural. Suppose the writer had Gina say this: "I am sorry, but you are badly mistaken, brother. You cannot run without falling down." Even Gina's use of the Italian term *fratello*, which means "brother," adds interest.

162 *Narrative Writing: Bringing History to Life*

Enabling Strategies

LEP Creating Conversation

Students learning English might benefit from writing original dialogue for comic strips. Blank out the speech balloons of simple comic strips and photocopy them for the students. First, have students provide written dialogue in their first languages. If fluent bilingual students are available, ask them to act as coaches in writing the dialogues in English. Partners can then read to each other the dialogues in both languages.

4.4 Writing Activities

Write a Dialogue

Do you think the men in this painting are talking to each other, or are they silent? If they are talking, what might they be saying? What are they doing in this open space? How does this painting make you feel? Write a dialogue between two students who are viewing the painting at an exhibition.

- Begin by jotting down some words or phrases you might use to react to the painting.
- Make your dialogue sound natural.

PURPOSE To create a realistic dialogue
AUDIENCE Your teacher and classmates
LENGTH 1–2 short paragraphs

Hughie Lee-Smith, *Man Standing on His Head,* 1969

▚▚ COMPUTER OPTION ▚▚

Use your computer and printer to prepare scripts. Your word-processing program allows you to indent actors' parts so that each character's name is clearly visible in the left margin.

Grammar Link

In dialogue, use quotation marks and other punctuation correctly.

"Most of my classmates have enlisted," said Hideyo. . . .

"You cannot go, Hideyo!" Mother told him.

Write each sentence below, using quotation marks and other punctuation where necessary.

1. You're leaving this house in that outfit over my dead body Mrs. Curphy announced.
2. But Mom! All the kids are wearing feathers in their noses Patty whined.
3. I don't care what the other kids are doing, Mrs. Curphy declared.
4. Mom! Patty cringed.
5. No daughter of mine is leaving my house looking like a bird, said Patty's mom, and that's final.

See Lesson 20.6, page 576.

4.4 Writing Realistic Dialogue **163**

Writing Activities Evaluation Guidelines

Write a Dialogue
Use these criteria when evaluating your students' writing.

- reflects an imaginative response to the painting
- reflects attention to mechanics
- sounds natural
- is correctly punctuated

See also the *Teacher's Guide to Writing Assessment.*

Computer Option
Work with students to make sure they know how to take advantage of the relevant word-processing features.

Grammar Link
(See Using the Grammar Link below.)

Reteaching
📁 *Composition Reteaching,* p. 28

Enrichment
📁 *Composition Enrichment,* p. 28

📷 Use *Fine Art Transparencies* 16–20 for enrichment activities also.

CLOSE

Ask students to look back at stories they have written and find one that might be improved by letting dialogue tell about a character. Encourage them to rework a section or two and to share before-and-after comparisons with the class.

Using the Grammar Link

Grammar Link Answers
1. "You're leaving…body!" Mrs. Curphy announced.
2. "But Mom!…noses," Patty whined.
3. "I don't…doing," Mrs. Curphy … .
4. "Mom!" Patty cringed.
5. "No daughter…bird," said Patty's mom. "And that's final."

About the Art

Hughie Lee-Smith, *Man Standing on His Head,* 1969
This work conveys a sense of isolation. You might ask the class to imagine who the two men in the painting are. Are they together or separate? This oil painting, 38 by 46 inches, is in the New Jersey State Museum in Trenton.

163

Setting the Purpose

Lesson 4.5 teaches students to create a character and story using research they have done about a historical event.

FOCUS

Lesson Overview

Objective: To synthesize fictional characters and a historical setting in creating an original narrative

Skills: creating characters; choosing a writing form; inventing a conflict

Critical Thinking: synthesizing; summarizing; making inferences; building background; visualizing

Speaking and Listening: note taking; discussing; questioning

🔔 Bellringer

When students enter the classroom, have this assignment on the board: *Write a few reasons why it may be more interesting to hear a personal account than a factual report of a historical event.*

Grammar Link to the Bellringer

As students discuss their answers to the Bellringer, ask for specific examples of historical events that could be made more interesting through personal accounts. Ask for student help in capitalizing nouns and adjectives that specify nationalities and languages.

Motivating Activity

Ask students to visualize living in another time and place. Encourage them to describe the settings they have pictured. Remind students that in historical fiction, a real setting often forms the background for a story about imaginary characters with made-up (though believable) problems.

164

LESSON

4.5

Narrative Writing
Relating a Historical Event

Andō Hiroshige, *The Wave*, c. 1850

Hannah Wilson read as much as she could find about Japanese immigrants of the 1920s. Then she created a character, gave her a problem, and let her tell her story.

Read this excerpt from Wilson's story. See what the point of view tells you about the character.

> ### Student Model
>
> **M**amma—I wish she were here now. I still miss her so much. I wish with all my heart she could be here to see this baby born. I remember how comforting she always was. I need that comfort now. Every day seems the same to me. Up at dawn, fix breakfast for Seiji and myself, off to work in the fields all day while Seiji goes fishing, hardly stopping to eat. The lonely nights when Seiji must stay on the fishing boats all night.
>
> I love America and Seiji, and I want a baby so much, but I miss Mamma and Papa and Sachiko and Akiko.
>
> Hannah Wilson, Newton Elementary School,
> Strafford, Vermont

What can you tell about the person whose voice you hear in this narrative?

164 *Narrative Writing: Bringing History to Life*

Teacher's Classroom Resources

The following resources can be used for planning, instruction, practice, reinforcement, assessment, reteaching, enrichment, or evaluation.

🔧 **Teaching Tools**
Lesson Plans, p. 36

📐 **Transparencies**
Fine Art Transparencies, 16–20
Writing Process Transparencies, 14–16B

Create a Character

If you, like Hannah Wilson, chose immigration as the subject for your narrative, your next step would be investigation. You might begin by reading immigration stories, jotting down details about ordinary people's lives. Then you might think of a character and imagine problems the character could face.

Can you see the germ of one or more story ideas in these prewriting notes?

Notes—Japanese Immigration to the U.S.

Many immigrated from the 1890s to 1920. Most entered the U.S. on the West Coast.

Issei: first-generation Japanese immigrants

Nisei: their chi... generation

Sensei: their ... third generation

World War I... internment ca...

Possible Topics
1. Leaving home forever
2. A rough sea voyage
3. First glimpse of land
4. Finding another home
5. First day in an American
   school...

● Male
■ Female

The Ikeda Family Tree

Mitsuo Ikeda   Sumiko Tanaka

Haruo Kiyo Masaru   Eiko Kenji Reiko

Yasuko Eiko Sadako Genzo Mitsuo

Journal Writing

Talk to a friend or family member about an immigration experience. Create a fictional character in the same time and place, and freewrite about problems your character might face.

4.5 Relating a Historical Event **165**

TEACH

Guided Practice

L2 Using the Model
You might explain that the best advice about writing believable historical fiction can be summed up in two words: *read* and *research*. No matter how wonderful the characters and how inventive the conflicts, historical fiction is not convincing if it lacks authentic details. Ask students which details in the model on page 164 show that the writer read and researched Japanese immigration experiences. Students will probably notice that the narrator in the model is a married woman, a mother-to-be, who is lonely because she's far from her home and family in Japan, and her husband's job takes him away for long hours.

L2 Using the Model
Examine the prewriting notes on page 165 with students. Point out that the notes at the left could have been taken from an encyclopedia article— a good starting point, though it lacks enough detail to be the writer's only source. Brainstorm other sources that a student might use in writing a story about Japanese immigration—interview notes or notes taken while reading a nonfiction immigration story, for example.

Journal Writing Tip

Formulating Questions Suggest that students create characters around their own age. It will be easier for them to create a conflict for someone with whom they have something in common. Once students have created their character, they can ask the person they have chosen to interview for details about what life was like for young teenagers.

📁 **Blackline Masters**
Thinking and Study Skills,
pp. 4, 23–24, 35, 37
Writing Across the Curriculum,
p. 14
Cooperative Learning Activities,
pp. 19–24

Speaking and Listening Activities, pp. 12, 21
Composition Practice, p. 29
Composition Reteaching, p. 29
Composition Enrichment, p. 29

Assessment
📁 *Teacher's Guide to Writing Assessment*

TEACH

Guided Practice

L2 Using the Model
Students might benefit from contrasting this model with the model on page 164. How do the characters' backgrounds differ? Why do the characters express different feelings? Point out that the journal entry format allowed both writers to express personal thoughts and feelings.

In discussing a possible future conflict, point out that the narrator's high expectations about *a land of amazing wealth* might eventually conflict with the reality of life in America.

Two-Minute Skill Drill

Challenge students to think of characters they might create based on these historical events.

the Revolutionary War

the drafting of the Constitution of the United States

the American Civil War

the Great Depression

Independent Practice

For further stimuli for narrative writing, see *Fine Art Transparencies* 16–20.

Writing Process Transparencies 14–16B

Writing Across the Curriculum, p. 14

Cooperative Learning Activities, pp. 19–24

Skills Practice

Thinking and Study Skills, pp. 4, 23–24, 35, 37

Speaking and Listening Activities, pp. 12, 21

Composition Practice, p. 29

166

Prewriting Tip

In prewriting look for details about the setting. You can use them to enrich your narrative with strong, colorful descriptions.

Choose Your Approach

After giving the character a problem or conflict, decide on an approach. You could write a short story, a series of journal entries, or some letters home. Formats such as these allow you to show a character's feelings and actions.

Like Hannah, Philip Garran wrote an immigration story. In his prewriting investigation, he researched the Irish potato crop failures, which led to famine and caused many to leave their homeland. Unlike Hannah, Philip focused on the early part of the experience, before his main character left home. He, too, made up the details, but they were based on his research. Read the model, and see why a journal entry was a logical approach for Philip to use.

Using sensory language, Philip paints a vivid word picture of the Irish countryside and conveys the narrator's feelings for his homeland.

What possible conflict is the writer setting up in these sentences?

Student Model

At last my father has found a ship. We have packed all of our belongings, and Dad has sold the cottage for a very small sum of money. However, it was almost enough to pay for the tickets, and we borrowed the rest from my Uncle Paul.

We will be leaving in three days. I will miss the green fields, the blue sky, and the sparkly rivers and lakes. But I will not miss the misery that has descended on us like fog. I hear that America is a land of amazing wealth, and the land there is incredibly cheap. I can't wait to see America.

Philip Garran, Newton Elementary School, Strafford, Vermont

166 *Narrative Writing: Bringing History to Life*

Enabling Strategies

LEP Sharing Histories
Pair students learning English with students proficient in English. Have them work together to generate ideas for historical fiction. Settings could be drawn from students' countries of origin.

This will allow all students to share information about their native countries, and it will allow students learning English to practice their new language with their peers.

4.5 Writing Activities

Write a Narrative Journal Entry

Invent a character who is fleeing by boat or ship from a country that has become dangerous to live in. Write an entry he or she would add to a personal journal while on board.

- Focus on the flight from home, the voyage itself, or hopes for the future.
- Convey feelings, as well as facts.

PURPOSE To reflect a historical event
AUDIENCE Yourself
LENGTH 1–2 paragraphs

Henry Bacon, *First Sight of Land*, 1877

Cross-Curricular: Art

Study the painting below. Write the next letter that the young woman will send home. Write it as a narrative that tells what she is seeing and feeling.

Grammar Link

Capitalize nouns and adjectives that specify nationalities and languages.

*first-generation **J**apanese immigrants*

Write each sentence below, using capital letters where necessary.

1. My uncle, a guatemalan by birth, speaks english, spanish, portuguese, and french.
2. In my neighborhood I hear more vietnamese than english.
3. Many italians who immigrated between 1899 and 1924 chose to return to their native land.
4. By 1910 the labor force in the West included native-born white americans, mexican americans, african americans, chinese americans, and tens of thousands of new mexican and japanese immigrants.
5. In later years many haitians and cubans settled in Florida.

See Lesson 19.4, page 556.

Using the Grammar Link

Grammar Link Answers
1. Guatemalan, English, Spanish, Portuguese, French
2. Vietnamese, English
3. Italians
4. Americans, Mexican Americans, African Americans, Chinese Americans, Mexican, Japanese
5. Haitians, Cubans

About the Art

Henry Bacon, *First Sight of Land*, 1877
Bacon's oil painting tells of another kind of immigration experience—the end of a voyage to America. The woman is a European immigrant whose port of entry was probably New York City.

ASSESS

Writing Activities Evaluation Guidelines

Write a Narrative Journal Entry
Use these criteria when evaluating your students' writing.

- establishes a setting
- explains the need for the flight
- includes observations about facts, events, and feelings
- incorporates correct capitalization of proper nouns and adjectives

See also the *Teacher's Guide to Writing Assessment*.

Cross-Curricular: Art
Students' responses should
- follow a friendly-letter format
- tell what the woman sees
- explain how the woman feels

Grammar Link
(See Using the Grammar Link below.)

Reteaching
Composition Reteaching, p. 29

Enrichment
Composition Enrichment, p. 29

Use *Fine Art Transparencies* 16–20 for enrichment activities also.

CLOSE

Encourage students to exchange papers. Peer reviewers could make three comments on the writer's work:
- praise for one particular item or quality, such as "This sentence paints a great word picture."
- a specific question, such as "Why does [character] say that…?"
- a specific suggestion, such as "You should show why [character] makes that choice."

Setting the Purpose

Lesson 4.6 teaches students how to write a news story.

FOCUS

Lesson Overview

Objective: To create a news-story lead and details that bring the event to life

Skills: formulating questions; identifying details that answer the "five Ws and an H"; identifying main ideas

Critical Thinking: establishing criteria; generating new information; identifying main idea; evaluating

Speaking and Listening: informal speaking; discussing

Bellringer

When students enter the classroom, have this assignment on the board: *You are a newspaper reporter covering a train accident. List the questions you would want to have answered before writing your article.*

Grammar Link to the Bellringer
Have students exchange their lists with a partner and point out any grammatical errors they find.

Motivating Activity

To emphasize the importance of getting the facts for a news story, decide on a news story to use in class. Ask students what they remember about the event from the news or from what other people have said. List the pieces of information on the board. Then display an actual newspaper story about the event. (An opaque projector works well here.) Compare the information on the board with that in the story. Which is more complete? Which details are verifiable? Would the students' information constitute a good news story?

LESSON
4.6

Narrative Writing
Writing a News Story

News stories, which record history as it happens, can become a resource for future historians. Strong news stories, such as the one below, answer these questions: What happened? When? Where? Who was involved? How did it happen? Why was the event important?

Collaborating on Computers

Computer Museum consults Martin Luther King Jr. Middle School students in developing new exhibit

By Teresa A. Martin
SPECIAL TO THE GLOBE

When the Computer Museum designed its new 3,600-square-foot, $1 million personal computer exhibit, it looked for inspiration in many places, including an eighth-grade class at the Martin Luther King Jr. Middle School in Dorchester, Massachusetts.

The collaboration was so successful that the museum is making such arrangements part of the development of all future exhibits.

"One of the things you often see is lip service to consulting with schools," said Greg Welch, director of exhibits at the museum. "But for us this was a concerted effort to find out their needs."

The exhibit in question, which opened last month and will be permanent, is called "Tools and Toys: The Amazing Personal Computer."

168 *Narrative Writing: Bringing History to Life*

Teacher's Classroom Resources

The following resources can be used for planning, instruction, practice, reinforcement, assessment, reteaching, enrichment, or evaluation.

Teaching Tools
Lesson Plans, p. 37

Transparencies
Fine Art Transparencies, 16–20
Writing Process Transparencies, 14–16B

Tell the Five Ws and an H

News writers try to answer all or most of these questions—*who? what? when? where? why?* and *how?*—in their lead, or opening. How many of the basic questions—five Ws and an H—are answered in each lead below?

FLORIDA BRACES FOR HURRICANE ANDREW
Associated Press

MIAMI–Hurricane Andrew surged relentlessly toward southern Florida Sunday, and forecasters warned it would be the most powerful storm to hit the United States in decades. More than 1 million residents were told to flee.

A SUMMER SEARCH
BY MARK FERENCHIK
Repository staff writer

LAKE TWP.–What did teacher Pete Esterle do for his summer vacation? He went slogging through a south Florida swamp, in search of an airplane wreck apparently undisturbed for about 50 years. Esterle, an art teacher at Lake High School, and his brother found it earlier this month.

RUNAWAY CHIMP FINDS UNWILLING PLAYMATE
NewYork Times News Service

INMAN, S.C.–A 78-year-old woman hanging sheets on a clothesline Monday became the unsuspecting playmate of a rambunctious chimpanzee that, along with two companions, escaped from nearby Hollywild Animal Park.

Some leads present only the basic facts; the details come later in the story. Other leads open with a question or an intriguing detail designed to get readers' attention. Which of the leads above opens with an attention grabber?

Journal Writing

Many things happen in a school day. Think about what happened yesterday, and choose one newsworthy event. Write answers to the five Ws and an H.

Grammar
Revising Tip

When you revise, use possessive pronouns where appropriate. For more information about possessive pronouns, see Lesson 11.4, page 408.

4.6 Writing a News Story **169**

📁 **Blackline Masters**
Thinking and Study Skills, pp. 4, 9, 13
Writing Across the Curriculum, p. 14
Cooperative Learning Activities, pp. 19–24
Speaking and Listening Activities, pp. 12, 21

Composition Practice, p. 30
Composition Reteaching, p. 30
Composition Enrichment, p. 30

Assessment
📁 *Teacher's Guide to Writing Assessment*

TEACH

Guided Practice

L2 Using the Model
Have a volunteer read aloud the headline from the model on page 168, including the subhead, and tell what information is given. Explain that the model is the beginning, or lead, for the story; the whole story provides much more information. Because this is a news story, however, the lead contains the essential information. Ask how students answered the questions in the paragraph at the top of the page. Should any additional information have been included?

L1 Identifying Five Ws and H
Have students create a chart to help them identify the five Ws and the H of news leads. Have them write, at the top of a sheet of paper, the headline of one of the news stories on page 169. Then, down the left margin, have them write the categories *Who? What? When? Where? Why?* and *How?* leaving about three vertical lines of space after each one. Have students fill in the chart with the answers to the questions, pointing out that not every lead answers all six questions.

 **Two-Minute Skill Drill**

Ask students to revise their Bellringer list of questions about the train accident to include the five Ws and H, if they did not include them all.

Journal Writing Tip

Recalling Events You may want to give students the option of recalling any school day they remember well, not necessarily yesterday.

TEACH

Guided Practice

L2 Using the Model

In discussing the Greenspan model, make sure students understand that today there are no longer "good guys" and "bad guys" because the USSR and the German Democratic Republic no longer exist and the Cold War is over. Clarify the meaning of the term *Olympic ideal* by having students answer the question about the photo. (*You'd cheer for the best athlete, no matter which country he or she represented.*)

L2 Cooperative Learning

To highlight the function of leads, have students work in pairs to identify the ideas presented in the model that they think will be expanded on in the rest of the article. Make sure they identify such ideas as the *Olympic ideal, good guys* and *bad guys,* and the end of *East-West rivalry.* Partners can share their lists with the rest of the class.

Independent Practice

For further stimuli for narrative writing, see *Fine Art Transparencies* 16–20.

Writing Process Transparencies 14–16B

Writing Across the Curriculum, p. 14

Cooperative Learning Activities, pp. 19–24

Skills Practice

Thinking and Study Skills, pp. 4, 9, 13

Speaking and Listening Activities, pp. 12, 21,

Composition Practice, p. 30

Go into Detail

In investigating a topic for a story, news reporters gather all the information they can. Then, after writing the lead, they bring their story to life with details they gathered. Read the opening section of this news story.

Literature Model

The national anthems played most often four years ago in Seoul—those of the USSR and the German Democratic Republic (GDR)—will be noticeably missing during the 25th Olympic Games that begin today. Now, the USSR and GDR no longer exist, and neither does the intense East-West rivalry that has marked the Games during the Cold War era.

This will be the first Olympics in decades with no "good guys" or "bad guys," and that could make these Games the most refreshing in recent memory—approaching the Olympic ideal of spectators cheering for the best athletes regardless of the country they represent.

Bud Greenspan, *Parade*

According to Bud Greenspan, why are there no "good guys" or "bad guys" in this Olympics?

Be sure to include details in your news story. Cover all sides of the story. Save your opinions for a letter to the editor. Finally, check the accuracy of your facts and the spelling of names.

If you were in this audience, how could you exemplify the "Olympic ideal"?

170   *Narrative Writing: Bringing History to Life*

Enabling Strategies

LEP Understanding the Five Ws and H

Pair students who are learning English with students proficient in English. Have them work together to review the leads from newspaper articles about major news events. Have students more proficient in English help others to explain the definitions of *who? what? when? where? why?* and *how?* in English. Then, as partners read the news articles, have the students try, with help as needed, to highlight or circle the information that answers the five *Ws* and *H.*

4.6 Writing Activities

Write a News Story

Write a news story about an important event in your school, such as a prom, football game, or band concert. Create a lead incorporating the 5Ws and an H. Make your lead grab the readers' attention. Also, write two paragraphs for the story, including important details about the event. A cluster diagram may be helpful in organizing your story.

- Include vivid language and specific details to make your story interesting.
- Cover all aspects of the event in your story.
- Make sure your story is based on fact, not opinion.
- Make sure your readers are well informed about the event.

PURPOSE   To create a lead and details for a news story
AUDIENCE   Readers of your school newspaper
LENGTH   2–3 paragraphs

COMPUTER OPTION

Most word-processing software allows you to print text in parallel columns as in a newspaper. Find out how to set up the format line for this option, and print out your story in newspaper format.

Grammar Link

Avoid double comparisons.

To form the comparative and superlative of modifiers of one syllable and some with two syllables, add the suffixes *-er* and *-est*. For most modifiers of two or more syllables, use the words *more* and *most*. Never use both techniques with the same modifier.

Esterle . . . and his brother found it **earlier** *this month.*
. . . forecasters warned it would be the **most powerful** *storm. . . .*

Write each sentence below, eliminating double comparisons.

1. Charlie Spradley was the most fastest sprinter in school.
2. He captured a more greater number of all-state titles than his brother.
3. Kate Shoemaker played more better tennis than ever before.
4. Nonetheless, she lost the match in straight sets to Shalewa Bigham, the most youngest player on the other team.
5. The audience applauded Kate's performance more longer than Shalewa's.

See Lesson 12.3, page 428, and Lesson 12.6, page 434.

4.6 Writing a News Story **171**

ASSESS

Writing Activities Evaluation Guidelines

Write a News Story
Use these criteria to evaluate your students' writing.
- The lead names the event and answers the five *Ws* and *H*.
- The lead is attention-grabbing.
- Detail paragraphs help bring the story to life.
- The writing is grammatically accurate.

See also the *Teacher's Guide to Writing Assessment*.

Computer Option
Discuss with students the benefits of printing news stories in parallel-column newspaper format.

Grammar Link
(See Using the Grammar Link below.)

Reteaching
📁 *Composition Reteaching*, p. 30

Enrichment
📁 *Composition Enrichment*, p. 30

CLOSE

Ask volunteers to read their news stories aloud while the rest of the class uses a checklist to see if the five *Ws* and *H* have been covered in each story. Also, discuss the strengths of the stories and the details that make them most effective.

Using the Grammar Link

Grammar Link Answers
1. Charlie Spradley was the fastest sprinter in McCullough Middle School.
2. He captured a greater number of all-state titles than his brother.
3. Kate Shoemaker played better tennis than ever before.
4. Nonetheless, she lost the match in straight sets to Shalewa Bigham, the youngest player on the other team.
5. The audience applauded Kate's performance longer than Shalewa's.

Setting the Purpose

Lesson 4.7 teaches students various ways to respond to their reading of historical fiction.

FOCUS

Lesson Overview

Objective: To respond to a historical narrative with one's own thoughts and feelings as well as with facts from the story

Skills: responding to literature; expressing thoughts and feelings; relating to others' experiences

Critical Thinking: synthesizing; contrasting; summarizing; comparing; making inferences; building background; visualizing; identifying

Speaking and Listening: discussing

Bellringer

When students enter the classroom, have this assignment on the board: *After watching a movie or reading a good book, do you like to talk about it with others? Write down why or why not.*

Grammar Link to the Bellringer

Ask students to check their answers to the Bellringer for the use of adjective clauses. Ask students who find them whether they used commas to set off nonessential adjective clauses.

Motivating Activity

Invite volunteers to name a novel or nonfiction narrative that moved them deeply. Encourage students to identify specific events or characters that impressed them and share what they felt and why. Discuss how a positive response could play a role in deciding whether to read another book by the same author.

LESSON

4.7

Writing About Literature
Responding to a Historical Narrative

The excerpt below is a young Jewish girl's firsthand account of Nazi Germany.

Anne Frank was born to a Jewish German family in 1929. The family went to the Netherlands to escape the Nazis but later went into hiding, when Anne was thirteen. In a secret room of an Amsterdam building, she wrote letters in a diary, named Kitty. After more than three years, the Nazis found the Frank family; Anne died in a concentration camp.

Literature Model

Wednesday, 29 March, 1944

Dear Kitty,

Bolkestein, an M.P. [Member of Parliament], was speaking on the Dutch News from London, and he said that they ought to make a collection of diaries and letters after the war. Of course, they all [Anne's family and the others in hiding with them] made a rush at my diary immediately. Just imagine how interesting it would be if I were to publish a romance of the "Secret Annexe." The title alone would be enough to make people think it was a detective story.

But, seriously, it would seem quite funny ten years after the war if we Jews were to tell how we lived and what we ate and talked about here. Although I tell you a lot, still, even so, you only know very little of our lives.

Anne Frank: *The Diary of a Young Girl*

Writer's Choice
172 - 187

ces

Transparencies
Fine Art Transparencies, 16–20
Writing Process Transparencies, 14–16B

Respond to Historical Events

Anne Frank's diary offers stark glimpses into wartime reality. Johanna Yngvason responded to Anne's diary by describing the terror of living in hiding. She focused on how historic events affected ordinary people, such as Anne Frank and her family.

> ### Student Model
>
> H ide! Hide! The Nazis are invading!" This was a terrifying sound heard by many Jews, many times, and caused them to go into hiding. A small closet became a bedroom, an attic became a home. . . . The Jews were rounded up like cattle and shipped off to concentration camps such as Auschwitz and Bergen-Belsen, where the majority of them died.
>
> Such a fate befell young Anne Frank. . . . The only surviving member of the party, Anne's beloved father, returned to the dusty attic after the war. There in the rubble was the diary, which he later published. . . . Although Anne didn't survive the Holocaust, her thoughts and memories live on.
>
> Johanna Yngvason, Canyon Park Junior High School,
> Bothell, Washington

Johanna reflects Anne's dread when she uses the word "terrifying."

What does this sentence reveal about Johanna's feelings?

Follow Johanna's example when you respond in writing to a nonfiction narrative. Tell what happened, but add your own thoughts and feelings.

Vocabulary
Revising Tip

As you revise, a thesaurus can help you locate just the right words to express your thoughts and feelings about a nonfiction historical narrative.

Journal Writing

Take a few moments to think about a narrative story that moved you. How did it make you feel? Write some words and phrases that best express your feelings.

4.7 Responding to a Historical Narrative **173**

TEACH

Guided Practice

L2 Using the Literature Model
Ask what students already know about *The Diary of a Young Girl*—either the book or the play based on it—including the historical background. Discuss any prior knowledge about Hitler and the Nazis in World War II Germany. Stress that, although Anne Frank and her family lived in daily fear of discovery, Anne could still write with amusement about her life. Invite the class to respond with personal feelings about Anne's diary entry.

L2 Using the Student Model
Point out that students can express their feelings about a piece of literature in several ways. The most obvious way is to state directly how they feel. Another way is illustrated in Johanna Yngvason's response.

Johanna doesn't name her feelings, but the reader understands them from her word choices and the details she includes. Have students identify words and phrases that convey Johanna's feelings. (Include the opening quotation and words such as *terrifying, such a fate,* and *the only surviving member of the party.*)

Journal Writing Tip

Synthesizing Remind students that the words and phrases they note in their journals might be words from the narrative they've chosen or words that occur to them as they sort out their feelings about the literature.

173

TEACH

Guided Practice

L2 Using the Model

Ask students to contrast Amy Groat's response to *Farewell to Manzanar* with a book report on that book. Help students to see that one important difference is that Amy Groat focuses on a single element of the book—a character whose story involves struggles familiar to most teenagers. Students might also mention that Amy uses words that reveal her sympathy for the main character—words such as *bombarded, discrimination, traumas, cultural gap,* and *generation gap.*

Two-Minute Skill Drill

Ask students to list three words they might use to express the following emotions:

sorrow	anger
joy	amazement

Independent Practice

For further stimuli for narrative writing, see *Fine Art Transparencies* 16–20.

Writing Process Transparencies, 14–16B

Writing Across the Curriculum, p. 14

Cooperative Learning Activities, pp. 19–24

Skills Practice

Thinking and Study Skills, pp. 5, 6, 22

Speaking and Listening Activities, pp. 12, 21

Composition Practice, p. 31

Respond to People Behind the Events

Amy Groat read and wrote about *Farewell to Manzanar.* This nonfiction narrative tells the story of Jeanne Wakatsuki, interned with her family in a wartime relocation camp for Asian Americans. Read it and see how Amy sympathizes with Jeanne.

Student Model

Farewell to Manzanar deals with a mixture of problems that bombarded the internees in the camp Manzanar. The minorities of today deal with the same discrimination but in a subtler form. By reading and discussing this book, eighth-graders in our district will have a better understanding of the events and traumas that rocked Japanese Americans during World War II. . . .

When the Wakatsuki family reentered the "real world," Jeanne faced a cultural gap between herself and her classmates. She wanted desperately to fit in but was discriminated against because of her ethnic background. She eventually was able to blend in with her classmates by joining after-school activities, but she was never able to deal with the generation gap in her family.

Amy Groat, Oak Creek Ranch School, Cornville, Arizona

> *Amy shows how important the book was to her by suggesting that everyone in the district should read it.*

> *Which words and expressions reveal Amy's sympathy for Jeanne Wakatsuki?*

One way of responding to a historical narrative—fiction or nonfiction—is to show how a character is like you. In reading *Farewell to Manzanar,* Amy discovered how the people from another time and place were like her.

174 *Narrative Writing: Bringing History to Life*

Enabling Strategies

LEP Organizing Responses

If students feel overwhelmed by the limited number of English words they know for expressing feelings and thoughts, help them organize their responses to make the task more approachable. They might answer a list of questions such as:

- What is the problem, and how does the main character try to solve the problem?
- How do I feel about what happens?
- What would I have done in the same situation?

4.7 Writing Activities

Responding to a Spoken Narrative

One type of narration is storytelling. Talk to a person who has survived a war. Have him or her describe fears, thoughts, and emotions of that time.

Write a one-page response. Tell how the survival story made you feel.

• Use precise language to describe your feelings about the story.
• Make sure your response addresses how the event affected his or her life.

PURPOSE To respond to a spoken narrative
AUDIENCE Your teacher and classmates
LENGTH 1 page

Diego Rivera, *Flower Vendor,* 1949

Cross-Curricular: History

The painting on this page shows women and children preparing to sell flowers in Mexico. Mexican peasants who gathered flowers often worked long hours in difficult conditions. Jot down ideas for a historical narrative about these workers. Then write a 3–4 paragraph narrative about them.

Grammar Link

Use commas to set off nonessential adjective clauses, but not ones that are essential to meaning.

There in the rubble was the diary, which he later published....

... the problems that bombarded the internees in the camp Manzanar.

Write the paragraph, using commas as needed.

In *The Road from Home* David Kherdian tells the story of his mother who grew up in the Armenian quarter of a Turkish town. Conflict raged in Turkey which was part of the Ottoman Empire. The Armenians who were often targeted by the Turks suffered terribly. Kherdian re-creates the tension that mounted in 1914 and 1915.

See Lesson 20.3, page 570.

4.7 Responding to a Historical Narrative **175**

Using the Grammar Link

Grammar Link Answers
In *The Road from Home* David Kherdian tells the story of his mother, who grew up ... Conflict raged in Turkey, which ... The Armenians, who were often targeted by the Turks, suffered terribly. Kherdian re-creates the tension that mounted in 1914 and 1915.

About the Art

Diego Rivera, *Flower Vendor,* 1949
Diego Rivera (1886–1957) is known for large, colorful murals that show activities and events in Mexican life. This piece, *Flower Vendor,* a 6-by-5-foot oil painting, is in the Museo Nacional, Centro de Arte, in Madrid, Spain.

ASSESS

Writing Activities Evaluation Guidelines

Write a Narrative
Use these criteria when evaluating your students' writing.
• The narrative conveys the writer's personal feelings about the war.
• The narrative describes how everyday actions are influenced by the nearby battle.

See also the *Teacher's Guide to Writing Assessment.*

Cross-Curricular: History
In addition to identifying the characters, setting, and situation, look for evidence that students have relied on some personal experience they have had—working on a shared task with family members, working when tired, gathering flowers, or feeling uncomfortable under the hot sun, for example.

Grammar Link
(See Using the Grammar Link below.)

Reteaching
📁 *Composition Reteaching,* p. 31

Enrichment
📁 *Composition Enrichment,* p. 31

✎ Use *Fine Art Transparencies* 16–20 for enrichment activities also.

CLOSE

Discuss other formats for responding to historical narratives, such as poetry or art. Additional historical narratives to suggest are *Oma* by Peter Hartling, *West Coast Chinese Boy* by Sing Lim, *Mukasa* by John Nagenda, and *The Alfred Summer* by Jan Slepian.

175

UNIT 4
WRITING PROCESS IN ACTION
NARRATIVE WRITING

Setting the Purpose

Students now have the opportunity to apply what they have learned about narrative writing to an independent writing project. They will use the stages of the writing process to create and present a finished piece.

FOCUS

Lesson Overview

Objective: To compose a historical narrative about a character whose life is important to the writer

Skills: Using the five stages of the writing process: prewriting, drafting, revising, editing, and presenting

Critical Thinking: building background; generating new information; using graphics as organizers

Speaking and Listening: discussing; evaluating

Bellringer

When students enter the classroom, have this assignment on the board: *Write and complete the following sentence: I would like to learn more about some people from history, including _____ and _____, because _____ .*

Grammar Link to the Bellringer

Have students exchange Bellringer answers with a partner and check capitalization.

Motivating Activity

Ask students to write questions they have about the people from history they named in the Bellringer. Remind them that writers research their topic to answer such questions. Note that the assignment permits either fiction or nonfiction writing, and students should decide which their piece will be.

In preceding lessons you've learned how time order, point of view, realistic details, and dialogue can make a historical narrative come to life. You've also had a chance to write narratives about people, places, and events in history. Now, in this lesson, you're invited to write a historical narrative about one of your ancestors or someone else whose life interests you.

• Assignment •

Context	You are going to write a historical narrative about an ancestor or someone else whose life is important to you. Although you may find facts about this person, you'll have to invent some likely—and lively—details about speech, actions, and attitudes.
Purpose	To make the past come alive in a historical narrative
Audience	Your family or friends
Length	4–5 paragraphs

The following pages can help you plan and write your historical narrative. Read through the pages, and then refer to them as you need to. Don't be tied down by them, however. You're in charge of your own writing process.

Teacher's Classroom Resources

The following resources can be used for planning, instruction, practice, reinforcement, assessment, reteaching, enrichment, or evaluation.

Teaching Tools
Lesson Plans, p. 39

Transparencies
Writing Process Transparencies, 14–16B

Prewriting

Is there a person in history whose life fascinates you? Would you like to know more about how an ancestor came to this country?

- Begin exploring ideas about an ancestor's life by interviewing relatives.
- Refer to old photo albums for pictures of where people lived, played, and worked in those days and to letters, diaries, and family records. Jot down notes and ideas in your journal. Begin thinking about where you might begin and end your narrative. Make a list of events, or simply begin writing where it feels right.

Option A
Interview people, look at photos, read letters.

Option B
Read about the period.

Option C
Jot down notes about a turning point in the story.

Krista given money on her eighteenth birthday. Not much—the farm in Denmark was too poor. Older children used money to move to the city to find work. Krista wanted to go to America.

Drafting

As you draft your historical narrative, include details to make the life of your subject real. Notice the details Katherine Paterson uses to portray a nineteenth-century factory.

Literature Model

Within five minutes, her head felt like a log being split to splinters. She kept shaking it, as though she could rid it of the noise, or at least the pain, but both only seemed to grow more intense. If that weren't trial enough, a few hours of standing in her proud new boots and her feet had swollen so that the laces cut into her flesh.

Katherine Paterson, *Lyddie*

Writing Process in Action **177**

TEACH

Prewriting

L2 Using Graphics in Writing
Point out the options on page 177, and have students note how their narratives can grow out of research they've done. Options A and B will yield facts about a person, event, or setting. Option C shows how these begin to turn into a story idea, including a problem and solution.

Suggest that students create graphics in their journals to help them develop and organize their narratives. Remind them that in addition to characters and settings, narratives must have

- a conflict or problem
- efforts to solve the conflict or problem
- an outcome showing how the problem is or is not solved

L3 Researching Genealogy
Students might enjoy research in genealogy. In many places the main library has records and facilities for genealogical research. Some cities, towns, and counties have staffed historical societies where records are kept. Remind students that the best sources for information on their genealogy are likely to be older family members.

Drafting

L2 Using the Model
Ask students to identify the details that make this narrative seem so real. Urge them to use such details as they write their draft.

L2 Using a Time Line
Remind students that a simple time line can prove helpful in keeping the chronological order straight as they write their drafts.

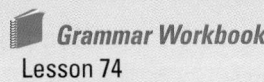 **Blackline Masters**
Thinking and Study Skills,
  pp. 3, 5, 9, 17, 22–24, 35–36
Composition Practice, p. 32
Composition Reteaching, p. 32
Composition Enrichment, p. 32

Grammar Workbook
Lesson 74

Assessment
Teacher's Guide to Writing Assessment

TEACH

Revising

L2 Peer Editing

Students can work in writing conferences with peer editors before they revise their writing. You may want to duplicate the Peer Response forms in the *Teacher's Guide to Writing Assessment.* Suggest that peer editors respond to the following questions:
- Is the chronology of the story clear?
- What details most captured your attention? Why?

Editing

L2 Peer Editing

After students have edited their own work, have them edit another student's writing. Remind them to refer to the Editing Checklist on page 179.

Presenting

Before students present their narrative writing, discuss how to prepare their papers for publication. Emphasize the importance of the final draft and that it must be neatly done.

Independent Practice

 *Writing Process Transparencies,* pp. 18–22

Skills Practice

📁 *Thinking and Study Skills,* pp. 3, 5, 9, 17, 22–24, 35–36
📁 *Composition Practice,* p. 32

📕 *Grammar Workbook,* Lesson 74

Journal Writing Tip

Talking It Over Suggest that students discuss answers with each other before writing them down. This will help to make answers more specific.

WRITING PROCESS IN ACTION

Drafting Tip

For a reminder about chronological order, review pages 152–155.

When drafting your historical narrative, use details that put your readers in the subject's shoes by making them feel part of the events and surroundings. Instead of simply saying, "the factory was noisy," or "Lyddie's feet hurt," Paterson takes her readers back to the mill to see her character and to feel her pain.

If you get stuck while drafting, look again at your prewriting notes for fresh ideas.

Revising

To begin revising, read over your draft to make sure that what you've written fits your purpose and audience. Then have a writing conference. Read your draft to a partner or small group. Use your audience's reactions to help you evaluate your work so far. The following questions can help you and your listeners.

Question A
Does every sentence contribute to my narrative?

Question B
Have I used specific details?

Question C
Have I established a clear point of view?

> Krista's feet were bleeding by the time she
> walked the nine miles from the station to the
> farm where she was to work. She wished she had
> heavy boots, instead of her Sunday
> brought old shoes instead of her best shoes, with
> to America.
> her This farm was bigger than the one she had
> left behind in Denmark. As she thought of the
> scrubbing, mending, and cooking
> hours of hard work that faced her, she became
> her heart sank.
> sad.

Enrichment and Extension

Follow-up Ideas
- Set aside a time for students to celebrate the conclusion of their writing projects.
- Consider class publication. Students' narrative writing can be collected, illustrated, bound, and placed in the school library.

Extending Narratives
- Brainstorm with students ways they can apply their expertise in narrative writing to other historical times.
- To spark additional writing ideas, ask students to invite older relatives and friends to share oral narrative histories with the class.

Editing

You've worked hard to figure out what you want to say and how to say it well. Since you'll be sharing this with your family or friends, you'll want them to pay attention to the story, not to any errors you might have made. During the editing stage, you'll want to **proofread** your work and eliminate mistakes that might detract from the ideas and feelings you want to share.

This checklist will help you catch errors you might otherwise overlook.

Editing Checklist

1. *Have I correctly punctuated appositives and adjective clauses?*
2. *Have I eliminated any double comparisons?*
3. *Do my verbs agree with their subjects?*
4. *Have I used standard spelling and capitalization?*

Presenting

You may wish to include a photograph or a drawing of your subject in your historical narrative. Pictures of a house or the city your subject lived in and of clothing or vehicles from your subject's era will also add interest to your narrative. If your computer software prints some old-fashioned type styles, they can also add a feeling of historical accuracy to your narrative.

Proofreading

For proofreading symbols, see page 81.

Journal Writing

Reflect on your writing process experience. Answer these questions in your journal: What do you like best about your narrative writing? What was the hardest part of writing it? What did you learn in your writing conference? What new things have you learned as a writer?

Writing Process in Action **179**

ASSESS

Evaluation Guidelines
Use the following criteria to evaluate students' finished writing.
- The narrative is based on family or other history.
- The facts are drawn from research.
- It is a story that uses the facts of history and adds descriptive details. Every detail makes a contribution.
- The story line fits the characters and setting.
- There is evidence of careful editing for grammar, spelling, and mechanics.

Refer to the *Teacher's Guide to Writing Assessment* for further help with evaluating student writing.

Reteaching
Composition Reteaching, p. 32

Enrichment
Composition Enrichment, p. 32

CLOSE

Ask volunteers to read their historical narratives to the class. Allow time for discussion about the writing strategies that make these stories interesting.

Setting the Purpose

In the Unit 4 Literature Model students read a literature passage that illustrates in a very real way effective narrative writing. Such readings serve as models for students as they create their own narrative writing.

About the Author

Katherine Paterson was born in China, where her father was a Christian missionary. This experience has inspired her to create characters who represent various cultural backgrounds. Although she treats her characters with sensitivity, Paterson doesn't usually place them in settings of great natural beauty. Instead, she tends to surround them with the gritty, realistic details of daily life.

Besides *Lyddie*, students might enjoy Paterson's award-winning historical novel *Jacob Have I Loved*.

FOCUS

Lesson Overview

Objective: To examine and appreciate how a professional writer uses the elements of narrative in a work of historical fiction
Skills: reading comprehension
Critical Thinking: comparing; contrasting; analyzing; visualizing; making inferences
Speaking and Listening: discussing

 **Bellringer**
When students enter the classroom, have this assignment on the board: *Write about an important first in your life, such as your first day in middle school.*

Motivating Activity

Invite students to read their "firsts" to the class.

180

Narrative Writing
Literature Model

Katherine Paterson
from

LYDDIE

In the mid-1800s the hope for a better life prompted many to join the ranks of factory laborers. Katherine Paterson's historical narrative relates how thirteen-year-old Lydia Worthen travels to Lowell, Massachusetts, seeking mill work and the chance for a new life. As you read, pay special attention to how Paterson tells Lydia's story. Then try the activities in Linking Writing and Literature on page 187.

The four-thirty bell clanged the house awake. From every direction, Lyddie could hear the shrill voices of girls calling to one another, even singing. Someone on another floor was imitating a rooster. From the other side of the bed Betsy groaned and turned over, but Lyddie was up, dressing quickly in the dark as she had always done in the windowless attic of the inn.

Her stomach rumbled, but she ignored it. There would be no breakfast until seven, and that was two and a half hours

---

Teacher's Classroom Resources

The following resources can be used for planning, instruction, or practice.

🔧 **Teaching Tools**
Lesson Plans, p. 40

📇 **Transparencies**
Fine Art Transparencies, 16–20

📁 **Blackline Masters**
Speaking and Listening Activities, pp. 12, 24
Thinking and Study Skills, pp. 6, 9, 13, 35–36

Assessment

📁 *Teacher's Guide to Writing Assessment*

away. By five the girls had crowded through the main gate, jostled their way up the outside staircase on the far end of the mill, cleaned their machines, and stood waiting for the workday to begin.

"Not too tired this morning?" Diana asked by way of greeting.

Lyddie shook her head. Her feet were sore, but she'd felt tireder after a day behind the plow.

"Good. Today will be something more strenuous, I fear. We'll work all three looms together, all right? Until you feel quite sure of everything."

Lyddie felt a bit as though the older girls were whispering in church. It seemed almost that quiet in the great loom room. The only real noise was the creaking from the ceiling of the leather belts that connected the wheels in the weaving room to the gigantic waterwheel in the basement.

Constantin Meunier, *In the Black Country*, c. 1860–80

Literature Model **181**

TEACH

L2 Guided Reading

- What information is given about Lyddie's workday schedule on pages 180 and 181? (*She gets up at four-thirty, but she doesn't get breakfast until seven; she's at the factory by five.*)
- What personal background information about Lyddie is given on pages 180 and 181? (*Lyddie used to live in an inn and had a room in the attic; she used to work on a farm, and she is younger than some of the other girls at the factory.*)

About the Art

Constantin Meunier, *In the Black Country*, c. 1860–80

Although Belgian artist Constantin Meunier (1831–1905) was known mainly as a sculptor, for a time he created paintings, including the one shown on this page. In both media, the artist demonstrates his deep sympathy for laborers who suffered long hours and backbreaking work for low wages in the hot, smoky mills and factories. *In the Black Country*, 31 3/5 by 36 7/8 inches, is in the Musée d'Orsay in Paris, France.

UNIT 4
Literature Model

TEACH

L2 Guided Reading

- Is this story told from first- or third-person point of view? (*third-person*) How can you tell? (*It contains pronouns such as* he *and* she.)
- What details does the author include about the atmosphere inside the mill so that readers can visualize it and its effect on Lyddie? (*looms…shuddered and groaned, head felt like a log being split, feet had swollen, air…laden with moisture and debris, window was nailed shut, glass seemed hot*) What sensations do these details impart about conditions in the mill? (*It is hot and noisy. The air is thick.*)

The overseer came in, nodded good morning, and pushed a low wooden stool under a cord dangling from the assembly of wheels and belts above his head. His little red mouth pursed, he stepped up on the stool and pulled out his pocket watch. At the same moment, the bell in the tower above the roof began to ring. He yanked the cord, the wide leather belt above him shifted from a loose to a tight pulley, and suddenly all the hundred or so silent looms, in raucous[1] concert, shuddered and groaned into fearsome life. Lyddie's first full day as a factory girl had begun.

Within five minutes, her head felt like a log being split to splinters. She kept shaking it, as though she could rid it of the noise, or at least the pain, but both only seemed to grow more intense. If that weren't trial enough, a few hours of standing in her proud new boots and her feet had swollen so that the laces cut into her flesh. She bent down quickly to loosen them, and when she found the right lace was knotted, she burst into tears. Or perhaps the tears were caused by the swirling dust and lint.

Now that she thought of it, she could hardly breathe, the air was so laden with moisture and debris.[2] She snatched a moment to run to the window. She had to get air, but the window was nailed shut against the April morning. She leaned her forehead against it; even the glass seemed hot. Her apron brushed the pots of red geraniums crowding the wide sill. They were flourishing in this hot house. She coughed, trying to free her throat and lungs for breath.

Then she felt, rather than saw, Diana. "Mr. Marsden has his eye on you," the older girl said gently, and put her arm on Lyddie's shoulder to turn her back toward the looms. She pointed to the stalled loom and the broken warp[3] thread that must be tied. Even though Diana had stopped the loom, Lyddie stood rubbing the powder into her fingertips, hesitating to plunge her hands into the bowels of the machine. Diana urged her with a light touch.

I stared down a black bear, Lyddie reminded herself. She took a deep breath, fished out the broken ends, and began to tie

1 **raucous** (rôʹkəs) hoarse; rough-sounding
2 **debris** (də brēʹ) bits of rubbish; litter
3 **warp** (wôrp) threads running lengthwise in a loom

Genre and Style

Reading Narrative Fiction

This passage from the historical novel *Lyddie* narrates the story of a girl who leaves a farm to work in the city. The setting is a New England textile mill in the late 1800s, and Lyddie is a typical worker. Katherine Paterson describes Lyddie's work in all its harsh, exhausting detail. As students read on, they will encounter long sentences that are full of parallel phrases and clauses, echoing the endless, repetitious labor they describe.

Eyre Crowe, *The Dinner Hour, Wigan*, 1874

the weaver's knot that Diana had shown her over and over again the afternoon before. Finally, Lyddie managed to make a clumsy knot, and Diana pulled the lever, and the loom shuddered to life once more.

How could she ever get accustomed to this inferno?[4] Even when the girls were set free at 7:00, it was to push and shove their way across the bridge and down the street to their boardinghouses, bolt down their hearty breakfast, and rush back, stomachs still churning, for "ring in" at 7:35. Nearly half the mealtime was spent simply going up and down the staircase, across the mill yard and bridge, down the row of houses—just getting to and from the meal. And the din[5] in the dining room was nearly as loud as the racket in the mill—thirty young women chewing and calling at the same time, reaching for the platters of flapjacks and pitchers of syrup, ignoring cries from the other end of the table to pass anything.

4 inferno (in fur′nō) hell or any place suggesting hell
5 din (din) a loud, continuous noise

Literature Model **183**

TEACH

L2 Guided Reading

- How does the scene portrayed in the painting differ from the description of breakfast in the passage? (*In the painting women are eating, relaxing, reading, and visiting. In the passage, the girls race to their meal, eat hurriedly, then race back to the mill.*)
- How does Lyddie's workday compare to a modern workday? (*Lyddie works longer hours than people do today; she is not supposed to take breaks. Such terrible working conditions would be illegal today.*)

About the Art

Eyre Crowe, *The Dinner Hour, Wigan*, 1874

The scene in the painting is similar to one that is often seen in today's cities and factories. On pleasant days, workers stream outside for their lunch break, when they read, write, visit, eat, or simply enjoy the outdoors. Like the novel *Lyddie*, this painting suggests how people strive to make the best of adverse working and living conditions. The painting is oil on canvas, 30 by 42 inches, and is in the Manchester City Art Gallery in Manchester, England.

TEACH

L2 Guided Reading

- Why might a meal of bark soup seem like a feast compared to the boardinghouse meals? (*Though the food was meager, Lyddie could take her time, the room was quiet, and there weren't many people around.*)
- How is Lyddie feeling at this point? (*She feels completely exhausted and is only interested in getting to bed.*) Why might the other girls be eager to talk in the parlor, while Lyddie only wants to go to her room and rest? (*This is Lyddie's first day on the job. The others are used to the pace and and the noise, and are eager for conversation.*)

Philip Evergood, *Lily and the Sparrows*, 1939

Her quiet meals in the corner of the kitchen with Triphena, even her meager bowls of bark soup in the cabin with the seldom talkative Charlie, seemed like feasts compared to the huge, rushed, noisy affairs in Mrs. Bedlow's house. The half hour at noonday dinner with more food than she had ever had set before her at one time was worse than breakfast.

At last the evening bell rang, and Mr. Marsden pulled the cord to end the day. Diana walked with her to the place by the door where the girls hung their bonnets and shawls, and handed Lyddie hers. "Let's forget about studying those regulations tonight," she said. "It's been too long a day already."

Lyddie nodded. Yesterday seemed years in the past. She couldn't even remember why she'd thought the regulations important enough to bother with.

She had lost all appetite. The very smell of supper made her nauseous [6]—beans heavy with pork fat and brown injun bread with orange cheese, fried potatoes, of course, and flapjacks with apple sauce, baked Indian pudding with cream and plum cake for dessert. Lyddie nibbled at the brown bread and washed it down with a little scalding tea. How could the others eat so heartily and with such a clatter of dishes and shrieks of conversation? She longed only to get to the room, take off her boots, massage her abused feet, and lay down her aching head. While the other girls pulled their chairs from the table and scraped them about to form little circles in the parlor area, Lyddie dragged herself from the table and up the stairs.

---

6 nauseous (nô'shəs) feeling sickness in the stomach

About the Art

Philip Evergood, *Lily and the Sparrows*, 1939
Philip Evergood (1901–1973) blends two sides of his work in this painting. Deeply moved by the effects of the Great Depression, he created works that deal with real social issues while expressing joy and imagination. *Lily and the Sparrows*, 30 by 24 inches, is in the Whitney Museum of American Art in New York City.

Betsy was already there before her, her current novel in her hand. She laughed at the sight of Lyddie. "The first full day! And up to now you thought yourself a strapping country farm girl who could do anything, didn't you?"

Lyddie did not try to answer back. She simply sank to her side of the double bed and took off the offending shoes and began to rub her swollen feet.

"If you've got an older pair"—Betsy's voice was almost gentle—"more stretched and softer . . ."

Lyddie nodded. Tomorrow she'd wear Triphena's without the stuffing. They were still stiff from the trip and she'd be awkward rushing back and forth to meals, but at least there'd be room for her feet to swell.

She undressed, slipped on her shabby night shift, and slid under the quilt. Betsy glanced over at her. "To bed so soon?"

Lyddie could only nod again. It was as though she could not possibly squeeze a word through her lips. Betsy smiled again. She ain't laughing at me, Lyddie realized. She's remembering how it was.

"Shall I read to you?" Betsy asked.

Lyddie nodded gratefully and closed her eyes and turned her back against the candlelight.

Betsy did not give any explanation of the novel she was reading, simply commenced to read aloud where she had broken off reading to herself. Even though Lyddie's head was still choked with lint and battered with noise, she struggled to get the sense of the story.

The child was in some kind of poorhouse, it seemed, and he was hungry. Lyddie knew about hungry children. Rachel, Agnes, Charlie—they had all been hungry that winter of the bear. The hungry little boy in the story had held up his bowl to the poorhouse overseer and said:

"Please sir, I want some more."

And for this the overseer—she could see his little rosebud mouth rounded in horror—for this the overseer had screamed out at the child. In her mind's eye little Oliver Twist looked exactly like a younger Charlie. The cruel overseer had screamed and hauled the boy before a sort of agent. And for what crime? For the monstrous crime of wanting more to eat.

Literature Model **185**

TEACH

L2 Guided Reading
- Who might Betsy be, and why does she read to Lyddie? (Students may infer that Betsy is another girl who works in the factory.)
- How could Lyddie's head still be *choked with lint and battered with noise* even though she's no longer in the mill? (*The bad conditions in the mill are so overwhelming that she is not able to get them out of her mind.*)

Connections Across the Curriculum

History

During the Industrial Revolution, many people left farms and sought work in the cities. Most farmers had produced only the food their families needed plus a little to trade with. When crops failed, farm families suffered.

Many other families produced goods by hand, but when factories began producing low-priced goods, people stopped buying the handmade goods. As a result, incomes for those families suffered, too.

TEACH

L2 Guided Reading

- How does Lyddie's distaste for food contrast with the appetite she has for the novel? (*Meals are part of the unpleasantness of her day. The novel takes her outside herself and makes her forget her life.*)
- Why is Lyddie so moved by the story of Oliver? (*She feels its connections to her own life. Oliver makes her think of her brother Charlie, and she knows about being hungry.*)

Independent Practice

Fine Art Transparencies 16–20

Skills Practice

Speaking and Listening Activities, pp. 21, 24

Thinking and Study Skills, pp. 6, 9, 13, 35–36

"That boy will be hung," the agent had prophesied. "I know that boy will be hung."

She fought sleep, ravenous[7] for every word. She had not had any appetite for the bountiful meal downstairs, but now she was feeling a hunger she knew nothing about. She had to know what would happen to little Oliver. Would he indeed be hanged just because he wanted more gruel?

She opened her eyes and turned to watch Betsy, who was absorbed in her reading. Then Betsy sensed her watching, and looked up from the book. "It's a marvelous story, isn't it? I saw the author once—Mr. Charles Dickens. He visited our factory. Let me see—I was already in the spinning room—it must have been in—"

But Lyddie cared nothing for authors or dates. "Don't stop reading the story, please, " she croaked out.

"Never fear, little Lyddie. No more interruptions," Betsy promised, and read on, though her voice grew raspy with fatigue, until the bell rang for curfew. She stuck a hair ribbon in the place. "Till tomorrow night," she whispered as the feet of an army of girls could be heard thundering up the staircase.

7 ravenous (rav′ə nəs) greedy

186 *Narrative Writing: Bringing History to Life*

Writers and Writing

Using Dialect

Many changes in word choices, grammar, and pronunciation have taken place since the 1800s. However, Paterson, like many writers of historical fiction, doesn't attempt to imitate the dialect of an earlier era, in pronunciation or word choice. Dialect would be hard to reproduce accurately and even harder to read. More important, its use might distract from Paterson's purpose—to tell a good story.

Linking Writing and Literature
Readers Respond to the Model

What makes Katherine Paterson's narrative come to life?

Explore Katherine Paterson's historical narrative by answering these questions. Then read what other students liked about her narrative.

1. Katherine Paterson's narrative tells the story of a young girl's experience in a factory during the nineteenth century. How does the opening paragraph draw the reader into the story?

2. From anywhere in the selection, choose a paragraph that is particu-larly realistic in creating the setting. What specific details make this setting realistic?

3. *I stared down a black bear, Lyddie reminded herself.* What does this line reveal about Lyddie's character? How does the line help the reader to identify with Lyddie?

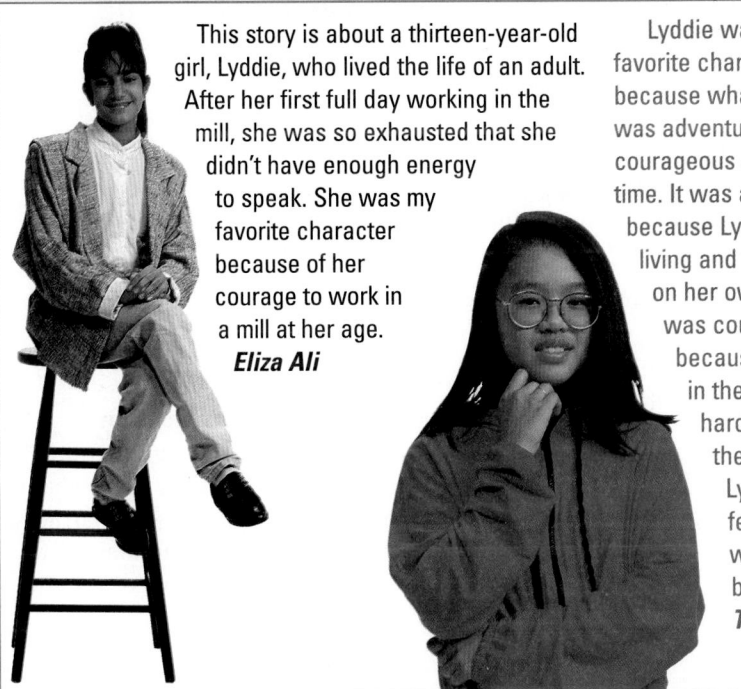

This story is about a thirteen-year-old girl, Lyddie, who lived the life of an adult. After her first full day working in the mill, she was so exhausted that she didn't have enough energy to speak. She was my favorite character because of her courage to work in a mill at her age.
Eliza Ali

Lyddie was my favorite character because what she did was adventurous and courageous at the same time. It was adventurous because Lyddie was living and working on her own. It was courageous because her job in the mill was hard. I liked the fact that Lyddie got to feel what it was like to be an adult.
Trina Cbu

Literature Model **187**

ASSESS

Evaluation Guidelines for Discussion

As your students discuss the selection, either in small groups or as a class, encourage them to begin with a personal response. The student responses on this page might be used as a starting point.

Look for evidence that students
• have read the selection
• can state some of the writer's ideas in their own words
• understand the writer's point of view
• have connected the content to their own knowledge and experiences
• understand the ideas and implications of the selection

Some possible responses to the discussion questions on this page:

1. In the opening paragraph, realistic details about the setting and characters, such as the 4:30 A.M. bell and the young girl imitating a rooster, draw the reader into the story.

2. The paragraph in which Lyddie looks out the nailed-down window, hoping for air, is particularly effective in helping readers get a sense of the stifling conditions of the mill.

3. This line reveals courage and self-reliance. We are able to identify with Lyddie because we have all had to find courage in frightening times by reminding ourselves of past moments of courage.

CLOSE

Enrichment and Extension

Listening and Responding
Have students listen to a recording of a part of *Oliver Twist*—any part that might give them a feel for the era. Alternatively, show the video of the movie *Oliver Twist*. As a response some students might make a diptych (a two-part picture) showing Oliver Twist on one side and Lyddie on the other, each in a typical setting. Exhibit the students' artwork and ask them to explain it to the class.

Invite students to discuss one of the following questions:
• How do you think Lyddie's story will turn out? Why?
• How can books make a difference in a person's life?

REVIEW

Reflecting on the Unit

You may have students respond to Reflecting on the Unit in writing or through discussion.

Writing Across the Curriculum

Before they begin writing, encourage students to order their events chronologically and to select and use appropriate transitions.

Adding to Your Portfolio

Ask students to choose their best narrative that integrates a real historical background with fictional characters and events. Suggest that they ask themselves the following questions:

- Which narrative did I most enjoy writing?
- Which piece is the most successful?
- Which piece best shows my ability to fulfill the objectives of the assignment?

Portfolio Evaluation

If you grade the portfolio selections, you may want to award two marks—one each for content and form. Explain your assessment criteria before students make their selections. Commend

- experimentation with creative prewriting techniques
- clear, concise writing in which the main idea, audience, and purpose are evident
- successful revisions
- work that shows a flair for language

Unit 4 Review

 **Reflecting on the Unit**

Summarize what you learned in this unit by answering the following questions.

- What is a narrative?
- Where can you get ideas for historical narratives?
- Why is the use of chronological order helpful?
- From what points of view can a narrative be told?
- How does dialogue help to enrich a narrative?
- On what facts do news stories focus?

 **Adding to Your Portfolio**

Choose a selection for your portfolio. Look over the narrative writing you did for this unit. Choose a piece of writing for your portfolio. The writing you choose should show one or more of the following:

- a realistic portrayal of a person, event, or setting from history
- an opening that introduces a person, event, or setting and that draws readers into the story
- lively dialogue that shows what the characters are like
- fictional but true-to-life characters to portray a historical era or event
- a lead that tells most or all of the five *W*s and an *H*

Reflect on your choice.
Attach a note to the piece you chose, explaining briefly why you chose it and what you learned from writing it.

Set goals.
How can you improve your writing? What skill will you focus on the next time you write?

 **Writing Across the Curriculum**

Make a History Connection.
Think of a historical event that took place during the lifetime of the character about whom you wrote your narrative. Write a paragraph telling some of the effects that event had on your character's life.

188 *Unit 4 Review*

Teacher's Classroom Resources

The following resources can be used for planning, assessment or evaluation.

Unit Assessment
📁 *Tests with Answer Key*
Unit 4 Choice A Test, p. 13
Unit 4 Choice B Test, p. 14
Unit 4 Composition Objective Test, pp. 15–16

Test Generator
Unit 4 Choice A Test
Unit 4 Choice B Test
Unit 4 Composition Objective Test

You may wish to administer one of these tests as a mastery test.

Expository Writing

EXPOSITORY WRITING IN THE REAL WORLD

189

UNIT GOALS

The goal of Unit 5 is to help students, through example and instruction, to develop an ability to understand and use the techniques of expository writing. The lessons focus on structuring supporting details; using comparison-contrast, step-by-step, and cause-effect organizations; and writing a report.

Unit Assessment

📁 *Tests with Answer Key*
Unit 5 Choice A Test, p. 17
Unit 5 Choice B Test, p. 18
Unit 5 Composition Objective Test,
  pp. 19–20

💿 *Test Generator*
Unit 5 Choice A Test
Unit 5 Choice B Test
Unit 5 Composition Objective Test

You may wish to administer either the Unit 5 Choice A Test or the Unit 5 Choice B Test as a pretest.

Key to Ability Levels

Enabling Strategies have been coded for varying learning styles and abilities.

L1 Level 1 activities are within the ability range of Learning Disabled students.

L2 Level 2 activities are basic-to-average activities and are within the ability range of average students.

L3 Level 3 activities are challenging activities and are within the ability range of above-average students.

LEP activities are within the ability range of Limited English Proficiency students.

UNIT

5

PREVIEW

Case
Study

Setting the Purpose

In the Unit 5 Case Study students see how an author collected, organized, and presented information for his traveler's guide.

FOCUS

Lesson Overview

Objective: To recognize how thorough research, clear organization, and appropriate presentation can result in interesting and effective expository writing

Skills: defining a purpose; collecting and organizing facts; varying writing styles; revising

Critical Thinking: analyzing; synthesizing; categorizing; recalling; summarizing; building background

Speaking and Listening: discussing; explaining a process

Bellringer

When students enter the classroom, have this assignment on the board: *What is a travel guide? What kinds of information would you expect to see in a travel guide? Who reads travel guides? Write down your answers.*

Grammar Link to the Bellringer

As students discuss travel guides, elicit descriptions of the types of sentence structures, phrases, and titles one might find in a travel guide. What are the chances of finding various forms of the adjective *good*? How might they be used?

Motivating Activity

Discuss why people might want to write guidebooks. How would someone get the idea to write such a book? Wouldn't the research task seem overwhelming? What are some possible motivations?

190

Expository Writing
in the Real World

McLain Guides Travelers

FOCUS:

Keeping in mind what the reader needs to know is important in expository writing.

On crisp winter days in 1989, Gary McLain walked for hours along the wooded banks of the Blue River in Kansas. McLain, a Choctaw-Irish author and artist, was writing *Indian America*, a traveler's guide to Native American tribes in the continental United States. Long walks helped him think about the book.

▲ *Guidebook author Gary McLain*

McLain hoped his guide would invite non-Indian travelers into his world. "We as Americans say that America is the melting pot of the world. Yet there are huge holes between cultures. We don't understand, or we aren't even interested in, each other at times. Most non-Indian people probably don't understand what it means to be Indian," he says. "So that's what I tried to do—explain what it means to be an Indian."

190 *Expository Writing: Finding Meaning*

Teacher's Classroom Resources

The following resources can be used for planning, instruction, practice, reinforcement, assessment, or evaluation.

Teaching Tools
Lesson Plans, p. 41

Transparencies
Writing Process Transparencies, 17–19B

Writing a Guidebook

Prewriting	Drafting	Revising
Collecting and Organizing the Facts	Writing the Book	Making the Story Complete

"I think we need to exchange ideas and information, take the best of all and . . . put it together—and maybe that will become what America is."

—Gary McLain (Eagle/Walking Turtle)

Prewriting

COLLECTING AND ORGANIZING THE FACTS

When McLain decided to write *Indian America,* he already knew a great deal about many Native American tribes. Even so, he needed to gather more information.

Using his knowledge and a list from the Bureau of Indian Affairs, McLain mailed 500 letters to tribal offices around the country. Three hundred tribal offices responded with information that travelers would need. Information included the tribe's name, address, tribal office phone number and location, as well as its public ceremonies and art forms. Some tribes even responded with histories written by tribal historians. McLain also

Case Study **191**

📂 **Blackline Masters**
Cooperative Learning Activities,
   pp. 25–30
Thinking and Study Skills,
   pp. 1–5, 11, 13, 35–37
*Research Paper and Report
Writing,* pp. 2–3, 36
*Case Studies: Writing in the
Real World,* pp. 17–20

Assessment
📂 *Teacher's Guide to Writing
Assessment*

TEACH

Building Background

Warm-Up:
Remind students that expository writing explains or informs. Ask students where they have seen explanations, or expository writing. In what kinds of situations would expository writing be useful? Start a list that students can add to throughout their reading of Unit 5.

Exposition in Speaking:
Remind students that they use expository language when they give directions to a place or when they explain how to make something. Ask for other examples of when people explain or give information in their speaking.

Exposition in Writing:
Discuss any expository writing students have read. Use prompts such as the following:
- How much of the reading you do for school is expository? What do you read for school that isn't expository?
- How much of the writing in a newspaper is expository? What in a newspaper isn't expository? How do you know?

Preview the Case Study
Have students preview the title, focus statement, illlustrations, and captions of the case study. Discuss students' predictions of what they will learn about McLain's process, and then have students read the case study.

🔁 **Cross-Reference: Writing**
For instruction and practice writing a business letter to request information, refer students to Lesson 5.8, pp. 224–227.

TEACH

Discussion Prompts

- Why might McLain have chosen to organize his information by dividing it into nine sections? How does it help the reader when the information is grouped into categories?
- Why might McLain have wanted to use two different writing styles? How might the variation make his book more interesting?

did library research. Before long he had a stack of material three feet high.

With the facts in hand, McLain next decided on the parts and organization of his guide. He says, "I divided the country into nine regions based mostly on how Indian

people live."

McLain planned to open the guidebook with information on Indian beliefs. The guide to the tribes would follow, organized by region. To help travelers picture locations, McLain decided to include regional maps.

▼ *In the Great Plains section of* Indian America, *McLain includes information about the traditions of the people—how the young and old cared for and taught one another.*

Drafting

WRITING THE BOOK

With his book plan in mind, McLain started writing, a job that would take him three months. For days at a time, he wrote from sunup to mid-morning, from mid-afternoon until 10:00 P.M.

As McLain worked with his material, he used two writing styles to present information. In the introduction to each region, he wrote in a conversational manner. For example, in his introduction to the Great Plains, McLain explained how

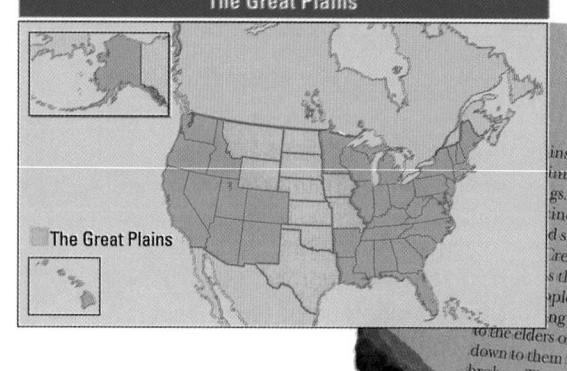

The Great Plains

The Great Plains

8 / Great Plains

...ins. And dances and songs and chants developed for s...
...ument and spiritual appreciation of the creation of al...
...gs.
...ines for the body and spirit evolved with time also. Sa...
...d sweetgrass were used in the sacred ceremonies of our p...
...reator provided the knowledge of how to use these sacr...
...s through the Medicine People found in every tribe.
...ple cared for each other, and the old were cared for in th...
...ng people were praised for their caring and for their a...
to the elders of the tribe. The elders taught the young the ways passe...
down to them from their elders in years gone by; the circle was never
broken. The sacred hoop of the people was whole and round. And
it was good. It was very, very good.
The men formed societies for the protection and well-being of the
whole of all the people. The women formed societies dedicated to
caring and embracing the welfare of all the people. And they bore
the babies and raised the children. And it was good. It was very, very
good.
The heartbeat of our Mother Earth was heard and felt with the
drum, and the flute from Father Sky played the prayers of the people. It is true that life could still be difficult and often was, but it was
difficult in an honorable and clean way. The people never forgot to
maintain their respect for the whole of all living things; they...
forgot to play the drum to keep the heartbeat of M...
they never forgot to pray...

192 *Expository*

Cultural Diversity

Appreciating Diversity Among Native Americans

Point out that Native Americans are themselves culturally diverse. People from different groups may have different physical characteristics, customs, governments, laws, and languages. At one time, more than five hundred different languages were spoken by Native American peoples. Although currently the largest concentration of native peoples is in the Southwest, every state has a Native American population.

people were bound together in a great sacred hoop.

McLain used a much different writing style for his guide to each tribe. Here he wrote in short sentences for travelers on the go. Then he organized the chunks of copy just as he had organized his letter: name, tribal office address, and phone number; details on ceremonies and art forms; and, finally, visitor information.

In the visitor-information section, McLain provided travelers with useful and intriguing facts. For the Taos Pueblo in New Mexico, he focused on photography rules for visitors. For the Cherokee in North Carolina,

he described a restored Cherokee village, a museum, and various tourist activities. By contrast, his section on the Comanches in Oklahoma discussed the tribe's history, not its modern life. The reason?

"There are no more reservations in Oklahoma," McLain explains. "The Comanches live in white frame houses that don't look much different from those in Ohio or Indiana. Yet the Comanches were hunters who lived up and down the central plains. They were great horsemen and great warriors and had much ceremony in their lives. I thought a little more attention to the history of the tribe could help visitors feel connected to these people."

TEACH

Discussion Prompts

- What seem to be the main priorities McLain used when deciding what information to include for each state? (Examples: what would make visitors feel connected to the Native Americans, what travelers would need to know)
- How much do you think a native people's past relates to who they are today? Why might the answer vary as it relates to different groups in different regions?

Connections Across the Curriculum

History

Point out that guides such as McLain's help to increase understanding among different groups of people who inhabit the United States. Although major civil rights laws were passed in 1875 and

1964, racial and ethnic issues still cause problems in our society. As a class or in small groups, discuss some of the ways people of diverse backgrounds can benefit from learning more about each other.

TEACH

Guided Practice

L2 Discussion

Stimulate a discussion of the case study. You may also want to invite students to talk about

- other ways in which one culture can tell others about itself.
- other modes of writing that could be used in an expository piece to make it more interesting.
- other sections McLain could add to his book if he were to print a revised edition.

Independent Practice

✍ *Writing Process Transparencies,* 17–19B

📁 *Case Studies: Writing in the Real World,* pp. 17–20

📁 *Cooperative Learning Activities,* pp. 25–30

Skills Practice

📁 *Thinking and Study Skills,* pp. 1–5, 11, 13, 35–37

📁 *Research Paper and Report Writing,* pp. 2–3, 36

Revising

MAKING THE STORY COMPLETE

▼ *In* Indian America *Gary McLain explains the use of sweetgrass and sage.*

Once McLain had his book on paper, he revised sections to make them clearer and more engaging. In some instances he took his editor's advice and clarified cloudy explanations. McLain's editor also asked him to expand his section on sweetgrass and sage, healing plants used by Medicine People in Plains ceremonies. McLain revised his brief comment to read: "The Medicine People use sage, cedar, and sweetgrass, and the sweet smell carries the healing forward from the past into the future . . . in the sacred dances of our people across the land."

Technology Tip

Using Quotations

Quotations from interviews with experts in a field can add sparkle to expository writing. Students who have access to portable tape recorders or to answering machines with recording features can record interviews. Later they can replay the tape and listen for the quotations that best illustrate the points they want to make. Remind students that writers must ask permission to use a tape recorder during an interview.

194

Responding to the Case Study

1. Discussion

Discuss these questions about Gary McLain's writing.

- Even before writers begin collecting facts for informational writing, they must choose an audience and a purpose for writing. What audience did Gary McLain choose for his book *Indian America*? What purpose for writing did he have in mind?
- McLain knew a great deal about Native American tribes. What two other sources of information did he use to collect his material? What did he have to do with all his material

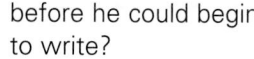

before he could begin to write?

- Explain the different writing styles McLain used in his guidebook and how each style matched a specific kind of information.
- Why did McLain not describe the modern life of the Comanches? What did he do instead?

2. Expository Writing

Make a plan for writing an explanation.

Choose a North American place, historical event, or cultural celebration—like the one in the photograph—with which you are familiar. Brainstorm a list of three or four key points. Organize them into an outline for a four-paragraph explanation of your topic. Make notes about what each paragraph might include.

Grammar Link

Use the correct forms of the adjective *good*.

The comparative and superlative forms of *good* are *better* and *best*.

It was very, very good. So I think we need to . . . take the best of all. . . .

Write a sentence based on each item below, using forms of the word *good*.

1. Compare opposing pitchers at a baseball game.
2. Compare the climate in three vacation spots.
3. Compare the winner of a singing competition with the other contestants.
4. Describe the tastes of foods you have eaten recently.

See Lesson 12.3, pages 428–429.

Case Study **195**

ASSESS

Responding to the Case Study

1. Discussion

- non-Indian travelers, to show what it means to be a Native American
- information from 300 tribal offices; library research; plan the parts and organization for his guide
- conversational style for the introduction to each region; for the guide to each tribe, short sentences for busy travelers to use easily
- it didn't differentiate them; he wrote about their heritage

2. Expository Writing

Answers will vary. Students might write about a local annual celebration including its origin and specific events.

See also the *Teacher's Guide to Writing Assessment.*

Grammar Link
(See Using the Grammar Link below.)

Reteaching

Invite students to locate another expository book at the library and identify its audience and purpose.

Enrichment

Suggest that students think of familial, ethnic, religious, organizational, or interest-based groups about which they have information. Ask students to create a presentation concerning their groups that will give listeners new information.

CLOSE

Discuss the purpose, audience, style, and organization of the case studies as a whole in *Writer's Choice: Composition and Grammar*. What makes them expository?

195

Using the Grammar Link

Grammar Link Answers

Answers will vary, but some suggestions are given below.

1. Our team has a good pitcher, but their pitcher was better.
2. Palm Springs is a good place to go if you need a break from the cold, although places in Florida could be better—especially the Keys, which are the best!
3. Maria sang better than the other contestants.
4. Olympic Pizza makes the best crust of all the pizzerias in town.

FOCUS

Lesson Overview

Objective: To organize an explanation with appropriate supporting details

Skills: choosing an appropriate approach; writing an explanation

Critical Thinking: analyzing; recalling; evaluating

Speaking and Listening: explaining a process

Bellringer

When students enter the classroom, have this assignment on the board: *Explain briefly how you get ready for school in the morning.*

Grammar Link to the Bellringer

Circle all of the pronouns in your list. Then draw arrows connecting them to the names they refer to. If no name is listed, draw an arrow to the margin and write the name there.

Motivating Activity

Compile a list of things students know how to do well. Encourage a variety of answers by suggesting such categories as sports, practical skills, or musical accomplishments. Challenge volunteers to explain how to do something on the list without using gestures. Emphasize that it may be difficult to explain a process using words alone.

196

Expository Writing
Conveying Information

Expository writing informs and explains. In the model below, the writer uses expository writing to convey information about a traditional Inuit game, the blanket toss.

> ### Literature Model
>
> **M**embers of the community grabbed hold of the edge of an animal skin. When everyone pulled at once, the center snapped up, propelling the person who sat or stood in the center of the skin into the air, just as if he or she were on a trampoline. The leader of the most successful whaling crew was often rewarded with the place on the skin; it was then a matter of pride to remain standing throughout the vigorous tossing.
>
> Kevin Osborn, *The Peoples of the Arctic*

196

Teacher's Classroom Resources

The following resources can be used for planning, instruction, practice, reinforcement, assessment, reteaching, enrichment, or evaluation.

Teaching Tools
Lesson Plans, p. 42

Transparencies
Fine Art Transparencies, 21–25
Writing Process Transparencies, 17–19B

Blackline Masters
Thinking and Study Skills, pp. 3, 5, 11, 13, 14
Writing Across the Curriculum, p. 17
Cooperative Learning Activities, pp. 25–30
Sentence Combining Practice, pp. 32–33

Write to Inform

The most familiar form of expository writing is the essay. An essay consists of an introduction, a body, and a conclusion. The introduction usually contains a thesis statement—a sentence that states the main idea of the essay. The body is made up of one or more paragraphs that include details supporting the thesis statement. The conclusion draws the essay to a close. It may restate what has been said or suggest a different way of looking at the material. Notice in the model below how Michele Casey begins her essay on sharks.

> *Student Model*
>
> A lthough shark attacks do occur, they are not so frequent that swimmers must arm themselves with shark repellents. Survivors of airplane or ship disasters, though, need an effective shark repellent, since they have practically no defenses. The most promising advances are sound/electronic barriers. All other methods have major drawbacks.
>
> Michele Casey, Glen Crest Junior High School,
> Glen Ellyn, Illinois

What is the thesis statement in Michele's essay?

The body of Michele's essay goes on to discuss various shark repellents. Her conclusion states, "Shark repellents of today and the future will help prevent further disaster for survivors at sea."

Journal Writing

Imagine that a friend has asked you how to play a game you know well. Write a thesis statement explaining the main goal of the game.

5.1 Conveying Information **197**

TEACH

Guided Practice

L2 Using the Model
Ask students to imagine they are in the Arctic Circle and someone suggests that they participate in a blanket toss. How would they begin? Explain that they might find the answer by reading Kevin Osborn's explanation of a blanket toss. After they read, ask students to identify specific details that help them understand how blanket toss is played. Help them recognize that such details as "pulled at once" and "vigorous tossing" make the action clear.

L3 Using the Model
Ask how Michele leads into the subject of shark repellents (by mentioning that only survivors of airplane or ship disasters need them). Why do such survivors need repellents? (They have practically no defenses.)

(Answer to callout: The most promising advances are sound/electronic barriers.)

Two-Minute Skill Drill

Have students order these sentences to match the parts of an essay:

A. Today we played basketball.

B. I won the game with my shot.

C. The score was tied many times.

Journal Writing Tip

Defining and Clarifying Topics
Suggest that students who are writing about team games might wish to decide first if they will focus on an individual's goal or on the team's goal.

Unit Assessment

Speaking and Listening Activities, pp. 12–13, 21
Research Paper and Report Writing, pp. 2–3, 9, 19–22
Composition Practice, p. 33
Composition Reteaching, p. 33
Composition Enrichment, p. 33

📁 *Teacher's Guide to Writing Assessment*
📁 *Tests with Answer Key*
Unit 5 Choice A Test, p. 17
Unit 5 Choice B Test, p. 18

⏱ *Test Generator*
Unit 5 Choice A Test
Unit 5 Choice B Test

You may wish to administer either the Unit 5 Choice A Test or the Unit 5 Choice B Test as a pretest.

TEACH

Guided Practice

L2 Finding Expository Writing
To help students recognize how common expository writing is, suggest that they look through a variety of printed materials and try to find examples of the four approaches. Encourage them to look at recipes, instructions, warning labels, and other forms of written communication.

L1 Discussing Approaches
Some students may have difficulty distinguishing among the types of expository writing. Discuss each kind of expository writing separately, if necessary, explaining the purpose of each. Ask students to volunteer their own examples for each type of expository writing.

(Answer to callout: According to the writer, people's respect and concern for the creatures have caused them to take protective measures.)

Independent Practice

📖 For further stimuli for expository writing, see *Fine Art Transparencies* 21–25.

📖 *Writing Process Transparencies,* 17–19B

📁 *Writing Across the Curriculum,* p. 17

📁 *Cooperative Learning Activities,* pp. 25–30

Skills Practice

📁 *Thinking and Study Skills,* pp. 3, 5, 11, 13, 14

📁 *Sentence Combining Practice,* pp. 32–33

📁 *Speaking and Listening Activities,* pp. 12–13, 21

📁 *Research Paper and Report Writing,* pp. 2–3, 9, 19–22

📁 *Composition Practice,* p. 33

Choose an Approach

The goal of expository writing is to explain or inform. The model on page 196 explains by describing the steps of a process. Expository writing can take other forms. The chart below explains four approaches to expository writing. These approaches can be used alone or combined in any expository piece. To explain about dolphins, the writer of the sample below chose the cause-and-effect approach.

> **Prewriting Tip**
> While prewriting, brainstorm a list of questions your essay should answer. Then answer the questions in your draft.

Approaches to Expository Writing	
Approach	**Sample Writing**
Definition	*Sivuquad,* a name for St. Lawrence Island, means squeezed dry. The islanders believed that a giant had made the island from dried mud.
Compare-Contrast	The boats in a coastal fishing fleet often stay at sea for days or weeks. Long-range fishing fleet vessels can remain at sea for months.
Process	To breathe, a whale surfaces in a forward rolling motion. For two seconds, it blows out and breathes in as much as 2,100 quarts of air.
Cause-Effect	The discovery of oil and gas in Alaska in 1968 led to widespread development in that region of the world.

> *According to the writer, why has the dolphin been protected?*

For centuries dolphins have fascinated people. Stories about dolphins that guided ships and rescued swimmers have led some people to idealize these creatures. Further, traditional respect and increasing public concern have resulted in measures intended to protect the dolphin.

198   *Expository Writing: Finding Meaning*

Enabling Strategies

LEP Understanding Terms: *Explanation* and *Detail*
Students may have trouble understanding abstract terms like *explanation* and *detail*. With an English proficient partner, have pairs make a list of daily processes, like brushing teeth or putting a cassette into a cassette player. The student who is learning English pantomimes one of the processes while the partner translates the actions into words. Point out that each action described is a detail and the whole description of the process is an explanation.

5.1 Writing Activities

Write an Explanation

A television program called *What in the World?* challenges viewers to send in answers to questions, such as "What is a solar eclipse?" or "How are a whale and a dolphin alike?" Choose one of these two questions, and write an essay that answers it.

• Choose an appropriate approach.
• Include an introduction, a body, and a conclusion.

PURPOSE To answer a question in an essay
AUDIENCE Television viewers (your classmates)
LENGTH 2 paragraphs

Hiroshige III, *Bank of Japan at Eitai Bridge*, 1884

Cross-Curricular: History

Like writing, some images clearly inform and explain. The Japanese print below reflects the influence of Western trade on Japan in the nineteenth century. Write two paragraphs describing influences that you notice in the print.

Grammar Link

Avoid using pronouns without clear antecedents.

To avoid confusion when using pronouns, you must be sure that the noun or group of words to which the pronoun refers–the antecedent–is clear.

*Stories about dolphins that guided ships and rescued swimmers have led some people to idealize **these creatures**.*

If this sentence ended "to idealize *them*," readers would not know if *them* referred to *dolphins, ships,* or *swimmers*.

Revise the paragraph below to eliminate confusing pronouns.

[1] Heather is helping Jen in the garden; Chad, Mike, and she are planting tomatoes. [2] They are proud of the garden. [3] Then Chad and Mike will weed his garden and the Wongs' garden.

See Lesson 11.2, pages 404–405.

5.1 Conveying Information **199**

Using the Grammar Link

Grammar Link Answers
1. ...is helping Chad, Mike, and Jen plant...
2. All four are proud...
3. ...will weed Mike's and the Wongs' gardens...

Choosing Clear Antecedents Write a paragraph about a favorite book, movie, or TV show. Use clear pronoun antecedents.

About the Art

Hiroshige III, *Bank of Japan at Eitai Bridge,* **1884**
Explain that Hiroshige III worked in the tradition of *Ukiyoe* ("pictures of the floating world") when he painted *Bank of Japan at Eitai Bridge* in 1884. The style depicted city life when Japan was almost totally cut off from the rest of the world.

FOCUS

Lesson Overview

Objective: To order information in an explanation
Skills: choosing a thesis statement; choosing and arranging details
Critical Thinking: identifying main idea; defining and clarifying
Speaking and Listening: speaking to persuade; explaining a process

Bellringer

When students enter the classroom, have this assignment on the board: *What is the main idea in the following passage? What details are given to support the main idea?*
More new homes are being built in Iola than in any other town in the state. The old schoolhouse has been reopened until extra class-rooms can be built. It's no surprise that Iola is the fastest-growing town in the state.

Grammar Link to the Bellringer
Ask volunteers to give the plural of *schoolhouse* (schoolhouses), the sin-gular of *classrooms* (classroom). Try to elicit that these are compound nouns.

Motivating Activity
Have students name favorite books and tell why they like them. Explain that details tell why a thing is enjoy-able and spark interest in it. Support-ing details in expository writing do the same thing: strengthen a writer's the-sis and capture a reader's attention.

LESSON
5.2
E x p o s i t o r y   W r i t i n g
Structuring an Explanation

Choosing and arranging details to support a statement are the foundations of expository writing. Notice how the writer of the model below uses supporting details to explain how computers tackle mountains of information in a flash.

Literature Model

Printed circuit boards are the heart of the com-puter. On them are mounted the transistors, capacitors, chips, and other electrical marvels that create a computer. Their undersides have ribbons of solder, through which electricity flows. It is not nec-essary for you to have the foggiest idea how all this works. But do consider how small, lightweight, and portable the printed circuit boards are. Each board has a special function: some provide memory for the computer; others provide the processing and arithmetic logic functions; still others convert the power supply to and from the required voltages.

Carol W. Brown, *The Minicomputer Simplified*

200 *Expository Writing: Finding Meaning*

Teacher's Classroom Resources

The following resources can be used for planning, instruction, practice, rein-forcement, assessment, reteaching, enrichment, or evaluation.

Teaching Tools
Lesson Plans, p. 43,

Transparencies
Fine Art Transparencies, 21–25
Writing Process Transparen-cies, 17–19B

Select Details

Supporting details are the heart of expository writing. They support the thesis statement in the introduction of your essay. The details you select for an essay will depend on the approach to expository writing you're using. If you're writing a cause-and-effect essay, you might use reasons as supporting details. In the model Carol W. Brown uses facts to define circuit boards. You can also use statistics, examples, or incidents to support what you say. Note the examples of the types of details listed in the chart below.

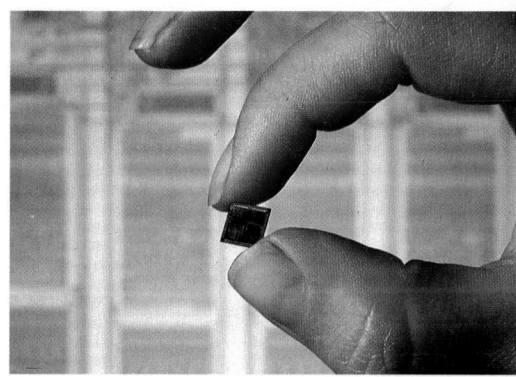

Details in Expository Writing	
Type	**Example**
Facts	Momenta International of California introduced a computer that can recognize and interpret printed handwriting.
Statistics	The processor inside a typical computer can carry out one million additions in only a second.
Examples/ Incidents	The optical processor is an example of a computer that uses light beams to process information.
Reasons	Computer manufacturers are developing smaller computers because businesspeople demand them for use when they travel.

Journal Writing

Think about something you would like to explain to a friend. Write your thesis statement, and list the details you would include, trying to use all four types of details.

Blackline Masters
Thinking and Study Skills,
  pp. 3, 9, 12
Writing Across the Curriculum,
  p. 17
Cooperative Learning Activities,
  pp. 25–30
Sentence Combining Practice,
  pp. 32–33

Speaking and Listening Activities, pp. 12–13, 21
Research Paper and Report Writing, pp. 2–3, 9, 19–22
Composition Practice, p. 34
Composition Reteaching, p. 34
Composition Enrichment, p. 34

Assessment
 Teacher's Guide to Writing Assessment

TEACH

Guided Practice

L2 Using the Model
Ask a volunteer to read the literature model and have other volunteers locate the details about printed circuit boards. Point out that these details support the writer's statement in the first sentence: "Printed circuit boards are the heart of the computer."

L1 Using the Model
If students have difficulty distinguishing among facts, statistics, examples, and reasons, provide samples of CD covers and the information included with a tape. Have students find a fact (can be proved or disproved), a statistic (numerical kind of fact), an example (instance or particular model), a reason (an explanation).

L3 Identifying Metaphorical Relationships
Ask students what two things Carol W. Brown compares in the first sentence (circuit boards and the heart). Encourage students to suggest ways in which printed circuit boards and the heart are alike.

L2 Visual Thinking
Point out that students might use a chart similar to the one on this page during the prewriting stage of writing. The chart could be used to classify supporting details that students might use in their expository writing.

Journal Writing Tip

Identifying Main Ideas If students are having difficulty locating the thesis statement, suggest that they work with partners. Students might swap articles, read them, summarize each in two or three sentences, and identify the main idea.

TEACH

Guided Practice

L2 Using the Model

Ask students to identify the thesis statement of the student model (the first sentence). As students discuss the types of details (facts, a statistic, an example, a reason), ask how these details are organized to support the main idea in the thesis statement (in chronological order).

Two-Minute Skill Drill

Have students write a paragraph explaining the features of a particular computer; explaining how to format a document on a computer; or recommending computer games. Ask them to decide what kind of organization to use for their details.

Independent Practice

For further stimuli for expository writing, see *Fine Art Transparencies* 21–25.

Writing Process Transparencies, 17–19B

Writing Across the Curriculum, p. 17

Cooperative Learning Activities, pp. 25–30

Skills Practice

Thinking and Study Skills, pp. 3, 9, 12

Sentence Combining Practice, pp. 32–33

Speaking and Listening Activities, pp. 12–13, 21

Research Paper and Report Writing, pp. 2–3, 9, 19–22

Composition Practice, p. 34

Arrange the Details

Grammar
Editing Tip

When editing an essay that uses time order, be sure the verb tenses reflect the order. For more on tenses, refer to Lessons 10.5–10.9, pages 376–385.

Once you've selected supporting details for your explanation, you're ready to organize them. Ask yourself what you're trying to do in your essay. For example, are you going to show the cause and effect of a tidal wave? Are you going to use a comparison-contrast essay to point out the similarities and differences between two comedians? Questions such as these can help you organize your ideas—the supporting details—logically.

You might choose a number of ways to arrange information and supporting details. If you're defining something, you might arrange features from most to least significant. If you're writing about a process, then chronological order, or time order, might be more logical. In the model below, notice the kinds of details that Emilie Baltz uses and how she arranges them.

Student Model

What types of details are in the writing?

What kind of organization does the writer use?

Thomas Edison's invention of the electric light bulb in 1879 came about only after a long, hard process. Finding the right material for the tiny filament inside the light bulb had been difficult. Edison tested 1,600 materials before finally using a piece of burned thread. Because it contained no air, the thread did not burn quickly inside the bulb. This invention would eventually bring light into the world.

Emilie Baltz, Hufford Junior High School, Joliet, Illinois

202 *Expository Writing: Finding Meaning*

Enabling Strategies

LEP Organizing Supporting Details

Students with limited English proficiency may need help writing and organizing supporting details. Suggest that they write and highlight what type of expository writing they will do: cause and effect, process, and so on. Pair students and have them write the highlighted word in the center of a piece of paper and then make a web of supporting details related to the highlighted word. Students can help each other translate difficult words into English.

5.2 Writing Activities

Write an Explanation

Imagine that a person from the 1800s has come to visit you. He wants to know how a computer works and what it does. Write a simple explanation of how a computer works and what it can be used for.

- Include reasons for using various features on the computer.
- Make sure your explanation is easy to understand.

PURPOSE To use reasons and supporting details to explain how a computer works and what it can be used for
AUDIENCE A person from the 1800s
LENGTH 2–3 paragraphs

COMPUTER OPTION

You can use a computer to illustrate your explanation with pictures, graphs, charts, and diagrams. Some word processing programs have graphic functions. Some programs can change statistics to graphs. Clip art—pictures you can copy and paste into your document—is also available.

Grammar Link

Form the plural of compound nouns correctly.

Add -s or -es to the end of one-word compound nouns and to the most important part of other compound nouns.

undersides

printed circuit boards

Use the plural form of each compound noun below in a sentence.

1. bookend
2. halfback
3. father-in-law
4. showcase
5. great-aunt
6. runner-up
7. storybook
8. basketball
9. pot of gold
10. paper plate
11. vice president
12. editor-in-chief
13. suitcase
14. brother-in-law
15. windowsill
16. nosebleed
17. groundhog
18. toothpaste
19. sunbeam
20. ice rink

See Lesson 9.2, pages 350–351.

5.2 Structuring an Explanation **203**

ASSESS

Writing Activities Evaluation Guidelines

Write an Explanation
Use these criteria when evaluating your students' writing.
- Does it explain what a computer can be used for?
- Does it explain how a computer works?
- Would a person from the 1800s understand the explanation?

See also the *Teacher's Guide to Writing Assessment.*

Computer Option
Hang up copies of students' computer-generated pictures, graphs, and so on. Discuss how these graphics can be used to support a thesis statement.

Grammar Link
(See Using the Grammar Link below.)

Reteaching
Composition Reteaching, p. 34

Enrichment
Composition Enrichment, p. 34

CLOSE

Ask some volunteers to read aloud the persuasive explanations they wrote. Have others in the class identify the main idea, supporting details, and types of details the students used.

Using the Grammar Link

Grammar Link Answers
Sentences will vary, but correct plurals are given below.

1. bookends
2. halfbacks
3. fathers-in-law
4. showcases
5. great-aunts
6. runners-up
7. storybooks
8. basketballs
9. pots of gold
10. paper plates
11. vice presidents
12. editors-in-chief
13. suitcases
14. brothers-in-law
15. windowsills
16. nosebleeds
17. groundhogs
18. toothpastes
19. sunbeams
20. ice rinks

FOCUS

Lesson Overview

Objective: To write a compare-and-contrast passage on two subjects
Skills: identifying similarities and differences; organizing compare-and-contrast writing
Critical Thinking: categorizing; classifying; comparing
Speaking and Listening: discussing; explaining similarities and differences

Bellringer

When students enter the classroom, have this assignment on the board: *Write these sentences:*
 1) Neither my brother nor my sister likes rock music.
 2) Either a tape or a CD is my birthday present to my mom.
Underline the compound subjects in each sentence and circle the verbs.

Grammar Link to the Bellringer

Have students discuss the Bellringer sentences. Make sure they understand that in sentences with compound subjects joined by *or* or *nor,* the verb agrees with the subject closer to it, as in the Bellringer sentences.

Motivating Activity

Ask students to write a paragraph about the differences between poor- and good-quality boom boxes. Have them base their writing on the absence or presence of specific features, such as a CD player.

204

LESSON

5.3 Expository Writing
Writing to Compare and Contrast

When you compare two things, you explain how they're similar. When you contrast two things, you explain how they're different. Comparing and contrasting two items can be a useful way of explaining them.

Tanya enjoys the songs of Patsy Cline. Classmate Ben prefers the music of Puerto Rico. These two kinds of music are different in some ways and alike in others. Think about two types of music. Jot down two or three things about them that are similar and two or three things that are different.

204 *Expository Writing: Finding Meaning*

Teacher's Classroom Resources

The following resources can be used for planning, instruction, practice, reinforcement, assessment, reteaching, enrichment, or evaluation.

Teaching Tools
Lesson Plans

Transparencies
Fine Art Transparencies, 21–25
Writing Process Transparencies, 17–19B

Identify Similarities and Differences

By looking carefully at two things, you see their similarities and differences. This close look often helps you understand each thing better. Comparing and contrasting requires an analytical approach.

Before you write a compare-and-contrast essay, you need to identify similarities and differences in your subjects. A Venn diagram, such as the one below, may help you. Be sure that your subjects are related, as two kinds of music are. Also, compare and contrast the same set of features, such as cultural sources and sound, that relate to the subjects.

Vocabulary

Drafting Tip

When drafting an opening sentence for a compare-and-contrast essay, choose words that will grab your reader's attention.

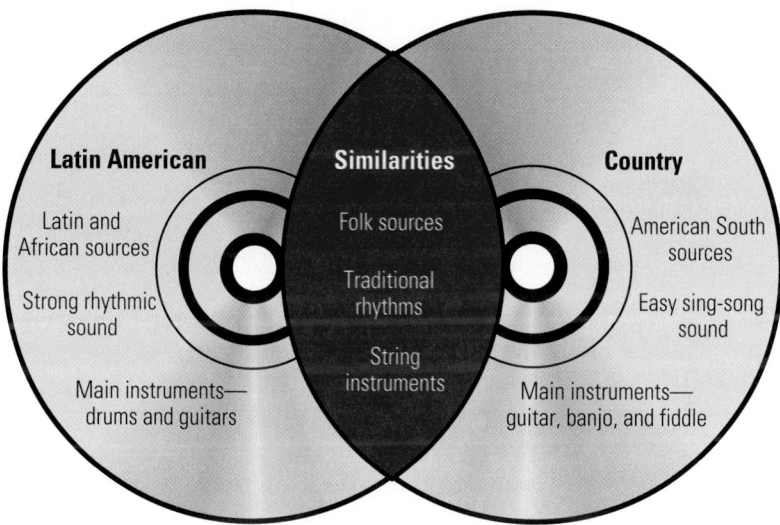

Latin American
- Latin and African sources
- Strong rhythmic sound
- Main instruments—drums and guitars

Similarities
- Folk sources
- Traditional rhythms
- String instruments

Country
- American South sources
- Easy sing-song sound
- Main instruments—guitar, banjo, and fiddle

Journal Writing

Think of two musical artists or groups that are related in some way. In your journal make a Venn diagram. Use the diagram to compare and contrast the musicians in terms of the same features.

5.3 Writing to Compare and Contrast **205**

TEACH

Guided Practice

L2 Using Similarities and Differences to Classify

Point out to students that noting similarities and differences is actually a form of classifying. Many professionals, such as librarians and biologists, use classifying in their work. For example, librarians classify books by similarities they share. Encourage students to suggest other examples.

L1 Identifying Similarities and Differences in Venn Diagrams

If students have difficulty identifying similarities and differences in the Venn diagram, ask them to trace a large circular object, such as a margarine lid, on a piece of paper. Tell them to color in the circle, then trace another circle, overlapping the first. Ask students to shade in the second circle using another color. Explain similarities and differences in terms of color. They may label the diagram to match the one on this page.

Two-Minute Skill Drill

List these compound subjects on the board and have students form sentences.

Neither jazz nor classical music
Either the guitar or the piano

Journal Writing Tip

Similarities and Differences
Suggest that students think of similarities first and differences second or that they think of as many details as possible first, separating them into similarities and differences later.

📁 **Blackline Masters**
Thinking and Study Skills, pp. 6, 9, 19
Writing Across the Curriculum, pp. 12, 19, 24
Cooperative Learning Activities, pp. 25–30
Sentence Combining Practice, pp. 32–33

Speaking and Listening Activities, pp. 12–13, 21
Research Paper and Report Writing, pp. 2–3, 9, 19–22
Composition Practice, p. 35
Composition Reteaching, p. 35
Composition Enrichment, p. 35

Assessment
📁 *Teacher's Guide to Writing Assessment*

TEACH

Guided Practice

L2 Using the Model

Before students read the model, point out that Yo-Yo Ma and Emanuel Ax have at least one thing in common—they are both musicians. Then ask students to read the model to find out why Yo-Yo and Manny are an unlikely pair.

(Answer to first callout: The model is organized by feature. Answer to second callout: The musicians' backgrounds are different, as are their feelings about playing music.)

Independent Practice

For further stimuli for expository writing, see *Fine Art Transparencies* 21–25.

Writing Process Transparencies, 17–19B

Writing Across the Curriculum, pp. 12, 19, 24

Cooperative Learning Activities, pp. 25–30

Skills Practice

Thinking and Study Skills, pp. 6, 9, 19

Sentence Combining Practice, pp. 32–33

Speaking and Listening Activities, pp. 12–13, 21

Research Paper and Report Writing, pp. 2–3, 9, 19–22

Composition Practice, p. 35

Organize by Subject or by Feature

You can organize compare-and-contrast writing either by subject or by feature. In organizing by subject, you discuss all the features of one subject and then the features of the other. For example, you might explain the sources and sound of Latin music and then discuss the contrasting sources and sound of country music. When organizing by feature, you discuss one feature at a time for both subjects. See the chart below.

Organizing by Subject or Feature	
Subject	Latin music sources are Latin American and African. The beat of the music is strong and rhythmic. Country music, on the other hand, comes from the American South.
Feature	Latin music comes from Latin America and Africa, while country music grew out of America's South. The sound of the two kinds of music is also different. Latin is rhythmic and country music is sing-songy.

How did Michael Shapiro organize the paragraph below on classical musicians Yo-Yo Ma and Emanual Ax?

Does the writer organize his contrast by feature or by subject?

How are Yo-Yo Ma and Emanuel Ax different?

Literature Model

They seem, on the surface, an unlikely pair, as is often the case with friends who never seem to lose the rhythm of their relationship. Ma was the child wonder who came of age musically in the warm embrace of such mentors as Isaac Stern and Leonard Rose. Ax grew up never knowing whether he would be able to become a concert pianist. For Ma playing the cello has always come easily. For Ax the musician's life is one for which he feels forever grateful.

Michael Shapiro, "Yo-Yo and Manny"

206

Enabling Strategies

LEP Distinguishing Between Subject and Feature

Students may have difficulty reading a section and distinguishing between subject and feature. If so, provide some concrete examples. Show some close-up pictures of human faces. Point out that these are subjects. Then suggest that a few volunteers describe the features of the subjects, such as eyes, mouth, and hair. Emphasize that these are features.

5.3 Writing Activities

Write a Compare-and-Contrast Essay

Write an essay about two people, places, or things that you are studying in school, such as two characters from a book or two cities.

- Identify similarities and differences. (Consider using a Venn diagram.)
- Organize by subject or by feature.

PURPOSE To compare and contrast items
AUDIENCE Your teacher or classmates
LENGTH 2–4 paragraphs

Cross-Curricular: Art

Study the painting below and the one on page 199. Imagine that they appear in an exhibit. Make a Venn diagram comparing and contrasting the subjects of the paintings.

John Biggers, *Jubilee—Ghana Harvest Festival,* 1959

5.3 Writing to Compare and Contrast **207**

Grammar Link

Make the verb agree with the closer subject when the parts of a compound subject are joined by *or* or *nor*.

Compound subjects are common in compare-and-contrast writing:

***Neither Ma nor Ax hides** his talent.*

Write the correct verb for each sentence.

1. Neither Mozart nor Haydn are very popular at my house.
2. Either the Beatles or the Grateful Dead were Mom's favorite.
3. Neither Jethro Tull nor Cat Stevens appeal to my parents.
4. Either my uncles or my dad rave about the Rolling Stones.

See Lesson 16.5, pages 516–517.

ASSESS

Writing Activities Evaluation Guidelines

Write a Compare-and-Contrast Essay
Use these criteria when evaluating your students' writing.
- The essay compares and contrasts at least two items.
- The essay is organized by subject or feature.

See also the *Teacher's Guide to Writing Assessment.*

Cross-Curricular: Art
The overlapping part of the Venn diagram should contain similarities students notice about both paintings. The outside areas should contain the differences between them.

Grammar Link
(See Using the Grammar Link below.)

Reteaching
📁 *Composition Reteaching,* p. 35

Enrichment
📁 *Composition Enrichment,* p. 35

📙 Use *Fine Art Transparencies* 21–25 for enrichment activities also.

CLOSE

Have students exchange their compare-and-contrast essays with a partner. Ask them to identify the items compared and contrasted and to tell whether the essay is organized by subject or feature.

Using the Grammar Link

Grammar Link Answers
1. is
2. was
3. appeals
4. raves

About the Art

John Biggers, *Jubilee—Ghana Harvest Festival,* 1959
John Biggers, grandson of a slave, believed art was not only personal expression but must reflect "the spirit and style" of his race. This 38 1/2-by-98 inch painting in the Houston Museum is mixed media on canvas.

Expository Writing
Writing About a Process

Everyday life is full of step-by-step processes. In this lesson you will learn to explain an everyday process so that others can understand how to complete it.

Making pizza dough may look difficult, but it isn't. There are, however, some basic steps you need to follow, in order. You also need a recipe, of course. The photos below break down the basic steps in making dough.

Making Pizza Dough in Four Steps

| Mix Ingredients | Knead Dough | Let Dough Rise | Shape Dough |

Have a Clear Purpose

Knowing how to do something does not guarantee that you can easily share that knowledge with others. Some people find it more difficult to explain a step-by-step process than to actually do it. The instructions in the model on the next page use clear and simple language to explain a rather complicated process: handling hot chilies.

208 *Expository Writing: Finding Meaning*

FOCUS

Lesson Overview

Objective: To order information to provide a clear explanation of a process
Skills: explaining; identifying purpose and audience; ordering information
Critical Thinking: visualizing; identifying main idea; activating prior knowledge; defining and clarifying
Speaking and Listening: discussing; explaining a process

Bellringer
When students enter the classroom, have this assignment on the board: *Do you have a way of explaining how to get to your house or some other place? Write it out.*

Grammar Link to the Bellringer
Discuss students' methods for giving directions. How often do they use precise verbs such as *turn* or *circle* to clarify their directions? Ask for suggestions of other applicable verbs and discuss how the verbs would need to change, depending on whether the visitor is planning to drive, walk, or take public transportation.

Motivating Activity
Ask students how they came up with the directions they wrote for the Bellringer. Talk about how helpful it is when describing a process to visualize going through the steps of the process.

Teacher's Classroom Resources

The following resources can be used for planning, instruction, practice, reinforcement, assessment, reteaching, enrichment, or evaluation.

Teaching Tools
Lesson Plans

Transparencies
Fine Art Transparencies, 21–25
Writing Process Transparencies, 17–19B

Literature Model

Wearing rubber gloves is a wise precaution, especially when you are handling fresh hot chilies. Be careful not to touch your face or eyes while working with them.

To prepare chilies, first rinse them clean in *cold* water. (Hot water may make fumes rise from dried chilies, and even the fumes might irritate your nose and eyes.) Working under cold running water, pull out the stem of each chili and break or cut the chilies in half. Brush out the seeds with your fingers. In most cases the ribs inside are tiny, and can be left intact, but if they seem fleshy, cut them out with a small, sharp knife. Dried chilies should be torn into small pieces, covered with boiling water and soaked for at least 30 minutes before they are used. Fresh chilies may be used at once, or soaked in cold, salted water for an hour to remove some of the hotness.

Recipes: Latin American Cooking

> *The word "first" helps identify what step to begin with.*

> *What are the steps in preparing fresh chilies?*

To explain a process, choose a topic that you understand well or can research if necessary. Then identify your audience and what they may already know. Locate terms they'll understand and those you'll have to explain. Be clear about your purpose. You may be helping readers make or do something themselves, such as making tacos. On the other hand, you may be explaining how something works or happens, such as how a Mexican chef makes tacos.

Grammar
Editing Tip

As you edit your essay, notice that some of your transitions can appear in adverb clauses. For information see Lesson 14.5, pages 480–481.

Journal Writing

In your journal use a cluster map to explore topics for a process explanation. You might choose a hobby or another activity you enjoy. Circle your three best ideas.

5.4 Writing About a Process **209**

TEACH

Guided Practice

L2 Using the Model
Discuss whether students think that they could follow the directions in the model. If not, do they think the explanation is meant for someone with more cooking experience than what they have? What clues from the model support their reasoning?

L1 Enacting and Explaining
Ask a volunteer to pantomime an action he or she might perform in the classroom, such as sharpening a pencil or throwing away a piece of paper. Encourage other students to guess what the student is doing. Then ask the volunteer to explain the steps in the process he or she pantomimed. Discuss which is easier—explaining something or actually doing it.

 **Two-Minute Skill Drill**

List these audiences on the board. Have students choose a process. How might they explain the process differently for each audience?

two-year-olds   grandparents
parents   your best friend

Journal Writing Tip

Brainstorming Encourage students to brainstorm topics of general interest, such as sports or life skills. As they generate topics, suggest that students circle the ones they know something about and have some interest in.

TEACH

Guided Practice

L2 Communicating a Process Visually

Discuss how good illustrations can clarify—or sometimes even replace—a written explanation of a process. Ask volunteers to read the words in the diagram on page 208 (or in another diagram of your choosing) and then to study the illustrations. Discuss what the words and pictures contribute to their understanding of the process.

L1 Using the Model

Discuss with students the importance of using correct chronological order in writing a recipe. For a pizza recipe, what might the writer say about the tomatoes in the beginning? What about the tomatoes should wait until later in the recipe?

Independent Practice

For further stimuli for expository writing, see *Fine Art Transparencies* 21–25.

Writing Process Transparencies, 17–19B

Writing Across the Curriculum, pp. 9, 10, 17

Cooperative Learning Activities, pp. 25–30

Skills Practice

Thinking and Study Skills, pp. 3, 11, 14, 23–24

Sentence Combining Practice, pp. 32–33

Speaking and Listening Activities, pp. 12–13, 21

Research Paper and Report Writing, pp. 2–3, 9, 19–22

Composition Practice, p. 36

Make the Order Clear

Before you write about a process, gather information through research, observation, or interviews. List the steps of the process in chronological order. Then write your draft. Use transition words, such as *first, next,* and *later,* to connect the steps. The chart shows a plan one student followed to write the explanation that appears below.

Relating a Process	
Organizing Your Writing	**Example**
Topic	How to make a pizza
Audience	Friends
What the audience needs to know	The steps in making the pizza
Gathering information	Watch the video I taped. Read a pizza cookbook.
Listing steps	1. Spread dough. 2. Spread cheese. 3. Add vegetables. 4. Top with fresh tomatoes.

Student Model

The writer lists the four steps in chronological order.

What transition words does the writer use in the explanation?

First, spread the dough so that you have an inch-wide rim around the sides. The rim keeps the filling from leaking out while the pizza's cooking. Now it's time to put in the fillings. Place the cheese on the dough to keep it from getting soggy. Then add peppers, onions, or other vegetables that could burn if they were on top. Place fresh chopped tomatoes over the vegetables. Your pizza's oven-ready.

Luke Lapenta Proskine, Wilmette Junior High School, Wilmette, Illinois

210 *Expository Writing: Finding Meaning*

Enabling Strategies

LEP Practicing Explanations

Give students who are learning English practice in explaining processes by pairing them with fluent English speakers. Students can use body language, gestures, and pictures as necessary to communicate the processes they have chosen to explain. Partners can then help by providing necessary words or grammatical forms.

5.4 Writing Activities

Write a Step-by-Step Guide

Select an ordinary task, such as how to tie your shoes or how to find a library book. Write a step-by-step explanation for someone who knows little or nothing about the task.

- Explain terms the reader may not know.
- Write the steps in chronological order.
- Use transition words to connect the steps.

PURPOSE To explain how to perform a simple task

AUDIENCE Someone who does not know how to perform the task

LENGTH 1/2 page

Cooperative Learning

In a small group, brainstorm different kinds of food that you know how to make. Choose a food from the list, and draft a brief but clear step-by-step explanation of how to make the food. If you need to do any research, individual students can take responsibility. Also, artistic students can draw some steps as an additional aid to understanding. Read your draft explanation in the group, and discuss how to revise the steps to make them clearer or more informative. Assemble your final explanation into a "How to Make It" booklet with other groups.

Grammar Link

Use precise verbs to clarify explanations.

Precise verbs tell your readers exactly what you mean.

. . . *pull* out the stem of each chili and *break* or *cut* the chilies in half.

Revise each sentence below, replacing general verbs with more specific ones.

1. To make sugar cookies, first put oil on a shiny cookie sheet.
2. After making the dough, get it to cool down for several hours in the refrigerator.
3. Cook the cookies at 350° for 10 minutes.
4. Enjoy the cookies with a glass of milk, but do not eat all of them at one time.
5. Be sure to clean up the counters afterward.

See Lesson 3.3, page 116, and Lesson 10.1, page 368.

5.4 Writing About a Process **211**

ASSESS

Writing Activities Evaluation Guidelines

Write a Step-by-Step Guide
Use these criteria when evaluating your students' writing. The guide should
- use chronological order of all important steps
- use transition words
- use basic explanations that require no prior knowledge of the task

See also the *Teacher's Guide to Writing Assessment*.

Cooperative Learning
Make sure that in each recipe
- every step is included
- steps are in chronological order

Computer-generated diagrams, charts, or illustrations may also be included.

Grammar Link
(See Using the Grammar Link below.)

Reteaching
📂 *Composition Reteaching*, p. 36

Enrichment
📂 *Composition Enrichment*, p. 36

CLOSE

Discuss experiences students have had with clear, understandable directions and experiences with confusing directions. What were the results in those situations? Ask students to use their knowledge about explaining a process to write about what made the directions clear or unclear, and how the unclear ones might have been improved.

Using the Grammar Link

Grammar Link Answers
Answers will vary, but some suggestions are given below.
1. bake; use oil to grease
2. mixing the dough; and place it in the refrigerator
3. bake
4. eat the cookies … but save a few of them
5. wipe off

Precise Verbs Ask volunteers to share with the class the precise verbs they chose to replace the originals. See how many replacements the class can collect for each verb. As you expand the lists, you might invite students to consult thesauruses to suggest even more verbs. Remind them that the verbs in a recipe should be exact.

211

FOCUS

Lesson Overview

Objective: To identify cause-and-effect relationships and patterns between and among things

Skills: identifying and using cause and effect

Critical Thinking: analyzing cause-and-effect relationships; identifying sequence of events

Speaking and Listening: discussing

Bellringer

When students enter the classroom, have this assignment on the board: *On a piece of paper, write the causes of two familiar events. For example, Why did the school's football team win or lose their last game? Why is your favorite singing group popular?*

Grammar Link to the Bellringer
Explain that noticing words or phrases such as *because, as a result,* and *due to* may help students determine which incidents caused other events.

Motivating Activity

Discuss students' answers to the Bellringer and possible causes of such recent events as new legislation, elections, plane crashes, or fires. Explore why people might want to know the cause of these events. (Knowing the causes might show how voters are leaning and/or help predict or prevent future disasters.)

Expository Writing
Explaining Connections Between Events

Sometimes events are connected—one event or situation causes another, and so on. The cause always comes before the effect, or result.

The skyscraper reflects billowing clouds. You ask yourself, What would cause an architect to use reflective glass in a skyscraper's windows? James Cross Giblin answers this question.

Literature Model

*T*he energy crisis of the 1970s presented yet another threat to the windows in homes, schools, and office buildings. The all-glass architectural styles of the postwar years had depended on a steady supply of inexpensive fuel for heating and air-conditioning. Now there was a danger that that supply might be cut off, or drastically reduced.

To conserve energy and meet the demand for even better climate control in buildings, manufacturers developed an improved window covering—reflective glass. Reflective glass was coated with a thin, transparent metallic film. This mirrorlike coating reflected the sun's rays away from the glass and lowered heat gain within the building much more than mere tinted glass could.

James Cross Giblin, *Let There Be Light*

212 *Expository Writing: Finding Meaning*

Teacher's Classroom Resources

Be Clear About Cause and Effect

Giblin uses cause and effect to explain the origins of mirror-like skyscraper windows. The cause (the energy crisis) led to an effect (the development of reflective-glass windows). A cause-and-effect explanation may show one cause and one effect. Or it may explain a series of effects resulting from a single cause. It can also present multiple causes and multiple effects.

Make sure that your topic describes true cause and effect. Because one event follows another doesn't mean that the first caused the second. Suppose you close a window, and then the phone rings. Shutting the window didn't make the phone ring. Nick Poole linked cause and effect correctly in the paragraph below.

Student Model

During the nineteenth century, Americans were part of a tremendous expansion westward. These pioneering Americans left their homes back east for at least three reasons. Some were seeking fertile soil for farming. Many were looking for economic development. Trade was one way of making money. The pioneers traded with Native Americans, especially for furs. Various goods were also available from Mexicans. Finally, other Americans just went west for the adventure.

Nick Poole, Wilmette Junior High School, Wilmette, Illinois

What three causes of westward expansion does Nick identify?

Journal Writing

Select a recent event that held some particular meaning for you. Identify the causes or effects of the event. In your journal list each cause or effect.

5.5 Explaining Connections Between Events **213**

TEACH

Guided Practice

L2 Using the Model

Have students identify the sequence of events in the literature model (the war, all-glass architecture, the energy crisis, the development of reflective glass). Explain that identifying the sequence of events can eliminate certain events as possible causes, since a later event cannot cause an earlier event.

L2 Using the Model

Ask students what reasons the writer gives for people moving west in the nineteenth century (desire for fertile soil, economic development, and adventure).

Explain that the activities of one culture can have profound effects on another. As the model shows, settlers moved west for various reasons. This, in turn, caused other effects. For example, many Navajo weavers began using different colors, patterns, and materials after they were exposed to settlers' fabrics and dyes.

Two-Minute Skill Drill

Write the word *skyscraper* on the board. Have students write four or five nouns naming things you could find in a skyscraper that you might not find in your home.

Journal Writing Tip

Cause-and-Effect Relationships Suggest that students start by noting the event and then asking themselves two separate questions: What caused this event? What effect or effects did this event produce?

TEACH

Guided Practice

L2 Visual Thinking

Ask volunteers to read each section of the chart. Point out that the arrow indicates an effect will follow. Encourage students to use pictures and arrows in their own notes or journals as they investigate causes and effects.

L1 Labeling Causes and Effects

Some students may find it easier to organize their essays by clearly labeling causes and effects during the prewriting stage. They might create columns with these headings; or they might note a single event and then list its causes or effects.

Independent Practice

For further stimuli for expository writing, see *Fine Art Transparencies* 21–25.

Writing Process Transparencies, 17–19B

Writing Across the Curriculum, p. 13

Cooperative Learning Activities, pp. 25–30

Skills Practice

Thinking and Study Skills, pp. 10, 14, 19

Sentence Combining Practice, pp. 32–33

Speaking and Listening Activities, pp. 12–13, 21

Research Paper and Report Writing, pp. 2–3, 9, 19–22

Composition Practice, p. 37

Choose an Organizational Pattern

Vocabulary
Revising Tip

When revising, use transitions such as the following to help you make cause-and-effect relationships clear: *so, if, then, since, because, therefore, as a result.*

The chart below shows steps you can take to organize a cause-and-effect essay. First, select a topic, and ask yourself if a clear cause-and-effect relationship exists. Next, explore the types of cause-and-effect relationships present. Is there one cause for several effects? Are there several causes leading to a single effect? Or are there multiple causes with multiple effects?

Finally, choose a pattern of organization for your writing. You can organize your cause-and-effect draft in one of two ways. One method involves identifying a cause and then explaining its effects. The other method involves stating an effect and then discussing its cause or causes. After you've completed your draft, review it to be sure the cause-and-effect relationships are clear.

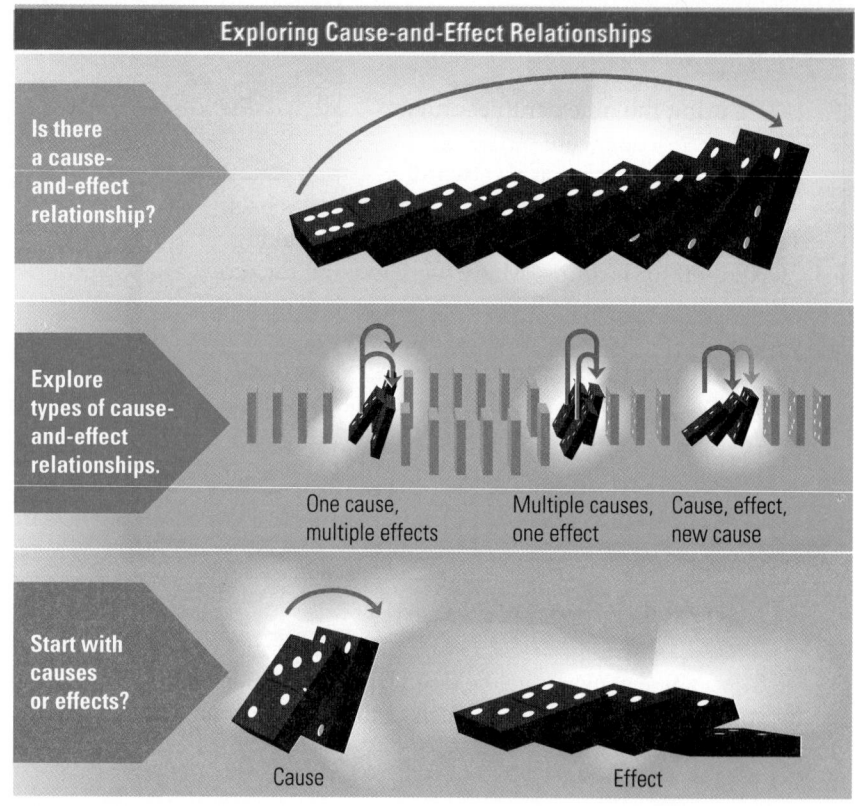

Exploring Cause-and-Effect Relationships

Is there a cause-and-effect relationship?

Explore types of cause-and-effect relationships.

One cause, multiple effects   Multiple causes, one effect   Cause, effect, new cause

Start with causes or effects?

Cause   Effect

214 *Expository Writing: Finding Meaning*

Enabling Strategies

LEP Recognizing Signal Words for Cause-and-Effect Relationships

Students whose first language is not English may have difficulty determining whether one event simply follows another or is actually caused by it. Have these students work with English-speaking partners to make a list of English words or phrases that can help determine when there is a cause-and-effect relationship. To get them started, remind students of the words and phrases *because, as a result,* and *due to* that were mentioned earlier in the lesson.

5.5 Writing Activities

Write a Cause-and-Effect Letter

You are concerned about the poor condition of the town's swimming pool and basketball courts. Write a letter to a town government official. Include what could be the result if no action is taken. Present some solutions.

- Establish a cause-and-effect relationship between equipment and accidents.
- Show any chain effects.
- Include facts to support your case.

PURPOSE To present a cause-and-effect explanation
AUDIENCE Town government official
LENGTH 3–4 paragraphs

David Hockney, *A Bigger Splash*, 1967

Cross-Curricular: Science

The painting on this page offers an artistic version of a cause-and-effect relationship that involves water. Explain cause and effect depicted in the painting. Write a two-paragraph cause-and-effect essay that explores the behavior of water.

Grammar Link

Watch out for confusing word pairs.

Be sure to choose the correct word in pairs like *than* and *then*.

. . . *lowered heat gain . . . much more **than** mere tinted glass could.*

Complete each sentence with the correct word.

I was ¹(laying, lying) down; ²(than, then) my sister's friends arrived for her party. I had to ³(raise, rise)—no more ⁴(quiet, quite) for me. I could ⁵(accept, except) that because Ann would ⁶(leave, let) me join the party. To help out, I ⁷(sat, set) the table; ⁸(all together, altogether) there were ten of us. Each would ⁹(choose, chose) food from a buffet. ¹⁰(Beside, Besides) sandwiches, we were offering Chinese dishes.

See Lessons 17.1–17.3, pages 526–531.

5.5 Explaining Connections Between Events **215**

ASSESS

Writing Activities Evaluation Guidelines

Write a Cause-and-Effect Letter
Use these criteria when evaluating your students' writing.
- Is the topic stated clearly?
- Do the details support the thesis?
- Are the causes and effects clearly stated?
- Do the details demonstrate a clear cause-and-effect relationship?
- Is the tone of the letter appropriate for the intended audience?

See also the *Teacher's Guide to Writing Assessment.*

Cross-Curricular: Science
The same guidelines used to evaluate the cause-and-effect letters can be used to evaluate each cause-and-effect essay on the behavior of water.

Grammar Link
(See Using the Grammar Link below.)

Reteaching
📁 *Composition Reteaching*, p. 37

Enrichment
📁 *Composition Enrichment*, p. 37

✋ Use *Fine Art Transparencies* 21–25 for enrichment also.

CLOSE

Encourage students to find answers to the *How?* questions that interest them. For example, How does an escalator work? How does a synthesizer produce music? If several students are interested in the same topic, encourage them to work together.

Using the Grammar Link

Grammar Link Answers
1. lying	6. let
2. then	7. set
3. rise	8. altogether
4. quiet	9. choose
5. accept	10. Besides

About the Art

David Hockney, *A Bigger Splash*, 1967
Hockney's acrylic painting, measuring 96 by 96 inches, is as noteworthy for what is not shown (a diver) as for what is visually included (the splash). The diving board and title suggest that the next diver, also not depicted, may create another change in the water.

LESSON
5.6
Expository Writing
Answering an Essay Question

How did the invention of the automobile change daily life in the United States?

Essay questions on tests call for explanations. Understanding what the question calls for will help you improve your answers.

Writing a good answer to an essay question takes some planning. First, read the question carefully. Then decide roughly how many minutes you'll spend on each of the following tasks: (1) underlining key words and jotting down key ideas to include in the answer; (2) developing a thesis statement and a brief outline; (3) drafting your answer; and (4) revising and editing as time permits.

Begin planning your answer. Look at the question for clue words that can help you compose your answer. Then identify key ideas you'll want to discuss. You might explore them by using a cluster diagram or organize them by renumbering. The facing page shows how a student organized some key ideas to answer the test question at the top of this page. The chart below the student model gives examples of clue words.

Revising Tip

When you revise your answer, cross out any unnecessary details. Insert details that will make your answer more complete.

216 *Expository Writing: Finding Meaning*

FOCUS

Lesson Overview

Objective: To write effective answers to questions on an essay test
Skills: activating prior knowledge; identifying main ideas
Critical Thinking: recalling; analyzing; synthesizing; planning an answer
Speaking and Listening: discussing; evaluating; explaining a process

Bellringer
When students enter the classroom, have this assignment on the board: *Describe the steps you should take when you are preparing to answer an essay question.*

Grammar Link to the Bellringer
Have volunteers read their answers aloud. Discuss strategies students used in organizing the answering process.

Motivating Activity
Discuss with students what their life would be like without a car. How would they get to school? How would they go shopping? Where and how would they go on vacation? Then ask students how they would organize the answers to these questions if they were asked to provide the information as an answer to a test question. Point out that they can benefit by learning a strategy for answering an essay question.

Teacher's Classroom Resources

The following resources can be used for planning, instruction, practice, reinforcement, assessment, reteaching, enrichment, or evaluation.

Teaching Tools
Lesson Plans, p. 47

Transparencies
Fine Art Transparencies, 21–25
Writing Process Transparencies, 17–19B

People
(Farmers) are no longer isolated. *Places*
Places like motels, drive-ins, and large
shopping malls are a part of daily life.
(People) within cities can travel to jobs many
miles from their homes.
(People) can drive many miles on short or
long vacations.

> The items in the list have been grouped as they will be discussed in the draft.

Clue Words in Essay Questions		
Clue Word	**Action to take**	**Example**
Describe	Use precise details to paint a picture of something.	Describe the appearance of the first Ford Model T.
Explain	Use facts, examples, or reasons to tell why or how.	Explain how the car was developed.
Compare	Tell how two or more subjects are alike.	Compare the steam car and the electric car.
Contrast	Tell how two or more subjects are different.	Contrast the Model T with a car of today.
Summarize	State main points in brief form.	Summarize how a four-cycle engine works.

Journal Writing

Use one clue word from the chart to write a question. Choose a topic that intrigues you. Take the notes you would need to answer the question.

5.6 Answering an Essay Question **217**

TEACH

Guided Practice

L2 **Identifying Key Ideas**
Students may benefit from identifying key ideas in content-area reading material. If possible give them copies of passages from textbooks they are having difficulty reading. Help them highlight key ideas in the passages. Alternatively, have them write key ideas from the passages on a piece of paper.

L1 **Using Graphic Devices**
Encourage students to organize their answers to essay questions by using visuals. Venn diagrams, for example, are useful for answers requiring comparing and contrasting.

 **Two-Minute Skill Drill**

Write three essay questions that you think the class would be interested in answering—one on school, one on outside hobbies or sports, and one on another subject.

Journal Writing Tip

Questions Before students begin taking notes, discuss what kinds of information a good answer should contain. These might include facts, descriptive details, or reasons.

TEACH

Guided Practice

L2 Using the Model

Refer students back to the question on page 216. Ask what content words from the question appear in the answer on page 218 ("the invention of the automobile" and "changed daily life in the United States").

(Answer to second callout: The writer used these details: city dwellers' and farmers' use of the car; travelers' use of the automobile; and places that cater to automobiles.)

L2 Restating Test Questions

To practice restating test questions, direct students in a partners activity. One member of each pair finds or creates an essay question that the other member restates as a topic sentence suitable for an answer. Teams then share both their questions and the topic sentences with other students.

Independent Practice

For further stimuli for expository writing, see *Fine Art Transparencies* 21–25.

Writing Process Transparencies, 17–19B

Writing Across the Curriculum, p. 16

Cooperative Learning Activities, pp. 25–30

Skills Practice

Thinking and Study Skills, pp. 11, 13, 41–42

Sentence Combining Practice, pp. 32–33

Speaking and Listening Activities, pp. 12–13, 21

Research Paper and Report Writing, pp. 2–3, 9, 19–22

Composition Practice, p. 38

Write Your Answer

Your answer should be a well-organized essay. The introduction to your essay should contain a statement of the main ideas in your answer. One effective way to begin is by restating the question.

Follow your introductory statement with the body of your answer. Include information from your notes as you write your supporting details. Then write a conclusion that restates your beginning statement and summarizes your answer. When you've finished your draft, see whether your content words match the content words of the question. Content words are the key words that relate to the subject matter. Finally, revise and edit your draft. Notice how one writer drafted an answer to the question on page 216.

The first sentence of the answer restates the question.

What details does the writer use in the body to show the change in Americans' daily life?

The conclusion restates the introductory statement.

> The invention of the automobile has changed daily life in the United States in two important ways. First, Americans are constantly on the move. City people can drive to jobs far from their homes. Farmers can travel to stores and offices miles away. Vacationers can drive to faraway places. Second, American businesses now provide services to go. Motels, drive-ins, and malls suit the needs of Americans on the run. Automobiles have changed America into a nation on wheels.

218   *Expository Writing: Finding Meaning*

Enabling Strategies

LEP Practicing Writing Answers

Allow students who are learning English to work with partners who are fluent in English to explain their answers to the essay question on page 216. Have the English-speaking partner assist by helping to supply words or phrases necessary to make the answer clear.

5.6 Writing Activities

Write a Question and Its Answer

Write an essay question and answer dealing with this image of an eagle. Keep in mind that Congress selected the eagle as the national bird and symbol of the spirit of the United States. The Latin words on the carving mean "Out of many, one."

• Plan your answer carefully.
• Include an introduction, a body, and a conclusion.

PURPOSE To answer an essay question
AUDIENCE Your history teacher
LENGTH 2 paragraphs

Cooperative Learning

With your group look through another textbook for a single essay question for everyone to answer. Take twenty minutes to answer the question. Then share your answers. Talk about the best parts of the organization and content of each essay. Discuss possible improvements.

Artist unknown, Eagle carved from one piece of pine, Salem, Massachusetts, c. 1900.

5.6 Answering an Essay Question **219**

Grammar Link

Use commas to separate items in a series.

Motels, drive-ins, and malls....

Write each sentence, adding commas where necessary.

1. Sound heat and light are all forms of energy.
2. Water wind and geothermal energy are used to generate electricity.
3. Environmentalists policymakers and consumers do not always agree on energy issues.
4. Ski resorts office buildings and airplanes all require large amounts of energy to operate.

See Lesson 20.2, pages 568–569.

ASSESS

Writing Activities Evaluation Guidelines

Write a Question and Its Answer
Use these criteria when evaluating your students' writing. Each question should
• link the art to American history

Each answer should
• respond to the key words in the question
• contain a statement identifying the main idea
• include an introduction, a body with specific details, and a conclusion

See also the *Teacher's Guide to Writing Assessment.*

Cooperative Learning
Shared discussion should focus on the organization and content of essay questions.

Grammar Link
(See Using the Grammar Link below.)

Reteaching
Composition Reteaching, p. 38

Enrichment
Composition Enrichment, p. 38

Use *Fine Art Transparencies* 21–25 for enrichment activities also.

CLOSE

Discuss past test experiences with students. Talk about how applying what students learned in this lesson can improve test results. Stress that having an organizational plan can reduce "test stress."

Using the Grammar Link

Grammar Link Answers
1. Sound, heat, and light ...
2. Water, wind, and geothermal energy are used to generate electricity.
3. Environmentalists, policymakers, and consumers ...
4. Ski resorts, office buildings, and airplanes ...

About the Art

Artist unknown, *Eagle carved from one piece of pine,* Salem, Massachusetts, c. 1900
Benjamin Franklin preferred the wild turkey, but Congress chose the eagle as a national symbol. American ships often displayed carvings like this one, which resides in the Shelburne Museum in Vermont.

219

FOCUS

Lesson Overview

Objective: To collect and gather information for a report

Skills: finding a research topic; narrowing a topic; considering purpose and audience; researching; note taking; attributing sources

Critical Thinking: analyzing; synthesizing; summarizing; generating new information; making inferences; building background

Speaking and Listening: discussing; questioning

Bellringer

When students enter the classroom, have this assignment on the board: *What resources do you go to first when researching a topic? Why do you like those resources? What other helpful resources have you found?*

Grammar Link to the Bellringer

After students list resources, suggest that they check their use of punctuation and capitalization in the titles.

Motivating Activity

Ask students which of these statements is true: The most poisonous spider is the black widow; polar bears can be green; ostriches bury their heads in the sand when they are frightened. (Only one is true: polar bears can turn green from algae inside their hairs.) Discuss different ways that students could find out about each topic.

LESSON
5.7

E x p o s i t o r y   W r i t i n g
Reports: Researching a Topic

Finding and narrowing a topic are the first tasks in preparing a research report.

On television you see a man flying an airplane, leading a flock of Canada geese. The man had raised these orphaned geese. Because they couldn't learn to fly on their own, the pilot is teaching them. Why do the geese follow the airplane? When are they ready to learn to fly? Where do they go in the winter?

Find a Research Topic

When you prepare to write a research report, think about things you'd like to know more about. Read your journal for thoughts, questions, and possible topics. Brainstorm a list of questions, such as the following, that you'd like to explore.

> *How do birds learn to fly?*
> *Do geese use all their feathers to help them fly?*
> *Why do birds migrate?*
> *How do they find their way? Do they use landmarks or the position of the sun, moon, and stars?*

Teacher's Classroom Resources

The following resources can be used for planning, instruction, practice, reinforcement, assessment, reteaching, enrichment, or evaluation.

Teaching Tools
Lesson Plans

Transparencies
Fine Art Transparencies, 21–25
Writing Process Transparencies, 17–19B

Sometimes it's difficult to know whether your questions pertain to one topic or to several. You can decide by considering the length of your report. Are you writing a two-page report or a twelve-page report? Whatever the amount of space, you must present your topic to your readers' satisfaction.

The list of questions on page 220 is about birds, but the general topic of birds is too large for one report. The topic of Canada goose feathers is probably too narrow. The topic of Canada goose migration is probably just the right size for a two-page report.

Next, consider your purpose and your audience. What do you want to explain? What information do you want to share? Decide who your readers will be and how much they already know about your topic. Can you provide all the necessary background information and facts?

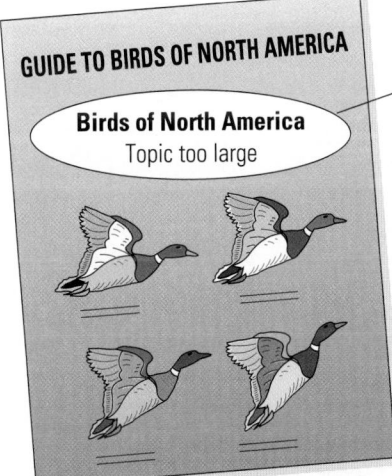

GUIDE TO BIRDS OF NORTH AMERICA

Birds of North America
Topic too large

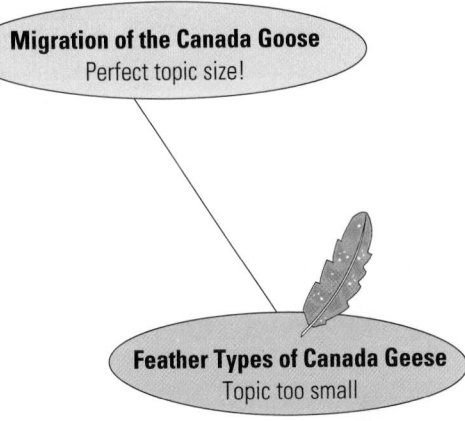

Migration of the Canada Goose
Perfect topic size!

Feather Types of Canada Geese
Topic too small

Journal Writing

Pick a news or sports event, and jot down some questions about it. Is there a report topic here? If so, summarize what you might include in the report.

5.7 Reports: Researching a Topic **221**

TEACH

Guided Practice

L2 Narrowing a Topic
Point out that students might narrow a broad topic, such as birds, by asking themselves questions that begin with *what, which, how,* or *why.* Provide practice by asking students to narrow a topic familiar to them, such as teenagers' fashions.

L1 Choosing Topics
Emphasize the importance of choosing a topic in which students have some interest. They might be put off researching topics they find uninteresting, and they might have trouble focusing on the material. To spark students' thinking, ask them if they have seen anything on television recently or heard something on the radio that they had questions about. Tell them to make a list of their questions and to save it as a source of possible topics.

Two-Minute Skill Drill

Write these topics on the board. Ask which topic would be most suitable for a two-page, seven-page, or twelve-page report. Discuss answers.

hot air balloons
weather
the first hot air balloon ride
becoming a hot air balloon pilot
buying a hot air balloon

Journal Writing Tip

Evaluating Topics Discuss the criteria students have used for identifying a valid report topic. You might also discuss how to expand or narrow a topic.

TEACH

Guided Practice

L2 Using Resources

Initiate a discussion on how the resources shown in the chart are used. (For example, encyclopedia indexes should be consulted for complete listings of subject coverage.) Also, talk about how the resources themselves can be located—through the card or computer catalog, *Readers' Guide to Periodical Literature*, etc.

L3 Expanding the Search

Encourage students to use a wider variety of sources than those shown in the chart. These might include microfilm, computer databases, a library's vertical files, or public documents. To learn how to use such materials, students can consult either a library assistant or reference books, such as *Finding Facts Fast*.

Independent Practice

For further stimuli for writing a research paper, see *Fine Art Transparencies* 21–25.

Writing Process Transparencies, 17–19B

Writing Across the Curriculum, p. 11

Cooperative Learning Activities, pp. 25–30

Skills Practice

Thinking and Study Skills, pp. 4, 13, 23–24, 35

Speaking and Listening Activities, pp. 12–13, 21

Sentence Combining Practice, pp. 32–33

Research Paper and Report Writing, pp. 2–3, 9, 19–22

Composition Practice, p. 39

Get the Facts

Now it's time to gather the facts you'll need to begin drafting your report. Find as many sources as you can. The chart below lists the kinds of sources available in the library and gives an example of each. It also shows the form in which you identify, or cite, your sources in your notes. You'll use the same form in your final paper. Pages 607–628 offer more information on using the library.

Many report writers use index cards to record notes from sources. Use one card for each note, and include your source. Read the source carefully so that you can summarize the information in your own words. You may also quote directly; but when you do, you must copy word for word the information you want to quote. Always use quotation marks when you quote directly. In your report you must let your readers know when you're using someone else's words or ideas.

Grammar
Editing Tip
When editing, check the spelling and capitalization of proper nouns. For more information see Lessons 19.2–19.4, pages 552–557.

Sources and Identification

Source	Examples	How to Identify Sources
Books	*Birds* / *Field Guide to the Birds* / *Bird Migration*	Mead, Chris. Bird Migration. New York: Facts on File Publications, 1983.
Magazines & Newspapers	*Audubon* / *Discover* / *Houston Chronicle*	Warden, J.W. "Migration! The Great Spring Event." Petersen's Photographic Magazine, April 1992: 22–25.
Encyclopedias	*The World Book Encyclopedia* / *The Illustrated Encyclopedia of the Animal Kingdom*	"Canada Goose." The World Book Encyclopedia. 1993 ed.
Video materials	*Audubon Society's Video-Guides to Birds of North America: Volume 1*	Audubon Society's VideoGuides to Birds of North America: 1. Godfrey-Stadin Productions, 1985.

222 *Expository Writing: Finding Meaning*

Enabling Strategies

LEP Choosing Words

Students may need help identifying key terms in the content area they are researching. Encourage them to find fluent English-speaking partners who will help them investigate confusing words. As students write the first draft of their reports, you might suggest that they use their home language for words they cannot translate. When they are finished, they can use a bilingual dictionary to translate all the words at once.

5.7 Writing Activities

Choose a Topic and Begin Your Research

Write down three or four topics that you would like to research. Take some time to think about which one you would most enjoy researching and writing about. Write your topic at the top of a piece of paper. Write the headings **Books, Magazines and Newspapers, People, Other Sources.** Beside each one, note specific research sources. Use the library, and talk to people who know about your subject to get more ideas for sources.

- Narrow the topic so that you can cover it thoroughly.
- Ask yourself three questions about your topic, and use your sources to answer the questions on note cards.

PURPOSE To gather information for a report
AUDIENCE Yourself
LENGTH 1 page of source ideas; at least 15 note cards

COMPUTER OPTION

Check to see if your local library has its card catalog on the computer. If so, ask the librarian to show you how to use it to search for books and magazine articles related to your topic.

Grammar Link

Punctuate and capitalize titles correctly.

"Migration! The Great Spring Event"

The World Book Encyclopedia

Write each title, adding capital letters, quotation marks, and italics (underlining) as needed.

1. a pictorial history of the civil war (book)
2. following in sherman's footsteps (magazine article)
3. minneapolis star tribune (newspaper)
4. funk and wagnall's new encyclopedia
5. robert m. stuart's guide to civil war battlegrounds (video)
6. the red badge of courage (book)
7. the journal of the civil war (magazine)
8. gettysburg as theme park? (newspaper article)
9. the battle hymn of the republic (song)
10. the battle of bull run (book chapter)

See Lesson 19.4, pages 556–557, and Lesson 20.6, pages 576–577.

5.7 Reports: Researching a Topic **223**

Using the Grammar Link

223

Setting the Purpose

Lesson 5.8 teaches students what information should be included in a business letter and how it should be presented.

FOCUS

Lesson Overview

Objective: To compose a concise, standard business letter

Skills: following a business letter format; requesting information; requesting an interview

Critical Thinking: synthesizing; identifying main idea; summarizing; building background; decision-making

Speaking and Listening: discussing

Bellringer

When students enter the classroom, have this assignment on the board: *Suppose that you find an article in the newspaper about your school basketball team. The article makes you really angry. What can you do about it?*

Grammar Link to the Bellringer

Talk about the option of sending a letter to the newspaper editor. Ask students how they think a letter might be received if it had several punctuation and spelling errors. What if the editor decided to print it with the errors intact? How might it come across?

Motivating Activity

Ask students what kinds of mail they most enjoy receiving. Encourage students to think of a question they have written in a letter. If they received a reply, how did it answer the question? Then ask if anyone has sent a letter to a business or other organization asking for information. If so, what did the writer want to know, and what was the answer?

LESSON

5.8

E x p o s i t o r y   W r i t i n g

Reports: Writing a Business Letter to Request Information

Writing a business letter can help you get answers to questions that other sources can't answer. As the model below shows, you can write a business letter to request information or to ask someone for an interview.

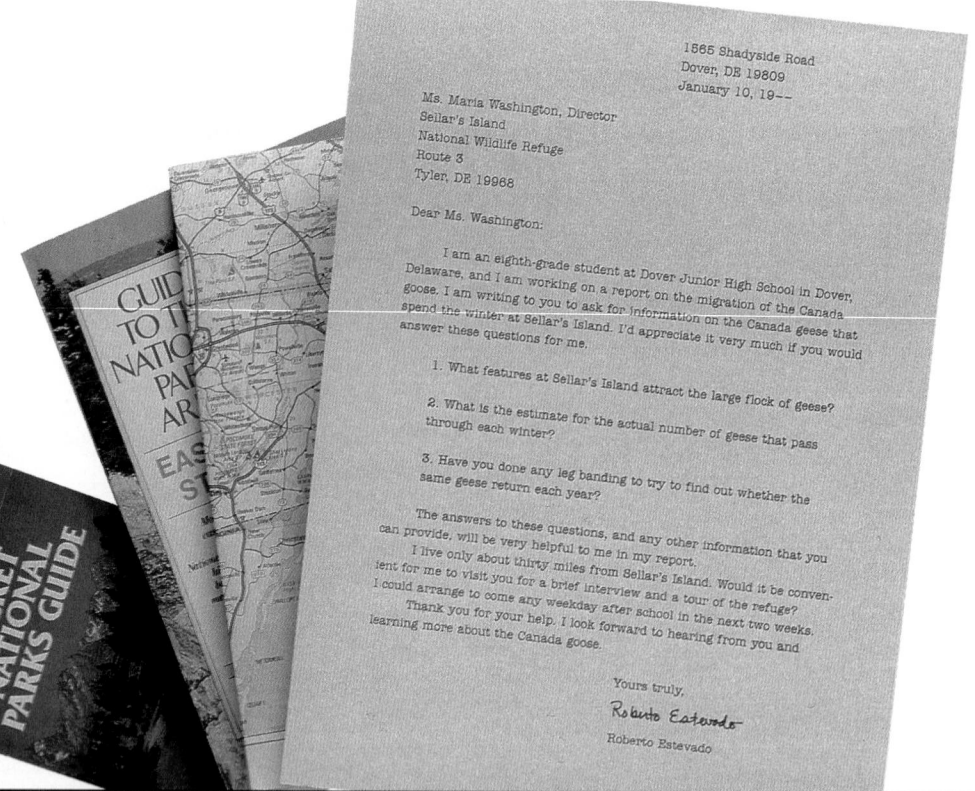

1865 Shadyside Road
Dover, DE 19809
January 10, 19--

Ms. Maria Washington, Director
Sellar's Island
National Wildlife Refuge
Route 3
Tyler, DE 19988

Dear Ms. Washington:

I am an eighth-grade student at Dover Junior High School in Dover, Delaware, and I am working on a report on the migration of the Canada goose. I am writing to you to ask for information on the Canada geese that spend the winter at Sellar's Island. I'd appreciate it very much if you would answer these questions for me.

1. What features at Sellar's Island attract the large flock of geese?

2. What is the estimate for the actual number of geese that pass through each winter?

3. Have you done any leg banding to try to find out whether the same geese return each year?

The answers to these questions, and any other information that you can provide, will be very helpful to me in my report.

I live only about thirty miles from Sellar's Island. Would it be convenient for me to visit you for a brief interview and a tour of the refuge? I could arrange to come any weekday after school in the next two weeks.

Thank you for your help. I look forward to hearing from you and learning more about the Canada goose.

Yours truly,

Roberto Estevado

Roberto Estevado

Teacher's Classroom Resources

The following resources can be used for planning, instruction, practice, reinforcement, assessment, reteaching, enrichment, or evaluation.

Teaching Tools
Lesson Plans, p. 49

Transparencies
Fine Art Transparencies, 21–25
Writing Process Transparencies, 17–19B

Know Why You're Writing a Business Letter

When you write a business letter, you should have a clear reason for writing. If you're writing a business letter to request information, state your questions clearly. Make your request specific and reasonable, and make sure you're asking for information you can't get anywhere else. If you're requesting an interview, explain what you want to discuss. Suggest some dates and times. Business letters have other uses, such as placing an order or lodging a complaint. A letter to the editor is a business letter written to express an opinion.

Grammar
Editing Tip

When editing, check your use of pronouns and antecedents. For more information see Lessons 11.1–11.7, pages 402–411.

Guidelines for Writing Business Letters

1. Use correct business-letter form. Some dictionaries and typing manuals outline different forms of business letters.
2. Be courteous, and use standard English.
3. Be brief and to the point. Explain why you need the information.
4. Use clean white or off-white paper. Make a neat presentation.
5. Be considerate. Request only information you can't get another way. If unsure where to find information, ask your librarian.
6. When requesting an interview, make it easy for the interviewee to meet with you. Suggest a few dates.

Don't hesitate to write business letters to request information. Many people will be happy to tell what they know.

Journal Writing

Look in your journal for a possible report topic. Brainstorm possible sources for this information other than the library and how to get the information.

5.8 Reports: Writing a Business Letter to Request Information **225**

UNIT 5
Lesson 5.8

TEACH

Guided Practice

L2 Writing a Letter
Ask students to think of reasons why written requests for items or information might be more effective than oral requests. (The receiver can consider the request when convenient and does not have to remember details; the sender can include several requests.) Point out that planning can improve the effectiveness of letters just as well as it improves other forms of writing.

L3 Trying It Out
Students can practice writing genuine letters of request for free samples, products, catalogs, or booklets. Ask them to collect names and addresses of sources for such items. Students can find these in books such as *Free Stuff for Kids*, magazines, newspaper columns, and advertisements. Invite each student to write a different letter requesting a specific item. Suggest that students have all items sent to the school for the class to examine.

Two-Minute Skill Drill

Write these occupations on the board, and ask students to give a reason for writing a letter to each.

restaurant manager
postal carrier
local sports hero
landlord

Journal Writing Tip

Brainstorming Resources Suggest that students consider individuals, representatives of organizations, or experts whom they might interview.

📁 **Blackline Masters**
Thinking and Study Skills, pp. 11, 13
Writing Across the Curriculum, pp. 4–8
Cooperative Learning Activities, pp. 25–30

Sentence Combining Practice, pp. 32–33
Speaking and Listening Activities, pp. 12–13, 21
Research Paper and Report Writing, pp. 2–3, 9, 19–22

Composition Practice, p. 40
Composition Reteaching, p. 40
Composition Enrichment, p. 40

Assessment
📁 *Teacher's Guide to Writing Assessment*

TEACH

Guided Practice

L2 Using the Model
Encourage students to consider the first impression that the model's appearance makes. Ask what contributes to the letter's businesslike appearance and what clues suggest that it was written with care. Then direct students to describe the appearance of a letter that would make a poor first impression (messy, error-filled, illegible). What might the recipient of such a letter think?

L2 Reviewing Peers' Letters
When peer reviewers look at drafts, suggest that they ask themselves the following questions: Is the writer identified early in the letter? Is the purpose of the letter clear? What response might be expected from the reader? Can the reader tell what action to take?

Independent Practice

- For further stimuli for letter writing, see *Fine Art Transparencies* 21–25.
- *Writing Process Transparencies,* 17–19B
- *Writing Across the Curriculum,* pp. 4–8
- *Cooperative Learning Activities,* pp. 25–30

Skills Practice
- *Thinking and Study Skills,* pp. 11, 13
- *Speaking and Listening Activities,* pp. 12–13, 21
- *Sentence Combining Practice,* pp. 32–33
- *Research Paper and Report Writing,* pp. 2–3, 9, 19–22
- *Composition Practice,* p. 40

226

Get Down to Business

Readers expect business letters to be clear and to follow certain rules. At the beginning of your letter, introduce yourself and your purpose for writing. Use the paragraphs that follow to support your purpose with details. Conclude by making it clear exactly what you want from the reader. Are you requesting an interview? Are you asking for answers to specific questions? Show your draft to a peer reviewer, and ask whether your message is clear. Noticing the care you took in writing to them, your readers will be more likely to respond to you.

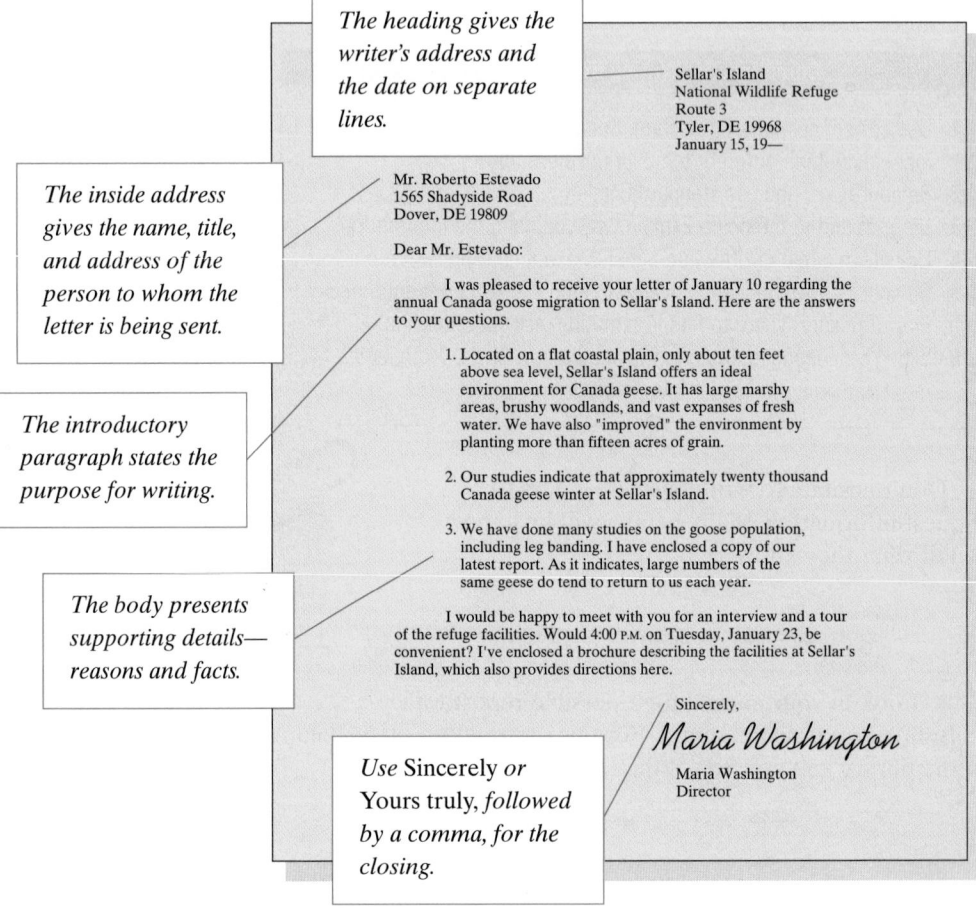

The heading gives the writer's address and the date on separate lines.

Sellar's Island
National Wildlife Refuge
Route 3
Tyler, DE 19968
January 15, 19—

The inside address gives the name, title, and address of the person to whom the letter is being sent.

Mr. Roberto Estevado
1565 Shadyside Road
Dover, DE 19809

Dear Mr. Estevado:

The introductory paragraph states the purpose for writing.

I was pleased to receive your letter of January 10 regarding the annual Canada goose migration to Sellar's Island. Here are the answers to your questions.

1. Located on a flat coastal plain, only about ten feet above sea level, Sellar's Island offers an ideal environment for Canada geese. It has large marshy areas, brushy woodlands, and vast expanses of fresh water. We have also "improved" the environment by planting more than fifteen acres of grain.

2. Our studies indicate that approximately twenty thousand Canada geese winter at Sellar's Island.

The body presents supporting details— reasons and facts.

3. We have done many studies on the goose population, including leg banding. I have enclosed a copy of our latest report. As it indicates, large numbers of the same geese do tend to return to us each year.

I would be happy to meet with you for an interview and a tour of the refuge facilities. Would 4:00 P.M. on Tuesday, January 23, be convenient? I've enclosed a brochure describing the facilities at Sellar's Island, which also provides directions here.

Sincerely,

Maria Washington

Maria Washington
Director

Use Sincerely *or* Yours truly, *followed by a comma, for the closing.*

226 *Expository Writing: Finding Meaning*

Enabling Strategies

LEP Beginning with Content
Some students may feel overwhelmed by details of form and by the need for standard English. Encourage such students to concentrate first on the content of their letters. They might orally rehearse their requests with fluent English-speaking partners, practicing how they will introduce themselves and how they will word their questions. After they feel comfortable with the content, they can focus on details of form.

5.8 Writing Activities

Write a Business Letter

Look again at the topic you chose in the Journal Writing activity on page 225. Somewhere there is a person who is an expert on that subject and can give you information that can be used in a report. Locate an expert on your topic; the librarian at your local library can help you with your search. After you have located an expert, write him or her a business letter. If the person lives in your area, use the letter to request an interview. Then prepare and carry out the interview. If your expert does not live near you, use the letter to ask the questions that you would ask in an interview.

PURPOSE To gain firsthand information for a report
AUDIENCE Your interviewer; yourself
LENGTH 1-page letter; 1–2 pages of notes from the interview

COMPUTER OPTION

Proofread your business letter carefully—even after your computer checks for spelling errors. Most programs can't catch errors caused by homophones, such as *to, too,* and *two.*

Grammar Link

Use correct punctuation in a business letter.

Remember to use a colon after the salutation and a comma between city and state, between day and year, and after the closing.

Write the business letter below, using the sample letter on page 226 as a guide.

4464 Rheims Place
Dallas TX 75205
January 20 19–

Dr. Cheryl Anne White
33 Parker Street
Cambridge MA 02138

Dear Dr. White

　　I heard you speak in Austin Texas on November 10 19– and was impressed with your advice on feeding birds. Please send me information about how I can order copies of your brochure, "Winter Feeding Stations."

　　Thank you for your assistance.

Yours truly

Aaron Jacobs

See Lesson 20.4, pages 572–573, and Lesson 20.5, pages 574–575.

5.8 Reports: Writing a Business Letter to Request Information **227**

Using the Grammar Link

Grammar Link Answers
1. Dallas, TX
2. January 20, 19—
3. Cambridge, MA
4. Dear Dr. White:
5. Austin, Texas,
6. November 10, 19—,
7. assistance.
8. Yours truly,

Punctuation Variations You might discuss variations students have seen in other business letters or business letter models, such as the abbreviation *St.* for *Street*, longer abbreviations for state names, and a comma instead of a colon after the salutation. Talk about which variations are acceptable.

Setting the Purpose

Lesson 5.9 teaches students to plan and draft a report based on notes taken from both oral and written sources.

FOCUS

Lesson Overview

Objective: To complete a written report through the draft stage
Skills: explaining; outlining; identifying purpose and audience; identifying main idea; writing a thesis statement; drafting
Critical Thinking: synthesizing information; finding main idea
Speaking and Listening: discussing

Bellringer

When students enter the classroom, have this assignment on the board: *Write a plan for a week-long camping trip you might take, and list all the things you need.*

Grammar Link to the Bellringer

Have students put their camping trip plans in outline form, including major heads for equipment, food, and so on. Have them circle any apostrophes that form possessives of plural nouns.

Motivating Activity

Ask students why people make specific plans when going on a vacation or taking a trip. To spark their thinking, suggest that planning might help realize the purpose of the trip: to relax and have a good time. Point out that even a rough draft of a plan can produce a better outcome than no plan at all. Explain that planning improves reports as well.

Expository Writing
Reports: Planning and Drafting

In this lesson, as you use research notes to begin planning and drafting, you will pull together all you've learned about reports.

© Watterson 1992. Universal Press Syndicate

Like Calvin, you've decided on a topic for your report. Unlike Calvin, however, you've done your research. Now that you've collected so much valuable information, it's time to learn a few strategies to help you begin your report.

Develop a Plan of Action

Before you begin planning and drafting a report, make sure you have a clear idea of your purpose for writing and of your audience. Knowing this information will help you focus your planning and drafting.

Review your notes, looking for a focus or a main idea that you can express in a sentence or two. This main idea is the angle or question that guided your research. Draft a thesis statement based on this main idea. Although your thesis statement may change, it can guide you as you write your outline.

228 *Expository Writing: Finding Meaning*

Teacher's Classroom Resources

The following resources can be used for planning, instruction, practice, reinforcement, assessment, reteaching, enrichment, or evaluation.

Teaching Tools
Lesson Plans, p. 50

Transparencies
Fine Art Transparencies, 21–25
Writing Process Transparencies, 17–19B

An outline and a thesis statement cover the main points of a report. Group your notes according to similar topics. These become your subtopics. In this model Roberto grouped his notes into subtopics. These appear as major outline headings. Roberto's thesis statement appears at the top of his outline.

The Canada goose's migration pattern has dramatically changed in recent years.

I. Characteristics of the Canada goose
   A. What the Canada goose looks and sounds like as it flies overhead
   B. What its traditional migration pattern used to be
   C. How the pattern has changed
II. Basic needs of the Canada goose, and how they relate to migration
   A. Food
   B. Water
   C. Protection
III. Why and where the Canada goose used to migrate

The thesis statement identifies the topic and the main idea of the report.

The major outline heads state the main ideas of the paragraphs. Subheads note supporting facts and details.

Like all wildlife, Canada geese have a few basic requirements for

Source: John Terborgh, *Where Have All the Birds Gone?*
Princeton

rld War I, corn harvested by ter harvested by machine—leave cent of crop in field. This will fe f birds. Therefore "the winter capacity for Canada geese has probably been raised many fold."

Journal Writing

Read a newspaper or magazine article. In your journal jot down the title and the main idea. Explain whether the article was clear. What subtopics did the writer use? Did the article hold your interest? Why?

TEACH

Guided Practice

L2 Using the Thesis Statement and Outline
Encourage students to ask questions raised by the thesis statement. For example: How has the migration pattern changed? Why has it changed? When did it change? Tell students to identify which questions the outline indicates it will answer and which it will not. This part of the outline, for example, does not tell where the Canada goose migrates to now. Discuss the kinds of details students would expect to find under each subhead.

L1 Identifying Main Ideas
Students may have difficulty identifying the main ideas in their notes. Have them look at each note and ask themselves "What is this about?" Students then might circle words in the note that answer the question. Suggest that students look for similar or common words in their other notes. They can use these words to write a sentence stating the main idea.

Two-Minute Skill Drill

Have students arrange these words into an outline:

baseball	sculpture	painting
sports	art	hockey

Journal Writing Tip

Main Ideas Remind students that the first and last few paragraphs of an article often contain statements of the main idea. Have them look for these paragraphs in their newspaper and magazine articles.

TEACH

Guided Practice

L2 Promoting Discussion

To help students understand the importance of an introduction, ask a volunteer to read aloud the introduction to the drafting facsimile. First have students identify how the author grabs the reader's attention. Then encourage volunteers to give personal responses to the introduction, explaining why they did or did not find it interesting.

L2 Improving Introductions

Have students write three possible introductions for their reports, and have them exchange papers with a partner. After a discussion, they should select the best introduction based on content and interest level.

Independent Practice

For further stimuli for expository writing, see *Fine Art Transparencies 21–25.*

Writing Process Transparencies, 17–19B

Writing Across the Curriculum, p. 11

Skills Practice

Thinking and Study Skills, pp. 23–24, 34–35

Cooperative Learning Activities, pp. 25–30

Sentence Combining Practice, pp. 32–33

Speaking and Listening Activities, pp. 12–13, 21

Research Paper and Report Writing, pp. 2–3, 9, 19–22

Composition Practice, p. 41

Put the Plan into Action

Drafting Tip

When drafting, refer to your outline and thesis statement to make sure you have included all your main ideas in your draft.

After you get your ideas organized, use your notes and outline to draft the three main parts of your report. The **introduction** presents your topic and thesis statement. It offers a chance to engage your readers and should grab their attention. Consider including a thought-provoking quotation, fact, statement, eyewitness account, or anecdote. The **body** supports your thesis statement with reasons and facts. The **conclusion** may reflect your thesis statement by summarizing main points. It should bring the report to a logical and graceful end. If your paper raises any new issues or questions, try including them in the conclusion.

Follow the process shown below in drafting a report from notes and an outline. Grammar and spelling errors will be corrected later.

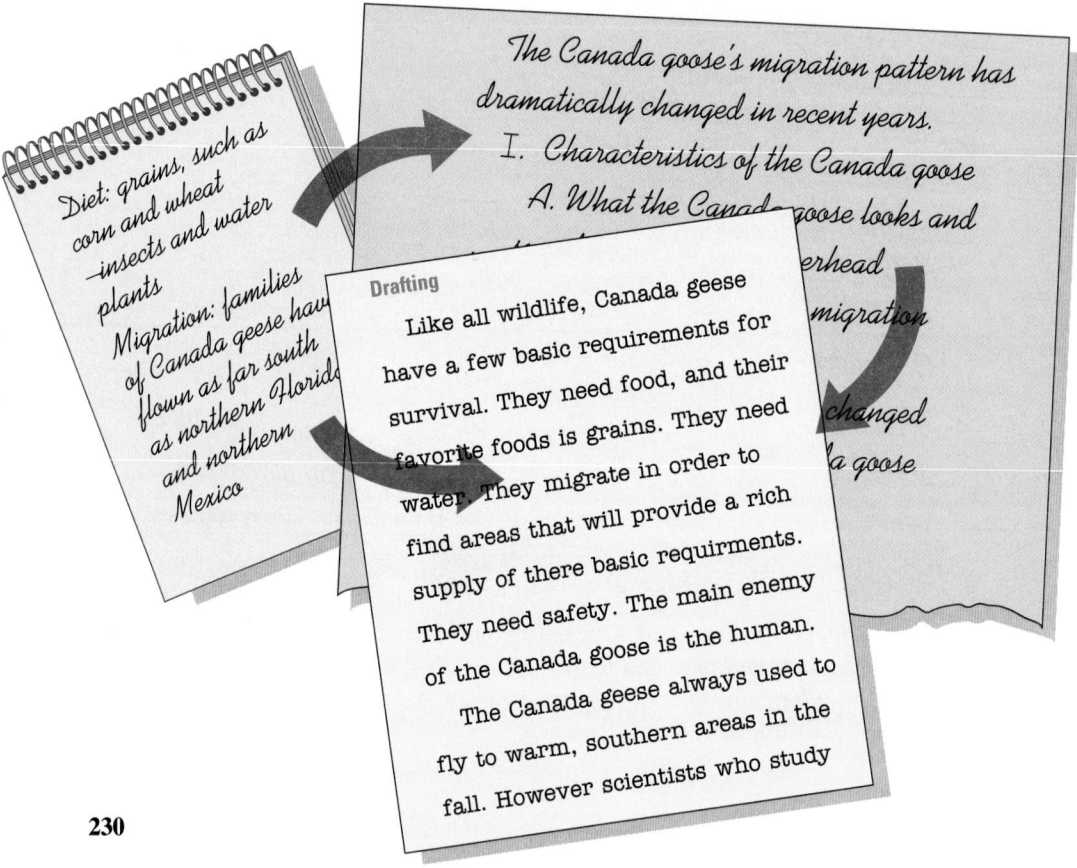

Diet: grains, such as corn and wheat —insects and water plants

Migration: families of Canada geese have flown as far south as northern Florida and northern Mexico

The Canada goose's migration pattern has dramatically changed in recent years.
I. Characteristics of the Canada goose
   A. What the Canada goose looks and ...
   ... erhead ... migration ... changed ... a goose

Drafting

Like all wildlife, Canada geese have a few basic requirements for survival. They need food, and their favorite foods is grains. They need water. They migrate in order to find areas that will provide a rich supply of there basic requirments. They need safety. The main enemy of the Canada goose is the human.

The Canada geese always used to fly to warm, southern areas in the fall. However scientists who study

230

Enabling Strategies

LEP Selecting Main Ideas

Students who are learning English may have problems grasping the concept of main ideas. Encourage English-proficient students to use a visual parallel to help them. Have them demonstrate that writers organize reports just as artists organize pictures. Like an artist, a writer must decide which details to focus upon and which to ignore, which to include and which to exclude. Help students learning English to use what they know about organizing to develop main ideas for their reports.

5.9 Writing Activities

Outline and Draft

Now you have the raw materials for your report. You have done your research and made your note cards. You are now ready to develop a plan of action and then write the draft of your report. Have your ideas changed as you researched? Are there new questions you would like to answer? Now is the time to finalize the focus of your report. Base your thesis statement on this focus or main idea. Create an outline from the notes you have taken, grouping the notes into similar topics or subtopics. Use your notes and outline to draft the three main parts of your report. Do not worry about spelling and grammar now; you will correct errors in these later.

- Write a thesis statement summarizing what you want to tell your readers.
- Create an outline, using your note cards.
- Draft your report, including an introduction and a conclusion.

PURPOSE To outline and draft a report
AUDIENCE Peer reviewers
LENGTH 2–3 pages

COMPUTER OPTION

Check to see whether your word-processing program has an Outlining feature to help you create an outline. Use it to organize your report.

Grammar Link

Use an apostrophe to form possessive nouns.

*The Canada **goose's** migration pattern. . . .*

To make the singular noun *goose* possessive, add *'s*. To make the plural noun *geese* possessive, also add *'s*: *geese's*. If a plural noun already ends in *-s*, add just an apostrophe: *birds'*.

Write each possessive phrase below, adding apostrophes where necessary.

1. the childrens playground
2. their parents voices
3. mices eating habits
4. a dogs life cycle
5. several students reports
6. the womens decision
7. my bosss orders
8. the planets orbits
9. universities research grants
10. peoples attitudes
11. the mens appointments
12. the gooses nest
13. the cities rail systems
14. their families vacation plans
15. his attorneys fees

See Lesson 20.7, pages 578–579.

5.9 Reports: Planning and Drafting **231**

Writing Activities Evaluation Guidelines

Outline and Draft
Use these criteria when evaluating your students' writing.
- The thesis statement should give the topic and main idea of the report.
- The outline should include the main ideas of the paragraphs as major heads as well as subheads with supporting facts and details.
- The draft should have a high-interest introductory paragraph, including a sentence that identifies the topic, a body with facts and reasons that support the thesis statement, and a logical conclusion that summarizes main points.

See also the *Teacher's Guide to Writing Assessment.*

Computer Option
Make sure students understand how to use the computer's outlining feature.

Grammar Link
(See Using the Grammar Link below.)

Reteaching
📁 *Composition Reteaching,* p. 41

Enrichment
📁 *Composition Enrichment,* p. 41

CLOSE

Encourage students to discuss the outlining and drafting processes they have just completed. Ask them what they had the most difficulty with, what they found easiest, and why. Ask volunteers to read their drafts aloud to the class.

Using the Grammar Link

Grammar Link Answers

1. children's
2. parents'
3. mice's
4. dog's
5. students'
6. women's
7. boss's
8. planets'
9. universities'
10. people's
11. men's
12. goose's
13. cities'
14. families'
15. attorney's
    or attorneys'

Using Apostrophes Ask students to work together to list additional plural nouns on the board. Have volunteers add apostrophes to form the plural possessives of these nouns.

FOCUS

Lesson Overview

Objective: To revise, edit, and present a report; to establish criteria for evaluating a report

Skills: using a checklist to make revisions; proofreading a report; making editorial comments on a peer's report

Critical Thinking: clarifying; summarizing; decision-making

Speaking and Listening: listening to a draft; presenting a draft; discussing

Bellringer

When students enter the classroom, have this assignment on the board: *Copy the following paragraph, and correct any errors you find.*

Contrary to legend Precident lincoln did not scrabble the Gettysburg Address on the back of an envelop. He revise it at least five tomes.

Grammar Link to the Bellringer

Ask students if they noticed any punctuation missing from the paragraph about the Gettysburg Address. (Contrary to legend, . . .)

Motivating Activity

Invite students to cite examples of situations in which someone temporarily lost an item and someone fresh on the scene discovered that it was "right under her nose." Point out that someone unfamiliar with a situation will often notice details that those involved will not observe.

Expository Writing
Reports: Revising, Editing, and Presenting

Revising and editing are crucial steps in presenting your topic clearly and effectively.

Sometimes writing your report can place you too close to it to evaluate it objectively. You need to read your report as if for the first time.

Read Between the Lines

After you've finished the first draft of your report, put it aside for a while so you can return to it with a fresh eye. Then you can begin revising. Start by reading for sense. Are your main ideas clear? Have you supported your ideas with strong facts, statistics, examples, incidents, and reasons? Have you used transitions to help your readers get from one main idea to the next? Put yourself in your readers' place. If they know little or nothing about the topic, imagine that you don't either. Read carefully. The hints in the following chart may help you.

232 *Expository Writing: Finding Meaning*

Teacher's Classroom Resources

The following resources can be used for planning, instruction, practice, reinforcement, assessment, reteaching, enrichment, or evaluation.

Teaching Tools
Lesson Plans

Transparencies
Fine Art Transparencies, 21–25
Writing Process Transparencies, 17–19B

Revising Checklist	
Question	**Example**
Do the main ideas in the paper support the thesis statement?	Summarize the main idea of each paragraph in the paper's body. Be sure that each main idea supports the thesis statement.
Do the main ideas appear in a logical sequence that builds to the conclusion?	List the main ideas in the order they appear. Can you think of a better order?
Does the conclusion sum up the main ideas and reflect the report's purpose?	Summarize the conclusion, and compare it with the thesis statement. The thesis statement should lead to the conclusion.

Like all wildlife, Canada geese have a few basic requirements for survival. They need food ^(an ample supply of) and their favorite foods is grains. They need water. They migrate to find areas that will provide a rich suply of there basic requirments. also ^(protection from their predators) They need safety. The main enemy of the Canada goose is the human. ^(predator)

The Canada geese always used to fly to warm, Southern areas in the fall. However scientists who study these birds have discovered a change.

Moving this sentence connects two important thoughts.

Journal Writing

Review some of your earliest journal writing. How would you revise your writing now? Jot down some notes, or revise a passage. Notice the difference a fresh eye can make.

eacher's Classroom Resources

TEACH

Guided Practice

L2 Asking Questions
Point out that the questions in the first column are limited. Help students create their own charts with questions such as the following: What transitions might make the connection between sentences or paragraphs clearer? What background information might make this report easier to understand? Work with students to apply these questions to their own writing.

L1 Creating a Checklist
Students may have difficulty keeping track of everything they need to look for as they revise their drafts. You might alleviate the problem by helping students make a checklist of revision steps, based on the questions posed in this lesson. Suggest that they draw a small square in front of each step on the list. As they complete each step, tell them to put a check in the square.

Two-Minute Skill Drill

List on the board these steps for developing a report. Have students reorder them into the sequence a writer would follow.

revise	plan	research
draft	present	edit

Journal Writing Tip

Revising Remind students that their writing should have a clear thesis statement. They should be rigorous in cutting material that does not support that statement.

233

TEACH

Guided Practice

L2 Discussing Revising

Point out that writer Ernest Hemingway once said, "Easy writing makes hard reading." Use this quotation as a springboard to discuss the difference between what a writer means to say and what the words actually say. Emphasize that revising helps ensure that writers' words say what writers intended.

L3 Examining a Revision

To emphasize the importance of revising and editing, encourage students to look for examples of revised and edited manuscript pages. These often appear as illustrations in biographies of authors, in books about writing, and in style guides. Encourage students to discuss any changes depicted and speculate about why the writer made them.

Independent Practice

For further stimuli for expository writing, see *Fine Art Transparencies*, 21–25.

Writing Process Transparencies, 17–19B

Writing Across the Curriculum, p. 11

Cooperative Learning Activities, pp. 25–30

Skills Practice

Thinking and Study Skills, pp. 14, 23–24, 34–35

Sentence Combining Practice, pp. 32–33

Speaking and Listening Activities, pp. 12–13, 21

Research Paper and Report Writing, pp. 2–3, 9, 19–22

Composition Practice, p. 42

Cross the *t*'s and Dot the *i*'s

Presenting Tip

When you hand in your report, make sure it is prepared neatly, clearly, and cleanly—for easier reading.

When you edit your report, you proofread for any errors in grammar, spelling, punctuation, and word use. For more information, review pages 80–83. For help with a particular problem, see the **Troubleshooter** Table of Contents on page 301. You may find it easier to proofread for one type of error at a time. Some word-processing programs will help you check for spelling errors. Remember, however, to read your draft for missing words and words that are easily confused, such as *their* and *there*. If you add a bibliography—a listing of your sources—follow the examples on page 222. Attach a clean cover sheet to your report, giving your name, the title of your report, and the date.

A spelling error is corrected.

Two nouns are changed to correct an error in subject-verb agreement.

> Like all wildlife, Canada geese have a few basic requirements for survival. They migrate to find areas that will provide a rich supply of there basic requirments. They need an ample supply of food. Their favorite foods is grains. They need water. They also need protection from their predators. The main predator of the Canada goose is the human.
>
> Canada geese always used to fly to warm, Southern areas in the fall. However, scientists who study these birds have discovered a change. Over the past few years, more and more Canada geese have remained in northern areas during the winter.

Migration Habits of Canada Geese
Roberto Estevado
February 28, 19–

234 *Expository Writing: Finding Meaning*

Enabling Strategies

LEP Naming Main Ideas

Remind students that the point of writing is to communicate, not to follow every rule exactly. Read the student facsimile aloud so that students can hear the writer's ideas instead of being distracted by minor errors. Then help students focus on their own messages by asking them to name the two or three most important ideas they want to communicate. Only after they have identified these ideas should students focus on the mechanics of writing them down.

5.10 Writing Activities

Revise, Edit, and Share Your Report

Now is the time to make sure your report says what you want it to say. Does it support your thesis statement? Will it interest your readers?

- Revise your report: Check it for clarity, accuracy, organization, and interest.
- Edit your report: Proofread for any errors in grammar, usage, or spelling.
- Present your report: Make a final copy that others will want to read and study.

PURPOSE To finish and share a research report
AUDIENCE Classmates, teacher, family
LENGTH 2–3 pages

Cooperative Learning

Work in a small group to practice your revising and editing skills. With other group members, choose a draft you have recently written. Take turns reading your drafts aloud. Then exchange papers with a partner in the group. Write revision suggestions for each other, and discuss each other's suggested changes. Make only the changes that you agree with. Exchange papers again, and edit for errors in spelling and sentence structure.

Grammar Link

Use a comma after introductory words or phrases.

However, scientists who study these birds have discovered a change.
Like all wildlife, Canada geese have a few basic requirements. . . .

Write each sentence, adding commas where necessary.

1. Indeed a human family that adopts a dog takes on a number of responsibilities.
2. Unlike wild dogs domestic dogs depend on people to meet their needs and to provide food and shelter.
3. Because of their long relationship with human beings domestic dogs also require human contact if they are to thrive.
4. Originally bred to work most domestic dogs today are nonworking dogs and thus need regular exercise.
5. In return for all this care domestic dogs give their owners companionship and fun.

See Lesson 20.2, pages 568–569.

5.10 Reports: Revising, Editing, and Presenting **235**

ASSESS

Writing Activities Evaluation Guidelines

Revise, Edit, and Share Your Report
Use these criteria when evaluating your students' writing:
- It is clear, accurate, organized, and interesting.
- There are no errors in grammar, usage, or spelling.
- It is cleanly presented.

See also the *Teacher's Guide to Writing Assessment*.

Cooperative Learning
Each student should
- bring a draft and read it aloud
- suggest and make revisions

Grammar Link
(See Using the Grammar Link below.)

Reteaching
📁 *Composition Reteaching*, p. 42

Enrichment
📁 *Composition Enrichment*, p. 42

CLOSE

Invite students to discuss why revising and editing help improve a report.

Using the Grammar Link

Grammar Link Answers
Answers will vary, but some suggestions are given below.
1. Indeed,…
2. Unlike wild dogs,…
3. …with human beings,…
4. …to work,…
5. …all this care,…

Using Commas Invite students to write a short speech for a gathering of school administrators. They might choose to write about what they would like to see changed at the school. The statement should start with introductory words followed by a comma.

5.11 Writing About Literature
Comparing Two Poems

Expository writing can be used to describe a piece of literature, answer an essay question about it, or compare and contrast two selections.

These two poems describe one part of fall—migration. As you read the poems, jot down some of your reactions.

Fall

The geese flying south
In a row long and V-shaped
Pulling in winter.

Sally Andresen

Something Told the Wild Geese

Something told the wild geese
    It was time to go.
Though the fields lay golden
    Something whispered,—"Snow."
Leaves were green and stirring,
    Berries luster-glossed,
But beneath warm feathers
    Something cautioned,—"Frost."
All the sagging orchards
    Steamed with amber spice,
But each wild breast stiffened
    At remembered ice.
Something told the wild geese
    It was time to fly,—
Summer sun was on their wings,
    Winter in their cry.

Rachel Field

236

FOCUS

Lesson Overview
Objective: To write an essay comparing and contrasting two poems on a single topic
Skills: organizing information; comparing and contrasting literature
Critical Thinking: visualizing; comparing; analyzing; synthesizing
Speaking and Listening: discussing

Bellringer
When students enter the classroom, have this assignment on the board: *If you read two books on the same topic, how do you decide which book is better? List the categories you use to compare them.*

Grammar Link to the Bellringer
Ask students to write sentences about the categories they listed in their Bellringer responses. As they write, tell them to use participial phrases if possible to enliven their sentences.

Motivating Activity
Discuss why a scientist might write about a bird and then why a poet might. Help students recognize that a scientist shares information, but a poet shares a feeling about an experience. Encourage students to recall specific poems that they have read and to remember the feelings the poems elicited. Ask them to jot down their reactions to the two poems on this page.

Teacher's Classroom Resources

The following resources can be used for planning, instruction, practice, reinforcement, assessment, reteaching, enrichment, or evaluation.

Teaching Tools
Lesson Plans, p. 52

Transparencies
Fine Art Transparencies, 21–25
Writing Process Transparencies, 17–19B

Write a Personal Reaction

Reading a poem is like listening to a song. It may create a picture in your mind, stir up feelings, or bring back a memory. Think about the pictures that come to your mind as you read the two poems on the previous page. Then jot down your responses to the following questions.

Questions About the Poems

1. In which poem do you see the geese from a distance? In which close up? Compare and contrast these views.

2. What sensory details does each poet use to describe the change of seasons from fall to winter?

3. How would you summarize the poems?

4. How would you compare their forms?

One student's answer to the second question appears below.

> In "Fall" I look at a _V_ of geese straining in the sky. They seem to be pulling in winter. In "Something Told the Wild Geese" I see the geese with summer sun on their wings. Below them I notice golden fields, shiny, sparkling berries, and orchards full of ripened fruit.

Journal Writing

Find two poems about the same topic. In your journal note any details that interest you. Which poem do you like better? Why? Write your impressions.

5.11 Writing About Literature: Comparing Two Poems **237**

Grammar
Editing Tip

When editing your comparison-contrast essay, be sure you have used comparative and superlative adjectives correctly. For more information see Lesson 12.3, pages 428–429.

TEACH

Guided Practice

L2 Using the Models
Remind students that poets use creative license to convey meaning. This means that they do not always follow the usual rules of grammar. Ask students to look for examples in both poems. For example, Rachel Field omits a verb twice ("Berries luster-glossed" and "Winter in their cry"), and Sally Andresen does not put a predicate in her poem.

L3 Identifying Poetry Elements
Students may benefit from a brief discussion about figurative language and the use of rhythm, rhyme, and form to create a comparison. You might use words and lines from the Field poem as examples of these elements. Challenge students to research other poetic terminology.

L1 Using the Facsimile
The student response in the facsimile focuses on the sense of sight. Point out that responses might also use other senses, such as hearing (*whispered, stirring leaves, cry*) or touch (*warm, steamed, stiffened*).

 Two-Minute Skill Drill

Have students brainstorm a list of adjectives to describe how each poem makes them feel.

Journal Writing Tip

Comparing Ask students to decide which of the two poems they prefer. Then suggest that they reread the preferred poem to identify and list specific words, phrases, or images that they liked.

📁 **Blackline Masters**
Thinking and Study Skills,
pp. 6, 9, 12
Writing Across the Curriculum,
pp. 18, 24
Cooperative Learning Activities,
pp. 25–30

Sentence Combining Practice,
pp. 32–33
Speaking and Listening Activities, pp. 12–13, 21
Research Paper and Report Writing, pp. 2–3, 9, 19–22
Composition Practice, p. 43
Composition Reteaching, p. 43
Composition Enrichment, p. 43

Assessment
📁 *Teacher's Guide to Writing Assessment*

237

TEACH

Guided Practice

L2 Using the Model
You may wish to point out that the writer used the words *different, however,* and *two* to emphasize differences between the poems. (Answer to callout: The student uses a subject-by-subject organization.)

L2 Identifying Responses to Poems
To help students identify the variety of responses people have to poems, organize a Roundtable activity. Divide the class into groups and then read aloud a poem with many images. Ask each student to note one response to the poem. Pass a sheet of paper around and have each student write a response and fold up the sheet to hide it from the next student. When every student has had a turn, ask a volunteer to read all the responses.

Independent Practice

🏳 For further stimuli for expository writing, see *Fine Art Transparencies,* 21–25.

🏳 *Writing Process Transparencies,* 17–19B

📁 *Writing Across the Curriculum,* pp. 18, 24

📁 *Cooperative Learning Activities,* pp. 25–30

Skills Practice

📁 *Thinking and Study Skills,* pp. 6, 9, 12

📁 *Sentence Combining Practice,* pp. 32–33

📁 *Speaking and Listening Activities,* pp. 12–13, 21

📁 *Research Paper and Report Writing,* pp. 2–3, 9, 19–22

📁 *Composition Practice,* p. 43

Compare and Contrast

To compare or contrast two poems in an essay, you might like to begin with a diagram such as the one below. Decide how to arrange your essay. You can write about the features of one poem and then write about the same kind of features in another. Or you can compare and contrast the poems one feature at a time.

Drafting Tip
For more information about compare and contrast writing, review Lesson 5.3, pages 204–206.

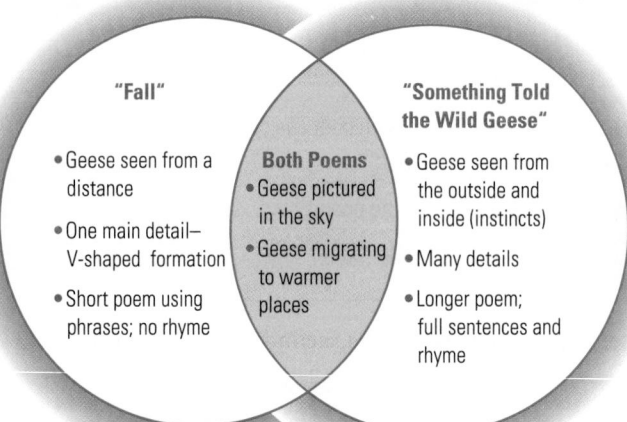

"Fall"
- Geese seen from a distance
- One main detail— V-shaped formation
- Short poem using phrases; no rhyme

Both Poems
- Geese pictured in the sky
- Geese migrating to warmer places

"Something Told the Wild Geese"
- Geese seen from the outside and inside (instincts)
- Many details
- Longer poem; full sentences and rhyme

The introduction identifies the two poems and states the thesis.

What method of organization did this student use to compare and contrast the two poems?

Student Model

"*F*all" and "Something Told the Wild Geese" are two very different poems about geese. "Something Told the Wild Geese" is a sixteen-line poem that rhymes. Using descriptive words, the poet paints pictures of geese, fields, and orchards. "Fall," however, is a short poem that does not rhyme. This poem shows geese flying, pulling in a different season. Reading the two poems is like looking at two different snapshots of geese.

John Moore, Wilmette Junior High School, Wilmettte, Illinois

238 *Expository Writing: Finding Meaning*

Enabling Strategies

LEP Understanding Poetic Language
Students may have difficulty with poetic language. First help them understand any words that are unfamiliar, such as *cautioned, sagging, amber,* and *stiffened.* Then tackle more difficult language, such as "*fields lay golden*" or "*Berries luster-glossed.*" For the former, you might ask questions such as, "What might make the fields golden?" For the latter, you might tell students to look up both *luster* and *glossed* and ask why berries might be *luster-glossed.*

5.11 Writing Activities

Write a Compare-and-Contrast Essay

Create a diagram to compare and contrast this poem with another poem about the sun. Then write an essay telling how the two poems are alike and different.

Sunset

The sun spun like
a tossed coin.
It whirled on the azure sky,
it clattered into the horizon,
it clicked in the slot,
and neon-lights popped
and blinked "Time expired,"
as on a parking meter.

> Oswald Mbuyiseni Mtshali

- Include similarities and differences.
- Organize your paragraphs to present the information clearly.

PURPOSE Compare two poems
AUDIENCE Yourself
LENGTH 3–4 paragraphs

Cross-Curricular: Art

Select a photograph of a dog from your home album or a magazine. Compare and contrast your photo with this one. Do they show the same objects? Is one animal posed and the other unposed? Are the moods similar? Write one or two paragraphs on similarities and differences between the photos.

Grammar Link

Use participial phrases to modify nouns or pronouns.

In "Fall" I look at a V of geese **straining in the sky.**

Use each participial phrase below as an adjective in a sentence.

1. compared to our old house
2. staring at the ground
3. recommended by my brother
4. hidden in the grass

See Lesson 15.1, pages 494–495.

William Wegman, *Blue Period*, 1981

5.11 Writing About Literature: Comparing Two Poems **239**

ASSESS

Writing Activities Evaluation Guidelines

Write a Compare-and-Contrast Essay
Use these criteria when evaluating your students' writing. The essay should
- compare two poems chosen by the student
- contain supporting details
- be organized by subject or by feature

See also the *Teacher's Guide to Writing Assessment.*

Cross-Curricular: Art
Each comparison should
- focus on the details in the photos
- identify similarities and differences

Grammar Link
(See Using the Grammar Link below.)

Reteaching
📁 *Composition Reteaching,* p. 43

Enrichment
📁 *Composition Enrichment,* p. 43

✍ Use *Fine Art Transparencies* 21–25 for enrichment activities also.

CLOSE

Discuss how students felt about the lesson and their essays. Ask volunteers to read their essays to the class, and discuss how different students organized their essays as well as what makes each essay effective.

Using the Grammar Link

Grammar Link Answers
Answers will vary, but some suggestions are given below.
1. Compared to our old house, our new house is huge.
2. I saw my friend staring at the ground.
3. We saw a movie recommended by my brother.
4. She found a bird's nest hidden in the grass.

About the Art

William Wegman, *Blue Period*, 1981
Wegman and Man Ray, his weimaraner, worked together on hundreds of projects. The dog, named after Surrealist artist and photographer Man Ray, died in 1982, and Wegman published a portfolio of photographs of him. The photograph on this page measures 23 ⅞ by 20 ½ inches.

Setting the Purpose

Students now have the opportunity to apply what they have learned about expository writing to an independent writing project. They will use the stages of the writing process to create and present a finished piece.

FOCUS

Lesson Overview

Objective: To write an essay explaining the origins and significance of a local memorial, building, or statue

Skills: Using the five stages of the writing process: prewriting, drafting, revising, editing, and presenting

Critical Thinking: analyzing; categorizing; decision making; summarizing

Speaking and Listening: discussing; evaluating; questioning

Bellringer

When students enter the classroom, have this assignment on the board: *Write the answer to this question in complete sentences: Why do you think Rhode Island might have built a monument to a chicken?* (Tell students that the chicken is Rhode Island's state bird and an important local product.)

Grammar Link to the Bellringer

Have students exchange Bellringer answers, checking to see that complete sentences are used and subjects and verbs agree.

Motivating Activity

Point out that students might act as detectives, unearthing the histories of monuments and sharing them. Have students discuss ideas for possible sources of information about these monuments. (library, Chamber of Commerce, state tourist bureau)

240

UNIT 5

WRITING PROCESS IN ACTION

EXPOSITORY WRITING

In preceding lessons you've learned about writing essays and the types of details to use to support various purposes, whether you are writing reports or answering test questions. You've also had the chance to write about a topic of interest to you. Now, in this lesson, you're invited to apply what you know to research and write information for a guidebook for travelers in your state.

• Assignment •

Context	*You have been asked to write about how a certain statue, memorial, or commemorative building came to be built in your neighborhood, city, or state. Your writing will be published in a guidebook for travelers.*
Purpose	*To inform travelers about the development and construction of a landmark*
Audience	*Visitors to your neighborhood, city, or state*
Length	*1 page*

The following pages can help you plan and write your essay. Read through them, and then refer to them as you need to. But don't be tied down by them. You're in charge of your own writing process.

240 *Expository Writing: Finding Meaning*

Teacher's Classroom Resources

The following resources can be used for planning, instruction, practice, reinforcement, assessment, reteaching, enrichment, or evaluation.

Teaching Tools
Lesson Plans, p. 54

Transparencies
Writing Process Transparencies, 17-19B

Prewriting

You might begin prewriting by listing your own first impressions of landmarks in your neighborhood, city, or state or by thinking about where you'd take friends or relatives from out of town. What places and details would most fascinate them?

Use the options at the right to help you, too. If you need more facts, do research at a library, historical society, or travel agency.

Option A

Make a cluster diagram of local places of interest.

Option B

List five or six of your favorite places.

Option C

Do some small-group brain-storming.

Freedom House, on Hamilton Pike— historic home, Underground Railroad, museum about slavery in America. Just celebrated its twentieth anniversary as official landmark. Others in area: Strauss Hall?

Drafting

Once you've gathered all your facts, begin drafting. First, decide which facts would be the most interesting and useful to your audience. Next, decide how to organize your writing. In the passage below, notice how the author organizes his writing around the steps for choosing a design for the Vietnam War memorial in Washington, D.C.

Literature Model

A total of 2,573 individuals and teams registered for the competition. They were sent photographs of the memorial site, maps of the area around the site and of the entire Mall, and other technical design information. The competitors had three months to prepare their designs, which had to be received by March 31, 1981.

Of the 2,573 registrants, 1,421 submitted designs, a record number for such a design competition. When the designs were spread out for jury selection, they filled a large airplane hangar.

Brent Ashabranner, *Always to Remember*

Drafting Tip

For more information about handling the details in an essay, see Lesson 5.2, pages 200–202.

241

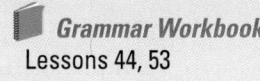
TEACH

Prewriting

L2 Finding Resources for Information

List the following resources on the board, and discuss with students how they might help to provide information: encyclopedias (general information about important monuments and buildings); government offices (statistics, dates, costs); back issues of newspapers (background information, stories about construction and people); historical societies (original documents, maps, pictures); history magazines (biographies, context); books about local and state history (details of local importance); community elders (first-person accounts). Then direct students to list questions about their topics. Discuss how the sources on the board might help them find answers to their questions.

Drafting

L2 Promoting Discussion

Point out that until recently, many contributions made by women and minorities were ignored by those who made statues and monuments. Discuss overlooked contributions such as pioneer women and the African-American military tank unit that fought under General George Patton. Ask students to brainstorm ways in which society might recognize such contributions.

L3 Organizing Details

Ask students to create outlines of the content of various magazine and newspaper articles, including details. Have them evaluate and critique whether the details were organized and ordered effectively in the writing. If they do not think the details were effectively placed in the writing, they should suggest a revised organization.

TEACH

Revising

L2 Peer Editing

Students can work in writing conferences with peer editors before they revise their work. You may want to duplicate the Peer Response forms in the *Teacher's Guide to Writing Assessment*. Suggest that peer editors respond to the following questions:

- Do you have questions after reading the draft?
- Can you suggest more vivid details?
- Which sections of the draft captured your attention most? Why?

Editing

L2 Peer Editing

After students have edited their own work, have them edit another student's writing. Remind them to refer to the Editing Checklist on student page 243.

Presenting

Before students present their expository writing, discuss how to prepare their papers for publication. Emphasize the importance of the final draft and that it must be neatly done.

Independent Practice

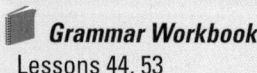 *Writing Process Transparencies*, 17–19B

Skills Practice

📁 *Thinking and Study Skills*, pp. 3–4, 23–24, 34–37
📁 *Sentence Combining Practice*, pp. 32–33
📁 *Composition Practice*, p. 44

📕 *Grammar Workbook* Lessons 44, 53

The purpose of the drafting stage is to get your thoughts and ideas on paper. If your writing contains many statistics, wait to check your facts later as part of the revising process. Do not worry about spelling, grammar, or punctuation at this point—just let the words flow. You will correct your errors in the revising and editing stages.

Revising

To begin revising, read over your draft to make sure that what you've written fits your purpose and audience. Then have a **writing conference**. Read your draft to a partner or small group. Use your audience's reactions to help you evaluate your work.

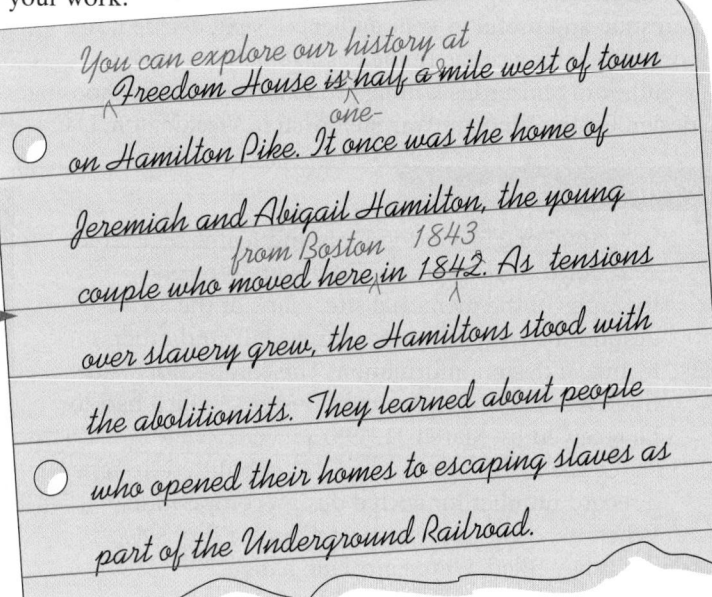

Question A
Will my introduction command attention?

Question B
Are details clear and accurate?

Question C
Does my conclusion reflect the main idea?

242 *Expository Writing: Finding Meaning*

Enrichment and Extension

Follow-Up Ideas
- Set aside time for students to celebrate the conclusion of their writing projects. Encourage them to share their finished pieces.
- If students are sending their work out of the classroom, make sure photocopies are retained.

Extending Expository Writing
- Brainstorm with students ways they can use their expertise in expository writing in other subject areas, such as writing a class newsletter.
- Explore opportunities for extending expository writing, such as creating a history of their school.

Editing

At this point you've put a lot of time and effort into the assignment. Don't let a few editing mistakes spoil the effect of an otherwise good piece of writing. When you **proofread** your revised draft, ask yourself questions like those listed on the right. If any part of the draft doesn't sound quite right, you may want to get additional advice from a teacher or friend.

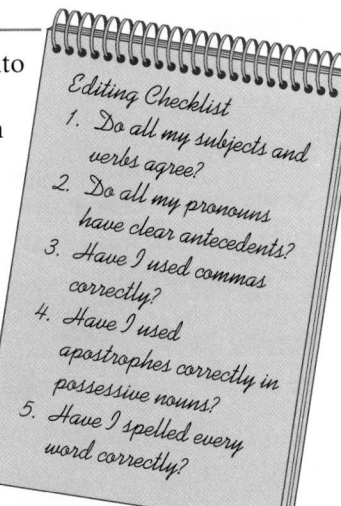

Editing Checklist
1. *Do all my subjects and verbs agree?*
2. *Do all my pronouns have clear antecedents?*
3. *Have I used commas correctly?*
4. *Have I used apostrophes correctly in possessive nouns?*
5. *Have I spelled every word correctly?*

Presenting

THEY THAT GO DOWN TO THE SEA IN SHIPS
1623 · 1923

Before you present your finished work, consider having someone at your chamber of commerce or local historical society read it. That person might be able to give you some little-known details that you could add to the paper. Also, you might consider attaching copies of authentic photos (people who inspired the memorial, a building being renovated, a statue being installed).

Proofreading

For proofreading symbols, see page 81.

Journal Writing

Reflect on your writing process experience. Answer these questions in your journal: What do you like best about your expository writing? What was the hardest part of writing it? What did you learn in your writing conference? What new things have you learned as a writer?

Writing Process in Action **243**

ASSESS

Evaluation Guidelines
Use the following questions to evaluate students' finished writing.
- Does the writing have an introduction, body, and conclusion?
- Is the main idea clearly defined as a thesis statement?
- Does the writing contain accurate factual information?
- Are the details organized in a logical way?

Refer to the *Teacher's Guide to Writing Assessment* for further help with evaluating student writing.

Reteaching
📁 *Composition Reteaching*, p. 44

Enrichment
📁 *Composition Enrichment*, p. 44

Journal Writing Tip

Reflecting Have students write about what they liked best about the writing process, and why.

CLOSE

Have students share and discuss the most interesting things they learned about the statue, memorial, or commemorative building they wrote about.

About the Author

Brent Ashabranner grew up in a small town in Oklahoma. An avid reader, he wrote his first story at age eleven. He taught English at a state university and published numerous pieces about the American West. He later spent years overseas working with people of different cultures. Most of his writing is nonfiction, and much of his current work centers on minority groups.

Ashabranner has said, "My books frequently examine complex social issues, but I think these issues can be made of interest to readers of all ages."

Three of Ashabranner's books were named American Library Association Best Books for Young Adults. His daughters have collaborated with him on several books, and one daughter, Jennifer, took the photographs for the book *Always to Remember*.

FOCUS

Lesson Overview

Objective: To explain a complex topic, using specific historical and biographical details for interest and clarity
Skills: reading comprehension
Critical Thinking: inferring
Speaking and Listening: informal speaking; discussing

Expository Writing
Literature Model

BRENT ASHABRANNER

from

Always to Remember

In 1980 Vietnam War veteran Jan Scruggs and lawyers Roberet Doubeck and John Wheeler persuaded Congress to approve the building of a Vietnam War memorial in Washington, D.C. They hoped that the memorial would help to heal the bitter feelings that still existed because of this country's involvement in that war, even though it had ended in 1973. Brent Ashabranner tells the story of the national competition to design the war memorial. As you read his essay, notice what he does to capture and hold your attention. Then try the activities in Linking Writing and Literature on page 251.

The memorial had been authorized by Congress "in honor and recognition of the men and women of the Armed Forces of the United States who served in the Vietnam War." The law, however, said not a word about what the memorial should be or what it should look like. That was left up to the Vietnam Veterans Memorial Fund, but the law did state that the memorial design and plans would have

244 *Expository Writing: Finding Meaning*

Teacher's Classroom Resources

The following resources can be used for planning, instruction, or practice.

Teaching Tools
Lesson Plans, p. 53

Transparencies
Fine Art Transparencies, 21–25

A section of the Vietnam Veterans Memorial

to be approved by the Secretary of the Interior, the Commission of Fine Arts, and the National Capital Planning Commission.

What would the memorial be? What should it look like? Who would design it? Scruggs, Doubek, and Wheeler didn't know, but they were determined that the memorial should help bring closer together a nation still bitterly divided by the Vietnam War. It couldn't be something like the Marine Corps Memorial showing American troops planting a flag on enemy soil at Iwo Jima. It couldn't be a giant dove with an olive branch of peace in its beak. It had to soothe passions, not stir them up. But there was one thing Jan Scruggs insisted on: the memorial, whatever it turned out to be, would have to show the name of every man and woman killed or missing in the war.

The answer, they decided, was to hold a national design competition open to all Americans. The winning design would receive a prize of $20,000, but the real prize would be the win-

Literature Model **245**

FOCUS

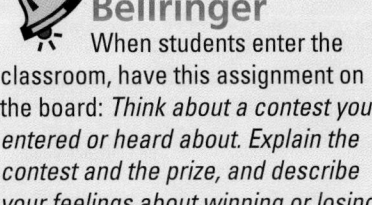

Bellringer
When students enter the classroom, have this assignment on the board: *Think about a contest you entered or heard about. Explain the contest and the prize, and describe your feelings about winning or losing.*

Motivating Activity
Tell students that sometimes people are surprised when a contest winner is young. Ask why they think that is so, and how they feel about it. Encourage them to provide examples of very young winners, such as Olympic medalists in their early teens.

TEACH

L2 Guided Reading
- Why did the planners want to avoid a design like the Marine Corps Memorial or a giant dove with an olive branch? (An image too associated with war or peace would anger some people.)
- Do you think holding a design competition was a good way to choose the designer of a national monument? Why? (It was a good idea because it opened up the competition to anyone who was interested.)

📁 **Blackline Masters**
Thinking and Study Skills,
  pp. 1–4, 8, 11, 13, 17, 23–24,
  35–37
Speaking and Listening Activities, pp. 12–13, 21

Assessment
📁 *Teacher's Guide to Writing Assessment*

TEACH

Guided Practice

L2 Guided Reading

- What aspect of expository writing is demonstrated on this page? (Facts and statistics are presented to inform the reader.)
- What facts are reported on this page? Start with the announcement of the competition. (October 1980—announcement of the competition; over 5,000 inquiries received; 2,573 registered for the competition; March 31, 1981—deadline for submissions; 1,421 designs received)

---

ner's knowledge that the memorial would become a part of American history on the Mall in Washington, D.C. Although fund raising was only well started at this point, the choosing of a memorial design could not be delayed if the memorial was to be built by Veteran's Day, 1982. H. Ross Perot contributed the $160,000 necessary to hold the competition, and a panel of distinguished architects, landscape architects, sculptors, and design specialists was chosen to decide the winner.

Announcement of the competition in October, 1980, brought an astonishing response. The Vietnam Veterans Memorial Fund received over five thousand inquiries. They came from every state in the nation and from every field of design; as expected, architects and sculptors were particularly interested. Everyone who inquired received a booklet explaining the criteria.[1] Among the most important: the memorial could not make a political statement about the war; it must contain the names of all persons killed or missing in action in the war; it must be in harmony with its location on the Mall.

A total of 2,573 individuals and teams registered for the competition. They were sent photographs of the memorial site, maps of the area around the site and of the entire Mall, and other technical design information. The competitors had three months to prepare their designs, which had to be received by March 31, 1981.

Of the 2,573 registrants, 1,421 submitted designs, a record number for such a design competition. When the designs were spread out for jury selection, they filled a large airplane hangar.[2] The jury's task was to select the design which, in their judgment, was the best in meeting these criteria:

- a design that honored the memory of those Americans who served and died in the Vietnam War.
- a design of high artistic merit.
- a design which would be harmonious with its site, including visual harmony with the Lincoln Memorial and the Washington Monument.

---

1 **criteria** (krī tir′ ē ə) standards, rules, or tests by which something is judged
2 **hangar** (hang′ər) a building or shed to keep airplanes in

---

Genre and Style

Reading Expository Writing

Always to Remember proves that straight expository writing can be as vivid and interesting as fiction. The book presents the events that led to the surprising announcement of the winner of the national design competition for the Vietnam Veterans Memorial. The selection then jumps back in time to take a biographical look at the young winner. Maya Ying Lin's own words personalize the story and make it vivid.

- a design that could take its place in the "historic continuity" of America's national art.
- a design that would be buildable, durable, and not too hard to maintain.

The designs were displayed without any indication of the designer's name so that they could be judged anonymously, on their design merits alone. The jury spent one week reviewing all the designs in the airplane hangar. On May 1 it made its report to the Vietnam Veterans Memorial Fund; the experts declared Entry Number 1,026 the winner. The report called it "the finest and most appropriate" of all submitted and said it was "superbly harmonious" with the site on the Mall. Remarking upon the "simple and forthright" materials needed to build the winning entry, the report concludes:

> This memorial, with its wall of names, becomes a place of quiet reflection, and a tribute to those who served their nation in difficult times. All who come here can find it a place of healing. This will be a quiet memorial, one that achieves an excellent relationship with both the Lincoln Memorial or Washington Monument, and relates the visitor to them. It is uniquely horizontal, entering the earth rather than piercing the sky.
>
> This is very much a memorial of our own times, one that could not have been achieved in another time and place. The designer has created an eloquent [3] place where the simple meeting of earth, sky and remembered names contain messages for all who will know this place.

The eight jurors signed their names to the report, a unanimous decision.

When the name of the winner was revealed, the art and architecture worlds were stunned. It was not the name of a nationally famous architect or sculptor, as most people had been sure it would be. The creator of Entry Number 1,026 was a twenty-one-year-old student at Yale University. Her name—unknown as yet in any field of art or architecture—was Maya Ying Lin.

---

3 eloquent (el′ə kwənt) having a strong effect on people's ideas and feelings

Literature Model **247**

TEACH

Guided Practice

L2 Guided Reading
- What is the meaning of the phrase "a design that could take its place in the 'historic continuity' of America's national art"? (This memorial would represent current American art in the body of significant works of national art.)
- What did you think when you found out the winner of the competition? (Answers will vary. Students may report being surprised.)

Thinking Skills

Inferring Author's Purpose
Ask students to infer why the author provided so many details about the criteria to be met as well as the specific number of registrants and of people who actually submitted designs. Lead them to conclude that the author might have provided so many details to emphasize the difficulty of the contest, the level of the competition, and the significance of Maya Ying Lin's accomplishment.

TEACH

Guided Practice

L2 Guided Reading

- Until this point, the selection has been about the competition. What happens here? (The author goes back in time to tell about Maya Lin and her background.) Why do you think the author does this? (He does it to answer the questions in people's minds about the unknown winner of the competition.)
- What in Maya Lin's background led her to design an outstanding memorial? (She grew up in an atmosphere where art was taken seriously. She had worked in sculpture. She was an excellent student and had become interested in cemetery architecture.)

How could this be? How could an undergraduate student win one of the most important design competitions ever held? How could she beat out some of the top names in American art and architecture? Who was Maya Ying Lin?

The answer to that question provided some of the other answers, at least in part. Maya Lin, reporters soon discovered, was a Chinese-American girl who had been born and raised in the small midwestern city of Athens, Ohio. Her father, Henry Huan Lin, was a ceramicist[4] of considerable reputation and dean of fine arts at Ohio University in Athens. Her mother, Julia C. Lin, was a poet and professor of Oriental and English literature. Maya Lin's parents were born to culturally prominent families in China. When the Communists came to power in China in the 1940s, Henry and Julia Lin left the country and in time made their way to the United States.

Maya Lin grew up in an environment of art and literature. She was interested in sculpture and made both small and large sculptural figures, one cast in bronze. She learned silversmithing and made jewelry. She was surrounded by books and read a great deal, especially fantasies such as *The Hobbit* and *Lord of the Rings.*

But she also found time to work at McDonald's. "It was about the only way to make money in the summer," she said.

A covaledictorian[5] at high school graduation, Maya Lin went to Yale without a clear notion of what she wanted to study and eventually decided to major in Yale's undergraduate program in architecture. During her junior year she studied in Europe and found herself increasingly interested in cemetery architecture. "In Europe there's very little space, so graveyards are used as parks," she said. "Cemeteries are cities of the dead in European countries, but they are also living gardens."

In France, Maya Lin was deeply moved by the war memorial to those who died in the Somme offensive in 1916 during World War I. The great arch by architect Sir Edwin Lutyens is considered one of the world's most outstanding war memorials.

---

4 ceramicist (sə ram'ə sist) an expert in making pottery

5 covaledictorian (cō' val ə dik tôr' ē ən) one who shares the position of the highest-ranking student in a class, who delivers the farewell address at graduation

Writers and Writing

Choosing Details

Ashabranner includes specific details of setting and characterization often found in fiction. Instead of merely accumulating facts and details, he puts them together to make an interesting and suspenseful story. "Recognizing good story material," said Ashabranner, "giving it shape and life, is a creative act that constantly renews the writer."

The Vietnam Veterans Memorial in Constitution Gardens, Washington, D.C.

Back at Yale for her senior year, Maya Lin enrolled in Professor Andrus Burr's course in funerary (burial) architecture. The Vietnam Veterans Memorial competition had recently been announced, and although the memorial would be a cenotaph—a monument in honor of persons buried someplace else—Professor Burr thought that having his students prepare a design of the memorial would be a worthwhile course assignment.

Surely, no classroom exercise ever had such spectacular results.

After receiving the assignment, Maya Lin and two of her classmates decided to make the day's journey from New Haven, Connecticut, to Washington to look at the site where the memorial would be built. On the day of their visit, Maya Lin remembers, Constitution Gardens was awash with a late November sun; the park was full of light, alive with joggers and people walking beside the lake.

"It was while I was at the site that I designed it," Maya Lin said later in an interview about the memorial with *Washington Post* writer Phil McCombs. "I just sort of visualized

Literature Model **249**

TEACH

Guided Practice

L2 Guided Reading
- What do you think was Maya Lin's impression of Constitution Gardens on her visit there? (It was a bright, sunny place. It was full of people.)
- Why does Ashabranner create a separate paragraph for the sentence beginning "Surely, no classroom exercise…"? (It gives the sentence added emphasis. It underscores the fact that a national monument was designed in response to a course assignment.)

Cultural Diversity

Remembering the Dead
Explain that various cultures have different ways of commemorating their dead. For instance, on Memorial Day, Americans remember their war dead. Other countries, including Mexico and Japan, honor ancestors on a special day. Mexico has a national holiday called the Day of the Dead, and people in Japan celebrate the Feast of Lanterns.

TEACH

Guided Practice

L2 Guided Reading
- What is the main idea of this selection? (The main idea of the selection is how Maya Ying Lin, a student, was able to win the competition.)
- Review the selection. Find a fact, a statistic, an example or incident, and a reason in the supporting details. What are they? (Answers will vary but should include one of each type of detail listed.)

Independent Practice

For further stimuli for expository writing, see *Fine Art Transparencies* 21–25.

Skills Practice
Thinking and Study Skills, pp. 1–4, 8, 11, 13, 17, 23–24, 35–37
Speaking and Listening Activities, pp. 12–13, 21

---

it. It just popped into my head. Some people were playing Frisbee. It was a beautiful park. I didn't want to destroy a living park. You use the landscape. You don't fight with it. You absorb the landscape. . . . When I looked at the site I just knew I wanted something horizontal that took you in, that made you feel safe within the park, yet at the same time reminding you of the dead. So I just imagined opening up the earth. . . ."

When Maya Lin returned to Yale, she made a clay model of the vision that had come to her in Constitution Gardens. She showed it to Professor Burr; he liked her conception and encouraged her to enter the memorial competition. She put her design on paper, a task that took six weeks, and mailed it to Washington barely in time to meet the March 31 deadline.

A month and a day later, Maya Lin was attending class. Her roommate slipped into the classroom and handed her a note. Washington was calling and would call back in fifteen minutes. Maya Lin hurried to her room. The call came. She had won the memorial competition.

Cooperative Learning

Word Webbing
To help students gain an understanding of the organization of a piece of expository writing, direct them in a Team Word-Webbing activity. Give each group a piece of chart paper, and ask the members to show graphically the main concepts of this piece, some supporting elements, and the relationship between the concepts and supporting elements. Encourage group discussion before actual webbing begins.

Linking Writing and Literature
Readers Respond to the Model

How does Brent Ashabranner make his essay a thought-provoking and meaningful story for his readers?

Explore Brent Ashabranner's writing by answering these questions. Then read what other students liked about his essay.

1. The first thing a writer must do is choose an appropriate topic for a particular audience. What makes the subject of Ashabranner's essay right on target for readers of your age?

2. What kind of order does Ashabranner use to present the facts and details in his essay? Why is this the best order for the information he is presenting?

3. The author has space for only a limited number of facts about Maya Ying Lin. Reread the facts about her background, and tell why you think the author chose to include them.

4. In the essay find two places where the author interrupts the events to ask a series of questions. In each case, what effect does this technique have on you as a reader?

I enjoyed reading about the competition to choose the memorial for the soldiers who served in Vietnam. I had never heard about it before. I was very surprised when I read that a student attending Yale won. I had predicted that one of the architects would win.

If I had written this selection, I would provide more details about the competition. I would write some background information about Maya Ying Lin.

I would recommend this selection to a friend. I think that they too would be surprised to hear who won the competition.
Faris Karadsheh

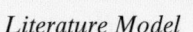

"Always to Remember" was a good selection. I was so surprised when I found out that a twenty-one-year-old unknown artist from Yale won an important competition.

I enjoyed reading everything about the memorial wall and what it took to make it.

I would recommend this selection, especially to friends who like history.
Shanna Breckenfeld

Literature Model **251**

ASSESS

Evaluation Guidelines For Discussion

As your students discuss the selection, either in small groups or as a class, encourage them to begin with a personal response. The student responses on this page might be used as a starting point.

Look for evidence that students
- have read the selection
- can state some of the writer's ideas in their own words
- understand the writer's point of view
- have connected the content to their own knowledge and experiences
- understand the ideas and implications of the selection.

Some possible responses to the discussion questions on this page:

1. The Vietnam War is an important subject for us to learn about. The competition and its results are exciting reading. The winner being a college student is inspiring.

2. The author uses time order to organize the information. Telling the events of the competition as a story helps to build anticipation until the winner is revealed. Then, the author tells the story from the viewpoint of the winner.

3. The author included facts about Maya Lin's family background, education, and talents so that you would know about what influenced her to enter the competition and what enabled her to win.

4. Sample: The first series of questions made me aware of the lack of details in the law authorizing the memorial. The second series of questions made me feel the disbelief the author and others felt at the announcement of the winner.

CLOSE

Invite students to write a paragraph speculating on Maya Ying Lin's feelings and actions when she heard that she had won the competition.

REVIEW

Reflecting on the Unit
You may have students respond to Reflecting on the Unit in writing or through discussion.

Writing Across the Curriculum
Before they begin writing their essays, remind students that the major focus of expository writing is to make information clear and interesting to a reader. Encourage students to sustain this focus from prewriting through revision.

Adding to Your Portfolio
Suggest that students look at their work in two different ways. First, they should think about which piece or pieces are the most successful overall. Then they should look for specific parts that are examples of good expository writing. One part of an essay, for instance, may be an example of clear, well-organized expository writing. Encourage students to confer with peer reviewers before they make their final choices.

Portfolio Evaluation
If you grade the portfolio selections, you may want to award two marks—one each for content and form. Explain your assessment criteria before students make their selections. Commend
- experimentation with creative prewriting techniques
- clear, concise writing in which the main idea, audience, and purpose are evident
- successful revisions
- work that shows a flair for language.

Unit 5 Review

Reflecting on the Unit

Summarize what you have learned in this unit by answering the following questions.

- What are the parts of an essay?
- Name four types of expository writing.
- How can you get your message across clearly?
- How should you answer an essay question?
- What are the stages in writing a report?
- What is one way to respond to poetry?

Adding to Your Portfolio

Choose a selection for your portfolio.
Look over the expository writing you did for this unit. Choose a piece of writing for your portfolio. The writing you choose should show one or more of the following:
- an introduction, body, and conclusion
- facts, statistics, examples, or reasons
- a strong organization and smooth transitions

Reflect on your choice.
Attach a note to the piece you chose, explaining briefly why you chose it and what you learned from writing it.

Set goals.
How can you improve your writing? What skill will you focus on the next time you write?

Writing Across the Curriculum

Make a music connection.
Choose two songs or other compositions by musicians with whom you are familiar. Write a one-page essay to compare and contrast the two compositions. Include information about the lyrics, rhythm, and melody, as well as your personal response to the two pieces. To review ways to organize information in comparison-contrast essays, see Lesson 5.3, pages 204–206, and Lesson 5.11, pages 236–238.

Teacher's Classroom Resources

The following resources can be used for assessment or evaluation.

Unit Assessment

📁 *Tests with Answer Key*
Unit 5 Choice A Test, p. 17
Unit 5 Choice B Test, p. 18
Unit 5 Composition Objective Test, pp. 19–20

💿 *Test Generator*
Unit 5 Choice A Test
Unit 5 Choice B Test
Unit 5 Composition Objective Test

You may wish to administer one of these tests as a mastery test.

UNIT 6

Persuasive Writing

Composition | **Lessons**

253

UNIT GOALS

The goal of Unit 6 is to help students, through example and instruction, to develop an understanding of and an ability to develop persuasive writing techniques for expressing opinions that will affect the way readers think and act. In the lessons, students practice the stages of persuasive writing, which include establishing a position and evaluating and using evidence.

Unit Assessment
📁 *Tests with Answer Key*
Unit 6 Choice A Test, p. 21
Unit 6 Choice B Test, p. 22
Unit 6 Composition Objective
   Test, pp. 23–24

💿 *Test Generator*
Unit 6 Choice A Test
Unit 6 Choice B Test
Unit 6 Composition Objective Test

You may wish to administer either the Unit 6 Choice A Test or the Unit 6 Choice B Test as a pretest.

Key to Ability Levels
Enabling Strategies have been coded for varying learning styles and abilities.

L1 Level 1 activities are within the ability range of Learning Disabled students.

L2 Level 2 activities are basic-to-average activities and are within the ability range of average students.

L3 Level 3 activities are challenging activities and are within the ability range of above-average students.

LEP LEP activities are within the ability range of Limited English Proficiency students.

UNIT

6

PREVIEW

Case
Study

Setting the Purpose

In the Unit 6 Case Study, students examine the use of persuasive writing in a real-life situation (in this case, a proposal). Students will explore and practice persuasive writing in the lessons that follow.

FOCUS

Lesson Overview

Objective: To explore how persuasive writing is used to develop a proposal
Skills: identifying examples of a concept
Critical Thinking: analyzing; relating content to audience; making inferences; building background
Speaking and Listening: discussing; informal speaking

Bellringer

When students enter the classroom, have this assignment on the board: *Write a definition (or an example) of a* proposal.

Grammar Link to the Bellringer
Have students look over their writing to make sure any proper nouns or adjectives are capitalized. Remind students that official names of most organizations and groups are capitalized.

Motivating Activity

Discuss students' Bellringer responses. Marriage, business, or political proposals are possible examples. Point out that *proposal* comes from the verb *propose,* (meaning "to put something forward for consideration." *Proposal* is also the technical term for a written application for money in support of a specific project. Ask students why it is necessary to be persuasive in a proposal. Have they ever tried to raise money for a project or cause? How did they go about it?

254

Persuasive Writing
in the Real World

Johnson Persuades with Proposals

F O C U S: When writing a persuasive proposal, you need to present your ideas and goals to a specific audience.

Struggle is central to artist Indira Freitas Johnson's work. In her drawings and sculptures she often creates images of hands, eyes, feet, and wheels to show the personal and physical challenges of going through life. In her current project, *Double Vision,* Johnson combines the artistic themes of struggle and action. She also combines the roles of visual artist and writer. Johnson's drawings will be used by SHARE, a group in Bombay, India, to fashion into quilts. She now writes proposals to obtain funding support for *Double Vision.*

◄ *Artist*
Indira Freitas Johnson

Teacher's Classroom Resources

The following resources can be used for planning, instruction, practice, reinforcement, assessment, or evaluation.

Teaching Tools
Lesson Plans

Transparencies
Writing Process Transparencies, 20–22B

Writing a Proposal

Prewriting	Drafting	Revising/Editing

Getting Started	Writing to the Audience	Getting Feedback

"Sometimes I think things click very quickly. And sometimes you really have to struggle with them. Certain parts don't say exactly what you want them to say, and it's hard to figure out why they're not saying that. So you have to keep working."

—Indira Freitas Johnson

Prewriting

GETTING STARTED

Johnson says, "I sometimes think that getting started is very difficult. You have all these ideas. I think that's when you just need to start." At this early stage,

when she is trying to describe her ideas for a project, she simply gets words down onto paper. She tries to explain her project ideas as clearly as possible. But she doesn't worry

◄ *Indira Johnson uses images of hands in a great deal of her work. This piece is titled* Charged Movement *(1990).*

Case Study **255**

TEACH

Building Background

Warm-up:
Explain to students that persuasive writing aims to make someone feel a certain way or do something. Have students make a brief list of occasions when they might need to use persuasive writing.

Persuasion in Speaking:
Invite students to think of examples of persuasion they hear in everyday language. These examples could include radio and television advertisements, teachers persuading students to do their work, parents persuading students to change their clothes or hairstyle, or classmates persuading students to attend a party or a school function.

Persuasion in Writing:
Invite students to discuss persuasive writing they have read, including
• magazine advertisements
• political campaign literature
• editorial articles
• product packaging

Preview the Case Study

Ask students to preview the title and focus of the Case Study. Invite students to point out the ways in which persuasive writing might be used in a proposal. Then have students read the Case Study.

📂 **Blackline Masters**
Cooperative Learning Activities,
 pp. 31–36
Thinking and Study Skills,
 pp. 5, 11, 13
Research Paper and Report Writing, pp. 3, 19–20, 25
Case Studies: Writing in the Real World, pp. 21–24

Assessment
📂 *Teacher's Guide to Writing Assessment*

TEACH

Discussion Prompts
- What kind of changes might Johnson make to her initial writing?
- Why does Johnson find library research helpful?

▲ *The ideas that Johnson generates in her drawings eventually appear in details of the quilts made by SHARE.*

that her prose isn't perfect or that her ideas aren't yet totally coherent. "I think from that initial writing you can say, 'This part is good' or 'This part needs reworking' or 'Juggle it around.' "

Research also helps Johnson to develop her ideas. "Very often," she says, "I'll go to the library and just read up on various aspects of a particular project that I want to do. For example, I'll ask myself, 'Has it been done before?'"

Research helps Johnson find out if ideas similar to her own have worked in other places. Sometimes her research even involves traveling to the site of the project.

Drafting

WRITING TO THE AUDIENCE

A successful proposal adapts to the concerns and interests of the audience.

Adapting to the audience involves adjusting the language and information of the

Cultural Diversity

Researching Cloth Art
In Johnson's proposal she states, "cloth and fiber arts have linked women all over the world for thousands of years." Indeed, archaeologists find that the earliest quilting dates back to prehistoric times. Patchwork quilting has a rich tradition in the United States. Fan-shape quilt patterns were especially popular fund-raising projects in the nineteenth century. Invite students to choose a region or culture in the world, research its cloth art traditions, and share their findings with the class.

proposal. Audiences made up of general readers have needs different from those of audiences of experts.

Johnson's art brings her into contact with many individuals and organizations, both in the United States and in India. "Who am I asking for support?" she asks herself as she writes. She then adapts her approach to persuade that audience. She matches the features of her project to the benefits her audience can

expect. If her readers are an arts-related group, Johnson stresses the artistic aspects of the project. If the audience is interested in social service or cultural issues, she emphasizes those points in the proposal.

Adapting to an audience also means that the writer pays attention to subtle suggestions of language. Often the writer must adapt the style of writing to communicate exactly what the project is about. In the proposal below, for example, Johnson avoided the pronoun *I*. She referred to herself as Indira because she wanted to stress that she was a member of a group effort and that this was not just her personal project.

▼ *In this proposal Indira Johnson emphasized the group effort for the project.*

TEACH

Discussion Prompts
- What are the most important things you need to know about the audience you are writing for?
- Why does Johnson focus on the benefits her audience can expect from the project?

Connections Across the Curriculum

Government

In recent years, there has been much debate about the role the government should play in providing funding for the arts. The National Endowment for the Arts, in particular, has come under attack. Interested students might want to look for articles presenting different

points of view on this issue. They might also find out how much money is appropriated for the arts in federal, state, and local budgets. Students may want to debate the issue of funding and censorship of the arts.

TEACH

Guided Practice

L2 Discussion

Stimulate a discussion of the Case Study. You may want to invite students to talk about

- how they would convince their school to exhibit Johnson's work. Whom would they need to convince? What type of argument would appeal to them? What type of language would students use?
- the importance of getting feedback from readers before sending a proposal.
- students' responses to the advice of Johnson's father. (*You have to rewrite.*) Ask students to relate the most helpful advice they ever received about writing.

Independent Practice

📖 *Writing Process Transparencies,* 20–22B
📁 *Case Studies: Writing in the Real World,* pp. 21–24
📁 *Cooperative Learning Activities,* pp. 31–36

Skills Practice

📁 *Thinking and Study Skills,* pp. 5, 11, 13
📁 *Research Paper and Report Writing,* pp. 3, 19–20, 25

258

Revising/Editing

GETTING FEEDBACK

▼ *When revising, Johnson felt that she must write as precisely as possible, especially since she was trying to persuade people to donate money. Support for the project depended on her ability to persuade.*

Johnson knows the stage of revising well. "When I was writing in school, my father always said that there was no way to write a good paper the first time. You have to rewrite," she recalls.

For Johnson rewriting sometimes means reseeing. As Johnson explains, "What happens very often is you become too close to a particular subject. You may have the sense that you're explaining it very clearly. But, because you know all the details, you could be skipping over important facts." Johnson likes to ask someone outside the project, often her son or the owner of the gallery that shows her work, to read her proposal in order to see if it makes sense.

Response from a reader helps Johnson avoid problems she knows that she sometimes has with her writing. "I have a tendency to write something that has beautiful words and sounds really nice, but is it really pinpointing the meaning?" After getting reader response, Johnson revises one more time.

258

Visual Thinking

Analyzing Audience

You might suggest that students use a chart to help them analyze their audience. The chart might include categories such as age, interests, concerns, language level, and knowledge of the subject. Students can use the chart as they review drafts and rewrite.

Responding to the Case Study

1. Discussion

Discuss these questions about Indira Johnson's writing.

- What does Johnson say is the best thing to do when you have difficulty getting your writing started?

- What other step does Johnson often take before she writes a draft?

- What key question does Johnson ask herself to ensure that her proposal is persuasive?

- What does Johnson usually do with her rough draft before she revises it?

2. Persuasive Writing

Write a short proposal to gain support for an art project.

Brainstorm to come up with a list of projects that would beautify your school or community, and then choose one to support. Do any research necessary. Decide whether you will try to persuade your principal, the mayor, or someone else, and with that audience in mind, write the proposal. Ask someone else from your school or community to read your proposal before you revise it.

Grammar Link

Capitalize proper nouns and proper adjectives.

*I*ndira *F*reitas *J*ohnson

the drawings of an *I*ndian-born *A*merican woman

Write each sentence, using capital letters where necessary.

1. A new exhibit is opening at the garcia gallery on friday.
2. It will feature native american, european, hispanic, and asian art.
3. This area was first settled by the navajo, then by germans, then by mexicans and laotians.
4. Gallery owner jose garcia calls the show "visions of home."
5. It will truly be an all-american exhibit.

See Lessons 19.2–19.4, pages 552–557.

Case Study **259**

ASSESS

Responding to the Case Study

1. **Discussion**
   - Just start getting ideas down on paper.
   - She researches her subject.
   - "Who am I asking for support?"
   - She has someone else read it.

2. **Persuasive Writing**

Evaluate students' proposals on the following:
   - a clear statement of the action that is desired
   - reasons why the reader should take that action
   - one or more benefits that would result from that action
   - language suitable for the audience

See also the *Teacher's Guide to Writing Assessment.*

Grammar Link
(See Using the Grammar Link below.)

Reteaching

Discuss ways of analyzing an audience's interests and concerns in order to make a proposal more appealing.

Enrichment

Have students interview a board member of a local arts group about writing grant proposals.

CLOSE

Have students work in teams to brainstorm ideas for a class trip and to write proposals to get approval for the trip.

Closing Note
Students can contact arts and social services groups to learn about people whose talents and needs could be brought together in a project.

Using the Grammar Link

Grammar Link Answers
1. … Garcia Gallery on Friday.
2. … Native American, European, Hispanic, and Asian art.
3. … Navajo, then by Germans, then by Mexicans and Laotians.
4. … Jose Garcia calls the show "Visions of Home."
5. … all-American exhibit.

About the Art

Discussing a Photograph
Have students discuss the photograph on this page. Who do they think the people are? Who painted the mural? Are there any murals in the students' community?

FOCUS

Lesson Overview

Objective: To develop a piece of persuasive writing

Skills: identifying issues; stating a position; supporting an opinion with facts

Critical Thinking: stating a main idea; relating cause and effect; defining and clarifying; identifying expert sources

Speaking and Listening: discussing; interviewing; questioning

🔔 Bellringer

When students enter the classroom, have this assignment on the board: *Have you heard the word* propaganda*? What do you think it means?*

Grammar Link to the Bellringer
Ask students to look over what they have written for the Bellringer. Do all the verbs agree with their subjects?

Motivating Activity

Point out to students that *propaganda* means a systematic effort (usually by a government) to persuade people to do or think something. The word often has negative connotations. Have students look at the poster on student page 260. How do they think it might have achieved its purpose? Would they consider it propaganda? Why or why not? Explain that the purpose of persuasive writing is to influence people's thoughts or actions. Have students ever bought something they read about in an advertisement? Was the ad propaganda? Why or why not?

When you write to persuade, you try to convince your audience to think or act in a particular way. Often an image can be a powerful form of persuasion. This poster helped convince many Americans to enlist during World War I.

State Your Case

In most persuasive writing, the writer states an opinion or urges an action and then offers reasons why readers should accept the opinion or support the action. Reasons are often supported by facts, examples, or stories. What kinds of support does the writer of the model on the next page use to back up her opinion?

260 *Persuasive Writing: Making a Difference*

Teacher's Classroom Resources

The following resources can be used for planning, instruction, practice, reinforcement, assessment, reteaching, enrichment, or evaluation.

🔧 **Teaching Tools**
Lesson Plans, p. 56

🖨 **Transparencies**
Fine Art Transparencies, 26–30
Writing Process Transparencies, 20–22B

📁 **Blackline Masters**
Thinking and Study Skills, pp. 4–6, 13–21
Writing Across the Curriculum, p. 16
Cooperative Learning Activities, pp. 31–36

Student Model

One of the most disturbing trends I see is the draining of wetlands. Thousand-year-old swamps are being destroyed in just days to build skyscrapers and shopping malls or to plant crops. Where are ducks, geese, and other wildfowl going to raise their families or find food and rest when migrating? The answer is simple: each species will slowly die. These animals' habitats are being taken from *all* of us. It is sad, it truly is, to know the birds I love are moving closer to extinction.

April wants her readers to take the problem personally, as she does. How does she appeal to their emotions?

April Barnes, Decatur, Alabama
First appeared in *Merlyn's Pen*

Your world is full of topics for persuasive writing. What changes would you like to see in your school and community and in the larger world? By exploring the following sources, you can discover some issues you care about.

Look for Issues in Your Reading

Look for Issues in Other Media

Look for Issues in Conversation

Journal Writing

List some changes you'd like to see, using the sources above for ideas. As you study this unit, add to your lists, and use the ideas in your persuasive writing.

6.1 Writing Persuasively **261**

TEACH

Guided Practice

L2 Using the Model
Ask students to identify the paragraph's topic sentence (the first sentence). Point out that the topic sentence states a problem that concerns the writer. Following the statement, the writer recites some unpleasant effects that she hopes will prompt her readers to share her concern. (Draining the wetlands leads to loss of habitat for wild birds. Loss of habitat means birds will die and their species perhaps become extinct.) Remind students that presenting a cause-and-effect relationship is one of many ways to make an argument. Students should note that the writer also appeals to readers' concern for wildlife by expressing her own strong feelings about the wild birds.

L2 Cooperative Learning
Have students use the Three-Step Interview strategy to generate topics for persuasive writing. Students should work in pairs, interviewing each other to find out what issues they feel strongly about. (What would you like to change about your own life? Your neighborhood? The school? The country? The environment? The world? Movies? Television? Sports? Music?) Have volunteers share with the rest of the class what they learned in their interviews.

Journal Writing Tip

Gathering Ideas To help students keep their lists active, you may want to start a class list of issues that students can add to as they study the unit. Students' ideas may develop or take new direction through sharing with classmates.

Unit Assessment

Speaking and Listening Activities, p. 22
Composition Practice, p. 45
Composition Reteaching, p. 45
Composition Enrichment, p. 45

📁 *Teacher's Guide to Writing Assessment*
📁 *Tests with Answer Key*
Unit 6 Choice A Test, p. 21
Unit 6 Choice B Test, p. 22
Unit 6 Composition Objective Test, p. 23

🖥 *Test Generator*
Unit 6 Choice A
Unit 6 Choice B Test
Unit 6 Composition Objective Test
You may wish to administer either the Unit 6 Choice A Test or the Unit 6 Choice B Test as a pretest.

TEACH

Guided Practice

L2 Using the Model
Ask students to consider what expert sources the writer uses to support his opinion (the U.S. government, Friends of the Illinois Prairie Path, citizen groups).

L3 Promoting Discussion
Ask what students would do if they found strong evidence opposing their viewpoint on an issue. What research would they do if their stand was the least popular or the most difficult to defend? (Encourage the interchange without focusing on a "right" answer.)

Two-Minute Skill Drill

Have students write the more appropriate word or phrase from each group to include in a persuasive letter to a governing body.

- bad, damaging
- awesome, helpful
- can of worms, situation

Independent Practice

 For further stimuli for persuasive writing, see *Fine Art Transparencies* 26–30.

Writing Process Transparencies, 20–22B

Writing Across the Curriculum, p. 16

Cooperative Learning Activities, pp. 31–36

Skills Practice
Thinking and Study Skills, pp. 4–5, 13–21

Speaking and Listening Activities, p. 22

Composition Practice, p. 45

262

Back It Up

Research is an important step in persuasive writing. Your opinions will carry weight only if you can back them up. To gather support, investigate your topic by reading, observing, and discussing, and sometimes by interviewing experts—those with special knowledge about the issue. Patrick MacRoy felt strongly about a local issue: an electric company's plan to run wires along a nature trail. He wrote the following article for his school paper.

> **Revising Tip**
> Even as you draft and revise, continue to seek information on your topic. Strengthen your case by adding any additional proof.

What information does Patrick include to show the usefulness of the path?

Notice that Patrick supports his opinion by referring to expert sources.

> ### Student Model
>
> The Prairie Path is one of the last areas around here in which to enjoy nature. It is used by cyclists, hikers, horseback riders, and even schools as a site for nature classes. It was even recognized by the U.S. government as a national recreation trail. Groups like Friends of the Illinois Prairie Path are working hard [to save] the trail by circulating petitions and holding public meetings. Citizen groups say there are alternate routes for the power lines, if [the electric company] is willing to find them.
>
> If you want to help save the path, there will be a petition to sign in the lunchroom for the next few days. Thanks for your help.
>
> Patrick MacRoy, Glen Ellyn, Illinois
> First appeared in *Call of the Wildcat*

262

Enabling Strategies

LEP Understanding Conventions
Some students may speak languages or come from cultures with different conventions of address. They may be used to using specific patterns or expressions that convey politeness. In some languages, even persuasion is accomplished indirectly. Point out that in American English, it is appropriate to be direct yet respectful in stating an opinion or position.

6.1 Writing Activities

Write a Persuasive Paragraph

Think of an environmental issue that affects your school or community. You might see an appropriate issue on the list you created for this lesson's Journal Writing activity. Research it, and discuss it with others. Make prewriting notes.

- State your position clearly.
- Use facts to back up your position.

PURPOSE To state and support a position
AUDIENCE Classmates; city council
LENGTH 1–2 paragraphs

Cross-Curricular: Art

Your city council is debating whether to install the sculpture shown on this page in a park near your home. Closely observe the sculpture. Based on your observation, state your opinion in writing. Offer reasons that will persuade the city council.

> ### Grammar Link
>
> **Make sure the verb agrees with the subject, not with a word in an intervening phrase.**
>
> ***One*** *of the most disturbing trends I see* ***is*** *the draining of wetlands.*
>
> Complete each sentence with the correct choice of verb.
>
> 1. The home of my ancestors (is, are) not for sale.
> 2. A classroom for small children (require, requires) toys.
> 3. Boys of my father's generation (was, were) routinely drafted at age eighteen.
> 4. Prairies in the midwestern United States (has, have) almost disappeared.
> 5. A path through the woods (offers, offer) many small pleasures.
>
> **See Lesson 16.2, page 510.**

Miriam Schapiro, *Anna and David*, 1987

6.1 Writing Persuasively **263**

Using the Grammar Link

Grammar Link Answers
1. is
2. requires
3. were
4. have
5. offers

About the Art

Miriam Shapiro, *Anna and David*, 1987
Anna and David, by Miriam Shapiro, is made of aluminum and painted stainless steel. Measuring 35 by 31 by 9 feet, the piece was commissioned by J. W. Kaempfer for an office building in Rosslyn, Virginia.

FOCUS

Lesson Overview

Objective: To explore ideas for persuasive writing

Skills: generating opinions and supporting reasons; writing for an audience

Critical Thinking: decision making; defining and clarifying; evaluating information

Speaking and Listening: discussing; listening to a persuasive speech

Bellringer

When students enter the classroom, have this assignment on the board: *Do you agree or disagree with the following statement?* The legal age for driving should be lowered to fifteen. *Explain briefly.*

Grammar Link to the Bellringer

Have students look over their responses. Did they put two reasons in one sentence? Do they need to add a comma between them?

Motivating Activity

Discuss the Bellringer. Ask students how they make up their minds about an issue. Do they listen to what their friends, parents, or teachers say; read about it; get information from television? Ask them to consider this issue: Should zoos exist? Take a class poll. Include positions *For, Against,* and *Undecided.* Then ask students to explain why they took the position they did.

264

LESSON
6.2
Persuasive Writing
Determining a Position

If you've visited a zoo, you've seen people of all ages looking at and learning about animals from around the world. Some people, however, claim that animals belong only in the wild, not in captivity. Other people defend zoos as humane, well-designed environments that preserve endangered species and educate visitors.

Take a Stand

Once you take a stand on an issue, you must find support for it. At the same time, you should also consider arguments your opponents might make against your position. During the prewriting step, list both *pros* (points that can be used to support your argument) and *cons* (points that might be used against it). Look at the example on page 265.

264 *Persuasive Writing: Making a Difference*

Teacher's Classroom Resources

The following resources can be used for planning, instruction, practice, reinforcement, assessment, reteaching, enrichment, or evaluation.

Teaching Tools
Lesson Plans

Transparencies
Fine Art Transparencies, 26–30
Writing Process Transparencies, 20–22B

Pro
1. Zoos protect endangered species.
2. Modern zoo environments resemble habitats.
3. Zoos educate public about conservation.
4. Zoos are run by professionals.

Con
1. Zoos are animal prisons.
2. Captivity changes animals' behavior.
3. Animals should not be entertainment.
4. Capture/confinement can hurt animals.

Student Model

Zoos today are important to the survival of many species. They do not abuse the animals, but instead they offer a safe and healthy environment. At the same time they provide an enjoyable viewing experience for people of all ages. This gives us an opportunity to better appreciate animals and learn more about their preservation. As stated in the *Utne Reader* [a general-interest magazine about ideas and issues], zoos are "institutions we should see not as abusers of the world's animals, but as vital forces saving animals from extinction."

Jacqueline Parks, Springman Junior High School,
Glenview, Illinois

According to Jacqueline, how do zoos benefit both animals and people?

Grammar
Editing Tip

In editing check for a comma before a coordinating conjunction, such as *and, but, or,* or *nor,* when it joins the two main clauses of a compound sentence. For more on compound sentences, see Lesson 14.1, page 472, and Lesson 20.3, page 570.

Journal Writing

Think of an issue on which someone disagrees with you. Create pro and con lists like the ones above. Try to include strong points on both sides.

6.2 Determining a Position **265**

TEACH

Guided Practice

L2 Using Graphic Organizers
Graphic devices can assist students in many different stages of the writing process. Pro and con lists, like the ones shown here, can help students in the prewriting stage explore opposing views on an issue. Students can refer to the lists later to make sure that each strong point in an opposing argument is countered or addressed in some way.

L3 Writing a Rebuttal
Have students write an argument to counter the argument made in the Student Model. Remind students that they may need to do some research to find evidence to support their opinions.

Two-Minute Skill Drill

Write *Pro* and *Con* on the board. Ask students to write two words or phrases with the same meaning as *pro* and two with the same meaning as *con*. (Samples: *for, in favor of; against, anti*)

Journal Writing Tip

Generating Information Students might brainstorm in small groups to come up with a list of popular issues on which to base the pro and con lists in their journals.

📁 **Blackline Masters**
Thinking and Study Skills, pp. 3, 5–7, 20, 21
Writing Across the Curriculum, p. 6
Cooperative Learning Activities, pp. 31–36

Speaking and Listening Activities, p. 22
Composition Practice, p. 46
Composition Reteaching, p. 46
Composition Enrichment, p. 46

Assessment
📁 *Teacher's Guide to Writing Assessment*

TEACH

Guided Practice

L2 Using the Models

Students should respond that Berry is countering the criticism that video games can be harmful to children. Turkle, on the other hand, is responding to the criticism that video games are mindless. Ask students to identify words that Turkle uses to make her point more persuasive (*mastering, skills, complex, differentiated, mastered, strategies, learning*).

L1 Identifying the Audience

If students have difficulty identifying the intended audience for each model, remind them to be sure to read the whole paragraph. Information in titles may also clarify the purpose or audience of the written piece.

Independent Practice

✍ For further stimuli for persuasive writing, see *Fine Art Transparencies* 26–30.

✍ *Writing Process Transparencies*, 20–22B

📂 *Writing Across the Curriculum*, p. 6

📂 *Cooperative Learning Activities*, pp. 31–36

Skills Practice

📂 *Thinking and Study Skills*, pp. 3, 5–7, 20, 21

📂 *Speaking and Listening Activities*, p. 22

📂 *Composition Practice*, p. 46

Consider Your Audience

Your audience is important in persuasive writing. When your goal is to influence opinions, you need to know who your readers are and how they think. Study the models below. The first, from the foreword of a book for children, is written to their parents. The second speaks to educators.

> *What criticism of video games is Berry answering?*

> *Who will do this encouraging?*

Literature Model

*I*t isn't that video games in and of themselves are harmful. Problems arise instead when the attitudes, priorities, or habits of their users are out of line. That's why children must be encouraged to view video games in a balanced, reasonable way and to take responsibility for their proper use.

Joy Wilt Berry, *What to Do When Your Mom or Dad Says . . ."Don't Overdo with Video Games!"*

> *What criticism of video games is Turkle answering?*

> *Why would this appeal to teachers?*

Literature Model

*T*here is nothing mindless about mastering a video game. The game demands skills that are complex and differentiated . . . and when one game is mastered, there is thinking about how to generalize strategies to other games. There is learning how to learn.

Dr. Sherry Turkle,
The Second Self: Computers and Human Spirit

Both writers defend video games but for different readers. Berry reassures worried parents and explains that attitudes and not video games are the problem. Turkle addresses educators and speaks about thinking skills.

266 *Persuasive Writing: Making a Difference*

Enabling Strategies

LEP Using Root Words

If students speak a Romance or Germanic language, they may already be familiar with *pro* and *con*. Point out that *pro* comes from the Greek for *before* and the Latin for *before* or *forward*. If you put forward an idea, you are for it, or pro. *Con* comes from the Latin word *contra*, meaning *against*. Words beginning with *contra-* usually imply *against* or *opposing*, as in *contrast, contrary, contraband,* or *contradiction*.

6.2 Writing Activities

Write a Position Paper

Think of a controversial issue on which you have not yet formed an opinion. Develop a list of supporting details for each side. Decide which side is stronger, and defend it in a persuasive piece directed at others who are still undecided.

- State your position clearly.
- Use facts and language that are targeted to your audience.

PURPOSE To defend a position
AUDIENCE Your classmates, readers of a newspaper
LENGTH 1 page

Cross-Curricular: Health and Safety

You've traveled back in time to the 1800s. You're aboard an English sailing ship docked in a Caribbean harbor. The sailors tell you that for months they've eaten nothing but hard biscuits and salt pork, with no fresh fruits or vegetables. Now their gums are bleeding. They've heard from other sailors that oranges will help the condition, but on this island, they find only limes, which they don't like. Using evidence that is easy to understand, write a conversation between yourself and a sailor. Try to persuade the sailor to eat the limes.

Grammar Link

Use a comma before a conjunction that links two main clauses.

They do not abuse the animals, **but** *instead they offer a safe and healthy environment.*

Write each sentence, adding commas where necessary.

1. Young people like the challenge of video games and that challenge can stimulate learning.
2. They can passively watch television or they can be active participants in a video game.
3. Some games are designed to be educational but even purely recreational games can spark the imagination.
4. Both young people and their parents should exercise good judgment for not all video games are appropriate for all ages.
5. Most young people do not become overly caught up in video games nor do the games make them neglect their responsibilities.

See Lesson 14.1, page 472, and Lesson 20.3, page 570.

6.2 Determining a Position **267**

ASSESS

Writing Activities Evaluation Guidelines

Write a Position Paper
Use these criteria when evaluating your students' writing.
- Is the writer's position stated clearly?
- Does the writing use audience-appropriate facts and language?

See also the *Teacher's Guide to Writing Assessment*.

Cross-Curricular: Health and Safety
The conversation should
- use easy-to-understand evidence
- convince the sailors that limes are as beneficial as oranges

Grammar Link
(See Using the Grammar Link below.)

Reteaching
Composition Reteaching, p. 46

Enrichment
Composition Enrichment, p. 46

CLOSE

Have students work in pairs to explore an issue for persuasive writing. Ask each pair to pick an issue and generate a pro and con list. Then each partner should take a side and write a persuasive piece defending it. (Remind students that they can defend a point of view as an exercise even if they don't share that point of view.) Pairs can present their arguments to the rest of the class in a Point/Counterpoint session.

Using the Grammar Link

Grammar Link Answers
Commas should fall between the following words:
1. games, and
2. television, or
3. educational, but
4. judgment, for
5. games, nor

Using Conjunctions Have students write a sentence using a conjunction and two main clauses. It may come from their writing activities or from work in their journals. Remind students that conjunctions include *and, but, or, yet, nor, although,* and others.

Persuasive Writing
Evaluating Evidence

Setting the Purpose

Lesson 6.3 teaches students to support a position with evidence and to connect and combine information in support of a position.

FOCUS

Lesson Overview

Objective: To support a position with evidence

Skills: supporting opinions; selecting evidence

Critical Thinking: evaluating; persuading; classifying; contrasting; visualizing

Speaking and Listening: interviewing; note taking; discussing; questioning

Bellringer

When students enter the classroom, have this assignment on the board: *In one sentence, write a slogan to persuade your friends to switch to your favorite breakfast cereal.*

Grammar Link to the Bellringer

Have students revise the following sentence by using the correct subject-verb agreement: *Super Bowl cereal and Yummy Chunk chocolate is good for you.*

Motivating Activity

Bring in boxes of several different brands of cereal. Ask students to examine the persuasive writing on each one. To what audiences do the different cereals try to appeal? What claims do they make? Are the claims supported by evidence? Which claims are most persuasive?

Advertisers and others who want to sell you products or services also use the techniques of persuasion. Even a cereal box can be a persuasive tool.

Nutrition information per one-ounce serving:

Calories	90
Protein	4 g
Carbohydrates	20 g
Fat	0 g
Cholesterol	0 mg
Sodium	0 mg
Potassium	105 mg

YOUR GOOD-HEALTH GAME PLAN

SUPER BOWL

"DELICIOUS"

FITNESS FLAKES

Your grocery list says "healthful cereal," so you hurry past Sugary Chunks and Sweet Treats. You spot an unfamiliar brand, Super Bowl Fitness Flakes. Read the labels on the box. What is the real difference between Fitness Flakes and Sweet Treats? When it's time to make your choice, will the box front or the labels be more helpful? Why?

Support Opinions with Evidence

The information on the cereal box illustrates two kinds of evidence—facts and opinions. Facts can be proved—the cereal could be tested for the number of calories per one-ounce serving. Opinions, such as "delicious," are personal judgments. They

268 *Persuasive Writing: Making a Difference*

Teacher's Classroom Resources

The following resources can be used for planning, instruction, practice, reinforcement, assessment, reteaching, enrichment, or evaluation.

Teaching Tools
Lesson Plans, p. 58

Transparencies
Fine Art Transparencies, 26–30
Writing Process Transparencies, 20–22B

can't be proved. When you state an opinion, back it up with evidence: facts, statistics, and examples.

Read the following paragraph, and notice the facts, opinions, and other kinds of evidence it contains. Then study the chart that follows.

Many Americans hate their bodies. "We have declared war on our bodies," charges Andrew Kimbrell, the author of The Human Body Shop. This war includes 34 percent of all men and 38 percent of all women. They spent $33 billion on diets in 1990. A preteen boy guzzles protein drinks, hoping to increase his size and strength, while a fifty-five-year-old woman gets a face-lift. Technology and social pressure are causing us to make extreme changes.

The opinion is stated first.

The writer supports the opinion with evidence.

The writer draws a conclusion.

Evidence in Persuasive Writing	
Kinds	**Examples**
Fact	Americans spent $33 billion on the diet industry in 1990.
Statistic	Thirty-four percent of men and 38 percent of women spent $33 billion on diets in 1990.
Example	A fifty-five-year-old woman gets a face-lift.

Journal Writing

Jot down the evidence that persuaded you to change your mind about something or someone. Label each piece of evidence as one or more of the three kinds shown above.

6.3 Evaluating Evidence **269**

📁 **Blackline Masters**
Thinking and Study Skills,
  pp. 5, 7, 14–15, 17, 19
Writing Across the Curriculum,
  pp. 6–7, 18, 21
Cooperative Learning Activities,
  pp. 31–36

Speaking and Listening
  Activities, p. 22
Composition Practice, p. 47
Composition Reteaching, p. 47
Composition Enrichment, p. 47

Assessment
📁 *Teacher's Guide to Writing Assessment*

TEACH

Guided Practice

L2 Using the Model
Point out the importance of identifying people quoted in a piece of persuasive writing. Here the writer quotes Andrew Kimbrell and identifies him as the author of a book about the body. Remind students that opinions carry weight only if they are the opinions of people who know something about the subject.

L2 Cooperative Learning
To evaluate the evidence used in persuasive writing, have students form teams of four, with two pairs on each team. Give each pair a different example of persuasive writing. One partner should analyze the example of persuasive writing and identify the types of evidence used in it while the other partner coaches. They can use a chart like the one on this page to organize their findings. Team pairs should then exchange examples, and partners should switch roles. Teams can then compare and discuss their findings.

Two-Minute Skill Drill

Ask students to scan the chart on this page and then to write down three sentences: one containing a fact, one containing a statistic, and one giving an example.

Journal Writing Tip

Analyzing Information Ask students which kinds of evidence seem most persuasive. Why? (Facts and statistics may seem most persuasive because they can be proved.)

269

TEACH

Guided Practice

L2 Using the Model

Ask students to identify Brody's position statement. (the second sentence) What evidence does she present to support it? (facts about the content of soft drinks) Point out how Brody uses words and phrases such as *probably*, *some*, and *for the most part* to limit her claims and keep them from becoming overgeneralizations. Note that the phrase *wet, sweet calories* echoes the phrase *empty calories* and vividly makes the point that soft drinks appeal to the senses but lack nutritional value.

L2 Selecting Evidence

Tell students that health educators use persuasive materials to attempt to influence people's ideas and behavior. Suggest that interested students contact the local health department or another health agency to get copies of brochures and other materials designed to promote good health. Have students evaluate the evidence presented in each one. Students might also want to interview health educators to discover what persuasive techniques the educators find most effective.

Independent Practice

🖎 For further stimuli for persuasive writing, see *Fine Art Transparencies* 26–30.

🖎 *Writing Process Transparencies*, 20–22B

📁 *Writing Across the Curriculum*, pp. 6–7, 18, 21

📁 *Cooperative Learning Activities*, pp. 31–36

Skills Practice

📁 *Thinking and Study Skills*, pp. 5, 7, 14–15, 17, 19

📁 *Speaking and Listening Activities*, p. 22

📁 *Composition Practice*, p. 47

270

Presenting Tip

When you present your persuasive writing, remember that charts, graphs, and other images can clarify your evidence and bring it to life.

Select Strong Evidence

Not all pieces of evidence are equally strong. Some "facts" are really opinions in disguise. When you write persuasively, check your facts, and make sure that they back up your point. In the model below, nutritionist Jane Brody says that choosing soft drinks over water "presents a . . . serious threat to good nutritional health." Does she persuade you? Why or why not?

Literature Model

No beverage in America gives water greater competition than flavored soft drinks. And probably no other choice presents a more serious threat to good nutritional health. Soft drinks are the epitome [ideal example] of empty calories. They contain water (with or without carbon dioxide), artificial colorings and flavorings, and sugar—as many as *6 teaspoons of sugar in one 8-ounce serving!* Nothing else. Some noncarbonated drinks add vitamin C, and "fruit" or "fruit-flavored" drinks may even contain some real fruit juice. But for the most part, they are just wet, sweet calories.

Jane Brody, *Jane Brody's Nutrition Book*

What kind of evidence does this sentence contain, facts or opinions?

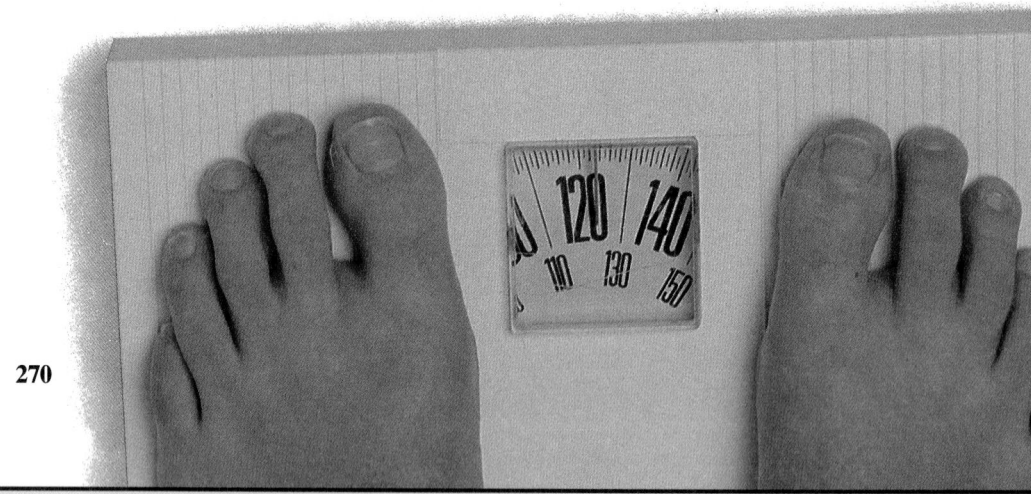

270

Enabling Strategies

LEP Using the Model

Students learning English may be unfamiliar with some of the more difficult vocabulary words in the Literature Model. You may want to read the model aloud, explaining words such as *beverage*, *epitome*, *calories*, *carbon dioxide*, *artificial*, and *noncarbonated*.

6.3 Writing Activities

Write a Persuasive Essay

Usually you look for evidence supporting a position you already hold. Sometimes, however, the reverse happens. A fact "grabs" you, and you want to learn enough to develop a position on the issue. Find a piece of evidence, such as the fact that some fast-food chains have switched from polystyrene containers to paper.

Brainstorm about what the evidence tells you. What questions does it raise? Try to connect this piece of evidence with what you already know. From this brainstorming, develop a persuasive piece of one page for an audience of your choice.

- Include facts, statistics, examples, and reasons as evidence.
- Examine your evidence critically to be sure that facts are correct and that they support your argument.

PURPOSE To persuade someone about an issue
AUDIENCE Your choice
LENGTH 1 page

Cooperative Learning

Has the world become warmer because of excess carbon dioxide and other gases? Are recent extreme temperatures simply normal climatic variations? Questions about the greenhouse effect remain unanswered.

With two or three classmates, research the existence and possible causes of the greenhouse effect. Prepare a short panel discussion for the class. Group members will use some current opinions to try to persuade the class to take a particular stand on the greenhouse effect. Afterwards, the class may discuss the presentation and its strengths and weaknesses.

Grammar Link

Use a plural verb with a compound subject joined by *and*.

Technology and social pressure are causing us to make extreme changes.

Write each sentence, correcting errors in subject-verb agreement.

1. At the end of this hilarious book, Perry's dog and his luggage ends up in China.
2. A sensible diet and an exercise program contributes to good health.
3. Three facts and one example supports the writer's opinion.
4. A sincere apology and a full refund has been sent to each angry customer.
5. Strong evidence and good organization makes your case more convincing.

See Lesson 16.5, page 516.

6.3 Evaluating Evidence **271**

Using the Grammar Link

Setting the Purpose

Lesson 6.4 teaches students effective ways to get a reader's attention and to organize an argument.

FOCUS

Lesson Overview

Objective: To organize persuasive evidence in the most effective order

Skills: identifying main idea and supporting details

Critical Thinking: organizing evidence; defining and clarifying

Speaking and Listening: speaking to persuade

Bellringer

When students enter the classroom, have this assignment on the board: *Rewrite the sentence below, using punctuation and capitalization as needed.*

stop we have a problem in our town to say nothing of the rest of the world that needs your attention

Grammar Link to the Bellringer

Ask volunteers to write their Bellringer answers on the board. Point out the use of commas to set off words that interrupt the flow of the sentence. (Sample: Stop! We have a problem in our town, to say nothing of the rest of the world, that needs your attention.)

Motivating Activity

Ask students what catches their attention when thumbing through a magazine or newspaper (striking photos, intriguing headlines, topics of interest, anything unusual). Explain that, as persuasive writers, they will try to catch a reader's attention. Have students recall any attention-getting strategies they already use in writing.

Persuasive Writing
Developing a Strategy

As Calvin demonstrates in the cartoon below, even a reluctant audience can be reached with the right attention-grabbing strategy. The first step in persuasion is to get the attention of your reader. Newspapers, magazines, television, and radio all compete for attention. You must find ways to make your message stand out from all the rest.

© Watterson 1992. Universal Press Syndicate

Get Attention

How can you capture your readers' attention? As many writers have discovered, a playful imagination can work wonders. The following student model brings an everyday object to life in a humorous, imaginative way; her serious purpose, however, is to draw attention to an important issue.

272 *Persuasive Writing: Making a Difference*

Teacher's Classroom Resources

The following resources can be used for planning, instruction, practice, reinforcement, assessment, reteaching, enrichment, or evaluation.

Teaching Tools
Lesson Plans, p. 59

Transparencies
Fine Art Transparencies, 26–30
Writing Process Transparencies, 20–22B

Student Model

A s one of the many cheap, unreliable, plastic department store bags, I'd like to speak out. Even though humans think of us as worthless, I wish they wouldn't throw us out their car windows, leaving us to fight for our lives on busy, treacherous highways. Wind gusts from cars going sixty miles an hour blow our flimsy bodies everywhere. Sometimes we land on windshields and cause accidents. Even worse, humans often leave us to baby-sit their small children. Don't get me wrong—we like kids, but not when they put us over their heads or in their mouths and begin to choke, turn blue, and die. . . .

So please, be careful when you dispose of us. Don't throw us out car windows or give us to babies. We like humans and definitely would not want to have them angry at us for wrecking their cars and killing their kids.

Dina Morrison, Pittsburgh, Pennsylvania
First appeared in *Merlyn's Pen*

The surprise of a talking plastic bag attracts the reader's attention and arouses interest.

What problems does the writer identify, and how does she suggest that people solve them?

Some lively formats for persuasive writing include real-life stories, fables, parables, ballads, and letters to people from the past or future. You might also use visuals, such as pictures, charts, and graphs, to call attention to the issue.

Journal Writing

Poet Robert Frost said that if there is no surprise for the writer, there will be no surprise for the reader. List some elements that have drawn your attention to persuasive messages. Analyze why they caught your attention.

TEACH

Guided Practice

L2 Using the Model
Discuss the writer's use of vivid language to create images in her readers' minds (the *flimsy bodies* of the plastic bags blowing on the highway, children who *turn blue, and die*). Point out that these images can be powerful persuaders. Students should respond that the writer identifies the dangers of plastic bags to automobile drivers and to children. She advises greater care in disposing of plastic bags.

L2 Connecting and Combining Information
Have students brainstorm a list of attention-getting strategies that they could use in persuasive writing (vivid descriptions, interesting anecdotes, questions, unusual facts, shocking statistics, humor, and so on).

Two-Minute Skill Drill

Ask students to brainstorm more attention-getting synonyms for *want*, *think*, and *agree* and use the synonyms in persuasive sentences.

Journal Writing Tip

Recalling Remind students to consider persuasive messages they have noticed on television, the radio, billboards, posters, and so on.

📂 **Blackline Masters**
Thinking and Study Skills,
  pp. 10, 11, 14, 17–19
Writing Across the Curriculum,
  p. 6
Cooperative Learning Activities,
  pp. 31–36

*Speaking and Listening
  Activities,* p. 22
Composition Practice, p. 48
Composition Reteaching, p. 48
Composition Enrichment, p. 48

Assessment
📂 *Teacher's Guide to Writing Assessment*

Guided Practice

L2 Using the Model
Point out how the writer addresses the opposition directly in the third sentence. Have students identify the main idea of the paragraph (rail passenger service should be an important part of America's future transportation system), and the evidence the writer presents (fourth, fifth, and sixth sentences). Explain that putting the strongest last makes it likely readers will remember it the best.

L1 Using Supporting Evidence
Use the Student Facsimile to demonstrate for students how evidence supports a position. Draw a diagram of building blocks on the board. Ask students to help place the topic sentence in a top block and supporting sentences in blocks "holding it up." In doing so, you will show the relationship between each piece of evidence and the topic sentence.

Independent Practice

For further stimuli for persuasive writing, see *Fine Art Transparencies* 26–30.

Writing Process Transparencies 20–22B

Writing Across the Curriculum, p. 6

Cooperative Learning Activities, 31–36

Skills Practice
Thinking and Study Skills, pp. 10, 11, 14, 17–19

Speaking and Listening Activities, p. 22

Composition Practice, p. 48

Organize Your Argument

Your case, or argument, consists of a statement of your position and supporting evidence arranged in an orderly manner. Notice how this writer includes an answer to an opposing idea.

This is the topic sentence, since it expresses the main idea. What is the main idea?

On quiet nights the sound of a distant train reminds me of a time when railroads provided our most reliable passenger transportation. Rail passenger service, vital to America's past, can be even more important to its future. But, you say, trains are slow. True, but with today's crowded airports and new "bullet-train" technology, rail service can compete with the airlines in speed as well as cost. Trains use less fuel per passenger-mile than planes, cars, or buses do. Most important, trains' fuel efficiency conserves oil and decreases air pollution.

The writer says this idea is the most important. Do you agree? Why might the writer have saved it for last?

First, the paragraph grabs attention with a nostalgic image involving trains. Then it presents its main point, answers opposition, and provides additional supporting evidence. The following chart summarizes what you should include in most arguments.

Grammar
Editing Tip

In editing make sure you use past and present tense correctly. For more information on verb tense, see Lesson 10.5, page 376.

How to Build Your Case
1. State your position clearly.
2. Present sound, relevant evidence.
3. Anticipate and answer the opposition.
4. Begin or end with your strongest point.

274 *Persuasive Writing: Making a Difference*

Enabling Strategies

LEP Getting Readers' Attention
Students who are new to English may benefit from additional work on attention-getting strategies. Encourage students to think about ways to interest readers (a photograph, an anecdote, a surprising statistic, a cartoon). Have newspapers and magazines available for students to use in finding examples of effective attention-getting strategies. Encourage students to bring in examples from newspapers or magazines they enjoy and explain why they find the examples effective.

6.4 Writing Activities

ASSESS

Write a Presentation

Your school system is considering ending athletic contests among schools in your district. Supporters of this view argue that the athletic program wastes money and takes time away from education. Write a presentation to your local school board making a case that supports your view of interscholastic athletics.

- Choose a strategy to gain attention and interest.
- Grab your readers' attention.
- State your position and evidence.
- Begin or end with your strongest point.
- Answer the opposition.

PURPOSE To persuade readers about school athletic contests
AUDIENCE Your school board
LENGTH 2–3 paragraphs

Cooperative Learning

With a group of classmates, brainstorm a list of charitable projects you might support (a book drive for the school library, meals for homeless families, and so on). Debate the merits of each, and choose one. Meet with the class to consider other groups' ideas. Then decide on a fund-raiser, such as a car wash, special athletic event, or bake sale. Create a flier to urge families to support the project. Decide on the content of the flier, and divide the tasks necessary to prepare it.

Grammar Link

Use commas to set off words that interrupt the flow of the sentence.

But, you say, trains are slow.

Rewrite the following, adding commas where necessary.

[1] Garbage and waste products you realize are always with us. They will not despite our closed eyes disappear.

[2] One way to reduce trash obviously is to reduce usage. Buying fewer objects you know means fewer discards.

[3] Another way of course is to recycle materials. Organic materials even kitchen garbage can go to a compost heap. Some materials like glass and aluminum are easily reused.

[4] Plastics and old tires on the other hand pose a challenge. Recycled plastic for example may be used in rugs.

[5] Unrecycled materials for the most part end up in landfills or incinerators.

See Lesson 20.2, page 568.

6.4 Developing a Strategy **275**

Writing Activities Evaluation Guidelines

Write a Presentation
Use these criteria when evaluating your students' writing. Each student's presentation should
- use an attention-getting strategy
- take a clear stand and support it
- present evidence that would appeal to school board members
- present the strongest evidence first or last
- answer the opposition

See also the *Teacher's Guide to Writing Assessment*.

Cooperative Learning
In evaluating the group's work, ask the following questions:
- Does the flier present enough information about the event?
- Does the flier present reasons that would make the audience want to support the fund-raiser?
- Did each group member contribute to the final product?

Grammar Link
(See Using the Grammar Link below.)

Reteaching
Composition Reteaching, p. 48

Enrichment
Composition Enrichment, p. 48

CLOSE

Suggest that students choose a historical or fictional character to present a position on an issue. One might choose a feminist such as Sarah Grimke to argue that girls' sports are entitled to the same support as boys' sports.

Using the Grammar Link

Grammar Link Answers
Commas should appear between the following words.
1. products, you; realize, are; not, despite; eyes, disappear
2. trash, obviously, is; objects, you; know, means
3. way, of; course, is; matter, even; garbage, can; materials, like; aluminum, are
4. tires, on; hand, pose; plastic, for; example, may
5. materials, for; part, end

275

FOCUS

Lesson Overview

Objective: To evaluate and revise a piece of persuasive writing
Skills: evaluating persuasive writing; peer reviewing
Critical Thinking: analyzing; contrasting; summarizing; establishing and evaluating criteria; decision-making
Speaking and Listening: discussing; questioning

Bellringer
When students enter the classroom, have this assignment on the board: *Write a few sentences explaining why it is important to revise your writing.*

Grammar Link to the Bellringer
Ask students to underline any subject and object pronouns used in the sentences from the Bellringer activity.

Motivating Activity
Discuss the revision strategies that students use. Ask: What are the advantages of having someone else review your work and comment on it? (The advantages are getting fresh ideas, a sense of how your audience may respond, and someone to discuss your work with.) What are the disadvantages? (Criticism can be hard to take.) How can the process be improved? (Emphasize the positive when reviewing another writer's work.)

Persuasive Writing
Strengthening Your Argument

Writing persuasively is a challenge. You can strengthen your argument by revising your work and filling in the gaps.

Just as the acrobats at the left must have sturdy equipment, your position must have strong support. And just as the acrobats have to synchronize their movements, you must organize your ideas so that they all work together to make your point.

Take Another Look

The word *revising* means "seeing again." To revise persuasive writing, set it aside for a time, and return to it later. You often have assignments that are due on a certain date, so you can't wait days or weeks to finish a piece of writing. However, if you begin your assignment several days before it is due, you will allow time for revision. Professional writers agree that setting your work aside, even if only for a day, will give you a fresh, new perspective. You may find that your best ideas will come during revision.

Peer reviewing is another helpful technique. Before you revise, ask a classmate to listen to your draft to help you identify any problems. To see how peer reviewing works, read the following draft. Then read the peer reviewer's comments, and decide whether you agree with them.

Teacher's Classroom Resources

The following resources can be used for planning, instruction, practice, reinforcement, assessment, reteaching, enrichment, or evaluation.

Teaching Tools
Lesson Plans

Transparencies
Fine Art Transparencies, 26–30
Writing Process Transparencies, 20–22B

Paragraph 1:
I like your opening paragraph. It grabs my attention. Are the slang words OK here?

Paragraph 2:
Good ideas, but you provide little evidence. Do you have any facts and examples?

Paragraph 3:
Is summer employment a reason why you don't want year-round school? Can you make this paragraph clearer?

I have something to say to those adults who want to keep schools open all year long. Give me a break! Please don't do anything so drastic! Eliminating summer vacation will cause enormous stress for everyone. Teachers will burn out faster. Nobody will pay attention in class in the middle of July, and the air-conditioning bills will be enormous. Also, additional salaries for teachers and janitors will be astronomical!

Year-round school will not help education, but it may reduce learning because many students take summer jobs to save for college tuition.

Notice that this peer review contains questions and suggestions—not commands. After peer review, it's up to you to read over the comments, decide which ones you agree with, and make those changes.

Vocabulary
Drafting Tip

When drafting, remember that slang is inappropriate for any but the most informal writing, such as a personal note or friendly letter.

Journal Writing

Describe one good and one unsatisfactory experience you've had with a peer reviewer. In your opinion what are the characteristics of a good peer reviewer?

6.5 Strengthening Your Argument **277**

TEACH

Guided Practice

L2 Using the Model
Emphasize the importance of peer reviewers making positive comments. Also point out that questions, like those shown here, can be a good way of directing a writer's attention to possible problems. Ask students what other suggestions for revisions they would make. Remind them to make their comments in a way that shows respect for the writer. Have them suggest sources the writer could use to get more convincing evidence (interviews with school administrators, articles on the issue of year-round school). Have them revise the final paragraph to make it clearer (by clarifying the connection between the need for some students to work during the summers and paying for higher education).

L1 Helping Peer Reviewers
Have students develop lists of Do's and Don'ts for peer reviewers using the Roundtable strategy. Let students work in small groups and use large sheets of paper with markers to make their group list. Each member of the group in turn should contribute to the list.

Two-Minute Skill Drill

Have students include each of the following sets of pronouns in a sentence:

I/them   They/him

Journal Writing Tip

Characterizing Good Reviewing Have students give examples of the kinds of peer reviewer comments they find most helpful.

TEACH

Guided Practice

L2 Using the Model
Suggest that students answer the questions in the chart to evaluate the model. In answer to the callout question, students should respond that Levine states the following position in the first sentence: *You'll be able to do far more with your life if you stay in school and graduate.*

L3 Writing Introductions
Remind students of the importance of getting the audience's attention in a piece of persuasive writing. Then have students write an attention-getting paragraph that might be used to introduce the Literature Model. (Possible strategies: a real-life story, a fable, startling statistics, questions addressed to the reader)

Independent Practice

For further stimuli for persuasive writing, see *Fine Art Transparencies* 26–30.

Writing Process Transparencies, 20–22B

Writing Across the Curriculum, pp. 7–8

Cooperative Learning Activities, pp. 31–36

Skills Practice

Thinking and Study Skills, pp. 14, 19, 20

Speaking and Listening Activities, pp. 22

Composition Practice, p. 49

Fill in the Gaps

Holes, or gaps, in the argument weaken a persuasive argument. The questions that follow will help you check your argument for adequate support.

Revising Persuasive Writing

1. Do I make my position clear?
2. Do I present enough evidence?
3. Is the evidence strong? Is it relevant?
4. Do I keep my audience in mind?
5. Are my ideas organized effectively?

Revision is far more than simply changing a word here and there. You may need to add, delete, or move whole sentences and paragraphs. During the revising stage, you must read, ask yourself questions, experiment, and revise some more. The paragraph below works well because David Levine supports his point with strong evidence.

Literature Model

> *What position does Levine state in the first sentence?*

> *Levine's evidence is powerful, solid, and relevant to his audience.*

Staying in school and graduating extends the range of options of what you can do with your life. It's also a fact that the consequences of dropping out are severe and the prospects for dropouts are bleak. According to the National Dropout Prevention Center, less than 50 percent of dropouts find jobs when they leave school. When they do, they earn 60 percent less than high school graduates (over a lifetime that adds up to $250,000).

David Levine, "I'm Outta Here"
First appeared in *Seventeen*

---

278 *Persuasive Writing: Making a Difference*

Enabling Strategies

LEP Evaluating Persuasive Writing
Give students an example of a piece of persuasive writing which they, as a group, can evaluate, using use the questions in the chart. Work through the questions one at a time to make sure students understand how to apply them to a specific piece of writing. You may need to give additional examples of relevant and irrelevant evidence to make the concepts clear.

6.5 Writing Activities

Revise a Persuasive Piece

Take another look at a writing assignment that you completed earlier in this unit or a persuasive piece that you wrote for a different class. Consider the five questions on the chart on the preceding page. Then revise the piece.

- Look at your piece with a new perspective. Ask yourself the five questions on the chart on page 278.
- Make sure there are no gaps in your argument.
- Add or change words and sentences as necessary.

PURPOSE To review and revise an earlier piece of persuasive writing

AUDIENCE Yourself

LENGTH 3–4 paragraphs

COMPUTER OPTION

Sometimes writers prefer to revise at their computer terminals. Having a revision checklist right on the screen, along with the piece of writing you want to revise, is helpful. Develop a list of ten or twelve items for the checklist, and use a split screen to keep the list available as you revise.

Grammar Link

Use subject pronouns in the subject of a sentence and object pronouns as the object of a verb or preposition.

I have something to say. . . .

*Give **me** a break!*

Be especially careful with compound elements: *Sue and **I** saw Joe and **him**.*
    Write each sentence, correcting errors in pronoun usage.

1. Rachel and me support the proposed art curriculum.
2. However, Rachel can better explain it to you and he.
3. Ginny was always available to help Ralph and she.
4. Here is a gift from Trudy and I.
5. Tell Martin and she the news.
6. Before she moved, her and I used to be best friends.
7. The song about Lance and she is very funny.
8. The Connors and us are vacationing together.
9. Them did better in school than anyone else.
10. Him and me don't talk much any more.

See Lesson 11.1, page 402, and Lesson 11.3, page 406.

6.5 Strengthening Your Argument **279**

ASSESS

Writing Activities Evaluation Guidelines

Revise a Persuasive Piece
Use these criteria when evaluating your students' writing.
- Is the writer's position stated clearly?
- Does the writer use language and sentence structure appropriate to the audience selected?
- Does the writer provide strong evidence to support his or her position?
- Does the writer order points in an effective manner?

See also the *Teacher's Guide to Writing Assessment.*

Grammar Link
(See Using the Grammar Link below.)

Reteaching
📂 *Composition Reteaching,* p. 49

Enrichment
📂 *Composition Enrichment,* p. 49

CLOSE

Have students choose a piece of their persuasive writing to submit to the school newspaper, the local newspaper, or another publication of their choice. Have students find out about submission guidelines and any additional information about the intended audience. Then have students use self-review and peer-review strategies to revise their writing for publication.

Using the Grammar Link

Grammar Link Answers
1. Rachel and I
2. you and him
3. Ralph and her
4. Trudy and me
5. Martin and her
6. she and I
7. Lance and her
8. The Connors and we
9. They
10. He and I

FOCUS

Lesson Overview

Objective: To identify the attributes of successful advertisements and to predict audience response to an advertisement

Skills: understanding attributes of advertising; distinguishing facts from an appeal to feelings; evaluating ads; writing persuasively

Critical Thinking: analyzing; comparing; synthesizing; contrasting; evaluating; making inferences; establishing and evaluating criteria; visualizing

Speaking and Listening: discussing

Bellringer

When students enter the classroom, have this assignment on the board: *In a brief paragraph, describe your favorite ad on TV.*

Grammar Link to the Bellringer Have students underline any possessive pronouns they used in their response to the Bellringer.

Motivating Activity

Have students read the first paragraph on this page and write down their thoughts about the billboard. Discuss with students whether or not the billboard is successful. Ask: Does it make you want to visit the Brookfield Zoo? Why or why not? Who is the likely audience for the ad? (parents) Do you think the ad would persuade its audience?

LESSON
6.6

Persuasive Writing
Creating an Ad

You find advertising almost everywhere you look. Ads try to sell products, places, candidates, and ideas. Advertising agencies use many approaches in their efforts to persuade.

At what audience is this ad aimed? Does the ad make you want to visit Brookfield Zoo? Jot down your reaction and some reasons for it. Consider why the ad works or doesn't work for you.

Write to Sell

All those catchy commercial slogans that pop up in ads—and in your memory—come from the minds of ad writers. Persuasive writing is their business.

Teacher's Classroom Resources

The following resources can be used for planning, instruction, practice, reinforcement, assessment, reteaching, enrichment, or evaluation.

Teaching Tools
Lesson Plans, p. 61

Transparencies
Fine Art Transparencies, 26–30
Writing Process Transparencies, 20–22B

In advertising audience is of the utmost importance. Ads are not aimed at the world in general but rather at particular groups. Market research provides ad writers with information about a group of potential buyers—their needs, their desires, and how they will probably spend their money.

Once the audience is defined, or targeted, the writing begins. Ad writing demands a lively imagination and a good feel for language. Getting the point across in as few words as possible is essential.

Writers in advertising are constantly reminded that ads should attract <u>A</u>ttention, arouse <u>I</u>nterest, create <u>D</u>esire, and cause <u>A</u>ction (AIDA). How well does the "tomato frogs" ad meet these standards?

Vocabulary
Prewriting Tip

You can create memorable ads by playing with words. For example, use figures of speech, such as person-ification ("Make your carpet happy").

AIDA in Action

Attention	"Tomato frogs! What an unusual name for an animal!"
Interest	*"Where imagination runs wild.* I certainly want to help my kids to develop their imaginations."
Desire	"I want my kids to learn about many things, including tomato frogs. Let's visit the zoo."
Action	"I'll call this number to find out what the zoo's hours are, what the cost is, and what's the best way to get there."

Journal Writing

Find a magazine or newspaper ad that you consider persuasive. Copy or paste it into your journal. Identify its audience, and analyze it with an AIDA chart.

6.6 Creating an Ad **281**

TEACH

Guided Practice

L2 Analyzing Advertisements
Bring in (or ask students to bring in) advertisements to analyze with the help of the AIDA chart. Be sure to include ads aimed specifically at teen-agers. Ask students to identify some of the techniques advertisers use to appeal to teen-agers (attractive young models; material that appeals to the desire to be popular, attractive, successful, rebellious; humor; celebrity spokespersons).

L3 Researching Ad History
Have students investigate how the style and content of advertisements have changed over the years. Suggest that students look at advertisements in old issues of magazines and newspapers. Let students discuss their findings with a partner and then put their ideas together in a presentation for the rest of the class.

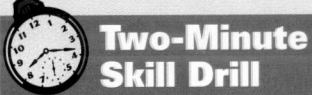

Two-Minute Skill Drill

Write two sentences—one with *its* and the other with *it's*.

Journal Writing Tip

Collecting and Gathering Information You may want to bring in a supply of magazines and newspapers for students to use. Have students present their ads and completed charts to the rest of the class.

📂 **Blackline Masters**
Thinking and Study Skills,
  pp. 16, 21, 22
Cooperative Learning Activities,
  pp. 31–36
Speaking and Listening Activities, p. 22

Composition Practice, p. 50
Composition Reteaching, p. 50
Composition Enrichment, p. 50

Assessment
📂 *Teacher's Guide to Writing Assessment*

TEACH

Guided Practice

L2 Using the Model
Answers to the callout question will vary. Some students might mention the appeal of such words as *pride, high-tech,* and *high style,* which suggest qualities many people desire. Students might also point out that the wearer of Power Pumps dominates the page. Have students think of other ads they have seen for athletic shoes. What words and images are used in those ads? What feelings or desires do the ads appeal to? How do the words and images work together?

L1 Understanding Ad Appeal
Use additional examples of advertisements to help students identify the needs or feelings that advertisers try to target. Discuss the examples, asking students questions such as the following: How does the ad make you feel? What feelings does the image suggest? What feelings do the words suggest?

Independent Practice

For further stimuli for persuasive writing, see *Fine Art Transparencies* 26–30.

Writing Process Transparencies, 20–22B

Cooperative Learning Activities, pp. 31–36

Skills Practice
Thinking and Study Skills, pp. 16, 21, 22

Speaking and Listening Activities, pp. 22

Composition Practice, p. 50

The slogan appeals to the consumer's desire for athletic and personal confidence.

How do the words and images in this ad work to persuade consumers to buy Power Pumps?

TWO POINTS FOR POWER PUMPS

HIGH-TECH DESIGN provides support, speed, and spring.

HIGH STYLE makes you a winner on and off the court.

Distinguish the Truthful from the Tricky

Advertising is tricky. As the AIDA chart shows, an ad can turn facts into feelings. It is a fact that children can see tomato frogs at the zoo, but the ad appeals to feelings of curiosity and parental concern. Ad writers know that consumers base decisions about what to buy on feelings more than on facts. Ads may appeal to either positive feelings (hope, love, duty) or negative feelings (guilt, fear, envy).

Sometimes ads use language more for the way it sounds than for what it means. Words may sound scientific, for example, but actually say nothing except "buy this product." What does "high-tech design" mean? Advertisers must maintain certain standards of truth, but measuring "truth" is a complicated task.

Now look at the Power Pumps ad again. What evidence does it use to persuade you to buy? What feelings does it appeal to? Do you think this ad would work?

282 *Persuasive Writing: Making a Difference*

Enabling Strategies

LEP Understanding Vocabulary
Some non-native English speakers may have difficulty with the vocabulary in the ad. Point out and define the words *pumps, high-tech, court,* and *stride.* Discuss the rhyme in "Put Pride in Your Stride."

What does the rhyme accomplish? Ask students to describe other ads, in English or in their first language, that use rhyme or other word associations so people will remember them.

6.6 Writing Activities

Write an Ad

An exhibit of works by artist Faith Ringgold will be shown at a local community center. Write a half-page newspaper ad to announce this exhibition. What can you say about the artist, based on a study of the story quilt below? Look closely at the work. Notice how Ringgold combines quilting and painting, figures and words. Are any of the figures real people? What words has she chosen?

Faith Ringgold, *Dream Two: King and the Sisterhood*, 1988

What significance can you find in the title? What can you say to persuade people to come to this exhibit?

- Select your audience
- Check that your ad draws attention, arouses interest, creates desire, and causes action.
- Appeal to people's feelings, but be truthful.

PURPOSE To persuade people to visit an exhibit
AUDIENCE Your choice
LENGTH ¹/₂ page

Grammar Link

Do not use apostrophes in possessive pronouns.

*Put Pride in **Your** Stride!*

Write each sentence, correcting any errors in possessive pronouns.

1. Notice it's quality.
2. If she takes our advice, the world is her's!
3. Travel with us—our's is a better way to go.
4. Compare and see—we can match theirs' any day, for less!
5. Remember, you're wish is our command.

See Lesson 11.4, page 408.

6.6 Creating an Ad **283**

Using the Grammar Link

Grammar Link Answers
1. its
2. hers
3. ours
4. theirs
5. your

Apostrophes in Pronouns Point out that an apostrophe indicates a missing letter or letters, and no letters are missing in 1–5 above.

About the Art

Faith Ringgold, *Dream Two: King and the Sisterhood*, 1988
The artwork is a quilt. It measures 94 by 60 inches and is made of painted, printed, and piece-dyed fabric. It is located in the collection of the artist.

FOCUS

Lesson Overview

Objective: To express an opinion in a letter to the editor

Skills: supporting an argument; expressing a viewpoint; using a reasonable tone

Critical Thinking: establishing and evaluating criteria; identifying main idea and details; analyzing; summarizing

Speaking and Listening: discussing; evaluating; questioning

🔔 Bellringer

When students enter the classroom, have this assignment on the board: *Which issue that you have written about in this unit do you feel most strongly about? Why?*

Grammar Link to the Bellringer

Have students circle any negative words they used in the Bellringer activity, such as *not, none, nobody, nothing*, and so on. If they circled more than one word in a sentence, they should check that their intended meaning is expressed in that sentence.

Motivating Activity

Discuss students' responses to the Bellringer, and write some of them on the board. How would students reach others with this piece of persuasive writing? (handing out copies, having it published) Point out that one way to reach a larger audience is by writing a letter to the editor of a newspaper or magazine.

LESSON
6.7

Persuasive Writing
Writing a Letter to the Editor

You may not be old enough to vote, but you can *have a voice in public decision making. One of the most influential public arenas is the editorial page, and it's open to everyone.*

Most newspapers and magazines invite letters from their readers. The following letter appeared in a popular magazine for young readers. Often in persuasive writing, the main idea comes at or near the beginning. This letter writer, however, has saved his main idea for the end. Why do you think he did that?

Dear Editor:

In the fall of 1989, I fractured one of my vertebrae playing football. I remained inactive for several months, wearing a full-body plastic jacket. The injury means no more football, no more soccer, no more baseball, or anything! As you may have noticed, my injury has a big effect on my life. Now I just go and watch my friends play.

I am not telling everybody to stop playing football. I'm just telling them to wear the right equipment.

Jon Good, Summit, New Jersey

First appeared in Sports Illustrated for Kids

284

Teacher's Classroom Resources

The following resources can be used for planning, instruction, practice, reinforcement, assessment, reteaching, enrichment, or evaluation.

📘 **Teaching Tools**
Lesson Plans, p. 62

📗 **Transparencies**
Fine Art Transparencies, 26–30
Writing Process Transparencies, 20–22B

Make and Support Your Point

A letter to the editor is really a letter to the readers of the newspaper or magazine. Like other persuasive writing, letters to the editor state a position and offer support for it. In the letter on the preceding page, Jon uses his own experience to support his argument that football players should use the right equipment. In the letter below, what does the writer want readers to think? What support does he offer?

> Dear Editor:
>
> I would like to tell readers that gymnastics is not only a sport for girls, but that it's also a sport for boys! Many people make fun of boys in this sport, but gymnastics is hard work, and all that hard work pays off when you get older. If you look at the men in the Olympics, you will see that they are fairly strong. So all you boys out there, don't tease us. Try gymnastics and see for yourselves: It's fun!
>
> Philip Trevino, Gilroy, California
> First appeared in <u>Sports Illustrated for Kids</u>

What is the writer's opinion, and what evidence does he use to support it?

Journal Writing

In a newspaper or magazine find a letter to the editor that persuades you to think or act as the writer wishes. Paste it in your journal. Make notes about what persuades you.

6.7 Writing a Letter to the Editor **285**

TEACH

Guided Practice

L2 Using the Model
Answers to the callout question will vary. Students should respond that the writer argues that gymnastics is for boys as well as girls. He supports his opinion with evidence that the hard work pays off later and that Olympic gymnasts are strong. Ask students to offer their own opinions on the issue.

L2 Cooperative Learning
Bring in copies of the editorial page from the local newspaper, a student newspaper, or other publications. Divide students into groups of three and ask them to evaluate letters to the editor. Each group should choose a letter that they find persuasive and identify its main point and supporting evidence. They should also choose a letter they believe is not persuasive, misses its audience, or is organized badly and make suggestions for ways to improve it.

Journal Writing Tip

Establishing Evaluation Criteria
Suggest that students use the revising chart on page 278 to help them evaluate the letter to the editor.

📁 **Blackline Masters**
Thinking and Study Skills,
pp. 1, 2, 5–7, 10–12, 17
Writing Across the Curriculum,
pp. 6, 22
Cooperative Learning Activities,
pp. 31–36

*Speaking and Listening
Activities,* p. 22
Composition Practice, p. 51
Composition Reteaching, p. 51
Composition Enrichment, p. 51

Assessment
📁 *Teacher's Guide to Writing
Assessment*

TEACH

Guided Practice

L2 Using the Model

Answers to the callout question will vary. Students might respond that by referring to the magazine's purpose, Kelinda's letter reminds the editors to consider all their subscribers, including those in North County.

Two-Minute Skill Drill

Letters to the editor should be sent to appropriate publications for the subject. Have students write the names of three publications they read or know of, and list an issue or topic that would be appropriate for a letter to the editor of each publication.

Independent Practice

For further stimuli for persuasive writing, see *Fine Art Transparencies* 26–30.

Writing Process Transparencies, 20–22B

Writing Across the Curriculum, pp. 6, 22

Cooperative Learning Activities, 31–36

Skills Practice

Thinking and Study Skills, pp. 1, 2, 5–7, 10–12, 17

Speaking and Listening Activities, p. 22

Composition Practice, p. 51

286

Watch Your Tone

Presenting Tip

When you write a letter to the editor, you are far more likely to see it in print if you use the correct business-letter form. For an example see Lesson 5.8, pages 224–226.

Frustration and anger have inspired many a letter to the editor. To make your letter persuasive, however, you need to keep uncontrolled emotion from weakening your message. Editors reject angry outbursts. The following letter expresses strong emotions but supports the writer's point in a calm, controlled way. Remember that there are usually at least two sides to an issue. You should express *your* viewpoint reasonably; if you do, your letter will be much more persuasive.

How might referring to the magazine's purpose make Kelinda's letter more persuasive?

Student Model

Dear Editor,

I am a thirteen-year-old native St. Louisan who lives in North County. I was extremely hurt when an article appeared in your April issue about plush and desirable places to live. To my surprise North County never appeared in the article. Why? North County is a beautiful place to live, filled with friendly faces. This to me, and probably many people, is extremely desirable.

The homes and subdivisions of this area are just as nice as the [ones] in the counties you featured. If you are *St. Louis Magazine*, then you should make a conscientious effort to represent *all* of the Metropolitan St. Louis area.

Kelinda Peaples, Florissant, Missouri
First appeared in *St. Louis Magazine*

286   *Persuasive Writing: Making a Difference*

Enabling Strategies

LEP Drafting a Letter

Let students put the first drafts of their letters to the editor on tape or dictate their letters to other students who have more experience with written English. Encourage students to be more concerned with getting their ideas down than about grammar, spelling, or punctuation in their drafts. Suggest that students get help from a peer reviewer at any stage in the writing process.

6.7 Writing Activities

Write a Letter to the Editor

Select an organization in your community that serves an important role or offers fine service but rarely receives public attention. Write a letter to the editor of the local newspaper in which you praise this organization and its service. Persuade the public to pay more attention to the organization and to support it. You might choose the local public library, a civic recreation center, a museum, or a service organization at your school.

- Place your main idea at the beginning or end—wherever it will be most effective.
- Support your views.
- Keep your tone reasonable.

PURPOSE Support a worthwhile organization
AUDIENCE Your community, especially adults
LENGTH 3–5 paragraphs

Cooperative Learning

In a small group, brainstorm about issues appropriate for letters to the editor of your school newspaper. As a group choose one of the issues that you have differing opinions about. Divide the group so members can write on the side of the issue with which they agree. Write letters to the editor. Then each group should pretend they are the editors of the paper. Read each other's letters, and evaluate them.

Consider how well each letter succeeded in presenting a strong argument in a calm, reasonable manner. Make specific suggestions for improving letters that need work.

Grammar Link

Avoid double negatives.

*The injury means **no** more football, **no** more soccer, **no** more baseball, **or anything!***

This sentence is a strong negative statement, but if the author had ended it "no nothing," he would have confused his meaning with a double negative.

Revise each sentence below to eliminate double negatives.

1. Sometimes football players don't have no protective equipment.
2. How people dress isn't none of your business.
3. He didn't have no reason to be so negative about everything.
4. Hardly nobody knows nothing about that.
5. I won't say nothing to him.

See Lesson 12.8, page 438.

Using the Grammar Link

Grammar Link Answers
1. …football players don't have any… OR …football players have no…
2. How people dress isn't any of… OR How people dress is none of…
3. He didn't have any reason… OR He had no reason…
4. Hardly anybody knows anything… OR Almost nobody knows anything…
5. I won't say anything… OR I will say nothing…

Using Double Negatives Explain that double negatives are correct in some other languages and are acceptable in many dialects. A usage in standard English such as "not incorrect" may sound like a double negative but is a qualified way of saying "right."

ASSESS

Writing Activities Evaluation Guidelines

Write a Letter to the Editor
Use these criteria when evaluating your students' writing.
- Is the main point in the most effective place in the letter?
- Is the position clearly stated?
- Is the position supported by reasons or facts?
- Is the tone appropriate for a letter to the editor?

See also the *Teacher's Guide to Writing Assessment*.

Cooperative Learning
Check to see that each group member writes a letter to the editor of the school newspaper and participates in the evaluation of the group's letters. Members of each group can then decide which of their letters to publish.

Grammar Link
(See Using the Grammar Link below.)

Reteaching
📁 *Composition Reteaching*, p. 51

Enrichment
📁 *Composition Enrichment*, p. 51

CLOSE

Students may use a local newspaper to select an article or a letter that they would like to respond to by writing a letter to the editor. Remind them to check the newspaper's submission guidelines for length and format of letters. Suggest that they use a peer reviewer to help them revise their letter. Encourage them to submit their finished letter to the publication.

Setting the Purpose

Lesson 6.8 teaches students to establish criteria to use in evaluating a book.

FOCUS

Lesson Overview

Objective: To develop a book review
Skills: writing a book review; personalizing a book review
Critical Thinking: defining; clarifying; identifying main idea and details
Speaking and Listening: speaking to persuade; discussing; explaining a process

🔔 Bellringer

When students enter the classroom, have this assignment on the board: *Jot down the name of a book you have read recently and liked.*

Grammar Link to the Bellringer

Ask students to revise the following sentence, using the correct form of the adjective *good* or *bad: The last book I read was the bestest ever.*

Motivating Activity

Ask students how they found out about the books they named in the Bellringer. (friends, librarians, teachers, advertisements, book reviews, and so on) How would they let others know that these were books worth reading? Explain that writing a book review is one way to let others know what you think about a book.

Writing About Literature
Writing a Book Review

Book reviews—you have probably written dozens. Book reviews can be persuasive. They help you decide what to read.

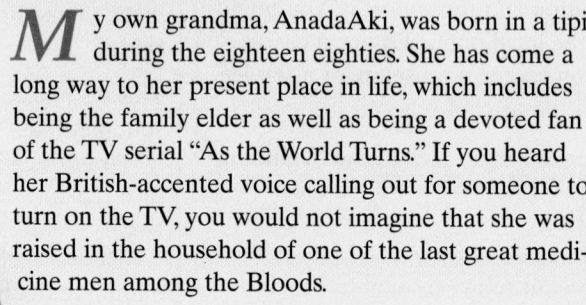

Literature Model

My own grandma, AnadaAki, was born in a tipi during the eighteen eighties. She has come a long way to her present place in life, which includes being the family elder as well as being a devoted fan of the TV serial "As the World Turns." If you heard her British-accented voice calling out for someone to turn on the TV, you would not imagine that she was raised in the household of one of the last great medicine men among the Bloods.

Beverly Hungry Wolf, *The Ways of My Grandmothers*

Beverly Hungry Wolf's grandmother has something to give you—stories of a past you may know nothing about. She speaks in the pages of the book *The Ways of My Grandmothers*. But how will readers find out about her and hear her wonderful stories? Sometimes people tell others about a book they liked, and the word spreads. Often, though, the best way to learn about new books is through book reviews.

Know Your Audience

Book reviews can help readers in two ways. The reviews summarize a book's contents and in that way answer every

288 *Persuasive Writing: Making a Difference*

Teacher's Classroom Resources

The following resources can be used for planning, instruction, practice, reinforcement, assessment, reteaching, enrichment, or evaluation.

🔖 **Teaching Tools**
Lesson Plans, p. 63

📖 **Transparencies**
Fine Art Transparencies, 26–30
Writing Process Transparencies, 20–22B

reader's first question: What's it about? Reviews also evaluate the book, telling whether, in the reviewer's opinion, the book is worth reading:

Literature Model

*I*t is a compilation of history, social life and customs. . . . There are stories . . . about the lives of her mother and grandmother, and others of her Elders, as well as accounts of some of her own experiences in learning how to live in the traditional [Blackfoot] manner. . . . Apart from its content, which is extremely valuable, one special quality of this work is its depiction of Native [American] people living a happy, normal and fulfilling existence—here are *anybody's* grandmothers, yours, mine, human beings. . . .

Beverly Hungry Wolf is a very good writer. Her book is interesting, moving, and, here and there, pretty funny.

Doris Seale, review of *The Ways of My Grandmothers*
First appeared in *Interracial Books for Children Bulletin*

> *Here the reviewer summarizes the book's contents, explaining what it is about.*

> *Here she evaluates the book. What does she consider its strengths?*

Different people look for different qualities in books. Some enjoy drama and suspense, while others read mainly for information. Some respond to the quality of the writing itself. Many look for new books by their favorite authors. When you review a book you've liked, you may have too much to say about it. Knowing your audience and their interests can help you decide what to include and what to leave out.

Journal Writing

Think of a book that you feel strongly about. List reasons why you like it or don't like it. Then list some people you could try to persuade to read—or not read—this book. Explain how you would persuade your audience.

6.8 Writing About Literature: Writing a Book Review **289**

TEACH

Guided Practice

L2 Using the Model
Point out that the writer identifies the following strengths: the book's content, its depiction of Native Americans, and the high quality of the writing.

L2 Analyzing Book Reviews
Ask students who they think the audience might be for the book review excerpt on this page (teachers, librarians, students). How does the writer take her audience's interests into account? (She focuses on the qualities of the book that would appeal to those interested in learning about other cultures.)

L2 Comparing Books
Explain that there are many different ways to focus a book review. Suggest that students try comparing books by the same writer, books on the same subject, or books of the same genre (such as science fiction, mystery, or adventure) in their book reviews.

Two-Minute Skill Drill

Ask students to write down what they think book reviews have in common with other types of persuasive writing. (The writer presents an opinion and supports it with evidence.)

Journal Writing Tip

Identifying Categories Help students think of categories to use to help them organize their thoughts about a book (subject, writing style, quality of writing, interest level, difficulty, characters, plot).

📁 **Blackline Masters**
Thinking and Study Skills, pp. 2–7, 19–20
Writing Across the Curriculum, pp. 1, 3
Cooperative Learning Activities, pp. 31–36

Speaking and Listening Activities, p. 22
Composition Practice, p. 52
Composition Reteaching, p. 52
Composition Enrichment, p. 52

Assessment
📁 *Teacher's Guide to Writing Assessment*

TEACH

Guided Practice

L2 Using the Model
Ask students whether they find this review persuasive. Why or why not? (Students may find the reviewer's honesty appealing. The review may seem convincing to students because the reviewer had an experience similar to the one in the book and found the author's account true to life.) Point out to students that the book reviewer was interested in the main character's experience of leaving a good friend behind, not knowing if they would ever meet again, because the reviewer had had a similar experience.

L1 Promoting a Book
Have students design a newspaper or magazine advertisement to promote a book they liked. In addition ask them to choose the image and write the text for a book jacket. (Have them look at examples of book jackets to get a feel for such writing.) Post the advertisements and book jackets. Students may measure the success of their work by seeing how many other students read the book they recommend.

Independent Practice

🎺 For further stimuli for persuasive writing, see *Fine Art Transparencies* 26–30.

🎺 *Writing Process Transparencies,* 20–22B

📁 *Writing Across the Curriculum,* pp. 1, 3

📁 *Cooperative Learning Activities,* pp. 31–36

Skills Practice

📁 *Thinking and Study Skills,* pp. 2–7, 19–20

📁 *Speaking and Listening Activities,* p. 22

📁 *Composition Practice,* p. 52

290

Personalize Your Review

Grammar
Editing Tip

When editing a book review, be sure to underscore the book title. Use italics if your word-processing program allows you to. See Lesson 20.6, page 576.

Some reviewers respond to books in a personal way. For example, *The China Year* tells of experiences similar to the reviewer's, so Melinda Eldridge also tells readers something about herself. Notice how Melinda's use of the first-person point of view makes her review all the more personal.

What particular part of the main character's experience interested Melinda? Why?

Student Model

T he best parts of the book . . . are the friendships that evolved during Henrietta's year in China. I know first-hand how much fun it is to have friends from another culture, but I also know how much more painful it is to leave them because you don't know if you'll ever see them again.

The *China Year* is an excellent book for people of all types and from all walks of life. It stands as great testimony to the wonderful adventures one can have by living outside one's own culture.

Melinda Eldridge, Arlington, Texas
First published in *Stone Soup*

As a book reviewer, you have a wide range of options. You can compare the book to others by the same author or to others of the same type. You can comment on whether the book holds your interest. You can suggest certain types of readers who would enjoy the book. You can relate the book to events in your own experience, as Melinda did. The choice is yours.

290 *Persuasive Writing: Making a Difference*

Enabling Strategies

LEP Using Diversity
Books are one way to learn about and share the experiences of people from different cultural backgrounds. Suggest that students who are learning English recall—or bring to class—books that they enjoyed reading in their native language. Students learning English might want to give their book reports on one of these books. If the books are classics, they may be available in translation for everyone to read.

6.8 Writing Activities

Write a Book Review

Think of a book you've read in the past that meant something special to you. Think especially of books in which you were able to identify with a character whose experiences were something like yours. Write a review, recommending the book to other readers of your own age.

- Tell what the story is about.
- Explain whether it is worthwhile to read the book.
- Keep your audience's preferences in mind.

PURPOSE To review your favorite book
AUDIENCE Your classmates
LENGTH 1 page

Carol Soatikee, *Students*, 1969

Cross-Curricular: Art

Study the painting below. Do the figures seem to be together or apart? How do colors and shapes create a certain mood? Write a review for a student art forum. Describe the painting's content, and give your opinion. Include your reasons.

Grammar Link

Use the correct forms of the adjectives *good* and *bad*.

*Beverly Hungry Wolf is a very **good** writer.*

A reviewer could also say that one writer is *better* than another or the *best* of several writers. Or she could call a book *bad, worse* than another, or the very *worst* of all.

Rewrite each sentence below, correcting errors in the use of adjectives.

1. Of the two stories, the writing in LeGuin's is more good.
2. The plot is totally unbelievable, the worstest I've ever read.
3. The dialogue is most good when it's most natural.
4. The descriptions are badder than the action scenes.

See Lesson 12.3, page 428.

6.8 Writing About Literature: Writing a Book Review **291**

Using the Grammar Link

Grammar Link Answers
Answers will vary, but some suggestions are given below.
1. better
2. worst
3. best
4. worse

About the Art

Carol Soatikee, *Students*, 1969
Native American artist Carol Soatikee, of Fort Sill Apache and Pima ancestry, teaches art at the U.S. Indian School in Coucho, Oklahoma. *Students* is painted in oil on canvas and measures 36 by 30 inches.

Setting the Purpose

Students now have the opportunity to apply what they have learned about persuasive writing to an independent writing project. They will use the stages of the writing process to create and present a finished piece.

FOCUS

Lesson Overview

Objective: To use the writing process to produce a sustained piece of persuasive writing
Skills: using the five stages of the writing process: prewriting, drafting, revising, editing, and presenting
Critical Thinking: recalling; synthesizing; summarizing; analyzing
Speaking and Listening: reading aloud and listening to a draft; discussing

Bellringer

When students enter the classroom, have this assignment on the board: *Imagine life in this country fifty years from now. Write two sentences describing what one aspect of life will be like.*

Grammar Link to the Bellringer

Have students look over their Bellringer responses and circle any words whose spelling they are unsure of. Allow time to look words up during class.

Motivating Activity

Ask students to think of books, films, or television programs that present a picture of life in the future. How is the future portrayed in these depictions? Which portrayals seem most plausible? Then ask students to share their own ideas about what the future might hold. Explain that in this assignment they will write about their visions of the future.

292

WRITING PROCESS IN ACTION

PERSUASIVE WRITING

In the preceding lessons you've learned how to state and support your opinions. You have had the opportunity to write a letter and a book review. Now, in this lesson, you're invited to write persuasively about how an important current issue might affect the future.

• Assignment •

Context	*Your class has decided to publish Our Future, a magazine that deals exclusively with how what people do today may affect the future.*
Purpose	*To persuade people to behave today in ways that will improve the future*
Audience	*Your classmates and the readers of your magazine*
Length	*1 page*

The following pages can help you plan and write your persuasive article. Read through them, and then refer to them as you need to. But don't be tied down by them. You're in charge of your own writing process.

292 *Persuasive Writing: Making a Difference*

Teacher's Classroom Resources

The following resources can be used for planning, instruction, practice, reinforcement, assessment, reteaching, enrichment, or evaluation.

Teaching Tools
Lesson Plans, p. 64

Transparencies
Writing Process Transparencies, 20–22B

Prewriting

One of the best ways to find a topic about the future is to look around you today. What if pollution continues at the current rate? Ask yourself *what if* questions until you hit on a topic. The chart on the right suggests more ways to find a topic.

Your next task is to research your topic to learn exactly how it might influence the future.

Consider your audience; would it be best to write a letter, a short essay, or perhaps a short story?

Option A

Explore your journal.

Option B

Brainstorm with a friend.

Option C

Freewrite for ideas.

Watching the cars and trucks pour in all day carrying their bottles, papers, and cans for recycling—You can't convince me that this doesn't help people and the environment. We just need to keep it up!

Drafting

Once you have gathered facts concerning your topic, you will need to organize them in a way that has a strong impact on the reader. Your goal is to change people's behavior. In order to do this, you must use specific, vivid language.

Notice how Rachel Carson focuses on the negative events that have happened, using words such as *misfortunes* and *disasters*. These present realitites influenced her fictional description of the world of tomorrow.

Drafting Tip

For more information about effectively making your case, see Lesson 6.4, pages 272–274.

Literature Model

I know of no community that has experienced all the misfortunes I describe. Yet every one of these disasters has actually happened somewhere, and many real communities have already suffered a substantial number of them.

Rachel Carson, *Silent Spring*

Writing Process in Action **293**

TEACH

Prewriting

L2 Developing Ideas for Persuasive Writing

To help students think about how the present may affect the future, lead a discussion about how the past has affected the present. You might keep the discussion focused by suggesting categories such as transportation, communication, food, clothing, school, or the environment. What trends can students identify that might provide clues about the future?

L2 Cooperative Learning

Have students work in pairs on prewriting. One student might play the role of a person from the future who has traveled back to the present. The other student could play the role of an interviewer from one of today's news magazines. Suggest that the interviewer come up with a list of questions about life in the future. At the end of the session, both students should discuss any ideas that emerged that could make good writing topics.

Independent Practice

Skills Practice
📁 *Thinking and Study Skills*, pp. 6, 9, 13, 14, 35, 37

Drafting

L1 Using a Diagram

Suggest that students use cause-and-effect diagrams to help them check the logic of their depictions of the future. They may want to review the use of such diagrams on page 214.

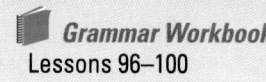
Blackline Masters
Thinking and Study Skills, pp. 6, 9, 13, 14, 35, 37
Composition Practice, p. 53
Composition Reteaching, p. 53
Composition Enrichment, p. 53

Grammar Workbook
Lessons 96–100

Assessment
📁 *Teacher's Guide to Writing Assessment*

TEACH

Revising

L2 Peer Editing

Students can work in writing conferences with peer editors before they revise their work. You may want to duplicate the Peer Response forms in the *Teacher's Guide to Writing Assessment.* Suggest that peer editors respond to the following questions:
- Are the predictions clear?
- Are reasons given to support the predictions?
- Do the reasons given make sense?

Editing

L2 Peer Editing

After students have edited their own work, have them edit another student's writing. Remind them to refer to the Editing Checklist on student page 295.

Presenting

Before students present their persuasive writing, discuss how to prepare their papers for publication. Emphasize the importance of the final draft and that it must be neatly done.

Independent Practice

Writing Process Transparencies, 20–22B

Skills Practice

Thinking and Study Skills, pp. 6, 9, 13, 14, 35, 37

Composition Practice, p. 53

Grammar Workbook, Lessons 96–100

WRITING PROCESS IN ACTION

Once you have all you need in order to write, think about the order in which you will present your ideas, facts, and examples. Then, using your notes, begin writing. At this stage just write steadily, and let your ideas flow.

Revising

To begin revising, read over your draft to make sure that what you have written fits your purpose and your audience. Then have a **writing conference.** Read your draft to a partner or a small group. Use your audience's reactions to help you evaluate your work so far. The questions below can help you and your listeners.

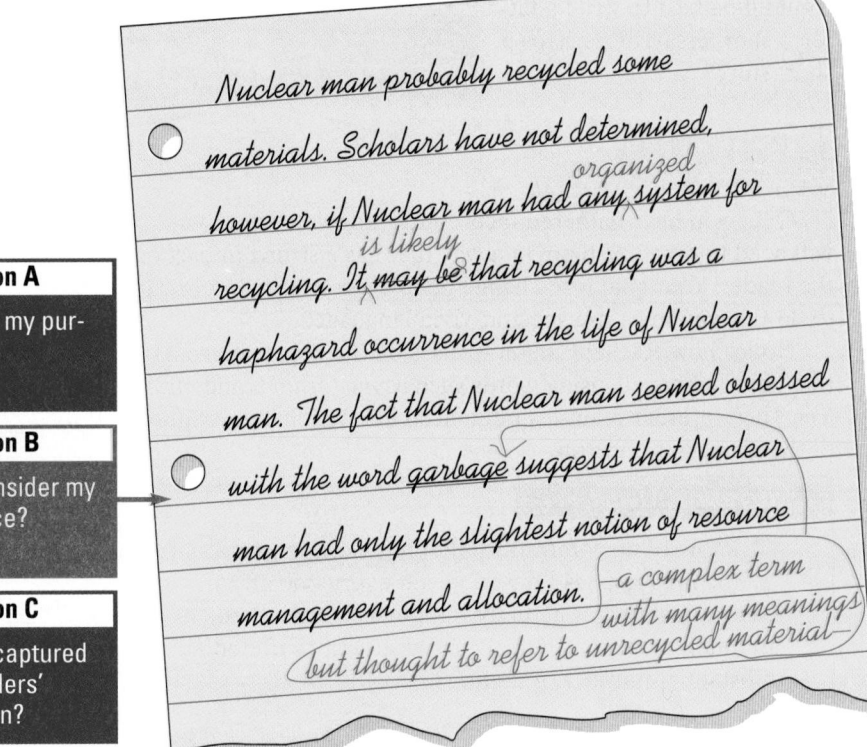

Question A
What is my purpose?

Question B
Do I consider my audience?

Question C
Have I captured my readers' attention?

294 *Persuasive Writing: Making a Difference*

Enrichment and Extension

Follow-up Ideas
- Set aside time for students to celebrate the conclusion of their writing projects.
- If students are sending their work out of the classroom for publication, make sure that photocopies are retained.

Extending Persuasion
Explore opportunities for extending persuasive writing skills beyond the classroom, such as students advocating change in the community, running for class office, or promoting a cause or an event.

Editing

Careful editing is essential to persuasive writing. Why? Given the chance to dismiss your argument—because of a misspelling or a grammatical error—some readers will. Check your sentences, and **proofread** for mechanics. Check for only one kind of error at a time.

Presenting

Once you've edited your composition, you are ready to submit your work to *Our Future*. Think about and discuss with your class what the cover of your magazine should look like.

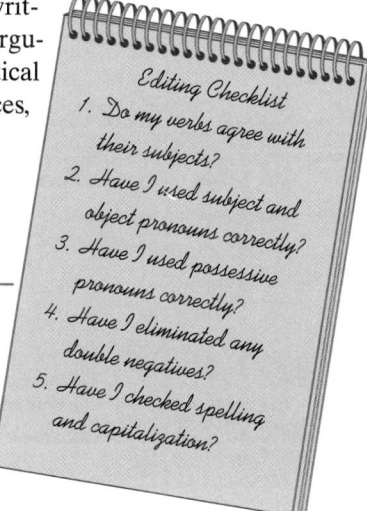

Editing Checklist
1. Do my verbs agree with their subjects?
2. Have I used subject and object pronouns correctly?
3. Have I used possessive pronouns correctly?
4. Have I eliminated any double negatives?
5. Have I checked spelling and capitalization?

Proofreading ►

For proofreading symbols, see page 81.

Journal Writing

Reflect on your writing process experience. Answer these questions in your journal: What do you like best about your persuasive writing? What was the hardest part of writing it? What did you learn in your writing conference? What new things have you learned as a writer?

Writing Process in Action **295**

Beyond the Classroom

The Power of the Word

Point out to students that Rachel Carson's book was successful in demonstrating the problems of pesticide use, revealing the power of the written word to bring about change. Following the publication of *Silent Spring*, President John F. Kennedy called on his Science Advisory Committee to study the issue. The committee found evidence to support Carson's warnings, and eventually legislation was passed to ban or limit the use of some pesticides.

UNIT 6
Persuasive Writing
Literature Model

Setting the Purpose

In the Unit 6 Literature Model students read a literature passage that illustrates in a very real way effective persuasive writing. Such readings serve as models for students as they create their own persuasive writing.

About the Author

Rachel Carson (1907–1964) was a marine biologist and science writer. For many years she worked for the U.S. Fish and Wildlife Service. She wrote *The Sea Around Us* (1951), which won the National Book Award, and *The Edge of the Sea* (1955). Through her work, Carson became aware of the hazards of pesticide use, in particular the extensive use of DDT, and the damage that had already been done to the environment. She felt compelled to sound the alarm. As she wrote to a friend, "There would be no peace for me if I kept silent."

FOCUS

Lesson Overview

Objective: To study the imaginative use of persuasive writing by a published author
Skills: reading comprehension
Critical Thinking: analyzing; contrasting; comparing
Speaking and Listening: discussing

Bellringer

When students enter the classroom, have this assignment on the board: *List the wild plants and animals that you most enjoy seeing and learning about.*

Motivating Activity

Have students share their Bellringer lists and tell why they chose those particular plants and animals.

296

Rachel Carson
from
Silent Spring

Written thirty years ago by scientist Rachel Carson, Silent Spring *begins with this fable that shows humanity's carelessness and irresponsibility. As you read, think about how the fable affects your view of current environmental problems. Then try the activities in Linking Writing and Literature on page 299.*

There was once a town in the heart of America where all life seemed to live in harmony with its surroundings. The town lay in the midst of a checkerboard of prosperous farms, with fields of grain and hillsides of orchards where, in spring, white clouds of bloom drifted above the green fields. In autumn, oak and maple and birch set up a blaze of color that flamed and flickered across a backdrop of pines. Then foxes barked in the hills and deer silently crossed the fields, half hidden in the mists of the fall mornings.

296 *Persuasive Writing: Making a Difference*

Teacher's Classroom Resources

The following resources can be used for planning, instruction, or practice.

Teaching Tools
Lesson Plans, p. 65

Transparencies
Fine Art Transparencies, 26–30

Blackline Masters
Speaking and Listening Activities, pp. 22, 24
Thinking and Study Skills, pp. 6, 12, 13, 24–25

Along the roads, laurel, viburnum and alder, great ferns and wildflowers delighted the traveler's eye through much of the year. Even in winter the roadsides were places of beauty, where countless birds came to feed on the berries and on the seed heads of the dried weeds rising above the snow. The countryside was, in fact, famous for the abundance and variety of its bird life, and when the flood of migrants was pouring through in spring and fall people traveled from great distances to observe them. Others came to fish the streams, which flowed clear and cold out of the hills and contained shady pools where trout lay. So it had been from the days many years ago when the first settlers raised their houses, sank their wells, and built their barns.

Then a strange blight crept over the area and everything began to change. Some evil spell had settled on the community: mysterious maladies swept the flocks of chickens; the cattle and sheep sickened and died. Everywhere was a shadow of death. The farmers spoke of much illness among their families. In the town the doctors had become more and more puzzled by new kinds of sickness appearing among their patients. There had been several sudden and unexplained deaths, not

Leonard Koscianski, *Whirlwind*, 1992

Literature Model **297**

TEACH

Guided Practice

L2 Guided Reading

- What is a fable? (A fable is a fictional story used to teach a lesson or moral. Often, the characters in fables are animals that act like humans.) Do you think Carson's choice of a fable to begin *Silent Spring* is effective? Tell why. (Using a fable to start her book is effective because it makes her message about dangers to the environment more universal.)

- In the first paragraph of the passage on page 296, how might the descriptive language Carson uses serve to persuade readers that the environment is worth their concern? (When Carson describes the fictional town, she uses positive, pleasant words and phrases such as *in the heart of America ... in harmony with its surroundings, prosperous farms ... white clouds of bloom, a blaze of color that flamed and flickered,* and *the mists of fall mornings.* By using this type of descriptive language, Carson conveys her feeling that the environment has value.)

Assessment
📁 *Teacher's Guide to Writing Assessment*

About the Art

Leonard Koscianski, *Whirlwind*, 1992
Whirlwind, an oil-on-canvas painting measuring 48 by 72 inches, is at the Phyllis Kind Gallery in New York City.

TEACH

Guided Practice

L2 Guided Reading

- What is Rachel Carson's central claim in this passage? (Carson claims that the irresponsible actions of humankind have harmed the environment.)
- What evidence does Carson present to support this claim? (Carson supports this claim by vividly describing the environmental disasters that have occurred, such as sickness and death among animals and humans; the absence of birds, remaining birds unable to fly; no chicks hatch, failure of young pigs to survive; no bees; withered vegetation; no fish.)

Independent Practice

Fine Art Transparencies, 26–30

Skills Practice

Speaking and Listening Activities, pp. 22, 24

Thinking and Study Skills, pp. 6, 12, 13, 24–25

---

only among adults but even among children, who would be stricken suddenly while at play and die within a few hours.

There was a strange stillness. The birds, for example—where had they gone? Many people spoke of them, puzzled and disturbed. The feeding stations in the backyards were deserted. The few birds seen anywhere were moribund; they trembled violently and could not fly. It was a spring without voices. On the mornings that had once throbbed with the dawn chorus of robins, catbirds, doves, jays, wrens, and scores of other bird voices there was now no sound; only silence lay over the fields and woods and marsh.

On the farms the hens brooded, but no chicks hatched. The farmers complained that they were unable to raise any pigs—the litters were small and the young survived only a few days. The apple trees were coming into bloom but no bees droned among the blossoms, so there was no pollination and there would be no fruit.

The roadsides, once so attractive, were now lined with browned and withered vegetation as though swept by fire. These, too, were silent, deserted by all living things. Even the streams were now lifeless. Anglers no longer visited them, for all the fish had died.

In the gutters under the eaves and between the shingles of the roofs, a white granular powder still showed a few patches; some weeks before it had fallen like snow upon the roofs and the lawns, the fields and streams.

No witchcraft, no enemy action had silenced the rebirth of new life in this stricken world. The people had done it themselves.

This town does not actually exist, but it might easily have a thousand counterparts in America or elsewhere in the world. I know of no community that has experienced all the misfortunes I describe. Yet every one of these disasters has actually happened somewhere, and many real communities have already suffered a substantial number of them. A grim specter has crept upon us almost unnoticed, and this imagined tragedy may easily become a stark reality we all shall know.

Genre and Style

Reading a Persuasive Essay
This is a persuasive essay in the form of a fable—a fictional story designed to teach. Carson uses vivid descriptions and precise language to convey the seriousness of the problem and to persuade people to take action.

Writers and Writing

Influencing Legislation
When *Silent Spring* was first published in 1962, the chemical industry tried to prevent its publication. These efforts failed, and the book became a bestseller, contributing to the passage of laws that protect the environment.

Linking Writing and Literature

Readers Respond to the Model

What makes Rachel Carson's fable persuasive?

Explore Rachel Carson's persuasive writing by answering these questions. Then read what other students liked about her writing.

1. Carson could have started her book by citing dramatic examples of the misuse of chemicals. Why do you think she chose to start with a fable instead?

2. What effect do the descriptions in the fable have on you?

3. From the selection choose one particular passage that you find especially persuasive. What specific words or phrases make this passage persuasive?

The fable from *Silent Spring* is a story about a beautiful town with peaceful surroundings. It seemed as if an evil plague crept over the town, for bad things started happening. The writer's point is that even though the story is fiction, many things like that are happening in America, and people are the cause of them.

I liked the descriptions the best. They were so vivid you could almost see what was happening. I would recommend this story to friends, because it gives them something to ponder.

Alina Braica

This story held my attention throughout. I think Rachel Carson wrote it as she did to let her readers know that everything beautiful doesn't have to stay that way and that we should take nothing for granted in this lifetime. I would recommend this story because I would want my friends to enjoy it as much as I have.

Tashaunda Jackson

Literature Model **299**

Connections Across the Curriculum

Health

Point out that the protection of the environment is a global issue. Many pesticides now banned in the United States are still produced and sold to other nations, where they may endanger the health of the people who use them.

These nations may use the pesticides on fruits and vegetables that are then imported by the United States. Have students discuss how they think nations can work together to keep people safe and protect the environment.

ASSESS

Evaluation Guidelines for Discussion

As your students discuss the passage, either in small groups or as a class, encourage them to begin with a personal response. The student responses on this page might be used as a starting point.

Look for evidence that students

- have read the selection
- can state some of the writer's ideas in their own words
- understand the writer's point of view
- have connected the content to their own knowledge and experiences
- understand the ideas and implications of the selection

Some possible responses to the discussion questions on this page:

1. The fable engages readers in a way that cold facts and examples might not have done.

2. Students may write about being drawn in by the very peaceful, beautiful imagery and then being hit all the harder by the deathly, poisonous images that follow.

3. Example: "No witchcraft, no enemy action had silenced the rebirth of new life in this stricken world. The people had done it themselves." "Witchcraft" and "enemy action" equate neglect of the environment with evil and violence. "Silenced the rebirth of new life" and "stricken" are forceful, emotional phrases.

CLOSE

Ask students to write a persuasive paragraph in which they encourage people to keep the environment clean. Ask volunteers to share their paragraphs with the class.

REVIEW

Reflecting on the Unit
You may have students respond to Reflecting on the Unit in writing or through discussion.

Writing Across the Curriculum
Before they begin, remind students that persuasive writing is most effective when writers state and support their opinions in a calm tone, relying on such evidence as facts, opinions, statistics, examples, and reasons to support their viewpoints.

Adding to Your Portfolio
As students decide what to include in their portfolios, remind them to consider pieces in which they stated a clear position; supported it with strong, relevant evidence; and used an effective attention-getting strategy to interest the audience in the topic. In making final selections, students might also want to consider their classmates' responses to the pieces.

Portfolio Evaluation
If you grade the portfolio selections, you may want to award two marks—one each for content and form. Explain your assessment criteria before students make their selections. Commend
- experimentation with creative prewriting techniques
- clear, concise writing in which the main idea, audience, and purpose are evident
- successful revisions
- work that shows a flair for language

300

Unit 6 Review

Reflecting on the Unit

Summarize what you have learned in this unit by answering the following questions.

- How does persuasive writing effect change?

- What kinds of evidence can you use to support your position?

- What do you need to keep in mind in order to write persuasively?

- What kinds of activities go into developing a strategy?

- What should you focus on when revising your persuasive writing?

Adding to Your Portfolio

Choose a selection for your portfolio.
Look over the writing you did for this unit. Choose a piece of writing for your portfolio. The writing you choose should show one or more of the following:

- an unusual or a surprising way of addressing a problem or an issue
- an opinion about a change you consider especially important
- words and ideas appropriate to a specific audience
- strong evidence gathered from at least two sources

Reflect on your choice.
Attach a note to the piece you chose, explaining briefly why you chose it and what you learned from writing it.

Set goals.
How can you improve your writing? What skill will you focus on the next time you write?

Writing Across the Curriculum

Make a science connection.
Think of a current environmental problem, such as ozone deterioration or destruction of the rain forest, that you have learned about in science class. Write a persuasive composition that states and supports your opinion about what we should do to remedy the problem.

Teacher's Classroom Resources

The following resources can be used for assessment or evaluation.

Unit Assessment
Tests with Answer Key
Unit 6 Choice A Test, p. 21
Unit 6 Choice B Test, p. 22
Unit 6 Composition Objective Test, pp. 23–24

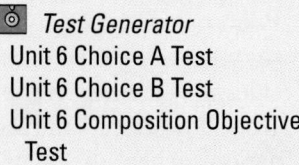 *Test Generator*
Unit 6 Choice A Test
Unit 6 Choice B Test
Unit 6 Composition Objective Test

You may wish to administer one of these tests as a mastery test.

UNIT 7

Troubleshooter

| Composition | Lessons |

Use Troubleshooter to help you correct common errors that you might make in your writing. You can indicate the errors on your paper using the handwritten codes in the left-hand column. Then the Table of Contents below will help you locate solutions to correct errors.

301

UNIT GOALS

The goal of **Troubleshooter** is to help students become more independent and competent writers and language users.

Key to Ability Levels
Enabling Strategies have been coded for varying learning styles and abilities.

L1 Level 1 activities are within the ability range of Learning Disabled students.

L2 Level 2 activities are basic-to-average activities and are within the ability range of average students.

L3 Level 3 activities are challenging activities and are within the ability range of above-average students.

LEP LEP activities are within the ability range of Limited English Proficiency students.

About the Troubleshooter

Teachers know that they mark some grammar, usage, and mechanics errors more often than others. Current research corroborates this experience. The *Writer's Choice* Troubleshooter, Grades 9–12, was prepared by Glencoe editors after they consulted one study by Robert J. Connors and Andrea Lunsford, reported in "Frequency of Formal Errors in Current College Writing, or Ma and Pa Kettle Do Research" (*College Composition and Communication*, December 1988). For the Grades 6–8 Troubleshooter, Glencoe editors selected pertinent errors and added errors common to middle school students.

FOCUS

Lesson Overview

Objective: To recognize the most common kinds of sentence fragments: those lacking a subject, those lacking a predicate, and those lacking both a subject and a predicate.

Bellringer

When students enter the classroom, have this assignment on the board: *Underline the subjects and circle the predicates in the following items:*

1. Jeff and Ian rode their bicycles in the park.
2. Took the wrong turn.
3. Got lost.
4. Their poor worried mothers.

Motivating Activity

Discuss which of the items from the Bellringer activity are not complete sentences (2, 3, and 4). What are they missing? (2 and 3 are missing subjects; 4 is missing a predicate) Elicit that 2, 3, and 4 are called *sentence fragments.* Ask students how often they notice sentence fragments in writing.

TEACH

Cross-reference: Grammar
For instruction and practice of the material in Problem 2, refer students to Lesson 8.2, pp. 328–329.

7.1 Sentence Fragment

PROBLEM 1

Fragment that lacks a subject

> *frag* Sol went to the airport. (Wanted to leave today.)
>
> *frag* Dora jogged to school. (Was late for class.)
>
> *frag* My car broke down today. (Couldn't start it.)

SOLUTION

Sol went to the airport. He wanted to leave today.

Dora jogged to school. She was late for class.

My car broke down today. I couldn't start it.

Add a subject to the fragment to make a complete sentence.

PROBLEM 2

Fragment that lacks a predicate

> *frag* Jo caught a plane yesterday. (The plane at noon.)
>
> *frag* Colin baked a cake today. (The cake in the oven.)
>
> *frag* Tatiana likes that court. (The tennis court in the park.)

302   *Troubleshooter*

Teacher's Classroom Resources

The following resources can be used for planning, instruction, practice, or reinforcement.

Teaching Tools
Lesson Plans, p. 66

Grammar Workbook
Lesson 3

SOLUTION

Jo caught a plane yesterday. The plane left at noon.

Colin baked a cake today. The cake is in the oven.

Tatiana likes that court. The tennis court in the park is the one she likes.

Add a predicate to make the sentence complete.

PROBLEM 3

Fragment that lacks both a subject and a predicate

frag   Sylvia played the violin. (In the symphony orchestra.)

frag   My cousin rode his bike. (To the store today.)

frag   Alex bought new skis. (From the sports store.)

SOLUTION

Sylvia played the violin in the symphony orchestra.

My cousin rode his bike to the store today.

Alex bought new skis from the sports store.

Combine the fragment with another sentence.

Need More Help? *If you need more help avoiding sentence fragments, turn to Lesson 8.2, pages 328–329.*

7.1 Sentence Fragment **303**

TEACH

☑ **Teaching Tip**
Have students work in pairs. Tell each student to write a brief paragraph containing sentence fragments. Suggest that they include a fragment that lacks a subject, one that lacks a predicate, and one that lacks both in their paragraphs. Students can then exchange papers and correct the sentence fragments.

 Two-Minute Skill Drill

Write the following paragraph on the board. Have students correct the sentence fragments by adding a subject or predicate or by combining the fragment with another sentence.
Jared likes to visit the pet store. The one in the mall. Saw a cute lab puppy there last week. With a glossy black coat. Sure wanted it! Too bad. Only had ten dollars.

Independent Practice
Skills Practice

 Grammar Workbook, Lesson 3

CLOSE

Challenge students to listen for sentence fragments in conversations on television or in person. Have them write down each fragment and then rewrite it to conform with the conventions of grammar and mechanics for written language. Students can collect their rewritten fragments for a bulletin board display. They might organize their collection under headings that indicate the three kinds of fragments.

Setting the Purpose

Lesson 7.2 teaches students to avoid using run-on sentences, thus clarifying their writing.

FOCUS

Lesson Overview

Objective: To recognize and revise run-on sentences

Bellringer
As students enter the classroom, have this assignment on the board: *Write a definition of a run-on sentence.*

Motivating Activity
Discuss the difference between run-on sentences in speech and in writing. Do students notice one more than the other? Do they think run-on sentences in speech are more acceptable than in writing? Why or why not?

TEACH

Cross-reference: Grammar
For instruction and practice of the material in this lesson, refer students to Lesson 8.6, pp. 336–337.

PROBLEM 1

Two main clauses separated only by a comma

run-on (Barb went water skiing, she skied behind the boat.)

run-on (I stopped reading, my eyes were tired.)

SOLUTION A

Barb went water skiing. She skied behind the boat.

Replace the comma with a period or other end mark, and begin the new sentence with a capital letter.

SOLUTION B

I stopped reading; my eyes were tired.

Place a semicolon between the main clauses.

PROBLEM 2

Two main clauses with no punctuation between them

run-on (My dog has fleas he scratches behind his ears.)

run-on (Husam bought that book he read it last week.)

304   *Troubleshooter*

Teacher's Classroom Resources

The following resources can be used for planning, instruction, practice, or reinforcement.

Teaching Tools
Lesson Plans, p. 66

Grammar Workbook
Lesson 6

SOLUTION A

My dog has fleas. He scratches behind his ears.

Separate the main clauses with a period or other end mark, and begin the second sentence with a capital letter.

SOLUTION B

Husam bought that book, and he read it last week.

Add a comma and a coordinating conjunction between the main clauses.

PROBLEM 3

Two main clauses with no comma before the coordinating conjunction

run-on Samantha went home (and she went to bed early.)

run-on I can go to Roberta's party (but I can't stay long.)

SOLUTION

Samantha went home, and she went to bed early.

I can go to Roberta's party, but I can't stay long.

Add a comma before the coordinating conjunction.

Need More Help? *If you need more help in avoiding run-on sentences, turn to Lesson 8.6, pages 336–337.*

7.2 Run-on Sentence **305**

TEACH

Two-Minute Skill Drill

Write this run-on sentence on the board and challenge students to correct it: *I eat the same thing for breakfast every day, that's the way I like it!*

Independent Practice

Skills Practice

Grammar Workbook, Lesson 6

CLOSE

Have each student write a run-on sentence on a piece of paper. On the back of the paper, have them correct the sentence. Then have students exchange papers with partners without displaying their corrections. Instruct students to revise their partners' run-on sentences and compare the corrections. Did they correct the sentences differently? Are both revisions correct? Why or why not?

Lesson 7.3 teaches students to avoid constructing sentences in which the subject and verb do not agree. Students will learn to recognize common errors in order to improve their writing and sentence sense.

FOCUS

Lesson Overview

Objective: To recognize the following constructions that lead to lack of subject-verb agreement: a subject separated from a verb by a prepositional phrase; a sentence that begins with *here* or *there;* an indefinite pronoun as the subject; a compound subject joined by *and, or,* or *nor*

Bellringer

When students enter the classroom, have this assignment on the board: *On a sheet of paper, write why this sentence is incorrect: Jackie run to get on the bus.*

Motivating Activity

Discuss students' answers to the Bellringer exercise. Have volunteers tell how they would correct the sentence, and write their corrections on the board. Then have them explain why they made the corrections.

TEACH

⇄ Cross-reference: Usage
For instruction and practice of the material in Problem 1, refer students to Lesson 16.2, pp. 510–511.

7.3	Lack of Subject-Verb Agreement

PROBLEM 1

A subject that is separated from the verb by an intervening prepositional phrase

> *agr*   One of the radios (are) broken.
>
> *agr*   The boys in the class (is) singing.

SOLUTION

One of the radios is broken.

The boys in the class are singing.

Ignore a prepositional phrase that comes between a subject and a verb. Make sure that the verb agrees with the subject of the sentence. The subject is never the object of the preposition.

PROBLEM 2

A sentence that begins with here *or* there

> *agr*   There (go) the local train.
>
> *agr*   Here (is) the students who will write the report.
>
> *agr*   There (is) oil paintings in the art gallery.

306 *Troubleshooter*

Teacher's Classroom Resources

The following resources can be used for planning, instruction, practice, or reinforcement.

𝄢 **Teaching Tools**
Lesson Plans, p. 66

📁 **Blackline Masters**
Sentence Combining Practice, pp. 16–17

📕 *Grammar Workbook*
Lesson 53

SOLUTION

There goes the local train.

Here are the students who will write the report.

There are oil paintings in the art gallery.

The subject is never *here* or *there*. In sentences that begin with *here* or *there*, look for the subject *after* the verb. The verb must agree with the subject.

PROBLEM 3

An indefinite pronoun as the subject

agr   Neither of the girls (have) their umbrella.

agr   Many of the books (is) old.

agr   All of my pleading (were) in vain.

Some indefinite pronouns are singular, some are plural, and some can be either singular or plural, depending upon the noun they refer to.

SOLUTION

Neither of the girls has her umbrella.

Many of the books are old.

All of my pleading was in vain.

Determine whether the indefinite pronoun is singular or plural, and make the verb agree.

7.3 Lack of Subject-Verb Agreement **307**

TEACH

▣ **Cross-reference: Usage**
For instruction and practice of the material in Problem 2, refer students to Lesson 16.2, pp. 510–511.

▣ **Cross-reference: Usage**
For instruction and practice of the material in Problem 3, refer students to Lesson 16.4, pp. 514–515.

TEACH

☑ **Teaching Tip**

If students experience difficulty, ask them to copy the sample exercises on note cards. Have students work in pairs to locate and underline the part that is the compound subject and then circle the verb. Then have them try replacing the subject with *he, she, it,* or *they.* Elicit the following generalization: If the subject can be replaced with *he, she,* or *it,* use a singular verb–if *they* can replace the subject, use a plural verb.

⇄ **Cross-reference: Usage**

For instruction and practice of the material in Problem 4, refer students to Lesson 16.5, pp. 516–517.

⇄ **Cross-reference: Usage**

For instruction and practice of the material in Problem 5, refer students to Lesson 16.4, pp. 514–515.

PROBLEM 4

A compound subject that is joined by **and**

> *agr* Posters and balloons (was) strewn around the gym.
>
> *agr* The star and team leader (are) Rico.

SOLUTION A

Posters and balloons were strewn around the gym.

If the parts of the compound subject do not belong to one unit or if they refer to different people or things, use a plural verb.

SOLUTION B

The star and team leader is Rico.

If the parts of the compound subject belong to one unit or if both parts refer to the same person or thing, use a singular verb.

PROBLEM 5

A compound subject that is joined by **or** *or* **nor**

> *agr* Either the actor or the actress (appear) onstage.
>
> *agr* Neither the tomato nor the bananas (looks) ripe.
>
> *agr* Either Mom or Dad (are) driving us to the movie.
>
> *agr* Neither my brother nor my uncles (likes) trains.

SOLUTION

Either the actor or the actress appears onstage.

Neither the tomato nor the bananas look ripe.

Either Mom or Dad is driving us to the movie.

Neither my brother nor my uncles like trains.

Make the verb agree with the subject that is closer to it.

 **Need More Help?** *If you need more help with subject-verb agreement, turn to Lessons 16.1–16.5, pages 508–517.*

TEACH

 **Two-Minute Skill Drill**

Write this sentence on the board: *Neither the coach nor the basketball players breaks team rules.* Have students rewrite the sentence so the subject and verb agree.

Independent Practice

Skills Practice
 Sentence Combining Practice, pp. 16–17

Grammar Workbook, Lesson 53

CLOSE

Ask students to write five sentences. Each sentence should demonstrate a different one of the problems illustrated in the lesson. Students can then exchange papers with a partner and correct the errors.

7.3 Lack of Subject-Verb Agreement **309**

FOCUS

Lesson Overview

Objective: To recognize the most common kinds of errors in verb tense or form, such as an incorrect or missing verb ending, an improperly formed irregular verb, and confusing the past form and the past participle

Bellringer

As students enter the classroom, have this assignment on the board: *On a sheet of paper, write what is wrong with this paragraph. Suggest how you might correct it.*

Last year, I travel with my parents to Arches National Monument. We singed in the car all the way. We had drove almost a day when we saw our first red mountain formations.

Motivating Activity

Discuss students' Bellringer responses. Tell students that this lesson will teach them the important skill of using verb tenses and forms correctly.

TEACH

Cross-reference: Grammar
For instruction and practice of the material in Problem 1, refer students to Lesson 10.5, pp. 376–377.

Cross-reference: Grammar
For instruction and practice of the material in this lesson, refer students to Lesson 10.11, pp. 388–389.

7.4 Incorrect Verb Tense or Form

PROBLEM 1

An incorrect or missing verb ending

tense	Have you (reach) all your goals?
tense	Last month we (visit) Yosemite National Park.
tense	The train (depart) an hour ago.

SOLUTION

Have you reached all your goals?

Last month we visited Yosemite National Park.

The train departed an hour ago.

Add *-ed* to a regular verb to form the past tense and the past participle.

PROBLEM 2

An improperly formed irregular verb

tense	The wind (blowed) the rain from the roof.
tense	The loud thunder (shaked) the house.
tense	Sophia (bringed) the horse back to the barn.

Teacher's Classroom Resources

The following resources can be used for planning, instruction, practice, or reinforcement.

Teaching Tools
Lesson Plans, p. 67

Grammar Workbook
Lessons 17, 20, and 23–24

The past and past participle forms of irregular verbs vary. Memorize these forms, or look them up.

SOLUTION

The wind blew the rain from the roof.

The loud thunder shook the house.

Sophia brought the horse back to the barn.

Use the correct past or past participle form of an irregular verb.

PROBLEM 3

Confusion between the past form and the past participle

tense   Mimi has rode the horse home from school.

SOLUTION

Mimi has ridden the horse home from school.

Use the past participle form of an irregular verb, not the past form, when you use the auxiliary verb *have.*

 **If you need more help with correct verb forms, turn to Lessons 10.1–10.12, pages 368–391.**

TEACH

 Two-Minute Skill Drill

Write this sentence on the board and ask students to correct it, changing "yesterday" and using as many correct verb tenses as possible: *I run a mile yesterday along the river before I eat my lunch.*

Independent Practice

Skills Practice

 *Grammar Workbook,* Lessons 17, 20, and 23–24

CLOSE

Ask students to write three sentences, each with a different type of error in verb tense or form. Have them exchange papers, identify the type of error, and revise each sentence using correct verb tenses and forms.

Setting the Purpose

Lesson 7.5 identifies three types of incorrect pronoun use and offers a correction for each.

FOCUS

Lesson Overview

Objective: To recognize the constructions that give rise to incorrect pronoun use

Bellringer

As students enter the classroom, have this assignment on the board: *How do you know when you've used or heard an incorrect pronoun in a sentence?*

Motivating Activity

Discuss how fluent English speakers often know when a pronoun has been incorrectly used, just because it sounds odd. Even if people can't list all of the subject pronouns and object pronouns, they still know "Him went to the store" sounds wrong.

TEACH

Cross-reference: Grammar

For instruction and practice of the material in Problem 1, refer students to Lesson 11.2, pp. 404–405.

PROBLEM 1

A pronoun that refers to more than one antecedent

pro   Sonia jogs with Yma, but (she) is more athletic.

pro   After the dogs barked at the cats, (they) ran away.

pro   When Sal called out to Joe, (he) didn't smile.

SOLUTION

Sonia jogs with Yma, but Yma is more athletic.

After the dogs barked at the cats, the cats ran away.

When Sal called out to Joe, Joe didn't smile.

Rewrite the sentence, substituting a noun for the pronoun.

PROBLEM 2

Personal pronouns as subjects

pro   Vanessa and (me) like to camp in the mountains.

pro   Georgianne and (them) drove to the beach.

pro   (Her) and Mark flew to London.

312   *Troubleshooter*

Teacher's Classroom Resources

The following resources can be used for planning, instruction, practice, or reinforcement.

Teaching Tools
Lesson Plans, p. 67

Grammar Workbook
Lessons 25–26

SOLUTION

Vanessa and I like to camp in the mountains.

Georgianne and they drove to the beach.

She and Mark flew to London.

Use a subject pronoun as the subject part of a sentence.

PROBLEM 3

Personal pronouns as objects

pro   Joel is coming with Manny and (she.)

pro   Please drive Rose and (I) to the store.

pro   The dog brought the stick to Chandra and (I.)

SOLUTION

Joel is coming with Manny and her.

Please drive Rose and me to the store.

The dog brought the stick to Chandra and me.

Use an object pronoun as the object of a verb or preposition.

 **Need More Help?** *If you need more help with the correct use of pronouns, turn to Lessons 11.1–11.7, pages 402–415.*

TEACH

 **Cross-reference: Grammar**
For instruction and practice of the material in Problems 2 and 3, refer students to Lesson 11.1, pp. 402–403.

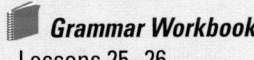 **Two-Minute Skill Drill**

Write these sentences on the board and ask students which shows the correct use of pronouns: *1. Taehoon and I walked up to the squirrel. 2. The squirrel walked up to Taehoon and I. 3. When the squirrel arrived, he chirped.* Discuss why sentences 2 and 3 have confusing pronouns.

Independent Practice
Skills Practice

Grammar Workbook, Lessons 25–26

CLOSE

Invite students to write a one-paragraph narrative in which they demonstrate correct usage of pronoun antecedents, subject pronouns, and object pronouns.

FOCUS

Lesson Overview

Objective: To recognize the most common kinds of errors in using regular and irregular comparative and superlative adjectives

 Bellringer
As students enter the classroom, have this assignment on the board: *What does the use of adjectives add to your writing?*

Motivating Activity

Discuss the Bellringer responses. Then have students write several sentences about their best friend, using the adjectives *good, better,* and *best* to describe her or him.

TEACH

 Cross-reference: Grammar
For an instruction and practice of the material in this lesson, refer students to Lesson 12.3, pp. 428–429.

7.6 Incorrect Use of Adjectives

PROBLEM 1

Incorrect use of good, better, best

> *adj*   Is mountain air (more good) than ocean air?
>
> *adj*   Marla is the (most good) babysitter I know.

SOLUTION

Is mountain air better than ocean air?

Marla is the best babysitter I know.

The comparative and superlative forms of *good* are *better* and *best*. Do not use *more* or *most* before irregular forms of comparative and superlative adjectives.

PROBLEM 2

Incorrect use of bad, worse, worst

> *adj*   Mandy's cold is the (baddest) cold I've ever seen.

SOLUTION

Mandy's cold is the worst cold I've ever seen.

Do not use *more* or *most* before irregular forms of comparative and superlative adjectives.

Teacher's Classroom Resources

The following resources can be used for planning, instruction, practice, or reinforcement.

Teaching Tools
Lesson Plans, p. 67

Grammar Workbook
Lesson 33

PROBLEM 3

Incorrect use of comparative adjectives

> *adj*   Twine is (more stronger) than thread.

SOLUTION

Twine is stronger than thread.

Do not use both *-er* and *more* at the same time.

PROBLEM 4

Incorrect use of superlative adjectives

> *adj*   This is the (most hardest) test I've ever taken.

SOLUTION

This is the hardest test I've ever taken.

Do not use both *-est* and *most* at the same time.

If you need more help with the incorrect use of adjectives, turn to Lesson 12.3, pages 428–429.

TEACH

 Teaching Tip

Ask students to work with partners to correct the use of adjectives in the following sentences and discuss why each correction was made.

1. Thalia is the most best soccer player in our class.
2. This year's floods in California were the most bad in history.
3. Tony's new kitten is much more younger than mine.
4. When we go camping, we bring the most warmest blankets that we have.

 **Two-Minute Skill Drill**

Write the following sentence on the board and ask students to correct the use of adjectives: *Although she is the most short player, Kim is the team's most highest scorer.*

Independent Practice

Skills Practice

 Grammar Workbook, Lesson 33

CLOSE

Ask students to write a paragraph using comparative adjectives to describe and compare three favorite foods or sports.

315

Lesson 7.7 teaches students to use commas to separate items in a series and to set off direct quotations, nonessential appositives, nonessential adjective clauses, and introductory adverb clauses.

FOCUS

Lesson Overview
Objective: To recognize when to use commas

🔔 Bellringer
When students enter the classroom, have this assignment on the board: *Can you read the following paragraph easily? Why or why not? What would you do to fix it?*

Mrs. Canfield who is my piano teacher has asked me to babysit her son Saturday afternoon. He likes to play checkers soccer and video games. Whenever I babysit him I am worn out!

Motivating Activity
Have various students suggest how they might correct the Bellringer paragraph. Discuss how using commas correctly will make their writing clearer and more interesting.

TEACH

▤ Cross-reference: Mechanics
For instruction and practice of the material in Problem 1, refer students to Lesson 20.2, pp. 568–569.

▤ Cross-reference: Mechanics
For instruction and practice of the material in Problem 2, refer students to Lesson 20.6, pp. 576–577.

7.7 Incorrect Use of Commas

PROBLEM 1

Missing commas in a series of three or more items

> *com*   We had fish vegetables and bread for dinner.
>
> *com*   Help me make the beds sweep the floor and wash the windows.

SOLUTION

We had fish, vegetables, and bread for dinner.

Help me make the beds, sweep the floor, and wash the windows.

When there are three or more items in a series, use a comma after each one including the item that precedes the conjunction.

PROBLEM 2

Missing commas with direct quotations

> *com*   "The concert," said Dora "was loud and boring."
>
> *com*   "Tomorrow," said Burton "I will read that book."

Teacher's Classroom Resources

The following resources can be used for planning, instruction, practice, or reinforcement.

🔧 **Teaching Tools**
Lesson Plans, p. 68

📁 **Blackline Masters**
Sentence Combining Practice, pp. 4, 6–8, 14–15, 18–20

📙 *Grammar Workbook*
Lessons 78, 81

SOLUTION

"The concert," said Dora, "was loud and boring."

"Tomorrow," said Burton, "I will read that book."

The first part of an interrupted quotation ends with a comma followed by quotation marks. The interrupting words are also followed by a comma.

PROBLEM 3

Missing commas with nonessential appositives

com   Mr. Unser͡our English teacher͡was born in England.

com   Ms. Charo͡my mother's boss͡is taking us to dinner.

SOLUTION

Mr. Unser, our English teacher, was born in England.

Ms. Charo, my mother's boss, is taking us to dinner.

Determine whether the appositive is truly not essential to the meaning of the sentence. If it is not essential, set off the appositive with commas.

7.7 Incorrect Use of Commas   **317**

TEACH

⮂ **Cross-reference: Mechanics**

For instruction and practice of the material in Problem 3, refer students to Lesson 20.2, pp. 568–569.

TEACH

Cross-reference: Mechanics

For instruction and practice of the material in Problems 4 and 5, refer students to Lesson 20.3, pp. 570–571.

Two-Minute Skill Drill

Have students correct the following sentences, using solutions from the lesson:

1. *That movie which Jake saw on Saturday was about space travel.*
2. *"I wonder" said Tia "why its reviews are so positive."*
3. *"When a movie is full of suspense a lot of people like it" answered Phil.*
4. *"I like adventure films comedies and musicals but not science fiction" said Tia.*

Independent Practice

Skills Practice

 Sentence Combining Practice, pp. 4, 6–8, 14–15, 18–20

Grammar Workbook, Lessons 78, 81

CLOSE

Have volunteers explain the five ways mentioned in this lesson in which writers mistakenly omit commas.

PROBLEM 4

Missing commas with nonessential adjective clauses

> *com* Devin who arose early smelled the eggs and bacon.

SOLUTION

Devin, who arose early, smelled the eggs and bacon.

Determine whether the clause is truly not essential to the meaning of the sentence. If it is not essential, set off the clause with commas.

PROBLEM 5

Missing commas with introductory adverb clauses

> *com* When the whistle blows the workday is over.

SOLUTION

When the whistle blows, the workday is over.

Place a comma after an introductory adverbial clause.

Need More Help?

If you need more help with commas, turn to Lessons 20.2–20.4, pages 568–573.

7.8 Incorrect Use of Apostrophes

PROBLEM 1

Singular possessive nouns

> *apos* (Beths) dress is from France.
>
> *apos* (My boss) report is on (Angelas) desk.
>
> *apos* (My gerbils) fur is brown and white.

SOLUTION

Beth's dress is from France.

My boss's report is on Angela's desk.

My gerbil's fur is brown and white.

Use an apostrophe and an -*s* to form the possessive of a singular noun, even one that ends in -*s*.

PROBLEM 2

Plural possessive nouns ending in -s

> *apos* The (boys) shirts are too big for them.
>
> *apos* My (horses) manes are long and thick.
>
> *apos* My (parents) friends joined them for dinner.

7.8 Incorrect Use of Apostrophes **319**

Setting the Purpose

Lesson 7.8 improves students' writing by teaching the correct use of the possessive apostrophe.

FOCUS

Lesson Overview

Objective: To recognize the most common instances in which possessive apostrophes are missing or misplaced, the inappropriate use of apostrophes and possessive pronouns, and the confusion between *its* and *it's*

Bellringer
As students enter the classroom, have this assignment on the board: *When do you use apostrophes in your writing? List two examples.*

Motivating Activity
Review the Bellringer responses and ask students to discuss anything they may think is wrong with this sentence: *Its the first day of school and its really too early for the bus according to it's route.* Discuss answers and correct the sentence together.

TEACH

Cross-reference: Mechanics
For instruction and practice of the material in Problems 1 and 2, refer students to Lesson 20.7, pp. 578–579.

eacher's Classroom Resources

The following resources can be used for planning, instruction, practice, or reinforcement.

Teaching Tools
Lesson Plans, p. 68

Blackline Masters
Sentence Combining Practice, p. 9

Grammar Workbook
Lesson 84

TEACH

Cross-reference: Mechanics

For instruction and practice of the material in Problem 3, refer students to Lesson 20.7, pp. 578–579.

Cross-reference: Grammar

For instruction and practice of the material in Problem 4, refer students to Lesson 11.4, pp. 408–409.

SOLUTION

The boys' shirts are too big for them.

My horses' manes are long and thick.

My parents' friends joined them for dinner.

Use an apostrophe alone to form the possessive of a plural noun that ends in -*s*.

PROBLEM 3

Plural possessive nouns not ending in -s

apos   The (childrens) books are in the library.

apos   The (womens) meetings are in this building.

SOLUTION

The children's books are in the library.

The women's meetings are in this building.

Use an apostrophe and an -*s* to form the possessive of a plural noun that does not end in -*s*.

PROBLEM 4

Possessive personal pronouns

apos   This new tape is (her's,) but the CD is (their's.)

SOLUTION

This new tape is hers, but the CD is theirs.

Do not use an apostrophe with any of the possessive personal pronouns.

PROBLEM 5

Confusion between its *and* it's

apos   The bird built (it's) nest in the oak tree.

apos   I want to know if (its) going to be sunny today.

SOLUTION

The bird built its nest in the oak tree.

I want to know if it's going to be sunny today.

Do not use an apostrophe to form the possessive of *it*. Use an apostrophe to form the contraction of *it is*.

 **Need More Help?** *If you need more help with apostrophes and possessives, turn to Lesson 20.7, pages 578–579.*

7.8 Incorrect Use of Apostrophes **321**

TEACH

 **Cross-reference: Grammar**
For instruction and practice of the material in Problem 5, refer students to Lesson 11.4, pp. 408–409.

 Two-Minute Skill Drill

Have students correct the use of apostrophes in the following sentences, using solutions from the lesson.

1. Jerrys' guitar is in it's case.
2. The skier's lodge is near my fathers home.
3. The womens' dresses are on the stores' fourth floor.
4. All of this land is their's, but that acre is her's.

Independent Practice
Skills Practice
Sentence Combining Practice, p. 9

Grammar Workbook, Lesson 84

CLOSE

Have students write five sentences, one for each of the five incorrect uses of apostrophes shown in the lesson problems. Ask them to trade their sentences with a partner and correct each other's sentences. Then have them discuss with their partner the type of error occurring in each sentence.

Lesson 7.9 teaches students the correct uses of capitalization in their writing.

FOCUS

Lesson Overview

Objective: To recognize correct capitalization when referring to ethnic groups, nationalities, and languages and when beginning direct quotations

 Bellringer

As students enter the classroom, have this assignment on the board: *List the use of capitalization in the following sentence and explain why you think each capital letter is needed:*

Maria said, "Some of my Japanese friends speak French as well as English."

TEACH

 Cross-reference: Mechanics
For instruction and practice of the material in Problem 1, refer students to Lesson 19.4, pp. 556–557.

 Cross-reference: Mechanics
For instruction and practice of the material in Problem 2, refer students to Lesson 19.1, pp. 550–551.

Independent Practice

Skills Practice

Grammar Workbook,
Lessons 73 and 76

CLOSE

Ask students to write a brief conversation between two foreign-exchange students discussing the challenges of speaking English. Have students exchange papers and correct any errors in capitalization.

7.9 Incorrect Capitalization

PROBLEM 1

Words referring to ethnic groups, nationalities, and languages

.cap   Many (canadian) citizens speak (french.)

SOLUTION

Many Canadian citizens speak French.

Capitalize proper nouns and adjectives that refer to ethnic groups, nationalities, and languages.

PROBLEM 2

The first word of a direct quotation

.cap   Devon said, ("the) new highway will run through town."

SOLUTION

Devon said, "The new highway will run through town."

Capitalize the first word in a direct quotation that is a complete sentence. A direct quotation gives the speaker's exact words.

 **Need More Help?**   *If you need more help in capitalizing, turn to Lessons 19.1–19.4, pages 550–557.*

Teacher's Classroom Resources

The following resources can be used for planning, instruction, practice, or reinforcement.

Teaching Tools
Lesson Plans, p. 68

Grammar Workbook
Lessons 73 and 76

Part 2

Grammar, Usage, and Mechanics

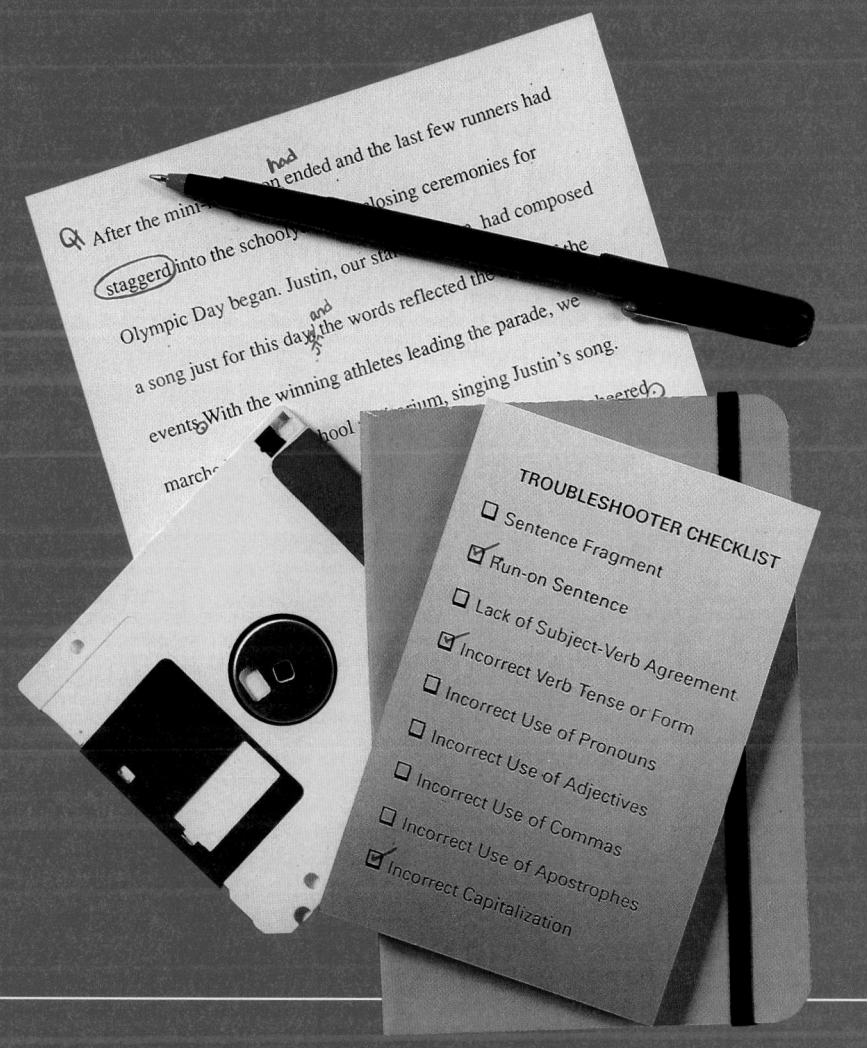

TROUBLESHOOTER CHECKLIST
- ☐ Sentence Fragment
- ☑ Run-on Sentence
- ☐ Lack of Subject-Verb Agreement
- ☑ Incorrect Verb Tense or Form
- ☐ Incorrect Use of Pronouns
- ☐ Incorrect Use of Adjectives
- ☐ Incorrect Use of Commas
- ☑ Incorrect Use of Apostrophes
- ☐ Incorrect Capitalization

Part 2 Grammar, Usage, and Mechanics

324

UNIT 8

Subjects, Predicates, and Sentences

Grammar	Lessons

325

UNIT GOALS

The goal of Unit 8 is to help students, through example and instruction, to develop an understanding of subjects and predicates and to use them in complete sentences. The lessons focus on kinds of sentences, sentence fragments, and run-on sentences; simple and complete subjects and predicates; normal word order and exceptions to it; and compound subjects and predicates.

Unit Assessment

📁 *Tests with Answer Key*
Unit 8 Pretest, pp. 29–30
Unit 8 Mastery Test, pp. 31–32

💿 *Test Generator*
Unit 8 Pretest
Unit 8 Mastery Test

You may wish to administer the Unit 8 Pretest at this point.

Key to Ability Levels

Enabling strategies have been coded for varying learning styles and abilities.

L1 Level 1 activities are within the ability range of Learning Disabled students.

L2 Level 2 activities are basic-to-average activities and are within the ability range of average students.

L3 Level 3 activities are challenging activities and are within the ability range of above-average students.

LEP LEP activities are within the ability range of Limited English Proficiency students.

Setting the Purpose

Lesson 8.1 teaches students how to use the four kinds of sentences—declarative, interrogative, exclamatory, and imperative.

FOCUS

Lesson Overview

Objective: To identify and correctly punctuate the four types of sentences

Bellringer

When students enter the classroom, have this assignment on the board: *Write an example of each type of sentence you know.*

Motivating Activity

Discuss the sentences students wrote. How many types of sentences were identified? How did they punctuate the different types of sentences?

TEACH

Speaking and Listening

Have students listen for intonation that indicates the kind of sentence being spoken. Discuss the correspondence between intonation and delete punctuation.

Cross-reference: Grammar

For information on diagraming the four kinds of sentences, refer students to Lesson 18.2, p. 539.

Two-Minute Skill Drill

Have students write each kind of sentence, using one of the following subjects:

horses	space shuttle
piano	basketball

8.1   Kinds of Sentences

A **sentence** is a group of words that expresses a complete thought.

Our class is reading "The Raven" by Edgar Allan Poe.

Different kinds of sentences have different purposes. A sentence can make a statement, ask a question, give a command, or express strong feeling. All sentences begin with a capital letter and end with a punctuation mark. The punctuation mark at the end of the sentence is determined by the purpose of that sentence.

Was it fun?

A **declarative sentence** makes a statement. It ends with a period.

> Edgar Allan Poe wrote suspenseful short stories.

It surely scared me!

An **interrogative sentence** asks a question. It ends with a question mark.

> Did Poe also write poetry?

An **exclamatory sentence** expresses strong feeling. It ends with an exclamation point.

> What a great writer Poe was!

An **imperative sentence** gives a command or makes a request. It ends with a period.

> Read "The Pit and the Pendulum."

Édouard Manet, Illustration to Poe's "The Raven," c. 1875

326   *Subjects, Predicates, and Sentences*

Teacher's Classroom Resources

The following resources can be used for planning, instruction, practice, reinforcement, assessment, reteaching, enrichment, or evaluation.

Teaching Tools
Lesson Plans, p. 69
Blackline Masters
Grammar Practice, p. 1
Grammar Reteaching, p. 1
Grammar Enrichment, p. 1

Grammar Workbook, Lessons 1–2

Unit Assessment

Tests with Answer Key
Unit 8 Pretest, pp. 29–30

Test Generator
Unit 8 Pretest

You may wish to administer the Unit 8 Pretest at this point.

Exercise 1 — Identifying Kinds of Sentences

Write whether each sentence is *declarative, interrogative, exclamatory,* or *imperative.*

1. Edgar Allan Poe was born in Boston in 1809.
2. Did you know that Poe lost his parents at a very early age?
3. How awful that must have been!
4. The boy lived with his foster parents.
5. Wasn't his foster father a wealthy merchant?
6. Poe was raised in Richmond, Virginia.
7. He attended college briefly.
8. Did he enlist in the army?
9. I can't believe that he went to West Point!
10. Read a biography of Poe.
11. Didn't he also edit magazines?
12. What impressive writing Poe produced!
13. Poe was a master of the short story.
14. How greatly he influenced other writers!
15. Tell me what you think about his writing.
16. Poe died at the age of forty.
17. Isn't that very young?
18. How sad that his life was so short!
19. What a tragedy!
20. Find out more about Poe.

Exercise 2 — Capitalizing and Punctuating Sentences

Write each sentence, adding capital letters and punctuation marks where needed.

1. is it true that Edgar Allan Poe wrote the first detective story
2. is private detective C. Auguste Dupin in one of Poe's tales
3. tell me if you have read Poe's famous poem about the raven
4. what a harrowing ending this poem has
5. Poe's writings are very popular in Europe
6. Did the young man go to college in Virginia
7. poe is also highly regarded for his literary criticism
8. he lived in Philadelphia during a part of his career
9. His writing includes mystery, suspense, fantasy, and humor
10. What a great adventure story "The Narrative of A. Gordon Pym" is

8.1 Kinds of Sentences **327**

Enabling Strategies

Forming Yes or No Questions
Point out that the way English forms yes-no questions may confuse students who speak a different language at home.
- Tag questions, used to confirm information, are built from declarative sentences. (For example: *Poe wrote "The Raven," didn't he?*)
- In other questions, the first helping verb (or *do,* if there is no helping verb) is placed before the subject. (For example: *Do people always try this?*)

327

FOCUS

Lesson Overview

Objective: To identify the sentence and its key elements, a subject and a predicate; to distinguish complete sentences from fragments.

Bellringer

When students enter the classroom, have this assignment on the board: *Identify these quotations from "The Raven" by Edgar Allan Poe as either sentences or sentence fragments, and explain your choice. (1) Ghastly grim and ancient Raven wandering from the Nightly shore— (2) Quoth the Raven, "Nevermore."*

(1 is a fragment; 2 is a sentence. 1 does not express a complete thought; 2 has a subject, *the Raven,* and a predicate, *Quoth ... 'Nevermore.)*

TEACH

☑ Grammar Tip

A good way to identify the subject is first to identify the verb. Then ask a *who* or *what* question using the verb. For example, the verb in the sentence *Emily Dickinson kept her unpublished poems in her attic* is easy to find: *kept.* Even though there are several nouns in the sentence, only one answers the question, *Who kept?* Thus, *Emily Dickinson* is the subject, of the sentence.

8.2 Sentences and Sentence Fragments

Every sentence has two parts: a subject and a predicate.

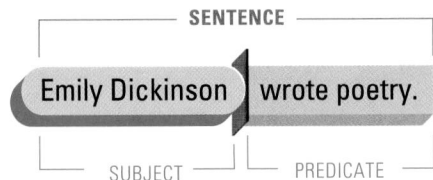

The **subject part** of a sentence names whom or what the sentence is about.

The **predicate part** of the sentence tells what the subject does or has. It can also describe what the subject is or is like.

A sentence must have both a subject and a predicate. It must also express a complete thought.

A **sentence fragment** does not express a complete thought. It may also be missing a subject, a predicate, or both.

You often use fragments when talking with friends or writing personal letters. Some writers use sentence fragments to produce special effects. You should use complete sentences, however, in anything you write for school or business.

Correcting Sentence Fragments		
Fragment	**Problem**	**Sentence**
Her sister.	The fragment lacks a predicate. *What did her sister do?*	Her sister discovered the poems in her bureau.
Wrote about her emotions.	The fragment lacks a subject. *Who wrote about her emotions?*	This gifted poet wrote about her emotions.
Of meaning.	The fragment lacks both a subject and a predicate.	Her poems contain many layers of meaning.

328   *Subjects, Predicates, and Sentences*

Teacher's Classroom Resources

The following resources can be used for planning, instruction, practice, reinforcement, reteaching, or enrichment.

Teaching Tools
Lesson Plans, p. 69

Blackline Masters
Grammar Practice, p. 1
Grammar Reteaching, p. 2
Grammar Enrichment, p. 1

Grammar Workbook,
Lesson 3

Exercise 3 — Identifying Sentences and Sentence Fragments

Write each sentence, underlining the subject part once and the predicate part twice. If it is a fragment, write *fragment*, and explain why it is a fragment.

1. Emily Dickinson lived in Amherst, Massachusetts.
2. At her parents' home.
3. Few of her poems were published during her lifetime.
4. Considered one of the greatest American poets.
5. You should study her poems carefully.
6. Dickinson's sister collected her poems.
7. This famous poet.
8. Insisted on complete privacy.
9. Her poems reflect her intensely emotional nature.
10. Many readers are attracted to her highly original style.
11. Dickinson's poetry comments on all matters of life.
12. Wrote about love and beauty.
13. Dickinson analyzes her emotions poetically.
14. So much fine work.
15. Found a world of her own.
16. With clear, precise observation.
17. Her writing style gives every word weight.
18. Her poetry uses sharp phrases and rich imagery.
19. Most of her poems include original insights.
20. To every possible human concern.

Exercise 4 — Correcting Sentence Fragments

Rewrite each sentence fragment to make it a complete sentence. Add a subject or a predicate or both.

1. Emily Dickinson author.
2. Lived from 1830 to 1886.
3. With clarity and style.
4. Began to retreat into herself at the age of twenty-three.
5. Moved quietly about the house.
6. Caught only glimpses of her.
7. In the nineteenth century.
8. Biographies of Dickinson.
9. Dickinson's poetry.
10. Observed the world and wrote about it.

8.2 Sentences and Sentence Fragments **329**

PRACTICE AND ASSESS

Answers: Exercise 3
1. <u>Emily Dickinson</u> <u>lived in Amherst, Massachusetts.</u>
2. fragment; lacks subject, predicate
3. <u>Few of her poems</u> <u>were published during her lifetime.</u>
4. fragment; lacks subject, predicate
5. <u>You</u> <u>should study her poems carefully.</u>
6. <u>Dickinson's sister</u> <u>collected her poems.</u>
7. fragment; lacks predicate
8. fragment; lacks subject
9. <u>Her poems</u> <u>reflect her intensely emotional nature.</u>
10. <u>Many readers</u> <u>are attracted to her highly original style.</u>
11. <u>Dickinson's poetry</u> <u>comments on all matters of life.</u>
12. fragment; lacks subject
13. <u>Dickinson</u> <u>analyzes her emotions poetically.</u>
14. fragment; lacks predicate
15. fragment; lacks subject
16. fragment; lacks subject, predicate
17. <u>Her writing style</u> <u>gives every word weight.</u>
18. <u>Her poetry</u> <u>uses sharp phrases and rich imagery.</u>
19. <u>Most of her poems</u> <u>include original insights.</u>
20. fragment; lacks subject, predicate

Answers: Exercise 4
Answers will vary but students should correctly add a subject or a predicate or both.

Independent Practice
Skills Practice
📁 *Grammar Practice,* p. 1
📁 *Grammar Reteaching,* p. 2
📁 *Grammar Enrichment,* p. 1
📖 **Grammar Workbook,** *Lesson 3*

Enabling Strategies
LEP **Finding Sentence Parts**
All sentences contain subjects and predicates, but the order in which they occur varies. Depending on the language, the verb or the entire predicate may come before the subject. In some languages, elements may even occur in any order, depending on the emphasis.

CLOSE
Have students recall a poem they have enjoyed reading. Ask them to describe in a paragraph what they like most about the poem. Tell them to be sure all their sentences have subjects and predicates.

329

FOCUS

Lesson Overview
Objective: To identify simple and complete subjects and simple and complete predicates

🔔 Bellringer
When students enter the classroom, have this assignment on the board: *Who is the doer and what action is done in the following sentence?*
Many students in my class have read books by Charles Dickens.

Motivating Activity
Discuss the Bellringer activity. Note that the doer (*students*) is the simple subject and what is done (*have read*) is the simple predicate. Explain that the words *Many* and *in my class* are part of the complete subject and the words *books by Charles Dickens* are part of the complete predicate.

TEACH

☑ Teaching Tip
To help students locate the subject of a sentence, tell them that the complete subject of a sentence can be replaced by a pronoun—*I, you, he, she, it, we,* or *they.* Have students take turns replacing the subjects of the sentences in Exercise 5 with pronouns.

8.3 Subjects and Predicates

A sentence consists of a subject and a predicate that together express a complete thought. Both a subject and a predicate may consist of more than one word.

Complete Subject	Complete Predicate
Dickens's **novels**	**are** still popular today.
My English **teacher**	**wrote** an article on Dickens.

The **complete subject** includes all of the words in the subject of a sentence.

The **complete predicate** includes all of the words in the predicate of a sentence.

Not all of the words in the subject or the predicate are of equal importance.

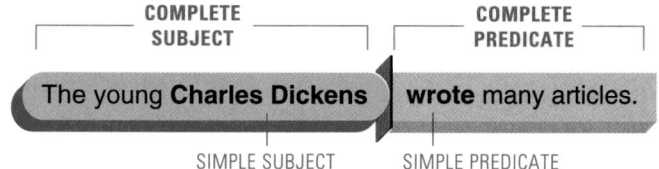

The **simple subject** is the main or most important word or group of words in the complete subject.

The simple subject is usually a noun or a pronoun. A **noun** is a word that names a person, a place, a thing, or an idea. A **pronoun** is a word that takes the place of one or more nouns.

The **simple predicate** is the main word or group of words in the complete predicate.

The simple predicate is always a verb. A **verb** is a word that expresses an action or a state of being.

Sometimes the simple subject is also the complete subject. Similarly, the simple predicate may also be the complete predicate.

330 *Subjects, Predicates, and Sentences*

Teacher's Classroom Resources

The following resources can be used for planning, instruction, practice, reinforcement, reteaching, or enrichment.

🔧 **Teaching Tools**
Lesson Plans

📁 **Blackline Masters**
Grammar Practice, p. 2
Grammar Reteaching, p. 3
Grammar Enrichment, p. 2

📘 ***Grammar Workbook***
Lesson 4

Exercise 5 — Identifying Subjects and Predicates

Write each sentence. Draw a line between the complete subject and the complete predicate.

1. Charles Dickens's first works consisted of articles about life in London.
2. These early works appeared under the name of Boz.
3. Their popularity led to publication of *Pickwick Papers*.
4. That first novel was highly successful.
5. Dickens wrote for the rest of his life.
6. Dickens's early experiences influenced much of his writing.
7. His only historical novel is *A Tale of Two Cities*.
8. *David Copperfield* is one of his most popular books.
9. The novel *Martin Chuzzlewit* reflects Dickens's trip to America.
10. The author gave dramatic readings of his works.

Exercise 6 — Identifying Subjects and Predicates

Write each item. Draw a vertical line between the complete subject and complete predicate. Underline the simple subject once and the simple predicate twice.

1. Charles Dickens wrote many great novels during his lifetime.
2. The English novelist remains a very popular writer.
3. He created memorable characters.
4. This very popular writer lived in poverty as a child.
5. Dickens lived with his family in London.
6. The youngster labored in a shoe polish factory at an early age.
7. The English courts sent Dickens's father to debtors' prison.
8. His family needed money then.
9. The young Dickens found work for a short while as a court stenographer.
10. He took notes at court for two years.
11. Dickens reported news for a local newspaper, too.
12. He published short articles on life in London.
13. His writing appeared first under a different name.
14. The best early articles appeared in *Sketches by Boz*.
15. His first novel was *Pickwick Papers*.
16. Most Dickens novels appeared in installments in periodicals.
17. People waited eagerly for each new chapter.
18. Dickens edited two periodicals.
19. My favorite Dickens novel is *Hard Times*.
20. Dickens's own favorite novel was *David Copperfield*.

8.3 Subjects and Predicates **331**

Answers: Exercise 5
In the actual sentences, all the words preceding the vertical line make up the complete subject and all of those following it make up the complete predicate.

1. works | consisted
2. works | appeared
3. popularity | led
4. novel | was
5. Dickens | wrote
6. experiences | influenced
7. novel | is
8. *David Copperfield* | is
9. *Martin Chuzzlewit* | reflects
10. author | gave

Answers: Exercise 6
1. Charles Dickens | wrote
2. novelist | remains
3. He | created
4. writer | lived
5. Dickens | lived
6. youngster | labored
7. courts | sent
8. family | needed
9. Dickens | found
10. He | took
11. Dickens | reported
12. He | published
13. writing | appeared
14. articles | appeared
15. novel | was
16. novels | appeared
17. People | waited
18. Dickens | edited
19. novel | is
20. novel | was

CLOSE

Write this sentence on the board: *My favorite Dickens character is Pip in Great Expectations.* Have one volunteer draw a vertical line between the complete subject and the complete predicate and another circle the simple subject and the simple predicate.

331

Enabling Strategies

LEP Identifying Simple Subjects and Predicates

Remind students that when people learn any language they generally begin with simple noun-verb sentences. Have students make a chart to help them determine the subject and predicate in the first five sentences in Exercise 5. Write all the nouns in one column and all the verbs in another column. For each sentence, have students find the words that go together in a simple noun-verb sentence that has the same meaning as the original sentence. These words are the simple subject and predicate.

FOCUS

Lesson Overview

Objective: To recognize the normal subject-predicate word order and the main exceptions to that order

🔔 Bellringer

When students enter the classroom, have this assignment on the board: *Explain the basic difference between these two sentences: Does Jeff's cat climb trees? and Jeff's cat climbs trees. Underline the subject of each sentence.*

Motivating Activity

Discuss students' answers in the Bellringer exercise. Explain that in an interrogative sentence, or one that begins with *Here* or *There,* part of the predicate precedes the subject.

TEACH

☑ Grammar Tip

Explain that students sometimes think the word *There*—as in the sentence *There are ghosts in Sleepy Hollow*—is the subject of the sentence. Note that *ghosts* is the real subject.

⮂ Cross-reference: Grammar

To help students identify interrogative and imperative sentences, refer them to Lesson 8.1, pp. 326–327. To help students identify *is* and *are* as linking verbs, refer them to Lesson 10.4, pp. 374–375.

8.4 | Identifying Subjects and Predicates

In most sentences the subject comes before the predicate.

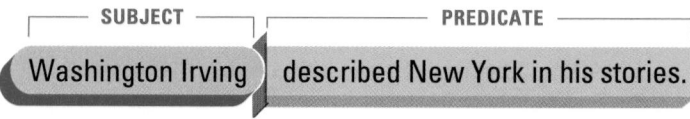

Other kinds of sentences, such as questions, begin with part or all of the predicate. The subject comes next, followed by the rest of the predicate.

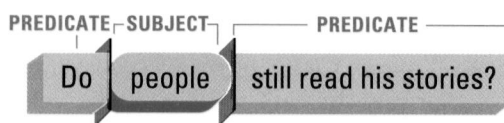

To locate the subject of a question, rearrange the words to form a statement.

Predicate	Subject	Predicate
Did	Irving	write many funny stories?
	Irving	did write many funny stories.

The predicate also precedes the subject in sentences with inverted word order and in declarative sentences that begin with *Here is*, *Here are*, *There is*, or *There are*.

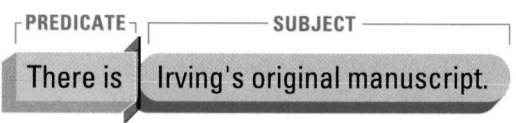

In requests and commands, the subject is usually not stated. The predicate is the entire sentence. The word *you* is understood to be the subject.

332 *Subjects, Predicates, and Sentences*

Teacher's Classroom Resources

The following resources can be used for planning, instruction, practice, reinforcement, reteaching, enrichment, or evaluation.

🔧 **Teaching Tools**
Lesson Plans

📁 **Blackline Masters**
Grammar Practice, p. 2
Grammar Reteaching
Grammar Enrichment, p.2

📘 *Grammar Workbook,*
Lessons 1, 2, and 4

Exercise 7 — Identifying the Subject in Sentences

Write the complete subject in each sentence. If the sentence is a command, write *(You)*.

1. Did Washington Irving achieve international fame?
2. Name two stories about Irving's childhood in New York.
3. There is a Washington Irving story with roots in German folklore.
4. Did Washington Irving live from 1783 to 1859?
5. Does Irving use a particular writing style in this tale?
6. Read Irving's satire on New York.
7. Examine Irving's humorous sketches of New York society first.
8. Did he write during his stay in England?
9. Did Irving devote himself completely to literature?
10. Has the class discussed his short story "The Legend of Sleepy Hollow"?
11. Here are Irving's two books on Columbus.
12. There are four books about his travels in Spain.
13. Study his style of writing.
14. Did Irving's *The Sketch Book* bring new importance to the short story?
15. Here is *The Sketch Book of Geoffrey Crayon*.
16. Do critics regard his short stories as his best achievement?
17. Discuss Irving's influence on other writers.
18. Here is a collection of his short stories.
19. There lies Irving's biography.
20. Did you read all of Irving's stories?

Exercise 8 — Identifying the Subjects and Predicates in Sentences

Write each sentence. If the sentence is a command, write *(You)* before it. Then, in each one, underline the complete subject once and the complete predicate twice.

1. Learn more about Washington Irving.
2. Was his life interesting?
3. Did Irving use the pen name Diedrich Knickerbocker?
4. There was *A History of New York* published under that name.
5. Find out the origin of his pen name.
6. Irving lived in Spain twice.
7. Was he interested in Spanish culture?
8. Did Irving represent the U.S. in Spain?
9. Tell about Irving's travels in the West.
10. Did Irving read his works to frontier audiences?

8.4 Identifying Subjects and Predicates **333**

PRACTICE AND ASSESS

Answers: Exercise 7
1. Washington Irving
2. You
3. a Washington Irving story with roots in German folklore
4. Washington Irving
5. Irving
6. You
7. You
8. he
9. Irving
10. the class
11. Irving's two books on Columbus
12. four books about his travels in Spain
13. You
14. Irving's *The Sketch Book*
15. *The Sketch Book of Geoffrey Crayon*
16. critics
17. You
18. a collection of his short stories
19. Irving's biography
20. you

Answers: Exercise 8
1. You learn more about Washington Irving.
2. Was his life interesting?.
3. Did Irving use the pen name Diedrich Knickerbocker?
4. There was *A History of New York* published under that name.
5. You Find out the origin of his pen name
6. Irving lived in Spain twice.
7. Was he interested in Spanish culture?
8. Did Irving represent the U.S. in Spain?
9. You Tell about Irving's travels in the West
10. Did Irving read his works to frontier audiences?

Independent Practice

Skills Practice
📁 *Grammar Practice*, p. 2
📁 *Grammar Reteaching*
📁 *Grammar Enrichment*, p. 2

📖 ***Grammar Workbook,***
Lesson 1, 2 and 4

Enabling Strategies

LEP Using Forms of Do
English uses the verb *do* for forming questions (*Did I see it?*) or tag questions (*You saw it, didn't you?*), for emphasis (*I did see it*), and for forming negatives (*He did not see it*). When a *do* question is turned into a statement, the *do* disappears. (*Did I see it?* becomes *I saw it.*)

CLOSE

Ask students to identify the kind of sentence, the subject, and the predicate of this quotation from Edgar Allan Poe's "The Raven": "*Take thy beak from out my heart and take thy form from off my door!*" (imperative sentence; both subjects: understood *you;* predicates: take thy beak from out my heart and take thy form from off my door)

Lesson 8.5 teaches students how to identify and use compound subjects and compound predicates in writing.

FOCUS

Lesson Overview

Objective: To make compound subjects agree with their predicates and compound predicates agree with their subjects

🔔 Bellringer

When students enter the classroom, have this assignment on the board: *What verb would you use for this sentence: Two dogs or a cat ___ all I want for my birthday.*

Motivating Activity

Talk about what verb students would use in the sentence above if the subject were only *two dogs*. What if it were *two dogs or two cats?* Why is it difficult to figure out which verb to use in the Bellringer sentence?

TEACH

Cooperative Learning

Have teams of students collect ten examples of compound subjects by looking at magazines, newspapers, and books. Each team can then hand their examples to another team. Have teams verify whether or not the examples show true compound subjects. They can check by asking *Who is doing the action?* For subjects joined by *and*, can *they* or *we* be substituted?

8.5 Compound Subjects and Compound Predicates

A sentence may have more than one simple subject or simple predicate.

A **compound subject** is two or more simple subjects that have the same predicate. The subjects are joined by *and*, *both . . . and*, *or*, *either . . . or*, *neither . . . nor*, or *but*.

COMPOUND SUBJECT

Charlotte Brontë and **Emily Brontë** were sisters.

When the two simple subjects are joined by *and* or by *both . . . and*, the compound subject is plural. Use the plural form of the verb to agree with this plural compound subject.

When the two simple subjects are joined by *or*, *either . . . or*, or *neither . . . nor*, however, the compound subject may be singular or plural. The verb must agree with the nearer simple subject.

Either **Charlotte** or **Emily** is my favorite author.
Neither **Charlotte** nor her **sisters** were outgoing.

In the first sentence, *Emily* is the nearer subject, and so the singular form of the verb is used. In the second sentence *sisters* is the nearer subject, and so the plural form is used.

A **compound predicate** is two or more simple predicates, or verbs, that have the same subject. The verbs are connected by *and*, *both . . . and*, *or*, *either . . . or*, *neither . . . nor*, or *but*.

COMPOUND PREDICATE

Many students **read** the novel *Jane Eyre* and **enjoy** it.

The compound predicate in this sentence consists of *read* and *enjoy*. Both verbs agree with the plural subject.

334 *Subjects, Predicates, and Sentences*

Teacher's Classroom Resources

Exercise 9   Identifying Compound Subjects and Predicates

Write whether each sentence has a *compound subject* or a *compound predicate*.

1. Either Charlotte or Emily Brontë will be the subject of my research paper entitled "A Great Nineteenth-century Novelist."
2. Neither Anne nor Emily is as well known as Charlotte.
3. Many readers have read and enjoyed their books.
4. Some scholars buy or sell rare editions of their books.
5. Neither the Brontë sisters nor their brother was long-lived.
6. The Brontë sisters lived and wrote in Yorkshire, England.
7. Charlotte's mother and sisters died early.
8. Anne Brontë both wrote novels and worked as a governess.
9. Scholars study and discuss the Brontës' novels.
10. Either *Wuthering Heights* or *Jane Eyre* is my favorite Brontë novel.

Exercise 10   Making Subjects and Verbs Agree

Write the correct form of the verb in parentheses.

1. Neither Emily Brontë's poems nor her one novel (deserve, deserves) to be forgotten.
2. Either *Wuthering Heights* or her poetic works (draw, draws) praise from critics everywhere.
3. Her writing (show, shows) an understanding of people and (reveal, reveals) her love of England.
4. Critics and other readers (discuss, discusses) and (praise, praises) her single novel.
5. Critics or other readers (pay, pays) more attention to Charlotte Brontë's works.
6. Charlotte's novel *Shirley* (paint, paints) a portrait of Emily and (show, shows) her feelings for her sister.
7. Charlotte's novels (reflect, reflects) her life experiences and (reveal, reveals) her dreams.
8. Both Anne Brontë's novel *Agnes Grey* and Charlotte's *The Professor* (tell, tells) love stories.
9. Charlotte's novels *Shirley* and *Villette* (receive, receives) less attention today.
10. Neither Anne's *The Tenant of Wildfell Hall* nor Charlotte's *Shirley* (attract, attracts) many readers today.

8.5 Compound Subjects and Compound Predicates   **335**

PRACTICE AND ASSESS

Answers: Exercise 9
1. compound subject
2. compound subject
3. compound predicate
4. compound predicate
5. compound subject
6. compound predicate
7. compound subject
8. compound predicate
9. compound predicate
10. compound subject

Answers: Exercise 10
1. deserves
2. draw
3. shows, reveals
4. discuss, praise
5. pay
6. paints, shows
7. reflect, reveal
8. tell
9. receive
10. attracts

Independent Practice

Skills Practice
📁 *Grammar Practice*, p. 2
📁 *Grammar Reteaching*, p. 3
📁 *Grammar Enrichment*, p. 2
📕 ***Grammar Workbook***, Lesson 5

CLOSE

Challenge students to write one sentence that has both a compound subject and a compound predicate. How did they decide which verb form to use?

Enabling Strategies

LEP Separating Compounds

To help students recognize the function of compound subjects and compound predicates, show them how to separate sentence 5 from Exercise 9 into two sentences: *The Brontë sisters were not long-lived. Their brother was not long-lived.*

Then have students make up sentences using *Either he or his sisters* and *Either his sisters or he* as a compound subject. Discuss why the verb changes.

Setting the Purpose

Lesson 8.6 teaches students how to write compound sentences using conjunctions and appropriate punctuation and how to correct run-on sentences.

FOCUS

Lesson Overview

Objective: To identify simple sentences, compound sentences, and run-on sentences

🔔 Bellringer

When students enter the classroom, have this assignment on the board: *Rewrite these two sentences to make one sentence: We planted corn and tomatoes. The rabbits and raccoons got most of them.*

TEACH

☑ Grammar Tip

Coordinating conjunctions (*and, but, or, for, yet, nor*) join words or groups of words of equal importance. They serve different functions: *and* introduces an addition, *but* a contrast, *or* a choice.

⇄ Cross-reference: Diagraming

For spatial presentation of compound sentences, see Lesson 18.7, p. 544.

⏱ Two-Minute Skill Drill

Correct the following run-on sentence: "I like avocados, they are especially good in guacamole".

336

8.6 Simple and Compound Sentences

A **simple sentence** has one subject and one predicate.

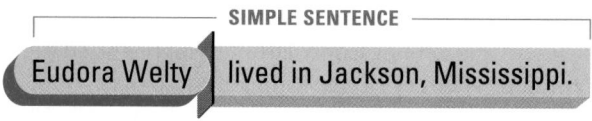

A simple sentence may have a compound subject, a compound predicate, or both, as in the following example.

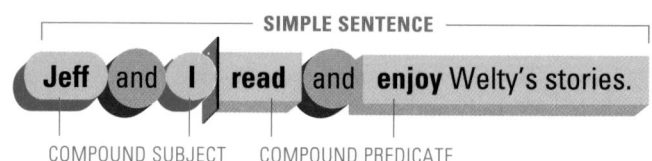

A **compound sentence** is a sentence that contains two or more simple sentences joined by a comma and a coordinating conjunction or by a semicolon.

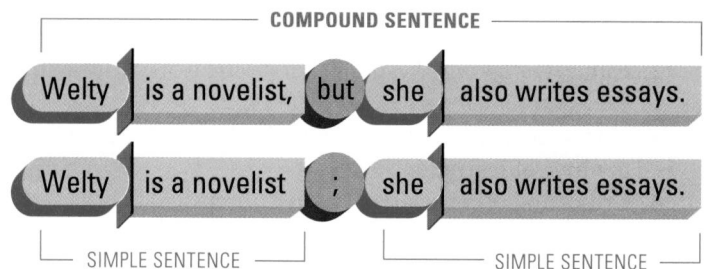

A run-on sentence is two or more sentences incorrectly written as one sentence. To correct a run-on, write separate sentences, or combine the sentences as shown below.

Correcting Run-on Sentences	
Run-on	**Correct**
Welty wrote novels she wrote essays.	Welty wrote novels. **S**he wrote essays.
Welty wrote novels, she wrote essays.	Welty wrote novels, **and** she wrote essays.
	Welty wrote novels**;** she wrote essays.

336   *Subjects, Predicates, and Sentences*

Teacher's Classroom Resources

The following resources can be used for planning, instruction, practice, reinforcement, reteaching, or enrichment.

🔧 **Teaching Tools**
Lesson Plans

📁 **Blackline Masters**
Grammar Practice, p. 3
Grammar Reteaching, p. 4
Grammar Enrichment, p. 3

📕 ***Grammar Workbook***
Lesson 6

Exercise 11   Identifying Simple and Compound Sentences

Write whether each sentence is *simple* or *compound*.

1. Elizabeth Barrett Browning and Robert Browning were poets.
2. They were famous for their poetry and their love.
3. Browning liked Elizabeth Barrett's poetry, and he wrote to her.
4. Elizabeth and Robert wrote hundreds of letters to each other.
5. Scholars and other people read and study these letters.
6. Elizabeth wanted to marry Robert, but her father forbade this.
7. The couple got married anyway, and they moved to Italy.
8. Her father never forgave her; he returned her letters unopened.
9. Elizabeth wrote love poems, and Robert wrote dramatic poems.
10. People still read and enjoy the couple's poems and letters.

Exercise 12   Identifying Simple, Compound, and Run-on Sentences

Write whether each sentence is *simple*, *compound*, or *run-on*. If it is a run-on sentence, rewrite it correctly.

1. Percy Bysshe Shelley lived and wrote in the nineteenth century.
2. He was a Romantic poet his wife, Mary Shelley, was a novelist.
3. Three of his poems are "Ozymandias," "Ode to a Skylark," and "Adonais."
4. *Frankenstein* was Mary Shelley's most famous novel.
5. Percy Shelley traveled in Europe and visited friends.
6. Shelley made friends with other poets; John Keats was Shelley's friend.
7. William Godwin was another friend, Shelley liked his daughter.
8. Mary Godwin and Percy Shelley met and fell in love.
9. Mary's father was a philosopher, her mother worked for women's rights.
10. Percy respected Mary's father and visited him often.
11. Percy and Mary married and went to Europe.
12. Mary and Percy were friendly with the poet Lord Byron.
13. Byron wrote long, beautiful poems; some of them are almost epic in scope.
14. Byron was one of the greatest Romantic poets students still study his work.
15. Byron, Keats, and Shelley were ranked together as great Romantic poets.
16. Poetry lovers and scholars read and discuss the men's poems.
17. I love Byron's lyrical poems, but some people prefer his satirical work.
18. *Childe Harold's Pilgrimage* and *Don Juan* are Byron's masterpieces.
19. Byron loved Greece, he traveled there.
20. He fell ill in Greece, and he died there.

8.6 Simple and Compound Sentences   **337**

Enabling Strategies

LEP Adding Commas
Some students may confuse conjunctions for other parts of speech and not add commas to their sentences. Have students cover words like *and*, *but*, *nor*, and *yet* in the sentence. If the two remaining parts are complete sentences, add a comma before the conjunction.

CLOSE

Write an explanation of how your state's tourist attractions could inspire a writer. Point out your state's best features. Use both simple and compound sentences.

TEACH

About the Literature

Explain that the review contains a passage from Russell Baker's *Growing Up,* followed by exercises on related topics. Russell Baker is probably best known as the author of the "Observer," a *New York Times* humorous commentary column. Baker was born in rural Virginia in 1925. His book *Growing Up* was published in 1982, and he received a Pulitzer Prize, his second, for it in 1983. Discuss how Russell Baker used various grammatical structures to convey his experience. How did he feel about having his writing enjoyed? What words tell about his feelings?

Linking Grammar and Literature

Speaking and Listening

Discuss how Baker's narrative would have been different if he had used only one or two types of sentence structure in his writing. For an example, read the highlighted compound sentence in the third paragraph. Then read it again as three simple sentences. Ask if that is the way people usually talk when they are telling a story. Talk about what makes listening to a story enjoyable.

Critical Thinking

To give students practice in classifying parts of speech and sentence structures, challenge them to find other elements in the passage that could have been highlighted and to suggest how they should be labeled.

338

Grammar Review

Subjects, Predicates, and Sentences

Russell Baker wrote about his early life in the memoir *Growing Up.* In this excerpt, he describes his reaction to having his work read publicly for the first time. The passage has been annotated to show some examples of the kinds of subjects, predicates, and sentences covered in this unit. Notice how he uses fragments for special effect.

Literature Model

from GROWING UP

by Russell Baker

"Now boys," he said, "I want to read you an essay. This is titled 'The Art of Eating Spaghetti.'"

And he started to read. My words! He was reading *my words* out loud to the entire class. What's more, the entire class was listening. Listening attentively. Then somebody laughed, then the entire class was laughing, and not in contempt and ridicule, but with openhearted enjoyment. Even Mr. Fleagle stopped two or three times to repress a small prim smile. . . .

For the first time, light shone on a possibility. It wasn't a very heartening possibility, to be sure. Writing couldn't lead to a job after high school, and it was hardly honest work, but Mr. Fleagle had opened a door for me. . . .

My mother was almost as delighted as I when I showed her Mr. Fleagle's A-Plus and described my triumph. Hadn't she always said I had a talent for writing?

Annotations (left margin):
- Fragment
- Complete predicate
- Fragment
- Simple subject
- Simple predicate
- Compound sentence
- Complete subject
- Interrogative sentence

338 *Subjects, Predicates, and Sentences*

Teacher's Classroom Resources

The following resources can be used for planning, instruction, practice, reinforcement, assessment, reteaching, enrichment, or evaluation.

Teaching Tools
Lesson Plans, p. 71

Grammar Workbook
Lessons 1–6
Unit 1 Review
Cumulative Review

Unit Assessment

Tests with Answer Key
Unit 8 Mastery Test, pp. 31–32

Test Generator
Unit 8 Mastery Test

Exercise 1

Identifying Sentences and Sentence Fragments   Write each sentence, and draw a line between the complete subject and the complete predicate. If it is a fragment, write *fragment*, and explain why it is a fragment.

SAMPLE   Said he could write.

ANSWER   fragment; no subject

1. Baker wrote an essay about eating spaghetti.
2. Mr. Fleagle read the essay out loud.
3. The entire class.
4. Laughed with genuine and honest good humor.
5. The author ranked Mr. Fleagle as one of the finest teachers.
6. He showed his mother the A-Plus on his paper.
7. Baker's proud mother.
8. Didn't think writing would lead to a job after high school.
9. This experience opened a door for him.
10. Baker's newspaper column is read by millions of people.

Exercise 2

Identifying Complete Subjects and Complete Predicates   Write each sentence. Underline the complete subject once and the complete predicate twice.

SAMPLE   The class studied English with Mr. Fleagle.

ANSWER   <u>The class</u> <u>studied English with Mr. Fleagle.</u>

1. Mr. Fleagle assigned the class an informal essay.
2. This form of writing seemed dull to Russell Baker.
3. A homework sheet listed a choice of topics.
4. Russell Baker chose "The Art of Eating Spaghetti."
5. That title brought up memories.
6. The young boy remembered a spaghetti dinner.
7. Not many people ate spaghetti in those days.
8. The family talked about this exotic dish.
9. Everyone had a good time that night.
10. Russell wrote about their funny arguments.

Grammar Review **339**

PRACTICE AND ASSESS

Answers: Exercise 1

1. Baker | wrote an essay about eating spaghetti.
2. Mr. Fleagle | read the essay out loud.
3. fragment; no predicate
4. fragment; no subject
5. The author | ranked Mr. Fleagle as one of the finest teachers.
6. He | showed his mother the A-plus on his paper.
7. fragment; no predicate
8. fragment; no subject
9. This experience | opened a door for him.
10. Baker's newspaper column | is read by millions of people.

Answers: Exercise 2

1. <u>Mr. Fleagle</u> assigned the class an informal essay.
2. <u>This form of writing</u> seemed dull to Russell Baker.
3. <u>A homework sheet</u> listed a choice of topics.
4. <u>Russell Baker</u> chose "The Art of Eating Spaghetti."
5. <u>That title</u> brought up memories.
6. <u>The young boy</u> remembered a spaghetti dinner.
7. <u>Not many people</u> ate spaghetti in those days.
8. <u>The family</u> talked about this exotic dish.
9. <u>Everyone</u> had a good time that night.
10. <u>Russell</u> wrote about their funny arguments.

UNIT 8
Review

Answers: Exercise 3
1. author; began
2. *Baltimore Sun;* hired
3. He; joined
4. reporter; covered
5. Baker; started
6. winner; received
7. columns; appear
8. humor; entertains
9. writer; became
10. Watchers; enjoy

Answers: Exercise 4
1. <u>Baker's mother</u> <u>had encouraged his writing skills.</u>
2. <u>Baker's teacher</u> <u>did like his essay.</u>
3. <u>The class</u> <u>did enjoy the essay.</u>
4. <u>The class</u> <u>was laughing at Baker's story</u>.
5. <u>Everyone</u> <u>did like the essay.</u>
6. <u>Baker</u> <u>did get an A-plus on his paper.</u>
7. <u>This experience</u> <u>did give Baker ideas about a career.</u>
8. <u>Mr. Fleagle</u> <u>had opened a door for Baker.</u>
9. <u>Mr. Fleagle</u> <u>was one of the finest teachers in Baker's school.</u>
10. <u>Baker's mother</u> <u>was pleased with her son.</u>

Exercise 3

Identifying Simple Subjects and Simple Predicates   Write the simple subject and the simple predicate for each sentence.

SAMPLE   Russell Baker wanted a career in newspapers.
ANSWER   Russell Baker wanted

1. The author began his career in journalism in 1947.
2. The *Baltimore Sun* hired the young journalist.
3. He joined the *New York Times* in 1954.
4. The new *Times* reporter covered the White House and Congress.
5. Baker started his "Observer" column in 1962.
6. The award winner received the Pulitzer Prize in 1979.
7. His columns appear in several collections.
8. Baker's humor entertains millions of people.
9. The writer became a television host.
10. Watchers of *Masterpiece Theater* enjoy Baker's introductions to the show.

Exercise 4

Identifying Subjects and Predicates in Questions   Rewrite each question to form a statement. Then underline each complete subject once and each complete predicate twice.

SAMPLE   Was the story about spaghetti?
ANSWER   <u>The story</u> <u>was about spaghetti.</u>

1. Had Baker's mother encouraged his writing skills?
2. Did Baker's teacher like his essay?
3. Did the class enjoy the essay?
4. Was the class laughing at Baker's story?
5. Did everyone like the essay?
6. Did Baker get an A-Plus on his paper?
7. Did this experience give Baker ideas about a career?
8. Had Mr. Fleagle opened a door for Baker?
9. Was Mr. Fleagle one of the finest teachers in Baker's school?
10. Was Baker's mother pleased with her son?

Exercise 5

Identifying Subjects and Predicates   Write the simple subject and the simple predicate in each sentence. If the sentence is a command, write *(You)*.

SAMPLE   Was Russell Baker born in Virginia?
ANSWER   Russell Baker   was born

1. Find out about Baker's early life.
2. Was Baker's father a stonemason?
3. Did his mother teach school?
4. Was Baker's sister named Doris?
5. Here is a picture of Baker's family.
6. Point to Baker in the picture.
7. Did Baker win a college scholarship?
8. Tell the name of his college.
9. There are many books by Russell Baker.
10. Read *Growing Up*.

Exercise 6

Identifying Compound Subjects and Compound Predicates   Write whether the sentence has a *compound subject* or a *compound predicate*.

SAMPLE   The cook boils spaghetti and adds sauce.
ANSWER   compound predicate

1. Russell Baker and his family ate spaghetti one night.
2. They enjoyed the food and argued about technique.
3. Both children and adults like spaghetti.
4. People all over the world prepare and eat pasta.
5. The Italians created and named dozens of different types of pasta.
6. The Chinese and the Japanese use noodles in many dishes.
7. My family and I eat ziti often.
8. Mom boils the ziti and covers it with sauce.
9. She adds cheese and bakes the ziti.
10. My sister and I wait with our forks ready!

Grammar Review   **341**

Answers: Exercise 5
1. You; find out
2. father; was
3. mother; did teach
4. sister; was named
5. picture; is
6. You; point
7. Baker; did win
8. You; tell
9. books; are
10. You; read

Answers: Exercise 6
1. compound subject
2. compound predicate
3. compound subject
4. compound predicate
5. compound predicate
6. compound subject
7. compound subject
8. compound predicate
9. compound predicate
10. compound subject

UNIT 8
Review

Answers: Exercise 7
1. attracts
2. praise
3. earn
4. create
5. interest
6. affect; delight
7. win
8. enjoy
9. appear; sell
10. proves

Answers: Exercise 8
1. compound
2. simple
3. compound
4. compound
5. simple
6. simple
7. compound
8. compound
9. simple
10. compound

Exercise 7

Making Compound Subjects and Verbs Agree Write the correct form of the verb in parentheses.

1. Russell Baker's wisdom or his humor (attract, attracts) readers.
2. Critics and other readers (praise, praises) his autobiography.
3. *Growing Up* or his other books (earn, earns) him fame.
4. Baker's childhood memories and stories (create, creates) a picture of his family.
5. His family and his life (interest, interests) readers.
6. His words and his voice (affect, affects) and (delight, delights) people.
7. His newspaper columns or his television appearances (win, wins) praise.
8. Critics or other viewers (enjoy, enjoys) his commentaries.
9. His columns and poems (appear, appears) regularly and (sell, sells) well.
10. The George Polk Award or the Pulitzer Prize (prove, proves) his worth.

Exercise 8

Identifying Simple and Compound Sentences Write whether each sentence is *simple* or *compound*.

1. Russell Baker began his journalism career at the age of eight; his mother got him a job.
2. He and his mother met and talked to a man from Curtis Publishing Company.
3. The man liked Russell, and he hired the boy.
4. Russell began his career at the bottom; he sold the *Saturday Evening Post.*
5. Russell placed the magazines in a bag and walked to a busy intersection.
6. He stood on a corner and waited for customers.
7. Russell waited for hours, but no one bought a single magazine.
8. Russell's mother was upset by this, and she taught Russell about salesmanship.
9. Russell's uncle felt sorry for the boy and bought a magazine.
10. Russell handed him a magazine, and Uncle Allen paid Russell a nickel.

Exercise 9

Identifying Compound Sentences and Run-on Sentences   Write whether each sentence is *compound* or *run-on*. If it is a run-on sentence, rewrite it correctly.

1. Russell Baker's mother wanted him to do well, and she encouraged him to study.
2. She didn't have much money, but she bought books and literary magazines for Russell.
3. Russell wasn't interested in literature he never read the books.
4. The magazines didn't appeal to him, he didn't read them either.
5. Russell's friend Charlie applied to Johns Hopkins University; he encouraged Russell to apply, also.
6. Russell's family couldn't afford college, but Charlie told him about scholarships.
7. Russell applied for a scholarship to Johns Hopkins he didn't expect to get it.
8. Many students wanted scholarships they had to pass an exam.
9. The exam lasted four hours, and Russell worried about passing it.
10. Two weeks later a letter came from Johns Hopkins, Russell had won the scholarship.

Exercise 10

Writing Compound Sentences   Combine each pair of simple sentences to form a compound sentence. Use the coordinating conjunction *and, but,* or *or.*

1. Russell Baker grew up in Baltimore. His first job was with a Baltimore newspaper.
2. Baker dreaded Mr. Fleagle's reaction. Mr. Fleagle liked Baker's story very much.
3. Mr. Fleagle read Baker's story to the class. The class enjoyed it.
4. Baker could have covered his ears. He could have left the room.
5. Baker needed a real job. He loved to write anyway.

Answers: Exercise 9
1. compound
2. compound
3. run-on—Russell wasn't interested in literature, and he never read the books.
4. run-on—The magazines didn't appeal to him; he didn't read them either.
5. compound
6. compound
7. run-on—Russell applied for a scholarship to Johns Hopkins, but he didn't expect to get it.
8. run-on—Many students wanted scholarship, but they had to pass an exam.
9. compound
10. run-on—Two weeks later a letter came from Johns Hopkins; Russell had won the scholarship.

Answers: Exercise 10
1. …Baltimore, and his first…
2. …reaction, but Mr. Fleagle liked…
3. …to the class, and the class enjoyed it.
4. …covered his ears, or he could…
5. …real job, but he…

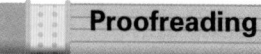

Exercise 11   **Proofreading**

The following passage is about American artist Joseph Raffael, whose work appears below. Rewrite the passage, correcting the errors in spelling, capitalization, grammar, and usage. Add any missing punctuation. There are ten errors. ➡

Joseph Raffael, *Joseph and Reuben,* **1984**

344   *Subjects, Predicates, and Sentences*

About the Art

Joseph Raffael, *Joseph and Reuben,* **1984**
Joseph Raffael, born in 1933, produced many photorealistic oil paintings during the 1960s. He then changed his media from oil to watercolor, pastel, and lithography and began creating a more impressionistic look. Of his work, Raffael has said: "I like to think I paint feeling. I am interested in spirit as expressed in nature, the invisible made visible." *Joseph and Reuben,* an oil-on-canvas painting, measures 84 1/4 inches by 72 1/4 inches. It is in the Nancy Hoffman Gallery in New York.

Joseph Raffael

[1] Joseph Raffael is an american artist known for his brightly colored paintings of landscapes, fish, flowers, and birds. [2] In the painting on the opposite page, however, Raffael has took a different approach. [3] Its a portrait of the artist and his son, who appear as if they were posing. [4] For a photograph

[5] The strong contrast between light and dark in the painting add to the effect and give it the accidental quality of a snapshot. [6] Raffael is experimanting with the different qualities of light and color. [7] The colors—from the warm yellow to the deep purple—are as much the subject of the painting as the artist and his' son. [8] What a dramatic portrait this is

Mixed Review

Exercise 12

Identify the underlined words as *complete* or *simple subjects* or *complete* or *simple predicates*. Write *C* beside any compound subjects or predicates.

1. Russell Baker <u>showed his talent in high school.</u>
2. His English <u>teacher</u> assigned the class an essay.
3. <u>Baker and the other students</u> had a choice of topics.
4. Baker <u>chose and wrote about the topic "The Art of Eating Spaghetti."</u>
5. <u>Another title for Baker's essay</u> might have been "How Not to Eat Spaghetti."
6. Baker's <u>teacher</u> returned everyone's paper but Baker's.
7. Mr. Fleagle <u>read</u> Baker's essay to the class.
8. <u>Mr. Fleagle's encouragement and support</u> gave Baker food for thought.
9. <u>The young writer</u> liked to make people laugh.
10. He <u>thought</u> about journalism as a career.
11. Journalism <u>couldn't lead to a job and wasn't honest work.</u>
12. Many people <u>write for a career.</u>
13. <u>Both magazines and newspapers</u> use many writers.
14. Newspaper reporters <u>gather information and write articles.</u>
15. <u>Columnists such as Russell Baker</u> present their opinions and ideas to the readers.
16. <u>Writers</u> for magazines write articles on a wide variety of topics.
17. Other writers <u>create</u> books of fiction and nonfiction.
18. Some writers <u>combine words with photography and create photo essays.</u>
19. <u>All these possibilities</u> are open to a young writer.
20. Russell Baker <u>finally realized his luck.</u>

Grammar Review **345**

CLOSE

Have students discuss what they have learned about sentences and sentence structure and how this helps them communicate effectively when speaking and writing. Make sure that students recognize that understanding and meaning develop when sentences and paragraphs contain the elements studied in this unit.

Answers: Exercise 11
Proofreading

This proofreading activity provides editing practice with (1) the current or previous units' skills, (2) the **Troubleshooter** errors, and (3) spelling errors. Students should be able to complete the exercise by referring to the units, the **Troubleshooter,** and a dictionary.

	Error (Type of Error)
1.	• American (proper adjective)
2.	• taken (verb form)
3.	• It's (contraction)
4.	• posing for (sentence fragment)
	• photograph. (end punctuation)
5.	• adds (subject–verb agreement)
	• gives (subject–verb agreement)
6.	• experimenting (spelling)
7.	• his (possessive pronoun)
8.	• is! (end punctuation)

Answers: Exercise 12
Mixed Review

1. complete predicate
2. simple subject
3. complete subject; compound subject
4. complete predicate; compound predicate
5. complete subject
6. simple subject
7. simple predicate
8. complete subject; compound subject
9. complete subject
10. simple predicate
11. complete predicate; compound predicate
12. complete predicate
13. complete subject; compound subject
14. complete predicate; compound predicate
15. complete subject
16. simple subject
17. simple predicate
18. complete predicate; compound predicate
19. complete subject
20. complete predicate

Sentence Patterns in Writing

Have students read the paragraph from *The Heart of a Woman* aloud without interruption. Then have them go back and discuss the sentence structures in relation to the Techniques with Sentence Patterns below.

Techniques with Sentence Patterns

Ask students to find other examples of repetitive or choppy sentence patterns in something they have read or written recently. Ask them how such patterns could have been avoided.

Practice

The answers to this challenging and enriching activity will vary. Refer to Techniques with Sentence Patterns as you evaluate student choices. Sample answer:

Last year my dad made me some shelves for my rock collection. <u>I watched as he cut and sanded the wood.</u> Perched up on top of some old boxes, <u>I could feel the vibrations of the saw as it sliced through each length of wood.</u> Buzzing filled the room. Sawdust piled up like blonde snow under the workbench. <u>I wanted to help, but Dad said why didn't I just keep him company.</u> So I told him stories <u>about my rocks, describing</u> where they came from. It was a special time together.

Writing Application

Sentence Patterns in Writing Maya Angelou varies both the length and the organization of her sentences in this passage from *The Heart of a Woman*. Pay particular attention to the sentence structure.

> I had worked two months for the SCLC, sent out tens of thousands of letters and invitations signed by Rev. King, made hundreds of statements in his name, but I had never seen him up close. He was shorter than I expected and so young. He had an easy friendliness, which was unsettling. Looking at him in my office, alone, was like seeing a lion sitting down at my dining-room table....

Techniques with Sentence Patterns Try to apply some of Maya Angelou's techniques when you write and revise your own work.

1. Mix short and long sentences to create variety. Compare the following:
Repetitive sentence pattern He had an easy friendliness. It was unsettling. I looked at him in my office. It was like seeing a lion sitting down at my dining-room table.
Improved version He had an easy friendliness, which was unsettling. Looking at him in my office, alone, was like seeing a lion sitting down at my dining-room table....

2. Combine two simple sentences into one compound sentence to communicate related ideas:
Choppy version I had made hundreds of statements in his name. I had never seen him up close.
Improved version I had made hundreds of statements in his name, but I had never seen him up close.

Practice Revise the following passage on a separate sheet of paper. Pay particular attention to the underlined words.
　　Last year my dad made some shelves for my rock collection. <u>I watched as he cut the wood. Then he sanded it.</u> Perched on top of some old boxes, <u>I could feel the vibrations of the saw. I watched it slice through each length of wood.</u> Buzzing filled the room. Sawdust piled up like blonde snow. <u>I wanted to help. Dad said why didn't I just keep him company.</u> So I told him stories <u>about my rocks. I described</u> where they came from. It was a special time together.

346 *Writing Application*

Teacher's Classroom Resources

The following resources can be used for assessment or evaluation.

Unit Assessment
📁 *Tests with Answer Key*
Unit 8 Mastery Test, pp. 31–32

📷 *Test Generator*
Unit 8 Mastery Test

You may wish to administer the Unit 8 Mastery Test at this point.

UNIT
9

Grammar

Nouns

Lessons

347

UNIT GOALS

The goal of Unit 9 is to help students, through example and instruction, to develop an understanding of the various kinds and forms of nouns and to use them appropriately. Lessons focus on common, proper, abstract, and concrete nouns; compound nouns and their plurals; possessive nouns; collective nouns; and appositives.

Unit Assessment

Tests with Answer Key
Unit 9 Pretest, pp. 33–34
Unit 9 Mastery Test, pp. 35–36

Test Generator
Unit 9 Pretest
Unit 9 Mastery Test

You may wish to administer the Unit 9 Pretest at this point.

Key to Ability Levels

Enabling Strategies have been coded for varying learning styles and abilities.

L1 Level 1 activities are within the ability range of Learning Disabled students.

L2 Level 2 activities are basic-to-average activities and are within the ability range of average students.

L3 Level 3 activities are challenging activities and are within the ability range of above-average students.

LEP LEP activities are within the ability range of Limited English Proficiency students.

347

FOCUS

Lesson Overview

Objective: To identify common and proper nouns, and concrete and abstract nouns

Bellringer

When students enter the classroom, have this assignment on the board: *List all the nouns in this excerpt from a letter in* Underground Railroad.

"Levi Coffin, by his devotion to the cause of the fugitive from boyhood to old age, gained the title of 'President of the Underground Railroad,' but he was not at the head of a formal organization. In truth the work was everywhere spontaneous."

TEACH

☑ Grammar Tip

Tell students that if a noun is something they can experience with any of their five senses—touch, sight, hearing, smell, taste—then it is a concrete noun. If they are unable to experience it with their senses, it is an abstract noun.

⇄ Cross-reference: Mechanics

To help students capitalize names and titles correctly, refer them to Lesson 19.2, pp. 552–553.

9.1 Kinds of Nouns

Look at the incomplete sentence below. Decide which of the words in the box that follows can complete the sentence.

The historian wrote about many famous _____

women	colorful	places	events
ago	ideas	did	pretty

The words *women, ideas, places,* and *events* can complete the sentence. These words are called nouns.

A **noun** is a word that names a person, place, thing, or idea.

There are two basic kinds of nouns: proper nouns and common nouns.

A **proper noun** names a *specific* person, place, thing, or idea.

A **common noun** names *any* person, place, thing, or idea.

The first word and all other important words in proper nouns are capitalized.

Common nouns can be either concrete or abstract.

Concrete nouns name things that you can see or touch.

Abstract nouns name ideas, qualities, or feelings that cannot be seen or touched.

Kinds of Nouns		
Common		Proper
Abstract	Concrete	
truth	document	Supreme Court
courage	crown	Queen Victoria
time	snow	December
history	museum	Museum of Anthropology
heritage	buffalo	Native American

348 *Nouns*

Teacher's Classroom Resources

The following resources can be used for planning, instruction, practice, reinforcement, assessment, reteaching, enrichment, or evaluation.

🔧 **Teaching Tools**
Lesson Plans

📁 **Blackline Masters**
Grammar Practice, p. 4
Grammar Reteaching, p. 4
Grammar Enrichment, p. 4

📕 *Grammar Workbook*
Lessons 7–8

Unit Assessment

📁 *Tests with Answer Key*
Unit 9 Pretest, pp. 33–34

💿 *Test Generator*
Unit 9 Pretest

You may wish to administer the Unit 9 Pretest at this point.

Exercise 1   Identifying Common and Proper Nouns

Write each noun that appears in the following sentences. Indicate whether each is a *common noun* or a *proper noun*. Remember to capitalize each proper noun.

1. A baby named isabella began life in slavery in the united states.
2. Slavery was allowed in the united states before the civil war.
3. Isabella worked very hard as a child.
4. The slaveholder chose a husband for isabella.
5. Isabella had thirteen children.
6. Isabella later became a free person.
7. Then isabella took the name sojourner truth.
8. This brave crusader worked for the freedom of women and african americans.
9. Sojourner truth traveled around the country.
10. Sojourner talked about the evils of slavery.
11. The brave woman spoke to large numbers of people in many states.
12. The speaker faced danger on many occasions.
13. Sojourner truth became famous as a result of her many speeches.
14. Sojourner met with president abraham lincoln at the white house.
15. After her visit with the president, sojourner stayed in washington, d.c.
16. She worked to improve conditions for african americans in the city.
17. She helped find work for other people who had once been enslaved who had come to washington.
18. Like sojouner truth, harriet tubman was also born in slavery in maryland.
19. Harriet tubman led her people to freedom on the underground railroad.
20. Sojourner truth and harriet tubman were important women in history.

Exercise 2   Identifying Concrete and Abstract Nouns

Write *abstract* or *concrete* for each underlined noun.
1. Born in <u>slavery</u>, Frederick Douglass escaped and fled to Massachusetts.
2. In 1841 he addressed a meeting and talked about <u>freedom</u>.
3. After he spoke, he was hired to talk to other <u>groups</u>.
4. It took <u>courage</u> for him to speak out as he did.
5. After his <u>autobiography</u> was published in 1845, he went to England.
6. When he returned, he continued to talk about his <u>beliefs</u>.
7. He helped <u>men</u>, <u>women</u>, and <u>children</u> flee to Canada.
8. Frederick Douglass is honored by many <u>people</u> in this <u>country</u>.
9. Douglass's books are appreciated for their <u>honesty</u>.
10. He was an important <u>person</u> in the <u>history</u> of the United States.

9.1 Kinds of Nouns **349**

PRACTICE AND ASSESS

Answers: Exercise 1
1. baby, life, slavery—common; Isabella, United States—proper
2. slavery—common; United States, Civil War—proper
3. Isabella—proper; child—common
4. slaveholder, husband—common; Isabella—proper
5. Isabella—proper; children—common
6. Isabella—proper; person—common
7. Isabella, Sojourner Truth—proper; name—common
8. crusader, freedom, women—common; African Americans—proper
9. Sojourner Truth—proper; country—common
10. Sojourner—proper; evils, slavery—common
11. woman, numbers, people, states—common
12. speaker, danger, occasions—common
13. Sojourner Truth—proper; result, speeches—common
14. Sojourner, President Abraham Lincoln, White House—proper
15. visit, president—common; Sojourner, Washington, D.C.—proper
16. conditions, city—common; African Americans—proper
17. work, people—common; Washington—proper
18. Sojourner Truth, Harriet Tubman, Maryland—proper; slavery—common
19. Harriet Tubman, Underground Railroad—proper; people, freedom—common
20. Sojourner Truth, Harriet Tubman—proper; women, history—common

Answers: Exercise 2
1. abstract
2. abstract
3. concrete
4. abstract
5. concrete
6. abstract
7. concrete
8. concrete
9. abstract
10. person—concrete; history—abstract

Independent Practice
Skills Practice
📁 *Grammar Practice,* p. 4
📁 *Grammar Reteaching,* p. 4
📁 *Grammar Enrichment,* p. 4

📁 **Grammar Workbook**
Lessons 7–8

Enabling Strategies

LEP Using Noncount Nouns
Students may have difficulty with nouns that cannot be counted, such as *homework*. Noncount nouns fall into the following groups: fluids, particles, gases, abstractions (such as *honesty*), phenomena (such as *weather*), and collections (such as *clothing*).

CLOSE

Have students write a paragraph using common and proper nouns and concrete and abstract nouns. Ask them to exchange paragraphs with a partner and check each other's work.

FOCUS

Lesson Overview

Objective: To identify different forms of compound nouns and to form plurals of compound nouns

Bellringer

When students enter the classroom, have this assignment on the board: *Write down three examples of nouns that are made up of two or more words. Example: homework*

Motivating Activity

Review students' answers to the Bellringer activity. Have them make the words they wrote plural. Discuss any irregular spelling changes.

TEACH

☑ Teaching Tip

There is no reliable way to predict whether a compound will be spelled as one word, hyphenated, or spelled as more than one word. Most compound nouns can be recognized by their unusual stress pattern of placing the emphasis on the first word. Compare: a *supermarket* is a grocery store, but a *super market* is a fantastic market.

9.2 | Compound Nouns

The noun *storybook* is made up of two words: *story* and *book*. Such a noun is called a compound noun.

Compound nouns are nouns made of two or more words.

A compound noun can be one word, like *storybook;* more than one word, like *ice cream;* or joined by hyphens, like *runner-up.*

Compound Nouns	
One word	housekeeper, showcase, bookmark, football, storybook
Hyphenated	mother-in-law, runner-up, great-grandmother, kilowatt-hour
More than one word	dining room, ice cream, maid of honor, music box

To form the plural of compound nouns written as one word, add -*s* or -*es*. To form the plural of compound nouns that are hyphenated or written as more than one word, make the most important part of the compound noun plural.

Forming Plural Compound Nouns		
	Singular	Plural
One word	Add **-s** to most words. Add **-es** to words that end in **ch, sh, s,** or **x.** Exception:	football**s**, headlight**s** strongbox**es**, rosebush**es** passer**s**by
Hyphenated	Make the most important part of the compound noun plural.	great-grandmother**s**, runner**s**-up, mother**s**-in-law
More than one word	Make the most important part of the compound noun plural.	maid**s** of honor, music box**es**

Whether the compound noun is singular or plural, the verb must agree with it.

> My sister-in-law **writes** books.   My sisters-in-law **write** books.

Teacher's Classroom Resources

The following resources can be used for planning, instruction, practice, reinforcement, reteaching, or enrichment.

🔧 **Teaching Tools**
Lesson Plans

📁 **Blackline Masters**
Grammar Practice, p. 4
Grammar Reteaching, p. 4
Grammar Enrichment, p. 4

📖 **Grammar Workbook**
Lesson 9

Exercise 3   Making Compound Nouns Plural

Write the plural form of each compound noun below.

1. lifeguard
2. vice-principal
3. golf club
4. master-at-arms
5. sweet potato
6. father-in-law
7. sheepskin
8. window sash
9. president-elect
10. clubhouse
11. textbook
12. police station
13. passerby
14. roller skate
15. headache
16. music box
17. flight deck
18. great-grandson
19. driving range
20. drugstore

Exercise 4   Using Plural Compound Nouns

Write each sentence, using the plural form of the compound noun in parentheses.

1. Voters go to (ballot box) to determine who is president.
2. The White House is the residence for each of our (commander in chief).
3. All (vice president) have had another residence.
4. Many (sergeant-at-arms) guard the White House.
5. John Adams was the first of the (chief executive) to live there.
6. (Sightseer) flock to the White House.
7. (Editor in chief) of newspapers must show passes to enter the White House.
8. President Franklin D. Roosevelt had small (swimming pool) added to the residence.
9. Under President John F. Kennedy, (guidebook) to the building's history were published.
10. Presidents can have daily (workout) in the gymnasium.
11. (Grandparent) sometimes visit the White House.
12. Overnight visitors sleep in (guest room) on the second floor.
13. In 1908 a meeting on the conservation of (natural resource) was held in the White House.
14. Many of the visitors to the White House are (jobholder).
15. In the West Wing are (workplace) for the president's staff.
16. Once a week the Cabinet, a group of (policymaker), gathers for a meeting.
17. Some presidents asked their daughters or (daughter-in-law) to serve as hostesses.
18. A meeting of (map maker) was held in the map room, a private area.
19. At the White House no (shortcut) are taken where security is concerned.
20. (Political scientist) study how the White House operates.

9.2 Compound Nouns   **351**

PRACTICE AND ASSESS

Answers: Exercise 3

1. lifeguards
2. vice-principals
3. golf clubs
4. masters-at-arms
5. sweet potatoes
6. fathers-in-law
7. sheepskins
8. window sashes
9. presidents-elect
10. clubhouses
11. textbooks
12. police stations
13. passersby
14. roller skates
15. headaches
16. music boxes
17. flight decks
18. great-grandsons
19. driving ranges
20. drugstores

Answers: Exercise 4

1. ballot boxes
2. commanders in chief
3. vice presidents
4. sergeants-at-arms
5. chief executives
6. Sightseers
7. Editors in chief
8. swimming pools
9. guidebooks
10. workouts
11. grandparents
12. guest rooms
13. natural resources
14. jobholders
15. workplaces
16. policymakers
17. daughters-in-law
18. map makers
19. shortcuts
20. Political scientists

Independent Practice

Skills Practice

📁 *Grammar Practice,* p. 4
📁 *Grammar Reteaching,* p. 4
📁 *Grammar Enrichment,* p. 4

📓 **Grammar Workbook,** Lesson 9

CLOSE

Have students describe what they would do if elected president of the United States. Ask them to use compound nouns in their writing.

Enabling Strategies

LEP Recognizing Compounds

Many languages do not form compounds in the same way that English does. Work with students to review the three types of compounds taught in the lesson. Encourage students to note the types in their journals for future reference. Students can circle the two (or more) words that make up each compound, confirm that each is a word, and write the meanings of the individual words and the compound word. Have students compare the way these compounds are formed with the way compounds are formed in their home languages.

FOCUS

Lesson Overview

Objective: To identify different forms of possessive nouns

🔔 Bellringer

When students enter the classroom, have this assignment on the board: *Rewrite the following sentence to include the word* has. *Jake's watch is broken.*

Motivating Activity

Discuss students' answers to the Bellringer activity. (*Jake has a broken watch.*) Ask what *has* and the *s* in *Jake's* have in common. (They both show possession.)

TEACH

☑ Grammar Tip

To see if a noun is possessive, try replacing the noun with a possessive personal pronoun: *his, her, its,* or *their.* If you can, the noun is likely to be possessive.

☑ Teaching Tip

You may wish to have students rewrite a sentence containing a possessive noun to include either *has* or *have.* For example, students can change the sentence *Ike's dog is happy* to *Ike has a happy dog.* While this takes some practice to learn, it's a reliable way to identify possessive nouns.

9.3 | Possessive Nouns

A noun can be singular, naming only one person, place, thing, or idea; or it can be plural, naming two or more. A noun can also show ownership or possession of things or qualities. This kind of noun is called a possessive noun.

A **possessive noun** names who or what owns or has something.

Possessive nouns can be common nouns or proper nouns. They can also be singular or plural. Notice the possessive nouns in the following sentences:

> **Rita** has a book on history.
> **Rita's** book is new.
>
> Read the **books**.
> Note the **books'** major themes.

Possessive nouns are formed in one of two ways. To form the possessive of most nouns, you add an apostrophe and -*s* (*'s*). This is true for all singular nouns and for plural nouns not ending in -*s*. To form the possessive of plural nouns already ending in -*s*, you add only an apostrophe. These rules are summarized in the chart below.

Forming Possessive Nouns		
Nouns	**To Form Possessive**	**Examples**
Most singular nouns	Add an apostrophe and **-s** (**'s**).	a girl—a girl**'s** name a country—a country**'s** products
Singular nouns ending in **-s**	Add an apostrophe and **-s** (**'s**).	Lewis—Lewis**'s** explorations Chris—Chris**'s** homework
Plural nouns ending in **-s**	Add an apostrophe (**'**).	animals—animals**'** habits the Joneses—the Joneses**'** car
Plural nouns not ending in **-s**	Add an apostrophe and **-s** (**'s**).	women—women**'s** history children—children**'s** history

352 *Nouns*

Teacher's Classroom Resources

The following resources can be used for planning, instruction, practice, reinforcement, reteaching, enrichment, or evaluation.

🔧 **Teaching Tools**
Lesson Plans, p. 73

📁 **Blackline Masters**
Grammar Practice, p. 5
Grammar Reteaching, p. 5
Grammar Enrichment, p. 5

📕 ***Grammar Workbook***
Lesson 9

Exercise 5 — Forming Possessive Nouns

Write the possessive form of each underlined word or group of words.

1. Queen Elizabeth reign
2. documents pages
3. Arizona landscape
4. citizens rights
5. Dickens work
6. people choice
7. King Charles laws
8. women rights
9. city law
10. children books
11. artists works
12. birds nests
13. car engine
14. New England weather
15. democracy benefits
16. whales bones
17. Cape Cod bicycle trails
18. song refrain
19. book theme
20. Andy Warhol soup cans

Exercise 6 — Using Possessive Nouns

For each sentence write the correct possessive form of the noun in parentheses.

1. Meriwether Lewis was one of (Virginia) famous people.
2. He shared many (children) love of exploring.
3. Lewis served as President (Jefferson) personal secretary.
4. Jefferson guided (Lewis) preparations for an expedition.
5. Lewis and William Clark explored the (nation) uncharted territory.
6. Lewis depended on (Clark) skill at map making.
7. The (expedition) route ran through the Louisiana Territory and the Oregon region.
8. With the (Native Americans) help, they were able to cross the Rocky Mountains.
9. The team spent more than two (years) time in the Northwest.
10. They followed the Columbia (River) waters to the Pacific Ocean.
11. The (explorers) friends in St. Louis thought they had died on their trek.
12. The (men) bravery won great praise.
13. Later John Charles Frémont followed in Lewis and (Clark) footsteps.
14. (Frémont) explorations took him to Oregon, Nevada, and California.
15. He inspired Americans to oppose (Mexico) control of California.
16. He served as (California) U.S. Senator from 1850–1851.
17. In 1856 he became the Republican (party) first candidate for president.
18. In the Civil War he commanded one of the Union (Army) departments.
19. Strongly antislavery, he took over (slaveholders) lands in Missouri.
20. Frémont was married to (Thomas Hart Benton) daughter.

9.3 Possessive Nouns **353**

PRACTICE AND ASSESS

Answers: Exercise 5

1. Queen Elizabeth's
2. documents'
3. Arizona's
4. citizens'
5. Dickens's
6. people's
7. King Charles's
8. women's
9. city's
10. children's
11. artists'
12. birds'
13. car's
14. New England's
15. democracy's
16. whales'
17. Cape Cod's
18. song's
19. book's
20. Andy Warhol's

Answers: Exercise 6

1. Virginia's
2. children's
3. Jefferson's
4. Lewis's
5. nation's
6. Clark's
7. expedition's
8. Native Americans'
9. years'
10. River's
11. explorers'
12. men's
13. Clark's
14. Frémont's
15. Mexico's
16. California's
17. party's
18. Army's
19. slaveholders'
20. Thomas Hart Benton's

Independent Practice

Skills Practice

📁 *Grammar Practice,* p. 5
📁 *Grammar Reteaching,* p. 5
📁 *Grammar Enrichment,* p. 5

📘 **Grammar Workbook,** Lesson 9

CLOSE

Have students use possessive nouns to write a short paragraph in which they imagine that they've been exploring the wilderness for the last two years. What would they miss the most? the least? Tell them to use some possessive nouns.

Enabling Strategies

LEP Practicing Writing Possessive Nouns

Ask groups of students to replace possessive phrases (the possessive noun plus the object that it possesses) with a *have* sentence, and then have them write the correct form of the possessive noun with its apostrophe.

Lesson 9. 4 teaches students how to form plurals, plural possessives, singular possessives, and contractions to use in their writing.

FOCUS

Lesson Overview

Objective: To distinguish between plurals, possessives, and contractions

Bellringer

When students enter the classroom, have this assignment on the board: *Copy the following sentences: Ian's house was just painted. The color's an odd shade of purple. It was his parents' choice. The painters worked on the house for a week.*

Underline the words that mean more than one or show possession.

Motivating Activity

Discuss students' answers to the Bellringer activity. (*Ian's* and *parents'* show possession; *painters* means more than one) Point out that the *'s* in *color's* indicates a contraction, not a plural or a possessive.

TEACH

☑ Teaching Tip

Tell students to identify possessive nouns by the *has* or *have* technique and contractions by expanding the contracted form back to the full form and then punctuating accordingly.

9.4 Distinguishing Plurals, Possessives, and Contractions

Most plural nouns, most possessive nouns, and certain contractions end with the letter -*s*. As a result they sound alike and can be easily confused. Their spellings and meanings are different, however.

Noun Forms and Contraction

	Example	Meaning
Plural Noun	The **students** wrote a play.	more than one student
Plural Possessive Noun	The **students'** play is good.	the play of the students
Singular Possessive Noun	I saw the **student's** play.	the play of one student
Contraction	The **student's** the author.	The student is the author.

A **contraction** is a word made by combining two words into one and leaving out one or more letters. An apostrophe shows where the letters have been omitted.

In the chart below, notice that the plural nouns do not have an apostrophe. The plural possessive nouns end with an apostrophe. The singular possessive nouns end with an apostrophe and an -*s*. You can tell these words apart by the way they are used in a sentence.

Noun Forms and Contractions

Plural Nouns	Contractions	Singular Possessive Nouns	Plural Possessive Nouns
speakers	speaker's	speaker's	speakers'
women	woman's	woman's	women's
echoes	echo's	echo's	echoes'
countries	country's	country's	countries'

354 *Nouns*

Teacher's Classroom Resources

The following resources can be used for planning, instruction, practice, reinforcement, reteaching, or enrichment.

Teaching Tools
Lesson Plans, p. 73

Blackline Masters
Grammar Practice, p. 5
Grammar Reteaching, p. 6
Grammar Enrichment, p. 5

Grammar Workbook
Lesson 11

Exercise 7   **Forming Possessives and Contractions**

Write each sentence, adding apostrophes to the possessive nouns and the contractions.

1. Woodrow Wilson was Americas twenty-eighth president.
2. As a student at Princeton, he joined the schools debating society.
3. Before becoming president, he served as Princeton Universitys president.
4. Wilsons regarded today as an educational and political reformer.
5. He was elected New Jerseys governor in 1910.
6. His success in New Jersey brought him to the Democrats attention.
7. Wilsons first term of office as president began in 1913.
8. The wars outbreak in Europe kept his attention on foreign affairs.
9. During his second term, he helped make the peace among Europes powers.
10. He had a stroke and was not able to fight for the peace treatys acceptance.

Exercise 8   **Using Plurals, Possessives, and Contractions**

Write the word in parentheses that correctly completes each sentence.

1. Herman (Melville's, Melvilles) a great American writer.
2. Herman (Melville's, Melvilles) life was full of adventure.
3. Melville traveled on sailing (ships, ship's) as a young man.
4. The (sailor's, sailors') lives were full of challenges.
5. Did Melville keep a record of his (experience's, experiences)?
6. Melville began his (adventures', adventures) as a cabin boy in 1837.
7. The young (man's, mans') destination was Liverpool.
8. (Liverpool's, Liverpools') an important city in Great Britain.
9. Special ships hunted (whales', whales) at this time.
10. These whaling (ships', ships) crews searched the world for whales.
11. (Whales, Whales') blubber provided many products.
12. (Nantucket's, Nantuckets) wealth depended on trade in whale products.
13. You can still visit the whaling (captains, captains') beautiful homes there.
14. Melville joined a whaling (ships, ship's) crew in 1841.
15. He visited the beautiful (islands, islands') of the Pacific Ocean.
16. Melville wrote (books', books) about his experience.
17. The public enjoyed this (writers', writer's) work.
18. In his masterpiece, *Moby Dick*, (sailors, sailors') hunt a great white whale.
19. The book describes the (dangers, dangers') of life aboard a whaling ship.
20. At the time, few people appreciated the (books, book's) power.

9.4 Distinguishing Plurals, Possessives, and Contractions   **355**

PRACTICE AND ASSESS

Answers: Exercise 7

1. America's	6. Democrat's
2. school's	7. Wilson's
3. University's	8. war's
4. Wilson's	9. Europe's
5. Jersey's	10. treaty's

Answers: Exercise 8

1. Melville's	11. Whales'
2. Melville's	12. Nantucket's
3. ships	13. captains'
4. sailors'	14. ship's
5. experiences	15. islands
6. adventures	16. books
7. man's	17. writer's
8. Liverpool's	18. sailors
9. whales	19. dangers
10. ships'	20. book's

Independent Practice

Skills Practice

 *Grammar Practice,* p. 5

Grammar Reteaching, p. 6

Grammar Enrichment, p. 5

Grammar Workbook, Lesson 11

CLOSE

Write the following sentences on the board: *That kitten's sure cute. The kitten's fur is the color of taffy. I wonder how many kittens were in the litter. The kittens' owners must be thrilled!* Have volunteers tell whether each underlined word is a plural noun, a plural possessive noun, a singular possessive noun, or a contraction.

Enabling Strategies

LEP **Writing Plural and Possessive Nouns**

Students whose first language is not English may experience difficulty in writing plural and possessive nouns correctly. Remind them to focus on the meaning of the noun in the sentence in order to determine if an apostrophe is needed. Pair students and have them find examples of plurals and possessives in one of their textbooks. Ask them to explain to each other the intended meanings of the examples. Then have them share their findings with the class.

FOCUS

Lesson Overview
Objective: To identify collective nouns and to understand that collective nouns can be singular or plural

Bellringer
When students enter the classroom, have this assignment on the board: *Correct these sentences:*
1. *My family like adventure movies the best.*
2. *My family likes to make their lunches themselves.*

Motivating Activity
Discuss students' answers to the Bellringer. Did they choose *like* for the second sentence? Explain that collective nouns are usually singular and treat the group that the noun refers to as a single unit. The problem arises when the members of the group act individually. Ask students if *My family like to make their own sandwiches* sounds funny—or incorrect—to them.

TEACH

Cross-reference: Grammar
For instruction and practice of matching verbs to collective nouns, refer students to Lesson 16.3, pp. 512–513.

9.5 Collective Nouns

A **collective noun** names a group that is made up of individuals.

Collective Nouns			
committee	audience	swarm	club
family	team	crowd	orchestra
flock	class	jury	herd

Nouns and verbs always must show agreement in sentences. Collective nouns, however, present special agreement problems. Every collective noun can have either a singular meaning or a plural meaning. If you speak about the group as a unit, then the noun has a singular meaning. If you want to refer to the individual members of the group, then the noun has a plural meaning.

The **crowd move** to their favorite spots.

The **crowd cheers.**

> The **crowd cheers** the passing parade. [refers to group as a unit, singular]
> The **crowd move** to their favorite spots along the parade route. [individual members, plural]

When you are thinking of the group as a unit, use a collective noun and the form of the verb that agrees with a singular noun. When you want to refer to the individual members of the group, use the collective noun and the form of the verb that agrees with a plural noun.

To help you determine whether a collective noun in a sentence is singular or plural, substitute the word *it* for the collective noun and any words used to describe it. If the sentence still makes sense, the collective noun is singular. If you can substitute *they*, the collective noun is plural.

> The **team** works on its project. [it, singular]
> The **team** work on their separate projects. [they, plural]

356 *Nouns*

Teacher's Classroom Resources

The following resources can be used for planning, instruction, practice, reteaching, reinforcement, or enrichment.

 Teaching Tools
Lesson Plans

 Grammar Practice, p. 4
 Grammar Enrichment, p. 4

 Grammar Workbook
Lesson 10

Exercise 9   Identifying Singular and Plural Collective Nouns

For each sentence write the collective noun. Write *singular* or *plural* to describe it.

1. The group received first place in the competition.
2. The crowd in the club danced the entire night.
3. The gaggle of geese made a tremendous racket.
4. The students were given a range of choices on the test.
5. After the program, the band played an encore.
6. The family received a memento of the event.
7. The jury returned to their seats.
8. Company came to dinner last night.
9. A majority of the players voted to cancel the game.
10. The infantry fought from a dangerous position.

Exercise 10   Using Collective Nouns

For each sentence write the collective noun. Then write the correct form of the verb in parentheses.

1. The class of seventh-graders (describes, describe) their vacations.
2. The entire class (meets, meet) at 2:00 P.M. every day.
3. The family (takes/take) their biggest towels with them to the beach.
4. The film club (devours/devour) its popcorn in the darkened theater.
5. Girl Scout Troop 39 (presents, present) a tribute to athletes.
6. The committee (argues, argue) among themselves over the suggestion.
7. The audience (cheers, cheer) its favorite contestants.
8. The orchestra (performs, perform) my favorite symphony.
9. The football team (eats/eat) its pregame meal in silence.
10. The herd (returns, return) to the same meadow each year.
11. The crowd of students (claps, clap) their hands to the music.
12. The public (supports, support) its local basketball team.
13. The whole wolf pack (roams, roam) the countryside.
14. The audience (shows/show) its approval by clapping and whistling.
15. The jury (reaches, reach) its verdict.
16. The battalion (marches, march) five miles each day.
17. The majority of stockholders (demands/demand) their ballots.
18. That family (takes, take) their responsibilities very seriously.
19. The whole litter (is, are) being given away to another family.
20. The flock of geese (grooms/groom) their feathers after the rain.

9.5 Collective Nouns   **357**

Enabling Strategies

LEP Comparing Usage

In American English, collective nouns are used in the singular when referring to an entire group; they are used in the plural when referring to all the individual members of a group. In British English, however, collective nouns are almost always used in the plural. Compare the following sentences. American: *The team is on the field.* British: *The team are on the field.* Students who have learned British English will tend to use all collective nouns in the plural.

FOCUS

Lesson Overview

Objective: To place and punctuate appositives accurately

🔔 Bellringer

When students enter the classroom, have this assignment on the board: *In the sentence "My friend Paula wants to go to Germany," what does the word* Paula *contribute to the sentence?*

Motivating Activity

Discuss how the sentence above would be different without the word *Paula.* Would the listener or reader know which friend is being discussed? Ask students if they sometimes forget to include necessary details when speaking or writing.

TEACH

☑ Grammar Tip

Point out that when deciding whether to use commas with an appositive, students can ask themselves, *Is the appositive essential to the meaning or not?* If not, they should use commas. If it is essential, commas are not necessary.

◖ Vocabulary Link

The word *appositive* comes from the Latin verb *apponere*, which means "to place near."

9.6　Appositives

An **appositive** is a noun that is placed next to another noun to identify it or add information about it.

> James Madison's wife **Dolley** was a famous first lady.

The noun *Dolley* adds information about the noun *wife* by giving the wife's name. *Dolley* in this sentence is an appositive.

An **appositive phrase** is a group of words that includes an appositive and other words that describe the appositive.

> Madison, **our fourth president**, held many other offices.

The words *our fourth* describe the appositive *president.* The phrase *our fourth president* is an appositive phrase. It adds information about the noun *Madison.*

An appositive or appositive phrase can appear anywhere in a sentence as long as it appears next to the noun that it identifies.

> **Our fourth president**, Madison held many other offices.
> Many historians have studied the life of Madison, **our fourth president**.

An appositive phrase is usually set off from the rest of the sentence with one or more commas. If, however, the appositive is needed to identify the noun or if it is a single word, you do not use commas.

> Madison's friend **Thomas Jefferson** was president before him.
> Madison's father, **James Madison,** was a plantation owner.

Since Madison had more than one friend, the name *Thomas Jefferson* is needed to identify this particular friend. No commas are needed. Since Madison had only one father, however, the father's name is not needed to identify him. Then commas are used.

358　*Nouns*

Teacher's Classroom Resources

Exercise 11 Identifying Appositive Phrases

Write each sentence. Underline each appositive noun or phrase, and draw an arrow to the noun it identifies. Add commas where they are needed.

1. Madison and his friend Jefferson formed a new political party.
2. This party the Democratic-Republican party was the forerunner of the present Democratic party.
3. Thomas Jefferson the author of the Declaration of Independence was the third president.
4. Jefferson appointed his friend James Madison as secretary of state.
5. The Louisiana Purchase one of Madison's most significant achievements took place in 1803.
6. Madison and his vice president George Clinton were elected in 1809.
7. Dolley Madison a vivacious and very pleasant hostess was known for her extravagant parties.
8. Britain and France two major powers were engaged in a trade war.
9. In 1812 the United States declared war on Great Britain a much stronger nation.
10. American forces tried to take Canada a British territory but they were unsuccessful.

Exercise 12 Using Appositives

Write each sentence, using commas around appositives where needed.

1. James Madison grew up on Montpelier a plantation.
2. He attended Princeton a college in New Jersey.
3. Madison a dedicated student completed college in two years.
4. He first held office in his home colony Virginia.
5. In 1776 Thomas Jefferson another young politician served in the first state assembly with Madison.
6. Madison a devoted patriot served in the Continental Congress.
7. He also represented his home state Virginia at the Constitutional Convention of 1787.
8. Madison a believer in strong government played an active role at the convention.
9. He wrote *The Federalist* with his colleagues Hamilton and Jay.
10. A series of letters to newspapers *The Federalist* still offers the best explanation of the Constitution.

9.6 Appositives **359**

PRACTICE AND ASSESS

Answers: Exercise 11
1. <u>Jefferson</u>—friend
2. , <u>the Democratic-Republican party</u>—party
3. , <u>the author of the Declaration of Independence</u>—Thomas Jefferson
4. <u>James Madison</u>—friend
5. , <u>one of Madison's most significant achievements</u>—The Louisiana Purchase
6. , <u>George Clinton,</u>—vice president
7. , <u>a vivacious and very pleasant hostess</u>—Dolley Madison
8. , <u>two major powers</u>—Britain and France
9. , <u>a much stronger nation</u>—Great Britain
10. , <u>a British territory</u>—Canada

Answers: Exercise 12
1. … Montpelier, a plantation.
2. … Princeton, a college …
3. Madison, a dedicated student, completed …
4. … in his home colony, Virginia.
5. … Thomas Jefferson, another young politician, served …
6. Madison, a devoted patriot, served …
7. … state, Virginia, at the …
8. Madison, a believer in strong government, played …
9. … colleagues, Hamilton and Jay.
10. … newspapers, *The Federalist*, still …

Independent Practice

Skills Practice
📁 *Grammar Practice,* p. 6
📁 *Grammar Reteaching,* p. 7
📁 *Grammar Enrichment,* p. 6
📖 *Grammar Workbook,* Lesson 12

Enabling Strategies

LEP Using Appositives
LEP students may experience difficulty using appositives and appositive phrases. Tell them to see if they can substitute the phrase for the word they are adding information about. If the word or phrase cannot be substituted, it is probably a noun modifier and not an appositive.

CLOSE

Ask volunteers to give examples of appositives that are essential and nonessential. Is there any disagreement? Why might that be?

359

TEACH

About the Literature

African American writer James Haskins, born in 1941 in Alabama, has written biographies of many important African Americans, including Barbara Jordan, Adam Clayton Powell, Scott Joplin, and Stevie Wonder. Haskins, who has also written about such topics as gang violence and Harlem night life, has received a Notable Children's Book award in the field of social studies. His interest in writing for young people is probably a carryover from his public school teaching days in New York City, from 1966 to 1968.

After students read the passage, discuss Jordan's groundbreaking speech as an African American representative. Ask students to focus on the highlighted words in the passage.

Linking Grammar and Literature

☑ Grammar Tip

If students have difficulty remembering the correct treatment of possessive nouns, explain that the apostrophe in the possessive form stands for the phrase *belongs to.* Write on the board a sentence that students can change so that it will contain a possessive noun. For example, you write *The chair belongs to John.* Then have a student change *John* to a possessive by writing *This is John's chair.*

UNIT

9

Unit Review

Grammar Review

Nouns

Barbara Jordan, by James Haskins, is a biography of the first African American woman from Texas to serve in the United States Congress. The following passage contains an excerpt from Jordan's keynote speech at the 1976 Democratic National Convention. The passage has been annotated to show some of the kinds of nouns covered in this unit.

Literature Model

from BARBARA JORDAN
by James Haskins

Common noun —— "One hundred and forty-four years ago, members of the Democratic Party first met in convention to select

Concrete noun —— a presidential candidate. Since that time Democrats have continued to convene once every four years and draft a party platform and nominate a presidential candidate. . . .

"But there is something different about tonight. There is something special about tonight. What is

Appositive —— different? What is special? I, Barbara Jordan, am a

Singular noun —— keynote speaker."

She was interrupted by wild applause and cheering, and she would be interrupted again and again as she

Plural noun —— spoke of the problems of the country and her hopes for

Proper noun —— America. . . . The overwhelming response was one of

Abstract noun —— pride, not just from women because she was a woman, not just from blacks because she was black, not just from Democrats or from Texans, but from all segments of the population, because she was an American.

360 *Nouns*

Teacher's Classroom Resources

The following resources can be used for planning, instruction, practice, reinforcement, assessment, reteaching, enrichment, or evaluation.

 Teaching Tools
Lesson Plans, p. 74

 Grammar Workbook
Lessons 7–12
Unit 2 Review
Cumulative Review: Units 1–2

Unit Assessment
 Tests with Answer Key
Unit 9 Mastery Test, pp. 35–36

 Test Generator
Unit 9 Mastery Test

Exercise 1

Identifying Kinds of Nouns   Write each noun that appears in the following sentences. Indicate whether each is a *common noun* or a *proper noun*. (Remember to capitalize each proper noun.)

SAMPLE   As keynote speaker, barbara jordan had an important role.
ANSWER   speaker, common; Barbara Jordan, proper; role, common

1. Texas is the birthplace of barbara jordan.
2. It gained independence from mexico in the last century.
3. It is bordered by the states of oklahoma, arkansas, and louisiana.
4. The rio grande forms the southern border.
5. Texas has many artificial lakes formed from dams on rivers.
6. The weather is usually very hot.
7. Some places average 48 inches of precipitation a year.
8. Oil fields produce many gallons of petroleum.
9. The arkansas national wildlife refuge is home to some rare birds.
10. Major cities include dallas, houston, and san antonio.

Exercise 2

Using Possessive Nouns   For each sentence write the correct possessive form of the singular or plural noun in parentheses.

SAMPLE   Washington, D.C., is our (nation) capital.
ANSWER   nation's

1. It is the (committee) decision to report out the bill.
2. Here is the minority (party) report on the bill.
3. Hearings will be held in a (month) time.
4. This new law will affect the (nation) postal system.
5. Senator (Jones) bill goes to the floor of the Senate tomorrow.
6. Not everyone agrees with the (bill) provisions.
7. Both (sides) opinions have to be taken into consideration.
8. The (members) votes were tallied by computer.
9. The House will now debate the (Senate) version of the bill.
10. The bill still requires the (president) signature.

Grammar Review **361**

PRACTICE AND ASSESS

Answers: Exercise 1
1. Texas, proper; birthplace, common; Barbara Jordan, proper
2. independence, common; Mexico, proper; century, common
3. states, common; Oklahoma, Arkansas, Louisiana: proper
4. Rio Grande, proper; border, common
5. Texas, proper; lakes, dams, rivers: common
6. weather, common
7. places, inches, precipitation, year: common
8. oil fields, gallons, petroleum: common
9. Arkansas National Wildlife Refuge, proper; home, birds: common
10. cities, common; Dallas, Houston, San Antonio: proper

Answers: Exercise 2
1. committee's
2. party's
3. month's
4. nation's
5. Jones's
6. bill's
7. sides'
8. members'
9. Senate's
10. president's

UNIT 9
Review

Answers: Exercise 3
1. party's
2. Democrats'
3. convention's
4. convention's
5. Style's
6. Democrats'
7. America's
8. women's
9. population's
10. Jordan's

Answers: Exercise 4
1. chooses
2. meets
3. state
4. nominates
5. deliver

Exercise 3

Using Plurals, Possessives, and Contractions The following sentences are based on the passage from *Barbara Jordan*. Write the word in parentheses that correctly completes the sentence.

SAMPLE The audience cheered (Jordans, Jordan's) speech.
ANSWER Jordan's

1. Barbara Jordan described the Democratic (parties, party's) first meeting.
2. She was welcomed by listeners at the (Democrats, Democrats') convention.
3. There is something special about being the (conventions, convention's) keynote speaker.
4. A (conventions, convention's) an important part of choosing a presidential candidate.
5. (Styles, Style's) an important aspect of public speaking.
6. The applause and cheers expressed the (Democrats, Democrats') pride in the congresswoman from Texas.
7. A better (Americas, America's) everyone's hope for the future, including Jordan's.
8. Jordan also talked about (womens, women's) rights.
9. This country's (populations, population's) impressed by speeches like Jordan's.
10. (Jordans, Jordan's) still a notable force in American politics.

Exercise 4

Using Collective Nouns Each sentence contains a collective noun. Write the form of the verb in parentheses that agrees with the noun.

SAMPLE The audience (roars, roar) its approval during the keynote speech.
ANSWER roars

1. A committee (chooses, choose) the convention city.
2. The group (meets, meet) to draft its party's policies.
3. Then the committee (states, state) their opinions.
4. During the convention, the party (nominates, nominate) its candidates for president and vice president.
5. After both candidates have been nominated, the team (delivers, deliver) their speeches.

Exercise 5

Using Appositives The following sentences are about Barbara Jordan. Write each sentence, adding the appositive or appositive phrase. Add a comma or commas where needed. In some cases more than one answer may be possible.

SAMPLE Barbara Jordan received her law degree from Boston University. (a lawyer)

ANSWER Barbara Jordan, a lawyer, received her law degree from Boston University. **OR**
A lawyer, Barbara Jordan received her law degree from Boston University.

1. When Jordan was born, Texas was segregated by race. (her home state)
2. In high school Jordan did very well in debating. (the art of formal discussion)
3. Her university had only African American teachers and students. (Texas Southern)
4. Jordan studied law at an integrated school. (Boston University)
5. After returing to Houston, Jordan became involved in local politics. (a lawyer with her own practice)
6. In 1960 Jordan campaigned for John F. Kennedy. (the Democratic nominee)
7. Kennedy's running mate was a Texan like Jordan. (Lyndon Johnson)
8. Jordan was asked to run for office in Texas. (a strong organizer and speaker)
9. Jordan was elected to the Texas State Senate in 1966. (a good campaigner)
10. The senate awarded her the Outstanding Senator Award her first year. (a body of thirty-one members)
11. Lyndon Johnson invited Jordan to a conference. (the vice president)
12. The participants discussed fair housing proposals. (civil rights leaders)
13. Jordan served in the House of Representatives. (a Texas Democrat)
14. She sat on the House Judiciary Committee. (a very important assignment)
15. Jordan took a firm stand when the committee voted to impeach Richard Nixon. (the president)
16. Jordan said that no one should lie to the American people. (freedom's champion)
17. Jordan has worked to promote the good of the country. (a role model)
18. She worked to pass legislation banning discrimination and dealing with another important issue. (the environment)
19. Jordan was also asked to address the Democratic National Convention in 1992. (a powerful speaker)
20. The audience's response to Jordan's speech was a tribute to a notable American. (a standing ovation)

Grammar Review **363**

18. She worked to pass legislation banning discrimination and dealing with the environment, another important issue.
19. A powerful speaker, Jordan was also asked to address the Democratic National Convention in 1992.
20. The audience's response to Jordan's speech, a standing ovation, was a tribute to a notable American.

Answers: Exercise 5

Answers will vary, but some suggestions are given below.

1. When Jordan was born, Texas, her home state, was segregated by race.
2. In high school Jordan did very well in debating, the art of formal discussion.
3. Her university, Texas Southern, had only African American teachers and students.
4. Jordan studied law at Boston University, an integrated school.
5. After returning to Houston, Jordan, a lawyer with her own practice, became involved in local politics.
6. In 1960 Jordan campaigned for John F. Kennedy, the Democratic nominee.
7. Kennedy's running mate, Lyndon Johnson, was a Texan like Jordan.
8. Jordan, a strong organizer and speaker, was asked to run for office in Texas.
9. Jordan, a good campaigner, was elected to the Texas State Senate in 1966.
10. The Senate, a body of thirty-one members, awarded her the Outstanding Senator Award her first year.
11. Lyndon Johnson, the vice president, invited Jordan to a conference.
12. The participants, civil rights leaders, discussed fair housing proposals.
13. Jordan, a Texas Democrat, served in the House of Representatives.
14. She sat on the House Judiciary Committee, a very important assignment.
15. Jordan took a firm stand when the committee voted to impeach Richard Nixon, the president.
16. Jordan, freedom's champion, said that no one should lie to the American people.
17. Jordan, a role model, has worked to promote the good of the country.

UNIT 9
Review

Answers: Exercise 6
Proofreading
This proofreading activity provides editing practice with (1) the current or previous units' skills, (2) the **Troubleshooter** errors, and (3) spelling errors. Students should be able to complete the exercise by referring to the units, the **Troubleshooter,** and a dictionary.

	Error (Type of Error)
1.	• Matisse, (nonessential appositive phrase)
2.	• century's (singular possessive)
3.	• painters' (plural possessive)
	• were (subject–verb agreement)
4.	• attempt (spelling)
5.	• Matisse's (singular possessive)
	• represent (subject–verb agreement)
6.	• shapes (plural noun)
7.	• birds (plural noun)
8.	• She's (contraction)

Exercise 6	Proofreading

The following passage is about the artist Henri Matisse, whose work appears below. Rewrite the passage, correcting the errors in spelling, grammar, and usage. Add any missing punctuation. There are ten errors.

Henri Matisse
[1] Henri Matisse a French artist, was the leader of the Fauves. [2] This group of painters began one of the twentieth centurys important art movements. [3] These painter's bright colors and simple designs was one of their trademarks.

[4] Matisse made no atempt to represent reality in his colorful paintings or in the compositions he made from paper cutouts. [5] Many of Matisses cutouts represents dancers. [6] In the cutout shown below, the vivid colors and bold shape's suggest an enormous energy. [7] The dancer stands proud and tall among the birds' and flowers. [8] Shes full of strength and dignity.

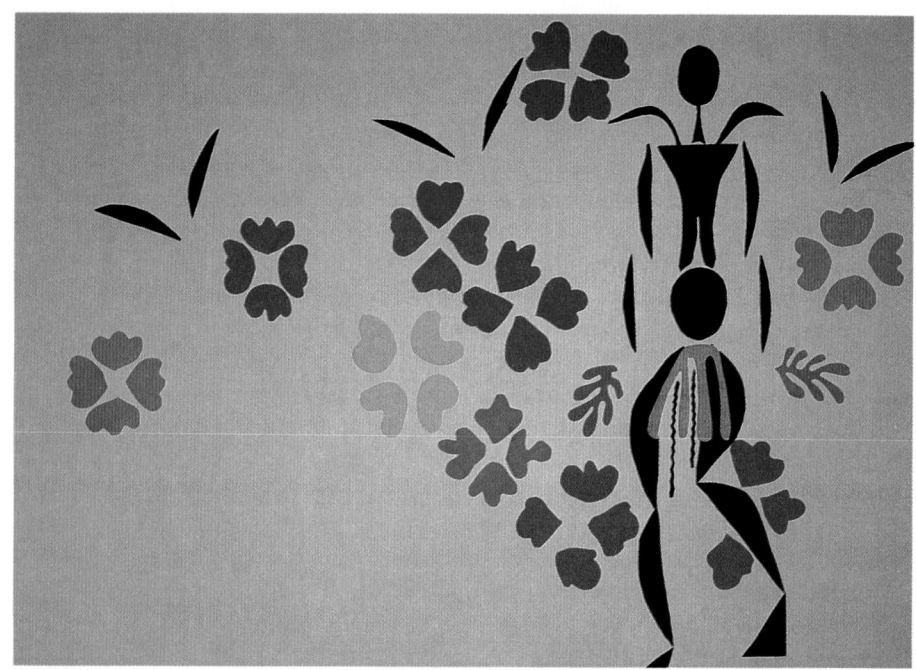

Henri Matisse, *La Négresse,* **1952**

364 *Nouns*

About the Art

Henri Matisse, *La Négresse,* **1952**
Although Henri Matisse's (1869–1954) favorite subjects included women, interior scenes, and still lifes, he thought design—not subject matter—was the important part of a piece of art.

Most of Matisse's artworks are paintings, but this piece was created from paper cutouts—a medium he turned to late in his life. The painting hangs in the National Gallery of Art, Washington, D.C.

Exercise 7

Mixed Review

Identify the underlined nouns in the paragraph as *common, proper, collective,* or *possessive.* More than one label may apply to a single noun.

Franklin Delano Roosevelt

[1]Franklin Delano Roosevelt inspired [2]Americans with his famous speeches, as well as with his actions. He became [3]president in 1933, when the country was in the depths of the [4]Great Depression. The [5]public was suffering, and many people were starving. His inaugural [6]address's words gave Americans [7]courage and confidence. His bold [8]words, "The only thing we have to fear is fear itself," called for faith in our [9]country.

Born into a wealthy [10]family, he believed strongly in public service. At the age of thirty-nine, Roosevelt was stricken with polio. His [11]legs were paralyzed, and he was never able to stand without help. Eleven years later he was elected president of the United States, following [12]President Herbert Hoover.

In [13]"The Hundred Days" after he first took office in 1933, Roosevelt launched his [14]New Deal. The laws that he introduced and that Congress passed helped the unemployed, farmers, [15]industry, and the common worker.

Though the Great Depression continued, Roosevelt won ordinary [16]citizens' admiration and affection. He was elected president four times—a [17]record unmatched by any other president.

Roosevelt knew how to reach voters. He was the first president to use the radio effectively to speak directly to the American [18]people. He often addressed the [19]nation in radio talks that were called "fireside chats." The public liked the sound of his [20]voice and gained [21]confidence in him and in the [22]ideals that he represented.

At the time of [23]Japan's attack on Pearl Harbor, Roosevelt, in his address before Congress, called December 7, "a date that will live in infamy." [24]Roosevelt's ringing words inspired Americans and helped prepare them for the long and very difficult [25]war that lay ahead. Roosevelt met many times during the war with Winston Churchill, the prime minister of [26]England, and with [27]Joseph Stalin, the premier of Russia.

Roosevelt died in April 1945, just before the end of the war. A huge [28]crowd gathered at the [29]White House as word of his death spread. He was deeply mourned by millions of people all over the [30]world.

Grammar Review **365**

Answers: Exercise 7
Mixed Review
Answers may vary, but some suggestions are given below.
1. proper
2. proper
3. common
4. proper
5. collective
6. common
7. common
8. common
9. common
10. common
11. common
12. proper
13. proper
14. proper
15. common
16. possessive, common
17. common
18. common
19. common
20. common
21. common
22. common
23. possessive, proper
24. possessive, proper
25. common
26. proper
27. proper
28. collective
29. proper
30. common

CLOSE

Pair students and have them choose an article from the newspaper. Then ask them to find examples of the various kinds of nouns they have studied in this unit. Ask students to highlight or underline their choices, and label each choice with its type of noun. Have students share and discuss their results with another pair of students.

Nouns in Writing

Have students read the passage from *Thrashin' Time* silently. You may wish to read it aloud without interruption, and then go back and discuss with students the italicized nouns. Discuss these nouns in relation to the Techniques with Nouns section below.

Techniques with Nouns

Discuss each of the techniques listed. You may want to analyze a previous example, such as the paragraphs about Franklin Delano Roosevelt, using these techniques.

Practice

When you give this assignment, tell students that they may use adjectives along with their stronger nouns.

The answers to this challenging and enriching activity will vary. Refer to **Techniques with Nouns** as you evaluate student choices. Sample answer:

Today I saw <u>the Pacific Ocean</u> for the first time. <u>Seagulls</u> dove and soared above the cliffs lining the <u>California coast.</u> Waves curled and crashed onto the beaches below. Out on the water, <u>bits</u> of white <u>froth</u> spread like lace across a huge blue <u>coverlet.</u> Amongst the crowds gathered at the edge of the scenic area I could see people wearing <u>San Francisco</u> T-shirts, <u>foreign visitors</u> struggling to read the <u>English signs,</u> and <u>parents</u> holding eager children away from the <u>cliff's edge</u>.

Writing Application

Nouns in Writing In this passage from *Thrashin' Time,* David Weiztman uses nouns to capture the excitement and details of an early twentieth-century farming event. Read the passage carefully, noting the italicized nouns.

The *engine* was quieter than I thought it would be. It was almost alive like the *horses* working everywhere round it. And the *horses.* Why, I'll betcha there were sixty *head,* big *horses—Belgians and Percherons—* coming and going that *afternoon. Teams* pulled *bundle wagons* heaped tall with *sheaves* of *wheat* from the *fields,* pulled *wagons* of yellow *grain* away from the *separator* to the *silo.* Another *team* hauled the *water wagon,* and another wagon brought *loads* of *cord* wood to keep the *engine* running sunup to sundown.

Techniques with Nouns Try to apply some of David Weiztman's techniques as you write and revise your own work.

1. When appropriate, use proper nouns to make your writing more exact:

Common nouns there were sixty head, big horses coming and going
Weitzman's version there were sixty head, big horses—*Belgians and Percherons—* coming and going

2. Make your writing more vivid by replacing general or abstract words with concrete specific nouns. Compare the following:

General words heaped tall with *crops*
Weitzman's version heaped tall with *sheaves* of *wheat* in from the *fields*

Practice Practice these techniques as you revise the following passage on a separate piece of paper. Instead of the underlined words, use proper nouns and more specific nouns to make the passage more vivid.

Today I saw <u>an ocean</u> for the first time. <u>Birds</u> dove and soared above the hills lining the <u>coast of the land</u>. Waves curled and crashed onto the beaches below. Out on the water, <u>pieces</u> of white <u>wave</u> spread like lace across a huge blue <u>piece of fabric</u>. Amongst the people gathered at the edge of the road I could see people wearing <u>city</u> T-shirts, <u>people</u> struggling to read the <u>signs in another language</u>, and <u>people</u> holding eager children away from the <u>side</u>.

Teacher's Classroom Resources

The following resources can be used for assessment or evaluation.

Unit Assessment
📁 *Tests with Answer Key*
Unit 9 Mastery Test, pp. 35–36

💿 *Test Generator*
Unit 9 Mastery Test

You may wish to administer the Unit 9 Mastery Test at this point.

UNIT

10

Grammar

Verbs

Lessons

367

UNIT GOALS

The goal of Unit 10 is to help students, through example and instruction, to develop an understanding of various kinds and forms of verbs and to use them appropriately in sentences. Lessons focus on action verbs, transitive and intransitive verbs, verbs with indirect objects, linking verbs with predicate nouns and adjectives, present and past tenses, main and helping verbs, progressive forms, perfect tenses, future tenses, active and passive voice, and irregular verbs.

Unit Assessment

📁 *Tests with Answer Key*
Unit 10 Pretest, pp. 37–38
Unit 10 Mastery Test, pp. 39–40

💿 *Test Generator*
Unit 10 Pretest
Unit 10 Mastery Test

You may wish to administer the Unit 10 Pretest at this point.

Key to Ability Levels

Enabling Strategies have been coded for varying learning styles and abilities.

L1 Level 1 activities are within the ability range of Learning Disabled students.

L2 Level 2 activities are basic-to-average activities and are within the ability range of average students.

L3 Level 3 activities are challenging activities and are within the ability range of above-average students.

LEP LEP activities are within the ability range of Limited English Proficiency students.

367

FOCUS

Lesson Overview

Objective: To identify action verbs

Bellringer

When students enter the classroom, have this assignment on the board: *If you were writing a dictionary, how would you define the word* action?

Motivating Activity

Discuss students' definitions of *action*. How much do they range in scope? Do students' ideas include mental activities, or only physical activities? Why?

TEACH

Cooperative Learning

Have partners ask each other "What did the subject do?" questions to identify action verbs. For example, in the sentence *The cat arrived in time for the show,* ask a *do* question to find out if the verb is an action verb.
Q: What did the cat *do*?
A: It arrived in time for the show.
Partners can take turns inventing sentences and asking the *do* questions.

Two-Minute Skill Drill

Have students write two sentences using one of the following verbs—first as an action verb, then as a helping (or nonaction) verb:

have   has   had

ACTION VERB

10.1 | Action Verbs

You may have heard of the movie director's call for "lights, camera, *action!*" The actions in movies and plays can be named by verbs. If a word expresses action and tells what a subject does, it is an action verb.

An **action verb** is a word that names an action. An action verb may contain more than one word.

Notice the action verbs in the following sentences.

> The director **shouts** at the members of the cast.
> The lights **are flashing** above the stage.
> The audience **arrives** in time for the performance.
> Several singers **have memorized** the lyrics of a song.

She **acted** as if . . .

Action verbs can express physical actions, such as *shout* and *arrive*. They can also express mental activities, such as *memorize* and *forget*.

Action Verbs	
Physical	shout, flash, arrive, own, talk, hit, applaud, praise
Mental	remember, memorize, forget, appreciate

Have, has, and *had* are action verbs, too, when they name what the subject owns or holds.

> The actors in this play already **have** their uniforms.
> The director **has** a script in her back pocket.
> The theater **has** a trapdoor.
> Rosa **had** a theater program from 1959.

. . . she **remembered** her lines.

368 *Verbs*

Teacher's Classroom Resources

The following resources can be used for planning, instruction, practice, reinforcement, assessment, reteaching, enrichment, or evaluation.

Teaching Tools
Lesson Plans, p. 75

Blackline Masters
Grammar Reteaching, p. 8

Grammar Workbook
Lesson 13

Unit Assessment

Tests with Answer Key
Unit 10 Pretest, pp. 37–38

Test Generator
Unit 10 Pretest

You may wish to administer the Unit 10 Pretest at this point.

Exercise 1 — Identifying Action Verbs

Write each action verb, and then write whether it expresses a *physical* or a *mental* action.

1. Eugene O'Neill's father, an actor, toured the country.
2. O'Neill learned about the theater from his father.
3. O'Neill's father sent him to Princeton University.
4. Soon O'Neill developed an interest in the sea.
5. He left home for two years of travel.
6. Later, a drama teacher at Harvard University inspired O'Neill.
7. O'Neill knew the value of his own work.
8. He journeyed to Cape Cod for the summer.
9. A group of friends admired this new playwright.
10. They used a stage in their town for theatrical productions.
11. O'Neill also wrote many plays while in Connecticut.
12. He joined a group of performers and writers.
13. The young O'Neill worked long hours.
14. On some days O'Neill walked along the wharves.
15. Sometimes he met friends along the way.
16. The playwright considered ideas for new plays.
17. In 1936 he won the Nobel Prize for literature.
18. Many theater groups perform his plays each year.
19. Audiences like the dramatic situations.
20. Most of the plays express dark moods.

Exercise 2 — Using Action Verbs

Write an appropriate action verb for each sentence. Answers will vary.

1. Our drama and history teachers _____ a joint project for our class.
2. First, our history teacher _____ us into four small groups.
3. Then he _____ the new assignment in detail.
4. The whole class _____ to the library every day for a week.
5. In our small groups, we _____ everyday life in colonial times.
6. Then the drama coach _____ us the next part of the assignment.
7. Each group _____ a one-act play set in the colonial period.
8. The coach _____ our play for an acting workshop.
9. All of us _____ our lines and movements over the weekend.
10. Finally, we _____ our play for the class and in a competition.

10.1 Action Verbs **369**

Enabling Strategies

🔷LEP Using Verbs in Context

To help students develop an understanding of action verbs that are either physical or mental, read the following paragraph. Have students discuss all the things that were done, telling which required physical action and which required mental action.

When I study for a test, I have to concentrate. I walk to the library and find a spot away from my friends. First I remember as much about the subject as I can. Then I open my notebook and review my class notes. If I don't understand something, I flip open my book and read about it there.

Setting the Purpose

Lesson 10.2 teaches students how to identify and use transitive and intransitive verbs in their writing.

FOCUS

Lesson Overview

Objective: To distinguish between transitive and intransitive verbs; identify direct objects; and to use these parts of speech correctly

🔔 Bellringer

When students enter the classroom, have this assignment on the board: *Read these two sentences and tell what Cathy did in each:*

1. Cathy returned.
2. Cathy returned the dishes.

Motivating Activity

Discuss students' answers to the Bellringer exercise. Point out that an action verb can be transitive or intransitive, resulting in a difference in meaning. The verb *return* as an intransitive verb means "to come back." As a transitive verb *return* means "to bring back something." Ask students which sentence tells what Cathy returned? The answer, *dishes,* is the direct object. Elicit that a transitive verb is an action verb that requires an object to make a complete sentence.

TEACH

Ⓐ Vocabulary Link

The word *transitive* is related to the Latin word *trans,* meaning "across." Reminding students that *trans-* has this meaning in words like *transport, transit,* and *transmit* will help them recall that transitive verbs carry their action across to an object.

370

10.2 | Transitive and Intransitive Verbs

In some sentences the predicate consists of only a verb.

> The actor **remembered**.

Usually sentences provide more information. The predicate often names who or what received the action of the verb.

The actor remembered **lines** from the play.

DIRECT OBJECT

In the sentence above, *lines* tells what was remembered. It is the direct object.

A **direct object** receives the action of a verb. It answers the question *whom?* or *what?* after an action verb.

Some sentences have a compound direct object. That is, a sentence may have more than one direct object.

> We saw **Maurice** and **Inez** in the audience.

When an action verb transfers action to a direct object, it is transitive. When an action verb has no direct object, it is intransitive.

A **transitive verb** has a direct object.

An **intransitive verb** does not have a direct object.

Many action verbs can be transitive or intransitive. Such verbs can be labeled transitive or intransitive only by examining their use in a particular sentence.

> The audience **applauds** the actors. [transitive]
> The audience **applauds** loudly. [intransitive]

370 *Verbs*

Teacher's Classroom Resources

The following resources can be used for planning, instruction, practice, reinforcement, assessment, reteaching, or enrichment.

🔧 **Teaching Tools**
Lesson Plans, p. 75

📋 **Blackline Masters**
Grammar Practice, p. 7
Grammar Reteaching, p. 9
Grammar Enrichment, p. 7

📙 *Grammar Workbook*
Lesson 14

| Exercise 3 | Identifying Transitive Verbs |

For each sentence write the action verb. If the verb is transitive, write the direct object.

1. Japanese kabuki theaters present popular scenes from dramas and dances.
2. Kabuki performers often wear very elaborate costumes.
3. Male actors perform all the female roles.
4. Characters make entrances and exits along the "flower way" aisle.
5. Instrumentalists behind a screen on stage provide the music.

| Exercise 4 | Distinguishing Transitive and Intransitive Verbs |

For each sentence write the action verb. If the verb has a direct object, write *T*. If it does not, write *I*.

1. The director remembered this fine old theater from past performances.
2. He loved its air of history and elegance.
3. Day after day, week after week, the cast rehearsed.
4. Finally, the day of the first performance arrived.
5. The director inspected the scenery, costumes, and lights.
6. Many people bought tickets to the new play.
7. The almost silent audience watched.
8. Nearly all the people liked the music and the drama.
9. At the end of the play, everyone clapped wildly.
10. Some enthusiastic spectators even cheered.
11. The majority of the critics enjoyed the performance.
12. They wrote favorable reviews.
13. The musical show succeeded.
14. In fact, the director won an award for it from a theater guild.
15. At the awards ceremony the director spoke.
16. The cast and their guests listened carefully.
17. He thanked the producers.
18. A newspaper reporter asked some questions.
19. The director complimented the stage crew for the scenery.
20. He praised the actors for their performances.

10.2 Transitive and Intransitive Verbs **371**

PRACTICE AND ASSESS

Answers: Exercise 3
1. present—verb; scenes—d.o.
2. wear—verb; costumes—d.o.
3. perform—verb; roles—d.o.
4. make—verb; entrances, exits—d.o.
5. provide—verb; music—d.o.

Answers: Exercise 4
1. remembered—T
2. loved—T
3. rehearsed—I
4. arrived—I
5. inspected—T
6. bought—T
7. watched—I
8. liked—T
9. clapped—I
10. cheered—
11. enjoyed—T
12. wrote—T
13. succeeded—I
14. won—T
15. spoke—I
16. listened—I
17. thanked—T
18. asked—T
19. complimented—T
20. praised—T

Independent Practice

Skills Practice
 Grammar Practice, p. 7
Grammar Reteaching, p. 9
Grammar Enrichment, p. 7

Grammar Workbook, Lesson 14

CLOSE

Think of the last play or concert you attended. Write a description of the performance, using transitive and intransitive verbs.

Enabling Strategies

LEP Adding Direct Objects
Point out to students that adding a direct object to a sentence helps clarify the meaning. They can change a sentence into a question beginning with *whom* or *what* to decide whether to add a direct object. For example, change

The actor remembers into a *what* question: *What did the actor remember?* The new sentence with more information could be *The actor remembered lines from the play.* Invite students to try the same with their own sentences.

Setting the Purpose

Lesson 10.3 teaches students to use direct and indirect objects appropriately.

FOCUS

Lesson Overview

Objective: To identify and distinguish between direct and indirect objects

🔔 Bellringer

When students enter the classroom, have this assignment on the board: *How are these two sentences different? Is there any difference in the meaning?*

1. *I sent my cousin a letter.*
2. *I sent a letter to my cousin.*

TEACH

☑ Teaching Tip

You might stress that one way to identify indirect objects is to try the *to* or *for* paraphrase. For example, change *Walter made the dog a bed* to *Walter made a bed for the dog* and *Tom sent his family a postcard* to *Tom sent a postcard to his family.* Be sure students notice that in the paraphrase the noun or pronoun that tells *to whom* or *for whom* is no longer an indirect object but the object of a preposition, and it no longer comes before the direct object but after it.

10.3 | Verbs with Indirect Objects

Words that answer the question *whom?* or *what?* after an action verb are called direct objects.

> Amalia wears a **costume**.

Sometimes both a direct object and an indirect object follow an action verb.

An **indirect object** answers the question *to whom?* or *for whom?* an action is done.

Friends sent the **actors** flowers.

to whom?

INDIRECT OBJECT

The direct object in the sentence above is *flowers*. The indirect object is *actors*. *Actors* answers the question *to whom?* after the action verb *sent*.

Some sentences have a compound indirect object.

> The audience gave the **cast** and the **orchestra** an ovation.

An indirect object appears only in a sentence that has a direct object. Two easy clues can help you recognize an indirect object. First, an indirect object always comes before a direct object. Second, you can add the preposition *to* or *for* before the indirect object and change its position. The sentence will still make sense, although there will no longer be an indirect object.

> Friends sent the **actors flowers**.   [*Actors* is an indirect object.]
> Friends sent flowers **to the actors**.   [*Actors* is not an indirect object.]

You know that in the first sentence *actors* is the indirect object because it comes before the direct object and because it can be placed behind the preposition *to,* as in the second sentence.

372   *Verbs*

Teacher's Classroom Resources

For Lesson 10.3, the following resources can be used for planning, instruction, practice, reinforcement, reteaching, enrichment, or evaluation.

🔧 **Teaching Tools**
Lesson Plans

📁 **Blackline Masters**
Grammar Practice, p. 8
Grammar Enrichment, p. 8

📗 ***Grammar Workbook***
Lesson 15

Exercise 5	Distinguishing Direct and Indirect Objects

For each sentence write the direct object. If the sentence contains an indirect object, write it and underline it.

1. None of the musicians know the composition.
2. The orchestra leader brings the musicians the music.
3. For several days the orchestra leader teaches the orchestra a song.
4. The sopranos learn their part first.
5. The audience loves the musical comedy.
6. That famous director frequently gives performers drama lessons.
7. She also gives children lessons in the afternoon.
8. She wrote plays and operas for many years.
9. Now she shows her students her special techniques.
10. The theater offers young people many opportunities.
11. Students ask actors and directors questions about different roles.
12. The expert director and producers bring the show success.
13. The director offers her students advice about their careers.
14. The actors memorize scripts.
15. One young writer sold a producer and a director his screenplay.
16. The theater club offers subscribers a discount.
17. The theater also sends subscribers performance information.
18. Subscribers often buy extra tickets for their friends.
19. Generous patrons give the theater large donations.
20. The theater usually gives generous patrons free tickets.

Exercise 6	Using Indirect Objects

Rewrite each sentence, changing each prepositional phrase into an indirect object.

SAMPLE   The cast members gave interviews to the press.
ANSWER   The cast members gave the press interviews.

1. The playwright gave a special tribute to her mother.
2. The youngest cast member handed a dozen roses to the star.
3. Cast members made a comical top hat for the director.
4. The audience offered thunderous applause to the entire cast.
5. The play's producer sent fifteen photographs of the event to the local newspaper.

10.3 Verbs with Indirect Objects **373**

Enabling Strategies

LEP Acting Out Direct and Indirect Objects

You might ask a student to help you act out the meanings of sentences with indirect objects such as *I threw Henry the ball* and *Mr. Scott handed Mark a pencil.* Point out that even though these verbs are different, their meanings are similar—someone gives something to someone. Invite students to think of other actions of this kind to act out for the class.

PRACTICE AND ASSESS

Answers: Exercise 5
1. (DO) composition
2. (IO) musicians; (DO) music
3. (IO) orchestra; (DO) song
4. (DO) part
5. (DO) comedy (or musical comedy)
6. (IO) performers; (DO) lessons
7. (IO) children; (DO) lessons
8. (DO) plays, operas
9. (IO) students; (DO) techniques
10. (IO) people; (DO) opportunities
11. (IO) actors, directors; (DO) questions
12. (IO) show; (DO) success
13. (IO) students; (DO) advice
14. (DO) scripts
15. (IO) producer, director; (DO) screenplay
16. (IO) subscribers; (DO) discount
17. (IO) subscribers; (DO) information
18. (DO) tickets
19. (IO) theater; (DO) donations
20. (IO) patrons; (DO) tickets

Answers: Exercise 6
1. The playwright gave her mother a special tribute.
2. The youngest cast member handed the star a dozen roses.
3. Cast members made the director a comical hat.
4. The audience offered the entire cast thunderous applause.
5. The play's producer sent the local newspaper fifteen photographs of the event.

Independent Practice

Skills Practice
📁 *Grammar Practice*, p. 8
📁 *Grammar Enrichment*, p. 8

📙 ***Grammar Workbook***, Lesson 15

CLOSE

Have students give examples of sentences with direct and indirect objects.

373

FOCUS

Lesson Overview

Objective: To identify linking verbs, predicate nouns, and predicate adjectives

🔔 Bellringer

When students enter the classroom, have this assignment on the board: *Write the answer to this question: How are the word* play *and the phrase* Romeo and Juliet *related in this sentence? My favorite Shakespeare play is* Romeo and Juliet.

Motivating Activity

Discuss students' answers to the Bellringer question. Point out that the term *linking verb* refers to the fact that linking verbs connect—or *link*—a subject with a word that defines it (predicate noun) or describes it (predicate adjective).

TEACH

☑ Grammar Tip

Tell students that one way to identify a linking verb in a sentence is to see whether a form of the verb *be* can be substituted for it. For example, *The night became still* can be changed to *The night was still.* This tells students that *becomes* is a linking verb.

⇄ Cross-reference: Diagraming

For information about how to diagram sentences with predicate nouns and predicate adjectives, refer students to Lesson 18.5, p. 542.

374

10.4 | Linking Verbs and Predicate Words

A **linking verb** connects the subject of a sentence with a noun or adjective in the predicate.

Bess Powell **was** the director.

LINKING VERB

LINKING
VERB

The verb *was* is a form of the verb *be.* It links the word *director* to the subject, telling what the subject is.

A **predicate noun** is a noun that follows a linking verb. It defines the subject by telling what it is.

A **predicate adjective** is an adjective that follows a linking verb. It describes the subject by telling what it is like.

A sentence may contain a compound predicate noun or a compound predicate adjective.

> The set designer was a **carpenter** and an **electrician.**
>   [compound predicate noun]
> He is **stern** but **kind.** [compound predicate adjective]

Some of the more common linking verbs are listed below.

Common Linking Verbs			
be	appear	turn	smell
become	look	taste	sound
seem	grow	feel	

Many of these verbs can be used as action verbs, also.

> The director grew angry. [linking verb]
> The director grew a beard. [action verb]

374   *Verbs*

Teacher's Classroom Resources

The following resources can be used for planning, instruction, practice, reinforcement, reteaching, or enrichment.

🔧 **Teaching Tools**
Lesson Plans

📁 **Blackline Masters**
Grammar Practice, p. 9
Grammar Reteaching, p. 10
Grammar Enrichment, p. 9

📗 *Grammar Workbook*
Lesson 16

Exercise 7 | Identifying Action and Linking Verbs

Write each verb. Then write whether it is an *action* verb or a *linking* verb.

1. Lorraine Hansberry became the first African American woman with a play on Broadway.
2. *A Raisin in the Sun* is the title of that play.
3. Hansberry used a line from a Langston Hughes poem for the title.
4. The play tells the story of an African American Chicago family and their dreams.
5. In the course of the play, the family grows stronger and closer.

Exercise 8 | Identifying Linking Verbs and Predicate Nouns and Adjectives

Write each verb and label it *action* or *linking*. If it is a linking verb, write the predicate word or words and add the label *predicate noun* or *predicate adjective*.

1. William Shakespeare was a great playwright and poet.
2. In fact, he is a giant in world literature.
3. Characters in Shakespeare's plays seem universal.
4. Some of the characters were actually historical figures.
5. Some costumes in Shakespeare's plays look odd.
6. The styles of earlier times appear strange today.
7. Shakespeare's language puzzles some modern listeners.
8. In time, however, that language becomes very clear and understandable.
9. Many of Shakespeare's plots sound exaggerated.
10. His stories thrill audiences all over the world with their power, beauty, and truth.
11. Some of the characters are more popular than others.
12. In *Romeo and Juliet* a character drinks poison.
13. In *Othello* the main character grows jealous.
14. In *The Merchant of Venice,* a clever young woman teaches other characters about justice and mercy.
15. Some members of Shakespeare's original casts were children.
16. The children played women's roles.
17. Films of Shakespeare's plays are plentiful and popular.
18. Great actors and actresses perform complex roles.
19. Laurence Olivier and John Barrymore were great Hamlets.
20. More recently Mel Gibson played Hamlet.

10.4 Linking Verbs and Predicate Words **375**

PRACTICE AND ASSESS

Answers: Exercise 7
1. became—linking verb
2. is—linking verb
3. used—action verb
4. tells—action verb
5. grows—linking verb

Answers: Exercise 8
1. was—linking; playwright, poet—PN
2. is—linking; giant—PN
3. seem—linking; universal—PA
4. were—linking; figures—PN
5. look—linking; odd—PA
6. appear—linking; strange—PA
7. puzzles—action
8. becomes—linking; clear, understandable—PA
9. sound—linking; exaggerated—PA
10. thrill—action
11. are—linking; popular—PA
12. drinks—action
13. grows—linking; jealous—PA
14. teaches—action
15. were—linking; children—PN
16. played—action
17. are—linking; plentiful, popular—PA
18. perform—action
19. were—linking; Hamlets—PN
20. played—action

Independent Practice

Skills Practice
📁 *Grammar Practice,* p. 9
📁 *Grammar Reteaching,* p. 10
📁 *Grammar Enrichment,* p. 9

📖 ***Grammar Workbook,*** Lesson 16

CLOSE

Have several volunteers give examples of sentences with linking verbs.

Enabling Strategies

LEP Linking Verbs in Other Languages

The verb *be* is irregular, as students can tell from its many forms: *am, is, are, was, were, be, being, been.* Have students from other language backgrounds tell about *be* in their original language. In some languages, such as Spanish and German, *be* is irregular, just as it is in English. It is important to note that many non-European languages do not have a word for *be.* If students need help recognizing linking verbs, refer them to the *Grammar Workbook,* Lesson 16.

FOCUS

Lesson Overview
Objective: To use the correct present-tense and past-tense verb forms

🔔 Bellringer
When students enter the classroom, have this assignment on the board: *Write the beginning of a fairy tale that is set not in the past or the future, but in the present.*

Motivating Activity
Ask volunteers to read their story beginnings. Discuss any complications that arose for students, and draw attention to the verb forms used.

TEACH

☑ Teaching Tip
The word *present* in the term *present tense* refers more accurately to the form of a verb than to the meaning of the word *present.* Only in special instances (sports broadcasts and stage directions) does this tense indicate actions taking place now. It is used more commonly for actions and conditions that are always true (*The moon revolves around the earth*), for repeated actions (*I listen to the news every morning*), and for continuous actions (*My pen leaks all the time*).

⇄ Cross-reference: Subject-Verb Agreement
For more information on subject-verb agreement, refer students to Lesson 7.3, pp. 306–309, and Lessons 16.1–16.5, pp. 508–517.

10.5 | Present and Past Tenses

The verb in a sentence tells what action takes place. It also tells you when the action takes place. The form of a verb that shows the time of the action is called the **tense** of the verb.

The **present tense** of a verb names an action that happens regularly. It can also express a general truth.

> A great actor **wins** awards.

In the present tense, the base form of a verb is used with all subjects except singular nouns and the words *he, she,* and *it.* When the subject is a singular noun or *he, she,* or *it, -s* is usually added to the verb. Remember that a verb in a sentence must agree in number with its subject.

Present Tense Forms	
Singular	**Plural**
I **walk.**	We **walk.**
You **walk.**	You **walk.**
He, she, *or* it **walks.**	They **walk.**

The **past tense** of a verb names an action that already happened.

The past tense of many verbs is formed by adding *-ed* to the verb.

> The actors **practiced** their lines.

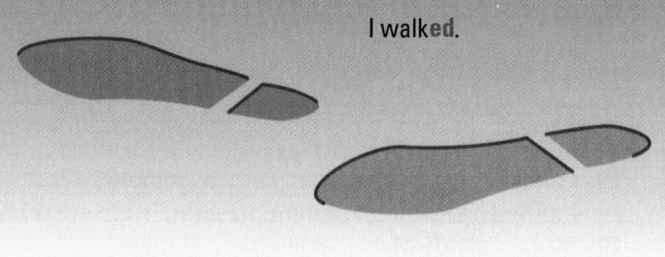

I walked.

I walk.

376 *Verbs*

Teacher's Classroom Resources

The following resources can be used for planning, instruction, practice, reinforcement, reteaching, or enrichment.

🔧 **Teaching Tools**
Lesson Plans, p. 77

📁 **Blackline Masters**
Grammar Practice, p. 10
Grammar Reteaching, p. 11
Grammar Enrichment, p. 10

📕 ***Grammar Workbook***
Lesson 17

Exercise 9   **Distinguishing Present and Past**

Write the correct form of the verb in parentheses. Then write whether it is in the *present tense* or *past tense.*

1. A month ago our music teacher (introduce) my sister and me to opera.
2. Opera is a form that (combine) music and drama into one production.
3. That combination (suit) my sister and me perfectly.
4. Last week we (attend) a light opera by Gilbert and Sullivan.
5. Every day that week the show (start) precisely on time.
6. However, we (arrive) late because of bus delays.
7. After the show we always (purchase) tickets for tomorrow's opera.
8. Yesterday a reviewer (compare) the lead performer with Caruso.
9. Enrico Caruso (live) at the beginning of the twentieth century.
10. In his lifetime, he (appear) in many operas throughout the world.
11. Caruso (arrive) in America in 1903.
12. Sometimes he (pass) out free tickets to poor people.
13. Caruso (earn) more money than any other singer at the time.
14. He always (maintain) a warm affection for his many fans.
15. Caruso often (play) tricks on his fellow performers.
16. He (possess) a dynamic personality.
17. Today singers still (talk) about his wonderful voice.
18. Now some people (listen) to his original recordings.
19. Some modern singers (copy) the great singer's style and technique.
20. That great Italian tenor (inspire) singers even today.

Exercise 10   **Using Past Tense**

For each sentence write the present tense verb. Then write its past tense form.

1. People in the audience chat with one another before the performance.
2. Several classes of students almost fill the second balcony.
3. The lights blink on and off, once, twice, three times.
4. Members of the audience settle into their seats.
5. Darkness descends on the theater except for the glow of safety lights.
6. Not a sound disturbs the silence.
7. Then a spotlight focuses on the heavy red curtain across the stage.
8. The curtains part and reveal a city street.
9. Suddenly actors and actresses appear on the stage.
10. The magic of theater captivates the audience.

10.5 Present and Past Tenses   **377**

Enabling Strategies

LEP Translating Verb Tenses
Ask students to describe how past and present are indicated in other languages. The class can compare and contrast the systems mentioned with the system used in English, discussing any complications or confusion that could arise when translating from one language to another.

L3 Shifting Tenses
Although students are told to avoid shifting tense for no reason, changes in tense are sometimes necessary. To illustrate, write the following sentence on the board: *Yesterday we hiked on the trail that runs along the ridge.* Discuss the shift from past to present tense.

FOCUS

Lesson Overview

Objective: To distinguish between main verbs and helping verbs; to recognize the four principal parts of a verb; and to identify the forms of the helping verbs *be* and *have*

🔔 Bellringer

When students enter the classroom, have this assignment on the board: *Copy the following sentences. Underline the verbs.*

My family has always loved national parks. We are going to Bryce Canyon next week. I have heard fantastic things about the rock formations.

Motivating Activity

Discuss students' answers to the Bellringer exercise. Make sure they underlined the helping verbs *has, are,* and *have* as well as the main verbs.

TEACH

☑ Teaching Tip

Stress that a verb's principal parts are forms, not tenses. The base form is used as the present tense except with *he, she, it,* and singular nouns, when *-s* or *-es* is added. Emphasize that present and past participles are also forms, not tenses. When used as a main verb, a participle follows a form of *be* (*is acting*) or *have* (*has acted*).

10.6 | Main Verbs and Helping Verbs

Verbs have four principal parts that are used to form all tenses. Notice how the principal parts of a verb are formed.

Principal Parts of Verbs			
Base Form	**Present Participle**	**Past Form**	**Past Participle**
act	acting	acted	acted

You can use the base form itself and the past form alone to form the present and past tenses. The present and past participles can be combined with helping verbs to form other tenses.

A **helping verb** helps the main verb tell about an action or make a statement.

A **verb phrase** consists of one or more helping verbs followed by a main verb.

> They **are acting** in another play right now.

In the sentence above, the word *are* is the helping verb, and the present participle *acting* is the main verb. Together they form a verb phrase.

The most common helping verbs are *be, have,* and *do.* Forms of the helping verb *be* include *am, is,* and *are* in the present and *was* and *were* in the past. They combine with the present participle of the main verb.

Forms of the helping verb *have* include *has* in the present and *had* in the past. They combine with the past participle form of a verb.

Have, Has, Had, and the Past Participle			
Singular	**Plural**	**Singular**	**Plural**
I **have** acted.	We **have** acted.	I **had** acted.	We **had** acted.
You **have** acted.	You **have** acted.	You **had** acted.	You **had** acted.
She **has** acted.	They **have** acted.	She **had** acted.	They **had** acted.

378 *Verbs*

Teacher's Classroom Resources

The following resources can be used for planning, instruction, practice, reinforcement, reteaching, or enrichment.

🔧 **Teaching Tools**
Lesson Plans

📁 **Blackline Masters**
Grammar Practice, p. 11
Grammar Reteaching, p. 12
Grammar Enrichment, p. 11

📕 **Grammar Workbook**
Lesson 18

Exercise 11   Identifying Helping Verbs and Participles in Verb Phrases

For each sentence write each verb phrase. Then circle the helping verbs.

1. Stagehands are preparing the scenery.
2. They had started their work before dawn.
3. One young woman is checking on the correct placement of all the props.
4. Earlier she had inspected all the backstage props and equipment.
5. The director had joined the crew later in the day, and now he is conducting his own last-minute check.
6. The star of the show has earned her fame by a number of huge successes.
7. The press and the public are expecting an excellent performance from this famous cast.
8. Theater has remained a popular form of entertainment.
9. People are buying tickets to many different shows.
10. Theater companies are staging plays, musicals, and revivals of older shows.

Exercise 12   Using Helping Verbs and Present and Past Participles

For each sentence choose and write the correct helping verb in parentheses. Then write the participle and label it *present participle* or *past participle*.

1. Now groups (are, have) performing dramas on television.
2. As a result, people (are, have) developing a taste for theater.
3. Television audiences (are, had) watching great performances, both comedies and tragedies.
4. Many of these productions (are, have) attracted huge numbers of viewers from all over the country.
5. The best of them (are, have) achieved very high ratings and rave reviews from critics and viewers alike.
6. Emmy awards (are, have) announced each year in the category Drama-Comedy Special.
7. The number and success of these productions (are, have) awakened substantial interest in drama.
8. Producers and advertisers (are, have) responding to people's interest in quality television programs.
9. Live theater (is, has) experienced a surge in interest.
10. Both professional companies and community theater groups (are, have) welcoming a new generation of theatergoers.

10.6 Main Verbs and Helping Verbs **379**

PRACTICE AND ASSESS

Answers: Exercise 11
1. (are) preparing
2. (had) started
3. (is) checking
4. (had) inspected
5. (had) joined; is conducting
6. (has) earned
7. (are) expecting
8. (has) remained
9. (are) buying
10. (are) staging

Answers: Exercise 12
1. are; performing; present
2. are; developing; present
3. are; watching; present
4. have; attracted; past
5. have; achieved; past
6. are; announced; present
7. have; awakened; past
8. are; responding; present
9. has; experienced; past
10. are; welcoming; present

Independent Practice

Skills Practice
📁 *Grammar Practice,* p. 11
📁 *Grammar Reteaching,* p. 12
📁 *Grammar Enrichment,* p. 11

 Grammar Workbook, Lesson 18

CLOSE

Imagine that you are a drama critic. You have just seen a performance of one of your favorite plays. Write a review of the performance. Use verb phrases.

Enabling Strategies

LEP Understanding Verb Phrases
A great confidence-building activity to help students with verb forms is to scramble the verbs in a verb phrase. Write a scrambled verb phrase, such as *have acting been*, on the board and invite students to use it in a sentence, reordering the words if necessary. Students quickly realize that there is usually only one possible way to order the verbs correctly. See *Grammar Reteaching*, p. 12.

FOCUS

Lesson Overview

Objective: To use present progressive and past progressive verb forms correctly

Bellringer

When students enter the classroom, have this assignment on the board: *Write a sentence that describes what you are doing right now. Rewrite that sentence in as many ways as you can.*

Motivating Activity

Discuss how many ways students structured their sentences for the Bellringer activity. For each sentence structure, collect several examples. Were there any structures that only one student thought of? Use the examples for your discussion of progressive forms.

TEACH

Vocabulary Link

The word *progressive* comes from a Latin word that means "to advance." The meaning of *progressive,* "moving forward," can remind students of the grammatical meaning, since the *-ing* forms are used for action in progress.

Critical Thinking

Ask students to contrast this use of the suffix *-ing* with other uses, such as for nouns (*the painting*), adjectives (*singing children*), and verbal nouns called gerunds (*Painting is my hobby*).

380

10.7 Progressive Forms

You know that the present tense of a verb names an action that occurs repeatedly. To describe an action that is taking place at the present time, you use the present progressive form of the verb.

The **present progressive form** of a verb names an action or condition that is continuing in the present.

> Althea **is finishing** her song.

The present progressive form of a verb consists of the present participle of the main verb and a form of *be*, such as *am, are,* or *is.*

Present Progressive Form	
Singular	**Plural**
I **am leaving**.	We **are leaving**.
You **are leaving**.	You **are leaving**.
He, she, *or* it **is leaving**.	They **are leaving**.

The past progressive names an action that was continuing at some point in the past.

The **past progressive form** of a verb names an action or condition that continued for some time in the past.

> The plot **was becoming** scary.

The past progressive form of a verb consists of the present participle and the helping verb *was* or *were.*

Past Progressive Form	
Singular	**Plural**
I **was following**.	We **were following**.
You **were following**.	You **were following**.
He, she, *or* it **was following**.	They **were following**.

380 *Verbs*

Teacher's Classroom Resources

The following resources can be used for planning, instruction, practice, reinforcement, reteaching, or enrichment.

Teaching Tools
Lesson Plans

Blackline Masters
Grammar Practice, p. 12
Grammar Reteaching, p. 13
Grammar Enrichment, p. 12

Grammar Workbook
Lesson 19

Exercise 13 — Using Present and Past Progressive Forms

For each sentence write the present progressive or past progressive form of the verb in parentheses.

1. This next semester my music class (go) to an opera production every week.
2. We (examine) the difference between nineteenth- and twentieth-century opera.
3. We (compare) German, French, Italian, and American operas.
4. The schedule (tire) for some students.
5. They (fall) behind in their schoolwork.
6. Our teacher (plan) a big party for us later.
7. She (praise) us yesterday for our patience and diligence.
8. At the end of this semester, we (expect) a period of relaxation.
9. Last month we (attend) two productions a week.
10. Together with our other responsibilities, that schedule (overwhelm) us.
11. Our parents said they (worry) about our lack of time for anything else.
12. Last year we (study) the comic operas of Gilbert and Sullivan.
13. From 1875 to 1895, the two men (collaborate) on a number of light operas.
14. William Gilbert (work) as a lawyer and a journalist.
15. Arthur Sullivan (write) music for various productions of Shakespeare.
16. Even today many theater groups (present) Gilbert and Sullivan.
17. Time and again new audiences (discover) the joys of these lively comedies.
18. Last year the city (prepare) a plan for a Gilbert and Sullivan festival.
19. As part of that festival, next spring we (stage) *The Pirates of Penzance*.
20. Many of us in the music class (hope) for good roles in that production.

Exercise 14 — Using Progressive Forms

In each sentence if the verb is in the present tense, change it to the present progressive form. If the verb is in the past tense, change it to the past progressive form.

1. The new theater season begins soon.
2. Local playwrights submitted their entries over a two-week period.
3. A committee reads the scripts.
4. Committee members hoped for a play with a large cast.
5. Last season this company attracted large audiences to its productions.
6. This year the members dream of an equally successful season.
7. One new play caused much excitement among the entries.
8. In this play a brother and sister investigate the story of a treasure.
9. Meanwhile, the children's parents organize a search for them.
10. Near the end of the play, everyone rushes to the same hilltop.

10.7 Progressive Forms **381**

Enabling Strategies

LEP Using Progressive Forms

Certain verbs, such as *doubt* and *love*, are not used in English in the present or past progressive tenses. These verbs refer to "timeless" mental states rather than action in a specific present or past time. Students whose first language is not English sometimes use progressive forms of verbs like *doubt* and *love* incorrectly in sentences like the following: *I am doubting the story* and *I was loving the baked beans.*

FOCUS

Lesson Overview

Objective: To identify the present perfect and past perfect tenses and to understand their meanings

🔔 Bellringer

When students enter the classroom, have this assignment on the board: *On a sheet of paper, write when the action took place in the following sentences:*

1. *Margaret has read* Gone With the Wind *three times.*
2. *Jonnie has practiced the guitar for an hour.*

Motivating Activity

Discuss students' answers to the Bellringer activity. Make sure they understand that the present tense can indicate both action completed in the past (first sentence) or action that has begun and is ongoing.

TEACH

☑ Teaching Tip

The word *perfect* means "complete," an appropriate term since the perfect tenses often refer to completed actions.

10.8 | Perfect Tenses

The **present perfect tense** of a verb names an action that happened at an indefinite time in the past. It also tells about an action that happened in the past and is still happening now.

> The actor **has rehearsed** for many hours.
> Nick and Maria **have seen** *Guys and Dolls* five times.

The present perfect tense consists of the helping verb *have* or *has* and the past participle of the main verb.

Present Perfect Tense	
Singular	**Plural**
I **have performed**.	We **have performed**.
You **have performed**.	You **have performed**.
He, she, *or* it **has performed**.	They **have performed**.

The **past perfect tense** of a verb names an action that happened before another action or event in the past.

The past perfect tense is often used in sentences that contain a past tense verb in another part of the sentence.

> We **had** just **arrived** when the play **began**.
> The play **had been rewritten** several times before it **opened**.

The past perfect tense of a verb consists of the helping verb *had* and the past participle of the main verb.

Past Perfect Tense	
Singular	**Plural**
I **had started**.	We **had started**.
You **had started**.	You **had started**.
He, she, *or* it **had started**.	They **had started**.

382 *Verbs*

Teacher's Classroom Resources

The following resources can be used for planning, instruction, practice, reinforcement, reteaching or enrichment.

🔧 **Teaching Tools**
Lesson Plans, p. 78

📁 **Blackline Masters**
Grammar Practice, p. 13
Grammar Reteaching, p. 14
Grammar Enrichment, p. 13

📗 ***Grammar Workbook***
Lesson 20

Exercise 15 — Identifying Present Perfect and Past Perfect Tenses

For each sentence write the verb phrase. Then write whether it is in the *present perfect* or the *past perfect* tense.

1. My favorite television show has earned six Emmy nominations this year.
2. Before this year it had collected three major Emmies for best drama, best actor, and best actress.
3. The actress had appeared in several other shows before this one.
4. All of her shows have challenged the boundaries of television.
5. This new one, however, has proved itself the best of all.

Exercise 16 — Using Present Perfect Tense

For each sentence write the present perfect tense of the verb in parentheses.

1. That actress (perform) in several award-winning plays.
2. Her drama coach (help) her a great deal.
3. The cast (learn) discipline and craft.
4. Our drama club (wait) for the opening of the opera season.
5. The members (plan) weekly theater parties.
6. Some new students (join) the club this year.
7. The club (elect) Tanya president.
8. She (appear) in most of our club's productions.
9. She (contribute) time and energy to every one of them.
10. All of us (benefit) from her work and good nature.

Exercise 17 — Using the Past Perfect Tense

For each sentence write the past perfect tense of the verb in parentheses.

1. Before the show began, the cast (rehearse) for weeks.
2. Artists (create) the scenery before the opening.
3. The costume designers (locate) boxes and boxes of Roaring '20s clothes.
4. Before the first rehearsal, our teacher (talk) to us.
5. She (warn) us of the hard work ahead.
6. Also, however, she (predict) an enjoyable, worthwhile activity for us.
7. Before opening night the cast (suffer) from stage fright.
8. We (present) only one show before last year.
9. Until last week every member of the cast (attend) every rehearsal.
10. The director (demonstrate) many valuable techniques.

10.8 Perfect Tenses **383**

Enabling Strategies

L3 Using Past and Past Perfect Tenses

Students whose first language is not English may experience difficulty with the two uses of the verb *have*: as a main verb and as a helping verb in the perfect tenses. Have students write sentences in their journals using the main verb *have*. Then introduce the perfect tenses and ask students how they would express past actions in their native language. Once students have drawn a parallel to familiar constructions, ask them to write sentences in their journals, using present perfect and past perfect verbs.

FOCUS

Lesson Overview

Objective: To identify some ways of expressing time in the future—using the future tense, using the future perfect tense, and using the present tense with time words

Bellringer

When students enter the classroom, have this assignment on the board: *Write a paragraph entitled "Where I Plan to Be in 15 Years."*

Motivating Activity

Discuss the Bellringer and have students circle all the words in their paragraphs that indicate future time.

TEACH

☑ Teaching Tip

Three ways of expressing future time in English are presented here. Students will be familiar with the use of *shall* and *will* as well as the present and present progressive tenses used with time words: *The show opens (or is opening) next week.* Less familiar is the future perfect tense, which relates two future events, showing that one precedes the other: *I will have had lunch by the time you come.* Notice the kind of time expressed—action completed before some future time.

10.9 | Expressing Future Time

The future tense of a verb is formed by using the helping verb *will* before the main verb. The helping verb *shall* is sometimes used when the subject is *I* or *we*.

There are other ways to show that an action will happen in the future. *Tomorrow, next year,* and *later* are all words that express a future time. These words are called **time words,** and they are used with the present tense to express future time. Read the sentences below.

> Our show **opens next week**.
> **Tomorrow** we **design** scenery and rehearse.

The present progressive form can also be used with time words to express future actions.

> **Next Friday** our show **is opening**.
> **Soon** we **are ending** rehearsals.

Another way to talk about the future is with the future perfect tense.

The **future perfect tense** of a verb names an action that will be completed before another future event begins.

The future perfect tense is formed by adding *will have* or *shall have* before the past participle of the verb.

> Thursday I **shall have performed** six times.
>
> By next week the production **will have closed**.

384 *Verbs*

Teacher's Classroom Resources

Exercise 18   Using the Future Perfect Tense

For each sentence change the underlined verb to the future perfect tense.

1. Until the show we <u>shall practice</u> every day.
2. Tomorrow I <u>will learn</u> my part by heart.
3. I <u>give</u> my first performance next Saturday.
4. By the time the show closes, I <u>shall perform</u> "Some Enchanted Evening" fifteen times.
5. My presence on stage <u>will startle</u> many skeptical people.

Exercise 19   Identifying Verb Tenses

For each sentence write the verb or verb phrase, and write whether it is in the *present, future, present progressive,* or *future perfect* tense.

1. All the dancers are practicing tomorrow morning.
2. That afternoon we will have our final dress rehearsal.
3. Tomorrow evening we are giving our first benefit performance for senior citizens.
4. By then Adam will have organized the ticket booth.
5. The O'Leary twins go today for another make-up lesson.
6. Tomorrow they demonstrate their techniques on the rest of us.
7. The day after tomorrow my new costume arrives.
8. Until then I am wearing a costume from last year's production.
9. Our official first night will come on Saturday.
10. By then we will have ironed out all the problems.
11. In the next few weeks we will stage six performances of our show.
12. Then next month we are going to the state drama competition.
13. At the state competition we present our play in front of a panel of expert judges.
14. They will have observed four other clubs before us.
15. Judges will score us on the basis of action, dialogue, and pace.
16. On the last day, we learn the names of the winners.
17. We shall cross our fingers very tightly.
18. After the competition we are changing our schedule completely.
19. Next year we are focusing on musical theater.
20. We will have gained considerable stage experience by then.

10.9 Expressing Future Time **385**

Enabling Strategies

LEP Using Modals

In English, a verb by itself cannot indicate future time. Future time is indicated by helping verbs, called *modals.* The modals are *can, may, must, shall,* and *will* (with their past-tense forms *could, might, should,* and *would*).

PRACTICE AND ASSESS

Answers: Exercise 18
1. shall have practiced
2. will have learned
3. will have given
4. shall have performed
5. will have startled

Answers: Exercise 19
1. are practicing—present progressive
2. will have—future
3. are giving—present progressive
4. will have organized—future perfect
5. go—present
6. demonstrate—present
7. arrives—present
8. am wearing—present progressive
9. will come—future
10. will have ironed—future perfect
11. will stage—future
12. are going—present progressive
13. present—present
14. will have observed—future perfect
15. will score—future
16. learn—present
17. shall cross—future
18. are changing—present progressive
19. are focusing—present progressive
20. will have gained—future perfect

Independent Practice

Skills Practice
 *Grammar Practice,* p. 13
 Grammar Reteaching, p. 14
 Grammar Enrichment, p. 13

 Grammar Workbook, Lesson 21

CLOSE

What kinds of future events does your school have planned? Write a paragraph using future tenses to describe one of these events.

Setting the Purpose

Lesson 10.10 teaches students the appropriate uses of the active and passive voices to enhance their writing.

FOCUS

Lesson Overview

Objective: To identify and distinguish between the active and passive voices

🔔 Bellringer

When students enter the classroom, have this assignment on the board: *List the verbs in the following following sentences and select the sentence you think is more exciting. Explain your choice.*

1. *Kim shifted the gears of her speeding race car.*
2. *The gears of her speeding race car were shifted by Kim.*

Motivating Activity

Discuss the Bellringer, explaining that although writers usually prefer the active voice because it is more dynamic, the passive voice is used to shift attention from the doer of an action to the receiver of an action.

TEACH

☑ Teaching Tip

Students will benefit from practice in turning passive sentences into active ones. One way to provide students with practice is to give them passive sentences that name the doer in a *by* phrase, with the preposition *by* underlined. Explain that the object of *by* becomes the subject of the new active sentence. For example, students turn *Lunch was prepared by Chris* into the active sentence *Chris prepared lunch.*

386

10.10 Active and Passive Voice

A sentence is in the **active voice** when the subject performs the action of the verb.

> George Bernard Shaw **wrote** that play.

A sentence is in the **passive voice** when the subject receives the action of the verb.

> That play **was written** by George Bernard Shaw.

In the first sentence above, the author, George Bernard Shaw, seems more important because *George Bernard Shaw* is the subject of the sentence. In the second sentence, *play* seems more important than the name of the author because *play* is the subject of the sentence.

Notice that the verbs in passive-voice sentences consist of a form of *be* and the past participle. Often a phrase beginning with *by* follows the verb in a passive-voice sentence.

> Plays are performed **by actors**.

The active voice is usually a stronger, more direct way of expressing your ideas. Use the passive voice only if you want to emphasize the receiver of the action or to de-emphasize the performer of the action or if you do not know who the performer is.

> *The Tempest* **was performed**. [You may want to emphasize the play.]
> The curtain **was drawn**. [You may not want to say who did it.]
> The theater **was burned**. [You may not know who did it.]

The curtain **was drawn** to reveal an empty stage.

386   *Verbs*

Teacher's Classroom Resources

The following resources can be used for planning, instruction, practice, reinforcement, assessment, reteaching, enrichment, or evaluation.

🔧 **Teaching Tools**
Lesson Plans, p. 78

📁 **Blackline Masters**
Grammar Practice, p. 15
Grammar Reteaching, p. 15
Grammar Enrichment, p. 15

📖 ***Grammar Workbook***
Lesson 22

Exercise 20 Distinguishing Active and Passive Voice

For each sentence write whether the sentence is in the *active* or *passive* voice. For passive-voice sentences, write the word that names the receiver of the action.

1. *Pygmalion* was written by George Bernard Shaw.
2. Shaw's play is based on an ancient Greek myth.
3. Many people saw the play at the theater.
4. A show at the playhouse was criticized by many in the audience.
5. Critics gave it poor reviews in the newspapers.
6. The script was written by a brilliant playwright.
7. She created strange and different characters.
8. The director did his very best with the material.
9. The director was praised by several critics.
10. The scenery was designed by the playwright's relatives.
11. Costumes were created by the cast members.
12. The show was produced by members of a local drama club.
13. Most people predicted a short run for the show.
14. The public was surprised by the show's long run.
15. The cast used the criticism as a way of improvement.
16. Many people liked the show.
17. They told their friends about it.
18. Critics reconsidered their reviews.
19. The show was awarded a prize.
20. Now it is performed everywhere.

Exercise 21 Using Active Voice

Rewrite each sentence, changing the verb from the passive to the active voice. Sentences will vary because some modifiers can be placed in more than one position.

1. In 1861 a church in Washington, D.C., was leased by John T. Ford.
2. The building was managed by Ford as a music hall.
3. It was destroyed by fire in 1862.
4. An architectural gem was built on the site by Ford.
5. On April 14, 1865, the theater was attended by President Abraham Lincoln.
6. That night *Our American Cousin* was performed by the theater company.
7. During the performance, Lincoln was assassinated by John Wilkes Booth.
8. In 1866 the building was bought by the federal government for office space.
9. It was restored to its original function by the government in 1968.
10. Today Ford's Theater and the basement museum are visited by many tourists.

10.10 Active and Passive Voice **387**

PRACTICE AND ASSESS

Answers: Exercise 20
1. passive; *Pygmalion*
2. passive; play
3. active
4. passive; show
5. active
6. passive; script
7. active
8. active
9. passive; director
10. passive; scenery
11. passive; costumes
12. passive; show
13. active
14. passive; public
15. active
16. active
17. active
18. active
19. passive; show
20. passive; it

Answers: Exercise 21
Answers will vary. Some samples are given.
1. In 1861 John T. Ford leased a . . .
2. Ford managed the building . . .
3. Fire destroyed it in 1862.
4. Ford built an architectural gem . . .
5. On April 14, 1865, President Abraham Lincoln attended the theater.
6. That night the theater company performed *Our American Cousin.*
7. During the performance, John Wilkes Booth assassinated Lincoln.
8. In 1866, the federal government bought the building for office space.
9. The government restored it . . .
10. Today many tourists visit Ford's . . .

Independent Practice

Skills Practice
 *Grammar Practice,* p. 15
Grammar Reteaching, p. 15
Grammar Enrichment, p. 15

Grammar Workbook, Lesson 22

CLOSE

Using the active voice, write a brief plot for a school play.

Enabling Strategies

LEP **Using Active and Passive Voice**

One tip-off that a sentence is passive is the *by* phrase (*John was seen at the party by Mary*). However, the *by* phrase is often left out (*John was seen at the party*). Students learning English can recognize passive sentences if they learn that they can change active to passive only in sentences with direct objects. You might list sentences such as *Leo created the poster* and have students make them passive: *The poster was created by Leo.* Then have them change sentences from passive to active, for example, *The wall was built by the Romans* becomes *The romans built the wall.*

10.11 Irregular Verbs

388

Setting the Purpose

Lesson 10.11 teaches students to use the correct forms of irregular verbs.

FOCUS

Lesson Overview

Objective: To identify the correct base, past tense, and past participle forms of irregular verbs

Bellringer

When students enter the classroom, have this assignment on the board: *Choose the right word* (sing, sang *or* sung) *for the sentences. Jamie first _____ that song two years ago. My cat wakes up when she hears the birds _____ .*

TEACH

☑ Teaching Tip

Some verbs have two past participle forms, and both are acceptable. Some examples are *hide, hid, (have) hid* or *hidden; bite, bit, (have) bit* or *bitten; swell, swelled, (have) swelled* or *swollen; beat, beat, (have) beat* or *beaten.* Assure students that alternative forms listed in a dictionary are equally acceptable, unless they have a label such as "archaic" or "informal."

Technology Tip

Students who use their computer's spelling checker need to know that the checker can't catch words that are spelled correctly but used incorrectly. If they use the wrong verb form, such as *I begun this book last night,* they will discover the error only by proofreading their writing carefully, line by line.

Irregular Verbs			
Pattern	Base Form	Past Form	Past Participle (have, had)
One vowel changes to form the past and the past participle.	begin	began	begun
	drink	drank	drunk
	ring	rang	rung
	shrink	shrank *or* shrunk	shrunk *or* shrunken
	sing	sang	sung
	spring	sprang *or* sprung	sprung
	swim	swam	swum
The past form and past participle are the same.	bring	brought	brought
	buy	bought	bought
	catch	caught	caught
	creep	crept	crept
	feel	felt	felt
	get	got	got *or* gotten
	keep	kept	kept
	lay	laid	laid
	lead	led	led
	leave	left	left
	lend	lent	lent
	lose	lost	lost
	make	made	made
	pay	paid	paid
	say	said	said
	seek	sought	sought
	sell	sold	sold
	sit	sat	sat
	sleep	slept	slept
	swing	swung	swung
	teach	taught	taught
	think	thought	thought
	win	won	won

Teacher's Classroom Resources

The following resources can be used for planning, instruction, practice, reinforcement, reteaching, or enrichment.

🔧 **Teaching Tools**
Lesson Plans

📁 **Blackline Masters**
Grammar Practice, p. 16
Grammar Reteaching, p. 16
Grammar Enrichment, p. 16

📙 *Grammar Workbook*
Lesson 23

Exercise 22 — Identifying the Past and Past Participle of Irregular Verbs

For each sentence write the verb or verb phrase. Then write whether it uses the *past form* or the *past participle*.

1. We had thought the old theater a good home for our production.
2. However, problems began with our first rehearsal there.
3. We had paid good money for renovation of the curtains.
4. Somehow, in the process, they shrank.
5. A number of us caught the habit of carelessness, too.
6. Before, we had kept our props and costumes in a member's barn.
7. A week after our arrival at the old theater, however, someone lost them.
8. We had made an examination of the electrical system some time ago.
9. We had sought out every possible problem.
10. Then bells in the sound system rang at odd moments.

Exercise 23 — Using the Past and Past Participle of Irregular Verbs

Write the correct form (either *past form* or *past participle*) of the verb in parentheses.

1. Earlier the first performance had (begin).
2. I had (lose) my way to the new theater.
3. The star had (sing) two songs before my arrival.
4. I already had (pay), but I could not find the ticket.
5. I have (sit) in the theater for a long time.
6. Unfortunately the manager (leave) for a few minutes.
7. He has (keep) me waiting for ten minutes.
8. Luckily I (bring) a book with me.
9. I finally have (catch) my breath by sitting quietly.
10. One of my friends (bring) me a copy of the program.
11. Finally I (get) in.
12. I (think) the show was superb.
13. A famous teacher had (teach) the performers well.
14. At the show's end, the members of the audience (spring) to their feet.
15. The leading actor had (win) our hearts.
16. I (feel) happy and sad at the same time.
17. After the performance we had (seek) autographs.
18. The shy star (shrink) from the crowd.
19. At last she (creep) away.
20. She (say) she wanted to rest.

10.11 Irregular Verbs **389**

Enabling Strategies

LEP Using Sentence Patterns

Students whose first language is not English may benefit from using irregular verbs in sentence patterns that help show their meaning (*Today, I begin . . .; Yesterday I began . . .; I have already begun . . .*).

Encourage students to work with a partner to determine which verb forms they are using incorrectly and to note those in their personal journal. One student can give the present tense in a sentence, and the other can adjust the sentence to use past and past participle forms.

FOCUS

Lesson Overview
Objective: To identify the correct base, past tense, and past participle forms of irregular verbs

Bellringer
When students enter the classroom, have this assignment on the board: *Select the appropriate verb form (grow, grew, or grown) for each of the sentences.*
I will (grow, grew, grown) tomatoes in my garden this year. Last year, I (grow, grew, grown) lettuce and carrots, too.

Motivating Activity
Discuss the Bellringer. Explain that there are many irregular verbs such as *grow,* for which the past form and the past participle are different. Assure students that they already know most of these forms.

TEACH

☑ Teaching Tip
Students are likely to use most irregular verbs correctly but have persistent usage problems with a few. You might encourage them to start a section of their notebook or journal for the irregular verbs that give them problems. They can write the correct forms at the top of a page; for example, *go, went, (have) gone.* Below this heading, they can write example sentences, adding others as they occur in their own speech or writing.

10.12   More Irregular Verbs

Irregular Verbs			
Pattern	**Base Form**	**Past Form**	**Past Participle**
The base form and the past participle forms are the same.	become come run	became came ran	become come run
The past form ends in *-ew,* and the past participle ends in *-wn.*	blow draw fly grow know throw	blew drew flew grew knew threw	blown drawn flown grown known thrown
The past participle ends in *-en.*	bite break choose drive eat fall give ride rise see speak steal take write	bit broke chose drove ate fell gave rode rose saw spoke stole took wrote	bitten broken chosen driven eaten fallen given ridden risen seen spoken stolen taken written
The past form and the past participle do not follow any pattern.	am, are, is do go tear wear	was, were did went tore wore	been done gone torn worn
The base form, past form, and past participle are the same.	cut let put	cut let put	cut let put

390   *Verbs*

Teacher's Classroom Resources

The following resources can be used for planning, instruction, practice, reinforcement, reteaching, or enrichment.

🔧 **Teaching Tools**
Lesson Plans

📁 **Blackline Masters**
Grammar Practice, p. 16
Grammar Reteaching, p. 16
Grammar Enrichment, p. 16

📕 *Grammar Workbook*
Lesson 24

| **Exercise 24** | Identifying the Past and Past Participles of Irregular Verbs |

For each sentence write the verb or verb phrase. Then write whether it uses the *past* form or the *past participle*.

1. Our class went on a field trip to Broadway in New York City.
2. For a long time, Broadway has been a symbol of American theater.
3. The name came from the Dutch *Brede Weg*, broad way.
4. The midtown section of the street is known as the Great White Way.
5. The many theaters in the area have run thousands of productions over the years.
6. The winds of fortune blew first one way, then another over these theaters.
7. Over the years some have fallen into disrepair.
8. Others rose to glory, elegance, and prominence.
9. Through Broadway's influence, the theater bug has bitten many young people.
10. Broadway has done a great deal for theater professionals and audiences.

| **Exercise 25** | Using the Past and Past Participle of Irregular Verbs |

Write the correct form (*past* or *past participle*) of the verb in parentheses.

1. A prominent actress has (write) about her experiences with stage fright.
2. One night onstage she (become) immobile.
3. Before her appearance on stage, she had (know) her lines by heart.
4. She (take) several slow, deep breaths.
5. She regained her confidence and (throw) herself into the part.
6. Her drama coach had (give) her good advice about stage fright.
7. The actress eventually (come) through with a fine performance.
8. She (draw) on her knowledge of the character's personality.
9. The actress (grow) into the part.
10. She (see) through her character's eyes.
11. She even (wear) similar clothes.
12. By the end of the play, the actress (speak) her lines flawlessly.
13. A majority of theater critics have (choose) her for an award.
14. They say she has (steal) the show.
15. She has (grow) more confident.
16. Awareness of her experiences has (drive) me to try again.
17. I have (let) the director assign me to a speaking role.
18. Before that I had (draw) away from any public performance.
19. I had (run) away from opportunities for personal growth.
20. Now with this new determination, I have (break) away from the old me.

10.12 More Irregular Verbs **391**

PRACTICE AND ASSESS

Answers: Exercise 24
1. went—past
2. has been—past participle
3. came—past
4. is known—past participle
5. have run—past participle
6. blew—past
7. have fallen—past participle
8. rose—past
9. has bitten—past participle
10. has done—past participle

Answers: Exercise 25

1. written	11. wore
2. became	12. spoke
3. known	13. chosen
4. took	14. stolen
5. threw	15. grown
6. given	16. driven
7. came	17. let
8. drew	18. drawn
9. grew	19. run
10. saw	20. broken

Independent Practice

Skills Practice
📁 *Grammar Practice,* p. 16
📁 *Grammar Reteaching,* p. 16
📁 *Grammar Enrichment,* p. 16

📖 *Grammar Workbook,* Lesson 24

CLOSE

Have students write briefly on this topic: *Imagine that you are a film-maker. Describe your latest movie. Use several irregular verbs in the past tense and one in one of the perfect tenses.*

Enabling Strategies

LEP Using Forms of Irregular Verbs
Tell the following joke: *A young boy had to stay after school to work on verb forms. When he finished, the teacher was out of the room, so he added this note: "I have written 'have gone' one hundred times and I have went home."* Write this last sentence on the board, and ask students to explain the joke. Point out that knowing the correct forms is important, but using them is what counts. For usage practice say some present tense verb forms as volunteers write the verbs' past participles on the chalkboard after *I have.*

TEACH

About the Literature

Thornton Wilder's (1897–1975) plays *Our Town* (1938) and *The Skin of Our Teeth* (1942) both won Pulitzer Prizes for drama. Although well known as a playwright, Wilder first gained recognition as a novelist when he won a Pulitzer for his novel *The Bridge of San Luis Rey* (1927). His plays and novels are still admired among critics as well as by the reading and theater going public.

In *Our Town,* as in his other plays and novels, Wilder goes beyond the surface of everyday life to explore a universal theme. In this passage the Stage Manager reflects on the changes brought by the passing of time. These changes affect not only the people of Grover's Corners, New Hampshire, where the play is set, but also people everywhere. Moreover, these changes affect not only humans, but the natural world as well.

Linking Grammar and Literature

☑ Grammar Tip

After students read the passage, have them refocus on the highlighted verbs. Ask if the shifts in verb tense and form help readers to understand the passage better. If so, how?

Cooperative Learning

Have students work in groups to plan a short dramatic skit called "Our Town," "Our City," or "Our School." Suggest that they think of events held by their own town, city, or school, such as an annual picnic or a holiday parade. Group members then brainstorm for ideas, assign roles, and write a script showing one brief episode from the event, such as deciding who will ride where on the float for the Labor Day parade. Suggest that students use lively verbs in the active voice.

392

Grammar Review

Verbs

The play *Our Town* by Thornton Wilder focuses on the fictional New England town of Grover's Corners, New Hampshire. The play consists of three acts, each with a single theme. These themes are a typical day in the town, love and marriage, and death. Each act is introduced by the Stage Manager, who also breaks into the action now and then to explain something about the town or its inhabitants. In the excerpt presented here, the Stage Manager sets the stage for the second act. The passage has been annotated to show examples of the kinds of verbs covered in this unit.

Literature Model

from OUR TOWN
by Thornton Wilder

Present perfect tense of an irregular verb

Action verb followed by a direct object

Past tense of a regular verb

Past tense of an irregular verb

Passive voice

STAGE MANAGER: Three years have gone by. Yes, the sun's come up over a thousand times. Summers and winters have cracked the mountains a little bit more and the rains have brought down some of the dirt. Some babies that weren't even born before have begun talking regular sentences already; and a number of people who thought they were right young and spry have noticed that they can't bound up a flight of stairs like they used to, without their heart fluttering a little. All that can happen in a thousand days. Nature's been pushing and contriving in other ways, too: a number of young people fell in love and got married. Yes, the mountain got bit away a few fractions of an inch; millions of gallons of water went by the mill; and here and there a new home was set up under one roof.

392 *Verbs*

Teacher's Classroom Resources

The following resources can be used for planning, instruction, practice, reinforcement, assessment, reteaching, enrichment, or evaluation.

🔧 **Teaching Tools**
Lesson Plans, p. 79

📓 **Grammar Workbook**
Lessons 13–24
Unit 3 Review
Cumulative Review: Units 1–3

Unit Assessment

📁 *Tests with Answer Key*
Unit 10 Mastery Test, pp. 39–40

💿 *Test Generator*
Unit 10 Mastery Test

Exercise 1

Identifying Action Verbs and Direct Objects   For each sentence write the action verb. Then write and circle each direct object.

SAMPLE   This semester we read Thornton Wilder's play.
ANSWER   read (play)

1. Thornton Wilder used unconventional forms in his plays.
2. For example, any production of *Our Town* requires very few props.
3. Wilder's words and the audience's imagination provide the scenery.
4. This technique emphasizes the characters in the play.
5. The Henry Miller Theater hosted the first New York performance in 1938.
6. Thornton Wilder won the Pulitzer Prize for drama that year.
7. He wrote other successful plays and novels, too.
8. In 1965 he received the first National Medal for literature.
9. Both critics and ordinary people enjoy his books.
10. Thornton Wilder truly deserves his high position in American literature.

Exercise 2

Distinguishing Transitive and Intransitive Verbs   For each sentence write the action verb. Then write any direct objects. Write whether the verb is *transitive* or *intransitive*.

SAMPLE   This edition of the play gives stage directions in italics.
ANSWER   gives, directions — transitive

1. Thornton Wilder includes few stage directions in the script of *Our Town*.
2. The audience arrives to a stage with nothing on it.
3. The Stage Manager brings tables, chairs, and a bench on stage.
4. Then he leans against a pillar on the left of the stage.
5. At that moment the theater darkens.
6. Now the Stage Manager speaks into the darkness.
7. He provides a verbal map of Grover's Corners.
8. He also introduces the major characters to the audience.
9. The tables and chairs remain on stage for Act II.
10. In this act the Stage Manager talks about the passage of time.

Grammar Review   **393**

PRACTICE AND ASSESS

Answers: Exercise 1
1. used (forms)
2. requires (props)
3. provide (scenery)
4. emphasizes (characters)
5. hosted (performance)
6. won (Pulitzer Prize)
7. wrote (plays,) (novels)
8. received (National Medal)
9. enjoy (books)
10. deserves (position)

Answers: Exercise 2
1. includes, directions—transitive
2. arrives—intransitive
3. brings, tables, chairs, bench—transitive
4. leans—intransitive
5. darkens—intransitive
6. speaks—intransitive
7. provides, map—transitive
8. introduces, characters—transitive
9. remain—intransitive
10. talks—intransitive

UNIT 10
Review

Answers: Exercise 3
1. activities
2. newspaper; <u>Dr. Gibbs</u>
3. future; <u>audience</u>
4. breakfast; <u>family</u>
5. children
6. mother
7. congratulations; <u>teacher</u>
8. antiques, beans
9. history; <u>audience</u>
10. question; <u>Mr. Webb</u>

Answers: Exercise 4
1. predicts, action verb; direct object
2. delivers, action verb; direct object
3. is, linking verb; predicate adjective
4. loves, action verb; direct object
5. offers, action verb; indirect object
6. promised, action verb; indirect object
7. became, linking verb; predicate noun
8. edits, action verb; direct object
9. seems, linking verb; predicate adjective
10. are, linking verb; predicate noun

Exercise 3

Distinguishing Direct and Indirect Objects   For each sentence write the direct object. If the sentence contains an indirect object, write it and then underline it.

1. In the first scene of *Our Town*, the audience sees morning activities.
2. Young Joe Crowell hands Dr. Gibbs a newspaper.
3. The Stage Manager shows the audience Joe's future.
4. Mrs. Webb serves her family a hearty breakfast.
5. Mrs. Webb and Mrs. Gibbs both scold their children for their misbehavior.
6. George Gibbs asks his mother for a larger allowance.
7. Mrs. Gibbs sends Rebecca's teacher her congratulations.
8. Mrs. Gibbs and Mrs. Webb discuss antiques and beans.
9. The Stage Manager tells the audience the history of Grover's Corners.
10. A woman in the balcony asks Mr. Webb a question.

Exercise 4

Identifying Action Verbs and Linking Verbs   For each sentence write each verb, and write whether it is an *action verb* or a *linking verb*. Then write whether each underlined word is a *predicate noun, predicate adjective, direct object*, or *indirect object*.

SAMPLE   Organist Simon Stimson directs the church <u>choir</u>.
ANSWER   directs, action verb; direct object

1. Joe Crowell's knee predicts the day's <u>weather.</u>
2. Howie Newsome delivers <u>milk</u> to local families.
3. Banker Cartwright is very <u>wealthy</u>.
4. Rebecca Gibbs loves <u>money</u> most of all.
5. A second-hand furniture man offers <u>Mrs. Gibbs</u> money for her highboy.
6. Long ago Mrs. Gibbs promised <u>herself</u> a trip to Paris, France.
7. Professor Willard became an <u>expert</u> on the history of Grover's Corners.
8. Charles Webb edits the local <u>newspaper</u>, the *Sentinel*.
9. In Mr. Webb's opinion, Grover's Corners seems very <u>ordinary</u>.
10. Emily Webb and George Gibbs are very good <u>friends</u>.

Exercise 5

Distinguishing Past and Present Tenses   Write the correct form of the verb in parentheses. Then write whether it is in the *present* or *past* tense.

SAMPLE   For eight years in childhood, Thornton Wilder (live) in China.
ANSWER   lived, past

1. Thornton Wilder was born in 1897 and (die) in 1975.
2. At the announcement of a new Wilder novel, buyers (line) up at bookstores.
3. Critics today still (applaud) Wilder's emphasis on ordinary people.
4. That emphasis (make) his work very appealing to us today.
5. Many new readers (comment) on Wilder's compassion.
6. Probably his most famous novel (remain) *The Bridge of San Luis Rey*.
7. He (publish) this book in 1927.
8. This story (explore) the lives of five people who die in a bridge collapse.
9. In 1944 Hollywood (release) a film version of *The Bridge of San Luis Rey*.
10. This movie (fail) at the box office.

Exercise 6

Using Present and Past Progressive Forms   For each sentence write the verb form indicated in italics.

SAMPLE   I (join) the community theater. *present progressive*
ANSWER   am joining

1. Our theater (consider) a production of *Our Town*. *present progressive*
2. Committee members (debate) between that play and *The Glass Menagerie* by Tennessee Williams. *present progressive*
3. At first they (lean) toward a musical production. *past progressive*
4. Then they (worry) about the cost of a musical. *past progressive*
5. Now they (look) for a regular drama. *present progressive*
6. I (hope) that they choose *Our Town*. *present progressive*
7. If so, I (try) out for the role of Emily. *present progressive*
8. My sister (tell) me about her experiences with the play. *past progressive*
9. Last year she and her friends (aim) for a production. *past progressive*
10. That project, however, (interfere) with other plans. *past progressive*

Grammar Review   **395**

Answers: Exercise 5
1. died, past
2. lined, past
3. applaud, present
4. makes, present
5. comment, present
6. remains, present
7. published, past
8. explores, present
9. released, past
10. failed, past

Answers: Exercise 6
1. is considering
2. are debating
3. were leaning
4. were worrying
5. are looking
6. am hoping
7. am trying
8. was telling
9. were aiming
10. was interfering

UNIT 10
Review

Answers: Exercise 7
1. will buy, future
2. will have flagged, future perfect
3. will wake up, future
4. will marry, future
5. will earn, future
6. will have broken out, future perfect
7. will have, future
8. will skip, future
9. will have canned, future perfect
10. will travel, future

Answers: Exercise 8
1. Thornton Wilder wrote …
2. The Stage Manager introduces …
3. Doc Gibbs delivered the baby.
4. Charles Webb publishes …
5. Simon Stimson directs the choir.
6. The living remember the dead.
7. Mrs. Webb fills the kitchen …
8. Rebecca Gibbs saved …
9. Archaeologists found fossils in …
10. A hundred years ago, the English settled …

Exercise 7

Identifying Future Tenses   For each sentence write the verb and write whether it is in the *future* or *future perfect*.

SAMPLE   By Act II we will have met the important characters.
ANSWER   will have met, future perfect

1. Mr. Cartwright will buy the first automobile in Grover's Corners in 1906.
2. By 6:00 A.M. Shorty Hawkins will have flagged the train to Boston.
3. Folks in town will wake up shortly.
4. Miss Foster will marry a man from Concord sometime soon.
5. According to the Stage Manager, Joe Crowell will earn a scholarship.
6. By the time of his college graduation, a world war will have broken out.
7. By ten o'clock Wally will have his head full of information about Canada.
8. Because of her sore throat, Mrs. Webb will skip choir this evening.
9. Mrs. Webb will have canned forty quarts of beans over the next few weeks.
10. In her dreams Mrs. Gibbs will travel to Paris, France, someday.

Exercise 8

Using Active Voice   Rewrite each sentence, changing the sentence from the passive voice to the active voice.

SAMPLE   The factory is owned by Banker Cartwright.
ANSWER   Banker Cartwright owns the factory.

1. *Our Town* was written by Thornton Wilder.
2. Each act is introduced by the Stage Manager.
3. The baby was delivered by Doc Gibbs.
4. The newspaper is published by Charles Webb.
5. The choir is directed by Simon Stimson.
6. The dead are remembered by the living.
7. The kitchen stove is filled with wood by Mrs. Webb.
8. Part of her allowance was saved by Rebecca Gibbs.
9. Fossils were found by archaeologists in Silas Peckham's cow pasture.
10. A hundred years ago, the area of Grover's Corners was settled by the English.

Exercise 9

Using the Past and Past Participle of Irregular Verbs   For each sentence write the appropriate form of the verb in parentheses.

SAMPLE   Emily (stand) rigidly, in her image of an elegant lady.

ANSWER   stood

1. Grover's Corners has (see) the comings and goings of many generations.
2. Not many young people (leave) Grover's Corners after graduation.
3. The Stage Manager has not (know) any remarkable people to come out of Grover's Corners.
4. Dr. Gibbs (bring) the Goruslawksi twins into the world—and most of the other babies in town, too.
5. The folks in town (sleep) later in the morning than those out on the farms.
6. The residents of Grover's Corners had (begin) their morning routine.
7. Rebecca Gibbs (wear) her blue gingham dress to school.
8. George Gibbs (eat) his breakfast with his geography book on the table.
9. Before her marriage, Miss Foster (teach) Joe Crowell's grade school class.
10. Mrs. Webb has (grow) enough beans to feed her family for the winter.
11. She (bite) into one to see if it was sweet and ripe.
12. That day Emily had (spoke) to her class about the Louisiana Purchase.
13. Despite criticism, George has again (throw) his ball into the air.
14. George had (break) one of his father's rules.
15. Dr. Gibbs had (take) his biannual trip to the Civil War battlefields.
16. By now he has (seek) out almost all of them.
17. The church bell (ring) out over the town of Grover's Corners.
18. Despite her poor voice, Mrs. Gibbs (sing) in the church choir.
19. According to the ladies in the choir, Mr. Stimson had (drink) too much before practice.
20. Dr. Gibbs worried that Mrs. Gibbs had (catch) cold on her way home from choir practice.
21. The Cartwright family has just (lay) the foundation for a new bank in Grover's Corners.
22. From her window Emily (give) George hints about his algebra homework.
23. Professor Willard had (come) over from the university for his lecture on the history of Grover's Corners.
24. As editor of the town newspaper, Mr. Webb had (become) the town's unofficial spokesperson.
25. A woman in the balcony had (rise) to her feet to ask Mr. Webb a question.

Grammar Review   **397**

Answers: Exercise 9
1. seen
2. left
3. known
4. brought
5. slept
6. begun
7. wore
8. ate
9. taught
10. grown
11. bit
12. spoken
13. thrown
14. broken
15. taken
16. sought
17. rang
18. sang
19. drunk
20. caught
21. laid
22. gave
23. come
24. become
25. risen

UNIT 10
Review

Answers: Exercise 10
Proofreading
This proofreading activity provides editing practice with (1) the current or previous units' skills, (2) the **Troubleshooter** errors, and (3) spelling errors. Students should be able to complete the exercise by referring to the units, the **Troubleshooter,** and a dictionary.

	Error (Type of Error)
1.	• done (verb form)
2.	• shows (subject-verb agreement)
3.	• lie (subject-verb agreement)
4.	• dunes, (nonessential appositive phrase)
5.	• shrunk *or* shrunken (verb form)
6.	• separately (spelling)
7.	• they think (verb tense)
8.	• moving (spelling)
9.	• swum (verb form)
10.	• cut (verb form)

398

The following passage is about artist Roger Brown, whose work appears below. Rewrite the passage, correcting the errors in spelling, grammar, and usage. Add any missing punctuation. There are ten errors.

Roger Brown

[1]The painting below was did by Chicago artist Roger Brown. [2]This work show a row of houses backed by sand dunes and palm trees. [3]The ocean and the setting or rising sun lies beyond the dunes and trees. [4]The dunes rigid mounds of sand, seem to be carved out of stone.

[5]The characters in this work have shrank to silhouettes. [6]They are either sitting seperately in their homes or walking alone along the sidewalk. [7]The walkers are moving fast; perhaps they will think they are late. [8]They are the only things moving in the picture. [9]The ocean looks as if no one has ever swam there. [10]Even the sun, cutted in half by the horizon, looks motionless.

Roger Brown, *Coast of California,* **1987**

About the Art

Roger Brown, *Coast of California,* **1987**

Students will see that *Coast of California* is not a realistic painting. Point out that it reflects twentieth-century artistic styles called Regionalism, Pop Art, and Patterning. The last dominates Brown's work. The silhouetted figures show some variations within the rigid patterns the artist has created. The viewer seems to be high above the scene. *Coast of California,* an oil on canvas, 48 by 72 inches, is in the Phyllis Kind Gallery in New York City.

Mixed Review

Exercise 11

For each numbered item write the appropriate form of the verb requested. Be sure that your completed sentences make sense. Some answers will vary.

The title of the play *Our Town* [1](*action verb, present tense*) a strong clue to the story's theme. Even though the action [2](*keep—present tense, passive voice*) in one small New Hampshire town, author Thornton Wilder is really giving [3](*indirect object*) the whole world. Other clues [4](*linking verb, present tense*) obvious, too. In Act I Rebecca notices that the same moon [5](*intransitive verb, present tense*) down on other countries. Later in the act she [6](*tell—future tense*) her brother the story of a letter addressed to Jane Crofut, Grover's Corners, the Universe.

Wilder once wrote that he deliberately [7](*emphasize—past tense*) big numbers like *thousands* and *millions*. By doing so he [8](*suggest—present progressive tense*) that the big and the small [9](*linking verb, present tense*) one. The Stage Manager is one [10](*predicate noun*) who comments on the big picture and the small.

Many universal events [11](*intransitive verb, present tense*). In Act I twin babies [12](*deliver—present tense, passive voice*) by Dr. Webb. In Act II Emily Webb and George Gibbs [13](*get—present progressive tense*) married, just as millions of people [14](*do—present perfect tense*) in the past and millions [15](*do—future tense*) in the future. Some characters in the play [16](*intransitive verb, present tense*) and are buried in the town cemetery.

Many scenes in the play emphasize ordinary [17](*direct object*). Families [18](*transitive verb, present tense*) meals together in every act. Children [19](*intransitive verb, present tense*) to school, and adults do chores. Wilder also stresses small daily [20](*direct object*), like the sound of birds, the scent of flowers, the smell of food, or the feel of newly ironed clothes. These joys, he suggests, are the real [21](*predicate noun*) of life. In Act III Emily [22](*learn—present tense*) anew to appreciate such joys. Dead people in the cemetery give [23](*indirect object*) advice about how to achieve peace and harmony. She [24](*learn—present perfect tense*) not to take life for granted.

By the end of the play the audience [25](*catch—future perfect tense*) a glimpse of their own lives.

Grammar Review **399**

Answers: Exercise 11
Mixed Review
Answers with asterisks may vary, but some suggestions are given below.
1. *provides
2. is kept
3. *us
4. *are
5. *shines
6. will tell
7. emphasized
8. is suggesting
9. *are
10. *character
11. *occur
12. are delivered
13. are getting
14. have done
15. will do
16. *die
17. *events
18. *eat
19. *go
20. *joys
21. *purpose
22. learns
23. *her
24. has learned
25. will have caught

CLOSE

Form small groups and have each choose a scribe. Ask each group to write several sentences in which they describe and reflect on one or more changes they have observed in their neighborhood, city, or town. Suggest that groups begin their paragraph with the Stage Manager's opening line: "Three years have gone by," from the *Our Town* passage. Then have each group discuss the kinds of verbs and verb tenses they used. Have them focus on the following questions: What do the different verb forms add to the meaning of the paragraph? How could students improve their paragraphs?

Verbs in Writing

Ask students to read the first section of this page silently. Then discuss Katherine Paterson's use of verbs in relation to the Techniques with Verbs section below. Does she use vague or vivid verbs? Are verb tenses formed correctly?

Techniques with Verbs

Discuss the two points listed. Then have students reread the passage on page 398. Quickly review the proofreading corrections students made to the passage. Next ask students whether they would have chosen to use a form of the verb *show* in the second sentence. Ask them to look through the rest of the passage and comment on the power of the rest of the verbs.

Practice

The answers to this challenging and enriching activity will vary. Refer to Techniques with Verbs as you evaluate student choices. Note that this activity is not limited to verbs. Sample answer:

Park and Noah strolled slowly along the sidewalk, deep in conversation. They evidenced no notice to their surroundings, not observing the hustle and bustle of busy commuters and the noise of cars speeding by on the street. An occasional pedestrian stole a glance at the two friends, but neither boy heeded. After several blocks, Park finally grasped Noah's shoulder and propelled him towards a small coffee shop. "Let's eat a bite. I haven't eaten since breakfast!" Then they commenced their conversation anew, heads close together.

Writing Application

Verbs in Writing As you read this passage from *Lyddie*, notice how Katherine Paterson's precise verbs and verb forms convey the sounds and actions of Lyddie's first day in the factory. Study the passage, focusing on the italicized words.

> His little red mouth *pursed,* he *stepped* up on a stool and *pulled* out his pocket watch. At the same moment, the bell in the tower above the roof *began* to *ring.* He *yanked* the cord, the wide leather belt above *shifted* from a loose to a tight pulley, and suddenly all the hundred or so silent looms, in raucous concert, *shuddered* and *groaned* into fearsome life. Lyddie's first full day as a factory girl *had begun.*

Techniques with Verbs Try to apply some of Katherine Paterson's writing techniques when you write and revise your own work.

1. Whenever possible, replace vague and common verbs with vivid and specific verbs. Compare the following:

Vague common verbs *moved* into fearsome life
Paterson's version *shuddered* and *groaned* into fearsome life

2. Keep the timing of your characters' actions clear by correctly forming the tenses of irregular verbs:

Incorrect verb tense Lyddie's first full day as a factory girl *had began.*
Paterson's version Lyddie's first full day as a factory girl *had begun.*

Practice Practice these techniques by revising the following passage, using a separate sheet of paper. Pay particular attention to the underlined words.

Park and Noah walked slowly along the sidewalk, deep in conversation. They took no notice of their surroundings, not noticing the hustle and bustle of busy commuters and the noise of cars driving by on the street. An occasional pedestrian made a glance at the two friends, but neither boy noticed. After several blocks, Park finally touched Noah's shoulder and turned him towards a small coffee shop. "Let's take a bite. I haven't eaten since breakfast!" Then they started their conversation again, heads close together.

Teacher's Classroom Resources

The following resources can be used for assessment or evaluation.

Unit Assessment

📂 *Tests with Answer Key*
Unit 10 Mastery Test, pp. 39–40

💿 *Test Generator*
Unit 10 Mastery Test

You may wish to administer the Unit 10 Mastery Test at this point.

UNIT 11

Pronouns

Grammar | **Lessons**

401

UNIT GOALS

The goal of Unit 11 is to help students, through example and instruction, to develop an understanding of the various kinds of pronouns and to use them appropriately in their writing. The lessons focus on personal pronouns (subject and object), pronoun antecedents, possessive pronouns, indefinite pronouns, reflexive and intensive pronouns, and interrogative and demonstrative pronouns.

Unit Assessment

📁 *Tests with Answer Key*
Unit 11 Pretest, pp. 41–42
Unit 11 Mastery Test, pp. 43–44

💿 *Test Generator*
Unit 11 Pretest
Unit 11 Mastery Test

You may wish to administer the Unit 11 Pretest at this point.

Key to Ability Levels

Enabling Strategies have been coded for varying learning styles and abilities.

L1 Level 1 activities are within the ability range of Learning Disabled students.

L2 Level 2 activities are basic-to-average activities and are within the ability range of average students.

L3 Level 3 activities are challenging activities and are within the ability range of above-average students.

LEP LEP activities are within the ability range of Limited English Proficiency students.

FOCUS

Lesson Overview
Objective: To identify several uses of personal pronouns

🔔 Bellringer
When students enter the classroom, have this assignment on the board: *When you read or hear a story about someone, is that person's name used in every sentence? Write other words that you might see in place of the person's name.*

Motivating Activity
Discuss students' answers to the Bellringer questions. How many pronouns are they able to list? Discuss the reasons for replacing some nouns with pronouns in writing.

TEACH

◖ Vocabulary Link
The prefix *pro-* comes from the Latin word *pro*, which means "before," "forward," or "for," so *pronoun* translates as "for the noun."

⏱ Two-Minute Skill Drill
Have students write a short paragraph using the following subject and object pronouns:

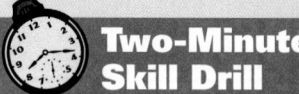

he	she	they
him	her	them

402

11.1 | Personal Pronouns

A **pronoun** is a word that takes the place of one or more nouns and the words that describe those nouns.

Pronouns that are used to refer to people or things are called **personal pronouns.**

Personal pronouns are singular or plural. Some personal pronouns are used as the subjects of sentences. Others are used as the objects of verbs or prepositions.

A **subject pronoun** is used as the subject of a sentence.

> Rita likes books. **She** particularly likes novels.

In the example above, the pronoun *She* replaces the noun *Rita* as the subject of the sentence.

An **object pronoun** is used as the object of a verb or a preposition.

> The novel amuses Rita. The novel amuses **her.** [direct object of the verb *amuses*]
>
> For Raul's birthday Rita gave **him** a novel. [indirect object of the verb *gave*]
>
> Rita presented a biography of Mark Twain to **us.** [object of the preposition *to*]

Personal Pronouns		
	Singular	**Plural**
Used as Subjects	I you he, she, it	we you they
Used as Objects	me you him, her, it	us you them

402 *Pronouns*

Teacher's Classroom Resources

The following resources can be used for planning, instruction, practice, reinforcement, assessment, reteaching, enrichment, or evaluation.

🔧 **Teaching Tools**
Lesson Plans, p. 80

📁 **Blackline Masters**
Grammar Practice, p. 17
Grammar Reteaching, p. 17
Grammar Enrichment, p. 17

📖 ***Grammar Workbook***
Lesson 25

Unit Assessment

📂 *Tests with Answer Key*
Unit 11 Pretest, pp. 41–42

💿 *Test Generator*
Unit 11 Pretest

You may wish to administer the Unit 11 Pretest at this point.

Exercise 1 — Identifying Personal Pronouns

Write each pronoun, and write whether it is a *subject* pronoun or an *object* pronoun.

1. Gwendolyn Brooks writes poems; they are about everyday life.
2. Slang and the rhythms of jazz and the blues are important to her.
3. She was born in Topeka, Kansas, but grew up in Chicago.
4. The poet Langston Hughes gave her literary advice.
5. Brooks always loved poetry; she wrote it from the age of seven.
6. Brooks taught poetry to students; she was a role model for them.
7. In 1949 she wrote a poetry collection called *Annie Allen.*
8. It made Brooks the first black poet to receive a Pulitzer Prize.
9. I have read the book, and the poems fascinate me.
10. The combination of street talk and American verse will amuse you.

Exercise 2 — Using Personal Pronouns

Write the pronoun you could use in place of each underlined word or words.

1. Sarah Orne Jewett was an American writer of the1800s.
2. The *Atlantic Monthly* first published Jewett.
3. This author wrote the stories at age nineteen.
4. These stories are about history and tradition.
5. The Jewetts lived amid Maine's many villages.
6. Sarah's father was a doctor with an interest in books and people.
7. Sarah studied books and people with her father.
8. Young Sarah observed people's ways of life.
9. She described the people in her stories.
10. She wrote stories about her experiences.
11. Readers learned about life in New England.
12. Bob wrote a research report on Sarah Jewett.
13. "A White Heron" is Sarah Jewett's best-known story.
14. The heron catches a young girl's attention.
15. The young girl approaches the nest.
16. The wild bird avoids the young girl.
17. "A White Heron" appeals to Robert.
18. Our class had difficulty with the story.
19. Luisa pointed out the theme to our class.
20. Rosa said, "Let Rosa help you."

11.1 Personal Pronouns **403**

Enabling Strategies

LEP Understanding *They*

Make sure students whose first language is not English understand that the plural *they* can indicate two or more of the singular words *he, she,* and *it.* The context indicates whom or what is being referred to. The format may be different in other languages. For example, the German word *sie* stands for *she, you,* and *they.* In Hungarian, one word stands for *he, she,* and *it.* In Spanish, sometimes the subject pronoun is indicated only in the verb form. Invite students to give additional examples from other languages.

FOCUS

Lesson Overview

Objective: To identify pronoun antecedents and to ensure that pronouns agree with their antecedents

Bellringer

When students enter the classroom, have this assignment on the board: *What is the subject of the second sentence below?*

Dave saw his brother Bill downtown. He was going into the movie theater.

Motivating Activity

Discuss the Bellringer and have students volunteer other sentences containing confusing pronouns.

TEACH

☑ Teaching Tip

An antecedent is a noun or group of words to which a pronoun refers. In writing, students must check that the antecedent, the *what* or *whom* to which a pronoun refers, is clear. The pronoun also must agree with its antecedent in number (singular or plural) and gender (masculine, feminine, or neuter).

Ⓐ Vocabulary Link

The word *antecedent* comes from the Latin word *antecedere,* which means "to go before." Other words derived from the same prefix are *anteroom* (room used before going into another room) and *antipasto* (food eaten before the meal).

11.2   Pronouns and Antecedents

Read the following sentences. Can you tell to whom the pronoun *She* refers?

> Louisa May Alcott wrote a novel about a young woman. **She** has three sisters.

The sentence is not clear because *She* could refer either to the *young woman* or to *Louisa May Alcott*. Sometimes you must repeat a noun or rewrite a sentence to avoid confusion.

> Louisa May Alcott wrote a novel about a young woman. **The young woman** has three sisters.

The noun or group of words that a pronoun refers to is called its **antecedent**.

When you use a pronoun, you should be sure that it refers to its antecedent clearly. Be especially careful when you use the pronoun *they*. Notice this pronoun in the following sentence.

> **WRONG: They** have two books by Alcott at the school library.

To whom does *They* refer? Its meaning is unclear. The sentence might be corrected in the following way.

> **RIGHT:** The school library has two books by Alcott.

Be sure every pronoun agrees with its antecedent in number (singular or plural) and gender. The gender of a noun or pronoun may be masculine, feminine, or neuter (referring to things). Notice the pronoun-antecedent agreement below.

> The Marches must face a death in their family. **They** face **it** with courage.

404   *Pronouns*

Teacher's Classroom Resources

The following resources can be used for planning, instruction, practice, reinforcement, reteaching, or enrichment.

Teaching Tools
Lesson Plans

Blackline Masters
Grammar Practice, p. 18
Grammar Reteaching, p. 18
Grammar Enrichment, p. 18

Grammar Workbook
Lesson 26

Exercise 3   **Using Pronouns and Antecedents Correctly**

Write the correct pronoun for the second sentence in each pair. Then write the antecedent the pronoun refers to.

1. Louisa May Alcott lived near Boston, Massachusetts. _____ had many famous neighbors.
2. Alcott came from a poor family. _____ wanted to help earn money.
3. Alcott worked as a teacher. Students learned history from _____.
4. But that job was not enough. _____ did not pay well.
5. Alcott also made dresses. Women paid Alcott money for _____.
6. The writer also tried housekeeping. That job didn't suit _____.
7. Alcott then tried writing. Finally _____ had found a career!
8. Alcott's first book contained stories for young children. _____ was called *Flower Fables*.
9. Two more books by Alcott appeared quickly. _____ describe her hospital work and her teaching days.
10. An editor asked Alcott to write a book for girls. The editor finally persuaded _____ .
11. In 1868 Alcott published the first part of *Little Women*. _____ was a success.
12. *Little Women* was very popular in the 1800s. _____ changed people's ideas about women's role in society.
13. In the novel Jo March is the main character. _____ eventually becomes a writer.
14. The father is a chaplain in the Civil War. _____ is away.
15. The girls and mother have little money. Life is hard for _____.
16. The March sisters attend school. _____ also earn money for their family.
17. Women had difficulty finding suitable work. _____ were not paid well.
18. Jo has an independent spirit. _____ is the most independent girl.
19. Jo turns down marriage to the boy next door. Jo says no to _____.
20. She tells her sisters. _____ are shocked.
21. Then Jo meets Fritz Bhaer. She ultimately falls in love with _____ .
22. Beth is a musician. _____ dies of a terrible illness.
23. Alcott relied on incidents from her own childhood. _____ seem realistic.
24. At the library I found Alcott's *An Old-Fashioned Girl*. _____ was published in 1870.
25. We have *Little Men* and *Jo's Boys*. I have read _____ .

11.2 Pronouns and Antecedents   **405**

PRACTICE AND ASSESS

Answers: Exercise 3
1. She—Louisa May Alcott
2. She—Alcott
3. her—Alcott
4. It—job
5. them—dresses
6. her—writer
7. she—Alcott
8. It—book
9. They—books
10. her—Alcott
11. It—part
12. It—*Little Women*
13. She—Jo March
14. He—father
15. them—girls and mother
16. They—sisters
17. They—Women
18. She—Jo
19. him—boy
20. They—sisters
21. him—Fritz Bhaer
22. She—Beth
23. They—incidents
24. It—*An Old-Fashioned Girl*
25. them—*Little Men* and *Jo's Boys*

Independent Practice

Skills Practice
 *Grammar Practice*, p. 18
📁 *Grammar Reteaching*, p. 18
📁 *Grammar Enrichment*, p. 18
📖 *Grammar Workbook*, Lesson 26

CLOSE

Ask students to write a brief summary of a book or screenplay they might like to write. Have them use pronouns in their writing, making sure that the pronouns refer clearly to and agree with their antecedents.

Enabling Strategies

LEP **Making Pronouns Agree with Antecedents**

A common error is the use of *them* to refer to a singular antecedent in order to avoid using *him or her* or using *him* or *her* alone. A good solution is to change the number of the antecedent noun so that *them* is appropriate. For example, change *If a customer comes to the counter, ask them what they want* to *If customers come to the counter, ask them what they want.*

Setting the Purpose

Lesson 11.3 helps students use subject pronouns and object pronouns appropriately.

FOCUS

Lesson Overview

Objective: To identify the use of subject and object pronouns in compounds, in incomplete comparisons, and after linking verbs

Bellringer

When students enter the classroom, have this assignment on the board: *Choose the correct pronoun.*
Tina and (I, me) liked the book.
Frank yelled at you and (I, me).

TEACH

☑ Teaching Tip

Many students have difficulty in choosing the correct form of a pronoun when it is the second element in a compound subject or object. Mistakes usually occur when the first part of the compound is a word that does not change form, such as a name or the pronoun *you.*

Two-Minute Skill Drill

List these pronouns on the board and have students identify the subject pronouns and the object pronouns:

you	I	her
she	me	them
he	they	it

11.3 Using Pronouns Correctly

Subject pronouns are used in compound subjects, and object pronouns are used in compound objects.

SUBJECT

Tina and Sam

she he

Tina and Sam recently read *Heidi.* **She** and **he** recently read *Heidi.* [*She* and *he* form the compound subject.]
Heidi appealed to Sam and Tina. *Heidi* appealed to **him** and **her.** [*Him* and *her* form the compound object.]

Whenever the subject pronoun *I* or the object pronoun *me* is part of the compound subject or object, *I* or *me* should come last.

Tina and **I** liked the book. [not *I and Tina*]

Sometimes a pronoun and a noun are used together for emphasis. The form of the pronoun depends on its function in the sentence.

We students read the book. [*We* is the subject.]
The book delighted **us** readers. [*Us* is the direct object.]

Some sentences make incomplete comparisons. The form of the pronoun can affect the meaning of such sentences. In any incomplete comparison, use the pronoun that would be correct if the comparison were complete.

Heidi liked Peter more than **she** [did]. [Heidi and Klara liked Peter, but Heidi liked him more than Klara did.]
Heidi liked Peter more than [she liked] **her.** [Heidi liked Peter and Klara, but Heidi liked Peter more than she liked Klara.]

In formal writing use a subject pronoun after a linking verb.

Heidi's closest friend is **he.**

read about

him her

Peter and Heidi.

OBJECT

406 *Pronouns*

Teacher's Classroom Resources

The following resources can be used for planning, instruction, practice, reinforcement, reteaching, or enrichment.

🔧 **Teaching Tools**
Lesson Plans

📁 **Blackline Masters**
Grammar Practice
Grammar Reteaching, p. 19
Grammar Enrichment

📘 *Grammar Workbook*
Lesson 27

| Exercise 4 | Identifying Subject and Object Pronouns |

Write the correct pronoun for each underlined noun. Then write whether each one is a *subject* pronoun or an *object* pronoun.

1. Eudora Welty and <u>William Faulkner</u> are famous writers from Mississippi.
2. Works by <u>Welty</u> and Faulkner are intimately connected to the atmosphere of the South.
3. Faulkner wrote in a more serious tone than <u>Welty</u>.
4. <u>Faulkner</u> demands much of us readers.
5. Important prizes were awarded to both Welty and <u>Faulkner</u>.

| Exercise 5 | Using Subject and Object Pronouns Correctly |

Write the correct word or words in parentheses. Then write whether each pronoun is a *subject* pronoun or an *object* pronoun.

1. *Heidi* entertained (we, us) readers.
2. Steffi and (me, I) read the story last weekend.
3. Heidi is an orphan; Grandfather takes care of (she, her).
4. (She, Her) and Grandfather live in the Swiss Alps.
5. Heidi and (he, him) tend goats together.
6. Peter and (her, she) love the mountains.
7. Peter becomes a friend to Heidi's grandfather and (she, her).
8. Grandfather is stern, although no one is kinder than (he, him).
9. (We, Us) readers grow fond of Grandfather.
10. My favorite character is (he, him).
11. Grandfather became almost real to (Juan and I, Juan and me).
12. (She, Her) and Peter tend goats.
13. Heidi says good-bye to (Peter and he, Peter and him).
14. (We, Us) readers feel very sympathetic toward Heidi.
15. In fact, I felt almost as sad as (she, her).
16. Between Peter and (she, her), they help Klara toward recovery.
17. Klara and (she, her) become friends in the city.
18. Heidi's dearest friends are Grandfather and (he, him).
19. Klara cannot walk, so Heidi aids the family and (she, her).
20. (Tom and I, Me and Tom) guessed the ending.

11.3 Using Pronouns Correctly   **407**

PRACTICE AND ASSESS

Answers: Exercise 4
1. he—subject
2. her—object
3. she—subject
4. He—subject
5. him—object

Answers: Exercise 5
1. us—object
2. I—subject
3. her—object
4. She—subject
5. he—subject
6. she—subject
7. her—object
8. he—subject
9. We—subject
10. he—subject
11. Juan and me—object
12. She—subject
13. Peter and him—object
14. We—subject
15. she—subject
16. her—object
17. she—subject
18. he—subject
19. her—object
20. Tom and I—subject

Independent Practice

Skills Practice

 Grammar Reteaching, p. 19

Grammar Workbook, Lesson 27

CLOSE

Have students write a paragraph describing what it would be like to form a special friendship. Ask them to use pronouns in compound subjects and in compound objects in their writing.

Enabling Strategies

LEP Using Pronouns Correctly

Suggest that students whose first language is not English create pronoun charts in their journals to help them determine which pronoun to use in a sentence. Have them list subject pronouns in one column (*I, you, he, she, it we,* *they*) and object pronouns in a second column (*me, you, him, her, it, us, them*). Tell students to refer to their charts and a simple sample sentence like "I know them" or "I like them" to decide which list of pronouns to use in sentences.

FOCUS

Lesson Overview

Objective: To identify the two forms of possessive pronouns

🔔 Bellringer

When students enter the classroom, have this assignment on the board: *What does the underlined word in each sentence indicate? In the first and third sentences, what is the relationship of the underlined word to the word that follows it?*

Does Bill know he left <u>his</u> book here?
Are you sure that one is <u>his</u>?
Yes; <u>his</u> name is on it.

Motivating Activity

Discuss students' answers to the Bell-ringer assignment. Emphasize that *his* indicates ownership. Point out that the word *whose* can help them determine if a word is a possessive pronoun. Say, "*Whose* book was left? Bill's book."

TEACH

☑ Teaching Tip

Make sure students do not confuse possessive pronouns such as *theirs* with contractions such as *there's*. Emphasize that possessive pronouns do not have apostrophes. Tell students that when a possessive pronoun is used before a noun, as in *his book*, it acts as an adjective. When a possessive pronoun stands alone, as in *Are you sure that one is* his? the word acts as a pronoun.

408

11.4 Possessive Pronouns

You often use pronouns to replace nouns that are subjects and nouns that are objects in sentences. You can use pronouns in place of possessive nouns, too.

A **possessive pronoun** is a pronoun that shows who or what has something. A possessive pronoun may take the place of a possessive noun.

Read the following sentences. Notice the possessive nouns and the possessive pronouns that replace them.

> Lisa's class put on a play. **Her** class put on a play.
> The idea was Lisa's. The idea was **hers.**

Possessive pronouns have two forms. One form is used before a noun. The other form is used alone. The chart below shows the two forms of possessive pronouns.

Possessive Pronouns		
	Singular	**Plural**
Used Before Nouns	my your her, his, its	our your their
Used Alone	mine yours hers, his, its	ours yours theirs

Unlike possessive nouns, such as *Mei's* or *cats'*, possessive pronouns do not contain an apostrophe.

Do not confuse the possessive pronoun *its* with the word *it's*. *It's* is a contraction, or shortened form, of the words *it is*.

> **Its** subject is William Shakespeare. [possessive pronoun]
> **It's** a famous play by Shakespeare. [contraction of *it is*]

408 *Pronouns*

Teacher's Classroom Resources

The following resources can be used for planning, instruction, practice, reinforcement, reteaching, or enrichment.

🔧 **Teaching Tools**
Lesson Plans, p. 81

📁 **Blackline Masters**
Grammar Practice, p. 19
Grammar Reteaching, p. 20
Grammar Enrichment, p. 19

📙 **Grammar Workbook**
Lesson 28

Exercise 6   **Identifying Possessive Pronouns**

Write each possessive pronoun. Then write *N* if the pronoun *comes before a noun* or *A* if it *stands alone*.

1. Our class is putting on a play by Shakespeare.
2. He wrote centuries ago, but his plays still thrill audiences.
3. *Hamlet* is Lian's favorite, but *Romeo and Juliet* is mine.
4. Have you seen your favorite play yet?
5. Gina was in *Hamlet,* but it's not a favorite of hers.
6. I know my part in the play, but some students may have trouble reading theirs.
7. The language of Shakespeare sounds strange to their ears.
8. To Shakespeare our English would seem like a foreign language.
9. Some of his words look odd in print; the spellings are unfamiliar.
10. The spoken words of Shakespeare are more eloquent than mine.

Exercise 7   **Using Possessive Pronouns**

Write the correct possessive pronoun for each underlined word or group of words.

1. The play's setting is the city of Verona.
2. Romeo was an uninvited guest at the feast of Romeo's enemy.
3. When Romeo and Juliet meet, Romeo and Juliet's love story begins.
4. Later Romeo sees Juliet and hears Juliet's confession of love for him.
5. A friar performs Romeo and Juliet's secret marriage the next day.
6. Mercutio, a friend of the bridegroom's, meets Tybalt, an enemy of Mercutio's.
7. Mercutio and Tybalt fight; Romeo stops Mercutio and Tybalt's fight.
8. Romeo draws his sword and kills Romeo's friend's murderer.
9. Romeo's sentence is banishment.
10. Romeo visits Juliet secretly; the meeting was Romeo and Juliet's alone.
11. Juliet refuses to marry Count Paris, but Juliet's father insists.
12. The night before the wedding, Juliet drinks a sleeping potion of Juliet's.
13. The potion's effects will render her apparently lifeless for forty hours.
14. The friar sends a message telling Romeo, "Rescue Romeo's wife; she is awake."
15. The friar's message gets mixed up; Romeo hears that Juliet is dead.
16. Romeo buys poison and goes to Juliet; "Death is Romeo and Juliet's," he says.
17. Thinking that Juliet is dead, Romeo drinks Romeo's poison and dies.
18. Juliet awakes and finds Romeo's dead body and the cup by her side.
19. Juliet guesses what has happened; she stabs Juliet's chest.
20. This story is a favorite of our class's.

11.4 Possessive Pronouns   **409**

PRACTICE AND ASSESS

Answers: Exercise 6

1. Our—N	6. my—N; theirs—A
2. his—N	7. their—N
3. mine—A	8. our—N
4. your—N	9. his—N
5. hers—A	10. mine—A

Answers: Exercise 7

1. Its	11. her
2. his	12. hers
3. their	13. Its
4. her	14. your
5. their	15. His
6. his	16. ours
7. their	17. his
8. his	18. his
9. His	19. her
10. theirs	20. ours

Independent Practice

Skills Practice

📁 *Grammar Practice,* p. 19
📁 *Grammar Reteaching,* p. 20
📁 *Grammar Enrichment,* p. 19

📕 **Grammar Workbook,** Lesson 28

CLOSE

Have several volunteers give examples of sentences containing possessive pronouns. Ask them whether the possessive pronoun acts as an adjective or a pronoun.

Enabling Strategies

LEP Knowing When to Use *Its* and *It's*

Students learning English may experience difficulty distinguishing between *its* (possessive) and *it's* (contraction). One helpful tip is to expand *it's* to the uncontracted form *it is* and restate the sentence. Encourage students to ask themselves,

Does the sentence have a subject and a verb? Ask students if the word *its* in the following sentences should have an apostrophe or not.

1. *Its* the first day of spring.
2. I was going to go to the grocery store, but *its* closed.

Lesson 11.5 teaches students about indefinite pronouns and how to make sure they agree with related verbs and possessive pronouns.

FOCUS

Lesson Overview

Objective: To use correct forms of indefinite pronouns and to ensure correct pronoun-verb agreement

Bellringer

When students enter the classroom, have this assignment on the board: *Would you use a singular or a plural verb after the word some-body? After the word anything? Write each in a sentence.*

Motivating Activity

Have students discuss their answers to the Bellringer questions. Do they agree that in both cases a singular verb is needed? Would they use a singular or plural verb after *everything, something, anybody, somebody?* Draw attention to the singular words *thing* and *body* that appear in the pronouns.

TEACH

☑ Teaching Tip

Indefinite pronouns may be confused with the same words used as adjectives. The following examples show the two usages:

1. Sam chose another car. (*Another* is an adjective modifying *car.*)
2. Sam chose another. (*Another* is an indefinite pronoun.)

Ask students for similar examples.

410

11.5 Indefinite Pronouns

An **indefinite pronoun** is a pronoun that does not refer to a particular person, place, or thing.

Each thinks about the plot.

Most indefinite pronouns are either singular or plural.

Some Indefinite Pronouns			
Singular			Plural
another	everybody	no one	both
anybody	everyone	nothing	few
anyone	everything	one	many
anything	much	somebody	others
each	neither	someone	several
either	nobody	something	

In addition, the indefinite pronouns *all, any, most, none,* and *some* are singular or plural, depending on the phrase that follows.

When an indefinite pronoun is used as the subject of a sentence, the verb must agree with it in number.

Everyone reads part of the novel. [singular]
Several enjoy it very much. [plural]
Most of the story **takes** place in England. [singular]
Most of the characters **are** memorable. [plural]

Possessive pronouns often have indefinite pronouns as their antecedents. In such cases the pronouns must agree in number. Note that the intervening prepositional phrase does not affect the agreement.

Several are presenting **their** interpretations of the novel.
Each of the students has **his** or **her** ideas about its meaning.

410 *Pronouns*

Teacher's Classroom Resources

The following resources can be used for planning, instruction, practice, reinforcement, reteaching, or enrichment.

🔧 **Teaching Tools**
Lesson Plans

📁 **Blackline Masters**
Grammar Practice, p. 19
Grammar Enrichment, p. 19

📘 **Grammar Workbook**
Lesson 28

Exercise 8   Choosing Indefinite Pronouns

Write the indefinite pronoun that agrees with the verb or possessive pronoun.

1. (Neither, All) of Robert Frost's poems are enjoyed by their readers.
2. (One, Many) of the poems have New England as their setting.
3. (Much, Many) of their narrators are people living close to nature.
4. (Much, Others) of the poetry has rhythm, and its lines rhyme.
5. (Both, Each) of these poems has its own rhyme.
6. (Somebody, Several) in this poem narrates his or her own tale.
7. (Most, Everyone) have their own interpretations of Frost's metaphors.
8. A bookstore had poem nights. (All, One) of the guests have read their poems.
9. (Both, One) of the guests has read her own poem about Frost.
10. (Each, Several) of the readers of Frost's poems has his or her favorite.

Exercise 9   Using Indefinite Pronouns

Write each sentence, using the correct verb or possessive pronoun in parentheses. Then underline the indefinite pronoun, and write whether the pronoun is *singular* or *plural*.

1. Everyone studies (his or her, their) section of *Alice's Adventures in Wonderland*.
2. Most of the characters (is, are) animals.
3. Some of them (attends, attend) a comical tea party.
4. Nothing (makes, make) sense in Wonderland.
5. Everything in Wonderland (confuses, confuse) Alice.
6. No one (answers, answer) her questions.
7. Many of the characters (talks, talk) peculiarly.
8. Some of them even (speaks, speak) in riddles.
9. The Cheshire cat disappears; nothing (is, are) left but its smile.
10. Few really (believes, believe) in disappearing cats.
11. None of the characters (looks, look) more bizarre than the Mock Turtle.
12. Several offer Alice (his or her, their) advice.
13. Each has (their, his or her) point of view.
14. Nothing predictable (happens, happen) in Wonderland.
15. Most of the story (occurs, occur) down a rabbit hole.
16. Everyone (know, knows) the story's author—British writer Lewis Carroll.
17. Much (has, have) been written about *Alice's Adventures in Wonderland*.
18. All of the critics (praises, praise) it.
19. None of them (gives, give) a bad review.
20. Everybody in class enjoys (his or her, their) reading of the book.

11.5 Indefinite Pronouns   **411**

PRACTICE AND ASSESS

Answers: Exercise 8

1. All	6. Somebody
2. Many	7. Most
3. Many	8. All
4. Much	9. One
5. Each	10. Each

Answers: Exercise 9

1. his or her—*Everyone*—s
2. are—*Most*—p
3. attend—*Some*—p
4. makes—*Nothing*—s
5. confuses—*Everything*—s
6. answers—*No one*—s
7. talk—*Many*—p
8. speak—*Some*—p
9. is—*nothing*—s
10. believe—*Few*—p
11. look—*None*—p
12. their—*Several*—p
13. his or her—*Each*—s
14. happens—*Nothing*—s
15. occurs—*Most*—s
16. knows—*Everyone*—s
17. has—*Much*—s
18. praise—*All*—p
19. give—*None*—p
20. his or her—*Everybody*—s

Independent Practice

Skills Practice

📁 *Grammar Practice,* p. 19
📁 *Grammar Enrichment,* p. 19

📘 **Grammar Workbook,** Lesson 28

CLOSE

Have pairs of students compose sentences with indefinite pronouns. One student starts a sentence with an indefinite pronoun; the other adds a verb that agrees with the subject. (Example: Student 1: "Most of us …"; student 2: "… like pizza.") Then have them switch places.

Enabling Strategies

LEP **Using Gender-free Pronouns**

Discuss how to avoid using a possessive pronoun that identifies only one gender. For example, ask students how they would complete this sentence: *Each applicant must include a picture of* _____ (*possessive pronoun*) *pet*. Point out that the correct answer—*his* or *her*—is awkward. Substituting plural words can avoid this awkwardness: <u>*All applicants*</u> *must include pictures of* <u>*their*</u> *pets*.

FOCUS

Lesson Overview

Objective: To identify and distinguish between reflexive and intensive pronouns and use each correctly

Bellringer

When students enter the classroom, have this assignment on the board: *Choose the words you would use in these sentences:*
I (me, myself) cleaned the garage.
I allowed (me, myself) several snack breaks because it took so long.

Motivating Activity

Ask students to look at the pronouns in the sentences in the Bellringer activity and determine if they are necessary or not. Point out that in the first sentence, the pronoun only adds emphasis to the sentence.

TEACH

☑ Teaching Tip

Tell students that one way to tell the difference between reflexive pronouns and intensive pronouns is to remember that reflexive pronouns are objects and are thus necessary words in a sentence; intensive pronouns are added for emphasis and are not necessary in a sentence.

11.6 Reflexive and Intensive Pronouns

A **reflexive pronoun** refers to a noun or another pronoun and indicates that the same person or thing is involved.

The woman bought **herself** a book by Horatio Alger.

REFLEXIVE PRONOUN

REFLEXIVE PRONOUN

Reflexive pronouns are formed by adding *-self* or *-selves* to certain personal and possessive pronouns.

Reflexive Pronouns	
Singular	**Plural**
myself	ourselves
yourself	yourselves
himself, herself, itself	themselves

Sometimes *hisself* is mistakenly used for *himself* and *theirselves* for *themselves*. Avoid using *hisself* and *theirselves*.

Reflexive pronouns can also add emphasis. When they are used for that purpose, they are called intensive pronouns.

An **intensive pronoun** is a pronoun that adds emphasis to a noun or pronoun already named.

> Horatio Alger **himself** wrote more than one hundred books.
> I **myself** have never read his books.

Reflexive and intensive pronouns have special uses. They should never be used as the subject of a sentence or as the object of a verb or preposition.

> Yolanda and **I** read *Sink or Swim*. [not *Yolanda and myself*]
> It pleased Yolanda and **me**. [not *Yolanda and myself*]

412 *Pronouns*

Teacher's Classroom Resources

The following resources can be used for planning, instruction, practice, reinforcement, reteaching, or enrichment.

🔧 **Teaching Tools**
Lesson Plans

📁 **Blackline Masters**
Grammar Practice, p. 20
Grammar Reteaching, p. 21
Grammar Enrichment, p. 20

📕 ***Grammar Workbook***
Lesson 29

Exercise 10 — Identifying Reflexive and Intensive Pronouns

Write each reflexive and intensive pronoun, and write whether it is a *reflexive pronoun* or an *intensive pronoun*.

1. You should occupy yourselves today by reading one of Edgar Allan Poe's tales.
2. His first three books of poetry were themselves not successful.
3. Poe did not think himself a writer of inferior material.
4. Poe himself had a high opinion of his abilities.
5. One of his first tales was superb; the tale itself won a $100 prize.
6. One of the contest judges himself got Poe a job as a magazine editor.
7. Edgar Allan Poe has endeared himself to readers of the macabre.
8. I myself would not read any of his short stories at night.
9. Poe may not be the author for you; only you yourself can decide.
10. You can get yourself a book of his stories and poems from the library.

Exercise 11 — Using Reflexive and Intensive Pronouns

Write the correct pronoun in parentheses. Write whether the pronoun is a *reflexive, intensive, subject,* or *object* pronoun.

1. I (me, myself) wrote a review of a book by Horatio Alger.
2. I found (me, myself) inspired by the characters' adventures.
3. Read a story (yours, yourself) about how to make hard work into a fortune.
4. Alger's life (it, itself) seems like one of his success stories.
5. Harvard Divinity School was near his home; Alger attended (it, itself).
6. He became a minister; his congregation thought (themselves, theirselves) lucky.
7. Alger thought (hisself, himself) ambitious and moved to New York.
8. He helped the homeless; (they, themself) became characters in his stories.
9. The characters improve (them, themselves) through work and a bit of luck.
10. Yusuf and Tony (themselves, theirselves) were impressed by Alger's books.
11. Horatio Alger (he, himself) lived from 1832 to 1899.
12. Alger's birthplace (it, itself) attracts visitors.
13. We enjoyed (us, ourselves) during a visit to his home.
14. Alger's stories (them, themselves) usually take place in large cities.
15. A friend and (I, myself) have read ten of Alger's books.
16. Alger's style seems warm and light to (me, myself).
17. For Alger ambition (it, itself) can bring about success.
18. According to (him, himself), any child could become a president or a millionaire.
19. (He or she, Themselves) just has to be intelligent, hard-working, and honest.
20. The Horatio Alger books became symbols of success (theirselves, themselves).

11.6 Reflexive and Intensive Pronouns **413**

PRACTICE AND ASSESS

Answers: Exercise 10
1. yourselves—reflexive pronoun
2. themselves—intensive pronoun
3. himself—reflexive pronoun
4. himself—intensive pronoun
5. itself—intensive pronoun
6. himself—intensive pronoun
7. himself—reflexive pronoun
8. myself—intensive pronoun
9. yourself—intensive pronoun
10. yourself—reflexive pronoun

Answers: Exercise 11
1. myself—intensive
2. myself—reflexive
3. yourself—intensive
4. itself—intensive
5. it—object
6. themselves—reflexive
7. himself—reflexive
8. they—subject
9. themselves—reflexive
10. themselves—intensive
11. himself—intensive
12. itself—intensive
13. ourselves—reflexive
14. themselves—intensive
15. I—subject
16. me—object
17. itself—intensive
18. him—object
19. He or she—subject
20. themselves—intensive

Independent Practice

Skills Practice
📁 *Grammar Practice,* p. 20
📁 *Grammar Reteaching,* p. 21
📁 *Grammar Enrichment,* p. 20
📕 **Grammar Workbook,** Lesson 29

Enabling Strategies

LEP Using Reflexive Pronouns
To help students learning English with reflexive pronouns, have them set up a chart. In one column under *Pronoun,* list *I, you, he, she, it, we, you, they.* In the second column have students list under *Reflexive Pronouns* the corresponding pronouns.

CLOSE

Ask students to write a paragraph about a city they would like to visit. Have them use reflexive and intensive pronouns.

FOCUS

Lesson Overview

Objective: To identify interrogative pronouns and demonstrative pronouns

 **Bellringer**

When students enter the classroom, have this assignment on the board: *Write the correct word in each question.*
(Who's, Whose) on first?
(Who's, Whose) book is under that desk?
About (who, whom) did Abigail Adams write?

TEACH

☑ Teaching Tip

Write the following questions on the chalkboard to show students when to use *who* and *whom: Who got the lead in the play? Whom are you going to visit?* Ask two volunteers to go to the chalkboard and each rewrite one sentence in statement form, replacing *who* or *whom* with an appropriate personal pronoun.

Point out that *who* takes the place of the subject pronouns (*I, you, he, she, it, we, they*). *Whom* takes the place of the object pronouns (*me, you, him, her, it, us, them*).

11.7 Interrogative and Demonstrative Pronouns

An **interrogative pronoun** is a pronoun used to introduce an interrogative sentence.

The interrogative pronouns *who* and *whom* both refer to people. *Who* is used when the interrogative pronoun is the subject of the sentence. *Whom* is used when the interrogative pronoun is the object of a verb or a preposition.

> **Who** borrowed the book? [subject]
> **Whom** did the librarian call? [direct object]
> For **whom** did you borrow the book? [object of preposition]

Which and *what* are used to refer to things and ideas.

> **What** interests you?   **Which** is it?

Whose shows that someone possesses something.

> I found a copy of *Great Expectations.* **Whose** is it?

When writing, be careful not to confuse *whose* with *who's. Who's* is the contraction of *who is.*

A **demonstrative pronoun** is a pronoun that points out something.

The demonstrative pronouns are *this, that, these,* and *those. This* (singular) and *these* (plural) refer to something nearby. *That* (singular) and *those* (plural) refer to something at a distance.

that

this

> **This** is an interesting book. [singular, nearby]
> **These** are interesting books. [plural, nearby]
> **That** is a long book. [singular, at a distance]
> **Those** are long books. [plural, at a distance]

414   *Pronouns*

Teacher's Classroom Resources

Exercise 12 | Using Interrogative and Demonstrative Pronouns

Write the correct word given in parentheses.

1. (These, This) is Arturo's favorite book.
2. From (who, whom) did you get that copy?
3. (That, Those) is the small orphan named Pip.
4. (That, Those) are Pip's students.
5. (Who, Whom) taught Pip about books?
6. With (who, whom) does Pip live?
7. (This, These) are Pip's sister and her husband.
8. (Who, Whom) does Pip meet?
9. (What, Who) does the stranger want?
10. (This, These) is food for the stranger.

Exercise 13 | Distinguishing Between Pronouns and Contractions

Write the correct word given in parentheses. Then write *I* if your choice is an *interrogative* pronoun, *D* if it is a *demonstrative* pronoun, or *C* if it is a *contraction*.

1. (Whose, Who's) Joe?
2. To (who, whom) was Joe married?
3. (Who's, Whose) Miss Havisham?
4. (This, These) is the mansion of Miss Havisham.
5. (That, These) was the time on the clocks.
6. (This, Those) are her bridal robes.
7. (Who, Whom) did Miss Havisham see?
8. (This, These) was the girl at Miss Havisham's home.
9. To (who, whom) did Estella get married?
10. (This, What) are Pip's great expectations?
11. (Who, Whom) becomes Pip's guardian?
12. (That, These) is a mystery.
13. (Who's, Which) school does Pip attend?
14. To (who, whom) does Pip turn for help?
15. (What, Who) did Lawyer Jaggers give Pip?
16. (Who, Whom) paid Lawyer Jaggers?
17. (This, These) are the payments from the stranger.
18. (What, Who) became of the stranger?
19. (What, Who's) helping Pip now?
20. (Whose, Who's) the author of this novel?

11.7 Interrogative and Demonstrative Pronouns **415**

Enabling Strategies

LEP Using Interrogative Pronouns
Students may have difficulty forming questions with interrogative pronouns that refer to the object of a verb. They may correctly begin with the interrogative pronoun but then fail to put the auxiliary verb before the subject. For example, students might ask, *Whom you are calling?* instead of *Whom are you calling?* or *What you should say?* instead of *What should you say?* Provide some statements containing interrogative pronouns and work with students to turn the statements into questions.

TEACH

About the Literature

The biography of Emily Dickinson by Bonita E. Thayer tells the story of a unique woman who devoted her life to writing poetry. Dickinson, who never married, was somewhat of a recluse. She lived what she called an "inner life"—going within herself to ponder and question life and then writing her reflections in poetic form. Tell students that this passage is from a biography of Emily Dickinson, one of the major poets of the nineteenth century. After students read the passage, initiate a discussion focusing on Dickinson's feelings about books.

Linking Grammar and Literature

☑ Teaching Tip

Point out to students how various kinds of pronouns covered in the unit are used in this literature passage. Review with students the highlighted pronouns and their uses. Ask students to identify other pronouns found in the passage and how they are used.

Speaking and Listening

Use the following paragraph to give students practice in identifying pronouns and their uses. First read the paragraph aloud, directing students to listen for meaning only. Then slowly reread the paragraph, this time having students point out the pronouns and their antecedents.

Bonita E. Thayer's biography of Emily Dickinson tells the story of a unique woman who devoted her life to writing poetry. Dickinson, who never married and she was somewhat of a recluse. She lived what she called an "inner life"—going within herself to ponder and question life and then writing her reflections in poetic form.

Grammar Review

Pronouns

The following passage is from a biography of Emily Dickinson by Bonita Thayer. In addition to writing nearly eighteen hundred poems, Dickinson wrote many letters to friends. These letters reveal much about her thinking at different periods of her life. In the passage below, Thayer quotes from Dickinson's letters to Colonel Higginson, a writer and abolitionist (someone who opposed slavery). The passage has been annotated to show examples of the kinds of pronouns covered in this unit.

> ### Literature Model
>
> #### from EMILY DICKINSON
>
> *by Bonita E. Thayer*
>
> Indefinite pronoun ——— Some of Emily's letters to Higginson reveal her feelings about the public in general. "Truth is such a rare thing, it is delightful to tell it," she says in one note.
>
> Subject pronoun agrees with its antecedent, *Emily* ——— Later she asks him, "How do most people live without any thoughts? There are many people in the world—you must have noticed them in the street—how do
>
> Object pronoun agrees with its antecedent, *many people* ——— they live? How do they get strength to put on their clothes in the morning?"
>
> She seemed satisfied with her life as she was living it. Her own thoughts filled her mind and were joined with the thoughts of others whose writings she studied.
>
> "There is no frigate like a book to take us lands away," she wrote. She felt that she could travel the world and meet all the people she wanted to through
>
> Possessive pronoun ——— books. She never had to leave her own home, which she considered to be the best and safest place for her.

416 *Pronouns*

Teacher's Classroom Resources

The following resources can be used for planning, instruction, practice, reinforcement, assessment, reteaching, or evaluation.

🔧 **Teaching Tools**
Lesson Plans

📔 **Grammar Workbook**
Lessons 25–30
Unit 4 Review
Cumulative Review: Units 1–4

Unit Assessment

🗁 *Tests with Answer Key*
Unit 11 Mastery Test, pp. 43–44

💿 *Test Generator*
Unit 11 Mastery Test

Exercise 1

Using Subject, Object, and Possessive Pronouns Write each sentence, replacing the underlined word or words with the correct pronoun. Write whether the pronoun you used is a *subject* pronoun, an *object* pronoun, or a *possessive* pronoun.

1. <u>Emily Dickinson</u> avoided having <u>Dickinson's</u> picture taken.
2. <u>Dickinson</u> had <u>one photograph</u> taken at about age sixteen.
3. <u>The author</u> craved biographies and portraits about <u>literary favorites.</u>
4. Dickinson started writing poetry in <u>Dickinson's</u> early twenties.
5. <u>The thought of publishing her poems</u> was abhorrent to <u>Dickinson</u>.

Exercise 2

Using Pronouns and Antecedents Write the second sentence in each of the following pairs, using the correct pronoun in each blank. Then write the antecedent of the pronoun with its number (singular or plural) and gender (masculine, feminine, or neuter).

SAMPLE After their mother's death, Emily and her sister, Lavinia, became recluses. Emily and _____ never left home.

ANSWER Emily and she never left home. Lavinia, singular, feminine

1. Emily Dickinson was born in Amherst, Massachusetts, in 1830. ____ was the daughter of Edward and Emily.
2. Dickinson's father was a Renaissance man. ____ was a lawyer, a politician, and a college treasurer.
3. The poet's brother, named William Austin, was always called Austin. ____ was the oldest child and only son.
4. The mother's job was care of the family. ____ was an important task.
5. Austin eventually became treasurer at the same college as the father. Austin succeeded ____.
6. Austin married Susan Gilbert. The father built ____ a house next door.
7. Dickinson and her sister, Lavinia, never married. ____ lived at home all their lives.
8. After the father died, the mother became paralyzed. ____ was confined to bed.
9. Emily and Lavinia shared the task of caring for the mother. Both took good care of ____.
10. The three children were close in age. ____ were devoted to one another.

Grammar Review **417**

PRACTICE AND ASSESS

Answers: Exercise 1

1. She, subject pronoun; her, possessive pronoun
2. She, subject pronoun; it, object pronoun
3. She, subject pronoun; them, object pronoun
4. her, possessive pronoun
5. It, subject pronoun; her, object pronoun

Answers: Exercise 2

1. She, Emily Dickinson, singular, feminine
2. He, father, singular, masculine
3. He, brother, singular, masculine
4. It, job, singular, neuter
5. him, father, singular, masculine
6. them, Austin and Susan Gilbert, plural, neuter
7. They, Dickinson and Lavinia, plural, neuter
8. She, mother, singular, feminine
9. her, mother, singular, feminine
10. They, children, plural, neuter

UNIT 11
Review

Answers: Exercise 3

1. she, subject pronoun
2. She, subject pronoun
3. he, subject pronoun
4. him, object pronoun
5. She, subject pronoun
6. They, subject pronoun
7. us, object pronoun
8. she, subject pronoun
9. Surya and I, subject pronoun
10. me, object pronoun

Answers: Exercise 4

1. consider, <u>Many</u>, plural
2. were, <u>Few</u>, plural
3. are, <u>Most</u>, plural
4. is, <u>All</u>, singular
5. were, <u>Some</u>, plural
6. reveals, <u>Everything</u>, singular
7. likes, <u>Everyone</u>, singular
8. has, <u>Much</u>, singular
9. enjoy, <u>Several</u>, plural
10. captures, <u>Something</u>, singular

Exercise 3

Using Subject and Object Pronouns Correctly Write the correct pronoun in parentheses. Then write whether each pronoun is a *subject* pronoun or an *object* pronoun.

1. Emily and (she, her) were sisters and friends.
2. (She, Her) and Charles Wadsworth were friends and correspondents.
3. Dickinson and (he, him) were friends and companions.
4. The poet and a friend corresponded with Thomas Higginson and (he, him).
5. (She, Her) and other poets wrote poems and letters.
6. (They, Them) and others are published in English and other languages.
7. Emily's poems and letters amused those students and (we, us).
8. An editor and (her, she) gave the poems numbers but no titles.
9. (Me and Surya, Surya and I) read poem 812 and poem 1017 today.
10. Poem 173 and poem 188 made Akim and (me, I) smile.

Exercise 4

Using Indefinite Pronouns Write each sentence, using the correct verb in parentheses. Then underline the indefinite pronoun, and write whether it is *singular* or *plural*.

SAMPLE Some of her poetry (is, are) deceptively simple.

ANSWER <u>Some</u> of her poetry is deceptively simple. *Singular*

1. Many (consider, considers) Dickinson one of the best American poets of the nineteenth century.
2. Few of her poems (was, were) published during her lifetime, perhaps only seven.
3. Most of her poems (is, are) very brief.
4. All of her work (is, are) interesting.
5. Some of her poems (was, were) circulated among her close friends.
6. Everything in her poems (reveal, reveals) her love of nature.
7. Everyone (like, likes) the spoofing fun of her valentines.
8. Much (has, have) been written about how she never left home.
9. Several of us (enjoy, enjoys) her work.
10. Something about her poetry (capture, captures) the reader's imagination.

Exercise 5

Using Subject, Object, Reflexive, and Intensive Pronouns Write the correct pronoun given in parentheses. Write whether the pronoun is a *reflexive, intensive, subject,* or *object* pronoun.

1. Dickinson (she, herself) knew that her words could attract readers.
2. But she did not want the readers (theirselves, themselves) at her door.
3. In midlife she rarely left the Dickinson property (it, itself).
4. Within the homestead (she, herself) had an active life.
5. The poet had many friends and wrote many letters to (them, themselves).
6. Friends and neighbors brought the outside world to (her, herself).
7. The garden needed tending in summer; she did that (itself, herself).
8. The cause of her reclusiveness (it, itself) is not fully understood.
9. She may have made the choice (her, herself) to remain in seclusion.
10. Emily Dickinson was devoted to her parents and took care of (them, themselves) until they died.

Exercise 6

Using Interrogative and Demonstrative Pronouns Write the correct word given in parentheses.

SAMPLE (Who, Whom) was the most important influence on her poetry?
ANSWER Who

1. To (who, whom) did Dickinson send the first samples of her poetry?
2. (This, These) are the first four poems she showed him.
3. (What, Whose) was his opinion of the poems?
4. (This, What) were the questions he asked of the poet?
5. (Which, Whom) are the three poems she sent in reply?
6. (What, Which) did writer Helen Hunt Jackson think of the poetry?
7. (Who's, Whose) poetry did Jackson praise?
8. (This, These) is the poetry Dickinson's niece brought to the publisher.
9. (Whose, Who's) idea was it to publish only some of them?
10. (That, Those) were the last of her poems to be published.

Grammar Review **419**

Answers: Exercise 5
1. herself, intensive
2. themselves, intensive
3. itself, intensive
4. she, subject
5. them, object
6. her, object
7. herself, intensive
8. itself, reflexive
9. herself, reflexive
10. them, object

Answers: Exercise 6
1. whom
2. These
3. What
4. What
5. Which
6. What
7. Whose
8. This
9. Whose
10. Those

UNIT 11
Review

Answers: Exercise 7
Proofreading

This proofreading activity provides editing practice with (1) the current or previous units' skills, (2) the **Troubleshooter** errors, and (3) spelling errors. Students should be able to complete the exercise by referring to the units, the **Troubleshooter**, and a dictionary. (Note: A run-on sentence counts as one error.)

	Error (Type of Error)
1.	• Havana, (nonessential appositive phrase)
2.	• him (object pronoun)
3.	• he and his family (subject pronoun)
4.	• 1963, (run-on sentence)
5.	• advertising (spelling)
6.	• his (possessive pronoun)
7.	• is seen (verb form)
8.	• themselves (intensive pronoun)
9.	• him (object pronoun)
10.	• reflect (subject–verb agreement)

Exercise 7

The following passage is about the artist Paul Sierra, whose work appears below. Rewrite the passage, correcting the errors in spelling, grammar, and usage. Add any missing punctuation. There are ten errors.

Paul Sierra

¹Paul Sierra was born in Havana the capital of Cuba. ²His parents wanted himself to become a doctor, but he wanted to be a painter. ³When Sierra was sixteen, him and his family immigrated to the United States and settled in Chicago.

⁴Sierra began his formal training as a painter in 1963 and he later went to work as a commercial layout artist. ⁵He still works in advertizing as a creative director. ⁶Because he does not have to rely on sales of paintings for ➡

Paul Sierra, *Degas' Studio,* **1990**

420 *Pronouns*

About the Art

Paul Sierra, *Degas' Studio,* **1990**

Paul Sierra, who was born in 1944, never knew the artist who inspired this work, since Degas lived from 1834–1917. The painting is an evocation of Degas and his work rather than a literal depiction of his studio. Although Degas himself is not shown, the horse and jockey recall his fascination with horse racing and the racetrack. The woman is done in the style of Degas's portrait of Emily Dickinson, the American poet. Sierra was born in Cuba and now resides in Chicago. His 48-by-70 inch oil on canvas is in a private collection.

his' livelihood, he is free to paint whatever he wants.
⁷Sierra's unusual use of color is saw in the painting on the opposite page. ⁸The images theirselves, however, are drawn from the paintings of Edgar Degas. ⁹The woman's head, for instance, is taken from a famous portrait done by he. ¹⁰The horse and jockey reflects Degas's fascination with the sport of racing.

Mixed Review

Exercise 8

After each sentence number, list in order the pronouns that appear in the sentence. Identify each pronoun as *personal, possessive, indefinite, reflexive, intensive, interrogative,* or *demonstrative.*

¹Emily Dickinson drew her last breath on May 15, 1886. ²She left a legacy of nearly eighteen hundred poems and a thousand remarkable letters. ³These were not published in their entirety until 1958.

⁴In the late 1850s Dickinson herself had copied dozens of finished poems into booklets. ⁵Dickinson had made them by sewing folded notepaper into sheaves. ⁶This was a way to organize the bits of scrap paper containing the drafts. ⁷What became of the booklets? ⁸Who found them?

⁹After Dickinson's death, Lavinia discovered the booklets; she persuaded Higginson and one of Austin's friends to edit a volume of the poetry. ¹⁰Reviews of the book were discouraging, but the public demand for it was heartening. ¹¹In 1945 the last of Dickinson's poetry was published, and virtually all of Dickinson's poems were finally in print, sixty years after her death!

¹²Dickinson's poetry itself is concise and intense. ¹³Most of the poems are brief. ¹⁴They usually are about nature and the themes of love, death, and immortality. ¹⁵She introduced new rhymes and rhythms, often within a single poem. ¹⁶Both give her poems originality and add richness. ¹⁷The phrases are themselves quite simple. ¹⁸Her diction is stripped to the fewest words. ¹⁹She delighted herself with paradox; the concrete and the abstract, the serious and the funny, the usual and the unusual exist side by side in Dickinson's work. ²⁰The style is easily recognized as hers.

Grammar Review **421**

Answers: Exercise 8
Mixed Review
1. her, possessive
2. She, personal
3. These, demonstrative; their, possessive
4. herself, intensive
5. them, personal
6. This, demonstrative
7. What, interrogative
8. Who, interrogative; them, personal
9. she, personal; one, indefinite
10. it, personal
11. all, indefinite; her, possessive
12. itself, intensive
13. Most, indefinite
14. They, personal
15. She, personal
16. Both, indefinite; her, possessive
17. themselves, intensive
18. Her, possessive
19. She, personal; herself, reflexive
20. hers, possessive

CLOSE

Have students, working in pairs, select a newspaper or magazine article. Ask them to highlight and label in the article the various kinds of pronouns they have studied in this unit. Then have them underline the word or words to which each pronoun refers.

Pronouns in Writing

Have students read the paragraphs silently. When all have finished, go back and discuss the italicized pronoun choices in the passage in relation to the **Techniques with Pronouns** below.

Techniques with Pronouns

Discuss each of the techniques listed. You may want to have students analyze an example using these techniques (the paragraphs about Emily Dickinson on page 421, for example).

Practice

The answers to this challenging and enriching activity will vary. Refer to **Techniques with Pronouns** as you evaluate student choices. Sample answer.

When the phone rang, Kay jumped quickly to answer it. "It's for me," she yelled. Just then, Mrs. Oliver entered the room carrying Will on her left hip and her briefcase in her right hand. "Good thing you were here to answer the phone, Kay. I might've dropped your brother trying to reach it," she said.

As Kay spoke, she waved her mother away and silently mouthed the words, "Just a minute, Mom." Then Kay quickly finished her call and hung up the phone.

Writing Application

Pronouns in Writing This passage from *The Game* includes references to many characters. Writer Walter Dean Myers uses different pronouns to lend variety to his prose and make the references to his characters clear. Review the passage below, noticing the italicized pronouns.

> *We* controlled the jump and Turk drove right down the lane and made a lay-up. Turk actually made the lay-up. Turk once missed seven lay-ups in a row in practice and *no one* was even guarding *him*. But *this* one *he* made. Then one of *their* men double-dribbled and *we* got the ball and *I* passed *it* to Leon, *who* threw up a shot and got fouled. The shot went in and when *he* made the foul shot *it* added up to a three-point play.

Techniques with Pronouns Try to apply some of Walter Dean Myers's writing techniques when you write and revise your own work.

1. When appropriate, use possessive pronouns to make your writing more concise. Compare the following:

Wordy version Then one of *the men on the other team* double-dribbled
Myers's version Then one of *their* men double-dribbled

2. Avoid confusing your readers. Be sure to choose correctly between subject and object pronouns.
Incorrect pronoun choice But this one *him* made.
Myers's version But this one *he* made.

Practice Apply these techniques as you revise the following passage on a separate sheet of paper. Pay particular attention to the underlined words.

When the phone rang, Kay jumped up quickly to answer it. "It's for <u>I</u>," <u>her</u> yelled. Just then, Mrs. Oliver entered the room, carrying Will on <u>the hip of her left side</u> and <u>she</u> briefcase <u>in the hand of her right side.</u> "Good thing you were here to answer the phone, Kay. <u>Me</u> might've dropped <u>this brother of yours</u> trying to reach it," she said.

As <u>her</u> spoke, Kay waved <u>she</u> away and silently mouthed the words, "Just a minute, Mom." Then <u>she</u> quickly finished <u>her call</u> and hung up the phone.

Teacher's Classroom Resources

The following resources can be used for assessment or evaluation.

Unit Assessment

📁 *Tests with Answer Key*
Unit 11 Mastery Test, pp. 43–44

💿 *Test Generator*
Unit 11 Mastery Test

You may wish to administer the Unit 11 Mastery Test at this point.

UNIT 12

Grammar | **Lessons**

Adjectives and Adverbs

423

UNIT GOALS

The goal of Unit 12 is to help students, through example and instruction, to develop an understanding of and an ability to use correctly the kinds and forms of adjectives and adverbs to add clarity, definition, and interest to their sentences. The lessons focus on modifying and predicate adjectives, articles and proper adjectives, demonstratives, comparative and superlative forms of adverbs and adjectives, modifying and intensifying adverbs, and double negatives.

Unit Assessment
📁 *Tests with Answer Key*
Unit 12 Pretest, pp. 45–46
Unit 12 Mastery Test, pp. 47–48

💿 *Test Generator*
Unit 12 Pretest
Unit 12 Mastery Test

You may wish to administer the Unit 12 Pretest at this point.

Key to Ability Levels
Enabling Strategies have been coded for varying learning styles and abilities.

L1 Level 1 activities are within the ability range of Learning Disabled students.

L2 Level 2 activities are basic-to-average activities and are within the ability range of average students.

L3 Level 3 activities are challenging activities and are within the ability range of above-average students.

LEP LEP activities are within the ability range of Limited English Proficiency students.

FOCUS

Lesson Overview

Objective: To use adjectives effectively to describe nouns and pronouns

Bellringer

When students enter the classroom, have this assignment on the board: *Write a list of words that you can think of to describe breakfast at your house.*

Motivating Activity

Discuss the words that students suggested and see if they can identify the words that are adjectives. Talk about students' use of adjectives in their own writing.

TEACH

Cooperative Learning

Have pairs of students collect a list of adjectives from a book. After they have written down 25 adjectives, ask them to note which of the words they have used before. Which words might they try using in the future?

Two-Minute Skill Drill

Have students use the following words as adjectives and predicate adjectives in sentences:

harmful   prehistoric

rejoicing   excessive

12.1 Adjectives

An adjective describes a person, place, thing, or idea. An adjective provides information about the size, shape, color, texture, feeling, sound, smell, number, or condition of a noun or a pronoun.

> The **eager, large** crowd of visitors examines the **huge** painting.

In the sentence above, the adjectives *eager* and *large* describe the noun *crowd,* and the adjective *huge* describes the noun *painting.*

An **adjective** is a word that modifies, or describes, a noun or a pronoun.

Most adjectives come before the nouns they modify. However, an adjective can be in the predicate and modify the noun or pronoun that is the subject of the sentence.

> The painting is **realistic** and **timeless.**

In the sentence above, the adjectives *realistic* and *timeless* follow the linking verb *is* and modify the subject, *painting.* They are called predicate adjectives.

A **predicate adjective** follows a linking verb and modifies the subject of the sentence.

The present participle and past participle forms of verbs may be used as adjectives and predicate adjectives.

> *Christina's World* is a **haunting** painting. [present participle]
>
> *Christina's World* is **inspired.** [past participle]

424 *Adjectives and Adverbs*

Teacher's Classroom Resources

The following resources can be used for planning, instruction, practice, reinforcement, assessment, reteaching, enrichment, or evaluation.

Teaching Tools
Lesson Plans, p. 84

Blackline Masters
Grammar Practice, p. 23
Grammar Reteaching, p. 23
Grammar Enrichment, p. 23

Grammar Workbook
Lesson 31

Unit Assessment

Tests with Answer Key
Unit 12 Pretest, pp. 45–46

Test Generator
Unit 12 Pretest

You may wish to administer the Unit 12 Pretest at this point.

Exercise 1   **Identifying Adjectives**

For each sentence below, write each adjective and the noun or pronoun it modifies. If any adjective is a participle form, circle it.

1. Georgia O'Keeffe is a major artist.
2. Her permanent residence was in the Southwest.
3. O'Keeffe's works hang in numerous museums.
4. The dry desert provided her with interesting material.
5. Georgia O'Keeffe spent several years in Wisconsin.
6. She studied art at a large school in Chicago in the early 1900s.
7. She lived for a short time in bustling New York City.
8. As a young woman O'Keeffe had not yet found the right subjects.
9. In 1912 she became aware of the interesting scenery in Texas.
10. She made an enlightening journey to Amarillo, Texas.
11. The bright flowers and whitened bones of the desert inspired her.
12. The endless landscape seemed filled with strange objects and ghostly figures.
13. Her unique style combined abstract design with realistic scenery.
14. O'Keeffe's best paintings were based on nature.
15. She might pick up an interesting shell on a sandy beach.
16. At first she made realistic paintings of what she found.
17. She would paint the white shape of the shell alongside a gray shingle.
18. Perhaps she would add two large green leaves to the objects.
19. She kept a large collection of shells under a glass tabletop.
20. O'Keeffe was recognized by leading museums as a major artist.

Exercise 2   **Identifying Predicate Adjectives**

Write each predicate adjective. Then write the noun or pronoun it modifies in parentheses.

1. The day was young.
2. The beach was deserted except for one lone walker.
3. The others were still asleep.
4. Even the waves were distant and respectful.
5. That silent woman was aware of everything around her.
6. She was curious about all she saw.
7. Everything around her was radiant in the morning light.
8. The colors were true and clear.
9. A piece of red coral was especially eye-catching.
10. Such a simple thing was wonderful to her.

12.1 Adjectives   **425**

PRACTICE AND ASSESS

Answers: Exercise 1
1. (A) major; (N) artist
2. (A) permanent; (N) residence
3. (A) numerous; (N) museums
4. (A) dry; (N) desert; (A) interesting; (N) material
5. (A) several; (N) years
6. (A) large; (N) school; (A) early; (N) 1900s
7. (A) short; (N) time; (A) bustling; (N) New York City
8. (A) young; (N) woman; (A) right; (N) subjects
9. (A) aware; (P) she; (A) interesting; (N) scenery
10. (A) enlightening; (N) journey
11. (A) bright; (N) flowers; (A) whitened; (N) bones
12. (A) endless; (N) landscape; (A) strange; (N) objects; (A) ghostly; (N) figures
13. (A) unique; (N) style; (A) abstract; (N) design; (A) realistic; (N) scenery
14. (A) best; (N) paintings
15. (A) interesting; (N) shell; (A) sandy; (N) beach
16. (A) realistic; (N) paintings
17. (A) white; (N) shape; (A) gray; (N) shingle
18. (A) two, large, green; (N) leaves
19. (A) large; (N) collection; (A) glass; (N) tabletop
20. (A) leading; (N) museums; (A) major; (N) artist

Answers: Exercise 2
1. young (day)
2. deserted (beach)
3. asleep (others)
4. distant, respectful (waves)
5. aware (woman)
6. curious (she)
7. radiant (everything)
8. true, clear (colors)
9. eye-catching (piece)
10. wonderful (thing)

Independent Practice
Skills Practice
📂 *Grammar Practice,* p. 23
📂 *Grammar Reteaching,* p. 23
📂 *Grammar Enrichment,* p. 23

📕 ***Grammar Workbook,*** Lesson 31

Enabling Strategies

LEP **Placing Adjectives**
Give LEP students noun phrases in which the adjectives and the noun are scrambled, such as *old cat ugly* or *day sunny bright.* Ask students to unscramble the words in each noun phrase so that it makes sense. Then ask them to identify the adjectives.

CLOSE

Ask students to use adjectives to write about a favorite painting or photograph.

425

FOCUS

Lesson Overview

Objective: To identify definite and indefinite articles and to recognize proper adjectives

Bellringer

When students enter the classroom, have this assignment on the board: *Look at the following sentences:*

1. *An apple a day keeps the doctor away.*
2. *April showers bring May flowers.*
3. *I like French fries.*

On a sheet of paper, answer these questions: What is the relationship of each underlined word to the word that follows it? What do you think the underlined words are?

Motivating Activity

Discuss students' answers to the Bell-ringer activity. Ask how they think *a* and *an* are used differently from *the.*

TEACH

☑ Grammar Tip

Proper adjectives with the endings *-an, -ese, -ian,* and *-ish* also can be nouns. For example, *Canadian* and *English* are nouns in these sentences:

1. The *Canadian* was happy with the outcome of the World Series.
2. A favorite food of the *English* is fish and chips.

🔁 Cross-reference: Grammar

For a review of proper nouns, refer students to Lesson 9.1, pp. 348–349.

426

12.2 Articles and Proper Adjectives

The words *a, an,* and *the* make up a special group of adjectives called **articles**. *A* and *an* are called **indefinite articles** because they refer to one of a general group of people, places, things, or ideas. *A* is used before words beginning with a consonant sound, and *an* before words beginning with a vowel sound. Don't confuse sounds with spellings. When speaking you would say *a university* but *an uncle.*

| **a** unit | **a** painting | **an** etching | **an** hour |

The is called a **definite article** because it identifies specific people, places, things, or ideas.

The valuable statue is **the** only one of its kind.

Proper adjectives are formed from proper nouns. A proper adjective always begins with a capital letter.

The **Italian** statue is on exhibit in the **Houston** museum.
The **February** exhibit follows a show of **French** paintings.

Although most proper adjectives are formed from proper nouns by adding one of the endings listed below, some are formed differently. Check the spellings in a dictionary.

Common Endings for Proper Adjectives				
-an	Mexico Mexic**an**	Morocco Morocc**an**	Alaska Alask**an**	Guatemala Guatemal**an**
-ese	China Chin**ese**	Bali Balin**ese**	Sudan Sudan**ese**	Japan Japan**ese**
-ian	Canada Canad**ian**	Italy Ital**ian**	Nigeria Niger**ian**	Asia As**ian**
-ish	Spain Span**ish**	Ireland Ir**ish**	Turkey Turk**ish**	England Engl**ish**

Teacher's Classroom Resources

The following resources can be used for planning, instruction, practice, reinforcement, reteaching, or enrichment.

📝 **Teaching Tools**
Lesson Plans

📁 **Blackline Masters**
Grammar Practice, p. 22
Grammar Enrichment, p. 22

📖 ***Grammar Workbook***
Lesson 32

Exercise 3   Using *A* and *An*

Write the correct indefinite article that would come before each word or group of words.

1. satellite
2. electrical storm
3. transmitter
4. vehicle
5. howling wind
6. expedition
7. unicorn
8. unique event
9. anonymous writer
10. unexplored part
11. unknown rock
12. typical day
13. masterpiece
14. awkward age
15. instrument
16. high-wire act
17. explanation
18. hourly report
19. honest effort
20. activity

Exercise 4   Forming Proper Adjectives

Rewrite each sentence, changing the proper noun into a proper adjective. You may have to change the article and eliminate other words.

1. The first exhibit included a drum from Africa.
2. One of my classmates was wearing a bracelet from Mexico.
3. Our class included an exchange student from China.
4. We braved a snowstorm in January to come to the show.
5. An artist from Poland was listening to an audio tape.
6. One painting represented a wedding in April.
7. A class favorite featured a bobsled from Alaska.
8. One parent arrived late in a car from Japan.
9. A snowy scene reminded the teacher of a winter in Minnesota.
10. A writer from Ireland introduced himself to the tour guide.
11. The furniture display included a clock from Taiwan.
12. Some of us chatted with a visitor from Italy.
13. Two people were copying a portrait of a dancer from Mexico.
14. I heard an art critic from Germany talking about the exhibit.
15. What he said puzzled a sailor from France.
16. A tourist from Egypt listened to her with interest.
17. At the museum restaurant the waitress offered us a tea from Australia.
18. A flag from Nigeria was displayed in the museum gift shop.
19. One postcard there showed a celebration in July.
20. The jewelry counter had a copy of a ring from Bolivia.

12.2 Articles and Proper Adjectives   **427**

PRACTICE AND ASSESS

Answers: Exercise 3

1. a	**6.** an	**11.** an	**16.** a
2. an	**7.** a	**12.** a	**17.** an
3. a	**8.** a	**13.** a	**18.** an
4. a	**9.** an	**14.** an	**19.** an
5. a	**10.** an	**15.** an	**20.** an

Answers: Exercise 4

1. … an African drum.
2. … a Mexican bracelet.
3. … a Chinese exchange student.
4. … a January snowstorm…
5. A Polish artist …
6. … an April wedding.
7. … an Alaskan bobsled.
8. … in a Japanese car.
9. … of a Minnesota winter.
10. An Irish writer …
11. … a Taiwanese clock.
12. … an Italian visitor.
13. … of a Mexican dancer.
14. … a German critic …
15. … a French sailor.
16. An Egyptian tourist …
17. … an Australian tea.
18. An Argentine flag …
19. … a July celebration.
20. … a Bolivian ring.

Independent Practice

Skills Practice

📁 *Grammar Practice,* p. 22
📁 *Grammar Reteaching*
📁 *Grammar Enrichment,* p. 22

📖 *Grammar Workbook,* Lesson 32

CLOSE

Tell students to write a paragraph describing a country they have studied, mentioning geographic features and neighboring countries. The paragraphs should contain both articles and proper adjectives.

Enabling Strategies

LEP Learning to Use Articles

Explain that English does not use any article when making a generalization about a plural noun (*Children are always noisy*) or a mass noun (*Milk is good for you*). *A* or *an* precedes a generalization about a singular noun (*A friend is always there for you*). *The* comes before the noun when the noun is something unique (*The moon is bright*), when the noun is one of a kind (*Derek is in the kitchen*), or when the hearer knows what is being talked about (*Who will win in the elections*). Have students write ten sentences using articles correctly with the words in Exercise 3.

427

FOCUS

Lesson Overview

Objective: To identify the comparative and superlative forms of adjectives and to form them correctly

Bellringer

When students enter the classroom, have this assignment on the board: *Write a sentence comparing the size of the following two animals: a lizard and a dinosaur.*

Motivating Activity

Discuss students' answers to the Bellringer exercise, listing any comparative and superlative forms of adjectives on the board. Try to point out patterns, such as adding *-er* or *-est* (*easier, easiest*) or using *more* or *most,* (*more afraid, most afraid*). Have students talk about the changes in meaning that occur.

TEACH

Cooperative Learning

Students might use a roundtable strategy to practice forming comparisons. One student writes a sentence that is part of a funny conversation. This sentence introduces a predicate adjective, for example, *My room is hot.* The next student writes a sentence that is a question using the same predicate adjective—*How hot is it?* Another student writes a third sentence using the comparative form of the adjective in a comic comparison, such as *My room is hotter than Arizona in a heat wave.*

12.3 Comparative and Superlative Adjectives

The **comparative form** of an adjective compares two things or people.

The **superlative form** of an adjective compares more than two things or people.

For most adjectives of one syllable and some of two syllables, *-er* and *-est* are added to form the comparative and superlative.

Comparative and Superlative Forms	
Comparative	She is **younger** than the other painter.
Superlative	She is the **youngest** painter in the entire group.

For most adjectives with two or more syllables, the comparative or superlative is formed by adding *more* or *most* before the adjective.

Comparative and Superlative Forms of Longer Adjectives	
Comparative	The one next to it is **more colorful.**
Superlative	The painting in the next room is the **most colorful.**

Never use *more* or *most* with adjectives that already end with *-er* or *-est.* This is called a double comparison.

Some adjectives have irregular comparative and superlative forms.

Irregular Comparative and Superlative Forms		
Adjective	**Comparative**	**Superlative**
good, well	better	best
bad	worse	worst
many, much	more	most
little	less	least

Teacher's Classroom Resources

The following resources can be used for planning, instruction, practice, reinforcement, reteaching, or enrichment.

Teaching Tools
Lesson Plans

Blackline Masters
Grammar Practice, p. 23
Grammar Enrichment, p. 23

Grammar Workbook
Lesson 33

Exercise 5   Identifying Correct Comparative and Superlative Forms

Rewrite each sentence, correcting the comparative or superlative form of the adjective.

1. You can't really say that my taste is worser than yours.
2. If someone has good taste in art, how can there be gooder taste?
3. You just don't like my favoritest painter.
4. Does that mean that the one you like is more good?
5. First of all, my favorite is more young than your favorite.
6. As she gets more older, her work improves.
7. Her bestest work has been done in the last ten years.
8. I know that critics have attacked her most early works.
9. The more large her paintings get, the more exciting they are.
10. The later paintings all sell for much more high prices.

Exercise 6   Using Comparative and Superlative Adjectives

Write the correct comparative or superlative form of the adjective in parentheses.

1. Michelangelo was one of the (great) artists of all time.
2. He was also the (famous) artist of his own time.
3. Are his statues (good) than his paintings?
4. Which is the (fine) statue, *David* or the *Pietà?*
5. Michelangelo's figures were (large) than life.
6. Few paintings are (beautiful) than the one on the ceiling of the Sistine Chapel.
7. His buildings may be (famous) than his renowned statues and paintings.
8. Pablo Picasso may be the (great) painter of our century.
9. His early paintings are (realistic) than his later work.
10. His (early) works were really quite traditional.
11. The work of Picasso's Blue Period included some of his (dark) views of life.
12. Picasso's (bleak) mood of all came during World War II.
13. During his Rose Period, though, his paintings were much (cheerful).
14. For Picasso painting was the (important) thing in his life.
15. His cubist works are probably the (famous) of all.
16. Cubism may have been the (original) of Picasso's many styles.
17. Critics argue over the question of his (good) style of all.
18. They also disagree on his (bad) style.
19. Few artists completed (many) paintings than he did.
20. Of all artists he showed the (quick) response to change.

12.3 Comparative and Superlative Adjectives   **429**

PRACTICE AND ASSESS

Answers: Exercise 5
1. worse
2. better
3. favorite
4. better
5. younger
6. older
7. best
8. earliest
9. larger
10. higher

Answers: Exercise 6

1. greatest	10. earliest
2. most famous	11. darkest
3. better	12. bleakest
4. finer	13. more cheerful
5. larger	14. most important
6. more beautiful	15. most famous
	16. most original
7. more famous	17. best
8. greatest	18. worst
9. more realistic	19. more
	20. quickest

Independent Practice

Skills Practice
 Grammar Practice, p. 23
 Grammar Enrichment, p. 23

📕 ***Grammar Workbook,*** Lesson 33

CLOSE

Have students imagine that they are movie critics. Ask them to write a brief comparison of three movies. Remind them to include both comparative and superlative adjectives in their writing.

Enabling Strategies

LEP Using Irregular Comparative and Superlative Forms

The words in the chart at the bottom of page 428 are frequently used. Suggest that students copy the chart in their learning logs. They might refer to it for help in using adjectives that have irregular comparative and superlative forms. They might also use it when they need to check the correct form to use with longer adjectives—*more* or *most, less* or *least.*

FOCUS

Lesson Overview

Objective: To identify demonstratives and to distinguish when they are used as adjectives and when they are used as pronouns

 **Bellringer**

When students enter the classroom, have this assignment on the board: *In which of these two sentences is the apple closer to you?*
This apple is mine.
That apple is yours.

Motivating Activity

Ask students to explain the difference in meaning between the two sentences.

TEACH

☑ **Teaching Tip**

You might use objects in the classroom to show when to use a particular demonstrative. For example, to show how to use *this* and *that,* you might hold up a book and say "This book is mine." Then hand it to someone and say, "That book is mine."

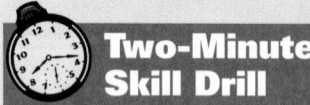 **Two-Minute Skill Drill**

Let students point to various objects and use *this, that, these,* and *those* appropriately.

430

That gallery has modern art.

This gallery contains Impressionist works.

12.4   Demonstratives

The words *this, that, these,* and *those* are called demonstratives. They "demonstrate," or point out, people, places, or things. *This* and *these* point out people or things near to you, and *that* and *those* point out people or things at a distance from you. *This* and *that* describe singular nouns, and *these* and *those* describe plural nouns.

This, that, these, and *those* are called demonstrative adjectives when they describe nouns.

Demonstrative adjectives point out something and describe nouns by answering the questions *which one?* or *which ones?*

The words *this, that, these,* and *those* can also be used as demonstrative pronouns. They take the place of nouns and call attention to, or demonstrate, something that is not named.

Notice the demonstratives in the following sentences.

| Demonstrative Words ||
Demonstrative Adjectives	Demonstrative Pronouns
This painting is my favorite.	**This** is my favorite painting.
I like **these** kinds of paintings.	**These** are the paintings I like.
That portrait is well known.	**That** was the first stage.
He draws **those** sorts of pictures.	**Those** are from his Cubist phase.

The words *here* and *there* should not be used with demonstrative adjectives. The words *this, these, that,* and *those* already point out the locations *here* and *there.*

This painting is by Matisse. [not *This here painting*]

The object pronoun *them* should not be used in place of the demonstrative adjective *those.*

I saw **those** pictures. [not *them pictures*]

430   *Adjectives and Adverbs*

Teacher's Classroom Resources

Exercise 7 **Identifying Demonstrative Adjectives and Pronouns**

Write the demonstrative from each sentence. Then write *adjective* or *pronoun* to tell what kind it is.

1. You can tell that this artist admired Cézanne's work.
2. All of these pictures show, in some way, Cézanne's influence.
3. This doesn't mean that the artist copied Cézanne's work.
4. Can you see how he uses these colors the same way?
5. Doesn't it remind you of those paintings of Cézanne's we just saw?
6. On the other hand, this one reminds me more of Van Gogh's work.
7. Now this is a painting I could look at every day.
8. All of those paintings by the Impressionists appeal to me.
9. I'm also interested in those abstract paintings in the next room.
10. This was a good day for seeing a wide variety of styles.

Exercise 8 **Using Demonstratives**

Write the correct word or words from the parentheses.

1. The artist saw (that, those) things in a new way.
2. (This, This here) painting shows her imaginative style.
3. This (kinds of, kind of) painting has become famous.
4. (This, That) painting over there shows an acrobat.
5. Usually (those, them) colors together would clash.
6. (This, These) are her brushes and palette.
7. (That there, That) painting by Paul Cézanne is influential.
8. (This, This here) is an early work.
9. Cézanne breaks up the dimensions of (this, these) objects.
10. Then he rearranges (these, these here) fragments.
11. This (kind of, kinds of) painting shows his technique.
12. (These, These here) are explorations of space.
13. The angles in (this, this here) picture seem to overlap.
14. These (kinds of, kind of) angles do form solids.
15. The *Pietà* is not (that, that there) kind of sculpture.
16. (This, These) is a fine example of abstract art.
17. Many are familiar with (that, that there) artist.
18. One artist produced all (this, these) works.
19. (Those, Them) paintings are older than his.
20. (These, These here) pieces are by an unknown artist.

12.4 Demonstratives **431**

Enabling Strategies

LEP Using Demonstratives

Explain to those new to English that the distinction between *this/these* and *that/those* is proximity to the speaker. To introduce a woman near us, we'd say, "This is Ms. Brown." If she were at a distance, we'd say, "That is Ms. Brown." Demonstrative pronouns can also indicate proximinty in time: *I saw him this afternoon* refers to today (near in time); *I saw him that afternoon* refers to some previous day (distant time). Have students write and share sentences using demonstrative pronouns.

FOCUS

Lesson Overview

Objective: To identify adverbs and to classify adverbs that answer such questions as *to what extent* (intensifiers), *when, where,* and *how* and that modify verbs, adjectives, or adverbs

🔔 Bellringer

When students enter the classroom, have this assignment on the board: *What difference in meaning do you find between "he is tall" and "he is extremely tall"?*

Motivating Activity

Discuss students' answers to the Bellringer exercise. Ask them, How tall is he? (*extremely* tall) Have students think of other words like *extremely* that answer the question *how.*

TEACH

☑ Teaching Tip

Adverbs are the most diverse part of speech. The most common kind of adverb modifies a verb. Adverbs that modify a verb fall into classes based on meaning—time, place, manner, and frequency. Each can be identified by asking a question using the words *when, where, how,* and *how often.* Most adverbs that modify verbs are easily moved from one position in the sentence to another. Intensifiers, which modify adjectives and adverbs, answer the question *to what extent.*

12.5 Adverbs

An **adverb** is a word that modifies, or describes, a verb, an adjective, or another adverb.

What Adverbs Modify	
Verbs	People handle old violins **carefully.**
Adjectives	**Very** old violins are valuable.
Adverbs	Some violins are played **extremely** rarely.

Some adverbs tell *to what extent* a quality exists. These adverbs are sometimes called **intensifiers**. *Very, quite,* and *almost* are intensifiers.

An adverb may tell *when, where,* or *how* about a verb. The adverbs in the sentences below all modify the verb *play.*

Ways Adverbs Modify Verbs	
How?	Many pianists play **well** with a large orchestra.
When?	Pianists **sometimes** play duets.
Where?	Some pianists play **everywhere** in the country.

When modifying an adjective or another adverb, an adverb usually comes before the word. However, when modifying a verb, an adverb can occupy different positions in a sentence.

Many adverbs are formed by adding *-ly* to adjectives. However, not all words that end in *-ly* are adverbs. The words *friendly, lively, kindly,* and *lonely* are usually adjectives. Similarly, not all adverbs end in *-ly.*

Adverbs Not Ending in *-ly*			
afterward	often	there	hard
sometimes	soon	everywhere	long
later	here	fast	straight

(handwritten note: Or to what extent?)

432   *Adjectives and Adverbs*

Teacher's Classroom Resources

The following resources can be used for planning, instruction, practice, reinforcement, reteaching, or enrichment.

🔧 **Teaching Tools**
Lesson Plans, p. 86

📁 **Blackline Masters**
Grammar Practice, p. 24
Grammar Reteaching, p. 24
Grammar Enrichment, p. 24

📙 *Grammar Workbook*
Lesson 35

Exercise 9   Identifying the Purpose of Adverbs

Write each adverb, and write whether it tells *how, when,* or *where.*

1. Our chorus finally has enough basses.
2. Unlike in previous years, our conductor can comfortably assign the parts.
3. Becky sometimes had to find choral arrangements with three parts.
4. Now she heads straight for the four-part works.
5. We've moved to another room because we have more space there.
6. She's arranged the seating differently, too.
7. Now each part sits in a wedge-shaped section.
8. That will give us better balance anywhere we sing.
9. She conducts us well, so we are happy.
10. We sing enthusiastically.

Exercise 10   Identifying Adverbs

Write each adverb and write the word it describes in parentheses.

1. The early Greeks studied music thoroughly.
2. To the Greeks music and mathematics were very similar.
3. Pythagoras strongly believed in the enormous power of music.
4. His ideas about music were certainly important.
5. People sang choral music often at ancient ceremonies.
6. The notes of each singer were exactly alike.
7. These choruses almost surely sang without accompaniment.
8. Composers later wrote separate parts for different voices.
9. Musicians of the Middle Ages developed part singing rather quickly.
10. Some unusually beautiful music resulted.
11. The parts were highly complex.
12. Modern choruses are very professional groups of singers.
13. These choruses perform everywhere.
14. Many choral singers are totally dedicated to their work.
15. People often overlook this kind of music.
16. Some people await major choral concerts eagerly.
17. Chorus singers are sometimes called choristers.
18. They generally sing pieces for four parts, or voices.
19. Tenors are sometimes female singers.
20. Some conductors always insist on male tenors.

12.5 Adverbs   **433**

PRACTICE AND ASSESS

Answers: Exercise 9
1. finally—when
2. comfortably—how
3. sometimes—when
4. Now—when
5. there—where
6. differently—how
7. Now—when
8. anywhere—where
9. well—how
10. enthusiastically—how

Answers: Exercise 10
1. thoroughly (studied)
2. very (similar)
3. strongly (believed)
4. certainly (important)
5. often (sang)
6. exactly (alike)
7. almost (surely); surely (sang)
8. later (wrote)
9. quickly (developed); rather (quickly)
10. unusually (beautiful)
11. highly (complex)
12. very (professional)
13. everywhere (perform)
14. totally (dedicated)
15. often (overlook)
16. eagerly (await)
17. sometimes (are called)
18. generally (sing)
19. sometimes (are)
20. always (insist)

Independent Practice

Skills Practice
🗀 *Grammar Practice,* p. 24
🗀 *Grammar Reteaching,* p. 24
🗀 *Grammar Enrichment,* p. 24

📕 **Grammar Workbook,** Lesson 35

CLOSE

Have students write a paragraph about a concert or play they have attended, using adverbs to describe the performance and the audience's reaction to it.

433

Enabling Strategies

LEP Identifying Adverbs

To help students locate adverbs, have them construct questions that ask *how, when, where,* and *how often,* using the sentence's simple subject and predicate. For example, for the sentence *Some pianists play everywhere in the country,* have students ask:

- How do pianists play?
- When do pianists play?
- Where do pianists play?
- How often do pianists play?

If students can answer one of these questions with a word from the sentence, then that word is an adverb. (Where do pianists play? *everywhere*)

FOCUS

Lesson Overview

Objective: To identify the comparative and superlative forms of adverbs and the correct use of each form

Bellringer

When students enter the classroom, have this assignment on the board: *Read this advertisement and write what it actually tells you about the toothpaste: "Bright-O-Dent toothpaste works better!"*

Motivating Activity

Invite students to discuss their responses to the Bellringer exercise and to suggest improvements to the advertisement.

TEACH

☑ Grammar Tip

To form the comparative and superlative forms of most one-syllable adverbs, simply add -er or -est (*faster, fastest*). To form the comparative and superlative of all adverbs that end in -ly, add *more* or *most* before the adverb (*more brightly, most brightly*). Almost all adverbs with more than one syllable end in -ly, so we can say that adverbs with two or more syllables follow the *more-most* pattern.

⇄ Cross-reference: Adverbs

For more information on comparative and superlative adverbs, refer students to Unit 3, Writing Process in Action, pp. 130–133.

434

12.6 Comparative and Superlative Adverbs

The **comparative form** of an adverb compares two actions.

The **superlative form** of an adverb compares more than two actions.

Long adverbs require the use of *more* or *most*.

Comparing Adverbs of More than One Syllable

Comparative	The audience listened **more attentively** last night than tonight.
Superlative	Last Sunday's audience responded **most enthusiastically** of all.

Shorter adverbs need *-er* or *-est* as an ending.

Comparing One-Syllable Adverbs

Comparative	Did the pianist play **louder** than the cellist?
Superlative	Did the drummer play the **loudest** of all?

Here are some irregular adverbs.

Irregular Comparative and Superlative Forms

Adverb	Comparative	Superlative
well	better	best
badly	worse	worst
little (amount)	less	least

The words *less* and *least* are used before both short and long adverbs to form the negative comparative and the negative superlative.

I play **less well**. I play **least accurately**.

Teacher's Classroom Resources

The following resources can be used for planning, instruction, practice, reinforcement, reteaching, or enrichment.

🔧 **Teaching Tools**
Lesson Plans, p. 86

📁 **Blackline Masters**
Grammar Practice, p. 25
Grammar Reteaching, p. 25
Grammar Enrichment, p. 25

📘 *Grammar Workbook*
Lesson 36

Exercise 11 — Forming the Comparative and Superlative

Write the comparative and superlative forms of each of the following adverbs.

1. tenderly	**6.** rapidly	**11.** soon	**16.** effectively	**21.** gracefully
2. fast	**7.** close	**12.** well	**17.** late	**22.** slow
3. little	**8.** gently	**13.** harshly	**18.** openly	**23.** frequently
4. easily	**9.** straight	**14.** eerily	**19.** negatively	**24.** effortlessly
5. violently	**10.** loud	**15.** hard	**20.** often	**25.** long

Exercise 12 — Using Comparative and Superlative Adverb Forms

For each sentence write the correct comparative or superlative form of the adverb in parentheses.

1. The performance began (late) tonight than last night.
2. My sister sat (far) from the stage than we did.
3. Several backup singers rehearsed (long) than the piano player.
4. The lead singer sang (badly) last year than this year.
5. The guitarists sang (little) during this concert than during their last one.
6. The drummer played (forcefully) during her solo than before.
7. We heard the first song (clearly) of all the songs.
8. The band played (energetically) of all at the end.
9. I clapped (loudly) during the second half than during the first.
10. I understand the band played (badly) at rehearsals than they ever had before.
11. (Often) than not, Miss Elly had to say, "Now, James, now!"
12. She expected (good) of him but couldn't be sure of it.
13. The night of the dress rehearsal came (quickly) than seemed possible.
14. There sat James in the percussion section as the music grew (fast).
15. He was staring even (blankly) into space than before.
16. "Now, James, now!" Miss Elly cried (desperately) than ever.
17. The entire band turned around and shouted even (loudly) than Miss Elly, "Now, James, now!"
18. The actual performance, however, went (well) than anyone expected.
19. James hit that triangle the (hard) he ever had, right on time.
20. The evening ended (soon) than expected.

12.6 Comparative and Superlative Adverbs **435**

PRACTICE AND ASSESS

Answers: Exercise 7

1. more or less, most or least tenderly
2. faster, fastest
3. less, least
4. more or less, most or least easily
5. more or less, most or least violently
6. more or less, most or least rapidly
7. closer, closest
8. more or less, most or least gently
9. straighter, straightest
10. louder, loudest
11. sooner, soonest
12. better, best
13. more or less, most or least harshly
14. more or less, most or least eerily
15. harder, hardest
16. more or less, most or least effectively
17. later, latest
18. more or less, most or least openly
19. more or less, most or least negatively
20. more or less, most or least often
21. more or less, most or least gracefully
22. slower, slowest
23. more or less, most or least frequently
24. more or less, most or least effortlessly
25. longer, longest

Answers: Exercise 8

1.	later	11.	More often
2.	farther	12.	better
3.	longer	13.	more quickly
4.	worse	14.	faster
5.	less	15.	more blankly
6.	more or less forcefully	16.	more desperately
7.	clearest	17.	louder
8.	most or least energetically	18.	better
9.	louder	19.	hardest
10.	worse	20.	sooner

Independent Practice

Skills Practice

Enabling Strategies

LEP Using Forms of Adverbs
Write a sentence on the board using the base form of an adverb, and ask LEP students to rewrite it, replacing the base form first with the comparative and then with the superlative. Example: *Tom replied **calmly**. Tom replied **more calmly** than any of his friends. Tom replied the **most calmly** of all.*

CLOSE

Ask students to choose five adverbs and write them along with their comparative and superlative forms.

FOCUS

Lesson Overview

Objective: To distinguish between predicate adjectives after linking verbs and adverbs after action verbs

🔔 Bellringer

When students enter the classroom, have this assignment on the board: *Complete each of these sentences with an adjective or adverb:*

I think jazz is _____.
I play piano _____.
Most people sing _____.
Our school band is _____.

Motivating Activity

Ask volunteers to read aloud their sentences from the Bellringer exercise. Have them describe how the adjectives or adverbs improve the sentences.

TEACH

Ⓐ Vocabulary Link

The word *well* can fill many roles in a sentence. One use of *well* is as an adverb that describes the manner in which an action is performed, for example: *They played well.* Another use of the word *well* is as an adjective that refers only to health, for example: *You look well.* There is a difference in meaning between the adjectives *well* and *good. You look good* refers to appearance. *You look well* refers to health only.

Louis Armstrong was a **real** innovator in jazz.

His music was **really** popular.

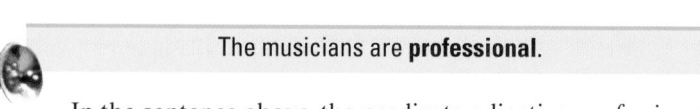

12.7 Using Adverbs and Adjectives

Adverbs and adjectives are often confused, especially when they appear after verbs. A predicate adjective follows a linking verb.

The musicians are **professional**.

In the sentence above, the predicate adjective *professional* describes *musicians*.

In the sentence below, the adverb *professionally* describes the action verb *behaved*.

The musicians behaved **professionally**.

People also sometimes confuse the words *bad, badly, good,* and *well. Bad* and *good* are both adjectives. They are used after linking verbs. *Badly* is an adverb. It is used after an action verb. *Well* can be either. When used to describe an adjective or verb, *well* is an adverb. When used after a linking verb to describe a person's health or appearance, *well* is an adjective.

| Distinguishing Adjective from Adverb ||
Adjective	Adverb
The sound is **bad**. The band sounds **good**. The soloist seems **well**.	The actor sang **badly**. The band played **well**.

People also confuse *real, really; sure, surely;* and *most, almost. Real, sure,* and *most* are adjectives. *Really, surely,* and *almost* are adverbs.

| Distinguishing Adjective from Adverb ||
Adjective	Adverb
Music is a **real** art. A pianist needs **sure** hands. **Most** pianos have eighty-eight keys.	Music is **really** popular. Piano music is **surely** popular. Piano strings **almost** never break.

436 *Adjectives and Adverbs*

Teacher's Classroom Resources

The following resources can be used for planning, instruction, practice, reinforcement, reteaching, or enrichment.

🎵 **Teaching Tools**
Lesson Plans, p. 87

📁 **Blackline Masters**
Grammar Reteaching, p. 26
Grammar Enrichment, p. 26

📘 ***Grammar Workbook***
Lesson 37

Exercise 13 — Using *bad*, *badly*, *good*, and *well*

For each sentence write the correct adjective or adverb given in parentheses.

1. The big bands did very (good, well) during the 1930s and 1940s.
2. As (good, well) as they were, they needed national radio to succeed.
3. Even (bad, badly) bands took advantage of the interest in this music.
4. The big bands' era is over, but their records still sell (good, well).
5. If you listen really (good, well), you'll still hear bands with that sound.

Exercise 14 — Identifying Adjectives and Adverbs

Write each sentence, and underline each verb. Circle the adverb or adjective that follows it, and draw an arrow to the word it modifies. Label each adjective or adverb.

1. Louis Armstrong was famous as a jazz trumpeter.
2. Armstrong began his music career early in the 1900s.
3. He played the trumpet well during his teens in New Orleans.
4. Armstrong listened carefully to other musicians' styles.
5. He seemed enthusiastic about a new singing style called "scat."
6. Scat was rhythmic in its use of syllables instead of words.
7. He seemed ready for a new career as an actor in motion pictures.
8. Big bands played everywhere.
9. They were popular in the 1930s.
10. Louis Armstrong traveled widely and made a number of hit records.
11. Both the soloists and the conductors of the big bands became widely known.
12. The Dorsey brothers were extremely successful as popular musicians.
13. They worked steadily throughout the 1940s.
14. Dinah Shore sang often with big bands.
15. Dinah became very popular as a solo artist.
16. The Spike Jones band is still popular with some people.
17. Spike's versions of some well-known songs were hilarious.
18. In some songs a fire whistle screamed wildly.
19. Meanwhile, the poor tenor sang unconcernedly in the background.
20. The Spike Jones band played well but sounded bad.

12.7 Using Adverbs and Adjectives **437**

PRACTICE AND ASSESS

Answers: Exercise 13
1. well 4. well
2. good 5. well
3. bad

Answers: Exercise 14
Arrows on student papers should point to the italicized words here.

1. *Louis Armstrong* was (famous)—adj.
2. *began* his music career (early)—adv.
3. *played* the trumpet (well)—adv.
4. *listened* (carefully)—adv.
5. *He* seemed (enthusiastic)—adj.
6. *Scat* was (rhythmic)—adj.
7. *He* seemed (ready)—adj.
8. *played* (everywhere)—adv.
9. *They* were (popular)—adj.
10. *traveled* (widely)—adv.
11. became (widely) *known*—adj.
12. were (extremely) *successful*—adj.
13. *worked* (steadily)—adv.
14. *sang* (often)—adv.
15. became (very) *popular*—adj.
16. is (still) *popular*—adj.
17. *versions* were (hilarious)—adj.
18. *screamed* (wildly)—adv.
19. *sang* (unconcernedly)—adv.
20. *played* (well) but *sounded* (bad)—adv.,adv.

Independent Practice
Skills Practice
Grammar Reteaching, p. 26
Grammar Enrichment, p. 26
Grammar Workbook, Lesson 37

CLOSE

Ask students to write a paragraph about their favorite musician or type of music. They should use both adjectives and adverbs.

Enabling Strategies

LEP Using Linking Verbs
To help students determine whether to use an adjective or adverb form in a sentence, review linking verbs with them. Have students create a chart of linking verbs on the board (for example, *is, are, were, look, grew*). They can also refer to Lesson 10.4 for more linking verbs.

Remind students that predicate adjectives are used with these linking verbs. Then have them practice writing sentences using linking verbs with the following predicate adjectives: *glad, beautiful, real, good,* and *awful*.

437

FOCUS

Lesson Overview
Objective: To identify contracted forms of *not* and to avoid using double negatives

🔔 Bellringer
When students enter the classroom, have this assignment on the board: *Write this sentence correctly: Aren't there no pizzas left?*

Motivating Activity
Discuss the Bellringer exercise with students. Ask them to identify the two words that should not be together in the same sentence and tell why.

TEACH

☑ Grammar Tip
Explain that a *no* word or a contraction with *not* is easily recognized as a negative. However, some words are not so easy to spot. Write *scarcely* and *hardly* on the board. Tell students that when these words are used in a sentence, no other negative can be used.

⏱ Two-Minute Skill Drill
Have a student write these words correctly in two similar sentences on the board: *nobody, anybody.* Have other students do the same with *ever, never* and *none, some.*

438

12.8 Avoiding Double Negatives

The adverb *not* is a **negative word**, expressing the idea of "no." *Not* often appears in a shortened form as part of a contraction. Study the words and contracted forms below.

Contractions with *Not*		
is not = isn't	cannot = can't	have not = haven't
was not = wasn't	could not = couldn't	had not = hadn't
were not = weren't	do not = don't	would not = wouldn't
will not = won't	did not = didn't	should not = shouldn't

The apostrophe replaces the *o* in *not* in all but two words. In *can't* both the letter *n* and the letter *o* are dropped. *Will not* becomes *won't*.

Other negative words are listed below. Each negative word has several opposites. These are **affirmative words**, or words that show the idea of "yes."

Negative and Affirmative Words	
Negative	**Affirmative**
never	ever, always
nobody	anybody, somebody
none	one, all, some, any
no one	everyone, someone, anyone
nothing	something, anything
nowhere	somewhere, anywhere

Be careful to avoid using two negative words in the same sentence. This is called a **double negative.** You can correct a double negative by removing one of the negative words or by replacing one with an affirmative word.

Incorrect:	The clarinet **isn't no** new instrument.
Correct:	The clarinet **isn't a** new instrument.
Correct:	The clarinet is **no** new instrument.

438   *Adjectives and Adverbs*

Teacher's Classroom Resources

The following resources can be used for planning, instruction, practice, reinforcement, reteaching, or enrichment.

🔧 **Teaching Tools**
Lesson Plans

📁 **Blackline Masters**
Grammar Practice, p. 26

📖 *Grammar Workbook*
Lesson 38

Exercise 15   Correcting Double Negatives

Rewrite each sentence, avoiding any double negatives.

1. My older brother doesn't take no piano lessons.
2. He plays the piano, but he can't hardly read music.
3. He plays by ear, but I haven't never been able to do that.
4. If we both want to play, we don't never agree who'll get the piano.
5. Sometimes I get there first, and he can't never stand it.
6. He hangs around, as though he doesn't have nothing to do.
7. Then he acts like he hasn't never wanted to play, just to sing.
8. But he starts singing so badly, I can't stand it no more.
9. I start laughing, and there isn't nothing can stop me.
10. Anyone laughing that hard can't hardly play the piano very well.

Exercise 16   Using Negative Words

Write the correct word or words given in parentheses.

1. Didn't (anyone, no one) play pipe organs before Roman times?
2. We (would, wouldn't) hardly recognize the Roman pipe organ today.
3. Aren't there (no, any) old Roman pipe organs still in existence?
4. The pipe organ (was, wasn't) scarcely used outside of churches.
5. Scarcely (no, any) ancient civilizations were without musical instruments.
6. The Egyptians (weren't, were) no exception.
7. Hardly (any, none) of their paintings leave out cymbals and drums.
8. The harp and flute weren't seen (nowhere, anywhere) until centuries later.
9. The zither (was, wasn't) heard nowhere before it was developed in China.
10. Hardly (no, any) ancient lyres are on public display.
11. If you haven't (ever, never) seen a lyre, try an art museum.
12. Some museums have instruments that are rarely played (anymore, no more).
13. They have instruments that can't be seen (nowhere, anywhere) else.
14. No one (should, shouldn't) have trouble understanding how music is made.
15. Didn't you (never, ever) learn that sounds come from making the air move?
16. Early stringed instruments weren't (ever, never) rubbed, only plucked.
17. Only later did (nobody, somebody) think of striking a string with a hammer.
18. Not all woodwind instruments (aren't, are) made of wood.
19. The brass instruments don't have (no, any) reeds at all.
20. Older percussion instruments aren't too different from ours (either, neither).

12.8 Avoiding Double Negatives   **439**

Enabling Strategies

LEP Identifying Negative Words

Students might have trouble distinguishing negative words from affirmative words. They may benefit from copying into their learning logs the chart of negative and affirmative words on page 438. Volunteers can read aloud each negative word and the corresponding affirmative words. Students can then circle the *n* or *no* in the negative words. Tell them that these letters are clues to identifying negative words.

TEACH

About the Literature

Explain that the review contains a passage from Elizabeth Borton de Treviño's *I, Juan de Pareja*. Treviño was born in Bakersfield, California, in 1904. She attended Stanford University, receiving a B.A. in Latin American history in 1925. She later studied violin at the Boston Conservatory of Music.

Treviño has written many novels for young people, several of them reflecting her interest in Latin America. In 1966 she won the Newbery medal—the most prestigious award in children's literature—for *I, Juan de Pareja*.

After students have read the passage, discuss the mood it creates and how the appropriate use of adjectives and adverbs enhances the writing.

Linking Grammar and Literature

☑ Teaching Tip

Ask students to find other adjectives and adverbs in the passage, such as *metallic, fine, softly,* and *daily.* Encourage students to tell how these words help them imagine how Juan ground the colors and prepared tools for his master. (*They help the reader see the process and understand how often certain tasks had to be done.*)

Critical Thinking

Have students categorize any adjectives in the passage that are articles, proper adjectives, comparative or superlative adjectives, or demonstratives.

Speaking and Listening

Ask a volunteer to read the passage to the class, excluding its adjectives and adverbs. Discuss the changes that the lack of adjectives makes in the passage and how this affects its quality.

Grammar Review

Adjectives and Adverbs

During the 1600s Juan de Pareja became enslaved to the great Spanish painter Diego Velázquez. *I, Juan de Pareja,* by Elizabeth Borton de Treviño, tells how Juan became the artist's friend and assistant. In this passage de Pareja explains his duties. The passage has been annotated to show some of the types of adjectives and adverbs covered in this unit.

> ### Literature Model
>
> #### *from* I, JUAN DE PAREJA
>
> *by Elizabeth Borton de Treviño*
>
> One by one, he taught me my duties. First, I had to learn to grind the colors. There were many mortars for **this** work, and pestles in varying sizes. I soon learned that the lumps of earth and metallic compounds had to be softly and **continuously** worked until there remained a powder as fine as the ground rice ladies used on their cheeks and foreheads. It took hours, and sometimes when I was sure the stuff was as fine as satin, Master would pinch and move it between his **sensitive** fingers and shake his head, and then I had to grind some more. Later **the** ground powder had to be incorporated into the oils, and well-mixed, and much later still, I arranged Master's palette for him, the little mounds of color each in its **fixed** place, and he had his preferences about how much of any one should be set out. And, of course, brushes were to be washed daily, in plenty of good **Castile** soap and water. Master's brushes all had to be clean and fresh every morning when he began to work.

Demonstrative adjective — *this*

Adverb — *continuously*

Adjective — *sensitive*

Article — *the*

Past participle used as an adjective — *fixed*

Proper adjective — *Castile*

440 *Adjectives and Adverbs*

Teacher's Classroom Resources

The following resources can be used for planning, instruction, practice, reinforcement, assessment, reteaching, enrichment, or evaluation.

🔧 **Teaching Tools**
Lesson Plans, p. 87

📕 **Grammar Workbook**
Lessons 31–38
Unit 5 Review
Cumulative Review: Units 1–5

Unit Assessment

📁 *Tests with Answer Key*
Unit 12 Mastery Test, pp. 47–48

💿 *Test Generator*
Unit 12 Mastery Test

Exercise 1

Identifying Adjectives   Write each adjective. Then write in parentheses the noun or pronoun it modifies . Do not include articles *a, an,* and *the.*

1. Velázquez painted in a large room on the second floor of the house.
2. A huge window let in a pure light from the north.
3. Juan learned to stretch the cotton canvas for the painter.
4. The artist never wrote down the secret formulas for preparing the canvas.
5. He called them professional secrets, and Juan had to memorize them.
6. Juan was a trustworthy assistant.
7. Velázquez liked the early light and would paint until late afternoon.
8. The painter's wife was a merry person and a thrifty housekeeper.
9. Juan had to arrange colorful backgrounds for Velázquez.
10. Juan always wore a gold earring.

Exercise 2

Using Comparative and Superlative Adjectives   Write the correct comparative or superlative form of the adjective in parentheses.

SAMPLE   De Pareja was (young) than Velázquez.
ANSWER   younger

1. Juan de Pareja ground the colors into the (fine) powder.
2. The artist's fingers were (sensitive) than Juan's.
3. He used the mounds of color on his palette to create some of the (beautiful) paintings of all.
4. Every day Juan de Pareja made sure the artist's brushes were (clean) and (fresh) than Velázquez had left them.
5. Velázquez used the (good) materials he could.
6. The painter often sat staring at his subject for the (long) time.
7. When asked why, the artist explained that this was the (good) way to feel the object's shape.
8. The (exciting) moment came when the king asked Velázquez to paint his portrait.
9. That meant the family would move in the (high) circles of society.
10. The king turned out to be (tall) and (pale) than Juan had expected.

PRACTICE AND ASSESS

Answers: Exercise 1
1. large (room); second (floor)
2. huge (window); pure (light)
3. cotton (canvas)
4. secret (formulas)
5. professional (secrets)
6. trustworthy (assistant)
7. early (light); late (afternoon)
8. merry (person); thrifty (housekeeper)
9. colorful (backgrounds)
10. gold (earring)

Answers: Exercise 2
1. finest
2. more sensitive
3. most beautiful
4. cleaner; fresher
5. best
6. longest
7. best
8. most exciting
9. highest
10. taller; paler

Grammar Review **441**

UNIT 12
Review

Answers: Exercise 3

1. continuously (modifies *worked*)
2. sometimes (modifies *ask*)
3. daily (modifies *washed*)
4. clumsily (modifies *worked*)
5. soon (modifies *cut, fit*)
6. occasionally (modifies *posed*)
7. usually (modifies *started*)
8. silently (modifies *drew*)
9. earnestly (modifies *asked*)
10. simply (modifies *answered*)

Answers: Exercise 4

1. more realistically
2. most clearly
3. most frequently
4. most heavily
5. farther
6. more calmly
7. most reluctantly
8. more softly
9. more freely
10. more easily

Exercise 3

Identifying Adverbs Write each sentence. Underline each adverb, and draw an arrow to the word it modifies.

1. The compounds had to be worked continuously.
2. Sometimes the painter would ask for more grinding.
3. Brushes had to be washed daily in soap and water.
4. Juan worked clumsily with his carpentry.
5. He could soon cut and fit the pieces.
6. Occasionally he posed so that the painter could draw or paint him.
7. The painter usually started work early in the morning.
8. Velázquez drew silently, making many drawings.
9. Juan earnestly asked the artist if he could learn to paint.
10. But Velázquez answered simply, "I cannot teach you."

Exercise 4

Using Comparative and Superlative Adverbs Write the correct comparative or superlative form of the adverb in parentheses.

SAMPLE He painted (boldly) than before.
ANSWER more boldy

1. Velázquez represented his subjects (realistically) than had many earlier artists.
2. Of all the techniques the artist's use of rich colors, light, and shadow (clearly) characterized his style.
3. Velázquez painted portraits (frequently) of all.
4. Although many artists have imitated his style, Velázquez (heavily) influenced modern painters.
5. He traveled (far) than many other artists of his day to study the art of ancient Rome.
6. Velázquez faced an upcoming trip to Italy (calmly) than did his family.
7. His wife stayed behind in Spain the (reluctantly) of all.
8. Velázquez found that the light shone (softly) in Italy than in Spain.
9. Juan moved around (freely) in Italy than in Spain.
10. He could buy paint supplies (easily) in Italy, too.

Exercise 5

Using Comparatives and Superlatives   Write the correct comparative or superlative form of the adverb or adjective in parentheses.

1. Fictional biography presents (interesting) problems than even straight fiction does.
2. Events must be evaluated (deliberately) than in straight fiction.
3. Biographers are (dependent) on written records than are writers of straight fiction.
4. Suppose that the main figure was one of the (famous) painters who ever lived.
5. Painters write (few) letters and diaries than do authors.
6. Velázquez wrote only a handful of letters, which makes things even (hard).
7. What is (difficult) than imagining conversations he might have had?
8. The (helpful) clues are in the artist's paintings.
9. The subjects of the paintings and how they are presented offer the (good) clues to the artist's interests and attitudes.
10. For de Pareja the clues are even (available) because he was less well known than his teacher.

Exercise 6

Distinguishing Between Adjectives and Adverbs   Write the correct adjective or adverb in parentheses.

1. Velázquez and de Pareja became (good, well) friends.
2. Velázquez recognized his assistant's (real, really) love for art.
3. The two worked (easy, easily) together.
4. Velázquez was never (harsh, harshly) with his assistant.
5. Juan was (frank, frankly) about his admiration of Velázquez.
6. He worked (eager, eagerly) to further Velázquez's career.
7. The portrait of de Pareja shows how (high, highly) he was regarded by Velázquez.
8. De Pareja had a (sure, surely) talent for painting.
9. Juan de Pareja served Velázquez (loyal, loyally) until the artist died.
10. De Pareja became a (true, truly) artist himself.

Grammar Review   **443**

Answers: Exercise 5
1. more interesting
2. more deliberately
3. more dependent
4. most famous
5. fewer
6. harder
7. more difficult
8. most helpful
9. best
10. less available

Answers: Exercise 6
1. good
2. real
3. easily
4. harsh
5. frank
6. eagerly
7. highly
8. sure
9. loyally
10. true

UNIT 12
Review

Answers: Exercise 7
Proofreading

This proofreading activity provides editing practice with (1) the current or previous units' skills, (2) the **Troubleshooter** errors, and (3) spelling errors. Students should be able to complete the exercise by referring to the units, the **Troubleshooter,** and a dictionary.

	Error (Type of Error)
1.	• Spanish (proper adjective)
2.	• an Italian (indefinite article before a vowel sound)
	• Italian (proper adjective)
	• artist, (nonessential appositive)
3.	• became (verb form)
4.	• family (spelling)
	• more like (comparative degree)
	• great (adjective)
5.	• skillfully (adverb)
6.	• omitted (verb tense)

Answers: Exercise 8
Mixed Review

1. many (adjective)
2. commissioned (adjective)
3. noncommissioned (adjective)
4. commissioned (adjective)
5. directly (adverb)
6. finished (adjective)
7. Sometimes (adverb)
8. Other (adjective)
9. painted (adjective)
10. dear (adjective)
11. official (adjective)
12. important (adjective)
13. noncommissioned (adjective)
14. usually (adverb)
15. that (adjective)
16. distinct (adjective)
17. sincere (adjective)
18. exactly (adverb)
19. honestly (adverb)
20. concerned (adjective)

Exercise 7 — Proofreading

The following passage is about Spanish artist Diego Velázquez, whose work appears on the next page. Rewrite the passage, correcting the errors in spelling, capitalization, grammar, and usage. Add any missing punctuation. There are ten errors.

Diego Rodriguez de Silva y Velázquez

[1]Diego Rodriguez de Silva y Velázquez (1599–1660) was born in the Spain city of Seville. [2]He studied a italian artist Caravaggio, whose realistic figures were painted in contrasting light and dark tones. [3]Velázquez become the official painter for Spain's King Philip IV in 1623. [4]However, the artist's portraits of the royal family looked most like pictures from a personal album than paintings advertising the greatly power of Spain.

[5]Velázquez skillful captures the personalities of his subjects. [6]When he painted his friend, Juan de Pareja, Velázquez omit neither his intelligence nor his dignity.

Exercise 8 — Mixed Review

On your paper write the twenty adjectives and adverbs that appear in the following paragraph. Do not include articles. Identify each word as an *adjective* or *adverb*.

Portraits

[1]Why do many painters do portraits? [2]There are commissioned portraits and noncommissioned portraits. [3]When an artist does a commissioned portrait, he or she has been asked directly to do so by someone who will pay for the finished work. [4]Sometimes it is the patrons, or buyers, who will sit for the portrait. [5]Other times they want a painted record of someone dear to them. [6]Or it may be an official portrait of an important person. [7]If artists do a noncommissioned portrait, it is usually because they have seen a face that they feel they have to capture. [8]That kind of portrait has a distinct advantage to sincere artists. [9]They can paint exactly what they see and do it honestly. [10]When artists are paid, the patron may be more concerned with appearances than honesty.

444 *Adjectives and Adverbs*

CLOSE

Have students look in magazine and newspaper ads for adjectives and adverbs and circle or highlight those words. Then discuss how vivid adjectives and adverbs can make a product appealing and may lead someone to buy it.

Diego Velázquez, *Juan de Pareja,* **1650**

About the Art

Diego Velázquez, *Juan de Pareja,* **1650**

This portrait is of Juan de Pareja, the slave of the artist Diego Velázquez. He assisted Velázquez by mixing his paints, arranging his palette, and cleaning his brushes. Velázquez learned to respect and admire de Pareja, and they became friends. Velázquez became the official court painter of King Philip IV of Spain in 1623, when Spain was enjoying its role as a colonial power.

Juan de Pareja, an oil on canvas measuring 32 by 27 1/2 inches, is in the Metropolitan Museum of Art in New York City.

Adjectives and Adverbs in Writing

Have students read the paragraph "On Summer" silently. Discuss the italicized adjective and adverb choices in relation to the Techniques with Adjectives and Adverbs below.

Techniques with Adjectives and Adverbs

Discuss the techniques described. Ask students how these techniques can be applied to the Proofreading passage on page 444.

Practice

The answers to this challenging and enriching activity will vary. Refer to Techniques with Adjectives and Adverbs as you evaluate student choices. Sample answer:

Every morning, Jason *eagerly* crossed off a day on his *giant basketball wall* calendar. Only five more until his *long-awaited* trip to Gona's house. Gona was *really* special, *especially* for a grown-up! Jason could reveal his *innermost* worries and she'd understand them *perfectly*. She never laughed or teased. Plus, just *next door* to Gona's creaky old house was the world's *most fabulous Chinese* restaurant. After his mom's *homemade spicy Italian* sausage, Jason was *positively nutty* for hot *Chinese* food.

446

Writing Application

Adjectives and Adverbs in Writing In this passage from "On Summer," Lorraine Hansberry uses adjectives and adverbs to convey the mood of summer nights in Chicago. As you read the passage, notice the italicized adjectives and adverbs.

Evenings were spent *mainly* on the *back* porches where screen doors slammed in the darkness with *those really very special summertime* sounds. And, *sometimes*, when *Chicago* nights got too *steamy*, the *whole* family got into the car and went to the park and slept out in the open on blankets. Those were, of course, the *best* times of all because the grownups were *invariably* reminded of having been children in *rural* parts of the country and told the *best* stories then.

Techniques with Adjectives and Adverbs Try to apply some of Lorraine Hansberry's writing techniques when you write and revise your own work.

1. Add detail and interest to your descriptions by combining several adjectives and adverbs in a group of descriptive words. Compare the following:

General Description special sounds
Hansberry's Version *those really very special summertime* sounds

2. When appropriate, use a proper adjective to make your descriptions more precise.

General Description when nights in *our city*
Hansberry's Version when *Chicago* nights

Practice Practice these techniques as you revise the following passage on a separate piece of paper. Experiment with adding one or more adjectives and adverbs in the blanks provided.

Every morning Jason _____ crossed off a day on his _____ calendar. _____ five more until his _____ trip to Gona's house. Gona was _____ special, _____ for a grown-up! Jason could reveal his _____ worries, and she'd understand them _____ . She never laughed or teased. Plus, just _____ to Gona's _____ house was the world's _____ restaurant. After his mom's _____ sausage, Jason was _____ for hot _____ food.

Teacher's Classroom Resources

The following resources can be used for assessment or evaluation.

Unit Assessment

📁 *Tests with Answer Key*
Unit 12 Mastery Test, pp. 47–48

💿 *Test Generator*
Unit 12 Mastery Test

You may wish to administer the Unit 12 Mastery Test at this point.

UNIT
13

Grammar

Prepositions, Conjunctions, and Interjections

Lessons

447

UNIT GOALS

The goal of Unit 13 is to help students, through example and instruction, to develop an understanding of and an ability to use prepositions, prepositional phrases, conjunctions, and interjections. Lessons focus on objects of prepositions, prepositional phrases as adjectives and adverbs, coordinating and correlative conjunctions, conjunctive adverbs, interjections, and other parts of speech.

Unit Assessment
📂 *Tests with Answer Key*
Unit 13 Pretest, pp. 49–50
Unit 13 Mastery Test, pp. 51–52

💿 *Test Generator*
Unit 13 Pretest
Unit 13 Mastery Test

You may wish to administer the Unit 13 Pretest at this point.

Key to Ability Levels
Enabling Strategies have been coded for varying learning styles and abilities.

L1 Level 1 activities are within the ability range of Learning Disabled students.

L2 Level 2 activities are basic-to-average activities and are within the ability range of average students.

L3 Level 3 activities are challenging activities and are within the ability range of above-average students.

LEP LEP activities are within the ability range of Limited English Proficiency students.

FOCUS

Lesson Overview

Objective: To identify prepositions and prepositional phrases and their correct use

🔔 Bellringer

When students enter the classroom, have this assignment on the board: *Write sentences that include the prepositional phrases "in the garden," "toward the car," and "throughout the day."*

Motivating Activity

Review the Bellringer and have students look at their sentences and identify the noun or pronoun to which each prepositional phrase refers.

TEACH

☑ Teaching Tip

Because prepositions exist as part of prepositional phrases, it is more effective to teach prepositions as part of the concept of prepositional phrases. Furthermore, since many words that function as prepositions can also be used as other parts of speech, such as coordinating conjunctions (*for*), subordinating conjunctions (*before, since*), or adverbs (*inside, past, underneath, up*), teaching prepositions alone can be confusing.

☑ Grammar Tip

A preposition is always the first word in a prepositional phrase. Prepositional phrases always include a noun or pronoun object.

448

13.1 | Prepositions and Prepositional Phrases

A **preposition** is a word that relates a noun or a pronoun to some other word in a sentence.

> The boy **by** the window is French.

The word *by* in the sentence above is a preposition. *By* shows the relationship of the word *boy* to the noun *window*.

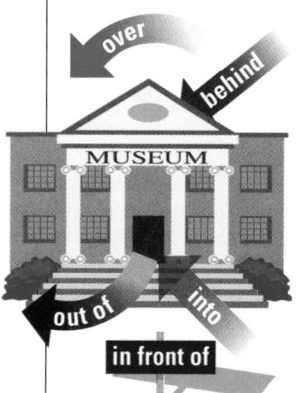

Commonly Used Prepositions

about	before	during	off	to
above	behind	for	on	toward
across	below	from	onto	under
after	beneath	in	out	until
against	beside	inside	outside	up
along	between	into	over	upon
among	beyond	like	since	with
around	by	near	through	within
at	down	of	throughout	without

A preposition can consist of more than one word.

> Yasmin will visit Trinidad **instead of** Jamaica.

Compound Prepositions

according to	aside from	in front of	instead of
across from	because of	in place of	on account of
along with	far from	in spite of	on top of

A **prepositional phrase** is a group of words that begins with a preposition and ends with a noun or pronoun, which is called the **object of the preposition**. The sentence below has two prepositional phrases.

> The painting **near you** is **by a Brazilian artist**.

448 *Prepositions, Conjunctions, and Interjections*

Teacher's Classroom Resources

The following resources can be used for planning, instruction, practice, reinforcement, assessment, reteaching, enrichment, or evaluation.

🔧 **Teaching Tools**
Lesson Plans, p. 88

📁 **Blackline Masters**
Grammar Practice, p. 27
Grammar Reteaching, p. 27
Grammar Enrichment, p.27

📖 ***Grammar Workbook***
Lesson 39

Unit Assessment

📁 *Tests with Answer Key*
Unit 13 Pretest, pp. 49–50

💿 *Test Generator*
Unit 13 Pretest

You may want to administer the Unit 13 Pretest at this point.

Exercise 1	Identifying Prepositional Phrases and Objects of Prepositions

Write each prepositional phrase. Draw a line under the preposition, and circle the object of the preposition.

1. The Louvre is a famous museum in Paris.
2. Do you know the history of this stately building?
3. The Louvre was once a residence for royalty.
4. Then the royal family moved to Versailles.
5. The galleries throughout the Louvre contain paintings and sculpture.
6. Paris, the French capital, is in northern France.
7. Vineyards stretch across the French countryside.
8. Picturesque old churches are scattered about the landscape.
9. Many harbors lie along the Mediterranean coast.
10. The largest French port, Marseilles, is on the Mediterranean Sea.
11. The high-speed Train à Grande Vitesse travels throughout France very quickly.
12. Ferries travel across the English Channel.
13. Cars and trains can also use a tunnel under the Channel.
14. The English held Calais for more than two centuries.
15. Many people enjoy winter sports in the French Alps.
16. Several resort cities cluster along the southern coast.
17. Most of the French kings were crowned at the cathedral in Reims.
18. Travelers to Europe will find many museums in Paris.
19. Each of these museums offers opportunity.
20. Visitors can also view many spacious and elegant gardens in European cities.

Exercise 2	Identifying Compound Prepositions

Write each prepositional phrase, and circle any compound prepositions.

1. According to our history book, a major change recently impacted Germany.
2. In place of two nations, West Germany and East Germany, Germany became one unified nation.
3. In spite of the challenges, most Germans celebrated becoming one nation again.
4. Visitors in front of the Brandenburg Gate can imagine the wall that once divided the city.
5. In eastern Berlin visitors will find old buildings instead of the modern additions of the western city.

13.1 Prepositions and Prepositional Phrases **449**

PRACTICE AND ASSESS

Answers: Exercise 1
1. … in (Paris.)
2. … of this stately (building?)
3. … for (royalty.)
4. … to (Versailles.)
5. … throughout the (Louvre)…
6. … in northern (France.)
7. … across the French (countryside.)
8. … about the (landscape.)
9. … along the Mediterranean (coast.)
10. … on the (Mediterranean Sea.)
11. … throughout (France)…
12. … across the (English Channel.)
13. … under the (Channel.)
14. … for more than two (centuries.)
15. … in the French (Alps.)
16. … along the southern (coast.)
17. … of the French (kings) … at the (cathedral) in (Reims.)
18. … to (Europe) … in (Paris)…
19. … of these (museums)…
20. … in European (cities.)

Answers: Exercise 2
1. (According to) our history book
2. (In place of) two nations
3. (In spite of) the challenges
4. (in front of) the Brandenburg Gate
5. In eastern Berlin, (instead of) the modern additions to the western city

Independent Practice

Skills Practice
📁 *Grammar Practice,* p. 27
📁 *Grammar Reteaching,* p. 27
📁 *Grammar Enrichment,* p. 27
📖 **Grammar Workbook,** Lesson 39

CLOSE

Have volunteers write sentences with prepositional phrases on the chalkboard. Ask other volunteers to underline the prepositional phrase, draw a second line under the preposition, and circle the preposition's object.

Enabling Strategies

LEP Using Prepositional Phrases
Write on the chalkboard several sentences containing prepositional phrases, such as *Mary plays in the band.* Ask students to work in pairs to substitute other prepositional phrases for the ones in the sentences, for example, *Mary plays across the street. Mary plays on the soccer team. Mary plays after school. Mary plays for fun. Mary plays with skill.*

FOCUS

Lesson Overview

Objective: To recognize the correct use of pronouns after prepositions

Bellringer

When students enter the classroom, have this assignment on the board: *What kind of phrase is underlined in each sentence?*
I gave my raisin cookies to Jan and Meg. I gave my raisin cookies to them.
(prepositional phrase)

Motivating Activity

Discuss the Bellringer activity. Ask students what part of speech *them* is. Help students see that the pronoun *them* is an object pronoun because it is the object of the preposition *to*.

TEACH

☑ Teaching Tip

Ask students to consider the following sentence: *Is Jim traveling with him or her?* To check whether the two pronouns in the compound object are used correctly, students can say the sentence with only one pronoun at a time.

13.2 Pronouns as Objects of Prepositions

When the object of a preposition is a pronoun, it should be an object pronoun and not a subject pronoun.

> Dan handed the tickets to Natalie. Dan handed the tickets to **her**.

In the example above, the object pronoun *her* is the object of the preposition *to*.

Sometimes a preposition will have a compound object: two nouns or a noun and a pronoun. The pronoun in a compound object must be an object pronoun.

> I borrowed the suitcase from **Ivan and Vera**. I borrowed the suitcase from **Ivan and her**.
>
> Natalie traveled with **Ivan and me**.

In the second sentence above, *Ivan and her* is the compound object of the preposition *from*. In the third sentence, *Ivan and me* is the compound object of the preposition *with*.

If you are unsure about whether to use a subject pronoun or an object pronoun, try saying the sentence aloud with only the object pronoun.

> I borrowed the suitcase from **her**.
> Natalie traveled with **me**.

Who is never the object of a preposition; only the object pronoun *whom* can be an object.

> The man **of whom** I spoke is from Colombia.
> To **whom** did you lend the guidebook?

Teacher's Classroom Resources

The following resources can be used for planning, instruction, practice, reinforcement, or reteaching, enrichment.

🔧 **Teaching Tools**
Lesson Plans, p. 88

📁 **Blackline Masters**
Grammar Practice, p. 28
Grammar Reteaching, p. 28
Grammar Enrichment, p. 28

📕 **Grammar Workbook**
Lesson 40

Exercise 3   Using Pronouns as Objects of Prepositions

Write the correct form of the pronoun in parentheses. Be sure each pronoun you choose makes sense in the sentence.

1. Carmen's aunt in Spain sent a postcard to David and (her, she).
2. This is the aunt about (who, whom) Carmen and David have told.
3. According to Carmen and (he, him), Spain is a great place to visit.
4. Carmen showed photographs of the Costa del Sol to Hector and (him, he).
5. There was one of David and (her, she) in front of the Alhambra in Granada.
6. The castle's magnificent gardens can be seen behind (them, they).
7. It was hard to distinguish between Carmen's cousin and (he, him); they look alike.
8. Because they look so much alike, Carmen's aunt could be mother to either of (them, they).
9. Aside from David, Carmen, and (he, him), no one in our class has been to Spain.
10. The Moors, who occupied Spain for 800 years, left architecture that impressed all of (us, we).
11. The description of the Alcázar given by Carmen and (her, she) was impressive.
12. Most of (us, we) thought the Alcázar was the Moors' best gift to Spain.
13. The Spanish lived alongside (them, they) for centuries.
14. The strong North African influences were described by David and (she, her).
15. Since only eight miles separate Spain from Africa at the narrowest point, this influence made perfect sense to (us, we).
16. Carmen explained to (me, I) that the Strait of Gibraltar is very narrow.
17. David showed the class how the Atlantic Ocean waters flow far beneath the surface while Mediterranean waters flow above (they, them).
18. Then Sheila asked why there were no pictures of (him, he) next to the water.
19. David pointed out to (her, she) that he had spent most of his trip inland.
20. Referring to the class map above (him, he), David located Barcelona.
21. Reaching across (I, me), Carmen gave Sheila a picture of a cathedral designed by Antonio Gaudí.
22. Carmen is standing between David and (him, he) in the first photograph.
23. The cathedral absolutely towers above (them, they) as they smile and point.
24. We were amazed to hear the history recounted by David and (her, she) of this never-finished wonder.
25. Some of (us, we) thought Gaudí's building looked a little like a sand castle.

Pronouns as Objects of Prepositions   **451**

PRACTICE AND ASSESS

Answers: Exercise 3

1.	her	14.	her
2.	whom	15.	us
3.	him	16.	me
4.	him	17.	them
5.	her	18.	him
6.	them	19.	her
7.	him	20.	him
8.	them	21.	me
9.	him	22.	him
10.	us	23.	them
11.	her	24.	her
12.	us	25.	us
13.	them		

Independent Practice

Skills Practice

📁 *Grammar Practice,* p. 28
📁 *Grammar Reteaching,* p. 28
📁 *Grammar Enrichment,* p. 28

 **Grammar Workbook,** Lesson 40

CLOSE

Have students describe the most interesting place they have ever visited. Tell them to use pronouns as objects of prepositions in their paragraphs.

Enabling Strategies

LEP **Using Pronouns in Compound Objects of Prepositions**

Have LEP students look at sentences 1, 3, 4, 5, 7, 9, 11, 14, 22, and 24 of Exercise 3. Tell them to practice using the test mentioned in the text to determine whether to use object or subject pronouns. Have them say each sentence aloud, omitting the proper noun or other nouns in the compound object and saying only the pronoun. Emphasize that pronouns used in compound objects have the same form as freestanding pronouns.

FOCUS

Lesson Overview

Objective: To use adjective phrases to describe nouns and pronouns; to use adverb phrases to describe verbs, adjectives, and adverbs

🔔 Bellringer

When students enter the classroom, have this assignment on the board: *Write down the following sentences and circle all the words that describe the underlined word in each sentence.*

1. I love the white <u>dress</u> with the blue satin sash.

2. My father <u>sings</u> loudly in the shower.

Motivating Activity

Ask students how many of the circled groups of words begin with a preposition. Are they prepositional phrases? How can they tell? Ask students to identify the word or words each phrase modifies.

TEACH

☑ Teaching Tip

Adverb phrases that modify verbs usually can be moved to other positions in sentences. For example, the adverb phrase *in the morning* in the sentence *They left the hotel in the morning* can be moved to the beginning of the sentence: *In the morning they left the hotel.* Adjective phrases, on the other hand, cannot be moved away from the nouns they modify.

13.3	**Prepositional Phrases as Adjectives and Adverbs**

A prepositional phrase is an **adjective phrase** when it modifies, or describes, a noun or pronoun.

> A temple **of great size** stands here.
>
> I noticed some men **with heavy suitcases**.

In the first sentence above, the prepositional phrase *of great size* modifies the subject of the sentence, *temple.* In the second sentence, the prepositional phrase *with heavy suitcases* describes a noun in the predicate, *men.*

Notice that, unlike most adjectives, an adjective phrase usually comes after the word it modifies.

A prepositional phrase is an **adverb phrase** when it modifies, or describes, a verb, an adjective, or another adverb.

Adverb Phrases Modifying a Verb, an Adjective, and an Adverb	
Describes a verb	The tourists travel **in a group**.
Describes an adjective	The temple is impressive **from this view**.
Describes an adverb	It has held up well **for its age**.

An adverb phrase tells *when*, *where*, or *how* an action occurs.

How Adverb Phrases Function	
When?	They left the hotel **in the morning**.
Where?	The curious visitors went **to Japan**.
How?	The large group traveled **by airplane**.

452 *Prepositions, Conjunctions, and Interjections*

Teacher's Classroom Resources

The following resources can be used for planning, instruction, practice, reinforcement, reteaching, or enrichment.

🔧 **Teaching Tools**
Lesson Plans, p. 89

📁 **Blackline Masters**
Grammar Practice, p. 29
Grammar Enrichment, p. 29

📘 ***Grammar Workbook***
Lesson 41

Exercise 4   Identifying Adjective and Adverb Phrases

Write each prepositional phrase, and write whether it is an *adjective phrase* or an *adverb phrase*.

1. Most people in Japan follow the traditional customs of their country.
2. The Japanese traditionally bow on certain occasions.
3. They show great respect for their elders.
4. Throughout their history the Japanese have also loved beauty.
5. Their gardens are models of grace and delicacy.
6. Japanese gardens are exceptional in their harmony.
7. Artificial and natural elements blend together in their gardens.
8. Soft woven mats cover the floors of many Japanese homes.
9. People customarily wear comfortable slippers inside their homes.
10. The guests of a family receive much kindness and consideration.
11. People sometimes cook on small charcoal stoves.
12. They often prepare bowls of noodles.
13. Diners frequently sit around very low tables.
14. Many Japanese people eat with chopsticks.
15. Hosts serve small cups of fragrant tea.
16. The Japanese tea ceremony has remained popular over the centuries.
17. We can enjoy our memories of Japan more fully with photos.
18. A guide translates the language with care.
19. Many people feel that Japanese is a language of great beauty.
20. When written, its letters are formed with graceful strokes.

Exercise 5   Writing Sentences with Prepositional Phrases

Rewrite each group of sentences, making a single sentence with adjective or adverb phrases.

1. Japan experienced little influence. The influence was from the outside.
2. Japan became an industrial nation. It became an industrial nation within fifty years.
3. We recently visited Nara. A Buddhist temple of historical significance can be seen at Nara.
4. Brightly colored plants dot the hills. The hills are below Kyushu's mountainous slopes.
5. The volcano Mount Aso stands. It stands at the island's highest point.

13.3 Prepositional Phrases as Adjectives and Adverbs   **453**

Answers: Exercise 4
1. in Japan—adj.; of their country—adj.
2. on certain occasions—adv.
3. for their elders—adj.
4. Throughout their history—adv.
5. of grace and delicacy—adj.
6. in their harmony—adv.
7. in their gardens—adv.
8. of many Japanese homes—adj.
9. inside their homes—adv.
10. of a family—adj.
11. on small charcoal stoves—adv.
12. of noodles—adj.
13. around very low tables—adv.
14. with chopsticks—adv.
15. of fragrant tea—adj.
16. over the centuries—adv.
17. of Japan—adj.; with photos—adv.
18. with care—adv.
19. of great beauty—adj.
20. with graceful strokes—adv.

Answers: Exercise 5
1. Japan experienced little influence from the outside.
2. Japan became an industrial nation within fifty years.
3. We recently visited a Buddhist temple of historical significance at Nara.
4. Brightly colored plants dot the hills below Kyushu's mountainous slopes.
5. The volcano, Mount Aso, stands at the island's highest point.

Independent Practice

Skills Practice
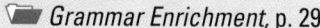 *Grammar Practice,* p. 29
 *Grammar Enrichment,* p. 29

📕 *Grammar Workbook,* Lesson 41

CLOSE

Have students use adjective and adverb phrases to write about a real or imagined trip to a place where the customs and practices were unfamiliar to them.

453

Enabling Strategies

LEP Using Prepositional Phrases

Virtually all languages use prepositional phrases, consisting of a preposition and its object in a fixed order. The order in which these two elements occur is not universal, however. In some languages, such as Japanese, the order is the reverse of that in English: the object of the preposition comes first and is followed by the preposition. One complication in English is that some constructions appear to be prepositions but lack objects, as in *He said he would stop by.*

Lesson 13.4 teaches students to use coordinating and correlative conjunctions correctly in their writing.

FOCUS

Lesson Overview
Objective: To recognize and distinguish between coordinating and correlative conjunctions

Bellringer
When students enter the classroom, have this assignment on the board: *On a sheet of paper explain the function of the underlined words in the sentences below.*

Sally and Fred love to ski. They have skied not only in Colorado but also in Utah. They would like to ski in Vermont also, but they've run out of money.

Motivating Activity
Discuss the Bellringer exercise. Ask students to identify the words or phrases each underlined word connects.

TEACH

☑ Grammar Tips
Tell students that coordinating conjunctions always join elements of the same kind—subject with subject, or verb with verb.

Remind students to be careful to place the first conjunction in a pair of correlative conjunctions correctly. This sentence is incorrect: *The different languages of Switzerland neither cause conflicts nor misunderstandings.* This one is correct: *The different languages of Switzerland cause neither conflicts nor misunderstandings.*

13.4　Conjunctions

A **coordinating conjunction** is a word used to connect parts of a sentence, such as words or phrases. *And*, *but*, *or*, *for*, and *nor* are coordinating conjunctions.

Using Coordinating Conjunctions	
Compound Subject	Allison **and** Rosita have lived in Mexico City.
Compound Predicate	Tourists shop **or** relax on the beaches.
Compound Object of a Preposition	Amiri went to Brazil **and** Peru.
Compound Sentence	Tom shopped every day, **but** we toured.

To make the relationship between words or groups of words especially strong, use a correlative conjunction.

Correlative conjunctions are pairs of words used to connect words or phrases in a sentence. Correlative conjunctions include *both . . . and*, *either . . . or*, *neither . . . nor*, and *not only . . . but also*.

> Examples of great architecture exist in **both** New York **and** Paris. **Neither** Carlo **nor** I have visited those cities.

When a compound subject is joined by the conjunction *and*, it is usually plural. The verb must agree with the plural subject.

When a compound subject is joined by *or* or *nor*, the verb must agree with the nearest part of the subject.

> Winema **and** Tanya **are** in Madrid this week.
> Neither the twins **nor** Ann **is** studying Spanish.

Teacher's Classroom Resources

The following resources can be used for planning, instruction, practice, reinforcement, reteaching, or enrichment.

Teaching Tools
Lesson Plans

Blackline Masters
Grammar Practice, p. 30
Grammar Reteaching, p. 29
Grammar Enrichment, p. 30

Grammar Workbook
Lesson 42

Exercise 6   Identifying Conjunctions

Write each conjunction. Write whether it forms a *compound subject*, a *compound predicate*, a *compound object of a preposition*, or a *compound sentence*.

1. Our teacher traveled to France and toured Paris.
2. The tour took a long time, but it was fascinating.
3. A cathedral or a museum in France may be very old.
4. Visitors spend hours in the bookstores and galleries.
5. After Paris, our teacher went to Normandy, which is between Paris and the English Channel.
6. This picturesque farming region is famous for delicious apples and cheeses.
7. Mr. King told us that he sampled some of the cheeses, but he enjoyed the fresh apple cider the most.
8. The leader and most of the participants voted for seeing the Loire Valley, a region known for its magnificent castles.
9. Our teacher agreed with us, but he requested that the group return to Dunkirk at the end of the tour.
10. Since Mr. King's trip, the tour company offers separate trips to one or the other of these regions.

Exercise 7   Making Compound Subjects and Verbs Agree

Write each sentence, using the correct verb form. Underline each coordinating or correlative conjunction.

1. An auto or a train (is, are) the best transportation for tourists.
2. Neither our teacher nor her companions (speaks, speak) French.
3. Both a subway and a bus system (serves, serve) Paris.
4. Either a taxi or a subway train (is, are) quick.
5. Two buses and a train (goes, go) to the Eiffel Tower.
6. Sometimes musicians and jugglers (performs, perform) in the subway stations in Paris.
7. Neither the Royal Palace nor the Louvre (is, are) open.
8. Still, Parisians and visitors alike (gathers, gather) outside these architectural points of interest.
9. Both the Left and the Right banks of the Seine (is, are) parts of Paris.
10. Either a tour boat or a stroll down the river banks (affords, afford) an intimate view of the city.

13.4 Conjunctions   **455**

Enabling Strategies

LEP Connecting Ideas

Have LEP students discuss the meaning in these sentences using conjunctions to connect compound predicates:

1. Jane plays baseball and soccer.
2. Jane plays both baseball and soccer.
3. Jane plays baseball, but she does not play soccer.
4. Jane not only plays baseball, but she also plays soccer.
5. Jane plays baseball or soccer.
6. Jane plays either baseball or soccer.
7. Jane plays neither baseball nor soccer.

Now ask students to rewrite the sentences using compound subjects.

FOCUS

Lesson Overview

Objective: To use conjunctive adverbs correctly

🔔 Bellringer

When students enter the classroom, have this assignment on the board: *Which of the following is easier to understand? Which conveys the more precise meaning?*

1. *DeVon is stingy with everybody. He often gets into arguments with his brother.*
2. *DeVon is stingy with everybody; therefore, he often gets into arguments with his brother.*

Motivating Activity

Discuss with students how the conjunctive adverb *therefore* in the second Bellringer sentence shows a causal relationship that is missed when the two sentences stand alone.

TEACH

☑ Teaching Tips

When two simple sentences are joined by a conjunctive adverb, a semicolon or a period must be used at the end of the first sentence. Explain to students that conjunctive adverbs show how the meaning of the second clause is related to that of the first.

13.5   Conjunctive Adverbs

You can use a special kind of adverb instead of a coordinating or correlative conjunction to join the simple sentences in a compound sentence.

> Many Asians use chopsticks, but some use forks.
> Many Asians use chopsticks; **however**, some use forks.

Conjunctive adverbs, such as *however* in the sentence above, are usually stronger and more precise than coordinating conjunctions.

Using Conjunctive Adverbs	
To replace *and*	also, besides, furthermore, moreover
To replace *but*	however, nevertheless, still
To state a result	consequently, therefore, so, thus
To state equality	equally, likewise, similarly

A **conjunctive adverb** may be used to join the simple sentences in a compound sentence.

When two simple sentences are joined with a conjunctive adverb, a semicolon always appears before the second sentence. The conjunctive adverb can appear at the beginning, at the end, or in the middle of the second sentence. When it comes at the beginning or end, it is set off with a comma. When it appears in the middle, one comma precedes it, and one follows it.

> Chinese people often stir-fry their food; **therefore,** they must cut it into very small pieces.
> Stir-frying should be done quickly; the wok must be very hot, **therefore.**
> Vegetables cook more quickly than meat; they must, **therefore,** be added to the wok last.

Teacher's Classroom Resources

The following resources can be used for planning, instruction, practice, reinforcement, reteaching, or enrichment.

🖉 Teaching Tools
Lesson Plans

📁 Blackline Masters
Grammar Practice, p. 30
Grammar Reteaching, p. 29
Grammar Enrichment, p. 30

📙 Grammar Workbook
Lesson 43

Exercise 8   Identifying Conjunctive Adverbs

Write each sentence. Underline each conjunctive adverb, and add any needed punctuation.

1. People in different lands often have different eating styles moreover they may use different utensils.
2. Many people in India use bread as a scoop some however use a fork.
3. Chinese cooks cut meat into bite-size pieces similarly they chop or slice most vegetables.
4. Food is bite-size thus a knife isn't needed.
5. Soup may be served without spoons it must however be sipped carefully.
6. In the United States, Chinese restaurants may offer diners chopsticks still forks are usually found at each place.
7. Europeans may push their food onto the fork they consequently hold both the knife and the fork while eating.
8. Each of these utensils has its own unique history a complete understanding of the topic consequently requires time and effort.
9. The fork was once used as a fishing tool likewise ancient people took their forks to battle as weapons.
10. The first known table fork in England was made of fragile glass thus it was kept with great care.

Exercise 9   Using Conjunctive Adverbs

Write a conjunctive adverb that makes sense in completing the sentence.

1. Cuisines differ from country to country; _____, they often feature similar dishes.
2. A crepe is a thin pancake around a filling; _____, an enchilada may feature cheese inside a pancake.
3. Each nation has its specialities; _____, these are the best foods to sample.
4. You can enjoy these foods in restaurants; _____, cookbooks offer recipes.
5. You could spend a week trying Asian foods; _____, you could spend a week on other international foods.
6. France is rich in dairy products; _____, French cooks use cream and cheese.
7. Indian food is sometimes vegetarian; _____, it is often spicy.
8. Rice is a staple of Chinese cooking; _____, it is a staple of Japanese cooking.
9. Italian cuisines vary from region to region; _____, each type is delicious.
10. Our school serves international foods; _____, American favorites appear on the menu.

13.5 Conjunctive Adverbs   **457**

PRACTICE AND ASSESS

Answers: Exercise 8
1. styles; <u>moreover,</u>
2. scoop; some, <u>however,</u>
3. pieces; <u>similarly,</u>
4. bite-size; <u>thus,</u>
5. spoons; it must, <u>however,</u>
6. chopsticks; <u>still,</u>
7. fork; they, <u>consequently,</u>
8. history; a complete understanding of the topic, <u>consequently,</u>
9. tool; <u>likewise,</u>
10. glass; <u>thus,</u>

Answers: Exercise 9
Answers will vary, but some suggestions are given below.
1. however
2. similarly
3. therefore
4. furthermore
5. likewise
6. consequently
7. also
8. similarly
9. however
10. nevertheless

Independent Practice

Skills Practice
Grammar Practice, p. 30
Grammar Reteaching, p. 29
Grammar Enrichment, p. 30

 Grammar Workbook, Lesson 43

CLOSE

Ask students to write a description of the various ethnic cuisines that comprise American cooking. Make sure they use conjunctive adverbs in their descriptions.

Enabling Strategies

LEP **Using Conjunctive Adverbs**
Some students whose primary languages do not use conjunctive adverbs may need extra help working with them. Make sure they understand how to punctuate conjunctive adverbs correctly, so they do not create run-on sentences. Have students write sentences using *however, therefore, besides, but,* and *nevertheless.* Have them exchange papers and correct them together in class.

FOCUS

Lesson Overview

Objective: To identify and correctly punctuate interjections

 **Bellringer**

When students enter the classroom, have this assignment on the board: *Which sentence in each pair shows more emphasis or emotion?*

a. *It's summer.*
   Yippee! It's summer.
b. *I want to get out of here.*
   Ugh! I want to get out of here.

TEACH

☑ Teaching Tip

Interjections seldom appear in formal writing. Their main use is to reflect the sound of spoken language in a written version of a conversation. Because interjections are not considered part of sentence grammar, personal preference may determine whether they are punctuated with a period or an exclamation point or are joined to the sentence with a comma. However, advise students not to use a dash.

⮂ Cross-reference: Writing

Interjections are used often in writing dialogue. For more information on writing dialogue, refer students to Unit 4, Writing to Tell a Story, p. 141–188.

13.6   Interjections

You can express very strong feelings in a short exclamation that may not be a complete sentence. These exclamations are called interjections.

An **interjection** is a word or group of words that expresses strong feeling. It has no grammatical connection to any other words in the sentence.

Interjections are used to express emotions, such as surprise or disbelief. They are also used to attract attention.

Any part of speech can be used as an interjection. Some of the more common interjections are listed below.

Common Interjections			
aha	good grief	oh	well
alas	ha	oh, no	what
awesome	hey	oops	whoops
come on	hooray	ouch	wow
gee	look	phew	yes

An interjection that expresses very strong feeling may stand alone either before or after a sentence. Such interjections are followed by an exclamation mark.

> We are taking a boat ride around Venice. **Hooray!**

When an interjection expresses a milder feeling, it can appear as part of a sentence. In that case, the interjection is separated from the rest of the sentence by a comma.

> **Wow**, that view of the skyline is spectacular.

You use interjections frequently when you speak. You should use them sparingly, however, when you write. Overusing interjections will spoil their effectiveness.

458   *Prepositions, Conjunctions, and Interjections*

Teacher's Classroom Resources

The following resources can be used for planning, instruction, practice, reinforcement, reteaching, or enrichment.

🛠 **Teaching Tools**
Lesson Plans, p. 90

📁 **Blackline Masters**
Grammar Reteaching, p. 30

📕 **Grammar Workbook**
Lesson 43

Exercise 10   Identifying Interjections

Write each sentence, adding punctuation where needed. Underline the interjection in each sentence.

1. Wow Doesn't Venice, Italy, have a lot of canals!
2. Imagine There are hardly any cars in Venice.
3. The city is built upon nearly 120 islands. Phew.
4. Alas we won't have time to visit every island.
5. There's a candy-striped pole up ahead. Oh, no
6. My goodness that was close.
7. Oops Look out for that gondola on your left.
8. Psst what is that bridge?
9. It is the famous Rialto Bridge. Yippee
10. No kidding Shall we visit it after lunch?
11. Good grief I can't believe I lost my camera.
12. Did you visit the Galleria dell'Accademia? Awesome
13. Come on There's a great outdoor restaurant very near the museum.
14. Hey Did you notice how the narrow, winding streets usually lead to a large, airy plaza?
15. Gee did you realize that the Grand Canal is so long?
16. Is rain in the forecast? Ugh
17. Hey the water is rough in this canal.
18. Eek Don't tip us over.
19. Oh, no Don't stand up in the gondola.
20. Whee Let's spend the whole day on this gondola.

Exercise 11   Identifying Interjections

Write an interjection that could complete each sentence. Make sure the sentence makes sense. Answers will vary.

1. _____! Our next stop in Italy will be the ancient city of Rome.
2. The city was first built during the great Roman Empire, more than 2,500 years ago. _____!
3. _____! Today's Romans live surrounded by remnants of an entirely different civilization.
4. _____! The Colosseum isn't one of the stops on today's tour.
5. We are planning instead to lunch on some of Italy's more than 200 kinds of pasta.

13.6 Interjections   **459**

PRACTICE AND ASSESS

Answers: Exercise 10
1. Wow!
2. Imagine!
3. Phew!
4. Alas, we …
5. Oh, no!
6. My goodness, that …
7. Oops!
8. Psst, what is…
9. Yippee!
10. No kidding!
11. Good grief!
12. Awesome!
13. Come on!
14. Hey!
15. Gee, did you …
16. Ugh!
17. Hey, the water …
18. Eek!
19. Oh, no!
20. Whee!

Answers: Exercise 11
Answers will vary, but some suggestions are given below.
1. Oh, boy
2. Wow
3. Imagine
4. Alas
5. Hooray

Independent Practice

Skills Practice
 *Grammar Reteaching,* p. 30

📖 **Grammar Workbook,** Lesson 43

CLOSE

Have students write a paragraph using interjections about the last time they went to an amusement park.

Enabling Strategies

LEP Using Interjections

To help students whose first language is not English, explain that an interjection commonly appears either at the beginning or at the end of a sentence. Then tell them that an adverb can also appear in those positions, but an adverb, unlike an interjection, can usually be moved to a different position. For example, we can rewrite *Reluctantly, the little boy replaced the candy* as *The little boy reluctantly replaced the candy.*

| 13.7 | Finding All the Parts of Speech |

Each separate word in a sentence performs a particular job. Each word belongs to a category called a **part of speech**. A word's part of speech depends on the job it performs in the sentence. You have learned all eight parts of speech. The sentence below contains an example of each category.

> Gee, Venice is astonishingly beautiful, and it has classic architecture in every quarter.

Parts of Speech		
Word	**Part of Speech**	**Function**
Gee	Interjection	Expresses strong feeling
Venice	Proper noun	Names a specific thing
is	Linking verb	Links *Venice* with the adjective *beautiful*
astonishingly	Adverb	Describes the adjective *beautiful*
beautiful	Adjective	Describes the subject, *Venice*
and	Conjunction	Joins two simple sentences
it	Pronoun	Takes the place of a noun
has	Action verb	Names an action
classic	Adjective	Describes the object, *architecture*
architecture	Common noun	Names a thing
in	Preposition	Relates *architecture* and *quarter*
every	Adjective	Describes the noun *quarter*
quarter	Common noun	Names a thing

460 *Prepositions, Conjunctions, and Interjections*

Setting the Purpose

Lesson 13.7 reviews the eight parts of speech and teaches students to use them correctly in their writing.

FOCUS

Lesson Overview
Objective: To identify and use the eight parts of speech correctly

Bellringer
When students enter the classroom, have this assignment on the board: *Identify as many parts of speech as you can in the following sentence:*
Gee, Venice is astonishingly beautiful, and it has classic architecture in every quarter.

Motivating Activity
Ask students to name the eight parts of speech they have learned. Discuss their list and then match the list to the words in the Bellringer sentence. Explain the function of each word in the sentence.

TEACH

☑ Teaching Tip
When doing a complete part-of-speech analysis of a sentence, begin by finding the most important words in the sentence—the simple subject (pronoun or noun) and the verb. Then identify the modifiers that go with these key words.

Speaking and Listening
Have students write down sentences they hear in conversations or on television and label the parts of speech.

Teacher's Classroom Resources

The following resources can be used for planning, instruction, practice, reinforcement, reteaching, or enrichment.

🔧 **Teaching Tools**
Lesson Plans

📂 **Blackline Masters**
Grammar Practice, p. 31
Grammar Reteaching, p. 31
Grammar Enrichment, p. 31

📕 ***Grammar Workbook***
Lessons 7, 13, 16, 25, 31, 35, 39, 42, 43

Exercise 12 — Identifying Parts of Speech

Write each underlined word and its part of speech.

1. Moira often <u>travels</u> to <u>foreign</u> countries.
2. <u>In</u> June <u>she</u> will go to Chile.
3. She <u>is</u> <u>especially</u> fond of Greece.
4. <u>Spain</u> is also close to her <u>heart</u>.
5. Next year she <u>plans</u> to visit Japan <u>and</u> Taiwan.

Exercise 13 — Using Parts of Speech

Complete each sentence below by supplying a word whose part of speech is indicated in parentheses. Be sure your finished sentences make sense.

1. Tony (conjunction) Sadie have been to more (common noun) than any other people I know.
2. (Pronoun) visited (proper noun) last year.
3. (Preposition) January they will (action verb) to Israel and Egypt.
4. Tony thought Portugal (linking verb) (adjective).
5. Tony went to (correlative conjunction) Peru (correlative conjunction) Chile.
6. He was (negative adverb) in Asia; Sadie, (conjunctive adverb), went to China.
7. She found (proper noun) amazing, and she (action verb) to go there again.
8. Africa reflects a patchwork of cultures; (conjunctive adverb), its climate varies from desert (preposition) tropical rain forest.
9. (Interjection)! How can that many climates exist within a (adjective) continent?
10. Kyle (adverb) visited Scandinavia, stopping in Norway (conjunction) Sweden.
11. It (linking verb) August, when days are long and the (common noun) is warm.
12. (Pronoun) flew to Lithuania, where he (action verb) this newly open nation.
13. (Correlative conjunction) Kyle (correlative conjunction) Sadie had studied Vilnius in detail.
14. (Interjection), their timetables allowed only two days to see this (adjective) city.
15. Tony, (time adverb), was in Brazil visiting the glorious (conjunction) vanishing rain forest.
16. He (linking verb) amazed by São Paulo, South America's largest (common noun).
17. This (adjective) city's factories produce (indefinite pronoun) from fabrics to electrical equipment.
18. (Preposition) Mexico City, these globe-trotters will (adverb) go home.
19. Good grief! I bet they'll be (adverb) to touch (proper adjective) soil again.
20. (Pronoun) is amazing how often they travel; (conjunctive adverb), they learn.

13.7 Finding All the Parts of Speech **461**

Enabling Strategies

LEP Identifying Main Parts of Speech

Students whose first language is not English can use these tips to help identify the main parts of speech. Common nouns follow articles (*a, an, the*) and can be made plural (*book—the book; books*). Verbs can follow *will* or can be put into the past tense form (*sing—will sing; sang*).

Predicate adjectives can be used in the comparative and superlative forms (*beautiful—more beautiful; most beautiful*). Adverbs that modify the verb can be moved (*John became worried soon; Soon John became worried*).

PRACTICE AND ASSESS

Answers: Exercise 12
1. travels, action verb; foreign, adj.
2. In, preposition; she, pronoun
3. is, linking verb; especially, adv.
4. Spain, proper noun; heart, common noun
5. plans, action verb; and, conjunction

Answers: Exercise 13
Answers will vary, but some suggestions are given below.
1. and, countries
2. They, Australia
3. In, travel
4. was, beautiful
5. both, and
6. never, however
7. China, plans
8. also, to
9. Gosh, single
10. recently, and
11. is, temperature
12. He, studied
13. Neither, nor
14. Wow, ancient
15. meanwhile, and
16. is, city
17. industrial, everything
18. After, probably
19. glad, U.S.
20. It, consequently

Independent Practice

Skills Practice
📂 *Grammar Practice*, p. 31
📂 *Grammar Reteaching*, p. 31
📂 *Grammar Enrichment*, p. 31

📕 **Grammar Workbook,**
Lessons 7, 13, 16, 25, 31, 35, 39, 42, 43

CLOSE

Challenge students to write their own sentences using every part of speech. Students can exchange sentences and identify the parts of speech.

TEACH

About the Literature

Michael Dorris, author of *Morning Girl*, is the son of a Modoc father. He has written another novel, *Yellow Raft in Blue Water*. His wife, Louise Erdrich, who is part Chippewa, has also written novels, including *Love Medicine* and *Tracks*. Dorris and Erdrich collaborated on *The Crown of Columbus*. *Morning Girl* is Dorris's first published book for children.

After students have read the passage, discuss the narrator's opinion about the strange visitors. Does she see them as dangerous? How are the Europeans in the "canoe" different from the narrator's own people?

Linking Grammar and Literature

☑ Teaching Tip

The prepositions *with* and *to* are sometimes paired incorrectly with *between* when the conjunction *and* should be used. Incorrect: *A comparison between Brazil to the other countries of South America shows the influence of Portuguese culture on Brazil.* Correct: *A comparison between Brazil and the other countries of South America shows the influence of Portuguese culture on Brazil.*

Speaking and Listening

Have students read the Literature Model aloud, substituting another word for each highlighted word. Encourage them to listen to the word's usage in the sentence for sense.

Grammar Review

Prepositions, Conjunctions, and Interjections

On a Caribbean island a young girl discovers Christopher Columbus's boat. The passage is annotated to show some of the parts of speech covered in this unit.

Literature Model

from MORNING GIRL

by Michael Dorris

Preposition → I forgot I was still beneath the surface until I

Prepositional phrase (adverb phrase) → needed air. But when I broke into the sunlight, the water sparkling all around me, the noise turned out to be nothing! Only a canoe! The breathing was the dip of many paddles! It was only *people* coming to visit, and since I could see they hadn't painted themselves to appear fierce, they must be friendly or lost.

Coordinating conjunction → I swam closer to get a better look and had to stop

Prepositional phrase (adjective phrase) → myself from laughing. The strangers had wrapped every part of their bodies with colorful leaves and cotton. Some had decorated their faces with fur and wore shiny rocks on their heads. Compared to us, they were very round. Their canoe was short and square, and,

Compound preposition → in spite of all their dipping and pulling, it moved so slowly. What a backward, distant island they must have come from. But really, to laugh at guests, no matter how odd, would be impolite, especially since I was the first to meet them. If I was foolish, they would think they

Noun as object of preposition → had arrived at a foolish place.

462   *Prepositions, Conjunctions, and Interjections*

Teacher's Classroom Resources

The following resources can be used for planning, instruction, practice, reinforcement, assessment, reteaching, enrichment, or evaluation.

🔧 **Teaching Tools**
Lesson Plans, p. 91

📖 **Grammar Workbook**
Lessons 39–43
Unit 6 Review
Cumulative Review: Units 1–6

Unit Assessment

📂 *Tests with Answer Key*
Unit 13 Mastery Test, pp. 51–52

💿 *Test Generator*
Unit 13 Mastery Test

Exercise 1

Identifying Prepositional Phrases and Objects of Prepositions Write each prepositional phrase. Draw a line under the preposition, and circle the object.

1. She swam beneath the blue waters.
2. Morning Girl saw an unusual canoe on its way toward her.
3. Its many paddles cut crisply through the clear water.
4. Until this day, Morning Girl had not known people could be so round.
5. The strangers did not look dangerous and wore no paint on their faces.
6. Morning Girl was curious about the new arrivals.
7. The strangers wore fur over their skin.
8. Torn between laughter and courtesy, Morning Girl chose courtesy and greeted the oddly dressed strangers warmly.
9. She wished her mother were beside her.
10. She would help Morning Girl behave correctly and would remind her of island customs.
11. Morning Girl could have called Star Boy from his work.
12. Since the storm, Star Boy had spent many days on his shell collection.
13. Morning Girl could not know how the boat and its occupants would change the lives of the island people.
14. Morning Girl wondered why the strangers were covered by those colorful leaves and cotton.
15. Perhaps they would tell her the meaning of these odd items.
16. The sun shone behind the canoe as the current gently cradled it.
17. Watching the travelers approach, Morning Girl saw her island through strangers' eyes.
18. How different the sparkling water and lush trees looked for the first time.
19. Morning Girl waved, as she had seen older people on her island do.
20. One stranger met Morning Girl's wave with a loud shout.
21. She explained who she was and gave her name and the names of her family members.
22. Morning Girl struggled for the correct words and invited the strangers ashore.
23. Although Morning Girl couldn't understand the strangers, she was sure they would all be friends before midday.
24. A meal shared among people usually created friendships.
25. As she turned up the path, Morning Girl observed the strangers in an argument.

Grammar Review **463**

PRACTICE AND ASSESS

Answers: Exercise 1
1. <u>beneath</u> the blue (waters)
2. <u>on</u> its (way) ; <u>toward</u> (her)
3. <u>through</u> the clear (water)
4. <u>Until</u> this (day)
5. <u>on</u> their (faces)
6. <u>about</u> the new (arrivals)
7. <u>over</u> their (skin)
8. <u>between</u> (laughter) and (courtesy)
9. <u>beside</u> (her)
10. <u>of</u> island (customs)
11. <u>from</u> his (work)
12. <u>Since</u> the (storm) ; <u>on</u> his shell collection
13. <u>of</u> the island (people)
14. <u>by</u> those colorful (leaves) and (cotton)
15. <u>of</u> these odd (items)
16. <u>behind</u> the (canoe)
17. <u>through</u> strangers' (eyes)
18. <u>for</u> the first (time)
19. <u>on</u> her (island)
20. <u>with</u> a loud (shout)
21. <u>of</u> her family (members)
22. <u>for</u> the correct (words)
23. <u>before</u> (midday)
24. <u>among</u> (people)
25. <u>up</u> the (path) ; <u>in</u> an (argument)

UNIT 13
Review

Answers: Exercise 2

1. her
2. whom
3. him
4. him
5. her
6. him
7. them
8. him
9. them
10. them

Answers: Exercise 3

1. them
2. them
3. her
4. them
5. them
6. them
7. him
8. him
9. him
10. them

Exercise 2

Using Pronouns as Objects of Prepositions Write the correct form of the pronoun in parentheses. Be sure each pronoun you choose makes sense in the sentence.

1. Morning Girl's visitors brought gifts to Star Boy and (her, she).
2. Morning Girl's story is based on the Native American people about (who, whom) Christopher Columbus wrote.
3. Columbus set sail from Spain in 1492 on a mission long cherished by (him, he).
4. Although Columbus believed in his journey, Queen Isabella was initially skeptical of the voyage planned by (him, he).
5. Columbus convinced the queen that his travels would bring riches and glory to (her, she).
6. Columbus thought that sailing west would bring India and its riches to (he, him).
7. As for the other explorers, most of (they, them) believed that India was to the east.
8. Columbus's men were discouraged, but they believed in (him, he).
9. At last the Caribbean Islands lay before (they, them).
10. The explorers met Native Americans who offered greetings to (they, them).

Exercise 3

Writing Sentences with Pronouns as Objects of Prepositions Write a pronoun form that would correctly complete the sentence.

1. He thought that these people occupied India, so "Indians" was the name Columbus gave to _____.
2. The Taino is the name we now give to _____.
3. The story could be based on Morning Girl and how change washed around _____ one day.
4. The Taino lived on the bounty of the land and sea around _____.
5. They caught giant turtles from the waters below _____.
6. Some Taino groups made hammocks from twisted cotton and slept in _____.
7. Each village had a chief, and its people looked to _____ for advice.
8. Because the chief was special, a special house was built for _____.
9. Therefore, when meeting Columbus, they gave ready welcome to _____.
10. Columbus started a colony among _____ before he left.

464 *Prepositions, Conjunctions, and Interjections*

Exercise 4

Identifying Adjective and Adverb Phrases   Write each prepositional phrase, and write *adjective phrase* or *adverb phrase* to tell how it is being used.

SAMPLE   She splashed through the surf.
ANSWER   through the surf (adverb phrase)

1. Morning Girl dove into the water.
2. In the distance she heard an unfamiliar sound.
3. The strangers were wrapped in leaves and cotton.
4. Some wore shiny rocks on their heads.
5. Morning Girl swam boldly toward the exotic visitors.
6. She hid her laughter and momentarily plunged beneath the waves.
7. Inside her mind, Morning Girl silently addressed the sister she'd named She Listens.
8. She Wins the Race, Morning Girl's mother, had said a new sister would soon add her smiles to the family.
9. Morning Girl had awaited her baby sister with great curiosity.
10. When her mother asked, Morning Girl had a name for the baby sister.
11. Her mother said, "A person isn't real without a name."
12. Morning Girl wondered what was happening when her mother made an unexpected visit to Grandmother's house.
13. She'd known that Father was worried by Mother's absence.
14. Morning Girl was disappointed when only her mother returned from Grandmother's house.
15. Throughout all the months, she had imagined her sister as a companion.
16. There would always be a perfect understanding between them.
17. This sister wouldn't complain about carrying heavy fruit.
18. If Morning Girl misbehaved, her sister would forgive her without hesitation.
19. Surely this friendly sister would always listen to Morning Girl.
20. Morning Girl felt almost as if this sister were really standing beside her.
21. She paused suddenly under the morning sky.
22. She Listens would be the name of her new sister.
23. As Morning Girl approached the strangers, she shared her thoughts with She Listens.
24. She chose her words with great care so she would make no mistakes.
25. Morning Girl kicked through the water.

Grammar Review **465**

Answers: Exercise 4

1. into the water—adverb phrase
2. In the distance—adverb phrase
3. in leaves and cotton—adverb phrase
4. on their heads—adverb phrase
5. toward the exotic visitors—adverb phrase
6. beneath the waves—adverb phrase
7. Inside her mind—adverb phrase
8. to the family—adverb phrase
9. with great curiosity—adverb phrase
10. for the baby sister—adjective phrase
11. without a name—adjective phrase
12. to Grandmother's house—adverb phrase
13. by Mother's absence—adverb phrase
14. from Grandmother's house—adverb phrase
15. Throughout all the months—adverb phrase
16. between them—adjective phrase
17. about carrying heavy fruit—adverb phrase
18. without hesitation—adverb phrase
19. to Morning Girl—adverb phrase
20. beside her—adverb phrase
21. under the morning sky—adverb phrase
22. of her new sister—adjective phrase
23. with She Listens—adverb phrase
24. with great care—adverb phrase
25. through the water—adverb phrase

UNIT 13
Review

Answers: Exercise 5

1. but—compound sentence
2. and—compound predicate
3. either...or—compound predicate
4. and—compound object of a preposition
5. and—compound subject

Answers: Exercise 6

1. were—<u>and</u>
2. are—<u>Both...and</u>
3. give—<u>and</u>
4. focus—<u>Neither...nor</u>
5. are—<u>Both...and</u>
6. remedy—<u>and</u>
7. influence—<u>Both...and</u>
8. greet—<u>both...and</u>
9. were—<u>and</u>
10. fail—<u>Neither...nor</u>

Exercise 5

Identifying Conjunctions   Write each conjunction, and write *compound subject, compound predicate, compound object of a preposition,* or *compound sentence* to tell what it forms.

SAMPLE   Their canoe was square, and it was shorter than any other canoes she had ever seen.

ANSWER   and (compound sentence)

1. She wanted to laugh, but she knew that would be impolite.
2. Morning Girl approached the strangers and called out a greeting.
3. The strangers either had come visit or were lost.
4. In spite of all their dipping and pulling, the canoe moved very slowly.
5. Morning Girl and her brother Star Boy often played together.

Exercise 6

Making Compound Subjects and Verbs Agree   Write each sentence, using the correct verb form from the parentheses. Then underline each coordinating or correlative conjunction.

SAMPLE   Neither Michael Dorris nor any other anthropologist (know, knows) all about the Taino people.

ANSWER   <u>Neither</u> Michael Dorris <u>nor</u> any other anthropologist knows all about the Taino people.

1. Christopher Columbus and the Taino people (was, were) real people.
2. Both Morning Girl and Star Boy (is, are) fictional characters.
3. Michael Dorris's Native American heritage and his anthropology training (give, gives) him strong ties to Morning Girl's story.
4. Neither history teachers nor history books (focus, focuses) often on the people who first met Christopher Columbus.
5. Both Native Americans and their experiences (is, are) overlooked.
6. *Morning Girl* and other works by Michael Dorris (remedy, remedies) this shortage of information.
7. Both Dorris's interests and background (influence, influences) his writing.
8. Sometimes both awards and high sales (greet, greets) Dorris's work.
9. He and Louise Erdrich (were, was) coauthors of *The Crown of Columbus*.
10. Neither the history nor the descriptions (fail, fails) to capture our interest.

Exercise 7

Using Conjunctive Adverbs   Substitute the conjunctive adverb in parentheses for each of the underlined conjunctions. Then write each compound sentence. Be sure to punctuate the resulting sentences correctly.

SAMPLE   Morning Girl swam near the ship, <u>but</u> the crew members didn't see her. (however)

ANSWER   Morning Girl swam near the ship, however, the crew didn't see her.

1. She had never seen people dressed as they were, <u>and</u> she didn't know what to make of them. (furthermore)
2. Star Boy collected shells, <u>but</u> he lost them all in a storm. (however)
3. Morning Girl was hot <u>and</u> she swam. (so)
4. The strangers were oddly dressed, <u>and</u> she thought they must have come from a backward island. (therefore)
5. Morning Girl knew it was impolite to laugh at strangers, <u>and</u> Morning Girl didn't want them to think she was foolish. (besides)

Exercise 8

Using Interjections   Write an interjection that could complete each sentence. More than one answer may be possible. Make sure your finished sentence makes sense.

SAMPLE   "_____!" cried Mother and Father when they discovered the necklaces I had carefully placed in their doorway.

ANSWER   Look

1. "_____!" thought Star Boy's mother as she realized the storm was worsening and her son still had not come home.
2. "_____! It's not like Star Boy to disappear like this. Where can he be?" asked She Wins the Race for the hundreth time that day.
3. "_____! I hear footsteps coming up the trail," said the villager who was watching for Star Boy with us.
4. "_____! We found him. We found him," shouted my father when he saw Star Boy stride into the village.
5. "_____!" said Morning Girl to herself, not realizing how worried she had been about her brother.

Grammar Review   **467**

Answers: Exercise 7
1. …were; furthermore, she…
2. …shells; however, he…
3. …hot; so, she swam.
4. … dressed; therefore, she…
5. …strangers; besides, Morning Girl …

Answers: Exercise 8
Answers will vary. Accept any interjections that make sense in context.
1. Oh, no
2. Good grief
3. Oh
4. Hooray
5. Phew

UNIT 13
Review

Answers: Exercise 9
Proofreading

This proofreading activity provides editing practice with (1) the current or previous units' skills, (2) the **Troubleshooter** errors, and (3) spelling errors. Students should be able to complete the exercise by referring to the units, the **Troubleshooter**, and a dictionary.

	Error (Type of Error)
1.	• was (verb tense)
2.	• behind her (object pronoun)
3.	• experience (spelling)
4.	• meanings; (sentences joined by conjunctive adverb)
	• moreover, (conjunctive adverb)
5.	• Spanish (proper noun)
6.	• refers (subject—verb agreement)
7.	• are (subject—verb agreement)
8.	• are (subject–verb agreement)
	• by her (object pronoun)

Exercise 9

The following passage is about the American artist Nereyda García-Ferraz, whose work appears below. Rewrite the passage, correcting the errors in spelling, grammar, and usage. Add any missing punctuation. There are ten errors.

Nereyda García-Ferraz

[1] Nereyda García-Ferraz is born in Havana, Cuba, in 1954. [2] She left Cuba behind she and immigrated to the United States when she was seventeen.

Nereyda García-Ferraz, *Without Hearing—Without Seeing,* 1991

468 *Prepositions, Conjunctions, and Interjections*

About the Art

Nereyda García-Ferraz, *Without Hearing—Without Seeing,* 1991

Nereyda García-Ferraz, born in Cuba in 1954, came to the United States when she was seventeen. García-Ferraz paints images that tell a story when viewed as a whole. This technique is apparent in this painting, which depicts fish swimming underneath an island. The fish—unhearing, unseeing—may be looking for home, unaware that it is all around them. This may refer to people who are disconnected from everything they once found familiar.

[3]García-Ferraz draws on her experence of living in Cuba for many of her works. [4]Her images have specific meanings moreover they often tell a story.

[5]García-Ferraz titled this painting *Without Hearing—Without Seeing*, which in spanish means *Sin Oir—Sin Ver*. [6]The word in the middle of the painting, *nadabas*, refer to swimming. [7]Words and bright colors is often part of García-Ferraz's work. [8]Both emotion and intellect is blended by she in her finished works of art.

Mixed Review

Exercise 10

Write a preposition, conjunction, or interjection that would make sense in each sentence. Use the clue in parentheses as a guide in choosing the appropriate word or words.

1. *Morning Girl*'s people called themselves the Taino; _____ , (conjunctive adverb) they are members of a larger group known as the Arawak people.
2. The Arawak lived on islands _____ (preposition) the Caribbean Sea.
3. These islands included three groups now called the Bahama Islands, the Greater Antilles, _____ (coordinating conjunction) the Lesser Antilles.
4. Since Christopher Columbus was searching for India when he discovered _____ (object pronoun), he named these islands the West Indies.
5. Although Columbus is often considered the first European to reach America, current research suggests that he may have been _____ (compound preposition) the first.
6. Historians believe that Columbus first landed _____ (adverb phrase) in the Bahama Group.
7. Both Watling Island and Samana Cay _____ (present-tense linking verb) among the possible first landing sites.
8. _____! (interjection) There are no longer any Arawaks living in the Caribbean Islands.
9. Many died from European diseases; _____, (conjunctive adverb) the poor living conditions under Spanish enslavement killed many more.
10. The Arawak were primarily a _____ (adjective) people and went to battle only when necessary.

Grammar Review **469**

Answers: Exercise 10
Mixed Review
Answers will vary. Accept any word that fits the part of speech and makes sense in context.
1. however
2. in
3. and
4. them
5. far from
6. on an island
7. are
8. Alas
9. moreover
10. peaceful

CLOSE

Ask students to write a paragraph describing a journey in or through another state or country. Remind them to use as many prepositions, conjunctions, and interjections as possible.

Conjunctions and Prepositions in Writing

Encourage students to read the passage in their books from *Living Up the Street* silently. Have them discuss how the relationships between events or ideas are conveyed through the use of conjunctions, and how information is added through the use of prepositions.

Techniques with Conjunctions and Prepositions

Have students talk about the difference between the two versions of each example; noting the use of conjunctions and prepositions. Which version is more inviting and captures the reader's interest? Have students review and discuss the Proofreading exercise on pages 468–469, looking for similar examples of these writing techniques.

Practice

The answers to this challenging and enriching activity will vary. Refer to Techniques with Conjunctions and Prepositions as you evaluate student choices. Sample answer:

Ethan suggested the latest horror film, <u>but</u> Doreen said she was sure to get nightmares. They then discussed every film <u>in</u> town until Doreen finally burst out, "Good grief! I don't care which film we see. Let's just go!" <u>Once inside</u> the theater, the two friends still couldn't agree on anything. "Look, Dorrie," insisted Ethan, "I'll sit <u>on the aisle or</u> in the back, <u>but</u> I can't see up close." The disputes began again the minute Doreen <u>and</u> Ethan emerged <u>from</u> the theater. "That was the most awful movie," pronounced Doreen. "I'll pick the next one, okay?"

Writing Application

Conjunctions and Prepositions in Writing   Sometimes the small words make a big difference. Notice how Gary Soto uses conjunctions and prepositions to link his ideas. As you read the passage below from *Living up the Street*, pay particular attention to the italicized words.

> I played *with* my grape knife, stabbing it into the ground, *but* stopped when Mother reminded me that I had better not lose it. I left the knife sticking up like a small, leafless plant. She then talked *about* school, the junior high I would be going to next fall, *and* then about Rick *and* Debra. . . . She stopped talking when she peeked *at* her watch, a bandless one she kept *in* her pocket.

Techniques with Conjunctions and Prepositions   Try to apply some of Gary Soto's writing techniques when you write and revise your own work.

1. Stress the relationship between ideas or events with appropriate use of conjunctions, such as *and, but*, and *or*. Study the following:

Events Linked   I played with my grape knife . . . I stopped when Mother reminded me.

Soto's Version   I played with my grape knife . . ., *but* stopped when Mother reminded me.

2. Use prepositions to add information to a sentence.

Bland Version   She talked.

Soto's Version   She talked about school . . . .

Practice   Apply some of Soto's techniques by revising the following passage, using a separate sheet of paper. Add conjunctions or prepositions in the places indicated by carets (∧). Answers will vary.

Ethan suggested the latest horror film, ∧ Doreen said she was sure to get nightmares. They then discussed every film ∧ town until Doreen finally burst out, "I don't care which film we see. Let's just go." ∧ the theater, the two friends still couldn't agree on anything. "Come on Dorrie," insisted Ethan, "I'll sit ∧ the back, ∧ I can't see up close." The disputes began again the minute Doreen ∧ Ethan emerged ∧ the theater. "That was the most awful movie," pronounced Doreen.

470   *Writing Application*

Teacher's Classroom Resources

The following resources can be used for assessment or evaluation.

Unit Assessment

📁 *Tests with Answer Key*
Unit 13 Mastery Test, pp. 51–52

📷 *Test Generator*
Unit 13 Mastery Test

You may wish to administer Unit 13 Mastery Test at this point.

UNIT 14

Clauses and Complex Sentences

Grammar | Lessons

UNIT GOALS

The goal of Unit 14 is to help students, through example and instruction, to develop an understanding of and an ability to use clauses and complex sentences. The lessons focus on main and subordinate clauses; essential and nonessential clauses; and adjective, adverb, and noun clauses.

Unit Assessment

Tests with Answer Key
Unit 14 Pretest, pp. 53–54
Unit 14 Mastery Test, pp. 55–56

Test Generator
Unit 14 Pretest
Unit 14 Mastery Test

You may wish to administer the Unit 14 Pretest at this point.

Key to Ability Levels

Enabling Strategies have been coded for varying learning styles and abilities.

L1 Level 1 activities are within the ability range of Learning Disabled students.

L2 Level 2 activities are basic-to-average activities and are within the ability range of average students.

L3 Level 3 activities are challenging activities and are within the ability range of above-average students.

LEP LEP activities are within the ability range of Limited English Proficiency students.

471

FOCUS

Lesson Overview

Objective: To identify simple and compound sentences and punctuate them correctly

🔔 Bellringer

When students enter the classroom, have this assignment on the board: *List the complete subjects and predicates in these sentences: 1. Ian kicked the soccer ball to the end of the field. 2. Kim baked cookies for the picnic, but her sisters left them at home.*

Motivating Activity

Review the Bellringer, explaining that the second sentence is a compound sentence because it contains two simple sentences. Ask students to name as many ways to connect two simple sentences into one as they can.

TEACH

☑ Teaching Tip

Help students understand that a clause contains a complete subject and a complete predicate. Every sentence must contain at least one free-standing (main) clause. A compound sentence contains two (or more) free-standing clauses joined by any of these: a comma plus a conjunction; a semicolon; or a semicolon plus a conjunctive adverb followed by a comma.

14.1 Sentences and Clauses

A **sentence** is a group of words that has a subject and a predicate and expresses a complete thought.

A **simple sentence** has one complete subject and one complete predicate.

The **complete subject** names whom or what the sentence is about. The **complete predicate** tells what the subject does or has. Sometimes it tells what the subject is or is like.

Complete Subject	Complete Predicate
The Cincinnati Reds	played their first baseball game in 1869.
This Ohio team	was the first professional baseball team.
The American League	played its first games in 1901.

A **compound sentence** contains two or more simple sentences. Each simple sentence is called a main clause.

A **main clause** has a subject and a predicate and can stand alone as a sentence.

Main clauses can be connected by a comma plus a conjunction, a semicolon, or a semicolon plus a conjunctive adverb. The conjunctive adverb is followed by a comma. In the compound sentences below, each main clause is in black; the connecting elements are highlighted in red.

> Abner Doubleday supposedly invented baseball, **but** some reject this claim. (comma plus coordinating conjunction)
> Alexander Joy Cartwright established rules; he was a good organizer. (semicolon)
> Cartwright improved the game; **moreover,** many now regard him as the inventor of modern baseball. (semicolon plus conjunctive adverb)

Teacher's Classroom Resources

The following resources can be used for planning, instruction, practice, reinforcement, assessment, reteaching, enrichment, or evaluation.

🔧 **Teaching Tools**
Lesson Plans

📁 **Blackline Masters**
Grammar Practice, p. 32
Grammar Reteaching, p. 32
Grammar Enrichment, p. 32

📖 *Grammar Workbook*
Lesson 44

Unit Assessment

📁 *Tests with Answer Key*
Unit 14 Pretest, pp. 53–54

💿 *Test Generator*
Unit 14 Pretest

You may wish to administer the Unit 14 Pretest at this point.

Exercise 1 — Identifying Simple and Compound Sentences

Identify each sentence as *simple* or *compound*.

1. Abner Doubleday or Alexander Cartwright invented baseball.
2. Cartwright wrote rules for the Knickerbocker Baseball Club.
3. The first modern baseball game took place in 1846.
4. One team brought the ball, and the other team provided the field.
5. Pitchers threw underhand, but their pitches were slow.
6. The first team with twenty-one runs would win the game.
7. Both teams played hard; however, only one team could win.
8. The game ended; two men were on third base.
9. The winners were the New York Nines.
10. The first teams were amateur; the players did not earn any money.
11. Baseball players were not paid until the end of the 1860s.
12. Today North American baseball teams are divided into two leagues.
13. One league is the National League, and the other is the American League.
14. The National League was organized in 1876; it had ten teams at that time.
15. The American League was founded in 1900; its first season began in 1901.
16. The Montreal Expos became the first Canadian team in the National League.
17. Some teams change cities, but they usually keep their names.
18. The Boston Braves moved to Milwaukee and became the Milwaukee Braves.
19. Later the Braves moved south to Atlanta.
20. The St. Louis Browns moved to Baltimore; they became the Orioles.

Exercise 2 — Punctuating Compound Sentences

Write each sentence, and underline each main clause. Add a comma or a semicolon as needed. If it is a simple sentence, write *simple*.

1. There are many theories about baseball's origin but the truth remains a mystery.
2. Ancient people played bat-and-ball games therefore these games could be ancestors of baseball.
3. Did baseball begin as rounders or did it come from cricket?
4. The British played rounders in the early nineteenth century.
5. Baseball resembles cricket however the rules of the game are very different.
6. Cartwright established the rules but Henry Chadwick improved them.
7. Baseball has many serious and devoted fans.
8. Some fans attend baseball games some listen to the games on the radio.
9. You can watch a game on television or you can read about it in the newspaper.
10. More than 50 million fans attend major league baseball games each year.

14.1 Sentences and Clauses **473**

Enabling Strategies

LEP Identifying Sentences

Have students practice distinguishing between a sentence and a fragment by turning a sentence into a question that can be answered with yes or no. Only sentences can be turned into questions without adding words. Demonstrate for students with the following sentence: *There were four of us. Were there four of us?*

473

FOCUS

Lesson Overview

Objective: To distinguish main and subordinate clauses in a complex sentence; to know that subordinate clauses function as adjectives, adverbs, or nouns

Bellringer

When students enter the classroom, have this assignment on the board: *Write this sentence:*

I enjoy taking long walks when spring has finally arrived.

Underline the main clause once. Locate the other clause—the one that cannot stand alone as a sentence— and underline it twice.

Motivating Activity

Explain that *when spring has finally arrived* in the Bellringer is a subordinate clause. Pair students to create sentences with subordinate clauses, with students taking turns creating main and subordinate clauses.

TEACH

☑ Teaching Tip

Subordinate clauses begin with tip-off words that signal that the clause is not a main clause: adjective clauses usually begin with relative pronouns, adverb clauses with subordinating conjunctions, and noun clauses with *that* or a *wh-* word (*when, what, where, who* and *whom*).

474

A **main clause** has a subject and a predicate and can stand alone as a sentence.

Sometimes sentences have a main clause and a subordinate clause.

A **subordinate clause** is a group of words that has a subject and a predicate but does not express a complete thought and cannot stand alone as a sentence. It is always combined with a main clause.

A **complex sentence** has a main clause and one or more subordinate clauses.

In each complex sentence below, the main clause is in light type, and the subordinate clause is in dark type.

> Many basketball fans visit Springfield, Massachusetts, **which was the birthplace of basketball.**
> Basketball has increased in popularity **since it began in Springfield.**
> Many people know **that basketball is played by men and women.**

The team waits on the sidelines, **while the substitute warms the bench.**

MAIN CLAUSE   SUBORDINATE CLAUSE

Subordinate clauses can function in three ways: as adjectives, as adverbs, or as nouns. In the examples above, the first sentence has an adjective clause that modifies the noun *Springfield,* the second has an adverb clause that modifies the verb *has increased,* and the third has a noun clause that is the direct object of the verb *know.* Such clauses can be used in the same ways that single-word adjectives, adverbs, and nouns are used.

474 *Clauses and Complex Sentences*

Teacher's Classroom Resources

The following resources can be used for planning, instruction, practice, reinforcement, reteaching, or enrichment.

✷ Teaching Tools
Lesson Plans, p. 92

☞ Blackline Masters
Grammar Practice, p. 32
Grammar Reteaching, p. 33
Grammar Enrichment, p. 32

📖 *Grammar Workbook*
Lesson 45

Exercise 3   **Identifying Complex Sentences**

Identify the main clause in each sentence. Then label each sentence *complex* or *simple*.

1. Professional basketball is played during the winter, which was once a dull season for sports.
2. James Naismith developed the game when he saw a need for an indoor sport.
3. He was an instructor for the YMCA in Massachusetts.
4. A soccer ball was the ball that was first used.
5. The first baskets were two half-bushel peach baskets that were hung from balconies.
6. Naismith planned a game with little physical contact because he did not envision basketball as a rough sport.
7. The rules of the game were drafted in 1891.
8. There were thirteen rules that penalized players for rough conduct.
9. Before the first official game was played in 1892, probably no one outside of Naismith's YMCA had heard of basketball.
10. Basketball still follows most of Naismith's original thirteen rules.
11. Although originally nine players were on each team, now each team has five players on the court at one time.
12. In the early 1900s the first women's teams were formed.
13. Do the rules of the game change when men and women play basketball together?
14. Although the rules for men's and women's basketball are similar, the ball is different.
15. The referee tosses the ball into the air.
16. After the referee tosses the ball, one player from each team jumps within the center circle.
17. Each player tries for the ball.
18. When a team scores, the opposing team takes the ball out of bounds from behind the base line.
19. The team then takes the ball to the basket that is at the other end of the court.
20. A team scores points when it gets the ball into its own basket.
21. The baskets at the top of ten-foot poles are usually called goals.
22. Behind each goal is a backboard, which can guide the ball down into the basket.
23. A special excitement belongs to basketball, which is a fast-moving game.
24. Basketball has won many fans who are dedicated basketball enthusiasts.
25. Many players who are popular have fan clubs.

14.2 Complex Sentences **475**

PRACTICE AND ASSESS

Answers: Exercise 3

1. Professional basketball… winter—c
2. James Naismith…game—c
3. He was…in Massachusetts—s
4. A soccer ball was the ball—c
5. The first baskets were… baskets—c
6. Naismith planned…contact—c
7. The rules…in 1891—s
8. There were thirteen rules—c
9. probably no one…basketball—c
10. Basketball…rules—s
11. now each team…time—c
12. In the early…formed—s
13. Do the rules…change—c
14. the ball is different—c
15. The referee tosses…air—s
16. one player…circle—c
17. Each…ball—s
18. the opposing team…line—c
19. The team…the basket —c
20. A team scores points—c
21. The baskets…goals—s
22. Behind…backboard—c
23. A special…basketball—c
24. Basketball…fans—c
25. Many…clubs—c

Independent Practice

Skills Practice
📁 *Grammar Practice,* p. 32
📁 *Grammar Reteaching,* p. 33
📁 *Grammar Enrichment,* p. 32

📖 ***Grammar Workbook,*** Lesson 45

Enabling Strategies

LEP Combining Sentences

Model how to combine two sentences into one complex sentence. Ask students to select pairs of short sentences from their own writing and combine them. Have them circle the tip-off word that introduces each subordinate clause.

CLOSE

Have students imagine that they are watching the first basketball game ever played. Tell them to describe this new game in a letter to a friend, using complex sentences.

FOCUS

Lesson Overview

Objective: To identify adjective clauses and the relative pronouns that usually introduce them

🔔 Bellringer

When students enter the classroom, have this assignment on the board: *Combine the following two sentences into one without losing any of the meaning:*

Agatha Christie wrote dozens of books.

The books are still popular today.

Motivating Activity

Discuss students' answers to the Bell-ringer activity. (Example: *Agatha Christie wrote dozens of books that are still popular today.*) Ask them what function *that are still popular today* has in the sentence. (It describes the books.) Point out that when the two sentences are combined, the first stays the same (stands alone), and the second changes so that it no longer can stand alone.

TEACH

☑ Teaching Tip

The tip-off word for adjective clauses is the relative pronoun that begins the clause. The relative pronoun must always refer to the noun in the main clause that the adjective clause modifies. The relative pronoun plays a noun role in its clause—it can be a subject, object, or possessive noun.

14.3 | Adjective Clauses

An **adjective clause** is a subordinate clause that modifies, or describes, a noun or pronoun in the main clause of a complex sentence.

> The Aqua-Lung, **which divers strap on**, holds oxygen.
>
> The divers breathe through a tube **that attaches to the tank.**

Each subordinate clause in dark type in these sentences is an adjective clause. An adjective clause adds information about a noun or pronoun in the main clause.

An adjective clause is usually introduced by a relative pronoun. Relative pronouns signal a subordinate clause, which cannot stand alone.

Relative Pronouns			
that	who	whose	what
which	whom	whoever	

An adjective clause can also begin with *where* or *when*.

> Divers search for reefs **where much sea life exists.**

A relative pronoun that begins an adjective clause can be the subject of the clause.

> Some divers prefer equipment **that is lightweight.**
> Willa is a new diver **who is taking lessons.**

In the first sentence above, *that* is the subject of the adjective clause. In the second sentence *who* is the subject.

476   *Clauses and Complex Sentences*

Exercise 4   Identifying Adjective Clauses

Write each adjective clause, and underline each relative pronoun. Write the noun or pronoun that each adjective clause modifies.

1. Scuba equipment, which is used for deep diving, gets its name from the phrase *self-contained underwater breathing apparatus.*
2. Jacques Cousteau, who is famous for underwater exploration, designed the Aqua-Lung.
3. Divers sometimes wear weights that they strap on.
4. Divers often wear wet suits, which are basic diving equipment.
5. Diving methods, which are now advanced, allow close observation of sea life.
6. Alexander the Great, who lived in the fourth century B.C., used a barrel for diving.
7. Leonardo da Vinci, who was a famous artist and inventor, designed a piece of diving equipment.
8. The equipment that da Vinci designed was a leather diving helmet.
9. The helmet, which had spikes on it for protection from monsters, had a long breathing tube.
10. At the end of the tube was a cork that kept the tube afloat.
11. Divers needed an apparatus that would protect them from high water pressure.
12. Diving bells were the earliest containers that were reliable.
13. The diving bells that were used in the 1500s were quite large.
14. Edmund Halley, who was an astronomer and mathematician, designed the first real diving bell in 1716.
15. Halley, whose most famous discovery was Halley's Comet, actually designed two very different diving bells.
16. One bell, which was made of wood, looked like an upside-down bucket.
17. Halley's other diving bell, which stood eight feet tall, could carry several divers.
18. It was the larger one that was made of lead.
19. Halley and four other divers could dive to a depth of ten fathoms, which is equal to sixty feet.
20. The five men, who were very brave, stayed at that depth for over an hour.
21. The only problem that they reported was a pain in their ears.
22. The pain that they felt was due to an increased pressure at that depth.
23. Auguste Piccard designed the bathyscaphe, which is a diving vehicle.
24. Jacques Piccard, who is Auguste's son, wanted to explore the Gulf Stream.
25. The Gulf Stream is a warm undersea current that flows through the Atlantic.

14.3 Adjective Clauses   **477**

PRACTICE AND ASSESS

Answers: Exercise 4
1. <u>which</u>…diving—equipment
2. <u>who</u> …exploration—Jacques Cousteau
3. <u>that</u>…on—weights
4. <u>which</u>…equipment—wet suits
5. <u>which</u>…advanced—methods
6. <u>who</u>…B.C.—Alexander the Great
7. <u>who</u>…inventor—Leonardo da Vinci
8. <u>that</u>…designed—equipment
9. <u>which</u> …monsters—helmet
10. <u>that</u>…afloat—cork
11. <u>that</u>…pressure—apparatus
12. <u>that</u>…reliable—containers
13. <u>that</u>…1500s—diving bells
14. <u>who</u>…mathematician—Edmund Halley
15. <u>whose</u>…comet—Halley
16. <u>which</u>…wood—bell
17. <u>which</u>…tall—diving bell
18. <u>that</u>…lead—one
19. <u>which</u>…feet—fathoms
20. <u>who</u>…brave—men
21. <u>that</u>…reported—problem
22. <u>that</u>…felt—pain
23. <u>which</u>…vehicle—bathyscaphe
24. <u>who</u>…son—Jacques Piccard
25. <u>that</u>…Atlantic—current

Independent Practice

Skills Practice
📁 *Grammar Practice,* p. 33
📁 *Grammar Reteaching,* p. 34
📁 *Grammar Enrichment,* p. 33

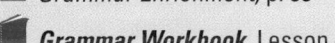 **Grammar Workbook,** Lesson 46

CLOSE

Tell students to imagine they're scuba diving in the ocean. Ask them to use adjective clauses in a paragraph describing their underwater adventure.

Enabling Strategies

LEP Using Sentence Combining

Use sentence combining to introduce subordinate adjective clauses. The first sentence must contain a noun identical to a noun in the second sentence: *Some divers prefer equipment. The equipment is lightweight.* Show students how to change the second sentence to an adjective clause by replacing the repeated noun (*equipment*) with the relative pronoun *that: Some divers prefer equipment that is lightweight.* Have students practice doing the same with other sentences.

477

FOCUS

Lesson Overview

Objective: To distinguish between essential and nonessential adjective clauses

Bellringer

When students enter the classroom, have this assignment on the board: *Write whether the underlined part of each sentence is necessary to understand its meaning.*

1. Nan and Dick, <u>who are twins</u>, are strong swimmers.
2. Their mother, <u>who never learned to swim herself</u>, had them take swimming lessons when they were young.
3. The program <u>that she took them to</u> starts teaching children at six months.

Motivating Activity

Discuss students' answers to the Bellringer exercise. Ask them what punctuation provides a clue to whether the underlined phrase is necessary.

TEACH

☑ Grammar Tip

Tell students that nonessential clauses, like appositives, give extra information about the nouns they follow. Dictate these sentences. Have students underline the appositive once and the nonessential clause twice, adding punctuation. *Esther Williams, a popular film star in the 1950s, was a graceful swimmer. Esther Williams, who was a popular film star in the 1950s, was a graceful swimmer.*

478

14.4   Essential and Nonessential Clauses

Read the sentence below. Is the adjective clause in dark type needed to make the meaning of the sentence clear?

The swimmer **who is in lane six** won last time.

Our team, **which is undefeated,** is favored to win the championship.

> The woman **who is near the pool** is a good swimmer.

The adjective clause here is essential, or necessary, to the meaning of the sentence. The clause identifies which woman is a good swimmer.

An **essential clause** is an adjective clause that is necessary to make the meaning of the sentence clear. Do not use commas to set off an essential clause from the rest of the sentence.

Notice, however, the adjective clauses in the sentences below.

> Swimmers enjoy the pool, **which is extremely clean.**
> The pool, **which is open all week,** is never crowded.

In the sentences above, the adjective clauses are set off by commas. The clauses are nonessential, or not necessary, to identify which pool the writer means. The clauses give only additional information about the noun that they modify.

A **nonessential clause** is an adjective clause that is not necessary to make the meaning of the sentence clear. Use commas to set off a nonessential clause from the rest of the sentence.

One way to tell whether some clauses are essential or nonessential is to look at the first word. For example, a clause that begins with *which* is usually nonessential. One that begins with *that* is essential.

> Did you see the meet **that** our team won yesterday? (essential)
> The meet, **which** began late, ended well after dark. (nonessential)

478   *Clauses and Complex Sentences*

Teacher's Classroom Resources

The following resources can be used for planning, instruction, practice, reinforcement, reteaching, or enrichment.

🔧 **Teaching Tools**
Lesson Plans, p. 93

📁 **Blackline Masters**
Grammar Practice, p. 33
Grammar Reteaching, p. 34
Grammar Enrichment, p. 33

📓 *Grammar Workbook*
Lesson 47

Exercise 5   Identifying Essential and Nonessential Clauses

Write each adjective clause. Identify the adjective clause as *essential* or *nonessential.*

1. The athletes whom I most admire are swimmers.
2. Swimming, which requires strength and stamina, is a challenging sport.
3. A swimmer who wishes to participate in serious swimming competitions must practice constantly.
4. Some swimmers are nervous before competitions, which are usually referred to as swim meets.
5. Our women's team, whose record stands, enters the pool area.
6. The team members, who hope for a win today, listen to the coach's advice.
7. Each race that the team members swim is called a heat.
8. The contestants, who are wearing special racing suits, will swim eight lengths of the pool in the first heat.
9. The racers stand on the starting blocks that are at the far end of the pool.
10. The signal that starts each race is a gunshot.

Exercise 6   Punctuating Essential and Nonessential Clauses

Write each sentence, and underline each adjective clause. Identify each as *essential* or *nonessential,* and add commas as needed.

1. In the 1800s the Australian crawl which replaced the breast stroke in popularity came into use.
2. In the 1920s Johnny Weissmuller whose other career was acting in movies perfected the front crawl.
3. The skillful athlete who portrayed Tarzan in twelve movies was known to many people as a swimmer rather than an actor.
4. Weissmuller whose swimming ability was quickly recognized began swimming at a young age.
5. He worked hard for the three gold medals that he won at the 1924 Olympics.
6. The two additional gold medals that Weissmuller won at the 1928 Olympic Games probably made all his long hours of practice seem worthwhile.
7. Weissmuller was the athlete who set sixty-five United States and world records.
8. In 1927 he swam to a new record which was 100 yards in 51 seconds.
9. In 1968 Jim Counsilman studied techniques that swimmers were using.
10. Counsilman whose observations were later published became a world-famous coach.

14.4 Essential and Nonessential Clauses   **479**

Enabling Strategies

LEP Distinguishing Between Clauses

Write this sentence on the board: *Did you see the meet that our swim team won yesterday?* Point out that the sentence is not about *any* meet but only about the meet *that our swim team won yesterday.* Explain that an essential clause changes the meaning of the noun it modifies by limiting it; a nonessential clause renames or adds information about the noun. Have students work in pairs to look at sentences 1, 2, 5, and 7 in Exercise 5 and decide whether the clause changes the meaning of the noun. Then ask pairs to write their own sentences.

PRACTICE AND ASSESS

Answers: Exercise 5
E—essential; N—nonessential
1. whom I most admire—E
2. which requires strength and stamina—N
3. who wishes to participate in serious swimming competitions—E
4. which are usually referred to as swim meets—N
5. whose records stands—N
6. who hope for a win today—N
7. that the team members swim—E
8. who are wearing special racing suits—N
9. that are at the far end of the pool—E
10. that starts each race—E

Answers: Exercise 6
1. , which replaced the breast stroke in popularity,—N
2. , whose other career was acting in movies,—N
3. , who portrayed Tarzan in twelve movies,—N. Also correct without commas—E
4. , whose swimming ability was quickly recognized,—N
5. that he won at the 1924 Olympics.—E
6. that Weissmuller won at the 1928 Olympic Games—E
7. who set sixty-five United States and world records.—E
8. , which was 100 yards in 51 seconds.—N
9. that swimmers were using.—E
10. , whose observations were later published,—N

CLOSE

Have students write a paragraph about a sport they like. Tell them to use both essential and nonessential clauses in their paragraphs and to punctuate them correctly.

FOCUS

Lesson Overview

Objective: To identify adverb clauses and the subordinating conjunctions that introduce them

Bellringer

When students enter the classroom, have this assignment on the board: *Make four columns across the top of a sheet of paper and label them* Time, Place, Cause, *and* Condition. *List each word or phrase below in the correct column:* if, because, where, when, until, unless, after, since, provided that, wherever.

Motivating Activity

Have students suggest sample adverb clauses that begin with each word they listed. Class members can add a main clause to each to make a complete sentence.

TEACH

☑ Teaching Tip

Tip-off words that help identify adverb clauses are called subordinating conjunctions. When an adverb clause modifies the verb (as most adverb clauses do), the subordinating conjunction can never be deleted. Subordinating conjunctions are bridge words that link the subordinate clause to the main clause.

14.5	Adverb Clauses

An **adverb clause** is a subordinate clause that often modifies, or describes, the verb in the main clause of a complex sentence.

An adverb clause tells *how, when, where, why,* or *under what conditions* the action occurs.

After she bought safe equipment, Lee explored the undersea world.

Scuba divers wear tanks **because they cannot breathe underwater.**

In the first sentence above, the adverb clause *After she bought safe equipment* modifies the verb *explored.* The adverb clause tells *when* Lee explored the undersea world. In the second sentence, the adverb clause *because they cannot breathe underwater* modifies the verb *wear.* The adverb clause tells *why* scuba divers wear tanks.

An adverb clause is introduced by a subordinating conjunction. Subordinating conjunctions signal a subordinate clause, which cannot stand alone.

Subordinating Conjunctions			
after	before	though	whenever
although	if	unless	where
as	since	until	whereas
because	than	when	wherever

You usually do not use a comma before an adverb clause that comes at the end of a sentence. However, you do use a comma after an adverb clause that introduces a sentence.

480   *Clauses and Complex Sentences*

Teacher's Classroom Resources

The following resources can be used for planning, instruction, practice, reinforcement, reteaching, or enrichment.

📂 **Teaching Tools**
Lesson Plans

📂 **Blackline Masters**
Grammar Practice, p. 34
Grammar Reteaching, p. 35
Grammar Enrichment, p. 34

📖 *Grammar Workbook*
Lesson 48

Exercise 7   Identifying Adverb Clauses

Write each sentence. Underline each adverb clause and circle each subordinating conjunction. Draw an arrow to the verb that each adverb clause modifies.

1. Divers wear wet suits and rubber fins when they swim.
2. They wear wet suits because the water might be cold.
3. Divers wear masks since they need them for underwater vision.
4. After you dive for the first time, you will have more confidence.
5. Divers wear weighted belts when they want to stay underwater for a long time.
6. When divers return to the surface, they should rise slowly and carefully.
7. Divers can suffer the bends if they rise to the surface too quickly.
8. Because this condition can occur, divers must learn how to control the ascent.
9. Although divers sometimes are in a hurry, they must rise slowly.
10. Divers should work with partners whenever they dive in unfamiliar waters.
11. Unless she has a buddy with her, a diver should not make a dive.
12. Because the deep sea is so mysterious, it fascinates people.
13. Interest in the deep seas began before Alexander the Great first went diving.
14. He sat inside a glass barrel as sailors lowered it into the sea.
15. Undersea quests progressed after Alexander the Great made his barrel dives.
16. Auguste Piccard flew in a balloon before he invented the bathyscaphe.
17. After Piccard designed this craft, he and his son Jacques descended in it.
18. Jacques used the bathyscaphe when he explored the Gulf of Mexico.
19. Until Jacques Costeau invented the Aqua-Lung, deep-sea diving was difficult.
20. Study of the oceans became much easier after scuba gear was invented.

Exercise 8   Punctuating Adverb Clauses

Write each sentence. Underline each adverb clause, and add a comma as needed.

1. Although diving may not seem easy it is not difficult for most people.
2. Hopeful divers can enroll in diving school when they are ready to learn.
3. Before students learn scuba diving they should learn snorkeling.
4. Trainers teach about the bends since this condition can be life-threatening.
5. The bends can occur when a diver surfaces too quickly.
6. If divers surface slowly they can avoid this problem.
7. After divers complete long training and many practice dives they are certified.
8. Can certified divers dive wherever they like?
9. New divers should dive only 130 feet since deeper dives can be dangerous.
10. If you dive in Belize you will have the ultimate diving experience.

14.5 Adverb Clauses   **481**

PRACTICE AND ASSESS

Answers: Exercise 7
1. (when)...swim—wear
2. (because)...cold—wear
3. (since)...vision—wear
4. (After)...time—will have
5. (when)...time—wear
6. (When)...surface—should rise
7. (if)...quickly—can suffer
8. (Because)...occur—must learn
9. (Although)...hurry—must rise
10. (whenever)...waters—should work
11. (Unless)...her—should make
12. (Because)...mysterious—fascinates
13. (before)...diving—began
14. (as)...sea—sat
15. (after)...dives—progressed
16. (before)...bathyscaphe—flew
17. (After)...craft—descended
18. (when)...Mexico—used
19. (Until)...Aqua-Lung—was
20. (after)...invented—became

Answers: Exercise 8
1. Although diving may not seem easy,
2. when they are ready to learn
3. Before students learn scuba diving,
4. since this condition can be life-threatening
5. when a diver surfaces too quickly
6. If divers surface slowly,
7. After divers complete long training and many practice dives,
8. wherever they like
9. since deeper dives can be dangerous
10. If you dive in Belize,

CLOSE

Ask students to imagine they are Alexander the Great and write a journal entry about their first dive in the barrel. Ask them to use some adverb clauses.

FOCUS

Lesson Overview

Objective: To identify noun clauses and to recognize their uses in sentences as subject, direct object, object of a preposition, and predicate noun

Bellringer

When students enter the classroom, have this assignment on the board: *Write the subject of this sentence.*

How high players jump is important in basketball.

Motivating Activity

Elicit from students that the subject of the sentence in the Bellringer activity is *How high players jump.* Remind students that the subject of a sentence can consist of more than just a noun. Ask volunteers to share a few of their own similar examples.

TEACH

☑ Teaching Tips

Explain that there are two kinds of noun clauses. The tip-off word for one kind is *that* (*That we have a test today was a shock*). The other kind begins with a *wh-* word (*who, whom, when, which,* and so on).

Point out the difference between a clause and a phrase. A clause has a subject and a verb that are in agreement; a phrase is a group of words lacking a predicate.

482

14.6 | Noun Clauses

A **noun clause** is a subordinate clause used as a noun.

Notice how the noun in dark type in the sentence below can be replaced by a clause.

> **Players** must skate extremely well.
> **Whoever plays ice hockey** must skate extremely well.

The clause in dark type, like the noun it replaces, is the subject of the sentence. Since this kind of clause acts as a noun, it is called a noun clause.

You can use a noun clause in the same ways that you can use any noun—as a subject, a direct object, an object of a preposition, or a predicate noun. With most sentences containing noun clauses, you could replace the noun clause with the word *it*, and the sentence would still make sense.

How Noun Clauses Are Used	
Subject	**What makes ice hockey exciting** is the speed.
Direct Object	Players know **that the game can be dangerous.**
Object of a Preposition	Victory goes to **whoever makes more goals.**
Predicate Noun	This rink is **where the teams will play.**

Following are some words that can introduce noun clauses.

Words That Introduce Noun Clauses		
how, however	where, whether	whom, whomever
that	which, whichever	whose
what, whatever	who, whoever	why, when

Teacher's Classroom Resources

The following resources can be used for planning, instruction, practice, reinforcement, reteaching, or enrichment.

🔧 **Teaching Tools**
Lesson Plans

📁 **Blackline Masters**
Grammar Practice, p. 35
Grammar Reteaching, p. 36
Grammar Enrichment, p. 35

📙 **Grammar Workbook**
Lesson 49

Exercise 9 Identifying Noun Clauses

Write each noun clause.

1. That ice hockey began in Canada is not surprising.
2. Where the sport began is not easily verified.
3. Three different cities claim that they hosted the first hockey game.
4. Most people believe that the game was played in Jamaica as early as 1830.
5. The fact is that the first recorded game occurred in Montreal around 1875.
6. You could argue that Canadians are still among the best hockey players.
7. There have been some changes in how ice hockey is played.
8. Whoever plays hockey today must wear protective equipment.
9. Do you know which sport is most dangerous?
10. Some people question whether hockey has to be so dangerous.

Exercise 10 Identifying Noun Clauses and Their Use

Write each noun clause, and label it *subject, direct object, object of a preposition,* or *predicate noun.*

1. Most people realize that ice hockey is a game of action.
2. Did you know that hockey is the fastest of all team sports?
3. Fast starts, stops, and turns are what the game demands.
4. What the players pursue is the puck.
5. Where they want to put the puck is inside the other team's goal.
6. That the puck often moves over one hundred miles an hour may surprise you.
7. The puck's speed is why hockey players must react so quickly.
8. The goalies know that their role is critical.
9. The goalie is who must block the other team's slap shots.
10. What is important to the team is a goalie's dependability.
11. Chris will demonstrate how a goalie drops to the ice and blocks shots.
12. Whoever stands and blocks shots is called a stand-up goalie.
13. The Vezina Trophy is awarded to whoever is the best goalie of the year.
14. Whoever asks can learn for whom the trophy was named.
15. The answer is that the trophy is awarded in honor of George Vezina.
16. Each year the Stanley Cup Playoffs determine which team is best.
17. That no team won the Stanley Cup in 1919 baffled me.
18. The truth is that a flu epidemic prematurely ended the finals.
19. How players respond can be crucial to the game.
20. Players must respond quickly to whatever happens.

14.6 Noun Clauses **483**

PRACTICE AND ASSESS

Answers: Exercise 9
1. That ice hockey began...Canada
2. Where the sport began
3. that they...hockey game.
4. that the game...1830.
5. that the first...1875.
6. that Canadians...hockey players.
7. how ice hockey is played.
8. Whoever plays hockey today
9. which sport is most dangerous?
10. whether hockey...dangerous.

Answers: Exercise 10
1. that ice hockey...action—DO
2. that hockey is...sports—DO
3. what the game demands—PN
4. What the players pursue—subj.
5. Where...the puck—subj.
6. that the puck...hour—subj.
7. why...quickly—PN
8. that their role is critical—DO
9. who...shots—PN
10. What...team—subj.
11. how a goalie...shots—DO
12. Whoever...shots—subj.
13. whoever...of the year—OP
14. Whoever asks—subj.; for whom...named—DO
15. that...Vezina—PN
16. which team is best—DO
17. That no team...1919—subj.
18. that...finals—PN
19. How players respond—subj.
20. whatever happens—OP

CLOSE

Tell students to imagine that they are watching a hockey game and write a paragraph describing what they might see and hear. Ask them to include some noun clauses.

Enabling Strategies

LEP Understanding *Wh-* Noun Clauses

Students tend to substitute the more common *wh-* question form for noun clauses beginning with *wh-* words. Compare (a) *I know what that means* (*wh-* type noun clause) with the incorrect (b) *I know what does that mean* or *I know what means that* (*wh-* question). The difference is in the verb. In *wh-* noun clauses, the verb does not move to a position preceding the subject; in *wh-* questions, the verb does move.

TEACH

About the Literature

In this passage, Mickey Mantle describes some of his problems as an outfielder, showing that even a Baseball Hall of Fame inductee did not always have an easy time on the diamond. Mickey Mantle's 536 home runs made him the greatest switch hitter in the history of baseball. He was named the American League's most valuable player in 1956, 1957, and 1962, and hit a record eighteen home runs during World Series games. The New York Yankees won eight World Series championships during the years Mantle played with them.

The exercises that follow are based on that passage and related topics.

As students read the passage, have them focus on the highlighted clauses and complex sentences. Ask them to discuss how these clauses add to the writing.

Linking Grammar and Literature

☑ Teaching Tip

Initiate a discussion to show how Mantle's description of his learning experiences in baseball relate to skills students have developed while learning to use English correctly and effectively. Then use the highlighted words in the passage to review the unit's grammar concepts.

Critical Thinking

Ask students to identify and categorize compound sentences, complex sentences, essential and nonessential adjective clauses, and adverb clauses found in the passage.

Grammar Review

Clauses and Complex Sentences

In this passage Mickey Mantle tells of his weaknesses in playing the field. The annotations show some of the types of clauses and sentences covered in this unit.

Literature Model

from THE EDUCATION OF A BASEBALL PLAYER

by Mickey Mantle

Main clause —

My fielding, I knew, was often sorry. I had learned to charge a ground ball well and if I could get an angle on a ball, I could field it cleanly and get off a fast throw. My arm was unusually strong, and my throws would really hum across the diamond.

Complex sentence —

But when a ball came straight at me, I was often undone. Somehow it was almost impossible for me to judge the speed or the bounce of a ground ball like that. I might back off foolishly, letting the ball play me, and then lose it altogether.

Adverb clause —

Or I would turn my head as it reached me, and the ball would skip by or bounce right into my face. I carried around uncounted fat lips in that day from stopping ground balls with my mouth. And the more often I got hit, the more I would shy at such a ball. Even the balls I

Adjective clause —

fielded cleanly did not always mean an out, for I had a habit of rejoicing so in the strength of my arm that I would not take the time to get a sure eye on the target.

Compound sentence —

I would just let fly with my full strength, and often the ball would sail untouched into the stands.

484 *Clauses and Complex Sentences*

Teacher's Classroom Resources

The following resources can be used for planning, instruction, practice, reinforcement, assessment, reteaching, enrichment, or evaluation.

🎬 **Teaching Tools**
Lesson Plan

📕 *Grammar Workbook,*
Lessons 44–49
Unit 7 Review
Cumulative Review: Units 1–7

Unit Assessment

📂 *Tests with Answer Key*
Unit 14 Mastery Test, pp. 55–56

💿 *Test Generator*
Unit 14 Mastery Test

Exercise 1

Identifying Simple and Compound Sentences   Write whether each sentence is *simple* or *compound*. If it is compound, write it and add commas where needed.

SAMPLE   Mickey Mantle's father loved baseball and he shared this love with his son.

ANSWER   Mickey Mantle's father loved baseball, and he shared this love with his son. (compound)

1. As a young boy Mantle frequently played ball from morning to night.
2. His father gave him a professional-model baseball glove for Christmas one year and he cared for it devotedly.
3. Mantle considered himself the worst player on his team.
4. His fielding was erratic and other boys hit better than he did.
5. Mantle was known for not only his powerful hitting but his fast running.
6. Mickey Mantle was a superb base runner but he stole few bases.
7. Base running and base stealing are two different skills.
8. A player may be a good base stealer but he may not be a good base runner.
9. Players like Ty Cobb were good at both.
10. Lou Brock was a great base stealer and he was an excellent base runner.

Exercise 2

Punctuating Simple and Compound Sentences   Write each sentence, and underline each main clause. Add a comma or a semicolon as needed.

SAMPLE   He stole fewer bases than Mantle each season but he was considered an excellent base runner.

ANSWER   <u>He stole fewer bases than Mantle each season</u>, but <u>he was considered an excellent base runner.</u>

1. Joe DiMaggio's father was a fisherman in San Francisco.
2. Joe did not like the smell of fish he chose baseball as a career.
3. His father wasn't thrilled but he wished his son luck.
4. Another DiMaggio son also played baseball.
5. Vince DiMaggio earned his living as a baseball player and he introduced Joe to the game.

Grammar Review   **485**

PRACTICE AND ASSESS

Answers: Exercise 1
1. simple
2. compound—His father gave him a professional-model baseball glove for Christmas one year, and he cared for it devotedly.
3. simple
4. compound—His fielding was erratic, and other boys hit better than he did.
5. simple
6. compound—Mickey Mantle was a superb base runner, but he stole few bases.
7. simple
8. compound—A player may be a good base stealer, but he may not be a good base runner.
9. simple
10. compound—Lou Brock was a great base stealer, and he was an excellent base runner.

Answers: Exercise 2
1. <u>Joe DiMaggio's father was a fisherman in San Francisco.</u>
2. <u>Joe did not like the smell of fish</u>; <u>he chose baseball as a career.</u>
3. <u>His father wasn't thrilled</u>, but <u>he wished his son luck.</u>
4. <u>Another DiMaggio son also played baseball.</u>
5. <u>Vince DiMaggio earned his living as a baseball player</u>, and <u>he introduced Joe to the game.</u>

UNIT 14
Review

Answers: Exercise 3
1. simple
2. complex; when he became a Giants player in 1951.
3. complex; which requires a powerful arm.
4. simple
5. complex; about who was the better player.
6. complex; that Mantle, with his speed and power, was the better of the two.
7. simple
8. complex; Since Mays was a terrific all-around player
9. simple
10. complex; Although he was often in pain

Answers: Exercise 4
1. compound
2. complex; that played for New York
3. complex; When the Dodgers and the Giants moved to California
4. complex; which is a National League team
5. complex; that some of baseball's best teams have come from New York.
6. complex; that from 1936 to 1964 the Yankees won sixteen World Series?
7. compound
8. compound
9. complex; who came to the Yankees in 1959
10. compound

Exercise 3

Distinguishing Between Simple and Complex Sentences   Label each sentence as *simple* or *complex*. If it is complex, write the subordinate clause.

SAMPLE   When Willie Mays joined the New York Giants, Mickey Mantle was playing center field for the American League Yankees.

ANSWER   (complex) When Willie Mays joined the New York Giants,

1. In the 1950s the Giants were the National League team from New York.
2. Willie Mays was twenty when he became a Giants player in 1951.
3. Mays played center field, which requires a powerful arm.
4. The arrival of Mays caused a controversy among baseball fans.
5. Fans argued all the time about who was the better player.
6. Some said that Mantle, with his speed and power, was the better of the two.
7. Mays, however, may have been the greatest player of all time.
8. Since Mays was a terrific all-around player, many agree with that opinion.
9. Injuries hindered Mickey Mantle's performance throughout his career.
10. Although he was often in pain, Mantle played well.

Exercise 4

Distinguishing Between Compound and Complex Sentences   Label each sentence as *compound* or *complex*. If it is complex, write the subordinate clause.

1. New York State has a long baseball history, and it has had many teams.
2. The teams that played for New York include the Yankees, Dodgers, and Giants.
3. When the Dodgers and the Giants moved to California, New York had no National League team.
4. The Mets, which is a National League team, was formed in 1962.
5. Fans agree that some of baseball's best teams have come from New York.
6. Did you know that from 1936 to 1964 the Yankees won sixteen World Series?
7. The Yankees had great teams then, but perhaps the best was the 1961 team.
8. That team had incredibly talented players; Mickey Mantle was one of them.
9. Roger Maris, who came to the Yankees in 1959, also starred on that team.
10. Maris and Mantle both hit more than fifty home runs that season, and they soon became known as the M & M boys.

486   *Clauses and Complex Sentences*

Exercise 5

Identifying Adjective Clauses   Write each sentence. Underline each adjective clause once and each relative pronoun twice. Circle the noun that each adjective clause modifies.

SAMPLE   In 1955 New York State had another team that is considered one of baseball's best.

ANSWER   In 1955 New York State had another (team) that is considered one of baseball's best.

1. You must mean the 1955 Brooklyn Dodgers, who later moved to Los Angeles.
2. Branch Rickey, whose courage and foresight brought amazing talent to the Dodgers' organization, was the manager of the team then.
3. It was one particularly courageous act that brought fame to Branch Rickey.
4. Branch Rickey signed Jackie Robinson, who was African American.
5. The major league color line, which had restricted African American players to the Negro League, was broken by Jackie Robinson in 1947.
6. Robinson soon proved his worth in the face of the jeers that surrounded him.
7. Insults that came from fans and opposing players surely must have hurt.
8. Jackie responded with the quiet dignity that marked his life and career.
9. Pee Wee Reese, who was a teammate, openly supported Jackie on the field.
10. In 1955 Robinson and the Dodgers won the World Series against the Yankees, whose roster included the young slugger Mickey Mantle.

Exercise 6

Identifying Essential and Nonessential Clauses   Write each adjective clause. Label the clause *essential* or *nonessential*, and add commas as needed.

1. Mickey was named after the catcher Mickey Cochrane who made it into the Hall of Fame.
2. Mantle's father who worked in the lead mines had played semi-pro ball.
3. The baseball glove that his father gave him one year cost twenty-two dollars.
4. Mantle who was named the Most Valuable Player three times also played in sixteen All-Star games.
5. Mantle hit 536 home runs during the years that he played with the Yankees.

Grammar Review   **487**

Answers: Exercise 5

1. (Brooklyn Dodgers); who later moved to Los Angeles
2. (Branch Rickey); whose courage and foresight brought amazing talent to the Dodgers' organization
3. (act); that brought fame to Branch Rickey
4. (Jackie Robinson); who was African American
5. (color line); which had restricted African American players to the Negro League
6. (jeers); that surrounded him
7. (insults); that came from fans and opposing players
8. (dignity); that marked his life and career
9. (Pee Wee Reese); who was a teammate
10. (Yankees); whose roster included the young slugger Mickey Mantle

Answers: Exercise 6

1. ..., who made it into the Hall of Fame.—nonessential
2. ..., who worked in the lead mines, had played...—nonessential
3. ...that his father gave him one year...—essential
4. ..., who was named the Most Valuable Player three times, also...—nonessential
5. ...that he played with the Yankees.—essential

Answers: Exercise 7

1. <u>When Mantle was just an infant,</u> his father Mutt (put) baseballs in his crib.
2. Mutt (talked) baseball to his infant son <u>whenever he got the chance.</u>
3. Mantle (considered) himself lucky <u>because his father pushed and encouraged him.</u>
4. Mantle (was) only nineteen years old <u>when the Yankees signed him.</u>
5. Mantle (hit) poorly <u>because he was confused by major league pitchers.</u>
6. <u>Since he was struggling,</u> the Yankees (sent) him down to the minor leagues.
7. <u>Although Mantle was now a professional,</u> he still (needed) his father's advice.
8. Mantle quickly (improved) <u>after his father gave him good advice.</u>
9. <u>While he played for the Yankees,</u> they (were) the dominant team in baseball.
10. Mantle (was elected) to the Hall of Fame <u>as soon as he became eligible.</u>

Answers: Exercise 8

1. What made the young Mickey Mantle so extraordinary; subject
2. how quickly he sped around the bases; object of preposition
3. that Mantle's speed was practically unbeatable; direct object
4. What made Mantle consult a doctor at age fifteen; subject
5. that Mickey had a serious bone infection; direct object
6. that Mickey would never play baseball again; predicate noun
7. what he had heard; direct object
8. how wrong the doctor was; direct object
9. Whoever knows about Mantle's illustrious career; subject
10. what kept Mantle's career hopes alive; predicate noun

Exercise 7

Identifying Adverb Clauses   Write each sentence. Underline the adverb clause, and circle the word that the clause modifies. Add commas where needed.

SAMPLE   When Mantle joined the Yankees Casey Stengel was the manager.
ANSWER   <u>When Mantle joined the Yankees</u>, Casey Stengel (was) the manager.

1. When Mantle was just an infant his father Mutt put baseballs in his crib.
2. Mutt talked baseball to his infant son whenever he got the chance.
3. Mantle considered himself lucky because his father pushed and encouraged him.
4. Mantle was only nineteen years old when the Yankees signed him.
5. Mantle hit poorly because he was confused by major league pitchers.
6. Since he was struggling the Yankees sent him down to the minor leagues.
7. Although Mantle was now a professional he still needed his father's advice.
8. Mantle quickly improved after his father gave him good advice.
9. While he played for the Yankees they were the dominant team in baseball.
10. Mantle was elected to the Hall of Fame as soon as he became eligible.

Exercise 8

Identifying Noun Clauses   Write each noun clause, and label it *subject*, *direct object*, *object of a preposition*, or *predicate noun*.

SAMPLE   Mantle's father knew that baseball could provide a future for his son.
ANSWER   that baseball could provide a future for his son; direct object

1. What made the young Mickey Mantle so extraordinary was his speed.
2. His coaches were amazed at how quickly he sped around the bases.
3. Opposing players knew that Mantle's speed was practically unbeatable.
4. What made Mantle consult a doctor at age fifteen was an injured ankle.
5. Mickey's doctor discovered that Mickey had a serious bone infection.
6. The doctor's conclusion was that Mickey would never play baseball again.
7. Mickey could hardly believe what he had heard.
8. Time and history proved how wrong the doctor was.
9. Whoever knows about Mantle's illustrious career knows the truth.
10. Courage and determination were what kept Mantle's career hopes alive.

488   *Clauses and Complex Sentences*

Exercise 9

Writing Complex Sentences Combine each pair of sentences below, using the relative pronoun or subordinating conjunction in parentheses. Put the subordinate clause where it makes sense, and add commas where they are needed.

1. I saw some films about baseball. I was home sick last week. (while)
2. One film was *Eight Men Out*. It was about the 1919 "Black Sox" scandal. (which)
3. Allegedly, eight players took money to lose the World Series. They were members of the Chicago White Sox. (who)
4. The eighth man never admitted guilt in the scheme. The scheme remained a black mark on the history of baseball. (which)
5. The movie was good. I didn't like it as much as others. (although)
6. *Field of Dreams* was my favorite. It starred Kevin Costner. (which)
7. Costner is an Iowa farmer. His character's name is Ray Kinsella. (whose)
8. Ray hears a voice. It says "If you build it, he will come." (that)
9. Ray ponders the mysterious message. He makes a discovery. (as)
10. The "he" in the message refers to Shoeless Joe Jackson. Jackson was one of the eight men in the Chicago "Black Sox" scandal. (who)
11. All the acquitted Chicago players come out of Ray's cornfield. Ray builds the baseball diamond. (when)
12. These men play baseball. These men have been dead for years. (who)
13. Another good film is *A League of Their Own*. You should see it. (that)
14. This story is about a special time in baseball during World War II. Women played professional baseball then. (when)
15. Many of the male players had been drafted into the armed forces. A women's professional baseball league was formed. (because)
16. The All-American Girls Professional Baseball League enlisted top female athletes. It was in existence from 1943 to 1954. (which)
17. Women had played baseball in school and at the amateur level. They had never played professional ball. (although)
18. The film's producer, Penny Marshall, interviewed some of the actual women players at a ceremony in Cooperstown. She made the movie. (after)
19. The women must have enjoyed seeing the movie. Their story is also told in a book by Sue Macy titled *A Whole New Ball Game*. (whose)
20. These women put up with taunts and jeers from men. The women loved baseball and were excellent players. (who)

Grammar Review **489**

19. The women, whose story is …
titled *A Whole New Ball Game*,
must have enjoyed seeing the
movie.
20. These women, who loved … players, put up with taunts … from
men.

Answers: Exercise 9
Answers will vary, but some suggestions are provided below.
1. I saw some films about baseball while I was home sick last week.
2. One film was *Eight Men Out*, which was about the … scandal.
3. Allegedly, eight players, who were members of the Chicago White Sox, took money to lose … Series.
4. The eighth man never admitted guilt in the scheme, which has remained a black mark … baseball.
5. The movie was good, although I didn't like it as much as others.
6. *Field of Dreams*, which … Kevin Costner, was my favorite.
7. Costner, whose character's name is Ray Kinsella, is an Iowa farmer.
8. Ray hears a voice that says, "If you build it, he will come."
9. Ray ponders the mysterious message as he makes a discovery.
10. The "he" in the message refers to Shoeless Joe Jackson, who was one of the eight men in … scandal.
11. When Ray builds the baseball diamond, all the acquitted … cornfield.
12. These men, who have been dead for years, play baseball.
13. Another good film that you should see is *A League of Their Own*.
14. This story is about a special time in baseball during World War II when women … baseball.
15. Because many of the male players had been drafted into the armed forces, a women's professional … formed.
16. The All-American Girls Professional Baseball League, which was in existence from 1943 to 1954, enlisted top female athletes.
17. Although women had played baseball in school and at the amateur level, they had never … ball.
18. After the film's producer, Penny Marshall, interviewed some of the actual women players at a ceremony in Cooperstown, she … movie.

489

UNIT 14
Review

Answers: Exercise 10
Proofreading

This proofreading activity provides editing practice with (1) the current or previous units' skills, (2) the **Troubleshooter** errors, and (3) spelling errors. Students should be able to complete the exercise by referring to the units, the **Troubleshooter,** and a dictionary. (Note: A run-on sentence counts as one error.)

	Error (Type of Error)
1.	• American (proper adjective)
2.	• training, (introductory adverb clause)
3.	• opposite (spelling)
	• page, (nonessential adjective clause)
4.	• father, (nonessential adjective clause)
	• time, (run-on sentence)
	• similar (spelling)
5.	• Mantle, (nonessential adjective clause)
	• hero, (nonessential adjective clause)
6.	• baseball, (introductory adverb clause)

Exercise 10 | Proofreading

The following passage is about the American artist Morris Kantor, whose work appears below. Rewrite the passage, correcting the errors in spelling, capitalization, grammar, and usage. Add any missing punctuation. There are ten errors.

Morris Kantor

[1]Morris Kantor was an american painter who lived during the early part of this century. [2]Although Kantor received formal art training his style seems primitive. ➡

Morris Kantor, *Baseball at Night,* **1934**

490 *Clauses and Complex Sentences*

About the Art

Morris Kantor, *Baseball at Night,* **1934**
Although Morris Kantor (1896–1974), who painted *Baseball at Night,* received formal art training, his 1930s style is more reminiscent of that of the American Primitives. Note the generalized, almost faceless figures and an oddly skewed perspective that shrinks the baseball field in relation to the players. The painting, an oil on canvas (37 by 47 1/4 inches), is in the National Museum of American Art in Washington, D.C. Suggest that students imagine themselves spectators and ask them to write a description of the game.

³*Baseball at Night*, which appears on the oposite page shows a group of people enjoying a game of semiprofessional baseball. ⁴Mutt Mantle, who was Mickey Mantle's father was playing baseball at about the same time and he probably played under similiar conditions.

⁵Mickey Mantle who became an American hero came from the world of small towns and sandlot baseball that Kantor depicts in *Baseball at Night*. ⁶Although Spavinaw, Oklahoma, may not have had night baseball it did produce at least one outstanding major league player.

Mixed Review

Exercise 11

Sentences and Clauses   Write whether each sentence is *simple, compound,* or *complex*. If a sentence is complex, write the subordinate clause. Then indicate whether the clause is an *adverb clause,* an *adjective clause*, or a *noun clause.*

¹While three-year-old Mickey Mantle was learning about baseball in Oklahoma, another future baseball star was born. ²He was Roberto Clemente from Carolina, Puerto Rico. ³Roberto, who had six older brothers and sisters, was shy as a young boy. ⁴In spite of this, Roberto eagerly helped others whenever he could. ⁵Roberto also had strong leadership qualities, which helped him enlist the aid of others. ⁶Young Roberto learned about baseball from his older brothers. ⁷They shared with him what they knew about the game. ⁸Roberto had very large hands; he could easily catch a ball. ⁹As his love for baseball grew, his talent also grew. ¹⁰The manager of a softball team for which sixteen-year-old Roberto played recognized this talent. ¹¹The manager believed that Roberto could be a professional. ¹²When major league scouts saw Roberto, they agreed. ¹³The boy had a powerful and accurate throwing arm; he also hit well. ¹⁴Clemente, whose major league career began with the Brooklyn Dodgers, ended up with the Pittsburgh Pirates. ¹⁵He played there until he died on Christmas Eve in 1972. ¹⁶At the time he was thirty-eight. ¹⁷The plane in which he was traveling crashed. ¹⁸He and others were on their way to Nicaragua, where there had been a terrible earthquake. ¹⁹The plane was carrying relief supplies. ²⁰Roberto Clemente had reached out to others all his life; this was true even at the time of his death.

Grammar Review   **491**

Answers: Exercise 11
Mixed Review
1. complex—While three-year-old Mickey Mantle was learning about baseball in Oklahoma—adverb clause
2. simple
3. complex—who had six older brothers and sisters—adjective clause
4. complex—whenever he could—adverb clause
5. complex—which helped him enlist the aid of others—adjective clause
6. simple
7. complex—what they knew about the game—noun clause
8. compound
9. complex—As his love for baseball grew—adverb clause
10. complex—for which sixteen-year-old Roberto played—adjective clause
11. complex—that Roberto could be a professional—noun clause
12. complex—When major league scouts saw Roberto—adverb clause
13. compound
14. complex—whose major league career began with the Brooklyn Dodgers—adjective clause
15. complex—until he died on Christmas Eve in 1972—adverb clause
16. simple
17. complex—in which he was traveling—adjective clause
18. complex—where there had been a terrible earthquake—adjective clause
19. simple
20. compound

CLOSE

Have students make up a game in which each kind of subordinate clause is used: *adjective, adverb,* and *noun.* Remind students that they must also include a brief description of the rules. Games can be created individually or with a group. Allow time in class for students to share their games.

Writing Application

Clauses in Writing

Encourage students to read the passage from *Silent Spring* by Rachel Carson silently. Then have them discuss the following: the use of adverb clauses to add detail to actions; the combining of related sentences into compound sentences in order to show the connection between events and ideas.

Techniques with Clauses

Have students talk about the two examples for using clauses in writing. Which version in each example expands or connects the ideas most effectively? Then have students review and discuss the Proofreading exercise on pages 490–491, looking for similar examples of these writing techniques.

Practice

The answers to this challenging and enriching activity will vary. Refer to Techniques with Clauses as you evaluate student choices. Sample answer:

Ben had never used a bank account before, but today he had made his first deposit. Since the creation of the Bank It! program, the students at Ben's school were learning all about deposits and withdrawals. Ben was eager to learn banking as he hoped to save enough money to buy a new bike. He'd been keeping his savings at home, where they were stashed in a shoe box under the bed. The box was getting full, and Ben knew that his money would be safer in the school bank.

Clauses in Writing   In *Silent Spring* Rachel Carson uses clauses to expand on her description of the natural world. Examine the passage, focusing on the italicized clauses.

> The countryside was, in fact, famous for the abundance and variety of its bird life, and *when the flood of migrants was pouring through in spring and fall* people traveled from great distances to observe them. Others came to fish the streams, *which flowed clear and cold out of the hills and contained shady pools where trout lay.* So it had been from the days many years ago *when the first settlers raised their houses, sank their wells, and built their barns.*

Techniques with Clauses   Try to apply some of Rachel Carson's writing techniques when you write.

1. Use adjective clauses to elaborate on details. Notice how Carson makes her writing interesting with the addition of an adjective clause.

Without extra detail Others came to fish the streams.

Carson's version Others came to fish the streams, *which flowed clear and cold out of the hills . . .*

2. Emphasize the relationship between events and ideas in your writing by combining related sentences into compound sentences. Compare the following:

Weaker connection The countryside was, in fact, famous for the abundance . . . and variety of its bird life. People traveled to observe them.

Carson's version The countryside was, in fact, famous for the abundance . . . of its bird life, *and when the flood of migrants was pouring through in spring and fall* people traveled . . .

Practice   Apply some of these techniques as you revise the following passage, using a separate sheet of paper. Reorganize or reword the sentences, combining clauses as appropriate to show the relationships among your ideas.

Ben had never used a bank account before. Today he made his first deposit. The Bank It! program was new at Ben's school. The students were learning all about deposits and withdrawals. Ben was eager to learn banking. He hoped to save enough money to buy a new bike. He'd been keeping his savings at home. They were stashed in a shoe box under the bed. The box was getting full. Ben knew that his money would be safer in the school bank.

Teacher's Classroom Resources

The following resources can be used for assessment or evaluation.

Unit Assessment

📁 *Tests with Answer Key*
Unit 14 Mastery Test, pp. 55–56

📷 *Test Generator*
Unit 14 Mastery Test

You may wish to administer the Unit 14 Mastery Test at this point.

UNIT

15 Verbals

Grammar | Lessons

493

UNIT GOALS

The goal of Unit 15 is to help students, through example and instruction, to develop an ability to identify and use verbals. Lessons focus on the three types of phrases—participles and participial phrases, gerunds and gerund phrases, and infinitives and infinitive phrases.

Unit Assessment
Tests with Answer Key
Unit 15 Pretest, pp. 57–58
Unit 15 Mastery Test, pp. 59–60

Test Generator
Unit 15 Pretest
Unit 15 Mastery Test

You may wish to administer the Unit 15 Pretest at this point.

Key to Ability Levels
Enabling Strategies have been coded for varying learning styles and abilities.

L1 Level 1 activities are within the ability range of Learning Disabled students.

L2 Level 2 activities are basic-to-average activities and are within the ability range of average students.

L3 Level 3 activities are challenging activities and are within the ability range of above-average students.

LEP LEP activities are within the ability range of Limited English Proficiency students.

Setting the Purpose

Lesson 15.1 teaches the use of present participles, past participles, and participial phrases, and tells how participial phrases should be punctuated.

FOCUS

Lesson Overview

Objective: To use present and past participles and participial phrases appropriately

Bellringer

When students enter the classroom, have this assignment on the board: *List all the suffixes you can think of that might be attached to a verb. Give two examples of each.*

Motivating Activity

Discuss the suffixes that might be attached to verbs. How many parts of speech are represented in the examples students give? Lead this discussion toward an explanation of present participles and past participles.

TEACH

☑ Grammar Tip

In grammar the term *verbal* is the collective term for a verb form used as another part of speech.

Two-Minute Skill Drill

Write these words on the board and have students identify them as present participles or past participles.

barked	tweeting
crowing	roared
snorting	meowed

494

15.1 Participles and Participial Phrases

A present participle is formed by adding *-ing* to the verb. A past participle is usually formed by adding *-ed* to the verb. A participle can act as the main verb in a verb phrase or as an adjective to describe, or modify, nouns or pronouns.

> The player has **kicked** the ball. [main verb in a verb phrase]
> The **kicked** ball soared. [adjective modifying *ball*]

Sometimes a participle that is used as an adjective is part of a phrase. This kind of phrase is called a participial phrase.

> **Cheering for the home team,** the fans were on their feet.
> The ball **kicked by Donnell** soared into the goal.

A **participial phrase** is a group of words that includes a participle and other words that complete its meaning.

A participial phrase that is placed at the beginning of a sentence is always set off with a comma.

> **Running for the ball,** a player slipped in the mud.

Other participial phrases may or may not need commas. If the phrase is necessary to identify the modified word, do not set it off with commas. If the phrase simply gives additional information about the modified word, set it off with commas.

> The player **kicking the ball** is Donnell.
> Donnell, **kicking the ball,** scored the final point.

A participial phrase can appear before or after the word it describes. Place the phrase as close as possible to the modified word; otherwise, the meaning of the sentence may be unclear.

The **kicked** ball soared . . .

. . . into the goal.

494 *Verbals*

Teacher's Classroom Resources

The following resources can be used for planning, instruction, practice, reinforcement, assessment reteaching, enrichment, or evaluation.

🖳 **Teaching Tools**
Lesson Plans

📁 **Blackline Masters**
Grammar Practice, p. 36
Grammar Reteaching, p. 37
Grammar Enrichment, p. 36

📖 ***Grammar Workbook***
Lesson 50

Unit Assessment

📁 *Tests with Answer Key*
Unit 15 Pretest, pp. 57–58

💾 *Test Generator*
Unit 15 Pretest

You may wish to administer the Unit 15 Pretest at this point.

Exercise 1   Identifying Participles

Write each participle. Write whether it is used as a *verb* or as an *adjective*.

1. Soccer can be a challenging game.
2. Many young people are participating in the sport.
3. The size of the playing field for soccer may vary.
4. Have rules for the sport changed over the years?
5. A player on our team has scored the winning goal.

Exercise 2   Using Participial Phrases

Write each sentence. Underline each participial phrase. Then draw two lines under the word that the phrase describes. Add commas if needed to set off the phrase.

1. Attracting huge crowds soccer is a popular sport.
2. The game consists of two teams competing for goals.
3. Playing within certain areas the goalkeepers can touch the ball with their hands.
4. For other players the only contact permitted by the rules is with their feet, heads, or bodies.
5. The two teams playing the game kick off.
6. The teams moving almost constantly during play kick the ball back and forth.
7. Varying their formations players move about the field.
8. By the 1800s English schools playing a similar game had drawn up the first set of rules.
9. Spreading throughout the world soccer became especially popular in Europe and Latin America in the late 1800s.
10. Spectators standing on the sidelines cheered the teams.
11. Representing two rival towns the teams took their places on the field.
12. Last year's champions defending their title played energetically.
13. Blowing a whistle the referee started the game.
14. The team dressed in blue tried to advance the ball toward the goal.
15. Kicking the ball out of bounds the blue team lost its advantage.
16. The team's star player dribbling the ball toward the goal suddenly tripped.
17. An opponent rushing toward the ball prevented a goal.
18. Passing the ball from player to player the team traveled down the field.
19. The goalkeeper jumping as high as possible was unable to catch the ball.
20. Kicking the ball high into the air a player on the blue team finally scored a goal.

15.1 Participles and Participial Phrases **495**

PRACTICE AND ASSESS

Answers: Exercise 1
1. challenging, adjective
2. participating, verb
3. playing, adjective
4. changed, verb
5. scored, verb; winning, adjective

Answers: Exercise 2
1. <u>Attracting huge crowds</u>, <u>soccer</u> …
2. … <u>teams</u>, <u>competing for goals</u>
3. <u>Playing within certain areas</u>, the <u>goalkeepers</u> …
4. … <u>contact</u> <u>permitted by the rules</u> …
5. … <u>teams</u> <u>playing the game</u> …
6. … <u>teams</u>, <u>moving almost constantly during play</u>, …
7. <u>Varying their formations</u>, <u>players</u> …
8. … <u>schools</u> <u>playing a similar game</u> …
9. <u>Spreading throughout the world</u>, <u>soccer</u> …
10. <u>Spectators</u> <u>standing on the sidelines</u> …
11. <u>Representing two rival towns</u>, the <u>teams</u> …
12. … <u>champions</u>, <u>defending their title</u>, …
13. <u>Blowing a whistle</u>, the <u>referee</u> …
14. The <u>team</u> <u>dressed in blue</u> …
15. <u>Kicking the ball out of bounds</u>, the blue <u>team</u> …
16. <u>player</u>, <u>dribbling the ball toward the goal</u>, …
17. An <u>opponent</u>, <u>rushing toward the ball</u>, …
18. <u>Passing the ball from player to player</u>, the <u>team</u> …
19. The <u>goalkeeper</u>, <u>jumping as high as possible</u>, …
20. <u>Kicking the ball high into the air</u>, a <u>player</u> …

Independent Practice

Skills Practice
📁 *Grammar Practice*, p. 36
📁 *Grammar Reteaching*, p. 37
📁 *Grammar Enrichment*, p. 36

📓 ***Grammar Workbook,*** Lesson 50

Enabling Strategies

LEP Checking Participles
To help students learning English decide whether a participle is an adjective or a verb, have students try *a*, *an*, or *the* in front of the word when reading the sentence. If the sentence still makes sense, the participle is an adjective.

CLOSE

Ask students to write a paragraph describing a successful experience they've had—winning a game, learning a new skill, overcoming a fear, making a new friend, for example. Ask them to use some participial phrases in their writing.

Setting the Purpose

Lesson 15.2 teaches students to use gerunds and gerund phrases appropriately in their writing.

FOCUS

Lesson Overview

Objective: To identify gerunds and gerund phrases and to distinguish between gerunds and participles

🔔 Bellringer

When students enter the classroom, have this assignment on the board: *On a sheet of paper, write down the subjects of these sentences:*

1. *Dancing is the love of Elisabeth's life.*
2. *Playing chess is Jonathan's favorite pastime. (Dancing; Playing chess)*

Motivating Activity

Discuss students' answers to the Bellringer assignment. Make sure students understand that the complete subject of the second sentence is *Playing* **chess.** Ask students what part of speech *dancing* and *playing* are. (verbs) Explain that *dancing* and *playing* are verbs but that they are used as nouns in these sentences.

TEACH

☑ Grammar Tip

Gerunds and gerund phrases can always be replaced by the pronoun *it;* participles and participial phrases never can. This replacement works because gerunds and gerund phrases are singular. Write *Rob enjoys swimming. Rob is swimming in a meet today.* Ask a volunteer to figure out which *swimming* is the gerund by replacing each with *it.* The sentence that makes sense with the *it* contains the gerund.

496

15.2 Gerunds and Gerund Phrases

The previous lesson explains that the present participle may be used as a verb or as an adjective. It may also be used as a noun, in which case it is called a *gerund.*

> The **playing** field is one hundred yards long. [adjective]
> **Playing** is our favorite activity. [gerund]

A **gerund** is a verb form that ends in *-ing* and is used as a noun.

Like other nouns a gerund can serve as the simple subject of a sentence. It can also be a direct object or the object of a preposition.

> **Blocking** requires strength. [subject]
> The athletes enjoy **exercising.** [direct object]
> They maintain endurance by **running.** [object of a preposition]

A **gerund phrase** is a group of words that includes a gerund and other words that complete its meaning.

> **Kicking the ball** takes skill.
> A team tries **scoring a touchdown.**
> A touchdown results from **moving the ball across the goal.**

You can identify the three functions of *-ing* verb forms if you remember that a present participle can serve as a verb, as an adjective, or as a noun, in which case it is called a gerund.

> The Giants are **winning** the game. [main verb]
> The **winning** team scores the most points. [adjective]
> **Winning** is always exciting. [gerund]

496 *Verbals*

Teacher's Classroom Resources

The following resources can be used for planning, instruction, practice, reinforcement, reteaching, or enrichment.

🔧 **Teaching Tools**
Lesson Plans

📁 **Blackline Masters**
Grammar Practice, p. 37
Grammar Reteaching, p.38
Grammar Enrichment, p. 37

📕 *Grammar Workbook*
Lesson 51

Exercise 3   Identifying Verbals

Copy each underlined word, and write *main verb*, *adjective*, or *gerund* to show how it is used in the sentence.

1. The coach or the captain chooses <u>playing</u> strategies.
2. The quarterback does not like <u>guessing</u> the next play.
3. The team members are <u>hoping</u> for a victory.
4. <u>Scoring</u> in football can occur in four different ways.
5. A team earns six points by <u>crossing</u> the opponent's goal line.

Exercise 4   Identifying Gerunds

Write each gerund or gerund phrase. Then write *subject, direct object,* or *object of a preposition* to show how it is used in the sentence.

1. A win means earning more points than the opponent.
2. Kicking earns points in two different ways in this sport.
3. A team earns three points by kicking a field goal.
4. Teams also try converting for one point after a touchdown.
5. Defending the team's own goal is crucial.
6. A team's defense features tackling.
7. Blocking is another important element of a good defense.
8. Passing makes football exciting.
9. Testing your skills is an important part of football.
10. Skilled players increase spectators' enjoyment by adding dramatic action to the game.
11. Watching football on television is a favorite pastime for many people.
12. The defense tries to keep its opponents from scoring a touchdown.
13. Enforcing the rules is the referee's job.
14. The home team advanced by passing the ball toward the goal line.
15. Playing well involves speed and teamwork.
16. Shoes with cleats prevent slipping.
17. Players can improve their skills with good coaching.
18. A coach's work involves deciding which positions team members will play and what plays will be used.
19. After preparing the game plan, a coach sometimes discusses ideas with the team's quarterback.
20. Kicking off is decided by flipping a coin.

15.2 Gerunds and Gerund Phrases **497**

PRACTICE AND ASSESS

Answers: Exercise 3
1. adjective   4. gerund
2. gerund   5. gerund
3. main verb

Answers: Exercise 4
1. earning more points than the opponent—d. o.
2. Kicking—subject
3. kicking a field goal—o. p.
4. converting . . . touchdown—d. o.
5. Defending . . . goal—subject
6. tackling—d. o.
7. Blocking—subject
8. Passing—subject
9. Testing your skills—subject
10. adding . . . to the game—o. p.
11. Watching . . . television—subject
12. scoring a touchdown—o. p.
13. Enforcing the rules—subject
14. passing . . . goal line—o. p.
15. Playing well—subject
16. slipping—d. o.
17. good coaching—o. p.
18. deciding . . . be used—d. o.
19. preparing the game plan—o. p.
20. Kicking off—subject; flipping a coin—o. p.

Independent Practice

Skills Practice
- *Grammar Practice,* p. 37
- *Grammar Reteaching,* p. 38
- *Grammar Enrichment,* p. 37

 **Grammar Workbook,** Lesson 51

CLOSE

Have students imagine that they are sportscasters and then write a paragraph describing an Olympic event. Tell them to use gerunds and gerund phrases in their writing.

Enabling Strategies

LEP Finding Gerunds

Students whose first language is not English may have difficulty determining whether a verb form ending in *-ing* is a verb or a gerund in a sentence. Have students first read the sentence with the *-ing* form. Then read it again, substituting *it* for the *-ing* word or group of words. If the sentence still makes sense with the word *it*, the *-ing* form is acting as a noun and is therefore a gerund.

FOCUS

Lesson Overview

Objective: To identify infinitives and infinitive phrases used as nouns, and to distinguish infinitives from prepositional phrases that begin with *to*

🔔 Bellringer

When students enter the classroom, have this assignment on the board: *List all the prepositional phrases that begin with* **to** *in the following sentences. Underline other* **to's**: Juan went to Europe to study. To learn other languages is his goal. Every day he goes to a university in Paris to learn French.* (prepositional phrases: to Europe, to a university)

TEACH

☑ Teaching Tips

Infinitives and infinitive phrases used as nouns are very similar to gerunds. In fact, infinitives and gerunds often may be interchanged, as shown here: *To stop is sometimes difficult. Stopping is sometimes difficult.* Infinitives and infinitive phrases used as nouns are singular and may be replaced by the pronoun *it.*

Infinitives and infinitive phrases may also function as adjectives or adverbs: *We met the challenge to win* (adjective modifying *challenge*). *We practice to win* (adverb modifying *practice*).

15.3 Infinitives and Infinitive Phrases

Another verb form that may function as a noun is an infinitive.

> **To referee** requires training.
> Trainees learn **to referee.**

An **infinitive** is formed from the word *to* together with the base form of a verb. It is often used as a noun in a sentence.

How can you tell whether the word *to* is a preposition or part of an infinitive? If the word *to* comes immediately before a verb, it is part of the infinitive.

> Those young players want **to win.** [infinitive]
> The coach is pointing **to the pitcher.** [prepositional phrase]

In the first sentence the words in dark type work together as a noun to name what the players want. In the second sentence the words in dark type are a prepositional phrase used as an adverb that tells *where* the coach is pointing.

Since infinitives function as nouns, they can be subjects and direct objects.

> **To referee** demands patience. [subject]
> Athletes often try **to argue.** [direct object]

An **infinitive phrase** is a group of words that includes an infinitive and other words that complete its meaning.

> A player may try **to influence the call.**
> **To go to every game of the season** is my dream.

INFINITIVE

The player starts **to run.**

She runs
to home base.

**PREPOSITIONAL
PHRASE**

498 *Verbals*

Teacher's Classroom Resources

The following resources can be used for planning, instruction, practice, reinforcement, reteaching, or enrichment.

🔧 **Teaching Tools**
Lesson Plans

📁 **Blackline Masters**
Grammar Practice, p. 38
Grammar Reteaching, p. 39
Grammar Enrichment, p. 38

📘 *Grammar Workbook*
Lesson 52

Exercise 5 — Identifying Infinitives

Write each underlined group of words and label it *infinitive* or *prepositional phrase*.

1. <u>To win</u> is the dream of every World Series player.
2. The top team in each division goes <u>to the play-offs</u>.
3. The two winners are invited <u>to the World Series</u>.
4. <u>To excel</u> is each team's goal at these games.
5. Millions of people plan <u>to watch</u> the World Series on television.
6. We went <u>to a baseball game</u> last Saturday.
7. Would you like <u>to become</u> a professional player?
8. <u>To begin</u> by playing Little League is good.
9. As players improve, they move from the rookie <u>to the minor leagues</u>.
10. <u>To sponsor</u> Little League teams local organizations pay for uniforms.

Exercise 6 — Identifying Infinitive Phrases

Write each infinitive or infinitive phrase. Label it *subject* or *direct object*.

1. To play in the American or National League is an accomplishment.
2. Most players prefer to play home games.
3. To leave means losing the support of all the home town fans.
4. To understand baseball requires knowledge of the structure of the game.
5. The players want to improve their strategies.
6. We've decided to root for the American League team in the World Series.
7. To attend a World Series game is one of my goals.
8. I want to go to Dodger Stadium.
9. Have you learned to pitch a fastball?
10. People began to play baseball in the 1800s.
11. Players learn to hit the ball.
12. To catch the ball is also very difficult.
13. The catcher needs to wear a mask, a chest protector, and shin guards.
14. To throw a variety of pitches is the goal of every pitcher.
15. Players need to check the batting order.
16. When the ball is hit, the player tries to run.
17. When the bases are loaded, the runner hopes to advance.
18. Try to tag the base!
19. To reach home plate is a wonderful feeling.
20. Would you like to join our team?

15.3 Infinitives and Infinitive Phrases **499**

PRACTICE AND ASSESS

Answers: Exercise 5
1. infinitive
2. prepositional phrase
3. prepositional phrase
4. infinitive
5. infinitive
6. prepositional phrase
7. infinitive
8. infinitive
9. prepositional phrase
10. infinitive

Answers: Exercise 6
1. To play in the American or National League—subject
2. to play home games—direct object
3. To leave—subject
4. To understand baseball—subject
5. to improve their strategies—direct object
6. to root for the American League team in the World Series—direct object
7. To attend a World Series game—subject
8. to go to Dodger Stadium—direct object
9. to pitch a fast ball—direct object
10. to play baseball in the 1800s—direct object
11. to hit the ball—direct object
12. To catch the ball—subject
13. to wear a mask, chest protector, and shin guards—direct object
14. To throw a variety of pitches—subject
15. to check the batting order—direct object
16. to run—direct object
17. to advance—direct object
18. to tag the base—direct object
19. To reach home plate—subject
20. to join our team—direct object

CLOSE

Ask students to write a brief sportscast using both infinitive and prepositional phrases. Have them exchange their work with a partner and identify and label the types of phrases.

Enabling Strategies

LEP Choosing Infinitives or Gerunds

Students learning English may be confused when forming objects for certain verbs. Some verbs permit only infinitives as objects: *I want **to swim***, not *I want **swimming***. Some verbs permit only gerunds as objects: *I coach **swimming***, not *I coach **to swim***. The verb *go* followed by a recreational activity takes a gerund: *I go **swimming** often*. Some verbs permit either gerunds or infinitives as objects: *I like **to swim**. I like **swimming***. However, the choice can change the meaning of the sentence: *I stopped **eating**. I stopped **to eat**.*

TEACH

About the Literature

The passage describes Wilma Rudolph's feelings after she lost a high school track meet. The passage relates how her confidence was shaken by losing, and how the loss created in her the determination to win.

Ask students whether they have ever had to struggle to overcome a loss. Encourage students to describe their experiences. What caused the loss? How did they feel after their loss? What did students do to get over the loss? Have students discuss each other's experiences, paying attention to whether their responses include verbals or verbal phrases.

Linking Grammar and Literature

☑ Grammar Tip

Help students distinguish between the infinitive phrases *to go out and die* and *to get back the next year and wipe them all out* and the prepositional phrase *to the track*. Write the sentences on the board: *Wilma wanted to ____. Wilma went to ____.* Let students complete the first sentence with single words, such as *win*. Explain that words that fit in the first sentence tell what Wilma wanted to do (verbs) and, when used with *to*, become an infinitive verb form. Students may complete the second sentence with two words, such as *the Olympics*. These words name places (nouns) and are objects of the preposition *to*.

Critical Thinking

After students have read the passage, discuss Rudolph's use of verbals and verbal phrases. Ask students to find and classify other verbals and verbal phrases in the passage. (Examples include the following: *to go out and die*—infinitive phrase; *Losing as badly as I did*—gerund phrase)

500

Grammar Review

Verbals

In 1960 Wilma Rudolph became the first American woman to win three gold medals in track and field at the Olympic games. Shortly before she competed in her first Olympics, however, Rudolph was defeated at a regional high school track meet in Tuskegee, Alabama. In the following passage from "Wilma," an autobiographical essay, Rudolph describes how the defeat at Tuskegee motivated her to win in the future. The passage has been annotated to show some of the types of verbals covered in this unit.

Literature Model

from WILMA
by Wilma Rudolph

I ran and ran and ran every day, and I acquired this sense of determination, this sense of spirit that I would never, never give up, no matter what else happened. That day at Tuskegee had a tremendous effect on me inside. That's all I ever thought about. Some days I just wanted to go out and die. I just moped around and felt sorry for myself. Other days I'd go out to the track with fire in my eyes and imagine myself back at Tuskegee, beating them all. Losing as badly as I did had an impact on my personality. Winning all the time in track had given me confidence; I felt like a winner. But I didn't feel like a winner any more after Tuskegee. My confidence was shattered, and I was thinking the only way I could put it all together was to get back the next year and wipe them all out.

Participial phrase used as adjective

Gerund phrase used as subject

Infinitive phrase

500 *Verbals*

Teacher's Classroom Resources

The following resources can be used for planning, instruction, practice, reinforcement, assessment, reteaching, enrichment, or evaluation.

🗐 Teaching Tools
Lesson Plans, p. 96

📕 Grammar Workbook
Lessons 50–52
Unit 8 Review
Cumulative Review Units 1–8

Unit Assessment

📁 Tests with Answer Key
Unit 15 Mastery Test, pp. 59–60

🖵 Test Generator
Unit 15 Mastery Test

Exercise 1

Identifying Participial Phrases   Write each sentence. Underline each participial phrase. Then draw two lines under the word that the phrase describes. Add commas as needed.

SAMPLE   The runner refusing to let her defeat stop her continued to train.

ANSWER   The <u>runner,</u> <u>refusing to let her defeat stop her</u>, continued to train.

1. Rudolph having won two gold medals tried for a third in the 400-meter relay.
2. Crouched at the starting line the runners waited for the signal to start.
3. Leading the field the first runner streaked over the track.
4. Taking the baton the second runner raced away.
5. One runner reaching for the baton nearly let it drop.
6. The spectators watched Rudolph pulling ahead.
7. The runner taking one final stride lunged through the tape.
8. Trying to break a record the runner felt exhilarated.
9. Roaring wildly the crowd rose from their seats.
10. Gasping for breath she knew she could win.

Exercise 2

Using Participles and Participial Phrases   Rewrite each sentence, inserting the participle or participial phrase in parentheses. Use commas as needed.

SAMPLE   Rudolph gained confidence. (running hard)

ANSWER   Running hard, Rudolph gained confidence.

1. The track meet at Tuskegee shocked the runner. (defeated)
2. Rudolph felt like quitting. (shattered by her defeat)
3. She briefly thought she might give up the sport. (discouraged at her failure)
4. She dreamed of winning the meet. (imagining herself back at Tuskegee)
5. The athlete never gave up. (fiercely determined)
6. She realized that a champion can try again, even after a defeat. (crushing)
7. Rudolph helped the 1956 Olympic relay team win a bronze medal. (having trained for just a year)
8. The young woman gained the respect of her coaches. (a talented athlete)
9. Rudolph won a trophy. (honoring her achievements)
10. Rudolph was pursued by reporters. (hoping for an interview)

Grammar Review   **501**

PRACTICE AND ASSESS

Answers: Exercise 1
1. <u>Rudolph</u>, <u>having won two gold medals</u>, tried…
2. <u>Crouched at the starting line</u>, the <u>runners</u> waited…
3. <u>Leading the field</u>, the first <u>runner</u>…
4. <u>Taking the baton</u>, the second <u>runner</u> …
5. One <u>runner</u>, <u>reaching for the baton</u>, …
6. …<u>Rudolph</u>, <u>pulling ahead</u>.
7. The <u>runner</u>, <u>taking one final stride</u>, lunged…
8. <u>Trying to break a record</u>, the <u>runner</u> …
9. <u>Roaring wildly</u>, the <u>crowd</u>…
10. <u>Gasping for breath</u>, <u>she</u> …

Answers: Exercise 2
1. The track meet at Tuskegee shocked the defeated runner.
2. Shattered by her defeat, Rudolph felt like quitting.
3. Discouraged at her failure, she briefly thought…
4. Imagining herself back at Tuskegee, she…
5. The fiercely determined athlete never gave up.
6. …again, even after a crushing defeat.
7. Having trained for just a year, Rudolph helped… *or* Rudolph, having trained for just a year, helped…
8. A talented athlete, the young woman gained… *or* The young woman, a talented athlete, gained…
9. Rudolph won a trophy honoring her achievements.
10. Rudolph was pursued by reporters hoping for an interview.

UNIT 15
Review

Answers: Exercise 3

1. Having polio when she was young; subject
2. learning to walk after her illness; object of a preposition
3. Her Olympic running; subject
4. playing basketball; direct object
5. setting a world record at the Olympics; object of a preposition
6. winning her third gold medal in the 1960 Olympics; object of a preposition
7. helping other women become runners; direct object
8. Winning a gold medal, subject
9. Taking part; subject
10. Participating in the Olympics; subject

Answers: Exercise 4

Answers may vary, but some suggestions are provided below.

1. Rudolph first achieved fame by competing in the 1956 Olympic games.
2. Another of Rudolph's achievements was setting world records in the 100-meter and 200-meter races.
3. Having polio as a young girl might have prevented Rudolph from pursuing a career in track.
4. Rudolph strengthened her muscles after her illness by running.
5. Rudolph's most recent challenge was working with young people in sports and educational programs.

Exercise 3

Identifying Gerund Phrases   Write each gerund phrase. Then write *subject*, *direct object*, or *object of a preposition* to tell how it is being used.

1. Having polio when she was young left Rudolph unable to walk without a special shoe.
2. Rudolph proved her determination by learning to walk after her illness.
3. Her Olympic running seemed like a miracle.
4. She had also tried playing basketball.
5. Before setting a world record at the Olympics, Rudolph ran many practice races.
6. After winning her third gold medal in the 1960 Olympics, Rudolph returned home a hero.
7. She anticipated helping other women become runners.
8. Winning a gold medal is not all that matters in the Olympics.
9. Taking part is a great honor.
10. Participating in the Olympics is the high point of an athlete's career.

Exercise 4

Using Gerunds and Gerund Phrases   Write a sentence that answers each question, using the word or words in parentheses.

SAMPLE   What is Wilma Rudolph best known for? (winning three gold medals at the Olympics)

ANSWER   Wilma Rudolph is best known for winning three gold medals at the Olympics.

1. By what means did Rudolph first achieve fame? (competing in the 1956 Olympic games)
2. What is another of Rudolph's achievements? (setting world records in the 100-meter and 200-meter races)
3. What might have prevented Rudolph from pursuing a career in track? (having polio as a young girl)
4. By what means did Rudolph strengthen her muscles after her illness? (running)
5. What was Rudolph's most recent challenge? (working with young people in sports and educational programs)

502   *Verbals*

Exercise 5

Identifying Infinitive Phrases Write each infinitive phrase. Then write *subject* or *direct object* to tell how it is being used.

1. To run a marathon tests the endurance and courage of even the most dedicated runners.
2. In the high jump an athlete needs to leap over a high bar.
3. Jumpers learn to kick their legs out at the end of their jump.
4. Pole vaulters need to thrust themselves into the air with a pole.
5. As the pole straightens, they try to twist their bodies.
6. Some athletes prefer to jump over hurdles.
7. To win a hurdle race requires speed, strength, and skill.
8. Broad jumpers like to land in a soft sand pit.
9. To throw the discus requires tremendous strength.
10. To measure jumps and throws accurately demands the skill of experienced and well-trained judges.

Exercise 6

Using Infinitives and Infinitive Phrases Write a sentence that answers each question, using the infinitive phrase in parentheses. Use the phrase as the part of speech indicated.

SAMPLE   What must a race walker learn?
(to maintain proper technique—direct object)
ANSWER   A race walker must learn to maintain proper technique.

1. What is the purpose of the hurdle race?
(to run and jump over obstacles placed on the track—subject)
2. What must relay racers learn?
(to pass the baton smoothly and quickly—direct object)
3. What does a high jumper attempt to do?
(to leap over an upraised bar—direct object)
4. What is an important skill in throwing events?
(to propel an object as far as possible—subject)
5. What requires years of training?
(to throw a discus—subject)

Grammar Review   **503**

Answers: Exercise 5
1. To run a marathon; subject
2. to leap over a high bar; direct object
3. to kick their legs out at the end of their jump; direct object
4. to thrust themselves into the air with a pole; direct object
5. to twist their bodies; direct object
6. to jump over hurdles; direct object
7. To win a hurdle race; subject
8. to land in a soft sand pit; direct object
9. To throw the discus; subject
10. To measure jumps and throws accurately; subject

Answers: Exercise 6
1. To run and jump over obstacles placed on the track is the purpose of the hurdle race.
2. Relay racers must learn to pass the baton smoothly and quickly.
3. A high jumper attempts to leap over an upraised bar.
4. To propel an object as far as possible is an important skill in throwing events.
5. To throw a discus requires years of training.

UNIT 15
Review

Answers: Exercise 7
Proofreading

This proofreading activity provides editing practice with (1) the current or previous units' skills, (2) the **Troubleshooter** errors, and (3) spelling errors. Students should be able to complete the exercise by referring to the units, the **Troubleshooter,** and a dictionary.

	Error (Type of Error)
1.	• grew (verb form)
2.	• programs, (introductory participial phrase)
	• achieved (spelling)
3.	• twenties, (introductory participial phrase)
	• became (verb form)
4.	• Lawrence's (singular possessive)
5.	• strain (subject–verb agreement)
6.	• determination, (introductory participial phrase)
7.	• artist, (nonessential participial phrase)
	• figures' (plural possessive)

Answers: Exercise 8
Mixed Review

1. held first in Olympia, Greece; participial phrase
2. training for the Games; gerund phrase
3. Reviving the Games; gerund phrase
4. to send athletes; infinitive phrase
5. desiring participation; participial phrase
6. to organize a committee; infinitive phrase
7. holding the Games; participial phrase
8. watching a runner with the Olympic flame; participial phrase
9. carrying their national flag; participial phrase
10. Dressed in their uniforms; participial phrase
11. to fly away; infinitive phrase
12. running around the track; participial phrase

13. Diving off a high board; gerund phrase
14. to watch skiers; infinitive phrase
15. talented in their sport; participial phrase
16. to bring home a medal; infinitive phrase
17. to win the gold; infinitive phrase

18. receiving three gold medals, participial phrase
19. Participating in the Games; gerund phrase

Exercise 7 — Proofreading

The following passage is about Jacob Lawrence, an African American artist whose work appears on the next page. Rewrite the passage, correcting the errors in spelling, grammar, and usage. Add any missing punctuation. There are ten errors.

Jacob Lawrence

[1]Jacob Lawrence was born in New Jersey in 1917 but growed up in Harlem. [2]Studying art in after-school programs he acheived success at an early age. [3]Gaining popularity in his twenties Lawrence becomed the first African American artist to have a one-person show at the Museum of Modern Art in New York.

[4]Vivid primary colors and highly stylized figures make Lawrences' work unique. [5]In the poster shown on the opposite page, for example, the relay racers visibly strains to cross the finish line. [6]Imitating Wilma Rudolph's determination each runner wants to win. [7]The artist using gestures and facial expressions, conveys his figure's emotions.

Exercise 8 — Mixed Review

Write *participial phrase, gerund phrase,* or *infinitive phrase* to tell how each underlined phrase is used.

The Olympics, held first in Olympia, Greece, began 3,500 years ago. Greek competitors underwent training for the Games. Reviving the Games was the idea of Pierre de Coubertin. In 1896 thirteen nations decided to send athletes. Each country desiring participation needs to organize a committee. The city holding the Games spends years preparing. As the Games begin, spectators love watching a runner with the Olympic flame. The athletes, carrying their national flag, enter the stadium. Dressed in their uniforms, they watch the release of pigeons. As the birds begin to fly away, the Games officially open. In summertime athletes, running around the track, demonstrate great speed. Diving off a high board is another event. In winter people like to watch skiers. Athletes talented in their sport want to bring home a medal, but few expect to win the gold. Even fewer are like Wilma Rudolph, receiving three gold medals. Participating in the Games is a dream come true.

504 *Verbals*

Jacob Lawrence, *Study for the Munich Olympic Games Poster*, 1971

Grammar Review **505**

CLOSE

Invite each student to share a brief thought about Wilma Rudolph or Jacob Lawrence's painting. Challenge them to include verbals in their remarks. Some students might relate their own experiences with the "agony and ecstasy" of competitive sports.

About the Art

Jacob Lawrence, *Study for the Munich Olympic Games Poster*, 1971

In this painting, Jacob Lawrence depicts relay racers, each with a team baton in hand, near the finish of a race. The artist's details convey the extreme physical exertion and pain involved in running to the limit of one's capacity. Ask students what the artwork and the passage from *Wilma* show about what it takes to succeed in sports. (Sample answers: determination, physical strength, ability to endure pain) The original artwork for the poster, which is in the Seattle Art Musuem collection, is gouache on paper and measures 35 1/2 by 27 inches.

Verbals in Writing

Have students read the passage from *Always to Remember* on page 506. Then ask them to review the different versions of each sentence offered in the Techniques with Verbals column. Do they agree that Ashabranner's versions are superior to the others given?

Techniques with Verbals

Ask students to rephrase the two points listed. Then have them turn to the Proofreading exercise on page 504. Ask students to listen for verbals as you read aloud a corrected version of the passage. Ask students what verbals they heard.

Practice

The answers to this challenging and enriching activity will vary. Refer to Techniques with Verbals as you evaluate student choices. Check that students use a variety of gerunds and participles in their paragraphs. Sample answer:

"<u>Working</u> on my science project without electricity will be <u>challenging</u>," said Sam to his teacher. "I know," Ms. Clayton replied. "The extra effort will expand your <u>learning</u> experience." She flashed Sam an <u>encouraging</u> grin. "Oh well," he thought, "<u>quitting</u> is not my style. <u>Inventing</u> new methods is <u>interesting</u>." Then, <u>gathering</u> what he needed to mix chemicals, he headed for home.

Writing Application

Verbals in Writing Brent Ashabranner uses participles and gerunds to bring a sense of action to his essay about the Vietnam War Memorial. As you read this passage from *Always to Remember*, pay special attention to the italicized verbals.

> The answer, they decided, was to hold a national design competition open to all Americans. The *winning* design would receive a prize of $20,000, but the real prize would be the winner's knowledge that the memorial would become a part of American history on the Mall in Washington, D.C. Although fund *raising* was only well started at this point, the *choosing* of a memorial design could not be delayed if the memorial was to be built by Veteran's Day, 1982.

Techniques with Verbals Try to apply some of Brent Ashabranner's writing techniques when you write and revise your work.

1. Use participle verb forms as adjectives to make your descriptions more lively and engaging. Compare the following:

Flat version The design *that won* would receive a prize.
Ashabranner's version The *winning* design would receive a prize. . . .

2. When appropriate, add a sense of action to your sentences by using gerunds.

Less active words They had only just started to raise funds.
Ashabranner's version Although fund *raising* was only well started. . . .

Practice Revise the following passage on a separate sheet of paper. Focusing on the underlined words, add gerunds and participles to make it more active.

"It will be <u>a real challenge</u> <u>to work</u> on my science project without electricity," said Sam to his teacher. "I know," Ms. Clayton replied. "The extra effort will expand <u>what you learn</u> from the experience." She flashed Sam a grin <u>that tried to encourage</u> him. "Oh well," he thought. "It's not my style <u>to quit</u>. It's <u>of interest</u> <u>to invent</u> new methods." He started <u>to gather</u> what he needed to mix chemicals and headed for home.

506 *Writing Application*

Teacher's Classroom Resources

The following resources can be used for assessment or evaluation.

Unit Assessment

📁 *Tests with Answer Key*
Unit 15 Mastery Test, pp. 59–60

💿 *Test Generator*
Unit 15 Mastery Test

You may wish to administer the Unit 15 Mastery Test at this point.

UNIT 16

Subject-Verb Agreement

Grammar | **Lessons**

UNIT GOALS

The goal of Unit 16 is to help students, through example and instruction, to develop an understanding of and an ability to use subject–verb agreement. Lessons also focus on collective and other special subjects, indefinite pronouns as subjects, and agreement with compound subjects.

Unit Assessment
📁 *Tests with Answer Key*
Unit 16 Pretest, pp. 61–62
Unit 16 Mastery Test, pp. 63–64

💿 *Test Generator*
Unit 16 Pretest
Unit 16 Mastery Test

You may wish to administer the Unit 16 Pretest at this point.

Key to Ability Levels
Enabling Strategies have been coded for varying learning styles and abilities.

L1 Level 1 activities are within the ability range of Learning Disabled students.

L2 Level 2 activities are basic-to-average activities and are within the ability range of average students.

L3 Level 3 activities are challenging activities and are within the ability range of above-average students.

LEP LEP activities are within the ability range of Limited English Proficiency students.

FOCUS

Lesson Overview

Objective: To use subject-verb agreement in written sentences

Bellringer

When students enter the classroom, have this assignment on the board: *Think of a topic that interests you. List five singular noun subjects and five singular verbs that are related to that topic. Pair the subjects with verbs to make five short sentences.*

Motivating Activity

Review students' answers to the Bellringer to see if the subjects and verbs agree. Point out that an -s at the end of a verb indicates singular, not plural as students might think. Example: Jane (singular) enjoy*s* embroidering.

TEACH

☑ Teaching Tip

In present-tense sentences all verbs must change form to agree with a third-person singular subject. In the past tense only the verb *be* changes form (*was, were*). Verb forms contrast with noun forms in that plural nouns usually end in -s, and singular verbs end in -s. In verb phrases, agreement depends on the first verb in the simple predicate.

16.1 Making Subjects and Verbs Agree

The basic idea of subject-verb agreement is a simple one—a singular noun subject calls for a singular form of the verb, and a plural noun calls for a plural form of the verb. The subject and its verb are said to *agree in number.* Read the sentences below. You can see that the subjects and verbs agree.

Notice that in the present tense the singular form of the verb usually ends in -*s* or -*es*.

The **frogs leap.**
PLURAL SUBJECT   PLURAL VERB

A **frog leaps.**
SINGULAR   SINGULAR
SUBJECT   VERB

Subject and Verb Agreement	
Singular Subject	**Plural Subject**
An **ecologist studies** nature.	**Ecologists study** nature.
The **boy learns** about ecology.	The **boys learn** about ecology.
Judy plants seedlings.	**Judy** and **Kim plant** seedlings.

The verb must also agree with a subject pronoun. Look at the chart below. Notice how the verb changes. In the present tense the -*s* ending is used with the subject pronouns *it, he,* and *she*.

Subject Pronoun and Verb Agreement	
Singular	**Plural**
I **hike**.	We **hike**.
You **hike**.	You **hike**.
He, she, *or* it **hikes**.	They **hike**.

The irregular verbs *be, do,* and *have* can be main verbs or helping verbs. They must agree with the subject, regardless of whether they are main verbs or helping verbs.

I **am** a ranger. They **are** tagging a bear. He **is** digging. She **does** well. She **does** climb cliffs. They **do** garden. He **has** gear. He **has** saved birds. They **have** traveled.

508   *Subject-Verb Agreement*

Teacher's Classroom Resources

The following resources can be used for planning, instruction, practice, reinforcement, assessment, reteaching, enrichment, or evaluation.

🔧 **Teaching Tools**
Lesson Plans

📁 **Blackline Masters**
Grammar Practice, p. 39
Grammar Reteaching, p. 40
Grammar Enrichment, p. 39

📕 *Grammar Workbook*
Lesson 53

Unit Assessment

📁 *Tests with Answer Key*
Unit 16 Pretest, pp. 61–62

💿 *Test Generator*
Unit 16 Pretest

You may wish to administer the Unit 16 Pretest at this point.

Exercise 1 — Making Subjects and Verbs Agree

Rewrite each sentence, changing singular subjects to plural and plural subjects to singular. Make the verbs agree with the subjects. Remember that other parts of the sentences might have to change when the subject changes.

1. The student plans a hike to the bog.
2. Bogs contain an interesting variety of organisms.
3. The state park is fun for everyone.
4. A leaflet explains the plants and animals in the park.
5. We are interested in learning more about the park's plants.
6. A ranger speaks to visitors every day at noon.
7. She identifies the various plants growing in the bog.
8. Guidebooks provide good information about the types of plants.
9. A bog offers opportunities for people hunting for fossils.
10. Bogs develop in former glacial lakes.

Exercise 2 — Using Correct Subject and Verb Agreement

Write the correct form of the verb in parentheses.

1. The day (is, are) perfect for a visit to the bog.
2. The students always (enjoy, enjoys) field trips.
3. Bogs (contain, contains) acidic soil and many mosses.
4. Swamps (is, are) similar to bogs in many ways.
5. The acidity (tell, tells) you about the type of bog.
6. A bog (is, are) usually smaller than a swamp.
7. Ecosystems (is, are) communities of living and nonliving factors.
8. An ecosystem (include, includes) the surrounding air.
9. An ecosystem (has, have) distinct cycles.
10. Water (is, are) an important part of all ecosystems.
11. An ecologist (do, does) a great deal of fieldwork.
12. Bogs often (provide, provides) interesting ecosystems.
13. This bog (have, has) supported a rare ecosystem.
14. A unique fungus (grow, grows) in this bog.
15. Many creatures (live, lives) in bogs.
16. Ecosystems (consist, consists) of many different plants and animals.
17. Our survival (do, does) depend upon the painstaking work of the ecologists.
18. Their research often (have, has) a great impact on our view of our planet.
19. We (rely, relies) on the research of ecologists.
20. They (has, have) changed our understanding of our planet.

16.1 Making Subjects and Verbs Agree   **509**

Enabling Strategies

LEP Practicing Subject-Verb Agreement

Students who speak a non-European language that does not require agreement between subjects and verbs may not see any logic in subject-verb agreement. Write these sentences on the board: *They like to run. They are good runners. They hope to be on the track team next year.* Have students change the *they* in each sentence to *he* or *she* and make the necessary change in verb form to show agreement.

Setting the Purpose

Lesson 16.2 teaches students to use the verb form that agrees with the subject when the subject does not immediately precede the verb.

FOCUS

Lesson Overview

Objective: To identify the subject of a sentence when it is separated from the verb by a prepositional phrase, when the sentence begins with *here* or *there,* or when the sentence is inverted, as in a question.

Bellringer

When students enter the classroom, have this assignment on the board: *List the subject and verb in each clause in this complex sentence. (subjects: season, land, they; verbs: turns, becomes, cannot)*

When the season turns and the land becomes warm and vital . . . they cannot hold still.

—N. Scott Momaday, *House Made of Dawn*

TEACH

Cooperative Learning

Divide the class into groups of two pairs. Give each pair of students the same two sentences with long and complicated complete subjects. Pairs should find the simple subject by starting with the first noun or pronoun in the sentence. The two pairs then compare their answers. They can check their work by rewriting the sentence, using only the simple subject with the predicate.

16.2 Problems with Locating the Subject

Making a subject and its verb agree is easy when the verb directly follows the subject. Sometimes, however, a phrase containing another noun comes between the subject and the verb.

In the sentence below, the phrase *except in the polar regions* contains a plural noun. The verb *becomes* must agree with the singular subject of the sentence, *desert,* not with the plural noun *regions,* which is the object of the preposition in the phrase.

> The **desert**, except in the polar regions, **becomes** very hot.

In inverted sentences the subject follows the verb. Inverted sentences often begin with a prepositional phrase. Do not mistake the object of the preposition for the subject of the sentence.

> In the desert **roam herds** of camels.

In inverted sentences beginning with *Here* or *There,* look for the subject after the verb. *Here* or *There* is never the subject.

> There **is** a high **mountain** near the desert.
> Here at the top **are** many damp **rocks**.

By rearranging each sentence so that the subject comes first, you see the subject and verb in their usual order.

> A high **mountain** there **is** near the desert.
> Many damp **rocks are** here at the top.

In some interrogative sentences an auxiliary verb comes before the subject. Look for the subject between the auxiliary verb and the main verb.

> **Do** any **deserts contain** large animals?

510   *Subject-Verb Agreement*

Teacher's Classroom Resources

The following resources can be used for planning, instruction, practice, reinforcement, reteaching, or enrichment.

Teaching Tools
Lesson Plans, p. 97

Blackline Masters
Grammar Practice, p. 40
Grammar Enrichment, p. 40

Grammar Workbook
Lesson 54

Exercise 3 — Making Subjects and Verbs Agree

Write each sentence. Underline the simple subject once and its verb twice. If they agree, write *correct.* If they do not agree, correct the verb.

1. The savanna, with its waving grasses, lie next to the desert.
2. It is on the margin of the trade-wind belts.
3. In the savanna lives many large animals.
4. The savanna, except in its rainy summers, are dry.
5. In Africa are the largest savannas.
6. Do savannas exist everywhere in the world?
7. There is many giraffes in the grassland.
8. Names for a savanna includes prairie, scrub, and veld.
9. Do much rain fall each year in a savanna?
10. The balance between grasses and woody plants is delicate.

Exercise 4 — Using the Correct Verb Form

Write the correct form of the verb in parentheses.

1. The plains near the North Pole (is, are) very cold.
2. The temperature in these zones (is, are) usually below zero.
3. In this area (live, lives) many animals.
4. During the brief summers (grow, grows) a rare moss.
5. In the moss (nest, nests) many birds.
6. There (is, are) little rainfall during the summer.
7. (Does, Do) snow provide the needed moisture?
8. Some areas of the Arctic (is, are) drier than the world's deserts.
9. There (is, are) several hundred species of plants in the Arctic.
10. Summer melting of icy areas (create, creates) nesting sites for birds.
11. Smog (accumulate, accumulates) over some Arctic areas.
12. Fish, such as cod and salmon, (live, lives) under the ice cap.
13. There (is, are) a reason for the white color of many Arctic animals.
14. (Does, Do) the absence of reptiles affect the ecosystem?
15. Along a well-traveled route (roam, roams) herds of caribou.
16. Here the threat to their habitat (is, are) from oil pipeline construction.
17. The dense, woolly coat of musk oxen (is, are) called *quivet.*
18. There (is, are) many uses for quivet, the world's most valuable raw fiber.
19. In summer (appear, appears) many types of grasses.
20. (Does, Do) lichens help create new soil?

16.2 Problems with Locating the Subject **511**

PRACTICE AND ASSESS

Answers: Exercise 3
1. <u>savanna</u>; <u>lies</u>
2. <u>It</u>; <u>is</u>; correct
3. <u>animals</u>; <u>live</u>
4. <u>savanna</u>; <u>is</u>
5. <u>savannas</u>; <u>are</u>; correct
6. <u>savannas</u>; <u>exist</u>; correct
7. <u>giraffes</u>; <u>are</u>
8. <u>names</u>; <u>include</u>
9. <u>rain</u>; <u>does fall</u>
10. <u>balance</u>; <u>is</u>; correct

Answers: Exercise 4
1. are	11. accumulates
2. is	12. live
3. live	13. is
4. grows	14. Does
5. nest	15. roam
6. is	16. is
7. Does	17. is
8. are	18. are
9. are	19. appear
10. creates	20. Do

Independent Practice

Skills Practice
📁 *Grammar Practice,* p. 40
📁 *Grammar Enrichment,* p. 40

📓 ***Grammar Workbook,*** Lesson 54

CLOSE

Have students write a paragraph describing preparations for a camping trip, keeping subject-verb agreement in mind as they write.

Enabling Strategies

LEP Finding the Subject

Some students have difficulty finding the subject of a sentence when an appositive or an appositive phrase appears between the subject and verb. Tell students that like an intervening prepositional phrase, the appositive does not affect the number of the verb.

Ask students to locate the subject and verb in the following sentence: *The dog, the smallest of the four animals,* shows *the greatest courage.* Point out that the appositive phrase, *the smallest of the four animals,* ends in a plural noun but does not affect the choice of verb form.

Setting the Purpose

Lesson 16.3 teaches students to use verbs that agree in number with special subjects, such as collective nouns, numbers, titles, and nouns with unusual endings.

FOCUS

Lesson Overview

Objective: To determine number when using collective nouns, numbers, titles, and other special subjects.

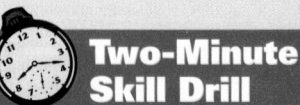

Bellringer

When students enter the classroom, have this assignment on the board: *Write sentences using the words* tools, scissors, *and* class *as subjects. Circle the verbs you use and mark them as singular or plural.*

TEACH

☑ Teaching Tip

Many nouns that end in *-cs* may be singular or plural, depending on their meaning in a particular sentence. Note the different meanings of *statistics* in the following sentences: *Statistics is an interesting branch of science.* (noun used as subject matter) *Statistics show that coal-burning industries pollute the environment.* (noun used to denote the application of the subject matter)

Two-Minute Skill Drill

Have students write sentences using the following as subjects:

shears	social studies
collection	five years

512

The team . . .

. . . **collect** cans and bottles at the shore.

The team . . .

. . . **collects** cans and bottles for recycling.

It is sometimes difficult to tell whether certain special subjects are singular or plural. For example, collective nouns follow special agreement rules. A **collective noun** names a group. The noun has a singular meaning when it names a group that acts as a single unit. The noun has a plural meaning when it refers to each member of the group acting as individuals. The meaning of the noun determines whether you use the singular or plural form of the verb.

> The **team agrees** to save papers. [one unit, singular]
> The **team agree** to store them in their homes. [individuals, plural]

Certain nouns, such as *mathematics* and *news*, end in *-s* but take a singular verb. Other nouns that end in *-s* and name one thing, such as *trousers* and *pliers*, take a plural verb.

> **Mumps is** a disease that is spread through the air. [singular]
> **Scissors are** not practical for shredding paper. [plural]

When the subject refers to an amount as a single unit, it is singular. When it refers to a number of individual units, it is plural.

> **Ten years seems** a long time. [single unit]
> **Ten years have passed** since you left. [individual units]
> **Five cents is** the deposit on one bottle. [single unit]
> **Five cents are** in my hand. [individual units]

A title of a book or work of art is considered singular even if a noun within the title is plural.

> ***Recycling Successes* is** now a best-selling book. [one book]

512 *Subject-Verb Agreement*

Teacher's Classroom Resources

The following resources can be used for planning, instruction, practice, reinforcement, reteaching, or enrichment.

🔧 **Teaching Tools**
Lesson Plans

📁 **Blackline Masters**
Grammar Practice, p. 41
Grammar Reteaching, p. 41
Grammar Enrichment, p. 41

📙 ***Grammar Workbook***
Lesson 55

Exercise 5   Identifying Verbs for Collective Nouns

Write each sentence. Underline the collective noun subject once and the verb twice. If they agree, write *correct*. If they do not agree, correct the verb.

1. *Recycling Tips* are a pamphlet of helpful ideas on ways to recycle.
2. Fifteen is the average number of refillings for a returnable bottle.
3. News about the town's recycling efforts are hopeful.
4. After lunch, the class empty their trays in the recycling bins.
5. Each week, the committee award a prize for the best recycling tip.
6. Two tons were the weight of last month's scrap metal collection.
7. Simple mathematics show the value of turning old paper into newsprint.
8. The cafeteria staff show their support by helping students recycle.
9. Scissors is in the desk drawer.
10. The parents' group have donated more recycling bins.

Exercise 6   Using the Correct Verb Form with Collective Nouns

Write the correct form of the verb in parentheses.

1. The committee (decide, decides) to recycle paper.
2. The committee (decide, decides) among themselves.
3. The audience (leave, leaves) when they are bored.
4. The audience (applaud, applauds) in unison.
5. News (is, are) being made at this town meeting.
6. Even eyeglasses (is, are) recyclable.
7. *Seven Ways to Recycle Newspapers* (is, are) the book we need.
8. The class (discuss, discusses) their different opinions about pollutants.
9. The group (discuss, discusses) the problem of landfills.
10. The herd of goats (graze, grazes) at the landfill.
11. The herd (is, are) all healthy.
12. One million gallons (is, are) a large amount of pollutants.
13. *Energy Alternatives* (is, are) an important book.
14. Five hundred dollars (is, are) available for a recycling program.
15. *Fragile Lands* (do, does) seem a significant film.
16. The class (is, are) working on a group project.
17. The group (see, sees) a movie about landfills.
18. Two years (seem, seems) a long time for recovery.
19. Trousers (is, are) recycled with other forms of clothing.
20. The class (draws, draw) posters showing their household recycling efforts.

16.3 Collective Nouns and Other Special Subjects   **513**

PRACTICE AND ASSESS

Answers: Exercise 5
1. Recycling Tips;   is
2. Fifteen;   is; correct
3. News;   is
4. class;   empty; correct
5. committee;   awards
6. tons;   was
7. mathematics;   shows
8. staff;   show; correct
9. Scissors;   are
10. group;   has

Answers: Exercise 6

1. decides	11. are
2. decide	12. is
3. leave	13. is
4. applauds	14. is
5. is	15. does
6. are	16. is
7. is	17. sees
8. discuss	18. seems
9. discusses	19. are
10. grazes	20. draw

Independent Practice

Skills Practice

📁 *Grammar Practice,* p. 41
📁 *Grammar Reteaching,* p. 41
📁 *Grammar Enrichment,* p. 41

📓 *Grammar Workbook,* Lesson 55

CLOSE

Have students sketch ideas for creating posters about a recycling drive, using sentences with the words *newspapers, teamwork,* and *pollutants* as subjects. Have them check their work to be sure their subjects and verbs agree.

Enabling Strategies

LEP Categorizing Plural Nouns

Some students, especially those whose first language is not English, have trouble with the surprisingly large number of nouns that are always used in plural. To improve students' memory of nouns that are always used in the plural, list on the board: *binoculars, glasses, clippers, pliers, jeans, pants, shorts, slacks, people, police, cattle.* Ask students to make up categories for the words (for example, "tools" or "clothing"), group the words by category, and use each word in a sentence.

FOCUS

Lesson Overview

Objective: To identify singular and plural indefinite pronouns and to use the correct verb forms

Bellringer

When students enter the classroom, have this assignment on the board: *Pick the verb: a. Several buses (stops, stop) here. b. Everybody (waits, wait) on this corner.*

TEACH

☑ Teaching Tip

It's easy to mistake the object of a preposition that follows the subject for the subject itself, causing an error in subject-verb agreement. In the sentence *Each of the candidates is bringing a résumé,* the object (*candidates*) may be mistaken for the subject. This results in the incorrect use of a plural verb with a singular subject.

⇄ Cross-reference: Grammar

For instruction and practice in indefinite pronouns, see Lesson 11.5, pp. 410–411.

16.4 | Indefinite Pronouns as Subjects

An **indefinite pronoun** is a pronoun that does not refer to a specific person, place, or thing.

Some indefinite pronouns are singular. Others are plural. When an indefinite pronoun is used as a subject, the verb must agree in number. Study the indefinite pronouns in the chart below.

Indefinite Pronouns			
Singular			**Plural**
another	everybody	no one	both
anybody	everyone	nothing	few
anyone	everything	one	many
anything	much	somebody	others
each	neither	someone	several
either	nobody	something	

A few indefinite pronouns take a singular or plural verb, depending on the phrase that follows. These pronouns include *all, any, most, none,* and *some.*

Notice how these indefinite pronouns are used below.

> **Most** of the forest **lies** to the east. [singular]
> **Most** of those scientists **study** the process of respiration. [plural]
> **Some** of her lawn **is** brown. [singular]
> **Some** of the ferns **are** large. [plural]

The prepositional phrases include names that are singular or plural. To determine whether the verb should be singular or plural, look at the object of the preposition. For example, in the third sentence above, *some* refers to *lawn.* Because *lawn* is singular, the verb is singular. In the fourth sentence *some* refers to *ferns.* Because *ferns* is plural, the verb is plural.

514   *Subject-Verb Agreement*

Teacher's Classroom Resources

The following resources can be used for planning, instruction, practice, reinforcement, reteaching, or enrichment.

Teaching Tools
Lesson Plans

Blackline Masters
Grammar Practice, p. 41
Grammar Reteaching, p. 41
Grammar Enrichment, p. 41

Grammar Workbook
Lesson 28

Exercise 7 — Identifying Indefinite Pronouns

Write the indefinite pronoun from each sentence. Then write *singular* or *plural* to tell what verb form it takes.

1. All of the students are working in the science laboratory.
2. All of the needed information is printed in the lab manual.
3. Most of the steps are easy to carry out.
4. None of the laboratory equipment is dangerous to use.
5. Some of the results need to be explained to the class.
6. Most of the experiment concerns respiration.
7. Any of the lab stations have the needed equipment.
8. Some of the underlying theory is written on the chalkboard.
9. None of the lab reports have been written yet.
10. All of the oxygen is used up as the candle burns.

Exercise 8 — Using the Correct Verb Form with Indefinite Pronouns

Write the correct form of the verb in parentheses.

1. Much of the process of respiration (is, are) complex.
2. Few completely (understand, understands) it.
3. Many (study, studies) the two types of oxygen exchange.
4. Much (happen, happens) during the two processes.
5. Someone (explain, explains) the respiratory system.
6. Another of our problems (is, are) water pollution.
7. One (need, needs) understanding of the solutions.
8. Some of them (improve, improves) the water supply immediately.
9. Many (provide, provides) sensible approaches.
10. Either of the processes (clean, cleans) the water equally well.
11. Both of them (call, calls) for further study.
12. Neither (is, are) apparently preferable.
13. Most of the higher animals (have, has) lungs.
14. All of the oxygen exchange (occur, occurs) there.
15. Most of the processes (is, are) clearly written.
16. Nobody (deny, denies) the value of the project.
17. Many of the volunteers (work, works) diligently.
18. Any of the projects (need, needs) extra volunteers.
19. Most of the people (support, supports) conservation.
20. Several of the volunteers (suggest, suggests) ideas.

16.4 Indefinite Pronouns as Subjects **515**

Enabling Strategies

LEP Using Indefinite Pronouns

The indefinite pronouns *much, any,* and *many* are sometimes difficult for LEP students to relate to. *Much* is used to refer to mass or noncount nouns (*Do you earn <u>much</u> money?*) *Many* is used with count nouns (*I have <u>many</u> jobs*). *Any* may refer to either count or noncount items. It is used often in questions and in sentences with negative meaning (*Do you have any work this weekend? I haven't received any calls*).

FOCUS

Lesson Overview

Objective: To identify compound subjects and use correct compound subject–verb agreement

Bellringer

When students enter the classroom, have this assignment on the board: *Choose the verb: a. Autos and buses (creates, create) smog. b. They (creates, create) smog.*

Motivating Activity

Lead into a discussion of compound subjects and verb agreement by reviewing the answers *(create, create)* to a. and b. above.

TEACH

☑ Teaching Tips

Agreement errors sometimes occur when compound subjects are joined by *and*. In the sentence *A lot of work **and** a little luck is necessary for success,* the writer may be thinking of *work* and *luck* as a single entity. If an article is, or can be, used before the second noun (***A** lot of work and **a** little luck),* then the individual subjects name separate items and require a plural verb.

16.5 Agreement with Compound Subjects

A compound subject contains two or more simple subjects for the same verb. Compound subjects take either a singular or a plural verb, depending on how the parts of the subject are joined. When the simple subjects are joined by the coordinating conjunction *and* or by the correlative conjunction *both . . . and,* the verb is plural.

In all of the sentences below, the reference is to more than one place, thing, or idea.

> New York, Denver, **and** London **have** smog.
> **Both** automobiles **and** factories **create** smog.
> Air inversion **and** the absence of wind **aid** the conditions.

Occasionally *and* is used to join two words that are part of one unit or refer to a single person or thing. In these cases the subject is considered to be singular. In the sentence below, notice that *captain* and *leader* refer to the same person. Therefore, the singular form of the verb is used.

> The captain **and** leader of the air-testing team **is** Joan.

When two or more subjects are joined by the conjunctions *or* or *nor, either . . . or,* or *neither . . . nor,* the verb agrees with the subject that is closer to it.

> The city **or** the state **responds** to pollution complaints.
> **Either** smoke **or** gases **cause** the smog.

In the first sentence *responds* agrees with *state,* which is the subject noun closer to the verb. The verb is singular because the subject is singular. In the second sentence, *cause* agrees with *gases,* which is closer. The verb is plural because *gases* is plural.

516 *Subject-Verb Agreement*

Teacher's Classroom Resources

The following resources can be used for planning, instruction, practice, reinforcement, reteaching, or enrichment.

🔧 **Teaching Tools**
Lesson Plans, p. 99

📁 **Blackline Masters**
Grammar Practice, p. 39
Grammar Reteaching, p. 42
Grammar Enrichment, p. 39

📓 *Grammar Workbook*
Lesson 5

Exercise 9   Using the Correct Verb Form with Compound Subjects

Write the correct form of the verb in parentheses.

1. A savanna and a desert (is, are) next to each other.
2. Rain forests and deserts (make, makes) good study sites.
3. Jungles, forests, and bogs (has, have) different characteristics.
4. Both Caldwell and the girls (want, wants) to study swamps.
5. The researcher and author (is, are) the opening speaker at the conference.
6. Food, water, and air (is, are) essential to life.
7. Both food and oxygen (come, comes) from plants.
8. Plants and animals in a community (is, are) interdependent.
9. Both days and seasons (change, changes) natural systems.
10. The wind, the sun, and the tides (is, are) sources of energy.
11. Oil and natural gas (forms, form) today's major energy supply.
12. The group's teacher and leader (is, are) an expert on ecological issues.
13. Too much rain and snow (do, does) affect the area.
14. States, cities, and towns (have, has) responsibilities.
15. Air pollution and water pollution (responds, respond) to clean-up actions.
16. The engineer and head of the hiking club (is, are) the pollution inspector.
17. Trout and salmon (need, needs) clean water to survive.
18. Both temperature and acidity (is, are) measured every day.
19. Environmental club members and their leader (helps, help) measure temperature.
20. Both club members and their families (participates, participate) in the program.

Exercise 10   Identifying Compound Subjects

Write the compound subjects for each sentence. Then write *singular* or *plural* to tell what verb form they take.

1. Neither rain nor snow is predicted for the weekend's weather.
2. Television bulletins or radio announcements warn people to evacuate.
3. Either high winds or heavy rains pose a danger of flooding.
4. The town or the state assists in the evacuation efforts.
5. Either a fire fighter or a rescue worker knocks on each resident's door.
6. Either a state helicopter or local boats are used to rescue the stranded.
7. The school gym or the town hall offers a refuge from the storm.
8. Hot chocolate or coffee warms those chilled by the weather.
9. Either soup or sandwiches are provided for the rescue workers.
10. Neither levees nor a dam has been built for flood control.

16.5 Agreement with Compound Subjects   **517**

PRACTICE AND ASSESS

Answers: Exercise 9

1. are	11. form
2. make	12. is
3. have	13. does
4. want	14. have
5. is	15. respond
6. are	16. is
7. come	17. need
8. are	18. are
9. change	19. help
10. are	20. participate

Answers: Exercise 10

1. Neither rain nor snow; singular
2. Television bulletins or radio announcements; plural
3. Either high winds or heavy rains; plural
4. The town or the state; singular
5. Either a fire fighter or a rescue worker; singular
6. Either a state helicopter or local boats; plural
7. The school gym or the town hall; singular
8. Hot chocolate or coffee; singular
9. Either soup or sandwiches; plural
10. Neither levees nor a dam; singular

Independent Practice

Skills Practice

📁 *Grammar Practice,* p. 39
📁 *Grammar Reteaching,* p. 42
📁 *Grammar Enrichment,* p. 39

📕 *Grammar Workbook,* Lesson 5

CLOSE

Tell students that people affect nature. Ask them to describe what they think their neighborhood looked like before people changed it. Have them use some compound subjects.

Enabling Strategies

LEP Using Compound Subjects

To help students whose first language is not English determine the number of compound subjects joined by *and*, write each of the following words on small strips of cardboard: *he, she, it, they.* Students may use these pronouns to replace compound subjects in these sentences: *Brittany and Adam have gone fishing. Their companion and teacher is Mrs. Phipps.* If the subject can be replaced with *he, she,* or *it,* use a singular verb. If *they* replaces the subject, use a plural verb.

TEACH

About the Literature

Tell students that Diane Ackerman wrote about bats in part to dispel some of the myths that surround the misunderstood mammals.

Have students read the passage and discuss its general content. Then have them focus on the variety of highlighted examples of subject-verb agreement in the passage. Ask students how varying the sentence types makes this expository passage more interesting to read.

Linking Grammar and Literature

☑ Teaching Tip

Invite volunteers to read aloud from Diane Ackerman's essay. Call on several students to locate the subject in various sentences and to identify it as singular or plural. Analyze the sentences in which students had the most difficulty locating the subjects. Which kinds of subjects were the most difficult to identify as singular or plural?

Critical Thinking

Ask students to recall the various types of subject-verb agreement taught in the unit and to categorize the sentences in the passage according to these types.

Speaking and Listening

Have volunteers select sentences from the passage and read them aloud, first with a singular subject then with a plural subject, while at the same time keeping the verbs as they appear in the selection. As each pair of sentences is read, have the rest of the students raise their hands when they hear the subject-verb agreement they think is correct.

518

UNIT

16

Unit Review

Grammar Review

Subject-Verb Agreement

To learn about bats, journalist Diane Ackerman accompanied a world authority on the subject to a cave in Texas. In the following excerpt from her essay "Bats," the writer observes an emergence of Mexican free-tailed bats. The passage has been annotated to show some examples of subject-verb agreement covered in this unit.

Literature Model

from BATS

by Diane Ackerman

Agreement between a singular subject and verb in an inverted sentence →

In the early evening, I take my seat in a natural amphitheater of limestone boulders, in the Texas hill country; at the bottom of the slope is a wide, dark cave mouth. Nothing stirs yet in its depths. But I have been promised one of the wonders of our age. Deep inside the cavern, twenty million Mexican free-tailed bats are hanging up by their toes. They are the largest known concentration of warm-blooded animals in the world. Soon, at dusk, all twenty million of them will fly out to feed, in a living volcano that scientists call an "emergence. . . ."

Agreement between a plural pronoun subject and a plural verb →

A hawk appears, swoops, grabs a stray bat out of the sky, and disappears with it. In a moment, the hawk returns, but hearing his wings coming, the bats in the column all shift sidewise to confuse him, and he misses. As wave upon wave of bats pours out of the cave, their collective wings begin to sound like drizzle on autumn leaves.

Agreement between a plural subject and a verb that have a prepositional phrase between them →

518 *Subject-Verb Agreement*

Teacher's Classroom Resources

The following resources can be used for planning, instruction, practice, reinforcement, assessment, reteaching, enrichment, or evaluation.

🗲 **Teaching Tools**
Lesson Plans, p. 99

📖 ***Grammar Workbook***
Lessons 53–57
Unit 9 Review
Cumulative Review: Units 1–9

Unit Assessment

🗁 *Tests with Answer Key*
Unit 16 Mastery Test, pp. 63–64

🖳 *Test Generator*
Unit 16 Mastery Test

Exercise 1

Making Verbs Agree with Noun and Pronoun Subjects   Write the correct form of the verb in parentheses.

1. Snakes (prowls, prowl) by the cave mouth, hunting for fallen bats.
2. A researcher (puts, put) on protective clothing before entering the cave.
3. Free-tailed bats (cruises, cruise) at thirty-five miles an hour.
4. The cave (stretches, stretch) 1,000 feet into the limestone hill.
5. It (averages, average) sixty feet in diameter.
6. Many researchers (comes, come) to see the emergence of the bats.
7. They (finds, find) the sight of the bats awe-inspiring.
8. A hawk (grabs, grab) a stray bat out of the sky.
9. The bats' wings (sounds, sound) like drizzle on autumn leaves.
10. Diane Ackerman (compares, compare) the emergence to a volcano.

Exercise 2

Making Forms of _Be, Do,_ and _Have_ Agree with Subjects   Write the correct form of the verb in parentheses.

SAMPLE   Diane Ackerman (is, are) interested in the behavior of bats.
ANSWER   is

1. Bats (is, are) warm-blooded animals.
2. Ackerman (does, do) seem interested in the study of bats.
3. This cave (is, are) a nursery full of mothers and their babies.
4. The cave mouth (is, are) at the bottom of the slope.
5. The spectators (has, have) a splendid view of the emerging bats.
6. Researchers (has, have) carried out many studies of this bat population.
7. Bats (does, do) sleep upside down.
8. A bat (is, are) the only mammal with the ability to fly.
9. A bat (do, does) have a good sense of smell.
10. Some people (has, have) a fear of bats.

Grammar Review   **519**

PRACTICE AND ASSESS

Answers: Exercise 1
1. prowl
2. puts
3. cruise
4. stretches
5. averages
6. come
7. find
8. grabs
9. sound
10. compares

Answers: Exercise 2
1. are
2. does
3. is
4. is
5. have
6. have
7. do
8. is
9. does
10. have

UNIT 16
Review

Answers: Exercise 3

1. In the cave <u>are</u> 20 million <u>bats</u>.
2. The <u>hawk</u>, a predator with keen eyes, <u>swoops</u> down upon a bat.
3. Here <u>is</u> a vivid <u>example</u> of a predator-prey relationship.
4. The <u>bats</u>, reacting to the hawk, <u>shift</u> their position sidewise.
5. <u>Do</u> the <u>bats</u> <u>rely</u> on echolocation to know the hawk's position?
6. The scientific <u>name</u> for bats <u>is</u> *Chiroptera,* meaning "hand wing."
7. There <u>are</u> forty different <u>kinds</u> of bats in North America.
8. <u>Is</u> there a <u>law</u> protecting colonies of bats?
9. The reproductive <u>rate</u> of bats <u>is</u> quite low.
10. Here <u>is</u> an important <u>reason</u> to protect bat colonies.

Answers: Exercise 4

1. give
2. take
3. raises
4. is
5. pass
6. is
7. cling
8. has
9. travels
10. represents

Exercise 3

Locating Subjects and Making Verbs Agree   Write each sentence, choosing the correct form of the verb in parentheses. Underline the simple subject once and the verb twice.

SAMPLE   The bats inside the dark cave (hangs, hang) upside down.
ANSWER   The <u>bats</u> inside the dark cave <u>hang</u> upside down.

1. In the cave (is, are) 20 million bats.
2. The hawk, a predator with keen eyes, (swoop, swoops) down upon a bat.
3. Here (is, are) a vivid example of a predator-prey relationship.
4. The bats, reacting to the hawk, (shifts, shift) their position sidewise.
5. (Does, Do) the bats rely on echolocation to know the hawk's position?
6. The scientific name for bats (is, are) *Chiroptera*, meaning "hand wing."
7. There (is, are) forty different kinds of bats in North America.
8. (Is, Are) there a law protecting colonies of bats?
9. The reproductive rate of bats (is, are) quite low.
10. Here (is, are) an important reason to protect bat colonies.

Exercise 4

Making Verbs Agree with Collective Nouns and Other Special Subjects
Write the correct form of the verb in parentheses.

1. Binoculars (gives, give) the researchers a clear view of the bats.
2. The research team (takes, take) their seats on the boulders.
3. The bat colony (raises, raise) the temperature inside the cave.
4. Twenty million (is, are) an estimate of the cave's bat population.
5. For those watching the bats, the hours (passes, pass) quickly.
6. "Bats" (is, are) an entertaining and informative essay.
7. The colony (clings, cling) to their roosts on the cave ceiling.
8. *National Geographic* (has, have) published several good articles on bats.
9. News (travels, travel) quickly among the individuals in a bat colony.
10. This colony (represents, represent) the world's largest concentration of warm-blooded animals.

Exercise 5

Making Verbs Agree with Indefinite Pronoun Subjects   Write the correct form of the verb in parentheses.

1. Everyone (has, have) an opinion about bats.
2. Many (fears, fear) the animals.
3. Few (knows, know) very much about them.
4. Most of the folklore (is, are) untrue.
5. Few (lives, live) in belfries.
6. Everyone (thinks, think) that bats get in people's hair.
7. Nobody (recognizes, recognize) how helpful bats are.
8. Much (remains, remain) to be learned about bats.
9. Some of the species (uses, use) high-frequency sounds to navigate in the dark.
10. Most of these sounds (extends, extend) beyond the range of human hearing.

Exercise 6

Making Verbs Agree with Compound Subjects   Write the correct form of the verb in parentheses.

1. Both snakes and hawks (preys, prey) on bats.
2. Neither the flying fox nor the vampire bat (hibernates, hibernate) in winter.
3. Fruit or insects (provides, provide) food for bats.
4. Either fear or ignorance (accounts, account) for the way many people react to seeing bats.
5. Caves and hollow trees (provides, provide) roosts for bats.
6. Both migration and hibernation (is, are) ways of coping with cold winter weather.
7. Either migration or hibernation (protects, protect) bats from the cold.
8. Both the sense of sight and the sense of smell (is, are) well developed in bats.
9. Either plant nectar or plant pollen (is, are) consumed by some bats.
10. The head scientist and leader of the bat research team (is, are) Dr. Tuttle.

Grammar Review   **521**

Answers: Exercise 5
1. has
2. fear
3. know
4. is
5. live
6. thinks
7. recognizes
8. remains
9. use
10. extend

Answers: Exercise 6
1. prey
2. hibernates
3. provide
4. accounts
5. provide
6. are
7. protects
8. are
9. is
10. is

UNIT 16
Review

Answers: Exercise 7
Proofreading

This proofreading activity provides editing practice with (1) the current or previous units' skills, (2) the **Troubleshooter** errors, and (3) spelling errors. Students should be able to complete the exercise by referring to the units, the **Troubleshooter**, and a dictionary. (Note: A run-on sentence counts as one error.)

	Error (Type of Error)
1.	• reflect (subject–verb agreement)
2.	• imposes (subject-verb agreement)
	• world. The *or* world; *or* world, and (run-on sentence)
	• is (subject–verb agreement)
3.	• hidden (spelling)
4.	• Mexican (proper adjective)
5.	• suggests (subject–verb agreement)
	• necessary (spelling)
6.	• fight (subject–verb agreement)
7.	• are (subject–verb agreement)

Answers: Exercise 8
Mixed Review

1. has
2. is
3. care
4. responds
5. is
6. distinguish
7. identifies
8. do
9. are
10. revolve

Exercise 7

This passage is about the artist Leonard Koscianski, whose work appears on the opposite page. Rewrite the passage, correcting the errors in spelling, capitalization, grammar, and usage. Add any missing punctuation. There are ten errors.

Leonard Koscianski

[1]Many of Leonard Koscianski's paintings reflects his concern with issues affecting the earth's future, such as environmental pollution. [2]The painter believes that human society impose an artificial order on the world, the result of such interference are a disruption of the balance of nature.

[3]In *Forest Spirit*, for example, the artist represents the natural order in the forest, where a hawk swoops down to attack hiden prey. [4]Like the mexican free-tailed bats in "Bats," the prey is seized and killed. [5]Koscianski suggest that such activities are neccesary to maintain the natural balance. [6]Besides, many animals fights back. [7]Most of the bats in Ackerman's essay is able to protect themselves and escape.

Mixed Review

Exercise 8

Write the correct verbs in parentheses.

Diane Ackerman, the author of "Bats," [1](has, have) also written essays about other animals. "White Lanterns" [2](is, are) the title of her essay about young penguins being raised at Sea World in California. Scientists and volunteers [3](care, cares) for the young animals by feeding and holding them.

A baby penguin exhibits thigmotaxis, the drive to press up hard against a parent. In the wild either the mother or the father [4](respond, responds) to the youngster. A colony of penguins [5](is, are) filled with the whistles of the young birds. Parents, in the midst of this noise, [6](distinguish, distinguishes) the whistles of their own offspring.

Everybody [7](identify, identifies) with penguins. Why [8](does, do) we have this reaction? There [9](is, are) many possible explanations. Most of these explanations [10](revolve, revolves) around the similarities between penguins and people. As Ackerman says, we see penguins "as little humanoids."

522 *Subject-Verb Agreement*

Leonard Koscianski, *Forest Spirit,* **1991**

Grammar Review **523**

CLOSE

Pair students and have them choose an article from the newspaper or a magazine. Ask them to highlight the subjects and verbs and discuss subject-verb agreement in the highlighted sentences. Invite them to share any errors or unusual examples they found.

About the Art

Leonard Koscianski, *Forest Spirit,*
1991

Leonard Koscianski conveys in his painting the primitive power of nature. In *Forest Spirit,* for example, the hawks are hunting and attacking their prey. The landscape in the painting, with its thick undergrowth and tangled trees, contributes to the sense of raw, overwhelming nature. This 1991 oil-on-canvas painting measures 48 by 36 inches and is in a private collection.

Subject-Verb Agreement in Writing

Have students read the passage from *Always to Remember* silently. Then ask them to discuss the subject-verb agreements in the passage.

Techniques with Subject-Verb Agreement

Discuss the writing techniques mentioned using the elements from the passage *Always to Remember*. Ask students to create their own examples for both of these techniques. Then ask them to apply the techniques to the Proofreading paragraphs on page 522.

Practice

The answers to this challenging and enriching activity will vary. Refer to Techniques with Subject-Verb Agreement as you evaluate student choices. Sample answers:

My family <u>supports</u> local sports. Both my parents <u>attend</u> most of the football, baseball, and soccer games that <u>are</u> played here. My brother Ken and I sometimes even <u>travel</u> with the team to road games. Citizens, especially those whose children participate in sports, <u>demonstrate</u> their support most effectively by being present. Burnsville's athletes <u>perform</u> better when their friends and family <u>rally</u> around them. We, the cheering squad for your local sports teams, <u>invite</u> you to join us at the next game.

Writing Application

Subject-Verb Agreement in Writing Lack of subject-verb agreement will distract readers from the information you wish to convey. Examine the passage below from *Always to Remember*, noting how Brent Ashabranner keeps his subjects and verbs in agreement. Focus especially on the italicized words.

> *Maya Lin,* reporters soon discovered, *was* a Chinese-American girl who had been born and raised in the small midwestern city of Athens, Ohio. *Her father,* Henry Huan Lin, *was* a ceramicist of considerable reputation and dean of fine arts at Ohio University in Athens. *Her mother,* Julia C. Lin, *was* a poet and professor of Oriental and English literature. Maya Lin's *parents were* born to culturally prominent families in China.

Techniques with Subject-Verb Agreement Check carefully for agreement when you write your work.

1. When checking for subject-verb agreement, remember to bypass phrases that come between a subject and its verb. Compare the following:
Harder to check *Maya Lin,* reporters soon discovered, *was* a Chinese American girl.
Easier to check *Maya Lin was* a Chinese American girl.

2. Be careful about subject-verb agreement when subjects include more than one word. Identify the most important words before checking for agreement:
Incorrect agreement Maya Lin's parents *was* born to
Correct agreement Maya Lin's *parents were* born to

Practice Complete the following passage on a separate sheet of paper. In each blank, write a present-tense verb that agrees with the subject noun or pronoun.

   My family _____ local sports. Both my parents _____ most of the football, baseball, and soccer games that _____ played here. My brother Ken and I sometimes even _____ with the team to road games. Citizens, especially those whose children participate in sports, _____ their support most effectively by being present. Burnsville's athletes _____ better when their friends and family _____ around them. We, the cheering squad for your local sports teams, _____ you to join us at the next game!

Teacher's Classroom Resources

The following resources can be used for assessment or evaluation.

Unit Assessment

📁 *Tests with Answer Key*
Unit 16 Mastery Test, pp. 63–64

📀 *Test Generator*
Unit 16 Mastery Test

You may wish to administer the Unit 16 Mastery Test at this point.

<table>
<tr><td>UNIT
17</td><td colspan="2">**Glossary of Special
Usage Problems**</td></tr>
<tr><td>Grammar</td><td>Lessons</td></tr>
</table>

525

UNIT GOALS

The goal of Unit 17 is to help students, through example and instruction, to develop an understanding of and an ability to use words and phrases that often present usage problems. Three glossaries provide definitions and examples of words that are commonly confused or misused because they sound alike or have similar meanings.

Unit Assessment
📁 *Tests with Answer Key*
Unit 17 Pretest, pp. 65–66
Unit 17 Mastery Test, pp. 67–68

💿 *Test Generator*
Unit 17 Pretest Test
Unit 17 Mastery Test

You may wish to administer the Unit 17 Pretest at this point.

Key to Ability Levels
Enabling Strategies have been coded for varying learning styles and abilities.

L1 Level 1 activities are within the ability range of Learning Disabled students.

L2 Level 2 activities are basic-to-average activities and are within the ability range of average students.

L3 Level 3 activities are challenging activities and are within the ability range of above-average students.

LEP LEP activities are within the ability range of Limited English Proficiency students.

Lesson 17.1 teaches students to distinguish between similar words that are often confused in writing.

FOCUS

Lesson Overview

Objective: To distinguish between confusingly similar words

Bellringer

When students enter the classroom, have this assignment on the board: *Make a list of pairs of similar words that you often confuse in your writing.*

Motivating Activity

Discuss students' answers to the Bellringer exercise and list pairs of similar words on the board. Have students give reasons why they confuse these words. Emphasize that thinking of the meaning of each word will help them to avoid confusion as they write a sentence.

TEACH

☑ Grammar Tip

Except is occasionally used as a verb meaning "to exclude," but it is more often used as a preposition.

⤭ Cross-reference: Dictionary and Thesaurus

Remind students that a dictionary is a good source for checking the correct usage of a word. For instruction and practice on how to use a dictionary, refer students to Lesson 22.7, pp. 623–626.

526

17.1 Using Troublesome Words I

Like all languages English contains a number of confusing expressions. The following glossary will help you understand some of the more troublesome ones.

Word	Meaning	Example
accept except	"to receive" "other than"	We do not readily **accept** new ideas. Few **except** scientists understand them.
all ready already	"completely prepared" "before" or "by this time"	They are **all ready** for new ideas. Ideas have **already** changed.
all together altogether	"in a group" "completely"	The planets **all together** weigh less than the sun. Most stars are **altogether** too distant to study.
a lot	"very much" *A lot* is two words. Its meaning is vague; avoid using it.	**A lot** of stars can't be seen. [vague] Thousands of stars can't be seen. [more precise]
beside besides	"next to" "in addition to"	In May the moon appeared **beside** Mars. **Besides** Saturn, Jupiter and Uranus have rings.
between among	Use *between* for two people or things. Use *among* when talking about groups of three or more.	Mercury is **between** Venus and the sun. Meteor trails are seen **among** the stars.
bring take	"to carry from a distant place to a closer one" "to carry from a nearby place to a more distant one"	Astronomers **bring** exhibits to schools. Students will **take** the model planets home.
can may	indicates ability expresses permission or possibility	We **can** see Pluto with a telescope. **May** we see the charts?
choose chose	"to select" "selected"	**Choose** a planet to study. Last year we **chose** Mars.

526   *Glossary of Special Usage Problems*

Teacher's Classroom Resources

The following resources can be used for planning, instruction, practice, reinforcement, assessment, reteaching, enrichment, or evaluation.

⚒ Teaching Tools
Lesson Plans, p. 100

📁 Blackline Masters
Grammar Practice, p. 42
Grammar Reteaching, p. 43
Grammar Enrichment, p. 42

📖 Grammar Workbook
Lessons 68–69

Unit Assessment

📁 Tests with Answer Key
Unit 17 Pretest, pp. 65–66

📷 Test Generator
Unit 17 Pretest

You may wish to administer the Unit 17 Pretest at this point.

Exercise 1   Choosing the Correct Word

For each sentence write the correct word or words in parentheses.

1. Our galaxy is one (among, between) many.
2. There may be more galaxies (beside, besides) the ones we know.
3. Many people (accept, except) the idea that space is endless.
4. (Can, May) we use that telescope?
5. (Bring, Take) a compass to the lab when you go.
6. Galaxies are (all together, altogether) too numerous.
7. The students were outdoors (all ready, already) to study the night sky.
8. The instructor (choose, chose) a hill away from the glare of city lights.
9. "Stand (beside, besides) me," he told the class.
10. We stood (all together, altogether), looking at the stars.

Exercise 2   Using the Correct Word

For each sentence write the correct word or words from the lesson. Use the clues in parentheses to help you.

1. We _____ see Pluto through this telescope. (have the ability)
2. Before today we'd observed every planet _____ Pluto. (other than)
3. Scientists have _____ learned a great deal about comets. (by this time)
4. They will _____ our class a meteorite. (carry to a closer place)
5. We will _____ the meteorite home. (carry to a farther place)
6. The instructor told us to _____ a partner. (select)
7. I _____ Marjorie Hall for my partner. (selected)
8. The partners were to share observations _____ themselves. (two people)
9. If you look over there, you _____ see the Big Dipper. (are able to)
10. There was a murmur of agreement _____ the students. (three or more people)
11. We learned the ancient Greeks named forty-eight constellations _____. (in all)
12. We _____ knew that the constellations have Latin names. (by this time)
13. The Big Dipper stars are _____ those of Ursa Major. (three or more things)
14. The instructor said, "You _____ use my telescope." (expresses permission)
15. I will gladly _____ his offer. (receive)
16. _____ the Big Dipper is the Little Dipper. (Next to)
17. There are two ways you might _____ to locate the North Star. (select)
18. Follow a line _____ the stars in the front of the Big Dipper's cup. (two things)
19. You _____ also see it as the end of the Little Dipper's handle. (are able to)
20. The students will _____ many ideas away with them. (carry to a farther place)

17.1 Using Troublesome Words I   **527**

PRACTICE AND ASSESS

Answers: Exercise 1

1. among	**6.** altogether
2. besides	**7.** all ready
3. accept	**8.** chose
4. May	**9.** beside
5. Take	**10.** all together

Answers: Exercise 2

1. can	**11.** altogether
2. except	**12.** already
3. already	**13.** among
4. bring	**14.** may
5. take	**15.** accept
6. choose	**16.** Beside
7. chose	**17.** choose
8. between	**18.** between
9. can	**19.** can
10. among	**20.** take

Independent Practice

Skills Practice

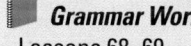 *Grammar Practice*, p. 42
Grammar Reteaching, p. 43
Grammar Enrichment, p. 42

Grammar Workbook,
Lessons 68–69

CLOSE

Have students work with a partner and write one sentence for each pair of words on page 526 that helps distinguish their respective meanings. (Sample: *I accept the most improved player award except I cannot attend the banquet to receive it.*) Have students share their sentences with the class.

Enabling Strategies

LEP Collecting Word Pairs

Ask students to create a class notebook of the sentences developed in the CLOSE activity. Pair students so that one member is more fluent in English. Have them practice reading the sentences to each other and explaining the meanings of the word pairs.

L2 Using Troublesome Words

Have students use their glossaries to complete Exercises 1 and 2. They choose the word they think is correct and read each sentence aloud, substituting the meaning from the glossary. If the sentence doesn't make sense, they try the definition for the other word in the pair.

Setting the Purpose

Lesson 17.2 teaches students to distinguish between similar words that are often confused in writing.

FOCUS

Lesson Overview

Objective: To help students distinguish between confusingly similar words

Bellringer

When students enter the classroom, have this assignment on the board: *On a piece of paper, write the word in each sentence that seems to be misused: 1. Marty can learn anyone to play the guitar. 2. Jill has had less lessons than Barb. 3. Yesterday Barb laid down for a nap and missed her lesson. 4. Phil always looses his music.*

Motivating Activity

Discuss students' answers in the Bellringer assignment. Point out that knowing when to use certain words can be confusing and that students need to pay special attention to these words when they write.

TEACH

☑ Teaching Tip

Tell students that *to lay* something down is "to cause it to lie." *To lie* means "to recline." Remind students that the past tense of *lie* is *lay*. Therefore, students need to decide whether an action is being caused in order to make the correct verb choice for a sentence. Using this strategy, have students read the following sentences, making corrections if needed. 1. *Lie* the book on the table, please. 2. Yesterday, Ben's dog *laid* down on my homework. 3. Ben *lay* the bone in Duffie's dish. (Answers: *lay, lay, lay*)

17.2 Using Troublesome Words II

Word	Meaning	Example
fewer	Use in comparisons with nouns that can be counted.	There are **fewer** sunspots this year than last year.
less	Use in comparisons with nouns that cannot be counted.	Mars has **less** gravitational force than Earth.
formally	the adverb form of *formal*	The sun is **formally** a star.
formerly	"in times past"	Pluto was **formerly** thought to be a moon
in	"inside"	Our sun is **in** the Milky Way.
into	indicates movement from outside to a point within	Meteorites fall **into** the atmosphere.
its	the possessive form of *it*	A comet wobbles in **its** orbit.
it's	the contraction of *it is*	**It's** difficult to see Neptune.
lay	"to put" or "to place"	**Lay** the charts on the table.
lie	"to recline" or "to be positioned"	Layers of dust **lie** on the moon.
learn	"to receive knowledge"	Astronauts **learn** astronomy as part of their training.
teach	"to give knowledge"	Many astronomers **teach** at colleges.
leave	"to go away"	We will **leave** after the eclipse.
let	"to allow"	The school **let** us use the telescope.
loose	"not firmly attached"	Scientists gather **loose** particles in space and bring them back to study.
lose	"to misplace" or "to fail to win"	Comets **lose** particles.
many	Use with nouns that can be counted.	We know the weight of **many** stars.
much	Use with nouns that cannot be counted.	**Much** of the weight is gas.
precede	"to go or come before"	Typewriters **preceded** computers.
proceed	"to continue"	*Voyager 2* will **proceed** to Neptune.

528 *Glossary of Special Usage Problems*

Teacher's Classroom Resources

The following resources can be used for planning, instruction, practice, reinforcement, reteaching, or enrichment.

🔧 **Teaching Tools**
Lesson Plans

📁 **Blackline Masters**
Grammar Practice, p. 42
Grammar Reteaching, p. 43
Grammar Enrichment, p. 42

📖 *Grammar Workbook*
Lessons 70–71

Exercise 3 — Choosing the Correct Word

For each sentence write the correct word in parentheses.

1. There are (many, much) kinds of telescopes.
2. Astronomers were (formally, formerly) limited by crude optics.
3. *Voyager 2* is traveling deep (in, into) space.
4. A telescope's power is determined by the size of (its, it's) lens.
5. Our astronomy club is (formally, formerly) organized.
6. Our astronomy club has (fewer, less) than five telescopes.
7. I write my astronomy notes (in, into) a notebook.
8. I (lay, lie) the notebook on the ground beside me while I use a telescope.
9. My young brother wants me to (learn, teach) him about the stars.
10. Tonight I will (precede, proceed) to give him his first lesson.

Exercise 4 — Using the Correct Word

For each sentence write the correct word from the lesson. Use the clues in parentheses to help you.

1. Volcanoes _____ erupted on the moon. (in times past)
2. I can _____ on the ground for hours, looking at the sky. (recline)
3. _____ that telescope stay where it is! (allow)
4. A _____ lens will make a telescope inoperable. (not firmly attached)
5. Astronomers _____ from space probes. (receive knowledge)
6. Astronomy involves _____ study. (amount that cannot be counted)
7. That study must _____ the field work. (go before)
8. Those not willing to study should _____ the class. (go away from)
9. More observation and _____ memory is needed. (amount that cannot be counted)
10. Like the stars, the earth was _____ a glowing sphere. (in times past)
11. Some planets have _____ moons. (amount that can be counted)
12. Our sun can be _____ defined as a giant ball of hot gases. (in a formal manner)
13. Planets are dark, solid bodies _____ space. (inside)
14. _____ than three are closer than Earth to the sun. (countable comparison)
15. Over time, stars _____ their heat and light. (misplace)
16. At night stars and planets look _____ alike. (amount that cannot be counted)
17. I can _____ you how to tell a star from a planet. (give knowledge)
18. A planet may glow, but _____ light is not like a star's. (possessive of *it*)
19. Relative to stars, planets do not always _____ in the same place. (be positioned)
20. You will _____ that our galaxy has 100 billion stars. (receive knowledge)

17.2 Using Troublesome Words II   **529**

TEACH

☑ **Teaching Tip**
Both *precede* and *proceed* have the same root word, *cede,* meaning "to go." The prefix *pre-* means "before." In the word *proceed,* the prefix *pro-* means "forward."

PRACTICE AND ASSESS

Answers: Exercise 3
1. many   6. fewer
2. formerly   7. in
3. into   8. lay
4. its   9. teach
5. formally   10. proceed

Answers: Exercise 4
1. formerly   11. many
2. lie   12. formally
3. Let   13. in
4. loose   14. Fewer
5. learn   15. lose
6. much   16. much
7. precede   17. teach
8. leave   18. its
9. less   19. lie
10. formerly 20. learn

Independent Practice

Skills Practice
📁 *Grammar Practice,* p. 42
📁 *Grammar Reteaching,* p. 43
📁 *Grammar Enrichment,* p. 42

📖 *Grammar Workbook,* Lessons 70–71

CLOSE

Have students choose five pairs of words from the chart on page 528 and use each correctly in a sentence.

Enabling Strategies

L2 **Using *Less* and *Fewer* Correctly**

Ask students to brainstorm a list of nouns having to do with *food* and *cooking*. Have them categorize the nouns into nouns that can be counted and nouns that cannot be counted. Then have them work in pairs to write sentences using the words *less* and *fewer* with nouns in their list. Provide the following examples as models: *I needed fewer eggs for the cookies than the recipe stated. It took me less time than I thought to mix the batter.* Point out that a general rule to follow is that *less* is used with nouns that cannot be counted, and *fewer* is used with plural nouns, items that can be counted.

529

Lesson 17.3 teaches students to distinguish between words that appear to be similar or the same and are often confused in writing.

FOCUS

Lesson Overview

Objective: To distinguish between confusingly similar words

Bellringer

When students enter the classroom, have this assignment on the board: *Write two words that sound like the word* there *but are spelled differently. Try using all three words in one sentence.*

Motivating Activity

Discuss various uses for the words *there, their,* and *they're.* Have students suggest how they might help themselves remember the appropriate use of each word.

TEACH

Critical Thinking

The verbs *lay, raise,* and *set* have something in common. They are all causative verbs, meaning to cause something to happen. For example, to *raise* is to cause something to *rise.* Invite students to devise a chart that compares and contrasts *lay* and *lie, raise* and *rise,* and *set* and *sit.*

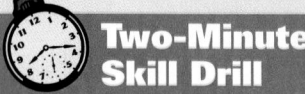

Two-Minute Skill Drill

Ask students to use one of these word pairs in a sentence: *quiet, quite; raise, rise; your, you're*

17.3   Using Troublesome Words III

Word	Meaning	Example
quiet	"silent" or "motionless"	It is very **quiet** in outer space.
quite	"completely" or "entirely"	It is **quite** dark in outer space.
raise	"to cause to move upward"	**Raise** heavy binoculars with a tripod.
rise	"to move upward"	The stars **rise** into view.
set	"to place" or "to put"	She **set** the camera down carefully.
sit	"to place oneself in a seated position"	Let's **sit** and watch the sky.
than	introduces the second part of a comparison	The sun is denser **than** the earth.
then	"at that time"	Choose a planet, and **then** locate it.
their	the possessive form of *they*	Ask **their** advice about lenses.
they're	the contraction of *they are*	**They're** using special night lenses.
theirs	"that or those belonging to them"	**Theirs** is a reflecting telescope.
there's	the contraction of *there is*	**There's** also a refracting telescope in our observatory.
to	"in the direction of"	Let's go **to** the observatory.
too	"also" or "excessively"	Why don't you come, **too**?
two	the number after one	We have only **two** telescopes in our observatory.
where at	Do not use *at* after *where* to indicate what place.	**Where** is the Milky Way? [not *Where is the Milky Way at?*]
who's	the contraction of *who is*	**Who's** a famous astronomer?
whose	the possessive form of *who*	**Whose** discoveries are the most significant?
your	the possessive form of *you*	I liked **your** essay about Mars.
you're	the contraction of *you are*	**You're** looking at the North Star.

530   *Glossary of Special Usage Problems*

Teacher's Classroom Resources

The following resources can be used for planning, instruction, practice, reinforcement, reteaching, or enrichment.

Teaching Tools
Lesson Plans

Blackline Masters
Grammar Practice, p. 42
Grammar Reteaching, p. 43
Grammar Enrichment, p. 42

Grammar Workbook
Lessons 71–72

Exercise 5 — Choosing the Correct Word

For each sentence write the correct word in parentheses.

1. Jupiter's moons look stationary, but (they're, their) always in orbit.
2. Pluto is smaller (than, then) the other planets.
3. (Who's, Whose) bringing the camera to the site?
4. (Set, Sit) the tripod over there.
5. Each of the planets is (quite, quiet) different in color.
6. (Your, You're) sure to see Venus tonight.
7. (Who's, Whose) count of Saturn's rings is correct?
8. Most observers (sit, set) in deck chairs.
9. (Theirs, There's) Venus now!
10. You can see it if you look (to, too, two) your right.

Exercise 6 — Using the Correct Word

For each sentence write the correct word from the lesson. Use the clues in parentheses to help you.

1. Our friends will bring _____ compass and camera. (possessive form of *they*)
2. The telescope is _____. (that belonging to them)
3. The observation site is on a _____ hill. (calm)
4. The night sky can be _____ stunning. (completely)
5. Venus will _____ soon. (move upward)
6. We will _____ our eyes and our spirits. (cause to move upward)
7. _____ our watch will begin. (at that time)
8. I hope it's not _____ cold. (excessively)
9. Mercury and Venus are _____ planets between Earth and the sun. (a number)
10. I wonder _____ turn it is to use the new telescope. (possessive of *who*)
11. You must _____ your telescope a few degrees to see Mars. (move upward)
12. It is very _____ here, away from the noise of the city. (silent)
13. Find the closest planets, _____ find the farthest ones. (at that time)
14. _____ going to make a model of the inner planets? (contraction of *who is*)
15. Outer planets are hard to model because _____ distant. (contraction of *they are*)
16. Which planets are _____ far away to see without a telescope? (excessively)
17. It looks as though _____ a white streak in the sky. (contraction of *there is*)
18. I think _____ referring to the Milky Way galaxy. (contraction of *you are*)
19. That's the galaxy _____ we live. (in what place)
20. It's bigger _____ it looks and contains billions of stars. (part of a comparison)

17.3 Using Troublesome Words III   **531**

UNIT 17
Lesson 17.3

PRACTICE AND ASSESS

Answers: Exercise 5

1. they're	6. You're
2. than	7. Whose
3. Who's	8. sit
4. Set	9. There's
5. quite	10. to

Answers: Exercise 6

1. their	11. raise
2. theirs	12. quiet
3. quiet	13. then
4. quite	14. Who's
5. rise	15. they're
6. raise	16. too
7. Then	17. there's
8. too	18. you're
9. two	19. where
10. whose	20. than

Independent Practice

Skills Practice
📁 *Grammar Practice*, p. 42
📁 *Grammar Reteaching*, p. 43
📁 *Grammar Enrichment*, p. 42

📓 **Grammar Workbook,**
Lessons 71–72

CLOSE

Have students write on an index card or small piece of paper those words in Unit 17 that they find problematic. Suggest that next to each word, they include a short clue or hint that will help them remember the correct usage. Encourage them to keep their cards in an accessible place so they can refer to them when writing.

Enabling Strategies

LEP Using *Set* Correctly

Set has several uses that can cause confusion for students whose first language is not English. Share and discuss the following examples: (a) *Please set the table*. (b) *The sun sets in the west*. Point out that in (a) *set* does not have the causative meaning of "causing the table to sit." It has an idiomatic meaning of "to prepare the table for eating." In (b) *set* tells the action of the subject *sun*. Have students write and share their own sentences using the word *set* to show its different uses and meanings.

TEACH

About the Literature

The passage from "Star Fever" by Judith Herbst discusses her and other people's fascination with stars and planets. The passage explains how the stars help people. After students read the passage, discuss how the context for each highlighted word gives clues about the word's meaning. Without the context, students could not know how the words should be spelled.

Linking Grammar and Literature

☑ Teaching Tip

Ask students to look up each word highlighted in the literature passage. Discuss the rule that governs the usage of each item. How might the sentences be rewritten to use another form of the highlighted words? For example, "*It's* not so crazy" could become, "To imagine a particular star and *its* terrain isn't so crazy."

Critical Thinking

Recalling the rules for special usage problems can be much easier if students use memory devices. For example, when deciding between the spellings *loose* and *lose*, a student might decide that *lose* has *lost* one of its *o*'s. Ask students to share with each other any devices they have created to recall rules for the highlighted words and other words in this unit.

UNIT

17

Unit Review

Grammar Review

Glossary of Special Usage Problems

In her essay "Star Fever," Judith Herbst discusses people's age-old fascination with stars. In the following passage, Herbst considers the worlds that may lie beyond our vision. She also explains the usefulness of the stars. The passage has been annotated to show some troublesome words covered in this unit.

Literature Model

from STAR FEVER
by Judith Herbst

Lie, meaning "to recline"

It's, contraction of *it is*

Rise, meaning "to move upward"

You're, contraction of *you are*

I love the stars. Sometimes I lie awake at night and think about them. I imagine that they all have planets with strange forms of life. I see red, rugged landscapes bathed in the glare of two suns, one swollen and scarlet, the other a cold steel blue. I see steamy tropical planets covered with silver vines that snake in and out of silver trees. I see planets with methane oceans and iron mountains. It's not so crazy. They could be out there, you know. . . .

The stars not only mark the seasons, they also tell you where north, south, east, and west are. Stars " rise " in the east and "set" in the west, so all you have to do is look for the appearance of a new constellation. If you see one that wasn't there an hour before, you're facing east. Once you know east it's a snap to find the other three directions. Just look behind you for west, to the right side for south, and to the left for north.

As you can imagine, without the compass the early sailors absolutely relied on the stars to find their way around. There are no landmarks on the high seas.

532 *Glossary of Special Usage Problems*

Teacher's Classroom Resources

The following resources can be used for planning, instruction, practice, reinforcement, assessment, reteaching, enrichment, or evaluation.

🔧 **Teaching Tools**
Lesson Plans

📖 **Grammar Workbook**
Lessons 68–72
Unit 11 Review
Cumulative Review: Units 1–11

Unit Assessment
📁 *Tests with Answer Key*
Unit 17 Mastery Test, pp. 67–68

💿 *Test Generator*
Unit 17 Mastery Test

Exercise 1

Making Usage Choices   For each sentence write the correct word in parentheses.

SAMPLE   (Beside, Besides) marking the seasons, stars can also be used to tell directions.

ANSWER   Besides

1. The stars (can, may) be used as a means to navigate only when the sky is clear.
2. On an overcast night, (fewer, less) stars are visible in the sky.
3. Chinese navigators were (all ready, already) using magnetic compasses to guide their ships by the 1100s.
4. Some of the objects we see (between, among) the stars are planets.
5. Do you (accept, except) the idea that there may be life on other planets?
6. (Many, Much) stars formed more than ten billion years ago.
7. The color of a star's light depends on (its, it's) surface temperature.
8. As a star dies, it slowly begins to (loose, lose) material and shrink.
9. About one hundred ball-like clusters of stars (lay, lie) around the center of the Milky Way galaxy.
10. People can (learn, teach) about stars at a planetarium.
11. The sun is nearer to the earth (than, then) any other star is.
12. Scientists have learned (quiet, quite) a bit about other stars by studying the sun.
13. (Theirs, There's) a solar telescope in Tucson, Arizona, that helps astronomers study the sun's light.
14. (Who's, Whose) studies in the early 1500s challenged earlier scientists' findings?
15. Polish astronomer Nicolaus Copernicus challenged (their, they're) beliefs about the sun.
16. Today scientists continue to (raise, rise) questions about the sun and its impact on people.
17. There are more than 200 billion billion stars (altogether, all together) in the universe.
18. A powerful telescope can (take, bring) distant stars close enough to view.
19. Stars eventually run out of hydrogen gas and (than, then) stop shining.
20. New stars form from (loose, lose) masses of gas and dust in space.

Grammar Review   **533**

PRACTICE AND ASSESS

Answers: Exercise 1

1. can
2. fewer
3. already
4. among
5. accept
6. Many
7. its
8. lose
9. lie
10. learn
11. than
12. quite
13. There's
14. Whose
15. their
16. raise
17. altogether
18. bring
19. then
20. loose

UNIT 17
Review

Answers: Exercise 2
Proofreading

This proofreading activity provides editing practice with (1) the current or previous units' skills, (2) the **Trouble-shooter** errors, and (3) spelling errors. Students should be able to complete the exercise by referring to the units, the **Troubleshooter**, and a dictionary.

	Error (Type of Error)
1.	• Léger, (nonessential appositive phrase) • style (spelling)
2.	• chooses (troublesome words)
3.	• to create (troublesome words)
4.	• to explore (troublesome words) • relationship between (troublesome words)
5.	• presents (subject-verb agreement) *or* presented (verb tense)
6.	• As it lies (troublesome words)
7.	• Perhaps many (troublesome words) • already (troublesome words)

Exercise 2 — Proofreading

The following passage is about Fernand Léger, whose work appears below. Rewrite the passage, correcting the errors in spelling, grammar, and usage. Add any missing punctuation. There are ten errors.

Fernand Léger

[1] Fernand Léger a French painter born in 1881, used an abstract stile of art. [2] An artist using this style choses many fragmented aspects of an object and combines them within a single picture. [3] Léger frequently chose cubes and other forms too create mechanical figures that represented the new machines developed in the early 1900s. [4] The artist used his talent two explore the relationship among a person and the industrial world.

[5] Léger present his vision of a world produced by machines in *The Creation of the World.* [6] As it lays beneath a moon and a handful of stars, Léger's world recalls the planets that Judith Herbst imagined in "Star Fever." [7] Perhaps much of the strange images in the painting all ready exist under some distant star.

Fernand Léger, *The Creation of the World,* c. 1925

534 *Glossary of Special Usage Problems*

About the Art

Fernand Léger, *The Creation of the World,* c. 1925

While *The Creation of the World* might seem to depict a distant planet, it could also be viewed as portraying the industrial, machine-age world here on Earth—a world created by human beings. In much of his art, Léger did explore the modern industrial world and people's place in it.

Invite students to identify some of the images in the painting. Ask whether Léger seems to be depicting a world of hope and progress or one of doom.

Mixed Review

Exercise 3

For each sentence, write the correct word or words in parentheses.

1. Migration is an important concept (between, among) the world's creatures.
2. Migration, (formally, formerly) defined, is movement from place to place.
3. Migration (in, into) the past was a way for people and animals to find better living conditions.
4. Today (a lot of, millions) of people still migrate.
5. Animals also migrate so that they (can, may) find better living conditions.
6. (Many, Much) different kinds of animals migrate, including birds, whales, fish, frogs, and toads.
7. In the autumn many birds gather in flocks (all ready, already) to migrate to warmer climates.
8. Although they may enjoy warm weather, (its, it's) plentiful food they seek.
9. Seasonal migrations of animals take place (to, too, two) times a year.
10. The distance that animals migrate (between, among) two habitats varies.
11. Some animals migrate (fewer, less) than a mile.
12. On the other hand, Arctic terns travel up to 22,000 miles each year between (their, they're) summer and winter residences.
13. Salmon migrate from small streams (to, too, two) the vast ocean.
14. They stay where (theirs, there's) a plentiful supply of food.
15. (Than, Then) they reverse the process and return to their home stream.
16. There the female will (lay, lie) her eggs, and the male will fertilize them.
17. The adult salmon may die after spawning, but their offspring (precede, proceed) to develop within the eggs.
18. Without anyone to (learn, teach) them, the young salmon repeat the pattern of their parents.
19. We must (accept, except) the mystery of animal migration.
20. What sense (brings, takes) animals away to another home?
21. What sense (brings, takes) them back to the exact spot where they once lived?
22. Humans can (choose, chose) the instruments that guide them.
23. They can (leave, let) the stars or a compass be their guide.
24. Electronic equipment will pinpoint (where at, where) they are sailing or flying.
25. Although humans have a great deal of knowledge, we still have much to (learn, teach) about animal migrations.

Grammar Review **535**

Answers: Exercise 3
Mixed Review
1. among
2. formally
3. in
4. millions
5. can
6. Many
7. all ready
8. it's
9. two
10. between
11. fewer
12. their
13. to
14. there's
15. Then
16. lay
17. proceed
18. teach
19. accept
20. takes
21. brings
22. choose
23. let
24. where
25. learn

CLOSE

Ask students to tell which of the usage rules covered in the review are most difficult for them to remember. Have them write those, along with an example. They might then meet with a partner or in a small group to share strategies and help each other remember the correct usage rules.

Usage in Writing
Have students read the paragraph from *Lyddie* aloud without interruption. Then discuss the italicized words in relation to the Techniques with Usage below.

Techniques with Usage
Ask students to identify other examples of word pairs and homophones in the Unit Review and in other readily available writings.

Practice
The answers to this challenging and enriching activity will vary. Refer to Techniques with Usage as you evaluate student choices. **Sample answer:**

"Edna and Tamara asked me to come to <u>their</u> house to help paint their treehouse. <u>May</u> I go, Dad?" asked Mari.

"If you <u>can</u> finish <u>your</u> chores before lunch, <u>it's</u> fine with me," replied her father. "The only question is, <u>who's</u> going to bring you home?"

"<u>Between</u> Edna's mom and Tamara's dad, I'm sure someone <u>can</u> do it. They asked me to bring a paintbrush. Will you help me <u>choose</u> one? We have so <u>many</u>," said Mari.

"No problem. Let's get started," answered her father.

536

Writing Application

Usage in Writing   Katherine Paterson chose her words carefully for this passage from *Lyddie* that uses troublesome words correctly. Read the passage, focusing especially on the italicized words.

Her stomach rumbled, but she ignored it. There would be no breakfast until seven, and that was *two* and a half hours away. By five the girls had crowded through the main gate, jostled their way up the outside staircase on the far end of the mill, cleaned their machines, and stood waiting for the workday *to* begin.

"Not *too* tired this morning?" Diana asked by way of greeting.

Techniques with Usage   Try to apply some of Katherine Paterson's writing techniques when you write and revise your own work.

1. Remember that some word pairs have related meanings, although their spellings and usages differ. Check each word against its context carefully before making your final choice:

Incorrect usage that was *too* and a half hours
Paterson's version that was *two* and a half hours

2. Homophones, or words with the same sound but different spellings and meanings, are easily confused. Be sure to choose the correct word and spelling for your intended meaning.

Incorrect usage Not *to* tired this morning?
Paterson's version Not *too* tired this morning?

Practice Try out these techniques on the following passage, revising it on a separate sheet of paper. Pay particular attention to the underlined words.

"Edna and Tamara asked me to come to <u>they're</u> house to help paint their treehouse. <u>Can</u> I go, Dad?" asked Mari.

"If you <u>may</u> finish <u>you're</u> chores before lunch, <u>its</u> fine with me," replied her father. "The only question is, <u>whose</u> going to bring you home?"

"<u>Among</u> Edna's mom and Tamara's dad, I'm sure someone <u>may</u> do it. They asked me to bring a paintbrush. Will you help me <u>chose</u> one? We have so <u>much</u>," said Mari.

"No problem. Let's get started," answered her father.

536   *Writing Application*

Teacher's Classroom Resources

The following resources can be used for assessment or evaluation.

Unit Assessment
📁 *Tests with Answer Key*
Unit 17 Mastery Test, pp. 67–68

💿 *Test Generator*
Unit 17 Mastery Test

You may wish to administer the Unit 17 Mastery Test at this point.

UNIT	Diagraming
18	**Sentences**
Grammar	Lessons

537

UNIT GOALS

The goal of Unit 18 is to help students, through example and instruction, to identify the various kinds of sentences and their parts, and to represent them in sentence diagrams that show how these components function as parts of sentences. Lessons focus on diagraming simple subjects and predicates; four kinds of sentences; direct and indirect objects; adjectives, adverbs, and prepositional phrases; predicate nouns and adjectives; compound sentences; complex sentences; noun clauses; and verbals.

Unit Assessment

📂 *Tests with Answer Key*
Unit 18 Pretest, pp. 69–70
Unit 18 Mastery Test, pp. 71–72

💿 *Test Generator*
Unit 18 Pretest
Unit 18 Mastery Test

You may wish to administer the Unit 18 Pretest at this point.

Key to Ability Levels

Enabling Strategies have been coded for varying learning styles and abilities.

L1 Level 1 activities are within the ability range of Learning Disabled students.

L2 Level 2 activities are basic-to-average activities and are within the ability range of average students.

L3 Level 3 activities are challenging activities and are within the ability range of above-average students.

LEP LEP activities are within the ability range of Limited English Proficiency students.

PRACTICE AND ASSESS

Answers: Exercise 1

1. People | arrived
2. They | started
3. people | were standing
4. women | have arrived
5. factories | are
6. lunchtime | arrived
7. workers | ate
8. Men | took
9. People | are watching
10. People | played
11. workers | returned
12. They | restarted
13. They | liked
14. supervisor | praises
15. workers | show
16. They | have worked
17. factory | resembles
18. People | care
19. They | work

538

18.1 Diagraming Simple Subjects and Simple Predicates

The basic parts of a sentence are the subject and the predicate. To diagram a sentence, first draw a horizontal line. Then draw a vertical line that crosses and extends below the horizontal line.

To the left of the vertical line, write the simple subject. To the right of the vertical line, write the simple predicate. Capitalize any words that are capitalized in the sentence. Do not include punctuation, however.

People are working.	People	are working

The positions of the subject and the predicate in a diagram always remain the same.

Operators sat by the machines.	Operators	sat
By the machines **sat operators.**	operators	sat

Exercise 1   Diagraming Simple Subjects and Simple Predicates

Diagram each simple subject and simple predicate.

1. People arrived early.
2. They started the machines.
3. Other people were standing around.
4. Four women have arrived late.
5. Most factories are busy.
6. Finally lunchtime arrived.
7. The workers ate lunch.
8. Men took walks.
9. People are watching a show.
10. People played games.
11. Then the workers returned.
12. They restarted the machines.
13. They liked their tasks.
14. The supervisor praises them.
15. The workers show loyalty.
16. They have worked for decades.
17. The factory resembles a home.
18. People care about one another.
19. They work together.
20. The workers help one another.

538   *Diagraming Sentences*

Answers: Exercise 1 (continued)

20. workers | help

CLOSE

Teacher's Classroom Resources

18.2 Diagraming the Four Kinds of Sentences

The simple subject and the simple predicate of the four kinds of sentences are diagramed below. Recall that in an interrogative sentence the subject often comes between the two parts of a verb phrase. In an imperative sentence the simple subject is the understood *you*.

Notice that the positions of the simple subject and the simple predicate in a sentence diagram are always the same, regardless of their positions in the original sentence.

DECLARATIVE
People use many machines.

People	use

INTERROGATIVE
Do people use many machines?

people	Do use

IMPERATIVE
Use this machine.

(you)	Use

EXCLAMATORY
What a loud noise **it makes!**

it	makes

Exercise 2   **Diagraming Simple Subjects and Predicates**

Diagram the simple subject and the simple predicate of each sentence.

1. Where do people use machines?
2. Machines exist in homes, office buildings, and hospitals.
3. What amazing things machines can do!
4. Listen to the radio.
5. Some machines perform several tasks.
6. Do you use a computer?
7. Try this program.
8. What a fast printer you have!
9. How long does it take?
10. This printer works beautifully.

18.2 Diagraming the Four Kinds of Sentences   **539**

Teacher's Classroom Resources

The following resources can be used for planning, instruction, practice, reinforcement, reteaching, or enrichment.

 **Teaching Tools**
Lesson Plans

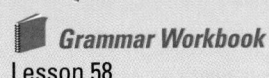 *Grammar Workbook*
Lesson 58

Setting the Purpose

Lesson 18.2 teaches students how simple subjects and simple predicates function in each of the four kinds of sentences.

FOCUS

Lesson Overview

Objective: To identify and diagram the four kinds of sentences—declarative, imperative, interrogative, and exclamatory

PRACTICE AND ASSESS

Answers: Exercise 2

1. | people | do use |
   |---|---|

2. | Machines | exist |
   |---|---|

3. | machines | can do |
   |---|---|

4. | (you) | Listen |
   |---|---|

5. | machines | perform |
   |---|---|

6. | you | Do use |
   |---|---|

7. | (you) | Try |
   |---|---|

8. | you | have |
   |---|---|

9. | it | does take |
   |---|---|

10. | printer | works |
    |---|---|

CLOSE

Have volunteers give examples of the four types of sentences for other students to diagram on the board.

539

Setting the Purpose

Lesson 18.3 teaches students how direct and indirect objects function as parts of sentences.

PRACTICE AND ASSESS

Answers: Exercise 3

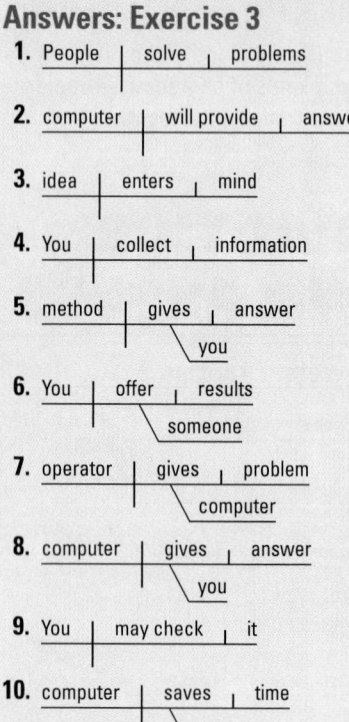

1. People | solve | problems

2. computer | will provide | answers

3. idea | enters | mind

4. You | collect | information

5. method | gives | answer
   you

6. You | offer | results
   someone

7. operator | gives | problem
   computer

8. computer | gives | answer
   you

9. You | may check | it

10. computer | saves | time
    us

CLOSE

Have volunteers write on the board sentences with direct or indirect objects—or both—in them. Tell them to leave enough space below each sentence for diagraming. Have other volunteers diagram the sentences.

540

18.3 Diagraming Direct and Indirect Objects

A direct object is part of the predicate. In a sentence diagram place the direct object to the right of the verb. The vertical line between the verb and the direct object should not extend below the horizontal line.

| Computers solve **problems**. | Computers | solve | problems |

| Computers process **data**. | Computers | process | data |

An indirect object is also part of the predicate. It usually tells to whom or for whom the action of a verb is done. An indirect object always comes before a direct object in a sentence. In a sentence diagram, place the indirect object on a line below and to the right of the verb. Then join it to the verb with a slanted line.

| Operators feed **computers** data. | Operators | feed | data |
| | | | computers |

Exercise 3   Diagraming Direct and Indirect Objects

Diagram the simple subject, the simple predicate, and the direct object of each sentence. Diagram any indirect objects as well.

1. People solve problems every day.
2. A computer will provide answers.
3. An idea enters your mind.
4. You collect the information.
5. The method gives you the answer.
6. You offer someone the results.
7. The operator gives the computer a problem.
8. The computer gives you an answer.
9. You may check it again.
10. The computer saves us time.

540 *Diagraming Sentences*

Teacher's Classroom Resources

The following resources can be used for planning, instruction, practice, reinforcement, reteaching, or enrichment.

🎵 **Teaching Tools**
Lesson Plans, p. 103

📖 *Grammar Workbook*
Lesson 59

18.4 Diagraming Adjectives, Adverbs, and Prepositional Phrases

In a diagram place adjectives and adverbs on slanted lines beneath the words they modify.

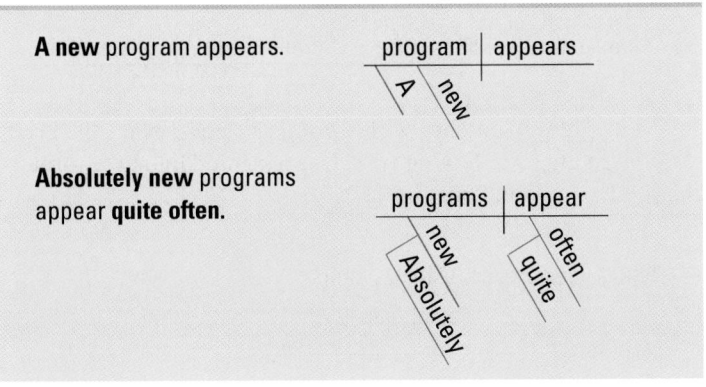

A prepositional phrase can function as either an adjective or an adverb. Study the diagram of a prepositional phrase below.

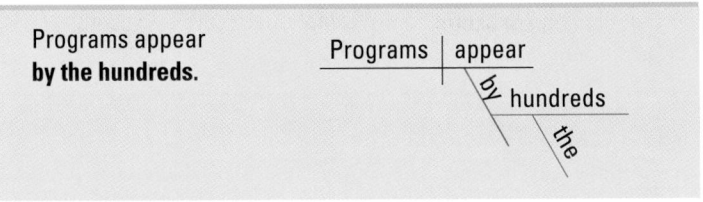

Exercise 4   Diagraming Sentences

Diagram each sentence.

1. Many people use computers regularly.
2. An extremely efficient computer works very quickly.
3. Businesses of all kinds need computers constantly.
4. Computers have changed our way of life.
5. People often play complicated games on personal computers.

18.4 Diagraming Adjectives, Adverbs, and Prepositional Phrases **541**

Setting the Purpose

Lesson 18.4 teaches students how adjectives, adverbs, and prepositional phrases function in simple sentences.

PRACTICE AND ASSESS

Answers: Exercise 4

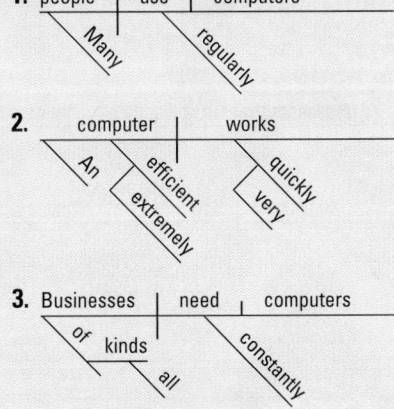

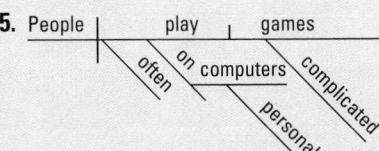

CLOSE

Have a volunteer tell, without looking at the lesson, where adjectives, adverbs, and prepositional phrases are placed when they are diagramed.

Teacher's Classroom Resources

The following resources can be used for planning, instruction, practice, reinforcement, reteaching, or enrichment.

🔧 **Teaching Tools**
Lesson Plans

📕 *Grammar Workbook*
Lessons 60–61

PRACTICE AND ASSESS

Answers: Exercise 5

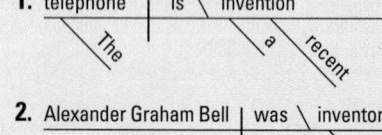

1. telephone | is \ invention
   The | a recent

2. Alexander Graham Bell | was \ inventor
   the

3. Telephones | have become \ common

4. calls | are \ international
   Many

5. telephones | looked \ odd
   Early

6. change | was \ dial
   The first big | the

7. improvement | was \ cable
   A much later | the undersea

8. cable | was \ benefit
   The | a real

9. world | grew \ smaller
   The | much

10. telephones | look \ sleek
    Some modern

18.5 Diagraming Predicate Nouns and Predicate Adjectives

You have learned that in a sentence diagram the direct object is placed after the action verb.

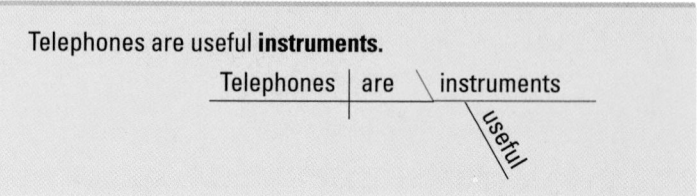

| People use telephones. | People | use | telephones |

To diagram a sentence with a predicate noun, place the predicate noun after the linking verb. Use a slanted line to separate the predicate noun from the verb.

Telephones are useful **instruments**.

Telephones | are \ instruments
useful

Diagram a predicate adjective in the same way.

Telephones are **useful**.   Telephones | are \ useful

Exercise 5   Diagraming Sentences

Diagram each sentence.

1. The telephone is a recent invention.
2. Alexander Graham Bell was the inventor.
3. Telephones have become common.
4. Many calls are international.
5. Early telephones looked odd.
6. The first big change was the dial.
7. A much later improvement was the undersea cable.
8. The cable was a real benefit.
9. The world grew much smaller.
10. Some modern telephones look sleek.

CLOSE

Have a volunteer explain why the line separating the predicate noun or adjective from the verb slants in the direction of the subject.

Teacher's Classroom Resources

18.6 Diagraming Compound Sentence Parts

Coordinating conjunctions such as *and, but,* and *or* are used to join compound parts: words, phrases, or sentences. When you diagram sentences with compound parts, place the second part of the compound below the first. Write the coordinating conjunction on a dotted line connecting the two parts.

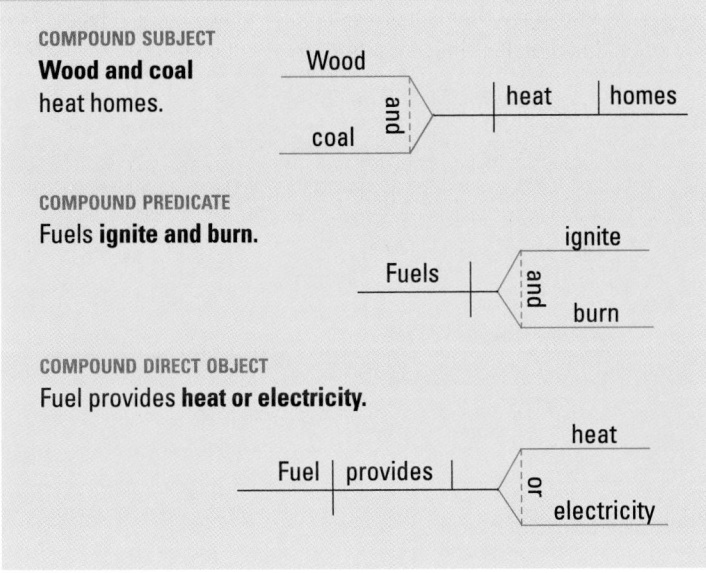

COMPOUND SUBJECT
Wood and coal heat homes.

COMPOUND PREDICATE
Fuels **ignite and burn.**

COMPOUND DIRECT OBJECT
Fuel provides **heat or electricity.**

Exercise 6   **Diagraming Sentences**

Diagram each sentence.

1. Oil or electricity heats most buildings.
2. Prices for fuels rise and fall.
3. Some families use windmills or solar energy.
4. Stoves and furnaces provide heat.
5. Heated air or heated water circulates through the house.

18.6 Diagraming Compound Sentence Parts   **543**

Teacher's Classroom Resources

The following resources can be used for planning, instruction, practice, reinforcement, reteaching, or enrichment.

🔧 **Teaching Tools**
Lesson Plans

📕 ***Grammar Workbook***
Lesson 62

Setting the Purpose

Lesson 18.6 teaches students how compound sentence parts function in simple sentences.

PRACTICE AND ASSESS

Answers: Exercise 6

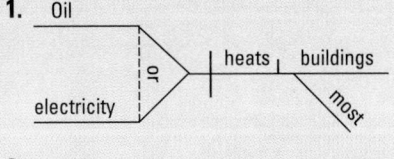

1.

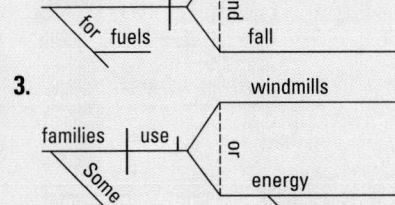

2.

3.

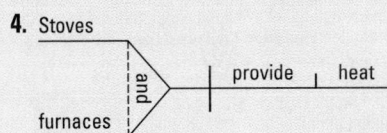

4.

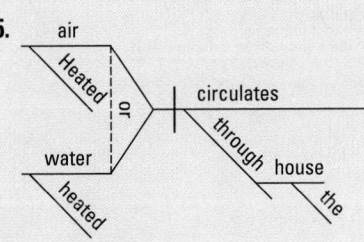

5.

CLOSE

Have students work in groups of three. The first student should think of a compound subject or predicate; the second should complete the sentence; the third should diagram it. Then have them switch assignments.

PRACTICE AND ASSESS

Answers: Exercise 7

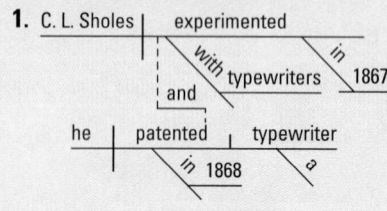

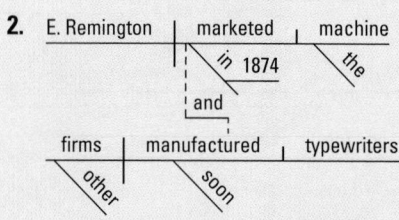

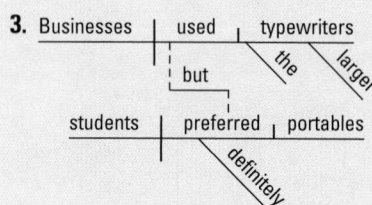

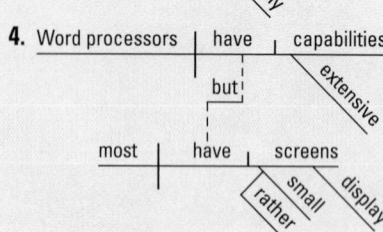

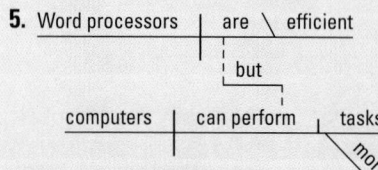

CLOSE

Have a volunteer explain what a compound sentence is. Have another student tell how to connect the sentences when they are diagramed.

544

18.7 | Diagraming Compound Sentences

When you diagram compound sentences, diagram each clause separately. If the main clauses are connected by a semicolon, use a vertical dotted line to connect the verbs of each clause. If the main clauses are connected by a conjunction such as *and, but,* or *or,* write the conjunction on a solid horizontal line, and connect it to the verbs of each clause by dotted lines.

An electric typewriter is more expensive than a manual typewriter, **but** the electric typewriter is more efficient.

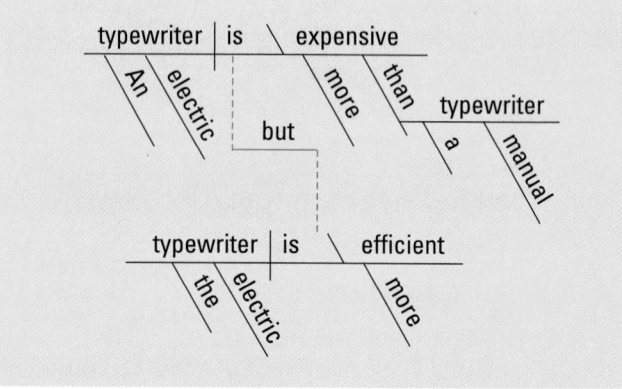

Exercise 7   **Diagraming Sentences**

Diagram each sentence.

1. C. L. Sholes experimented with typewriters in 1867, and he patented a typewriter in 1868.
2. E. Remington marketed the machine in 1874, and soon other firms manufactured typewriters.
3. Businesses used the larger typewriters, but students definitely preferred portables.
4. Word processors have extensive capabilities, but most have rather small display screens.
5. Word processors are efficient, but computers can perform more tasks.

Teacher's Classroom Resources

The following resources can be used for planning, instruction, practice, reinforcement, reteaching, or enrichment.

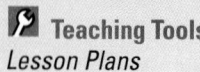 **Teaching Tools**
Lesson Plans

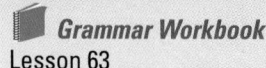 *Grammar Workbook*
Lesson 63

18.8 Diagraming Complex Sentences with Adjective and Adverb Clauses

When you diagram a sentence with an adjective clause, diagram each clause separately. Draw a dotted line between the adjective clause and the word it modifies in the main clause. In the adjective clause, diagram the relative pronoun according to its function in its own clause. In the sentence below, *who* is the subject of the verb *cooked*.

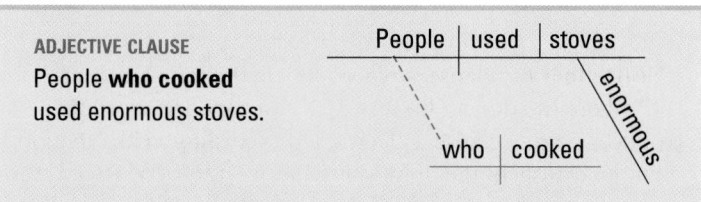

ADJECTIVE CLAUSE
People **who cooked** used enormous stoves.

When you diagram a sentence with an adverb clause, follow the same process. Then write the subordinating conjunction on the dotted connecting line.

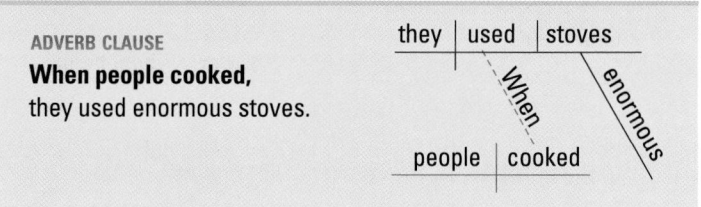

ADVERB CLAUSE
When people cooked, they used enormous stoves.

Exercise 8   Diagraming Sentences

Diagram each sentence.

1. People once used only stoves that burned wood.
2. Such stoves required attention while they were hot.
3. People who cooked on those stoves worked hard.
4. Families inserted the wood that these stoves required.
5. As the wood burned, ashes and dirt accumulated.

18.8 Diagraming Complex Sentences with Adjective and Adverb Clauses   **545**

Teacher's Classroom Resources

The following resources can be used for planning, instruction, practice, reinforcement, reteaching, or enrichment.

🔧 **Teaching Tools**
Lesson Plans

📖 *Grammar Workbook*
Lesson 64

Setting the Purpose

Lesson 18.8 teaches students how adjective and adverb clauses function as parts of complex sentences.

PRACTICE AND ASSESS

Answers: Exercise 8

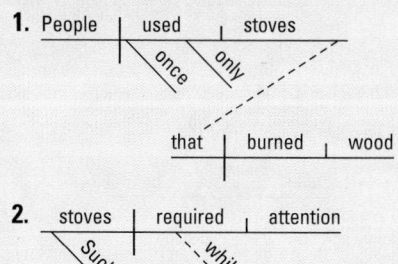

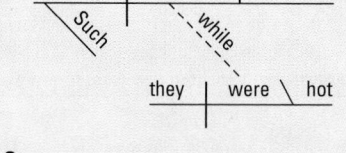

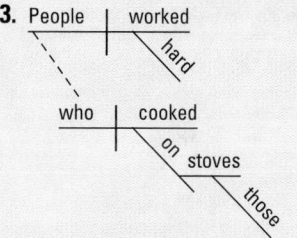

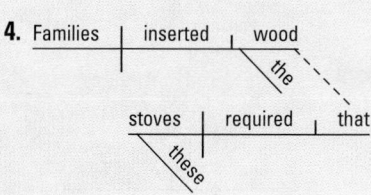

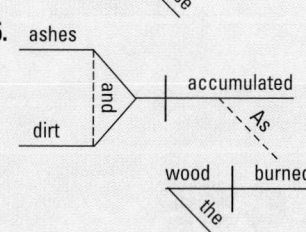

CLOSE

Have volunteers explain what adjective and adverb clauses are. Ask a student to diagram the following sentence on the board: *When I was young, I had a pet monkey.*

PRACTICE AND ASSESS

Answers: Exercise 9

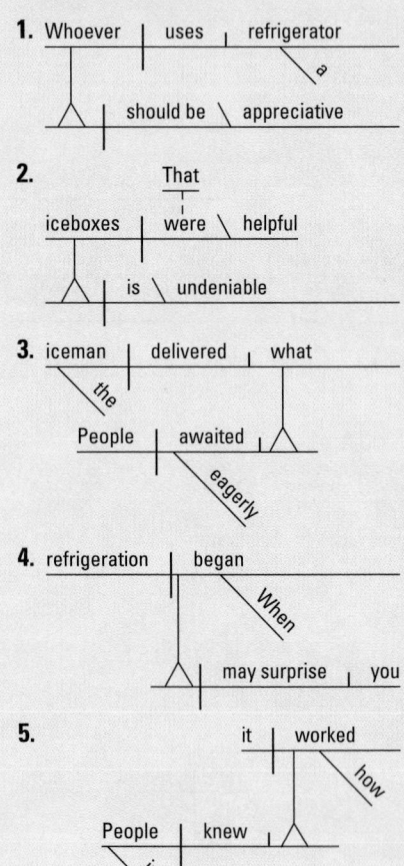

1. Whoever | uses | refrigerator — should be \ appreciative

2. That — iceboxes | were \ helpful — is \ undeniable

3. iceman | delivered | what — the / People | awaited — eagerly

4. refrigeration | began — When — may surprise | you

5. it | worked — how / People | knew — in / century / the last

CLOSE

Have a volunteer explain why students must decide what role the noun clause plays in a sentence before they begin to diagram the noun clause.

18.9 Diagraming Noun Clauses

Noun clauses can be used in sentences as subjects, direct objects, objects of prepositions, or predicate nouns. In the sentence below, the noun clause is a direct object.

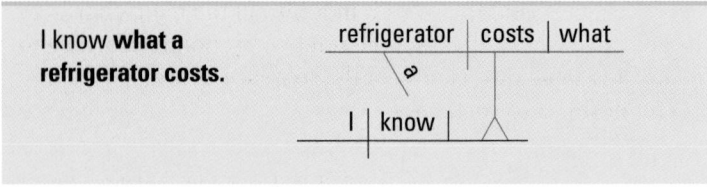

I know **what a refrigerator costs.**

refrigerator | costs | what

I | know

Notice that the clause is placed above the base line on a "stilt" where the direct object usually appears. The word that introduces a noun clause is diagramed according to its function within the clause. In the noun clause above, the word *what* is the direct object. If the word that introduces the noun clause is not truly part of either the noun clause or the main clause, place the word on its own line.

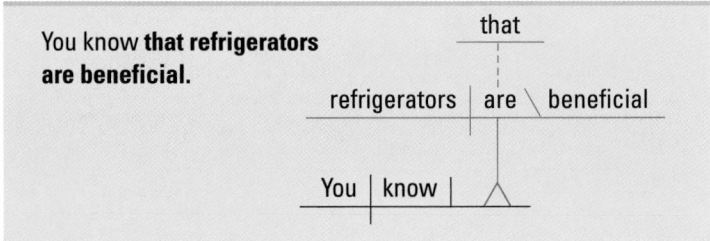

You know **that refrigerators are beneficial.**

that

refrigerators | are \ beneficial

You | know

Exercise 9   **Diagraming Sentences**

Diagram each sentence.

1. Whoever uses a refrigerator should be appreciative.
2. That iceboxes were helpful is undeniable.
3. People eagerly awaited what the ice wagon delivered.
4. When refrigeration began may surprise you.
5. People in the last century knew how it worked.

546 *Diagraming Sentences*

Teacher's Classroom Resources

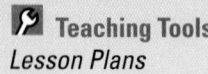
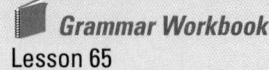

18.10 Diagraming Verbals I

When diagraming a participle or a participial phrase, make a line that descends diagonally from the word the participle modifies and then extends to the right horizontally. Write the participle along that angled line, as shown below.

The machine, **humming loudly**, cooled the air rapidly.

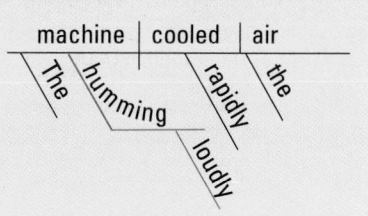

When diagraming a gerund or a gerund phrase, make a "stilt" located according to the role of the gerund. (A gerund can be a subject, an object of a verb or a preposition, or an appositive.) Then write the gerund on a "step" above the stilt.

Cleaning the air is another job of the machine.

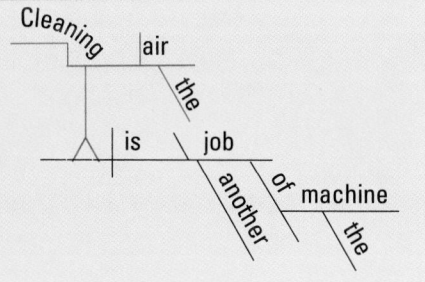

Exercise 10 — Diagraming Sentences

Diagram each sentence.

1. Cooling the air was the subject of much research.
2. The machines cool the heated air.
3. Controlling the temperature is not an easy task.
4. The circulating air cools everyone.
5. Working people appreciate this modern invention.

18.10 Diagraming Verbals I   **547**

Teacher's Classroom Resources

The following resources can be used for planning, instruction, practice, reinforcement, reteaching, or enrichment.

🔧 **Teaching Tools**
Lesson Plans

📕 **Grammar Workbook**
Lesson 66

Setting the Purpose

Lesson 18.10 teaches students how participles, participial phrases, gerunds, and gerund phrases function as parts of sentences.

PRACTICE AND ASSESS

Answers: Exercise 10

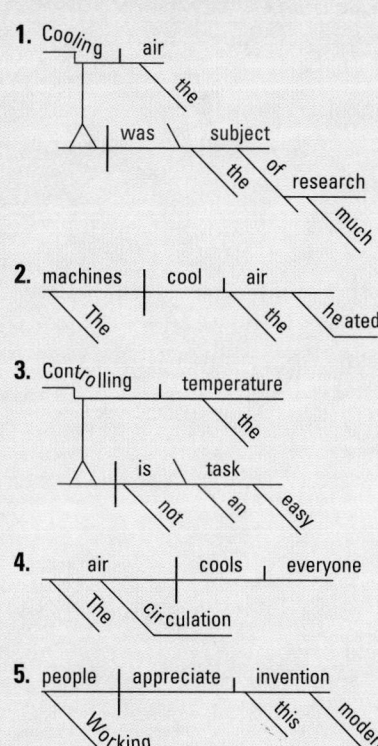

CLOSE

Have students explain the difference between participial and gerund phrases, giving examples of each. Ask volunteers to diagram the sentences as they are suggested.

Setting the Purpose

Lesson 18.11 teaches students how infinitives and infinitive phrases function as parts of sentences.

PRACTICE AND ASSESS

Answers: Exercise 11

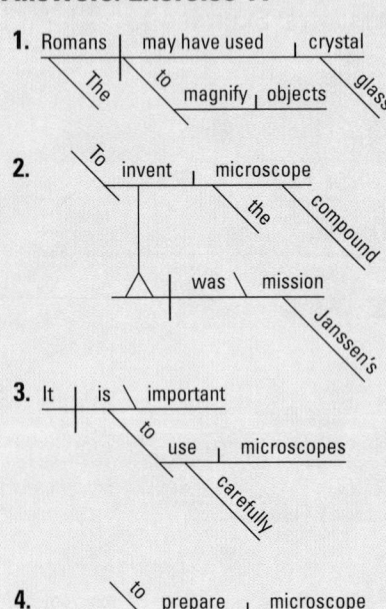

1. Romans | may have used | crystal
The / to magnify | objects / glass

2. To invent | microscope
the / compound / was \ mission / Janssen's

3. It | is \ important
to use | microscopes / carefully

4. to prepare | microscope
for use / the
job | is / Sloan's

5. work | governs | preparation
The / to do / the

CLOSE

Have a student show the difference in how prepositional phrases and infinitive phrases are diagramed.

18.11 Diagraming Verbals II

When diagraming an infinitive or an infinitive phrase that is used as either an adjective or an adverb, diagram it like a prepositional phrase.

The microscope **to choose** depends upon your needs.

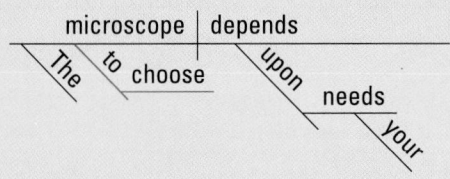

microscope | depends
The / to choose / upon
needs / your

When diagraming an infinitive or an infinitive phrase that is used as a noun, make a "stilt" in the appropriate position. Then diagram the phrase as you would a prepositional phrase.

The function of the microscope is **to magnify objects.**

to magnify | objects
function | is
The / of microscope / the

Exercise 11 — Diagraming Sentences

Diagram each sentence.

1. The Romans may have used glass crystal to magnify objects.
2. To invent the compound microscope was Janssen's mission.
3. It is important to use microscopes carefully.
4. Sloan's job is to prepare the microscope for use.
5. The work to do governs the preparation.

Teacher's Classroom Resources

The following resources can be used for planning, instruction, practice, reinforcement, assessment, reteaching, enrichment, or evaluation.

Teaching Tools
Lesson Plans

Grammar Workbook
Lesson 67

Unit Assessment

Tests with Answer Key
Unit 18 Mastery Test, pp. 71–72

Test Generator
Unit 18 Mastery Test

You may wish to administer the Unit 18 Mastery Test at this point.

UNIT
GOALS

The goal of Unit 19 is to help students, through example and instruction, to become familiar with and use the rules for capitalization. Lessons focus on capitalizing sentences, quotations, and salutations; names and titles of persons; names of places; and other proper nouns and adjectives.

Unit Assessment

📁 *Tests with Answer Key*
Unit 19 Pretest, pp. 73–74
Unit 19 Mastery Test, pp. 75–76

◎ *Test Generator*
Unit 19 Pretest
Unit 19 Mastery Test

You may wish to administer the Unit 19 Pretest at this point.

Key to Ability Levels

Enabling Strategies have been coded for varying learning styles and abilities.

L1 Level 1 activities are within the ability range of Learning Disabled students.

L2 Level 2 activities are basic-to-average activities and are within the ability range of average students.

L3 Level 3 activities are challenging activities and are within the ability range of above-average students.

LEP LEP activities are within the ability range of Limited English Proficiency students.

UNIT	
19	**Capitalization**
Grammar	Lessons

549

Setting the Purpose

Lesson 19.1 teaches students how to correctly capitalize sentences, quotations, and salutations.

FOCUS

Lesson Overview

Objective: To use capital letters to indicate the beginnings of sentences, quotations, and salutations

Bellringer

When students enter the classroom, have this assignment on the board: *Write all the reasons you can think of for capitalizing a word.*

Motivating Activity

List and discuss responses to the Bell-ringer activity. Have students find examples of each in their textbooks. Remind them to find examples of capital letters in quotations and salutations.

TEACH

Critical Thinking

Have students distinguish between direct and indirect quotes by determining whether the word *that* is used after the verb that introduces the quote. They might compare *Travis said that another man rode with Paul Revere* (indirect) with *Travis said, "Another man rode with Paul Revere"* (direct).

Two-Minute Skill Drill

Have students use each of these words in two sentences—one that requires capitalizing the word and one that doesn't.

    can   dear   sheep   it

19.1 Capitalizing Sentences, Quotations, and Salutations

A capital letter appears at the beginning of a sentence. A capital letter also marks the beginning of a direct quotation and the salutation and closing of a letter.

RULE 1: Capitalize the first word of every sentence.

Many people helped our country gain independence.
Among them were George Washington, Thomas Jefferson, and Benjamin Franklin.

RULE 2: Capitalize the first word of a direct quotation that is a complete sentence. A direct quotation gives a speaker's exact words.

Travis said, "Another one of those people was Paul Revere."

RULE 3: When a quoted sentence is interrupted by explanatory words, such as *she said*, do not begin the second part of the sentence with a capital letter.

"I read a famous poem," said Kim, "about Paul Revere."

When the second part of a quotation is a new sentence, put a period after the explanatory words, and begin the second part of the quotation with a capital letter.

"I know that poem," said Sarah. "My class read it last week."

RULE 4: Do not capitalize an indirect quotation. Because an indirect quotation does not repeat a person's exact words, it does not appear in quotation marks. It is often preceded by the word *that*.

The teacher said the poem was written by Longfellow.
Travis said that another man rode with Paul Revere.

RULE 5: Capitalize the first word in the salutation and closing of a letter. Capitalize the title and name of the person addressed.

Dear Mrs. Adams,   Yours truly,

Teacher's Classroom Resources

The following resources can be used for planning, instruction, practice, reinforcement, assessment, reteaching, enrichment, or evaluation.

Teaching Tools
Lesson Plans

Blackline Masters
Grammar Practice, p. 43
Grammar Reteaching, p. 44
Grammar Enrichment, p. 43

Grammar Workbook
Lesson 73

Unit Assessment

Tests with Answer Key
Unit 19 Pretest, pp. 73–74

Test Generator
Unit 19 Pretest

You may wish to administer the Unit 19 Pretest at this point.

Exercise 1   Capitalizing Sentences, Quotations, and Salutations

Write each word that needs to be capitalized. If a sentence contains no error, write *correct*.

1. our class was learning about heroes of the American Revolution.
2. we wanted to learn more about Paul Revere.
3. he came from Boston and lived in a house that is now open to the public.
4. "let's go to the library," said Lisa, "and see what we can find."
5. one book about Paul Revere says, "he designed the first issue of Continental money."
6. Hasan said that Paul Revere was a silversmith and an engraver.
7. "my aunt," said Hasan, "visited a Boston museum that had a Revere teapot."
8. "he designed the colonies' first official seal," said Hasan. "then he engraved it."
9. "did you know that he took part in the Boston Tea Party?" asked Lisa.
10. about fifty other American patriots went to the harbor in December 1773.
11. "he is best known," said Hasan, "for warning the people that the British were coming."
12. on April 18, 1775, he rode through Lexington toward Concord shouting, "the British are coming! the British are coming!"
13. lanterns were used as signals in the steeple of the Old North Church.
14. we read that on his famous ride Paul Revere was assisted by William Dawes.
15. "isn't it funny," said Hasan, "that Dawes is not known for this deed?"
16. "yes, it is," Lisa agreed. "the famous poem about the ride mentions only Paul Revere."
17. "did you know," asked Hasan, "that the poem was written by Henry Wadsworth Longfellow, who lived in Cambridge?"
18. we also learned that the poem was written more than eighty years after that important ride happened.
19. "because of Paul Revere's ride," said Lisa, "the Minutemen were prepared."
20. we thought we had discovered many interesting facts about this famous hero.
21. we decided to submit our report to a magazine.
22. Hasan began the letter, "dear sir or madam."
23. "we have written a report on Paul Revere," he wrote. "we would like to submit it to you."
24. a few weeks later we received a reply from the magazine.
25. they said that they would publish it.

19.1 Capitalizing Sentences, Quotations, and Salutations   **551**

PRACTICE AND ASSESS

Answers: Exercise 1
1. Our
2. We
3. He
4. "Let's
5. One
6. Correct
7. "My
8. "He—Then
9. "Did
10. About
11. "He
12. On; "The—The—"
13. Lanterns
14. We
15. "Isn't
16. "Yes—"The
17. "Did
18. We
19. "Because
20. We
21. We
22. "Dear
23. "We—"We
24. A
25. They

Independent Practice
Skills Practice
 Grammar Practice, p. 43
Grammar Reteaching, p. 44
Grammar Enrichment, p. 43

Grammar Workbook, Lesson 73

CLOSE

Have students write down and correctly punctuate an imagined dialogue with a historical figure.

Enabling Strategies

LEP Understanding Capitalizations in Direct Quotations

Students whose first language is not English may be confused about what words to capitalize when using direct quotations. Form groups to read a book with dialogue. Ask students to note the word in direct quotations that follows explanatory words such as *he said, she said happily,* and so on. Then have them discuss when the first word is capitalized (when a period precedes the quote) and when it is not (when a comma precedes the direct quote).

A common noun is the general name of a person, place, or thing. A common noun is not capitalized. A proper noun names a particular person, place, or thing and is capitalized.

RULE 1: Capitalize the names of people and the initials that stand for their names.

Lucretia Mott   E. C. Stanton

RULE 2: Capitalize a title or an abbreviation of a title when it comes before a person's name or when it is used in direct address.

In 1918 President Wilson planned the League of Nations.
"Has peace been declared, General?"

Do not capitalize a title that follows or is a substitute for a person's name.

Woodrow Wilson was president during World War I.

RULE 3: Capitalize the names and abbreviations of academic degrees that follow a person's name. Capitalize *Jr.* and *Sr.*

Martin Greer, Ph.D.   Eve Tanaka, M.D.   Carl Healy Sr.

RULE 4: Capitalize words that show family relationships when used as titles or as substitutes for a person's name.

We have pictures of Aunt Meg marching for women's rights.
In 1902 Grandmother was a suffragist.

Do not capitalize words that show family relationships when they follow a possessive noun or pronoun.

Maria's cousin wrote about women's suffrage.
My aunt has told me about the women's movement.

RULE 5: Always capitalize the pronoun *I*.

History is the subject I like best.

552 *Capitalization*

FOCUS

Lesson Overview
Objective: To use proper capitalization of people's names and titles

🔔 Bellringer
When students enter the classroom, have this assignment on the board: *Write the first and last name of someone in your class. If that person were a doctor, how would you write his or her name?*

Motivating Activity
Discuss students' answers to the Bellringer activity. Have students brainstorm other titles that are capitalized.

TEACH

☑ Teaching Tip
In using someone's title after a possessive noun or pronoun, the title is a common noun and not capitalized. *My brother usually works late.* In using a title to directly address someone, the title is a proper noun and capitalized. *Are you tired, Aunt Margie?*

⇄ Cross-reference: Mechanics
Encourage students to pay attention to rules of capitalization when proofreading their work. For instruction and practice of proofreading, refer students to Lesson 2.9, Editing: Finetuning Your Work, pp. 80–82.

Teacher's Classroom Resources

The following resources can be used for planning, instruction, practice, reinforcement, reteaching, or enrichment.

🔲 **Teaching Tools**
Lesson Plans, p. 108

📁 **Blackline Masters**
Grammar Practice, p. 43
Grammar Reteaching, p. 45
Grammar Enrichment, p. 43

📔 *Grammar Workbook*
Lesson 74

Exercise 2
Capitalizing Proper Names and Titles

Write each item, using capital letters where needed.

1. miss lucy stone
2. benjamin davis jr.
3. sonia fox, d.d.s.
4. edward r. murrow
5. beth parker, ph.d.
6. peter ashike, m.a.
7. dr. michael thomas
8. general robert e. lee
9. sir walter raleigh
10. j. p. slaughter
11. aunt martha
12. ben casey, m.d.
13. mayor riley
14. private bailey
15. gerald r. ford
16. uncle dexter
17. hillary r. clinton
18. pablo cruz sr.
19. mr. ted dover
20. king george

Exercise 3
Using Capital Letters for Names, Titles, and Abbreviations

Write each item from the following sentences that needs a capital letter. If a sentence is correct, write *correct*.

1. Without susan b. anthony, women might not have the vote today.
2. Unfortunately, miss anthony died before women were allowed to vote.
3. With elizabeth cady stanton and m. j. gage, anthony wrote *History of Woman Suffrage.*
4. miss anthony met elizabeth cady stanton in New York.
5. esther p. newton, my great-grandmother, was a suffragist.
6. My great-grandmother once met miss anthony.
7. At the time most people knew about miss anthony.
8. Later she met president wilson.
9. "Should women vote, mr. wilson?" she asked.
10. A shy man, woodrow wilson did not care to comment.
11. warren g. harding was the first president elected after women could vote.
12. Because harding died in office, calvin coolidge became president in 1923.
13. My great-grandmother knew the importance of the right to vote.
14. My grandmother, beverly newton walsh, says that her mother always voted.
15. She served in the army under general dwight d. eisenhower.
16. A colonel in the army, aunt helen owes a debt of gratitude to the women's movement.
17. In the army she also met charles lindbergh and general george c. patton.
18. aunt helen smiled and replied, "Yes, sir!"
19. My uncle and i often tease, "Do you think women belong in the military?"
20. I'm sure esther p. newton would have been proud of aunt helen.

19.2 Capitalizing Names and Titles of People   **553**

PRACTICE AND ASSESS

Answers: Exercise 2
1. Miss Lucy Stone
2. Benjamin Davis Jr.
3. Sonia Fox, D.D.S.
4. Edward R. Murrow
5. Beth Parker, Ph.D.
6. Peter Ashike, M.A.
7. Dr. Michael Thomas
8. General Robert E. Lee
9. Sir Walter Raleigh
10. J. P. Slaughter
11. Aunt Martha
12. Ben Casey, M.D.
13. Mayor Riley
14. Private Bailey
15. Gerald R. Ford
16. Uncle Dexter
17. Hillary R. Clinton
18. Pablo Cruz, Sr.
19. Mr. Ted Dover
20. King George

Answers: Exercise 3
1. Susan B. Anthony . . .
2. Miss Anthony . . .
3. Elizabeth Cady Stanton . . . M.J. Gage, Anthony
4. Miss Anthony . . . Elizabeth Cady Stanton
5. Esther P. Newton
6. Miss Anthony
7. Miss Anthony
8. President Wilson
9. Mr. Wilson
10. Woodrow Wilson
11. Warren G. Harding
12. Harding . . . Calvin Coolidge
13. Correct
14. Beverly Newton Walsh
15. General Dwight D. Eisenhower
16. Aunt Helen
17. Charles Lindbergh . . . General George C. Patton
18. Aunt Helen
19. I
20. Esther P. Newton . . . Aunt Helen

Independent Practice

Skills Practice
📂 *Grammar Practice, p. 43*
📂 *Grammar Reteaching, p. 45*
📂 *Grammar Enrichment, p. 43*

📓 **Grammar Workbook,** Lesson 74

Enabling Strategies

LEP Practicing Capitalization
Some students whose first language is not English may have difficulty with capitalization. Have them list ten people they know: relatives, teachers, and so forth. Then have them exchange papers with a partner and check names for correct capitalization.

CLOSE

Write a brief paragraph about a well-known event in American history, such as the signing of the Declaration of Independence, the Gettysburg Address, or D-Day near the end of World War II. Include the names of those involved and capitalize them correctly.

FOCUS

Lesson Overview

Objective: To identify names of specific places as proper nouns and to punctuate them correctly

🔔 Bellringer

When students enter the classroom, have this assignment on the board: *Write the names of the following: a) the name of the country in which you were born, and b) the name of a nearby body of water.*

Motivating Activity

Ask volunteers to write their Bellringer answers on the board. Be sure to point out the appropriate capitalization of place names. Correct any errors students may have made.

TEACH

☑ Teaching Tip

Names of geographical features are capitalized if they are part of a name: *Idaho Falls, Cedar Rapids, Lake Pontchartrain, Pipe Spring National Monument, Oak Park, Walden Pond, Nile Delta, Great Barrier Reef.*
If the geographical feature is merely descriptive, it is not capitalized: *the Maine coast, the Mississippi valley.*

19.3   Capitalizing Names of Places

The names of specific places are proper nouns and are capitalized. Do not capitalize articles and prepositions that are part of geographical names, however.

RULE 1:   Capitalize the names of cities, counties, states, countries, and continents.

> Chicago   Dade County   Hawaii

RULE 2:   Capitalize the names of bodies of water and other geographical features.

> Dead Sea   Gulf of Mexico   Rocky Mountains

RULE 3:   Capitalize the names of sections of a country.

> New England   Midwest   the South

RULE 4:   Capitalize compass points when they refer to a specific section of a country.

> the West Coast   the West   the Northwest

Do not capitalize compass points when they indicate direction.

> Milwaukee is north of Chicago.

Do not capitalize adjectives derived from words indicating direction.

> southerly wind   northern Texas

RULE 5:   Capitalize the names of streets and highways.

> River Road   West Side Highway

RULE 6:   Capitalize the   names of buildings, bridges, monuments,   and other structures.

> Golden Gate Bridge
> Lincoln Memorial

Teacher's Classroom Resources

Exercise 4 — Capitalizing Place Names

Write each item, using capital letters where needed.

1. northern illinois
2. world trade center
3. spain
4. arabian desert
5. northern california
6. front street
7. national boulevard
8. carlsbad caverns
9. nebraska
10. atlantic ocean
11. yellowstone river
12. yankee stadium
13. fifth avenue
14. mediterranean sea
15. ford's theater
16. bryce canyon
17. caspian sea
18. dallas
19. great britain
20. lake erie

Exercise 5 — Using Capital Letters for Place Names

Write each geographical name, using capital letters where needed. Write "correct" if none are needed.

1. The louisiana purchase covered 827,987 square miles.
2. The united states bought the land from france.
3. At that time Napoleon Bonaparte was the leader of france, and Thomas Jefferson was our president.
4. It extended from canada to mexico.
5. Some of the states that were once part of this territory are arkansas, kansas, nebraska, and oklahoma.
6. The land was bordered by the mississippi river on the east and by the rocky mountains on the west.
7. The platte river and the missouri river are also in this region.
8. new orleans was an important city.
9. It is located on the gulf of mexico.
10. The purchase of the land doubled the size of the united states of america.
11. It also ended French control of the mississippi valley.
12. spain still owned parts of florida and texas.
13. General Andrew Jackson defeated the British in new orleans in 1815.
14. The Americans had wanted only a small piece of land that allowed access to the west.
15. Leaving from st. louis, missouri, Lewis and Clark explored this region.
16. They traveled to what is now bismarck, north dakota.
17. Meanwhile, people in washington, d.c., were thinking of these men.
18. Lewis and Clark reached the pacific ocean by traveling down the columbia river.
19. Now Americans could move farther westward.
20. Someday the country might extend to the west coast.

19.3 Capitalizing Names of Places **555**

PRACTICE AND ASSESS

Answers: Exercise 4

1. northern Illinois
2. World Trade Center
3. Spain
4. Arabian Desert
5. northern California
6. Front Street
7. National Boulevard
8. Carlsbad Caverns
9. Nebraska
10. Atlantic Ocean
11. Yellowstone River
12. Yankee Stadium
13. Fifth Avenue
14. Mediterranean Sea
15. Ford's Theater
16. Bryce Canyon
17. Caspian Sea
18. Dallas
19. Great Britain
20. Lake Erie

Answers: Exercise 5

1. Louisiana Purchase
2. United States; France.
3. France
4. Canada; Mexico
5. Arkansas; Kansas; Nebraska; Oklahoma
6. Mississippi River; Rocky Mountains
7. Platte River; Missouri River
8. New Orleans
9. Gulf of Mexico
10. United States of America
11. Mississippi
12. Spain; Florida; Texas
13. New Orleans
14. West
15. St. Louis, Missouri
16. Bismarck, North Dakota
17. Washington, D.C.
18. Columbia River
19. Correct
20. West Coast

Independent Practice

Skills Practice
📁 *Grammar Practice,* p. 44
📁 *Grammar Reteaching,* p. 45
📁 *Grammar Enrichment,* p. 44

📕 *Grammar Workbook,* Lesson 75

CLOSE

Direct students to write a brief paragraph about the place where they live. Have them name the region of the country in which it is located, and any nearby landmarks.

Enabling Strategies

LEP Capitalizing Names of Places

For students having difficulty capitalizing place names, write the name of each state capital, uncapitalized, on a small piece of paper. Pin the names on the appropriate states on a United States map. Invite students to come forward, read the name of the capital, write it, capitalized properly, on the back of the paper, and pin the corrected name on the map. To extend the activity, include the oceans, rivers, Great Lakes, and mountain ranges.

Lesson 19.4 teaches students to correctly capitalize proper nouns and adjectives.

FOCUS

Lesson Overview

Objective: To use correct capitalization of proper nouns and adjectives

Bellringer

When students enter the classroom, have this assignment on the board: *Write the names of the following: a) our school, and b) one of the school clubs.*

Motivating Activity

Review students' answers to the Bellringer by asking volunteers to write their answers on the board. Have them give other examples of proper nouns that should be capitalized.

TEACH

☑ Grammar Tip

Important events generally are capitalized, but there are many exceptions: *cold war, civil rights movement, the gold rush.* Examples of the kinds of events that are most often capitalized are acts and treaties *(the Mayflower Compact; the Treaty of Paris)*; events of religious significance *(Passover, the Hijrah, the Crusades, the Flood)*; wars and battles *(the Civil War, the Battle of the Bulge).* Historical eras with commonly accepted names should be capitalized, such as *the Age of Reason* or *the Middle Ages.* However, names not commonly accepted by historians, such as an "age of despair" or "the golden age of the sailing ship," are not capitalized.

556

19.4 Capitalizing Other Proper Nouns and Adjectives

Many nouns besides the names of people and places are proper nouns. Adjectives that are formed from proper nouns are called proper adjectives. For example, the proper adjective *Cuban* is formed from the proper noun *Cuba.*

RULE 1: Capitalize the names of clubs, organizations, businesses, institutions, and political parties.

American Bar Association   Farragut Middle School

RULE 2: Capitalize brand names but not the nouns following them.

Smoothies lotion   Neato sneakers

RULE 3: Capitalize the names of important historical events, periods of time, and documents.

Vietnam War   Renaissance   Gettysburg Address

RULE 4: Capitalize the names of days of the week, months of the year, and holidays. Do not capitalize names of the seasons.

Friday   July   Thanksgiving Day   winter

RULE 5: Capitalize the first word, the last word, and all important words in the title of a book, play, short story, poem, essay, article, film, television series, song, magazine, newspaper, and chapter of a book.

Profiles in Courage   "The Necklace"   *Newsweek*

RULE 6: Capitalize the names of ethnic groups, nationalities, and languages.

Vietnamese   Chilean   German

RULE 7: Capitalize proper adjectives that are formed from the names of ethnic groups and nationalities.

Chinese cooking   Japanese flag

Teacher's Classroom Resources

The following resources can be used for planning, instruction, practice, reinforcement, reteaching, or enrichment.

Teaching Tools
Lesson Plans, p. 109

Blackline Masters
Grammar Practice, p. 44
Grammar Reteaching, p. 45
Grammar Enrichment, p. 44

Grammar Workbook
Lesson 76

Exercise 6 — Capitalizing Proper Nouns and Adjectives

Write the following items, using capital letters where needed.

1. sunnyvale school
2. *reader's digest*
3. english
4. magna carta
5. "yankee doodle"
6. egyptian history
7. american red cross
8. girl scouts
9. wheatola cereal
10. *boston globe*
11. boston tea party
12. memorial day
13. chrysler corporation
14. campbell soup
15. mexican food
16. *the red pony*
17. world war II
18. colby college
19. treaty of paris
20. russian literature

Exercise 7 — Using Capital Letters

Write each proper noun and adjective needing capitalization. Write *correct* if the sentence has no errors.

1. The emancipation proclamation ended slavery in the South.
2. President Abraham Lincoln wrote this document in the summer of 1862.
3. Lincoln issued it during the civil war.
4. It became official in the winter of 1863.
5. It is as well known as the declaration of independence and the bill of rights.
6. These three writings are vital documents of american history.
7. Lincoln is also famous for the Gettysburg address, a short speech he delivered in november 1863.
8. The french, the english, and other peoples around the world have read them.
9. In march 1861 the russians freed their serfs.
10. The Thirteenth Amendment, ratified in december 1865, ended slavery in the United States.
11. *uncle tom's cabin*, a book by Harriet Beecher Stowe, helped end slavery.
12. She wrote the novel while her husband taught at bowdoin college.
13. The book was printed in *national era*, a popular magazine before the civil war.
14. The book was an american best seller.
15. The Fourteenth Amendment to the constitution was also ratified soon after the war.
16. Before each amendment became law, congress had to pass it.
17. The *new york times* printed articles about these amendments.
18. The fourteenth amendment gave african americans the right to vote.
19. The civil war was well documented in *harper's weekly*.
20. Today we can read about the civil war in books like *the blue and the gray*.

19.4 Capitalizing Other Proper Nouns and Adjectives **557**

Enabling Strategies

LEP Using Capitalization

Students learning English may not always recognize words that need capitalization. Have student pairs look through a newspaper or magazine and find proper nouns or adjectives that have been capitalized. Have students explain to their partners why the words are capitalized in each case.

TEACH

About the Literature

Explain that the review contains a passage from Brent Ashabranner's *Morning Star, Black Sun,* followed by exercises on related topics. After students read the passage, initiate a discussion focusing on what students know about the relocation of Native Americans to reservations.

Brent Ashabranner was born in 1921 in Shawnee, Oklahoma. He's worked with the U.S. Agency for International Development and the Peace Corps in Nigeria, Ethiopia, Libya, and India. With Russell Davis he has coauthored books for young people about the cultures of these countries. The two authors have also written about Native Americans of the West and Southwest.

Linking Grammar and Literature

☑ Teaching Tip

Generate a discussion about some reasons for capitalization: to indicate proper nouns and adjectives, to show beginnings of sentences, and to identify place names.

Ask students to note the highlighted capitalized words in the passage. Point out examples of capitalization used for titles, names, and places.

Speaking and Listening

Use a passage from a book students are reading, especially one with many proper names, and ask someone to read it to the class. Have students listen to the reading and indicate the words they think are capitalized. Without capitalization of the words *Joe Little Coyote* in the passage in their books, for example, a reader would be confused about the name of the speaker.

Grammar Review

Capitalization

Morning Star, Black Sun by Brent Ashabranner details the efforts of the Northern Cheyenne to preserve their cherished homeland. In the following passage from the book, Joe Little Coyote, a young Northern Cheyenne man, relates the story of how his people had obtained their reservation. The passage has been annotated to show some of the rules of capitalization covered in this unit.

> **Literature Model**
>
> *from* MORNING STAR, BLACK SUN
>
> *by Brent Ashabranner*
>
> "When General Miles—the Indians called him Bear Coat—decided to help my ancestors get a reservation," Joe Little Coyote said, "he picked a group of Cheyenne under Chief Two Moons and a troop of soldiers and told them to ride through the country until they found good land for a reservation. The Cheyenne rode straight to the Tongue River, and they said that was the land they wanted. The soldiers wanted them to look further, to be sure they had found the best place. They were afraid General Miles might think they hadn't done their job right. But the Cheyenne said, 'No. This will be our land.' "
>
> Then Joe Little Coyote said, "Our spiritual history is here, in this land, and in Bear Butte where Sweet Medicine received the Sacred Arrows. This is more than a reservation. This is our homeland." And he added, "You don't sell your homeland."

Title coming before a person's name

Name of a person

Name of a body of water

First word of a direct quotation that is a complete sentence

Place name

558 *Capitalization*

Teacher's Classroom Resources

The following resources can be used for planning, instruction, practice, reinforcement, assessment, reteaching, enrichment, or evaluation.

🔎 **Teaching Tools**
Lesson Plans, p. 109

📒 *Grammar Workbook*
Lessons 73–76
Unit 12 Review
Cumulative Review: Units 1–12

Unit Assessment

📁 *Tests with Answer Key*
Unit 19 Mastery Test, pp. 75–76

💿 *Test Generator*
Unit 19 Mastery Test

Exercise 1

Capitalizing Sentences and Quotations   Write each sentence, correcting any errors in capitalization.

SAMPLE   Joe Little Coyote said, "our spiritual history is in this land."
ANSWER   Joe Little Coyote said, "Our spiritual history is in this land."

1. "My ancestors got the reservation," he explained, "With the help of General Miles."
2. general Miles said that we should look for reservation land.
3. "soon a group of Cheyenne headed for a good place to live," Joe said.
4. Chief Two Moons said That they wanted the land along the Tongue River.
5. the Cheyenne were interested in living on this land.
6. the soldiers asked the Cheyenne, "do you want to look further?"
7. "my ancestors were afraid they hadn't looked carefully enough," said Joe.
8. the Cheyenne said that the land near the Tongue River would be their home.
9. "our spiritual history is here," said Joe. "the land is sacred to us."
10. Joe Little Coyote said, " you don't sell your homeland."

Exercise 2

Capitalizing Direct Quotations   Write each sentence, correcting any errors in capitalization.

1. Brendan said, "many Navajo who live in places like Monument Valley and Canyon de Chelly still live as their ancestors did."
2. "some make jewelry," said Jason. "they use silver, turquoise, and coral."
3. "did you know," asked Jennifer, "that they are also weavers?"
4. "yes," said Brendan. "they raise their own sheep and spin the wool."
5. "when they weave," said Jason, "their designs are based on ancient patterns."
6. Jennifer said, "once I saw a sand painting that was made by a Navajo."
7. "did you know," she added, "that there are more than 500 designs?"
8. "no, I didn't," said Brendan. "how big are they?"
9. "some are small and take only an hour or two to make," said Jennifer. "others are so large that several people work for hours."
10. "these pictures are not made from paint at all," added Jason.

Grammar Review **559**

PRACTICE AND ASSESS

Answers: Exercise 1
1. … with the help of General Miles."
2. General Miles said …
3. "Soon a group…
4. … said that they wanted the land …
5. The Cheyenne were …
6. The soldiers asked the Cheyenne, "Do you …
7. "My ancestors …
8. The Cheyenne said that …
9. "Our spiritual … said Joe. "The land is …
10. … said, "You don't …

Answers: Exercise 2
1. Brendan said, "Many …
2. "Some … "They use …
3. "Did you …
4. "Yes," said … "They raise …
5. "When they …
6. … said, "Once I saw …
7. "Did you …
8. "No, I … Brendan. "How big …
9. "Some are small … Jennifer. "Others are so …
10. "These pictures …

UNIT 19
Review

Answers: Exercise 3

1. Howard W. Hill, Ph.D., Pocahontas
2. Captain John Smith
3. John Rolfe, Rebecca
4. J. N. Barker, Walt Disney, *Pocahontas*
5. Squanto, Sir Ferdinando Gorges
6. William Bradford, Squanto
7. Captain Miles Standish, Governor John Carver
8. Sacajawea, Meriwether Lewis, William Clark
9. President Thomas Jefferson
10. John White

Answers: Exercise 4

1. Russia, Alaska
2. Southwest, East, United States
3. Columbia River
4. Plymouth Rock
5. Narragansett Bay, Atlantic Ocean
6. Route 6, Cape Cod
7. Boston, Faneuil Hall
8. Santa Fe Trail
9. Monument Valley, Utah, Arizona
10. Cree, Sioux

Exercise 3

Capitalizing Names and Titles of People   Write only names and titles of people, using capital letters as needed.

SAMPLE   sitting bull isn't the only famous Native American.
ANSWER   Sitting Bull

1. According to howard w. hill, ph.d., pocahontas was always well known.
2. Legend says that she saved the life of captain john smith.
3. Later she married john rolfe and was baptized under the name rebecca.
4. She is the main character in an old play by j. n. barker and is also the star of the walt disney animated movie called *pocahontas*.
5. squanto, who helped the Pilgrims, was captured by sir ferdinando gorges.
6. william bradford was surprised to find that squanto spoke English.
7. He helped settlers like captain miles standish and governor john carver.
8. Much later, sacajawea helped meriwether lewis and william clark.
9. president thomas jefferson wanted them to find a way to the Pacific Ocean.
10. Artist john white depicted scenes of Native American life.

Exercise 4

Capitalizing Names of Places   Write any place names that need capital letters.

SAMPLE   People first came to north america by crossing over from asia.
ANSWER   North America; Asia

1. During the Ice Age, there was a land bridge between russia and alaska.
2. People settled in the southwest, the east, and other areas of the united states.
3. The first people to see the columbia river were Native Americans.
4. At plymouth rock the Wampanoag greeted the Pilgrims.
5. narragansett bay, a Native American name, is part of the atlantic ocean.
6. In those days there was no route 6 winding through cape cod.
7. Many years later the colonists in boston built Faneuil hall.
8. Soon settlers headed west, traveling along the santa fe trail.
9. Monument valley in utah and arizona was sacred to the Native Americans.
10. Other Native American nations include the cree and the sioux.

Exercise 5

Capitalizing Other Proper Nouns   Write each item, using capital letters where needed.

SAMPLE   girl scouts of america
ANSWER   Girl Scouts of America

1. speed king sneakers
2. monday, september 6
3. *reader's digest*
4. korean war
5. memorial day
6. american medical association
7. general motors
8. "the open window"
9. *the red badge of courage*
10. middle ages
11. kennedy middle school
12. treaty of paris
13. irish
14. republicans and democrats
15. *the lion king*
16. victorian age
17. cadillac sedan
18. fourth of july
19. new york historical society
20. declaration of independence

Exercise 6

Capitalizing Proper Adjectives   Write the proper noun from each item correctly. Then write each group of words, changing the proper noun to a proper adjective.

SAMPLE   the language of spain
ANSWER   Spain, the Spanish language

1. a poodle from france
2. the capital of egypt
3. music of germany
4. cars from japan
5. clothes from india
6. antiques from england
7. a bank in korea
8. a lantern from china
9. wood from south america
10. elephants from africa
11. food from brazil
12. the language of norway
13. a beach in hawaii
14. a glacier in alaska
15. a boomerang from australia
16. the mountains of switzerland
17. a doll from russia
18. a song from greece
19. a book from nigeria
20. a palm tree in samoa

Grammar Review   **561**

Answers: Exercise 5
1. Speed King sneakers
2. Monday, September 6
3. *Reader's Digest*
4. Korean War
5. Memorial Day
6. American Medical Association
7. General Motors
8. "The Open Window"
9. *The Red Badge of Courage*
10. Middle Ages
11. Kennedy Middle School
12. Treaty of Paris
13. Irish
14. Republicans and Democrats
15. *The Lion King*
16. Victorian Age
17. Cadillac sedan
18. Fourth of July
19. New York Historical Society
20. Declaration of Independence

Answers: Exercise 6
1. France, the French poodle
2. Egypt, the Egyptian capital
3. Germany, German music
4. Japan, Japanese cars
5. India, Indian clothes
6. England, English antiques
7. Korea, a Korean bank
8. China, a Chinese lantern
9. South America, South American wood
10. Africa, African elephants
11. Brazil, Brazilian food
12. Norway, the Norwegian language
13. Hawaii, a Hawaiian beach
14. Alaska, an Alaskan glacier
15. Australia, an Australian boomerang
16. Switzerland, the Swiss mountains
17. Russia, a Russian doll
18. Greece, a Greek song
19. Nigeria, a Nigerian book
20. Samoa, a Samoan palm tree

UNIT 19
Review

Answers: Exercise 7
Proofreading
This proofreading activity provides editing practice with (1) the current or previous units' skills, (2) the **Troubleshooter** errors, and (3) spelling errors. Students should be able to complete the exercise by referring to the units, the **Troubleshooter**, and a dictionary.

	Error (Type of Error)
1.	• American (proper adjective)
2.	• artist (common noun)
3.	• era (common noun)
4.	• was (subject-verb agreement)
	• feeling, (commas in a series)
5.	• through (spelling)
6.	• subject, (nonessential adjective clause)
7.	• Like (first word in a sentence)
	• Joe (proper noun)
	• *Morning* (first word in a book title)

Answers: Exercise 8
Mixed Review
1. Massasoit … Governor John Carver of Plymouth Colony
2. Crazy Horse defeated Lt. Col. George A. Custer in the Battle of Little Bighorn on June 25, 1876
3. Geronimo, an Apache … Sierra Madre in Mexico
4. United States
5. He … San Carlos Indian Reservation.
6. Sitting Bull, a Sioux … Grand River in South Dakota
7. Jim Thorpe … Olympic Games … Jill
8. He … Cincinnati Reds, a National League
9. An … Football Hall of Fame in Canton, Ohio.
10. William Cody presented "Buffalo Bill's Wild West Show" in the East.

562

Exercise 7

Proofreading

The following passage is about artist Robert Henri, whose work appears on the next page. Rewrite the passage, correcting the errors in spelling, capitalization, grammar, and usage. Add any missing punctuation. There are ten errors.

Robert Henri

[1]Robert Henri (1865–1929) was an american portrait and cityscape painter whose subjects sparkle with life. [2]The Artist painted ordinary and exotic people rather than the rich and famous. [3]His paintings of urban life helped portray a newer, more modern Era.

[4]Henri's aim in painting were to capture feeling sensation, and character. [5]*Portrait of Po Tse (Water Eagle)* conveys this spirit thru the subject's expressive, dignified face. [6]The subject who is dressed in traditional clothes, shows pride in his Native American heritage. [7]like joe Little Coyote in *morning Star, Black Sun,* the subject in the portrait cherishes his homeland.

Exercise 8
Mixed Review

Write each sentence, correcting any errors in capitalization.

SAMPLE there have been many famous native americans in our history.
ANSWER There; Native Americans

1. massasoit signed a treaty in 1621 with governor john carver of plymouth colony.
2. crazy horse defeated lt. col. george a. custer in the battle of little bighorn on june 25, 1876.
3. geronimo, an apache, once fled to the sierra madre in mexico.
4. He later returned to the united states.
5. he lived on the san carlos indian reservation.
6. sitting bull, a sioux, was born near the grand river in south dakota.
7. "jim thorpe won gold medals in the 1912 olympic games," said jill.
8. he played baseball for the cincinnati reds, a national league baseball team.
9. an excellent football player, too, he is enshrined in the football hall of fame in canton, ohio.
10. william cody presented "buffalo bill's wild west show" in the east.

562 *Capitalization*

Robert Henri, *Portrait of Po Tse (Water Eagle),* **c. 1916–1925**

Grammar Review **563**

CLOSE

Have volunteers restate the rules for capitalization that they applied in the exercises in the Unit 19 Review. Reteach rules with which students had difficulty.

About the Art

Robert Henri, *Portrait of Po Tse (Water Eagle),* **c. 1916–1925**

Robert Henri lived from 1865 to 1929. Henri was a leader of the Ashcan School, which rejected the conservative tradition and espoused strong realism. Instead of using the social elite as artistic subjects, Henri painted portraits that sparkle with the lives of ordinary people—often children—and unusual people, such as the woman shown on this page. This 40-by-32 inch oil on canvas is housed in the Gerald Peters Gallery in Santa Fe, New Mexico.

Capitalization in Writing

Have students read the passage from *So Far from the Bamboo Grove*. Then discuss it in terms of the points mentioned in the Techniques with Capitalization section below.

Techniques with Capitalization

Discuss with students each of the techniques listed. You may want to have students analyze a previous example—such as the passage from *Morning Star, Black Sun* on page 558 or the proofreading practice earlier in the Unit 19 Review—using these techniques.

Practice

The answers to this challenging and enriching activity will vary. Refer to Techniques with Capitalization as you evaluate students' choices. A sample follows.

"I have never been to New Haven," said Eve.

"Of course you have," replied Aunt Petra. "Don't you remember the cranes we saw while crossing the bridge?"

"Father told me about them, but I can't recall what they look like," insisted Eve. "How about you, Marty? Can you describe them?" asked Eve, turning toward her cousin Marty.

"Yes," said Marty. "I think they were painted bright red. You always said they looked like giant grasshopper legs, only red."

"Oh, yeah!" exploded Eve. "Now I remember."

Writing Application

Capitalization in Writing   Examine the following passage from *So Far from the Bamboo Grove*, noting how Yoko Kawashima Watkins uses capitalization to identify characters. Pay particular attention to the italicized words.

> "Most of my classmates have enlisted," said *Hideyo*, serious for once. "*I* have decided to go to help our country."
>
> "*You* cannot go, *Hideyo*!" *Mother* told him. "*You* must talk with *Father*. *You* just cannot make such a decision alone."
>
> "*Mother*, *I* have already sent in my application," said *Hideyo*. "*I* will take the written and physical examinations!"
>
> "How could *you*?" *Mother* moaned. "Why didn't *you* tell me?"
>
> "*I* am eighteen. Big enough to make my own decision."

Techniques with Capitalization
Try to apply some of Yoko Kwashima Watkins's writing techniques when you write and revise your own work.

1. Remember to capitalize people's names, including names describing family relationships if they replace a specific person's name:
Incorrect capitalization "How could you?" *his Mother* moaned.
Watkins's version "How could you?" *Mother* moaned.
2. Always capitalize the pronoun *I*, regardless of where in a sentence it appears. Other pronouns should be capitalized only when they begin a sentence:
Incorrect capitalization "Why didn't *You* tell me?"
"*i* am eighteen."
Watkins's version "Why didn't *you* tell me?"
"*I* am eighteen."

Practice   Practice these capitalization techniques as you revise the following passage, using a separate sheet of paper. Focus especially on the underlined words.

> "<u>i</u> have never been to New Haven," said <u>eve</u>.
>
> "Of course <u>You</u> have," replied <u>aunt petra</u>. "Don't <u>You</u> remember the cranes we saw while crossing the bridge?"
>
> "<u>father</u> told me about them, but <u>i</u> can't recall what they look like," insisted <u>eve</u>. "How about <u>You</u>, <u>marty</u>? Can <u>You</u> describe them?" asked <u>eve</u>, turning toward her <u>Cousin marty</u>.
>
> "Yes," said <u>marty</u>. "<u>i</u> think they were painted bright red. <u>you</u> always said they looked like giant grasshopper legs, only red."
>
> "Oh, yeah!" exploded <u>eve</u>. "Now <u>i</u> remember."

564   *Writing Application*

Teacher's Classroom Resources

The following resources can be used for assessment or evaluation.

Unit Assessment

📁 *Tests with Answer Key*
Unit 19 Mastery Test, pp. 75–76

💿 *Test Generator*
Unit 19 Mastery Test

You may wish to administer the Unit 19 Mastery Test at this point.

UNIT 20

Punctuation

Grammar Lessons

565

UNIT GOALS

The goal of Unit 20 is to help students, through example and instruction, to develop an understanding of and an ability to use standard rules of punctuation. Lessons focus on endmarks of punctuation; commas, colons, and semicolons; quotation marks and underscoring; apostrophes; hyphens, dashes, and parentheses; writing numbers; and abbreviations.

Unit Assessment

📁 *Tests with Answer Key*
Unit 20 Pretest, pp. 77–78
Unit 20 Mastery Test, pp. 79–80

💿 *Test Generator*
Unit 20 Pretest
Unit 20 Mastery Test

You may wish to administer the Unit 20 Pretest at this point.

Key to Ability Levels

Enabling Strategies have been coded for varying learning styles and abilities.

L1 Level 1 activities are within the ability range of Learning Disabled students.

L2 Level 2 activities are basic-to-average activities and are within the ability range of average students.

L3 Level 3 activities are challenging activities and are within the ability range of above-average students.

LEP LEP activities are within the ability range of Limited English Proficiency students.

Lesson 20.1 teaches students to use correct end marks in punctuating sentences.

FOCUS

Lesson Overview

Objective: To use periods, exclamation points, and question marks correctly in a variety of sentences

Bellringer

When students enter the classroom, have this assignment on the board: *Write these sentences adding end punctuation:*
The track meet is today
Are you going to watch it
Yeah, we won

Motivating Activity

Talk about what it might be like to read without having end marks or other punctuation for guidance. Explain that punctuation was invented much later than writing; the oldest manuscripts have no punctuation marks at all. Punctuation marks evolved to help people read aloud.

TEACH

Using End Marks

Speaking and Listening

Discuss how, when reading aloud, the end marks tell readers how to express the sentences. Have volunteers demonstrate the different tones of voice for various end marks.

☑ Grammar Tip

Remind students that the word *you* is the understood subject of all imperative sentences.

20.1 Using the Period and Other End Marks

Three punctuation marks signal the end of sentences. The period is used for declarative and mild imperative sentences. The question mark is used for interrogative sentences. The exclamation point is used for exclamatory sentences, strong imperatives, and interjections.

RULE 1: Use a period at the end of a declarative sentence. A declarative sentence makes a statement.

Tractors perform many jobs on a farm.
I worked on a farm last summer.

RULE 2: Use a period at the end of an imperative sentence that does not express strong feeling. An imperative sentence gives a command or makes a request.

Turn the key. [command]
Please start the motor. [request]

RULE 3: Use a question mark at the end of an interrogative sentence. An interrogative sentence asks a question.

When was the first tractor built?
Were you aware of that?
Do modern tractors have both speed and power?

RULE 4: Use an exclamation point at the end of an exclamatory sentence or a strong imperative. An exclamatory sentence expresses strong feeling.

What a powerful tractor that is!
Get out of the way!

RULE 5: Use an exclamation point at the end of an interjection. An interjection is a word or group of words that expresses strong emotion.

Wow!	My goodness!	Hi!	Hey!
Hooray!	Oh, boy!	Oops!	Phew!

Teacher's Classroom Resources

The following resources can be used for planning, instruction, practice, reinforcement, assessment, reteaching, enrichment, or evaluation.

Teaching Tools
Lesson Plans

Blackline Masters
Grammar Practice, p. 45
Grammar Reteaching, p. 46
Grammar Enrichment, p. 45

Grammar Workbook
Lesson 77

Unit Assessment

Tests with Answer Key
Unit 20 Pretest, pp. 77–78

Test Generator
Unit 20 Pretest

You may wish to administer the Unit 20 Pretest at this point.

Exercise 1 — Using End Marks

Write the last word of each sentence, and add the correct end mark. Then write whether each sentence is *declarative*, *imperative*, *interrogative*, or *exclamatory*.

1. Please tell me about the history of tractors
2. Read about tractors in your book
3. The first tractor was used in the 1870s
4. This tractor was driven by steam and required a licensed steam engineer to operate and repair it
5. Was this machine very large
6. Could it haul and pull heavy loads
7. Can you believe that this tractor could pull as many as forty plows at one time
8. What an amazing sight it must have been
9. Internal combustion tractors were built in the 1890s but did not become practical until about 1920
10. Both early tractors and tractors today are used to move or operate other equipment, such as combines, threshers, or post-hole diggers
11. Do some research to find out what else these kinds of equipment do
12. Please tell me about the early days of farming
13. Open your history book
14. Read about the fascinating techniques used by ancient farmers
15. Did you know that the first cultivated crops were probably grasses grown from wild seed
16. The early Egyptians developed the first large-scale irrigation system, which allowed them to distribute water efficiently over a large area
17. What a tremendous advancement this was
18. Each year the Nile River overflowed its banks
19. Farmers discovered they could grow crops by using this water
20. Did farmers prosper when the Nile overflowed
21. In 3000 B.C. Egyptian farmers invented the ox-drawn plow
22. This plow helped Egyptian farmers produce a great deal of food
23. Did your history teacher tell you that they not only fed their own people but also exported huge quantities to other countries
24. Can you imagine the work involved to grow, harvest, and ship 20 million bushels of grain to Rome each year
25. Look at the stylized pictures on Egyptian pottery to see how they raised poultry and cared for their sheep

20.1 Using the Period and Other End Marks **567**

PRACTICE AND ASSESS

Answers Exercise 1
1. … tractors.—imp.
2. … book.—imp.
3. … 1870s.—dec.
4. … it.—dec.
5. … large?—int.
6. … loads?—int.
7. … time?—int.
8. … been!—excl.
9. … 1920.—dec.
10. … diggers.—dec.
11. … do.—imp.
12. … farming.—imp.
13. … book.—imp.
14. … farmers.—imp.
15. … seed?—int.
16. … area.—dec.
17. … was!—excl.
18. … banks.—dec.
19. … water.—dec.
20. … overflowed?—int.
21. … plow.—dec.
22. … food.—dec.
23. … countries?—int.
24. … year?—int.
25. … sheep.—imp.

Independent Practice

Skills Practice
- *Grammar Practice,* p. 45
- *Grammar Reteaching,* p. 46
- *Grammar Enrichment,* p. 45
- **Grammar Workbook,** Lesson 77

Unit Assessment
- *Tests with Answer Key* Unit 20 Pretest, pp. 77–78
- *Test Generator* Unit 20 Pretest

Enabling Strategies

LEP **Correct Punctuation**
Encourage students to compare punctuation in English to that used in their primary language if it punctuates sentences differently. For example, Spanish uses an upside down question mark at the beginning of an interrogative sentence as well as one at the end.

CLOSE

Photocopy a paragraph onto a transparency. Before showing it to the class, read it aloud slowly. Have students work in groups to decide how to correctly punctuate the paragraph. Then have them compare their paragraph against the original shown on an overhead projector.

FOCUS

Lesson Overview

Objective: To use commas appropriately

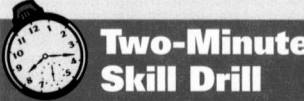

Bellringer

When students enter the classroom, have this assignment on the board: *Where do commas belong in this sentence?*

Tom Dick and Harry our best blockers all received football scholarships.

Motivating Activity

Discuss students' use of commas in their own writing. Then talk about how commas help them when they read. What do they do when they come across a comma while reading?

TEACH

Speaking and Listening

Point out that not every natural pause in a sentence requires a comma. For example, even when there seems to be a pause between the complete subject and complete predicate of a sentence, a comma is not needed.

Two-Minute Skill Drill

Challenge students to write a sentence using commas according to one of the following pairs of rules:

Rules 2 and 7
Rules 1 and 3
Rules 5 and 6

20.2 Using Commas I

Commas signal a pause between parts of a sentence.

and clog city streets.

RULE 1: Use commas to separate three or more items in a series.

Cars, buses, and trucks clog city streets.

RULE 2: Use commas to show a pause after an introductory word and to set off names used in direct address.

Yes, most cities have few parking garages.
Tony, are you going downtown?

RULE 3: Use a comma after two or more introductory prepositional phrases when the prepositional phrase is very long, or when the comma is needed to make the meaning clear. A comma is not needed after a single, short prepositional phrase, but it is acceptable to use one.

In the fall of 1991, Frank M. Jordan was elected mayor.

RULE 4: Use a comma after an introductory participle and an introductory participial phrase.

Plagued by deficits, many cities need state aid.

RULE 5: Use commas to set off words that interrupt the flow of thought in a sentence.

A large city, as you can see, employs many police officers.

RULE 6: Use a comma after conjunctive adverbs such as *however, moreover, furthermore, nevertheless,* and *therefore.*

The city is growing; therefore, the city payroll must grow.

RULE 7: Use commas to set off an appositive if it is not essential to the meaning of a sentence.

Alpine Inc., this city's oldest company, joined a large cartel.

568 *Punctuation*

Teacher's Classroom Resources

The following resources can be used for planning, instruction, practice, reinforcement, reteaching, or enrichment.

Teaching Tools
Lesson Plans

Blackline Masters
Grammar Practice, p. 46
Grammar Reteaching, p. 47
Grammar Enrichment, p. 46

Grammar Workbook
Lesson 78

Exercise 2 — Using Commas

Write each sentence, adding a comma or commas where needed. If the sentence needs no changes, write *correct*.

1. Yes cities offer many different places to live.
2. People can live in apartment buildings private homes town houses residential hotels or rooming houses.
3. In the middle of the city you can see skyscrapers.
4. Some buildings are neat clean and attractive.
5. Other buildings are dirty and neglected.
6. The city has a large population.
7. In the tiny yards behind some city buildings the residents have created charming "pocket gardens."
8. Yolanda did you know that San Diego is one of the nation's fastest-growing cities?
9. A big city in my opinion is the best place to live.
10. No I do not mind the crowding; the hustle and bustle in my opinion are part of a city's appeal.
11. Norm do you prefer the city or the country?
12. Does Jo your new friend enjoy living in the city?
13. Pausing a moment to consider my answer I responded that she likes the city.
14. Moreover she has never lived in the country.
15. Eva dislikes the city; nevertheless she refuses to move.
16. Traveling away from the center of the city you can find less crowded living conditions.
17. Country houses you might imagine have more land.
18. I hope Maya that you can find a big house in the country.
19. The suburbs I suppose would be a good alternative Maya.
20. The town of Ridgemont a northern suburb offers some of the advantages of both city and country.
21. From the top of the ridge in the town cemetery you can see the lights and towers of the city.
22. The center of town the commercial district offers convenient services.
23. Around the square at the very center you can find a drug store a bakery a restaurant a hardware store a clothing shop and a shoe store.
24. In most areas outside the city's center grass and trees dominate the landscape.
25. The residents are inspired by this landscape; consequently many take up gardening as a hobby.

20.2 Using Commas I   **569**

PRACTICE AND ASSESS

Answers: Exercise 2
1. Yes, cities offer …
2. … buildings, private homes, town houses, residential hotels, or …
3. … of the city, you …
4. … neat, clean, and attractive.
5. correct
6. correct
7. buildings, the …
8. Yolanda, did …
9. … city, in my opinion, is the …
10. No, … bustle, in my opinion, …
11. Norm, do you …
12. Does Jo, your new friend, …
13. … my answer, I …
14. Moreover, she …
15. … nevertheless, she …
16. … of the city, you …
17. … houses, you might imagine, …
18. I hope, Maya, that you …
19. The suburbs, I suppose, would … alternative, Maya.
20. … Ridgemont, a northern suburb, offers …
21. … cemetery, you …
22. … town, the commercial district, offers …
23. … center, … store, a bakery, a restaurant, a hardware store, a clothing shop, and a shoe store.
24. … center, grass …
25. … consequently, …

Independent Practice

Skills Practice
📁 *Grammar Practice,* p. 46
📁 *Grammar Reteaching,* p. 47
📁 *Grammar Enrichment,* p. 46
📓 **Grammar Workbook,** Lesson 78

CLOSE

Have students write examples of sentences that require commas on the board.

Enabling Strategies

LEP Punctuating Verbals

Some students may have difficulty understanding when to punctuate verbals, especially if they are punctuated differently in students' primary languages. Briefly review verbals. Remind students that if a verbal (such as *plagued by deficits*) is placed within a sentence, no commas are needed: *Many cities plagued by deficits need state aid.* If, however, the verbal begins a sentence, it must be punctuated with a comma: *Plagued by deficits, many cities need state aid.*

Lesson 20.3 teaches students to use commas appropriately as they write both compound and complex sentences.

FOCUS

Lesson Overview

Objective: To recognize appropriate use of commas in compound sentences, after introductory adverb clauses, and with nonessential adjective clauses

Bellringer

When students enter the classroom, have this assignment on the board: *Rewrite the following sentences, inserting commas where you think they are needed.*

1. *I really wanted to attend the play but I had to work instead.*
2. *Before making that important decision consider all your options.*
3. *Jeremy who works at the library called me last night.*

(Students should insert commas after *play,* after *decision,* after *Jeremy,* and before *called.*)

TEACH

☑ Grammar Tip

When an adverb clause is at the end of a sentence, as in *A crop can be ruined when rain comes at the wrong time,* do not use a comma. The adverb clause acts like a single adverb or adverb phrase. When the adverb clause is moved to a position in front of the main clause, as in *When rain comes at the wrong time, a crop can be ruined,* a comma is required.

570

20.3 | Using Commas II

Commas clarify meaning in sentences with more than one clause. A clause is a group of words that has a subject and a predicate and is used as part of a sentence.

RULE 9: Use a comma before *and, or,* or *but* when it joins main clauses.

> Farming is a business, and farmers need to make a profit.
> Farmers must sell their crops, or they cannot afford to replant.
> Farming can be rewarding, but it is hard work.

RULE 10: Use a comma after an introductory adverb clause. Adverb clauses begin with subordinating conjunctions, such as *after, although, as, because, before, considering (that), if, in order that, since, so that, though, unless, until, when, whenever, where, wherever, whether,* or *while.*

> When the weather is too dry, farmers have problems.
> If there is no rain, crops can be ruined.

In most cases, do not use a comma with an adverb clause that comes at the end of a sentence.

> Farmers have problems when the weather is too dry.
> Crops can be ruined if there is no rain.

RULE 11: Use a comma or a pair of commas to set off an adjective clause that is not essential to the meaning of a sentence. This means that the clause merely gives additional information. Adjective clauses often begin with the relative pronouns *who, whom, whose, which,* or *that.*

> Dairy cows, which are common on farms, are raised for their milk.

Do not use a comma or pair of commas to set off an essential clause from the rest of the sentence. An adjective clause is essential when it is necessary to the meaning of the sentence.

> An animal that is raised for milk is the dairy cow.

Teacher's Classroom Resources

The following resources can be used for planning, instruction, practice, reinforcement, reteaching, or enrichment.

🔧 **Teaching Tools**
Lesson Plans

📁 **Blackline Masters**
Grammar Practice, p. 47
Grammar Reteaching, p. 48
Grammar Enrichment, p. 47

📖 ***Grammar Workbook***
Lesson 79

Exercise 3 — Using Commas with Main Clauses

Write each sentence. Find the main clauses and the conjunction. Add commas where necessary. If the sentence needs no commas, write *correct*.

1. Farmers prepare the soil and then they plant crops in the fields.
2. Sometimes they plant a cover crop and plow it into the soil in spring.
3. They sometimes add organic material, which helps build the soil.
4. They maintain a compost pile from which they add finished compost to the soil.
5. Some seeds are planted directly in the ground but others are started indoors.
6. Some seeds are started in a greenhouse and they are planted outdoors when it's warm.
7. The farmers can buy the seeds fresh or they can save them from a previous crop.
8. Even when the plants are in the ground, the farmers' work is not done.
9. Weeds of all kinds suddenly appear and the farmers must act quickly.
10. They must remove the weeds carefully or they will disturb the young plants.

Exercise 4 — Using Commas with Subordinate Clauses

Write the subordinate clause in each sentence, adding commas where needed.

1. Whenever farmers grow crops insects move in for the feast.
2. IPM which stands for Integrated Pest Management helps control insects.
3. Because insects flourish in debris farmers try to keep their fields clean.
4. They make sure that seedlings are insect-free before they plant them.
5. They rotate crops so that soil insects don't have a chance to multiply.
6. They choose varieties that can hold their own against insects.
7. Breeders whose job it is to develop such varieties watch for resistant plants.
8. They isolate these plants which are then used to produce seed.
9. When insects are large another effective control is handpicking them.
10. Physical barriers that keep insects away are also helpful.
11. An example is a row cover which discourages maggots and beetles.
12. If an insect responds to visual or chemical cues it can be caught in a trap.
13. A bright red plastic apple lures apple maggots which stick to its surface.
14. Electronic lures that zap bugs are not very effective.
15. Strong pesticides are avoided because they kill beneficial insects.
16. These insects which include lady bugs and praying mantises eat other insects.
17. Although many people fear wasps some wasps help control harmful insects.
18. If all else fails farmers must rely on pesticides.
19. When they do they limit application to the exact problem area.
20. The safest kind is insecticidal soap which doesn't linger in the soil.

20.3 Using Commas II   **571**

PRACTICE AND ASSESS

Answers: Exercise 3
1. … soil, and …
2. correct
3. correct
4. correct
5. … ground, but …
6. … greenhouse, and …
7. … fresh, or …
8. correct
9. … appear, and …
10. … carefully, or …

Answers: Exercise 4
1. Whenever farmers grow crops, …
2. IPM, which … Management, …
3. Because … in debris, …
4. … before they plant them.
5. … so that … chance to multiply.
6. … that can … against insects.
7. breeders, whose … varieties, …
8. … plants, which … seed.
9. When insects are large, …
10. … that keep insects away …
11. … cover, which … beetles.
12. If an insect … chemical cues, …
13. … maggots, which … surface.
14. … that zap bugs …
15. because … insects.
16. … insects, which … mantises, …
17. Although … fear wasps, …
18. If all else fails, …
19. When they do, …
20. … soap, which … in the soil.

Independent Practice

Skills Practice
📁 *Grammar Practice*, p. 47
📁 *Grammar Reteaching*, p. 48
📁 *Grammar Enrichment*, p. 47

 **Grammar Workbook,** Lesson 79

Enabling Strategies

LEP Reviewing Main and Adverb Clauses

To help students practice using main clauses and adverb clauses, write examples of main clauses on one color paper, adverb clauses on another, and commas on a third. Have students assemble sentences and punctuate them correctly.

CLOSE

Have students write three original examples for each of the three rules about using commas taught in this lesson. Ask them to exchange their sentences with a partner to check each other's work.

FOCUS

Lesson Overview

Objective: To recognize several special conventions for comma use, including commas with dates and addresses, commas with titles or degrees, and commas in direct quotations

🔔 Bellringer

When students enter the classroom, have this assignment on the board: *Write answers to the questions below, inserting commas as needed.*

What is the date of your birth?
What is your mailing address?

Motivating Activity

Review students' answers to the Bellringer. Then write this sentence on the board and have students suggest where commas are needed: *Hank asked "Was the Magna Carta signed June 15 1215?"* (Commas are needed after *asked* and after *15.*)

TEACH

Cooperative Learning

Ask students to work in pairs to write two additional sample sentences for Rules 12 and 13—punctuating dates and addresses. Then have pairs volunteer to write their sample sentences on the board, omitting commas. Have the rest of the class write each sentence, placing commas as needed. Then allow each pair of students to write in the commas on the board and compare answers.

| 20.4 | Using Commas III |

Several rules for using commas—among those the rules for punctuating dates and addresses—are a matter of standard usage.

RULE 12: Use commas before and after the year when it is used with both the month and the day. If only the month and the year are given, do not use a comma.

> The antipollution project began on May 25, 1992, and lasted a year.
> The first meeting was held in July 1992 and made headlines.

RULE 13: Use commas before and after the name of a state or a country when it is used with the name of a city. Do not use a comma after the state if it is used with a ZIP code.

> Speakers came from Palo Alto, California, to speak at the meeting.
> The address on the envelope was as follows: 123 Ridge Road, Orange, CT 06477.

RULE 14: Use a comma or pair of commas to set off an abbreviated title or degree following a person's name.

> One expert on pollution and health is Jay Carr, M.D.
> Peter Fujita, Ph.D., wrote a book on pollution.

RULE 15: Use a comma or commas to set off *too* when *too* means "also."

> Air pollution creates problems, too. The courts, too, are involved.

RULE 16: Use a comma or commas to set off a direct quotation.

> Dr. Flores said, "Pollution causes serious problems in our cities."
> "We will try," said Joan, "to fight pollution."

RULE 17: Use a comma after the salutation of a friendly letter and after the closing of both a friendly and a business letter.

> Dear Sharon,   Your friend,   Yours truly,

RULE 18: Use a comma for clarity in reading a sentence.

> Instead of three, four panelists discussed pollution.

Teacher's Classroom Resources

The following resources can be used for planning, instruction, practice, reinforcement, reteaching, or enrichment.

🔧 **Teaching Tools**
Lesson Plans, p. 111

📁 **Blackline Masters**
Grammar Practice, p. 48
Grammar Reteaching, p. 49
Grammar Enrichment, p. 48

📕 *Grammar Workbook*
Lessons 80–81

Exercise 5 — Using Commas with Names, Titles, Dates, and Quotations

Write each sentence below, adding commas where necessary, or write *correct* if the sentence needs no changes.

1. Larry said "Our conference on pollution is sure to be successful."
2. A letter from Austin Texas arrived today.
3. It said that Jean Loubet Ph.D. will be attending too.
4. "Is Dr. Jean Loubet" asked Evan "a physician?"
5. His most famous book appeared in June 1995.
6. His letter told us that dozens of boxes of materials will be sent ahead by train.
7. We must prepare them for distribution at the conference.
8. Dr. Loubet will arrive at the conference on November 5 1996 and depart a week later.
9. He and Sarah McInerney M.D. will be our featured speakers.
10. Dr. McInerney has written many books and articles too.
11. She does research in Ann Arbor Michigan at the university.
12. Dr. McInerney asked "Should I send materials ahead, too?"
13. She doesn't have a Ph.D. but is as famous as Dr. Loubet.
14. Larry told both speakers "We're delighted to have you here."
15. Both Dr. McInerney and Jean Loubet, Ph.D. agreed to attend the 1997 conference to deliver speeches.

Exercise 6 — Using Commas in Letters

Write each numbered item below, adding commas where necessary.

¹109 National Boulevard
²Los Angeles CA 90034
³September 30 1993

⁴Dear Aunt Patricia

    ⁵Last week my teacher said "We can all do more to stop pollution." ⁶I think that students can help too. ⁷I said to Yoko "Let's make posters for the Stop Pollution Fair." ⁸The fair will be like the one that was held on January 5 1992 in Denver Colorado. ⁹Alex Gafar M.A. will speak on recycling.

¹⁰Much love
Antonia

20.4 Using Commas III **573**

Enabling Strategies

LEP Replacing Commas

A good way to help students whose primary languages punctuate differently is to remove all of the commas from the sentences in a paragraph.

Divide the students into groups, including one student who is fluent in English in each group. Give each group a paragraph from which all the commas have been removed. At the end of the paragraph, tell each group how many commas they should put back in.

Have students work in groups, replacing commas in their paragraph. Have the groups compare answers.

Lesson 20.5 teaches students the proper use of semicolons and colons. These punctuation marks help writers express complex ideas.

FOCUS

Lesson Overview

Objective: To use semicolons and colons appropriately

Bellringer

As students enter the classroom, have this assignment on the board: *Punctuate these sentences: Efrat thought English was difficult to learn however she speaks very well. I have to pack these items for my trip a sleeping bag, a small camping stove, and a pup tent.*

Motivating Activity

Review students' responses to the Bellringer activity. Have students suggest other uses for the colon.

TEACH

☑ Teaching Tip

Write on the board the sentence below. Point out that the semicolon indicates a more definite break in thought than a comma does. Read the sentence aloud. Ask students if they can "hear" where the semicolon belongs. How? (The semicolon calls for a longer pause than a comma.)

Eagerly he hurried along, now slipping on a rotten log or a loose stone, but making headway; night was beginning to settle down on the island.

—Richard Connell, "The Most Dangerous Game"

574

20.5 Using Semicolons and Colons

RULE 1:   Use a semicolon to join the parts of a compound sentence when a coordinating conjunction, such as *and, or, nor,* or *but,* is not used.

> Many people in Africa farm small pieces of land; these farmers raise food for their families.

RULE 2:   Use a semicolon to join parts of a compound sentence when the main clauses are long and are subdivided by commas. Use a semicolon even if these clauses are already joined by a coordinating conjunction.

> Herding is an important job for the Dinka, Masai, and Turkana; but plowing, planting, and harvesting are also crucial tasks.

RULE 3:   Use a semicolon to separate main clauses joined by a conjunctive adverb, such as *consequently, furthermore, however, moreover, nevertheless,* or *therefore.* Be sure to use a comma after a conjunctive adverb.

> Many African farmers grow crops on family-owned farms; however, in some areas farmers work on land owned by the government.

RULE 4:   Use a colon to introduce a list of items that ends a sentence. Use a phrase such as *these, the following,* or *as follows* to signal that a list is coming.

> African farmers grow the following: corn, millet, and sorghum.

Do not use a colon immediately after a verb or a preposition.

> Some farmers work with hoes, knives, and digging sticks.

RULE 5:   Use a colon to separate the hour and the minute when you write the time of day.

> Many farmers start working at 5:15 in the morning.

RULE 6:   Use a colon after the salutation of a business letter.

> Dear Sir or Madam: Dear Ms. Ngai:

Teacher's Classroom Resources

The following resources can be used for planning, instruction, practice, reinforcement, reteaching, or enrichment.

⚙ Teaching Tools
Lesson Plans, p. 112

📁 Blackline Masters
Grammar Practice, p. 49
Grammar Reteaching, p. 50
Grammar Enrichment, p. 49

📕 Grammar Workbook
Lesson 82

Exercise 7 — Using Semicolons and Colons

Write each sentence. Add a semicolon or a colon where needed. Remember to use a comma after a conjunctive adverb.

1. I was bored at 330 in the afternoon then the mail arrived.
2. It included these items two bills, three ads, and a letter from my cousin.
3. Jill wrote about her work in Africa she is teaching English in Tanzania.
4. Africa can be divided into these regions deserts, jungles, grasslands, and farmlands.
5. The equator cuts through Africa however most land lies north of the equator.
6. Some areas are not very hospitable nevertheless most are inhabited.
7. There is a strip of fertile land along the Mediterranean Sea in North Africa however the Sahara dominates that area.
8. The southern edge of the desert merges into grassland further south the grassland merges into a tropical rain forest.
9. Southern Africa lies in the temperate zone snow falls there occasionally.
10. Africa is rich in resources thus it supports a variety of life styles.
11. Rubber trees flourish in the rain forest olive trees grow near the Mediterranean.
12. In the grasslands farmers grow wheat and barley they also raise sheep.
13. South Africa is a major wool producer its main crops are corn and sugar.
14. Spectacular rivers flowing through Africa include the following the mighty Nile in the east, the Congo in Central Africa, and the Niger in the west.
15. Agriculture dominates the economy mining is another important activity.
16. Jill mentioned the following Tanzanian products cotton, coffee, and sugar.
17. Some areas are quite poor consequently farmers must struggle to survive.
18. Subsistence farmers depend on corn they may also raise cattle or goats.
19. Jill finds life in Africa fascinating nevertheless she misses home.
20. Now at 345 I am no longer bored Jill's letter has sparked my imagination.

Exercise 8 — Using Semicolons and Colons in Letters

Write the following numbered items, adding a semicolon or a colon where needed.

[1]Dear Mr. Bishop

[2]I am buying a farm for my venture I will need farming equipment. [3]I will have to buy plows, tractors, and spreaders. [4]In the near future I will also need the following seed, fertilizer, and more machinery. [5]I am now pricing equipment therefore, if you are interested in doing business with me, please send me a list of your prices.

Sincerely yours,
Eleni Ruiz

20.5 Using Semicolons and Colons **575**

Answers: Exercise 7
1. … 3:30 … afternoon;
2. … items: two …
3. … Africa; …
4. … regions:
5. … Africa; however,
6. … hospitable; nevertheless, …
7. … Africa, however,
8. … grassland; …
9. … zone; …
10. … resources; thus,
11. … forest; …
12. … barley;
13. … producer; …
14. … following:
15. … economy; …
16. … products: …
17. … poor; consequently,
18. … corn; …
19. … fascinating; nevertheless,
20. … 3:45 … bored;

Answers: Exercise 8
1. Dear Mr. Bishop:
2. …farm, for my venture; I will need …
3. correct as written
4. … following: seed, …
5. … equipment; therefore, …

Independent Practice

Skills Practice
📁 *Grammar Practice,* p. 49
📁 *Grammar Reteaching,* p. 50
📁 *Grammar Enrichment,* p. 49

📖 **Grammar Workbook,** Lesson 20.5

CLOSE

Have students write a brief business letter requesting information. It should have a colon in the salutation and include a compound sentence joined by a semicolon.

Enabling Strategies

LEP Combining Sentences

Some students may have difficulty punctuating conjunctive adverbs, especially if they are punctuated differently in their primary languages. Sentence combining can show students how to join sentences with a semicolon and a conjunctive adverb. Write two sentences on the board, such as

Greg went to the park. Chidi stayed home. Have students combine the two sentences using a semicolon, one of the conjunctive adverbs listed in Rule 6, and a comma. Then have students combine two sentences of their own.

FOCUS

Lesson Overview

Objective: To recognize the correct use of quotation marks and related punctuation and to recognize the correct use of italics (or underlining)

Bellringer

When students enter the classroom, have this assignment on the board: *Write the next sentence, inserting quotation marks and other needed punctuation.*

Mr. Hill announced Tomorrow is a holiday

Motivating Activity

Discuss students' answers to the Bellringer. Then write these sentences on the board, and have volunteers suggest how to punctuate them.

1. My pet iguana said Karl likes to sit on my shoulder
2. Cosette read Les Miserables long before the play became popular.

TEACH

☑ **Teaching Tip**

In teaching the use of end punctuation in quotations, explain that if the quoted sentence is a question or emphatic statement, the end punctuation goes inside the quotation marks. If the main sentence is a question or emphatic statement, the question mark or exclamation point goes outside the quotation marks, and there's no punctuation inside them.

20.6 Using Quotation Marks and Italics

Quotation marks enclose a person's exact words, as well as the titles of some works. Italic type—a special slanted type that is used in printing—identifies titles of other works. In handwriting, use underlining to show italic type.

RULE 1: Use quotation marks before and after a direct quotation.

"A nomad is a person who wanders," May said.

RULE 2: Use quotation marks with both parts of a divided quotation.

"Most nomads," said Ali, "travel by animal or on foot."

RULE 3: Use a comma or commas to separate a phrase such as *he said* from the quotation itself. Place the comma inside closing quotation marks.

"Most nomads," Betsy explained, "raise animals."

RULE 4: Place a period inside closing quotation marks.

José said, "Some nomads move their animals through deserts."

RULE 5: Place a question mark or an exclamation point inside the quotation marks when it is part of the quotation.

Bo asked, "Do nomads travel to find water for their herds?"

RULE 6: Place a question mark or an exclamation point outside the quotation marks when it is part of the entire sentence.

Did Ms. McCall say, "Write an essay on nomads"?

RULE 7: Use quotation marks for the title of a short story, essay, poem, song, magazine or newspaper article, or book chapter.

"Dusk" [short story]   "Mending Wall" [poem]   "Skylark" [song]

RULE 8: Use italics (underlining) for the title of a book, play, film, television series, magazine, newspaper, or work of art.

The Sea Wolf [book]   *Julius Caesar* [play]   *Newsweek* [magazine]

576   *Punctuation*

Teacher's Classroom Resources

The following resources can be used for planning, instruction, practice, reinforcement, reteaching, or enrichment.

🎿 **Teaching Tools**
Lesson Plans

📁 **Blackline Masters**
Grammar Practice, p. 50
Grammar Reteaching, p. 51
Grammar Enrichment, p. 50

📖 *Grammar Workbook*
Lesson 83

Exercise 9 — Punctuating Titles

Write each item below, adding quotation marks or underlining for italics where needed.

1. Nanook of the North (film)
2. New York Times (newspaper)
3. The Eternal Nomad (poem)
4. The Old Man and the Sea (book)
5. Dream-Children (essay)
6. Star Trek (television series)
7. The Skin of Our Teeth (play)
8. Scientific American (magazine)
9. The Coldest Land (magazine article)
10. To Build a Fire (short story)

Exercise 10 — Using Quotation Marks and Italics

Write the following sentences, adding quotation marks, underlining for italics, and other punctuation marks where needed.

1. Frieda asked Have you read the assignment in our textbook
2. Bonnie shouted What an interesting article on nomads that was
3. I didn't know said Barry that some nomads live in northern Europe
4. Yes said Ms. Ito Lapland lies in Russia, Finland, Sweden, and Norway
5. Did Ms. Ito say The people of Lapland are called Lapps
6. Barry asked Have you read the article on Lapps in National Geographic
7. No I answered but I read about them in another magazine
8. The Lapps have two seasons said Frieda day and night
9. Does the night season really last nine months asked Barry
10. The book The Far North says Lapland has only six weeks of warm weather a year
11. Did the book say Only mosses and a few trees grow in Lapland
12. Why are the Lapps considered nomads asked George
13. Bonnie answered The people live by hunting and fishing
14. During the summer season I said they lay in supplies for the winter
15. Reindeer and dogs added Frieda are their only domestic animals
16. Do the people follow the reindeer all summer asked George
17. Bonnie replied The herds must keep moving to find enough to eat
18. Tim asked What do the Lapps do with the reindeer
19. The filmstrip The Land of the Lapps says they use the milk, meat, and hides
20. Did you know asked Ms. Ito that both male and female reindeer have antlers

20.6 Using Quotation Marks and Italics **577**

PRACTICE AND ASSESS

Answers: Exercise 9

1. <u>Nanook of the North</u>
2. <u>New York Times</u>
3. "The Eternal Nomad"
4. <u>The Old Man and the Sea</u>
5. "Dream-Children"
6. <u>Star Trek</u>
7. <u>The Skin of Our Teeth</u>
8. <u>Scientific American</u>
9. "The Coldest Land"
10. "To Build a Fire"

Answers: Exercise 10

1. Frieda asked, "Have ... textbook?"
2. Bonnie shouted, "What ... was!"
3. "I ... know," said Barry, "that ... Europe."
4. "Yes," said Mrs. Ito. "Lapland ... Norway."
5. ...say, "The ... Lapps"?
6. Barry asked, "Have ... <u>National Geographic</u>?"
7. "No," I answered, "but ... magazine."
8. "The ... seasons," said Freida, "day and night."
9. "Does ...months?" asked Barry.
10. The book, <u>The Far North</u>, says ... year.
11. ... say, "Only ... Lapland"?
12. "Why ... nomads?" asked George.
13. ... answered, "The ... fishing."
14. "During ... season," I said, "they... winter."
15. "Reindeer and dogs," added Freida, "are ... animals."
16. "Do ... summer?" asked George.
17. Bonnie replied, "The ... eat."
18. Tim asked, "What ... reindeer?"
19. ... filmstrip, "The ... Lapps," says ... hides.
20. "Did you know," asked Mrs. Ito, "that ... antlers?"

Enabling Strategies

LEP Shifting Verb Tenses

Students may have difficulty with verb tenses in indirect quotations because the tense in the reported speech usually shifts backward. Compare the following: *Kamisha said, "I am tired."* Indirect: *Kamisha said that she was tired.* Elicit examples from students.

CLOSE

Ask students to write a brief dialogue. Have them feel free to use slang and idiomatic expressions for realism. However, stress that correctly punctuating dialogue will make the dialogue—and their stories—easier to follow.

Setting the Purpose

Lesson 20.7 teaches students to use the apostrophe to indicate possession and contraction and with certain plurals.

FOCUS

Lesson Overview

Objective: To recognize the correct use of the apostrophe

🔔 Bellringer
When students enter the classroom, have this assignment on the board: *Tom and Mary's cat is lost.* Who owns the cat?

Motivating Activity
Lead into the lesson by explaining that "Tom and Mary's cat" means the cat belongs to both of them. Ask students what indicates that both Tom and Mary own the cat.

TEACH

☑ Teaching Tip
Explain that if a thing is jointly owned by two or more individuals, only the last name takes the apostrophe: *Tim and Lisa's house.* If the ownership is not joint, each name takes an apostrophe: *Aaron's and Marsha's houses.*

⇄ Cross-reference: Grammar
For a review of possessive nouns, refer students to Lesson 9.3, pp. 352–353. To help students distinguish among plural nouns, possessive nouns, and contractions, see Lesson 9.4, pp. 354–355.

To help students understand other troublesome words that are often confused in their possessive forms and as contractions, refer them to Lessons 17.2 and 17.3, pp. 526–531.

578

| 20.7 | **Using Apostrophes** |

An apostrophe shows possession as well as the missing letters in a contraction. It can also signal the plural of letters, numbers, or words.

RULE 1: Use an apostrophe and an *s* (*'s*) to form the possessive of a singular noun.

girl + **'s** = girl**'s**   Francis + **'s** = Francis**'s**

RULE 2: Use an apostrophe and an *s* (*'s*) to form the possessive of a plural noun that does not end in *s*.

women + **'s** = women**'s**   mice + **'s** = mice**'s**

RULE 3: Use an apostrophe alone to form the possessive of a plural noun that ends in *s*.

girls + **'** = girls**'**   Johnsons + **'** = Johnsons**'**

RULE 4: Use an apostrophe and an *s* (*'s*) to form the possessive of an indefinite pronoun.

anyone + **'s** = anyone**'s**   somebody + **'s** = somebody**'s**

Do not use an apostrophe in a possessive pronoun.

That map is **theirs**.   Is this mark **mine**?
The books on the table are **hers**.   The bird flapped **its** wings.

RULE 5: Use an apostrophe to replace letters that have been omitted in a contraction.

it + is = it**'s**   you + are = you**'re**
there + is = there**'s**   did + not = didn**'t**

RULE 6: Use an apostrophe to form the plural of letters, figures, and words when they are used as themselves.

three *t***'s**   five *6***'s**   no *and***'s**, *if***'s**, or *but***'s**

RULE 7: Use an apostrophe to show missing numbers in a date.

the class of **'87**

Teacher's Classroom Resources

The following resources can be used for planning, instruction, practice, reinforcement, reteaching, or enrichment.

🔧 **Teaching Tools**
Lesson Plans

📁 **Blackline Masters**
Grammar Practice, p. 51
Grammar Reteaching, p. 52
Grammar Enrichment, p. 51

📓 *Grammar Workbook*
Lesson 84

Exercise 11   Using Apostrophes in Possessives

Write the possessive form of each of the words below.

1. cities	9. woman	17. the Gilsons
2. nation	10. geese	18. landowners
3. everybody	11. classes	19. managers
4. children	12. teacher	20. people
5. Mr. Schultz	13. Alex	21. rooster
6. dogs	14. someone	22. family
7. man	15. oxen	23. nobody
8. Sharice	16. Jim	24. Ms. Tremon
		25. clowns

Exercise 12   Using Apostrophes

Write each plural, possessive, or contraction. Use apostrophes where needed. Write *correct* if the sentence needs no changes.

1. This citys outlook is uncertain.
2. Ours is an uncertain future.
3. Today cities arent built beneath the earth.
4. Its strange to think of underground cities.
5. Perhaps well see cities floating on the water.
6. Many city planners ideas are unusual.
7. Their reports usually are filled with too many *if*s.
8. Tomorrows cities are a mystery to us.
9. No city can plan its future exactly.
10. All of our visions are full of *maybe*s.
11. What will actually happen to cities is anybodys guess.
12. These authors new book predicts the end of cities.
13. The Murrays idea is that we wont need cities.
14. In their view computers will let us live anywhere.
15. I can do my job at my house, you can do yours at your house, and other people can work out of their houses, too.
16. Ill believe that when I see it.
17. Other peoples dreams take them to space.
18. One of Arthur C. Clarks books is about a city in a space station.
19. The residents lives would be very different from ours.
20. Someone elses book predicts that cities will expand outward.

20.7 Using Apostrophes   **579**

Two-Minute Skill Drill

Have students spell the possessive form of *no one (no one's), women (women's), birds (birds')*.

PRACTICE AND ASSESS

Answers: Exercise 11

1. cities'	14. someone's
2. nation's	15. oxen's
3. everybody's	16. Jim's
4. children's	17. the Gilsons'
5. Mr. Schultz's	18. landowners'
6. dogs'	19. managers'
7. man's	20. people's
8. Sharice's	21. rooster's
9. woman's	22. family's
10. geese's	23. nobody's
11. classes'	24. Ms. Tremon's
12. teacher's	25. clowns'
13. Alex's	

Answers: Exercise 12

1. city's	11. anybody's
2. correct	12. authors'
3. aren't	13. Murrays', won't
4. It's	14. correct
5. we'll	15. correct
6. planners'	16. I'll
7. *if*s	17. people's
8. Tomorrow's	18. Clark's
9. correct	19. residents'
10. *maybe*s	20. else's

Independent Practice

Skills Practice

📁 *Grammar Practice*, p. 51
📁 *Grammar Reteaching*, p. 52
📁 *Grammar Enrichment*, p. 51

📖 *Grammar Workbook,* Lesson 84

CLOSE

Tell students: *The year is 2238. Use apostrophes in a sentence to describe what you see.*

579

Enabling Strategies

LEP Using the Apostrophe

Students whose primary language is not English may be confused by the use of the apostrophe. Have them use these rules in sentences 1, 3–6, 12, 13, and 17 in Exercise 12 to determine whether a noun is possessive:

• replacing the -*s* or -'*s* with *have* (children's toys = the children have toys)
• replacing the -*s* or -'*s* with *of* (children's toys = the toys of the children)
• replacing the possible possessive noun with a possessive pronoun (children's toys = their toys).

Setting the Purpose

Lesson 20.8 teaches students to correctly use hyphens, dashes, and parentheses.

FOCUS

Lesson Overview

Objective: To use hyphens, dashes, and parentheses appropriately

🔔 Bellringer

When students enter the classroom, have this assignment on the board: *When do you use hyphens, dashes, and parentheses in writing? List the situations.*

Motivating Activity

Discuss students' answers to the Bellringer exercise. Then write the following sentence on the board and ask students what effect the parentheses and hyphen have on the meaning of the passage.

> We lived with our grandmother and uncle in the rear of the Store (it was always spoken of with a capital s), which she had owned some twenty-five years.
>
> —Maya Angelou, *I Know Why the Caged Bird Sings*

TEACH

☑ Grammar Tip

The general guidelines for dividing words at the ends of lines are as follows: (a) division is usually made according to pronunciation; (b) division should be made after a vowel; (c) one-letter divisions are not permissible; (d) proper nouns should not be divided if possible.

RULE 1:   Use a hyphen to show the division of a word at the end of a line. Always divide the word between its syllables.

Forests and their products are of the greatest importance to people.

RULE 2:   Use a hyphen in compound numbers.

eighty-seven   thirty-nine

RULE 3:   Use a hyphen in a fraction that is used as a modifier. Do not use a hyphen in a fraction used as a noun.

Forest rangers receive **one-half** pay upon retirement. [modifier]
One half of all tree diseases are caused by fungi. [noun]

RULE 4:   Use a hyphen or hyphens in certain compound nouns.

great-grandfather   brother-in-law   attorney-at-law

RULE 5:   Hyphenate a compound modifier only when it precedes the word it modifies.

It's a **well-maintained** park.   It is **well maintained**.

RULE 6:   Use a hyphen after the prefixes *all-*, *ex-*, and *self-*. Use a hyphen to separate any prefix from a word that begins with a capital letter.

all-powerful   ex-wife   self-educated   pre-Columbian

RULE 7:   Use a dash or dashes to show a sudden break or change in thought or speech.

Mrs. Poulos—she lives nearby—helps the park attendants.

RULE 8:   Use parentheses to set off words that define or helpfully explain a word in the sentence.

In tropical rain forests dozens of species of plants may grow in one square mile (2.6 square kilometers) of land.

Teacher's Classroom Resources

The following resources can be used for planning, instruction, practice, reinforcement, reteaching, or enrichment.

🔧 **Teaching Tools**
Lesson Plans, p. 113

📁 **Blackline Masters**
Grammar Practice, p. 51
Grammar Reteaching, p. 52
Grammar Enrichment, p. 51

📓 *Grammar Workbook*
Lesson 85

Exercise 13   Using Hyphens

Write each item. Use a hyphen where needed. Write *correct* if the item needs no hyphens.

1. two thirds majority
2. one half of the pie
3. exchampion
4. self knowledge
5. well loved author
6. all inclusive
7. Great aunt Katie
8. sixty five
9. mid American
10. postwar
11. one quarter finished
12. father in law
13. well known author
14. seventy three
15. pro Irish

Exercise 14   Using Hyphens, Dashes, and Parentheses

Write the following sentences, adding any needed hyphens, dashes, or parentheses. Write *correct* if the sentence needs no changes.

1. Before people began to clear the forest for farms and cities, forests covered about one half of the earth.
2. Dr. Orzeck he is an expert on ecology spoke about deforestation.
3. His presentation was well documented.
4. People have used wood products since the beginning of time but more about that later.
5. One tree may have as many as forty two uses.
6. In pre Columbian America vast all pine forests were common.
7. Some pines were huge, up to 240 feet tall and 2 feet in diameter.
8. British law see text on page 311 reserved these huge trees for the Crown.
9. The super straight trunks were perfect for the masts of sailing ships.
10. In 1947 a month long fire in a Maine forest provided a forest laboratory.
11. At first sun loving flowers and shrubs grew up to fill the new clearings.
12. Now evergreens trees that don't shed their leaves are shading out the birches.
13. These shade tolerant trees will again dominate the forest.
14. About 748 species of trees are native in the continental United States.
15. The National Register of Big Trees page 221 lists champion trees.
16. A sequoia truly a giant at eighty-three feet in circumference is the largest tree.
17. Some sequoias in California have been growing for three thousand years.
18. Others want to protect the remaining old growth forests in the country.
19. Forests grow only where there is at least fifteen inches thirty-eight centimeters of rainfall per year.
20. Forests also require a frost free growing period of at least three months.

20.8 Using Hyphens, Dashes, and Parentheses **581**

PRACTICE AND ASSESS

Answers: Exercise 13
1. two-thirds majority
2. correct
3. ex-champion
4. self-knowledge
5. well-loved author
6. all-inclusive
7. Great-aunt Katie
8. sixty-five
9. mid-American
10. correct
11. one-quarter finished
12. father-in-law
13. well-known author
14. seventy-three
15. pro-Irish

Answers: Exercise 14
1. correct
2. Dr. Orzeck—he is an expert on ecology—spoke …
3. correct
4. … of time—but more …
5. … forty-two uses.
6. In pre-Columbian … all-pine …
7. correct
8. … law (see text on page 311) …
9. The super-straight …
10. … month-long …
11. At first sun-loving …
12. correct
13. These shade-tolerant …
14. correct
15. … Big Trees (page 221) …
16. A sequoia—truly … circumference—is …
17. correct
18. … remaining old-growth …
19. … inches (thirty-eight centimeters) …
20. … a frost-free …

Independent Practice

Skills Practice
📁 *Grammar Practice*, p. 51
📁 *Grammar Reteaching*, p. 52
📁 *Grammar Enrichment*, p. 51
📒 ***Grammar Workbook***, Lesson 85

Enabling Strategies

LEP Hyphenating Compound Modifiers

Guide students in using this format: *The park is well maintained.* What kind of a park is it? *It is a well-maintained park.* Other examples are *straight-sided, dust-catching, thirst-quenching, interest-bearing, well-read, well-grounded, half-hidden.*

CLOSE

Have students write a paragraph discussing some of the products that can be made from things provided by forests. Remind students to use hyphens, dashes, and parentheses.

Setting the Purpose

Lesson 20.9 teaches students to use abbreviations correctly in six situations.

FOCUS

Lesson Overview

Objective: To use the correct form of abbreviations

Bellringer

When students enter the classroom, have this assignment on the board: *List all the situations you can think of in which abbreviations are used.*

Motivating Activity

Discuss when and how abbreviations are used. Do students know of times when it is better to spell out than to abbreviate? Why might that be?

TEACH

Speaking and Listening

Encourage students to use abbreviations—even invented ones—when they take notes in class. Explain that this method will allow them to jot down notes quickly and keep up with the discussion.

Cross-reference: Mechanics

For instruction and practice of the rules for capitalizing names and titles of people, refer students to Lesson 19.2, pp. 552–553 and Lesson 19.4, pp. 556–557.

National
Aeronautics and
Space
Administration

20.9　Using Abbreviations

RULE 1: Abbreviate the titles *Mr., Mrs., Ms.,* and *Dr.* before a person's name. Also abbreviate any professional or academic degree that follows a name, along with the titles *Jr.* and *Sr.*

Mr. Roy Sims **Jr.**　　Rita Mendez, **M.D.**　　Hugo Allen **Sr.**

RULE 2: Use capital letters and no periods with abbreviations that are pronounced letter by letter or as words. Exceptions are *U.S.* and *Washington, D.C.,* which do use periods.

WHO World Health Organization　**JV** junior varsity
ROTC Reserve Officers' Training Corps

RULE 3: With exact times use *A.M.* (*ante meridiem,* "before noon") and *P.M.* (*post meridiem,* "after noon"). For years use *B.C.* (before Christ) and, sometimes, *A.D.* (*anno Domini,* "in the year of the Lord," after Christ).

7:15 **A.M.**　9:30 **P.M.**　　40 **B.C.**　**A.D.** 476

RULE 4: Abbreviate days and months only in charts and lists.

Sun.　Tues.　Wed.　　Feb.　Jul.　Aug.　Sept.

RULE 5: In scientific writing abbreviate units of measure. Use periods with English units but not with metric units.

inch(es) **in.**　pound(s) **lb.**　gallon(s) **gal.**
kilometer(s) **km**　liter(s) **l**　milliliter(s) **ml**

RULE 6: On envelopes only, abbreviate street names and state names. In general text, spell out street names and state names.

Street **St.**　Avenue **Ave.**　Road **Rd.**　Drive **Dr.**
Boulevard **Blvd.**　Parkway **Pkwy.**　Place **Pl.**
Arizona **AZ**　Colorado **CO**　Hawaii **HI**　Oklahoma **OK**
Kentucky **KY**　Utah **UT**　Virginia **VA**　Missouri **MO**

[on an envelope]　Mrs. Emily Anderson
　　　　　　　　　3117 Chelsea **Ave.**
　　　　　　　　　Norfolk, **VA** 23503

but　We still live on Chelsea **Avenue** in Norfolk, **Virginia.**

582　*Punctuation*

Teacher's Classroom Resources

The following resources can be used for planning, instruction, practice, reinforcement, reteaching, or enrichment.

Teaching Tools
Lesson Plans

Blackline Masters
Grammar Practice, p. 52
Grammar Enrichment, p. 52

Grammar Workbook
Lesson 86

Exercise 15   Using Abbreviations

Write the correct abbreviation for each underlined item.

1. *anno Domini* 2000
2. David Parker <u>Junior</u>
3. 153 <u>kilometers</u>
4. <u>February</u> 23
5. <u>Wednesday</u>
6. 1066 <u>before Christ</u>
7. <u>Young Women's Christian Association</u>
8. <u>Mister</u> Al Moreno
9. ninety-eight <u>pounds</u>
10. Saratoga <u>Road</u>
11. 67 Ryer <u>Avenue</u>
12. Sam Blie <u>Senior</u>
13. Phoenix, <u>Arizona</u>
14. Lewis Wright, <u>Medical Doctor</u>
15. <u>Students Against Driving Drunk</u>
16. *post meridiem*
17. Ann Carey, <u>Doctor of Philosophy</u>
18. Cato <u>Boulevard</u>
19. Denver, <u>Colorado</u>
20. <u>Columbia Broadcasting System</u>

Exercise 16   Using Abbreviations in Sentences

Write the correct abbreviation for each underlined item in the following sentences. Write "correct" if there are no changes.

1. The address on the envelope read 48 Bolton <u>Street</u>, Madison, <u>Wisconsin</u>.
2. It contained information from <u>Doctor</u> Rita Tapahonso.
3. <u>Mister</u> Ed Jones is teaching ecology.
4. Last year classes met from 9:30 <u>in the morning</u> until 3:30 <u>in the afternoon</u>.
5. Scheduled speakers included <u>Doctor</u> Robin Oren.
6. Also present will be a representative of the <u>Geological Society of America</u>.
7. Classes begin in <u>September</u>.
8. My adviser will see me on <u>Tuesday</u>.
9. Do you know the purpose of most <u>United Nations</u> agencies?
10. I know <u>United Nations International Children's Emergency Fund</u> helps children and mothers in developing nations.
11. Also, the <u>International Labor Organization</u> promotes employment and fair labor conditions.
12. The President lives at 1600 Pennsylvania <u>Avenue</u>, Washington, <u>District of Columbia</u>.
13. I was born on <u>February</u> 29, 1980, at 6:50 *ante meridiem*.
14. Madeline Jefferson, <u>Master of Arts</u>, is our English teacher.
15. Mix 3 <u>gallons</u> of Substance A with 2 <u>pounds</u> of Substance B.
16. Salt Lake City, <u>Utah</u>, and Tulsa, <u>Oklahoma</u>, are often compared.
17. Kim Yang, <u>Doctor of Dental Surgery</u>, has been my dentist for three years.
18. His office address is 412 Mullins <u>Road</u>, Kalamazoo, <u>Michigan</u>.
19. Mexico, <u>Missouri</u>, and Paris, <u>Kentucky</u>, are both <u>United States</u> cities.
20. What is the sum of 12 <u>liters</u> and 48 <u>milliliters</u>?

20.9 Using Abbreviations   **583**

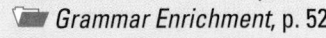

Enabling Strategies

LEP Understanding Abbreviations

Explain to students whose primary language is not English that people living in the United States tend to abbreviate more than other English-speakers and speakers of other languages. Make a list of common abbreviations in one column and the names they stand for, in a different order, in another column. Include such abbreviations as JFK, RPM, NASA, TV, VCR, and CD. Have students match the abbreviations with their meanings. Ask volunteers who are proficient in English to create similar lists for these students to practice matching.

FOCUS

Lesson Overview

Objective: To use numerals and spelled-out numbers appropriately

Bellringer

When students enter the classroom, have this assignment on the board: *List the current date and time, your birthdate, phone number, street address, and zip code.*

Motivating Activity

Discuss students' answers to the Bellringer activity. Discuss which words they spelled out and which they left as numerals.

TEACH

☑ Teaching Tip

Two-word numbers ending in *hundred, thousand, million,* and *billion* should be spelled out; for example, *eight hundred, twelve thousand.*

⇄ Cross-reference: Mechanics

For a review of the use of hyphens in compound numbers, refer students to Lesson 20.8, pp. 580–581

⇄ Cross-reference: Mechanics

For a review of the rules for capitalizing the first word of a sentence, refer students to Lesson 19.1, pp. 550–551.

20.10 Writing Numbers

In charts and tables, numbers are always written as figures. However, in an ordinary sentence some numbers are spelled out and others are written as numerals.

RULE 1: Spell out numbers that you can write in one or two words.

My dad had not visited his hometown for **twenty-five** years.

RULE 2: Use numerals for numbers of more than two words.

Approximately **250** people used to live in his hometown.

RULE 3: Spell out any number that begins a sentence, or reword the sentence so that it does not begin with a number.

Nine thousand two hundred people now live in Dad's hometown.

RULE 4: Write very large numbers as a numeral followed by the word *million* or *billion*.

The population of the United States is about **263 million**.

RULE 5: If related numbers appear in the same sentence, use all numerals.

Of the **435** graduates, **30** have received a scholarship to college.

RULE 6: Spell out ordinal numbers (*first, second,* and so forth).

Jan is the **sixth** person to use the new library.

RULE 7: Use words to express the time of day unless you are writing the exact time or using the abbreviation A.M. or P.M.

Classes begin at **nine o'clock**.
They end at **2:45 P.M.**

RULE 8: Use numerals to express dates, house and street numbers, apartment and room numbers, telephone numbers, page numbers, amounts of money of more than two words, and percentages. Write out the word *percent*.

May **24, 1887**   **62** Oak Drive   Room **307**   **98** percent

584   *Punctuation*

Teacher's Classroom Resources

The following resources can be used for planning, instruction, practice, reinforcement, reteaching, enrichment.

⚡ Teaching Tools
Lesson Plans

📁 Blackline Masters
Grammar Practice, p. 52
Grammar Enrichment, p. 52

📙 Grammar Workbook
Lesson 87

Exercise 17 — Writing Numbers

Write the sentences below, using the correct form for writing numbers. Write *correct* if a sentence needs no changes.

1. My father graduated from Red Bank Regional High School with the class of nineteen hundred sixty-one.
2. His class recently had a reunion after thirty years.
3. The reunion was scheduled for April ninth.
4. The party began at seven-thirty P.M.
5. Dad was the 13th person to arrive that evening.
6. The reunion was held in room forty-two, the old cafeteria.
7. 220 people came to the reunion.
8. Of these, 180 guests were graduates and forty were spouses.
9. More than 50% of the graduates attended.
10. There were three hundred thirty-four students in his graduating class.
11. Dad was happy to see his old best friend, whom he had not seen in 27 years.
12. He learned that Mr. Elton has moved back to town, to One Eighteen Jay Rd.
13. Dad, Mr. Elton, and 2 other old friends agreed to get together in the coming year.
14. They figure three hundred sixty-five days gives them enough time to plan something.
15. Each alumnus contributed twenty dollars.
16. The committee collected 4 thousand 4 hundred dollars.
17. The party lasted until one o'clock.
18. My father graduated 5th in his class.
19. 75% of the class went on to college.
20. Of these students, 41 did not complete college.

Exercise 18 — Writing Numbers

In the following paragraph, use the correct form for writing numbers.

¹In nineteen hundred ninety-one the population of the United States was approximately 248 million. ²The estimated population of North America was three hundred ninety million. ³North America has the 3rd largest population of the world's continents. ⁴Asia has the largest, with fifty-nine percent. ⁵More than three billion people live in Asia. ⁶Africa ranks 2nd in the world's population. ⁷Close to seven hundred million people live there. ⁸Australia and New Zealand account for only 20,000,000 people. ⁹Antarctica has no permanent population, and fewer than 1,000 scientists stay the winter. ¹⁰Overall, more than five point three billion people inhabit the earth.

20.10 Writing Numbers **585**

Enabling Strategies

LEP Choosing Singular Verbs

Expressions of time, money, and distance usually require singular verbs. Students new to English often use plural verbs with expressions such as the ones below because the nouns take plural forms:

• Time: *Two hours of swimming is too much.*

• Money: *Five dollars is the price of that toy.*
• Distance: *Six hundred miles is a long day's drive.*

Ask students to write their own sentences using expressions of time, money, and distance as subjects with singular verbs.

TEACH

About the Literature

This passage from Jamaica Kincaid's book, *A Small Place,* is written from the perspective of a typical tourist in Antigua. Jamaica Kincaid understands why people are attracted to her homeland. Throughout the book, however, Kincaid expresses contempt for those who find the customs, culture, and poverty of Antigua "quaint."

After students read the passage, initiate a discussion of its style and tone. Have a student locate Antigua on a map or globe. Ask if Kincaid makes Antigua seem attractive? How?

Linking Grammar and Literature

☑ Teaching Tip

Continue discussion of the passage by asking: *Do the short sentences and repeating word patterns contribute to making Antigua sound attractive? Why or why not?* Then focus students on the highlighted punctuation. Ask: *What would happen if the punctuation were removed from the passage? Would it still be easy to read?*

Critical Thinking

Ask students to write a brief description of the place where they live. Their descriptions should make tourists interested in visiting there. (As an alternative, students could write a description of an imaginary place that would discourage visits by tourists.) Encourage students to vary the length and structure of sentences in their descriptions, paying careful attention to punctuation. Have students share their work and discuss how the writer made the place sound attractive (or unattractive).

586

UNIT

20

Unit Review

Grammar Review

Punctuation

Tourists see a place differently from the way local inhabitants do. In *A Small Place,* Jamaica Kincaid writes about her homeland, the small Caribbean island of Antigua. In the following passage from the book, Kincaid looks at the island through the eyes of a tourist. She describes the island's beauty and discusses its history. She also expresses her hopes for the future of Antigua. The passage has been annotated to show some of the rules of punctuation covered in this unit.

Literature Model

from A SMALL PLACE

by Jamaica Kincaid

Comma before *and* used to join main clauses

Semicolon to join parts of a compound sentence without a conjunction

Dash to show an interrupted thought

Comma after two introductory prepositional phrases

Oh, but by now you are tired of all this looking , and you want to reach your destination—your hotel, your room. You long to refresh yourself ; you long to eat some nice lobster, some nice local food. You take a bath, you brush your teeth. You get dressed again; as you get dressed, you look out the window. That water — have you ever seen anything like it? Far out, to the horizon, the color of the water is navy-blue; nearer, the water is the color of the North American sky. From there to the shore , the water is pale, silvery, clear, so clear that you can see its pinkish-white sand bottom. Oh, what beauty! Oh, what beauty! You have never seen anything like this. You are so excited. You breathe shallow. You breathe deep.

586 *Punctuation*

Teacher's Classroom Resources

The following resources can be used for planning, instruction, practice, reinforcement, assessment, reteaching, enrichment, or evaluation.

🔧 **Teaching Tools**
Lesson Plans, p. 114

📘 ***Grammar Workbook***
Lessons 77–87
Unit 13 Review
Cumulative Review: Units 1–13

Unit Assessment
📁 *Tests with Answer Key*
Unit 20 Mastery Test, pp. 79–80

💿 *Test Generator*
Unit 20 Mastery Test

PRACTICE AND ASSESS

Exercise 1

Using Commas Write each sentence, adding commas where needed.

1. Tourists come for the white sand beaches colorful reefs and balmy climate.
2. Antigua unlike other islands of the Lesser Antilles is not mountainous.
3. Most of the island is flat; however there are hills in the Southwest.
4. These hills the remnants of ancient volcanoes bear patches of rain forest.
5. Did you know Catherine that Antigua was once covered by rain forest?
6. It was deforested by its original inhabitants British planters and modern developers.
7. Antigua does not have much rainfall; therefore rain seldom interferes with tourists' plans.
8. Mangroves tidal flats salt ponds and freshwater pools are found near the shore.
9. These watery habitats as you can imagine host a great variety of wildlife.
10. Magnificent frigate birds black seabirds with long wings soar the cliffs.

Exercise 2

Using Commas with Introductory Words and Phrases Write each sentence, adding commas where needed.

SAMPLE Lying among the Leeward Islands Antigua is a Caribbean jewel.
ANSWER Lying among the Leeward Islands, Antigua is a Caribbean jewel.

1. Blessed with low humidity and year-round trade winds Antigua has an ideal climate for tourists.
2. Fringed by coral reefs the island is a snorkeler's paradise.
3. With its miles of undulating coastline it appeals to beach lovers from all over the world.
4. Shimmering in the tropical sun the turquoise waters are very inviting.
5. Indeed all kinds of water sports are popular with both natives and tourists.
6. In the sheltered water of English Harbor sailboats find safe haven.
7. From old military installations on Shirley Heights Antiguans and visitors can view fabulous sunsets.
8. No the capital is not at English Harbor.
9. Situated on the northwest coast St. John's Harbor welcomes cruise ships.
10. Yes that irregular coastline also provides many smaller bays for swimming.

Answers: Exercise 1

1. …beaches, colorful reefs, and…
2. Antigua, unlike…Antilles, is…
3. …however, there…
4. …hills, the…volcanoes, bear…
5. …know, Catherine, that…
6. …inhabitants, British planters, and…
7. …therefore, rain…
8. Mangroves, tidal flats, salt ponds, and freshwater pools…
9. …habitats, as you can imagine, host…
10. …birds, black seabirds with long wings, soar…

Answers: Exercise 2

1. …winds, Antigua…
2. …reefs, the…
3. …coastline, it…
4. …sun, the…
5. Indeed, all…
6. …Harbor, sailboats…
7. …Heights, Antiguans…
8. No, the…
9. …coast, St. John's…
10. Yes, that…

Grammar Review **587**

UNIT 20
Review

Answers: Exercise 3

1. ...shallow, it...
2. ...sea, brown...
3. correct
4. ...down, you...
5. correct
6. ...water, it...
7. correct
8. everywhere, Potswork...
9. ...evergreens, visit...
10. correct

Answers: Exercise 4

1. correct
2. Paradise Reef, which offers a mile of coral, is...
3. ...boats, which...the reef, are...
4. ...hawksbill, whose...
5. The hawksbill, which... jawbone, is...
6. correct
7. ...Drive, which...fig, is...
8. correct
9. ...Nelson, who... admiral, served...
10. ...Hill, which...

Exercise 3

Using Commas with Adverb Clauses   Write each sentence, adding commas where needed. Write *correct* if the sentence is correct.

SAMPLE   If you want to see mahogany trees stroll through Walling Woodlands.
ANSWER   If you want to see mahogany trees, stroll through Walling Woodlands.

1. Because McKinnon's Salt Pond is very shallow it appeals to sandpipers.
2. Where Indian Creek flows into the sea brown pelicans dive for tarpon.
3. You won't find a tropical rain forest unless you drive up Boggy Peak.
4. Before you drive back down you should look for scarlet tanagers.
5. Visit the lovely beaches of Carlisle Bay after you leave Boggy Peak.
6. Since Farley Bay is accessible only by foot or by water it is very peaceful.
7. Look for unusual shells when you go to Rendezvous Bay.
8. Although blue herons are everywhere Potswork Reservoir attracts the most.
9. If you want to see a mature stand of evergreens visit Weatheralls Hill.
10. In hotel gardens you will see hummingbirds because they want the nectar in the resort's tropical flowers and fruit trees.

Exercise 4

Using Commas with Adjective Clauses   Write each sentence, adding commas if needed. Write *correct* if the sentence is correct.

SAMPLE   Christopher Columbus who arrived in 1493 named Antigua.
ANSWER   Christopher Columbus, who arrived in 1493, named Antigua.

1. Tourists who like to explore have many options on Antigua.
2. Paradise Reef which offers a mile of coral is popular with snorkelers.
3. Glass-bottomed boats which let nonswimmers see the reef are also popular.
4. You may see the hawksbill whose shell is used for tortoiseshell jewelry.
5. The hawksbill which is named for its beaky upper jawbone is a sea turtle.
6. On Green Castle Hill are rock formations that may date to ancient times.
7. Fig Tree Drive which is named for the Antiguan fig is lush with trees.
8. Devil's Bridge is a natural formation that was created by pounding waves.
9. Captain Horatio Nelson who later became a famous British admiral served for a time in Antigua and gave his name to Nelson's Dockyard.
10. A strenuous hike leads to Monk Hill which overlooks two harbors.

Exercise 5

Using Commas   Write each sentence, adding commas where needed.

1. Leona's home is at 1147 Schyler Street Gary Indiana.
2. Her aunt Jo lives in Falmouth Antigua.
3. Josephine Susannah Hardy M.D. is her aunt's full name.
4. Leona arrived for a visit on July 15 1995.
5. Leona's brother Conrad came too.
6. "It's great to be here" said Leona "because I love to swim."
7. "You'll have lots of beaches to choose from" said Aunt Jo.
8. Among these three are especially recommended.
9. Leona and Conrad swam every day and studied Antiguan birdlife too.
10. On August 2 1995 they regretfully waved goodbye to Antigua.

Exercise 6

Using Commas, Semicolons, and Colons   Write each sentence, adding commas, semicolons, and colons where needed.

SAMPLE   Old towns can be revived the story of English Harbor proves it.
ANSWER   Old towns can be revived; the story of English Harbor proves it.

1. English Harbor bustled for two centuries but then its glory faded.
2. The English navy sailed for home and traders found different ports.
3. Nelson's Dockyard itself was badly decayed old buildings had fallen in.
4. In 1951 the governor founded the Society of the Friends of English Harbor its purpose was to restore the harbor.
5. The group unearthed original plans consequently their restoration is historically accurate.
6. They tried to get these details right hand-hewn beams, pegged wood, and old glass.
7. Interest among natives, sailors, and business people grew and soon old-timers, visitors, and new residents made the streets bustle again.
8. Now Nelson's Dockyard is full of shops the Galley, the Saw Pit, the Cooper and Lumber Store, and more.
9. Tourists flock to these shops therefore the economy has steadily grown.
10. Charter boats and private boats crowd the harbor it once again welcomes travelers from the sea.

Grammar Review   **589**

Answers: Exercise 5
1. …Street, Gary, Indiana.
2. …Falmouth, Antigua.
3. …Hardy, M.D., is…
4. …July 15, 1995.
5. …came, too.
6. …here," said Leona, "because…
7. …from," said…
8. Among these, three…
9. …birdlife, too.
10. On August 2, 1995, they…

Answers: Exercise 6
1. …centuries, but…
2. …home, and…
3. …decayed; old…
4. …Harbor; its…
5. …plans; consequently, their…
6. right: hand-hewn…
7. …grew, and…
8. …shops: the Galley…
9. …shops; therefore, the…
10. …harbor; it…

UNIT 20
Review

Using Commas and End Marks in Direct Quotations Write each sentence, adding commas and end marks where needed.

SAMPLE "Let's visit an Arawak dig" suggested Ann.
ANSWER "Let's visit an Arawak dig," suggested Ann.

1. "The Caribbean Islands are just like stepping stones from Venezuela to Florida" said Ron
2. Keisha added "Most of the first inhabitants came from South America"
3. "Among those who settled Antigua" said Mr. Hays "were the Arawaks"
4. Did you say "The Arawaks lived in wooden houses"
5. "Yes" said Mr. Hays "the houses were wood with thatched roofs"
6. "Didn't the Arawaks play an early kind of soccer" asked Ron
7. "The object of the game" said Keisha "was to keep the ball in the air"
8. "And you couldn't use your hands" exclaimed Ann
9. Ron asked "How were the points scored"
10. "If you let the ball touch ground, the other side scored a point" said Ann

Answers: Exercise 7

1. …Florida," said Ron.
2. Keisha added, "Most…South America."
3. …Antigua," said Mr. Hays, "were the Arawaks."
4. …say, "The …houses"?
5. "Yes," said Mr. Hays, "the …roofs."
6. …soccer?" asked Ron.
7. …game," said Keisha, "was …air."
8. …hands!" exclaimed Ann.
9. Ron asked, "How…scored?"
10. …point," said Ann.

Punctuating Direct Quotations Write each sentence, adding quotation marks, underlining for italics, commas, and end marks where needed.

SAMPLE Who were the first people on Antigua asked Tony
ANSWER "Who were the first people on Antigua?" asked Tony.

1. I have been reading about the Arawaks and Caribs in a beautiful book called Lost Empires
2. In it there is a chapter about the Caribbean called Crossroads Cultures
3. I told the class The Arawaks used sophisticated farming methods
4. They knew how to control erosion and irrigate their fields explained Tim
5. Manioc was their chief crop I said but they also grew other foods
6. Tony asked What's manioc
7. It's a starchy, edible root like cassava answered Mr. Hays
8. The sea I said provided the Arawaks with fish and turtles
9. Tim asked Weren't the Arawaks eventually conquered by the Caribs
10. The Caribs were cannibals I exclaimed

Answers: Exercise 8

1. …<u>Lost Empires</u>.
2. …"Crossroads Cultures."
3. …class, "The…methods."
4. "They…fields," explained Tim.
5. "Manioc…crop," I said, "but …foods."
6. Tony asked, "What's manioc?"
7. "It's…cassava," answered Mr. Hays.
8. "The sea," I said, "provided… turtles."
9. Tim asked, "Weren't…Caribs?"
10. "The…cannibals!" I exclaimed.

590 *Punctuation*

Exercise 9

Using Apostrophes, Hyphens, Dashes, and Parentheses   Write each sentence, inserting apostrophes, hyphens, dashes, and parentheses where needed.

SAMPLE   Antigua has a well developed educational system.
ANSWER   Antigua has a well-developed educational system.

1. The country of Antigua and Barbuda has a total land area of 171 square miles 442 square kilometers.
2. Barbuda is a game preserve, and its anyones guess how many species of birds live there.
3. Redonda an uninhabited island is also part of the island country.
4. The country has been a self governing nation since 1981.
5. The three islands terrain is mostly flat.
6. Most of the countrys population live on the island of Antigua.
7. The majority of the people descendants of Africans speak English.
8. The peoples main foods include beans, fish, lobsters, and sweet potatoes.
9. On their jobs theyre bankers, shopkeepers, hotel workers, taxi drivers, farmers, and manufacturers.
10. Drought often harms farmers crops of sugar cane and cotton.

Exercise 10

Using Abbreviations and Numbers   Write each sentence, correcting the errors in abbreviations and numbers.

1. Mister Vere Cornwall is the prime minister of Antigua and Barbuda.
2. About two percent of the people live on Barbuda, the smaller island.
3. The islands receive about 45 in. of rain annually.
4. 2 deaths and 80 million dollars in property damage resulted when Hurricane Hugo struck in 1989.
5. The island's hospitals need qualified Drs.
6. Slavery was abolished on Antigua in eighteen thirty-four.
7. Forests cover 15.9% of Antigua, and 59.1% of the land is agricultural.
8. When it's 2 o'clock in VA, it's 3 o'clock in Antigua.
9. Tourists can choose from among three hundred sixty-five beaches on Antigua.
10. Summer Carnival is celebrated in late Jul. and early Aug.

Grammar Review   **591**

Answers: Exercise 9
1. …miles (442 square kilometers).
2. …and it's anyone's guess…
3. Redonda—an uninhabited island—is… *or* Redonda (an uninhabited island) is…
4. …self-governing nation…
5. …islands' terrain…
6. …country's population…
7. …people—descendants of Africans—speak…*or* …people (descendents of Africans) speak…
8. The people's main…
9. …they're bankers, …
10. …farmers' crops…

Answers: Exercise 10
1. Mr. Vere Cornwall…
2. About 2 percent…
3. …about forty-five inches…
4. Two deaths…
5. …qualified doctors.
6. in 1834.
7. …cover 15.9 percent of Antigua, and 59.1 percent of the land…
8. …two o'clock in Virginia, it's three o'clock…
9. …among 365 beaches…
10. …in late July and early August.

UNIT 20
Review

Answers: Exercise 11
Proofreading

This proofreading activity provides editing practice with (1) the current or previous units' skills, (2) the **Troubleshooter** errors, and (3) spelling errors. Students should be able to complete the exercise by referring to the units, the **Troubleshooter,** and a dictionary.

	Error (Type of Error)
1.	• sits (subject-verb agreement)
2.	• sea, (comma after two or more introductory prepositional phrases)
3.	• bathes (subject-verb agreement)
4.	• pinks, (commas in a series)
5.	• *Place*, (comma after two or more introductory prepositional phrases) • moment (spelling)
6.	• picture—(dash to show change in thought) • duplicates (subject-verb agreement)
7.	• drawn (verb form)
8.	• *Nice*? (end punctuation)

Answers: Exercise 12
Mixed Review

1. …1949, young…read; one…<u>Jane Eyre</u>.
2. …childhood, Kincaid…family— her mother, father, and three brothers—underestimated her abilities; she…
3. By sixteen she…self-directed young woman, and…
4. …colleges, but…
5. …teenagers' magazines, she… <u>The New Yorker</u> magazine.
6. …articles; however, now…"Girl," a short story.
7. …ten stories in <u>At the Bottom of the River</u>, which…1983, deal…
8. …following: "Girl," "My Mother," and "In the Night."
9. Kincaid's second book, <u>Annie John,</u> is
10. … <u>A Small Place</u>, which…

Exercise 11 — Proofreading

Rewrite the following passage, correcting the errors in spelling, grammar, and usage. Add any missing punctuation. There are ten errors.

Interior at Nice

[1] The young woman in the picture on the opposite page sit in front of a window on a hotel balcony in France. [2] With her back to the sea she gazes at the observer. [3] The sun reflects off the sea and bathe the room in silvery light. [4] Intense pinks blues, and grays help convey the atmosphere of warmth.

[5] Like Jamaica Kincaid in the passage from *A Small Place* Henri Matisse has captured a momant by the sea. [6] The picture on the hotel wall—a picture within the picture duplicate the figure of the woman on the balcony. [7] The observer's attention is drawed to the woman. [8] What differences can you find between *A Small Place* and *Interior at Nice*

Exercise 12 — Mixed Review

Write each sentence, correcting all errors in punctuation and numbers.

[1] Born on May 25, 1949 young Jamaica Kincaid loved to read, one of her favorite books was Jane Eyre. [2] Although she had a happy childhood Kincaid realized that her family her mother father and three brothers underestimated her abilities she also felt stifled by the island. [3] By 16 she was a very self directed young woman and she left Antigua for a job in New York. [4] She attended several colleges but she never earned a degree. [5] After she had written articles for teenagers magazines she became a staff writer for The New Yorker magazine. [6] She wrote gardening articles however now her interest in fiction motivated her to write Girl, a short story. [7] Most of the 10 stories in At the Bottom of the River, which was published in 1983 deal with mothers and daughters. [8] Among the stories are the following Girl My Mother and In the Night. [9] Kincaid's 2nd book Annie John, is about a young Antiguan girl who grows from childhood to adolescence. [10] Kincaid also wrote A Small Place which criticizes British colonialism and the government of Antigua.

Henri Matisse, *Interior at Nice,* **1921**

Grammar Review **593**

CLOSE

Ask students to name the types of punctuation demonstrated in the Unit 20 Review. Discuss any types with which students had difficulty.

About the Art

Henri Matisse, *Interior at Nice,* **1921**
Artists often try to evoke a particular mood or feeling by using different colors. Ask students to list some of the colors Henri Matisse used in *Interior at Nice* (pink, gray, blue, coral). Then ask the class to describe the feelings these colors evoke in relation to what is seen in the painting (warmth, relaxation, a holiday spirit).

Matisse's oil-on-canvas painting measures 52 by 35 inches and is in the Art Institute of Chicago.

593

Apostrophes in Writing

Have students read the passage from *Thrashin' Time* silently. Then discuss it in terms of the points mentioned in the Techniques with Apostrophes section below.

Techniques with Apostrophes

Discuss with students each of the techniques listed. You may want to have students analyze a previous example—such as the passage from *A Small Place* or the Proofreading on page 592—using these techniques.

Practice

The answers to this challenging and enriching activity will vary. Refer to Techniques with Apostrophes as you evaluate student choices. Sample answers:

"Nothin' doin', Fred," said Mr. Felters. "I can't accept this wood. It's not cut short enough."

"Come on, Felters, we've been workin' together for goin' on ten years. Trust me. I'll come tomorrow and cut it shorter for you," implored Fred.

"Nope! 'Fore I take it, it's got to be right. Cut 'em down to two-foot lengths and I'll be a happy man," insisted Mr. Felters.

"If I must," sighed Fred, "I guess I may as well get goin' on it."

Writing Application

Apostrophes in Writing David Weitzman uses apostrophes in this passage from *Trashin' Time* to make his farming characters' dialogue sound realistic. Study the passage, paying close attention to the italicized words.

> "What do you think about all this, Peter, steam power instead of horse power?"
> I *wasn't* sure. "If the engine took the place of the horses, I think *I'd* miss Annie and Lulu and Quinn. *Wouldn't* you, Pa?"
> "I would, but, you know, horse-power *thrashin'* is awful hard on them, son. Sure, *I'd* miss them, but we work them hard all year *plowin'* and *diskin'*, and *seedin'* and *mowin'*. Then just when *they're* so tuckered out, about to drop and *needin'* a good rest, we put them to *thrashin'.*"

Techniques with Apostrophes Try to apply some of David Weitzman's writing techniques when you write.

1. Use apostrophes to create contractions and help your writing flow more smoothly:

Awkward version I *was not* sure.
Weitzman's version I *wasn't* sure.

2. Dialogue conveys information about a character. When appropriate, show characters' natural speech patterns by replacing missing letters with apostrophes. The first version, although correct, is not how Pa really speaks:

Less information we work them hard all year *plowing* and *disking*, and *seeding* and *mowing*
Weitzman's version we work them hard all year *plowin'* and *diskin'*, and *seedin'* and *mowin'*

Practice Rewrite the following passage, adding apostrophes to the underlined words to make the dialogue sound more natural.

"<u>Nothing doing</u>, Fred," said Mr. Felters. "I <u>cannot</u> accept this wood. <u>It is</u> not cut short enough."
"Come on, Felters, <u>we have</u> been <u>working</u> together for <u>going</u> on ten years. Trust me. <u>I will</u> come tomorrow and cut it shorter for you," implored Fred.
"Nope! <u>Before I</u> take it, <u>it has</u> got to be right. Cut <u>them</u> down to two foot lengths and <u>I will</u> be a happy man," insisted Mr. Felters.
"If I must," sighed Fred, "I guess I may as well get <u>going</u> on it."

Teacher's Classroom Resources

The following resources can be used for assessment or evaluation.

Unit Assessment
📂 *Tests with Answer Key*
Unit 20 Mastery Test, pp. 79–80

⊙ *Test Generator*
Unit 20 Mastery Test

You may wish to administer the Unit 20 Mastery Test at this point.

UNIT 21

Grammar

Grammar Through Sentence Combining

Lessons

595

UNIT GOALS

The goal of Unit 21 is to help students, through example and instruction, to develop an ability to combine short sentences into longer, more complex ones in order to give their writing style greater clarity of thought, conciseness, and variety. Lessons focus on using prepositional phrases, appositives, adjective clauses, and adverb clauses.

Unit Assessment

📁 *Tests with Answer Key*
Unit 21 Pretest, pp. 81–82
Unit 21 Mastery Test, pp. 83–84

💿 *Test Generator*
Unit 21 Pretest
Unit 21 Mastery Test

You may wish to administer the Unit 21 Pretest at this point.

Key to Ability Levels
Enabling Strategies have been coded for varying learning styles and abilities.

L1 Level 1 activities are within the ability range of Learning Disabled students.

L2 Level 2 activities are basic-to-average activities and are within the ability range of average students.

L3 Level 3 activities are challenging activities and are within the ability range of above-average students.

LEP LEP activities are within the ability range of Limited English Proficiency students.

Setting the Purpose

Lesson 21.1 teaches students to combine related sentences using prepositional phrases.

FOCUS

Lesson Overview

Objective: To recognize prepositional phrases and use them in writing

Bellringer

When students enter the classroom, have this assignment on the board: *Make a list of the reasons why you would want to combine sentences in your writing.*

Motivating Activity

Discuss students' answers to the Bellringer exercise. Pair students and ask them to write two or three short sentences. Then ask students to combine the sentences and write the new ones on the board. Point out those sentences that were combined by using prepositions or prepositional phrases.

TEACH

☑ Teaching Tip

Remind students that there are many ways to revise, and encourage them to consider their options. Lead students to realize that they may be more successful if they read over an entire paragraph before they begin to revise it. Also encourage students to read various versions of their sentences aloud to determine which ones sound the clearest and most natural.

☑ Grammar Tip

A prepositional phrase that modifies a verb may precede or follow the verb in a sentence.

21.1 | Prepositional Phrases

Prepositional phrases are effective tools for sentence combining. They describe nouns and verbs, just as single-word adjectives and adverbs do. Furthermore, because they show relationships between words, prepositional phrases can express complicated ideas.

EXAMPLE
  a. The landscape has undergone a change.
  b. This change is **for the worse**.
  c. This is **according to Rachel Carson**.

According to Rachel Carson, the landscape has undergone a change **for the worse**.

The new information from sentences *b* and *c* is added to sentence *a* in the form of prepositional phrases. In the new sentence, the prepositional phrase *According to Rachel Carson* modifies the verb *has undergone,* and the prepositional phrase *for the worse* modifies the noun *change.* Prepositional phrases follow the nouns they modify. Prepositional phrases that modify verbs can precede or follow the verbs they modify. (For a list of common prepositions, see page 448.)

A **prepositional phrase** is a group of words that begins with a preposition and ends with a noun or pronoun. Prepositional phrases modify nouns, verbs, and pronouns.

Exercise 1   **Combining Sentences with Prepositional Phrases**

The following sentences are based on an excerpt from *Silent Spring* by Rachel Carson, which you can find on pages 296–298. Combine each group of sentences so that the new information is turned into a prepositional phrase. In the first few items the new information is in dark type.

  1. a. Carson describes a mythical town.
     b. The town was one **of great natural beauty**.
  2. a. Prosperous farms surrounded the town.
     b. The farms were dotted **with rich productive fields.**➡

596   *Grammar Through Sentence Combining*

Teacher's Classroom Resources

The following resources can be used for planning, instruction, practice, reinforcement, assessment, reteaching, enrichment, or evaluation.

🔧 **Teaching Tools**
Lesson Plans, p. 115

📁 **Blackline Masters**
Sentence Combining Practice,
  pp. 1–3

📘 *Grammar Workbook*
Lesson 39

Unit Assessment

📂 *Tests with Answer Key*
Unit 21 Pretest, pp. 81–82

⏱ *Test Generator*
Unit 21 Pretest

You may wish to administer the Unit 21 Pretest at this point.

3. a. Birds filled the trees and bushes.
  b. The birds were **of many different kinds.**
4. a. People visited this town.
  b. They came from miles away.
  c. They came on account of the romantic beauty of this special place.
5. a. A blight covered the land.
  b. The blight was one of unknown origin.
6. a. A powdery chemical snow fell.
  b. It fell on buildings and land alike.
7. a. Strange sicknesses were in the human and animal communities.
  b. Doctors studied the strange sicknesses.
  c. The doctors studied with the latest medical tools.
8. a. The vegetation was dead or dying.
  b. The dying vegetation was beside the roads.
  c. The dying vegetation was in the orchards.
9. a. Silence now reigned in the springtime.
  b. It reigned after the disappearance of the birds.
10. a. The countryside changed dramatically.
  b. It turned into a scene of mysterious mourning.

| Exercise 2 | **Combining Sentences** |

Rewrite the following paragraphs. Use prepositional phrases to combine sentences. Make any other changes in wording that you feel are necessary.

Rachel Carson describes some tragedies caused by people. She describes them in her book *Silent Spring.* These tragedies were not caused by any alien or mysterious agent. Her mythical town faced a bright and hopeful future. Then people destroyed the land. They destroyed it with their thoughtless actions. Now the land was dying. Everything on it was dying. There were no new young plants and animals to replace those that had died. Therefore, the only prospect was despair.

No one place has suffered all the tragedies described by Carson. However, each blight has occurred somewhere. The blights are upon the environment. Each one might have occurred in this country, or it might have been in other parts of the world. Many communities have undergone several of these misfortunes. This fact is without exaggeration. Carson writes of a "grim specter." This specter is upon our landscape. Carson writes in her book *Silent Spring.* The tragedy might become a reality. The tragedy is that of the mythical town. The reality is for all of us. This is according to Rachel Carson.

21.1 Prepositional Phrases **597**

PRACTICE AND ASSESS

Answers: Exercise 1
Answers will vary, but some suggestions are given below.
1. Carson describes a mythical town of great natural beauty.
2. Prosperous farms with rich productive fields surrounded the town.
3. Birds of many different kinds filled the trees and bushes.
4. People visited this town from miles away on account of the romantic beauty of this special place.
5. A blight of unknown origin covered the land.
6. A powdery chemical snow fell on buildings and land alike.
7. Doctors with the latest medical tools studied the strange sicknesses in the human and animal communities.
8. Beside the roads and in the orchards, the vegetation was dead or dying.
9. Silence now reigned in the springtime as the birds disappeared.
10. The countryside changed dramatically into a scene of mysterious mourning.

Answers: Exercise 2
Answers will vary, but some suggestions are given below.
In her book, *Silent Spring,* Rachel Carson describes some tragedies caused by people, not by any alien or mysterious agent. Her mythical town faced a bright and hopeful future until people destroyed the land with their thoughtless actions. Now everything on the land was dying. Without young plants and animals to replace those that had died, the only prospect was despair.

No one place has suffered all the tragedies described by Carson. However, each blight upon the environment has occurred somewhere in this country or in other parts of the world. Without exaggeration, many communities have undergone several of these misfortunes. In her book *Silent Spring* Carson writes of a "grim specter" upon our landscape. According to Rachel Carson, the tragedy of the mythical town might become a reality for all of us.

Independent Practice
Skills Practice
📁 *Sentence Combining Practice,* pp. 1–3

📕 *Grammar Workbook,* Lesson 39

Enabling Strategies

LEP Meanings of Prepositions
Write the following on the board: [*For, Within, In*] her book Rachel Carson alerted millions of people [*into, to, by*] the tragic results [*of, from, after*] pollution. Ask students to choose the best preposition in each set of options by thinking of the meaning of the sentence.

CLOSE

Ask students to imagine a *what if...?* situation. For example, what would it be like if there were no television? Have students write two paragraphs describing their *what if* situation and its effects.

FOCUS

Lesson Overview

Objective: To recognize appositives and appositive phrases and to use them in combining sentences correctly and effectively

🔔 Bellringer

When students enter the classroom, have this assignment on the board: *Which of these two options do you think is more interesting? Explain your answer in writing.*
  Option 1: Dr. Chang, a noted archaeologist, scaled the ruins of the ancient pyramid.
  Option 2: Dr. Chang is a noted archaeologist. Dr. Chang scaled the ruins of the ancient pyramid.

TEACH

☑ Grammar Tip

As students work on combining sentences, remind them that appositives help writers present information in a tighter, more compact way. The hesitancy of some students to use appositives in sentence combining may arise from doubt as to how to punctuate them. Review the answers to Exercise 3, stressing that commas are needed for all appositives that supply extra, nonessential information.

⮂ Cross-reference: Grammar

For instruction and practice on appositives and how to punctuate them, refer students to Lesson 9.6, pp. 358–359.

21.2 Appositives

Appositives allow you to combine sentences in a compact and informative way. Appositives and appositive phrases identify or reveal something new about a noun or pronoun.

EXAMPLE
a. Maya Lin designed the Vietnam Veterans Memorial.
b. Maya Lin was **an architecture student**.

Maya Lin, **an architecture student**, designed the Vietnam Veterans Memorial.

The appositive phrase *an architecture student* tells us more about *Maya Lin*. The appositive is set off with commas because it gives additional information. If an appositive supplies essential information, it is not set off with commas. (For more information about appositives, see pages 358–359.)

An **appositive** is a noun placed next to another noun to identify it or give additional information about it. An **appositive phrase** includes an appositive and other words that describe it.

Exercise 3   Combining Sentences with Appositives

The following sentences are based on "Always to Remember" by Brent Ashabranner, which you can find on pages 244–250. Combine each group of sentences so that the new information is turned into an appositive or appositive phrase. In the first few items, the new information is in dark type. Add commas when necessary to your new sentences.

1. **a.** Congress had authorized the Vietnam Veterans Memorial.
   b. The memorial was to be **a monument to the war's dead and missing soldiers**.
2. **a.** Over one thousand contestants submitted plans.
   b. This number of contestants was **a record number for a design competition**. ➡

598 *Grammar Through Sentence Combining*

Teacher's Classroom Resources

The following resources can be used for planning, instruction, practice, reinforcement, reteaching, or enrichment.

🖉 **Teaching Tools**
Lesson Plans

📁 **Blackline Masters**
Sentence Combining Practice, pp. 7–8

📙 *Grammar Workbook*
Lesson 12

3. **a.** The winner was Maya Lin.
   b. She was **the daughter of the dean of fine arts at Ohio University.**
   c. The dean was **Henry Huan Lin.**
4. **a.** She was the child of cultured and educated parents.
   b. Maya Lin felt that art and literature were always beside her.
   c. Art and literature were her childhood friends.
5. **a.** Maya Lin studied architecture at Yale University.
   b. She was valedictorian in high school.
6. **a.** Lin was a student in Europe.
   b. There she became interested in the architecture of cemeteries.
   c. Cemeteries are also called "cities of the dead."
7. **a.** In France she was impressed by a memorial.
   b. The memorial was the work of the architect.
   c. The architect was Sir Edwin Lutyens.
8. **a.** Maya learned of the Memorial Competition from Andrus Burr.
   b. She was a Yale student.
   c. He was a professor of funerary (burial) architecture.
9. **a.** During a visit to the site Maya Lin envisioned the winning design.
   b. The site was in Constitution Gardens.
   c. Maya Lin was an architecture student.
10. **a.** The winner described her feelings to a *Washington Post* writer.
    b. Maya Lin was the winner.
    c. The writer was Phil McCombs.

Exercise 4 **Combining Sentences**

Rewrite the paragraph below. Use appositives and appositive phrases to combine sentences. Make any changes in wording you feel necessary.

Before making her design, Maya Lin visited the monument's proposed site. The site was Constitution Gardens in Washington, D.C. During her visit the park was being enjoyed by many people. These people were Washington, D.C., residents and tourists. Lin did not want to destroy a living, beautiful park with a grim monument. That monument would be a structure out of harmony with its surroundings. Upon returning to Yale, Lin made a clay model of her vision. The vision she had in Constitution Gardens. Professor Burr had been the catalyst to Lin's involvement. He liked her ideas. She plunged onward, and finally her design was ready to submit. It took her six weeks of work to complete. Lin's design fits in with the park's landscape. Her final design was a long wall of polished black stone.

21.2 Appositives **599**

PRACTICE AND ASSESS

Answers: Exercise 3
Answers will vary, but some suggestions are given below:
1. Congress…Memorial, a monument…soldiers.
2. Over…contestants, a record…competition, submitted plans.
3. The winner…Lin, the daughter…Lin, the dean of fine arts at Ohio University.
4. The child…parents, Maya Lin felt that art and literature, her childhood friends, were…her.
5. Maya Lin, valedictorian in high school, studied…at Yale University.
6. As a student in Europe, Lin became interested…cemeteries, also called "cities of the dead."
7. In…memorial, the work of the architect Sir Edwin Lutyens.
8. Maya, a Yale student, learned…Burr, a professor…architecture.
9. During…site in Constitution Gardens, Maya Lin, an architecture student, envisioned…design.
10. The winner, Maya Lin, described…writer, Phil McCombs.

Answers: Exercise 4
Answers will vary, but some suggestions are given below:
Before…site, Constitution Gardens in Washington, D.C. During her…people, both Washington,…and tourists. Lin did…monument, a structure out…surroundings. Upon returning to Yale, Lin made…vision, the one she had…Gardens. Professor Burr, the catalyst to Lin's involvement, liked her ideas. She plunged onward, and finally her design, taking six weeks of work to complete, was ready to submit. Lin's design, a long wall of polished black stone, fits in with the park's landscape.

Enabling Strategies

LEP Combining Sentences Using Appositives
Combining sentences can be difficult for students new to English. Have them write two or three facts about someone they know. Then have them combine all three facts in one sentence, using appositives and appositive phrases.

CLOSE

Have students write a paragraph describing either a memorial they have seen, or one they might design. Tell them to use appositives and appositive phrases in their descriptions.

FOCUS

Lesson Overview

Objective: To recognize and use adjective clauses

Bellringer

When students enter the classroom, have this assignment on the board: *On a piece of paper, write the following sentence.* My piano teacher, <u>who is always very helpful,</u> suggested that I listen to "The Moonlight Sonata." *How is the underlined phrase related to the words "My piano teacher"?*

Motivating Activity

Discuss students' answers to the Bellringer exercise. Point out that the whole phrase modifies, or describes, "my piano teacher." Have students substitute simple adjectives for the phrase.

TEACH

☑ Teaching Tip

Explain to students that an adjective clause must immediately follow the word it modifies. Ask students to work in pairs to correct the following sentences: **1.** Lyddie feared the overseer who had never worked in a factory before. (*Lyddie, who had never worked in a factory before, feared the overseer.*) **2.** *Oliver Twist* fascinated Lyddie, which described the hardships of a poor boy. (*Oliver Twist, which described the hardships of a poor boy, fascinated Lyddie.*)

21.3 | Adjective Clauses

Adjective clauses are useful in combining sentences. When two sentences share information, one of them can be made into an adjective clause that modifies a word or phrase in the other.

> **EXAMPLE**
> **a.** Lyddie began her working day long before breakfast.
> **b.** Lyddie **labored in a cloth factory.** [, who . . . ,]
>
> Lyddie, **who labored in a cloth factory,** began her working day long before breakfast.

The new information from sentence *b*, *labored in a cloth factory*, becomes an adjective clause modifying *Lyddie* in sentence *a*. The pronoun *who* now connects the clauses. Notice the commas in the new sentence. Adjective clauses that add nonessential information require commas. Adjective clauses that add essential information do not require commas. (For more information about adjective clauses, see pages 476–477.)

An **adjective clause** is a subordinate clause that modifies a noun or pronoun in the main clause. The relative pronouns *who, whom, whose, which, that,* and *what* tie the adjective clause to the main clause.

Exercise 5   **Combining Sentences with Adjective Clauses**

The following sentences are based on an excerpt from *Lyddie* by Katherine Paterson, which you can find on pages 180–186. Combine each group of sentences so that the new information is turned into an adjective clause. In the first three items the new information is in dark type. The information in brackets indicates the relative pronoun to use and whether a comma or commas are needed.

1. **a.** The girls began their working day long before breakfast.
   b. The girls **labored in the cloth factory.** [who]
2. **a.** Lyddie found a job in a cloth factory.
   b. Lyddie **had come from the country.** [, who . . . ,]
3. **a.** The overseer pulled the cord to the leather belt.
   b. The belt **set the factory machinery into motion.** [that]➡

Teacher's Classroom Resources

The following resources can be used for planning, instruction, practice, reinforcement, reteaching, or enrichment.

🔧 **Teaching Tools**
Lesson Plans, p. 116

📁 **Blackline Masters**
Sentence Combining Practice, pp. 14–15

📖 **Grammar Workbook**
Lesson 46

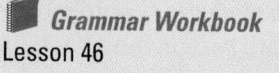

4. **a.** The girls had to rush back at seven-thirty.
   b. The girls were released at seven for breakfast.
5. **a.** Lyddie examined her boots.
   b. Her boots had knotted laces.
6. **a.** Lyddie ran to the window for a breath of fresh air.
   b. Lyddie's eyes were filled with tears.
   c. She needed the breath of fresh air so desperately.
7. **a.** The window was nailed shut.
   b. It was the window Lyddie reached first.
8. **a.** Diana gently guided Lyddie back to the loom.
   b. Diana had already been a great friend to Lyddie.
9. **a.** The day now seemed an endless nightmare.
   b. The day had begun with so much hope.
10. **a.** By the end of the day, Lyddie was too tired to think about the regulations.
    b. These were the rules that all the girls had to learn.

| Exercise 6 | Combining Sentences |

Rewrite the paragraphs below, using adjective clauses to combine sentences. Make any other changes in wording or punctuation you think necessary.

The bountiful supper table made Lyddie nauseated tonight. It might otherwise appeal to Lyddie. Finally, after sitting listlessly through the meal, Lyddie reached her bed. There she began to undress. She struggled with her clothes. She had donned the clothes so quickly and deftly just that morning. The boots were now a sore burden to her. The boots had been her special pride. Triphena's old boots sat on the floor near Lyddie's bed. She had left them there the night before. Maybe these old boots would give Lyddie's swollen feet some breathing space. These boots were stiff and awkward.

Betsy felt Lyddie's pain. She was a fellow sufferer. She remembered the horrors of her own first day. Maybe reading would make Lyddie feel better as well. It always helped Betsy to escape. With this thought in mind, Betsy picked up a book. She hoped Lyddie would enjoy this book.

Betsy read out loud from the novel *Oliver Twist*. *Oliver Twist* was written by Charles Dickens. The novel tells the story of a hungry boy. The boy is punished for asking for more food at a poorhouse. Lyddie heard the description of Oliver's punishment. The man reminded her of the factory overseer. The man scolded Oliver. The overseer had frightened her that very day. Lyddie now wanted to hear the whole story of Oliver. Lyddie had before been too tired to speak. Betsy read on until the curfew bell. Betsy's voice grew hoarse with fatigue.

21.3 Adjective Clauses **601**

PRACTICE AND ASSESS

Answers: Exercise 5

Answers will vary, but some suggestions are given below.

1. The girls who labored in the cloth factory began...breakfast.
2. Lyddie, who had...country, found a job in a cloth factory.
3. The overseer...belt that set the factory machinery into motion.
4. The girls, who were released...breakfast, had to...seven-thirty.
5. Lyddie examined her boots, which had knotted laces.
6. Lyddie, whose eyes...tears, ran to the window for a breath of fresh air that she needed so desperately.
7. The window that Lyddie reached first was nailed shut.
8. Diana, who had...Lyddie, gently guided her back to the loom.
9. The day, which had...hope, now seemed an endless nightmare.
10. By...day, Lyddie was...regulations that all the girls had to learn.

Answers: Exercise 6

Answers will vary, but some suggestions are given below.

The bountiful supper, which might...to Lyddie, made her nauseated tonight. Finally, after sitting ...meal, Lyddie reached her bed, where...undress. She...clothes that she... morning. The boots, which...pride, were...to her. Triphena's old boots...bed where she... before. Maybe these old boots, which were stiff and awkward, would...space. Betsy, a fellow sufferer who felt Lyddie's pain, remembered... day. Maybe reading, which...escape, would... as well. With...mind, Betsy picked up a book that she...enjoy. Betsy...Twist, which was... Dickens. The novel...boy who is...poorhouse. Lyddie...punishment. The man who scolded Oliver reminded her...overseer who had...day. Lyddie, who had...speak, now wanted...Oliver. Betsy, whose voice grew...fatigue, read...bell.

Enabling Strategies

LEP **Using Relative Pronouns**
Students whose first language is not English may need practice in the use of the relative pronouns that introduce adjective clauses. Remind them that *who* and *whom* are used with people, while *which* and *that* are used with animals and objects. *That* can also be used to refer to people.

CLOSE

Ask students to write two positive sentences describing a person they know well. Then have them exchange papers with a partner, who will then combine the sentences, using an adjective clause.

FOCUS

Lesson Overview

Objective: To recognize adverb clauses

🔔 Bellringer

When students enter the classroom, have this assignment on the board: *Write the adverb clause in this excerpt.* (Answer is underlined.)

> Although I was much entertained by the spectacle of one of this continent's most powerful carnivores hunting mice, I did not really take it seriously.
>
> —Farley Mowat, *Never Cry Wolf*

Motivating Activity

Review with students the answer to the Bellringer. Discuss the function of adverbs and adverb clauses in writing.

TEACH

☑ Teaching Tip

Adverb clauses offer students a wide range of choices in sentence combining. Encourage students to work in pairs to brainstorm different subordinating conjunctions they might use, such as *while, when, as, before, after, since,* and *because.* Have them work together to write sentences using subordinating conjunctions.

21.4 Adverb Clauses

Adverb clauses are a frequently used and highly effective way to combine sentences. Adverb clauses help you establish clear relationships between two or more ideas or actions. For example, you can use adverb clauses to show that one action causes another or results from another.

> EXAMPLE
> **a.** Mr. Reese drilled the team thoroughly.
> **b.** They would soon be playing for the championship. [**since**]
>
> Mr. Reese drilled the team thoroughly **since they would soon be playing for the championship**.

In the new sentence, the adverb clause *since they would soon be playing for the championship* explains why Mr. Reese drilled the team so thoroughly. Note that the subordinating conjunction *since* makes the cause-effect relationship very clear. An adverb clause can occupy several positions within a sentence. If it begins the sentence, it is followed by a comma. (For more information about adverb clauses, see pages 480–481.)

An **adverb clause** is a subordinate clause that often modifies or describes the verb in the main clause. Adverb clauses are introduced by subordinating conjunctions such as *after, although, as, before, if, since, when, whenever, wherever,* and *while.*

Exercise 7   Combining Sentences with Adverb Clauses

The following sentences are based on "The Game" by Walter Dean Myers, which you can find on pages 92–96. Use adverb clauses to combine each group of sentences. In the first few items the information in brackets signals the subordinating conjunction and the punctuation you should use.

1. a. The narrator's team was warming up for the championship game. [As ...,]
     b. They tried not to look at their opponents at the other end of the court. ➡

Teacher's Classroom Resources

2. **a.** The other team dominated the game's opening minutes.
   b. They passed and shot the ball extremely well. [**because**]
3. **a.** The narrator's team made a few mistakes. [**When . . . ,**]
   b. Mr. Reese, the coach, called timeout to give the players a rest.
4. **a.** Mr. Reese seemed as calm and reassuring as he usually was.
   b. His team was not playing well. [**although**]
5. **a.** The team returned to the floor [**When . . . ,**]
   b. They began to play much better.
6. **a.** The other team took the ball and immediately tried a slick move.
   b. The narrator's team was ready and handily outmaneuvered them.
7. **a.** The narrator was in the right place at just the right time.
   b. He made his first basket.
8. **a.** Mr. Reese urged the team to stay cool.
   b. They were losing by seven points.
9. **a.** A basketball player is fouled in the process of making a shot.
   b. He gets two foul shots, not one.
10. **a.** The narrator's teammates were happy and proud.
    b. They had beaten a very rough team.

Exercise 8   **Combining Sentences**

Rewrite the following paragraphs. Use adverb clauses to combine sentences. Make any other changes in punctuation or wording that you feel are necessary to improve the flow of the paragraph.

    The opposing side was tricked by the "Foul him!" strategy. The narrator's team got the ball. The score was tied. The narrator did not realize it at the time. There were just four minutes left in the game. Sam and Chalky, two good players, came back in. They outscored the other team by four points. The narrator's team won the championship.

    The narrator's teammates were given their first-place trophies. They began to jump up and down and slap each other on the back. They had an extra trophy. They gave it to their cheerleaders. The coach shook each player's hand. Then he invited the players' parents and the cheerleaders into the locker room. Mr. Reese made a little speech to the group. He said he was proud of the team. They had worked so hard to win. Mr. Reese finished speaking. The parents and cheerleaders gave the team a round of applause. The narrator started to cry. He often did this. However, this time he was not embarrassed. Leon was crying even more. For the next few days the narrator and his friends were walking on air. They saw someone in the street. They would just "walk up and be happy."

21.4 Adverb Clauses **603**

603

UNIT 21
Lesson 21.4

Answers: Exercise 9
Mixed Review

Answers will vary, but some suggestions are given below.

1. In his autobiography, Gary Soto describes the experience of his first day picking grapes.
2. Gary had trouble keeping up with his mother, with whom he was picking.
3. Mother, an experienced picker, worried that Gary would get tired before the day was over.
4. Gary ate the sandwich that he had brought for lunch.
5. Mother remembered long ago days when she worked in the fields of Texas and Michigan.
6. Gary played with his knife, which he was careful not to lose because it was the tool necessary to his job.
7. Gary thought longingly of the swimming pool, the one at the YMCA, when he felt the hot sun.
8. Mother glanced gratefully at Gary, whose singing entertained them as they worked.
9. Whenever he closed his eyes, Gary saw the new jeans that his earnings would buy.
10. After he and Scott made several shopping trips, Gary finally chose a pair of pants.

Independent Practice

Skills Practice

 Sentence Combining Practice, pp. 18–20

Grammar Workbook, Lesson 48

Mixed Review

Exercise 9

The following sentences are based on *Living up the Street* by Gary Soto, which you can find on pages 34–38. Combine each group of sentences using a phrase or clause, as indicated in brackets. The bracketed directions also indicate any pronouns or punctuation that is needed.

1. **a.** Gary Soto describes the experience.
   b. The experience is that of his first day picking grapes. **[prepositional phrase]**
   c. This information appears in his autobiography. **[prepositional phrase; +,]**
2. **a.** Gary had trouble keeping up.
   b. It is with his mother that he had this trouble. **[prepositional phrase]**
   c. She is the person with whom he was picking. **[prepositional phrase; ,+,]**
3. **a.** Mother worried that Gary would get tired.
   b. She is an experienced picker. **[appositive phrase; ,+,]**
   c. He may feel that way before the day is over. **[prepositional phrase]**
4. **a.** Gary ate the sandwich.
   b. He had brought the sandwich for lunch. **[adjective clause; that . . .]**
5. **a.** Mother remembered long ago days.
   b. Those days she worked in the fields. **[adverb clause; when . . .]**
   c. These were the fields of Texas and Michigan. **[prepositional phrase]**
6. **a.** Gary played with his knife.
   b. It was the tool necessary to his job. **[adverb clause; because . . .]**
   c. He was careful not to lose it. **[adjective clause; which . . .]**
7. **a.** Gary thought longingly of the swimming pool.
   b. It was the swimming pool at the YMCA. **[appositive]**
   c. He felt the hot sun. **[adverb clause; when . . .]**
8. **a.** Mother glanced gratefully at Gary.
   b. It was his singing that entertained them. **[adjective clause; , whose . . .]**
   c. They worked at this time. **[adverb clause; as . . .]**
9. **a.** Gary saw the new jeans.
   b. He saw them whenever he closed his eyes. **[adverb clause; Whenever . . . ,]**
   c. These were the jeans that his earnings would buy. **[adjective clause; that . . .]**
10. **a.** He and Scott made several shopping trips. **[adverb clause; After . . . ,]**
    b. Gary finally chose a pair.
    c. It was a pair of pants. **[prepositional phrase]**

CLOSE

Ask students to write a paragraph describing a game or competitive event. Have them try to make their readers feel as if they were actually present at the event. Students can use the rewritten paragraphs in Exervse 8 as models for sentence combining.

Enabling Strategies

LEP Building Vocabulary

Students who are new to English may have difficulty with some of the basketball terms in the exercises relating to "The Game." You may wish to have students familiar with basketball summarize the action and explain the meaning of such terms as *foul shot.*

Part 3

Resources and Skills

PART 3 GOALS

The goal of Part 3 is to help students, through example and instruction, to develop an understanding of the resources available within a library, vocabulary and spelling through context and structural analysis, as well as effective study and test-taking skills.

Unit Assessment

📁 *Tests with Answer Key*
Units 22–26 Pretests, pp. 85–104
Units 22–26 Mastery Tests, pp. 85–104

💿 *Test Generator*
Units 22–26 Pretests
Units 22–26 Mastery Tests

See each unit's Teacher's Classroom Resources information for specific Pretest and Mastery Test page references.

Key to Ability Levels

Enabling Strategies have been coded for varying learning styles and abilities.

L1 Level 1 activities are within the ability range of Learning Disabled students.

L2 Level 2 are basic-to-average activities and are within the ability range of average students.

L3 Level 3 are challenging activities that are within the ability range of above-average students.

LEP LEP activities are within the ability range of Limited English Proficiency students.

Part 3 Resources and Skills

UNIT 22

Library and Reference Resources

22.1 The Sections of a Library

Learning how a library is organized can help you unlock a wealth of information. Although no two libraries are exactly alike, all libraries group like things together. Adult books are in one section. Children's books are in another. Novels and stories are usually separate from information books. Magazines and newspapers have their own section. So do videos and audio-tapes. Turn the page to see how a typical library is organized.

22.1 The Sections of a Library **607**

Setting the Purpose

Lesson 22.1 teaches students that a library is divided into different sections. Students learn how these sections are set up in a typical library so that they have better access to any library's resources.

FOCUS

Lesson Overview
Objective: To become familiar with the sections of the library
Skills: identifying the various sections of the library
Critical Thinking: classifying; visualizing; recalling
Speaking and Listening: discussing

Bellringer
When students enter the classroom, have this assignment on the board: *List five types of resources you might find in a library.*

Motivating Activity
Ask volunteers to share what they listed in the Bellringer exercise. How easily can they find a book or other library items they listed when they are in the library? How much time does it take them? Do they ask the librarian for help? Explain that this lesson will help them find books and other resources in a library more easily and quickly.

Teacher's Classroom Resources

For Lesson 22.1, the following resources can be used for planning, instruction, practice, assessment, reinforcement, or evaluation.

Teaching Tools
Lesson Plans, p. 117

Blackline Masters
Vocabulary and Spelling Practice, pp. 35–40
Thinking and Study Skills, pp. 23–29

Unit Assessment
Tests with Answer Key
Unit 22 Pretest, pp. 85–86

Test Generator
Unit 22 Pretest

You may wish to administer the Unit 22 Pretest at this point.

TEACH

Guided Practice

L2 Drawing a Diagram

With students' help, draw a bird's-eye diagram of the school library on the board. Ask students how the school library is similar to the one shown in their books. Does it have the same sections? Does their library have other sections that are not shown in the book diagram? Ask students to suggest reasons for the differences they identify.

L1 Finding Library Resources

Some students can be overwhelmed by the number of resources in a library and may have trouble finding materials they need. Ask students if they know where the resources mentioned on page 607 are located in their school library. Take them to the library and help them identify and locate the resource sections they do not know. Then ask them to identify new sections of the library.

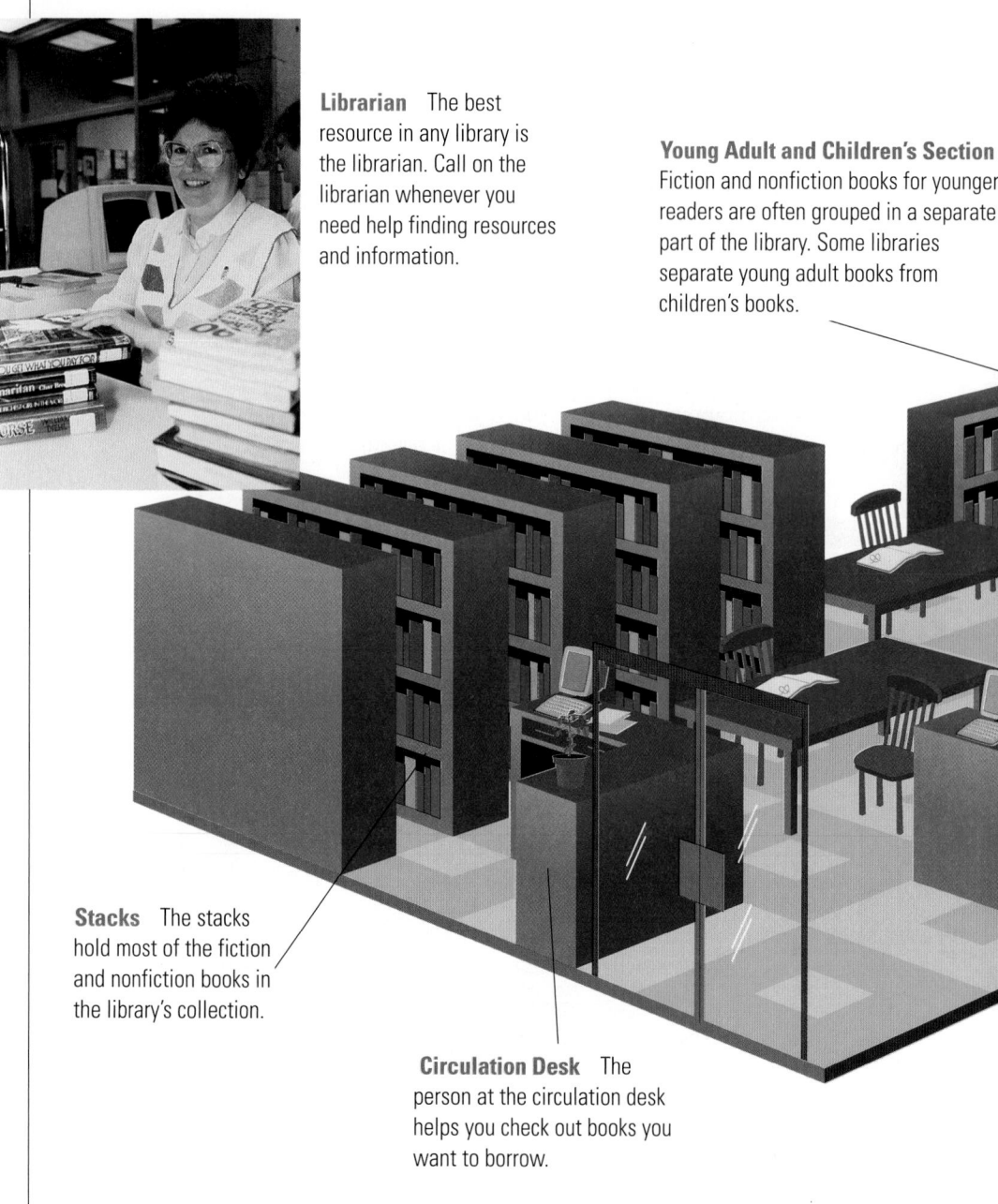

Librarian The best resource in any library is the librarian. Call on the librarian whenever you need help finding resources and information.

Young Adult and Children's Section Fiction and nonfiction books for younger readers are often grouped in a separate part of the library. Some libraries separate young adult books from children's books.

Stacks The stacks hold most of the fiction and nonfiction books in the library's collection.

Circulation Desk The person at the circulation desk helps you check out books you want to borrow.

608 *Library and Reference Resources*

Connections Across the Curriculum

History

The first free, tax-supported library in the United States was established in Boston in 1849. The number of public libraries grew slowly until 1881. In that year, Andrew Carnegie began financing the building of public libraries. Between 1889 and the 1920s, he helped build 1,679 public libraries in 1,412 communities across the United States. In all, he donated $56 million to build 2,509 library buildings throughout the English-speaking world. About 740 of the original Carnegie libraries remain in operation in the United States.

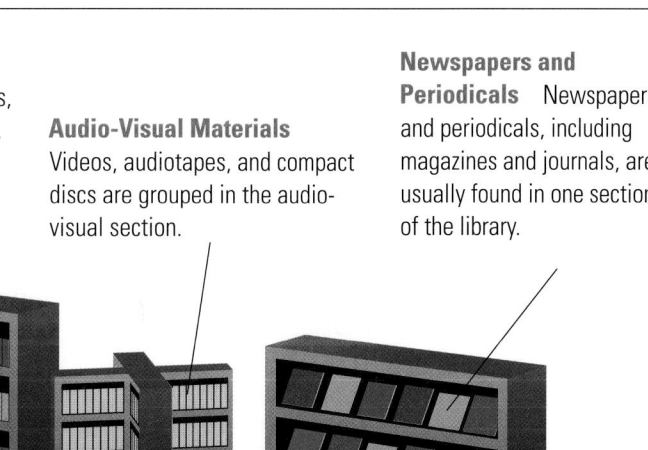

Reference In the reference area you can find encyclopedias, dictionaries, atlases, almanacs, and other reference works.

Audio-Visual Materials Videos, audiotapes, and compact discs are grouped in the audio-visual section.

Newspapers and Periodicals Newspapers and periodicals, including magazines and journals, are usually found in one section of the library.

Catalog A library catalog, whether on computer or cards, contains information about each book in the library, including its location.

Exercise 1

In which section of the library might you find these items?

1. A compact disc of the musical *Cats*
2. The magazine *American Heritage*
3. *To Kill a Mockingbird* (a novel)
4. The *Dictionary of American Biography*
5. The video of *The Call of the Wild*

22.1   The Sections of a Library   **609**

PRACTICE AND ASSESS

Answers: Exercise 1
1. audio-visual
2. newspapers and periodicals
3. fiction stacks and young adult section
4. reference
5. audio-visual

Independent Practice

Skills Practice
📁 *Vocabulary and Spelling Practice,* pp. 35–40
📁 *Thinking and Study Skills,* pp. 23–29

CLOSE

Have students reiterate what the terms *stacks, circulation desk,* and *catalog* mean. Then have them describe the various sections of a library.

Enabling Strategies

LEP Comparing Libraries

If any of your students have just recently come to the United States, encourage them to describe libraries in their home countries. How are the school and public libraries organized? Do they have the same sections as the library shown in their books? Ask the students to point out as many similarities and differences as possible. Encourage other students to provide assistance in speaking English when needed.

FOCUS

Lesson Overview

Objective: To become familiar with the Dewey Decimal and Library of Congress classification systems
Skills: categorizing books in the library; comparing the Dewey Decimal and the Library of Congress classification systems
Critical Thinking: categorizing; analyzing
Speaking and Listening: discussing

Bellringer

When students enter the classroom, have this assignment on the board: *How would you locate books about science in the library?*

TEACH

Guided Practice

L2 Exploring Subcategories
Divide the class into ten teams and assign each team one major category from the classification system used by your school library. Take students to the library to look at the range of books in their category. Have them list the subcategories they discover. Then have teams share what they found.

610

22.2 Call Number Systems

If you walk through the stacks in the library, you will see that the books are labeled with numbers and letters. These numbers and letters are part of the system the library uses to organize its collection.

Many libraries use the Dewey Decimal System. Under this system, a library uses numbers to group books into ten categories of knowledge. Other libraries use the Library of Congress System. The Library of Congress System uses letters, then numbers, to group books.

Find out which system your library uses. You don't have to memorize the letters and numbers for these systems. It's best, however, to know how each system works. You also should know where your library has posted the chart that identifies and explains the system they use. Both systems are shown in the chart below.

Library Classification Systems			
Dewey Decimal System		**Library of Congress System**	
Numbers	**Major Categories**	**Letters**	**Major Categories**
000–099	General works	A, Z	General works
100–199 200–299	Philosophy Religion	B	Philosophy, religion
300–399	Social sciences	H, J, K, L	Social sciences, political science, law, education
400–499	Language	P	Language
500–599	Science	Q	Science
600–699	Technology	R, S, T, U, V	Medicine, agriculture, technology, military and naval sciences
700–799	The arts, recreation	M, N	Music, fine arts
800–899	Literature	P	Literature
900–999	History, geography	C-G	History, geography, recreation

610 *Library and Reference Resources*

Teacher's Classroom Resources

For Lesson 22.2, the following resources can be used for planning, instruction, practice, or reinforcement.

Teaching Tools
Lesson Plans, p. 117

Blackline Masters
Vocabulary and Spelling Practice, pp. 35–40
Thinking and Study Skills, pp. 23–29

Each general category contains subcategories. The first number or letter always indicates the main category and will be followed by other numbers or letters. The diagram below shows how each system works.

How the Two Systems Work		
Dewey Decimal	Description	Library of Congress
700	A book about art	N
750	A book about painting (a subcategory of art)	ND
759	A book about Spanish painting (a subcategory of painting)	ND800
759.609	*The Story of Spanish Painting*	ND804

Exercise 2

1. Suppose a library used the Dewey Decimal System. What number (in the hundreds) would it use to show the category of each of the following books?

   a. *A History of Colonial America*
   b. *Science for the Nonscientist*
   c. *Language Made Easy*
   d. *World Religions*
   e. *The Novels of Charles Dickens*

2. At your school or neighborhood library, find an interesting book in each section listed below. Write down the book's title, topic, and full Dewey Decimal or Library of Congress call number.

   a. 200–299 or B   c. 400–499 or P   e. 900–999 or C
   b. 300–399 or H   d. 500–599 or Q

PRACTICE AND ASSESS

Answers: Exercise 2
1. a. 900s (history)
   b. 500s (science)
   c. 400s (language)
   d. 200s (religion)
   e. 800s (literature)
2. Students should include a title, an inference about the book's topic, and a complete call number. The books should represent the following categories:
   a. religion
   b. social sciences
   c. language
   d. sciences
   e. history and geography

Independent Practice

Skills Practice
📁 *Vocabulary and Spelling Practice*, pp. 35–40
📁 *Thinking and Study Skills*, pp. 23–29

CLOSE

Ask students to think of and discuss problems that would occur if every library used its own system of organizing books as they used to do. Talk about the advantages of being able to walk into any library in the United States and understand how the books are arranged.

Connections Across the Curriculum

History
Encourage students to investigate the Dewey Decimal System, which is used by about 95 percent of all school and public libraries and 25 percent of all university libraries. The first modern classification scheme for libraries, it was invented in 1873 by Melvin Dewey. The Library of Congress, established in 1800, at first classified books by size. In 1815, it bought Thomas Jefferson's private library and reorganized all of its holdings using Jefferson's classification system, which was by subject. The present Library of Congress Classification System began in 1897.

611

FOCUS

Lesson Overview

Objective: To learn how to use a computer or card catalog at the library
Skills: using a catalog; comparing a computer catalog with a card catalog
Critical Thinking: generating new information; explaining a process
Speaking and Listening: explaining a process

Bellringer

When students enter the classroom, have this assignment on the board: *Answer this question on a sheet of paper: If you were looking for a certain book in the library, what information would you need to find it? How would you use this information to find the book?*

Motivating Activity

Discuss students' answers to the Bellringer questions. Ask them if they have used a computer catalog to locate a book in the library. Was it easier or more difficult to use than a card catalog? Tell them that many libraries are eliminating card catalogs and relying only on computer catalogs. Discuss the advantages and disadvantages of making this change.

22.3 Library Catalogs

So many books, so little time! Maybe you've had this thought as you begin your research at the library. The library catalog makes searching for books easier and saves you time.

Using a Computer Catalog

Many libraries use computers to catalog their books. Computer catalogs allow readers to search for books by author, by title, or by subject. For example, suppose you are looking for books by the writer Milton Meltzer.

1. Type in the author's name: *Meltzer, Milton.*
2. You will see a list of all the books in the library by this author. Each book will have a call number.
3. Type the call number of the book you are interested in to get more information about it.
4. Information about the book will appear, as shown below.

Computer catalogs give step-by-step instructions for each kind of search. Just follow the on-screen directions to use the catalog. If you run into trouble, ask a librarian for help.

```
GRANVILLE----------LIBRARIES----------ITEM SCREEN
Call number----973.3 AME
Title---The American revolutionaries: a history in
        their own words
Copy-------1
Look for-------973.3 AME
Location-------GRA Child nonfic
Loan period-------28 days
Item status is: AVAILABLE
Type C and press RETURN for ADDITIONAL COPIES
OF OTHER VOLUMES
  or type CA and press RETURN for
  cataloging information
```

Teacher's Classroom Resources

For Lesson 22.3, the following resources can be used for planning, instruction, practice, or reinforcement.

Teaching Tools
Lesson Plans, p. 117

Blackline Masters
Vocabulary and Spelling Practice, pp. 35–40
Thinking and Study Skills, pp. 23–29

Using a Card Catalog

In libraries that use card catalogs, you will find groups of deep, narrow drawers. The drawers contain rows of cards like those below. These catalog cards are in alphabetical order according to title, author, and subject.

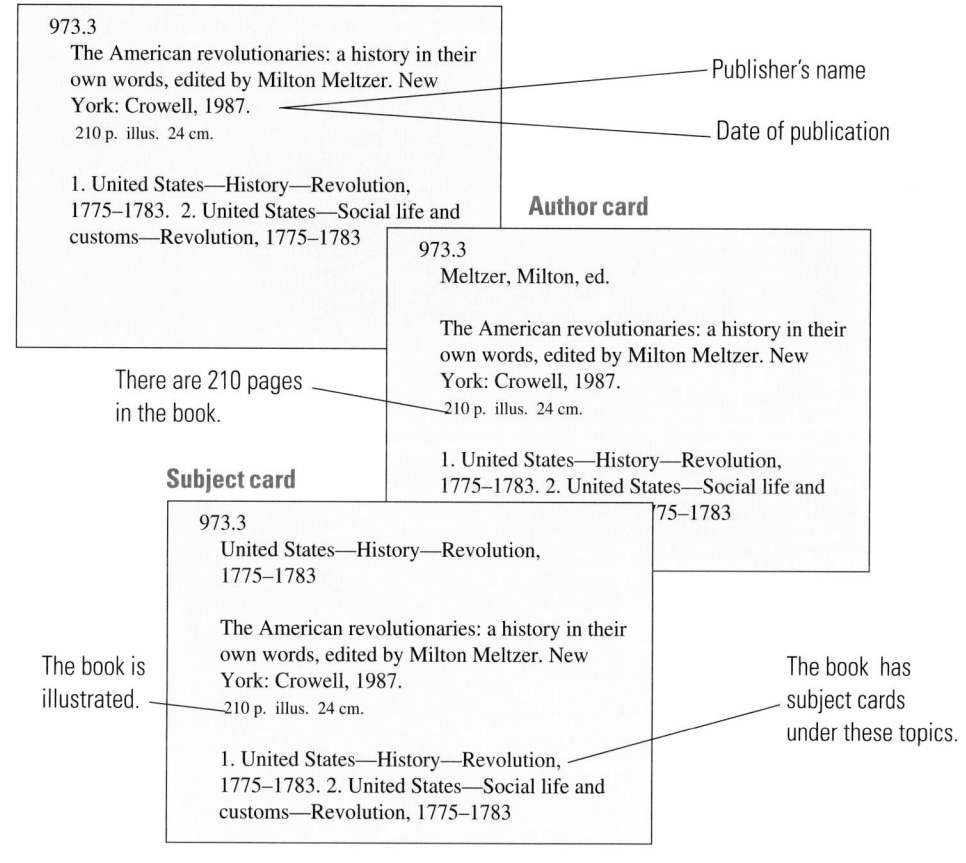

Title card

973.3
The American revolutionaries: a history in their own words, edited by Milton Meltzer. New York: Crowell, 1987.
210 p. illus. 24 cm.

1. United States—History—Revolution, 1775–1783. 2. United States—Social life and customs—Revolution, 1775–1783

— Publisher's name
— Date of publication

Author card

973.3
Meltzer, Milton, ed.

The American revolutionaries: a history in their own words, edited by Milton Meltzer. New York: Crowell, 1987.
210 p. illus. 24 cm.

1. United States—History—Revolution, 1775–1783. 2. United States—Social life and ...75–1783

There are 210 pages in the book.

Subject card

973.3
United States—History—Revolution, 1775–1783

The American revolutionaries: a history in their own words, edited by Milton Meltzer. New York: Crowell, 1987.
210 p. illus. 24 cm.

1. United States—History—Revolution, 1775–1783. 2. United States—Social life and customs—Revolution, 1775–1783

The book is illustrated.

The book has subject cards under these topics.

Nonfiction books usually have three catalog cards: an author card, a title card, and one or more subject cards. Most fiction books have an author card and a title card. The call number of the book is near the upper-left corner of each card. The same call number is on the spine of the actual book.

22.3   Library Catalogs   **613**

Connections Across the Curriculum

History

Students may notice a second—and often a third—line of letters and numbers in the call number of a book. Some libraries that use the Dewey Decimal System add these numbers to further classify books. The second row of numbers is called the Cutter number (after C. A. Cutter, a pioneer in library science). The first letter of the code is the first initial of the author's last name. The final part of the code is the first letter from the title of the book. For example, *Life on the Mississippi* by Mark Twain might have this call number: 817 T969L.

TEACH

Guided Practice

L2 Creating Catalog Cards

Bring a nonfiction book from the library to class, describe it briefly, and help students create a subject card for it on the board. Ask them to suggest other subject cards that could be made for the book. Help students understand that many subject cards could be made for the book, but usually only a few will actually appear in a card catalog. Point out that when using the card catalog or computer catalog for research, they may have to brainstorm for possible subject headings that will lead them to the books they need. Suggest that they try to generalize about a topic and to think of related topics.

L1 Using Call Numbers

Make certain that all students understand that the call number on the library catalog entry is the same number that appears on the spine of the book. Copy the card of a library book from the catalog. Bring the book from the library and copy the information from the card onto the board. Remind students that books are arranged on the shelves by these call numbers. Provide practice by giving each student the title of a library book and having the student find the book and check it out.

L3 Making a Computer Guide

Ask some students to learn as much as they can about the computer catalog. They should talk with the librarian and learn about any special search functions the computer may have. Have them prepare a simple, step-by-step guide for using the computer catalog and share it with the class.

PRACTICE AND ASSESS

Answers: Exercise 3

Students should include complete information: author, title, and call number. The most likely call number categories are

1. 500s (science) or 600s (technology—medicine)
2. 600s (technology)
3. 800s (literature)
4. 500s (science)
5. 400s (language)
6. 700s (recreation)
7. 900s (geography)
8. 100s (philosophy—psychology)

Independent Practice

Skills Practice

📁 *Vocabulary and Spelling Practice,* pp. 35–40

📁 *Thinking and Study Skills,* pp. 23–29

CLOSE

Have students discuss how they would go about finding a book about whales for a report. Make sure that they understand how to use both a computer and a card catalog and that they can distinguish among the three different types of catalog cards.

Finding a Book

When you have located a book you want in the catalog, write down the call number shown on the card or computer screen. Note the area in the library where the book is shelved. You will use this information to locate the book.

In the stacks, signs on the shelves tell which call numbers are included in each row. Books with the same call number are alphabetized by the author's last name or by the first author's last name when there is more than one author.

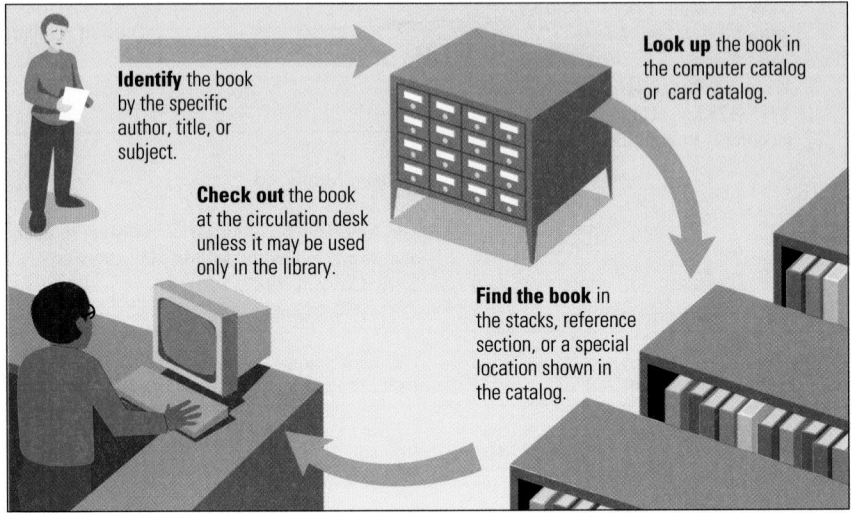

Identify the book by the specific author, title, or subject.

Look up the book in the computer catalog or card catalog.

Check out the book at the circulation desk unless it may be used only in the library.

Find the book in the stacks, reference section, or a special location shown in the catalog.

Exercise 3

Use the card catalog or computer catalog to find a book about any five of the following topics. List the author, title, and call number of each book you find.

1. The brain
2. The development of television
3. Poetry by X. J. Kennedy
4. Marsupials
5. The Spanish language
6. Professional football
7. Mountains
8. The mind

Technology Tip

Learning About Microfilm Catalogs

Some libraries use a microfilm catalog for their book collections as an alternative to both computer and card catalogs. Information is organized similarly to a card catalog, but the data is stored on microfilm, which is viewed by the library user on a microfilm reader.

22.4 Types of Reference Works

When you look up the answer to a question or read a book to find information for social studies class, you are doing research. When you check with friends who know more than you do about your bike, you are doing research. For research you need experts. You'll find the opinions and discoveries of many experts in the reference materials in your library.

Reference works are designed to help you locate specific information quickly. You may be doing research for a class project, looking for a single fact, or just feeling curious about a topic. Whatever your purpose is, the reference area offers many interesting resources.

The chart below describes some general types of reference sources found in most libraries. Find out where each of these kinds of references is kept in your public library. Locate those references that are available in your school library or classroom as well.

Using General Reference Works to Answer Questions		
Questions	**Where to Look for an Answer**	**Examples of Sources**
When did Henry Ford introduce the Model T?	**Encyclopedias** include general information on a variety of topics.	• *World Book Encyclopedia* • *Grolier Encyclopedia* • *Encyclopaedia Britannica*
What major cities are on the Ohio River?	**Atlases** are collections of maps. They often include special maps on climate, population, and other topics.	• *Hammond Contemporary World Atlas* • *The Rand McNally Atlas of World Exploration*
Who received the Nobel Peace Prize in 1979?	**Almanacs** provide lists, statistics, and other information on recent and historical topics.	• *Information Please Almanac* • *Guinness Book of World Records*
Where was Mark Twain born?	**Biographical reference works** include biographies of notable persons, both past and present.	• *Dictionary of American Biography* • *Webster's Biographical Dictionary*

22.4 Types of Reference Works **615**

Setting the Purpose

Lesson 22.4 describes the general types of reference sources available and teaches students how to use them so that they can find information quickly.

FOCUS

Lesson Overview
Objective: To become familiar with basic reference sources
Skills: differentiating between encyclopedias, atlases, almanacs, and biographical dictionaries
Critical Thinking: contrasting different reference sources; evaluating which reference source fits a particular information need
Speaking and Listening: note taking; discussing

Bellringer
When students enter the classroom, have this assignment on the board: *Choose a country in South America and list four reference sources you would use to write a report about it. Write what kind of information you would use from each source.*

Motivating Activity
Discuss students' responses to the Bellringer exercise. Then show the class a one-volume encyclopedia or one book of a multivolume encyclopedia, an atlas, an almanac, and a biographical dictionary. Ask students to suggest any additional kinds of information they would expect to find in each resource.

Teacher's Classroom Resources

For Lesson 22.4, the following resources can be used for planning, instruction, practice, or reinforcement.

🔧 **Teaching Tools**
Lesson Plans, p. 118

📁 **Blackline Masters**
Vocabulary and Spelling Practice, pp. 35–40
Thinking and Study Skills, pp. 23–29

TEACH

Guided Practice

L2 Using Encyclopedias

Stress that using encyclopedias is only one step in the research process. Point out that encyclopedias give overviews of topics and frequently provide suggestions that can guide further research. Have students examine as many different encyclopedias as possible and share what they learn with the class. Ask them to explain what types of research aids—such as outlines of topics and bibliographic citations—are included in the different encyclopedias.

L1 Looking at Reference Sources

Emphasize that the chart on page 615 shows just a few of the general reference sources available in a library. Take students to the reference section of the school library. Show them where the references listed in the chart are located. Ask them to find and examine one or two other reference sources in the reference section. Then have students compile a list of these sources.

L3 Exploring Atlases

Ask students to work in small groups to explore the atlases available in the school library. Tell them to examine each book and record its title and copyright date. Suggest that students note the differences in content, organization, size, quality, and use of photos in the various atlases. Then ask each group to write a brief summary of the contents of each atlas, including descriptions of any unique features. Have the groups share what they learn about atlases with the rest of the class.

Encyclopedias

You will find one-volume encyclopedias and sets made up of many volumes. Encyclopedias may be either general or specialized. General encyclopedias contain articles about all branches of knowledge. Specialized encyclopedias present articles in a specific area of knowledge, such as history, science, or the arts. Two examples of specialized encyclopedias are the *McGraw-Hill Encyclopedia of Science and Technology,* and *The New York Times Encyclopedia of Film.*

Most encyclopedias are organized alphabetically. To find all of the articles with information on your topic, look up the topic in the index. The index is usually the last volume of a multi-volume encyclopedia. It contains an alphabetical listing of topics. After each topic you will find the subjects related to the topic you are investigating. The index tells you the volume and page number of the article where you will find the information. Sometimes the index refers you to a different topic heading for a list of articles.

Many encyclopedia entries end with a list of books that contain additional information. These books may be available at your library. The entry may also list other related articles in the encyclopedia.

Atlases

Atlases are collections of maps. General atlases contain maps of all parts of the world. In a general atlas, you can find map information about population, industry, farming, and other topics for all parts of the world. These atlases may also contain graphs, charts, and pictures. For example, the *National Geographic Atlas of the World* includes satellite images of the earth's major regions.

Some atlases are specialized. They may cover one part of the world, such as a single country. Others have maps on a special topic, such as population, the environment, or animals. Travelers often rely on atlases that show highways, national parks, and places of interest to tourists. Historical atlases contain maps for different periods in history and various parts of the world.

616 *Library and Reference Resources*

Enabling Strategies

LEP Focusing on Visual Resources

Have students refer to reference resources that are primarily visual in nature, such as atlases. Make sure that students understand the kind of information available from the sources including the map legend. Students shsould also become familiar with other, less text-heavy sources, such as almanacs and yearbooks. Students should be encouraged to work in pairs with encyclopedias, to help maximize their understanding of the text, and to work with encyclopedias on CD-ROM, if available.

Almanacs and Yearbooks

If you're looking for very current information or statistics, consult almanacs and yearbooks. These references contain the most recent available information on a variety of topics. A new edition is published every year.

Two widely used almanacs are the *Information Please Almanac* and the *World Almanac and Book of Facts.* Both cover a wide range of information, from baseball statistics to the latest scientific discoveries. Much of the information is presented in the form of lists or tables.

A yearbook is a book issued each year by some encyclopedia publishers to update their regular encyclopedia volumes. It contains articles about events and developments of that year. The yearbooks for an encyclopedia generally follow the *Z* volume or the Index volume on the reference shelf.

22.4 Types of Reference Works **617**

TEACH

Guided Practice

L2 Using an Almanac
Provide an almanac for students to use to find two facts about the biggest, fastest, lightest, longest anything, or about winners of awards or athletes who have set sports records. Then have students write two questions on the board about the information they've found. Challenge other students to find the answers.

L3 Using Almanacs and Yearbooks
Bring several current almanacs and yearbooks to class and ask students to examine them. Name a world event of the previous year, and have students race to see who can find the answer first. Ask students questions such as, Who won the Wimbledon men's singles championship in 1975? (Arthur Ashe) Ask students to describe the major differences between almanacs and yearbooks. (Almanacs have more concise information and far more statistical data. Yearbooks provide extensive discussions of the past year.)

Technology Tip

Researching with CD-ROMs
Personal computers with CD-ROM (compact disc players specially designed for use with computers) have made it possible to have entire reference resources—including encyclopedias, atlases, and dictionaries—available on a single compact disc. Many public libraries now have these systems available. In addition to the small disc size, CD-ROM technology makes it possible to search rapidly for specific topics or entries, enabling users to easily find even minor mentions of topics.

PRACTICE AND ASSESS

Answers: Exercise 4

1. a. almanac
   b. atlas or encyclopedia
   c. encyclopedia or biographical dictionary
   d. enclopedia, atlas, or almanac
   e. encyclopedia
2. Any two of the following:
   a. Jackie Joyner-Kersee (United States)
   b. Indonesia
   c. printer, riverboat pilot, reporter, prospector
   d. Arizona
   e. *Sputnik* was the name of the first space satellite launched by the Soviet Union in 1957. Its launching surprised the United States, hastening the United States's entry into the space race.

Independent Practice

Skills Practice

📂 *Vocabulary and Spelling Practice,* pp. 35–40

📂 *Thinking and Study Skills,* pp. 23–29

CLOSE

Have students work together to create a chart of the basic reference sources taught in this lesson. Encourage them to add to the chart other reference sources they have discovered. Students may want to use the chart on page 615 as a model.

Biographical Dictionaries

Biographical dictionaries contain information on important people. Some of these dictionaries include living persons as well as persons from history. These references may have many volumes or may be contained in a single book.

In the larger, multivolume dictionaries, such as the *Dictionary of American Biography,* entries are lengthy and give a detailed life history. An example of a shorter reference is *Webster's Biographical Dictionary.* In this work the entries are much briefer, sometimes only a few lines long. An example is shown below. Biographical dictionaries are useful when you need information about particular people.

Cra´zy Horse´ (krā´zē hôrs´) Indian name **Tashunca-Uitco.** 1849?–1877. American Indian chief, of the Oglala tribe of the Sioux, in battle of Little Big Horn, in which Custer was killed (1876); surrendered; killed while resisting imprisonment (Sept. 5, 1877).

Exercise 4

1. Name the type of reference work in which you would expect to find answers to the following:

   a. Who was the Olympic champion in the women's long jump in 1988?
   b. Of what country is Jakarta the capital?
   c. What occupations did Samuel Clemens follow before becoming a writer?
   d. In what state is the Painted Desert located?
   e. What was *Sputnik,* and why was it important?

2. Use a library reference to write the answers to any *two* of the above questions.

Connections Across the Curriculum

History

Almanacs, which originated in the Middle East, were used to record the positions of stars and the weather at given locations. The idea of recording such information spread to Europe in the Middle Ages, where publishers added folklore, advice, and other information to weather and astronomical data. The shape and content of almanacs continued to evolve until the middle of the nineteenth century. Today there are two major almanacs in the United States: *The World Almanac and Book of Facts* and *Information Please Almanac.*

22.5 The *Readers' Guide*

Sometimes you may want up-to-date information about a topic. A magazine may be an interesting and useful reference in this case. One of the best sources for finding magazine articles on almost any subject is the *Readers' Guide to Periodical Literature*. The guide indexes articles from over 175 magazines by author and subject.

Using the *Readers' Guide*

Each hard-bound volume of the *Readers' Guide* contains a year's entries. New paperback indexes are published every two weeks, and larger paperback indexes are published every three months. The following annotated excerpt from the *Readers' Guide* shows you how to read the information in the index.

BLACK HIGH SCHOOL STUDENTS *See* Black students ——— Cross-reference
BLACK HISTORY *See* Blacks—History
BLACK HISTORY MONTH ——————————— Subject
    Black History Month calendar. H. C. Harrison. il
      American Visions 7:54–64 F/Mr '92
    Black History Month cites discovery, exploration of
      America by heroic blacks. il *Jet* 81:22–3 F 17 '92
    Black History Month fete at White House boosts Bush's
      spirits. il por *Jet* 81:4–5 Mr 9 '92 ——————— Date
    Black History Month: stars reveal their favorite heroes
      in black history. C. Waldron. il *Jet* 81:60–2 F 24 '92
    Now you see them. . . [books published during Black His- ——— Article title
      tory Month] il *Newsweek* 119:60–2 Mr 9 '92
BLACK HOLES (ASTRONOMY)
    How to find a black hole. F. Flam. il *Science* 255:794–5 F 14 '92
    Hubble captures a violent universe [core of two galaxies] ——— Volume
      R. Cowen. il *Science News* 141:52 Ja 25 '92
    New evidence for black holes in Milky Way. R. Cowen. ——— Author
      Science News 141:101 F 15 '92
    New strategy in the hunt for black holes [Hubble Space
      Telescope photographs core of M87 galaxy; study by
      Todd Lauer and Sandra Faber] F. Flam. il *Science* ——— Magazine title
      255:537–8 Ja 31 '92 ————————————————— Pages
    No black hole in SS 433. il *Sky and Telescope* 83:249–50 Mr '92
      Caricatures and cartoons ——————————— Subheading
    Science Classics. L. Gonick. il *Discover* 13:78–79 Ja '92

22.5 The Readers' Guide **619**

Teacher's Classroom Resources

For Lesson 22.5, the following resources can be used for planning, instruction, practice, or reinforcement.

📑 **Teaching Tools**
Lesson Plans

🗂 **Blackline Masters**
Vocabulary and Spelling Practice, pp. 35–40
Thinking and Study Skills, pp. 23–29

Setting the Purpose

Lesson 22.5 teaches students how to use the *Readers' Guide to Periodical Literature* and how to find articles in periodicals.

FOCUS

Lesson Overview
Objective: To learn how to use the *Readers' Guide* as a research tool
Skills: researching magazine articles; using the *Readers' Guide*
Critical Thinking: recalling; synthesizing; defining; clarifying
Speaking and Listening: discussing; explaining a process

Bellringer
When students enter the classroom, have this assignment on the board: *How might you go about finding a magazine article on computer software?*

TEACH

Guided Practice
L1 Using the *Readers' Guide*
Some students may be easily overwhelmed by the density of information packed into the *Readers' Guide.* Reassure them that the *Readers' Guide* is well organized by both subject and author and that they can use it just as they use the card catalog. Give students a topic and an author's name, and help them use the *Readers' Guide* to locate one article for each.

PRACTICE AND ASSESS

Answers: Exercise 5

1. *Sky and Telescope*
2. African-American students
3. Yes. An article is listed under the subheading "Caricatures and cartoons."
4. pages 54–64
5. R. Cowen, *Science News*

Independent Practice

Skills Practice

📁 *Vocabulary and Spelling Practice,* pp. 35–40

📁 *Thinking and Study Skills,* pp. 23–29

CLOSE

Ask students how information from periodicals can enhance a report. (Periodicals cover events that have occurred recently.) Ask a volunteer to describe the process he or she must go through to find a periodical for a report.

Finding an Article in a Periodical

The *Readers' Guide* lists more magazines than any single library owns. Check to see which periodicals are available at your library. Then look up the topic that interests you. Find an entry you would like to investigate. Write the name of the magazine, its date, the article title, and the page numbers. This is the information you will use to locate the article.

If the article is from a recent issue, you will probably find it on open shelves in the periodicals section. Articles from older issues are generally stored as bound volumes or microforms. Microforms are tiny photographs of printed pages arranged on small film cards (called microfiche) or on strips of film (called microfilm). Each type of microform is viewed on a special machine that enlarges the pages so they can be read or printed. A librarian can help you locate microforms and use the viewing equipment.

Exercise 5

Using the excerpts from the *Readers' Guide* on the previous page, answer the following questions:

1. What is the name of the magazine that contains the article "No Black Hole in SS 433"?
2. Under what topic would you find articles about black high school students?
3. Could you use this excerpt of the *Readers' Guide* to find a cartoon about black holes? Explain.
4. On what pages of *American Visions* would you find a calendar of events for Black History Month?
5. Who wrote an article about the Hubble telescope photographing the core of two galaxies? In what magazine was the article published?

620 *Library and Reference Resources*

Enabling Strategies

LEP Interpreting the *Readers' Guide*

Some students may have difficulty interpreting entries in the *Readers' Guide* due to the abbreviations and shortened magazine titles used. Show students the list of abbreviations and the list of magazines that appear in the front of every guide. Help students interpret several entries.

22.6 Other Print and Nonprint Media

While books are the heart of most library collections, libraries offer several kinds of media. The word *media* (singular *medium*) means methods of communication, such as newspapers, magazines, movies, and television. The media are often divided into two types—print and nonprint.

Print Media

Magazines and newspapers, like books, are print media. Both news magazines, such as *Time,* and special-interest magazines, such as *Photography,* are good sources for up-to-date information. Since they are printed often (usually weekly or monthly), magazines can provide more recent information than most books. Whatever special interests or research needs you have, there's likely to be a magazine that can help you.

Current newspapers cover recent events of national and local interest, but older issues can also be a good source of information. Some libraries keep copies of local newspapers from as far back as the 1800s. These old issues can be useful if you are doing research on a historical period. Check your library to find out what newspapers are available there. Microforms are used to store back issues of both newspapers and magazines. For more information on using microforms, see page 620.

Some Types of Magazines	
Types of Magazines	Examples
News magazines	*Newsweek, U.S. News and World Report, Time*
General-interest magazines	*Reader's Digest, National Geographic, Atlantic*
Special-interest magazines	*Photography, House and Garden, Bicycling, MacUser*
Magazines for younger readers	*National Geographic World, Zillions, Sports Illustrated for Kids*

22.6 Other Print and Nonprint Media **621**

Teacher's Classroom Resources

For Lesson, 22.6, the following resources can be used for planning, instruction, practice, or reinforcement.

Teaching Tools
Lesson Plans, p. 118

Blackline Masters
Vocabulary and Spelling Practice, pp. 35–40
Thinking and Study Skills, pp. 23–29

Setting the Purpose

Lesson 22.6 teaches students that most libraries carry a variety of print and nonprint media that can provide students with useful information when writing a report.

FOCUS

Lesson Overview

Objective: To become familiar with a variety of print and nonprint media
Skills: categorizing types of media; analyzing types of information in print and nonprint media
Critical Thinking: classifying; categorizing
Speaking and Listening: informal speaking; questioning

Bellringer
When students enter the classroom, have this assignment on the chalkboard: *Make a list of magazines with which you are familiar. What subjects are covered in each magazine?*

Motivating Activity
Discuss students' answers to the Bellringer. Have students compile a chart of the magazines they suggested.

TEACH

Guided Practice

L2 Finding Information in Nonprint Media
Tell students that not all information is obtained by reading. Point out that audio-visual materials can be useful when looking for information for reports. Send students to the school library to explore nonprint resources. Ask them to make a list of the nonprint resources they find.

Nonprint Media

Most libraries now offer videotapes of movies, travelogues, and instructional (how-to-do-it) films. Audiotapes and compact discs (CDs) contain sound recordings. Besides music of all types, they hold plays and readings of poetry and fiction. Compact discs also store printed information such as periodical indexes and encyclopedias. These CDs are fed into a computer, which provides very fast searches for information.

Using Nonprint Media		
Type of Media	**Information Available**	**Equipment Needed**
Microforms	Back issues of newspapers and magazines	Microform viewer or viewer/printer (at the librar
Videotapes	Movies, documentaries, travel and instructional films	VCR and television set
Laser discs	Movies, documentaries, travel and instructional films	Laser disc player and television set
Audiotapes	Music, readings, dramas, language lessons	Audiocassette player
Compact discs	Same as audiotapes Information sources	CD player and stereo syste CD player and computer

Exercise 6

In which print or nonprint medium would you expect to find each of the following items? More than one answer may be appropriate in some cases.

1. An article describing a new type of computer
2. Recorded Russian lessons for travelers
3. A documentary about the canal era in Ohio
4. An article about a student from your school who just won a national award
5. *The Grolier Encyclopedia* on computer

Enabling Strategies

LEP Learning About Popular Magazines

Some students may not be familiar with many popular American magazines, such as those given as examples in the chart on page 621. You may want to bring examples of some of these magazines to class to give students a chance to become familiar with them.

22.7 The Dictionary

You English words
I know you:
You are light as dreams,
Tough as oak,
Precious as gold,
As poppies and corn,
Or an old cloak . . .

These lines by Edward Thomas hint at the richness of the English language. You can enrich your knowledge of English by frequent use of the dictionary—an essential tool for a writer.

The Dictionary

A dictionary is an alphabetical listing of words with definitions and often with word origins and other information. Most dictionaries fall into one of the categories below.

Types of Dictionaries		
Type	**Characteristics**	**Examples**
Unabridged Dictionaries	• 250,000 or more entries • Detailed word histories • Detailed definitions • Found mostly in libraries	• *Random House Dictionary of the English Language* • *Webster's Third New International Dictionary*
College Dictionaries	• About 150,000 entries • Detailed enough to answer most questions on spelling or definitions • Widely used in schools, homes, and businesses	• *Random House Webster's College Dictionary* • *American Heritage Dictionary of the English Language* • *Webster's New World Dictionary*
School Dictionaries	• 90,000 or fewer entries • Definitions suitable for students' abilities • Emphasizes common words	• *The Scribner's Dictionary* • *Webster's School Dictionary*

22.7   The Dictionary   **623**

Setting the Purpose

Lesson 22.7 teaches students the differences between various types of dictionaries and the types of information they contain. Students also learn the basic elements of an entry so that they can make better use of the dictionary when writing.

FOCUS

Lesson Overview
Objective: To become familiar with dictionaries
Skills: distinguishing between various types of dictionaries; identifying the basic elements of an entry
Critical Thinking: comparing and contrasting dictionaries; identifying characteristics
Speaking and Listening: explaining the process of using various dictionaries

Bellringer
When students enter the classroom, have this assignment on the chalkboard: *You want to buy a dictionary. Write a paragraph that describes why you want a dictionary and the type of information you will be looking for.*

Motivating Activity
Bring several school and college dictionaries and, if possible, an unabridged dictionary to class. Have volunteers read aloud the entry for the same word in each of the dictionaries. Ask students to discuss the differences among the definitions and information given. When might they use a school dictionary? an unabridged dictionary?

Teacher's Classroom Resources

For Lesson 22.7, the following resources can be used for planning, instruction, practice, or reinforcement.

🔧 **Teaching Tools**
Lesson Plans, p. 119

📁 **Blackline Masters**
Vocabulary and Spelling Practice, pp. 35–40
Thinking and Study Skills, pp. 23–29

623

TEACH

Guided Practice

L2 Finding Dictionary Aids

Have students use their classroom dictionaries to find the guide words and pronunciation key. Tell them to turn to the front of their dictionaries and locate the complete pronunciation key and list of abbreviations. What other information is in the front and back of their dictionaries? (Answers will depend upon the dictionary used.) Then ask students to look up *Samuel Johnson* and *Hartford, Connecticut*. Where did they locate the information?

L1 Using the Pronunciation Key

The pronunciation key in a dictionary can baffle some students. Write the pronunciation for several common words that appear in your classroom dictionary. Help students identify each word by sounding it out. Then give students some unfamiliar words. Have them use their dictionaries to find the correct pronunciation of each word.

Guide words show the first and last entry on the page. Use them to zero in on the word you are seeking.

The illustrations show how to use two helpful dictionary features. Guide words help you locate words quickly. The pronunciation key can help you sound out a word.

> **foot soldier / fore-and-aft**
>
> **foot soldier,** a soldier trained or equipped to fight on foot; infantryman.
> **foot·sore** (foot′sôr′) *adj.* having sore or tired feet, as from much walking.
> **foot·step** (foot′step′) *n.* **1.** a step or tread of the foot: *a baby's first awkward footsteps.* **2.** the sound made by this: *I heard his footsteps in the hall.* **3.** the distance covered in a step.
> **to follow in someone's footsteps.** to imitate or follow the same course as someone: *Dan followed in his father's footsteps and became a teacher.*
>
> **for·bid·ding** (fer bid′ing) *adj.* looking unfriendly or dangerous; frightening; grim: *The old house was dark and forbidding.* —**for·bid′ding·ly,** *adv.*
> **for·bore** (fôr bôr′) the past tense of **forbear** .
> **for·borne** (fôr bôrn′) the past participle of **forbear** .
> **force** (fôrs) *n.* **1.** power, strength, or energy: *The batter struck the ball with great force. The force of the explosion broke windows in the nearby buildings.* **2.** the use of such power, strength, or energy; violence: *The sheriff dragged the outlaw off by force.* **3.** the power to convince, or control: *The force of her argument won*

The pronunciation key uses well-known words to interpret the pronunciation symbols.

> oneself from (doing something): refrain from: *Tom could not forbear smiling at his embarrassed friend.* [Old English forberan to hold back.]
> **for·bear**² (fôr′ber) another spelling of **forebear.**
> **for·bear·ance** (fôr berʹəns) *n.* **1.** the act of forbearing. **2.** self-control or patience: *Jim showed great forbearance during his long illness.*
> **for·bid** (fer bid′) *v.t.,* **for·bade** or **for·bad, for·bid·den** or (*archaic*) **for·bid, for·bid·ding.** to order not to do something; refuse to allow; prohibit: *I forbid you to go out. The school forbids eating in the classrooms.*
>
> **fore-and-aft** (fôr′en aft′) *adj.* from bow to stern of a ship: *a fore-and-aft sail.*
>
> at; āpe; cär; end; mē; it; īce; hot; ōld; fôrk; wood; ̄oo̅l; oil; out; up; turn; sing; thin; this; hw in white; zh in treasure. The symbol ə stands for the sound of **a** in about, **e** in taken, **i** in pencil, **o** in lemon, and **u** in circus.

Other useful features are located in the front and back pages of the dictionary. In the front you can find a complete pronunciation key, a list of abbreviations used in entries, and information about punctuation and capitalization. Some dictionaries include a short history of the English language. In the back of the dictionary you may find sections with biographical and geographical entries. Some dictionaries include such information with the regular word listings.

Entry Word

A dictionary entry packs a great deal of information into a small space. By becoming familiar with the basic elements of an entry, you'll find it easier to explore new words.

The entry word is the first element in each entry. It is printed in bold type, which makes it easy to find the beginning of an entry. The entry word shows how to divide a word of more than one syllable. Notice how *flourish* is divided by the dot. Not every dictionary entry is a single word. Some entries

624 *Library and Reference Resources*

Enabling Strategies

LEP Using Bilingual Dictionaries

Students learning English may find it helpful to discuss how they use a bilingual dictionary to learn the meanings of English words. Help them to see that those same skills relate to how they use an English dictionary. If possible, pair students who speak the same language

so that one member is more fluent in English. Ask pairs to find two unfamiliar words in a newspaper article and look up the words in their bilingual dictionaries. Then have them use the same process with an English dictionary. Have them discuss how the process is similar.

are two words, such as *cuckoo clock,* and some, such as *T-shirt,* are hyphenated.

————— Entry word

flour (~~flour~~, flou ər) *n.* **1.** soft, powdery substance obtained by grinding and sifting grain, esp. wheat, used chiefly as a basic ingredient in baked goods and other foods. **2.** any soft powdery substance. —*v.t.* to cover or sprinkle with flour. [Form of FLOWER in the sense of "finest part" (of the grain).]

flour·ish (flur´ish) *v.i.* **1.** to grow or develop vigorously or prosperously; thrive: *Crops flourish in rich soil. His business is flourishing.* **2.** to reach or be at the peak of development or achievement: *a civilization that flourished thousands of years ago.* —*v.t.* **1.** to wave about with bold or sweeping gestures; brandish: *to flourish a sword; to flourish a baton.* **2.** to display ostentatiously; flaunt. —*n.* **1.** a brandishing: *He bowed to her with a flourish of his hat.* **2.** ostentatious or dramatic display or gesture: *She entered the room with a flourish.* **3.** decorative stroke or embellishment in writing. **4.** elaborate, ornamental passage or series of notes, as a trill or fanfare, added to a musical work. [Old French *floriss-*, a stem of *florir* to flower, bloom, going back to Latin *florere* to flower, bloom] —**Syn.** *v.i.* see **prosper.**

————— Definition

————— Pronunciation

————— Part of speech

————— Word origin

Synonym reference. You can find a list of synonyms for flourish *in the entry for* prosper.

Pronunciation

The pronunciation of a word follows the entry word. It is written in special symbols that allow you to sound out the word. If you are not sure how to pronounce a syllable, check the pronunciation key, which is usually at the bottom of the page. The simple words in the key show the sounds of the most common symbols. To see a complete pronunciation key, turn to the front pages of the dictionary. Some words have more than one pronunciation; the most common is generally shown first.

Part of Speech

Every dictionary entry indicates a word's part or parts of speech. For example, in the entry for *flourish, v.i.* stands for *intransitive verb* and *v.t.* for *transitive verb.* The letter *n.* stands for *noun.* What would you expect the abbreviations for adjective and adverb to be? A list of the abbreviations is located in the front of the dictionary.

22.7 The Dictionary **625**

TEACH

L2 Reading a Dictionary Entry
Divide students into groups. Provide each group with a dictionary. Have them look up the word *flourish* and compare the entry with the one shown on page 625. Ask students to find the guide words, the entry word, the pronunciation, the part of speech, the definition, and the origin of the word. Be sure they understand any symbols or abbreviations unique to their dictionaries.

Cross-reference: Grammar
For more information on correct forms of irregular verbs, refer students to lessons 10.11–10.12, pp. 388–391.

Cross-reference: Spelling
For more information on the spelling of irregular plural nouns, refer students to Lesson 23.6, pp. 647–654.

Enrichment and Extension

Learning About the *OED*
The *Oxford English Dictionary* (*OED*) traces the history of each word before it entered English. Then it gives the date, a quote of the word's earliest known usage in English, and additional quotations from the earliest English writers to modern times.

Beyond the Classroom

Using Specialized Dictionaries
Besides standard English dictionaries, many other specialized dictionaries are found in libraries. These include dictionaries of slang, music, biography, geography, law, medicine, science, and sports. Ask students to find and examine as many of these in their library as they can.

Answers: Exercise 7
1. four (two intransitive and two transitive)
2. to wave about boldly (*v.t.*)
3. flurry
4. to cover or sprinkle with flour (*v.t.*)
5. to flower, bloom

Independent Practice

Skills Practice
📂 *Vocabulary and Spelling Practice,* pp. 35–40
📂 *Thinking and Study Skills,* pp. 23–29

CLOSE

Ask students to discuss what they have learned about the various types of dictionaries available to them and to discuss the types of information that can be found in a dictionary.

626

Definition

The definition, or meaning, of the word is the heart of the entry. Many words have more than one meaning. These meanings are usually numbered from most common to least common. Some unabridged and college dictionaries, however, use a different method. They give definitions from the earliest-known meaning to the most recent meaning. Look at the sample entries on page 625 to see how the definitions of *flourish* are numbered.

Word Origins

The word origin is a brief account of how the word entered the English language. Many words, like *flourish,* were used in more than one language before entering English. For example, look at the *flourish* entry. The source of the word is Latin. The word then moved into Old French. English speakers borrowed it from Old French. Many dictionaries use abbreviations for the language from which a word comes, such as *L.* for Latin. A list of these abbreviations is located at the front of the dictionary.

Exercise 7

Use the dictionary entries in this lesson to answer the following questions:

1. How many definitions does this dictionary include for the verb form of the word *flourish?*
2. Which meaning of *flourish* is implied in the following sentence? *The students flourished their hand-made signs at the rally.*
3. Does the first syllable of *flourish* rhyme with the first syllable of *flower, flurry,* or *Florence?*
4. Which of the meanings shown for *flour* do you find in the following sentence? *I floured the chicken before putting it into the oven.*
5. What was the meaning of the Latin word that was the original source of *flourish?*

---

626 *Library and Reference Resources*

Cooperative Learning

Determining Word Origins

Explain that word origins may help students understand the exact meanings of words that distinguish them from their synonyms. Many words share common origins, so knowing the origin of a word can help students with the meanings of related words. Ask teams of students to look up word origins for five different words. (For example, *tentacle, industrious, scuba, contradict, visor*) Then have the groups mime their words for the class. When the class figures out a word, ask them to brainstorm the word origin, and then check it in the dictionary.

22.8 The Thesaurus

More than 150 years ago a British doctor, Peter Mark Roget [rō zhā´], developed a thesaurus. A thesaurus is a dictionary of synonyms—words with similar meanings. Since that time, the thesaurus has grown and changed.

Using a Thesaurus

Roget organized his thesaurus by categories. Then he listed the categories in an index. When you use this type of thesaurus, you find the category you want in the index. The index will refer you to the lists of synonyms you want.

The excerpt below is from another kind of thesaurus, one in which the words are arranged like those in a dictionary. In a dictionary-style thesaurus the word entries are in alphabetical order.

Clever *adjective*
1. Mentally quick and original: *The child is clever but not brilliant.*
   Syns: alert, bright, intelligent, keen, quick-witted, sharp, sharp-witted, smart.
   —*Idiom* smart as a tack (*or* whip).
2. Amusing or pleasing because of wit or originality: *made the audience laugh with a few clever, offbeat comparisons.*
   Syns: scintillating, smart, sparkling, sprightly, witty.
3. DEXTEROUS.
4. SHARP.
clew *noun* SEE **clue.**
cliché *noun*
A trite expression or idea: *a short story marred by clichés.*
   Syns: banality, bromide, commonplace, platitude, stereotype, truism.
cliché *adjective* TRITE.
click *noun* SNAP.
   click *verb*
   1. RELATE.
   2. SNAP.
   3. SUCCEED.

Part of speech is indicated.

Synonyms are grouped by definition.

Usage examples are given.

In this thesaurus capital letters indicate a cross-reference to another entry. More synonyms are found under the cross-reference entry.

22.8 The Thesaurus **627**

Teacher's Classroom Resources

For Lesson 22.8, the following resources can be used for planning, instruction, practice, assessment, reinforcement, or evaluation.

Teaching Tools
Lesson Plans, p. 119

Blackline Masters
Vocabulary and Spelling Practice, pp. 35–40
Thinking and Study Skills, pp. 23–29

Unit Assessment
Tests with Answer Key
Unit 22 Mastery Test, pp. 87–88

Test Generator
Unit 22 Mastery Test

You may wish to administer the Unit 22 Mastery Test at this point.

FOCUS

Lesson Overview

Objective: To become familiar with the thesaurus
Skills: identifying the basic information found in a thesaurus entry; using alphabetical order to locate words
Critical Thinking: defining and clarifying; recalling
Speaking and Listening: discussing

Bellringer

When students enter the classroom, have this assignment on the board:

Read the following sentences:

Mark blabbed to everyone about the surprise party.

Mark tattled to everyone about the surprise party.

Do the sentences have the same meaning? What are the differences? Write your answers.

TEACH

Guided Practice

L2 Using Synonyms
Have students review a paragraph from a recent writing assignment. Ask them to rewrite the paragraph, replacing five words with more precise or vivid synonyms. Students should exchange their rewrites with partners and discuss how the paragraph improved.

PRACTICE AND ASSESS

Answers: Exercise 8

Sentences should convey the appropriate meaning of the word. Some possible synonyms include the following:

1. talk, utter, verbalize, address
2. dash, scurry, bolt, rush
3. scrawny, twiggy, slender, gaunt
4. fizz, froth, lather, suds
5. glistening, glassy, gleaming, polished

Independent Practice

Skills Practice

📁 *Thinking and Study Skills*, pp. 23–29

📁 *Vocabulary and Spelling Practice*, pp. 35–40

CLOSE

Ask students to discuss how they plan to use a thesaurus in their next writing assignment.

Finding Synonyms

Knowing how the thesaurus is arranged can help you find the exact word you need. You can see from the samples on the previous page that each definition is followed by several synonyms or by a cross-reference to another entry. Synonyms, you recall, are words that have *similar* meanings. The thesaurus can help you distinguish among many synonyms to find the most exact one.

The words in capital letters lead you to further synonyms. If you look up a word shown in capital letters, you will find a definition and many additional synonyms. *Dexterous*, for example, means *clever*, but in a specific way: exhibiting or possessing skill or ease in performance. Your expert handling of a bike might be called dexterous. Conversation on a talk show may be clever, but it is not necessarily dexterous.

Most libraries will have more than one type of thesaurus available. A similar resource, a dictionary of synonyms, is also available to help you locate the most precise word. Two examples are *Webster's New Dictionary of Synonyms* and *Webster's New World Dictionary of Synonyms*.

Many thesauruses list antonyms—words with opposite meanings—as well as synonyms. Your library may have *Webster's Collegiate Thesaurus*, which includes antonyms. For more information on synonyms and antonyms, see pages 641–642.

> **Exercise 8**
>
> Use a thesaurus to find two synonyms for each word below. Then write an original sentence to illustrate the meaning of each synonym. Check the exact meaning of each word in a dictionary before you use it in a sentence.
>
> 1. speak (verb)
> 2. run (verb)
> 3. thin (adjective)
> 4. foam (noun)
> 5. shiny (adjective)

Enabling Strategies

LEP Distinguishing Shades of Meaning

Distinguishing shades of meaning among synonyms may be difficult for students whose first language is not English. Suggest that these students use a thesaurus to make a list of synonyms for a simple word such as *pretty*, *large*, or *happy*. They may need to look up definitions for the synonym to identify differences in meaning. The synonyms notes that appear with many entries in the *American Heritage Dictionary* are particularly helpful in identifying shades of meaning.

UNIT 23 Vocabulary and Spelling

23.1 Words from American English

People all over the world use the word *okay*. It began, however, as an American-English word. How did *okay* become so widespread? Citizens of many nations borrowed this word from American travelers. Speakers of one language will often borrow words from speakers of another language they come into contact with.

Words from Native Americans

English colonists began settling in North America in the early 1600s. They often borrowed Native American words to name foods, plants, and animals new to them. Some examples are the words *pecan*, *hickory*, *squash*, *moose*, *chipmunk*, and *skunk*.

Europeans also borrowed Native American words to name natural features and places. The Mississippi River's name, for example, comes from Algonquian words meaning "great water." More than half the states and many cities and counties have names with Native American origins. Hawaii's name came from its original Polynesian settlers.

Kayak

Raccoon

States with Native American Names		
Alabama	Kansas	Oklahoma
Alaska	Kentucky	Oregon
Arizona	Massachusetts	North Dakota
Arkansas	Michigan	South Dakota
Connecticut	Minnesota	Tennessee
Idaho	Mississippi	Texas
Illinois	Missouri	Utah
Indiana	Nebraska	Wisconsin
Iowa	Ohio	Wyoming

23.1 Words from American English **629**

Teacher's Classroom Resources

For Lesson 23.1, the following resources can be used for planning, instruction, practice, assessment, reinforcement, or evaluation.

🔧 **Teaching Tools**
Lesson Plans

📂 **Blackline Masters**
Vocabulary and Spelling Practice, pp. 13–26

Unit Assessment

📂 *Tests with Answer Key*
Unit 23 Pretest, pp. 89–90

💿 *Test Generator*
Unit 23 Pretest

You may wish to administer the Unit 23 Pretest at this point.

In Lesson 23.1 students learn that many words in English were borrowed from other languages. They also learn that many words originated in the United States and are used all over the world.

FOCUS

Lesson Overview

Objective: To gain insight into the sources of many English words
Skills: learning how words become a part of a language; identifying words that come from other languages
Critical Thinking: analyzing; synthesizing; relating
Speaking and Listening: discussing; questioning; note taking

🔔 **Bellringer**
When students enter the classroom, have this assignment on the board: *Where do you think these words came from: moccasin, fast food, croissant, home run?*

Motivating Activity

Discuss students' answers to the Bellringer. Make sure that students understand that *croissant* (French) and *moccasin* (Native American) have been borrowed from other languages and that *home run* and *fast food* originated in the United States. Discuss how understanding where words come from can help people better understand the meanings of words and increase their vocabularies.

629

TEACH

Guided Practice

L1 Discussing Loan Words

Encourage students to name some common words having to do with food—such as *pizza* or *taco*—that came from other languages. Then have them think of at least one word they know that comes from a Native American language, such as *tomahawk* or *papoose*. Talk about why students think some words get incorporated into English while others do not. What might be some influential factors?

L3 Considering How Trade and Immigration Affect Vocabulary

Ask students what they have observed about the role of immigration and trade in the introduction of foreign words into English. For example, how many foreign words do they know as a result of foreign imports? Discuss how advances in technology, transportation, and communication accelerate this process. Encourage students to name ethnic foods, music, and imported goods that are in the vocabulary of most English speakers. Do students know of any words exported to other languages from the United States?

Other Early Loan Words

Europeans from France and Spain were in America even before the English. English speakers had already borrowed many words from the French in Europe. As American English developed, its speakers borrowed more French words in North America. Other new English words came from the Spanish and from Spanish-speaking Mexicans in the Southwest. Some examples of these words of French and Spanish origin are included in the chart below.

Some American-English Loan Words	
Sources	**Words**
French	toboggan, pumpkin, bayou, prairie, dime, chowder
Spanish	mustang, ranch, rodeo, stampede, cafeteria, canyon
Dutch	sleigh, cole slaw, Santa Claus, cookie, boss, waffle
African	gumbo, voodoo, juke, jazz, tote
German	hamburger, noodle, pretzel, kindergarten, semester
Yiddish	kosher, bagel, klutz, kibitzer, schmaltz
Italian	macaroni, spaghetti, pizza, ravioli

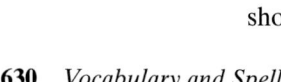
Rodeo

Americans are often called Yankees or Yanks. The word came from Dutch colonists in America in the 1600s. The Dutch called New Englanders Yankees. (The name was considered an insult at the time.) The Dutch colony of New Netherland and its port city, New Amsterdam, were taken over by the British. The British renamed the colony and the city New York. The Dutch lost their American colony, but they left a number of their words in American English.

Most of the Africans in colonial America were brought here as slaves. Their contribution to the English language included such words as *gumbo*, *voodoo*, and *juke* (as in *juke box*). The origin of the word *jazz* is uncertain, but it, too, may have come from an African language. These and some other words that became part of American English are shown in the chart above.

630 *Vocabulary and Spelling*

Enabling Strategies

LEP Understanding Where Words Come From

Students who are not proficient in English may need support doing Exercise 1. Place them in groups with students who are more comfortable speaking English. If students are unfamiliar with English words that come from other languages, suggest that they think of words in their original languages that are now used in English or, conversely, English words that are commonly used in their original languages.

Words from Immigrants

Over the centuries millions of immigrants—Italians, Poles, Czechs, Greeks, Chinese, Filipinos, Haitians, Cubans, and many more—came to America. They passed on some of their customs and some of their words to Americans. These words became part of American English. Often the use of the words spread from the United States throughout the English-speaking world. Some examples are included in the chart on the previous page.

Juke box

Words Made in America

Americans have also contributed new words that did not originate in another language. *Okay* is an example of a word that was "made in the U.S.A." Inventions and customs that started in America often led to new words. Some examples are *refrigerator*, *telephone*, *jeep*, *inner city*, *flow chart*, *zipper*, *laser*, and *airline*. Like *okay*, these words are now used throughout the world. Can you think of any other words that were probably made in America?

Exercise 1

Work with a small group. Develop a list of more English words that originated in America. The words can have come from Native American languages or from the languages of immigrants to America. They might be words invented by Americans.

Begin by looking at the place names in your area. Where did the names of mountains, rivers, counties, or cities come from? Look in your library for books or articles on the origins of place names. Think about the names of foods you eat that originated in other countries. If family members or friends are recent immigrants, ask them if they know of any American English words that came from their language. Use your dictionary to check the origins of words on your list.

23.1   Words from American English   **631**

PRACTICE AND ASSESS

Evaluation Guidelines: Exercise 1
Be sure students list appropriate English words from America, appropriate ethnic food names, and appropriate place names from the surrounding area.

Independent Practice

Skills Practice
📁 *Vocabulary and Spelling Practice,* pp. 13–26

CLOSE

Discuss how students can tell that a word comes from another language. What clues do they usually look for? Invite the class to keep a list of words they find throughout the year that come from other languages. They might note each word's origin, its pronunciation, and where they first found it.

Enrichment and Extension

Discussing Place Origins
In sections of the United States that were first colonized by Spain, such as California and New Mexico, many streets and cities have Spanish names—Los Angeles and Santa Fe, for example. In sections that were once part of the Louisiana Purchase, many places have French names.

The city of New Orleans, for instance, was named for Orleans, France. Have students brainstorm names of regions, streets, geographical features, towns, and cities that reflect the culture of the people who settled there.

Lesson Overview

Objective: To understand that many words are formed as a result of advancements in technology
Skills: identifying word origins
Critical Thinking: analyzing; synthesizing; recalling; classifying; defining
Speaking and Listening: discussing

TEACH

Discussion

Have students read Wordworks, page 632, and discuss the following question: Why might the word *computer* be recognized by non-English speakers?

L3 Listing Inventions

Encourage students to list inventions they think are used throughout the world. Emphasize the most recent technologies. Then suggest that they list all the related words that come to mind. For example, computer technologies gave birth to terms such as *FAX, E-mail, modem, hacker,* and *computer virus.*

PRACTICE AND ASSESS

Answers: Challenge

The most recent meaning of the word *silo* is "a sunken shelter for a missile, with facilities for launching it." One type of silo used for fodder storage was a pit dug in the ground, somewhat like the modern missile silo.

A *tweeter* is the speaker that produces the high-frequency sounds in a high-fidelity speaker system. The word *tweet* is associated with high-pitched sounds, such as those made by small birds.

Wordworks

Techno-Talk

What do the words *nylon, silo,* and *gearshift* have in common? All these words—and countless others—entered the English language as a result of developing technology. New machines, products, and processes required a new vocabulary.

Technical words enter the language by different routes. Some words are coined. A coined word is simply created—none of its parts have any meaning by themselves. For instance, in 1938 scientists developed synthetic fiber, and the word *nylon* was coined as a name for it.

Another route into English is through borrowing. The word *silo* was borrowed into English in 1881 as a name for an airtight container for fodder. The word is Spanish in origin and carries the same meaning in that language.

Another way languages gain new technical words is by compounding. The word parts *gear* and *shift* have existed in English for a long time. It was only because of developing technology that they were combined to name a part of an automobile transmission. Other examples of combining include *transmission* (from Latin word parts) and *telephone* (from Greek word parts). Some words for new inventions originated as names of people; *Ferris wheel* is an example.

CHALLENGE

What new technology uses the word silo? *Think of another technology that named a product a* tweeter. *How do the original meanings of these words fit the new ways in which they are used?*

Tele—
far off
or distant
television
telephone
telescope
telecast
telephoto

Name That Invention

Create several names for the imaginary inventions listed below. Use any of the sources for word formation.

1. a car for air, water, and all surfaces
2. a thermal container that will biodegrade within twelve hours
3. earphones that don't "leak" noise and that allow for loud music without damage to hearing

632 *Vocabulary and Spelling*

Answers: Name That Invention

Students should demonstrate an understanding of borrowing words, compounding word parts, coining words, or using proper names to identify a new invention. Possible answers include the following:

1. omnimobile
2. ecojar
3. safesound

CLOSE

Ask students if they have ever coined a word or a phrase. Invite students who have to tell the story of how and why they did it. Ask for similar stories about words students or their friends have borrowed or compounded for their own uses.

23.2 Context Clues

Do you check your dictionary every time you read or hear a new word? Probably not—most people don't. The best way to build your vocabulary is to learn new words as you come across them. However, you don't have to have a dictionary in your pocket at all times. You often can learn the meaning of a new word by looking for clues in the context. The words and sentences around the word are its context.

Using Specific Context Clues

Context clues help you unlock the meaning of an unfamiliar word. Sometimes the context actually tells you what the word means. The following chart shows three types of specific context clues. It also gives examples of words that help you identify the type of context clue.

Using Specific Context Clues		
Type of Context Clue	**Clue Words**	**Example**
Comparison The thing or idea named by the unfamiliar word is compared with something more familiar.	also same likewise similarly identical	A *rampant* growth of weeds and vines surrounded the old house. The barn was likewise covered with uncontrolled and wild growth.
Contrast The thing or idea named by the unfamiliar word is contrasted with something more familiar.	but on the other hand on the contrary unlike however	Thank goodness Martin didn't *bungle* the arrangements for the party; on the contrary, he handled everything very smoothly and efficiently.
Cause and effect The unfamiliar word is explained as a part of a cause-and-effect relationship.	because since therefore as a result	Because this rubber raft is so *buoyant*, it will float easily, and we won't have to worry about its sinking.

Setting the Purpose

Lesson 23.2 teaches students to figure out the meaning of new words by using context clues. They learn to use three specific kinds of context clues: comparison, contrast, and cause and effect.

FOCUS

Lesson Overview

Objective: To use context clues to figure out the meaning of new words
Skills: determining the meaning of words using context clues; identifying specific clue words
Critical Thinking: analyzing; extrapolating; defining and clarifying; relating to similar words; inferring
Speaking and Listening: discussing; questioning; evaluating

Bellringer

When students enter the classroom, have this assignment on the board: *Write the meaning of the underlined word in this sentence: Our porch is falling apart because it was jerrybuilt. How did you figure out what the word meant?*

TEACH

Guided Practice

L1 Using Context Clues
Provide additional practice with each type of context clue, giving several examples, such as this use of contrast: *The speaker rarely* digressed; *he stayed on the subject throughout his speech.* Then invite students to generate their own examples, using words related to class work, hobbies, or other interests.

Teacher's Classroom Resources

For Lesson 23.2, the following resources can be used for planning, instruction, practice, or reinforcement.

Teaching Tools
Lesson Plans, p. 120

Blackline Masters
Vocabulary and Spelling Practice, pp. 13–26

Answers: Exercise 2
Sentences should contain context clues of the types discussed in the lesson and reflect the following definitions:

1. depreciate—to make less valuable
2. collaborate—to work together on a specific project
3. fathom (noun)—a unit of measure used in nautical measurements
4. adobe—sun-dried brick made of clay and straw
5. crucial—having great importance
6. olfactory—relating to the sense of smell
7. refulgence—brightness, radiance
8. fathom (verb)—to understand fully
9. omnipotent—all powerful
10. brinkmanship—the practice of giving the impression that one is willing to take a crisis to the brink of war

Independent Practice

Skills Practice

📁 *Vocabulary and Spelling Practice,* pp. 13–26

CLOSE

Encourage students to discuss strategies they use when they are reading to figure out unfamiliar words. Ask them to apply those strategies to this sentence: *Women had been disenfranchised for most of history, but in 1920 they finally won the right to vote.* (denied voting rights)

Using the General Context

How do you figure out an unfamiliar word if there are no specific context clues? With a little extra detective work you often can find general clues in the context. Look at the two sentences below. What context clues help you understand the meaning of the word *liaison*?

Note that the word communication *helps you figure out that being a liaison means acting as a line of communication between two groups.*

Joel was chosen student <u>liaison</u> to the faculty. Everyone hoped his appointment would improve communication between the students and the teachers.

Joel is a liaison from one group (the students) to another (the faculty).

Exercise 2

Divide the words below between you and a partner. Use a dictionary if necessary to find the meanings of your words. Then write a sentence using each one. Your sentences should contain context clues to help a reader figure out the meanings of the words. Try to use different types of context clues in the sentences.

Next, exchange papers with your partner and read his or her sentences. Try to use your partner's context clues to understand the words from the list. Discuss whether and how your context clues helped you and your partner understand the meanings of each other's words.

1. depreciate	6. olfactory
2. collaborate	7. refulgence
3. fathom (noun)	8. fathom (verb)
4. abode	9. omnipotent
5. crucial	10. brinkmanship

Enabling Strategies

LEP **Understanding Words and Creating Context Clues**

Provide help as needed with dictionary definitions for the words in Exercise 2. For students with limited knowledge of English, provide sample sentences, such as *Paul, will you collaborate on this assignment with Raphael?* Pair LEP students with students who can help them understand the words and create context clues. Then have that set of partners complete the activity with another set of partners.

Wordworks

As Stale as Day-old Bread

If you listen to a cassette tape over and over, most likely you'll get tired of listening to it. Hearing a cliché is something like listening to that cassette tape.

Clichés are expressions your reader has heard many times before. All clichés, though, were once fresh and original. In fact, they were so fresh and original that people used them over and over. Some clichés have been in use for centuries. For example, the phrase *sweeter than honey* originated around 700 B.C. That's when the ancient Greek poet Homer said, "From his tongue flowed speech sweeter than honey."

Another person whose original phrases have turned into clichés was the English poet and playwright William Shakespeare (1564–1616). If you've ever been stubborn about something, you might have said, "I'm not going to budge an inch." That idea comes from Shakespeare's play *The Taming of the Shrew*. Sometimes clichés are slight alterations of the writer's original words. *Cool as a cucumber*, for example, can be traced to the playwrights Francis Beaumont and John Fletcher. Their phrase in the seventeenth-century play *Cupid's Revenge* was "cold as cucumbers."

One way or another, we all get edited.

CHALLENGE

Rewrite the following without the clichés:

Beyond a shadow of a doubt, too many clichés will put you in hot water. Sad but true, a cliché sticks out like a sore thumb. Avoid clichés like the plague.

Do These Clichés Ring a Bell?

Look up the following clichés in *Bartlett's Familiar Quotations* or another reference book, and record the sources.

1. as old as the hills
2. a word to the wise
3. busy as a bee
4. few and far between
5. all in all

"I'm not going to budge an inch."

23.2 Context Clues **635**

CLOSE

Make sure students understand that a cliché was once a new saying that called an image to mind so effectively that people loved it and began to use it over and over again. Have them think of original expressions from a movie, a television show, or a song. Discuss with students why clichés lose their effectiveness—and even their meanings—with overuse.

635

Lesson 23.3 teaches students how to form new words using prefixes, roots, and suffixes. Students learn to analyze the meanings of word parts and to change the spellings when necessary.

FOCUS

Lesson Overview

Objective: To understand how prefixes and suffixes can be used to form new words

Skills: identifying prefixes, roots, and suffixes; combining word parts

Critical Thinking: comparing; contrasting; synthesizing; recalling

Speaking and Listening: discussing

Bellringer

When students enter the classroom, have this assignment on the board: *How many prefixes and suffixes do you know? Make as long a list as you can.*

Motivating Activity

Ask volunteers to name some of the prefixes and suffixes they wrote down for the Bellringer activity, identifying each suggestion as a prefix or suffix. List the suggestions on the board in two columns, with enough space between them to insert root words. As a class, brainstorm root words that could be inserted between the prefixes and suffixes listed to make new, sensible words. Ask, What do the new words mean?

23.3 Prefixes and Suffixes

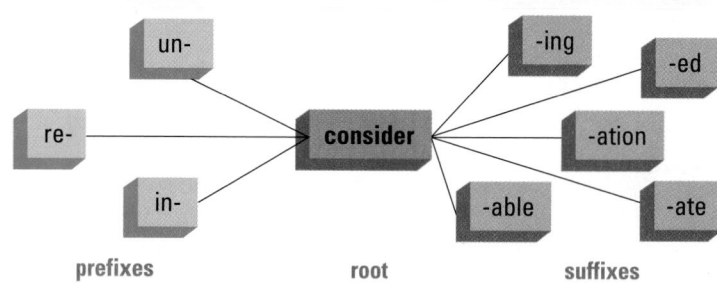

prefixes   root   suffixes

The illustration above shows how words parts can be put together to form many different words. These word parts are called roots, prefixes, and suffixes.

Roots

The root of a word carries the main meaning. Some roots (like the word *consider* above) can stand alone. Others (like *lect*, shown in the chart below) make little or no sense without a prefix or suffix. Knowing the meanings of roots can help you figure out the meanings of unfamiliar words.

Word Roots		
Roots	**Words**	**Meanings**
bio means "life"	biography biosphere	the story of a person's life part of the atmosphere where living things exist
dent means "tooth"	dentist trident	person who treats diseases of the teeth spear with three prongs, or teeth
flex or *flec* means "to bend"	flexible reflect	easily bent to bend back (light)
lect means "speech"	lecture dialect	a speech form of a language spoken in a certain region
tele means "distant"	television telescope	device for receiving pictures from a distance device for viewing distant things

---

Teacher's Classroom Resources

For Lesson 23.3, the following resources can be used for planning, instruction, practice, or reinforcement.

Teaching Tools
Lesson Plans, p. 120

Blackline Masters
Vocabulary and Spelling Practice, pp. 13–26

Prefixes

Adding a prefix can change, or even reverse, the meaning of a root word (for example, *belief—disbelief*). In English, a number of prefixes have the same, or nearly the same, meaning. For example, *dis-*, *un-*, and *in-* all can mean "not" or "the opposite of." On the other hand, some prefixes have more than one meaning. The prefix *in-* can also mean "into," as in the word *incise* ("to cut into").

The chart below shows some common prefixes and their meanings. Notice in the example words how the prefixes change the root words' meanings. Learning these prefixes can help you figure out unfamiliar words.

Prefixes			
Categories	**Prefixes**	**Words**	**Meanings**
Prefixes that reverse meaning	*un-* means "not" or "the opposite of"	unnatural unhappy	not natural not happy
	in- means "not" or "the opposite of"	inconsiderate intolerant	not considerate not tolerant
	il- means "not" or "the opposite of"	illegal illogical	not legal not logical
	im- means "not" or "the opposite of"	immoderate imbalance	not moderate lacking balance
	ir- means "not" or "the opposite of"	irregular irreplaceable	not regular not able to be replaced
Prefixes that show relations	*pre-* means "before"	prepay prearrange	to pay in advance to arrange beforehand
	post- means "after"	postdate postpone	to assign a later date to delay until a later time
	sub- means "below" or "beneath"	submarine subway	an underwater boat an underground way or passage
	co- means "with" or "partner"	copilot cooperate	relief or second pilot to work with others

23.3   Prefixes and Suffixes   **637**

TEACH

Guided Practice

L2 Using Word Parts to Understand Meanings of Words

Explain that the meanings of word parts provide clues to the meanings of new words. On the chalkboard, write the word *postdate* and ask a volunteer to identify the root word and the prefix (*date, post-*). Tell students they may not find this word in a dictionary, but they can figure out when "a postdated check" would be dated. Call on volunteers to attempt definitions and explain how they used their understanding of word parts to arrive at them. Write the word *remoisturize* on the chalkboard. This word is not in the dictionary, but volunteers will be able to explain that it means to make something moist again by analyzing the word parts.

L1 Understanding Prefix and Suffix Meanings

To help students remember the meanings of prefixes and suffixes discussed by the class and listed in the book, you may wish to provide more examples of how the prefixes and suffixes are used. Students could search books and periodicals for words using these affixes. Dictionaries are good sources of words with specific prefixes, and some rhyming dictionaries list words with common suffixes.

Enabling Strategies

LEP Developing the Word-Part Concept

Some students may speak a first language in which prefixes and suffixes do not exist. In Chinese, for example, all words are made of roots of one syllable. Some Semitic languages, such as Arabic, do not use affixes. Such students may not easily conceptualize and use affixes. Provide additional examples and additional practice in combining word parts to create new words. Search various types of literature for examples, and discuss how an affix contributes meaning in each example.

TEACH

Guided Practice

L2 Avoiding Jargon

As students create new words by adding prefixes and suffixes, they may need to develop a sense of whether a word they've created is conventional or not. Discuss jargon (words such as *uncool* or *weatherwise)* that students have heard, and help them understand how to determine whether a word is acceptable to use in writing. (You might decide that it is better to avoid words that are not found in a dictionary.)

⬄ Cross-reference: Spelling

For more information on spelling rules that apply when adding prefixes or suffixes to words, refer students to Lesson 23.6, pp. 649–651.

Suffixes

Like prefixes, suffixes change the meanings of roots. Like prefixes, they can have more than one meaning. They can have the same meaning as one or more other suffixes. Unlike prefixes, however, suffixes can also change the part of speech of a root word. For example, adding the suffix *-ness* to *quick* (an adjective) makes it into *quickness* (a noun). Adding *-ly* to *quick* makes *quickly* (an adverb).

Learning suffixes and how they change a root word can help build your vocabulary. The following chart shows a sample of common suffixes. As you look at it, try to think of other words to which each suffix might be added.

Suffixes			
Categories	**Suffixes**	**Words**	**Meanings**
Suffixes that mean "one who does [something]"	*-er, -or*	worker sailor	one who works one who sails
	-ee, -eer	employee profiteer	one who is employed one who profits
	-ist	pianist chemist	one who plays the piano one who works at chemistry
	-ian	physician	one who practices medicine (once called "physic")
Suffixes that mean "full of"	*-ful*	joyful wonderful	full of joy full of wonder
	-ous	furious courageous	full of fury (anger) full of courage
Suffixes that mean "in the manner of" or "having to do with"	*-ly*	happily secretly	in the manner of being happy in the manner of a secret
	-y	windy icy	having to do with wind having to do with ice
	-al	musical formal	having to do with music having to do with form

638 *Vocabulary and Spelling*

Cultural Diversity

Learning Indo-European Linguistic History

English is one of many European and Asian languages that are descended from an ancient parent language now called Indo-European. Prefixes and suffixes are used in all Indo-European languages. Semitic languages, such as Arabic, Amharic, and Hebrew, however, use only consonants in writing root words. Instead of using a prefix or suffix, the vowels are changed between the consonants to change meaning. Examples of this practice in English include the change of *drink* to *drank* and *woman* to *women*.

When suffixes are added to words, the spelling of the word may change. For example, when -*ous* is added to *fury*, the *y* in *fury* is changed to *i* to make the word *furious*. See pages 649–651 to learn more about the spelling of words that have suffixes added to them.

Exercise 3

Write a word containing each root listed below. Try to use a word that is not used in the word-roots chart. Then write a definition of each word. Check your dictionary if necessary.

1. bio
2. dent
3. flec or flex
4. tele

Exercise 4

Write a word to fit each of the definitions below. Each word should have a prefix or a suffix or both. Underline the suffixes and prefixes in the words. Use the charts in this lesson and a dictionary for help.

1. full of beauty
2. to behave badly
3. to fail to function correctly
4. below the earth
5. one who is a specialist in mathematics
6. a note written at the end of a letter, after the main part of the letter is complete (often abbreviated)
7. not able to be measured
8. in the manner of being not perfect
9. to live or exist together at the same time and in the same place
10. in the manner of being not happy

23.3 Prefixes and Suffixes **639**

PRACTICE AND ASSESS

Answers: Exercise 3
Examples follow. Accept other valid words that use the roots properly, and make sure they are defined properly.
1. bio: biology
2. dent: denture
3. flec or flex: reflex, reflection
4. tele: telegram

Answers: Exercise 4
Examples are given. Accept other valid words.
1. beauti<u>ful</u>
2. <u>mis</u>behave
3. <u>mal</u>function
4. <u>sub</u>terranean
5. mathematic<u>ian</u>
6. <u>post</u>script
7. <u>im</u>measur<u>able</u>
8. <u>im</u>perfect<u>ly</u>
9. <u>co</u>exist
10. <u>un</u>happi<u>ly</u>

Independent Practice

Skills Practice
📁 *Vocabulary and Spelling Practice,* pp. 13–26

CLOSE

List several words that include prefixes and/or suffixes and that may be unfamiliar to students, such as *indefensible, subsist, nonconformist,* and *cellist.* Ask students to work together to figure out the meanings of the words, using what they know about the word parts included.

Cooperative Learning

Making Words from Prefixes

Divide students into cooperative groups for a Simultaneous Roundtable learning activity. Assign each group a different prefix. Each student has two minutes to write as many words as possible from the prefix. Repeat the process with suffixes.

Then students compare their lists and choose a recorder to prepare a master list of all the words generated by the group. Have groups share their word parts and the words they generated.

Lesson Overview

Objective: To recognize the impermanence of words and word meanings
Skills: recognizing word roots; examining how cultural changes affect language; considering trends
Critical Thinking: analyzing patterns; comparing
Speaking and Listening: discussing

TEACH

Discussion

Have students read Wordworks, page 640, and discuss the following questions: *What words have you heard that are seldom used today? What words do we use now to mean the same thing?*

L3 **Collecting Obsolete Words**
Challenge students interested in words no longer in use to interview older people they know and research old books that might contain words no longer in use. They might make a booklet or a "Word Graveyard" bulletin board display with the words they find.

PRACTICE AND ASSESS

Answers: Challenge
joyance: *enjoyment*
impressure: *impression*
argument: *symptom, evidence*

Answers : Gone but Not Forgotten
1. gruesome
2. grueling
3. forlorn
4. yolk

CLOSE

Start a class list of trendy words that students have seen go out of fashion. End the list with words that are popular now.

Wordworks

Weird Old Words

If someone called you a popinjay, would you be pleased? Do you like to show off a little when you know you look good? A popinjay is a vain, strutting person. The word is old-fashioned and not used much today, but the type of personality it describes isn't old-fashioned at all.

Words come and go in any language. If there's no evidence that a word has been used since about 1750, some dictionaries label it obsolete. An example of an obsolete word is an older definition of *popinjay*: a "parrot." No one today uses *popinjay* instead of *parrot*. So this meaning for the word is obsolete.

Many words have disappeared from English. Some vanish completely: *egal* once meant "equal," and a *prest* was money one person was forced to lend another. Neither word is used now. Other obsolete words leave traces. For example, a horse that could be hired out for riding was called a hackney or hack. This meaning of *hack* is now obsolete, but modern English does have a related word. Taxis are often called hacks. It's easy to trace this connection, since people hire taxis today, not riding horses, when they want to get around town.

The next time you pick up your dictionary, keep in mind that it's a work in progress.

CHALLENGE

Words vanish, and one reason may be that they aren't really needed to do the job. List a synonym for each of these obsolete words: joyance, impressure, argument *(meaning an outward sign).*

Gone but Not Forgotten

Think of a modern word related to each of the old words below. The definitions in parentheses should give you a clue or two. A college dictionary will also help.

1. grue (to shiver)
2. gruel (to exhaust)
3. lorn (forsaken, abandoned)
4. yelk (yellow)

Enabling Strategies

LEP **Narrowing Choices**
If students' first language is not English, the correct words to complete the exercise may not be in their vocabulary. For items 1 and 2, suggest that they look up words beginning with *grue-* and *gruel,* and then choose from subsequent entries. For items 3 and 4, they may pick from the following multiple choice options: 3. rejected, forsaken, forlorn. 4. lemon, yolk, canary. Direct them to use dictionaries to verify their choices. You may wish to have them work with students whose first language is English.

23.4 Synonyms and Antonyms

You want your writing to be as clear as you can make it. How can you be sure you have written just the right word to express exactly what you mean? Becoming familiar with synonyms and antonyms—and knowing how to locate them—can help you in your writing. At the same time, you can increase your vocabulary.

Synonyms

Partly because of the borrowings from other languages, English speakers can choose from many words to express the same idea. These words that have the same, or nearly the same, meanings are called synonyms.

The important thing to remember is that synonyms rarely mean *exactly* the same thing. When searching for just the right word, the best place to find synonyms is in a thesaurus. (See pages 627–628 for information on how to use a thesaurus.) To use the right word, not *almost* the right word, check your dictionary for the definitions of synonyms, and notice the usage examples given.

For example, suppose you're writing about someone who spoke before a group. You look up synonyms for the word *speech* and find *address* and *oration. Speech* is a more general choice than *address* and *oration.* A speech may or may not be formal. An address is a prepared formal speech. An oration is even more formal and is always given at a special occasion. For example, you may have read Abraham Lincoln's Gettysburg Address. Before Lincoln gave that famous address, another speaker gave a two-hour oration.

Knowing synonyms also helps make your writing more interesting. Writing that uses tired, colorless clichés—no matter how precise—is almost always boring. Use your knowledge of synonyms to substitute lively verbs and adjectives for lifeless, dried-out words.

fast
rapid
quick
fleet
speedy
swift

23.4   Synonyms and Antonyms   **641**

Teacher's Classroom Resources

For Lesson 23.4, the following resources can be used for planning, instruction, practice, or reinforcement.

Teaching Tools
Lesson Plans, p. 121

Blackline Masters
Vocabulary and Spelling Practice, pp. 13–26

Setting the Purpose

Lesson 23.4 discusses the value of using synonyms and antonyms in one's writing. It also explains how to choose synonyms and antonyms using a thesaurus or dictionary.

FOCUS

Lesson Overview

Objective: To encourage the use of synonyms and antonyms
Skills: distinguishing between different synonyms; using synonyms to enliven writing; creating antonyms using prefixes and suffixes
Critical Thinking: comparing and contrasting synonyms; synthesizing information
Speaking and Listening: discussing

Bellringer
When students enter the classroom, have this assignment on the board: *List three synonyms and three antonyms for* hot.

TEACH

Guided Practice

L2 Choosing Synonyms to Be Precise
Some students waste words by relying on modifiers to qualify weak or general nouns and verbs. Demonstrate how replacing a verb such as *run* with one such as *sprint* can eliminate a modifier such as *fast.* Encourage students to use their thesauruses regularly to find possible synonyms for unspecific nouns, verbs, and modifiers. Suggest that as they read, they note and record examples of well-chosen words or phrases.

PRACTICE AND ASSESS

Independent Practice

Skills Practice
📂 *Vocabulary and Spelling Practice,* pp. 13–26

CLOSE

Group the class into teams. List on the chalkboard several words that have many synonyms, such as *talk, angry, happy, throw,* and *big.* Allow two minutes after writing each word for groups to make a list of as many synonyms as possible. When they have finished, ask groups to share and compare their lists. Discuss the meanings and connotations of any unusual words that were chosen.

642

Antonyms

fast

slow

Antonyms are words with opposite or nearly opposite meanings. The easiest way to form antonyms is by adding a prefix meaning "not." *Un-, il-, dis-, in-,* and *non-* are all prefixes that reverse the meaning of a root. They form antonyms, such as *untrue, illegible, disbelief, insufficient,* and *nonfat.* Sometimes an antonym can be made by changing the suffix. For example, *cheerful* and *cheerless* are antonyms.

As with synonyms, the important thing to keep in mind when choosing an antonym is finding exactly the right word. You need to check your dictionary to make sure you are using the right word for your context. When making an antonym by adding a prefix, make sure you check the dictionary. Be sure you are using the right prefix.

Exercise 5

For each of the following words, write two synonyms. Then write a sentence using one of the synonyms in each group. Use your dictionary and thesaurus as needed.

1. difficulty   **3.** confusion   **5.** slow (adjective)
2. nice   **4.** idea

Exercise 6

Replace the underlined word or words in each of the following sentences with an antonym. Use a thesaurus and a dictionary if you wish.

1. Jeremy's <u>good health</u> seems to be changing.
2. Andrea looks especially <u>pale</u> tonight.
3. That was the <u>most difficult</u> test I've ever taken.
4. Jake <u>closed</u> his eyes and saw the man who had been chasing him for so many days.
5. This fruit is so <u>dried out</u> I can't eat it.

Enabling Strategies

LEP Using a Dictionary or Thesaurus
Students who have not yet developed a large English vocabulary may have trouble thinking of synonyms and antonyms for some words. For example, when asked to think of synonyms and antonyms for *hot,* they might write down the translation they know for *hot* in the language with which they are most familiar. They could list synonyms and antonyms they know in their home language, and then use a bilingual dictionary to help them translate those words into English.

Wordworks

Eating Your Words–a Great Diet?

Can you ever gain weight from eating your words? As a matter of fact, people don't generally sit down to a meal of their words. That's because they know that the expression *eat your words* really means "to take back something you've said." It's an idiom.

Let's look at some idioms and pull them apart. If you have decided to *put up with* something, where do you put it? If you *go back on* a promise, where have you gone? The point is, you can't understand an idiom just by putting together the meanings of the parts.

Idioms are a pretty big part of everybody's vocabulary. Some idioms are so ordinary that we hardly give them a thought—such as *to put over (a trick* or *a joke)*, or *to come down with (a sickness)*. Others add color to language. For example, you might keep a secret *up your sleeve* or *under your hat*.

Idioms arise in various ways. Some are translations from other languages. Many more probably started out having a word-for-word meaning. Later, people changed the meaning to include other situations. For example, at one time *to break the ice* only meant "to cut through river ice in the winter to make a path for ships and boats." In the 1700s the phrase's meaning extended to the process of starting a conversation.

CHALLENGE

English has many idioms that contain the names of animals. How many idioms can you think of that use the names of the following animals?

cat duck crow bird

Idio-Matic

How many idioms do you know? Test your idiom vocabulary. Match the following idioms with their meanings.

1. in the pink	a. gloomy
2. draw the line	b. get angry
3. in the dumps	c. healthy
4. a good egg	d. set a limit
5. hit the ceiling	e. nice person

643

Enabling Strategies

LEP Understanding Idioms

Students with a limited knowledge of English may have difficulty completing the exercise. Use phrase dictionaries from languages your students know to give examples of idioms. Once they understand what an idiom is, invite them to share with the class English translations of other idioms they know. Discuss similarities between the idioms suggested and any related English idioms.

If you're like most people, you may have to think for a minute about whether to write *principal* or *principle* when you're talking about the head of your school. Or you might write *there* in your essay when you mean *their*. When someone points out your mistake, you think, "I knew that!" Some words sound alike but are spelled differently. Others are spelled the same but have different meanings.

Homographs

Words that are spelled alike but have different meanings and sometimes different pronunciations are called homographs. The root *homo* means "same," and *graph* means "write" or "writing." *Homograph*, therefore, means "written the same" (in other words, spelled alike).

Fly and *fly* are homographs. You can swat a fly or fly a plane. Although the two words are spelled alike, they have different meanings. The following chart shows some common homographs used in sample sentences. See if you can tell how the homographs in each group differ in meaning.

Homographs
Ed finished the test with one *minute* left before the bell. To build very small model airplanes, one must enjoy *minute* details.
It's difficult to *row* a canoe upstream. We sat in the third *row* of seats in the balcony. We had a terrific *row* yesterday, but today we're getting along fine.
I hope I pick the winning *number*. This snow is making my feet *number* by the minute.
Abby tried to *console* her little sister when their cat died. The television *console* has speakers built into it.
Don't let that *wound* on your arm get infected. Jim *wound* the rope around the tree branch.

644 *Vocabulary and Spelling*

Setting the Purpose

Lesson 23.5 teaches students about homographs and homophones.

FOCUS

Lesson Overview

Objective: To become familiar with homographs and homophones

Skills: inferring different meanings of homographs and homophones; identifying homographs and homophones

Critical Thinking: contrasting; inferring

Speaking and Listening: listening to the context of words to determine if the words are homographs or homophones

Bellringer

When students enter the classroom, have this assignment on the board: *Write two words that are spelled alike but have different meanings. (These words may or may not sound alike.) Then write two words that sound alike but are spelled differently and have different meanings.*

TEACH

Guided Practice

L3 Researching Literary Homophones

Some students may enjoy researching literature and folk sayings for word plays using homophones. Many writers include homophones for humorous effect. Most puns are homophones or use words that are nearly homophones. Students working in teams can make lists of homophones and share their favorites with the class.

Teacher's Classroom Resources

For Lesson 23.5, the following resources can be used for planning, instruction, practice, or reinforcement.

Teaching Tools
Lesson Plans, p. 121

Blackline Masters
Vocabulary and Spelling Practice, pp. 13–26

Homophones

Homophones are words that *sound* alike but are spelled differently and have different meanings. *Write* and *right* are homophones. The chart below shows some common homophones with their spellings and meanings.

Homophones			
Words	**Meanings**	**Words**	**Meanings**
sight	act of seeing or ability to see	scent	an odor
site	a location	cent	one one-hundredth of a dollar
cite	to quote an authority	sent	past tense of *send*
read	the act of reading	bore	to tire out with dullness
reed	the stalk of a tall grass	boar	a male pig
four	the number following three	main	most important
fore	located at the front	mane	long hair on an animal's neck
mail	letters delivered by post	blue	the color of a clear sky
male	the sex opposite the female	blew	past tense of *blow*
real	actual, not artificial	would	past tense of *will*
reel	a spool used to wind on	wood	hard material that makes up a tree

Exercise 7

Write the homophone from the parentheses that best completes each of the following sentences.

1. Jackie tried to (real, reel) in the fish.
2. The lion is the (main, mane) attraction at the zoo.
3. Chiyo thought that the speech was a (boar, bore).
4. This is the (cite, sight, site) on which the museum will be built.
5. What is that strange (scent, cent, sent) in the air?
6. A wild (bore, boar) can be dangerous if it attacks.
7. Sol (sighted, sited, cited) a thesaurus as his source.
8. Do I detect the (scent, cent, sent) of roses?

23.5 Homographs and Homophones **645**

PRACTICE AND ASSESS

Answers: Exercise 7
1. reel
2. main
3. bore
4. site
5. scent
6. boar
7. cited
8. scent

Independent Practice

Skills Practice

📁 *Vocabulary and Spelling Practice,* pp. 13–26

CLOSE

Write these sentences on the chalkboard:

1. "I'm not your maid!" Mom said as she made the bed.
2. I felt the sweat pour out of every pore of my body.
3. Don't write on red paper if you expect the writing to be read!

Challenge students to pick out the homophones—the words that sound alike but have different meanings and usually different spellings (*maid/made; pour/pore; red/read*).

Enabling Strategies

LEP Practicing with Homographs

Write this sentence on the board: *Raphael tried to lead the hike, but his legs felt like lead after the first three miles.* Ask students: What words are spelled alike? Are they pronounced alike? Do they have the same meaning? Explain that many words in English look alike but have different meanings and often different pronunciations. These words are called homographs. Invite students to think of examples of homographs from their home languages.

645

Lesson Overview

Objective: To learn about words that can function as two parts of speech—nouns as verbs or adjectives and verbs as nouns

Skills: classifying words as nouns, verbs, or adjectives; inferring a word's part of speech

Critical Thinking: classifying; inferring; contrasting

Speaking and Listening: composing sentence pairs

TEACH

Discussion

Have students read Wordworks, page 646, and discuss the following questions:

- How can you tell whether a word like *park* is a noun or a verb? (by looking at its context in a sentence)
- Name some other words that can be used as more than one part of speech.

L2 **Using Nouns as Verbs and Verbs as Nouns**

Call on students to compose sentence pairs, using each of the following words as both a noun and a verb: *lecture, return, run, swim.*

PRACTICE AND ASSESS

Answers: Challenge

The ship sails today.
Ship the sails today.
The words *ship* and *sail* can be used as either nouns or verbs.

Answers: Double Duty

1. baby
2. march
3. project

CLOSE

Ask students to suggest additional words that can function as more than one part of speech. Then invite volunteers to use them in sentence pairs.

Wordworks

When Is a Noun Not a Noun?

The labels on the figure below are nouns that name body parts. English lets you put these same words into action as verbs. Here's how—from head to toe.

You can *head* a committee, *eye* a bargain, or *nose* a car into a parking space. You can *shoulder* a burden, *elbow* your way through a crowd, *hand* over the key, *knuckle* down to work, *thumb* a ride, *back* into a room, *foot* the bill, and *toe* the mark.

For hundreds of years, speakers of English have used these nouns and many others as verbs. Some words shifted in the other direction, from verb to noun. Today you can *walk* on a *walk, park* in a *park,* and *pitch* a wild *pitch.* Some shifts involve pronunciation. Notice which syllable you accent:

Will you *perMIT* me to drive?
Yes, when you get a *PERmit.*

Does your garden *proDUCE* carrots?
No, I buy *PROduce* at the market.

Still another shift involves nouns that became adjectives, as in the following: Sara unlocked the *steel* door. Tom wore a *straw* hat. Marty made *onion* soup.

So, when is a noun not a noun? When it's used as a verb or an adjective. The only way to identify such a word is to use it in a sentence.

CHALLENGE

Suppose you got this written message: Ship sails today. *What does it mean? Put the* before *ship; then put the* before *sails. Why can this sentence have two different meanings?*

shoulder
head
nose
hand
elbow
thumb
toe
foot

646

Double Duty

Use these clues to identify some words that have two functions.

1. *noun:* a very young person
   verb: to pamper
2. *verb:* to walk with regular steps
   noun: music with a steady beat
3. *verb:* throw pictures onto a screen
   noun: special work in science class

23.6 Spelling Rules

You may not know it, but you might have something in common with Noah Webster (of dictionary fame). He wanted to simplify the spelling of American English. He convinced people that the British *gaol* should be spelled *jail* in American English. He also got rid of the *k* in the British *picnick*, *musick*, and *frolick*. Webster especially disliked silent letters. He tried to get people to accept *iland* (*island*), *hed* (*head*), and *bilt* (*built*), among others.

However, most people didn't like Webster's spelling reforms. So today we have a system of spelling filled with rules and exceptions and words spelled nothing like the way they are pronounced. Using a dictionary to check spelling is the best way to avoid mistakes.

Common Spelling Rules

You won't always have a dictionary handy to check your spelling. Memorizing some of the following spelling rules will ensure that you spell most words correctly even when you don't have a dictionary.

Spelling *ie* and *ei* The letter combinations *ie* and *ei* are found in many English words, and they often cause confusion in spelling. The problem is that two words might have the same vowel sound—long *e*— but one word might be spelled *ie* while the other is spelled *ei*. You can master the spelling of these words by memorizing the rhyme below.

Rule	Examples
Put *i* before *e*	achieve, retrieve, grieve
except after *c*	deceive, receipt, ceiling
or when sounded like *a*, as in *neighbor* and *weigh*.	eighty, veil, freight
Exceptions: species, weird, either, neither, seize, leisure, protein, height	

23.6   Spelling Rules   **647**

Teacher's Classroom Resources

For Lesson 23.6, the following resources can be used for planning, instruction, practice, or reinforcement.

🔧 **Teaching Tools**
Lesson Plans

📁 **Blackline Masters**
Vocabulary and Spelling Practice, pp. 13–26

Lesson 23.6 teaches students the spelling rules for *ie* and *ei*, unstressed vowels, adding prefixes and suffixes, and forming plurals.

FOCUS

Lesson Overview
Objective: To learn spelling rules
Skills: memorizing and applying rules to common spelling problems; recognizing exceptions
Critical Thinking: memorizing; analyzing; recalling; visualizing; categorizing; patterning
Speaking and Listening: note taking; discussing; explaining process

🔔 Bellringer
When students enter the classroom, have this assignment on the board: *Correct the incorrect spelling in this paragraph.*

I recieved good care in the hospitel when I broke my leg, which occured while I was sking. Often when I'm sick, I can be disagreable, so it's amazeing that the nurses were nice rather than aweful! The Hendrixs brought me some delicious strawberrys. Although everyone was wonderful, I was still gratful to go home.

Motivating Activity
Go over students' corrections in the Bellringer exercise. (Correct spellings: received, hospital, occurred, skiing, disagreeable, amazing, awful, Hendrixes, strawberries, grateful.) Ask volunteers to name some frequently misspelled words. (They can name the words themselves or categories of words.) Tell them that this lesson will help them learn rules that govern frequently misspelled words.

TEACH

Guided Practice

L1 Spelling Unstressed Vowels

Some students may have trouble spelling unstressed vowel sounds. Review with them the strategy of thinking of a related word in which the vowel is stressed. Guide students through the words on the chart using the strategy. Help them recall other words with unstressed vowels and have them use the spelling strategy on those words. Examples might include: *confidential/confide, observant/observation, human/humanity.*

Spelling Unstressed Vowels   The unstressed vowel sound in many English words can cause spelling problems. Dictionary pronunciation guides represent this unstressed vowel sound by a special symbol called a schwa(ə). Listen to the unstressed vowel sound in the word *about.* This vowel sound can be spelled in more than a dozen ways—with any vowel letter and with several combinations of vowel letters—but it always sounds the same. Here are a few examples. Pronounce each word, and listen for the sound represented by the underlined letter or letters:

> *canvas, angel, pencil, ridicule, carton, medium, enormous, ancient, pigeon, courageous.*

Notice that you hear the schwa sound only in unstressed syllables.

As always, the best way to make sure of your spelling is to check a dictionary. When you can't use a dictionary, you might be able to figure out the spelling of the unstressed vowel sound. Think of a related word in which the vowel is stressed. For example, the word *informative* has an unstressed vowel, which happens to be spelled *a.* However, if you don't know that, you might think of the related word *information,* in which the vowel is stressed and sounds like an *a.* The chart below shows some additional examples of how to apply this process.

Spelling Unstressed Vowels		
Unknown Word	**Related Word**	**Word Spelled Correctly**
popul_rize	popul**a**rity	popularize
plur_l	plur**a**lity	plural
aut_mation	aut**o**	automation
influ_nce	influ**e**ntial	influence
not_ble	not**a**tion	notable
form_l	form**a**lity	formal
practic_l	practic**a**lity	practical
pol_r	pol**a**rity	polar
inhabit_nt	habit**a**tion	inhabitant
hospit_l	hospit**a**lity	hospital

Enabling Strategies

LEP Discerning Syllables

Students who have trouble hearing the number of syllables or discerning which syllable is accented may benefit from tapping their feet to the rhythm of the words, as they might to music or rap. Demonstrate with the word *strategy* by saying the word and clapping loudly on the first syllable and more softly on the second and third syllables. Then ask students to repeat the word and the clapping with you.

Another way you can help students recognize the number of syllables is by counting vowel sounds.

Adding Prefixes   Adding prefixes to words usually doesn't present any spelling problems. Keep the spelling of the word, and attach the prefix. If the prefix ends in the same letter as the first letter of the word, keep both letters. Some common examples include the following:

co- + pilot = copilot   dis- + service = disservice
il- + legal = illegal   co- + operate = cooperate

Suffixes and the Final *y*   Adding suffixes to words that end in *y* can often cause spelling problems. The following rules will help you:

- When a word ends in a consonant + *y*, change the *y* to *i*.
  imply + -es = implies   reply + -ed = replied
  pry + -ed = pried   apply + -es = applies

- If the suffix begins with an *i*, keep the *y*.
  supply + -ing = supplying   fly + -ing = flying

- When a word ends in a vowel + *y*, keep the *y*.
  toy + -ing = toying   stay + -ing = staying
  delay + -ed = delayed   prey + -ed = preyed

Doubling the Final Consonant   When adding suffixes to words that end in a consonant, you sometimes double the final consonant. In other cases you simply add the suffix without doubling the consonant.

Double the final consonant when a word ends in a single consonant following one vowel and

- the word is one syllable
  strip + -ed = stripped   sad + -er = sadder
  shop + -ing = shopping   ship + -ed = shipped
  war + -ing = warring   tap + -ed = tapped

- the word has an accent on the last syllable, and the accent remains there after the suffix is added
  occur + -ence = occurrence   repel + -ing = repelling
  forget + -able = forgettable   commit + -ed = committed
  upset + -ing = upsetting   refer + -ed + referred

23.6   Spelling Rules   **649**

TEACH

Guided Practice

L1 Adding Suffixes

Some students may need extra practice with suffixes. Form small groups and have students look through newspapers or magazines and circle words with suffixes that match the examples studied on this page. Ask students to create a class chart by writing the rules from this page at the top of columns. Then have them add the words they have found under the appropriate columns. Students may want to continue adding other words to the chart during the year or create individual spelling notebooks that follow the same model.

Cross-reference: Spelling

For more information on words ending in suffixes, refer students to Lesson 23.3, pp. 636–639.

Technology Tip

Using Handheld Electronic "Spelling Dictionaries"

In addition to software for checking spelling on computers, handheld spelling dictionaries with keyboards and display screens are available. They operate much like computer programs for checking spelling. Many of them, however, do not have enough memory to store the number of words contained in a good dictionary or to operate searches speedily. Anyone interested in these "spell checkers" should compare the number of entries and searching speed of competing brands.

TEACH

Guided Practice

L2 Using Suffix Rules

Dictate the following words, pausing after each one: *haunting, equipment, robbing, development, cranky, wed-ded, preference, raining.* Ask volunteers to spell them correctly. Then have students tell which spelling rule on pages 649–650 each word follows.

Do not double the final consonant when

- the accent is not on the last syllable
  flavor + -ing = flavoring
  envelop + -ment = envelopment
  remember + -ing = remembering

- the accent moves when the suffix is added
  refer + -ence = reference
  fatal + -ity = fatality

- two vowels come before the final consonant
  remain + -ed = remained   floor + -ing = flooring
  lead + -ing = leading   train + -ed = trained

- the suffix begins with a consonant
  master + -ful = masterful   dark + -ness = darkness
  tear + -less = tearless   leader + -ship = leadership
  loyal + -ty = loyalty   flat + -ly = flatly
  great + -ness = greatness

- the word ends in two consonants
  bring + -ing = bringing   stick + -ing = sticking
  inspect + -or = inspector   hunt + -ed = hunted
  attach + -ment = attachment
  great + -ness = greatness

  SPECIAL CASE: When a word ends in *ll,* and the suffix *-ly* is added, drop one *l.*
  dull + -ly = dully   full + -ly = fully

  Suffixes and the Silent e   Noah Webster did his best to get rid of the silent letter *e* in American-English spelling. He succeeded in changing *axe* to *ax.* However, he lost the battle to change *give* to *giv,* and he failed to change the spellings of other words ending in silent *e.* The public was not willing to give up spellings with which they were familiar.
  The silent *e* can still cause spelling problems, especially when you add a suffix to a word that ends in a silent *e.* Sometimes the silent *e* is dropped when adding a suffix, and sometimes it is kept. The following chart shows the rules for adding suffixes to words that end in silent *e.*

650   *Vocabulary and Spelling*

Beyond the Classroom

Using Newspapers to Find Suffixes

Pair students and ask them to choose an article in the newspaper. Have them underline words that have suffixes. Then ask students to make a chart that includes their underlined words and matching root words. Challenge students to star those words that do not double the final consonant.

Adding Suffixes to Words That End in Silent *e*	
Rule	**Examples**
When adding a suffix that begins with a consonant to a word that ends in silent *e*, keep the *e*.	state + -ment = statement
	complete + -ly = completely
Common exceptions	awe + -ful = awful
	judge + -ment = judgment
When adding *-ly* to a word that ends in *l* plus a silent *e*, always drop the *e*.	able + -ly = ably
	sensible + -ly = sensibly
	remarkable + -ly = remarkably
When adding *y* or a suffix that begins with a vowel to a word that ends in a silent *e*, usually drop the *e*.	state + -ing = stating
	nose + -y = nosy
Common exceptions	lime + -ade = limeade
	mile + -age = mileage
When adding a suffix that begins with *a* or *o* to a word that ends in *ce* or *ge*, keep the *e* so the word will retain the soft *c* or *g* sound.	exchange + -able = exchangeable
	trace + -able = traceable
When adding a suffix that begins with a vowel to a word that ends in *ee* or *oe*, keep the *e*.	disagree + -able = disagreeable
	shoe + -ing = shoeing
	flee + -ing = fleeing

Forming Compound Words   The rule for spelling compound words is very simple. In most cases, just put the two words together. Seeing two consonants together, such as *hh*, *kk*, or *kb*, may seem odd. The English language does not have many words with these combinations. However, the rule is to keep the original spelling of both words, no matter how the words begin or end.

foot + lights = footlights	fish + hook = fishhook
busy + body = busybody	book + keeper = bookkeeper
book + bag = bookbag	light + house = lighthouse

Some compound words, such as *hand-me-down* and *forty-niners*, are hyphenated. Others, like *honey bear* (but not *honeybee*), are spelled as two words. Use a dictionary when in doubt.

23.6   Spelling Rules   **651**

TEACH

Guided Practice
L2 Adding Suffixes to Verbs
Challenge students to write short action stories using at least five verbs that end with suffixes such as *-ing* and *-ed*. Remind them to use the spelling rules they have been studying to add the suffixes correctly.

L1 Adding Suffixes to Root Words
Some learners have trouble transferring spelling rules to writing. For additional practice, have them look through books and periodicals and pick root words like the ones listed in the chart on page 651. Tell them to try to choose root words that represent each group in the chart. Pair students and have them challenge each other to write each word they picked out, adding suffixes correctly and using the new words in sentences.

Enabling Strategies

LEP Using Compounds
Some students whose first languages are not English may be accustomed to different types of compounds. For example, in German many words are combined to make a very long compound word. A comparable English example might be *fortallmendiscountclothingstore*. You may need to explain that compounds are not formed as freely or as often in English. Point out that an English compound word often has a meaning different from that of its separate parts; for example, *freelance*, *joystick*, *piggyback*, *ponytail*, or *shortcut*.

TEACH

Guided Practice

L2 Categorizing Plural Forms

On the board list categories of common things, such as animals, plants, people, and units of measure. Ask students to suggest words for each category and to give the plural form of each word. List their suggestions on the board. Then discuss the ways these plurals are formed, and group the words again according to plural form. For example, correct groupings might include *geese, mice, women, feet; players, roses, yards; wishes, inches, boxes.*

Forming Plurals The way plurals are formed in English is generally simple, and the rules are fairly easy to remember. The most common way to form plurals is to add *-s* or *-es*. The following chart shows the basic rules, their exceptions, and example words.

Rules for Plurals		
If the Noun Ends in	**Then Generally**	**Examples**
ch, *s,* *sh,* *x,* or *z*	add *-es*	witch → witches toss → tosses flash → flashes ax → axes buzz → buzzes
a consonant + *y*	change *y* to *i* and add *-es*	story → stories folly → follies
a vowel + *y*	add *-s*	play → plays jockey → jockeys
a vowel + *o*	add *-s*	studio → studios rodeo → rodeos
a consonant + *o*	generally add *-s* **Common exceptions** but sometimes add *-es*	piano → pianos photo → photos hero → heroes veto → vetoes echo → echoes
f or *ff*	add *-s* **Common exceptions** change *f* to *v* and add *-es*	staff → staffs chief → chiefs thief → thieves leaf → leaves
lf	change *f* to *v* and add *-es*	self → selves half → halves
fe	change *f* to *v* and add *-s*	life → lives knife → knives

652 *Vocabulary and Spelling*

Enabling Strategies

LEP Practicing Plurals

Students who speak a first language that does not use plural forms may have difficulty understanding the concept of plural nouns and cultivating the habit of changing singular nouns to the plural form. Some Asian languages, for example, do not have plural forms of nouns.

Some other languages have plural forms of adjectives that modify plural nouns. Provide additional practice and rules for the formation of plurals for such students. You may wish to team them with peers who can dictate sentences.

A few nouns form plurals in a special way. Most of these special cases should not give you any problems in spelling. If you do not already know the irregular forms, such as *goose—geese*, you can memorize them. The following chart lists the special rules for plurals and gives some examples.

Special Rules for Plurals	
Special Case	**Examples**
To form the plural of proper names, add either -s or -es, following the general rules for plurals.	Smith → Smiths Jones → Joneses Perez → Perezes
To form the plural of one-word compound nouns, follow the general rules for plurals.	homemaker → homemakers blackberry → blackberries latchkey → latchkeys
To form the plural of hyphenated compound nouns or compound nouns of more than one word, generally make the most important word plural.	father-in-law → fathers-in-law lunch box → lunch boxes chief of state → chiefs of state
Some nouns have irregular plural forms and do not follow any rules.	goose → geese mouse → mice tooth → teeth child → children
Some nouns have the same singular and plural forms.	deer → deer sheep → sheep fish → fish

Improving Spelling Skills

Spelling rules will help you spell new words correctly. You can further improve your spelling skills by developing a method for learning these words.

Keep a notebook of unfamiliar words or words that are hard to spell. When you write, take note of any words you have trouble spelling, and add them to your notebook. As you come across new words, add them to your list. When you master the spelling of a word, cross the word off your list. Follow the steps on the next page to learn to spell those difficult words.

23.6   Spelling Rules   **653**

TEACH

Guided Practice

L1 **Writing a Story Using Plurals**

Some students may need additional practice with spelling rules for plurals. Tell them to write a story about a visit to a zoo, describing all the people, animals, plants, and objects they see. Have them exchange their stories with a partner. The partner should list all the plurals the other student used, verify the spellings using the rules presented in this chapter, and note the spelling rule that applies to each plural.

Cross-reference: Grammar

For more information on plural nouns, refer students to Lesson 9.4, pp. 354–355.

Enrichment and Extension

Putting on a Spelling Bee

Divide the class into two teams for a spelling bee. Pronounce words that use the various rules taught in this lesson. When a student spells a word correctly, he or she must state the rule that applies. As an alternative, team members may take turns generating words to challenge the opposing team. Make sure that each challenge word fits one of the rules presented in this lesson. If a team member challenges the other team with a word that fails to fit one of the rules studied, that counts as an error for that team.

PRACTICE AND ASSESS

Answers: Exercise 8
1. applied
2. lives
3. fully
4. Walshes
5. remaining
6. transferring
7. reference
8. completely
9. sheep
10. upsetting

Independent Practice

Skills Practice

📂 *Vocabulary and Spelling Practice,* pp. 13–26

CLOSE

Have different volunteers summarize the rules governing spelling in this lesson and give an example for each. Students may want to create a classroom chart for visual reference.

Say It	**Visualize It**	**Write It**	**Check It**
Look at the printed word or the word as it is written in your notebook. Say it out loud. Say it a second time, pronouncing each syllable clearly.	Close your eyes, and imagine seeing the word printed or written. Picture how the word is spelled.	Look at the printed word again, and write it two or three times. Then write it again without looking at the printed word.	Check what you have written against the printed word. Did you spell it correctly? If not, go through the process again until you can spell it correctly.

Exercise 8

Find the misspelled word in each sentence and write its correct spelling.

1. Mr. Harrison, the bookkeeper, has applyed for a government grant to buy new computers.
2. The book describes the lifes of famous artists.
3. Hector is fullly aware that we have to proceed with the polar expedition.
4. Stefanie spends her leisure time with the Walshs.
5. Kevin should be in the barnyard shoeing one of the remainning horses.
6. The zookeeper believes he will succeed in transfering the monkeys from the old cages without any problems.
7. The librarian has suggested two referrence books that should contain photos of wolves.
8. The summer weather has been so changeable that everyone is completly convinced we will have an unusually bad winter.
9. The puffs of clouds in the springtime sky reminded me of sheeps in a meadow.
10. The recent recurrence of fighting between the two warring nations is upseting to everyone who hopes for a peaceful settlement.

654 *Vocabulary and Spelling*

Cooperative Learning

Forming Spelling Groups

Suggest that students form groups and create a spelling exercise similar to the one above. Then have groups exchange and complete them. Let groups score the responses.

Wordworks

Vowel Switch

Spelling in English can be a real mystery. Why should the first vowel sounds in *pleasant* and *please* be spelled the same even though they are pronounced differently? Why not spell the sound in *pleasant* with just an *e*, as in *pen* and *red*?

Here's the scoop: Sometime between 1400 and 1600 the pronunciation of certain vowels underwent a change. The vowel in *please* was pronounced like the e in *pen,* only it was longer. This sound gradually shifted to a long ā sound as in *pane*. Meanwhile, the long vowel ā had begun to take on the long ē sound as in *feed,* while the long vowel ē had begun to take on the long i sound as in *ride*. Similar changes occurred in the other long vowels. These pronunciation changes are called the Great Vowel Shift.

Meanwhile, the short vowels (as in *pleasant*) did not change. Because spelling didn't always keep up with pronunciation changes, the words *please* and *pleasant* were still spelled with the same vowel even though *please* was now pronounced like *plays*. Later some words like *please* changed again. By about 1700 most people pronounced *please* the way you pronounce it today.

So the next time you're puzzled by English spelling, remember that the way a word is spelled sometimes holds a clue to its history.

CHALLENGE

Some spellings have changed to reflect pronunciation changes. One example appears several times on this page. Can you find it?

Shifty Vowels

Which of the following word pairs demonstrate the Great Vowel Shift?

1. crime, criminal
2. mouse, mice
3. breathe, breath
4. serene, serenity
5. die, death

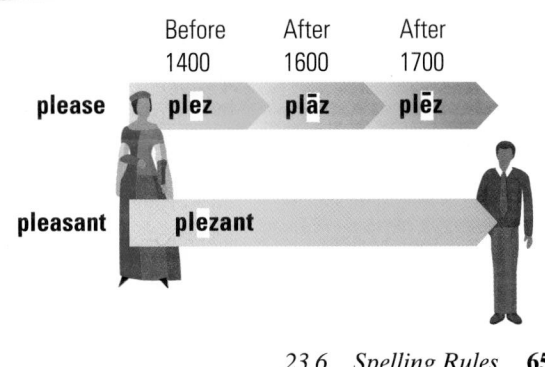

	Before 1400	After 1600	After 1700
please	plez	plāz	plēz
pleasant	plezant		

23.6 Spelling Rules **655**

Enabling Strategies

LEP Distinguishing Hard-to-Hear English Vowels

Students new to English have difficulty spelling, and sometimes hearing, English vowels. For example, the difference between *pen* and *pane* is difficult for Spanish-speaking students to discriminate. Provide auditory practice with additional pairs, such as *met/mate*. Encourage students to keep notebooks that classify irregular vowel spellings within regular families. For example, they could list *bread, head, thread, dead, dread,* and *spread* as one family in which sounds are regular.

Lesson Overview
Objective: To learn that many of the difficulties in spelling words in English are a result of changes in pronunciation of certain vowels
Skills: distinguishing words affected by the Great Vowel Shift
Critical Thinking: analyzing; synthesizing; classifying; comparing
Speaking and Listening: discussing

TEACH

Discussion

Have students read *Wordworks,* page 655, and discuss the following question: How do the irregular spellings of English vowel sounds make learning to read and write difficult?

L2 Pronouncing Words Affected by the Great Vowel Shift

Write the following word groups on the chalkboard: *bread, lead, read, head; give, alive, live, olive.* Ask students how they might pronounce these words if they were seeing them for the first time.

PRACTICE AND ASSESS

Answers: Challenge
The spelling of the word *pronunciation,* used several times on this page, reflects a change in the pronunciation of the vowels in *pronounce*.

Answers: Shifty Vowels
Word pairs 1, 3, and 4 demonstrate the Great Vowel Shift.

CLOSE

Ask a volunteer to explain the Great Vowel Shift. Have others give examples of words with vowels that demonstrate this shift.

655

656

Setting the Purpose

Lesson 23.7 teaches students strategies for remembering how to spell commonly used words. Students practice these strategies and use them on words they find troublesome.

FOCUS

Lesson Overview

Objective: To become a better speller
Skills: applying common spelling strategies; distinguishing between words that are often confused
Critical Thinking: establishing criteria for spelling words; analyzing; recalling
Speaking and Listening: using special clues; discussing

Bellringer

When students enter the classroom, have this assignment on the board: *List five words you have a hard time remembering how to spell correctly and explain why.*

Motivating Activity

Encourage students to share strategies they have used to remember how to spell troublesome words. For example, they may be able to remember how to spell *environment* by remembering that the word *iron* appears in it. Or, they may use rhymes or other memory techniques.

23.7   Becoming a Better Speller

Spelling the *really* difficult words—such as *pusillanimous* (meaning "cowardly")—is usually not too much of a problem. The reason is that when you use such words (which is not often), you will probably look them up in the dictionary.

What about the less difficult but more common words that you use often? Following is a list of such words. See if any of them are words you have had trouble spelling. What words would you add to the list?

Words Often Misspelled

absence	curiosity	incidentally	pneumonia
accidentally	develop	incredibly	privilege
accommodate	definite	jewelry	pronunciation
achievement	descend	laboratory	receipt
adviser	discipline	leisure	recognize
alcohol	disease	library	recommend
all right	dissatisfied	license	restaurant
analyze	eligible	maintenance	rhythm
answer	embarrass	mischievous	ridiculous
attendant	environment	misspell	schedule
ballet	essential	molasses	separate
beautiful	February	muscle	sincerely
beginning	fulfill	necessary	souvenir
beneficial	foreign	neighborhood	succeed
business	forty	niece	technology
cafeteria	funeral	noticeable	theory
canceled	genius	nuisance	tomorrow
canoe	government	occasion	traffic
cemetery	grammar	original	truly
changeable	guarantee	pageant	unanimous
choir	height	parallel	usually
colonel	humorous	permanent	vacuum
commercial	hygiene	physical	variety
convenient	imaginary	physician	various
courageous	immediate	picnic	Wednesday

656   *Vocabulary and Spelling*

Teacher's Classroom Resources

For Lesson 23.7, the following resources can be used for planning, instruction, practice, assessment, reinforcement, or evaluation.

Teaching Tools
Lesson Plans, p. 122

Blackline Masters
Vocabulary and Spelling Practice, pp. 13–26

Unit Assessment

Tests with Answer Key
Unit 23 Mastery Test, pp. 91–92

Test Generator
Unit 23 Mastery Test

You may wish to administer the Unit 23 Mastery Test at this point.

Spelling and Misspelling

Do you have trouble remembering the spellings of common words? How many *c*'s and *m*'s are in *recommend* and *accommodate*? Is it *separate* or *seperate*? Words like these cause many people problems. The following techniques will help you learn to spell troublesome words.

- Use rhymes (such as "*i* before *e* except after *c* . . .") and memory tricks (such as "there's *a rat* in *separate*").
- Pay special attention to words likely to be confused with other words. Below are some examples. You can find more in the list of homophones on page 645.

Words Often Confused	
accept except	Marianne will not *accept* the nomination for class president. All the students *except* Barry were on time.
affect effect	This cold weather can *affect* my sinuses. The space program could have an *effect* on future generations.
formally formerly	The new president was *formally* introduced to the student body. Ananda *formerly* lived in southern California.
its it's	Since *its* walls collapsed, the mine entrance has been closed. *It's* been a long time since I saw Winston so happy.
stationary stationery	The radio transmitting station is mobile, not *stationary*. Her *stationery* is decorated with tiny blue flowers.
thorough through	They completed a *thorough* revision of the student handbook. *Through* the window we could see them coming up the path.
than then	The final draft of my story is much better *than* the first draft. What happened *then*?
their there they're	What was the outcome of *their* first game? The address you are looking for is over *there*. The team members say *they're* happy with the new gym.
weather whether	I hope the *weather* stays nice for the picnic. I'm not sure *whether* it was luck or skill, but I made the team.

23.7   Becoming a Better Speller   **657**

TEACH

Guided Practice

L2 Using Context Clues
Ask students to explain why words such as *its, knew, scent, led,* and *right* cannot be spelled with certainty if they are heard out of context. Encourage them to list other easily confused words that are difficult to spell out of context.

L1 Interpreting Meanings
Some students may not identify the sentences in the chart on page 657 as examples of how the words are used. Discuss the difference between the aid provided by a definition and the aid provided by a sentence that uses the word in context. If students are still unclear about a word's meaning after reading the sentence in the chart, encourage them to find an appropriate definition in a dictionary. Challenge them to suggest a new sentence that would make the word's meaning clear.

Enabling Strategies

LEP Using Pronunciation Keys
Students whose first language is not English may mispronounce many of the words used in this lesson—for example, *foreign* and *colonel*—if they rely on the spellings. Review difficult words using the pronunciation keys in your classroom dictionaries. Give students practice listening to and pronouncing words.

PRACTICE AND ASSESS

**Evaluation Guidelines:
Exercise 9**

Answers will vary. Students will develop their own lists of words. Memory aids should show an understanding of the spelling problem involved and a realistic and easily memorized tactic to help with correct spelling.

Answers: Exercise 10

1. its
2. effect
3. formerly
4. there
5. its
6. stationery
7. you're
8. thorough
9. whether
10. their
11. formally
12. they're

Independent Practice

Skills Practice

📂 *Vocabulary and Spelling Practice,* pp.13–26

CLOSE

Have students discuss the spelling strategies that they are most likely to use in their writing. Ask them to give examples of particular words they find troublesome and tell how they will remember the correct spelling of these words.

658

Exercise 9

Work with one or two other students. Choose three words from the list of Words Often Misspelled on page 656 of this lesson. Develop a memory aid that will help you spell each word. Share your completed memory aids with the class.

Exercise 10

Write the word in the parentheses that correctly completes each sentence.

1. The school decided to change the name of (its, it's) football team.
2. One of the test questions asked for an (effect, affect) of the Civil War.
3. Pete (formerly, formally) played on a soccer team at his old school.
4. If you leave your books (their, there, they're), they may get lost.
5. The cat pushed (its, it's) way through the swinging door.
6. Use your best (stationery, stationary) for the thank-you notes.
7. Have you decided what dress (your, you're) going to wear to the party?
8. The detective was very (thorough, through) in his investigation of the crime.
9. We would like to know (whether, weather) it will rain or be sunny on the day of our field trip.
10. The two dogs need to have (their, there, they're) coats brushed after being out all day.
11. I've never been (formerly, formally) introduced to the new counselor.
12. The three girls said that (their, there, they're) going to go swimming.

Connections Across the Curriculum

History

Some irregularities of English spelling resulted when foreign words entered the language, spelled as they were originally pronounced. People later modified the pronunciation to fit English speech sounds. Words of recent French origin, such as *chivalrous* and *chef*, retain the French pronunciation of *ch*. However, in words taken from French in the distant past, such as *chain*, the sound of *ch* has been changed. The *ch* in words from Greek, as in *chorus* and *character*, is now pronounced with a simple *k* sound instead of the original *kh*. Words beginning in *ps* are also of Greek origin.

UNIT 24 · Study Skills

24.1 Using Book Features

Imagine you're writing a research paper on the Civil War. You've narrowed your topic to the Battle of Gettysburg, focusing on Pickett's Charge, a key event in the three-day battle. You find that the library has many books on the Battle of Gettysburg—but you certainly can't read them all.

How do you decide which books will be the most useful? Looking at certain pages in the front or back of a book will help you narrow your choice.

The pages shown below are valuable tools in discovering which books may hold the material you need. The title page and table of contents appear in the front, before the main text of the book. You'll find the index in the back.

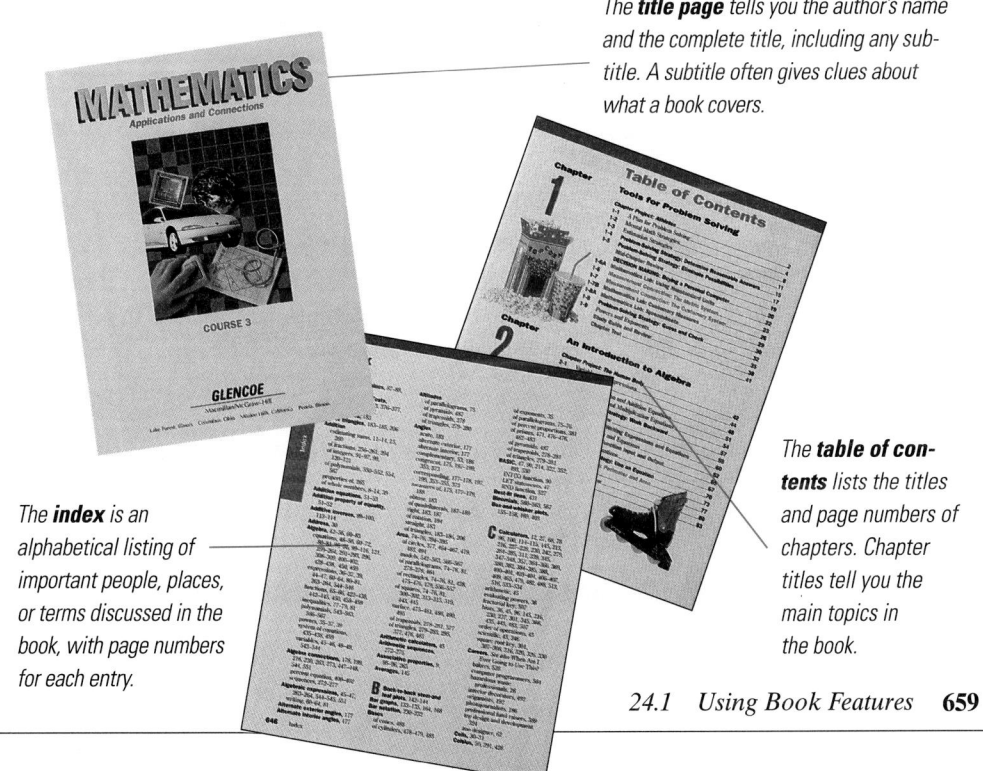

*The **title page** tells you the author's name and the complete title, including any subtitle. A subtitle often gives clues about what a book covers.*

*The **index** is an alphabetical listing of important people, places, or terms discussed in the book, with page numbers for each entry.*

*The **table of contents** lists the titles and page numbers of chapters. Chapter titles tell you the main topics in the book.*

24.1   Using Book Features   **659**

Teacher's Classroom Resources

For Lesson 24.1, the following resources can be used for planning, instruction, practice, assessment, reinforcement, or evaluation.

🔧 **Teaching Tools**
Lesson Plans, p. 123

📁 **Blackline Masters**
Thinking and Study Skills,
pp. 2, 8, 18, 39–40

Unit Assessment

📁 *Tests with Answer Key*
Unit 24 Pretest, pp. 93–94

💿 *Test Generator*
Unit 24 Pretest

You may wish to administer the Unit 24 Pretest at this point.

FOCUS

Lesson Overview
Objective: To develop skills for locating and researching information
Skills: understanding information found on the title page; determining the relevance of a book to a topic
Critical Thinking: defining and clarifying; decision making
Speaking and Listening: questioning; evaluation

🔔 Bellringer
When students enter the classroom, have this assignment on the board: *List where you would look in a book to decide if it has material for a research paper on Labrador retrievers. What would help you decide?*

TEACH

Guided Practice
L2 **Identifying Sections in a Book**
Provide students with a variety of nonfiction books. Tell them to preview each book and identify a topic the book would address. Give them five minutes to scan the book for special features and prepare a one-minute summary. They should include the book's title, author, copyright date, and special features and at least one topic addressed in the book. Have pairs share what they found, discussing what features were the most useful in determining their topic.

PRACTICE AND ASSESS

Answers: Exercise 1
1. glossary
2. pages 628, 641
3. 1996
4. Verbs
5. yes; page 644

Independent Practice

Skills Practice

📁 *Thinking and Study Skills,* pp. 2, 8, 18, 39–40

CLOSE

Have students review the terms *title page, table of contents,* and *index.* Then have them work in pairs using a real book to create a chart indicating where each of these sections would be found. Encourage students to include other book features they have learned about. They may also want to create a classroom chart for reference.

Many books include other informative sections separate from the main text. The copyright page follows the title page. It tells you the year in which the book was published. Also in the front of a book, you may find a foreword, a preface, or an introduction. In the back of some books are glossaries for definitions and pronunciations of unusual words. The chart below shows you how to use some of these parts of a book.

Using a Book Effectively	
Questions	**Where to Look for the Answer**
Who is the author of this book?	The title page contains the author's name and the complete title.
Will this book contain information about my topic?	The table of contents identifies the main topics.
Will this book contain recent information about my topic?	The copyright page tells when a book was published or updated.
Will I find the people, places, and events I'm researching in this book?	The index is an alphabetical listing of people, places, events, and other topics covered in the book.

Exercise 1

Use this textbook to answer all but the first of the following questions:

1. Suppose you were studying how the human heart functions and wanted to find a definition of *atrium*. In what part of a science book would you look?
2. On what page or pages of this book are synonyms discussed?
3. In what year was this book published?
4. What is the title of Unit 10?
5. Does this book discuss homographs and, if so, on what pages?

660 *Study Skills*

Enabling Strategies

LEP **Learning Book Feature Terms**

To reinforce students' understanding of the terms *topic, copyright, publisher, preface, table of contents, index,* and *glossary,* ask them to work in pairs to make up questions about these terms, referring to page numbers in their own textbooks. Have students ask each other, or another pair, for the answers to their questions.

24.2 Skimming, Scanning, and Careful Reading

What if you needed information about the structure of the human heart? What would you do? Most likely, you would read a book about your topic. There are several different ways to read for information. Using the right reading style for a particular purpose can save valuable time.

Skimming

When you want to know if a book covers the information you need, skimming is a good technique. Skimming can be very helpful in your research or when previewing or reviewing. While skimming, you glance over the text to find the main ideas. To skim a text, you look at the chapter titles, words in italic or bold type, and the topic sentence of each paragraph. Without taking too much time, you can grasp the most important ideas in a given chapter. For instance, the sample notes below might be made by skimming a detailed chapter on the makeup of the human heart.

Heart has two sections—right and left sides.
Right side pumps blood from body through lungs.
Left side pumps blood from lungs through body.
Blood enters right side, or *atrium*, through two veins, called *superior vena cava* and *inferior vena cava*.
Blood carrying oxygen flows from lungs to left atrium through *pulmonary veins*.

Scanning

When you are searching for specific information, you can use the technique of scanning. Scanning is a rapid form of skimming. While scanning, you move your eyes quickly over a page, looking for key words. When you locate the information you want, you read carefully for specific details.

24.2 Skimming, Scanning, and Careful Reading **661**

Teacher's Classroom Resources

For Lesson 24.2, the following resources can be used for planning, instruction, practice, or reinforcement.

🔧 **Teaching Tools**
Lesson Plans, p. 123

📁 **Blackline Masters**
Thinking and Study Skills, pp. 2, 8, 18, 39–40

Setting the Purpose

Lesson 24.2 teaches students how to use three styles of reading to find information: skimming, scanning, and careful reading.

FOCUS

Objective: To read in different ways for different purposes
Skills: skimming to find overall content; scanning to find information; careful reading
Critical Thinking: identifying characteristics; predicting; inferring; using prior knowledge
Speaking and Listening: discussing

🔔 Bellringer

When students enter the classroom, have this assignment on the board: *List five different purposes for reading something. Provide examples of each.*

TEACH

Guided Practice

L2 Skimming Headings
Make copies of a page from *Time* or *Newsweek* magazine to show to the class. Choose a page with clear headings and subheadings. Underline the heading and have students identify and read aloud the boldfaced subheading and captions. Discuss what clues these features provide about content.

PRACTICE AND ASSESS

Answers: Exercise 2

1. skimming
2. careful reading
3. scanning

Explanations should reflect an understanding of how skimming and scanning differ.

Independent Practice

Skills Practice

📂 *Thinking and Study Skills,* pp. 2, 8, 18, 39–40

CLOSE

Lead a discussion on the ways in which life today may not seem geared to the careful acquisition of information. The discussion may cite examples of the fast pace of living—fast food, rapid transportation, immediate availability of world news. Ask students how scanning and skimming can be best used in such an atmosphere.

Careful Reading

Careful reading is a third way to read for information. When you use this technique, you read the text slowly. You pay close attention to all details to make sure you clearly understand the information presented. Read carefully when learning material for the first time, such as when studying a new chapter in a science textbook. If you just skim or scan your textbook chapter the first time you read it, you won't learn as much as you need to. You also probably won't understand the technical terms you read. Then, when you have a quiz or a test, you'll find yourself in trouble.

You also practice careful reading when preparing to explain material to someone else. Suppose you were going to present an oral report on the human circulatory system. Any book you find explaining the circulatory system would probably include medical information unfamiliar to you. The only way to fully understand the content is to read slowly and carefully. Read a passage several times until you fully understand it. If you don't understand what you will be speaking or writing about, your audience won't understand it either. Also, keep a dictionary nearby so you can look up any unfamiliar words.

Exercise 2

Decide which reading technique—skimming, scanning, or careful reading—should be used in each of the following situations. Explain each decision.

1. You find a library book on a topic that interests you. You wonder whether the book is worth reading.
2. You've been asked to read the first half of a chapter in your science textbook before tomorrow's class.
3. You need information about the causes of the American Revolution for a report you are writing. You need to decide which of the ten books on the American Revolution you've found would best fit your needs.

Enrichment and Extension

Reading for a Purpose

To help students to see the difference between a quick skimming of material and a closer reading, tell them to select a short piece of fiction. Ask them to skim it for 30 seconds or less, and then summarize the story. Next, tell them to go back to the same story and read it more carefully. They will probably see details they missed the first time. Discuss how reading quickly may tell them what happens in a story, while reading more carefully can tell them how and why it happens.

24.3 Summarizing

Explaining the main ideas of something in your own words is called summarizing. Every time you tell a friend about a movie you saw or a book you read, you are summarizing. You might summarize yesterday's science lesson to a friend who was sick that day. Summarizing saves time. You also might find that explaining or summarizing something for someone else helps you understand it better.

When to Summarize

Though you often make informal summaries, there are also times when you need to make formal ones. When researching material for a report, for instance, you need to summarize the important ideas. You also might summarize information you hear in a lecture, speech, or film presented in class. After you take notes on what you read or hear, you can summarize the main ideas for reference or review.

You can also use summarizing as a study tool when reading or reviewing material in your text. Writing passages from a textbook in your own words can help you better understand and remember the material. The following chart shows when and why you might summarize material.

When to Summarize	
Situation	**Purpose**
Preparing a written or oral research report	To include important ideas from your reading in your report
Reading textbook material	To better understand and remember ideas from the textbook
Listening to lectures or speeches	To write a report or prepare for a test on ideas from the lecture or speech
Viewing a film or video documentary	To write a report or prepare for a test on ideas from the film

24.3 Summarizing **663**

Teacher's Classroom Resources

For Lesson 24.3, the following resources can be used for planning, instruction, practice, or reinforcement.

🔧 **Teaching Tools**
Lesson Plans, p. 123

📂 **Blackline Masters**
Thinking and Study Skills, pp. 2, 8, 18, 39–40

Setting the Purpose

Lesson 24.3 teaches students when and how to summarize information they have read or heard.

FOCUS

Lesson Overview
Objective: To become familiar with summarizing
Skills: paraphrasing; taking notes; organizing and presenting a summary
Critical Thinking: establishing and evaluating criteria; analyzing
Speaking and Listening: listening accurately; discussing

🔔 Bellringer
When students enter the classroom, have this assignment on the board: *Write the main events for the plot of "The Three Little Pigs."*

Motivating Activity
To prompt a discussion about summarizing, have students review their responses to the Bellringer. Explain that the events they described in "The Three Little Pigs" could be used to develop a summary of the plot.

TEACH

Guided Practice

L2 Summarizing a Topic
Have students turn to the table of contents on pages xi and xii. Ask volunteers to summarize what they know about nouns (Unit 9), verbs (Unit 10), or another unit topic. As they respond, you may wish to write notes on the board. Afterward, ask students to mention any details they chose to leave out of their summaries and why.

663

PRACTICE AND ASSESS

Evaluation Guidelines: Exercise 3
Answers will vary, but summaries should contain clear statements of the main ideas of the written or audio-visual material.

Independent Practice

Skills Practice
📁 *Thinking and Study Skills,*
pp. 2, 8, 18, 39–40

CLOSE

Point out that students are often asked to summarize something in their own words. Discuss how one student's "own words" may be very different from another's. Inform students that both versions would be correct as long as they included the important facts.

How to Summarize

When you write a summary, put the ideas in your own words. Concentrate on the main ideas, leaving out examples and supporting details. Look below at the example of an original text and one student's summary of it. Notice what details are left out and how the student's language differs from the original.

Abraham Lincoln (1809–1865), considered one of our greatest presidents, preserved the Union at a time of unrest during the Civil War. With the United States facing disintegration, he showed that a democratic form of government can endure.

One of Lincoln's most important qualities was his understanding. Lincoln realized that the Union and democracy had to be preserved. Lincoln was also a remarkable communicator, able to clearly and persuasively express ideas and beliefs in speech and writing. His most famous speech was the brief but powerful Gettysburg Address. His first and second inaugural addresses were also very significant.

> *Abraham Lincoln, one of our greatest presidents, is best remembered for holding the Union together through the Civil War. He is noted for his understanding and his ability to communicate effectively and persuasively.*

Exercise 3

With a partner, choose a film or television documentary, a lesson or chapter from a book, or an encyclopedia article about a subject that interests you. Read or discuss the material, and then work together to write a summary. Identify the main ideas, and put them in your own words. Decide whether to use any direct quotes. Share your completed summary with the class.

664 *Study Skills*

Connections Across the Curriculum

History
Initiate a discussion about direct quotations by telling students about the astronaut Neil Armstrong, whose words as he stepped onto the moon's surface were meant to be "One small step for a man, one giant leap for mankind." Armstrong left out the *a* in delivering the words, but many printed sources include it. Which version do students think should stand? Why? Ask students what other famous historical quotations they may recall. Then have them check the exact words in a book of quotations or a history textbook.

24.4 Making Study Plans

Studying may not be your favorite activity but, like it or not, studying is essential to doing well in school. But what about free time? Everyone would like more time off each week. Practicing good study habits will improve your schoolwork and increase your free time.

Setting Goals

A good study plan begins with goal setting. Review your assignments, and then set your goals for each class. Break down your assignments into short-term and long-term goals. Short-term goals can be completed in one study session; long-term goals will take several sessions. Break down your long-term goals into smaller tasks. Be realistic about what you can get done in each study session.

The chart below shows some short-term and long-term goals, and how long-term goals can be broken down.

Setting Goals	
Short-Term Goals	1 learning a short list of spelling or vocabulary words
	2 reading several pages in your textbook
	3 completing a math exercise for homework
Long-Term Goals	1 completing a research report *short-term tasks* • find library materials • do prewriting • write rough draft • revise draft • prepare final report
	2 preparing for a unit test *short-term tasks* • read Chapter 22 • read Chapter 23 • review key terms

24.4 Making Study Plans **665**

Teacher's Classroom Resources

For Lesson 24.4, the following resources can be used for planning, instruction, practice, or reinforcement.

🔧 **Teaching Tools**
Lesson Plans, p. 124

📁 **Blackline Masters**
Thinking and Study Skills,
pp. 2, 8, 18, 39–40

Setting the Purpose

Lesson 24.4 emphasizes the importance of setting study goals and gives students tips for studying effectively.

FOCUS

Lesson Overview

Objective: To learn how to make study plans
Skills: setting goals; establishing good study habits; creating an environment conducive to studying
Critical Thinking: analyzing; synthesizing; evaluating; establishing and evaluating criteria
Speaking and Listening: discussing; explaining a process

🔔 Bellringer

When students enter the classroom, have this assignment on the board: *Answer the following questions about your study habits: How often do you study? What time(s) of the day do you study? Where do you study?*

TEACH

Guided Practice

L1 Planning a Calendar
To help students visualize short-term and long-term goals, have them draw a large one-month calendar on a sheet of paper. Advise students to indicate the due dates for current assignments. Have them figure out the number of days it will take to complete each assignment. Then encourage them to break each assignment down into small tasks, such as reading a specific number of pages each day.

PRACTICE AND ASSESS

Evaluation Guidelines: Exercise 4

Answers will vary, but completed assignments should reflect students' ability to objectively analyze their study habits and recognize productive ones.

Independent Practice

Skills Practice

📁 *Thinking and Study Skills,* pp. 2, 8, 18, 39–40

CLOSE

Ask students why it is important to break a long-term study goal into short-term goals. Help them see that any long-term project will seem less overwhelming if it is divided into several focused tasks that can be accomplished in stages.

Effective Study Time

Once you've determined your goals, set a reasonable deadline for reaching each goal. Write the deadline in a study-plan calendar that includes your regular activities and assignments. When you schedule your study time, keep your deadlines and your other activities in mind. Don't schedule too many deadlines for the same day. Look at the following studying tips. What other tips could you add?

Tips on Studying

1. Study at the same time and in the same place each day. Also, keep your study tools, such as pencils, pens, notepads, and dictionaries, in the same place.

2. Take a short break after reaching each goal.

3. Begin study time with your most difficult assignment.

4. Focus on one assignment at a time.

5. Try a variety of study methods, such as reading, summarizing what you have read, developing your own graphic aids (like clusters), or discussing material with a study partner.

Exercise 4

Keep a "study log" for two weeks. Record the beginning and ending time of each study session, even if it's only fifteen minutes at lunch. Write down what you study each day, and comment on how effective your studying is. You may want to include observations on circumstances that affect your study on a particular day. (For example: It was raining, so I was glad to be inside studying; I had headache, so I had trouble concentrating.) At the end of the two weeks, take a good look at your study log. Identify the factors that contributed to your most effective use of study time.

Cooperative Learning

Discussing Study Habits

Have groups of students discuss their study habits. Use these questions:

• Where do you study and what reference books do you use?
• When is the most effective time for you to study?

• What method do you use to memorize information or study for a test?
• What do you consider distractions?
• How can you avoid them?
• What do you do for a study break?

Encourage group members to take notes on tactics they might like to try.

24.5 The SQ3R Method

Do you sometimes spend hours reading your textbook only to find that you immediately forget most of what you read? Do you find that, even though you study hard, you often do not do well on tests? The SQ3R method can help make your study time more productive.

SQ3R is an effective method for improving your ability to read and remember written information. SQ3R stands for the steps in the process: survey, question, read, record, and review. Using this method can help you study more efficiently and remember more of what you read. The diagram shows how the SQ3R method works.

Survey	Question	Read	Record	Review
Preview the material by skimming. Read heads, highlighted terms, and the first sentence of each paragraph. Look at all pictures and graphs.	Ask questions about the material. Your questions might begin with *who, what, when, where, why,* and *how.*	Read the selection carefully. Identify the main idea of each section. Take notes, and add questions to your list.	Write answers to your questions without looking at the text. Make brief notes about additional main ideas and facts.	Check your answers in the text. Continue to study the text until you can answer all questions correctly.

The SQ3R method works with any subject. Practice the method, and make it a habit. Once you thoroughly learn the SQ3R method and use it regularly, you will

- remember more of what you read,
- better understand the material by developing specific questions about it, and
- be better prepared to participate in class.

Survey

The purpose of surveying, or previewing, the material is to get a general idea of what it is about. The main ideas are sometimes contained in section headings or subheadings. Read each heading and subheading, and skim the entire material. (See page 661

24.5 The SQ3R Method **667**

Teacher's Classroom Resources

For Lesson 24.5, the following resources can be used for planning, instruction, practice, or reinforcement.

🔧 **Teaching Tools**
Lesson Plans, p. 124

📁 **Blackline Masters**
Thinking and Study Skills, pp. 2, 8, 18, 39–40

Setting the Purpose

Lesson 24.5 explains the SQ3R method for studying written information. Students learn and practice the five steps—Survey, Question, Read, Record, and Review.

FOCUS

Lesson Overview

Objective: To learn how to read difficult material and remember what is read by employing the SQ3R reading strategy

Skills: surveying; questioning; reading; recording; and reviewing

Critical Thinking: analyzing; synthesizing; categorizing; classifying; contrasting; recalling; determining main idea; evaluating; summarizing; comparing; inferring; visualizing

Speaking and Listening: note taking; discussing; evaluating; questioning; giving oral reports

🔔 Bellringer

When students enter the classroom, have this assignment on the board: *List the steps you take to remember and understand difficult reading material.*

Motivating Activity

Point out that there are strategies readers can use to remember and understand what they read. Discuss the strategies students listed for the Bellringer activity. Then explain that one common strategy is called the SQ3R method. Challenge students to guess what the name stands for if they don't know.

TEACH

Guided Practice

L2 Employing the SQ3R Method

Give students one minute to skim and scan a page they are currently studying in their science or social studies texts. Have them write at least two questions about the material. Then tell them to read the section carefully and answer the questions. Discuss how this method compares with quickly reading the page once.

L1 Practicing the SQ3R Method

Choose several composition and grammar sections from this book for small groups to examine. Assign a different section to each group and instruct groups to use the SQ3R study method. Each group member can survey the section and then contribute a question to a sheet of paper circulated by the group. Each student will then read the section and answer another group member's question.

L3 Evaluating the SQ3R Method

Show students several textbooks to which they might apply the SQ3R method. You might use pages from a science book, a mathematics book, a history book, and an English book. Ask students to evaluate which texts they would understand and remember better by employing the SQ3R method. Is it easier to understand a chapter when they skim and scan first? Does asking and answering questions clarify the material? Discuss the differences in reading materials that may require variations in study techniques.

⇄ Cross-reference: Writing

To model the SQ3R method, refer students to Unit 2, Case Study: Documentary Writing, pp. 74–79.

668

---

for hints on skimming.) If the material does not include headings, skim each paragraph to find its topic sentence. It will often be the first sentence of the paragraph.

Sometimes important ideas in the text are shown in bold or italic print. Make sure you note these carefully. When previewing, also take note of all pictures, charts, graphs, and maps. Examine them to see how the graphic aids fit in with the text. Read the title and caption for each one.

Question

Before you read, prepare a list of questions you want to be able to answer after reading the material. Having a list of questions before you begin helps you focus on the important ideas. Use questions that begin with *who, what, when, where, why,* and *how.* For example, suppose you're reading a chapter on the Battle of Gettysburg for your history class. You might write questions such as these: Who were the opposing generals in the battle? When did the battle take place? What was the outcome? Develop at least one question for each main idea before you read. Also, look at any review questions at the end of each chapter or lesson.

Read

Once you have prepared your list of questions, you are ready to read through the material carefully. (See page 662 for tips on careful reading.) As you read, look for answers to the questions on your list. Take brief notes about the main ideas. (See pages 670–671 for more information on taking notes.) For example, your notes might include "Battle of Gettysburg fought July 1–3, 1863. Confederate General Robert E. Lee; Union General George G. Meade. Turning point of Civil War." Add more questions to your list as they are raised during your reading. Make sure you thoroughly understand all the ideas. If the ideas are complicated and you are having difficulty, read the material through two or three times. Don't go on to the next chapter or section until you have mastered the material in your current reading.

668 *Study Skills*

Enabling Strategies

LEP Defining Terms

Check students' understanding of the meaning of the terms *survey, question, read, record,* and *review.* Students might work in pairs or small groups to write each word and its meaning on a separate three-by-five card and quiz each other. Some students may prefer to translate the words into their native languages, creating a new abbreviation with letters that stand for the translated words.

Record

When you complete your reading, write the answers to your questions without looking at the book or article. If there is a large amount of material, you may wish to stop and answer your questions after you finish reading each section. Answering the questions from your memory will test whether you have thoroughly learned the material. If you have difficulty answering the questions, reread the material. Then try to answer the questions again without looking at the text. Make sure your questions apply to the material. If the material you're studying does not thoroughly answer the questions, revise your questions to fit the text.

Review

Check the answers to your questions against the material you've read. Did you answer them all correctly? If not, review the material to find the answers. Try rewriting some of the questions you missed, or write several new questions that cover the same material. Review the material again, and then answer the new questions. Check your answers against the material. If you miss some of these questions, go through the process again, rewriting questions and reviewing the material until you are able to correctly answer all questions. Save your review questions and answers. You can use them later to study or review for tests.

Exercise 5

Work with a small group of classmates. Each member should choose an event from American history, then find an encyclopedia article or a passage from a book about that event. Study your material, using the SQ3R method. Allow each member to give a brief oral report to the group on the material studied. Group members may evaluate one another's reports and discuss how the SQ3R method helped them.

24.5   The SQ3R Method   **669**

PRACTICE AND ASSESS

Evaluation Guidelines: Exercise 5
Answers will vary.
- When students evaluate the oral reports, they should take into consideration whether the report is clear and easily understood.
- When discussing how the SQ3R method helped them, students should think about which of the five techniques was most helpful to them (surveying, questioning, reading, recording, or reviewing).

Independent Practice

Skills Practice
📁 *Thinking and Study Skills,* pp. 2, 8, 18, 39–40

CLOSE

Have students think about how they can most effectively use the SQ3R method in their other classes. In which classes will the method be most useful? Why? How would they modify the method for other classes?

Technology Tip

Using a Tape Recorder
Tell students that they can use a tape recorder to review material they have read. After surveying the material, they can tape-record their questions. They can then read the material carefully and tape their answers to the questions. To review the material, students can play back the tape.

Setting the Purpose

Lesson 24.6 teaches students how to prepare for a research paper or presentation by taking notes and creating an outline.

FOCUS

Lesson Overview

Objective: To become familiar with gathering and organizing data
Skills: summarizing; taking notes; creating an outline
Critical Thinking: establishing and evaluating criteria; analyzing
Speaking and Listening: listening for special clues; discussing

Bellringer

When students enter the classroom, have this assignment on the board: *Write down any words you can remember from a conversation you heard just before class.*

Motivating Activity

To help students gain experience taking notes while listening, you might play a portion of an audiotape of a famous speech, a short story, or a novel. Tell students to jot down key words, phrases, or ideas as they listen. You might want to have peer reviewers check one another's notes. Encourage classroom discussion of the message of the speech or the story's plot, theme, and other features.

24.6 Gathering and Organizing Information

Can you remember the important ideas from a discussion you heard two weeks ago? Probably not. Unless you took notes, you've probably forgotten what was said. Note taking is important, because people usually forget most of what they hear. Taking notes and organizing them helps clarify what you hear or read. Well-written notes also come in handy when you're studying for a test or writing a report.

Taking Notes

Taking notes isn't always easy, whether you are working from a lecture, a film or video shown in class, or from research material. You may find you are either trying to write down too much or not enough. Taking notes requires special skill.

The notes you take while listening are important for your later review. They'll help you understand and remember what you hear. The notes you take while reading will allow you to review the important ideas from a source. With good notes, you won't have to go back to a source and reread it.

Tips for Taking Notes

While Listening
1. Take down only main ideas and key details.
2. Listen for transitions and signal words.
3. Use numerals, abbreviations, and symbols for speed, making sure that later you can understand what you have written.

While Writing
1. Take notes only on material that applies directly to your topic.
2. Use a card for each piece of information, and record the source of the information at the top of the card.
3. Summarize as much as possible.
4. Use direct quotations only for colorful language or something that's particularly well phrased.

Teacher's Classroom Resources

For Lesson 24.6, the following resources can be used for planning, instruction, practice, or reinforcement.

Teaching Tools
Lesson Plans, p. 125

Blackline Masters
Thinking and Study Skills, pp. 2, 8, 18, 39–40

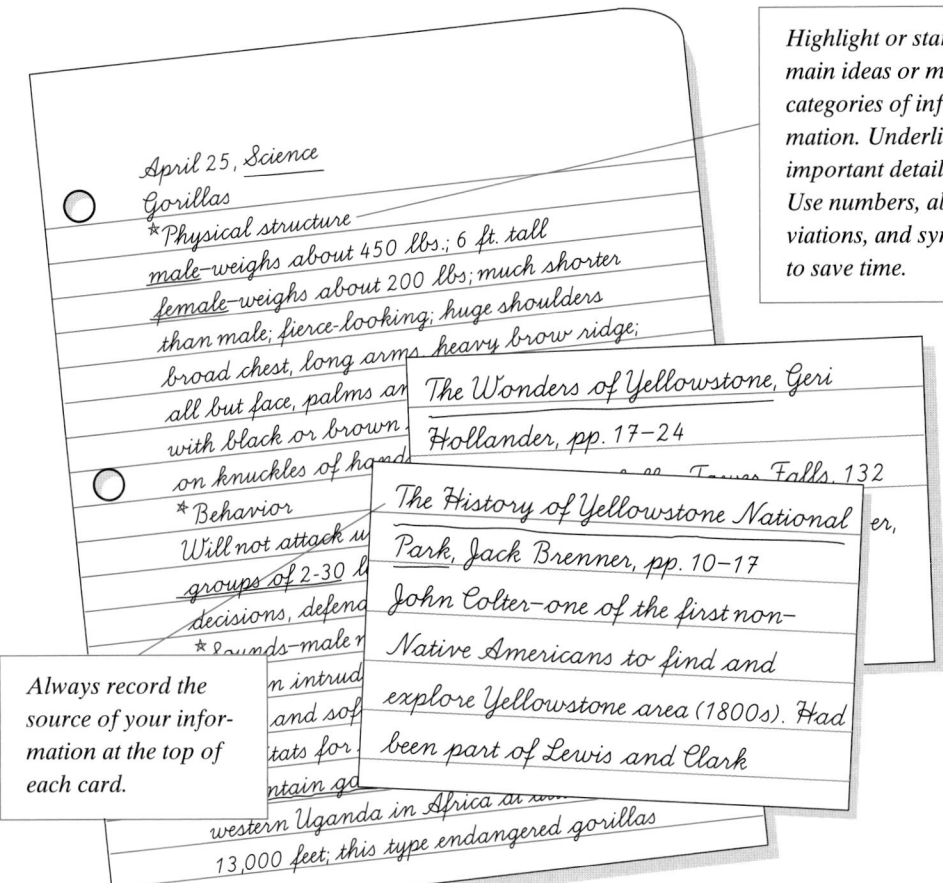

Highlight or star main ideas or major categories of information. Underline important details. Use numbers, abbreviations, and symbols to save time.

April 25, Science
Gorillas
*Physical structure
male—weighs about 450 lbs.; 6 ft. tall
female—weighs about 200 lbs; much shorter
than male; fierce-looking; huge shoulders
broad chest, long arms, heavy brow ridge;
all but face, palms an...
with black or brown...
on knuckles of hand...
*Behavior
Will not attack u...
groups of 2-30 l...
decisions, defend...
*Sounds—male...
...n intrud...
...and sof...
...tats for...
...ntain ga...
western Uganda in Africa at...
13,000 feet; this type endangered gorillas

The Wonders of Yellowstone, Geri
Hollander, pp. 17-24
...Tower Falls, 132

The History of Yellowstone National
Park, Jack Brenner, pp. 10-17
John Colter—one of the first non-
Native Americans to find and
explore Yellowstone area (1800s). Had
been part of Lewis and Clark

Always record the source of your information at the top of each card.

Outlining

Once you complete your research, put your note cards in order and prepare an outline. The order you use depends on the kind of paper you are writing. If you're writing a paper on historical events, you might use chronological order, or the order in which events happen. A science paper might be ordered by cause and effect.

Group together your note cards that cover similar topics. Each group will become a main topic. Within each group put similar cards into subgroups. These will become your subtopics.

24.6   Gathering and Organizing Information   **671**

Guided Practice

L2 Using Abbreviations

Inform students that no one can write fast enough to take down a speaker's every word without using some method of shorthand. That's why abbreviations can be helpful when taking notes. Some people use *w/* for *with* and *e.g.* for *for example.* Ask students to suggest other abbreviations that can be used while taking notes. Point out that the abbreviations they use may be conventional abbreviations, personal ones, or a combination of the two.

L3 Creating an Outline

Have students develop an outline based on a newspaper article. You might use articles about colorful cities or countries from the Sunday travel section. Ask volunteers to write parts of their completed outlines on the chalkboard.

Thinking Skills

Critical Thinking

Ask students to read the notes and note cards on this page. Then ask them to look at the chart on page 670 and to compare and contrast the tips for listening and writing. Are there any tips they would add to the chart?

PRACTICE AND ASSESS

Evaluation Guidelines: Exercise 6

Answers will vary, but student outlines should contain accurate main ideas and subtopics from the article. Comparison of notes and outlines should yield discussion of completeness of information presented in students' work and correct use of the outline form.

Independent Practice

Skills Practice

☞ *Thinking and Study Skills,* pp. 2, 8, 18, 39–40

CLOSE

In art, the word *outline* indicates an object's outer edge or contour. Discuss how, in writing, an outline gives the contour or profile of a body of material.

672

As your outline develops, you may find that you need to do more research. You may also find that you do not need all the notes you have taken. Set aside any note cards that don't apply to your outline. Examine the sample outline below.

Use Roman numerals to number the main topics, or big ideas of your paper.

Indent and use letters and numbers for subtopics and their divisions. Do not use subtopics or divisions unless you have at least two.

Yellowstone National Park

I. The History of Yellowstone

    A. Earliest Explorers

        1. John Colter
           a. member of the earlier Lewis and Clark expedition
           b. first non-Native American to see Yellowstone
           c. visited in early 1800s

        2. Jim Bridger
           a. famous "mountain man" and explorer
           b. visited the region about 1830

    B. Washburn Expedition

        1. confirmed earlier reports of natural wonders

        2. worked to make area a national park

II. Yellowstone's Natural Beauty

Exercise 6

Working with a small group of classmates, look through a magazine such as *National Geographic* or *Discover.* Choose an article that interests all of you. Have each member of the group read the article individually, take notes on it, and write a detailed outline. Then compare notes and outlines, discussing the differences.

Thinking Skills

Visual Thinking

Explain that during note taking, most people simply write sentences, phrases, lists, and numbers; this is using mainly the left part of the brain. Students can learn to use the right part of the brain, which involves imagination and association, to take better notes and recall more information. They can do this by drawing key images during note taking. Ask students to find an idea, a fact, or a concept in one of their textbooks and draw an image that would help them memorize the idea. Ask them to share their drawings with the class.

24.7 Graphic Information

Imagine trying to explain to someone, using just words, how a car engine works. A simple description of a process may seem confusing or incomplete. However, a picture or diagram can make it much easier for people to understand how something works.

Tables and Graphs

Many books use graphic aids such as tables and graphs to present figures or other data that are hard to explain with words alone. Table and graphs organize information and make it more understandable.

Tables Tables allow you to group facts or numbers into categories so that you can compare information easily. The left-hand column of a table lists a set of related items. Across the top of the table are column headings that describe the items in each column. With this arrangement, you can read a table horizontally or vertically, and you don't have to read all the information to find the piece you need. For example, in the table below, you can easily find the population growth of the five largest U.S. cities. Looking across the rows, you can see how a particular city's population increased or decreased over the years. Looking down the columns, you can compare the populations in the different years listed.

Population of Largest U.S. Cities						
Rank	City	1950	1960	1970	1980	1986
1	New York City	7,891,984	7,781,984	7,895,563	7,071,639	7,262,700
2	Los Angeles	1,970,358	2,479,015	2,811,801	2,966,850	3,259,340
3	Chicago	3,620,962	3,550,404	3,369,357	3,005,072	3,009,530
4	Houston	596,163	938,219	1,233,535	1,595,138	1,728,910
5	Philadelphia	2,071,605	2,002,512	1,949,996	1,688,210	1,642,900

Source: *U.S. Bureau of the Census*

Setting the Purpose

In Lesson 24.7 students explore various graphic forms of information presentation.

FOCUS

Objective: To become familiar with graphic information
Skills: using and creating graphs, tables, and diagrams
Critical Thinking: using criteria; comparing and contrasting; classifying; analyzing; identifying patterns
Speaking and Listening: explaining a process; discussing; giving oral reports

Bellringer
When students enter the classroom, have this assignment on the board: *Tally the number of people in this room wearing each of the following colors: red, blue, green, purple, black, white.*

Motivating Activity
Ask students to read their tallies for who is wearing various colors of clothing. Ask them how interesting it is to read or listen to a list of numbers. Explain that graphic information is a way to present numeric or technical information in a clear, concise, engaging way. Students might brainstorm ways to present their tallies graphically in forms they have seen before, such as tables, circle graphs, picture graphs, or bar graphs.

Teacher's Classroom Resources

For lesson 24.7, the following resources can be used for planning, instruction, practice, or reinforcement.

Teaching Tools
Lesson Plans, p. 125

Blackline Masters
Thinking and Study Skills
pp. 2, 8, 18, 39–40

TEACH

Guided Practice

L2 Making a Bar Graph

Point out that using a bar graph can be a quick and clear way to compare amounts. Help the class make a bar graph showing how many people are wearing certain colors. Volunteers can write the number of students wearing each color (for example, *5 red, 8 blue* and so forth) in a column on the left side of the chalkboard. Then write the numbers 1 to 20 across the bottom of the board. Help them create bars representing the different amounts. Ask the class what comparisons can easily be made by looking at the chart.

L1 Preparing Steps to Follow

Using graph paper, lead students in making a bar graph. Begin by writing the data they have collected on the chalkboard. Show them where the heading should be written, where the horizontal and vertical axes should go, where to place numbers on the scale, and how to measure each of the bars using the scale. You might want to have a prepared model for students to follow.

Each bar represents a different type of athletic shoe. The height of each bar shows the total sales for one type of shoe.

By comparing the lengths of the bars, you see that gym shoes, or sneakers, outsold all other types of athletic shoes in 1987.

Amounts are shown along the vertical axis. Horizontal lines make it easy to locate the amount for a given year.

Years are shown along the horizontal axis. Vertical lines on the graph make it easy to see where the year intersects the graph line.

Bar Graphs   In bar graphs each quantity is shown as a bar. The length of the bar indicates the amount, making it easy to visually compare the amounts. Bar graphs can have horizontal bars or vertical bars, depending on how many categories are being compared. Look at the bar graph below. Use the graph to compare the sales figures for different types of athletic shoes sold in the United States.

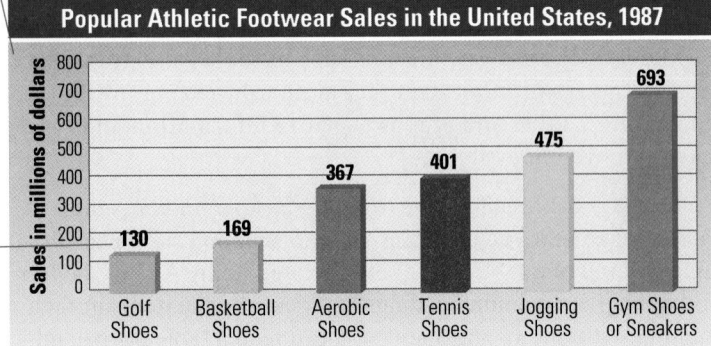

Popular Athletic Footwear Sales in the United States, 1987

Source: *Statistical Abstract of the United States,* 1989

Line Graphs   Line graphs help the reader to see at a glance whether certain numbers are rising, falling, or going up and down. They also show the period of time in which these changes take place. The line graph at the left shows the amount of solid waste thrown away between 1960 and 1985. The amount of garbage, in millions of tons, is listed along the left-hand side, or vertical axis. The years are shown along the bottom, or horizontal axis. By following the line, you can

U.S. Public Solid Waste, 1960–1985

Source: *Statistical Abstract of the United States,* 1989

674 *Study Skills*

Enabling Strategies

LEP Finding Examples of Graphics

Ask students to find examples of graphic aids in newspapers and magazines written in their first languages. Ask other students to try to determine from the visual aid what information is being presented, even though they may not be able to translate the labels. Then ask the students who brought the examples to explain briefly the graphic aid and the information it is presenting.

quickly see that the amount of garbage thrown away in the United States kept rising over the years given.

Circle Graphs   Circle graphs, or pie charts, begin with a circle representing the whole of something. The parts are shown as slices of a pie, with each slice representing part of the whole. Because a circle graph shows parts of a whole, information is often presented as percentages. For instance, instead of representing the population of North America in numbers of people, a circle graph might show it as a percentage of the total world population.

The circle graph on this page uses the same information as the bar graph on the opposite page. The whole circle represents the total of athletic shoes sold in the United States in 1987. The graph is then divided into the different types of athletic shoes. The sizes of the slices allow you to easily compare the portions of total sales for each type of shoe.

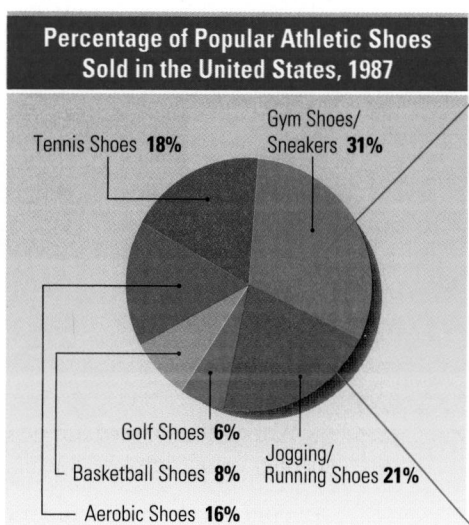

Percentage of Popular Athletic Shoes Sold in the United States, 1987

Tennis Shoes **18%**
Gym Shoes/ Sneakers **31%**
Golf Shoes **6%**
Basketball Shoes **8%**
Jogging/ Running Shoes **21%**
Aerobic Shoes **16%**

Source: *Statistical Abstract of the United States,* 1989

Ordinary gym shoes, or sneakers, are represented by a slice that is 31 percent of all athletic shoes sold in 1987.

The next largest slice, representing jogging or running shoes, accounts for 21 percent of all athletic shoes sold in 1987.

Diagrams

Diagrams may illustrate the steps in a process or show how the parts of an object work together. You might find it difficult to learn about a complex process by reading about it or by listening to someone give an explanation. You might not be able to follow all the stages or understand all the parts without the help of a diagram.

In a diagram each part of the object or process is labeled, sometimes with an explanation of its function. The diagram on the next page, for example, shows how heat energy is turned into electricity. Notice how each important part is labeled. Note also how the arrows show the movement of water and energy.

24.7   Graphic Information   **675**

Technology Tip

Creating Graphic Aids

Students may want to investigate computer software programs that create graphic aids. For example, spreadsheet programs and even some word processors can be used to create a wide variety of graphs. If possible, schedule a demonstration of one of these programs on a school computer.

PRACTICE AND ASSESS

Evaluation Guidelines: Exercise 7

Answers will vary, but should include the following:

1. The graph should be a line graph. (A bar graph is acceptable, but students should realize that a line graph is better for showing changes in numbers or quantities over time.) The finished work should be accurate in graphing the data.

2. The graphic aid could be a bar graph or a table. Both the graphic and the paragraph that it accompanies should reflect correct information.

Independent Practice

Skills Practice
📂 *Thinking and Study Skills,* pp. 2, 8, 18, 39–40

CLOSE

Discuss jobs in which people make use of graphic aids, such as weather forecasting, scientific research, or technical illustration. How do graphic aids improve reports in these professions?

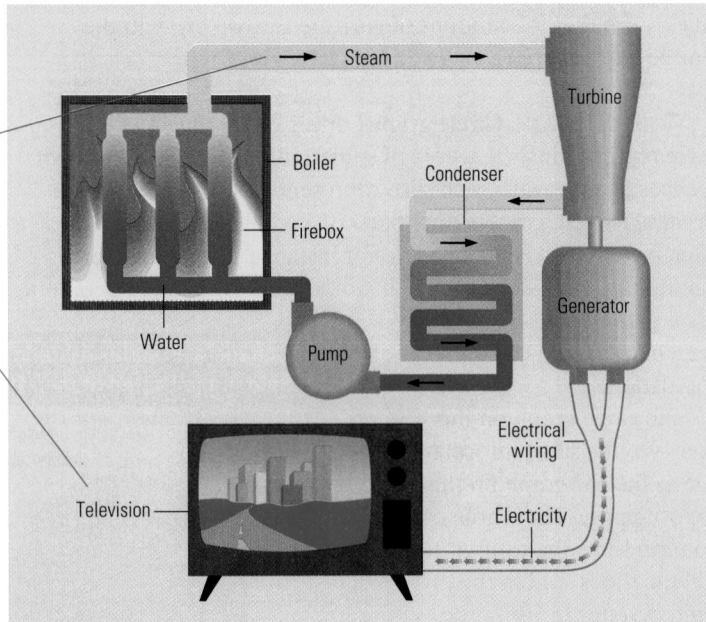

Arrows show movement of water through its complete cycle.

Diagram labels tell the name of each part of the process, but not all the details within that process.

Steam • Turbine • Boiler • Condenser • Firebox • Generator • Water • Pump • Electrical wiring • Television • Electricity

Exercise 7

Work with a classmate on one of the following projects. Display your completed project in class.

1. Find out the high temperature for each day of the preceding week. Draw the appropriate graph showing the week's temperatures. Then write a brief paragraph explaining the graph.

2. Find the total number of games won by five competing athletic teams this season. Develop an appropriate graphic showing the number of games won by each of the five teams. Then write a brief paragraph explaining your graphic.

676 *Study Skills*

Thinking Skills

Visual Thinking

A picture graph conveys information by using picture symbols instead of bars or lines. For example, to show numbers of unemployed people, the graph might employ a figure of a person. Each figure might represent a hundred, a thousand, or a hundred thousand people.

Provide or ask students to find examples of picture graphs from newspapers or magazines. Students might want to create their own picture graphs about topics of their choice.

24.8 Memorizing

Do you ever call your best friend on the phone? Of course you do. Friends call each other all the time. Do you look up your friend's number in the phone book every time you call? Not if you have it memorized. Memorizing phone numbers is easy, but what about things you need to know in school? You can memorize information for school as easily as you memorize a friend's phone number.

How to Memorize

Different people have different "learning styles," or methods, of memorizing. One thing may work for one person, but not for someone else. The following are two techniques for memorizing. Try them and see what works better for you.

The most common technique for memorizing is repetition. You keep reading a passage aloud until you've got it memorized. You could also write the material over and over. If you combine your writing with reading aloud, you may memorize even more quickly. If you learn better by hearing, tape record as you read. Play back the tape as many times as necessary until you have memorized the information.

Visualizing is another method of memorizing. Use it to memorize small pieces of information, such as phone numbers, formulas, or the spelling of words. Look at the information. Then close your eyes and "see" the number or word in your mind. Visualize it in an interesting or humorous way. If you can get a unique picture in your mind, you're more likely to be able to visualize it again.

Tricks for Memorizing

Using memory games or tricks is another way to remember information. There are many different tricks or games you can use. Try making a sentence out of words that start with the first letter of each item in a list you want to memorize. Or make up a name using those same letters. You could also try writing a rhyme. Look at the chart below. When you need to

24.8 Memorizing **677**

Teacher's Classroom Resources

For Lesson 24.8, the following resources can be used for planning, instruction, practice, assessment, reinforcement, or evaluation.

🔧 **Teaching Tools**
Lesson Plans, p. 125

📁 **Blackline Masters**
Thinking and Study Skills
pp. 2, 8, 18, 39–40

Unit Assessment

📁 *Tests with Answer Key*
Unit 24 Mastery Test, pp. 95–96

💿 *Test Generator*
Unit 24 Mastery Test

You may wish to administer the Unit 24 Mastery Test at this point.

Setting the Purpose

Lesson 24.8 teaches students methods of memorization.

FOCUS

Lesson Overview

Objective: To develop a method for memorizing
Skills: identifying characteristics; using organizational patterns; using graphic organizers
Critical Thinking: recalling; identifying patterns
Speaking and Listening: repeating passages; listening to recording

🔔 **Bellringer**
When students enter the classroom, have this assignment on the board: *From memory, write the twelve months of the year and how many days are in each. How do you remember this?*

TEACH

Guided Practice

L1 **Experimenting with Memorization Devices**
Invite students to try out these additional memory devices:
1. Acronyms: Use the first letters of words to be memorized to spell out a word or a phrase.
2. Chunking: Break information into small groups. Telephone numbers are an example of chunking—memorize the first three numbers separately from the last four.

PRACTICE AND ASSESS

Evaluation Guidelines: Exercise 8

Responses should reflect an understanding of mnemonic devices in general and those described in the lesson specifically.

Evaluation Guidelines: Exercise 9

Responses should reflect an understanding of the kinds of mnemonic devices described in the lesson. Look for particularly imaginative solutions, and remind students that the device should be easier to remember than the information it is meant to recall.

Independent Practice

Skills Practice

📂 *Thinking and Study Skills,* pp. 2, 8, 18, 39–40

CLOSE

Have students invent a rap (rhythmic talk-singing) for one of the memory aids listed on page 678 or create their own rap memory aid. Invite volunteers to share the rap with the class and discuss whether it helps with memorizing.

---

memorize something, try some of these memory tricks to remember the material.

Tricks for Remembering	
Purpose	**Memory Aid**
To remember the number of days in each month of the year	Thirty days has September, April, June, and November. All the rest have thirty-one, Except February alone, Which has twenty-eight. In leap year, coming once in four, February then has one day more.
To remember the year Columbus sailed to the Americas	In fourteen hundred and ninety-two, Columbus sailed the ocean blue.
To remember the order of the planets from the sun : **M**ercury, **V**enus, **E**arth, **M**ars, **J**upiter, **S**aturn, **U**ranus, **N**eptune, and **P**luto	**M**y **v**ery **e**xcellent **m**other **j**ust **s**erved **u**s **n**ine **p**izzas.
To remember that the person who runs a school is a *principal*, not a *principle*	The princip**al** is my p**al**.

Exercise 8

Develop a memory trick to remember the parts of the sun: core, photosphere, chromosphere, corona. Work on your own or with a classmate or two.

Exercise 9

With a partner choose at least two words from the list of Easily Confused Words on page 657 in Lesson 23 .7. Develop ways to memorize each word.

678 *Study Skills*

Cooperative Learning

Developing Memorization Strategies
Invite students to form small groups to discuss strategies for memorizing information. Encourage them to apply one strategy to material they want to learn or will need to remember for an exam. Visit students as they brainstorm within the groups, and suggest that they write down their ideas for remembering the material. Strategies might include reading aloud, asking each other questions, and writing notes on key ideas. When they have finished, have groups share with the class what they have memorized. Ask them if memorizing together was easier or more difficult. Why?

UNIT 25 Taking Tests

25.1 Strategies

No one said it would be easy. Studying for and taking a test is hard work. Still, you can learn some strategies that will help you prepare for and take tests. These strategies can help make you less uncomfortable and perhaps more confident in a test-taking situation.

Preparing for a Test

Preparing for a test begins well before the day of the test. Before you study, try to find out what information will be on the test. Then make a test-studying schedule. Include time for reviewing your class notes, homework, quizzes, and textbook. As you study, jot down questions that you think might be on the test. Try to answer these questions after writing them. If some questions are difficult to answer, spend some extra time looking up the answers.

When you think you know the material, work with another student or a group of students. Test these students with your study questions. Explaining the answers to someone else will help you learn the information. In addition, ask the students in your group to test you with questions they wrote. They may have come up with some you hadn't thought of yourself.

Taking a Test

You need to make careful use of the limited time for a test. First, make sure you understand all the test directions. Then estimate how much time each test section will take. Begin with the sections that will take less time, and don't spend too much time on one section. Planning your test time wisely may help you answer all of the questions. The chart on the following page offers suggestions for budgeting your time.

25.1 Strategies **679**

Teacher's Classroom Resources

For Lesson 25.1, the following resources can be used for planning, instruction, practice, assessment, reinforcement, or evaluation.

📄 **Teaching Tools**
Lesson Plans

📁 **Blackline Masters**
Standardized Test Practice Thinking and Study Skills,
  pp. 41–42

Unit Assessment
📁 *Tests with Answer Key*
Unit 25 Pretest, pp. 97–98

💿 **Software**
Test Generator
  Unit 25 Pretest

You may wish to administer the Unit 25 Pretest at this point.

Setting the Purpose

Lesson 25.1 teaches students how to prepare to take tests so they will become more effective test takers.

FOCUS

Lesson Overview
Objective: To become familiar with test-taking strategies
Skills: making a schedule; budgeting test time
Critical Thinking: establishing and evaluating test-taking criteria; decision making; recalling
Speaking and Listening: discussing; note taking

🔔 **Bellringer**
When students enter the classroom, have this assignment on the board: *List the steps you take to prepare for a test.*

TEACH

L2 Guided Practice

Understanding Directions
Explain to students that they should read test directions carefully, especially when a test contains more than one set of directions. Encourage them to ask for help with any directions they do not understand. Provide sample test directions for pairs of students to read. Have students check their understanding of the directions by asking them to explain the directions to each other. Then ask each pair to write a test item with directions, using information in one of their textbooks. Have a pair of students exchange their test item with another pair and discuss whether each other's directions are clear.

679

PRACTICE AND ASSESS

Answers: Exercise 1
1. b
2. c
3. a

Independent Practice

Skills Practice

📁 *Standardized Test Practice*
📁 *Thinking and Study Skills,*
pp. 41–42

CLOSE

Ask students to discuss which of the strategies presented in this lesson they feel will be most helpful to them the next time they take a test and why. Have each student develop their own chart of these strategies, writing them in a notebook or on an index card for quick reference.

Tips for Budgeting Time During a Test

1. Read the directions carefully. Be sure you understand them before you begin the test.

2. Begin with the section of the test that will take the least amount of time.

3. Answer easier items first. Skip the ones you can't answer.

4. Return to the more difficult items when you have answered everything else.

5. Use any time left over to check your answers. Check the numbers to be sure you didn't write an answer in the wrong place.

Exercise 1

Practice using the test-taking skills you have learned in this lesson. Write the letter of the response that best answers these questions.

1. Which of these strategies is a good way to prepare for a test?
   a. Save all studying until the night before you take the test.
   b. Allow plenty of time to review the material.
   c. Sleep with your book under your pillow.
   d. none of the above
2. Which items should you answer first on a test?
   a. the last ones
   b. the first ones
   c. the easy ones
   d. the difficult ones
3. Which of these is *not* a good test-taking strategy?
   a. Skip the items you know.
   b. Read the directions carefully.
   c. Begin with a section that won't take much time.
   d. Check your answers.

680 *Taking Tests*

Enabling Strategies

LEP **Time-budgeting Tips**

Discuss with students the tips presented in the chart. Discuss why it is best to answer the easy items first. Ask students what might happen if they try to answer all the items in a test in the order in which they are listed.

25.2 Classroom Tests

You have just found out that your upcoming exam in science will include true-false, multiple-choice, matching, fill-in, short-answer, and essay questions. Don't panic. Learning a few simple strategies for answering these types of questions can help you deal with them.

True-False Items

True-false items can be tricky. A single item may include both true and untrue information. You must read the whole statement carefully before answering. If *any* part of the statement is not true, the answer to the item should be *false*. Look at the statement below.

> California has more people and more land than any other state in the United States.

California does have more people than any other state. However, Alaska is the largest state in area. The statement is false.

Multiple-Choice Items

Multiple-choice items include either an incomplete sentence or a question, and three or four responses. You need to pick the response that best completes the sentence or answers the question. Read the tips below for answering multiple-choice items. Then answer the question that follows.

- Read each item carefully to know what information you are looking for.
- Read all responses before answering. Sometimes an answer may seem correct, but a response that follows it may be better.
- If permitted, cross out answers you know are incorrect.
- Be careful about choosing responses that contain absolute words, such as *always*, *never*, *all*, or *none*. Since most statements have exceptions, absolute statements are often incorrect.

25.2 Classroom Tests **681**

Setting the Purpose

Lesson 25.2 teaches students classroom test-taking strategies to help them become more effective test takers.

FOCUS

Lesson Overview

Objective: To become familiar with different classroom test formats
Skills: identifying test item clues; applying self-tests; budgeting time
Critical Thinking: analyzing; recalling; relating; making inferences; identifying a main idea
Speaking and Listening: note taking; discussing

Bellringer

When students enter the classroom, have this assignment on the board: *What kinds of tests do you do best on—multiple-choice, true-false, matching, fill-in, short-answer, or essay? What kinds do you do worst on?*

Motivating Activity

Explain to students that true-false, multiple-choice, matching, short-answer, and fill-in test items are considered objective because there is one correct answer to each question. Have students offer three advantages of objective tests.

Teacher's Classroom Resources

For Lesson 25.2, the following resources can be used for planning, instruction, practice, or reinforcement.

Teaching Tools
Lesson Plans

Blackline Masters
Standardized Test Practice
Thinking and Study Skills,
pp. 41–42

TEACH

Guided Practice

L2 Creating Multiple-Choice Questions

Ask students what they know about Sandra Day O'Connor, Shirley Chisholm, and Barbara Jordan. Does anyone know what "firsts" these women are famous for? (O'Connor is the first woman to become a justice of the U.S. Supreme Court; Chisholm was the first African American woman elected to the U.S. Congress; Jordan was the first African American woman to represent a Southern state in the U.S. Congress.) Ask students to write a multiple-choice question for each of these women similar to the question at the top of page 682.

L3 Creating Matching Items

Using the test item at the bottom of the page as a guide, challenge students to create a matching item using other historical events or documents. When they have finished, they can exchange papers and complete each other's items.

All these women were first in some way. Geraldine Ferraro was the first woman nominated for vice president by a major party.

Who was the first woman nominated by a major political party to be vice president of the United States?

a. Sandra Day O'Connor

b. Shirley Chisholm

c. Geraldine Ferraro

d. Barbara Jordan

Matching Items

To complete a matching item, you must match items found in one group to items in another. For example, you might have to match terms with their definitions, cities with countries, or causes with their effects. A good way to tackle these types of questions is to compare the groups. Do they contain the same number of items? Will every item be used only once? Complete easier items first. If you are allowed to write on your test copy, cross out each item after you use it. When you get to the harder items, you will have fewer choices left.

Read the following example. Match the events or documents in the first column with the dates in the second. Use each date only once.

The number of items in each column is not the same. One item in column 2 will not be used.

The answers to the matching items are: 1. c; 2. a; 3. d; 4. e

___ 1. U.S. Civil War begins	a. 1950
___ 2. Korean War begins	b. 1945
___ 3. U.S. Constitution	c. 1861
___ 4. Emancipation Proclamation	d. 1789
	e. 1863

682 *Taking Tests*

Enabling Strategies

LEP Using a Tape Recorder

You may wish to record passages and test items with a cassette recorder so students can listen to the tape as they follow along with the written text. This approach helps students who comprehend oral language better than written language. They can practice their test-taking strategies while also learning to recognize the written forms of familiar words.

Fill-in Items

To complete a fill-in item, you need to fill in a blank or blanks in a sentence. Your answer must make the sentence true and must be grammatically correct. Rereading the sentence with your answer included will help you determine whether you have made the correct choice. Look at the fill-in question below.

> 1. A cold–blooded vertebrate that has gills early in life and then develops lungs later in life is an _____.
>
> 2. The three states in which matter exists are _____, _____, and _____.

The blank is preceded by the word an, so the answer must be singular and begin with a vowel. The answer is amphibian.

Note that three responses are called for and that their order is not important. The correct answers are solid, liquid, and gas.

Short-Answer Items

In responding to short-answer items, you must provide specific information. Your answer should be clear and easy to understand. The best way to write it is in complete sentences. For example, look at the question and answer below.

> Why are the first ten amendments to the United States Constitution known as the Bill of Rights?

The question asks for an explanation. In your answer you must tell why the amendments are called the Bill of Rights.

> The first ten amendments are called the Bill of Rights because they preserve and protect specific rights of the people.

Note that the answer is written in a complete sentence.

*25.2   Classroom Tests   **683***

TEACH

Guided Practice

L3 Writing Fill-in and Short-Answer Test Items

Write this limerick on the board:

*An epicure dining at Crewe
Once found a large mouse in his stew.
   Said the waiter, "Don't shout
   And wave it about,
Or the rest will be wanting one, too!"*

Have students help you fill in short-answer items about the limerick. Samples: *Another word for epicure is _____. Why did the waiter want the epicure to be quiet about the mouse?* Have students discuss what those test items showed about their understanding of the limerick. Then, have students find another limerick, copy it, and write at least one fill-in and one short-answer item about it. Allow time to share the limericks and test items.

Cooperative Learning

Writing a Test

Divide students into small groups. From a lesson in another unit, prepare a brief test that includes examples of each type of test discussed to this point. Ask students to reread the earlier lesson. As you write each test item on the board, students in each group will consult with one another to choose the correct answer. Call on a volunteer from one group to answer. If an incorrect answer is given, call on a member of another group. When the correct answer is given, ask the class why it's correct.

PRACTICE AND ASSESS

Answers: Exercise 2

1. False
2. d
3. bark
4. 1. c; 2. d; 3. a
5. Sample: It is important to use recycled paper because doing so saves trees.

Independent Practice

Skills Practice

📂 *Standardized Test Practice*
📂 *Thinking and Study Skills,*
pp. 41–42

CLOSE

Have students discuss how they will be able to apply the test-taking strategies discussed in this lesson in other classes.

684

Essay Questions

Essay questions usually require an answer that is at least one paragraph long. To answer an essay question, take time to think about your main idea and the details that will support it. Also allow yourself time to write and revise your answer.

Exercise 2

Read the passage below. Use the test-taking strategies you have learned to answer the questions that follow.

Most of the paper we use today comes from trees. After the bark has been removed, the wood is ground up and mixed with water. This mixture is called wood pulp. The wet pulp is pressed into layers by machines, which dry the pulp on a series of screens and large rollers. The dried paper is then wound onto rolls.

Different types of paper are made from a variety of materials that are mixed with the pulp. These include wax, plastic, rags, and wastepaper. Making wastepaper into usable paper products is called recycling. Recycling is an important way to save trees.

1. Is the following statement true or false?
   Paper comes from paper plants.
2. Which of the following is not normally used in the making of paper?
   a. wax   **b.** plastic   **c.** wood pulp   **d.** bark
3. Fill in the correct response: Before paper is made, the
   _____ of a tree must be removed.
4. Correctly match the items in the first column with those in the second.
   1. wood pulp   **a.** added to wood pulp
   2. screens   **b.** saves trees
   3. wax, plastic, rags **c.** ground wood plus water
                         d. what the pulp is dried on
5. What is an important reason why you should use recycled paper?

Enabling Strategies

LEP Making Essay Questions Easier

Students who find it hard to write in English may be intimidated by essay questions. Encourage them to ask questions if they do not understand an essay question. Tell them that before they write their essay answer, they should jot down the information that they will need to include in it. In some cases, you may wish to allow these students to answer essay questions orally.

25.3 Standardized Tests

Standardized tests, such as the Iowa Test of Basic Skills and the California Test of Basic Skills, are given to groups of students around the country. Knowing what kinds of questions might be on the tests can help you relax and concentrate on doing well.

Reading Comprehension

Reading-comprehension items measure how well you understand what you read. Each reading-comprehension section includes a written passage and questions about the passage. Some questions will ask you to identify the main idea. Others will ask you to draw conclusions from information in the passage. Practice your skills by reading the passage below and answering the questions.

If you have ever been to a sushi bar, you have had an experience that is new to most Americans. Sushi is a Japanese delicacy created from raw fish, seasoned rice, pickles, seaweed, and horseradish. At a sushi bar customers sit at long counters and watch expert chefs prepare sushi by hand. The chefs shape some pieces one at a time. They slice other pieces from a long roll of rice, fish, and seaweed.

1. What is the best title for this paragraph?
   a. Japanese Traditions
   b. What Is a Sushi Bar?
   c. Raw Fish Is Good for You
   d. Japanese Cooking

2. What is sushi made of?
   a. horseradish
   b. raw fish and rice
   c. seaweed and pickles
   d. all of the above

The paragraph focuses on describing a sushi bar. The best title is b.

If you reread the paragraph's second sentence carefully, you will see that d is the correct choice.

25.3   Standardized Tests   **685**

Setting the Purpose

Lesson 25.3 teaches students about standardized tests.

FOCUS

Lesson Overview

Objective: To become familiar with standardized tests
Skills: categorizing and understanding different types of questions/examples found in standardized tests
Critical Thinking: analyzing; recalling; evaluating; making decisions
Speaking and Listening: discussing

Bellringer

When students enter the classroom, have this assignment on the board: *List three things you might do to help yourself perform well on a standardized test.*

Motivating Activity

Ask students to recall the experience of taking a standardized test. Did they enjoy themselves, or did they worry about how they would do? Have students brainstorm a list of tips for those who have never taken a standardized test. The list should include things they would recommend doing prior to, during, and after testing.

Teacher's Classroom Resources

For Lesson 25.3, the following resources can be used for planning, instruction, practice, assessment, reinforcement, or evaluation.

Teaching Tools
Lesson Plans, p. 126

Blackline Masters
Standardized Test Practice
Thinking and Study Skills,
pp. 41–42

Unit Assessment

Tests with Answer Key
Unit 25 Mastery Test,
pp. 99–100

Test Generator
Unit 25 Mastery Test

You may wish to administer the Unit 25 Mastery Test at this point.

685

TEACH

Guided Practice

L2 **Discussing Vocabulary Items on Standardized Tests**

List on the chalkboard several challenging vocabulary words, such as *stalagmite, frenetic, cursory,* and *monotone.* Work with students to create vocabulary items similar to the ones shown in the sample test on page 686 for each word. Write the items on the board. Call on volunteers to answer each item and to explain how they figured out the correct answer. For example, students may have used context clues from the sentence, or they may have used their knowledge of prefixes, suffixes, and roots to choose the correct meaning.

Cross-reference: Vocabulary

For more information on context clues, refer students to Lesson 23.2, pp. 633–634.

Cross-reference: Vocabulary

For more information on prefixes and suffixes, refer students to Lesson 23.3, pp. 636–639.

Vocabulary

Vocabulary items are usually multiple-choice. Some items ask you to choose the correct meaning of a word used in a sentence. Others may ask you to choose the word that best completes a sentence or a definition. If you are unfamiliar with the word, look for context clues to help you with the meaning. Also, look for prefixes, suffixes, and roots that may be familiar. For example, you may not know what the word *dentifrice* means. If you recognize the root *dent,* you might guess that it is related to *denture* and *dentist.* If you were asked to choose among *boardwalk, can opener, toothpaste,* or *sherbet,* which definition would you choose?

Now try these sample test questions.

The correct answer would be toothpaste.

Context clues can help you guess the meaning of ambivalent. *Jeremy can't decide between two things. The answer is* c.

Note that Mae Ling wants her brother to make sense. Rational *probably means "sensible." Choice* a *is correct.*

The word biplane *contains two parts: the prefix* bi-, *meaning "two," and the root word. Choice* b *makes the most sense.*

Choose the letter of the correct definition of or the synonym for each underlined word.

1. Jeremy could not make up his mind whether to go to the circus or to the baseball game. He was <u>ambivalent.</u>

   a. carefree
   b. feeling angry
   c. having two conflicting wishes
   d. having no energy

2. "Please be <u>rational</u>!" insisted Mae Ling. It annoyed her when her brother made no sense at all.

   a. sensible b. confused c. eager d. polite

3. Samuel planned to perform tricks with his <u>biplane</u> in the county fair competition.

   a. a plane with three sets of wings
   b. a plane with two sets of wings
   c. a glider
   d. a car with two sets of wheels

686 *Taking Tests*

Enabling Strategies

LEP **Preparing for a Standardized Vocabulary Test**

For students concerned about their ability to perform well on standardized vocabulary tests, point out that the best way to prepare for these tests is to work constantly on expanding their vocabularies. Encourage students always to be on the lookout for new words and to use a variety of strategies to figure out their meanings. Suggest that jotting down unfamiliar words in a personal dictionary is a good way to increase one's vocabulary.

Analogies

Analogy items test your understanding of the relationships between things or ideas. On a standardized test you may see an analogy written as *animal : whale :: tool : hammer.* The single colon stands for "is to"; the double colon reads "as." The relationship among the words is that the category *animal* includes the whale, and the category *tool* includes the hammer.

This chart shows some word relationships you might find in analogy tests.

Word Relationships in Analogy Tests		
Type	Definition	Example
Synonyms	Two words have the same general meaning.	vivid : bright :: dark : dim
Antonyms	Two words have opposite meanings.	night : day :: tall : short
Use	Words name a user and something used.	writer : pen :: chef : spoon
Cause and Effect	Words name a cause and its effect.	heat : boil :: cold : freeze
Category	Words name a category and an item in it.	fruit : pear :: flower : rose
Description	Words name an item and a characteristic of it.	baby : young :: sky : blue

Try to complete these sample analogies.

1. violin : orchestra :: clown : ___

   a. saxophone b. juggler c. make-up   d. circus

2. weeping : sadness :: laughter : ___

   a. comedian   b. joy   c. yelling   d. discomfort

Identify the relationship. A violin is a part of an orchestra. A clown is a part of a ___. The correct answer is circus, *or* d.

Although a *may seem like the right choice, it is not a feeling, as is* sadness. *The correct answer is* b.

25.3 Standardized Tests **687**

TEACH

Guided Practice

L1 Answering Analogy Items
Write the following on the board: *violin : orchestra :: clown : _____.* Explain that students can figure out the relationship between the first pair of words in an analogy by putting the words into a sentence: "A violin is part of an orchestra." Ask them to read through the responses in item 1 on page 687 to find the word that correctly completes this sentence: "A clown is part of a _____." You may wish to practice this strategy with students using analogy items other than those listed on this page.

Enrichment and Extension

Writing Analogies

Challenge students to write at least one analogy item for each of the types shown in the chart on page 687. They can then compile their items in a folder and create an answer key. Students who need extra practice in answering analogy items can complete the items in the folder.

TEACH

Guided Practice

L2 **Examining Items on Standardized Grammar Tests**

Ask students to give some examples of similarities between proofreading their own writing, or the writing of a classmate, and completing items on standardized grammar tests. Make sure they understand that in each case they are looking for the types of errors shown in the list on page 688. Which types of errors do individual students consider the easiest to find? Which types seem to be more difficult to detect? Why?

Cross-reference: Usage

For more information on subject-verb agreement, refer students to Lesson 16.1, pp. 516–517.

Grammar, Usage, and Mechanics

Standardized tests measure your understanding of correct grammar, usage, and mechanics by asking you to identify errors. You will be given a sentence with portions underlined and lettered. Or you will be given a sentence with numbered sections. In either case you will be asked to identify the section that contains an error. Most tests include one choice that states the sentence has no errors.

Before you complete the sample questions, study this list of common errors included in standardized grammar tests:

- errors in grammar
- incorrect use of pronouns
- subject-verb agreement
- wrong verb tenses
- misspelled words
- incorrect capitalization
- punctuation mistakes

Now choose the section in each item that contains an error.

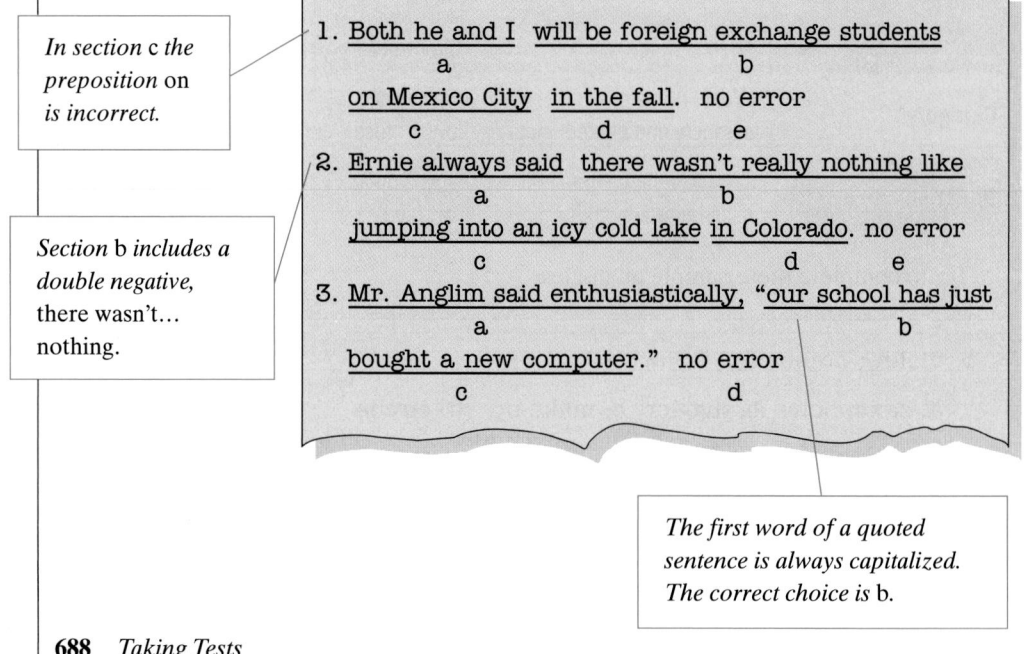

In section c the preposition on *is incorrect.*

1. Both he and I will be foreign exchange students
   a   b
   on Mexico City in the fall. no error
   c   d   e

Section b includes a double negative, there wasn't… nothing.

2. Ernie always said there wasn't really nothing like
   a   b
   jumping into an icy cold lake in Colorado. no error
   c   d   e

3. Mr. Anglim said enthusiastically, "our school has just
   a   b
   bought a new computer." no error
   c   d

The first word of a quoted sentence is always capitalized. The correct choice is b.

688   *Taking Tests*

Speaking and Listening

Listening for Common Errors

Call on volunteers to read aloud each item on the sample test shown on page 688. Tell students to listen for the section in each item that contains an error. Ask if anyone can explain why the section "sounds wrong," and how to correct each error. Point out to students that when practicing answering these test items, reading the sentences aloud sometimes makes it easier to find the errors. Point out that even though they cannot read aloud during a test, practice in listening for errors will help them "listen" to themselves as they read test items silently.

4. Frida Kahlo was a Mexican artist who painted
   <u>a</u>

   beautiful, dreamlike senes of her life. no error
   <u>b</u>   <u>c</u>   <u>d</u>

The word scenes *is misspelled in the third section. Therefore,* c *is the correct choice.*

5. When John Henry was a little baby, he sat on his
   <u>a</u>   <u>b</u>

   father's knee and plays with a hammer. no error
                      <u>c</u>   <u>d</u>

6. We really should ought to thank Grandma for the
   <u>a</u>   <u>b</u>

   presents she sent to us. no error
   <u>c</u>   <u>d</u>

The phrase should ought to *is incorrect.* Either should *or* ought to *could be used, but not both. So* a *is the answer.*

The action in this sentence is taking place in the past. The verb should be played, *not* plays. *Choice* c *is correct.*

Taking a Standardized Test

Standardized tests are different from classroom tests. Instead of writing your answers on the test itself, you will be provided with a separate answer sheet. Since answer sheets are usually graded electronically, you should be careful to avoid stray marks that might be misread.

Some standardized tests do not subtract points for incorrect answers. If this is true for the test you are taking, try to give an answer for every item. You might improve your test score by guessing correctly. But don't just guess wildly. Eliminate options that you know are wrong before making a guess.

If you can't answer a question, don't waste time thinking about it. Go on to the next one. You can come back to the unanswered question later if you have time.

25.3 Standardized Tests **689**

TEACH

Guided Practice

L1 Making Proofreading Manageable

Suggest that students can organize the way they proofread for errors in different ways. Using a short check-list, such as the one on page 688, students can determine the easiest way for them to check for each type of error. Suggest these ways.

- Students can read one sentence at a time and find all the kinds of errors shown before moving on to the next sentence.
- Students can read all the sentences checking for one type of error at a time, and then reread each sentence to check for each kind of error.

Have students discuss the pros and cons of each method, and suggest other methods that may work better for individuals.

Cross-reference: Spelling

For a discussion of spelling rules, refer students to Lesson 23.6, pp. 647–654.

Enrichment and Extension

Taking a Standardized Test

Share with students a blank answer sheet from a standardized test (or a facsimile from a book about standardized testing). Ask, *Why is it important to erase any stray marks from your answer sheet?* (They may be counted as answers by the machine doing the grading.) What can happen if you skip an item? (You may forget to skip that number on the answer sheet.) Why should you always find out if you will be penalized for incorrect answers? (It's better to leave those questions unanswered than to guess at them.)

PRACTICE AND ASSESS

Answers: Exercise 3

1. a		**4.** b
2. a		**5.** c
3. a		

Independent Practice

Skills Practice

📁 *Standardized Test Practice*
📁 *Thinking and Study Skills,*
pp. 41–42

CLOSE

Have students work in pairs. Partners can review together the sample test items presented in this lesson and the test-taking strategies suggested for the various items.

Exercise 3

Reading-Comprehension Items   Read the passage below and answer the questions that follow it.

> Medical Research Secretary. Two years' experience in related field required. Must type 50 words per minute. Please send resumé and salary requirements to Tulane University.

1. Where would you most likely find the above paragraph?
   a. the help-wanted page of a newspaper
   b. a teen diary
   c. a science textbook
   d. the front page of a newspaper

2. What experience would be most acceptable?
   a. a typist in a bank
   b. a chemist at a laboratory
   c. a cashier at a supermarket
   d. all of the above

Vocabulary Item   Find the best synonym for the underlined word.

3. We have to make a <u>unified</u> effort, or we will never win the election.
   a. shared   b. difficult   c. untried   d. mighty

Analogy Item   Complete the analogy.

4. flock : geese :: _____ : wolves
   a. herd   b. pack   c. collection   d. sheep

Grammar, Usage, and Mechanics Item   Identify the section that contains an error.

5. <u>The entire side of the mountain</u> <u>exploded into the</u>
             a   b
   <u>air when Mt. St. Helens was erupted.</u> no error
                  c   d

Technology Tip

⊙ Using the Test Generator

An accompanying Test Generator is available to teachers. The floppy disk—for either IBM, Apple, or Macintosh—contains a file of individual test items for you to choose from. Any or all of these items can be printed out and duplicated for students to use in practicing the test-taking strategies covered in this unit. If students have access to a computer, you may wish to allow them to practice their test-taking skills directly on screen.

Listening and Speaking

26.1 Effective Listening

Understanding what you hear begins with good listening skills. It's often hard to listen when people are talking and moving around or when other noises attract your attention. But you can learn how to tune out distractions and tune in to what is being said. You can improve your listening skills and increase your ability to understand.

Listening in Class

What happens when you don't understand how to do your homework assignment? It's difficult to do a good job when you don't understand what's expected of you. Learning how to listen better will make tasks that depend on understanding directions much simpler. The following tips will help you improve your listening skills to better understand what you hear.

Tips for Effective Listening

1. First, determine the type of information you are hearing. Are you listening to a story, or is someone giving you directions? Knowing what you are listening for makes understanding easier.

2. Take notes. Identify the main ideas as you hear them, and write them in your own words.

3. Take a note if you hear a statement that tells when you will need the information you are listening to.

4. If you don't understand something, ask a question. Asking questions right away helps avoid confusion later on.

5. Review your notes as soon as possible after the listening experience. Reviewing them soon afterward will allow you to fill in any gaps in your notes.

26.1 Effective Listening **691**

Teacher's Classroom Resources

For Lesson 26.1, the following resources can be used for planning, instruction, practice, assessment, reinforcement, or evaluation.

Teaching Tools
Lesson Plans, p. 127

Blackline Masters
Speaking and Listening Activities, pp. 6–8
Thinking and Study Skills, p. 33

Unit Assessment
Tests with Answer Key
Unit 26 Pretest, pp. 101–102

Test Generator
Unit 26 Pretest

You may wish to administer the Unit 26 Pretest at this point.

Setting the Purpose

Lesson 26.1 teaches students to listen to spoken presentations with an active mind and ask questions to evaluate information.

FOCUS

Lesson Overview

Objective: To develop the ability, when listening to a presentation, to identify important information and information that is incomplete or biased

Skills: listening in class; listening to persuasive speech; listening to radio and television news

Critical Thinking: classifying; recalling; analyzing; evaluating; establishing and evaluating criteria

Speaking and Listening: discussing; note taking; listening to persuasive speech; evaluating; questioning

Bellringer

When students enter the classroom, have this assignment on the board: *What kinds of things do you think about as you listen to a presentation in class or on television?*

Motivating Activity

Ask students to share what they think about when listening to a presentation. How many students mentioned more than simply taking in information? Discuss the challenges of thinking and listening at the same time. How much thinking can one do without missing parts of a presentation? Explain that this lesson will suggest effective listening skills.

TEACH

Guided Practice

L1 Listening Critically
Ask students to list situations in which persuasive speaking is used. Can they explain why it is important to listen critically to persuasive speeches? Point out that listening critically involves questioning. Go over the questions in the chart on this page. Have students recall political speeches that they have heard or read—or have them bring in campaign materials to analyze. Help them formulate questions to identify faulty thinking.

L3 Using Emotional Appeals
Encourage students to consider why emotional appeals work and to what extent they should be used in a persuasive speech. Do students think such appeals are always manipulative, or do they think there is an appropriate use for them?

⇄ Cross-reference: Writing
For more information on analyzing, refer students to Lesson 6.3, Evaluating Evidence, pp. 268–271.

Listening to Persuasive Speech

What type of argument most easily persuades you? Is it one that includes facts and logical conclusions or one that appeals to your emotions? Speakers who want to persuade you may concentrate on emotional appeals. They may even use faulty thinking to persuade you to accept their opinions.

Faulty Thinking   Faulty thinking may be intentional or unintentional. That is, the speaker may be trying to deceive you or simply may not be thinking clearly. It's up to you, the listener, to analyze the speaker's statements and arguments. Are they well thought out, or are they flawed? Following are some examples of statements you might hear from a political candidate. However, you can find examples of faulty thinking in other kinds of persuasive speeches as well.

Questioning What You Hear	
Statements	**Questions**
Every child in America will have food on the table if I'm elected.	This is a broad statement. Do you think any one candidate can keep such a promise?
Don't vote for my opponent. His brother was investigated by the IRS two years ago.	What was the nature of the investigation? What were its results? Should a candidate be judged by someone else's activities?
I have the support of the great governor of our state in my campaign for senator.	Does the support of the governor prove a person is qualified to be senator? Is the governor a political ally of the candidate?
Voters in three states claim health care is important. I listen to America.	Might voters in some other states have different needs?

Speaker's Bias   Speakers may try to persuade audiences to agree with them by presenting only one side of an issue. Such speeches are biased, or slanted, in favor of one opinion. Always listen with a questioning attitude. Ask yourself if the speaker is dealing with all sides of the issue. Maybe the speaker is giving only the facts that support one opinion.

692   *Listening and Speaking*

Enabling Strategies

LEP Recognizing a Speaker's Bias
Students who are not proficient in English may not easily recognize words that indicate a speaker's bias. The class might work together to compile a list of words and phrases that often accompany a person's opinion, such as *I think that, I feel that,* and exaggerations such as *always* and *never*. Make sure each suggestion is explained and elaborated upon when necessary.

Be alert for speeches that show bias, such as the first example below. The other example is more objective. As you read, notice the facts each speaker uses.

BIASED SPEAKER: You should vote in favor of the proposed tax increase on gasoline. This tax will give the government enough revenue to rebuild the nation's crumbling highway system. It will provide many thousands of new jobs in the construction industry. It also will help us reduce the national debt. Our country needs this tax increase.

UNBIASED SPEAKER: This tax increase has faults as well as benefits. True, it will help rebuild highways and provide more jobs in highway construction. But it will also place a burden on those who must drive to make a living. The added cost of gas may drive many independent truckers and drivers out of work. People who take buses may find themselves paying higher fares.

The biased speaker gives only arguments in favor of the tax increase. The unbiased speaker admits that the arguments of the biased speaker are valid. However, this speaker points out that the increase will also have some negative effects.

Listening to Radio and Television News

Do you ask questions when you listen to the news? You might be surprised at how much there is to question. It's important to sort out facts from opinions in print, radio, and television news coverage. Doing so will help you evaluate the news coverage for truthfulness and accuracy. It will help you form your own unbiased opinion about what's being said.

Journalists are supposed to be objective. This means that they should not let their own opinions affect what they report and how they report it. This is sometimes a difficult thing to do. For example, a news commentator may call someone an "influential senator." Is the senator really influential, or is the commentator only expressing an opinion? The answer will help you evaluate anything the senator says. It will also help you evaluate what the commentator says about the senator.

26.1   Effective Listening   **693**

TEACH

Guided Practice

L1 Distinguishing Fact from Opinion
Some students may have trouble differentiating between facts and opinions. Explain that facts are pieces of information that can be proven. ("He was convicted of fraud.") Opinions are value judgments. ("It was an unfair trial.") Point out that even facts can be misleading if they are taken out of context or if they represent only a part of the truth. Encourage students to look through newspapers to practice identifying facts and opinions in articles.

L3 Showing Both Sides
Discuss the tendency for people to avoid or hide any opposing arguments when giving a persuasive speech. Point out that although the speaker may feel safer doing this, listeners are left wondering what to think about the other side's arguments. An effective persuasive speaker will present both sides of the argument, telling exactly how the audience should respond to the opposition's arguments.

Civic Literacy

Identifying Biased Statements
Challenge students to begin a class collection of newspaper and magazine clippings, as well as quotes they have written down, of biased statements. They might attach captions that address the following:

- What questions do the statements leave unanswered?
- What effects could the biased statements have on the intended audience?

TEACH

Guided Practice

L2 Evaluating a News Broadcast

Ask students to listen to and evaluate a brief report on a television or radio news broadcast. Students should listen for the following: completeness (Does it answer *what? who? when? where? how?* and *why?*), sources (Does the journalist provide sources for information?), and objectiveness (Does the journalist interject his or her opinions and biases into the report?). Tell students to take notes as they listen and to present their evaluations in small groups.

L1 Analyzing News Broadcasts

If students need help analyzing news broadcasts, help them create a chart in which they can keep track of who, what, when, where, how and why. Create a second chart or two columns to keep track of opinions and facts. Students may wish to first practice this by analyzing written news reports.

L3 Researching Faulty Thinking

Students may enjoy researching specific kinds of faulty thinking, such as circular reasoning and overgeneralization. Invite volunteers to give brief persuasive speeches in which they demonstrate different types of faulty thinking. Ask them to lead a class discussion to discover individual reactions to various kinds of faulty reasoning.

⬳ Cross-reference: Writing

For more information on what a news article should cover, refer students to Lesson 4.6, Writing a News Story, pp. 168–171.

Journalists are taught to provide sources for their information. Often it's important to know where the information in a news item came from. For example, suppose you heard the following two items on a newscast. Which would you be more likely to believe?

- Certain unnamed sources reported today that the President would not seek a second term of office.
- The President's chief of staff announced this afternoon that the President plans to seek a second term.

Journalists also try to present information that is complete. In their reports they usually try to answer the questions *what, who, when, where, how,* and *why.* If you carefully read or listen to almost any news story, you will see that it answers questions such as these:

- *What* happened?
- *Who* was involved?
- *When* did it happen?
- *Where* did it happen?
- *How* did it happen?
- *Why* did it happen? (or *Why* is it important?)

The questions may not always follow the above order, but they will all be answered. They'll usually be answered in the first paragraph of a newspaper story or the first minute or so of a radio or television newscast.

When you listen to a news broadcast, you can evaluate the quality of the reporting. Ask yourself some questions, such as the following:

- Was the report complete?
- Is all the information provable, or are some statements only opinions?
- Is any of the report based on faulty thinking?
- If an opinion is expressed, does the reporter tell whose opinion it is?
- Did the reporter identify the sources of the information?

Following are some other examples of how asking questions will help you evaluate a news broadcast.

694 *Listening and Speaking*

Speaking and Listening

Analyzing Media for Bias

Videotape a segment of a news analysis television program, such as *Nightline* or *60 Minutes.* Play the tape for students, and discuss aspects that have been covered in class. Ask students to:
- identify possible biases of speakers
- distinguish between the facts and opinions presented
- identify whether the report tells what, who, when, where, how, and why
- identify whether the speakers provide sources for their facts

Encourage students to ask each other questions as they discuss their perceptions.

Evaluating News Statements

Sample Statements	Questions to Ask
The candidate has a liberal voting record on defense spending.	What is a liberal voting record? Who defines *liberal?* Does the candidate's record match the definition?
A reliable source stated that the company has been dumping toxic waste into the river.	Who is the source? How reliable is he or she? Did the source actually see the dumping?
One eyewitness stated that the defendant fired three shots.	Who is this witness? Where was the witness at the time? Does the witness know the defendant?
An expert claims we are in a recession.	Who is the expert? In what field is he or she an expert? Was any proof provided? Do other experts agree?
The tobacco company denies any proven relationship between smoking and illness.	Doesn't the company have an interest in denying the relationship? On what facts does the company base its statement?
Last winter's frost is driving the price of fruit upward.	Is there a proven relationship between the frost and rising fruit costs? Are there other possible reasons for the rising costs?

Exercise 1

Divide into small groups. Each group will form a news broadcast team. Select one person to be the news anchor. Other members of the group can be reporters on special assignments.

Decide which current events in your school or neighborhood to cover. Assign a story to each person. Students should research their stories and write short reports to deliver during a news broadcast of no more than ten minutes. Rehearse your newscast within the group, then present it to the class. Other members of the class should evaluate each broadcast.

26.1   Effective Listening   **695**

PRACTICE AND ASSESS

Evaluation Guidelines: Exercise 1

Broadcasts should be evaluated for the following criteria:
- The news anchor and reporters should speak clearly.
- News reports should tell what, who, where, when, how, and why.
- Reporters should cite sources for their information.
- Facts and opinions should be differentiated.
- Reports should be objective and unbiased; all sides of an issue should be presented.

Independent Practice

Skills Practice
📁 *Thinking and Study Skills*, p. 33
📁 *Speaking and Listening Activities*, pp. 6–8

CLOSE

Revisit the discussion from the beginning of this lesson. Ask, *What kinds of things might go through your mind now when you listen to a presentation in class or on television?*

Cooperative Learning

Writing a News Statement
Arrange students in groups of four or five. Tell each group to brainstorm a news statement, such as those in the chart on this page, to share with the class. Groups should write statements that are precise and leave no questions unanswered. After each group presents their news statement to the class, ask students to assess whether any questions need to be answered to make the statement more straightforward and clear.

FOCUS

Lesson Overview

Objective: To develop effective interviewing skills

Skills: formulating questions; summarizing a topic

Critical Thinking: summarizing; defining and clarifying; generating new information

Speaking and Listening: discussing; interviewing; note taking

Bellringer

When students enter the classroom, have this activity on the board: *List topics you would like to know more about. Write down whom you could interview in order to get information about one of the topics on your list.*

Motivating Activity

Talk over students' responses to the Bellringer activity and write them on the board. Then discuss the different kinds of interviews: telephone, letter, and in-person. Ask students which type of interview they would conduct to gather information on the topics listed. What are the advantages and disadvantages of each type of interview?

26.2 Interviewing Skills

If you wanted answers to three or four questions on the topic of fly fishing, what would be an efficient way to get them? Would you read about the topic in an encyclopedia or interview a neighbor who is a fly fisher? In an encyclopedia you'd have to sift through much information to get to the facts you want. In an interview your questions could be answered directly as you asked them. An interview with an expert can often provide you with exactly the right amount of information on exactly the right topic.

Whom to Interview

Who is an expert? An expert usually is someone who has very precise, in-depth, and up-to-date information. More importantly, the expert probably has first-hand knowledge about a topic. Look at the topics and the list of people in the chart. People like these might have interesting information you could use in an oral report.

People to Interview	
Topic	**Source**
Local government	mayor, city council member, governor, state legislator
Scuba diving	local diving expert or instructor, equipment shop owner
Automobile engines	auto mechanic, auto designer, school shop teacher
The circulatory system	doctor, nurse, medical student, science teacher
Portrait photography	fashion photographer, portrait studio photographer
Caring for infants	parent, day-care worker, nurse, pediatrician

When you have determined that interviewing an expert will add to your report, you must decide on the kind of interview you want to set up. If the person lives far from you, you might arrange a telephone or letter interview. If the subject is nearby, consider an in-person interview. Whichever form you choose, be sure to keep the following things in mind during the early contacts with your subject.

Teacher's Classroom Resources

For Lesson 26.2, the following resources can be used for planning, instruction, practice, or reinforcement.

Teaching Tools
Lesson Plans

Blackline Masters
Speaking and Listening Activities, pp. 12–13
Thinking and Study Skills, p. 33

Setting Up the Interview

1. Make sure you clearly state who you are and why you are seeking the interview.

2. Tell the person if you have a deadline, but respect the fact that your interviewee may be very busy.

3. Ask the subject to suggest times for an interview.

4. Give the person the option of an in-person, written, or telephone interview. You can state your preference, but leave the decision to the subject of the interview.

Preparing to Interview

Before you meet with your subject, research your topic thoroughly. Try to learn all you can about the topic before the interview. This preparation will help you to think on your feet during the questioning. You will be able to ask more intelligent questions if you are familiar with the topic. You also will be able to take advantage of interesting information that your subject might reveal. If you know how a new fact fits into the whole picture, you'll be better able to use it or to discard it as irrelevant.

Also try to learn as much as you can about the person you will interview. If the person is a public figure or is in business, you might ask his or her secretary for biographical information. Or you might request it from the person before the interview. You should know about the person to whom you are talking. This information will help you formulate good questions. It also saves you the trouble of asking questions that can be answered in a biographical handout.

Before you conduct the interview, write out the questions you plan to ask. It helps if you have the general outline of the interview in your mind as well as on paper. Try to make your questions open-ended. Don't ask questions that have a yes or no answer. Instead, encourage your subject to talk freely. A *Why?* may bring out important and interesting information. Look at these questions you might ask a marathon runner:

26.2   Interviewing Skills   **697**

TEACH

Guided Practice

L2 Planning the Interview
Arrange students in groups for a cooperative activity. Invite each group to choose a topic to research. Have group members think of a specific expert they might interview and write out a list of interview questions. Let each group report to the class its topic, interviewee, and questions. Encourage the rest of the class to comment on the questions and to suggest additional ones that could be asked in the interview.

L3 Formulating Questions
Explain that open-ended questions allow for in-depth and sometimes colorful answers. Ask a volunteer to explain why an interviewer should avoid asking questions that can be answered with *yes* or *no.* If students were interviewing the people included on the chart on the previous page, what questions could become conversational dead ends? What open-ended questions could they ask instead?

Enabling Strategies

LEP Interviewing by Letter
Some students may be hesitant to conduct an interview for fear of faltering, because of limited English proficiency, while asking questions and trying to understand answers. Suggest that they try a letter interview. A letter interview will allow them time to double-check the wording of their questions and remove the problem of having to ad-lib in English. Tell them that well-thought-out and clearly stated questions will result in useful, easily understood answers.

TEACH

Guided Practice

L3 Preparing to Conduct an Interview

Some students may be ready to conduct a telephone or in-person interview. They can select a topic, research it, pinpoint an expert, and write interview questions. You may wish to look over their questions before they conduct their interviews. Invite students to share with the class the information and experience they gained.

Cross-reference: Writing

For more information on researching a topic, refer students to Lesson 5.7, pp. 220–222.

1. How many marathons have you run? Where did you place?
2. How do you prepare for a marathon?
3. What is your weekly running schedule?
4. What types of terrain do you run on when you are in training?
5. What kind of special equipment do you wear?
6. What kind of diet do you eat?
7. What are the three most important aspects of your training?

Conducting the Interview

Your manner during an interview should be serious and respectful, but relaxed. You will put the person you are interviewing at ease if you appear comfortable and confident. This attitude will make the interview flow smoothly. It's much more pleasant to talk in a relaxed atmosphere.

Study the journalist's questions covered in the last lesson. Remember how you used them to evaluate how well a reporter covered a story? See how many *what, who, when, where, how,* and *why* questions you can use in your interview. You'll find that *how* and *why* questions are particularly good for probing deeply into a topic.

Sometimes a person being interviewed will get side-tracked onto something that really doesn't apply to your topic. In this case, it's your job to politely but firmly lead the discussion back to the topic at hand.

Talk as little as possible yourself. Your job as an interviewer is to ask questions clearly and briefly. Then listen to the response. If the interviewee mentions something interesting that you hadn't thought about, ask some follow-up questions. You might bring out an unexpected piece of information— something that might not have been revealed otherwise. That's when an interview can get exciting.

During the interview you have two jobs to perform. You need to keep track of the questions you've prepared, so you don't forget something important. At the same time, you need to listen carefully to what the person is telling you. Be open to new information you didn't think about and that may raise new questions. You can develop this "thinking on your feet" skill by following some tips.

698 *Listening and Speaking*

Technology Tip

Taping Phone Interviews

A simple and inexpensive telephone recording jack, plugged into a cassette recorder, makes it possible to record phone interviews so that time isn't wasted writing and transcribing extensive notes.

Tell students to be sure to notify the interviewee that the conversation is being recorded. Explain that some people may not want to be recorded and that their wishes must be honored.

Tips for Interviewing

1. State your topic and the general scope of the discussion you'd like to have. This will give the person you are interviewing an idea of the boundaries that can be expected during the questioning.

2. Look at the person you're interviewing. Nothing cuts the connection between reporter and subject more quickly than the loss of eye contact. If you're conducting a telephone interview, comment briefly after each point the subject makes.

3. Be courteous at all times, even if your subject wanders away from the topic.

4. If you are unclear about anything the person says, ask a question right away. Then you can build on information you understand.

5. Follow up interesting statements quickly by asking another question. Don't wait, or you might forget the importance of the statement.

6. Take notes. At the end of the interview, glance over them. If something is unclear, ask a question.

7. Thank the person for the interview. Ask if you can call back if you have a follow-up question or if something is not clear. Review your notes thoroughly when you are alone. If you need to call the person back, do so as soon as you can.

Exercise 2

Work in pairs, and take turns playing the roles of expert and interviewer. Each interviewer should choose a topic. The interviewer's job is to ask good questions and to lead the expert back gently and politely if he or she wanders from the topic. Use one of the following topics or one of your own choosing:

- Why it's important to do well in mathematics
- How to have a great vacation in your own backyard
- The most important person in your life

26.2 Interviewing Skills **699**

PRACTICE AND ASSESS

Evaluation Guidelines: Exercise 2

Interviewers should
- state their topic at the beginning of the interview
- try to put the interviewee at ease
- ask relevant, open-ended questions
- be courteous
- maintain eye contact
- take brief notes
- immediately follow up interesting statements with more questions
- keep the interview on track, leading the interviewee back to the topic with pertinent questions

Independent Practice

Skills Practice

📁 *Speaking and Listening Activities,* pp. 12–13

📁 *Thinking and Study Skills,* p. 33

CLOSE

Have students discuss the usefulness of good interviewing skills—for school reports, job interviews, video features or profiles; for careers in journalism, radio, and TV; and even in informal contexts, such as conversation with new friends.

Beyond the Classroom

Conducting an Interview

Pair students for an activity in which they will conduct interviews of students, teachers, administrators, and other school staff. Partners will select a topic and think of appropriate questions. During the interview, one partner will be in charge of asking questions as the other takes notes and makes sure that the interview stays on track. Either student may ask impromptu follow-up questions to interesting answers. Partners can report their findings to the class.

FOCUS

Lesson Overview

Objective: To develop informal speaking skills

Skills: differentiating between types of informal speaking situations; following guidelines for presenting information orally; role-playing various informal speaking situations

Critical Thinking: analyzing; comparing and contrasting

Speaking and Listening: speaking informally; making announcements and introductions; explaining a process

Bellringer

When students enter the classroom, have this assignment on the board: *Write a sentence describing how you feel in two of the following situations: talking with a group of friends, giving directions, telling jokes, or talking to someone on the telephone.*

Motivating Activity

Have students share their responses to the Bellringer activity. Then have them brainstorm a list of the types of problems that can arise in ordinary conversations and discussions. Encourage them to look back at this list as they learn about being an effective participant in informal speaking situations.

26.3   Informal Speech

Someone stops you on the street and asks directions to the nearest grocery store. You talk with your friends on the way to school. You respond to a question the teacher asks in class. All of these situations call for informal speech. They are spontaneous and unrehearsed. They are among the most common speech situations.

There are other kinds of informal speech—discussions and announcements, for example. Four types of informal speech are included on the chart below. The chart describes each type and includes some hints that will help you be an effective participant in that type of speaking.

Tips on Informal Speaking

Type	Description	Hint
Conversations	Conversations can occur at almost any time and in almost any place. Each person involved contributes and responds to the others.	Be courteous to the person speaking. Taking turns enables everyone to air his or her thoughts.
Discussions	Discussions can occur in many settings, including classrooms. Usually one person leads the discussion, and all are asked to share their thoughts in an orderly manner.	Stick closely to the topic and follow the directions of the discussion leader. Following these rules will ensure an interesting and productive discussion.
Announcements	Announcements summarize the most important information about an activity or event.	List the information you want to include before you make your announcement. Double-check it for accuracy and completeness.
Demonstrations	Demonstrations explain and show a process—how something works, for example. They are useful in many settings, including classrooms.	Number the steps in the process you will demonstrate to make sure the sequence is clear.

Teacher's Classroom Resources

For Lesson 26.3, the following resources can be used for planning, instruction, practice, or reinforcement.

Teaching Tools
Lesson Plans, p. 128

Blackline Masters
Speaking and Listening Activities, pp. 16–18
Thinking and Study Skills, p. 33

The purpose of all speech should be to communicate clearly. To take part in a discussion, you must be prepared and familiar with the topic the group is going to discuss. For example, to answer a question, you must have the information being asked for. In a conversation, on the other hand, you do not need to prepare in advance. You may cover many topics. Your answer to a question may very well be, "I don't know."

Another factor is attitude. Which of the following words describes how you feel when you talk to friends, family, and teachers?

> shy   enthusiastic   confident   eager   uninterested

Once you've identified your attitude, you can build on your strengths. You can change whatever gets in the way of good communication. It may take practice, but it will benefit you in the end.

Making Introductions

Everyone is a newcomer at one time or another. Entering into a new situation is much easier if someone in the group knows how to make correct introductions. With practice, that someone can be you.

Keep the following points in mind when introducing two people: First, be sure you look at each person. Don't let either party feel left out. You may be introducing one person to a group of people. In this case, make eye contact with the new person and with members of the group. Also, gesture from one person to another as you make the introduction. This will help point out which person you are referring to.

State each person's full name. You might say, "Evan, I'd like to introduce you to Miguel Hernandez. Miguel, this is Evan Schmit." If there are several people in the group, you might mention first names only for people your own age. First and last names are more appropriate when introducing adults. First and last names are also best used when introducing an adult and a younger person.

Tell each person something interesting about the other. If they have something in common, share that. It will become a natural conversation starter.

26.3   Informal Speech   **701**

TEACH

Guided Practice

L2 Introducing Strangers
Ask volunteers to introduce two people to each other in front of the class. Point out the section at the bottom of this page on making introductions. Encourage them to put those tips into practice. Urge volunteers to talk to the two people first to find out any unique information they can include in their introductions.

L3 Recording a Conversation
In order to pinpoint their own speech habits, students can record a conversation with a friend or record themselves talking naturally about a familiar topic. Students can use the tapes to analyze their strengths and weaknesses as informal speakers. Encourage students to take notes as they listen to the tapes.

Enabling Strategies

LEP Rehearsing Making Introductions
Suggest that students with language difficulties prepare to introduce people by writing and rehearsing phrases they will use ahead of time. For example, _____ , I'd like to introduce you to _____ .

_____ is a friend of mine from school. Give students plenty of time to practice the phrases until they feel comfortable using them.

TEACH

Guided Practice

L2 Giving Directions

Have students work together in small groups to prepare and present simple process explanations. Encourage students to think of humorous topics, such as How to Wash a Hippopotamus. Remind students to list any materials they will use and to number the steps of the process in the correct order. After each student's presentation, have groups discuss any suggestions they have for making the presentation better.

Participating in a Discussion

Rules of the game exist for discussions as well. A discussion usually has a leader, whose job it is to guide the discussion and keep it on track. The leader may be appointed for the group or chosen by the group. Sometimes a group member just takes over as leader.

As a discussion becomes lively and members of the discussion group get excited about what they are saying, the discussion becomes more difficult to organize. For this reason, it's important that you help the leader by managing your own comments. Be sure they contribute to the topic.

Discussions can focus on any topic. The idea is to come together in an organized group to share ideas and draw conclusions about the subject. A discussion depends totally on the comments of those involved. Before you enter a discussion, have a thorough knowledge of your subject. That way you can be a valuable participant. The following chart has a few more tips about how to act responsibly in a discussion.

Tips for Taking Part in a Discussion

1. Come prepared. Review important information, and bring visual aids or research you can use to illustrate the points you want to make.

2. Be polite. Take turns speaking and listening. You're there to learn as well as to contribute.

3. Go into the discussion willing to modify your opinion. That's the best way to learn.

4. Let the discussion leader take the lead. Concentrate on your part in the discussion—expressing yourself and listening to others.

5. Make your comments brief and concise. People will pay attention to your ideas if they are well thought out and clearly presented.

6. When you state your opinions, back them up with reasons or examples. You'll be much more convincing if you do this.

7. If a member of the group says something you don't understand, ask about it. It's likely that you aren't the only one confused.

702 *Listening and Speaking*

Connections Across the Curriculum

Social Science

The Gallup organization conducted a poll to discover what people think are the most annoying speaking habits. The habits that people found highly annoying include interrupting (88 percent), swearing (84 percent), talking too softly (80 percent), talking too loudly (73 percent), and using filler words, such as "and um" (69 percent).

Explaining a Process

If you want to explain how to bake a cake, you must do several things. First, you should tell the type of cake the recipe is for. Next, you need to list the ingredients. Then you'll explain the steps to follow.

An explanation of almost any process has the same parts: materials needed, steps to follow, and the result. If the process is long or complicated, you may need to number the steps. Or you might simply use words such as *before, next,* and *finally* to make the sequence of steps clear.

Correct order is all-important. For example, if the steps for building a model airplane are out of sequence, the plane may be incorrectly assembled. To be sure you don't leave out a part of the process, take time to prepare well. Write your explanation in the proper order. Review your instructions to make sure you haven't left out a step or put one in the wrong place.

Making Announcements

When you're asked to make an announcement, think first about what information your listeners need. If you're planning an announcement for an activity, the important facts include the date, the time, the place, and the price of a ticket.

26.3   Informal Speech   **703**

TEACH

Guided Practice

L1 Making a Checklist
Some students may be uncomfortable in any speaking situation. Work with students to make a checklist of things that will help them present themselves in a confident manner. For example, standing or sitting straight and speaking up are ways that students can appear as confident speakers. Encourage students to consult their checklist whenever they are feeling uneasy about speaking before others.

Cross-reference: Writing
For tips on explaining a process, refer students to Lesson 5.4, pp. 208–211.

Technology Tip

Using a Microphone
Many announcements require the use of a microphone. Before using a microphone, students should make sure to turn the microphone on, adjust it to the proper height (chin level), and test it to be sure it is set at the proper volume. A speaker should also stand a few inches away from the microphone.

PRACTICE AND ASSESS

Evaluation Guidelines: Exercise 3

Answers will vary. Announcements should
- be brief
- include all necessary information (who, what, where, when, and so on)
- appeal to the intended audience— the students in the school

Independent Practice

Skills Practice

📂 *Thinking and Study Skills,* p. 33
📂 *Speaking and Listening Activities,* pp. 16–18

CLOSE

Ask students how they would handle the following informal speaking situations:
- making an announcement in front of a noisy, crowded auditorium
- explaining how to build a bookcase to a group of first graders
- conducting a class discussion on a topic that generates a great deal of controversy

---

Next, try to determine the briefest way to deliver your information. Announcements should always be short and to-the-point. They are no-fuss pieces of information. You'll want to include just enough information to interest the audience and convey the important facts.

Below are two examples of how the same information might be conveyed. Which is the better announcement?

Example 1
Tryouts for cheerleaders are coming soon. Get in shape now! Don't miss this once-in-a-school-year opportunity!

Example 2
Tryouts for cheerleaders will be this Wednesday afternoon in the gym right after school. Wear loose clothing and plan to stay a few hours. No need to sign up—just show up Wednesday for this once-in-a-school-year opportunity!

Finally, don't forget your audience! Speak so everyone can understand you. That means you must think about who is listening. You might word an announcement one way for preschoolers and another way for their parents.

Exercise 3

Divide into small groups. Let each member of the group select one of the events listed below. Jot down information about the event, including the date, time, and place. Fold the papers and mix them together. Each group member will select a topic at random, then write a short announcement based on the information on the paper. If you need additional pieces of information, invent them. Read your announcements to the group. Discuss how helpful and effective each announcement is.

- Band tryouts
- Countries of the World Festival
- Square-dancing lessons
- Debate Club meeting

704 *Listening and Speaking*

Speaking and Listening

Taking Time to Respond

Dr. Lillian Glass recommends that people practice the In-Hold-Out technique in conversations. In this technique, you inhale for three seconds, hold your breath for three seconds, and then speak. The time the technique takes shows the speaker that your response is thought out.

26.4 Oral Reports

What image comes to mind when you think about giving an oral report? For some students the image might be exciting; for others, a little scary. However you feel, you can make the experience more enjoyable by preparing well.

You can prepare to give an oral report in three ways. First, you must prepare the content of your report. Make sure you understand everything you will be saying about your topic. Second, you need to prepare your presentation. Practice is the key here. Finally, you need to prepare yourself mentally so that you feel good about your presentation.

Preparing the Report

Think for a few moments about the purpose of your report. Is it to inform, persuade, explain, narrate, or entertain? Perhaps you have more than one purpose. An oral report can inform, persuade, and entertain, but one purpose should be the main one.

Another important consideration is your audience. To whom will you be speaking? Students your own age? Younger people? Older people? A mixed audience? What is the best way to reach your particular audience?

When you've thought about your purpose and audience, think a little further about your topic. Is it sufficiently narrowed down? If not, can you narrow it further? A precisely defined topic is easier to research than one that is unfocused. It is also easier to write about.

Now begin your research. Read articles in newspapers, magazines, encyclopedias, and other sources. You may also want to interview an expert in the field. Take notes. Develop an outline. Check the relationship of your main ideas and supporting details.

When you feel comfortable with the amount of information you've gathered, prepare your notes for the report. You may want to write out the entire report as you'd like to deliver it. Or you may write the key ideas and phrases on note cards. You might want to note the transitions you'll use to get from one main idea to the next. The transitions will jog your memory as you speak and help you move through your report smoothly.

26.4 Oral Reports **705**

Teacher's Classroom Resources

For Lesson 26.4, the following resources can be used for planning, instruction, practice, or reinforcement.

Teaching Tools
Lesson Plans

Blackline Masters
Speaking and Listening Activities, pp. 20–24
Thinking and Study Skills, p. 33

Setting the Purpose

Lesson 26.4 teaches students how to prepare, practice, and present an oral report.

FOCUS

Lesson Overview
Objective: To develop skills for presenting oral reports
Skills: narrowing a topic; researching a topic; public speaking
Critical Thinking: recalling; identifying a main idea; defining and clarifying
Speaking and Listening: giving oral reports

Bellringer
When students enter the classroom, have this assignment on the board: *Write about a time you gave an oral report. How did you feel before, during, and after? What would you do differently next time?*

Motivating Activity
Invite students to share experiences they have had giving oral reports. Discuss what is easiest and hardest for students. Although some students might find public speaking easier than others, do students think anyone can learn to give an interesting report?

TEACH

Guided Practice
Cross-reference: Study Skills
For more information on researching and note taking, refer students to Lesson 24.6, pp. 670–672.

TEACH

Guided Practice

L2 Analyzing Gestures

Discuss with students how gestures can clarify or emphasize a speaker's words. Ask students to recall a presentation or speech where the speaker's waving arms or swaying body proved distracting. Ask students to create a list of dos and don'ts for speakers. Their list should give speakers tips on ways to use gestures effectively. Tips can also provide speakers with strategies for overcoming their bad habits.

L1 Practicing Public Speaking

To help students get past a fear of speaking in front of an audience, divide the class into small groups for a speaking game. Each student must come up with a silly topic for a story, such as The Day I Rode an Ostrich or Why the Banana Wears a Peel. Tell them to write their ideas on strips of paper and place them in a bag. Each student will then draw a topic and tell a story about it on the spot to his or her group. Afterwards, remind students that most public speaking is best accomplished when planned and rehearsed; explain that this activity is a quick exercise to overcome fear.

⇄ Cross-reference: Writing

For more information on investigating a topic, refer students to Lesson 2.3, pp. 56–59.

Practicing the Report

Practicing your report is important. Practice will help you understand and remember your main ideas and supporting details. In addition, practice will give you confidence about your presentation. You will know how you want to speak the words, make the gestures, and display any visual materials you've decided to use.

Begin practicing alone. Speak in front of a mirror. Use the voice and gestures you would use if you were in front of a live audience. Time your report as you practice so that you can adjust the length if necessary.

The more you practice, the more natural the report will sound. Practice glancing from your note cards to the audience. You don't want to read your report word for word, but you'll probably want to memorize parts of it.

When you feel comfortable with your report, ask a friend or family member to listen to your delivery. Then try giving it before more than one person.

Ask your practice audience to listen *and* watch you. You'll want feedback about both the content of the report and your presentation. If the audience thinks the content or delivery needs work, make the changes you think are necessary. Then begin your practice sessions over again. If you need work on the delivery of your report, try using the following tips.

Tips on Delivering an Oral Report
1. Make eye contact with the audience. This helps people feel involved in what you are saying.
2. Use your voice to emphasize main points. You can raise or lower it, depending upon the effect you want to achieve.
3. Stop a moment after you've made an important point. This stresses the point and allows people to think about what you've said.
4. Use gestures if you've practiced them.
5. If they relate to your topic, use visual aids to help your audience understand your ideas.

706 *Listening and Speaking*

Enrichment and Extension

Using Sign Language

Remind students that some people communicate not by speaking aloud, but by signing. In what ways would it be easier to give a presentation using sign language instead of speaking? In what ways would it be more difficult?

Presenting the Report

When it's time to deliver your report, relax. (You'll find some tips for relaxing on page 711.) Deliver your report just as you've practiced it. Speak in a clear, natural voice, and use gestures when they are appropriate.

As you speak, show that you find your information interesting. Be enthusiastic. Think of your audience as people who are there because they're interested in what you have to say. Speak to them as if they were friends. They'll respond to your positive attitude.

When you conclude your report, ask for questions. Remain in front of the audience until you have answered everyone's questions.

Exercise 4

Select a topic from the following list, or use one of your own choosing. Write how you would narrow the topic. Then write your ideas for researching it.

Share the ideas you've developed with a partner. Ask for comments and suggestions. Then look at your partner's work, and make constructive comments about how he or she narrowed the topic and planned to research it.

- The migration of the monarch butterfly
- How our Constitution provides for the election of a president
- How to navigate by compass
- *Kente* cloth from Ghana

26.4   Oral Reports   **707**

PRACTICE AND ASSESS

Evaluation Guidelines: Exercise 4
Answers will vary. Make sure students have properly narrowed their topic and have listed a broad range of possible research material. Partners should give constructive comments and ideas for further narrowing the topic, including additional avenues of research.

Independent Practice

Skills Practice
📁 *Speaking and Listening Activities,* pp. 20–24
📁 *Thinking and Study Skills,* p. 33

CLOSE

Have students use their knowledge to present an oral report in class, perhaps on a topic they're studying in another course. Use their presentations as an opportunity for other students to practice their listening and evaluation skills.

Enabling Strategies

LEP Choosing Words

If students are still overwhelmed by the idea of preparing and presenting an oral report, ease them toward this goal by having them present short oral summaries of interesting news or feature stories from newspapers or magazines. If students later wish to do an oral report on the same subject, they could use the newspaper or magazine article as one of their sources.

FOCUS

Lesson Overview

Objective: To prepare and deliver a speech using a five-stage process
Skills: preparing, practicing, and delivering a speech; developing an awareness of audience
Critical Thinking: analyzing; establishing and evaluating criteria
Speaking and Listening: speaking formally; listening to a prepared speech

Bellringer
When students enter the classroom, have this assignment on the board: *List the steps you would follow in order to give a speech announcing that you are running for a class office.*

Motivating Activity
Discuss students' answers to the Bellringer exercise. Ask them how a speaker makes his or her audience feel comfortable and attentive. Discuss the importance of speakers knowing their audiences. Ask students to brainstorm a list of things speakers would need to know about their audience if they were running for a class office (age of students, school issues they are concerned with, and so on).

708

26.5 Formal Speeches

Delivering a formal speech in front of a live audience is the last stage of a five-stage process. You can think of it as the reward for successfully completing the earlier steps in the process. Once you've prepared thoroughly, delivering the speech can be fun and rewarding.

Preparing a Speech

You are familiar with the stages of writing a report: prewriting, drafting, revising, editing, and presenting. Formal speaking depends on a similar five-stage process. In preparing a speech, however, the editing stage becomes practicing. In effect, you edit your speech as you practice giving it. You are preparing for an audience of listeners rather than of readers.

Each step builds on the work done in the previous step. However, you may find it necessary to move back and forth during the drafting, revising, and practicing stages. For example, you might find during the practicing stage that your speech is too short or too long. To shorten it, you can back up to the revising stage or even the drafting stage to prepare a shorter version. The chart shows the process in detail.

Before you move to the practicing stage you'll want to have a speech you feel confident about. Word it in a way that will be easy to deliver.

Prewrite
- Define and narrow your topic.
- Remember your purpose and your audience.
- Complete your research.

Draft
- Make an outline, using main ideas and supporting details.
- Write your speech, or jot down the main points on note cards.

Revise
- Make sure your ideas are in order.
- Mark transitions on cards.
- Change wording until it is the way you want it.

Practice
- Give the speech in front of a mirror.
- Time your speech.
- Deliver it to a practice audience.
- Use the suggestions you receive.

Present
- Relax, and deliver your speech just as you've practiced it.

Teacher's Classroom Resources

For Lesson 26.5, the following resources can be used for planning, instruction, practice, assessment, reinforcement, or evaluation.

Teaching Tools
Lesson Plans

Blackline Masters
Speaking and Listening Activities, p. 19
Thinking and Study Skills, p. 33

Unit Assessment

Tests with Answer Key
Unit 26 Mastery Test, pp. 103–104

Test Generator
Unit 26 Mastery Test

You may wish to administer the Unit 26 Mastery Test at this point.

You don't want words you'll stumble over or phrases that sound awkward. If you aren't sure how to pronounce a term, look it up. If you still aren't comfortable with it, find another term that means the same thing.

Practicing a Speech

Practicing also involves several steps. When you practice your speech out loud, you want to make sure it sounds natural. The first time you practice it, just listen to the words as you speak. Listening to yourself on a tape recorder can be helpful. The rhythm of the speech should feel comfortable to you. If you don't like a phrase, rework it out loud until you come up with another way to express the idea.

The next time through, try looking in a mirror and using a few hand gestures to emphasize main points. Don't force the gestures. Try to think about what you're saying, and let your gestures develop spontaneously. Once you see where you need emphasis, make a point of practicing the gestures while speaking until they feel comfortable to you.

Finally, ask friends or relatives to listen to your delivery. Use their responses to fine-tune your speech. Below are a few more tips for practicing your speech.

Tips for Practicing a Speech

1. Each time you deliver your speech in practice, act just as if you were giving it before a live audience. Try to imagine the audience in front of you. This will help cut down on nervousness when you actually present the speech before a real audience.

2. Practice making eye contact with your imaginary audience. Let your eyes sweep slowly across the room from one side to the other, making contact with each member of the audience. Focus on talking to them, rather than on practicing your speech.

3. Make sure your gestures feel comfortable and fit with the points in the speech. Emphasize main points, or direct attention to visual aids, using gestures that are natural to you.

26.5 Formal Speeches **709**

TEACH

Guided Practice

L2 Using Gestures
Arrange students in groups for a round-robin-type activity to reinforce the effectiveness of gestures in communication. Tell students to think of simple statements or questions that they can communicate to the group through gestures and facial expressions only. (Give examples such as these: "What did you say?" "I don't know." "That is ridiculous.") After each student has had a turn to gesture, the group should discuss what they think the message was.

L1 Preparing a Speech
If students experience difficulty preparing their speeches, guide them in a careful review of the chart at the bottom of page 708 to make sure they understand the different steps. Suggest that the drafting stage might be made simpler if students mentally divide their speeches into three parts: the introduction, the body, and the conclusion. The body can be further divided into the three or four main ideas of the speech.

Cross-reference: Writing
For additional help in understanding the stages of the writing process, refer students to Lesson 2.1, pp. 48–51.

Enabling Strategies

LEP Practicing Speaking
Students who are not fluent English speakers will benefit from reading aloud to themselves or to family members. Encourage them to read aloud stories and newspaper and magazine articles—anything that interests them. If possible, they should also read to a friend who is fluent in English and who is willing to help them with their pronunciation and inflection.

TEACH

Guided Practice

L1 Preparing Visual Aids

Encourage students to try using visual aids. They can draw simple charts or pictures to use for each point of their speech. Suggest that if they first illustrate their speech, their written outlines will develop much more easily. Using visual aids will also help them deliver their speech more smoothly and confidently.

Cross-reference: Writing

For a discussion of adapting material for an audience, refer students to Lesson 2.2, pp. 52–55.

Delivering a Speech

Formal speaking is like conversation. Although you are the only one talking, your audience is communicating with you. Your success depends in part on how well you can interpret and use the signals they are sending you.

Keep your mind on your speech, and read the audience's response at the same time. A good speaker does both. The best speakers add a third element: They can change what they're doing to accommodate the needs of the audience.

710

Enrichment and Extension

Interviewing Experts

Invite a member of a local Toastmasters International club to talk to the class about the club's purpose and to discuss the benefits of public speaking. Have students prepare a list of questions based on their experiences during this lesson.

Tips for Relaxing

1. Take a few deep, slow breaths before you begin speaking. When you pause at important points in your speech, you can repeat the process to keep yourself relaxed.

2. When you deliver your speech, talk to people in the audience as individuals rather than to the group as a whole. This will help personalize your message and make you feel comfortable. Some speakers like to pick out and concentrate on a few friendly faces in the audience.

3. Speak in a tone that is normal for you. Speak loudly enough to be heard throughout the room, but don't shout.

4. Let your voice rise and fall naturally at key points in your speech. The idea is to sound comfortable and natural.

5. Keep alert. Don't let your thoughts wander. Focus on the content of your speech and on sharing it with your audience.

Focusing on the audience can help you feel less nervous. The charts on this page can give you some help. The one above contains some tips for relaxing. The chart below offers some suggestions for communicating with your audience.

Communicating with Your Audience	
Audience Signals	**Speaker Response**
People are yawning, stretching, or moving restlessly. They seem not to be paying attention to you.	You may have lost the attention of your audience. Try adding some enthusiasm to what you are saying.
People look confused or seem to want to ask a question.	You may have confused your audience. Try asking if there are questions or if what you've said is clear to them.
People are sitting forward in their chairs, trying to hear you.	People may be having trouble hearing you. Speak more loudly, and note whether or not that eliminates this audience response.
People look pleased with what you are saying. They nod in agreement.	You are doing a great job. Finish your speech in the same manner.

26.5   Formal Speeches   **711**

Speaking and Listening

Speaking Naturally

Beginning public speakers often try to change their personalities when they are in front of a group of people. Tell students that it's important that they be themselves when they give a speech. They should speak and move naturally.

Tell them that audiences warm up to speakers who reveal their own personalities and who let their enthusiasm for their subject show in their words and body language.

PRACTICE AND ASSESS

Evaluation Guidelines: Exercise 5

Answers will vary. Evaluate each group, using the following criteria:

- Group discussions should demonstrate an awareness of the listening and speaking skills covered in this unit.
- Each group should select a variety of television or radio programming to watch or listen to and evaluate.

Evaluation Guidelines: Exercise 6

Answers will vary. Evaluate each student, using the following criteria:

1. Each student should include the five stages of writing a speech: prewriting, drafting, revising, practicing, and presenting. Speakers should maintain a confident posture, speak clearly, and use gestures naturally.
2. Each student should put the traded speech into his or her own words, using the same basic content but different or additional facial expressions and body gestures.

Independent Practice

Skills Practice

📁 *Speaking and Listening Activities,* p. 19

📁 *Thinking and Study Skills,* p. 33

CLOSE

Using the charts from this unit, help students list important tips for listening and speaking effectively. Encourage them to add to their lists as they deliver speeches and oral reports during the year.

Exercise 5

With a small group, brainstorm ways to become better listeners. Work together to create a list of common listening problems. Then agree on one or two hours of television or radio programming that all of you will watch or listen to in the next few days. Include drama, news, music, comedy, talk shows, and other types of programming.

Listen to the television or radio programs your group selected for you. After each program write comments telling why you found the listening easy or difficult. When you meet again as a group, compare notes, and discuss kinds of programming that are easy to listen to and those that are more challenging. Discuss distractions and ways to listen more carefully to programming with which you had difficulties.

Exercise 6

1. Prepare a two-minute speech on a topic of your choice. Go through each of the steps outlined in this lesson. Then break into small groups, and take turns delivering your speeches within the groups. Discuss each speech. Share ideas you can all use to improve the presentation and content of your speeches. Then make revisions, and deliver the revised speeches to the class.
2. Exchange copies of speeches with someone in your group. If you have notes instead of a complete written speech, exchange the note cards. Try to develop a speech, and practice delivering it. Alter the speech to suit your manner of speaking, but keep the content the same. Join your group, and take turns delivering your new speeches. Discuss how and why they differ from the originals.

Enabling Strategies

LEP Using Visual Aids in Speeches

If students have trouble writing two-minute speeches for Exercise 6, encourage them to try using visual aids. They can draw simple charts or pictures to use for each point of their speeches. Point out to them that if they first "write" their speeches using pictures, their written outlines will develop much more easily. Using visual aids will also help them deliver their speeches more smoothly and confidently.

Index

A

A, an, the, 426
Abbreviations, 582
  academic degrees, 582
  capitalization of, 552, 582
  commas with, 572
  days of the week, 582
  government agencies, 582
  of months, 582
  of organizations, 582
  for states, 582
  of street names, 582
  time, 582, 584
  titles of persons, 552, 572, 582
  units of measure, 582
  with ZIP codes, 582
Abstract nouns, 348
Academic degrees
  abbreviations for, 582
  capitalizing names of, 552, 582
  commas to set off, 572
Accept, except, 526, 657
Action verbs, 368, 370, 372, 374
Active voice, 386
Addresses
  abbreviations in, 582
  in business letters, 226
  commas in, 572
  numerals in, 584
Adjective clauses, 474, 476, 600
  commas to set off, 478, 570, 600
  definition of, 476, 600
  diagraming, 545
  essential and nonessential, 478, 570, 600
  Troubleshooter for, 318
Adjective phrases, 452
Adjectives
  articles as, 426
  bad and *badly,* 436
  choosing precise, 114–115
  colorful, 150
  comparative form of, 237, 428

  compound, 580
  definition of, 424
  demonstrative, 430
  diagraming, 541
  distinguishing from adverbs, 436
  good and *well,* 432, 436
  irregular, 428
  after linking verb, 374, 436
  participles as, 424, 494
  predicate, 374, 424, 436, 542
  prepositional phrases as, 452
  proper, 426, 556
  superlative form of, 237, 428
  Troubleshooter for, 314–315
Ads, creating, 280–283
Adverb clauses, 209, 474, 480, 602
  commas after introductory, 570, 602
  definition of, 480, 602
  diagraming, 545
  Troubleshooter for, 318
Adverb phrases, 452
Adverbs
  choosing precise, 116
  comparative form of, 434
  conjunctive, 456, 472, 568, 574
  contractions, 438
  definition of, 432
  diagraming, 541
  distinguishing from adjectives, 436
  intensifiers, 432
  irregular, 434
  negatives as, 438
  prepositional phrases as, 452
  superlative form of, 434
Advertising, as persuasion, 280–282
Affect, effect, 657
Agencies, abbreviations for, 582
Agreement. *See* Pronoun-antecedent agreement; Subject-verb agreement

All ready, already, 526
All together, altogether, 526
Almanacs, 615, 617
A lot, 526
Already, all ready, 526
Among, between, 526
Analogies, on standardized tests, 687
Announcements, making, 703–704
Antecedents, pronoun, agreement with, 225, 404
Antonyms, 642, 687
Apostrophes
  in contractions, 354, 578
  with possessives, 354, 578
  to show missing numbers in date, 578
  with special plurals, 578
  Troubleshooter for, 319–321
Appositive, 358, 598
  commas to set off, 358, 568, 598
  Troubleshooter for, 317
Argument, strengthening, in persuasive writing, 276–279
Art, *See* Cross-curricular writing topics; Fine art
Articles, definite and indefinite, 426
Assessment. *See* Peer review; Study skills; Tests
Atlases, 615, 616
Audience
  in expository writing, 240
  in descriptive writing, 130
  determining, 52–55
  in narrative writing, 176
  in personal writing, 30
  in persuasive writing, 256–257, 266, 292
  in the writing process, 88
Audiotapes, 622
Autobiography, 22–25
Auxiliary verbs. *See* Helping verbs

Dates *(continued)*
  commas in, 572
  numerals in, 584
Days, capitalization of, 556
Declarative sentences, 326, 566
  diagraming, 539
Definite articles, 426
Definitions,
  in dictionary, 623–626
  in expository writing, 198
Demonstrative adjectives, 430
Demonstrative pronouns,
  414, 430
Dependent clauses. *See* subordinate clauses
Descriptive writing, 105,
  106–109
  describing subject of a
    biography, 126–129
  describing things, 122–125
  details in, 102, 110–113,
    118–121, 123, 124, 130
  drafting, 102, 131
  editing, 108, 133
  focusing on subject in, 128
  forming strong impressions
    in, 127
  literature models in, 106, 107,
    111, 119, 124, 126, 134–138
  note taking in, 123, 131
  orienting reader in, 120
  precise language in,
    114–117
  presenting, 116
  prewriting, 101–102, 113,
    115, 131
  revising, 103–104, 124, 132
  spatial order in, 118–121
  transitions in, 120
  word choice in, 114, 116
Details
  choosing, 123
  in descriptive writing, 102,
    110–113, 118–121, 123,
    124, 130
  for comparison-contrast, 239
  in expository writing,
    201–202, 203
  in narrative writing, 150,
    166, 170
  order of importance, 118–119

organizing, 61, 120
  in personal writing, 58
  spatial ordering of, 118–121
Dewey Decimal System, 610
Diagraming sentences,
  538–548
Diagrams, 675–676
Dialogue
  editing, 161
  in narrative writing, 160–163
  punctuating, 576
  and quotation marks, 576
Diaries. *See* Journal writing
Dictionary
  bibliographical, 618
  checking pronunciation
    in, 116
  college, 623
  definition in, 626
  entry word in, 624–625
  part of speech in, 625
  pronunciation in, 625
  school, 623
  unabridged, 623
  word origins in, 626
Direct address, commas to
  set off, 568
Direct object, 370
  diagraming, 540, 543
Direct quotations, 128, 572, 576
  capitalizing, 550
  comma to set off, 572
  quotation marks with, 576
Directions, giving, 208–210
Discussion, participating in, 702
Double comparisons, 428
Double negatives, 438
Drafting, 45–46, 64–67, 89–90
  of compare-and-contrast
    essay, 205
  in descriptive writing,
    102–103, 131
  of documentary writing,
    45–46
  in expository writing,
    192–193, 230, 241–242
  in narrative writing, 144–145,
    150, 177–178
  in news story, 169–170
  in personal writing, 7,
    31–32, 49

in persuasive writing,
    256–257, 277, 293–294
  of speech, 708

E

Editing, 46, 80–83, 91
  book review, 290
  checklist for, 33, 91, 133, 179,
    243, 295
  comparison-contrast
    essay, 237
  in descriptive writing, 108, 133
  of dialogue, 161
  in expository writing, 202,
    234, 243
  for grammar, 108, 128
  for mechanics, 82, 222
  in narrative writing, 158, 179
  in personal writing, 33, 49
  in persuasive writing, 258,
    274, 295
  in writing process, 46, 80–83,
    91
  See also Proofreading; Revis-
    ing
Effect, affect, 657
Emphasis, pronouns used for,
  406, 412
Encyclopedias, 615, 616
End marks
  definition of, 566
  exclamation point, 566
  period, 566
  question mark, 566
  and run-on sentence, 566
English language, history of,
  629–632
  See also Vocabulary; Words
Essay, 197. *See also* Expository
    writing
Essay question
  answering, 216–219
  clue words in, 217
  on tests, 684
Essential clauses, 478
Evidence, evaluating, in
    persuasive writing, 268–271
Examples
  in expository writing, 201
  in persuasive writing, 269

Quotation marks *(continued)*
  with other marks of
    punctuation, 576
  with titles of short
    works, 576
Quotations
  capitalization of, 550
  direct, 129, 576

R

Radio news, listening to,
  693–695
Raise, rise, 530
Read, reed, 645
Reading
  careful, 662
  scanning, 661
  skimming, 661
Reading comprehension, 685
Real, reel, 645
Reasons
  in expository writing, 201
  in persuasive writing, 269
Reed, read, 645
Reel, real, 645
Reference works
  almanacs, 615, 617
  atlases, 615, 616
  biographical reference
    works, 615, 618
  dictionaries, 623–626
  encyclopedias, 615, 616
  thesauruses, 627–628
Reflecting, 33, 91, 133, 179,
  243, 295
Reflexive pronouns, 412
Relative pronouns, 476, 600
Reports, oral, 705–707
Research, in persuasive
  writing, 262
Research reports, 220–223
  drafting, 230, 231
  editing, 234
  prewriting, 220–222,
    228–229
  revising, 232–233, 235
Responding to literature. *See*
  Literature, responding to
Revising, 46, 68–71, 72–75,

76–79, 90
checklist for, 32, 90, 132, 178,
  242, 294
for clarity and sense, 68–69
in descriptive writing,
  103–104, 124, 132
in documentary writing, 46
in expository writing, 194,
  216, 232–233, 242
in narrative writing, 144, 173,
  178
in personal writing, 8, 32–33, 49
in persuasive writing, 258,
  262, 294–295
of speech, 708
writing unified
  paragraphs, 72–75
writing varied sentences, 76–79
See also Editing; Proofreading
Rise, raise, 530
Roots, 636
Run-on sentences, 304–305

S

Salutations
  capitalization of, 550
  colon after, in business
    letter, 574
  comma after, 572
Scanning, 661
Scent, cent, sent, 645
Semicolons
  in compound sentences, 472,
    574
  with conjunctive adverb, 456,
    472
Senses, appealing to, 110, 111,
  112
Sensory details, in descriptive
  writing, 110–113
Sent, scent, cent, 645
Sentence fragments, 328
  Troubleshooter for, 302–303
Sentences
  capitalization of, 550
  choppy, 78
  complex, 474
  compound, 336, 454, 472
  declarative, 326, 566

definition of, 326, 472
diagraming, 538–548
exclamatory, 326, 566
imperative, 326, 566
interrogative, 326, 566
inverted, 510
monotonous, 78
predicate in, 328, 330, 332, 334,
  472
run-on, 304–305, 336
simple, 336, 472
subject in, 328, 330, 332, 334,
  472
topic, 73, 228–229. *See also*
  Thesis statement
variety in, 76
word order in, 332, 510
Sentence combining. *See* Combining sentences
Series, commas in, 568
Set, sit, 530
Several, both, few, many, 410,
  514
Short-answer tests, 683
Sight, site, cite, 645
Simple predicates, 330
Simple sentences, 336, 472
Simple subjects, 330
Sit, set, 530
Site, sight, cite, 645
Skimming, 661
Slang, 277
Spatial order, 62, 118–121
Speaker's bias, 692–693
Speaking
  critical listening, 691–695
  explaining process, 703
  formal, 708–711
  informal, 700–707
  interviewing, 696–699
  making announcements,
    703–704
  making introductions, 701
  oral reports, 705–707
  participating in discussion, 702
  in writing conference, 32, 90,
    132, 178, 242, 294
  See also Listening
Spelling, 647–654
  adding prefixes, 649
  compound words, 651
  dictionary used for, 623–626

Y

Acknowledgments (continued from page iv)

Text

4 From the book *The Lost Garden* by Laurence Yep. Copyright © 1991. Used by permission of the publisher, Julian Messner/A division of Silver Burdett Press, Inc. Simon & Schuster, Englewood Cliffs, NJ. **12** Reprinted with the permission of Four Winds Press, an Imprint of Macmillan Publishing Company from *Louisa May: The World and Works of Louisa May Alcott* by Norma Johnston. Copyright © 1991 by Dryden Harris St. John, Inc. **20** Excerpt from *Letters Home by Sylvia Plath* edited by Aurelia Schober Plath. Copyright © 1975 by Aurelia Schober Plath. Reprinted by permission of HarperCollins Publishers. **22** From *The Heart of a Woman* by Maya Angelou. Copyright © 1981 by Maya Angelou. Published by Random House, Inc. **24** Reprinted with permission from *Stone Soup, the magazine by children,* copyright © 1992 (1990 for "The Shellster") by the Children's Art Foundation. **26** "The Clouds Pass" by Richard Garcia. Copyright © 1975 by Richard Garcia. **29** "Jukebox Showdown" by Victor Hernandez Cruz. Copyright © 1976 by Victor Hernandez Cruz. Reprinted by permission. **31, 34** From *Living Up the Street: Narrative Reflections* by Gary Soto. Copyright © 1985 by Gary Soto. Published by Dell Publishing, a division of Bantam, Doubleday Dell Publishing Group, Inc. **53** The following article is reprinted courtesy of *Sports Illustrated* from the June 12, 1989 issue. Copyright © 1989, Time Inc. "Tigers Burning Bright" by Merrell Noden. All Rights Reserved. **53** The following article is reprinted courtesy of *Sports Illustrated for Kids* from the March, 1991 issue. Copyright © 1991, Time Inc. "Fly, Hollis, Fly!" **54** Reprinted by permission of *Cricket* Magazine, August 1987 Vol. 14, No. 12, © 1987 by Carus Corporation. **73** © 1989. *The Washington Post.* Reprinted with permission. **78** From *Barrio Boy* by Ernesto Galarza. © 1971 by University of Notre Dame Press. Reprinted by permission. **89, 92** "The Game" from *Fast Sam, Cool Clyde, and Stuff* by Walter Dean Myers. Copyright © 1975 by Walter Dean Myers. Published by Viking Penguin, a division of the Penguin Group. **100** From *How the Garcia Girls Lost Their Accents* by Julia Alvarez. Copyright © 1991 by Julia Alvarez. Published by the Penguin Group. **106** From "On Summer" by Lorraine Hansberry. Copyright © 1960 by Robert Nemiroff. All rights reserved. Reprinted by permission of Robert Nemiroff. **107** From *In Nueva York* by Nicholasa Mohr. Copyright © 1977 by Nicholasa Mohr. Published by The Dial Press. **108** From *Merlyn's Pen: The National Magazine of Student Writing,* February/March, 1990. Copyright © 1991. Published by Merlyn's Pen, Inc. **111** Text excerpt from *A Girl From Yamhill* by Beverly Cleary. Copyright © 1988 by Beverly Cleary. By permission of Morrow Junior Books, a division of William Morrow & Co., Inc. **119** From *The Lost Garden* by Laurence Yep. Copyright © 1991. Used by permission of the publisher. Julian Messner/A division of Silver Burdett Press, Inc. Simon & Schuster, Englewood Cliffs, NJ. **122** From "Teddy" by Amanda Morgan from *Treasures: Stories & Art by Students in Oregon* collected by Chris Weber. Copyright © 1985 by Chris Weber. Published by Oregon Students Writing and Art Foundation. **124** From "Private Property" by Leslie Marmon Silko. Published by Wylie, Aitken & Stone, Inc. Reprinted by permission. **126** From *Thurgood Marshall* by Lisa Aldred. Reprinted by permission of Chelsea House Publishers, a division of Main Line Book Co. **131, 134** From *Thrashin' Time* by David Weitzman. Copyright © 1991. Published by Godine. **149** From *Sojourner Truth: A Self-Made Woman* by Victoria Ortiz. Copyright © 1974 by Victoria Ortiz. Published by J.B. Lippincott Company. **153** From *Homesick* by Jean Fritz. Copyright © 1982 by Jean Fritz. Published by Dell Publishing Company, Inc. **158** From "Revolutionary Tea" from *I Hear America Singing: Great Folk Songs From the Revolution to Rock* by Hazel Arnett. Copyright © 1975 by Hazel Arnett. Published by Praeger Publishers, Inc. **161** From *So Far From the Bamboo Grove* by Yoko Kawashima Watkins. Copyright © 1986 by Yoko Kawashima Watkins. Published by William Morrow & Co.

168 From "Collaborating on Computers" by Theresa A. Martin from *The Boston Sunday Globe,* July 19, 1992. Copyright © 1992. Published by The Globe Newspaper Co. **169** From "A Summer Search" by Mark Ferenchik from *The Repository.* Copyright © 1992. Published by The Repository. **169** From "Runaway Chimp Finds Unwilling Playmate" from *Chicago Tribune,* Wednesday, August 26, 1992, Section 1, Page 3. Copyright © 1992 by National News Service. Published by *Chicago Tribune.* **169** From "Florida Braces for Hurricane Andrew" *Daily Herald,* DuPage County Edition, Monday, August 24, 1992. Copyright © 1992 by Associated Press. Published by *Daily Herald.* **170** From "Best Hopes for the Gold" by Bud Greenspan from *Parade,* July 26, 1992. Copyright © 1992. Published by Parade Publications, Inc. **172** From *Anne Frank: Diary of a Young Girl* by Anne Frank. Copyright © 1952 by Otto H. Frank. Published by Simon & Schuster, Inc. **177, 180** From *Lyddie* by Katherine Paterson. Copyright © 1991 By Katherine Paterson. Published by Lodestar Books. **190** From *Indian America: A Traveler's Companion* by Eagle/Walking Turtle. Copyright © 1989 by Gary McLain. Published by John Muir Publications. **196** Reprinted by permission of Chelsea House Publishers, a division of Main Line Book Co. **200** From *The Minicomputer Simplified: An Executive's Guide to the Basics* by Carol W. Brown. Copyright © 1980 by Carol W. Brown. Reprinted with the permission of The Free Press, A Division of Macmillan, Inc. **206** From "Yo-Yo and Manny" by Michael Shapiro from *World Monitor The Christian Science Monitor Monthly.* Copyright © 1991 by Michael Shapiro. Published by The Christian Science Publishing Society. **209** From *Foods of the World: Latin American Cooking* by Jonathan Norton Leonard and the Editors of Time-Life Books. © 1969 Time-Life Books, Inc. **212** From *Let There Be Light: A Book About Windows* by James Cross Giblin. Copyright © 1988 by James Cross Giblin. Published by Thomas Y. Crowell, HarperCollins Publishers. **236** "Fall" by Sally Andresen from *A New Treasury of Children's Poetry: Old Favorites and New Discoveries* edited by Joanna Cole. Copyright © 1984 by Joanna Cole. Published by Doubleday & Company. **236** "Something Told the Wild Geese" by Rachel Field from *Reflections on a Gift of Watermelon Pickle . . . And Other Modern Verse* compiled by Stephen Dunning, Edward Lueders and Hugh Smith. Copyright © 1967. Published by Scott, Foresman, and Company. **241, 244** "The Vision of Maya Ying Lin" from *Always to Remember* by Brent Ashabranner. Copyright © 1988. Published by Putnam, Berkley Group. **261** "Progress or Plunder " by April Barnes from *Merlyn's Pen: The National Magazine of Student Writing,* Vol. 4, No. 1, October/November 1988. Copyright © 1991. Published by Merlyn's Pen, Inc. **262** From "Save the Prairie Path" by Patrick MacRoy. First appeared in *Call of the Wildcat,* April, 1991. **265** From "Should Animals Be Held In Captivity" by Jacqueline Parks. Copyright © 1992 by Jacqueline Parks. **266** From *What to Do When Your Mom or Dad Says . . . "Don't Overdo with Video Games!"* by Joy Wilt Berry. Copyright © 1983 by Joy Wilt Berry. Published by Children's Press. **266** From *The Second Self: Computers and the Human Spirit* by Sherry Turkle. Copyright © 1984 by Sherry Turkle. Published by Simon & Schuster. **270** From *Jane Brody's Nutrition Book: A Lifetime Guide to Good Eating for Better Health and Weight Control by the Personal Health Columnist of The New York Times* by Jane E. Brody. Copyright © 1981 by Jane E. Brody. Published by W. W. Norton & Company. **273** From "Plastic Bags, Cars and Kids" by Dina Morrison from *Merlyn's Pen: The National Magazine of Student Writing,* Vol. 2, No. 3, February/March, 1987. Copyright © 1987. Published by Merlyn's Pen. **278** From "I'm Outta Here" by David Levine from *Seventeen,* March 1992. Copyright © 1992 by *Seventeen*/David Levine. Published by *Seventeen.* **280** Reprinted by permission of Brookfield Zoo. **284** From *Sports Illustrated for Kids,* September, 1990. Copyright © 1990. Published by Time, Inc. Reprinted by permission of Philip Trevino. **285** From *Sports Illustrated for Kids,* September, 1990. Copyright © 1990. Published by Time, Inc. **286** From "North by Northwest" by Kelinda Peaples from *St. Louis Magazine,* June 1, 1992. Copyright © 1992. Published by St. Louis Magazine.

288 From *The Ways of My Grandmothers* by Beverly Hungry Wolf. Copyright © 1980 by Beverly Hungry Wolf. Published by William Morrow & Company. **290** Reprinted with permission from *Stone Soup, the magazine by children*, copyright © 1992 (1990 for "The Shellster") by the Children's Art Foundation. **293, 296** From *Silent Spring* by Rachel Carson. Copyright © 1978. Published by Houghton Mifflin Company. **338** From *Growing Up* by Russell Baker. Copyright © 1982 by Russell Baker. Published by Congdon & Weed, Inc. **346** From *The Heart of a Woman* by Maya Angelou. Copyright © 1981 by Maya Angelou. Published by Random House, Inc. **360** From *Barbara Jordan* by James Haskins. Copyright © 1977. Published by Dial Press. **366** From *Thrashin' Time* by David Weitzman. Copyright © 1991. Published by Godine. **392** From *Our Town: A Play in Three Acts* by Thorton Wilder. Copyright © 1985. Published by Harper Collins. **400** From *Lyddie* by Katherine Paterson. Copyright © 1991 by Katherine Paterson. Published by Lodestar. **416** From *Emily Dickinson* by Bonita Thayer. Copyright © 1990. Published by Watts. **422** From "The Game" from *Fast Sam, Cool Clyde, and Stuff* by Walter Dean Myers. Copyright © 1975 by Walter Dean Myers. Published by Viking Penguin, a division of the Penguin Group. **440** From *I, Juan de Pareja* by Elizabeth Borton de Trevino. Copyright © 1987. Published by Farrar, Straus and Giroux. **446** From "On Summer" by Lorraine Hansberry. Copyright 1960 by Robert Nemiroff. All rights reserved. Reprinted by permission of Robert Nemiroff. **462** From *Morning Girl* by Michael Dorris. Copyright © 1992 by Michael Dorris. Published by Hyperion Books for Children. **470** From *Li ing up the Street: Narrati e Reflections* by Gary Soto. Copyright © 1985 by Gary Soto. Published by Dell Publishing, a division of Bantam, Doubleday Dell Publishing Group, Inc. **484** From *The Education of a Baseball Player* by Mickey Mantle. Copyright © 1967. Published by Simon & Schuster. **492** From *Silent Spring* by Rachel Carson. Copyright © 1978. Published by Houghton Mifflin Company. **506** From *Always to Remember* by Brent Ashabranner. Copyright © 1988. Published by Putnam, Berkley Group. **536** From *Lyddie* by Katherine Paterson. Copyright © 1991 by Katherine Paterson. Published by Lodestar. **558** From *Morning Star, Black Sun* by Brent Ashabranner. Copyright © 1982. Published by Putnam Publishing Group. **564** From *So Far from the Bamboo Gro e* by Yoko Kawashima Watkins. Copyright © 1986 by Yoko Kawashima Watkins. Published by William Morrow & Company. **586** From *A Small Place* by Jamaica Kincaid. Copyright © 1988 by Jamaica Kincaid. Published by Farrar, Straus, and Giroux. **594** From *Thrashin' Time* by David Weitzman. Copyright © 1991. Published by Godine. **618** By Permission. From *Webster's New Biographical Dictionary* © 1988 by Merriam-Webster, Inc., publisher of the Merriam-Webster (R) dictionaries. **619** *Readers' Guide to Periodical Literature,* May 1992, Volume 92, No, 5, pages 33 and 83. Copyright © 1992 by the H.W. Wilson Company. Material reproduced with permission of the publisher. **623** "Words" from *Collected Poems* by Edward Thomas. Copyright © 1974 by Edward Thomas. Published by W. W. Norton & Co., Inc. **625** From *Dictionary*. Copyright © 1977. Published by Macmillan Publishing Company. **627** From *Roget's II: The New Thesaurus*. Copyright © 1984 by Houghton Mifflin Company. Published by Berkley Books by arrangement with Houghton Mifflin Company.

Photos

Front Cover: Mark E. Gibson/The Stock Market; Aaron Haupt **4** Laurence Yep. **5** Allan Landau. **6** Laurence Yep(l); Allan Landau(r). **7** Laurence Yep. **8** Allan Landau. **9** Allan Landau. **10** Allan Landau. **11** David Madison 1991. **12** Allan Landau. **13** Copyright by Leonard Von Matt, photographer, Buochs Switzerland. **14-15** Allan Landau. **18** Art Wise. **20** Art Wise. **21** Edward Owen/Art Resource 1977. **22** UPI/Bettmann (t); UPI/Bettmann (b). **25** Courtesy Bernice Steinbaum Gallery, NYC. **26** Courtesy of Ray Vinella. **28** Allan Landau. **30** ©Tony Freeman/PhotoEdit. **35** Courtesy of Susan Moore. **37** Courtesy of the artist. **39** Art Wise (t)(b). **42** Courtesy Kurtis Productions Ltd. **43** Courtesy Kurtis Productions Ltd.(t)(b). **44** Allan Landau(t); Courtesy Kurtis Productions Ltd.(b). **45** Allan Landau. **46** Courtesy Kurtis Productions Ltd. **47** Allan Landau. **48** Art Wise. **51** Courtesy of Claes Oldenburg Studio(l)(r). **52** Art Wise. **55** Collection of The Grand Rapids Art Museum Gift of Mrs. Cyrus E. Perkins, 1911.1.4. **56** Art Wise. **58** Art Wise. **60** Art Wise. **64** © Jeff Dunn/Stock, Boston. **66** ©Larry Kolvoord/The Image Works. **67** Located in San Francisco at the Pacific Stock Exchange. Dirk Bakker, Photographer. **68** Art Wise. **72** ©Barbara Alper/Stock, Boston(l); © Charle Fell/Stock, Boston(r). **75** The Jamison Galleries, Sante Fe, New Mexico. **76** Art Wise. **80** Art Wise. **82** The Far Side cartoon by Gary Larson is reprinted by permission of Chronicle Features, San Francisco, CA. **84** Art Wise. **86** Art Wise. **88** Tom McCarthy/PhotoEdit. **91** Glennon Donahue/Tony Stone Worldwide. **94** © 1992 Red Grooms/ARS, New York. **97** Art Wise(t)(b). **100** Tad Merrick. **101** © 1992 Martha Cooper/Peter Arnold, Inc. **102** Ralph Brunke. **103** Ralph Brunke. **104** Ralph Brunke. **105** ©Joe Sohm/Chromosohm/The Image Works. **106** ©Larry Kolvoord/The Image Works. **107** Robert Frerck/Odyssey Productions/Chicago. **109** Courtesy American Federation of The Arts. **110** The Saint Louis Art Museum Museum Purchase. **111** Allen Landau. **114** Allan Landau. **115** Cindy Brodie(c); Alex Murdoch(r). **118** © Erich Lessing/Art Resource, NY. **121** Courtesy Nancy Hoffman Gallery. **122** Allan Landau. **126** UPI/Bettmann. **128** Princeton University Library. **129** Courtesy of Frumkin/Adams Gallery, New York. **130** Bob Daemmrich/The Image Works. **135** From "Thrashin' Time: Harvest Days in the Dakotas" by David Weitzman © 1991 by David Weitzman. Reprinted by permission of David R. Godine, Publisher, Inc. **137** The Metropolitan Museum of Art, George A. Hearn Fund, 1943 (43.159.1). **139** Art Wise(t)(b). **142** Tom Green. **144** Tom Green(l)(r); Culver Pictures(c). **145** Tom Green. **146** Courtesy of The Colonial Williamsburg Foundation. **147** Culver Pictures. **148** Hampton University Museum. **149** The Bettmann Archive. **152** Art Wise. **154** "Rape of the Records" by Les Schrader/Naper Settlement Village Museum. **156** ©1979 Vernon Merritt/Black Star. **157** Focus on Sports. **159** Robert Miller Gallery, New York. **160** Courtesy of the artist. **163** Courtesy June Kelly Gallery, New York. Photo: Manu Sassoonian. **164** Giraudon/Art Resource, NY. **166** Statute of Liberty National Monument, National Park Service. **167** Private Colllection/Laura Platt Winfrey, Inc. **168** Neal Hamburg. **170** Focus on Sports. **172** UPI/Bettmann(t); ©Joe Viesti/Viesti Associates(b). **174** David Young-Wolff/PhotoEdit. **175** Archivo fotográfico, Museo Nacional Centro de Arte Reina Sofia. **176** Tom Prettyman/PhotoEdit. **181** Erich Lessing/Art Resource, NY. **183** Manchester City Art Galleries. **184** Phillip Evergood. "Lily and the Sparrows" 1939. oil on composition board. 30 x 24 inches. (76.2 cm x 61 cm). Collection of Whitney Museum of American Art. Purchase 41.42. **187** Art Wise(t)(b). **190** Courtesy Gary McLain. **191** © 1991 Greg Probst/Allstock. **192-3** Art Wise. **193** Stephen Trimble(l); Courtesy Cherokee Historical Association(r). **194** Allan Landau. **195** David Young-Wolf/PhotoEdit. **196** ©Clark Mishler/Alaska Stock Images. **199** Art Wise. **200** ©Charles Feil/Stock, Boston. **202** The Bettman Archive. **204** Art Wise. **207** The Museum of Fine Arts, Houston; museum purchase with funds provided by Panhandle Eastern Corporation. **208** Art Wise. **210** ©Jon Elliott. **212** Edith G. Haun/Stock, Boston. **213** Culver Pictures. **215** © David Hockney Ref: 67A34. **216, 218** ©J. Pickerell/The Image Works. **219** Shelburne Museum, Shelburne, Vermont, Photograph by Ken Burris. **220** William Lishman and Associates. **224** Art Wise. **225** Art Wise. **228** Calvin and Hobbes ©1990 Watterson. Reprinted with permission of Universal Press Syndicate. All rights reserved. **232** Sharon Hoogstraten. **236** © 1992 Roger and Donna Aitkenhead/ Animals Animals(t); ©Jack Wilburn/Animals Animals(b). **239** Courtesy Holly Solomon Gallery, New York. **240** ©Holt Confer/The Image Works. **243** Tom Wurl/Stock, Boston. **245** Bill Barley/Super Stock, Inc. **249** ©David M. Doody/Uniphoto. **251** Art Wise(t)(b). **254** Art Wise. **255** Courtesy Indira Freitas Johnson. **256** Ralph Brunke.

257 Courtesy of Indira Freitas Johnson(tc); Ralph Brunke(b).
258 Courtesy Indira Freitas Johnson. **259** Cathlyn Melloan/Tony Stone Worldwide. **260** Historical Pictures/Stock Montage, Inc.
262 ©David Young-Wolf/PhotoEdit. **263** Courtesy Bernice Steinbaum Gallery, NYC. **264** ©Leonard Lee Rue III/Stock, Boston(l); ©Herb Snitzer/Stock, Boston(r). **270** Art Wise.
272 Calvin and Hobbes ©1986 Waterson. Reprinted with permission of United Press Syndicate. All rights reserved. **273** Art Wise.
276 ©1992 R. Fukuhara/Westlight. **280** Courtesy Brookfield Zoo.
282 Art Wise. **283** © Faith Ringgold. **284** Art Wise. **285** © Mitchell B. Reibel/Sports Photo Masters, Inc. **286** Art Wise. **288** Art Wise.
290 Alain Le Garsmeur/Tony Stone Worldwide. **291** U.S. Department of The Interior Indian Arts and Crafts Board Southern Plains Indian Museum and Crafts Center. **292** Peter Menzel/Stock, Boston. **295** Dean Abramson/Stock, Boston. **297** Phyliss Kind Gallery, New York/Chicago. **299** Art Wise(t)(b). **326** Gift of W. G. Russell Allen. Courtesy, Museum of Fine Arts, Boston. ©1992.
344 Courtesy Nancy Hoffman Gallery, New York. **356** Myrleen Ferguson/PhotoEdit. **364** Henri Matisse, La Negresse, Ailsa Mellon Bruce Fund, © 1992 National Gallery of Art, Washington, 1952. Collage on canvas/paper collage on canvas, 4.539 x 6.233 (178 3/4 x 245 1/2). **368** ©Rhonda Sidney/Stock, Boston. **398** Phyliss Kind Gallery, New York/Chicago. **420** Phyllis Kind Gallery, Chicago.
436 ©Dennis Stock/Magnum. **445** The Metropolitan Museum of Art, Fletcher Fund, Rogers Fund, and Bequest of Miss Adelaide Milton de Groot (1876-1967), by exchange, supplemented by gifts from friends of the Museum, 1971. (1971.86) Photograph by Malcolm Varon. **458** Joan Messerschmidt/Leo de Wys Inc.
460 Julie Houck/TSW. **468** Courtesy of the artist and Deson Saunders Gallery, Chicago. **478** Focus on Sports. **490** National Museum of American Art, Washington D.C./Art Resource, NY.
471 Giraudon/Art Resource © 1992 ARS, New York/ADAGP, Paris. **505** Seattle Art Museum. Photo Credit: Paul Macapia.
512 Jon Riley/ Tony Stone Worldwide(t); David Young-Wolff/PhotoEdit(b). **523** Phyliss Kind Gallery, New York/Chicago.
534 Giraudon/Art Resource, NY © 1992 ARS, New York/SPA-DEM, Paris. **563** Robert Henri, "Portrait of Po Tse (Water Eagle)" Oil on Canvas, 40 x 32 inches Photograph courtesy of the Gerald Peters Gallery, Santa Fe, New Mexico. **593** Henri Matisse, French, 1869-1954, Interior at Nice, oil on canvas, 1921, 132.1 x 88.9 cm, Charles H. and Mary F. S. Worcester Collection, 1956.339. **607** Allan Landau. **608** © 1992 Cathy Ferris. **617** Allan Landau. **620** Allan Landau. **629** © 1992 Frank Oberle/ Photo Resource. **630** ©Bob Daemmrich/Stock, Boston. **631** ©Richard Pasley/Stock, Boston.
640 Steve Bentsen/Natural Selection. **641** Lori Adamski Peek/Tony Stone Worldwide. **642** ©George Chan/Tony Stone Worldwide(t); Pete Seaward/Tony Stone Worldwide(b). **646** David Young-Wolf/PhotoEdit. **659** Ralph Brunke. **707** Billy E. Barnes/ Stock, Boston. **710** Ralph Brunke(t); Ralph Brunke(c); Ralph Brunke(b).
Back Cover: Aaron Haupt